ZANICHELLI Compact ITALIAN and ENGLISH Dictionary

English-Italian/Italian-English

Edited by Edigeo

NTC Publishing Group

Library of Congress Cataloging-in-Publication Data

Zanichelli compact Italian and English dictionary / edited by Edigeo.
p. cm.
ISBN 0-8442-2249-6
1. Italian language—Dictionaries—English. 2. English language—Dictionaries—Italian. I. Edigeo.
PC1640.Z33 1999
453'.21—dc21 99-13123
CIP

This edition based on *INGLESE—Dizionario Compatto Inglese-Italiano Italiano-Inglese* published in Italy by Zanichelli editore

This edition published 1999 by NTC Publishing Group
A division of NTC/Contemporary Publishing Group, Inc.
4255 West Touhy Avenue, Lincolnwood (Chicago), Illinois 60646-1975 U.S.A.

Printed in the United States of America
International Standard Book Number: 0-8442-2249-6
99 00 01 02 03 04 MV 19 18 17 16 15 14 13 12 11 10 9 8 7 6 5 4 3 2 1

CONTENTS

INTRODUCTION

The *Zanichelli Compact Italian and English Dictionary* contains more than 34,000 entries and is a convenient, practical reference for students, travelers, businesspeople, and others seeking knowledge of the Italian language.

In the Italian-English section, acute and grave accents identify the stressed syllables of the Italian entry words and also distinguish between "open" and "closed" vowels. In the English-Italian section, the pronunciation of each English entry word is given in the International Phonetic Alphabet. In both sections, entries include the part of speech and feature concise definitions, useful examples, and many idiomatic phrases and compounds. Abbreviations used in the dictionary are listed at the end of the book.

This compact bilingual dictionary also provides an appendix of useful phrases for travelers.

ENGLISH-ITALIAN
INGLESE-ITALIANO

A

a [eɪ, ə] (**an** *davanti a vocale e 'h' muta*) *art. indeterm.* **1** uno, una (ES: **I see a man and a house** vedo un uomo e una casa; **Bob is an old man** Bob è un uomo anziano) **2** il, lo, la (ES: **a rose is a flower** la rosa è un fiore, **to smoke a pipe** fumare la pipa) **3** un certo, una certa, un tale, una tale (ES: **in a sense** in un certo senso, **do you know a Mrs Smith?** conosci una certa signora Smith?) **4** stesso, stessa (ES: **to be of a height** essere della stessa altezza) **5** (*distributivo*) per, al, ogni (ES: **once a year** una volta all'anno) **6** (*idiom.*) (ES: **what a pity!** che peccato!)
aback [ə'bæk] *avv.* all'indietro ♦ **to be taken a.** essere colto alla sprovvista
abacus ['æbəkəs] *s.* (*arch.*) abaco *m.*
abandon [ə'bændən] *s.* abbandono *m.*, effusione *f.*
to abandon [ə'bændən] *v. tr.* abbandonare, lasciare
to abash [ə'bæʃ] *v. tr.* confondere, sconcertare
abashed [ə'bæʃt] *agg.* confuso, imbarazzato
to abate [ə'beɪt] **A** *v. tr.* diminuire **B** *v. intr.* placarsi, calmarsi
abbey ['æbɪ] *s.* abbazia *f.*
abbot ['æbət] *s.* abate *m.*
to abbreviate [ə'bri:vɪeɪt] *v. tr.* abbreviare
abbreviation [əˌbri:vɪ'eɪʃ(ə)n] *s.* abbreviazione *f.*
to abdicate ['æbdɪkeɪt] *v. tr. e intr.* abdicare
abdication [ˌæbdɪ'keɪʃ(ə)n] *s.* abdicazione *f.*
abdomen ['æbdəmɛn] *s.* addome *m.*
abdominal [æb'dəmɪn(ə)l] *agg.* addominale
to abduct [æb'dʌkt] *v. tr.* rapire
abductor [æb'dʌktə^r] *s.* rapitore *m.*
aberration [ˌæbə'reɪʃ(ə)n] *s.* aberrazione *f.*
to abet [ə'bɛt] *v. tr.* appoggiare, spalleggiare ♦ **to aid and a. sb.** essere complice di qc.
abeyance [ə'bɛ(ɪ)əns] *s.* **1** sospensione *f.* **2** (*dir*) disuso *m.* ♦ **to be in a.** essere messo da parte, essere sospeso
to abide [ə'baɪd] (*pass. e p. p.* **abode**) *v. tr.* **1** sopportare **2** resistere a ♦ **to a. by** attenersi a, rispettare
ability [ə'bɪlɪtɪ] *s.* abilità *f.*
abject ['æbdʒɛkt] *agg.* abietto, spregevole
ablaze [ə'bleɪz] *agg.* **1** in fiamme **2** splendente
able ['eɪbl] *agg.* capace ♦ **a.-bodied** sano, robusto; **to be a. to** essere in grado di, potere, riuscire a
abnormal [æb'nɜ:m(ə)l] *agg.* anormale
aboard [ə'bɜ:d] **A** *avv.* a bordo **B** *prep.* a bordo di ♦ **to go a.** imbarcarsi
abode (1) [ə'bɒʊd] *s.* dimora *f.*, domicilio *m.*
abode (2) [ə'bɒʊd] *pass. e p. p. di* **to abide**
to abolish [ə'bəlɪʃ] *v. tr.* abolire, sopprimere
abolitionism [ˌæbə'lɪʃənɪz(ə)m] *s.* abolizionismo *m.*
abominable [ə'bəmɪn(ə)bl] *agg.* abominevole, pessimo
aboriginal [ˌæbə'rɪdʒənl] *agg. e s.* aborigeno *m.*
aborigine [ˌæbə'rɪdʒɪnɪ] *s.* aborigeno *m.*
to abort [ə'bɜ:t] *v. tr. e intr.* abortire
abortion [ə'bɜ:ʃ(ə)n] *s.* aborto *m.*
abortive [ə'bɜ:tɪv] *agg.* **1** abortivo **2** (*fig.*) fallito, mancato
to abound [ə'baʊnd] *v. intr.* abbondare ♦ **to a. in/with** avere in abbondanza
about [ə'baʊt] **A** *avv.* **1** quasi, circa, pressappoco **2** intorno, attorno **3** nei pressi **B** *prep.* **1** circa, riguardo a **2** intorno a **3** vicino a, nei pressi di ♦ **to be a. to** accingersi, prepararsi a; **a.-face/turn** dietrofront
above [ə'bʌv] **A** *avv.* **1** sopra, di sopra **2** precedentemente **B** *prep.* su, sopra, al di sopra di ♦ **a. all** soprattutto; **a.-mentioned** suddetto; **see a.** vedi sopra
abrasion [ə'breɪʒ(ə)n] *s.* abrasione *f.*
abrasive [ə'breɪzɪv] *agg. e s.* abrasivo *m.*
abreast [ə'brɛst] *avv.* a fianco ♦ **to keep a. of** tenersi aggiornato su
to abridge [ə'brɪdʒ] *v. tr.* ridurre, riassumere, accorciare ♦ **abridged edition** edizione ridotta, compendio
abroad [ə'brɜ:d] *avv.* all'estero
to abrogate ['æbrɒ(ʊ)geɪt] *v. tr.* abrogare
abrupt [ə'brʌpt] *agg.* **1** improvviso **2** bru-

sco, sbrigativo **3** ripido, scosceso
abscess ['æbsɪs] *s.* ascesso *m.*
to abscond [əb'skənd] *v. intr.* scappare
absconder [əb'skəndər] *s.* fuggiasco *m.*, latitante *m. e f.*
absence ['æbs(ə)ns] *s.* **1** assenza *f.* **2** mancanza *f.* **3** contumacia *f.*
absent ['æbs(ə)nt] *agg.* assente ♦ **a.-minded** distratto; **a.-mindedly** distrattamente; **a.-mindedness** distrazione
absentee [ˌæbs(ə)n'tiː] *s.* assente *m. e f.*
absolute ['æbsəluːt] *agg.* assoluto, completo, totale
absolutely ['æbs(ə)luːtlɪ] *avv.* **1** assolutamente, completamente **2** senz'altro, certamente
to absolve [əb'zəlv] *v. tr.* **1** assolvere **2** liberare da
to absorb [əb'sɜːb] *v. tr.* **1** assorbire **2** assimilare
absorbing [əb'sə(ː)bɪŋ] *agg.* **1** assorbente **2** avvincente
absorption [əb'sɜːpʃ(ə)n] *s.* **1** assorbimento *m.*, assimilazione *f.* **2** dedizione *f.*
to abstain [əb'steɪn] *v. intr.* astenersi
abstemious [æb'stiːmjəs] *agg.* astemio
abstinence ['æbstɪnəns] *s.* astinenza *f.*
abstract ['æbstrækt] **A** *agg.* astratto **B** *s.* **1** estratto *m.*, riassunto *m.* **2** astrazione *f.*
to abstract [æb'strækt] *v. tr.* **1** astrarre **2** sottrarre **3** riassumere **4** rimuovere
abstraction [æb'strækʃ(ə)n] *s.* **1** astrazione *f.* **2** sottrazione *f.* **3** rimozione *f.*
abstractionism [æb'strækʃ(ə)nɪz(ə)m] *s.* astrattismo *m.*
abstractionist [æb'strækʃ(ə)nɪst] *s.* astrattista *m. e f.*
absurd [əb'sɜːd] *agg.* **1** assurdo **2** ridicolo
abundance [ə'bʌndəns] *s.* abbondanza *f.*
abundant [ə'bʌndənt] *agg.* abbondante
abuse [ə'bjuːs] *s.* **1** abuso *m.* **2** insulti *m. pl.*, ingiurie *f. pl.*
to abuse [ə'bjuːz] *v. tr.* **1** abusare di **2** insultare, ingiuriare
abusive [ə'bjuːsɪv] *agg.* offensivo, ingiurioso
abysmal [ə'bɪzm(ə)l] *agg.* abissale
abyss [ə'bɪs] *s.* abisso *m.*
acacia [ə'keɪʃə] *s.* acacia *f.*
academic [ˌækə'dɛmɪk] **A** *agg.* **1** accademico **2** formale **B** *s.* accademico *m.*
academy [ə'kædəmɪ] *s.* accademia *f.*
acanthus [ə'kænθəs] *s.* acanto *m.*
to accelerate [æk'sɛləreɪt] *v. tr. e intr.* accelerare
accelerator [æk'sɛləreɪtər] *s.* acceleratore *m.*
accent ['æks(ə)nt] *s.* **1** accento *m.* **2** enfasi *f.*, tono *m.*
to accept [ək'sɛpt] *v. tr.* accettare
acceptable [ək'sɛptəbl] *agg.* accettabile
acceptance [ək'sɛpt(ə)ns] *s.* **1** accettazione *f.* **2** approvazione *f.*
access ['æksɛs] *s.* accesso *m.*
accessible [æk'sɛsəbl] *agg.* accessibile
accessory [æk'sɛsərɪ] *s.* **1** accessorio *m.* **2** (*dir.*) complice *m. e f.*
accident ['æksɪd(ə)nt] *s.* **1** incidente *m.*, infortunio *m.* **2** caso *m.* ♦ **by a.** per caso
accidental [ˌæksɪ'dɛntl] *agg.* accidentale
accidentally [ˌæksɪ'dɛntlɪ] *avv.* accidentalmente, per caso
acclaim [ə'kleɪm] *s.* acclamazione *f.*
to acclaim [ə'kleɪm] *v. tr.* acclamare
to acclimatize [ə'klaɪmətaɪz] *v. tr.* ambientare, acclimatare ♦ **to get acclimatized** ambientarsi
accolade ['ækəleɪd] *s.* elogio *m.*
to accomodate [ə'kəmədeɪt] *v. tr.* **1** alloggiare, sistemare **2** adattare **3** favorire
accomodating [ə'kəmədeɪtɪŋ] *agg.* accomodante, compiacente
accomodation [əˌkəmə'deɪʃ(ə)n] *s.* **1** alloggio *m.*, sistemazione *f.* **2** accordo *m.* **3** comodità *f.*
to accompany [ə'kʌmp(ə)nɪ] *v. tr.* **1** accompagnare **2** scortare
accomplice [ə'kəmplɪs] *s.* complice *m. e f.*
to accomplish [ə'kəmplɪʃ] *v. tr.* compiere, realizzare
accomplished [ə'kəmplɪʃt] *agg.* **1** compiuto **2** esperto
accomplishment [ə'kəmplɪʃmənt] *s.* **1** compimento *m.*, realizzazione *f.* **2** impresa *f.* **3** *al pl.* dote *f.*, talento *m.*
accord [ə'kɜːd] *s.* accordo *m.* ♦ **of one's own a.** spontaneamente, di propria iniziativa; **with one a.** di comune accordo
to accord [ə'kɜːd] *v. tr.* accordare, concedere
accordance [ə'kɜːd(ə)ns] *s.* concordanza *f.* ♦ **in a. with** in conformità con
accordingly [ə'kɜːdɪŋlɪ] *avv.* di conseguenza, perciò
according to [ə'kɜːdɪŋtuː] *prep.* secondo, in base a, in conformità con
accordion [ə'kɜːdjən] *s.* fisarmonica *f.*
to accost [ə'kəst] *v. tr.* avvicinare, abbor-

dare
account [ə'kaʊnt] *s.* **1** conto *m.* **2** (*banca*) conto *m.*, deposito *m.* **3** acconto *m.* **4** relazione *f.*, descrizione *f.* **5** vantaggio *m.*, tornaconto *m.* **6** importanza *f.*, considerazione *f.* ♦ **a. number** numero di conto; **by all accounts** a detta di tutti; **current a.** conto corrente; **of no a.** di nessuna importanza; **on a.** in acconto; **to take into a.** tener conto di
to account [ə'kaʊnt] *v. tr. e intr.* considerare ♦ **to a. for** spiegare, rendere conto di, influire, (*fam.*) distruggere
accountable [ə'kaʊntəbl] *agg.* responsabile
accountancy [ə'kaʊntənsɪ] *s.* contabilità *f.*, ragioneria *f.*
accountant [ə'kaʊntənt] *s.* contabile *m. e f.*
accounting [ə'kaʊntɪŋ] *s.* contabilità *f.*, ragioneria *f.*
to accrue [ə'kruː] *v. intr.* derivare, provenire ♦ **accrued interest** interesse maturato
to accumulate [ə'kjuːmjʊleɪt] *v. tr. e intr.* accumulare, accumularsi
accumulator [ə'kjuːmjʊleɪtəʳ] *s.* accumulatore *m.*
accuracy ['ækjʊrəsɪ] *s.* accuratezza *f.*, precisione *f.*
accurate ['ækjʊrɪt] *agg.* accurato, preciso, esatto
accusation [ˌækjʊ(ː)'zeɪʃ(ə)n] *s.* accusa *f.*, incriminazione *f.*
to accuse [ə'kjuːz] *v. tr.* accusare, incriminare
to accustom [ə'kʌstəm] *v. tr.* abituare ♦ **to a. oneself to** abituarsi a
accustomed [ə'kʌstəmd] *agg.* **1** abituato, avvezzo **2** abituale ♦ **to become a. to doing st.** abituarsi a fare q.c.
ace [eɪs] *s.* asso *m.*
acephalous [ə'sɛfələs] *agg.* acefalo
ache [eɪk] *s.* dolore *m.*
to ache [eɪk] *v. intr.* **1** far male, dolere **2** (*fam.*) desiderare ardentemente
achievable [ə'tʃiːvəbl] *agg.* raggiungibile
to achieve [ə'tʃiːv] *v. tr.* **1** compiere **2** raggiungere, conseguire
achievement [ə'tʃiːvmənt] *s.* **1** risultato *m.* positivo, successo *m.* **2** impresa *f.*, realizzazione *f.*
acid ['æsɪd] *agg. e s.* acido *m.*
acidulous [ə'sɪdjʊləs] *agg.* acidulo
acinus ['æsɪnəs] *s.* acino *m.*
to acknowledge [ək'nɒlɪdʒ] *v. tr.* **1** ammettere **2** riconoscere **3** mostrare apprezzamento per ♦ **to a. receipt** accusare ricevuta
acknowledg(e)ment [ək'nɒlɪdʒmənt] *s.* **1** riconoscimento *m.*, ammissione *f.* **2** riconoscenza *f.* **3** ricevuta *f.*
acne ['æknɪ] *s.* acne *f.*
acorn ['eɪkɜːn] *s.* ghianda *f.*
acoustic [ə'kuːstɪk] *agg.* acustico
acoustics [ə'kuːstɪks] *s. pl.* (*v. al sing.*) acustica *f.*
to acquaint [ə'kweɪnt] *v. tr.* informare, mettere al corrente ♦ **to a. sb. with st.** informare qc. di q.c.; **to be acquainted with** conoscere
acquaintance [ə'kweɪnst(ə)ns] *s.* **1** conoscenza *f.* **2** conoscente *m. e f.*
to acquiesce [ˌækwɪ'ɛs] *v. intr.* acconsentire, aderire
to acquire [ə'kwaɪəʳ] *v. tr.* acquisire, procurarsi
acquisition [ˌækwɪ'zɪʃ(ə)n] *s.* acquisizione *f.*
to acquit [ə'kwɪt] *v. tr.* assolvere ♦ **to a. oneself well** dare una buona prova di sé, comportarsi bene
acquittal [ə'kwɪtl] *s.* assoluzione *f.*
acquittance [ə'kwɪtəns] *s.* **1** pagamento *m.*, saldo *m.* **2** quietanza *f.*, ricevuta *f.*
acre ['eɪkəʳ] *s.* acro *m.*
acrid ['ækrɪd] *agg.* acre, pungente
acrimonious [ˌækrɪ'məʊnjəs] *agg.* aspro, astioso
acrobat ['ækrəbæt] *s.* acrobata *m. e f.*
acrobatics [ˌækrə'bætɪks] *s. pl.* acrobazia *f.*
acropolis [ə'krɒpəlɪs] *s.* acropoli *f.*
across [ə'krɒs] **A** *prep.* **1** attraverso **2** dall'altro lato di, oltre **B** *avv.* da una parte all'altra, in larghezza ♦ **a. from** di fronte a; **to go a.** passare dall'altra parte
acrylic [ə'krɪlɪk] *agg.* acrilico
act [ækt] *s.* **1** atto *m.*, azione *f.* **2** decreto *m.*, legge *f.*, documento *m.* **3** (*teatro*) atto *m.*
to act [ækt] **A** *v. intr.* **1** agire, comportarsi **2** funzionare **3** recitare **4** fingere **B** *v. tr.* recitare (la parte di) ♦ **to a. as/for** fungere da, agire per conto di; **to a. up** comportarsi male
acting ['æktɪŋ] **A** *agg.* facente funzione, sostituto **B** *s.* **1** recitazione *f.* **2** funzionamento *m.*

action ['ækʃ(ə)n] *s.* **1** azione *f.*, atto *m.* **2** funzionamento *m.*, moto *m.* **3** (*dir.*) processo *m.*, causa *f.* **4** (*mil.*) combattimento *m.* ♦ **out of a.** fuori uso, fuori combattimento, fuori servizio
to activate ['æktɪveɪt] *v. tr.* attivare
active ['æktɪv] *agg.* attivo, operoso
activity [æk'tɪvɪtɪ] *s.* attività *f.*
actor ['æktəʳ] *s.* attore *m.*
actress ['æktrɪs] *s.* attrice *f.*
actual ['æktjʊəl] *agg.* reale, effettivo
actually ['æktjʊəlɪ] *avv.* realmente, effettivamente
aculeus [ə'kjʊ(ː)lɪəs] *s.* aculeo *m.*
acumen [ə'kjuːmɛn] *s.* acume *m.*
acupuncture ['ækjʊˌpʌŋktʃəʳ] *s.* agopuntura *f.*
acute [ə'kjuːt] *agg.* acuto
ad [æd] *s.* (*abbr. di* **advertisement**) annuncio *m.* pubblicitario
adamant ['ædəmənt] *agg.* inflessibile, irremovibile
to adapt [ə'dæpt] *v. tr.* adattare ♦ **to a. oneself** adattarsi
adaptable [ə'dæptəbl] *agg.* **1** adattabile **2** che sa adattarsi
adaptation [ˌædæp'teɪʃ(ə)n] *s.* adattamento *m.*
adapter [ə'dæptəʳ] *s.* adattatore *m.*
to add [æd] **A** *v. tr.* **1** aggiungere **2** addizionare, sommare **B** *v. intr.* aggiungersi, aumentare ♦ **to a. in** includere; **to a. up** sommare, fare una somma; **to a. up to** ammontare a
adder ['ædəʳ] *s.* vipera *f.*
addict ['ædɪkt] *s.* **1** tossicomane *m. e f.* **2** fanatico *m.*, maniaco *m.*
addicted [ə'dɪktɪd] *agg.* dedito ♦ **to be a. to drugs** essere tossicodipendente
addiction [ə'dɪkʃ(ɛ)n] *s.* dipendenza *f.* ♦ **drug a.** tossicodipendenza
addictive [ə'dɪktɪv] *agg.* che dà assuefazione
addition [ə'dɪʃ(ə)n] *s.* **1** addizione *f.*, somma *f.* **2** aggiunta *f.*, supplemento *m.* ♦ **in a.** inoltre; **in a. to** oltre a
additional [ə'dɪʃən(ə)l] *agg.* addizionale, supplementare
additive ['ædɪtɪv] *s.* additivo *m.*
address [ə'drɛs] *s.* **1** indirizzo *m.*, recapito *m.* **2** discorso *m.* ♦ **a. book** rubrica
to address [ə'drɛs] *v. tr.* **1** indirizzare **2** rivolgersi a, fare un discorso a
addressee [ˌædrɛ'siː] *s.* destinatario *m.*
addresser [ə'drɛsəʳ] *s.* mittente *m.*
adept [ə'dɛpt] *agg. e s.* esperto *m.*, perito *m.*
adequate ['ædɪkwɪt] *agg.* adeguato, sufficiente
to adhere [əd'hɪəʳ] *v. intr.* aderire
adherent [əd'hɪərənt] **A** *agg.* aderente, attaccato **B** *s.* aderente *m. e f.*, seguace *m. e f.*
adhesive [əd'hiːsɪv] *agg.* adesivo
adjacent [ə'dʒeɪs(ə)nt] *agg.* adiacente, attiguo
adjective ['ædʒɪktɪv] *s.* aggettivo *m.*
to adjoin [ə'dʒəɪn] *v. tr.* confinare con
adjoining [ə'dʒəɪnɪŋ] *agg.* adiacente, contiguo
to adjourn [ə'dʒɜːn] **A** *v. tr.* aggiornare, rinviare **B** *v. intr.* aggiornarsi
to adjudicate [ə'dʒuːdɪkeɪt] **A** *v. intr.* (*dir.*) giudicare **B** *v. tr.* aggiudicare
to adjust [ə'dʒʌst] **A** *v. tr.* **1** sistemare, aggiustare **2** regolare, adattare **B** *v. intr.* adattarsi a
adjustable [ə'dʒʌstəbl] *agg.* adattabile, regolabile
adjustment [ə'dʒʌstmənt] *s.* **1** adattamento *m.*, sistemazione *f.* **2** modifica *f.* **3** conguaglio *m.*
to administer [əd'mɪnɪstəʳ] *v. tr.* **1** amministrare **2** somministrare
administration [ədˌmɪnɪs'treɪʃ(ə)n] *s.* **1** amministrazione *f.* **2** somministrazione *f.*
administrative [əd'mɪnɪstrətɪv] *agg.* amministrativo
administrator [əd'mɪnɪstreɪtəʳ] *s.* amministratore *m.*
admirable ['ædm(ə)rəbl] *agg.* ammirevole
admiral ['ædm(ə)r(ə)l] *s.* ammiraglio *m.*
admiralty ['ædm(ə)r(ə)ltɪ] *s.* ammiragliato *m.*
admiration [ˌædmə'rəɪʃ(ə)n] *s.* ammirazione *f.*
to admire [əd'maɪəʳ] *v. tr.* ammirare
admirer [əd'maɪərəʳ] *s.* ammiratore *m.*
admissible [əd'mɪsəbl] *agg.* ammissibile
admission [əd'mɪʃ(ə)n] *s.* **1** ammissione *f.* **2** riconoscimento *m.*, confessione *f.* **3** ingresso *m.*, entrata *f.* ♦ **a. fee** prezzo del biglietto d'ingresso; **a. free** ingresso gratuito
to admit [əd'mɪt] *v. tr.* **1** ammettere, far entrare **2** ammettere, riconoscere **3** contenere, aver posto per ♦ **to a. of** lasciar adito a
admittance [əd'mɪt(ə)ns] *s.* ammissione

f., accesso *m.*, ingresso *m.* ♦ **no a.** vietato l'ingresso
admittedly [əd'mɪtɪdlɪ] *avv.* per ammissione generale
to admonish [əd'mɒnɪʃ] *v. tr.* ammonire, esortare
ado [ə'du:] *s.* rumore *m.*, confusione *f.*
adolescence [ˌædə'lɛs(ə)ns] *s.* adolescenza *f.*
adolescent [ˌædə'lɛs(ə)nt] **A** *agg.* adolescente, adolescenziale **B** *s.* adolescente *m. e f.*
to adopt [ə'dɒpt] *v. tr.* adottare
adoption [ə'dɒpʃ(ə)n] *s.* adozione *f.*
adoptive [ə'dɒptɪv] *agg.* adottivo
to adore [ə'dɜ:ʳ] *v. tr.* adorare
to adorn [ə'dɜ:n] *v. tr.* adornare, imbellire
adrift [ə'drɪft] *avv. e agg. pred.* alla deriva
adult ['ædʌlt] *agg. e s.* adulto *m.*
to adulterate [ə'dʌltəreɪt] *v. tr.* adulterare, contraffare
adultery [ə'dʌltərɪ] *s.* adulterio *m.*
advance [əd'va:ns] *s.* **1** avanzamento *m.*, progresso *m.* **2** aumento *m.* **3** acconto *m.*, anticipo *m.* ♦ **in a.** in acconto
to advance [əd'va:ns] **A** *v. intr.* **1** avanzare, progredire **2** (*di prezzo*) aumentare, salire **B** *v. tr.* **1** anticipare **2** far avanzare, spostare avanti **3** avanzare, presentare **4** promuovere, far progredire **5** (*prezzo*) aumentare
advanced [əd'va:nst] *agg.* **1** avanzato, progredito **2** (*di studio*) superiore
advantage [əd'va:ntɪdʒ] *s.* vantaggio *m.*, profitto *m.* ♦ **to take a. of** approfittare di
advantageous [ˌædvən'teɪdʒəs] *agg.* vantaggioso
advent ['ædvənt] *s.* avvento *m.*
adventure [əd'vɛntʃəʳ] *s.* avventura *f.*
adventurer [əd'vɛntʃ(ə)rəʳ] *s.* avventuriero *m.*
adventurous [əd'vɛntʃ(ə)rəs] *agg.* avventuroso
adverb ['ædvɜ:b] *s.* avverbio *m.*
adversary ['ædvəs(ə)rɪ] *s.* avversario *m.*
adverse ['ædvɜ:s] *agg.* avverso, contrario
adversity [əd'vɜ:sɪtɪ] *s.* avversità *f.*
to advertise ['ædvəˌtaɪz] **A** *v. tr.* fare pubblicità a **B** *v. intr.* fare un'inserzione pubblicitaria ♦ **to a. for** mettere un annuncio per
advertisement [əd'vɜ:tɪsmənt] *s.* inserzione *f.*, annuncio *m.* pubblicitario
advertiser ['ædvəˌtaɪzəʳ] *s.* inserzionista *m. e f.*
advertising ['ædvəˌtaɪzɪŋ] *s.* pubblicità *f.*
advice [əd'vaɪs] *s.* **1** consiglio *m.* **2** consulenza *f.* **3** avviso *m.*, notizia *f.*
advisable [əd'vaɪzəbl] *agg.* consigliabile
to advise [əd'vaɪz] *v. tr.* **1** consigliare **2** avvisare, notificare
advisedly [əd'vaɪzɪdlɪ] *avv.* deliberatamente, di proposito
adviser [əd'vaɪzəʳ] (o **advisor**) *s.* consigliere *m.*, consulente *m. e f.*
advisory [əd'vaɪz(ə)rɪ] *agg.* consultivo
advocate ['ædvəkɪt] *s.* difensore *m.*, sostenitore *m.*
to advocate ['ædvəkeɪt] *v. tr.* sostenere, patrocinare
to aerate ['ɛ(ɪ)əreɪt] *v. tr.* aerare, ventilare
aeration [ˌɛ(ɪ)ə'reɪʃ(ə)n] *s.* aerazione *f.*, ventilazione *f.*
aerial (1) ['ɛərɪəl] *agg.* aereo ♦ **a. photography** aerofotografia
aerial (2) ['ɛərɪəl] *s.* antenna *f.*
aerobic [ɛər'ɒʊbɪk] *agg.* aerobico
aerobics [ɛər'ɒʊbɪks] *s. pl.* (*v. al sing.*) (ginnastica) aerobica *f.*
aerodrome ['ɛərədrɒʊm] *s.* aerodromo *m.*
aerodynamic ['ɛərɒ(ʊ)daɪ'næmɪk] *agg.* aerodinamico
aeronautic [ˌɛərə'nɜ:tɪk] *agg.* aeronautico
aeronautics [ˌɛərə'nɜ:tɪks] *s. pl.* (*v. al sing.*) aeronautica *f.*
aeroplane ['ɛərəpleɪn] *s.* aeroplano *m.*
aerosol ['ɛərɒ(ʊ)ˌsəl] *s.* aerosol *m.*
aerospace ['ɛərɒ(ʊ)speɪs] *agg.* aerospaziale
aesthetic [i:s'θɛtɪk] *agg.* estetico
aestheticism [i:s'θɛtɪsɪz(ə)m] *s.* estetismo *m.*
aesthetics [i:s'θɛtɪks] *s. pl.* (*v. al sing.*) estetica *f.*
afar [ə'fa:ʳ] *avv.* lontano ♦ **from a.** da lontano
affair [ə'fɛəʳ] *s.* **1** faccenda *f.*, affare *m.* **2** relazione *f.* amorosa
to affect (1) [ə'fɛkt] *v. tr.* **1** riguardare, interessare, influenzare **2** (*di malattia*) colpire **3** commuovere
to affect (2) [ə'fɛkt] *v. tr.* **1** fingere, simulare **2** preferire
affectation [ˌæfɛk'teɪʃ(ə)n] *s.* affettazione *f.*, ostentazione *f.*
affected [ə'fɛktɪd] *agg.* **1** commosso, afflitto **2** affettato, lezioso **3** (*med.*) affetto
affection [ə'fɛkʃ(ə)n] *s.* affezione *f.*

affectionate [ə'fɛkʃnɪt] *agg.* affezionato, affettuoso
affective [ə'fɛktɪv] *agg.* affettivo
affinity [ə'fɪnɪtɪ] *s.* affinità *f.*
to affirm [ə'fɜːm] *v. tr.* **1** affermare **2** (*dir.*) convalidare
affirmative [ə'fɜːmətɪv] *agg.* affermativo
affirmatory [ə'fɜːmət(ə)rɪ] *agg.* affermativo
to affix [ə'fɪks] *v. tr.* **1** affiggere, attaccare **2** apporre
to afflict [ə'flɪkt] *v. tr.* affliggere
affluence ['æflʊəns] *s.* abbondanza *f.*, ricchezza *f.*
affluent ['æflʊənt] *agg.* **1** ricco, opulento **2** abbondante ♦ **a. society** società del benessere
to afford [ə'fɜːd] *v. tr.* **1** permettersi **2** offrire, fornire
to afforest [æ'fərɪst] *v. tr.* imboschire
affront [ə'frʌnt] *s.* affronto *m.*, insulto *m.*
afield [ə'fiːld] *avv.* **far a.** lontano
afloat [ə'flɒʊt] *avv.* **1** a galla **2** in mare
afoot [ə'fʊt] *avv.* **1** (*mil.*) in marcia **2** in atto
aforesaid [ə'fɜːsɛd] *agg.* predetto, suddetto
afraid [ə'freɪd] *agg. pred.* spaventato, pauroso ♦ **to be a.** temere, dispiacersi; **to be a. of st.** temere q.c.
afresh [ə'frɛʃ] *avv.* di nuovo, da capo
African ['æfrɪkən] *agg. e s.* africano *m.*
aft [aːft] *avv.* a poppa
after ['aːftəʳ] **A** *agg.* **1** posteriore, successivo **2** di poppa **B** *prep.* **1** dopo **2** dietro, di seguito a **3** secondo, alla maniera di **C** *avv.* **1** dopo, in seguito, successivamente **2** dietro **D** *cong.* dopo che ♦ **a. all** dopotutto; **a. lunch** dopo pranzo; **ever a.** da allora in poi; **never a.** mai più; **the day a.** il giorno dopo
aftereffect ['aːftəɪˌfɛkt] *s.* effetto *m.* collaterale
aftermath ['aːftəmæθ] *s.* **1** conseguenza *f.* **2** (*med.*) postumi *m. pl.*
afternoon [aːftə'nuːn] *s.* pomeriggio *m.*
afters ['aːftəs] *s. pl.* (*fam.*) dessert *m. inv.*
aftershave ['aːftəʃeɪv] *s.* dopobarba *m. inv.*
afterthought ['aːftəθɜːt] *s.* ripensamento *m.*
afterwards ['aːftəwədz] *avv.* dopo, più tardi, successivamente
again [ə'gɛn] *avv.* **1** ancora, nuovamente **2** inoltre, d'altra parte ♦ **a. and a.** ripetutamente; **as much a.** altrettanto; **never a.** mai più; **over a.** ancora una volta
against [ə'gɛnst] *prep.* **1** contro **2** in senso contrario **3** su, a contatto con **4** in previsione di ♦ **as a.** di fronte a, a paragone di; **over a.** in contrasto con; **to be a.** osteggiare
agave [ə'geɪvɪ] *s.* agave *f.*
age [eɪdʒ] *s.* **1** età *f.* **2** epoca *f.*, era *f.* ♦ **middle a.** mezz'età; **the Middle Ages** il Medioevo; **to be of a.** essere maggiorenne; **to come of a.** diventare maggiorenne
to age [eɪdʒ] *v. tr. e intr.* invecchiare
aged ['eɪdʒɪd] *agg.* **1** anziano **2** dell'età di **3** stagionato
ageing ['eɪdʒɪŋ] *s.* **1** invecchiamento *m.* **2** stagionatura *f.*
agency ['eɪdʒ(ə)nsɪ] *s.* **1** agenzia *f.*, ente *m.* **2** (*comm.*) rappresentanza *f.* **3** azione *f.*, agente *m.*, impulso *m.*
agenda [ə'dʒɛndə] *s.* agenda *f.*
agent ['eɪdʒ(ə)nt] *s.* **1** agente *m.* **2** concessionario *m.*, rappresentante *m.*
agglomerate [ə'glɒmərɪt] *s.* agglomerato *m.*
to aggravate ['ægrəveɪt] *v. tr.* aggravare
aggregate ['ægrɪgɪt] *agg. e s.* aggregato *m.*
aggressive [ə'grɛsɪv] *agg.* aggressivo
aggressiveness [ə'grɛsɪvnɪs] *s.* aggressività *f.*
aggressor [ə'grɛsəʳ] *s.* aggressore *m.*
aggrieved [ə'griːvd] *agg.* addolorato, offeso
aghast [ə'gaːst] *agg. pred.* **1** inorridito **2** stupefatto
agile ['ædʒaɪl] *agg.* agile
agility [ə'dʒɪlɪtɪ] *s.* agilità *f.*, scioltezza *f.*
to agitate ['ædʒɪteɪt] **A** *v. tr.* **1** agitare, scuotere **2** turbare **B** *v. intr.* agitarsi
agitation [ˌædʒɪ'teɪʃ(ə)n] *s.* agitazione *f.*
agnostic [æg'nəstɪk] *agg.* agnostico
ago [ə'gɒʊ] *avv.* fa, in passato, or sono ♦ **long a.** molto tempo fa
agog [ə'gɒg] *agg. pred.* impaziente, eccitato
agonistic(al) [ˌægə'nɪstɪk((ə)l)] *agg.* agonistico
agonizing ['ægənaɪzɪŋ] *agg.* angoscioso, straziante
agony ['ægənɪ] *s.* **1** agonia *f.* **2** tormento *m.*, supplizio *m.*, angoscia *f.*
agrarian [ə'grɛərɪən] *agg.* agrario, agricolo
to agree [ə'griː] **A** *v. tr.* accettare, ammettere **B** *v. intr.* **1** convenire, essere d'accordo **2** acconsentire **3** andare d'accordo **4**

(*gramm.*) concordare **5** confarsi, andare bene per
agreeable [ə'grɪəbl] *agg.* **1** gradevole, simpatico **2** consenziente, ben disposto
agreed [ə'grɪ(ː)d] *agg.* convenuto, pattuito
agreement [ə'griːmənt] *s.* **1** accordo *m.*, patto *m.* **2** contratto *m.* **3** (*gramm.*) concordanza *f.*
agricultural [ˌægrɪ'kʌltʃʊr(ə)l] *agg.* agricolo
agriculture ['ægrɪkʌltʃəʳ] *s.* agricoltura *f.*
agronomics [ˌægrə'nəmɪks] *s. pl.* (*v. al sing.*) agronomia *f.*
aground [ə'graʊnd] *agg. pred.* arenato, in secco
ahead [ə'hɛd] **A** *avv.* **1** davanti, avanti **2** in anticipo **B** *agg. pred.* in vantaggio
aid [eɪd] *s.* **1** aiuto *m.*, soccorso *m.* **2** assistenza *f.*, sovvenzione *f.* ♦ **first a.** pronto soccorso
to aid [eɪd] *v. tr.* aiutare, assistere ♦ **to a. and abet sb.** essere complice di qc.
aide [eɪd] *s.* aiutante *m.* di campo
aileron ['eɪlərən] *s.* alettone *m.*
ailing ['eɪlɪŋ] *agg.* malaticcio, sofferente
ailment ['eɪlmənt] *s.* malattia *f.*, indisposizione *f.*
aim [eɪm] *s.* **1** mira *f.* **2** scopo *m.*, finalità *f.*
to aim [eɪm] **A** *v. tr.* **1** puntare **2** indirizzare **B** *v. intr.* **1** puntare, mirare **2** aspirare a, tendere a ♦ **to a. at st.** mirare a q.c., aspirare a q.c.
aimless ['eɪmlɪs] *agg.* senza scopo
air [ɛəʳ] *s.* aria *f.* ♦ **a. conditioned** aria condizionata; **by a.** per via area; **on the a.** in onda
to air [ɛəʳ] *v. tr.* **1** arieggiare, ventilare **2** rendere noto, diffondere
airborne ['ɛəbɜːn] *agg.* aerotrasportato
aircraft ['ɛəkraːft] *s.* velivolo *m.* ♦ **a.-carrier** portaerei
airfield ['ɛəfiːld] *s.* campo *m.* di aviazione
airforce ['ɛəfɜːs] *s.* aeronautica *f.* militare
airlift ['ɛəlɪft] *s.* ponte *m.* aereo
airline ['ɛəlaɪn] *s.* linea *f.* aerea
airliner ['ɛəlaɪnəʳ] *s.* aereo *m.* di linea
airmail ['ɛəmeɪl] *s.* posta *f.* aerea
airplane ['ɛəpleɪn] *s.* aereo *m.*, aeroplano *m.*
airport ['ɛəpɜːt] *s.* aeroporto *m.*
airsickness ['ɛəsɪknɪs] *s.* mal *m.* d'aria
airspace ['ɛəspeɪs] *s.* spazio *m.* aereo
airtight ['ɛətaɪt] *agg.* ermetico
airway ['ɛəweɪ] *s.* **1** aerovia *f.* **2** compagnia *f.* aerea
airy ['ɛərɪ] *agg.* **1** arioso, ventilato **2** gaio, lieve **3** superficiale, noncurante
aisle [aɪl] *s.* **1** navata *f.* **2** passaggio *m.*, corridoio *m.*
ajar [ə'dʒaːʳ] *agg. pred.* socchiuso
akin [ə'kɪn] *agg.* consanguineo, affine
alabaster ['æləbaːstəʳ] *s.* alabastro *m.*
alacrity [ə'lækrɪty] *s.* alacrità *f.*
alarm [ə'laːm] *s.* allarme *m.* ♦ **a. clock** sveglia
alarming [ə'laːmɪŋ] *agg.* allarmante, inquietante
alarmism [ə'laːmɪzm] *s.* allarmismo *m.*
alas [ə'laːs] *inter.* ahimè
albeit [ɜːl'biːɪt] *cong.* sebbene
album ['ælbəm] *s.* album *m. inv.*
albumen ['ælbjʊmɪn] *s.* albume *m.*
alcohol ['ælkəhəl] *s.* alcol *m.*
alcoholic [ˌælkə'həlɪk] *agg.* **1** alcolico **2** alcolizzato
alcoholism ['ælkəhəlɪz(ə)m] *s.* alcolismo *m.*
ale [eɪl] *s.* birra *f.*
alert [ə'lɜːt] **A** *agg.* vigile, attento **B** *s.* allarme *m.*
to alert [ə'lɜːt] *v. tr.* mettere in guardia, avvertire
Alexandrian [ˌælɪg'zaːndrɪən] *agg.* alessandrino
alga ['ælgə] (*pl.* **algae**) *s.* alga *f.*
algebra ['ældʒɪbrə] *s.* algebra *f.*
alias ['eɪlɪæs] **A** *s.* pseudonimo *m.* **B** *avv.* alias, altrimenti detto
alibi ['ælɪbaɪ] *s.* alibi *m. inv.*
alien ['eɪljən] **A** *agg.* **1** straniero **2** alieno **B** *s.* **1** straniero *m.* **2** alieno *m.*, extraterrestre *m. e f.*
to alienate ['eɪljəneɪt] *v. tr.* alienare
alienation [ˌeɪljə'neɪʃ(ə)n] *s.* alienazione *f.*
alight [ə'laɪt] *agg. pred.* acceso
to alight [ə'laɪt] *v. intr.* scendere, smontare ♦ **to a. on** posarsi su
to align [ə'laɪn] *v. tr. e intr.* allineare, allinearsi
alike [ə'laɪk] **A** *agg. pred.* simile **B** *avv.* ugualmente, parimenti
alimentary [ˌælɪ'mɛntərɪ] *agg.* alimentare
alimony ['ælɪmənɪ] *s.* (*dir.*) alimenti *m. pl.*
alive [ə'laɪv] *agg. pred.* **1** vivo, in vita **2** attivo, vivace **3** attuale ♦ **any man a.** chiunque; **to be a. to** essere consapevole di; **to be a. with** essere pieno di, brulicare di
all [ɜːl] **A** *agg.* **1** tutto, intero **2** ogni **3**

totale, completo **B** *pron.* **1** tutto, ogni cosa **2** *pl.* tutti **C** *avv.* del tutto, completamente **D** *s.* il tutto *m.* ♦ **above a.** soprattutto; **after a.** dopotutto; **a. but** pressoché; **a. clear** cessato allarme; **a. day** tutto il giorno; **a.-in** tutto compreso; **a. of us** tutti noi; **a. right** bene, va bene; **a. the better/more** tanto meglio/più; **a. up** senza speranza; **most of a.** soprattutto; **not at a.** niente affatto, non c'è di che
to allay [ə'leɪ] *v. tr.* diminuire, alleviare
allegation [ˌælɛ'geɪʃ(ə)n] *s.* asserzione *f.*
to allege [ə'lɛdʒ] *v. tr.* asserire, dichiarare
alleged [ə'lɛdʒd] *agg.* presunto
allegiance [ə'liːdʒ(ə)ns] *s.* fedeltà *f.*, devozione *f.*
allegory ['ælɪgərɪ] *s.* allegoria *f.*
allergic [ə'lɜːdʒɪk] *agg.* allergico
allergy ['ælədʒɪ] *s.* allergia *f.*
to alleviate [ə'liːvɪeɪt] *v. tr.* alleviare, lenire, attenuare
alley ['ælɪ] *s.* vicolo *m.*
alliance [ə'laɪəns] *s.* alleanza *f.*
allied ['ælaɪd] *agg.* **1** alleato **2** connesso, affine
alligator ['ælɪgeɪtəʳ] *s.* alligatore *m.*
to allocate ['æləkeɪt] *v. tr.* distribuire, assegnare
to allot [ə'lɔt] *v. tr.* assegnare
allotment [ə'lɔtmənt] *s.* **1** assegnazione *f.* **2** porzione *f.* assegnata
all-out ['ɔːlaʊt] *agg.* (*fam.*) completo, totale
to allow [ə'laʊ] *v. tr.* **1** permettere **2** ammettere **3** concedere, accordare ♦ **to a. sb. to do st.** permettere a qc. di fare q.c.; **to a. for** tener conto di; **to be allowed** avere il permesso
allowance [ə'laʊəns] *s.* **1** indennità *f.*, assegno *m.* **2** concessione *f.* **3** sconto *m.*, detrazione *f.* **4** razione *f.* ♦ **to make allowances for st.** tenere conto di
alloy ['ælɔɪ] *s.* (*metall.*) lega *f.*
all-purpose ['ɔːlˌpɜːpəs] *agg.* per tutti gli usi
all-round ['ɔːlraʊnd] *agg.* completo, globale
all-time ['ɔːltaɪm] *agg.* massimo, assoluto
to allude [ə'luːd] *v. intr.* alludere
all-up ['ɔːlʌp] *agg. pred.* senza scampo, senza speranza
to allure [ə'ljʊəʳ] *v. tr.* attrarre, affascinare
allurement [ə'ljʊəmənt] *s.* allettamento *m.*
allusion [ə'luːʒ(ə)n] *s.* allusione *f.*
alluvial [ə'luːvjəl] *agg.* alluvionale
alluvion [ə'luːvjən] *s.* alluvione *f.*
ally [ə'laɪ] *s.* alleato *m.*
almanac ['ɔːlmənæk] *s.* almanacco *f.*
almighty [ɔːl'maɪtɪ] *agg.* onnipotente
almond ['aːmənd] *s.* mandorla *f.*
almost ['ɔːlmɒʊst] *avv.* pressoché, quasi
alms [aːmz] *s. pl.* carità *f.*, elemosina *f.* ♦ **to give a.** fare l'elemosina
aloft [ə'lɔft] *agg. pred. e avv.* in alto
alone [ə'lɒʊn] *agg. e avv.* **1** solo, da solo **2** soltanto ♦ **let a.** per non parlare di; **to leave a.** lasciare in pace
along [ə'lɔŋ] **A** *prep.* lungo, per **B** *avv.* **1** avanti, in avanti **2** insieme ♦ **all a.** per tutto il tempo, fin dall'inizio; **a. with** insieme con
alongside [əˌlɔŋ'saɪd] **A** *avv.* accanto **B** *prep.* **1** di fianco a, lungo **2** a fianco di, insieme a
aloof [ə'luːf] **A** *agg.* appartato, distaccato **B** *avv.* in disparte, a distanza, alla larga
aloud [ə'laʊd] *avv.* ad alta voce
alphabet ['ælfəbɪt] *s.* alfabeto *m.*
alpine ['ælpaɪn] *agg.* alpino
alpinism ['ælpɪnɪzəm] *s.* alpinismo *m.*
alpinist ['ælpɪnɪst] *s.* alpinista *m. e f.*
already [ɔːl'rɛdɪ] *avv.* già
also ['ɔːlsɒʊ] *avv.* anche, inoltre
altar ['ɔːltəʳ] *s.* altare *m.* ♦ **a.-piece** pala d'altare
to alter ['ɔːltəʳ] **A** *v. tr.* alterare, cambiare, modificare **B** *v. intr.* cambiare, modificarsi
alteration [ˌɔːltə'reɪʃ(ə)n] *s.* alterazione *f.*, cambiamento *m.*, modifica *f.*
altercation [ˌɔːltə'keɪʃ(ə)n] *s.* alterco *m.*, diverbio *m.*
alternate ['ɔːltɜːnɪt] *agg.* **1** alterno, alternato **2** alternativo, sostitutivo
to alternate ['ɔːltəneɪt] *v. tr. e intr.* alternare alternarsi ♦ **alternating current** corrente alternata
alternation [ˌɔːltə'neɪʃ(ə)n] *s.* alternanza *f.*
alternative [ɔːl'tɜːnətɪv] **A** *agg.* alternativo **B** *s.* alternativa *f.*
alternator ['ɔːltəneɪtəʳ] *s.* alternatore *m.*
although [ɔːl'ðɒʊ] *cong.* benché, sebbene nonostante
altitude ['æltɪtjuːd] *s.* altitudine *f.*
alto ['æltɒʊ] *s.* (*mus.*) contralto *m.*
altogether [ˌɔːltə'gɛðəʳ] *avv.* **1** del tutto, completamente **2** tutto considerato, nell'insieme

alto-rilievo [ˌæltɒʊrɪlɪˈeɪvɒʊ] *s.* altorilievo *m.*
altruism [ˈæltrʊɪz(ə)m] *s.* altruismo *m.*
aluminium [ˌæljʊˈmɪnjəm] (*USA* **aluminum**) *s.* alluminio *m.*
always [ˈɜːlwəz] *avv.* sempre
to amalgamate [əˈmælgəmeɪt] *v. tr. e intr.* amalgamare, amalgamarsi
to amass [əˈmæs] *v. tr.* ammassare, accumulare
amateur [ˈæmətɜːʳ] *agg.* dilettante
amateurish [ˌæməˈtɜːrɪʃ] *agg.* dilettantesco
to amaze [əˈmeɪz] *v. tr.* meravigliare, sorprendere ♦ **to be amazed at st.** stupirsi di q.c.
amazement [əˈmeɪzmənt] *s.* meraviglia *f.*, stupore *m.*
amazing [əˈmeɪzɪŋ] *agg.* sorprendente, sbalorditivo
ambassador [æmˈbæsədəʳ] *s.* ambasciatore *m.*
amber [ˈæmbəʳ] *s.* ambra *f.*
ambergris [ˈæmbəgrɪ(ː)s] *s.* ambra *f.* grigia
ambience [ˈæmbjəns] *s.* ambiente *m.*, atmosfera *f.*
ambiguity [ˌæmbɪˈgjʊɪtɪ] *s.* ambiguità *f.*
ambiguous [æmˈbɪgjʊəs] *agg.* ambiguo
ambition [æmˈbɪʃ(ə)n] *s.* ambizione *f.*
ambitious [æmˈbɪʃəs] *agg.* ambizioso
amble [ˈæmbl] *s.* ambio *m.*
to amble [ˈæmbl] *v. intr.* **1** andare all'ambio **2** camminare lentamente
ambulance [ˈæmbjʊləns] *s.* ambulanza *f.*
ambulatory [ˈæmbjʊlətərɪ] **A** *agg.* ambulatorio **B** *s.* (*arch.*) ambulacro *m.*
ambush [ˈæmbʊʃ] *s.* imboscata *f.*
to ambush [ˈæmbʊʃ] *v. tr.* tendere un'imboscata a
amenable [əˈmiːnəbl] *agg.* **1** responsabile **2** soggetto a **3** riferibile, riconducibile
to amend [əˈmɛnd] *v. tr.* emendare, correggere
amends [əˈmɛndz] *s. pl.* ammenda *f.*
amenity [əˈmiːnɪtɪ] *s.* **1** amenità *f.* **2** *al pl.* attrattive *f. pl.*
American [əˈmɛrɪkən] *agg. e s.* americano *m.*
Amerind [ˈæmərɪnd] *agg. e s.* amerindio *m.*
amethyst [ˈæmɪθɪst] *s.* ametista *f.*
amiable [ˈeɪmjəbl] *agg.* affabile, simpatico
amiantus [æmɪˈæntəs] *s.* amianto *m.*
amicable [ˈæmɪkəbl] *agg.* amichevole
amid(st) [əˈmɪd(st)] *prep.* fra, tra, nel mezzo di
amiss [əˈmɪs] **A** *agg.* **1** sbagliato **2** fuori luogo, inopportuno **B** *avv.* **1** male, erroneamente **2** inopportunamente ♦ **to take it a.** aversene a male
ammonia [əˈmɒʊnjə] *s.* ammoniaca *f.*
ammunition [ˌæmjʊˈnɪʃ(ə)n] *s.* **1** (*mil.*) munizioni *f. pl.* **2** (*fig.*) materiale *m.*
amnesia [æmˈniːzjə] *s.* amnesia *f.*
amnesty [ˈæmnɛstɪ] *s.* amnistia *f.*
among(st) [əˈmʌŋ(st)] *prep.* **1** fra, tra, in mezzo a **2** rispetto a
amoral [æˈmərəl] *agg.* amorale
amorous [ˈæmərəs] *agg.* amoroso
amortization [əˌmɜːtɪˈzeɪʃ(ə)n] *s.* ammortamento *m.*
to amortize [əˈmɜːtaɪz] *v. tr.* ammortizzare
amount [əˈmaʊnt] *s.* **1** ammontare *m.*, importo *m.* **2** quantità *f.*
to amount [əˈmaʊnt] *v. intr.* **1** ammontare **2** equivalere
ampersand [ˈæmpəsænd] *s.* 'e' *f.* commerciale (&)
amphetamine [æmˈfɛtəmiːn] *s.* anfetamina *f.*
amphibian [æmˈfɪbɪən] *agg.* anfibio
amphitheatre [ˈæmfɪˌθɪətəʳ] *s.* anfiteatro *m.*
amphora [ˈæmfərə] *s.* anfora *f.*
ample [ˈæmpl] *agg.* **1** ampio, spazioso **2** sufficiente, bastevole
amplifier [ˈæmplɪfaɪəʳ] *s.* amplificatore *m.*
to amplify [ˈæmplɪfaɪ] *v. tr.* **1** aumentare, allargare **2** amplificare
to amputate [ˈæmpjʊteɪt] *v. tr.* amputare
amulet [ˈæmjʊlɪt] *s.* amuleto *m.*
to amuse [əˈmjuːz] *v. tr.* divertire
amusement [əˈmjuːzmənt] *s.* divertimento *m.*, svago *m.* ♦ **a. arcade** sala giochi; **a. park** lunapark
amusing [əˈmjuːzɪŋ] *agg.* divertente
an [æn, ən] *art. indeterm.* → **a**
anachronism [əˈnækrənɪz(ə)m] *s.* anacronismo *m.*
anachronistic [əˌnækrəˈnɪstɪk] *agg.* anacronistico
an(a)emia [əˈniːmjə] *s.* anemia *f.*
an(a)emic [əˈniːmɪk] *agg.* anemico
an(a)esthesia [ˌænɪsˈθiːzjə] *s.* anestesia *f.*
an(a)esthetic [ˌænɪsˈθɛtɪk] *agg. e s.* anestetico *m.*
to an(a)esthetize [æˈniːsθɪtaɪz] *v. tr.* anestetizzare

anagram ['ænəgræm] *s.* anagramma *m.*
analgesic [ˌænæl'dʒiːsɪk] *agg. e s.* analgesico *m.*, antidolorifico *m.*
analogous [ə'næləgəs] *agg.* analogo
analog(ue) ['ænəlæg] *agg.* analogico
analogy [ə'nælədʒɪ] *s.* analogia *f.*
to analyse ['ænəlaɪz] (*USA* **analyze**) *v. tr.* **1** analizzare **2** (*USA*) psicoanalizzare
analysis [ə'næləsɪs] (*pl.* **analyses**) *s.* analisi *f.*
analyst ['ænəlɪst] *s.* analista *m. e f.*
anarchism ['ænəkɪz(ə)m] *s.* anarchia *f.*
anarchist ['ænəkɪst] *s.* anarchico *m.*
anarchy ['ænəkɪ] *s.* anarchia *f.*
anathema [ə'næθɪmə] *s.* **1** anatema *m.* **2** cosa *f.* detestabile
anatomy [ə'nætəmɪ] *s.* anatomia *f.*
ancestor ['ænsɪstəʳ] *s.* antenato *m.*
ancestry ['ænsɪstrɪ] *s.* ascendenza *f.*, schiatta *f.*
anchor ['æŋkəʳ] *s.* ancora *f.* ♦ **to drop a.** ancorare, gettare l'ancora; **to weigh a.** salpare, levare l'ancora
to anchor ['æŋkəʳ] *v. tr. e intr.* ancorare, ancorarsi
anchorage ['æŋkərɪdʒ] *s.* ancoraggio *m.*
anchovy ['æntʃɒvɪ] *s.* acciuga *f.*
ancient ['eɪnʃ(ə)nt] *agg.* antico ♦ **in a. times** anticamente
ancillary [æn'sɪlərɪ] *agg.* ausiliario, accessorio
and [ænd, ən(d)] *cong.* **1** e, ed **2** (*tra due comp.*) sempre più (ES: **farther a. farther** sempre più lontano) **3** (*tra due v.*) a, di (ES: **try a. come next Friday** cerca di venire venerdì) ♦ **a. so on** eccetera; **a. yet** eppure
anecdote ['ænɪkdɒʊt] *s.* aneddoto *m.*
anemometer [ˌænɪ'məmɪtəʳ] *s.* anemometro *m.*
aneurism ['ænjʊ(ə)rɪz(ə)m] *s.* aneurisma *m.*
anew [ə'njuː] *avv.* di nuovo ♦ **to begin a.** ricominciare
angel ['eɪn(d)ʒ(ə)l] *s.* angelo *m.*
anger ['æŋgəʳ] *s.* collera *f.*, rabbia *f.*
angina [æn'dʒaɪnə] *s.* angina *f.*
angle ['æŋgl] *s.* angolo *m.*
Anglican ['æŋglɪkən] *agg.* anglicano
anglicism ['æŋglɪsɪz(ə)m] *s.* anglicismo *m.*, inglesismo *m.*
angling ['æŋglɪŋ] *s.* pesca *f.* con la lenza
Anglo-Saxon [ˌæŋglɒ(ʊ)'sæks(ə)n] *agg. e s.* anglosassone *m. e f.*
angora [æŋ'gɜːrə] *s.* angora *f.*
angry ['æŋgrɪ] *agg.* arrabbiato, rabbioso ♦ **to be a. with sb., at st.** essere arrabbiato con qc., per q.c.; **to get a.** arrabbiarsi; **to make sb. a.** far arrabbiare qc.
anguish ['æŋgwɪʃ] *s.* angoscia *f.*
angular ['æŋgjʊləʳ] *agg.* angolare
animal ['ænɪm(ə)l] *agg. e s.* animale *m.*
animate ['ænɪmɪt] *agg.* animato
animated ['ænɪmeɪtɪd] *agg.* animato, movimentato
animator ['ænɪmeɪtəʳ] *s.* animatore *m.*
anise ['ænɪs] *s.* anice *m.*
aniseed ['ænɪsiːd] *s.* semi *m. pl.* di anice
ankle ['æŋkl] *s.* caviglia *f.*
to annex [ə'nɛks] *v. tr.* **1** allegare **2** annettere
to annihilate [ə'naɪəleɪt] *v. tr.* annientare, annichilire
anniversary [ˌænɪ'vɜːs(ə)rɪ] *s.* anniversario *m.*
annotation [ˌænɒ(ʊ)'teɪʃ(ə)n] *s.* annotazione *f.*, nota *f.*
to announce [ə'naʊns] *v. tr.* annunciare
announcement [ə'naʊnsmənt] *s.* avviso *m.*, annuncio *m.*
announcer [ə'naʊnsəʳ] *s.* annunciatore *m.*, presentatore *m.*
to annoy [ə'nəɪ] *v. tr.* importunare, infastidire
annoyance [ə'nəɪəns] *s.* seccatura *f.*, fastidio *m.*
annoyed [ə'nəɪd] *agg.* infastidito ♦ **to get a.** infastidirsi, irritarsi
annoying [ə'nəɪɪŋ] *agg.* fastidioso, molesto, seccante
annual ['ænjʊəl] **A** *agg.* annuale **B** *s.* **1** pianta *f.* annuale **2** annuario *m.*
annually ['ænjʊəlɪ] *avv.* annualmente
annuity [ə'njʊɪtɪ] *s.* annualità *f.*, rendita *f.* annua ♦ **life a.** vitalizio
to annul [ə'nʌl] *v. tr.* annullare
annulment [ə'nʌlmənt] *s.* annullamento *m.*
anomalous [ə'nəmələs] *agg.* anomalo
anonymous [ə'nənɪməs] *agg.* anonimo
anorak ['ænəræk] *s.* giacca *f.* a vento
anorexia [ˌænɒ(ʊ)'rɛksɪə] *s.* anoressia *f.*
another [ə'nʌðəʳ] **A** *agg.* **1** un altro, uno in più **2** diverso, differente **3** un altro simile, un secondo **B** *pron. indef.* **1** un altro, uno in più **2** un altro, differente ♦ **one a.** l'un l'altro, reciprocamente
answer ['aːnsəʳ] *s.* risposta *f.*, responso *m.*

to answer ['aːnsəʳ] *v. tr. e intr.* rispondere (a) ♦ **to a. back** controbattere; **to a. for** essere responsabile di; **to a. the telephone** rispondere al telefono; **answering machine** segreteria telefonica
answerable ['aːns(ə)rəbl] *agg. pred.* responsabile
ant [ænt] *s.* formica *f.*
antagonism [æn'tægənɪz(ə)m] *s.* antagonismo *m.*
antagonist [æn'tægənɪst] *s.* antagonista *m. e f.*, avversario *m.*
antagonistic [æn,tægə'nɪstɪk] *agg.* antagonistico
to antagonize [æn'tægənaɪz] *v. tr.* contrapporsi a, inimicarsi
Antarctic [ænt'aːktɪk] *agg.* antartico
antecedent [,æntɪ'siːd(ə)nt] *agg.* antecedente
antechamber ['æntɪ,tʃeɪmbəʳ] *s.* anticamera *f.*
antelope ['æntɪlɒʊp] *s.* antilope *f.*
antenatal [,æntɪ'neɪtl] *agg.* prenatale
anteroom ['æntɪrʊm] *s.* anticamera *f.*
anthem ['ænθəm] *s.* inno *m.*
anthology [æn'θələdʒɪ] *s.* antologia *f.*
anthropological [,ænθrəpə'lədʒɪk(ə)l] *agg.* antropologico
anthropologist [,ænθrə'pələdʒɪst] *s.* antropologo *m.*
anthropology [,ænθrə'pələdʒɪ] *s.* antropologia *f.*
anthropomorphous [,ænθrəpə'mɜːfəs] *agg.* antropomorfo
antiallergic [,æntɪə'lɜːdʒɪk] *agg. e s.* antiallergico *m.*
antibiotic [,æntɪbaɪ'ətɪk] *agg. e s.* antibiotico *m.*
antibody ['æntɪ,bədɪ] *s.* anticorpo *m.*
to anticipate [æn'tɪsɪpeɪt] *v. tr.* **1** anticipare **2** prevedere, pregustare **3** prevenire, precedere
anticipation [æn,tɪsɪ'peɪʃ(ə)n] *s.* anticipo *m.*
anticlerical [,æntɪ'klɛrɪkl] *agg.* anticlericale
anticlockwise [,æntɪ'kləkwaɪz] *agg. e avv.* in senso antiorario
anticonstitutional [,æntɪ,kənstɪ'tjʊʃən(ə)l] *agg.* anticostituzionale
antics ['æntɪks] *s. pl.* buffonate *f. pl.*
anticyclone [,æntɪ'saɪklɒʊn] *s.* anticiclone *m.*
antidepressant [,æntɪdɪ'prɛs(ə)nt] *agg. e s.* antidepressivo *m.*
antifreeze [,æntɪ'friːz] *s.* antigelo *m.*
antifreezing [,æntɪ'friːzɪŋ] *agg.* anticongelante
antihistamine [,æntɪ'hɪstəmiːn] *agg. e s.* antistaminico *m.*
antineuralgic [,æntɪnjʊ'rældʒɪk] *agg e s.* antinevralgico *m.*
antiquarian [,æntɪ'kwɛərɪən] *s.* antiquario *m.*
antiquated [æntɪ'kweɪtɪd] *agg.* antiquato
antique [æn'tiːk] **A** *agg.* antico **B** *s.* antichità *f.* ♦ **a. trade** antiquariato
antiquity [æn'tɪkwɪtɪ] *s.* antichità *f.*
antirabic [,æntɪ'ræbɪk] *agg.* antirabbico
antirheumatic [,æntɪruː'mætɪk] *agg. e s.* antireumatico *m.*
antirust [,æntɪ'rʌst] *agg.* antiruggine
anti-Semitism [,æntɪ'sɛmɪtɪz(ə)m] *s.* antisemitismo *m.*
antiseptic [,æntɪ'sɛptɪk] *agg.* antisettico
antisocial [,æntɪ'sɒʊʃ(ə)l] *agg.* antisociale
antonomasia [,æntənɒʊ'meɪʃɪə] *s.* antonomasia *f.*
anus ['eɪnəs] *s.* ano *m.*
anvil ['ænvɪl] *s.* incudine *f.*
anxiety [æŋ'zaɪətɪ] *s.* ansia *f.*
anxious ['æŋ(k)ʃəs] *agg.* ansioso
any ['ɛnɪ] **A** *agg.* **1** (*in frasi neg., interr., dubit. e condiz.*) alcuno, alcuna, alcuni, alcune, del, della, dei, delle, un po' di (ES: **have you got a. cigarettes?** hai delle sigarette?) **2** (*in frasi afferm.*) qualsiasi, qualunque (ES: **come at a. time** vieni in qualunque momento) **B** *pron. indef.* **1** (*in frasi neg., interr., dubit. e condiz.*) alcuno, qualcuno, nessuno, ne (ES: **I haven't a.** non ne ho) **2** (*in frasi afferm.*) chiunque, uno, una, qualunque (ES: **take a. of these books** prendi uno qualsiasi di questi libri) **C** *avv.* un po', in qualche misura (ES: **is he a. better today?** sta un po' meglio oggi?)
anybody ['ɛnɪ,bədɪ] *pron. indef.* **1** (*in frasi neg., interr., dubit. e condiz.*) qualcuno, taluno, nessuno (ES: **is a. coming with me?** c'è qualcuno che viene con me?) **2** (*in frasi afferm.*) chiunque (ES: **a. can understand that** chiunque può capirlo)
anyhow ['ɛnɪhaʊ] *avv.* **1** comunque, non importa come **2** in ogni caso, a ogni modo
anyone ['ɛnɪwʌn] *pron. indef.* → **anybody**
anything ['ɛnɪθɪŋ] *pron. indef.* **1** (*in frasi neg., interr., dubit. e condiz.*) qualche cosa, alcuna cosa, niente (ES: **can you hear a.?**

senti niente?) **2** (*in frasi afferm.*) qualunque cosa, qualsiasi cosa (ES: **a. is better than nothing** qualunque cosa è meglio di niente)
anytime ['ɛnɪtaɪm] *avv.* in qualsiasi momento
anyway ['ɛnɪweɪ] *avv.* → **anyhow**
anywhere ['ɛnɪwɛəʳ] *avv.* **1** (*in frasi neg., interr., dubit. e condiz.*) in qualche luogo, da qualche parte, in nessun luogo, da nessuna parte (ES: **are you going a.?** stai andando da qualche parte?) **2** (*in frasi afferm.*) dovunque, in qualsiasi luogo (ES: **you can stay a.** puoi stare ovunque)
apart [ə'paːt] *avv.* **1** a parte, a una certa distanza **2** separatamente ♦ **a. from** oltre a; **to take a machine a.** smontare una macchina; **to tell a.** distinguere
apartment [ə'paːtmənt] *s.* appartamento *m.*, camera *f.* ♦ **a. building** condominio
apathetic [ˌæpə'θɛtɪk] *agg.* apatico
ape [eɪp] *s.* scimmia *f.*
aperitif [ɑ(ː)pərɪ(ː)'tiːf] *s.* aperitivo *m.*
aperture ['æpətjʊəʳ] *s.* apertura *f.*
apex ['eɪpɛks] *s.* apice *m.*
aphorism ['æfərɪz(ə)m] *s.* aforisma *m.*
aphrodisiac [ˌæfrɒ(ʊ)'dɪzɪæk] *agg. e s.* afrodisiaco *m.*
apiculture ['eɪpɪkʌltʃəʳ] *s.* apicoltura *f.*
apiece [ə'piːs] *avv.* a testa, per ciascuno
apnea [æp'niːə] *s.* apnea *f.*
apocryphal [ə'pɒkrɪfəl] *agg.* apocrifo
apologetic [əˌpɒlə'dʒɛtɪk] *agg.* di scusa
to apologize [ə'pɒlədʒaɪz] *v. intr.* scusarsi, chiedere scusa
apology [ə'pɒlədʒɪ] *s.* scusa *f.* ♦ **to make an a.** fare le proprie scuse
apostle [ə'pɒsl] *s.* apostolo *m.*
apostrophe [ə'pɒstrəfɪ] *s.* apostrofo *m.*
to appal [ə'pɜːl] *v. tr.* atterrire, spaventare
appalling [ə'pɜːlɪŋ] *agg.* orrendo, terribile
apparatus [ˌæpə'reɪtəs] *s.* apparato *m.*
apparel [ə'pær(ə)l] *s.* **1** paramenti *m. pl.* **2** (*USA*) abbigliamento *m.*, vestiti *m. pl.*
apparent [ə'pær(ə)nt] *agg.* **1** evidente, manifesto **2** apparente
apparently [ə'pær(ə)ntlɪ] *avv.* **1** evidentemente, ovviamente **2** apparentemente
apparition [ˌæpə'rɪʃ(ə)n] *s.* apparizione *f.*
appeal [ə'piːl] *s.* **1** appello *m.*, supplica *f.* **2** attrattiva *f.*
to appeal [ə'piːl] *v. intr.* **1** fare appello **2** attrarre, piacere
to appear [ə'pɪəʳ] *v. intr.* **1** apparire, sembrare **2** (*dir.*) comparire, presentarsi (in giudizio) **3** apparire, mostrarsi
appearance [ə'pɪər(ə)ns] *s.* **1** apparizione *f.*, comparsa *f.* **2** parvenza *f.*, aspetto *m.*
to appease [ə'piːz] *v. tr.* calmare, placare
to append [ə'pɛnd] *v. tr.* **1** apporre **2** aggiungere, allegare, attaccare
appendicitis [əˌpɛndɪ'saɪtɪs] *s.* appendicite *f.*
appendix [ə'pɛndɪks] (*pl.* **appendices, appendixes**) *s.* appendice *f.*
appetite ['æpɪtaɪt] *s.* appetito *m.*
appetizer ['æpɪtaɪzəʳ] *s.* antipasto *m.*
appetizing ['æpɪtaɪzɪŋ] *agg.* appetitoso
to applaud [ə'plɜːd] *v. tr. e intr.* applaudire
applause [ə'plɜːz] *s.* applauso *m.*
apple ['æpl] *s.* mela *f.* ♦ **a.-pie** torta di mele
appliance [ə'plaɪəns] *s.* apparecchio *m.*, strumento *m.* ♦ **household a.** elettrodomestico
applicant ['æplɪkənt] *s.* candidato *m.*
application [ˌæplɪ'keɪʃ(ə)n] *s.* **1** applicazione *f.* **2** richiesta *f.*, istanza *f.* ♦ **a. form** modulo di domanda
applied [ə'plaɪd] *agg.* applicato
to apply [ə'plaɪ] **A** *v. tr.* **1** applicare **2** azionare **B** *v. intr.* **1** rivolgersi, inoltrare domanda **2** riguardare, concernere ♦ **to a. for** fare domanda per; **to a. to** rivolgersi a, riferirsi a; **to a. oneself** applicarsi, indirizzarsi
to appoint [ə'pɔɪnt] *v. tr.* **1** designare, nominare, eleggere **2** stabilire, fissare **3** prescrivere, ordinare
appointee [əpɔɪn'tɪ] *s.* incaricato *m.*
appointment [ə'pɔɪntmənt] *s.* **1** appuntamento *m.* **2** nomina *f.* **3** incarico *m.*, carica *f.* **4** prescrizione *f.*, decreto *m.*
appraisal [ə'preɪz(ə)l] *s.* perizia *f.*, stima *f.*
to appraise [ə'preɪz] *v. tr.* valutare, stimare
to appreciate [ə'priːʃɪeɪt] **A** *v. tr.* **1** apprezzare, stimare **2** rendersi conto di **B** *v. intr.* aumentare di valore
appreciation [əˌpriːʃɪ'eɪʃ(ə)n] *s.* **1** apprezzamento *m.*, valutazione *f.* **2** (*fin.*) rivalutazione *f.*
to apprehend [ˌæprɪ'hɛnd] *v. tr.* **1** arrestare **2** afferrare, comprendere
apprehension [ˌæprɪ'hɛnʃ(ə)n] *s.* apprensione *f.*
apprehensive [ˌæprɪ'hɛnsɪv] *agg.* apprensivo
apprentice [ə'prɛntɪs] *s.* apprendista *m.*

e *f.*
apprenticeship [ə'prɛntɪʃɪp] *s.* apprendistato *m.*, tirocinio *m.*
approach [ə'prɒʊtʃ] *s.* **1** avvicinamento *m.*, approccio *m.* **2** accesso *m.*
to approach [ə'prɒʊtʃ] **A** *v. intr.* avvicinarsi **B** *v. tr.* **1** avvicinare, accostare **2** rivolgersi a
approachable [ə'prɒʊtʃəbl] *agg.* **1** accessibile, avvicinabile **2** disponibile
appropriate [ə'prɒʊprɪɪt] *agg.* appropriato, opportuno
to appropriate [ə'prɒʊprɪeɪt] *v. tr.* **1** appropriarsi, impadronirsi di **2** accantonare, stanziare
approval [ə'pruːv(ə)l] *s.* **1** approvazione *f.* **2** prova *f.*, esame *m.*
to approve [ə'pruːv] *v. tr. e intr.* approvare
approximate [ə'prəks(ɪ)mɪt] *agg.* **1** approssimato **2** approssimativo
approximately [ə'prəksɪmɪtlɪ] *avv.* approssimativamente, circa
après-ski [ˌæpreɪ'skiː] *agg.* doposcì
apricot ['eɪprɪkət] *s.* albicocca *f.*
April ['eɪpr(ə)l] *s.* aprile *m.*
apron ['eɪpr(ə)n] *s.* **1** grembiule *m.* **2** (*teatro*) ribalta *f.*
apse [æps] *s.* abside *f.*
apt [æpt] *agg.* **1** adatto **2** pronto, intelligente **3** propenso, soggetto
apterous ['æptərəs] *agg.* aptero
aptitude ['æptɪtjuːd] *s.* **1** abilità *f.* **2** attitudine *f.*, propensione *f.* **3** prontezza *f.*
aqualung ['ækwəlʌŋ] *s.* autorespiratore *m.*
aquamarine [ˌækwəmə'riːn] *s.* acquamarina *f.*
aquarium [ə'kwɛərɪəm] *s.* acquario *m.*
Aquarius [ə'kwɛərɪəs] *s.* (*astr.*) acquario *m.*
aquatic [ə'kwætɪk] *agg.* acquatico
aqueduct ['ækwɪdʌkt] *s.* acquedotto *m.*
Arab ['ærəb] *agg. e s.* arabo *m.*
arabesque [ˌærə'bɛsk] *s.* arabesco *m.*
Arabian [ə'reɪbjən] *agg.* arabo, arabico
Arabic ['ærəbɪk] **A** *agg.* arabo, arabico **B** *s.* arabo *m.* (*lingua*) ♦ **A. numerals** numeri arabi
arbiter ['aːbɪtəʳ] *s.* arbitro *m.*
arbitrary ['aːbɪtrərɪ] *agg.* arbitrario
to arbitrate ['aːbɪtreɪt] *v. tr. e intr.* arbitrare
arboreal [aː'bɜːrɪəl] *agg.* arboreo
arboriculture ['aːbərɪˌkʌltʃəʳ] *s.* arboricoltura *f.*
arc [aːk] *s.* arco *m.*
arcade [aː'keɪd] *s.* **1** arcata *f.* **2** galleria *f.*, porticato *m.*
Arcadian [aː'keɪdjən] *agg.* arcadico
arcane [aː'keɪn] *agg.* arcano
arch (1) [aːtʃ] *s.* arco *m.*, arcata *f.*
arch (2) [aːtʃ] *agg.* **1** arci-, principale, superiore **2** astuto, malizioso
archaeologic [ˌaːkɪə'lədʒɪk] *agg.* archeologico
archaeologist [ˌaːkɪ'ələdʒɪst] *s.* archeologo *m.*
archaeology [ˌaːkɪ'ələdʒɪ] *s.* archeologia *f.*
archaic [aː'keɪɪk] *agg.* arcaico
archangel ['aːkˌeɪn(d)ʒ(ə)l] *s.* arcangelo *m.*
archbishop [ˌaːtʃ'bɪʃəp] *s.* arcivescovo *m.*
archer ['aːtʃəʳ] *s.* arciere *m.*
archery ['aːtʃərɪ] *s.* tiro *m.* con l'arco
archetype ['aːkɪtaɪp] *s.* archetipo *m.*
archipelago [ˌaːkɪ'pɛlɪgɒʊ] *s.* arcipelago *m.*
architect ['aːkɪtɛkt] *s.* architetto *m.*
architectonic [ˌaːkɪtɛk'tənɪk] *agg.* architettonico
architecture ['aːkɪtɛkʃəʳ] *s.* architettura *f.*
architrave ['aːkɪtreɪv] *s.* architrave *m.*
archive ['aːkaɪv] *s.* archivio *m.*
archivolt ['aːkɪvɒʊlt] *s.* archivolto *m.*
Arctic ['aːktɪk] *agg.* artico
ardent ['aːdənt] *agg.* ardente, appassionato, fervente
arduous ['aːdjʊəs] *agg.* arduo, difficile
are [aːʳ] *s.* (*misura*) ara *f.*
area ['ɛərɪə] *s.* area *f.*, zona *f.* ♦ **a. code** prefisso telefonico
arena [ə'riːnə] *s.* arena *f.*
argil ['aːdʒɪl] *s.* argilla *f.*
arguable ['aːgjʊəb(ə)l] *agg.* sostenibile, discutibile
to argue ['aːgjuː] **A** *v. intr.* **1** ragionare, argomentare **2** disputare, discutere, litigare **B** *v. tr.* **1** provare, dimostrare **2** persuadere ♦ **to a sb. into doing st.** persuadere qc. a fare q.c.
argument ['aːgjʊmənt] *s.* **1** argomento *m.* **2** contesa *f.*, disputa *f.*
argumentative [ˌaːgjʊ'mɛntətɪv] *agg.* polemico, litigioso
arid ['ærɪd] *agg.* arido
Aries ['ɛəriːz] *s.* (*astr.*) ariete *m.*
to arise [ə'raɪz] (*pass.* **arose**, *p. p.* **arisen**) *v. intr.* **1** sorgere, alzarsi, levarsi **2** risultare,

derivare **3** presentarsi
aristocracy [ˌærɪs'tɔkrəsɪ] *s.* aristocrazia *f.*
aristocrat ['ærɪstəˌkræt] *s.* aristocratico *m.*
aristocratic(al) [ˌærɪstə'krætɪk((ə)l)] *agg.* aristocratico
arithmetic [ˌərɪθ'mətɪk] *s.* aritmetica *f.*
arithmetic(al) [ˌærɪθ'mɛtɪk((ə)l)] *agg.* aritmetico
ark [aːk] *s.* arca *f.*
arm (1) [aːm] *s.* **1** braccio *m.* **2** bracciolo *m.* **3** manica *f.*
arm (2) [aːm] *s.* **1** *al pl.* armi *f. pl.*, armamenti *m. pl.* **2** arma *f.* (*dell'esercito*) ♦ **to bear arms** essere sotto le armi; **to take up arms** prendere le armi
to arm [aːm] *v. tr. e intr.* armare, armarsi
armament ['aːməmənt] *s.* armamento *m.*
armchair ['aːmˌtʃɛəʳ] *s.* poltrona *f.*
armed [aːmd] *agg.* armato ♦ **a. robbery** rapina a mano armata
armful ['aːmfʊl] *s.* bracciata *f.*
armistice ['aːmɪstɪs] *s.* armistizio *m.*
armour ['aːməʳ] *s.* armatura *f.*, corazza *f.*
to armour ['aːməʳ] *v. tr.* corazzare, blindare ♦ **armoured car** autoblindo
armoury ['aːmərɪ] *s.* armeria *f.*
armpit ['aːmpɪt] *s.* ascella *f.*
armrest ['aːmˌrɛst] *s.* bracciolo *m.*
army ['aːmɪ] *s.* esercito *m.* ♦ **a. corps** corpo d'armata
aroma [ə'rɒʊmə] *s.* aroma *m.*
aromatic [ˌærɒ(ʊ)'mætɪk] *agg.* aromatico
arose [ə'rɒʊz] *pass. di* **to arise**
around [ə'raʊnd] **A** *avv.* **1** intorno, da ogni parte **2** in giro **3** circa **B** *prep.* attorno a, intorno a ♦ **all a.** tutt'intorno
to arouse [ə'raʊz] *v. tr.* **1** svegliare **2** provocare, suscitare
to arrange [ə'reɪn(d)ʒ] **A** *v. tr.* **1** ordinare, sistemare **2** preparare, disporre, stabilire **3** (*mus.*) arrangiare **B** *v. intr.* accordarsi ♦ **to a. to do st.** accordarsi per fare q.c.
arrangement [ə'reɪn(d)ʒmənt] *s.* **1** sistemazione *f.*, disposizione *f.*, ordinamento *m.* **2** piano *m.*, progetto *m.*, preparativo *m.* **3** accordo *m.* **4** (*mus.*) arrangiamento *m.*
array [ə'reɪ] *s.* **1** assortimento *m.* **2** (*mil.*) schieramento *m.*, spiegamento *m.* **3** schiera *f.* **4** insieme *m.*
to array [ə'reɪ] *v. tr.* **1** ordinare, disporre, schierare **2** adornare, addobbare
arrear [ə'rɪəʳ] **A** *agg.* arretrato **B** *s.* **1** *al pl.* arretrati *m. pl.* **2** lavoro *m.* arretrato
arrest [ə'rɛst] *s.* **1** arresto *m.*, fermo *m.* **2** fermata *f.* ♦ **under a.** in arresto
to arrest [ə'rɛst] *v. tr.* **1** arrestare, catturare **2** fermare **3** attirare (l'attenzione)
arrival [ə'raɪv(ə)l] *s.* arrivo *m.*
to arrive [ə'raɪv] *v. intr.* **1** arrivare, giungere **2** raggiungere il successo, arrivare
arrogant ['ærəgənt] *agg.* arrogante, prepotente
arrow ['ærɒʊ] *s.* freccia *f.*
arsenal ['aːsɪnl] *s.* arsenale *m.*
arson ['aːs(ə)n] *s.* (*dir.*) incendio *m.* doloso
art [aːt] *s.* arte *f.* ♦ **a. gallery** galleria d'arte; **Arts** lettere; **a. school** scuola d'arte
artefact [ˌaːtɪ'fækt] (*USA* **artifact**) *s.* manufatto *m.*
arterial [aː'tɪərɪəl] *agg.* arterioso
arteriosclerosis [aːˌtɪərɪɒʊsklɪə'rɒʊsɪs] *s.* arteriosclerosi *f.*
artery ['aːtərɪ] *s.* arteria *f.*
artful ['aːtf(ʊ)l] *agg.* **1** astuto, furbo **2** abile
arthritis [aː'θraɪtɪs] *s.* artrite *f.*
artichoke ['aːtɪtʃɒʊk] *s.* carciofo *m.*
article ['aːtɪkl] *s.* **1** articolo *m.* **2** *spec. al pl.* regolamenti *m. pl.*, statuto *m.*
articulate [aː'tɪkjʊlɛt] *agg.* **1** articolato **2** (*di parola*) distinto **3** (*di persona*) eloquente
to articulate [aː'tɪkjʊleɪt] *v. tr.* **1** articolare **2** pronunciare distintamente, scandire
articulated [aː'tɪkjʊleɪtɪd] *agg.* articolato
artifact ['aːtɪfækt] *s.* (*USA*) → **artefact**
artifice ['aːtɪfɪs] *s.* artificio *m.*, stratagemma *m.*
artificial [ˌaːtɪ'fɪʃ(ə)l] *agg.* artificiale
artillery [aː'tɪlərɪ] *s.* artiglieria *f.*
artisan [ˌaːtɪ'zæn] *s.* artigiano *m.*
artist ['aːtɪst] *s.* artista *m. e f.*
artistic [aː'tɪstɪk] *agg.* artistico
artless ['aːtlɪs] *agg.* semplice, ingenuo
as [æz, ëz] **A** *avv. e cong.* **1** (*in frasi comp.*) come **2 as ... as, so ... as** così ... come, tanto ... quanto **B** *cong.* **1** (*temporale*) quando, mentre (ES: **as he was eating** mentre mangiava) **2** (*causale*) poiché, dal momento che (ES: **as it was raining, we caught a bus** poiché pioveva, prendemmo l'autobus) **3** (*concessiva*) sebbene (ES: **handsome as he is, he is not happy** sebbene sia bello, non è felice) **4** (*modale*) come, secondo (ES: **do as I did** fa' come me) **5** in qualità di, come (ES: **I'm talking**

to you as a friend ti parlo come amico) **6** (*relativo*) che, quale (ES: **you have the same chances as I had** hai le stesse possibilità che ho avuto io) ♦ **as far as** fino a, per quanto; **as if** come se; **as long as** per tutto il tempo che; **as many** altrettanti; **as much** altrettanto; **as soon as** appena; **as usual** come al solito; **as well as** come pure
to ascend [ə'sɛnd] *v. tr.* **1** salire, ascendere **2** risalire
ascending [ə'sɛndɪŋ] *agg.* ascendente
ascent [ə'sɛnt] *s.* **1** ascensione *f.*, ascesa *f.* **2** salita *f.*, pendio *m.*
to ascertain [ˌæsə'teɪn] *v. tr.* accertare, constatare
asceticism [ə'sɛtɪsɪz(ə)m] *s.* ascetismo *m.*
ascribable [əs'kraɪbəbl] *agg.* attribuibile
to ascribe [əs'kraɪb] *v. tr.* attribuire
ash (1) [æʃ] *s.* frassino *m.*
ash (2) [æʃ] *s.* cenere *f.* ♦ **A. Wednesday** mercoledì delle ceneri
ashamed [ə'ʃeɪmd] *agg.* vergognoso ♦ **to be a. of st.** vergognarsi di q.c.
ashen ['æʃn] *agg.* cinereo, livido
ashlar ['æʃlərʳ] *s.* (*arch.*) bugnato *m.*
ashore [ə'ʃɜːʳ] *avv.* a riva, a terra
ashtray ['æʃtreɪ] *s.* portacenere *m. inv.*
Asian ['eɪʃ(ə)n] *agg. e s.* asiatico *m.*
Asiatic [ˌeɪʃɪ'ætɪk] *agg. e s.* asiatico *m.*
aside [ə'saɪd] **A** *avv.* da parte, a parte **B** *s.* digressione *f.* ♦ **a. from** a parte, eccetto
to ask [aːsk] *v. tr.* **1** domandare, chiedere **2** invitare ♦ **to a. after/for sb.** chiedere di qc.; **to a. a question** fare una domanda; **to a. for st.** chiedere (per avere) q.c.; **to a. sb. to dinner** invitare qc. a pranzo; **to a. sb. st.** chiedere q.c. a qc.
askance [əs'kæns] *avv.* sospettosamente, di traverso
askew [əs'kjuː] **A** *agg.* storto, obliquo **B** *avv.* di traverso
asleep [ə'sliːp] *agg. pred.* addormentato ♦ **to be a.** dormire; **to fall a.** addormentarsi
asparagus [əs'pærəgəs] *s.* asparago *m.*
aspect ['æspɛkt] *s.* **1** aspetto *m.*, apparenza *f.* **2** (*di edificio*) esposizione *f.*
aspersion [əs'pɜːʃ(ə)n] *s.* diffamazione *f.*
asphalt ['æsfælt] *s.* asfalto *m.*
to asphalt ['æsfælt] *v. tr.* asfaltare
to asphyxiate [æs'fɪksɪeɪt] *v. intr.* asfissiare
asphyxiation [æsˌfɪksɪ'eɪʃ(ə)n] *s.* asfissia *f.*
to aspire [əs'paɪəʳ] *v. intr.* aspirare
aspirin [əs'p(ə)rɪn] *s.* aspirina *f.*
ass [æs] *s.* asino *m.*, somaro *m.* ♦ **to make an a. of oneself** rendersi ridicolo
to assail [ə'seɪl] *v. tr.* assalire, attaccare
assailant [ə'seɪlənt] *s.* assalitore *m.*
assassin [ə'sæsɪn] *s.* assassino *m.*
to assassinate [ə'sæsɪneɪt] *v. tr.* assassinare
assassination [əˌsæsɪ'neɪʃ(ə)n] *s.* assassinio *m.*
assault [ə'sɜːlt] *s.* attacco *m.*, assalto *m.*, aggressione *f.*
to assault [ə'sɜːlt] *v. tr.* assaltare, aggredire
to assemble [ə'sɛmbl] **A** *v. tr.* **1** riunire **2** montare, assemblare **B** *v. intr.* riunirsi
assembly [ə'sɛmblɪ] *s.* **1** assemblea *f.*, riunione *f.* **2** montaggio *m.*
assent [ə'sɛnt] *s.* assenso *m.*, approvazione *f.*
to assent [ə'sɛnt] *v. intr.* acconsentire, assentire
to assert [ə'sɜːt] *v. tr.* **1** asserire, affermare, sostenere **2** rivendicare, far valere ♦ **to a. oneself** far valere i propri diritti
assertion [ə'sɜːʃ(ə)n] *s.* **1** asserzione *f.* **2** rivendicazione *f.*
to assess [ə'sɛs] *v. tr.* **1** accertare **2** gravare d'imposta **3** valutare
assessment [ə'sɛsmənt] *s.* accertamento *m.*, valutazione *f.*
asset ['æsɛt] *s.* **1** bene *m.*, vantaggio *m.*, risorsa *f.* **2** *al pl.* (*econ.*) attivo *m.*
assiduous [ə'sɪdjʊəs] *agg.* assiduo
to assign [ə'saɪn] *v. tr.* **1** assegnare **2** designare, incaricare **3** stabilire, fissare
assignment [ə'saɪnmənt] *s.* **1** assegnazione *f.* **2** designazione *f.* **3** compito *m.*
to assist [ə'sɪst] *v. tr.* assistere, aiutare
assistance [ə'sɪst(ə)ns] *s.* assistenza *f.*, soccorso *m.*
assistant [ə'sɪst(ə)nt] *s.* assistente *m. e f.* ♦ **shop a.** commesso
associate [ə'sɒʊʃɪɪt] **A** *agg.* associato **B** *s.* socio *m.*, collega *m. e f.*
to associate [ə'sɒʊʃɪeɪt] **A** *v. tr.* **1** associare **2** unire, congiungere **B** *v. intr.* associarsi ♦ **to a. with sb.** frequentare qc.
association [əˌsɒʊsɪ'eɪʃ(ə)n] *s.* associazione *f.*
assorted [ə'sɜːtɪd] *agg.* assortito
assortment [ə'sɜːtmənt] *s.* assortimento *m.*

to **assume** [ə'sjuːm] *v. tr.* **1** supporre **2** assumere, prendere
assumption [ə'sʌm(p)ʃ(ə)n] *s.* **1** supposizione *f.* **2** premessa *f.*, ipotesi *f.* **3** assunzione *f.*
assurance [ə'ʃʊər(ə)ns] *s.* **1** assicurazione *f.* **2** fiducia *f.*, certezza *f.*
to **assure** [ə'ʃʊəʳ] *v. tr.* assicurare
asthma ['æsmə] *s.* asma *f. o m.*
asthmatic [æs'mætɪk] *agg.* asmatico
astigmatic [ˌæstɪg'mætɪk] *agg.* astigmatico
astir [ə'stɜːʳ] *avv. e agg. pred.* **1** in agitazione, in moto **2** in piedi
to **astonish** [əs'tənɪʃ] *v. tr.* meravigliare, sorprendere, stupire
astonished [əs'tənɪʃt] *agg.* stupito ♦ **to be a. at st.** stupirsi di q.c.
astonishing [əs'tənɪʃɪŋ] *agg.* stupefacente
astonishment [əs'tənɪʃmənt] *s.* stupore *m.*, meraviglia *f.*
to **astound** [əs'taʊnd] *v. tr.* sbalordire
astounding [əs'taʊndɪŋ] *agg.* sbalorditivo
astragal ['æstrəg(ə)l] *s.* (*arch.*) astragalo *m.*
astragalus [æs'trægələs] *s.* (*anat., bot.*) astragalo *m.*
astray [əs'treɪ] *avv. e agg. pred.* fuori strada
astride [əs'traɪd] **A** *avv.* a cavalcioni **B** *prep.* a cavalcioni di
astringent [əs'trɪn(d)ʒ(ə)nt] *agg.* astringente
astrolabe ['æstrɒ(ʊ)leɪb] *s.* astrolabio *m.*
astrologer [əs'trələdʒəʳ] *s.* astrologo *m.*
astrologic [ˌæstrə'lədʒɪk] *agg.* astrologico
astrology [əs'trələdʒɪ] *s.* astrologia *f.*
astronaut ['æstrənɜːt] *s.* astronauta *m. e f.*
astronautical [ˌæstrə'nɜːtɪk(ə)l] *agg.* astronautico
astronautics [ˌæstrə'nɜːtɪks] *s. pl.* (*v. al sing.*) astronautica *f.*
astronomer [əs'trənəməʳ] *s.* astronomo *m.*
astronomic(al) [ˌæstrə'nəmɪk((ə)l)] *agg.* astronomico
astronomy [əs'trənəmɪ] *s.* astronomia *f.*
astute [əs'tjuːt] *agg.* astuto
asylum [ə'saɪləm] *s.* **1** asilo *m.*, rifugio *m.* **2** casa *f.* di ricovero ♦ **lunatic a.** manicomio
asymmetric [ˌæsɪ'metrɪk] *agg.* asimmetrico
at [æt, ət] *prep.* **1** (*luogo, direzione*) a, in, da, presso, verso, contro (ES: **at school** a scuola, **he threw a shoe at the cat** tirò una scarpa al gatto) **2** (*tempo*) a, di (ES: **at night** di notte) **3** (*condizione*) a, in (ES: **at work** al lavoro) **4** (*misura, valore*) a (ES: **at a low price** a basso prezzo) **5** (*modo*) a, con (ES: **at leisure** con comodo) **6** (*causa*) per (ES: **surprised at st.** sorpreso per q.c.) ♦ **at all** affatto; **at best** nella migliore delle ipotesi; **at first** dapprima; **at hand** a portata di mano; **at last** finalmente; **at least** almeno; **at most** al massimo; **at once** subito; **at times** a volte
atavic [ə'tævɪk] *agg.* atavico
ate [ɛt] *pass. di* **to eat**
atheism ['eɪθɪɪz(ə)m] *s.* ateismo *m.*
atheist ['eɪθɪɪst] *s.* ateo *m.*
athlete ['æθliːt] *s.* atleta *m. e f.*
athletic [æθ'lɛtɪk] *agg.* atletico
athletics [æθ'lɛtɪks] *s. pl.* (*v. al sing.*) atletica *f.*
athwart [ə'θwɜːt] **A** *prep.* attraverso **B** *avv.* di traverso
Atlantic [ət'læntɪk] *agg.* atlantico
atlas ['ætləs] *s.* atlante *m.*
atmosphere ['ætməsfɪəʳ] *s.* atmosfera *f.*
atmospheric [ˌætməs'fɛrɪk] *agg.* atmosferico
atoll ['ætəl] *s.* atollo *m.*
atom ['ætəm] *s.* atomo *m.*
atomic [ə'təmɪk] *agg.* atomico
atomizer ['ætəmaɪzəʳ] *s.* vaporizzatore *m.*, nebulizzatore *m.*
to **atone** [ə'tɒʊn] *v. intr.* espiare
atop [ə'təp] *avv. e prep.* in cima (a)
atrocious [ə'trɒʊʃəs] *agg.* **1** atroce **2** (*fam.*) pessimo, orribile
atrocity [ə'trəsɪtɪ] *s.* atrocità *f.*
to **attach** [ə'tætʃ] *v. tr.* **1** attaccare, unire **2** allegare **3** apporre
attaché [ə'tæʃeɪ] *s.* addetto *m.*
attached [ə'tætʃt] *agg.* **1** attaccato, unito **2** legato, devoto **3** addetto, assegnato
attachment [ə'tætʃmənt] *s.* **1** attaccatura *f.* **2** attaccamento *m.*, devozione *f.* **3** (*mecc.*) accessorio *m.*
attack [ə'tæk] *s.* attacco *m.* ♦ **heart a.** attacco cardiaco
to **attack** [ə'tæk] *v. tr.* **1** attaccare **2** iniziare **3** aggredire
attacker [ə'tækəʳ] *s.* **1** aggressore *m.* **2** attaccante *m.*
to **attain** [ə'teɪn] *v. tr.* ottenere, raggiungere, conseguire ♦ **to a. to** arrivare a
attainable [ə'teɪnəbl] *agg.* raggiungibile

attainment [ə'teɪnmənt] *s.* **1** risultato *m.*, conseguimento *m.* **2** *al pl.* cognizioni *f. pl.*, cultura *f.*
attempt [ə'tɛm(p)t] *s.* **1** tentativo *m.*, sforzo *m.* **2** attentato *m.*
to attempt [ə'tɛm(p)t] *v. tr.* **1** osare, tentare, provare **2** attentare a
to attend [ə'tɛnd] **A** *v. tr.* **1** assistere a, frequentare, partecipare a **2** assistere, curare **3** accompagnare **B** *v. intr.* **1** occuparsi di, prendersi cura di **2** badare, prestare attenzione
attendance [ə'tɛndəns] *s.* **1** frequenza *f.*, presenza *f.* **2** servizio *m.* **3** assistenza *f.* **4** pubblico *m.*, spettatori *m. pl.*
attendant [ə'tɛndənt] **A** *agg.* **1** connesso, concomitante **2** dipendente, al servizio di **3** presente **B** *s.* guardiano *m.*, custode *m. e f.*, inserviente *m. e f.*
attention [ə'tɛnʃ(ə)n] *s.* attenzione *f.*
attentive [ə'tɛntɪv] *agg.* **1** attento **2** premuroso
to attest [ə'tɛst] *v. tr.* attestare, testimoniare
attic ['ætɪk] *s.* **1** (*arch.*) attico *m.* **2** soffitta *f.*
attitude ['ætɪtju:d] *s.* **1** atteggiamento *m.* **2** opinione *f.* **3** assetto *m.*
attorney [ə'tɜ:nɪ] *s.* **1** procuratore *m.* **2** avvocato *m.*
to attract [ə'trækt] *v. tr.* attirare, attrarre
attraction [ə'trækʃən] *s.* **1** attrattiva *f.* **2** attrazione *f.*
attractive [ə'træktɪv] *agg.* attraente
attributable [ə'trɪbjʊtəbl] *agg.* attribuibile
attribute ['ætrɪbju:t] *s.* attributo *m.*
to attribute [ə'trɪbjʊ(:)t] *v. tr.* attribuire, ascrivere
attrition [ə'trɪʃ(ə)n] *s.* attrito *m.*, logoramento *m.*
atypical [ə'tɪpɪk(ə)l] *agg.* atipico
aubergine ['ɒʊbəʒi:n] *s.* melanzana *f.*
auction ['ɜ:kʃ(ə)n] *s.* asta *f.*
to auction ['ɜ:kʃ(ə)n] *v. tr.* vendere all'asta
auctioneer [ˌɜ:kʃə'nɪəʳ] *s.* banditore *m.*
audible ['ɜ:dɪbl] *agg.* udibile
audience ['ɜ:djəns] *s.* **1** pubblico *m.*, spettatori *m. pl.* **2** udienza *f.*
audio ['ɜ:dɪɒʊ] *agg. e s.* audio *m. inv.*
audiovisual [ˌɜ:dɪɒ(ʊ)'vɪʒʊəl] *agg.* audiovisivo
audit ['ɜ:dɪt] *s.* (*comm.*) revisione *f.* (dei conti)
to audit ['ɜ:dɪt] *v. tr.* (*comm.*) rivedere, verificare
audition [ɜ:'dɪʃ(ə)n] *s.* audizione *f.*
auditor ['ɜ:dɪtəʳ] *s.* (*di società*) sindaco *m.*, (*dei conti*) revisore *m.*
auditorium [ˌɜ:dɪ'tɜ:rɪəm] *s.* auditorio *m.*
to augment [ɜ:g'mɛnt] *v. tr.* aumentare
to augur ['ɜ:gəʳ] *v. intr.* essere di auspicio
August ['ɜ:gəst] *s.* agosto *m.*
aunt [a:nt] *s.* zia *f.*
auricle ['ɜ:rɪkl] *s.* (*anat.*) padiglione *m.*
aurora [ɜ:'rɜ:rə] *s.* aurora *f.* ♦ **a. borealis** aurora boreale
auspicious [ɜ:s'pɪʃəs] *agg.* propizio, fausto
austere [əs'tɪəʳ] *agg.* austero
austerity [əs'tɛrɪtɪ] *s.* austerità *f.*
austral ['ɜ:str(ə)l] *agg.* australe
Australian [əs'treɪljən] *agg. e s.* australiano *m.*
Austrian ['əstrɪən] *agg. e s.* austriaco *m.*
authentic [ɜ:'θɛntɪk] *agg.* autentico, genuino
to authenticate [ɜ:'θɛntɪkeɪt] *v. tr.* autenticare, vidimare
authenticity [ˌɜ:θɛn'tɪsɪtɪ] *s.* autenticità *f.*
author ['ɜ:θəʳ] *s.* autore *m.*
authoritarian [ɜ:ˌθərɪ'tɛərɪən] *agg.* autoritario
authoritative [ɜ:'θərɪtətɪv] *agg.* **1** autorevole **2** autoritario
authority [ɜ:'θərɪtɪ] *s.* **1** autorità *f.* **2** autorizzazione *f.*
authorization [ˌɜ:θ(ə)raɪ'zeɪʃ(ə)n] *s.* autorizzazione *f.*
to authorize ['ɜ:θəraɪz] *v. tr.* autorizzare
auto ['ə(:)tɒʊ] **A** *agg.* automobilistico **B** *s.* (*USA*) automobile *f.*
autobiographic(al) [ˌɜ:tɒ(ʊ)ˌbaɪɒ(ʊ)'græfɪk((ə)l)] *agg.* autobiografico
autobiography [ˌɜ:tɒ(ʊ)baɪ'əgrəfɪ] *s.* autobiografia *f.*
autograph ['ɜ:təgra:f] *agg. e s.* autografo *m.*
to autograph ['ɜ:təgra:f] *v. tr.* firmare
automatic [ˌɜ:tə'mætɪk] *agg.* automatico
automation [ˌɜ:tə'meɪʃ(ə)n] *s.* automazione *f.*
automaton [ɜ:'təmət(ə)n] *s.* automa *m.*
autonomous [ɜ:'tənəməs] *agg.* autonomo
autonomy [ɜ:'tənəmɪ] *s.* autonomia *f.*
autumn ['ɜ:təm] *s.* autunno *m.*
autumnal [ɜ:'tʌmnəl] *agg.* autunnale
auxiliary [ɜ:g'zɪljərɪ] *agg.* ausiliario, di riserva

to avail [ə'veɪl] *v. intr.* servire, favorire ♦ **to a. oneself of** servirsi di
availability [əˌveɪlə'bɪlɪtɪ] *s.* disponibilità *f.*
available [ə'veɪləbl] *agg.* **1** disponibile, utilizzabile **2** libero
avalanche ['ævəlaːnʃ] *s.* valanga *f.*
avant-garde [ˌævɜːŋ'gaːd] *s.* avanguardia *f.*
to avenge [ə'vɛn(d)ʒ] *v. tr.* vendicare
avenue ['ævɪnjuː] *s.* **1** viale *m.* **2** via *f.*, strada *f.*
average ['ævərɪdʒ] **A** *agg.* medio, comune **B** *s.* **1** (*mat.*) media *f.* **2** (*naut.*) avaria *f.*
to average ['ævərɪdʒ] *v. tr.* **1** calcolare la media **2** fare in media ♦ **to a. out at** aggirarsi su
averse [ə'vɜːs] *agg.* contrario
aversion [ə'vɜːʃ(ə)n] *s.* riluttanza *f.*
to avert [ə'vɜːt] *v. tr.* **1** distogliere **2** evitare
aviary ['eɪvjərɪ] *s.* voliera *f.*
aviation [ˌeɪvɪ'eɪʃ(ə)n] *s.* aviazione *f.*
aviculture ['eɪvɪkʌltʃə^r] *s.* avicoltura *f.*
avid ['ævɪd] *agg.* avido, bramoso
avifauna [ˌeɪvɪ'fɜːnə] *s.* avifauna *f.*
avocado [ˌævə'kaːdɒʊ] *s.* avocado *m. inv.*
to avoid [ə'vɔɪd] *v. tr.* evitare, fuggire, scansare
avoidable [ə'vɔɪdəbl] *agg.* evitabile
avowal [ə'vaʊəl] *s.* ammissione *f.*
avuncular [ə'vʌŋkjʊlə^r] *agg.* di zio
to await [ə'weɪt] *v. tr.* aspettare, attendere
to awake [ə'weɪk] (*pass.* **awoke, awaked,** *p. p.* **awoken, awaked**) *v. tr. e intr.* svegliare, svegliarsi
awakening [ə'weɪk(ə)nɪŋ] *s.* risveglio *m.*
award [ə'wɜːd] *s.* **1** premio *m.* **2** risarcimento *m.*
to award [ə'wɜːd] *v. tr.* assegnare, attribuire, aggiudicare
aware [ə'wɛə^r] *agg. pred.* **1** consapevole **2** informato ♦ **to be a. of st.** rendersi conto di q.c.
awash [ə'wɔʃ] *avv.* a galla
away [ə'weɪ] *avv.* **1** via **2** lontano **3** da parte **4** continuamente, via via **5** (*sport*) fuori casa ♦ **far and a.** moltissimo; **right a.** subito
awe [ɜː] *s.* timore *m.*
awesome ['ɜːsəm] *agg.* imponente
awful ['ɜːfʊl] *agg.* terribile, tremendo
awhile [ə'waɪl] *avv.* per un po'
awkward ['ɜːkwəd] *agg.* **1** goffo **2** scomodo **3** inopportuno
awning ['ɜːnɪŋ] *s.* tendone *m.*
awoke [ə'wɒʊk] *pass. di* **to awake**
awoken [ə'wɒʊkən] *p. p. di* **to awake**
awry [ə'raɪ] **A** *agg. pred.* storto, bieco **B** *avv.* di traverso
axe [æks] *s.* scure *f.*, ascia *f.*
axis ['æksɪs] (*pl.* **axes**) *s.* (*mat., fis.*) asse *m.*
axle ['æksl] *s.* asse *f.* ♦ **a.-shaft** (*autom.*) semiasse
ay(e) [aɪ] **A** *avv.* sì **B** *s.* voto *m.* favorevole
azalea [ə'zeɪljə] *s.* azalea *f.*
azimuth ['æzɪməθ] *s.* azimut *m. inv.*
azote [ə'zɒʊt] *s.* azoto *m.*

B

to baa [bɑː] (*pass. e p. p.* **baaed**) *v. intr.* belare
to babble [bæbl] **A** *v. tr.* balbettare, farfugliare **B** *v. intr.* **1** balbettare, farfugliare **2** cianciare, parlare a vanvera
baboon [bə'buːn] *s.* babbuino *m.*
baby ['beɪbɪ] *s.* neonato *m.*, bambino *m.* ♦ **b. carriage** carrozzina
babyhood ['beɪbɪhʊd] *s.* prima infanzia *f.*
to baby-sit ['beɪbɪ,sɪt] *v. intr.* fare da baby-sitter
baby-sitter ['beɪbɪ,sɪtəʳ] *s.* baby-sitter *f. e m. inv.*
bachelor ['bætʃ(ə)ləʳ] *s.* **1** scapolo *m.* **2** laureato *m.*
back [bæk] **A** *agg.* **1** posteriore **2** remoto, lontano **3** arretrato **B** *s.* **1** dorso *m.*, schiena *f.* **2** schienale *m.* **3** retro *m.*, parte *f.* posteriore **4** fondo *m.*, sfondo *m.* **C** *avv.* **1** indietro **2** di ritorno **3** prima **4** di rimando ♦ **b. to front** alla rovescia; **to be b.** essere di ritorno
to back [bæk] **A** *v. tr.* **1** far indietreggiare **2** sostenere, spalleggiare **3** puntare su, scommettere su **4** sottoscrivere, controfirmare **B** *v. intr.* indietreggiare, fare marcia indietro ♦ **to b. down** indietreggiare; **to b. out of st.** ritirarsi da q.c.; **to b. up** appoggiare, sostenere
backache ['bækeɪk] *s.* mal *m.* di schiena
backbone ['bækbɒʊn] *s.* colonna *f.* vertebrale
backcloth ['bækkləθ] *s.* **1** (*teatro*) fondale *m.* **2** sfondo *m.*
to backdate [,bæk'deɪt] *v. tr.* retrodatare
backfire ['bækfaɪəʳ] *s.* ritorno *m.* di fiamma
background ['bækgraʊnd] **A** *s.* **1** sfondo *m.* **2** ambiente *m.*, retroterra *m. inv.* **3** antefatto *m.* **B** *agg.* di fondo
backhand ['bæk,hænd] *s.* (*tennis*) rovescio *m.*
backhanded ['bæk,hændɪd] *agg.* **1** (*tennis*) dato di rovescio **2** ambiguo, a doppio senso
backing ['bækɪŋ] *s.* **1** rinforzo *m.* (posteriore) **2** sostegno *m.*, appoggio *m.* **3** (*mus.*) sottofondo *m.*
backlash ['bæklæʃ] *s.* **1** (*mecc.*) rinculo *m.* **2** ripercussione *f.*
backlog ['bækləg] *s.* (lavoro) arretrato *m.*
backpack [,bæk'pæk] *s.* zaino *m.*
backside [,bæk'saɪd] *s.* parte *f.* posteriore
backstage [,bæk'steɪdʒ] *s.* retroscena *f.*
backstairs [,bæk'stɛəz] *s. pl.* scala *f.* di servizio
back-stitch ['bækstɪtʃ] *s.* impuntura *f.*
backstroke ['bæk,strɒʊk] *s.* **1** contraccolpo *m.* **2** nuoto *m.* sul dorso
backup ['bækʌp] **A** *s.* **1** riserva *f.* **2** supporto *m.*, appoggio *m.* **B** *agg. attr.* di riserva
backward ['bækwəd] *agg.* **1** volto all'indietro, a rovescio **2** arretrato **3** ritardato, sottosviluppato
backwards ['bækwədz] *avv.* indietro, all'indietro
backwash ['bækwəʃ] *s.* risacca *f.*
bacon ['beɪk(ə)n] *s.* pancetta *f.*
bacterium [bæk'tɪərɪəm] *s.* batterio *m.*
bad [bæd] (*comp.* **worse**, *sup. rel.* **worst**) **A** *agg.* **1** cattivo **2** brutto **3** dannoso **4** andato a male, guasto **B** *s.* male *m.*, rovina *f.* ♦ **b. luck** sfortuna; **b. mood** malumore; **b. weather** maltempo; **to feel b.** sentirsi male; **to go b.** andare a male; **to go to the b.** andare in rovina
bade [beɪd] *pass. di* **to bid**
badge ['bædʒ] *s.* distintivo *m.*, insegna *f.*
badger ['bædʒəʳ] *s.* (*zool.*) tasso *m.*
badly ['bædlɪ] *avv.* **1** male, malamente **2** duramente **3** grandemente ♦ **b.-off** povero, spiantato
bad-tempered ['bæd,tɛmpəd] *agg.* irritabile, irascibile
to baffle ['bæfl] *v. tr.* **1** sconcertare, confondere **2** frustrare, impedire **3** (*tecnol.*) deviare
bag [bæg] *s.* **1** sacco *m.*, sacchetto *m.* **2** borsa *f.*, borsetta *f.* **3** carniere *m.* ♦ **bags of** un sacco di; **sleeping b.** sacco a pelo; **shoulder b.** borsa a tracolla
to bag [bæg] *v. tr.* **1** insaccare **2** (*fam.*) intascare **3** (*fam.*) accaparrare
baggage ['bægɪdʒ] *s.* bagaglio *m.* ♦ **b. car** bagagliaio; **b. claim** ritiro bagagli; **b. room** deposito bagagli
baggy ['bægɪ] *agg.* gonfio, cascante
bagpipe ['bægpaɪp] *s.* cornamusa *f.*
bail [beɪl] *s.* cauzione *f.* ♦ **to be on b.** essere in libertà provvisoria (su cauzione)

to bail (1) [beɪl] *v. tr.* dar garanzia per ♦ **to b. sb. out** ottenere la libertà provvisoria di qc.
to bail (2) [beɪl] *v. tr.* (*naut.*) sgottare
bailer ['beɪlər] *s.* (*naut.*) sassola *f.*
bailiff ['beɪlɪf] *s.* ufficiale *m.* giudiziario
bain-marie [ˌbænˌmɑ'riː] *s.* bagnomaria *m.*
bait [beɪt] *s.* esca *f.*
to bait [beɪt] *v. tr.* **1** fornire di esca **2** adescare, lusingare
to bake [beɪk] *v. tr. e intr.* cuocere al forno
baker ['beɪkər] *s.* fornaio *m.* ♦ **b.'s (shop)** panetteria
bakery ['beɪkərɪ] *s.* panificio *m.*, panetteria *f.*
baking ['beɪkɪŋ] *s.* cottura *f.* al forno ♦ **b. pan** stampo; **b. powder** lievito in polvere; **b. tin** teglia, tortiera
balance ['bæləns] *s.* **1** bilancia *f.* **2** equilibrio *m.* **3** bilancio *m.*, saldo *m.* **4** contrappeso *m.* ♦ **b. of trade** bilancia commerciale; **b. sheet** bilancio di esercizio
to balance ['bæləns] **A** *v. tr.* **1** bilanciare, equilibrare **2** pesare, valutare **3** pareggiare, saldare **B** *v. intr.* **1** stare in equilibrio **2** (*comm.*) quadrare, essere in pareggio
balanced ['bælənst] *agg.* bilanciato, equilibrato
balancing ['bælənsɪŋ] *s.* equilibratura *f.*
balcony ['bælkənɪ] *s.* **1** balcone *m.* **2** (*teatro*) balconata *f.*, galleria *f.*
bald [bɜːld] *agg.* **1** calvo, pelato **2** spoglio, disadorno **3** esplicito, immediato
baldachin ['bɜːldəkɪn] *s.* baldacchino *m.*
baldly ['bɜːldlɪ] *avv.* chiaramente, schiettamente
baldness ['bɜːldnɪs] *s.* **1** calvizie *f.* **2** nudità *f.* **3** schiettezza *f.*
baldric ['bɜːldrɪk] *s.* bandoliera *f.*
bale [beɪl] *s.* (*di merce*) balla *f.*
baleful ['beɪlf(ʊ)l] *agg.* funesto
ball (1) [bɜːl] *s.* **1** palla *f.*, pallone *m.* **2** sfera *f.* **3** gomitolo *m.* ♦ **b. bearings** cuscinetti a sfere; **b.-pen** penna a sfera
ball (2) [bɜːl] *s.* ballo *m.*
ballad ['bæləd] *s.* ballata *f.*
ballast ['bæləst] *s.* **1** zavorra *f.* **2** equilibrio *m.* **3** massicciata *f.*
ballet ['bæleɪ] *s.* balletto *m.* ♦ **b. dancer** ballerino
balloon [bə'luːn] *s.* pallone *m.* ♦ **hot-air b.** mongolfiera
ballot ['bælət] *s.* **1** scheda *f.* (per votazione) **2** voto *m.* ♦ **b. box** urna elettorale
ballroom ['bɜːlrʊm] *s.* sala *f.* da ballo
balm [baːm] *s.* balsamo *m.*
balmy ['baːmɪ] *agg.* **1** balsamico **2** (*pop.*) svanito, sventato
balsam ['bɜːlsəm] *s.* balsamo *m.*
balsamic [bɜːl'sæmɪk] *agg.* balsamico
balustrade [ˌbæləs'treɪd] *s.* balaustra *f.*
bamboo [bæm'buː] *s.* bambù *m.*
ban [bæn] *s.* **1** bando *m.*, proclama *m.* **2** interdizione *f.*
to ban [bæn] *v. tr.* proibire, interdire
banal [bə'naːl] *agg.* banale
banana [bə'naːnə] *s.* banana *f.*
band (1) [bænd] *s.* **1** benda *f.*, fascia *f.*, nastro *m.* **2** (*radio*) banda *f.*
band (2) [bænd] *s.* (*mus.*) banda *f.*, orchestra *f.*
bandage ['bændɪdʒ] *s.* benda *f.*, fascia *f.*
to bandage ['bændɪdʒ] *v. tr.* bendare
bandaging ['bændɪdʒɪŋ] *s.* bendaggio *m.*, fasciatura *f.*
bandit ['bændɪt] *s.* bandito *m.*
bandy ['bændɪ] *agg.* arcuato ♦ **b.-legged** con le gambe storte
to bandy ['bændɪ] *v. tr.* scambiare (*parole, accuse, colpi*)
bang (1) [bæŋ] *s.* **1** colpo *m.*, botta *f.* **2** scoppio *m.*
bang (2) [bæŋ] *s.* (*di capelli*) frangia *f.*
to bang [bæŋ] **A** *v. tr.* **1** colpire, battere **2** sbattere **B** *v. intr.* **1** scoppiare, esplodere **2** sbattere
bangle ['bæŋgl] *s.* braccialetto *m.*
to banish ['bænɪʃ] *v. tr.* bandire
banisters ['bænɪstəz] *s. pl.* balaustra *f.*
bank (1) [bæŋk] *s.* **1** argine *m.*, riva *f.*, sponda *f.* **2** banco *m.*, cumulo *m.*
bank (2) [bæŋk] *s.* **1** banca *f.*, banco *m.* **2** (*gioco*) banco *m.* ♦ **b. holiday** giorno di festa; **b. note** banconota; **b. robber** scassinatore; **b. statement** estratto conto; **b. transfer** bonifico bancario
to bank (1) [bæŋk] **A** *v. tr.* ammucchiare, ammassare **B** *v. intr.* **1** ammucchiarsi, ammassarsi **2** (*aer.*) inclinarsi in virata
to bank (2) [bæŋk] **A** *v. tr.* depositare in banca **B** *v. intr.* **1** avere un conto in banca **2** (*gioco*) tenere il banco ♦ **to b. on** fare affidamento su
banker ['bæŋkər] *s.* banchiere *m.*
banking ['bæŋkɪŋ] **A** *agg.* bancario **B** *s.* attività *f.* bancaria ♦ **b. hours** orario di banca

bankrupt ['bæŋkrʌpt] *agg.* fallito ♦ **to go b.** fallire
bankruptcy ['bæŋkrʌptsɪ] *s.* bancarotta *f.*, fallimento *m.*
banner ['bænəʳ] *s.* **1** bandiera *f.*, stendardo *m.* **2** striscione *m.*, insegna *f.*
banns [bænz] *s. pl.* pubblicazioni *f. pl.* di matrimonio
banquet ['bæŋkwɪt] *s.* banchetto *m.*
to banter ['bæntəʳ] *v. tr.* stuzzicare, canzonare
baptism ['bæptɪz(ə)m] *s.* battesimo *m.*
baptismal [bæp'tɪzm(ə)l] *agg.* battesimale
baptistery ['bæptɪst(ə)rɪ] *s.* battistero *m.*
to baptize [bæp'taɪz] *v. tr.* battezzare
bar (1) [baːʳ] *s.* **1** barra *f.*, spranga *f.*, tavoletta *f.* **2** ostacolo *m.*, restrizione *f.* **3** barra *f.* (di sabbia) **4** banco *m.*, bar *m. inv.* **5** (*dir.*) sbarra *f.*, tribunale *m.* ♦ **b. code** codice a barre; **the Bar** professione forense
bar (2) [baːʳ] *prep.* eccetto, tranne
to bar [baːʳ] *v. tr.* **1** sbarrare, chiudere **2** ostacolare, impedire **3** vietare
barbarian [baː'bɛərɪən] *agg. e s.* barbaro *m.*
barbaric [baː'bærɪk] *agg.* barbaro, barbarico
barbarization [ˌbaːbəraɪ'zeɪʃ(ə)n] *s.* imbarbarimento *m.*
barbarous ['baːb(ə)rəs] *agg.* barbaro
barbecue ['baːbɪkjuː] *s.* barbecue *m. inv.*
barbed wire [ˌbaːbd'waɪəʳ] *s.* filo *m.* spinato
barber ['baːbəʳ] *s.* barbiere *m.* ♦ **b.'s shop** barbiere (*bottega*)
barbiturate [baː'bɪtjʊrɪt] *s.* barbiturico *m.*
bare [bɛəʳ] *agg.* **1** nudo, spoglio, brullo **2** vuoto, privo di **3** semplice
to bare [bɛəʳ] *v. tr.* **1** scoprire, denudare **2** (*fig.*) rivelare, mostrare
bareback ['bɛəbæk] *agg.* senza sella
barefaced ['bɛəfeɪst] *agg.* sfacciato
barefoot ['bɛəfʊt] *agg.* scalzo
barely ['bɛəlɪ] *avv.* **1** appena **2** chiaramente, apertamente **3** poveramente
bargain ['baːgɪn] *s.* **1** affare *m.* **2** accordo *m.*, transazione *f.* ♦ **into the b.** per di più
to bargain ['baːgɪn] *v. tr. e intr.* trattare, contrattare ♦ **to b. for** aspettarsi
barge [baːdʒ] *s.* chiatta *f.*
to barge [baːdʒ] **A** *v. tr.* trasportare su chiatta **B** *v. intr.* muoversi pesantemente ♦ **to b. in** intromettersi a sproposito
baritone ['bærɪtɒʊn] *s.* baritono *m.*
bark (1) [baːk] *s.* corteccia *f.*
bark (2) [baːk] *s.* abbaio *m.*, latrato *m.*
to bark [baːk] *v. intr.* abbaiare
barley ['baːlɪ] *s.* orzo *m.*
barmaid ['baːmeɪd] *s.* barista *f.*
barman ['baːmən] *s.* (*pl.* **barmen**) barista *m.*
barn [baːn] *s.* fienile *m.*, granaio *m.*
barometer [bə'rəmɪtəʳ] *s.* barometro *m.*
baron ['bær(ə)n] *s.* barone *m.*
baroness ['bær(ə)nɪs] *s.* baronessa *f.*
baroque [bə'rɒʊk] *agg. e s.* barocco *m.*
barracks ['bærəks] *s. pl.* caserma *f.*
barrage ['bæraːʒ] *s.* **1** sbarramento *m.* **2** serie *f.* continua
barred [baːd] *agg.* **1** sbarrato, ostruito **2** vietato
barrel ['bær(ə)l] *s.* **1** barile *m.*, botte *f.* **2** (*di fucile*) canna *f.* **3** (*di rivoltella*) tamburo *m.* ♦ **b. vault** volta a botte
barren ['bær(ə)n] *agg.* **1** sterile **2** arido
barrenness ['bær(ə)nnɪs] *s.* **1** sterilità *f.* **2** aridità *f.*
barricade ['bærɪkeɪd] *s.* barricata *f.*
barrier ['bærɪəʳ] *s.* barriera *f.*, transenna *f.* ♦ **sound b.** muro del suono
barrister ['bærɪstəʳ] *s.* avvocato *m.*
barrow (1) ['bærɒʊ] *s.* **1** carriola *f.* **2** barella *f.*
barrow (2) ['bærɒʊ] *s.* **1** altura *f.* **2** tumulo *m.*
bartender ['baːˌtɛndəʳ] *s.* (*USA*) barista *m. e f.*
barter ['baːtəʳ] *s.* baratto *m.*, permuta *f.*
to barter ['baːtəʳ] *v. tr.* barattare, scambiare
base [beɪs] **A** *s.* **1** base *f.* **2** zoccolo *m.*, basamento *m.* **B** *agg.* basso, ignobile, vile
to base [beɪs] *v. tr.* basare, fondare
baseball ['beɪsbɜːl] *s.* baseball *m. inv.*
basement ['beɪsmənt] *s.* **1** seminterrato *m.* **2** basamento *m.*
to bash [bæʃ] *v. tr.* colpire con violenza
bashful ['bæʃf(ʊ)l] *agg.* timido
basic ['beɪsɪk] *agg.* fondamentale, essenziale, di base
basically ['beɪsɪklɪ] *avv.* fondamentalmente
basil ['bæzl] *s.* basilico *m.*
basilica [bə'zɪlɪkə] *s.* basilica *f.*
basin ['beɪsn] *s.* **1** bacino *m.* **2** bacinella *f.*, vasca *f.*
basis ['beɪsɪs] *s.* (*pl.* **bases**) base *f.*
to bask [baːsk] *v. intr.* crogiolarsi
basket ['baːskɪt] *s.* cestino *m.*, canestro *m.*
basketball ['baːskɪtˌbɜːl] *s.* pallacanestro *f.*
bas-relief ['bæsrɪˌliːf] *s.* bassorilievo *m.*

bass [bæs] *s.* (*mus.*) basso *m.*
bassoon [bə'suːn] *s.* (*mus.*) fagotto *m.*
bastard ['bæːstəd] *agg.* bastardo
to **baste** [beɪst] *v. tr.* **1** imbastire **2** (*cuc.*) ungere **3** (*fam.*) battere
bastion ['bæstɪən] *s.* bastione *m.*
bat (1) [bæt] *s.* pipistrello *m.*
bat (2) [bæt] *s.* **1** racchetta *f.* **2** mazza *f.*
to **bat** [bæt] *v. tr.* battere (le palpebre)
batch [bætʃ] *s.* **1** infornata *f.* **2** (*di merce*) gruppo *m.*, partita *f.*
to **bate** [beɪt] *v. tr.* **1** diminuire **2** trattenere ♦ **with bated breath** col fiato sospeso
bath [baːθ] *s.* **1** bagno *m.* **2** *al pl.* bagni *m. pl.* pubblici, terme *f. pl.* ♦ **b. towel** asciugamano; **b. tub** vasca da bagno; **bubble b.** bagnoschiuma; **to have a b.** fare il bagno
to **bathe** [beɪð] **A** *v. tr.* bagnare **B** *v. intr.* nuotare
bather ['beɪðəʳ] *s.* bagnante *m. e f.*
bathing ['beɪðɪŋ] *s.* il bagnarsi, i bagni *m. pl.* ♦ **b. hut** cabina; **b. suit** costume da bagno
bathrobe ['baːθˌrɒʊb] *s.* accappatoio *m.*
bathroom ['baːθrʊm] *s.* stanza *f.* da bagno
baton ['bæt(ə)n] *s.* **1** sfollagente *m. inv.*, bastone *m.* **2** bacchetta *f.*
to **batter** ['bætəʳ] *v. tr. e intr.* battere, picchiare ♦ **to b. down** abbattere; **battered** sformato, malconcio
battery ['bætərɪ] *s.* batteria *f.*, pila *f.*
battle ['bætl] *s.* battaglia *f.* ♦ **b.-field** campo di battaglia; **b.-ship** nave da guerra
bawdy ['bɜːdɪ] *agg.* osceno
bawl [bɜːl] *s.* urlo *m.*
to **bawl** [bɜːl] *v. tr. e intr.* **1** urlare **2** piangere ♦ **to b. out** sgridare
bay (1) [beɪ] *s.* baia *f.*
bay (2) [beɪ] *s.* **1** (*arch.*) campata *f.* **2** recesso *m.*
bay (3) [beɪ] *s.* (*bot.*) alloro *m.*
bay-window [ˌbeɪ'wɪndɒʊ] *s.* bovindo *m.*
to **be** [biː, bɪ] (*pass.* **was**, *p. p.* **been**) *v.* **1** (*copula, ausiliare nelle forme passive*) essere (ES: **this is a dictionary** questo è un dizionario, **he was not chosen** non fu prescelto) **2** essere, esistere, stare, trovarsi, andare, venire, fare (ES: **to be or not to be** essere o non essere, **to be at school** essere a scuola, **he has been to Paris twice** è stato a Parigi due volte, **has anyone been here?** è venuto qualcuno?, **it is five o'clock** sono le cinque) **3** (*seguito da gerundio*) stare (ES: **what are you drinking?** cosa stai bevendo?) **4** (*preceduto da 'there'*) esserci (ES: **there was no one** non c'era nessuno) **5** stare (di salute) (ES: **how are you?** come stai?) **6** costare (ES: **how much is it?** quanto costa?) **7** avvenire, avere luogo (ES: **the party is tomorrow** la festa avrà luogo domani) **8** essere, fare (*di professione*) (ES: **he's a doctor** fa il medico) **9** (*seguito da inf.*) dovere, essere da (ES: **you are not to see him again** non devi vederlo più)
beach [biːtʃ] *s.* spiaggia *f.*, lido *m.* ♦ **b. umbrella** ombrellone
to **beach** [biːtʃ] *v. tr.* (*naut.*) tirare in secco
beacon ['biːk(ə)n] *s.* **1** segnale *m.* **2** faro *m.*, meda *f.* ♦ **radio b.** radiofaro
bead [biːd] *s.* perlina *f.*, grano *m.*
beak [biːk] *s.* **1** becco *m.* **2** rostro *m.*
beam [biːm] *s.* **1** trave *f.* **2** raggio *m.* **3** (*naut.*) baglio *m.*
to **beam** [biːm] *v. intr.* sfavillare, brillare
beaming ['biːmɪŋ] *agg.* splendente
bean [biːn] *s.* fagiolo *m.* ♦ **French b.** fagiolino
bear [bɛəʳ] *s.* **1** orso *m.* **2** (*Borsa*) ribasso *m.*
to **bear** [bɛəʳ] (*pass.* **bore**, *p. p.* **borne, born**) *v. tr.* **1** portare, reggere **2** tollerare, sopportare **3** generare, partorire, produrre ♦ **to b. away** portar via; **to be born** nascere; **to b. down** premere, sconfiggere; **to b. on** influire; **to b. oneself** comportarsi; **to b. out** convalidare; **to b. up** farsi forza
bearable ['bɛərəbl] *agg.* sopportabile
beard [bɪəd] *s.* barba *f.*
bearded ['bɪədəd] *agg.* barbuto
bearer ['bɛərəʳ] *s.* portatore *m.*, latore *m.*
bearing ['bɛərɪŋ] *s.* **1** rapporto *m.*, attinenza *f.* **2** condotta *f.*, comportamento *m.* **3** (*naut.*) rilevamento *m.* **4** supporto *m.* **5** (*mecc.*) cuscinetto *m.*
beast [biːst] *s.* bestia *f.*, animale *m.*
beastly ['biːs(t)lɪ] *agg.* **1** bestiale **2** orribile, abominevole
beat [biːt] *s.* **1** colpo *m.* **2** battito *m.* **3** (*mus.*) battuta *f.*, ritmo *m.*
to **beat** [biːt] (*pass.* **beat**, *p. p.*, **beaten, beat**) *v. tr.* battere, colpire, percuotere ♦ **to b. about** perlustrare; **to b. off** respingere; **to b. up** picchiare (*una persona*), sbattere (*le uova*)
beaten ['biːtn] **A** *p. p. di* **to beat** **B** *agg.* **1** battuto, picchiato **2** abbattuto
beating ['biːtɪŋ] *s.* **1** percosse *f. pl.* **2** scon-

fitta *f.*
beautician [bjuː'tɪʃ(ə)n] *s.* estetista *m. e f.*
beautiful ['bjuːtəf(ʊ)l] *agg.* bello, piacevole
beauty ['bjuːtɪ] *s.* bellezza *f.*
beaver ['biːvəʳ] *s.* castoro *m.*
became [bɪ'keɪm] *pass. di* **to become**
because [bɪ'kəz] *cong.* perché, poiché ♦ **b. of** a causa di
beck (1) [bɛk] *s.* cenno *m.*, segno *m.*
beck (2) [bɛk] *s.* ruscello *m.*
to beckon ['bɛk(ə)n] *v. tr.* chiamare con un cenno
to become [bɪ'kʌm] (*pass.* **became**, *p. p.* **become**) **A** *v. intr.* **1** diventare **2** accadere **B** *v. tr.* adattarsi a
becoming [bɪ'kʌmɪŋ] *agg.* adatto, conveniente
bed [bɛd] *s.* **1** letto *m.* **2** fondo *m.*, fondamento *m.*, strato *m.* sottostante **3** aiuola *f.* ♦ **b. and board** vitto e alloggio; **b. and breakfast** alloggio e prima colazione; **b. clothes** biancheria da letto; **b. cover** copriletto; **double b.** letto matrimoniale; **single b.** letto a una piazza
bedding ['bɛdɪŋ] *s.* biancheria *f.* da letto
bedlam ['bɛdləm] *s.* pandemonio *m.*
bedridden ['bɛd,rɪdn] *agg.* costretto a letto
bedroom ['bɛdrʊm] *s.* camera *f.* da letto
bedside ['bɛdsaɪd] *s.* capezzale *m.* ♦ **b. carpet** scendiletto; **b. table** comodino
bedsitter [,bɛd'sɪtəʳ] *s.* monolocale *m.*
bedspread ['bɛdsprɛd] *s.* copriletto *m.*
bedtime ['bɛdtaɪm] *s.* ora *f.* di andare a letto
bee [biː] *s.* ape *f.*
beech [biːtʃ] *s.* faggio *m.*
beef [biːf] *s.* manzo *m.*
beehive ['biːhaɪv] *s.* alveare *m.*
beeline ['biːlaɪn] *s.* linea *f.* retta
been [biːn] *p. p. di* **to be**
beep [biːp] *s.* trillo *m.*, bip *m. inv.*
beeper [biːpəʳ] *s.* cicalino *m.*
beer [bɪəʳ] *s.* birra *f.* ♦ **draught b.** birra alla spina
beet [biːt] *s.* barbabietola *f.*
beetle ['biːtl] *s.* scarafaggio *m.*
beetroot ['biːtruːt] *s.* barbabietola *f.* rossa
before [bɪ'fɜːʳ] **A** *avv.* prima, in passato, già **B** *prep.* **1** prima di **2** davanti a, di fronte a **C** *cong.* prima che, prima di ♦ **b. long** presto, prossimamente
beforehand [bɪ'fɜːhænd] **A** *avv.* in anticipo, prima **B** *agg.* precipitoso
to beg [bɛg] **A** *v. tr.* **1** pregare, supplicare **2** chiedere **B** *v. intr.* chiedere l'elemosina ♦ **I b. your pardon** chiedo scusa
began [bɪ'gæn] *pass. di* **to begin**
beggar ['bɛgəʳ] *s.* **1** accattone *m.*, mendicante *m. e f.* **2** (*fam.*) individuo *m.*
to begin [bɪ'gɪn] (*pass.* **began**, *p. p.* **begun**) *v. tr. e intr.* cominciare, incominciare, iniziare ♦ **to b. again** ricominciare; **to b. with** per cominciare, anzitutto
beginner [bɪ'gɪnəʳ] *s.* principiante *m. e f.*
beginning [bɪ'gɪnɪŋ] *s.* inizio *m.*, principio *m.*
begonia [bɪ'gɒʊnjə] *s.* begonia *f.*
to begrudge [bɪ'grʌdʒ] *v. tr.* **1** lesinare **2** invidiare
to beguile [bɪ'gaɪl] *v. tr.* ingannare, illudere
begun [bɪ'gʌn] *p. p. di* **to begin**
behalf [bɪ'haːf] *s.* **1 on b. of** per conto di **2 in b. of** a favore di
to behave [bɪ'heɪv] *v. intr.* **1** comportarsi **2** funzionare
behaviour [bɪ'heɪvjəʳ] (*USA* **behavior**) *s.* **1** comportamento *m.*, condotta *f.* **2** funzionamento *m.*
to behead [bɪ'hɛd] *v. tr.* decapitare
beheld [bɪ'hɛld] *pass. e p. p. di* **to behold**
behind [bɪ'haɪnd] **A** *avv.* **1** dietro, indietro **2** in ritardo **B** *prep.* dietro a
to behold [bɪ'hɒʊld] (*pass. e p. p.* **beheld**) *v. tr.* vedere, scorgere, guardare
being ['biːɪŋ] *s.* l'essere *m.*, esistenza *f.*
belated [bɪ'leɪtɪd] *agg.* tardivo, tardo
to belay [bɪ'leɪ] *v. tr.* (*naut.*) legare, assicurare ♦ **belaying pin** caviglia
to belch [bɛltʃ] **A** *v. tr.* eruttare **B** *v. intr.* ruttare
belfry ['bɛlfrɪ] *s.* campanile *m.*
Belgian ['bɛldʒ(ə)n] *agg. e s.* belga *m. e f.*
to belie [bɪ'laɪ] *v. tr.* smentire
belief [bɪ'liːf] *s.* **1** credenza *f.*, fede *f.* **2** opinione *f.*, parere *m.* ♦ **beyond b.** incredibile
believable [bɪ'liːvəbl] *agg.* credibile
to believe [bɪ'liːv] **A** *v. tr.* **1** credere, prestar fede a **2** ritenere, pensare **B** *v. intr.* credere, aver fede, aver fiducia
believer [bɪ'liːvəʳ] *s.* credente *m. e f.*
belittle [bɪ'lɪtl] *v. tr.* sminuire
bell [bɛl] *s.* **1** campana *f.* **2** campanello *m.* ♦ **b. tower** campanile
belligerent [bɪ'lɪdʒər(ə)nt] *agg. e s.* belligerante *m.*
bellow ['bɛlɒʊ] *s.* **1** muggito *m.* **2** urlo *m.* **3** fragore *m.*
bellows ['bɛlɒʊz] *s. pl.* soffietto *m.*

belly ['bɛlɪ] *s.* pancia *f.*, ventre *m.* ♦ **b. ache** mal di pancia
bellyful ['bɛlɪfʊl] *s.* mangiata *f.*, scorpacciata *f.*
to belong [bɪ'lɔŋ] *v. intr.* **1** appartenere, far parte di **2** concernere, spettare **3** stare di posto
belongings [bɪ'lɔŋɪŋz] *s. pl.* roba *f.*, effetti *m. pl.* personali
beloved [bɪ'lʌvd] *agg.* adorato
below [bɪ'lɒʊ] **A** *avv.* sotto, in basso, giù **B** *prep.* sotto, al di sotto di ♦ **see b.** vedi oltre
belt [bɛlt] *s.* **1** cintura *f.*, cinghia *f.* **2** fascia *f.*, zona *f.* ♦ **safety b.** cintura di sicurezza
to belt [bɛlt] *v. tr.* **1** cingere con una cinghia **2** (*fam.*) percuotere, picchiare
beltway ['bɛltweɪ] *s.* (*USA*) circonvallazione *f.*
to bemuse [bɪ'mju:z] *v. tr.* confondere, stupire
bench [bɛn(t)ʃ] *s.* **1** panca *f.*, panchina *f.* **2** banco *m.* **3** seggio *m.* ♦ **the B.** la magistratura
bend [bɛnd] *s.* curva *f.*
to bend [bɛnd] (*pass. e p. p.* **bent**) **A** *v. tr.* **1** curvare, flettere, piegare **2** sottomettere **B** *v. intr.* piegarsi, curvarsi
beneath [bɪ'ni:θ] **A** *avv.* sotto, di sotto **B** *prep.* **1** sotto a **2** inferiore a, indegno di
benediction [ˌbɛnɪ'dɪkʃ(ə)n] *s.* benedizione *f.*
benefactor ['bɛnɪfæktəʳ] *s.* benefattore *m.*
beneficence [bɪ'nɛfɪs(ə)ns] *s.* beneficenza *f.*
beneficial [bɛnɪ'fɪʃəl] *agg.* che giova, che fa bene, vantaggioso
benefit ['bɛnɛfɪt] *s.* **1** beneficio *m.*, giovamento *m.* **2** indennità *f.*
to benefit ['bɛnɪfɪt] *v. tr.* giovare a, beneficare ♦ **to b. by** giovarsi di, trarre vantaggio da
benevolent [bɪ'nɛvələnt] *agg.* **1** benevolo **2** benefico
benign [bɪ'naɪn] *agg.* benigno, benevolo
bent (1) [bɛnt] *s.* tendenza *f.*, attitudine *f.*
bent (2) [bɛnt] **A** *p. p. di* **to bend** **B** *agg.* **1** piegato, curvo **2** propenso **3** corrotto, disonesto **4** (*pop.*) omosessuale ♦ **to be b. on doing st.** essere propenso a fare q.c.
bequest [bɪ'kwɛst] *s.* (*dir*) lascito *m.*
bereavement [bɪ'ri:vmənt] *s.* perdita *f.*, lutto *m.*
beret ['bɛreɪ] *s.* berretto *m.*
berry ['bɛrɪ] *s.* **1** bacca *f.* **2** chicco *m.*
berth [bɜ:θ] *s.* **1** cuccetta *f.* **2** ancoraggio *m.*, ormeggio *m.*
to berth [bɜ:θ] *v. tr. e intr.* attraccare, ormeggiare
to beseech [bɪ'si:tʃ] (*pass. e p. p.* **besought**) *v. tr.* supplicare
to beset [bɪ'sɛt] (*pass. e p. p.* **beset**) *v. tr.* **1** circondare **2** assalire
beside [bɪ'saɪd] *prep.* presso, accanto ♦ **to be b. oneself** essere fuori di sé
besides [bɪ'saɪdz] **A** *avv.* inoltre **B** *prep.* oltre a
to besiege [bɪ'si:dʒ] *v. tr.* **1** assediare **2** importunare, tempestare
besought [bɪ'sɜ:t] *pass. e p. p. di* **to beseech**
bespoke [bɪ'spɒʊk] *agg.* fatto su misura
best [bɛst] **A** *agg.* (*sup. di* **good**) (il) migliore **B** *avv.* (*sup. di* **well**) meglio **C** *s.* il meglio *m.* ♦ **at b.** nella migliore delle ipotesi, tutt'al più; **b. man** testimone (dello sposo); **the b.** il migliore, il meglio; **the b. part of** la maggior parte di
bestiary ['bɛstɪərɪ] *s.* bestiario *m.*
to bestow [bɪ'stɒʊ] *v. tr.* concedere, conferire
bestowal [bɪ'stɒ(ʊ)əl] *s.* concessione *f.*
bet [bɛt] *s.* **1** scommessa *f.* **2** puntata *f.*
to bet [bɛt] (*pass. e p. p.* **bet**) *v. tr. e intr.* **1** scommettere **2** puntare
to betray [bɪ'treɪ] *v. tr.* tradire
betrayal [bɪ'trɛ(ɪ)əl] *s.* tradimento *m.*
betrayer [bɪ'treɪəʳ] *s.* traditore *m.*
better (1) ['bɛtəʳ] **A** *agg.* (*comp. di* **good**) migliore, meglio **B** *avv.* (*comp. di* **well**) **1** meglio **2** di più **C** *s.* il meglio *m.* ♦ **all the b.** tanto meglio; **b. and b.** sempre meglio; **b. still** ancora meglio; **I had b.** farei meglio a; **to get b.** migliorare; **to have the b. of** avere la meglio su; **to like b.** preferire; **you had b.** ti converrebbe
better (2) ['bɛtəʳ] *s.* scommettitore *m.*
to better ['bɛtəʳ] *v. tr. e intr.* migliorare, migliorarsi
betting ['bɛtɪŋ] *s.* scommesse *f. pl.* ♦ **b. shop** sala corse
between [bɪ'twi:n] **A** *prep.* fra, tra **B** *avv.* **1** nel mezzo **2** nel frattempo
beverage ['bɛvərɪdʒ] *s.* bevanda *f.*
to beware [bɪ'wɛəʳ] *v. tr. e intr.* guardarsi da, stare attento a ♦ **b. the dog** attenti al cane
to bewilder [bɪ'wɪldəʳ] *v. tr.* disorientare,

confondere
bewilderment [bɪ'wɪldəmənt] *s.* confusione *f.*, perplessità *f.*
to bewitch [bɪ'wɪtʃ] *v. tr.* incantare, affascinare
bewitching [bɪ'wɪtʃɪŋ] *agg.* affascinante
beyond [bɪ'jənd] **A** *prep.* oltre, al di là di, al di sopra di **B** *avv.* oltre, al di là ♦ **b. belief** incredibile; **b. doubt** senza dubbio
bias ['baɪəs] *s.* pregiudizio *m.*, prevenzione *f.*
bias(s)ed ['baɪəst] *agg.* prevenuto, parziale
bib [bɪb] *s.* bavaglino *m.*
Bible ['baɪbl] *s.* bibbia *f.*
biblical ['bɪblɪk(ə)l] *agg.* biblico
bibliographic(al) [ˌbɪblɪə'græfɪk((ə)l)] *agg.* bibliografico
bibliography [ˌbɪblɪ'əgrəfɪ] *s.* bibliografia *f.*
bibliophile ['bɪblɪɒ(ʊ)faɪl] *s.* bibliofilo *m.*
bicarbonate [baɪ'kaːbənɪt] *s.* bicarbonato *m.*
to bicker ['bɪkəʳ] *v. intr.* litigare
bicoloured [ˌbaɪ'kʌləd] *agg.* bicolore
bicycle ['baɪsɪkl] *s.* bicicletta *f.*
bid [bɪd] *s.* **1** offerta *f.* **2** tentativo *m.*
to bid [bɪd] (*pass.* **bid**, **bade**, *p. p.* **bidden**, **bid**) **A** *v. tr.* **1** dire, augurare **2** ordinare **B** *v. intr.* (*a un'asta*) fare un'offerta ♦ **to b. sb. farewell** dire addio a qc.; **to b. up** fare un'offerta superiore
bidder ['bɪdəʳ] *s.* offerente *m. e f.*
to bide [baɪd] (*pass.* **bode**, *p. p.* **bided**) *v. tr.* (*letter.*) aspettare
biennial [baɪ'ɛnɪəl] *agg.* biennale
bifocal [baɪ'fɒʊk(ə)l] *agg.* bifocale
big [bɪg] *agg.* **1** grande, grosso **2** importante ♦ **b. dipper** montagne russe; **b. toe** alluce; **b. top** tendone da circo
bigamist ['bɪgəmɪst] *s.* bigamo *m.*
bigamy ['bɪgəmɪ] *s.* bigamia *f.*
big-headed [ˌbɪg'hɛdɪd] *agg.* presuntuoso
big-hearted [ˌbɪg'haːtɪd] *agg.* generoso
bike [baɪk] *s.* bicicletta *f.*
bilberry ['bɪlb(ə)rɪ] *s.* mirtillo *m.*
bilge [bɪldʒ] *s.* sentina *f.*
bilingual [baɪ'lɪŋgw(ə)l] *agg.* bilingue
bilingualism [baɪ'lɪŋgwəlɪz(ə)m] *s.* bilinguismo *m.*
bill (1) [bɪl] *s.* **1** conto *m.*, fattura *f.*, parcella *f.* **2** manifesto *m.*, locandina *f.* **3** (*USA*) banconota *f.* **4** (*comm.*) effetto *m.*, cambiale *f.* **5** bolla *f.*, bolletta *f.*, documento *m.* ♦ **b. of credit** lettera di credito; **b. of fare** lista delle vivande; **b. of sale** atto di vendita; **to ask for the b.** chiedere il conto
bill (2) [bɪl] *s.* becco *m.*
to bill [bɪl] *v. tr.* **1** (*comm.*) fatturare **2** mettere in programma
billboard ['bɪlˌbɜːd] *s.* tabellone *m.*
billet ['bɪlɪt] *s.* (*mil.*) alloggio *m.*
billfold ['bɪlˌfɒʊld] *s.* (*USA*) portafoglio *m.*
billiards ['bɪljədz] *s. pl.* (*v. al sing.*) biliardo *m. sing.*
billion ['bɪljən] *s.* **1** bilione *m.* **2** (*USA*) miliardo *m.*
billionaire [ˌbɪljən'ɛəʳ] *s.* (*USA*) miliardario *m.*
bimonthly [baɪ'mʌnθlɪ] **A** *agg.* bimestrale **B** *avv.* ogni due mesi
bin [bɪn] *s.* bidone *m.*, recipiente *m.*
to bind [baɪnd] (*pass. e p. p.* **bound**) **A** *v. tr.* **1** legare, fissare **2** rilegare **3** obbligare, impegnare **B** *v. intr.* **1** legare **2** (*mecc.*) grippare ♦ **to b. oneself to do st.** impegnarsi a fare q.c.
binder ['baɪndəʳ] *s.* **1** rilegatore *m.* **2** cartella *f.*, fascetta *f.*
binding ['baɪndɪŋ] **A** *agg.* **1** legante **2** impegnativo, obbligatorio **B** *s.* **1** copertina *f.*, rilegatura *f.* **2** legame *m.*, legatura *f.*
binge [bɪndʒ] *s.* (*pop.*) baldoria *f.*
binoculars [bɪ'nəkjʊləz] *s. pl.* binocolo *m.*
biochemistry [ˌbaɪɒ(ʊ)'kɛmɪstrɪ] *s.* biochimica *f.*
biodegradable [ˌbaɪɒ(ʊ)dɪ'greɪdəb(ə)l] *agg.* biodegradabile
biographer [baɪ'əgrəfəʳ] *s.* biografo *m.*
biographical [ˌbaɪɒ(ʊ)'græfɪk(ə)l] *agg.* biografico
biography [baɪ'əgrəfɪ] *s.* biografia *f.*
biological [ˌbaɪə'lədʒɪk(ə)l] *agg.* biologico
biologist [baɪ'ələdʒɪst] *s.* biologo *m.*
biology [baɪ'ələdʒɪ] *s.* biologia *f.*
birch [bɜːtʃ] *s.* betulla *f.*
bird [bɜːd] *s.* uccello *m.*, volatile *m.* ♦ **b.'s eye view** veduta dall'alto; **to be an early b.** essere in anticipo
biro ['baɪrɒʊ] *s.* biro *f. inv.*
birth [bɜːθ] *s.* **1** nascita *f.* **2** origine *f.* ♦ **b. control** controllo delle nascite; **b. rate** indice di natalità; **to give b. to** partorire, procreare, causare
birthday ['bɜːθdeɪ] *s.* compleanno *m.*
birthplace ['bɜːθpleɪs] *s.* luogo *m.* di nascita
biscuit ['bɪskɪt] *s.* biscotto *m.*

to bisect [baɪ'sɛkt] *v. tr.* tagliare in due
bisexual [baɪ'sɛksjʊəl] *agg.* bisessuale
bishop ['bɪʃəp] *s.* **1** vescovo *m.* **2** (*scacchi*) alfiere *m.*
bishopric ['bɪʃəprɪk] *s.* vescovado *m.*
bison ['baɪsn] *s.* bisonte *m.*
bistoury ['bɪstʊrɪ] *s.* bisturi *m.*
bit (1) [bɪt] *s.* **1** morso *m.*, boccone *m.* **2** pezzo *m.*, pezzetto *m.*, un poco *m.* **3** (*inf.*) bit *m. inv.* ♦ **b. by b.** a poco a poco; **not a b.** niente affatto
bit (2) [bɪt] *pass. di* **to bite**
bitch [bɪtʃ] *s.* **1** cagna *f.*, lupa *f.* **2** (*volg.*) puttana *f.*
bite [baɪt] *s.* **1** morso *m.*, puntura *f.* **2** boccone *m.*, spuntino *m.*
to bite [baɪt] (*pass.* **bit**, *p. p.* **bitten**) **A** *v. tr.* mordere, pungere **B** *v. intr.* abboccare ♦ **to get bitten** farsi imbrogliare
biting ['baɪtɪŋ] *agg.* pungente, tagliente
bitten ['bɪtn] *p. p. di* **to bite**
bitter ['bɪtəʳ] **A** *agg.* **1** amaro **2** pungente **3** aspro, duro **4** accanito **B** *s. al pl.* amaro *m.* ♦ **b.-sweet** agrodolce
bitterness ['bɪtənɪs] *s.* amarezza *f.*, gusto *m.* amaro
biweekly [baɪ'wiːklɪ] **A** *agg.* bisettimanale **B** *avv.* ogni due settimane
biyearly [baɪ'jɪəlɪ] **A** *agg.* biennale **B** *avv.* ogni due anni
bizarre [bɪ'zaːʳ] *agg.* bizzarro
to blab [blæb] **A** *v. tr.* spifferare **B** *v. intr.* fare la spia
black [blæk] *agg.* **1** nero, buio, scuro **2** clandestino, sommerso **3** lugubre, triste
blackberry ['blækb(ə)rɪ] *s.* mora *f.*
blackbird ['blækbɜːd] *s.* merlo *m.*
blackboard ['blækbɜːd] *s.* lavagna *f.*
blackcurrant [ˌblæk'kʌrənt] *s.* ribes *m.* nero
to blacken ['blæk(ə)n] *v. tr.* annerire, oscurare
blackleg ['blæklɛg] *s.* **1** imbroglione *m.* **2** crumiro *m.*
blackmail ['blækmeɪl] *s.* ricatto *m.*
to blackmail ['blækmeɪl] *v. tr.* ricattare
blackmailer ['blækmeɪləʳ] *s.* ricattatore *m.*
blackout ['blækaʊt] *s.* **1** oscuramento *m.* **2** svenimento *m.* **3** interruzione *f.* di corrente
blacksmith ['blæksmɪθ] *s.* fabbro *m.* ferraio, maniscalco *m.*
blackthorn ['blækθɜːn] *s.* pruno *m.*
bladder ['blædəʳ] *s.* vescica *f.*
blade [bleɪd] *s.* **1** lama *f.*, lametta *f.* **2** pala *f.* **3** filo *m.* d'erba ♦ **b.-bone** scapola
blame [bleɪm] *s.* **1** riprovazione *f.* **2** colpa *f.*, responsabilità *f.*
to blame [bleɪm] *v. tr.* **1** biasimare **2** incolpare ♦ **to be to b.** essere colpevole
bland [blænd] *agg.* **1** gentile **2** blando
blank [blæŋk] **A** *agg.* **1** vuoto, in bianco, non riempito **2** vacuo **3** totale, completo **B** *s.* **1** lacuna *f.* , spazio *m.* vuoto **2** (*USA*) modulo *m.*
blanket ['blæŋkɪt] *s.* coperta *f.*
blare [blɛəʳ] *s.* squillo *m.*
blasphemous ['blæsfɪməs] *agg.* blasfemo
blasphemy ['blæsfɪmɪ] *s.* bestemmia *f.*
blast [blaːst] *s.* **1** raffica *f.* **2** scoppio *m.*, esplosione *f.*
to blast [blaːst] *v. tr.* **1** far esplodere **2** rovinare, distruggere **3** inaridire
blasted ['blaːstɪd] *agg.* maledetto
blatant ['bleɪtənt] *agg.* **1** chiassoso **2** vistoso, plateale
blaze [bleɪz] *s.* **1** fiammata *f.*, vampata *f.* **2** incendio *m.* **3** splendore *m.*
to blaze [bleɪz] *v. intr.* ardere, bruciare, sfavillare, risplendere
blazer ['bleɪzəʳ] *s.* blazer *m. inv.*
bleach [bliːtʃ] *s.* candeggio *m.*
to bleach [bliːtʃ] *v. tr.* candeggiare
bleaching ['bliːtʃɪŋ] *s.* candeggio *m.*
bleak [bliːk] *agg.* **1** brullo **2** squallido, triste
bleary ['blɪərɪ] *agg.* offuscato, ottenebrato ♦ **b.-eyed** con lo sguardo annebbiato
to bleat [bliːt] *v. intr.* **1** belare **2** piagnucolare
to bleed [bliːd] (*pass. e p. p.* **bled**) *v. intr.* sanguinare
bleeding ['bliːdɪŋ] *s.* dissanguamento *m.*, emorragia *f.*
bleeper ['bliːpəʳ] *s.* cicalino *m.*
blemish ['blɛmɪʃ] *s.* macchia *f.*, imperfezione *f.*
blend [blɛnd] *s.* mescolanza *f.*, miscela *f.*
to blend [blɛnd] **A** *v. tr.* mescolare, fondere **B** *v. intr.* mescolarsi, fondersi
blending ['blɛndɪŋ] *s.* miscela *f.*, mescolanza *f.*
to bless [blɛs] (*pass. e p. p.* **blessed, blest**) *v. tr.* benedire
blessing ['blɛsɪŋ] *s.* benedizione *f.*
blew [bluː] *pass. di* **to blow**
to blight [blaɪt] *v. tr.* **1** danneggiare **2** deludere
blimey ['blaɪmɪ] *inter.* (*pop.*) accidenti

blind [blaɪnd] **A** *agg.* **1** cieco **2** chiuso, nascosto, senza aperture **B** *s.* cortina *f.*, persiana *f.*
to blind [blaɪnd] *v. tr.* **1** accecare **2** oscurare
blindfold ['blaɪn(d)fɒʊld] **A** *agg.* con gli occhi bendati **B** *avv.* a occhi bendati, alla cieca **C** *s.* benda *f.*
to blindfold ['blaɪn(d)fɒʊld] *v. tr.* bendare gli occhi a
blindness ['blaɪndnɪs] *s.* cecità *f.*
to blink [blɪŋk] *v. intr.* **1** ammiccare **2** lampeggiare
bliss [blɪs] *s.* beatitudine *f.*
blister ['blɪstəʳ] *s.* vescica *f.*, bolla *f.*
blithe [blaɪð] *agg.* allegro
blizzard ['blɪzəd] *s.* bufera *f.* di neve
to bloat [blɒʊt] *v. tr. e intr.* gonfiare, gonfiarsi
blob [bləb] *s.* **1** goccia *f.* **2** macchia *f.*, grumo *m.*
block [blək] *s.* **1** blocco *m.* **2** ingorgo *m.*, intasamento *m.* **3** grande edificio *m.*, isolato *m.* ♦ **b. letters** stampatello; **b. of flats** caseggiato; **road b.** posto di blocco
to block [blək] *v. tr.* bloccare, ostruire
blockade [blə'keɪd] *s.* blocco *m.*
to blockade [blə'keɪd] *v. tr.* bloccare ♦ **to run the b.** forzare il blocco
blockhouse ['bləkhaʊs] *s.* fortino *m.*
bloke [blɒʊk] *s.* (*fam.*) individuo *m.*, tipo *m.*
blond [blənd] *agg.* biondo
blood [blʌd] *s.* sangue *m.* ♦ **b. group** gruppo sanguigno; **b. heat** temperatura corporea; **b. poisoning** setticemia; **b. test** analisi del sangue
bloodhound ['blʌdhaʊnd] *s.* segugio *m.*
bloodshed ['blʌdʃɛd] *s.* spargimento *m.* di sangue, massacro *m.*
bloodshot ['blʌdʃət] *agg.* iniettato di sangue
bloody ['blʌdɪ] *agg.* **1** sanguinante **2** sanguinoso, cruento **3** sanguinario **4** (*fam.*) dannato, maledetto ♦ **b.-minded** scontroso, indisponente
bloom [bluːm] *s.* fiore *m.*, fioritura *f.*
to bloom [bluːm] *v. intr.* fiorire
blooming ['bluːmɪŋ] *agg.* fiorente
blossom ['bləsəm] *s.* fiore *m.*, fioritura *f.*
to blossom ['bləsəm] *v. intr.* fiorire, essere in fiore
blot [blət] *s.* **1** macchia *f.* **2** difetto *m.*
to blot [blət] *v. tr.* **1** macchiare **2** assorbire, asciugare ♦ **blotting-paper** carta assorbente; **to b. out** offuscare, nascondere; **to b. up** prosciugare
blotch [blətʃ] *s.* macchia *f.*
to blotch [blətʃ] **A** *v. tr.* macchiare **B** *v. intr.* coprirsi di macchie
blouse [blaʊz] *s.* camicetta *f.*
blow (1) [blɒʊ] *s.* soffio *m.*, raffica *f.* ♦ **b.-dry** asciugatura dei capelli con il fon
blow (2) [blɒʊ] *s.* colpo *m.*, percossa *f.*, pugno *m.*
to blow [blɒʊ] (*pass.* **blew**, *p. p.* **blown**) **A** *v. intr.* **1** soffiare **2** ansimare **3** (*di pneumatico*) scoppiare **B** *v. tr.* **1** soffiare, spingere (*soffiando*) **2** far saltare **3** (*strumento a fiato*) suonare ♦ **to b. away** volare via; **to b. down** abbattere; **to b. out** spegnere, scoppiare; **to b. over** esaurirsi; **to b. up** esplodere, far saltare in aria, gonfiare, (*fot.*) ingrandire
blue [blʊ] **A** *agg.* **1** azzurro, blu **2** depresso, triste **3** (*fam.*) (*di film*) osceno, pornografico **B** *s.* **1** blu *m.* **2** *al pl.* (*fam.*) tristezza *f.*, depressione *f.* ♦ **out of the b.** all'improvviso
bluebell ['blʊ(ː)bɛl] *s.* campanula *f.*
bluebottle ['bluːˌbətl] *s.* **1** (*zool.*) moscone *m.* **2** (*bot.*) fiordaliso *m.*
bluff (1) [blʌf] **A** *agg.* **1** ripido, scosceso **2** brusco **B** *s.* **1** scogliera *f.* **2** promontorio *m.*
bluff (2) [blʌf] *s.* bluff *m. inv.*
to bluff [blʌf] *v. tr.* bluffare, ingannare
blunder ['blʌndəʳ] *s.* errore *m.*, strafalcione *m.*
blunt [blʌnt] *agg.* **1** smussato, spuntato **2** ottuso **3** brusco
blur [blɜːʳ] *s.* apparenza *f.* confusa
blurb [blɜːb] *s.* (*fam.*) **1** trafiletto *m.* pubblicitario **2** (*di libro*) fascetta *f.*
to blurt [blɜːt] *v. tr.* lasciarsi sfuggire, dire senza riflettere
blush [blʌʃ] *s.* rossore *m.*
to blush [blʌʃ] *v. intr.* arrossire
blustering ['blʌst(ə)rɪŋ] *agg.* **1** rumoroso **2** infuriato
boar [bɜːʳ] *s.* cinghiale *m.*
board [bɜːd] *s.* **1** asse *f.*, tavola *f.* **2** cartellone *m.* **3** mensa *f.*, vitto *m.* **4** comitato *m.*, consiglio *m.* **5** (*naut.*) bordo *m.* **6** *al pl.* (*teatro*) palcoscenico *m.* ♦ **b. and lodging** vitto e alloggio; **full b.** pensione completa; **half b.** mezza pensione; **ironing b.** asse da stiro; **on b.** a bordo
to board [bɜːd] **A** *v. tr.* **1** ospitare **2** imbarcarsi su **B** *v. intr.* **1** essere a pensione **2** imbarcarsi

boarding ['bɜːdɪŋ] *s.* **1** tavolato *m.* **2** imbarco *m.* ♦ **b. card/pass** carta d'imbarco; **b. house** pensione; **b. school** collegio
boast [bɒʊst] *s.* vanto *m.*
to boast [bɒʊst] *v. tr. e intr.* vantare, vantarsi
boaster ['bɒʊstəʳ] *s.* gradasso *m.*, spaccone *m.*, sbruffone *m.*
boat [bɒʊt] *s.* barca *f.*, battello *m.*, imbarcazione *f.*, nave *f.* ♦ **b. race** regata; **fishing b.** peschereccio; **motor b.** barca a motore; **row(ing) b.** barca a remi; **sail(ing) b.** barca a vela
boating ['bɒʊtɪŋ] *s.* canottaggio *m.*
boatman ['bɒʊtmən] *s.* (*pl.* **boatmen**) barcaiolo *m.*
boatswain ['bɒʊs(ə)n] *s.* nostromo *m.*
to bob [bəb] *v. tr. e intr.* muovere, muoversi avanti e indietro ♦ **to b. for** cercare di afferrare; **to b. up** saltar fuori
bobby ['bəbɪ] *s.* (*fam.*) poliziotto *m.*
to bode [bɒʊd] *v. intr.* presagire ♦ **to b. well** essere di buon augurio
bodily ['bədɪlɪ] **A** *agg.* fisico, corporale **B** *avv.* **1** in persona **2** in massa **3** interamente
body ['bədɪ] *s.* **1** corpo *m.*, struttura *f.* **2** busto *m.*, tronco *m.* **3** massa *f.* **4** carrozzeria *f.*, fusoliera *f.* **5** corporazione *f.*, società *f.* **6** (*miner.*) giacimento *m.* ♦ **(dead) b.** cadavere; **b. work** carrozzeria
bodyguard ['bədɪgaːd] *s.* guardia *f.* del corpo
bog [bəg] *s.* acquitrino *m.*, palude *f.*
to bog [bəg] *v. intr.* impantanarsi
to boggle ['bəgl] *v. intr.* **1** trasalire **2** esitare
boggy ['bəgɪ] *agg.* paludoso
bogus ['bɒʊgəs] *agg.* artefatto, finto
to boil [bəɪl] *v. tr. e intr.* bollire, lessare ♦ **boiled beef** lesso; **to b. away** evaporare bollendo; **to b. down** ridursi; **to b. over** traboccare bollendo; **to b. up** riscaldare
boiler ['bəɪləʳ] *s.* caldaia *f.*, scaldabagno *m.* ♦ **b. suit** tuta da lavoro
boiling ['bəɪlɪŋ] **A** *agg.* bollente **B** *s.* ebollizione *f.* ♦ **b. point** punto di ebollizione
boisterous ['bəɪst(ə)rəs] *agg.* **1** chiassoso **2** turbolento
bold [bɒʊld] *agg.* **1** baldo, audace **2** sfacciato
boldface ['bɒʊldfeɪs] *s.* neretto *m.*
bollard ['bələd] *s.* bitta *f.*
to bolster ['bɒʊlstəʳ] *v. tr.* sostenere ♦ **to b. up** rinforzare
bolt [bɒʊlt] *s.* **1** chiavistello *m.*, spranga *f.* **2** bullone *m.* **3** freccia *f.* **4** fulmine *m.* **5** balzo *m.* **6** rotolo *m.*
to bolt [bɒʊlt] **A** *v. tr.* **1** sprangare **2** imbullonare **3** (*USA*) disertare, abbandonare **B** *v. intr.* scappare ♦ **to b. down** trangugiare
bomb [bəm] *s.* bomba *f.*
bombardment [bəm'baːdmənt] *s.* bombardamento *m.*
bombastic [bəm'bæstɪk] *agg.* ampolloso
bomber ['bəməʳ] *s.* bombardiere *m.*
bombing ['bəmɪŋ] *s.* bombardamento *m.*
bombshell ['bəmʃɛl] *s.* **1** bomba *f.* **2** (*fig.*) notizia *f.* esplosiva
bond [bənd] *s.* **1** legame *m.*, vincolo *m.* **2** impegno *m.*, accordo *m.* **3** (*econ.*) obbligazione *f.* **4** cauzione *f.* ♦ **goods in b.** merci in attesa di sdoganamento
bondage ['bəndɪdʒ] *s.* schiavitù *f.*
bone [bɒʊn] *s.* **1** osso *m.* **2** lisca *f.*, spina *f.* **3** *al pl.* scheletro *m.*, ossatura *f.* ♦ **b. china** porcellana
to bone [bɒʊn] *v. tr.* **1** disossare **2** togliere le spine a ♦ **to b. up** (*USA, fam.*) sgobbare
bonfire ['bən,faɪəʳ] *s.* falò *m.*
bonnet ['bənɪt] *s.* **1** cuffia *f.* **2** cofano *m.*
bonus ['bɒʊnəs] *s.* **1** indennità *f.*, premio *m.* **2** (*econ.*) dividendo *m.* straordinario
bony ['bɒʊnɪ] *agg.* **1** osseo **2** ossuto **3** pieno di lische
to boo [buː] *v. tr. e intr.* fischiare, disapprovare
booby ['buːbɪ] *s.* sciocco ♦ **b. trap** trappola, scherzo
book [bʊk] *s.* **1** libro *m.*, volume *m.* **2** registro *m.* **3** blocchetto *m.* ♦ **b. mark** segnalibro; **b. reset** leggio; **note b.** quaderno per appunti
to book [bʊk] *v. tr.* **1** annotare **2** prenotare, fissare **3** multare ♦ **b. a seat on a train** prenotare un posto in treno; **to b. in** riservare una stanza (*in albergo*)
bookbindery ['bʊk,baɪndərɪ] *s.* legatoria *f.*
bookcase ['bʊkkeɪs] *s.* libreria *f.*, scaffale *m.* per libri
booking ['bʊkɪŋ] *s.* prenotazione *f.* ♦ **b. office** biglietteria, ufficio prenotazioni; **to cancel a b.** annullare una prenotazione
bookish ['bʊkɪʃ] *agg.* libresco
book-keeper ['bʊk,kiːpəʳ] *s.* contabile *m. e f.*
booklet ['bʊklɪt] *s.* libretto *m.*, opuscolo *m.*
bookmaker ['bʊk,meɪkəʳ] *s.* allibratore *m.*
bookseller ['bʊk,sɛləʳ] *s.* libraio *m.*

bookshop ['bʊkʃəp] *s.* libreria *f.*
bookstall ['bʊkˌstɜːl] *s.* edicola *f.*
bookstore ['bʊkˌstɜː] *s.* (*USA*) libreria *f.*
boom (1) [buːm] *s.* **1** (*econ.*) boom *m. inv.* **2** aumento *m.* improvviso
boom (2) [buːm] *s.* **1** (*naut.*) boma *m.* **2** (*TV*) giraffa *f.*
boom (3) [buːm] *s.* rimbombo *m.*
to boom (1) [buːm] *v. intr.* prosperare, espandersi
to boom (2) [buːm] *v. intr.* rimbombare
boon [buːn] *s.* vantaggio *m.*
boor [bʊəʳ] *agg.* maleducato, cafone
boorish ['bʊərɪʃ] *agg.* maleducato, cafone
boost [buːst] *s.* **1** spinta *f.*, impulso *m.* **2** aumento *m.*
boot [buːt] *s.* **1** stivale *m.*, scarpone *m.* **2** (*autom.*) bagagliaio *m.*
booth [buːð] *s.* **1** cabina *f.* **2** bancarella *f.*
booty ['buːtɪ] *s.* bottino *f.*
booze ['buːz] *s.* (*pop.*) bevanda *f.* alcolica
boozer ['buːzəʳ] *s.* (*pop.*) bevitore *m.*
border ['bɜːdəʳ] *s.* **1** bordo *m.*, confine *m.*, orlo *m.* **2** frontiera *f.*
to border ['bɜːdəʳ] *v. tr.* **1** orlare, delimitare **2** confinare con ♦ **to b. on** rasentare
borderline ['bɜːdəlaɪn] **A** *s.* linea *f.* di demarcazione **B** *agg.* **1** di confine, ai limiti del consentito **2** incerto
bore (1) [bɜːʳ] *s.* **1** foro *m.* **2** (*mecc.*) alesaggio *m.*
bore (2) [bɜːʳ] *s.* scocciatore *m.*
bore (3) [bɜːʳ] *pass. di* **to bear**
to bore (1) [bɜːʳ] *v. tr.* trivellare, perforare, trapanare
to bore (2) [bɜːʳ] *v. tr.* seccare, annoiare ♦ **to be bored** annoiarsi
boredom ['bɜːdəm] *s.* noia *f.*, uggia *f.*
boring ['bɜːrɪŋ] *agg.* noioso, seccante
born [bɜːn] **A** *p. p. di* **to bear** **B** *agg.* nato, generato
borne [bɜːn] *p. p. di* **to bear**
borough ['bʌrə] *s.* **1** borgo *m.*, cittadina *f.* **2** (*di città*) circoscrizione *f.* amministrativa
to borrow ['bərɒʊ] *v. tr.* prendere in prestito
bosom ['bʊzəm] *s.* **1** seno *m.* **2** affetto *m.*
boss [bəs] *s.* padrone *m.*, capo *m.*
bossy ['bəsɪ] *agg.* prepotente, autoritario
botanic(al) [bə'tænɪk((ə)l)] *agg.* botanico
both [bɒʊθ] *agg. e pron.* entrambi, entrambe ♦ **b. ... and** sia ... sia, insieme
bothany ['bətənɪ] *s.* botanica *f.*
bother ['bəðəʳ] *s.* disturbo *m.*, seccatura *f.*
to bother ['bəðəʳ] **A** *v. tr.* assillare, disturbare **B** *v. intr.* disturbarsi, preoccuparsi
bothersome ['bəðəsəm] *agg.* fastidioso
bottle ['bətl] *s.* **1** bottiglia *f.* **2** bombola *f.* **3** biberon *m. inv.* ♦ **b. feeding** allattamento artificiale; **b. neck** collo di bottiglia, strozzatura; **b. opener** apribottiglie
to bottle ['bətl] *v. tr.* imbottigliare ♦ **to b. up** bloccare (il traffico), contenere
bottom ['bətəm] **A** *agg.* inferiore, ultimo (*in basso*) **B** *s.* **1** fondo *m.*, parte *f.* inferiore **2** carena *f.* **3** (*fam.*) sedere *m.*
bottomless ['bətəmlɪs] *agg.* sfondato
bough [baʊ] *s.* ramo *m.*
bought [bɜːt] *pass. e p. p. di* **to buy**
bouillon ['buːjəŋ] *s.* brodo *m.* ♦ **b. cube** dado da brodo
boulder ['bɒʊldəʳ] *s.* masso *m.*
boulevard ['buːl(ə)vaːd] *s.* viale *m.*
boulter ['bɒʊltəʳ] *s.* palamito *m.*
to bounce [baʊns] **A** *v. tr.* **1** far rimbalzare **2** respingere **B** *v. intr.* **1** rimbalzare **2** balzare **3** (*di assegno*) essere respinto
bound (1) [baʊnd] **A** *pass. e p. p. di* **to bind** **B** *agg.* **1** legato **2** costretto, obbligato **3** rilegato ♦ **b. to** destinato a; **to be b. for** essere diretto a
bound (2) [baʊnd] *s.* limite *m.*, confine *m.*
bound (3) [baʊnd] *s.* salto *m.*, balzo *m.*
boundary ['baʊnd(ə)rɪ] *s.* confine *m.*, frontiera *f.*, contorno *m.*
boundless ['baʊndlɪs] *agg.* illimitato
bouquet [buː'keɪ] *s.* mazzetto *m.*
bourgeois ['bʊəʒwaː] *agg.* borghese
bourgeoisie [ˌbʊəʒwaː'ziː] *s.* borghesia *f.*
bout [baʊt] *s.* **1** prova *f.* **2** (*med.*) attacco *m.* **3** incontro *m.*, gara *f.*
bovine ['bɒʊvaɪn] *agg.* bovino
bow (1) [bɒʊ] *s.* **1** arco *m.* **2** (*mus.*) archetto *m.* **3** fiocco *m.*, nodo *m.* ♦ **b. tie** cravatta a farfalla
bow (2) [bɒʊ] *s.* inchino *m.*
bow (3) [bɒʊ] *s.* (*naut.*) prua *f.*
to bow [bɒʊ] **A** *v. tr.* piegare, curvare **B** *v. intr.* **1** chinarsi, curvarsi **2** sottomettersi
bowel ['baʊəl] *s.* intestino *m.*
bower ['baʊəʳ] *s.* pergolato *m.*
bowl [bɒʊl] *s.* **1** coppa *f.*, ciotola *f.*, scodella *f.* **2** boccia *f.* ♦ **game of bowls** gioco delle bocce
bowler ['bɒʊləʳ] *s.* bombetta *f.*
bowling ['bɒʊlɪŋ] *s.* bowling *m. inv.* ♦ **b. green** bocciodromo
bowman ['bɒʊmən] *s.* (*pl.* **bowmen**) arciere *m.*

bowsprit ['bɒʊsprɪt] *s.* bompresso *m.*
box (1) [bɔks] *s.* **1** cassa *f.*, cassetta *f.* **2** scatola *f.* **3** palco *m.* **4** riquadro *m.*, casella *f.* **5** cabina *f.* **6** (*USA*, *fam.*) televisione *f.* ♦ **b. office** botteghino; **letter b.** cassetta per le lettere; **P.O. b.** casella postale
box (2) [bɔks] *s.* pugno *m.*, schiaffo *m.*
box (3) [bɔks] *s.* bosso *m.*
to box (1) [bɔks] *v. tr.* inscatolare
to box (2) [bɔks] *v. intr.* **1** fare a pugni **2** fare il pugile
boxer ['bɔksəʳ] *s.* pugile *m.*
boxing (1) ['bɔksɪŋ] *s.* imballaggio *m.*, inscatolamento *m.*
boxing (2) ['bɔksɪŋ] *s.* pugilato *m.*
boy [bɔɪ] *s.* **1** ragazzo *m.* **2** figlio *m.* **3** garzone *m.* ♦ **little b.** bambino
to boycott ['bɔɪkɔt] *v. tr.* boicottare
boyfriend ['bɔɪfrɛnd] *s.* ragazzo *m.*, fidanzato *m.*
boyhood ['bɔɪhʊd] *s.* fanciullezza *f.*
bra [brɑː] *s.* reggiseno *m.*
brace [breɪs] *s.* **1** sostegno *m.* **2** *al pl.* bretelle *f. pl.*
to brace [breɪs] *v. tr.* **1** sostenere **2** rinforzare ♦ **to b. oneself** farsi coraggio
bracelet ['breɪslɪt] *s.* braccialetto *m.*
bracing ['breɪsɪŋ] *agg.* tonificante
bracken ['brækən] *s.* felce *f.*
bracket ['brækɪt] *s.* **1** parentesi *f.* **2** supporto *m.*, mensola *f.*
bradyseism ['brædɪsaɪz(ə)m] *s.* bradisismo *m.*
to brag [bræ] *v. tr. e intr.* vantare, vantarsi
to braid [breɪd] *v. tr.* intrecciare
brain [breɪn] *s.* **1** cervello *m.* **2** *al pl.* ingegno *m.*
brainchild ['breɪntʃaɪld] *s.* (*fam.*) idea *f.*, creazione *f.*
brainwashing ['breɪn,wɔʃɪŋ] *s.* lavaggio *m.* del cervello
braise [breɪz] *v. tr.* brasare
brake [breɪk] *s.* freno *m.*
to brake [breɪk] *v. tr.* frenare
bramble ['bræmbl] *s.* rovo *m.*
bran [bræn] *s.* crusca *f.*
branch [brɑːn(t)ʃ] *s.* **1** ramo *m.* **2** diramazione *f.* **3** sezione *f.*, succursale *f.*
to branch [brɑːn(t)ʃ] *v. intr.* **1** ramificare **2** diramarsi ♦ **to b. out** intraprendere una nuova attività
brand [brænd] *s.* **1** marca *f.* **2** marchio *m.* ♦ **b. new** nuovo di zecca
to brand [brænd] *v. tr.* marcare
to brandish ['brændɪʃ] *v. tr.* brandire
brandy ['brændɪ] *s.* acquavite *f.*
brash [bræʃ] *agg.* insolente, arrogante
brass [brɑːs] **A** *agg.* di ottone **B** *s.* **1** ottone *m.* **2** *al pl.* (*mus.*) ottoni *m. pl.* ♦ **b. band** fanfara
brassiere ['bræsɪɛəʳ] *s.* reggiseno *m.*
brat [bræt] *s.* (*spreg.*) marmocchio *m.*
brave [breɪv] *agg.* coraggioso, valoroso
to brave [breɪv] *v. tr.* sfidare, affrontare
brawl [brɜːl] *s.* rissa *f.*, tafferuglio *m.*
to brawl [brɜːl] *v. intr.* litigare, schiamazzare
brawny ['brɜːnɪ] *agg.* muscoloso
bray [breɪ] *s.* raglio *m.*
to bray [breɪ] *v. intr.* ragliare
brazen ['breɪzn] *agg.* sfacciato, sfrontato
brazier ['breɪzjəʳ] *s.* braciere *m.*
breach [briːtʃ] *s.* **1** rottura *f.*, breccia *f.* **2** violazione *f.*, infrazione *f.*
bread [brɛd] *s.* pane *m.* ♦ **wholemeal b.** pane integrale
to bread [brɛd] *v. tr.* (*cuc.*) impanare
breadstick ['brɛdstɪk] *s.* grissino *m.*
breadth [brɛdθ] *s.* larghezza *f.*, ampiezza *f.*
breadwinner ['brɛd,wɪnəʳ] *s.* il sostegno *m.* della famiglia
break [breɪk] *s.* **1** rottura *f.* **2** interruzione *f.*, intervallo *m.*, pausa *f.* **3** (*fam.*) opportunità *f.* **4** violazione *f.*, irregolarità *f.*
to break [breɪk] (*pass.* **broke**, *p. p.* **broken**) **A** *v. tr.* **1** rompere, spezzare **2** infrangere, venir meno a **3** (*un record*) battere, superare **4** interrompere **5** rovinare **B** *v. intr.* **1** rompersi, spezzarsi **2** interrompersi, fare una pausa **3** diffondersi **4** (*di tempesta*) scoppiare ♦ **to b. away** allontanarsi; **to b. down** (*mecc.*) guastarsi, fallire, abbattere, crollare; **to b. even** chiudere in pareggio; **to b. in** irrompere, interrompere; **to b. off** staccare, interrompere; **to b. out** scoppiare, liberarsi da; **to b. through** sfondare, superare; **to b. up** distruggere, fare a pezzi, disperdere
breakage ['breɪkɪdʒ] *s.* **1** rottura *f.* **2** danni *m. pl.*
breakdown ['breɪkdaʊn] *s.* **1** (*mecc.*) guasto *m.*, (*naut.*) avaria *f.* **2** collasso *m.*, esaurimento *m.* **3** insuccesso *m.*, rottura *f.*
breakfast ['brɛkfəst] *s.* (prima) colazione *f.*
break-in ['breɪkɪn] *s.* irruzione *f.*
breaking ['breɪkɪŋ] *s.* **1** rottura *f.*, frattura *f.* **2** infrazione *f.* ♦ **b. and entering** violazione di domicilio con effrazione; **b.-**

point punto di rottura
breakthrough ['breɪkθruː] *s.* **1** (*mil.*) sfondamento *m.* **2** passo *m.* in avanti
breakup ['breɪk'ʌp] *s.* disfacimento *m.*
breakwater ['breɪk,wɜːtəʳ] *s.* frangiflutti *m. inv.*
breast [brɛst] *s.* petto *m.*, seno *m.* ♦ **b. pocket** taschino
to breast [brɛst] *v. tr.* **1** affrontare, tener testa a **2** scalare
breastbone ['brɛs(t)bɒʊn] *s.* sterno *m.*
to breast-feed ['brɛs(t)fiːd] (*pass. e p. p.* **breast-fed**) *v. tr.* allattare al seno
breaststroke ['brɛs(t),strɒʊk] *s.* nuoto *m.* a rana
breath [brɛθ] *s.* **1** fiato *m.*, respiro *m.* **2** soffio *m.* **3** mormorio *m.* ♦ **to be out of b.** essere senza fiato
to breathe [briːð] *v. tr. e intr.* respirare ♦ **to b. in/out** inspirare/espirare
breathing ['briːðɪŋ] *s.* respirazione *f.*, respiro *m.*
breathless ['brɛθlɪs] *agg.* **1** senza fiato, ansante **2** esanime
breathtaking ['brɛθ,teɪkɪŋ] *agg.* mozzafiato
bred [brɛd] *pass. e p. p. di* **to breed**
breed [briːd] *s.* (*zool.*) razza *f.*, (*bot.*) varietà *f.*
to breed [briːd] (*pass. e p. p.* **bred**) **A** *v. tr.* **1** generare, riprodurre **2** allevare, educare **B** *v. intr.* **1** (*di animali*) riprodursi, generare **2** originarsi
breeding ['briːdɪŋ] *s.* **1** allevamento *m.* **2** procreazione *f.*, riproduzione *f.* **3** educazione *f.*
breeze [briːz] *s.* brezza *f.*
breezy ['briːzɪ] *agg.* **1** ventilato **2** allegro
brew [bruː] *s.* **1** infuso *m.*, miscela *f.* **2** (*di birra*) fermentazione *f.*
to brew [bruː] **A** *v. tr.* **1** fare un infuso **2** fare la birra **3** preparare il tè **B** *v. intr.* **1** essere in fermentazione, essere in infusione **2** prepararsi
brewer ['bruːəʳ] *s.* birraio *m.*
briar ['braɪəʳ] *s.* **1** erica *f.* **2** pipa *f.* di radica
bribe [braɪb] *s.* bustarella *f.*, tangente *f.*
bribery ['braɪbərɪ] *s.* corruzione *f.*
brick [brɪk] *s.* mattone *m.*, laterizio *m.*
bricklayer ['brɪk,lɛ(ɪ)əʳ] *s.* muratore *m.*
bridal ['braɪdl] *agg.* nuziale
bride [braɪd] *s.* sposa *f.* ♦ **b.'s cake** torta nuziale
bridegroom ['braɪdgrʊm] *s.* sposo *m.*
bridesmaid ['braɪdzmeɪd] *s.* damigella *f.* d'onore
bridge [brɪdʒ] *s.* **1** ponte *m.* **2** (*gioco*) bridge *m. inv.* ♦ **swing b.** ponte girevole
to bridge [brɪdʒ] *v. tr.* **1** costruire un ponte su, collegare con un ponte **2** (*fig.*) colmare ♦ **to b. over** essere d'aiuto a
bridle ['braɪdl] *s.* briglia *f.*
brief [briːf] **A** *agg.* breve **B** *s.* **1** riassunto *m.* **2** (*dir.*) memoria *f.*, fascicolo *m.* **3** direttive *f. pl.*, istruzioni *f. pl.* **4** *al pl.* mutande *f. pl.*
to brief [briːf] *v. tr.* **1** riassumere **2** dare istruzioni a, ragguagliare
briefcase ['briːfkeɪs] *s.* cartella *f.* (portadocumenti)
briefing ['briːfɪŋ] *s.* briefing *m. inv.*
brig [brɪg] *s.* (*naut.*) brigantino *m.*
bright [braɪt] *agg.* **1** luminoso, brillante **2** vivace, sveglio (*fig.*)
to brighten ['braɪtn] **A** *v. tr.* **1** ravvivare, far brillare **2** rallegrare **B** *v. intr.* **1** illuminarsi, schiarirsi **2** rallegrarsi
brightness ['braɪtnɪs] *s.* **1** luminosità *f.* **2** vivacità *f.*, intelligenza *f.*
brights [braɪts] *s. pl.* (*USA*) (*autom.*) abbaglianti *m. pl.*
brilliance ['brɪljəns] *s.* **1** brillantezza *f.*, splendore *m.* **2** vivacità *f.*
brilliant ['brɪljənt] *agg.* **1** brillante **2** splendido
brim [brɪm] *s.* **1** orlo *m.*, margine *m.* **2** (*di cappello*) falda *f.*
brine [braɪn] *s.* salamoia *f.*
to bring [brɪŋ] (*pass. e p. p.* **brought**) *v. tr.* **1** portare, prendere con sé **2** causare, produrre **3** persuadere ♦ **to b. about** causare, determinare; **to b. along** condurre con sé; **to b. back** riportare, restituire; **to b. down** far calare, abbattere; **b. forward** anticipare, avanzare (*proposte*); **to b. off** portare a termine; **to b. out** tirare fuori, far uscire (*un prodotto, un libro*); **to b. round** convincere; **b. up** allevare, educare, sollevare (*una questione*)
brink [brɪŋk] *s.* orlo *m.*, margine *m.*
brisk [brɪsk] *agg.* svelto, vivace
bristle ['brɪsl] *s.* setola *f.*
British ['brɪtɪʃ] *agg.* britannico
brittle ['brɪtl] *agg.* fragile
broach [brɒʊtʃ] *s.* **1** spiedo *m.* **2** guglia *f.*
to broach [brɒʊtʃ] *v. tr.* **1** (*una botte*) spillare **2** (*una bottiglia*) stappare **3** (*un argomento*) affrontare

broad [brɜːd] *agg.* **1** largo, esteso **2** evidente, chiaro **3** marcato, spiccato **4** generale, essenziale ♦ **b.-minded** tollerante

broadcast ['brɜːdkaːst] *s.* (*radio, TV*) trasmissione *f.*

to broadcast ['brɜːdkaːst] (*pass. e p. p.* **broadcast**) *v. tr.* (*radio, TV*) trasmettere

to broaden ['brɜːdn] **A** *v. tr.* allargare **B** *v. intr.* allargarsi

broadness ['brɜːdnɪs] *s.* larghezza *f.*

brocade [brə'keɪd] *s.* broccato *m.*

broccoli ['brəkəlɪ] *s.* broccolo *m.*

brochure ['brɒʊʃjʊəʳ] *s.* opuscolo *m.*

to broil [brɔɪl] **A** *v. tr.* cuocere (*allo spiedo, alla griglia*) **B** *v. intr.* bruciare, arrostirsi

broken ['brɒʊk(ə)n] **A** *p. p. di* **to break** **B** *agg.* **1** rotto, spezzato **2** interrotto **3** indebolito ♦ **b. ground** terreno accidentato; **b.-hearted** dal cuore spezzato; **b. sleep** sonno agitato

broker ['brɒʊkəʳ] *s.* mediatore *m.*, agente *m.*, broker *m. inv.*

brolly ['brəlɪ] *s.* (*pop.*) ombrello *m.*

bronchitis [brəŋ'kaɪtɪs] *s.* bronchite *f.*

bronchopneumonia [ˌbrəŋkɒ(ʊ)njʊ(ː)'mɒʊnjə] *s.* broncopolmonite *f.*

bronze [brənz] *s.* bronzo *m.*

brooch [brɒʊtʃ] *s.* spilla *f.*

brood [bruːd] *s.* nidiata *f.*, covata *f.*

to brood [bruːd] *v. tr. e intr.* **1** covare **2** (*fig.*) meditare, rimuginare

brook [brʊk] *s.* ruscello *m.*

broom [brʊm] *s.* **1** ginestra *f.* **2** ramazza *f.*, scopa *f.*

broth [brəθ] *s.* brodo *m.*

brothel ['brəθl] *s.* postribolo *m.*

brother ['brʌðəʳ] *s.* fratello *m.* ♦ **b.-in-law** cognato

brought [brɜːt] *pass. e p. p. di* **to bring**

brow [braʊ] *s.* **1** fronte *f.* **2** *al pl.* sopracciglia *f. pl.* **3** orlo *m.*

brown [braʊn] **A** *agg.* bruno, castano **B** *s.* marrone *m.* ♦ **b. bread** pane nero

to browse [braʊz] *v. intr.* **1** brucare **2** girellare

bruise [bruːz] *s.* ammaccatura *f.*, contusione *f.*, livido *m.*

to bruise [bruːz] *v. tr. e intr.* ammaccare, farsi un livido

brunt [brʌnt] *s.* urto *m.*

brush [brʌʃ] *s.* **1** spazzola *f.*, spazzolino *m.* **2** pennello *m.* **3** boscaglia *f.* ♦ **hair b.** spazzola per capelli; **shaving b.** pennello da barba

to brush [brʌʃ] *v. tr.* **1** spazzolare **2** sfiorare ♦ **to b. away/aside** cacciar via, scostare; **to b. off** rifiutare seccamente, ignorare; **to b. up** dare una ripassata

brusque [brʊ(ː)sk] *agg.* brusco

Brussels sprouts [ˌbrʌs(ə)lz'spraʊts] *s. pl.* cavolini *m. pl.* di Bruxelles

brutal ['bruːtl] *agg.* brutale

brute [bruːt] *agg.* bruto

bubble ['bʌbl] *s.* bolla *f.* ♦ **b. bath** bagno schiuma

to bubble ['bʌbl] *v. intr.* gorgogliare, spumeggiare

buck [bʌk] *s.* **1** (maschio di) daino *m.*, cervo *m.*, antilope *f.*, coniglio *m.*, lepre *f.* **2** (*USA, fam.*) dollaro *m.*

to buck [bʌk] *v. intr.* **1** (*di cavallo*) impennarsi **2** fare resistenza ♦ **to b. off** disarcionare; **to b. up** rallegrare, rianimarsi

bucket ['bʌkɪt] *s.* secchiello *m.*

buckle ['bʌkl] *s.* fibbia *f.*

to buckle ['bʌkl] **A** *v. tr.* allacciare (*con fibbia*) **B** *v. intr.* (*mecc.*) deformarsi, piegarsi

buckskin ['bʌkskɪn] *s.* pelle *f.* di camoscio

bucolic [bjʊ(ː)'kəlɪk] *agg.* bucolico

bud [bʌd] *s.* **1** bocciolo *m.* **2** gemma *f.*

to bud [bʌd] *v. intr.* **1** sbocciare **2** germogliare

Buddhism ['bʊdɪz(ə)m] *s.* buddismo *m.*

budding ['bʌdɪŋ] *agg. attr.* in erba

buddy ['bʌdɪ] *s.* (*USA, fam.*) amico *m.*, compagno *m.*

to budge [bʌdʒ] **A** *v. tr.* spostare, muovere **B** *v. intr.* spostarsi, scostarsi

budget ['bʌdʒɪt] *s.* bilancio *m.* preventivo

to budget ['bʌdʒɪt] **A** *v. tr.* preventivare, programmare **B** *v. intr.* fare un bilancio preventivo

buff [bʌf] *s.* **1** pelle *f.* scamosciata **2** (*fam.*) appassionato *m.*

buffalo ['bʌfəlɒʊ] *s.* bufalo *m.*

buffer ['bʌfəʳ] *s.* **1** (*ferr.*) respingente *m.* **2** (*mecc., inf.*) tampone *m.*

buffet (1) ['bʌfɪt] *s.* **1** credenza *f.* **2** buffet *m. inv.* ♦ **b. car** vagone ristorante

buffet (2) ['bʌfɪt] *s.* schiaffo *m.*, colpo *m.*

to buffet ['bʌfɪt] *v. tr.* **1** colpire, schiaffeggiare **2** urtare

buffoon [bʌ'fuːn] *s.* buffone *m.*

bug [bʌg] *s.* **1** cimice *f.* **2** (*USA*) insetto *m.* **3** (*fam.*) microbo *m.*, germe *m.* **4** (*fam.*) problema *m.* **5** (*inf.*) errore *m.*, difetto *m.*

6 (*fam.*) microspia *f.*
buggy ['bʌgɪ] *s.* **1** carrozzino *m.* **2** passeggino *m.*
bugle ['bjuːgl] *s.* corno *m.* da caccia, tromba *f.*
build [bɪld] *s.* **1** struttura *f.* **2** corporatura *f.*
to build [bɪld] (*pass. e p. p.* **built**) *v. tr.* costruire, edificare ♦ **to b. in** incassare, incorporare; **to b. up** aumentare, sviluppare, accumulare
builder ['bɪldəʳ] *s.* costruttore *m.*
building ['bɪldɪŋ] **A** *s.* **1** costruzione *f.* **2** edificio *m.* **B** *agg.* edile, edilizio ♦ **b. code** regolamento edilizio
built [bɪlt] *pass. e p. p. di* **to build** ♦ **b.-in** incassato, incorporato; **b.-up** costruito
bulb [bʌlb] *s.* **1** (*bot.*) bulbo *m.* **2** lampadina *f.* ♦ **b. socket** portalampada
Bulgarian [bʌl'gɛərɪən] *agg.* bulgaro
bulge [bʌldʒ] *s.* rigonfiamento *m.*
to bulge [bʌldʒ] *v. tr. e intr.* gonfiare, gonfiarsi
bulk [bʌlk] *s.* **1** mole *f.*, volume *m.* **2** la maggior parte *f.*
bulkhead ['bʌlkhɛd] *s.* (*naut.*) paratia *f.*
bulky ['bʌlkɪ] *agg.* massiccio, voluminoso
bull (1) [bʊl] *s.* **1** toro *m.* **2** (*di grandi mammiferi*) maschio *m.* **3** (*Borsa*) rialzo *m.*
bull (2) [bʊl] *s.* bolla *f.*, editto *m.*
bulldozer ['bʊlˌdɒʊzəʳ] bulldozer *m. inv.*
bullet ['bʊlɪt] *s.* proiettile *m.*
bulletin ['bʊlɪtɪn] *s.* bollettino *m.*
bulletproof ['bʊlɪtˌpruːf] *agg.* antiproiettile, blindato
bullfight ['bʊlˌfaɪt] *s.* corrida *f.*
bullion ['bʊljən] *s.* oro *m.* (in lingotti), argento *m.* (in lingotti)
bullock ['bʊlək] *s.* manzo *m.*
bully ['bʊlɪ] *agg.* prepotente
bulwark ['bʊlwək] *s.* **1** baluardo *m.* **2** frangiflutti *m. inv.* **3** (*naut.*) murata *f.*
bum [bʌm] *s.* (*volg.*) sedere *m.*
to bum [bʌm] (*pass. e p. p.* **bummed**) **A** *v. intr.* (*USA*) oziare, fare il vagabondo **B** *v. tr.* (*USA, fam.*) scroccare
bump [bʌmp] *s.* **1** urto *m.*, colpo *m.*, scossone *m.* **2** protuberanza *f.*, bernoccolo *m.*
to bump [bʌmp] *v. tr. e intr.* **1** urtare, collidere **2** tamponare ♦ **to b. into** sbattere contro, imbattersi in
bumper [bʌmpəʳ] **A** *s.* paraurti *m. inv.*, respingente *m.* **B** *agg.* eccezionale, abbondante
bumptious ['bʌm(p)ʃəs] *agg.* presuntuoso
bumpy ['bʌmpɪ] *agg.* accidentato, dissestato
bun [bʌn] *s.* focaccia *f.*, ciambella *f.*, panino *m.* dolce
bunch [bʌn(t)ʃ] *s.* **1** mazzo *m.*, grappolo *m.* **2** gruppo *m.*
bundle ['bʌndl] *s.* **1** fascio *m.* **2** involto *m.*, fagotto *m.*
to bundle ['bʌndl] *v. tr.* **1** affastellare, impacchettare **2** spingere a forza ♦ **to b. off** spingere via
bungalow ['bʌŋgəlɒʊ] *s.* bungalow *m. inv.*
to bungle ['bʌŋgl] *v. tr.* pasticciare, abborracciare
bunion ['bʌnjən] *s.* callo *m.* (*al piede*)
bunk [bʌŋk] *s.* cuccetta *f.* ♦ **b. bed** letto a castello
bunker ['bʌŋkəʳ] *s.* **1** serbatoio *m.* di combustibile **2** bunker *m. inv.*
bunny ['bʌnɪ] *s.* coniglietto *m.*
bunting ['bʌntɪŋ] *s.* pavese *m.*
buoy [bəɪ] *s.* boa *f.*, gavitello *m.*
to buoy [bəɪ] *v. tr.* **1** far galleggiare, tenere a galla **2** sostenere
buoyancy ['bəɪənsɪ] *s.* galleggiabilità *f.*
buoyant ['bəɪənt] *agg.* **1** galleggiante **2** allegro, vivace
burden ['bɜːdn] *s.* peso *m.*, carico *m.*
to burden ['bɜːdn] *v. tr.* caricare, gravare
burdensome ['bɜːdnsəm] *agg.* gravoso, oneroso
bureau ['bjʊ(ə)rɒʊ] *s.* (*pl.* **bureaux**) **1** ufficio *m.* **2** scrittoio *m.*, scrivania *f.* **3** (*USA*) dipartimento *m.*
bureaucracy [bjʊ(ə)'rəkrəsɪ] *s.* burocrazia *f.*
bureaucratic [ˌbjʊərɒ(ʊ)'kræt ɪk] *agg.* burocratico
burglar ['bɜːgləʳ] *s.* scassinatore *m.* ♦ **b. alarm** (allarme) antifurto
burglary ['bɜːglərɪ] *s.* furto *m.* con scasso
to burgle ['bɜːgl] *v. tr.* scassinare, svaligiare
burial ['bɛrɪəl] *s.* sepoltura *f.* ♦ **b. ground** cimitero
burlesque [bɜː'lɛsk] *agg.* burlesco
burly ['bɜːlɪ] *agg.* corpulento
burn [bɜːn] *s.* scottatura *f.*, ustione *f.*
to burn [bɜːn] (*pass. e p. p.* **burnt**, *raro* **burned**) **A** *v. tr.* **1** bruciare, incendiare **2** ustionare, scottare **B** *v. intr.* **1** bruciare, incendiarsi **2** scottare **3** divampare ♦ **to b. down** distruggere col fuoco; **to b. out** estinguersi, consumarsi
burner ['bɜːnəʳ] *s.* bruciatore *m.*

burning ['bɜːnɪŋ] **A** *s.* bruciore *m.*, bruciatura *f.* **B** *agg.* rovente, scottante
burnt [bɜːnt] *pass. e p. p. di* **to burn**
burrow ['bʌrɒʊ] *s.* tana *f.*
to burrow ['bʌrɒʊ] **A** *v. tr.* scavare (una tana) **B** *v. intr.* rintanarsi, nascondersi
burst [bɜːst] *s.* esplosione *f.*, scoppio *m.*
to burst [bɜːst] (*pass. e p. p.* **burst**) *v. intr.* esplodere, scoppiare, saltare in aria ♦ **to b. in** interrompere; **to b. into, to b. out** scoppiare a (*ridere, piangere*)
to bury ['bɛrɪ] *v. tr.* seppellire ♦ **to b. away** nascondere
bus [bʌs] *s.* autobus *m. inv.* ♦ **b. line** autolinea; **b.-stop** fermata d'autobus
bush [bʊʃ] *s.* **1** cespuglio *m.* **2** boscaglia *f.*
busily ['bɪzɪlɪ] *avv.* alacremente
business ['bɪznɪs] *s.* **1** affare *m.*, affari *m. pl.* **2** lavoro *m.*, occupazione *f.* **3** commercio *m.* ♦ **b. consultant** commercialista; **b.-like** efficiente; **b. trip** viaggio d'affari
businessman ['bɪznɪsm(ə)n] *s.* (*pl.* **businessmen**) uomo *m.* d'affari
busker ['bʌskəʳ] *s.* suonatore *m.* ambulante
bust (1) [bʌst] *s.* busto *m.*
bust (2) [bʌst] **A** *s.* (*fam.*) fallimento *m.*, rovina *f.* **B** *agg.* rotto ♦ **to go b.** fallire
bustle ['bʌsl] *s.* trambusto *m.*
to bustle ['bʌsl] *v. intr.* agitarsi, darsi da fare
busy ['bɪzɪ] *agg.* **1** attivo, indaffarato **2** (*di telefono*) occupato
busybody ['bɪzɪˌbɒdɪ] *s.* intrigante *m.*, ficcanaso *m.*
but [bʌt, bət] **A** *cong.* ma, però, tuttavia, eppure **B** *prep.* eccetto, tranne **C** *avv.* soltanto ♦ **b. for** se non fosse stato per
butcher ['bʊtʃəʳ] *s.* macellaio *m.* ♦ **b.'s shop** macelleria
butler ['bʌtləʳ] *s.* maggiordomo *m.*
butt (1) [bʌt] *s.* botte *f.*
butt (2) [bʌt] *s.* **1** impugnatura *f.*, estremità *f.* **2** mozzicone *m.* **3** bersaglio *m.*
to butt [bʌt] *v. tr. e intr.* cozzare, urtare ♦ **to b. in** intromettersi
butter ['bʌtəʳ] *s.* burro *m.*
to butter ['bʌtəʳ] *v. tr.* imburrare
buttercup ['bʌtəkʌp] *s.* ranuncolo *m.*
butterfly ['bʌtəflaɪ] *s.* farfalla *f.*
buttock ['bʌtək] *s.* natica *f.*
button ['bʌtn] *s.* **1** bottone *m.* **2** pulsante *m.* **3** (*USA*) distintivo *m.* **4** germoglio *m.*
to button ['bʌtn] *v. tr.* abbottonare
buttonhole ['bʌtnhɒʊl] *s.* asola *f.*, occhiello *m.*
buttress ['bʌtrɪs] *s.* **1** sostegno *m.* **2** contrafforte *m.*
buxom ['bʌksəm] *agg.* (*di donna*) formosa
to buy [baɪ] (*pass. e p. p.* **bought**) *v. tr.* comprare ♦ **to b. back** ricomprare; **to b. by instalments** comprare a rate; **to b. out** rilevare; **to b. up** accaparrarsi
buyer ['baɪəʳ] *s.* compratore *m.*
to buzz [bʌz] *v. intr.* ronzare
buzzer ['bʌzəʳ] *s.* cicalino *m.*
by [baɪ] **A** *prep.* **1** (*luogo*) presso, davanti, accanto a, attraverso, per, via, verso (ES: **by the river** presso il fiume) **2** (*tempo*) di, per, entro (**by night** di notte, **by tomorrow** entro domani) **3** (*mezzo*) con, a, per, per mezzo di, in (ES: **by train** in treno, **by cheque** con assegno) **4** (*modo*) per, di, a, secondo, da (ES: **to judge by appearances** giudicare dalle apparenze) **5** (*agente*) da (ES: **Penicillin was discovered by Fleming** la penicillina fu scoperta da Fleming) **6** (*misura*) per, a, di (ES: **2 feet by 3** 2 piedi per 3) **B** *avv.* **1** vicino, accanto **2** da parte, in disparte ♦ **by chance** per caso; **by hand** a mano; **by all means** senz'altro; **by now** ormai; **by the way** a proposito, incidentalmente; **by then** allora; **one by one** uno per volta
bye(-bye) ['baɪbaɪ] *inter.* ciao
bygone ['baɪgən] *agg.* passato, antico
bylaw ['baɪlɔː] *s.* (*dir.*) legge *f.* locale
bypass ['baɪˌpaːs] *s.* **1** tangenziale *f.*, circonvallazione *f.* **2** derivazione *f.* **3** deviazione *f.*, by-pass *m. inv.*
by-product ['baɪˌprədəkt] *s.* **1** sottoprodotto *m.* **2** effetto *m.* secondario
byroad ['baɪrɒʊd] *s.* strada *f.* secondaria
bystander ['baɪˌstændəʳ] *s.* spettatore *m.*
by-way ['baɪˌweɪ] *s.* **1** strada *f.* appartata **2** scorciatoia *f.*
by-word ['baɪwɜːd] *s.* **1** detto *m.*, proverbio *m.* **2** personificazione *f.*
by-work ['baɪwɜːk] *s.* lavoro *m.* secondario

C

cab [kæb] *s.* **1** (*USA*) taxi *m. inv.* **2** (*ferr., di camion*) cabina *f.*
cabal [kə'bæl] *s.* **1** congiura *f.*, intrigo *m.* **2** combriccola *f.*
cabaret ['kæbəˌreɪ] *s.* cabaret *m. inv.*
cabbage ['kæbɪdʒ] *s.* cavolo *m.*
cab(b)ala [kə'baːlə] *s.* cabala *f.*
cab(b)alistic [ˌkæbə'lɪstɪk] *agg.* cabalistico
cabin ['kæbɪn] *s.* **1** cabina *f.* **2** capanna *f.* ♦ **c. boy** mozzo
cabinet ['kæbɪnɪt] *s.* **1** stipo *m.*, mobiletto *m.* **2** (*pol.*) gabinetto *m.*, consiglio *m.* dei ministri
cable ['keɪbl] *s.* **1** cavo *m.* **2** cablogramma *m.* ♦ **c. car** funivia; **c. television** televisione via cavo
cableway ['keɪblweɪ] *s.* **1** teleferica *f.* **2** funivia *f.*
cabman ['kæbmən] *s.* (*USA*) tassista *m. e f.*
cabotage ['kæbətɪdʒ] *s.* cabotaggio *m.*
cacao [kə'kaːɒʊ] *s.* cacao *m.*
cache [kæʃ] *s.* nascondiglio *m.*
to cache [kæʃ] *v. tr.* nascondere
to cackle ['kækl] *v. intr.* schiamazzare
cactus ['kæktəs] *s.* cactus *m. inv.*
cad [kæd] *s.* mascalzone *m.*
cadastre [kə'dæstrəʳ] *s.* catasto *m.*
cadence ['keɪd(ə)ns] *s.* cadenza *f.*
cadet [kə'dɛt] *s.* cadetto *m.*
to cadge [kædʒ] **A** *v. intr.* mendicare **B** *v. tr.* scroccare
cadre ['kaːdrə] *s.* **1** (*pol., mil.*) quadro *m.* **2** schema *m.*
café ['kæfeɪ] *s.* caffè *m. inv.*
cafeteria [ˌkæfɪ'tɪərɪə] *s.* tavola *f.* calda, mensa *f.*, self-service *m. inv.*
caffeine ['kæfiːn] *s.* caffeina *f.*
cage [keɪdʒ] *s.* **1** gabbia *f.* **2** recinto *m.*
cagey ['keɪdʒɪ] *agg.* (*fam.*) cauto, riluttante
cake [keɪk] *s.* **1** torta *f.*, focaccia *f.*, pasticcino *m.* **2** tavoletta *f.* ♦ **c. of soap** saponetta
to cake [keɪk] *v. tr. e intr.* incrostare, incrostarsi
calamity [kə'læmɪtɪ] *s.* calamità *f.*
calcareous [kæl'kɛərɪəs] *agg.* calcareo
calcium ['kælsɪəm] *s.* (*chim.*) calcio *m.*
to calculate ['kælkjʊleɪt] **A** *v. tr.* calcolare **B** *v. intr.* **1** fare affidamento su **2** (*USA*) credere, ritenere
calculation [ˌkælkjʊ'lɛʃ(ə)n] *s.* **1** (*mat.*) calcolo *m.*, conto *m.* **2** congettura *f.*
calculator ['kælkjʊleɪtəʳ] *s.* calcolatrice *f.*
calculus ['kælkjʊləs] *s.* (*med., mat.*) calcolo *m.*
calendar ['kælɪndəʳ] *s.* calendario *m.* ♦ **c. year** anno civile
calf (1) [kaːf] (*pl.* **calves**) *s.* vitello *m.*
calf (2) [kaːf] (*pl.* **calves**) *s.* polpaccio *m.*
to calibrate ['kælɪbreɪt] *v. tr.* calibrare
calibre ['kælɪbəʳ] (*USA* **caliber**) *s.* **1** (*mecc.*) calibro *m.* **2** (*fig.*) importanza *f.*
calix ['kælɪks] *s.* calice *m.*
call [kɜːl] *s.* **1** richiamo *m.* **2** chiamata *f.*, telefonata *f.*, comunicazione *f.* **3** breve visita *f.* **4** scalo *m.*, (*di treno*) fermata *f.* **5** richiesta *f.* **6** necessità *f.*, motivo *m.* ♦ **c. box** cabina telefonica; **charge c.** (*USA* **collect c.**) telefonata a carico del destinatario; **self-dialled c.** chiamata in teleselezione; **trunk c.** (*USA* **long distance c.**) telefonata interurbana
to call [kɜːl] **A** *v. tr.* **1** chiamare **2** annunciare **3** telefonare a **4** convocare, far venire **B** *v. intr.* **1** chiamare, gridare **2** telefonare **3** fare una visita, passare **4** fare scalo, fare una fermata ♦ **to c. attention** richiamare l'attenzione; **to c. back** richiamare; **to c. for** passare a prendere, richiedere; **to c. in** far intervenire, richiamare; **to c. off** disdire, annullare; **to c. on** fare una visita a; **to c. out** urlare, chiamare a voce alta; **to c. up** telefonare a, richiamare alle armi
caller ['kɜːləʳ] *s.* visitatore *m.*
calligraphy [ˌkælɪ'grəfɪ] *s.* calligrafia *f.*
calling ['kɜːlɪŋ] *s.* **1** occupazione *f.*, professione *f.* **2** vocazione *f.* ♦ **c. card** biglietto da visita
callous ['kæləs] *agg.* **1** calloso **2** (*fig.*) insensibile
callus ['kæləs] *s.* callo *m.*
calm [kaːm] **A** *agg.* calmo, tranquillo **B** *s.* calma *f.*
to calm [kaːm] *v. tr.* calmare, placare ♦ **to c. down** calmarsi, calmare
calmative ['kælmətɪv] *agg. e s.* tranquillante *m.*

calmly ['kaːmlɪ] *avv.* con calma
caloric [kə'lɒrɪk] *agg.* calorico
calorie ['kælərɪ] *s.* caloria *f.*
Calvinism ['kælvɪnɪz(ə)m] *s.* calvinismo *m.*
Calvinist ['kælvɪnɪst] *s.* calvinista *m. e f.*
camber ['kæmbəʳ] *s.* (*tecnol.*) curvatura *f.*
came [keɪm] *pass. di* **to come**
camel ['kæməl] *s.* cammello *m.*
camellia [kə'miːljə] *s.* camelia *f.*
cameo ['kæmɪɒʊ] *s.* cammeo *m.*
camera ['kæmərə] *s.* **1** macchina *f.* fotografica **2** cinepresa *f.*, telecamera *f.*
camisole ['kæmɪsɒʊl] *s.* maglietta *f.*
camomile ['kæməmaɪl] *s.* camomilla *f.*
camouflage ['kæmʊflaːʒ] *s.* travestimento *m.*, mimetizzazione *f.*
to camouflage ['kæmʊflaːʒ] *v. tr.* mimetizzare, camuffare
camp (1) [kæmp] *s.* **1** (*mil.*) campo *m.*, accampamento *m.* **2** campeggio *m.* **3** (*fig.*) campo *m.*, partito *m.*
camp (2) [kæmp] *agg.* (*fam.*) affettato, effeminato
to camp [kæmp] *v. intr.* **1** accamparsi **2** campeggiare
campaign [kæm'peɪn] *s.* campagna *f.*
to campaign [kæm'peɪn] *v. intr.* fare una campagna
camper ['kæmpəʳ] *s.* **1** campeggiatore *m.* **2** camper *m. inv.*
camping ['kæmpɪŋ] *s.* (il fare) campeggio *m.*
campsite ['kæmpsaɪt] *s.* campeggio *m.* (*luogo*)
campus ['kæmpəs] *s.* campus *m. inv.*
campy ['kæmpɪ] *agg.* effeminato
can (1) [kæn, k(ə)n] (*congiuntivo pass. e condiz.* **could**; *forme neg.* **cannot**, **can not**, **can't**, **couldn't**, **could not**) *v. difett.* **1** (*possibilità, capacità*) potere, riuscire a, essere in grado di, sapere (ES: **I can write the report today** posso scrivere la relazione oggi, **can he speak Italian?** sa parlare italiano?) **2** (*permesso*) potere, essere permesso (ES: **you cannot go outside Europe without your passport** non puoi uscire dall'Europa senza il passaporto) **3** (*per chiedere informazioni, permesso e sim.*) potere (ES: **can I use the phone?** posso usare il telefono?, **could you open the window?** potresti aprire la finestra?) **4** (*supposizione*) essere possibile (ES: **c. it be true?** possibile che sia vero?) **5** (*idiom.*) (ES: **can you see that woman at the window?** vedi quella donna alla finestra?)
can (2) [kæn] *s.* barattolo *m.*, latta *f.*, lattina *f.*, tanica *f.*, scatola *f.* ♦ **c. opener** apriscatole
to can [kæn] *v. tr.* inscatolare
Canadian [kə'neɪdjən] *agg.* canadese
canal [kə'næl] *s.* canale *m.*
canalization [ˌkænəlaɪ'zeɪʃ(ə)n] *s.* canalizzazione *f.*
to canalize ['kænəlaɪz] *v. tr.* **1** canalizzare **2** incanalare
canary [kə'nɛərɪ] *s.* canarino *m.*
canasta [kə'næstə] *s.* canasta *f.*
to cancel ['kæns(ə)l] *v. tr.* **1** cancellare **2** annullare, disdire
cancellation [ˌkænsə'leɪʃ(ə)n] *s.* cancellazione *f.*, annullamento *m.*
cancer ['kænsəʳ] *s.* cancro *m.*
candelabrum [ˌkændɪ'laːbrəm] *s.* candelabro *m.*
candid ['kændɪd] *agg.* sincero, schietto
candidate ['kændɪdɪt] *s.* candidato *m.*
candidature ['kændɪdɪtʃəʳ] *s.* candidatura *f.*
candied ['kændɪd] *agg.* candito
candle ['kændl] *s.* candela *f.*
candlelight ['kændllaɪt] *s.* lume *m.* di candela
candlestick ['kændlstɪk] *s.* candeliere *m.*, bugia *f.*
candour ['kændəʳ] (*USA* **candor**) *s.* franchezza *f.*, candore *m.*
candy ['kændɪ] *s.* **1** zucchero *m.* candito **2** (*USA*) caramella *f.*, dolciume *m.* ♦ **c. floss** zucchero filato
cane [keɪn] *s.* **1** canna *f.*, giunco *m.* **2** bastone *m.* (*da passeggio*) **3** verga *f.*
to cane [keɪn] *v. tr.* bastonare, fustigare
canine ['kænaɪn] *agg. e s.* canino *m.*
canister ['kænɪstəʳ] *s.* scatola *f.* metallica
canna ['kænə] *s.* (*bot.*) canna *f.*
canned [kænd] *agg.* in scatola ♦ **c. food** scatolame
cannibal ['kænɪb(ə)l] *s.* cannibale *m.*
cannibalism ['kænɪbəlɪz(ə)m] *s.* cannibalismo *m.*
cannon ['kænən] *s.* cannone *m.*
cannot ['kænət] → **can (1)**
canny ['kænɪ] *agg.* circospetto, astuto
canoe [kə'nuː] *s.* canoa *f.*
canon ['kænən] *s.* **1** canone *m.* **2** canonico *m.*

canonical [kə'nɒnɪk(ə)l] *agg.* canonico
canopy ['kænəpɪ] *s.* baldacchino *m.*
to cant [kænt] *v. intr.* inclinarsi, curvarsi
cantankerous [kən'tæŋk(ə)rəs] *agg.* (*fam.*) irascibile, litigioso
cantata [kæn'tɑːtə] *s.* (*mus.*) cantata *f.*
canteen [kæn'tiːn] *s.* **1** mensa *f.* **2** posto *m.* di ristoro **3** servizio *m.* di posate
canter ['kæntəʳ] *s.* piccolo galoppo *m.*
cantilever ['kæntɪˌliːvəʳ] *s.* mensola *f.*, trave *f.* a sbalzo ♦ **c. roof** pensilina
canvas ['kænvəs] *s.* tela *f.*
canvass ['kænvəs] *s.* **1** propaganda *f.* elettorale, sollecitazione *f.* (di voti) **2** analisi *f.*
to canvass ['kænvəs] *v. tr.* **1** sollecitare voti, fare propaganda **2** esaminare a fondo
canyon ['kænjən] *s.* canyon *m. inv.*
cap [kæp] *s.* **1** berretto *m.* **2** tappo *m.*, cappuccio *m.* **3** (*di fungo*) cappella *f.*
to cap [kæp] *v. tr.* **1** tappare, coprire **2** coronare **3** superare
capability [ˌkeɪpə'bɪlɪtɪ] *s.* capacità *f.*, facoltà *f.*
capable ['keɪpəbl] *agg.* **1** capace, abile **2** suscettibile di
capacious [kə'peɪʃəs] *agg.* capiente, spazioso
capacity [kə'pæsɪtɪ] *s.* **1** capacità *f.*, capienza *f.*, portata *f.* **2** capacità *f.*, abilità *f.*
cape [keɪp] *s.* **1** capo *m.*, promontorio *m.* **2** cappa *f.*, mantellina *f.*
caper (1) ['keɪpəʳ] *s.* cappero *m.*
caper (2) ['keɪpəʳ] *s.* **1** capriola *f.*, salto *m.* **2** monelleria *f.*
to caper ['keɪpəʳ] *v. intr.* saltellare, fare capriole
capillarity [ˌkæpɪ'lærɪtɪ] *s.* capillarità *f.*
capillary [kə'pɪlərɪ] *agg.* capillare
capital (1) ['kæpɪt(ə)l] **A** *agg.* **1** capitale **2** (*econ.*) relativo al capitale **3** (*di lettera*) maiuscolo **B** *s.* **1** (*di città*) capitale *f.* **2** (lettera) maiuscola *f.* **3** (*econ.*) capitale *m.* ♦ **c. punishment** pena capitale; **share c.** capitale azionario
capital (2) ['kæpɪt(ə)l] *s.* (*arch.*) capitello *m.*
capitalism ['kæpɪtəlɪz(ə)m] *s.* capitalismo *m.*
capitalist ['kæpɪtəlɪst] *s.* capitalista *m. e f.*
to capitalize [kə'pɪtəlaɪz] **A** *v. tr.* capitalizzare **B** giovarsi di
to capitulate [kə'pɪtjʊleɪt] *v. intr.* capitolare, arrendersi
caprice [kə'priːs] *s.* capriccio *m.*
caprine ['kæpraɪn] *agg.* caprino
to capsize [kæp'saɪz] *v. tr. e intr.* capovolgere, capovolgersi
capsule ['kæpsjuːl] *s.* capsula *f.*
captain ['kæptɪn] *s.* capitano *m.*, comandante *m.*
caption ['kæpʃ(ə)n] *s.* didascalia *f.*, titolo *m.*
to captivate ['kæptɪveɪt] *v. tr.* avvincere, attrarre
captive ['kæptɪv] *agg. e s.* prigioniero *m.*
captivity [kæp'tɪvɪtɪ] *s.* cattività *f.*
capture ['kæptʃəʳ] *s.* **1** cattura *f.* **2** preda *f.*, bottino *m.*
to capture ['kæptʃəʳ] *v. tr.* catturare
Capuchin ['kæpjʊʃɪn] *s.* (frate) cappuccino *m.*
car [kɑːʳ] *s.* **1** automobile *f.*, macchina *f.*, vettura *f.* **2** vagone *m.* ♦ **c. body repairer** carrozziere; **c. electrician** elettrauto; **c. hire** autonoleggio; **c. park** parcheggio; **c. wash** autolavaggio; **sleeping c.** vagone letto
carafe [kə'rɑːf] *s.* caraffa *f.*
caramel ['kærəmɛl] *s.* **1** caramello *m.* **2** caramella *f.*
caravan ['kærəvæn] *s.* **1** carovana *f.* **2** roulotte *f. inv.*
carbohydrate [ˌkɑːbɒ(ʊ)'haɪdreɪt] *s.* carboidrato *m.*
carbon ['kɑːbən] *s.* carbonio *m.*
to carbonize ['kɑːbənaɪz] *v. tr.* carbonizzare
carburettor [ˌkɑːbjʊ'rɛtəʳ] (*USA* **carburator**) *s.* carburatore *m.*
carcinogenic [ˌkɑːsɪnɒ(ʊ)'dʒɛnɪk] *agg.* cancerogeno
card [kɑːd] *s.* **1** scheda *f.*, tessera *f.* **2** biglietto *m.* da visita ♦ **c. holder** schedario; **c. member** tesserato; **identity c.** carta d'identità; **playing cards** carte da gioco; **post c.** cartolina
cardboard ['kɑːdbɜːd] *s.* cartone *m.*
cardiac ['kɑːdɪæk] *agg.* cardiaco
cardigan ['kɑːdɪgən] *s.* cardigan *m. inv.*
cardinal ['kɑːdɪn(ə)l] *agg. e s.* cardinale *m.*
cardiogram ['kɑːdɪɒʊgræm] *s.* cardiogramma *m.*
cardiologist [ˌkɑːdɪ'ələdʒɪst] *s.* cardiologo *m.*
cardiopath ['kɑːdɪɒ(ʊ)pɑːθ] *s.* cardiopatico *m.*
care [kɛəʳ] *s.* **1** cura *f.*, attenzione *f.* **2** vigilanza *f.*, custodia *f.* **3** preoccupazione *f.*

♦ **c. of** (*abbr.* **c/o**) (*negli indirizzi*) presso; **to take c. of** curare, occuparsi di
to care [kɛəʳ] *v. intr.* **1** preoccuparsi, importare, interessarsi **2** voler bene ♦ **to c. for** prendersi cura di, piacere
career [kə'rɪəʳ] *s.* carriera *f.*
carefree ['kɛəfriː] *agg.* spensierato
careful ['kɛəf(ʊ)l] *agg.* **1** accurato **2** attento, sollecito ♦ **be c.!** attenzione!
carefully ['kɛəflɪ] *avv.* attentamente
careless ['kɛəlɪs] *agg.* **1** disattento, incurante **2** spensierato
carelessness ['kɛəlɪsnɪs] *s.* **1** disattenzione *f.* **2** incuria *f.*
caress [kə'rɛs] *s.* carezza *f.*
to caress [kə'rɛs] *v. tr.* accarezzare
caretaker ['kɛəˌteɪkəʳ] *s.* custode *m. e f.*
caricature [ˌkærɪkə'tjʊəʳ] *s.* caricatura *f.*
caries ['kɛərɪiːz] *s. inv.* carie *f.*
caring ['kɛərɪŋ] *agg.* premuroso, altruista
carnation [kaː'neɪʃ(ə)n] *s.* garofano *m.*
carnival ['kaːnɪv(ə)l] *s.* carnevale *m.*
carnivorous [kaː'nɪv(ə)rəs] *agg.* carnivoro
carol ['kær(ə)l] *s.* canto *m.* (*gioioso, religioso*) ♦ **Christmas c.** canzone di Natale
to carp [kaːp] *v. intr.* cavillare, trovare da ridire
carpenter ['kaːpɪntəʳ] *s.* falegname *m.*, carpentiere *m.*
carpet ['kaːpɪt] *s.* tappeto *m.*, moquette *f. inv.* ♦ **c.-slippers** ciabatte; **c. sweeper** battitappeto
carriage ['kærɪdʒ] *s.* **1** carrozza *f.*, vettura *f.* **2** trasporto *m.* **3** carrello *m.* **4** portamento *m.* ♦ **c. way** carreggiata
carrier ['kærɪəʳ] *s.* **1** corriere *m.*, spedizioniere *m.* **2** portapacchi *m. inv.* **3** supporto *m.*, sostegno *m.* **4** (*med.*) portatore *m.* ♦ **c. bag** sacchetto; **c. pigeon** piccione viaggiatore
carrot ['kærət] *s.* carota *f.*
to carry ['kærɪ] (*pass. e p. p.* **carried**) **A** *v. tr.* **1** portare, trasportare **2** (*malattie*) trasmettere, diffondere **3** comportare **B** *v. intr.* raggiungere, farsi sentire ♦ **to be carried away** lasciarsi trascinare dall'entusiasmo; **to c. back** riportare, ricordare; **to c. off** rapire, cavarsela; **to c. on** proseguire, mandare avanti; **to c. out** effettuare, eseguire; **to c. through** portare a termine
carry-on [ˌkærɪ'ən] *s.* (*fam.*) confusione *f.*
cart [kaːt] *s.* carro *m.*, carrozzino *m.*
cartilage ['kaːtɪlɪdʒ] *s.* cartilagine *f.*
cartographic(al) [ˌkaːtə'græfɪk((ə)l)] *agg.* cartografico
cartography [kaː'təgrəfɪ] *s.* cartografia *f.*
carton ['kaːtən] *s.* **1** cartone *m.*, scatola *f.* di cartone **2** (*di sigarette*) stecca *f.*
cartoon [kaː'tuːn] *s.* **1** vignetta *f.*, fumetto *m.* **2** cartone *m.* animato
cartoonist [kaː'tuːnɪst] *s.* vignettista *m. e f.*, disegnatore *m.* (*di fumetti, cartoni animati*)
cartridge ['kaːtrɪdʒ] *s.* **1** cartuccia *f.* **2** (*di registratore*) cassetta *f.*
to carve [kaːv] *v. tr.* **1** incidere, intagliare **2** scolpire **3** trinciare, affettare ♦ **to c. out** ottenere con sforzo; **to c. up** suddividere
carving ['kaːvɪŋ] *s.* intaglio *m.*
caryatid [ˌkærɪ'ætɪd] *s.* cariatide *f.*
cascade [kæs'keɪd] *s.* cascata *f.*
case (1) [keɪs] *s.* **1** caso *m.*, fatto *m.*, avvenimento *m.* **2** (*dir.*) causa *f.*, processo *m.* ♦ **c. history** anamnesi, casistica; **in any c.** in ogni caso; **in c. of** in caso di
case (2) [keɪs] *s.* **1** cassa *f.* **2** astuccio *m.*, custodia *f.*
cash [kæʃ] *s.* **1** cassa *f.* **2** (denaro) contante *m.*, moneta *f.* ♦ **c. desk** cassa; **c. dispenser** cassa di prelievo automatico; **c. register** registratore di cassa
to cash [kæʃ] *v. tr.* incassare, riscuotere
cashemere [kæʃ'mɪəʳ] *s.* cachemire *m. inv.*
cashew [kæ'ʃuː] *s.* anacardio *m.*
cashier [kæ'ʃɪəʳ] *s.* cassiere *m.*
casing ['keɪsɪŋ] *s.* involucro *m.*, rivestimento *m.*
cask [kaːsk] *s.* barile *m.*, botte *f.*
casket ['kaːskɪt] *s.* scrigno *m.*, cofanetto *m.*
casserole ['kæsərɒʊl] *s.* casseruola *f.*, tegame *m.*
cassette [kæ'sɛt] *s.* cassetta *f.* ♦ **c. player** mangianastri; **c. recorder** registratore a cassetta
cassock ['kæsək] *s.* tonaca *f.*
cast [kaːst] *s.* **1** tiro *m.*, lancio *m.* **2** (*teatro*) cast *m. inv.*
to cast [kaːst] (*pass. e p. p.* **cast**) *v. tr. e intr.* **1** lanciare, buttare **2** (*teatro*) assegnare una parte ♦ **to c. off** liberarsi di; **to c. out** buttare fuori
castaway ['kaːstəweɪ] *s.* naufrago *m.*
casting vote ['kaːstɪŋvɒʊt] *s.* voto *m.* decisivo
cast iron [ˌkaːst'aɪən] *s.* ghisa *f.*

castle ['kaːsl] *s.* **1** castello *m.* **2** (*scacchi*) torre *f.*
castor oil [ˌkaːstər'ɔɪl] *s.* olio *m.* di ricino
to castrate [kæs'treɪt] *v. tr.* castrare
casual ['kæʒjʊəl] *agg.* **1** casuale, accidentale, occasionale **2** indifferente, noncurante **3** informale, disinvolto
casually ['kæʒjʊəlɪ] *avv.* **1** casualmente **2** con noncuranza
casualty ['kæʒjʊəltɪ] *s.* **1** ferito *m.*, vittima *f.* **2** infortunio *m.*, incidente *m.* ♦ **c. ward** pronto soccorso
cat [kæt] *s.* gatto *m.* ♦ **c.'s eye** catarifrangente
cataclysm ['kætəklɪz(ə)m] *s.* cataclisma *m.*
catacomb ['kætəkɒʊm] *s.* catacomba *f.*
catalogue ['kætələg] (*USA* **catalog**) *s.* catalogo *m.*
to catalogue ['kætələg] (*USA* **to catalog**) *v. tr.* catalogare
catalyst ['kætəlɪst] *s.* catalizzatore *m.*
catamaran [ˌkætəmə'ræn] *s.* catamarano *m.*
catapult ['kætəpʌlt] *s.* **1** catapulta *f.* **2** fionda *f.*
cataract ['kætərækt] *s.* cateratta *f.*
catarrh [kə'taːʳ] *s.* catarro *m.*
catastrophe [kə'tæstrəfɪ] *s.* catastrofe *f.*
catastrophic [ˌkætə'strəfɪk] *agg.* catastrofico
catch [kætʃ] *s.* **1** presa *f.*, cattura *f.* **2** pesca *f.*, retata *f.* **3** gancio *m.*, fermo *m.* **4** inganno *m.*, trucco *m.*
to catch [kætʃ] (*pass. e p. p.* **caught**) **A** *v. tr.* **1** prendere, afferrare, sorprendere **2** attirare, attrarre **3** agganciare **4** raggiungere **B** *v. intr.* **1** impigliarsi, restar preso **2** far presa **3** essere contagioso ♦ **to c. a cold** raffreddarsi; **to c. on** capire, diventare di moda; **to c. out** cogliere in fallo; **to c. up** catturare, mettersi in pari
catching ['kætʃɪŋ] *agg.* **1** contagioso, infettivo **2** attraente
catchphrase ['kætʃfreɪz] *s.* slogan *m. inv.*, frase *f.* fatta
catchy ['kætʃɪ] *agg.* orecchiabile
catechism ['kætɪkɪz(ə)m] *s.* catechismo *m.*
category ['kætɪgərɪ] *s.* categoria *f.*
to cater ['keɪtəʳ] *v. intr.* **1** fornire (*cibi, bevande*), organizzare il servizio (*per ricevimenti*) **2** provvedere a, considerare
caterpillar ['kætəˌpɪləʳ] *s.* bruco *m.*
cathedral [kə'θiːdr(ə)l] *s.* cattedrale *f.*
Catherine-wheel ['kæθ(ə)rɪnwiːl] *s.* girandola *f.*
catholic ['kæθəlɪk] *agg.* **1** universale, generale **2** cattolico
Catholicism [kə'θəlɪsɪz(ə)m] *s.* cattolicesimo *m.*
catlike ['kætlaɪk] *agg.* felino
cattle ['kætl] *s.* **1** bestiame *m.* **2** (*spreg.*) marmaglia *f.*
catty ['kætɪ] *agg.* dispettoso, malizioso
caucus ['kɜːkəs] *s.* comitato *m.* (politico)
caught [kɜːt] *pass. e p. p. di* **to catch**
cauliflower ['kəlɪflaʊəʳ] *s.* cavolfiore *m.*
causal ['kɜːz(ə)l] *agg.* causale
cause [kɜːz] *s.* causa *f.*, ragione *f.*
to cause [kɜːz] *v. tr.* causare, procurare, produrre ♦ **to c. sb. to do st.** far fare q.c. a qc.
caustic ['kɜːstɪk] *agg.* caustico
caution ['kɜːʃ(ə)n] *s.* **1** cautela *f.*, circospezione *f.* **2** cauzione *f.* **3** avvertimento *m.*
to caution ['kɜːʃ(ə)n] *v. tr.* mettere in guardia, avvertire
cautious ['kɜːʃəs] *agg.* prudente, cauto
cavalier [ˌkævə'lɪəʳ] *agg.* superbo, altezzoso
cavalry ['kæv(ə)lrɪ] *s.* cavalleria *f.*
cave [keɪv] *s.* caverna *f.*, grotta *f.*
to cave [keɪv] *v. tr.* incavare, scavare ♦ **to c. in** sprofondare, crollare
caveman ['keɪvmæn] (*pl.* **cavemen**) *s.* uomo *m.* delle caverne
cavern ['kævən] *s.* caverna *f.*, grotta *f.*
caviar(e) ['kævɪaːʳ] *s.* caviale *m.*
cavil ['kævɪl] *s.* cavillo *m.*
cavity ['kævɪtɪ] *s.* cavità *f.*
to cavort [kə'vɜːt] *v. intr.* saltellare, fare capriole
to cease [siːs] *v. tr. e intr.* cessare
cease-fire ['siːsfaɪəʳ] *s.* cessate il fuoco *m.*
ceaseless ['siːslɪs] *agg.* incessante
cedar ['siːdəʳ] *s.* cedro *m.*
ceiling ['siːlɪŋ] *s.* **1** soffitto *m.* **2** (*fig.*) tetto *m.*, plafond *m. inv.*
celebrant ['sɛlɪbr(ə)nt] *s.* celebrante *m.*
to celebrate ['sɛlɪbreɪt] *v. tr. e intr.* **1** celebrare **2** festeggiare
celebrated ['sɛlɪbreɪtɪd] *agg.* celebre
celebration [ˌsɛlɪ'breɪʃ(ə)n] *s.* celebrazione *f.*, festeggiamento *m.*
celebrity [sɪ'lɛbrɪtɪ] *s.* celebrità *f.*
celery ['sɛlərɪ] *s.* sedano *m.*

celestial [sɪ'lɛstjəl] *agg.* **1** celeste **2** celestiale
cell [sɛl] *s.* **1** cella *f.* **2** cellula *f.* **3** (*elettr.*) pila *f.*
cellar ['sɛləʳ] *s.* **1** cantina *f.* **2** scantinato *m.*, sotterraneo *m.*
cellular ['sɛljʊləʳ] *agg.* cellulare
Celtic ['kɛltɪk] *agg.* celtico
cement [sɪ'mɛnt] *s.* cemento *m.*
cemeterial [ˌsɛmɪ'tɪərɪəl] *agg.* cimiteriale
cemetery ['sɛmɪtrɪ] *s.* cimitero *m.*
censor ['sɛnsəʳ] *s.* **1** censura *f.* **2** censore *m.*
to censor ['sɛnsəʳ] *v. tr.* censurare
censorship ['sɛnsəʃɪp] *s.* censura *f.*
to censure ['sɛnʃəʳ] *v. tr.* riprovare, biasimare
census ['sɛnsəs] *s.* censimento *m.*
cent [sɛnt] *s.* (*USA*) centesimo *m.* (*di dollaro*) ♦ **per c.** per cento
centaur ['sɛntɜːʳ] *s.* centauro *m.*
centenarian [ˌsɛntɪ'nɛərɪən] *agg. e s.* (*di persona*) centenario *m.*
centenary [sɛn'tiːnərɪ] *agg. e s.* centenario *m.*
centennial [sɛn'tɛnjəl] **A** *agg.* centennale **B** *s.* centenario *m.* (*anniversario*)
center ['sɛntəʳ] → **centre**
centigrade ['sɛntɪgreɪd] *agg.* centigrado
centimetre ['sɛntɪˌmiːtəʳ] (*USA* **centimeter**) *s.* centimetro *m.*
central ['sɛntr(ə)l] *agg.* centrale
to centralize ['sɛntrəlaɪz] *v. tr.* accentrare, centralizzare
centre ['sɛntəʳ] (*USA* **center**) *s.* centro *m.* ♦ **c. field** centrocampo; **c. forward** centravanti, centrattacco; **c. piece** centrotavola
to centre ['sɛntəʳ] **A** *v. tr.* **1** centrare **2** incentrare, concentrare **B** *v. intr.* **1** convergere, concentrarsi **2** basarsi, imperniarsi
centreboard ['sɛntəbɜːd] *s.* (*naut.*) deriva *f.* mobile
centrifugal [sɛn'trɪfjʊg(ə)l] *agg.* centrifugo
centrifuge ['sɛntrɪˌfjuːdʒ] *s.* centrifuga *f.*
centring ['sɛntrɪŋ] *s.* **1** centina *f.* **2** centraggio *m.*, centratura *f.*
centripetal [sɛn'trɪpɪt(ə)l] *agg.* centripeto
century ['sɛntʃʊrɪ] *s.* secolo *m.*
cephalalgy [ˌsəfə'lædʒɪ] *s.* cefalea *f.*
ceramics [sɪ'ræmɪks] *s. pl.* (*v. al sing.*) ceramica *f.*
ceramist [sɪ'ræmɪst] *s.* ceramista *m. e f.*
cereal ['sɪərɪəl] *s.* cereale *m.*
cerebellum [ˌsɛrɪ'bɛləm] *s.* cervelletto *m.*
cerebral ['sɛrɪbr(ə)l] *agg.* cerebrale
ceremony ['sɛrɪmənɪ] *s.* cerimonia *f.*
certain ['sɜːtn] *agg.* certo, sicuro ♦ **for c.** di sicuro; **to make c. of st.** accertarsi di q.c.
certainly ['sɜːtɪnlɪ] *avv.* certamente
certainty ['sɜːtntɪ] *s.* certezza *f.*, sicurezza *f.*
certificate [sə'tɪfɪkɪt] *s.* certificato *m.*, diploma *m.*
certified ['sɜːtɪfaɪd] *agg.* certificato, attestato
to certify ['sɜːtɪfaɪ] *v. tr.* **1** certificare, attestare, dichiarare **2** autenticare
cervical ['sɜːvɪk(ə)l] *agg.* cervicale
cervix ['sɜːvɪks] *s.* cervice *f.*
to chafe [tʃeɪf] **A** *v. tr.* **1** sfregare, logorare **2** irritare **B** *v. intr.* **1** sfregarsi, logorarsi **2** irritarsi
chaff [tʃɑːf] *s.* pula *f.*, paglia *f.*
chafing-dish ['tʃeɪfɪŋdɪʃ] *s.* scaldavivande *m. inv.*
chagrin ['ʃægrɪn] *s.* imbarazzo *m.*, disappunto *m.*
chain [tʃeɪn] *s.* catena *f.* ♦ **c. reaction** reazione a catena
to chain [tʃeɪn] *v. tr.* incatenare
chair [tʃɛəʳ] *s.* **1** sedia *f.* **2** seggio *m.*, cattedra *f.* ♦ **c. lift** seggiovia; **to take the c.** assumere la presidenza
chairman ['tʃɛəmən] (*pl.* **chairmen**) *s.* presidente *m.*
chairmanship ['tʃɛəmənʃɪp] *s.* presidenza *f.*
chalet ['ʃæleɪ] *s.* chalet *m.*, villetta *f.*
chalice ['tʃælɪs] *s.* calice *m.*
chalk [tʃɜːk] *s.* gesso *m.*
challenge ['tʃælɪn(d)ʒ] *s.* sfida *f.*
to challenge ['tʃælɪn(d)ʒ] *v. tr.* **1** sfidare, provocare **2** contestare
challenging ['tʃælɪn(d)ʒɪŋ] *agg.* **1** sfidante **2** impegnativo, stimolante
chamber ['tʃeɪmbəʳ] *s.* **1** sala *f.*, aula *f.* **2** camera *f.* **3** cavità *s.* ♦ **c. maid** cameriera d'albergo; **c. music** musica da camera
chamois ['ʃæmwɑː] *s.* camoscio *m.*
champion ['tʃæmpjən] *agg. e s.* campione *m.*
championship ['tʃæmpjənʃɪp] *s.* campionato *m.*
chance [tʃɑːns] **A** *s.* **1** caso *m.*, combinazione *f.*, fortuna *f.*, probabilità *f.* **2** occa-

sione *f.*, opportunità *f.* **B** *agg.* casuale, fortuito, occasionale ♦ **by c.** per caso; **to take a c.** correre un rischio
to chance [tʃaːns] *v. tr.* rischiare, arrischiare
chancellery ['tʃaːnsələrɪ] *s.* cancelleria *f.* (*ufficio*)
chancellor ['tʃaːnsələʳ] *s.* cancelliere *m.*
chandelier [ˌʃændɪ'lɪəʳ] *s.* lampadario *m.*
change [tʃeɪn(d)ʒ] *s.* **1** cambiamento *m.*, cambio *m.* **2** spiccioli *m. pl.*, resto *m.*
to change [tʃeɪn(d)ʒ] *v. tr. e intr.* **1** cambiare, modificare **2** sostituire ♦ **to c. into** trasformarsi in; **to c. over** passare a, scambiarsi i ruoli
changeable ['tʃeɪn(d)ʒəbl] *agg.* variabile, instabile
changeover ['tʃeɪn(d)ʒˌɒʊvəʳ] *s.* cambiamento *m.*, trasformazione *f.*
changing ['tʃeɪn(d)ʒɪŋ] *agg.* mutevole, cangiante ♦ **c. room** camerino, spogliatoio
channel ['tʃænl] *s.* **1** canale *m.*, stretto *m.* **2** alveo *m.* **3** condotto *m.* **4** (*TV, radio*) canale *m.* **5** scanalatura *f.* ♦ **English Channel** la Manica
chant [tʃaːnt] *s.* canto *m.* (*liturgico*)
chaos [kɛ(ɪ)əs] *s.* caos *m.*
chaotic [kɛ(ɪ)'ɔtɪk] *agg.* caotico
chap (1) [tʃæp] *s.* screpolatura *f.*
chap (2) [tʃæp] *s.* (*zool.*) mascella *f.*
chap (3) [tʃæp] *s.* (*fam.*) tipo *m.*, individuo *m.*
to chap [tʃæp] *v. tr. e intr.* screpolare, screpolarsi
chapel ['tʃæp(ə)l] *s.* cappella *f.*
chaplain ['tʃæplɪn] *s.* cappellano *m.*
chappy ['tʃæpɪ] *agg.* screpolato
chapter ['tʃæptəʳ] *s.* capitolo *m.*
to char (1) [tʃaːʳ] *v. tr.* carbonizzare
to char (2) [tʃaːʳ] *v. intr.* lavorare a ore, a giornata
character ['kærɪktəʳ] *s.* **1** carattere *m.* **2** personaggio *m.*
characteristic [ˌkærɪktə'rɪstɪk] **A** *s.* caratteristica *f.* **B** *agg.* caratteristico
to characterize ['kærɪktəraɪz] *v. tr.* caratterizzare
charade [ʃə'raːd] *s.* sciarada *f.*
charcoal ['tʃaːkɒʊl] *s.* **1** carbonella *f.* **2** carboncino *m.*
chard [tʃaːd] *s.* bietola *f.*
charge [tʃaːdʒ] *s.* **1** carica *f.*, incarico *m.*, onere *m.* **2** cura *f.*, sorveglianza *f.* **3** addebito *m.*, spesa *f.*, prezzo *m.* richiesto **4** (*dir.*) accusa *f.* **5** (*elettr.*) carica *f.*
to charge [tʃaːdʒ] **A** *v. tr.* **1** addebitare, far pagare **2** accusare **3** caricare **4** incaricare **B** *v. intr.* **1** lanciarsi, precipitarsi **2** andare alla carica
chariot ['tʃærɪət] *s.* cocchio *m.*
charioteer [ˌtʃærɪə'tɪəʳ] *s.* auriga *m.*
charismatic [ˌkærɪz'mætɪk] *agg.* carismatico
charitable ['tʃærɪtəbl] *agg.* caritatevole
charity ['tʃærɪtɪ] *s.* **1** carità *f.*, elemosina *f.* **2** beneficenza *f.*, istituzione *f.* benefica
charlady ['tʃaːˌleɪdɪ] *s.* domestica *f.* a ore
charlatan ['ʃaːlətən] *s.* ciarlatano *m.*
charm [tʃaːm] *s.* **1** incantesimo *m.* **2** fascino *m.* ♦ **lucky c.** portafortuna
to charm [tʃaːm] *v. tr.* incantare, affascinare
charming ['tʃaːmɪŋ] *agg.* affascinante, avvincente, incantevole
chart [tʃaːt] *s.* **1** diagramma *m.*, grafico *m.* **2** carta *f.* nautica **3** *al pl.* hit-parade *f.*
charter ['tʃaːtəʳ] **A** *s.* statuto *m.* **B** *agg.* a noleggio ♦ **c. flight** volo charter
to charter ['tʃaːtəʳ] *v. tr.* noleggiare
charterer ['tʃaːtərəʳ] *s.* noleggiatore *m.*
chartreuse [ʃaː'trɜːz] *s.* certosa *f.*
chase [tʃeɪs] *s.* caccia *f.*, inseguimento *m.*
to chase [tʃeɪs] **A** *v. tr.* cacciare, inseguire **B** *v. intr.* affrettarsi
chasm ['kæz(ə)m] *s.* baratro *m.*, voragine *f.*
chassis ['ʃæsɪ] *s.* châssis *m. inv.*, telaio *m.*
chaste [tʃeɪst] *agg.* castigato
chastity ['tʃæstɪtɪ] *s.* castità *f.*
chat [tʃæt] *s.* chiacchierata *f.*
to chat [tʃæt] *v. intr.* chiacchierare
chatter ['tʃætəʳ] *s.* **1** chiacchiera *f.*, ciarla *f.* **2** cinguettio *m.* **3** il battere i denti
to chatter ['tʃætəʳ] *v. intr.* **1** chiacchierare **2** cinguettare **3** battere i denti
chatterbox ['tʃætəbɔks] *s.* chiacchierone *m.*
chatty ['tʃætɪ] *agg.* **1** chiacchierone **2** familiare, amichevole
chauvinism ['ʃɒʊvɪnɪz(ə)m] *s.* sciovinismo *m.*
cheap [tʃiːp] **A** *agg.* **1** economico, conveniente **2** dozzinale, grossolano **3** meschino, volgare **B** *avv.* a basso prezzo
cheapish ['tʃiːpɪʃ] *agg.* dozzinale
cheat [tʃiːt] *s.* **1** imbroglione *m.*, truffatore *m.* **2** imbroglio *m.*, truffa *f.*
to cheat [tʃiːt] *v. tr. e intr.* imbrogliare, truffare
check [tʃɛk] *s.* **1** controllo *m.*, verifica *f.*,

ispezione *f.* **2** ostacolo *m.*, arresto *m.* **3** (*USA*) assegno *m.* **4** (*USA*) (al ristorante) conto *m.* **5** scontrino *m.* **6** scacco *m.*
to check [tʃɛk] **A** *v. tr.* **1** controllare, verificare **2** frenare, impedire **3** contrassegnare **4** depositare, lasciare in custodia **B** *v. intr.* concordare ♦ **to c. in** (*in albergo, aeroporto*) registrarsi; **to c. out** controllare, saldare il conto dell'albergo; **to c. up** verificare, controllare
checkmate ['tʃɛk,meɪt] *s.* scaccomatto *m.*
to checkmate ['tʃɛk,meɪt] *v. tr.* dare scaccomatto a
cheek [tʃiːk] *s.* **1** guancia *f.* **2** sfacciataggine *f.*
cheekbone ['tʃiːkbɒʊn] *s.* zigomo *m.*
cheeky ['tʃiːkɪ] *agg.* impertinente, sfacciato
to cheep [tʃiːp] *v. intr.* pigolare
cheer ['tʃɪəʳ] *s.* grido *m.* di incoraggiamento, evviva *m. inv.*
to cheer ['tʃɪəʳ] **A** *v. tr.* rallegrare **B** *v. intr.* applaudire, incoraggiare ♦ **c. up!** coraggio!; **to c. up** rallegrarsi
cheerful ['tʃɪəf(ʊ)l] *agg.* allegro, contento
cheerfulness ['tʃɪəf(ʊ)lnɪs] *s.* allegria *f.*, contentezza *f.*
cheering ['tʃɪrɪŋ] *s.* applauso *m.*
cheese [tʃiːz] *s.* formaggio *m.* ♦ **c. factory** caseificio *m.*
cheetah ['tʃiːtə] *s.* ghepardo *m.*
chemical ['kɛmɪk(ə)l] **A** *agg.* chimico **B** *s.* prodotto *m.* chimico
chemist ['kɛmɪst] *s.* **1** chimico *m.* **2** farmacista *m. e f.* ♦ **c.'s shop** farmacia
chemistry ['kɛmɪstrɪ] *s.* chimica *f.*
cheque [tʃɛk] *s.* assegno *m.* ♦ **blank c.** assegno in bianco; **c. book** libretto degli assegni; **c. card** carta assegni; **uncovered c.** assegno scoperto
to cherish ['tʃɛrɪʃ] *v. tr.* aver caro, curare
cherry ['tʃɛrɪ] *s.* ciliegia *f.*
chess [tʃɛs] *s.* scacchi *m. pl.* ♦ **c. board** scacchiera
chest [tʃɛst] *s.* **1** cassa *f.*, cassapanca *f.* **2** scatola *f.* **3** torace *m.*, petto *m.* ♦ **c. of drawers** cassettone
chestnut ['tʃɛsnʌt] *s.* castagna *f.*
to chew [tʃuː] *v. tr.* masticare
chewing gum ['tʃʊ(ː)ɪŋgʌm] *s.* gomma *f.* da masticare
chick [tʃɪk] *s.* pulcino *m.*
chicken ['tʃɪkɪn] *s.* pollo *m.* ♦ **c. pox** varicella; **roast c.** pollo arrosto
chickpea ['tʃɪkpiː] *s.* cece *m.*
chicory ['tʃɪkərɪ] *s.* cicoria *f.*
chief [tʃiːf] **A** *s.* capo *m.*, comandante *m.* **B** *agg.* principale ♦ **c. town** capoluogo
chiefly ['tʃiːflɪ] *avv.* principalmente
child [tʃaɪld] (*pl.* **children**) bambino *m.*, figlio *m.* ♦ **c. birth** parto; **only c.** figlio unico
childhood ['tʃaɪldhʊd] *s.* infanzia *f.*
childish ['tʃaɪldɪʃ] *agg.* puerile
chill [tʃɪl] *agg. e s.* freddo *m.*
to chill [tʃɪl] *v. tr. e intr.* raffreddare, raffreddarsi
chilli ['tʃɪlɪ] *s.* peperoncino *m.*
chilly ['tʃɪlɪ] *agg.* **1** freddo **2** freddoloso
to chime [tʃaɪm] *v. intr.* scampanare, rintoccare
chimney ['tʃɪmnɪ] *s.* camino *m.*, comignolo *m.*, ciminiera *f.* ♦ **c.-sweep(er)** spazzacamino
chimpanzee [,tʃɪmpən'ziː] *s.* scimpanzé *m.*
chin [tʃɪn] *s.* mento *m.*
china ['tʃaɪnə] *s.* porcellana *f.* ♦ **c. clay** caolino
chinaware ['tʃaɪnəwɛəʳ] *s.* stoviglie *f. pl.* di porcellana
Chinese [tʃaɪ'niːz] *agg. e s.* cinese *m. e f.*
chip [tʃɪp] *s.* **1** scheggia *f.*, scaglia *f.*, pezzetto *m.* **2** *al pl.* patatine *f. pl.* fritte **3** gettone *m.* **4** (*elettron.*) chip *m. inv.*
to chip [tʃɪp] **A** *v. tr.* scalpellare, scheggiare **B** *v. intr.* scheggiarsi ♦ **to c. in** interloquire, contribuire
chiromancer ['kaɪərəmænsəʳ] *s.* chiromante *m. e f.*
chiropodist [kɪ'rəpədɪst] *s.* pedicure *m. e f. inv.*
to chirp [tʃɜːp] *v. intr.* cinguettare, frinire
to chirrup ['tʃɪrəp] *v. intr.* cinguettare, frinire
chisel ['tʃɪzl] *s.* cesello *m.*, scalpello *m.*
to chisel ['tʃɪzl] *v. tr.* cesellare, scalpellare
chit [tʃɪt] *s.* (*fam.*) biglietto *m.*
chivalrous ['ʃɪv(ə)l(r)əs] *agg.* cavalleresco
chivalry ['ʃɪv(ə)lrɪ] *s.* cavalleria *f.*
chive [tʃaɪv] *s.* erba *f.* cipollina
chlorine ['klɜːriːn] *s.* cloro *m.*
chlorophyl ['klərəfɪl] *s.* clorofilla *f.*
chock-a-block [,tʃəkə'blək] *agg.* pieno zeppo
chocolate ['tʃək(ə)lɪt] **A** *agg.* di cioccolato **B** *s.* cioccolato *m.*, cioccolata *f.*, cioccolatino *m.* ♦ **milk c.** cioccolato al latte; **plain c.** cioccolato fondente

choice [tʃɔɪs] **A** *agg.* scelto **B** *s.* scelta *f.* ♦ **at c.** a volontà
choir ['kwaɪəʳ] *s.* coro *m.*
choke [tʃɒʊk] *s.* **1** soffocamento *m.* **2** ingorgo *m.*, intasamento *m.* **3** (*autom.*) valvola *f.* dell'aria
to choke [tʃɒʊk] **A** *v. tr.* **1** soffocare, strozzare **2** intasare, ingolfare **B** *v. intr.* soffocare
choking ['tʃɒʊkɪŋ] **A** *agg.* soffocante **B** *s.* soffocamento *m.*
cholera ['kələrə] *s.* colera *m.*
cholesterol [kə'lɛstərəl] *s.* colesterolo *m.*
to choose [tʃuːz] (*pass.* **chose**, *p. p.* **chosen**) *v. tr. e intr.* **1** scegliere **2** gradire, preferire
choosy [tʃuːzɪ] *agg.* (*fam.*) schizzinoso
chop (1) [tʃəp] *s.* **1** costata *f.* **2** taglio *m.* ♦ **lamb c.** costata d'agnello; **pork c.** costata di maiale
chop (2) [tʃəp] *s.* mascella *f.*
to chop [tʃəp] *v. tr.* **1** tagliare, fare a pezzi **2** tritare ♦ **to c. off** recidere
chopping-board ['tʃəpɪŋ,bɜːd] *s.* tagliere *m.*
choppy ['tʃəpɪ] *agg.* (*di mare*) increspato
choral ['kɜːr(ə)l] *agg.* corale
chord [kɜːd] *s.* (*mus.*) accordo *m.*
choreography [,kərɪ'əgrəfɪ] *s.* coreografia *f.*
chorister ['kərɪstəʳ] *s.* corista *m. e f.*
chorus ['kɜːrəs] *s.* **1** coro *m.* **2** corpo *m.* di ballo ♦ **c. girl** ballerina di fila
chose [tʃɒʊz] *pass. di* **to choose**
chosen ['tʃɒʊzn] *p. p. di* **to choose**
chowder ['tʃaʊdəʳ] *s.* zuppa *f.* (*di pesce*) ♦ **clam c.** zuppa di vongole
to christen ['krɪsn] *v. tr.* battezzare
Christendom ['krɪsndəm] *s.* cristianità *f.*
Christian ['krɪstjən] *agg.* cristiano ♦ **C. name** nome (di battesimo)
Christianity [,krɪstɪ'ænɪtɪ] *s.* cristianesimo *m.*
Christmas ['krɪsməs] *s.* Natale *m.* ♦ **C. Eve** vigilia di Natale; **merry C.** buon Natale
chromatic [krə'mætɪk] *agg.* cromatico
chrome [krɒʊm] *s.* cromo *m.*
chromium ['krɒʊmjəm] *s.* cromo *m.* ♦ **c. plating** cromatura
chronic ['krənɪk] *agg.* cronico
chronicle ['krənɪkl] *s.* cronaca *f.*, cronistoria *f.*
chronicler ['krənɪkləʳ] *s.* cronista *m. e f.*
chronologic(al) [,krənə'lədʒɪk((ə)l)] *agg.* cronologico
chronometer [krə'nəmɪtəʳ] *s.* cronometro *m.*
chubby ['tʃʌbɪ] *agg.* paffuto
to chuck [tʃʌk] *v. tr.* gettare, buttare ♦ **to c. out** sbattere fuori
to chuckle ['tʃʌkl] *v. intr.* ridacchiare, sogghignare
chum [tʃʌm] *s.* compagno *m.*, amico *m.*
chunk [tʃʌŋk] *s.* pezzo *m.* (*grosso*)
church [tʃɜːtʃ] *s.* chiesa *f.* ♦ **c.-officer** sagrestano; **c. tower** campanile
churchyard ['tʃɜːtʃjaːd] *s.* **1** cimitero *m.* (*presso una chiesa*) **2** sagrato *m.*
churlish ['tʃɜːlɪʃ] *agg.* villano, rozzo
churn [tʃɜːn] *s.* **1** zangola *f.* **2** bidone *m.* (*per latte*)
chute [ʃuːt] *s.* **1** scivolo *m.* **2** canale *m.* di scarico **3** cascata *f.*
cicada [sɪ'kaːdə] *s.* cicala *f.*
cicerone [,tʃɪtʃə'rɒʊnɪ] *s.* cicerone *m.*
cider ['saɪdəʳ] *s.* sidro *m.*
cigar [sɪ'gaːʳ] *s.* sigaro *m.*
cigarette [,sɪgə'rɛt] *s.* sigaretta *f.* ♦ **c. end** mozzicone; **c. holder** bocchino
cinecamera ['sɪnɪ,kæm(ə)rə] *s.* cinepresa *f.*
cinema ['sɪnɪmə] *s.* cinema *m. inv.*
cinematographic [,sɪnɪ,mætə'græfɪk] *agg.* cinematografico
cinerary ['sɪnərərɪ] *agg.* cinerario
cinnabar ['sɪnəbaːʳ] *s.* cinabro *m.*
cinnamon ['sɪnəmən] *s.* cannella *f.*
circle ['sɜːkl] *s.* **1** cerchio *m.* **2** circolo *m.*, anello *m.* **3** (*teatro*) galleria *f.* **4** cerchia *f.*
to circle ['sɜːkl] **A** *v. tr.* **1** circondare **2** girare intorno a **B** *v. intr.* muoversi in cerchio
circuit ['sɜːkɪt] *s.* **1** circuito *m.* **2** giro *m.*
circuitous [sə(ː)'kjuːɪtəs] *agg.* tortuoso, indiretto
circular ['sɜːkjʊləʳ] **A** *agg.* circolare **B** *s.* (lettera) circolare *f.*
to circulate ['sɜːkjʊleɪt] **A** *v. intr.* **1** circolare **2** diffondersi **B** *v. tr.* far circolare
circulation [,sɜːkjʊ'leɪʃ(ə)n] *s.* **1** circolazione *f.* **2** diffusione *f.*
circumcision [,sɜːkəm'sɪʒ(ə)n] *s.* circoncisione *f.*
circumference [sə'kʌmf(ə)r(ə)ns] *s.* circonferenza *f.*
to circumscribe ['sɜːkəmskraɪb] *v. tr.* circoscrivere
circumstance ['sɜːkəmstəns] *s.* circo-

stanza *f.*
to circumvent [ˌsɛːkəm'vɛnt] *v. tr.* **1** circuire **2** eludere
circus ['sɜːkəs] *s.* circo *m.*
Cistercian [sɪs'tɜːʃən] *agg.* cistercense
cistern ['sɪstən] *s.* cisterna *f.*, serbatoio *m.*
citadel ['sɪtədl] *s.* cittadella *f.*
citation [saɪ'teɪʃ(ə)n] *s.* citazione *f.*
to cite [saɪt] *v. tr.* citare
citizen ['sɪtɪzn] *s.* cittadino *m.*
citizenship ['sɪtɪz(ə)nʃɪp] *s.* cittadinanza *f.*
citron ['sɪtr(ə)n] *s.* cedro *m.* (*frutto*)
city ['sɪtɪ] *s.* città *f.* ♦ **c. planner** urbanista; **c. planning** urbanistica
civic ['sɪvɪk] *agg.* civico
civil ['sɪvl] *agg.* civile ♦ **c. servant** impiegato statale; **c. service** pubblica amministrazione
civility [sɪ'vɪlɪtɪ] *s.* civiltà *f.*, educazione *f.*
civilization [ˌsɪvɪlaɪ'zeɪʃ(ə)n] *s.* civiltà *f.*, civilizzazione *f.*
clad [klæd] *agg.* (*arc.*) vestito, rivestito
claim [kleɪm] *s.* **1** richiesta *f.*, rivendicazione *f.* **2** reclamo *m.* **3** affermazione *f.*
to claim [kleɪm] *v. tr.* **1** pretendere, rivendicare **2** reclamare **3** sostenere
claimant ['kleɪmənt] *s.* richiedente *m. e f.*
clam [klæm] *s.* **1** vongola *f.* **2** mollusco *m.* (bivalve)
to clamber ['klæmbər] *v. intr.* arrampicarsi (*con mani e piedi*)
clammy ['klæmɪ] *agg.* viscido, appiccicaticcio
clamorous ['klæm(ə)rəs] *agg.* clamoroso
clamour ['klæmər] (*USA* **clamor**) *s.* **1** clamore *m.* **2** rimostranza *f.*
to clamour ['klæmər] (*USA* **to clamor**) *v. intr.* **1** strepitare **2** chiedere a gran voce
clamp [klæmp] *s.* morsetto *m.*, pinza *f.*
clan [klæn] *s.* clan *m. inv.*
clandestine [klæn'dɛstɪn] *s.* clandestino *m.*
to clang [klæŋ] *v. intr.* produrre un suono metallico
to clap [klæp] **A** *v. tr.* **1** applaudire **2** dare un colpo con la mano **3** (*fam.*) mandare **B** *v. intr.* applaudire ♦ **to c. on** infilarsi
to clarify ['klærɪfaɪ] *v. tr.* **1** chiarire **2** (*tecnol.*) raffinare
clarinet [ˌklærɪ'nɛt] *s.* clarinetto *m.*
clarity ['klærɪtɪ] *s.* chiarezza *f.*
clash [klæʃ] *s.* **1** cozzo *m.*, urto *m.*, rumore *m.* metallico **2** (*fig.*) scontro *m.*
to clash [klæʃ] *v. intr.* **1** cozzare, urtare, stridere **2** (*fig.*) scontrarsi
clasp [klaːsp] *s.* **1** fermaglio *m.*, fibbia *f.* **2** stretta *f.*
to clasp [klaːsp] *v. tr.* **1** affibbiare, agganciare **2** stringere, serrare
class [klaːs] *s.* **1** classe *f.*, categoria *f.* **2** corso *m.*, lezione *f.* ♦ **first c.** prima classe; **middle c.** ceto medio
to class [klaːs] *v. tr.* classificare
classic ['klæsɪk] *agg. e s.* classico *m.*
classical ['klæsɪkl] *agg.* classico
classicism ['klæsɪsɪz(ə)m] *s.* classicismo *m.*
classicist ['klæsɪsɪst] *s.* classicista *m. e f.*
classification [ˌklæsɪfɪ'keɪʃ(ə)n] *s.* classificazione *f.*
classified ['klæsɪfaɪd] *agg.* **1** (*di documento*) segreto, riservato **2** classificato
to classify ['klæsɪfaɪ] *v. tr.* classificare
classmate ['klaːsmeɪt] *s.* compagno *m.* di classe
classroom ['klaːsrʊm] *s.* aula *f.*
clatter ['klætər] *s.* **1** acciottolio *m.* **2** scalpitio *m.*
clause [klɜːz] *s.* **1** clausola *f.* **2** (*gramm.*) proposizione *f.*
claustrophobia [ˌklɜːstrə'fɒʊbjə] *s.* claustrofobia *f.*
clavicle ['klævɪkl] *s.* clavicola *f.*
claw [klɜː] *s.* **1** artiglio *m.* **2** chela *f.*, pinza *f.* **3** zampa *f.*
to claw [klɜː] *v. tr.* artigliare ♦ **to c. at** afferrarsi a; **to c. off** prendere il largo
clay [kleɪ] *s.* argilla *f.*, creta *f.*
clean [kliːn] **A** *agg.* **1** pulito, puro, limpido **2** armonioso **3** accurato, preciso **B** *avv.* completamente
to clean [kliːn] *v. tr. e intr.* pulire, pulirsi ♦ **to c. out** ripulire; **to c. up** pulire, raccogliere
clean-cut [ˌkliːn'kʌt] *agg.* **1** ben delineato, marcato **2** (*di persona*) pulito, per bene
cleaner ['kliːnər] *s.* **1** addetto *m.* alle pulizie **2** depuratore *m.* ♦ **c.'s** tintoria
cleaning ['kliːnɪŋ] *s.* pulizia *f.*
to cleanse [klɛnz] *v. tr.* **1** pulire, detergere **2** (*fig.*) purificare
clean-shaven [ˌkliːn'ʃeɪvn] *agg.* ben rasato
cleansing ['klɛnzɪŋ] *agg.* detergente
clear [klɪər] *agg.* **1** chiaro, limpido, nitido **2** aperto, libero, sgombro **3** (*di somma*) netto **4** sicuro

to clear [klɪəʳ] **A** *v. tr.* **1** chiarire, schiarire **2** discolpare **3** liberare, svuotare sgomberare **4** superare **5** sdoganare **B** *v. intr.* diventare chiaro, rasserenarsi ♦ **to c. off** squagliarsela; **to c. out** andarsene; **to c. up** chiarire, ripulire
clearing ['klɪərɪŋ] *s.* radura *f.*
clearly ['klɪəlɪ] *avv.* chiaramente
clearness ['klɪənɪs] *s.* limpidezza *f.*
clearway ['klɪəweɪ] *s.* strada *f.* con divieto di sosta
to cleave [kli:v] (*pass. e p. p.* **cleaved, cleft**) *v. tr.* fendere, spaccare
cleaver ['kli:vəʳ] *s.* mannaia *f.*
clef [klɛf] *s.* (*mus.*) chiave *f.*
cleft [klɛft] **A** *pass. e p. p. di* **to cleave B** *s.* crepaccio *m.*, fessura *f.*
to clench [klɛn(t)ʃ] *v. tr.* stringere, serrare
clepsydra ['klɛpsɪdrə] *s.* clessidra *f.*
clergy ['klɜ:dʒɪ] *s.* clero *m.*
clergyman ['klɜ:dʒɪmən] *s.* ecclesiastico *m.*
cleric ['klɛrɪk] *s.* chierico *m.*
clerical ['klɛrɪkl] *agg.* **1** clericale **2** di impiegato, di scrivano
clerk [kla:k] *s.* **1** impiegato *m.* **2** (*USA*) commesso
clever ['klɛvəʳ] *agg.* **1** bravo, abile, intelligente **2** eseguito con abilità
cleverness ['klɛvənɪs] *s.* ingegnosità *f.*, abilità *f.*, intelligenza *f.*
clew [klu:] *s.* **1** gomitolo *m.* **2** (*naut.*) bugna *f.*
click [klɪk] *s.* scatto *m.*
to click [klɪk] *v. tr. e intr.* **1** battere, far scattare, schioccare **2** (*fam.*) riuscire
client ['klaɪənt] *s.* cliente *m. e f.*
cliff [klɪf] *s.* rupe *f.*, scogliera *f.*
climate ['klaɪmɪt] *s.* clima *m.*
climatic [klaɪ'mætɪk] *agg.* climatico
climax ['klaɪmæks] *s.* culmine *m.*, apice *m.*
climb [klaɪm] *s.* salita *f.*, arrampicata *f.*
to climb [klaɪm] *v. tr. e intr.* arrampicarsi, scalare, salire ♦ **to c. down** scendere
climber ['klaɪməʳ] *s.* **1** scalatore *m.*, arrampicatore *m.* **2** (*bot.*) rampicante *m.*
climbing ['klaɪmɪŋ] **A** *agg.* rampicante **B** *s.* **1** alpinismo *m.* **2** arrampicata *f.* ♦ **free c.** arrampicata libera
to clinch [klɪn(t)ʃ] *v. tr.* concludere
to cling [klɪŋ] (*pass. e p. p.* **clung**) *v. intr.* aggrapparsi, attaccarsi
clinging ['klɪŋɪŋ] *agg.* **1** attillato, aderente **2** appiccicoso
clinic ['klɪnɪk] *s.* clinica *f.*
clinical ['klɪnɪk(ə)l] *agg.* clinico
clip [klɪp] *s.* **1** fermaglio *m.*, molletta *f.* **2** spilla *f.*
to clip (1) [klɪp] *v. tr.* unire, attaccare
to clip (2) [klɪp] *v. tr.* **1** tosare **2** (*una siepe*) potare
clipper ['klɪpəʳ] *s.* **1** *al pl.* forbici *f. pl.*, cesoie *f. pl.* **2** (*naut.*) clipper *m. inv.*
clipping ['klɪpɪŋ] *s.* **1** taglio *m.*, tosatura *f.* **2** (*di giornale*) ritaglio *m.*
clique [kli:k] *s.* conventicola *f.*
cloak [klɒʊk] *s.* mantello *m.* ♦ **c. room** guardaroba (*in locale pubblico*), gabinetti
to cloak [klɒʊk] *v. tr.* avvolgere, nascondere
clock [klək] *s.* orologio *m.* ♦ **alarm c.** sveglia
to clock [klək] *v. tr.* cronometrare ♦ **to c. in (on)/off (out)** timbrare il cartellino all'entrata/uscita
clockwise ['kləkwaɪz] *avv.* in senso orario
clog [kləg] *s.* **1** zoccolo *m.* **2** impedimento *m.*, ostacolo *m.*
to clog [kləg] **A** *v. tr.* **1** inceppare, impedire **2** ostruire **B** *v. intr.* intasarsi, otturarsi
cloister ['kləɪstəʳ] *s.* chiostro *m.*
close [klɒʊs] **A** *agg.* **1** vicino **2** intimo **3** chiuso, serrato, ristretto **4** nascosto, riservato, appartato **5** afoso **B** *avv.* vicino ♦ **c. on** quasi; **c. to** vicino a
to close [klɒʊz] **A** *v. tr.* **1** chiudere **2** concludere **B** *v. intr.* **1** chiudere, chiudersi **2** finire ♦ **to c. about/around** avvolgere; **to c. down** chiudere, cessare l'attività; **to c. up** ostruire, serrare; **closing time** ora di chiusura
closely ['klɒʊslɪ] *avv.* **1** strettamente **2** attentamente
closet ['kləzɪt] *s.* stanzino *m.*, bugigattolo *m.*, armadio *m.*
close-up ['klɒʊsʌp] *s.* (*fot.*, *cine.*) primo piano *m.*
closure ['klɒʊʒəʳ] *s.* chiusura *f.*
clot [klət] *s.* **1** grumo *m.*, coagulo *m.* **2** (*pop.*) stupido *m.*
to clot [klət] *v. tr. e intr.* coagulare, coagularsi
cloth [kləθ] *s.* **1** stoffa *f.*, tela *f.* **2** straccio *m.* ♦ **table c.** tovaglia
clothes [klɒʊðz] *s. pl.* **1** abbigliamento *m.*, vestiti *m. pl.* **2** biancheria *f.* (da letto) ♦ **c. hanger** gruccia; **c. hook** attaccapanni; **c. peg** molletta per panni
clothing ['klɒʊðɪŋ] *s.* abbigliamento *m.*,

vestiario *m.*
cloud [klaʊd] *s.* **1** nube *f.*, nuvola *f.* **2** macchia *f.* ♦ **c. burst** nubifragio
to cloud [klaʊd] *v. intr.* **1** annuvolarsi **2** macchiarsi, intorbidarsi
cloudy ['klaʊdɪ] *agg.* **1** nuvoloso **2** di cattivo umore **3** torbido
clove (1) [klɒʊv] *s.* chiodo *m.* di garofano
clove (2) [klɒʊv] *s.* (*di aglio*) spicchio *m.*
clover ['klɒʊvəʳ] *s.* trifoglio *m.*
clown [klaʊn] *s.* clown *m. inv.*, pagliaccio *m.*
to cloy [klɔɪ] *v. tr.* saziare, stuccare, nauseare
club [klʌb] *s.* **1** mazza *f.*, randello *m.* **2** club *m. inv.*, circolo *m.*, associazione *f.* **3** (carta di) fiori *m. pl.*
to club [klʌb] **A** *v. tr.* bastonare **B** *v. intr.* raccogliersi in un circolo ♦ **to c. with** associarsi
to cluck [klʌk] *v. intr.* chiocciare
clue [kluː] *s.* **1** indizio *m.*, indicazione *f.* **2** (*di cruciverba*) definizione *f.* **3** (*naut.*) bugna *f.*
clumsy ['klʌmzɪ] *agg.* goffo, maldestro
clung [klʌŋ] *pass. e p. p. di* **to cling**
cluster ['klʌstəʳ] *s.* **1** grappolo *m.*, mazzo *m.*, ammasso *m.* **2** sciame *m.*
to cluster ['klʌstəʳ] *v. intr.* raggrupparsi
clutch [klʌtʃ] *s.* **1** presa *f.*, stretta *f.* **2** (*mecc.*) frizione *f.*
to clutch [klʌtʃ] **A** *v. tr.* afferrare, stringere **B** *v. intr.* aggrapparsi
to clutter ['klʌtəʳ] *v. tr.* ingombrare, mettere in disordine
coach [kɒʊtʃ] *s.* **1** carrozza *f.*, pullman *m.*, vettura *f.* **2** insegnante *m.* privato **3** (*sport*) allenatore *m.*
coagulant [kɒ(ʊ)'ægjʊlənt] *s.* coagulante *m.*
coal [kɒʊl] *s.* carbone *m.*
coalition [ˌkɒ(ʊ)ə'lɪʃən] *s.* coalizione *f.*
coalmine ['kɒʊlmaɪn] *s.* miniera *f.* di carbone
coarse [kɜːs] *agg.* **1** grossolano, volgare **2** (*di tessuto e sim.*) ruvido, grezzo
coast [kɒʊst] *s.* costa *f.*, litorale *m.*
to coast [kɒʊst] *v. intr.* costeggiare
coastal ['kɒʊstl] *agg.* costiero
coat [kɒʊt] *s.* **1** giacca *f.*, soprabito *m.*, mantello *m.* **2** pelo *m.*, pelliccia *f.* **3** rivestimento *m.* **4** (*di vernice*) mano *f.* ♦ **c. hanger** attaccapanni; **c. of arms** stemma
to coat [kɒʊt] *v. tr.* rivestire
coating ['kɒʊtɪŋ] *s.* **1** rivestimento *m.* **2** (*di vernice*) mano *f.* **3** tessuto *m.*
coauthor [kɒʊ'ɜːθəʳ] *s.* coautore *m.*
to coax [kɒʊks] *v. tr. e intr.* persuadere, indurre
cob [kəb] *s.* pannocchia *f.*
cobble ['kəbl] *s.* ciottolo *m.*
cocaine [kɒʊ'keɪn] *s.* cocaina *f.*
cock [kək] *s.* **1** gallo *m.* **2** (*di uccelli*) maschio *m.*
cockerel ['kək(ə)r(ə)l] *s.* galletto *m.*
cockeyed ['kəkaɪd] *agg.* **1** strabico **2** strampalato
cockpit ['kəkpɪt] *s.* **1** abitacolo *m.*, cabina *f.* di pilotaggio **2** (*naut.*) pozzetto *m.*
cockroach ['kəkrɒʊtʃ] *s.* scarafaggio *m.*
cocktail ['kəkteɪl] *s.* cocktail *m. inv.*
cocoa ['kɒʊkɒʊ] *s.* cacao *m.* (in polvere)
coconut ['kɒʊkənʌt] *s.* (noce di) cocco *m.*
cocoon [kə'kuːn] *s.* bozzolo *m.*
cod [kəd] *s.* merluzzo *m.* ♦ **dried c.** stoccafisso; **salted c.** baccalà
code [kɒʊd] *s.* **1** codice *m.* **2** prefisso *m.* ♦ **dialling c.** (*USA* **area c.**) prefisso telefonico; **postal c.** (*USA* **zip c.**) codice postale
codification [ˌkədɪfɪ'keɪʃ(ə)n] *s.* codifica *f.*
coefficient [ˌkɒ(ʊ)ɪ'fɪs(ə)nt] *s.* coefficiente *m.*
to coerce [kɒ(ʊ)'ɜːs] *v. tr.* costringere
coercion [kɒʊ'ɜːʃ(ə)n] *s.* coercizione *f.*
coeval [kɒ(ʊ)'iːv(ə)l] *agg.* coevo
coexistent [kɒ(ʊ)ɪg'zɪstənt] *agg.* coesistente
coffee ['kəfɪ] *s.* caffè *m.* ♦ **black c.** caffè nero; **c. break** pausa per il caffè; **c. cup** tazzina; **c. table** tavolino (*da salotto*); **instant c.** caffè solubile; **strong c.** caffè ristretto; **weak c.** caffè lungo
coffeepot ['kəfɪpət] *s.* caffettiera *f.*
coffer ['kəfəʳ] *s.* **1** cofano *m.*, forziere *m.*, scrigno *m.* **2** (*arch.*) cassettone *m.*
coffin ['kəfɪn] *s.* bara *f.*
cog [kəg] *s.* (*mecc.*) dente *m.*, ingranaggio *m.*
cogent ['kɒʊdʒ(ə)nt] *agg.* persuasivo, convincente
to cohabit [kɒ(ʊ)'hæbɪt] *v. intr.* convivere
cohabitation [ˌkɒ(ʊ)hæbɪ'teɪʃ(ə)n] *s.* coabitazione *f.*
to cohere [kɒ(ʊ)'hɪəʳ] *v. tr.* aderire a
coherent [kɒ(ʊ)'hɪərənt] *agg.* coerente
coil [kəɪl] *s.* **1** spira *f.* **2** (*elettr*) avvolgimento *m.*
to coil [kəɪl] *v. tr.* avvolgere, attorcigliare

coin [kɔɪn] *s.* moneta *f.*
to **coin** [kɔɪn] *v. tr.* coniare
to **coincide** [ˌkɒ(ʊ)ɪn'saɪd] *v. intr.* coincidere, concordare
coincidence [kɒ(ʊ)'ɪnsɪd(ə)ns] *s.* coincidenza *f.*, combinazione *f.*
coke [kɒʊk] **1** (carbone) coke *m. inv.* **2** Coca-Cola *f.* **3** cocaina *f.*
colander ['kʌləndəʳ] *s.* colino *m.*
cold [kɒʊld] **A** *agg.* freddo **B** *s.* **1** freddo *m.* **2** raffreddore *m.*, infreddatura *f.* ♦ **in c. blood** a sangue freddo; **to be c.** aver freddo, far freddo; **to catch a c.** prendere un raffreddore
coldly ['kɒʊldlɪ] *avv.* freddamente
cole [kɒʊl] *s.* ravizzone *m.*
colic ['kəlɪk] *s.* colica *f.*
colitis [kə'laɪtɪs] *s.* colite *f.*
to **collaborate** [kə'læbəreɪt] *v. intr.* cooperare, collaborare
collaboration [kəˌlæbə'rɛʃ(ə)n] *s.* collaborazione *f.*
collaborator [kə'læbəˌreɪtəʳ] *s.* collaboratore *m.*
collapse [kə'læps] *s.* **1** crollo *m.* **2** (*med.*) collasso *m.*
to **collapse** [kə'læps] *v. intr.* **1** crollare, franare, sprofondare **2** (*med.*) avere un collasso
collar ['kələʳ] *s.* **1** colletto *m.* **2** collare *m.*
collarbone ['kələbɒʊn] *s.* clavicola *f.*
collateral [kə'læt(ə)r(ə)l] *agg.* collaterale
colleague ['kəliːg] *s.* collega *m. e f.*
collect [kə'lɛkt] *agg. e avv.* (*USA*) con tassa a carico ♦ **c. call** telefonata a carico del destinatario
to **collect** [kə'lɛkt] **A** *v. tr.* **1** raccogliere, radunare **2** riscuotere, incassare **3** collezionare **B** *v. intr.* **1** raccogliersi, radunarsi **2** raccogliere offerte, fare una colletta ♦ **to c. up** riunire
collection [kə'lɛkʃ(ə)n] *s.* **1** collezione *f.*, raccolta *f.* **2** colletta *f.*
collective [kə'lɛktɪv] *agg.* collettivo
collectivity [ˌkəlɛk'tɪvɪtɪ] *s.* collettività *f.*
collector [kə'lɛktəʳ] *s.* **1** collezionista *m. e f.* **2** esattore *m.*
college ['kəlɪdʒ] *s.* **1** istituto *m.*, scuola *f.* secondaria **2** (*USA*) università *f.* **3** collegio *m.* (*edificio*)
to **collide** [kə'laɪd] *v. intr.* urtare, scontrarsi
colliery ['kəljərɪ] *s.* miniera *f.* di carbone
collision [kə'lɪʒ(ə)n] *s.* **1** collisione *f.*, scontro *m.* **2** conflitto *m.*
colloquial [kə'lɒʊkwɪəl] *agg.* colloquiale
colon (1) ['kɒʊlən] *s.* colon *m. inv.*
colon (2) ['kɒʊlən] *s.* due punti *m. pl.* (*segno di punteggiatura*)
colonel ['kɜːnl] *s.* colonnello *m.*
colonial [kə'lɒʊnjəl] *agg.* coloniale
colonialism [kə'lɒʊnjəlɪz(ə)m] *s.* colonialismo *m.*
colonialist [kə'lɒʊnjəlɪst] *s.* colonialista *m. e f.*
to **colonize** ['kələnaɪz] *v. tr.* colonizzare
colonnade [ˌkələ'neɪd] *s.* colonnato *m.*
colony ['kələnɪ] *s.* colonia *f.*
colour ['kʌləʳ] (*USA* **color**) *s.* colore *m.* ♦ **c. bar** segregazione razziale; **c. blind** daltonico; **in (full) c.** a colori
to **colour** ['kʌləʳ] (*USA* **to color**) *v. tr. e intr.* colorare, colorarsi
coloured ['kʌləd] *agg.* **1** colorato **2** (*di persona*) di colore
colourful ['kʌləf(ʊ)l] *agg.* **1** colorato **2** colorito, pittoresco
colt [kɒʊlt] *s.* puledro *m.*
column ['kələm] *s.* **1** colonna *f.* **2** (*di giornale*) rubrica *f.*
columnist ['kələmnɪst] *s.* giornalista *m. e f.* (*che cura una rubrica*), cronista *m.* mondano
coma ['kɒʊmə] *s.* coma *m. inv.*
comb [kɒʊm] *s.* pettine *m.*
to **comb** [kɒʊm] *v. tr.* **1** pettinare **2** perlustrare
combat ['kəmbæt] *s.* combattimento *m.*
to **combat** ['kəmbæt] *v. tr. e intr.* combattere
combination [ˌkəmbɪ'neɪʃ(ə)n] *s.* combinazione *f.*, associazione *f.*
combine [kəm'baɪn] *s.* associazione *f.*
to **combine** [kəm'baɪn] **A** *v. tr.* **1** combinare, unire **2** associare **B** *v. intr.* **1** combinarsi, unirsi **2** associarsi
to **come** [kʌm] (*pass.* **came**, *p. p.* **come**) *v. intr.* **1** venire **2** arrivare, giungere **3** provenire **4** accadere ♦ **to c. about** accadere; **to c. across** imbattersi in; **to c. along** presentarsi; **to c. away** venir via; **to c. back** ritornare; **to c. by** procacciarsi; **to c. before** precedere; **to c. down** scendere, crollare; **to c. forward** farsi avanti; **to c. from** derivare; **to c. in** entrare; **to c. into** entrare, ereditare; **to c. off** staccarsi, venir via; **to c. on** affrettarsi, progredire, sopraggiungere, entrare in campo, entrare in azione; **to c. out** uscire, risultare; **to c. round** ritornare in sé; **to**

c. up salire, spuntare
comedian [kə'miːdjən] *s.* comico *m.*, commediante *m. e f.*
comedy ['kəmɪdɪ] *s.* commedia *f.*
comet ['kəmɪt] *s.* cometa *f.*
comfort ['kʌmfət] *s.* **1** comfort *m. inv.*, comodità *f.* **2** conforto *m.*, consolazione *f.*
to **comfort** ['kʌmfət] *v. tr.* confortare, consolare
comfortable ['kʌmf(ə)təbl] *agg.* **1** confortevole, accogliente **2** agiato
comforting ['kʌmfətɪŋ] *agg.* confortante
comic ['kəmɪk] **A** *agg.* comico **B** *s.* **1** comico *m.* **2** (attore) comico *m.* **3** giornale *m.* a fumetti, *al pl.* fumetti *m. pl.* ♦ **comics strip** striscia (di fumetti)
comicality [ˌkəmɪ'kælɪtɪ] *s.* comicità *f.*
coming ['kʌmɪŋ] **A** *agg.* prossimo, futuro **B** *s.* arrivo *m.* ♦ **c. and going** viavai
comma ['kəmə] *s.* virgola *f.*
command [kə'maːnd] *s.* **1** comando *m.* **2** padronanza *f.*
to **command** [kə'maːnd] **A** *v. tr.* **1** comandare, ordinare **2** disporre di **B** *v. intr.* avere il comando
commander [kə'maːndəʳ] *s.* comandante *m.* ♦ **c. in chief** comandante in capo
to **commemorate** [kə'mɛməreɪt] *v. tr.* commemorare
commemoration [kəˌmɛmə'reɪʃ(ə)n] *s.* commemorazione *f.*
to **commence** [kə'mɛns] *v. tr. e intr.* cominciare
to **commend** [kə'mɛnd] *v. tr.* **1** lodare **2** raccomandare
comment ['kəmɛnt] *s.* **1** commento *m.* **2** critica *f.*
to **comment** ['kəmɛnt] *v. tr.* **1** commentare **2** criticare
commentary ['kəmənt(ə)rɪ] *s.* **1** commento *m.* **2** (*radio, TV*) cronaca *f.*
commentator ['kəmɛnteɪtəʳ] *s.* **1** commentatore *m.* **2** (*radio, TV*) cronista *m. e f.*
commercial [kə'mɜːʃ(ə)l] **A** *agg.* commerciale **B** *s.* annuncio *m.* pubblicitario
to **commiserate** [kə'mɪzəreɪt] **A** *v. tr.* commiserare **B** *v. intr.* dolersi
commission [kə'mɪʃ(ə)n] *s.* **1** commissione *f.* **2** (*mil.*) grado *m.* da ufficiale ♦ **out of c.** (*di nave*) in disarmo, fuori servizio
to **commit** [kə'mɪt] *v. tr.* **1** commettere **2** affidare
commitment [kə'mɪtmənt] *s.* **1** impegno *m.* **2** responsabilità *f.*
committee [kə'mɪtɪ] *s.* comitato *m.*, commissione *f.*
commodity [kə'mədɪtɪ] *s.* **1** merce *f.*, prodotto *m.* **2** *al pl.* comodità *f. pl.*
common ['kəmən] **A** *agg.* **1** comune, usuale, corrente **2** generale, condiviso **3** ordinario **B** *s.* **1** (ciò che è) comune *m.* **2** terreno *m.* demaniale ♦ **c. law** diritto consuetudinario; **c. sense** buon senso
commoner ['kəmənəʳ] *s.* cittadino *m.* (*non nobile*)
commonly ['kəmənlɪ] *avv.* comunemente
commonplace ['kəmənpleɪs] **A** *agg.* banale **B** *s.* banalità *f.*, luogo *m.* comune
commotion [kə'mɒʊʃ(ə)n] *s.* confusione *f.*, tumulto *m.*
communal ['kəmjʊnl] *agg.* comunale, della comunità
to **commune** [kə'mjuːn] *v. intr.* comunicare, essere in comunione (spirituale)
to **communicate** [kə'mjuːnɪkeɪt] **A** *v. tr.* comunicare, trasmettere **B** *v. intr.* essere in comunicazione
communication [kəˌmjuːnɪ'keɪʃ(ə)n] *s.* comunicazione *f.* ♦ **c. cord** (*ferr.*) segnale d'allarme
communion [kə'mjuːnjən] *s.* **1** comunione *f.*, comunanza *f.* **2** (*relig.*) comunione *f.*, eucaristia *f.*
communism ['kəmjʊnɪz(ə)m] *s.* comunismo *m.*
communist ['kəmjʊnɪst] *agg. e s.* comunista *m. e f.*
community [kə'mjuːnɪtɪ] *s.* comunità *f.*, collettività *f.* ♦ **c. center** centro ricreativo
to **commute** [kə'mjuːt] **A** *v. tr.* commutare **B** *v. intr.* fare il pendolare
commuter [kə'mjʊ(ː)təʳ] *s.* pendolare *m. e f.*
compact [kəm'pækt] *agg.* compatto ♦ **c. car** utilitaria
companion [kəm'pænjən] *s.* compagno *m.*
companionship [kəm'pænjənʃɪp] *s.* compagnia *f.*, amicizia *f.*
company ['kʌmp(ə)nɪ] *s.* **1** compagnia *f.* **2** società *f.* ♦ **insurance c.** compagnia d'assicurazioni; **to keep sb. c.** tenere compagnia a qc.
comparable ['kəmp(ə)rəbl] *agg.* comparabile, paragonabile
comparative [kəm'pærətɪv] *agg.* **1** relativo **2** (*gramm.*) comparativo **3** compara-

to
to compare [kəm'pɛəʳ] **A** *v. tr.* confrontare, paragonare **B** *v. intr.* reggere il confronto
comparison [kəm'pærɪsn] *s.* **1** paragone *m.* **2** (*gramm.*) comparazione *f.*
compartment [kəm'pɑːtmənt] *s.* compartimento *m.*, scompartimento *m.*
compass ['kʌmpəs] *s.* **1** bussola *f.* **2** *al pl.* compasso *m.* **3** ambito *m.*, portata *f.* ♦ **c. card** rosa dei venti
compassion [kəm'pæʃ(ə)n] *s.* compassione *f.*
compatible [kəm'pætəbl] *agg.* compatibile
to compel [kəm'pɛl] *v. tr.* costringere, forzare, obbligare
compelling [kəm'pɛlɪŋ] *agg.* irresistibile, attraente
to compensate ['kəmpɛnseɪt] *v. tr.* compensare, ricompensare
compensation [ˌkəmpɛn'seɪʃ(ə)n] *s.* compensazione *f.*, risarcimento *m.*
compere ['kəmpɛəʳ] *s.* (*radio, TV*) presentatore *m.*
to compete [kəm'piːt] *v. intr.* competere, gareggiare
competence ['kəmpɪtəns] *s.* competenza *f.*
competent ['kəmpɪtənt] *agg.* competente
competition [ˌkəmpɪ'tɪʃ(ə)n] *s.* **1** competizione *f.*, gara *f.* **2** concorrenza *f.*
competitive [kəm'pɛtɪtɪv] *agg.* **1** competitivo **2** concorrenziale
competitiveness [kəm'pɛtɪtɪvnɪs] *s.* competitività *f.*
competitor [kəm'pɛtɪtəʳ] *s.* concorrente *m. e f.*
compilation [ˌkəmpɪ'leɪʃ(ə)n] *s.* compilazione *f.*
to compile [kəm'paɪl] *v. tr.* compilare, redigere
complacence [kəm'pleɪsns] *s.* compiacimento *m.*
to complain [kəm'pleɪn] *v. intr.* **1** lagnarsi, lamentarsi **2** reclamare **3** (*dir.*) citare in giudizio
complaint [kəm'pleɪnt] *s.* **1** lagnanza *f.*, lamentela *f.* **2** reclamo *m.*, protesta *f.* **3** (*dir.*) citazione *f.*, denuncia *f.* **4** malattia *f.*
complement ['kəmplɪmənt] *s.* complemento *m.*
complementary [ˌkəmplɪ'mɛnt(ə)rɪ] *agg.* complementare
complete [kəm'pliːt] *agg.* completo
to complete [kəm'pliːt] *v. tr.* **1** completare, finire **2** riempire
to completely [kəm'pliːtlɪ] *avv.* completamente
completion [kəm'pliːʃ(ə)n] *s.* completamento *m.*, compimento *m.*
complex ['kəmplɛks] *agg. e s.* complesso *m.*
complexion [kəm'plɛkʃ(ə)n] *s.* carnagione *f.*, colorito *m.*
complexity [kəm'plɛksɪtɪ] *s.* complessità *f.*
compliance [kəm'plaɪəns] *s.* **1** condiscendenza *f.*, conformità *f.* **2** sottomissione *f.* ♦ **in c. with** in conformità di
to complicate ['kəmplɪkeɪt] *v. tr. e intr.* complicare, complicarsi
complicated ['kəmplɪkeɪtɪd] *agg.* complicato
compliment ['kəmplɪmənt] *s.* **1** complimento *m.* **2** *al pl.* ossequi *m. pl.*, omaggi *m. pl.* ♦ **to pay a c.** fare un complimento
to compliment ['kəmplɪmənt] *v. tr.* congratularsi con, complimentarsi con
complimentary [ˌkəmplɪ'mɛnt(ə)rɪ] *agg.* **1** complimentoso **2** gratuito, in omaggio
to comply [kəm'plaɪ] *v. intr.* accondiscendere, conformarsi a
component [kəm'pɒʊnənt] *agg. e s.* componente *m. e f.*
to compose [kəm'pɒʊz] *v. tr.* **1** comporre, costituire, disporre **2** (*mus., letter.*) comporre **3** calmare
composer [kəm'pɒʊzəʳ] *s.* compositore *m.*
composite ['kəmpəzɪt] *agg.* composito
composition [ˌkəmpə'zɪʃ(ə)n] *s.* componimento *m.*, composizione *f.*
compost ['kəmpəst] *s.* concime *m.*
compound (1) ['kəmpaʊnd] **A** *agg.* composto **B** *s.* miscuglio *m.*, composto *m.*
compound (2) ['kəmpaʊnd] *s.* recinto *m.*
to compound [kəm'paʊnd] **A** *v. tr.* **1** comporre, mescolare **2** (*una vertenza*) conciliare **B** *v. intr.* accordarsi, effettuare una transizione
comprehend [ˌkəmprɪ'hɛnd] *v. tr.* comprendere
comprehension [ˌkəmprɪ'hɛnʃ(ə)n] *s.* comprensione *f.*
comprehensive [ˌkəmprɪ'hɛnsɪv] *agg.* comprensivo, globale
compress ['kəmprɛs] *s.* compressa *f.* (*di garza*)
to compress [kəm'prɛs] *v. tr.* comprimere

compressor [kəm'prɛsəʳ] *s.* compressore *m.*
to **comprise** [kəm'praɪz] *v. tr.* comprendere
compromise ['kəmprəmaɪz] *s.* compromesso *m.*
to **compromise** ['kəmprəmaɪz] **A** *v. tr.* **1** compromettere **2** transigere **B** *v. intr.* venire a un compromesso
compulsion [kəm'pʌlʃ(ə)n] *s.* costrizione *f.*
compulsive [kəm'pʌlsɪv] *agg.* **1** coercitivo **2** incontrollabile
compulsory [kəm'pʌls(ə)rɪ] *agg.* obbligatorio
to **compute** [kəm'pjuːt] *v. tr.* calcolare
computer [kəm'pjuːtəʳ] *s.* computer *m. inv.* ♦ **c. science** informatica
comrade ['kəmrɪd] *s.* compagno *m.*, camerata *m.*
comradely ['kəmrɪdlɪ] *agg.* cameratesco
con [kən] (*pop.*) truffa *f.*
concatenation [kən,kætɪ'neɪʃ(ə)n] *s.* concatenazione *f.*
concave [kən'keɪv] *agg.* concavo
to **conceal** [kən'siːl] *v. tr.* nascondere
to **concede** [kən'siːd] *v. tr.* **1** concedere **2** ammettere, riconoscere
conceit [kən'siːt] *s.* presunzione *f.*, vanità *f.*
conceited [kən'siːtɪd] *agg.* presuntuoso, vanitoso
conceivable [kən'siːvəbl] *agg.* concepibile, plausibile
to **conceive** [kən'siːv] **A** *v. tr.* **1** concepire, generare **2** ideare, immaginare **B** *v. intr.* immaginare
to **concentrate** ['kənsɛntreɪt] *v. tr. e intr.* concentrare, concentrarsi
concentration [,kənsɛn'treɪʃ(ə)n] *s.* concentrazione *f.*
concentric [kən'sɛntrɪk] *agg.* concentrico
concept ['kənsɛpt] *s.* concetto *m.*
conception [kən'sɛpʃ(ə)n] *s.* **1** concezione *f.*, concetto *m.* **2** concepimento *m.*
conceptual [kən'sɛptjuəl] *agg.* concettuale
concern [kən'sɜːn] *s.* **1** affare *m.*, interesse *m.* **2** ansietà *f.*, preoccupazione *f.*
to **concern** [kən'sɜːn] *v. tr.* **1** concernere, riguardare **2** preoccupare
concerning [kən'sɜːnɪŋ] *prep.* riguardo a
concert ['kənsət] *s.* **1** (*mus.*) concerto *m.* **2** accordo *m.*
concerted [kən'sɜːtɪd] *agg.* convenuto
concertina [,kənsə'tiːnə] *s.* piccola fisarmonica *f.*
concerto [kən'tʃɜːtɒʊ] *s.* (*mus.*) concerto *m.*
concession [kən'sɛʃ(ə)n] *s.* concessione *f.*
concessionaire [kən,sɛʃə'nɛəʳ] *s.* concessionario *m.*
conch [kəŋk] *s.* conchiglia *f.*
to **conciliate** [kən'sɪlɪeɪt] *v. tr.* **1** conciliare **2** accattivarsi
concise [kən'saɪs] *agg.* conciso, sintetico
to **conclude** [kən'kluːd] *v. tr. e intr.* concludere, concludersi
conclusion [kən'kluːʒ(ə)n] *s.* conclusione *f.*
conclusive [kən'klʊsɪv] *agg.* conclusivo
to **concoct** [kən'kəkt] *v. tr.* **1** mescolare, mettere insieme **2** ordire, architettare
concoction [kən'kəkʃ(ə)n] *s.* **1** miscuglio *m.* **2** macchinazione *f.*
concomitant [kən'kəmɪtənt] *agg.* concomitante
concourse ['kəŋkɜːs] *s.* **1** concorso *m.*, affluenza *f.* **2** (*USA*) atrio *m.*
concrete ['kənkriːt] **A** *agg.* **1** concreto, reale **2** di calcestruzzo **B** *s.* calcestruzzo *m.*
concreteness [kən'kriːtnɪs] *s.* concretezza *f.*
to **concur** [kən'kɜːʳ] *v. intr.* **1** concordare, essere d'accordo **2** concorrere, contribuire
concurrent [kən'kʌr(ə)nt] *agg.* **1** concorrente, simultaneo **2** concordante
concurrently [kən'kʌr(ə)ntlɪ] *avv.* simultaneamente
concussion [kən'kʌʃ(ə)n] *s.* **1** (*med.*) commozione *f.* cerebrale **2** (*dir*) concussione *f.*
to **condemn** [kən'dɛm] *v. tr.* **1** condannare **2** dichiarare inagibile
condemnation [,kəndɛm'neɪʃ(ə)n] *s.* condanna *f.* ♦ **c. by default** condanna in contumacia
condensation [,kəndɛn'seɪʃ(ə)n] *s.* condensazione *f.*
to **condense** [kən'dɛns] *v. tr. e intr.* condensare, condensarsi
condescending [,kəndɪ'sɛndɪŋ] *agg.* condiscendente
condescension [,kəndɪ'sɛnʃ(ə)n] *s.* condiscendenza *f.*
condiment ['kəndɪmənt] *s.* condimento *m.*

condition [kən'dɪʃ(ə)n] *s.* condizione *f.* ♦ **on c. that** a condizione che
to condition [kən'dɪʃ(ə)n] *v. tr.* **1** pattuire, stipulare **2** condizionare, influenzare
conditional [kən'dɪʃənl] *agg.* condizionale
conditioner [kən'dɪʃ(ə)nəʳ] *s.* **1** condizionatore *m.* **2** (*per capelli*) balsamo *m.* **3** (*per tessuti*) ammorbidente *m.*
conditioning [kən'dɪʃ(ə)nɪŋ] *s.* condizionamento *m.*
condolence [kən'dɒʊləns] *s.* condoglianza *f.*
condom ['kəndəm] *s.* preservativo *m.*
condominium [ˌkəndə'mɪnɪəm] *s.* **1** condominio *m.* **2** (*USA*) appartamento *m.*
to condone [kən'dɒʊn] *v. tr.* condonare
condor ['kəndɜːʳ] *s.* condor *m. inv.*
conducive [kən'djuːsɪv] *agg.* tendente
conduct ['kəndəkt] *s.* **1** condotta *f.* **2** gestione *f.*
to conduct [kən'dʌkt] *v. tr.* **1** condurre, guidare **2** (*un'orchestra*) dirigere ♦ **to c. oneself** comportarsi
conductor [kən'dʌktəʳ] *s.* **1** (*d'orchestra*) direttore *m.* **2** (*su mezzi pubblici*) bigliettaio *m.*, controllore *m.* **3** accompagnatore *m.* (turistico) **4** (*fis.*) conduttore *m.*
conduit ['kəndɪt] *s.* **1** condotto *m.*, tubazione *f.* **2** passaggio *m.*
cone [kɒʊn] *s.* cono *m.*
confectioner [kən'fɛkʃənəʳ] *s.* pasticciere *m.* ♦ **c.'s shop** pasticceria
confectionery [kən'fɛkʃən(ə)rɪ] *s.* **1** confetteria *f.*, pasticceria *f.* **2** dolci *m. pl.*
confederation [kənˌfɛdə'reɪʃ(ə)n] *s.* confederazione *f.*
to confer [kən'fɜːʳ] **A** *v. tr.* conferire, accordare **B** *v. intr.* conferire, consultarsi
conference ['kənf(ə)r(ə)ns] *s.* conferenza *f.*
to confess [kən'fɛs] *v. tr.* confessare
confessional [kən'fɛʃənl] *agg. e s.* confessionale *m.*
confetti [kən'fɛtɪ(ː)] *s.* coriandoli *m. pl.*
to confide [kən'faɪd] *v. tr.* **1** confidare **2** affidare ♦ **to c. in** confidare in, confidarsi con
confidence ['kənfɪd(ə)ns] *s.* **1** fiducia *f.* **2** confidenza *f.*, familiarità *f.* **3** sicurezza *f.* (di sé) ♦ **c. trick** truffa; **no-c.** (*pol.*) sfiducia
confident ['kənfɪdənt] *agg.* **1** fiducioso **2** sicuro di sé
confidential [ˌkənfɪ'dɛnʃ(ə)l] *agg.* confidenziale, riservato
configuration [kənˌfɪgjʊ'reɪʃ(ə)n] *s.* configurazione *f.*, composizione *f.*
to confine [kən'faɪn] *v. tr.* **1** confinare, relegare, imprigionare **2** limitare
confined [kən'faɪnd] *agg.* ristretto, limitato
confinement [kən'faɪnmənt] *s.* reclusione *f.*, prigionia *f.*
to confirm [kən'fɜːm] *v. tr.* **1** confermare **2** (*relig.*) cresimare
confirmation [ˌkənfə'meɪʃ(ə)n] *s.* **1** conferma *f.* **2** (*relig.*) cresima *f.*
confirmed [kən'fɜːmd] *agg.* **1** inveterato, cronico **2** (*relig.*) cresimato
confiscable [kən'fɪskəbl] *agg.* confiscabile
to confiscate ['kənfɪskeɪt] *v. tr.* confiscare
confiscation [ˌkənfɪs'keɪʃ(ə)n] *s.* confisca *f.*
conflict ['kənflɪkt] *s.* conflitto *m.*
to conflict [kən'flɪkt] *v. intr.* essere in conflitto
conflicting [kən'flɪktɪŋ] *agg.* contraddittorio, contrastante
confluence ['kənflʊəns] *s.* confluenza *f.*
to conform [kən'fɜːm] **A** *v. tr.* conformare, adattare **B** *v. intr.* conformarsi, adeguarsi, concordare
conformism [kən'fɜːmɪz(ə)m] *s.* conformismo *m.*
to confound [kən'faʊnd] *v. tr.* confondere
to confront [kən'frʌnt] *v. tr.* **1** affrontare **2** stare di fronte a **3** mettere a confronto, paragonare
confrontation [ˌkənfrən'teɪʃ(ə)n] *s.* confronto *m.*, scontro *m.*
to confuse [kən'fjuːz] *v. tr.* confondere ♦ **to get confused** confondersi
confusion [kən'fjuːʒ(ə)n] *s.* confusione *f.*
to confute [kən'fjuːt] *v. tr.* confutare
to congeal [kən'dʒiːl] *v. tr. e intr.* **1** congelare, congelarsi **2** coagulare, coagularsi
congenial [kən'dʒiːnjəl] *agg.* **1** congeniale, affine **2** simpatico
to congest [kən'dʒɛst] *v. tr.* congestionare
congestion [kən'dʒɛstʃ(ə)n] *s.* congestione *f.*
to conglobate ['kənglɒ(ʊ)beɪt] *v. tr.* conglobare
conglomerate [kən'gləmərɪt] *agg. e s.* conglomerato *m.*
to congratulate [kən'grætjʊleɪt] *v. tr.* congratularsi, felicitarsi, complimentarsi

congratulations [kən,grætjʊ'leɪʃ(ə)nz] *s. pl.* congratulazioni *f. pl.*, felicitazioni *f. pl.*
to congregate ['kɔŋgrɪgeɪt] *v. tr. e intr.* riunire, riunirsi
congregation [,kɔŋgrɪ'geɪʃ(ə)n] *s.* **1** congregazione *f.* **2** riunione *f.*
congress ['kɔŋgrɛs] *s.* congresso *m.*
congruency ['kɔŋgrʊənsɪ] *s.* congruenza *f.*
conical ['kɔnɪkl] *agg.* conico
conifer ['kɒ(ʊ)nɪfə] *s.* conifera *f.*
conjecture [kən'dʒɛktʃəʳ] *s.* congettura *f.*
to conjugate ['kɔn(d)ʒʊgeɪt] *v. tr.* coniugare
conjunction [kən'dʒʌŋkʃ(ə)n] *s.* congiunzione *f.*
conjunctivitis [kən,dʒʌŋktɪ'vaɪtɪs] *s.* congiuntivite *f.*
to conjure ['kʌn(d)ʒəʳ] *v. intr.* fare giochi di prestigio ♦ **to c. up** evocare, rievocare, far apparire
conjurer ['kʌn(d)ʒərəʳ] *s.* prestigiatore *m.*
to conk [kɔŋk] *v. tr.* (*pop.*) dare un colpo in testa a ♦ **to c. out** incepparsi, guastarsi
to connect [kə'nɛkt] **A** *v. tr.* connettere, collegare **B** *v. intr.* **1** connettersi, collegarsi **2** (*di mezzi di trasporto*) fare coincidenza ♦ **to be connected with** essere imparentato con, aver rapporti con
connected [kə'nɛktɪd] *agg.* **1** connesso, collegato **2** imparentato
connection [kə'nɛkʃ(ə)n] *s.* **1** collegamento *m.*, connessione *f.* **2** relazione *f.*, rapporto *m.* **3** (*di mezzi di trasporto*) coincidenza *f.* **4** (*elettr*) contatto *m.*
to connive [kə'naɪv] *v. intr.* essere connivente
connoisseur [,kɔnɪ'sɜːʳ] *s.* conoscitore *m.*, intenditore *m.*
to conquer ['kɔŋkəʳ] **A** *v. tr.* conquistare **B** *v. intr.* vincere
conquest ['kɔŋkwɛst] *s.* conquista *f.*
conscience ['kɔnʃ(ə)ns] *s.* coscienza *f.*
conscientious [,kɔnʃɪ'ɛnʃəs] *agg.* coscienzioso ♦ **c. objector** obiettore di coscienza
conscious ['kɔnʃəs] *agg.* cosciente, consapevole
consciousness ['kɔnʃəsnɪs] *s.* coscienza *f.*, consapevolezza *f.*
conscription [kən'skrɪpʃ(ə)n] *s.* **1** coscrizione *f.* **2** precettazione *f.*
to consecrate ['kɔnsɪkreɪt] *v. tr.* consacrare
consecutive [kən'sɛkjʊtɪv] *agg.* consecutivo
consent [kən'sɛnt] *s.* consenso *m.*
to consent [kən'sɛnt] *v. intr.* acconsentire
consequence ['kɔnsɪkwəns] *s.* **1** conseguenza *f.* **2** importanza *f.*
consequent ['kɔnsɪkwənt] *agg.* conseguente
conservation [,kɔnsə(ː)'vəɪʃ(ə)n] *s.* conservazione *f.*
conservative [kən'sɜːv(ə)tɪv] *agg.* **1** conservatore **2** prudente
conservatory [kən'sɜːvətrɪ] *s.* **1** serra *f.* **2** conservatorio *m.*
conserve ['kɔnsɜːv] *s.* conserva *f.* (di frutta)
to consider [kən'sɪdəʳ] *v. tr.* **1** considerare **2** tener conto di ♦ **to c. doing st.** pensare di fare q.c.
considerable [kən'sɪd(ə)rəbl] *agg.* considerevole
considerably [kən'sɪd(ə)rəblɪ] *avv.* considerevolmente, notevolmente
considerate [kən'sɪd(ə)rɪt] *agg.* premuroso
consideration [kən,sɪdə'reɪʃ(ə)n] *s.* **1** considerazione *f.*, riflessione *f.* **2** riguardo *m.* **3** rimunerazione *f.*
considering [kən'sɪdərɪŋ] **A** *prep.* in considerazione di, tenendo conto di, in vista di **B** *cong.* considerato che
to consign [kən'saɪn] *v. tr.* **1** consegnare, spedire **2** affidare **3** relegare
to consist [kən'sɪst] *v. intr.* consistere, constare
consistency [kən'sɪst(ə)nsɪ] *s.* **1** coerenza *f.* **2** compattezza *f.*
consistent [kən'sɪstənt] *agg.* **1** coerente, conforme **2** costante
consolation [,kɔnsə'leɪʃ(ə)n] *s.* consolazione *f.*
console ['kɔnsɒʊl] *s.* **1** (*arch.*) mensola *f.* **2** console *f. inv.*, quadro *m.* di comando
to console [kən'sɒʊl] *v. tr.* consolare
to consolidate [kən'sɔlɪdeɪt] *v. tr. e intr.* consolidare, consolidarsi
consolidation [kən,sɔlɪ'deɪʃ(ə)n] *s.* consolidamento *m.*
consonant ['kɔnsənənt] *s.* consonante *f.*
consort ['kɔnsɜːt] *s.* consorte *m. e f.*
consortium [kən'sɜːtjəm] *s.* consorzio *m.*
conspicuous [kən'spɪkjʊəs] *agg.* cospicuo
conspiracy [kən'spɪrəsɪ] *s.* cospirazio-

ne *f.*
conspirator [kən'spɪrətəʳ] *s.* cospiratore *m.*
constable ['kʌnstəbl] *s.* **1** agente *m.* di polizia **2** (*stor.*) conestabile *m.*, governatore *m.*
constabulary [kən'stæbjʊlərɪ] *s.* corpo *m.* di polizia
constant ['kənst(ə)nt] **A** *agg.* **1** costante, invariabile **B** *s.* (*mat., fis.*) costante *f.*
constellation [ˌkənstə'leɪʃ(ə)n] *s.* costellazione *f.*
constipated ['kənstɪpeɪtɪd] *agg.* stitico
constipation [ˌkənstɪ'peɪʃ(ə)n] *s.* costipazione *f.*, stitichezza *f.*
constituency [kən'stɪtjʊənsɪ] *s.* collegio *m.* elettorale
constituent [kən'stɪtjʊənt] **A** *agg.* costituente **B** *s.* elettore *m.*
to constitute ['kənstɪtjuːt] *v. tr.* costituire
constitution [ˌkənstɪ'tjuːʃ(ə)n] *s.* costituzione *f.*
constitutional [ˌkənstɪ'tjuːʃənl] *agg.* costituzionale
to constrain [kən'streɪn] *v. tr.* costringere
constraint [kən'streɪnt] *s.* costrizione *f.*
to constrict [kən'strɪkt] *v. tr.* costringere, comprimere
constriction [kən'strɪkʃ(ə)n] *s.* costrizione *f.*, compressione *f.*
to construct [kən'strʌkt] *v. tr.* costruire, edificare
construction [kən'strʌkʃ(ə)n] *s.* costruzione *f.*
constructive [kən'strʌktɪv] *agg.* costruttivo
consul ['kəns(ə)l] *s.* console *m.*
consulate ['kənsjʊlɪt] *s.* consolato *m.*
to consult [kən'sʌlt] *v. tr. e intr.* consultare, consultarsi
consultant [kən'sʌltənt] *s.* **1** consulente *m.* **2** medico *m.* specialista
consultation [ˌkəns(ə)l'teɪʃ(ə)n] *s.* consultazione *f.*, consulto *m.*
to consume [kən'sjuːm] *v. tr.* consumare
consumer [kən'sjuːməʳ] *s.* **1** consumatore *m.* **2** utente *m. e f.* ♦ **c. goods** beni di consumo
consummation [ˌkənsə'meɪʃ(ə)n] *s.* compimento *m.*, completamento *m.*
consumption [kən'sʌm(p)ʃ(ə)n] *s.* consumo *m.*
contact ['kəntækt] *s.* **1** contatto *m.*, relazione *f.* **2** conoscenza *f.* ♦ **c. lenses** lenti a contatto
to contact ['kəntækt] *v. tr.* mettere in contatto, contattare
contagion [kən'teɪdʒ(ə)n] *s.* contagio *m.*
contagious [kən'teɪdʒəs] *agg.* contagioso
to contain [kən'teɪn] *v. tr.* **1** contenere, comprendere **2** trattenere, reprimere
container [kən'teɪnəʳ] *s.* **1** contenitore *m.*, recipiente *m.* **2** container *m. inv.*
to contaminate [kən'tæmɪneɪt] *v. tr.* contaminare
contamination [kənˌtæmɪ'neɪʃ(ə)n] *s.* contaminazione *f.*
to contemplate ['kəntɛmpleɪt] *v. tr.* **1** contemplare **2** prevedere
contemplative [kən'tɛmplətɪv] *agg.* contemplativo
contemporary [kən'tɛmp(ə)rərɪ] **A** *agg.* contemporaneo **B** *s.* coetaneo *m.*, contemporaneo *m.*
contempt [kən'tɛm(p)t] *s.* **1** disprezzo *m.* **2** (*dir.*) inosservanza *f.*
contemptible [kən'tɛm(p)təbl] *agg.* spregevole
to contend [kən'tɛnd] **A** *v. intr.* contendere, combattere **B** *v. tr.* asserire
contender [kən'tɛndəʳ] *s.* contendente *m. e f.*, concorrente *m. e f.*
content (1) ['kəntɛnt] *s.* contenuto *m.* **(table of) contents** (*di libro*) indice
content (2) ['kəntɛnt] **A** *agg.* contento, soddisfatto **B** *s.* **1** contentezza *f.* **2** voto *m.* favorevole
contention [kən'tɛnʃ(ə)n] *s.* **1** contesa *f.*, controversia *f.* **2** opinione *f.*
contest ['kəntɛst] *s.* competizione *f.*, concorso *m.*
to contest [kən'tɛst] *v. tr.* **1** contestare **2** contendere, disputare **3** (*dir.*) impugnare
contestant [kən'tɛstənt] *s.* concorrente *m. e f.*
context ['kəntɛkst] *s.* contesto *m.*
continent ['kəntɪnənt] *s.* continente *m.*
continental [ˌkəntɪ'nɛntl] *agg.* continentale
contingency [kən'tɪn(d)ʒ(ə)nsɪ] *agg.* contingenza *f.*, eventualità *f.*
continual [kən'tɪnjʊəl] *agg.* continuo
continually [kən'tɪnjʊəlɪ] *avv.* continuamente
continuation [kənˌtɪnjʊ'eɪʃ(ə)n] *s.* continuazione *f.*
to continue [kən'tɪnjʊ(ː)] *v. tr. e intr.* continuare, proseguire

continuity [ˌkɒntɪ'njuːɪtɪ] *s.* **1** continuità *f.* **2** (*cine.*) sceneggiatura *f.*
continuous [kən'tɪnjʊəs] *agg.* continuo
to contort [kən'tɜːt] *v. tr.* contorcere
contortion [kən'tɜːʃ(ə)n] *s.* contorcimento *m.*, contorsione *f.*
contour ['kɒntʊəʳ] *s.* contorno *m.* ♦ **c. lines** curve di livello
contraband ['kɒntrəbænd] *s.* contrabbando *m.*
contraceptive [ˌkɒntrə'sɛptɪv] *agg. e s.* contraccettivo *m.*
contract ['kɒntrækt] *s.* contratto *m.*
to contract [kən'trækt] **A** *v. tr.* contrarre, restringere **B** *v. intr.* **1** contrarsi, restringersi **2** impegnarsi **3** prendere in appalto ♦ **to c. in/out** associarsi/dissociarsi
contraction [kən'trækʃ(ə)n] *s.* contrazione *f.*
contractor [kən'træktəʳ] *s.* **1** contraente *m. e f.* **2** imprenditore *m.*, appaltatore *m.*
to contradict [ˌkɒntrə'dɪkt] *v. tr. e intr.* contraddire
contradiction [ˌkɒntrə'dɪkʃ(ə)n] *s.* contraddizione *f.*
contraindication [ˌkɒntrəˌɪndɪ'keɪʃ(ə)n] *s.* controindicazione *f.*
contraposition [ˌkɒntrəpə'zɪʃ(ə)n] *s.* contrapposizione *f.*
contraption [kən'træpʃ(ə)n] *s.* (*fam.*) congegno *m.*
contrary ['kɒntrərɪ] *agg. e s.* contrario *m.*, opposto *m.* ♦ **on the c.** al contrario; **c. to** contrariamente a
contrast ['kɒntræst] *s.* contrasto *m.*
to contrast [kən'træst] **A** *v. tr.* mettere in contrasto **B** *v. intr.* contrastare
contravention [ˌkɒntrə'vɛnʃ(ə)n] *s.* contravvenzione *f.*
to contribute [kən'trɪbjʊt] **A** *v. intr.* **1** contribuire **2** (*con un giornale*) collaborare **B** *v. tr.* **1** contribuire con **2** scrivere (*un articolo*)
contribution [ˌkɒntrɪ'bjuːʃ(ə)n] *s.* **1** contributo *m.* **2** (*con un giornale*) collaborazione *f.*
contrivance [kən'traɪv(ə)ns] *s.* **1** espediente *m.* **2** congegno *m.*
to contrive [kən'traɪv] **A** *v. tr.* **1** escogitare **2** fare in modo di **B** *v. intr.* fare piani
control [kən'trɒʊl] *s.* **1** controllo *m.* **2** (dispositivo di) comando *m.* ♦ **to be in c. of** avere il controllo di
to control [kən'trɒʊl] *v. tr.* **1** controllare, dirigere **2** trattenere, dominare
controller [kən'trɒʊləʳ] *s.* **1** sovrintendente *m.* **2** (*USA*) direttore *m.* amministrativo
controversial [ˌkɒntrə'vɜːʃ(ə)l] *agg.* **1** controverso **2** polemico
controversy ['kɒntrəvɜːsɪ] *s.* **1** controversia *f.*, polemica *f.* **2** (*dir.*) vertenza *f.*
to convalesce [ˌkɒnvə'lɛs] *v. intr.* essere in convalescenza
convalescence [ˌkɒnvə'lɛsns] *s.* convalescenza *f.*
convalescent [ˌkɒnvə'lɛs(ə)nt] *agg. e s.* convalescente *m. e f.*
convection [kən'vɛkʃ(ə)n] *s.* (*fis.*) convezione *f.*
to convene [kən'viːn] **A** *v. tr.* convocare, adunare **B** *v. intr.* convenire, adunarsi
convenience [kən'viːnjəns] *s.* **1** convenienza *f.*, vantaggio *m.* **2** comodità *f.*
convenient [kən'viːnjənt] *agg.* **1** conveniente, comodo **2** (*di luogo*) vicino
convent ['kɒnv(ə)nt] *s.* convento *m.*
convention [kən'vɛnʃ(ə)n] *s.* **1** convenzione *f.*, accordo *m.* **2** convegno *m.*
conventional [kən'vɛnʃənl] *agg.* convenzionale, comune
to converge [kən'vɛːdʒ] *v. intr.* convergere, confluire
convergence [kən'vɜːdʒ(ə)ns] *s.* convergenza *f.*
conversant [kən'vɜːs(ə)nt] *agg.* pratico, al corrente
conversation [ˌkɒnvə'seɪʃ(ə)n] *s.* conversazione *f.*, discorso *m.*
conversational [ˌkɒnvə'seɪʃənl] *agg.* **1** loquace **2** discorsivo
converse ['kɒnvɜːs] *agg.* contrario
to converse [kən'vɜːs] *v. intr.* conversare
conversely [kən'vɜːslɪ] *avv.* invece, al contrario, per converso
conversion [kən'vɜːʃ(ə)n] *s.* conversione *f.*
to convert [kən'vɜːt] *v. tr.* convertire
convertible [kən'vɜːtəbl] *agg.* convertibile
convex [ˌkɒn'vɛks] *agg.* convesso
to convey [kən'veɪ] *v. tr.* **1** trasmettere **2** trasportare
conveyance [kən'vɛ(ɪ)əns] *s.* trasmissione *f.*
conveyor [kən'veɪəʳ] *s.* trasportatore *m.* ♦ **c. belt** nastro trasportatore
convict ['kɒnvɪkt] *s.* condannato *m.*, dete-

nuto *m.*
to **convict** [kən'vɪkt] *v. tr.* condannare, dichiarare colpevole
conviction [kən'vɪkʃ(ə)n] *s.* **1** condanna *f.*, verdetto *m.* di colpevolezza **2** convinzione *f.*
to **convince** [kən'vɪns] *v. tr.* convincere
convincing [kən'vɪnsɪŋ] *agg.* convincente
convocation [ˌkənvə'keɪʃ(ə)n] *s.* convocazione *f.*
convoluted ['kənvəlju:tɪd] *agg.* **1** ritorto **2** involuto, contorto
convoy ['kənvəɪ] *s.* scorta *f.*, convoglio *m.*
convulsion [kən'vʌlʃ(ə)n] *s.* convulsione *f.*
to **coo** [ku:] *v. intr.* tubare
cook [kʊk] *s.* cuoco *m.*
to **cook** [kʊk] *v. tr. e intr.* cucinare, cuocere
cookbook ['kʊkbʊk] *s.* ricettario *m.*
cooker ['kʊkəʳ] *s.* **1** fornello *m.*, cucina *f.* **2** pentola *f.* ♦ **pressure c.** pentola a pressione
cookery ['kʊkərɪ] *s.* arte *f.* culinaria, gastronomia *f.*
cookie ['kʊkɪ] *s.* (*USA*) biscotto *m.*
cooking ['kʊkɪŋ] *s.* **1** cottura *f.* **2** cucina *f.*, arte *f.* culinaria
cool [ku:l] *agg.* **1** fresco **2** (*di persona*) tranquillo, freddo, compassato **3** impudente, sfacciato
to **cool** [ku:l] *v. tr.* **1** raffreddare, rinfrescare **2** calmare ♦ **to c. down** raffreddarsi; **cool it!** calma!
coolness ['ku:lnɪs] *s.* **1** fresco *m.* **2** freddezza *f.*
coop [ku:p] *s.* stia *f.*
to **coop** [ku:p] *v. tr.* rinchiudere
to **cooperate** [kɒ(ʊ)'əpəreɪt] *v. intr.* cooperare, collaborare
cooperation [kɒ(ʊ)ˌəpə'reɪʃ(ə)n] *s.* cooperazione *f.*, collaborazione *f.*
cooperative [kɒ(ʊ)'əp(ə)rətɪv] *s.* cooperativa *f.*
coordinate [kɒ(ʊ)'ɜ:dnɪt] **A** *agg.* **1** uguale **2** coordinato **B** *s.* coordinata *f.*
coordination [kɒ(ʊ)ˌɜ:dɪ'neɪʃ(ə)n] *s.* coordinazione *f.*
coordinator [kɒ(ʊ)'ɜ:dɪneɪtəʳ] *s.* coordinatore *m.*
coowner [kɒ(ʊ)'ɒʊnəʳ] *s.* comproprietario *m.*
to **cope** [kɒʊp] *v. intr.* tener testa, far fronte
copper ['kəpəʳ] *s.* rame *m.*
coppice ['kəpɪs] *s.* bosco *m.* ceduo
copse [kəps] *s.* bosco *m.* ceduo
copy ['kəpɪ] *s.* copia *f.* ♦ **c. book** quaderno
to **copy** ['kəpɪ] *v. tr.* **1** copiare **2** imitare **3** riprodurre ♦ **to c. down** trascrivere
copyright ['kəpɪraɪt] *s.* copyright *m. inv.*, diritto *m.* d'autore
coral ['kər(ə)l] **A** *s.* corallo *m.* **B** *agg.* corallino ♦ **c. reef** barriera corallina
cord [kɜ:d] *s.* **1** corda *f.* **2** filo *m.*, cordone *m.* **3** velluto *m.* a coste
cordial ['kɜ:djəl] *agg.* cordiale
cordiality [ˌkɜ:dɪ'ælɪtɪ] *s.* cordialità *f.*
cordon ['kɜ:dn] *s.* cordone *m.*
core [kɜ:ʳ] *s.* **1** nucleo *m.*, centro *m.* **2** torsolo *m.*
coriaceous [ˌkərɪ'eɪʃəs] *agg.* coriaceo
Corinthian [kə'rɪnθɪən] *agg.* corinzio
cork [kɜ:k] *s.* **1** sughero *m.* **2** tappo *m.* ♦ **c. oak** quercia da sughero; **c. skrew** cavatappi
to **cork** [kɜ:k] *v. tr.* tappare, turare
cormorant ['kɜ:m(ə)r(ə)nt] *s.* cormorano *m.*
corn (1) [kɜ:n] *s.* **1** cereale *m.*, granaglie *f. pl.* **2** grano *m.* **3** (*USA*) mais *m.* ♦ **c. cob** pannocchia; **c.-flakes** fiocchi di mais
corn (2) [kɜ:n] *s.* callo *m.*
to **corn** [kɜ:n] *v. tr.* conservare (sotto sale), salare ♦ **corned beef** carne in scatola
cornea ['kɜ:nɪə] *s.* cornea *f.*
corner ['kɜ:nəʳ] *s.* **1** angolo *m.*, spigolo *m.* **2** (*di merce*) accaparramento *m.*
to **corner** ['kɜ:nəʳ] **A** *v. intr.* curvare, svoltare **B** *v. tr.* **1** mettere alle strette **2** accaparrare, imboscare
cornet ['kɜ:nɪt] *s.* **1** (*mus.*) cornetta *f.* **2** cartoccio *m.* (*a cono*) **3** cono *m.* gelato
cornflower ['kɜ:nˌflaʊəʳ] *s.* fiordaliso *m.*
cornice ['kɜ:nɪs] *s.* (*arch.*) cornicione *m.*
cornucopia [ˌkɜ:njʊ'kɒʊpjə] *s.* cornucopia *f.*
corny ['kɜ:nɪ] *agg.* **1** di grano, ricco di grano **2** trito, banale
corolla [kə'rələ] *s.* corolla *f.*
coronary ['kərənərɪ] **A** *agg.* coronario **B** *s.* trombosi *f.* coronaria
coronation [ˌkərə'neɪʃ(ə)n] *s.* incoronazione *f.*
coronet ['kərənɪt] *s.* corona *f.*, diadema *m.*
corporal (1) ['kɜ:p(ə)r(ə)l] *agg.* corporale
corporal (2) ['kɜ:p(ə)r(ə)l] *s.* (*mil.*) caporale *m.*
corporate ['kɜ:p(ə)rɪt] *agg.* **1** corporativo **2** societario, aziendale ♦ **c. name** ragione

sociale
corporation [ˌkɔːpə'reɪʃ(ə)n] *s.* compagnia *f.*, società *f.* ♦ **municipal c.** consiglio comunale
corps [kɔːʳ] *s. inv.* **1** (*mil.*) corpo *m.* **2** (*di persone*) gruppo *m.*
corpse [kɔːps] *s.* cadavere *m.*
corpuscle ['kɔːpʌsl] *s.* corpuscolo *m.*
corral [kə'raːl] *s.* recinto *m.* per bestiame
correct [kə'rɛkt] *agg.* **1** corretto, giusto **2** adatto, opportuno
to correct [kə'rɛkt] *v. tr.* correggere
correction [kə'rɛkʃ(ə)n] *s.* correzione *f.*
correctly [kə'rɛktlɪ] *avv.* **1** correttamente, giustamente **2** opportunamente
correlation [ˌkɔrɪ'leɪʃ(ə)n] *s.* correlazione *f.*
to correspond [ˌkɔrɪs'pɔnd] *v. intr.* corrispondere
correspondence [ˌkɔrɪs'pɔndəns] *s.* **1** corrispondenza *f.*, carteggio *m.* **2** accordo *m.*
corresponding [ˌkɔrɪs'pɔndɪŋ] *agg. e s.* corrispondente *m. e f.*
corridor ['kɔrɪdɔːʳ] *s.* corridoio *m.*
to corroborate [kə'r(ə)bəreɪt] *v. tr.* corroborare, avvalorare
to corrode [kə'rɒʊd] *v. tr. e intr.* corrodere, corrodersi
corrosive [kə'rɒʊsɪv] *agg.* corrosivo
corrugated ['kɔrʊgeɪtɪd] *agg.* corrugato, increspato ♦ **c. iron** lamiera ondulata
to corrupt [kə'rʌpt] *v. tr.* **1** corrompere **2** alterare
corruption [kə'rʌpʃ(ə)n] *s.* corruzione *f.*
corset ['kɔːsɪt] *s.* busto *m.*
cortisone ['kɔːtɪzɒʊn] *s.* cortisone *m.*
corvée ['kɔːveɪ] *s.* corvè *f. inv.*
cosh [kɔʃ] *s.* manganello *m.*
cosmetic [kɔz'mɛtɪk] **A** *agg.* **1** cosmetico **2** apparente, superficiale **B** *s.* cosmetico *m.*
cosmic ['kɔzmɪk] *agg.* cosmico
cosmopolitan [ˌkɔzmə'pɔlɪt(ə)n] *agg.* cosmopolita
cosmos ['kɔzməs] *s.* cosmo *m.*
to cosset ['kɔsɪt] *v. tr.* vezzeggiare, coccolare
cost [kɔst] *s.* costo *m.*, prezzo *m.* ♦ **at all costs** a ogni costo; **c.-effective** efficace, conveniente; **c. price** prezzo di costo
to cost [kɔst] (*pass. e p. p.* **cost**) **A** *v. intr.* costare **B** *v. tr.* valutare i costi
costly ['kɔstlɪ] *agg.* costoso, caro
costume ['kɔstjuːm] *s.* **1** costume *m.* **2** tailleur *m. inv.* ♦ **c. ball** ballo in costume; **c. jewellery** bigiotteria; **swimming c.** costume da bagno
cosy ['kɒʊzɪ] (*USA* **cozy**) *agg.* accogliente, confortevole
cot [kɔt] *s.* **1** culla *f.*, lettino *f.* **2** branda *f.*
coterie ['kɒʊtərɪ] *s.* circolo *m.*, cenacolo *m.*
cottage ['kɔtɪdʒ] *s.* casetta *f.*, villetta *f.*
cotton ['kɔtn] *s.* cotone *m.* ♦ **c. wool** cotone idrofilo
to cotton ['kɔtn] *v. intr.* fraternizzare ♦ **to c. on** afferrare, iniziare a capire
couch [kaʊtʃ] *s.* divano *m.*
couchette [kuː'ʃɛt] *s.* cuccetta *f.*
cough [kɔf] *s.* tosse *f.* ♦ **c.-drop** pasticca per la tosse
to cough [kɔf] *v. intr.* tossire
could [kʊd, kəd] *pass. di* **can**
council ['kaʊnsl] *s.* **1** (*adunanza di persone*) consiglio *m.* **2** (*relig.*) concilio *m.* ♦ **city/town c.** consiglio comunale; **c. house** casa popolare; **c. estate** quartiere popolare
councillor ['kaʊnsɪləʳ] *s.* consigliere *m.*
counsel ['kaʊns(ə)l] *s.* **1** consiglio *m.*, consultazione *f.* **2** (*dir.*) avvocato *m.*, consulente *m. e f.*
to counsel ['kaʊns(ə)l] *v. tr.* consigliare
counsellor ['kaʊnsələʳ] *s.* **1** consigliere *m.*, consulente *m. e f.* **2** (*USA*) avvocato *m.*
count (1) [kaʊnt] *s.* conto *m.*, conteggio *m.*
count (2) [kaʊnt] *s.* conte *m.*
to count [kaʊnt] **A** *v. tr.* **1** contare, calcolare **2** considerare, annoverare **B** *v. intr.* **1** contare **2** avere importanza ♦ **to c. down** fare il conto alla rovescia; **to c. in** includere; **to c. on** fare assegnamento
countenance ['kaʊntɪnəns] *s.* **1** espressione *f.*, aria *f.* **2** approvazione *f.*, appoggio *m.*
to countenance ['kaʊntɪnəns] *v. tr.* approvare, appoggiare
counter (1) ['kaʊntəʳ] *s.* (*tecnol.*) contatore *m.*, misuratore *m.*
counter (2) ['kaʊntəʳ] *s.* **1** gettone *m.* **2** banco *m.*, cassa *f.* ♦ **telephone c.** gettone telefonico
counter (3) ['kaʊntəʳ] *avv.* contrariamente
to counter ['kaʊntəʳ] *v. tr. e intr.* **1** opporsi a **2** respingere, mandare a vuoto **3** replicare
to counteract [ˌkaʊntə'rækt] *v. tr.* **1** agire contro **2** contrastare

counterclockwise [ˌkaʊntə'kləkwaɪs] *agg.* antiorario
countercurrent [ˌkɑntə'kʌrənt] *s.* controcorrente *f.*
counterfeit ['kaʊntəfɪt] **A** *agg.* falso, contraffatto **B** *s.* contraffazione *f.*, falsificazione *f.*
to counterfeit ['kaʊntəfiːt] *v. tr.* contraffare, falsificare
counterfoil ['kaʊntəfəɪl] *s.* matrice *f.*
countermand [ˌkaʊntə'maːnd] *s.* contrordine *m.*
to countermand ['kaʊntəˌmaːnd] *v. tr.* annullare, revocare
counterpart ['kaʊntəpaːt] *s.* **1** controparte *f.* **2** duplicato *m.*, copia *f.*
counterproductive ['kaʊntəprəˌdʌktɪv] *agg.* controproducente
Counter-Reformation ['kaʊntərɛfəˌmeɪʃ(ə)n] *s.* controriforma *f.*
countersign ['kaʊntəsaɪn] *s.* contrassegno *m.*, controfirma *f.*
to countersign ['kaʊntəsaɪn] *v. tr.* contrassegnare, controfirmare
countess ['kaʊntɪs] *s.* contessa *f.*
countless ['kaʊntlɪs] *agg.* innumerevole
country ['kʌntrɪ] **A** *s.* **1** paese *m.*, nazione *f.*, regione *f.* **2** patria *f.* **3** campagna *f.* **B** *agg.* di campagna
countryman ['kʌntrɪmən] (*pl.* **countrymen**) *s.* **1** campagnolo *m.*, contadino *m.* **2** compatriota *m.*
countryside ['kʌntrɪsaɪd] *s.* campagna *f.*
countrywide ['kʌntrɪwaɪd] *agg.* esteso a tutto il territorio nazionale
county ['kaʊntɪ] *s.* contea *f.*
couple ['kʌpl] *s.* coppia *f.*, paio *m.*
to couple ['kʌpl] *v. tr.* **1** accoppiare, abbinare **2** unire insieme
coupon ['kuːpən] *s.* buono *m.*, scontrino *m.*, tagliando *m.*
courage ['kʌrɪdʒ] *s.* coraggio *m.*
courageous [kə'reɪdʒəs] *agg.* coraggioso
courgette [ˌkʊə'ʒɛt] *s.* zucchino *m.*
courier ['kʊrɪəʳ] *s.* **1** corriere *m.*, messaggero *m.* **2** guida *f.* (turistica)
course [kɜːs] *s.* **1** corso *m.*, decorso *m.* **2** direzione *f.*, rotta *f.* **3** pietanza *f.*, portata *f.* **4** (*sport*) campo *m.*, percorso *m.* **5** *al pl.* mestruazioni *f. pl.* ♦ **of c.** naturalmente, senz'altro
court [kɜːt] *s.* **1** corte *f.*, cortile *m.* **2** (*dir*) corte *f.*, tribunale *m.* **3** castello *m.*, dimora *f.* **4** (*sport*) campo *m.* (di gioco) **5** corteggiamento *m.* ♦ **c.-martial** corte marziale; **c. of inquiry** commissione d'inchiesta; **c. room** aula di tribunale
to court [kɜːt] *v. tr.* corteggiare
courteous ['kɜːtjəs] *agg.* cortese
courtesy ['kɜːtɪsɪ] *s.* cortesia *f.* ♦ **by c. of** per gentile concessione di
courtier ['kɜːtjəʳ] *s.* cortigiano *m.*
courtyard ['kɜːtˌjaːd] *s.* cortile *m.*
cousin ['kʌzn] *s.* cugino *m.*
cove [kɒʊv] *s.* baia *f.*, caletta *f.*
covenant ['kʌvɪnənt] *s.* convenzione *f.*, accordo *m.*
cover ['kʌvəʳ] *s.* **1** copertura *f.*, coperchio *m.*, coperta *f.*, fodera *f.* **2** (*di libro, giornale*) copertina *f.* **3** riparo *m.* **4** (*econ.*) copertura *f.* **5** coperto *m.* ♦ **c. charge** prezzo del coperto; **c. girl** fotomodella; **to take c.** mettersi al riparo
to cover ['kʌvəʳ] *v. tr.* **1** coprire **2** ricoprire, rivestire **3** comprendere ♦ **to c. up** coprire, nascondere
coverage ['kʌvərɪdʒ] *s.* **1** copertura *f.* **2** (*radio, TV*) zona *f.* di ricezione **3** servizio *m.* d'informazione
covering ['kʌvərɪŋ] *s.* rivestimento *m.*
to covet ['kʌvɪt] *v. tr.* agognare, bramare
cow [kaʊ] *s.* mucca *f.* ♦ **c. house** stalla
to cow [kaʊ] *v. tr.* intimorire
coward ['kaʊəd] *agg.* vigliacco
cowardice ['kaʊədɪs] *s.* vigliaccheria *f.*
cowl [kaʊl] *s.* **1** cappuccio *m.* **2** tonaca *f.*
cowslip ['kaʊslɪp] *s.* primula *f.*
cox(wain) ['kəks(weɪn)] *s.* timoniere *m.*
coy [kəɪ] *agg.* schivo, riservato
cozy ['kɒʊzɪ] *agg.* (*USA*) → **cosy**
crab (1) [kræb] *s.* granchio *m.*
crab (2) [kræb] *s.* melo *m.* selvatico
crack [kræk] **A** *agg.* di prim'ordine, scelto **B** *s.* **1** rottura *f.*, crepa *f.* **2** schianto *m.*, esplosione *f.* **3** crollo *m.*, tracollo *m.*
to crack [kræk] **A** *v. tr.* **1** rompere, incrinare **2** schioccare **3** (*fam.*) decifrare **4** (*pop.*) scassinare **B** *v. intr.* **1** rompersi, incrinarsi **2** schioccare ♦ **to c. a joke** dire una barzelletta; **to c. on** darci dentro; **to c. up** rompere, andare in mille pezzi
cracker ['krækəʳ] *s.* **1** cracker *m. inv.* **2** petardo *m.*
to crackle ['krækl] *v. intr.* **1** crepitare, scricchiolare **2** screpolarsi
cradle ['kreɪdl] *s.* culla *f.* ♦ **c. song** ninnananna

craft [kraːft] *s.* **1** mestiere *m.* **2** corporazione *f.*, categoria *f.* **3** abilità *f.* **4** imbarcazione *f.*
craftsman ['kraːftsmən] (*pl.* **craftsmen**) *s.* artigiano *m.*
crafty ['kraːftɪ] *agg.* astuto
crag [kræg] *s.* picco *m.*, dirupo *m.*
to cram [kræm] **A** *v. tr.* riempire, rimpinzare **B** *v. intr.* **1** rimpinzarsi, ingozzarsi **2** ammassarsi
cramp [kræmp] *s.* crampo *m.*
cramped [kræmpt] *agg.* **1** ristretto, limitato **2** contratto
crampon ['kræmpən] *s.* rampone *m.*
crane [kreɪn] *s.* (*zool., mecc.*) gru *f. inv.* ♦ **bridge c.** carroponte
cranial ['kreɪnjəl] *agg.* cranico
cranium ['kreɪnjəm] *s.* cranio *m.*
crank [kræŋk] *s.* **1** manovella *f.* **2** (*fam.*) persona *f.* eccentrica ♦ **c. shaft** albero a gomiti
crash [kræʃ] *s.* **1** fragore *m.*, schianto *m.* **2** scontro *m.*, collisione *f.* **3** crollo *m.*, caduta *f.* ♦ **c. barrier** guardrail; **c. helmet** casco di protezione; **c. landing** atterraggio di fortuna; **c.-proof** a prova d'urto
to crash [kræʃ] **A** *v. tr.* rompere, fracassare **B** *v. intr.* **1** schiantarsi, precipitare **2** (*autom.*) scontrarsi **3** crollare, precipitare
crate [kreɪt] *s.* cassa *f.*, cesta *f.*
crater ['kreɪtəʳ] *s.* cratere *m.*
to crave [kreɪv] **A** *v. intr.* desiderare fortemente **B** *v. tr.* scongiurare, chiedere con insistenza
craving ['kreɪvɪŋ] *s.* desiderio *m.*, brama *f.*
crawl [krɜːl] *s.* crawl *m. inv.*
to crawl [krɜːl] *v. intr.* **1** strisciare **2** avanzare carponi
crayfish ['kreɪˌfɪʃ] *s.* **1** gambero *m.* **2** aragosta *f.*
crayon ['krɛ(ɪ)ən] *s.* pastello *m.*
craze [kreɪz] *s.* mania *f.*
crazy ['kreɪzɪ] *agg.* **1** matto **2** entusiasta, maniaco **3** (*pop.*) fantastico
creak [kriːk] *s.* scricchiolio *m.*
cream [kriːm] *s.* **1** panna *f.* **2** crema *f.* ♦ **whipped c.** panna montata
creamy ['kriːmɪ] *agg.* cremoso
crease [kriːs] *s.* piega *f.*, grinza *f.*
to crease [kriːs] *v. tr.* stropicciare, spiegazzare
to create [kriː'eɪt] *v. tr.* creare
creation [kriː'eɪʃ(ə)n] *s.* creazione *f.*
creative [krɪ(ː)'eɪtɪv] *agg.* creativo
creature ['kriːtʃəʳ] *s.* creatura *f.*
crèche [kreɪʃ] *s.* asilo *m.* infantile
credence ['kriːd(ə)ns] *s.* credenza *f.*, credito *m.* ♦ **to give c. to st.** prestar fede a q.c.
credentials [krɪ'dɛnʃ(ə)lz] *s. pl.* credenziali *f. pl.*
credit ['krɛdɪt] *s.* **1** credito *m.* **2** merito *m.* ♦ **c. card** carta di credito; **to give c. to** prestar fede a; **to place c. in** aver fiducia in
to credit ['krɛdɪt] *v. tr.* **1** prestar fede **2** attribuire **3** accreditare ♦ **to c. sb. with st.** attribuire q.c. a qc.
creditor ['krɛdɪtəʳ] *s.* creditore *m.*
creed [kriːd] *s.* (*relig.*) credo *m.*
creek [kriːk] *s.* **1** insenatura *f.* **2** (*USA*) torrente *m.*
to creep [kriːp] (*pass. e p. p.* **crept**) *v. intr.* **1** strisciare **2** avanzare furtivamente **3** rabbrividire, avere la pelle d'oca ♦ **to c. away** allontanarsi furtivamente; **to c. in** prendere piede; **to c. up** salire lentamente, insinuarsi
creeper ['kriːpəʳ] *s.* **1** verme *m.* **2** (*bot.*) rampicante *m.* **3** (*naut.*) grappino *m.*
creeping ['kriːpɪŋ] *agg.* rampicante
creepy ['kriːpɪ] *agg.* **1** strisciante **2** che fa accapponare la pelle
to cremate [krɪ'meɪt] *v. tr.* cremare
cremation [krɪ'meɪʃ(ə)n] *s.* cremazione *f.*
crematorium [ˌkrɛmə'tɔːrɪəm] *s.* forno *m.* crematorio
crepe [kreɪp] *s.* crespo *m.*
crept [krɛpt] *pass. e p. p. di* **to creep**
crepuscular [krɪ'pʌskjʊləʳ] *agg.* crepuscolare
crescendo [krɪ'ʃɛndɒʊ] *s.* crescendo *m.*
crescent ['krɛsnt] **A** *agg.* **1** crescente **2** a mezzaluna **3** a semicerchio **B** *s.* **1** luna *f.* crescente, falce *m.* di luna **2** mezzaluna *f.*
cress [krɛs] *s.* crescione *m.*
crest [krɛst] *s.* **1** cresta *f.*, ciuffo *m.* **2** (*arald.*) cimiero *m.* **3** crinale *m.*
crestfallen ['krɛstˌfɜːlən] *agg.* abbattuto, mortificato
crevasse [krɪ'væs] *s.* crepaccio *m.*
crevice ['krɛvɪs] *s.* crepa *f.*, fenditura *f.*
crew [kruː] *s.* equipaggio *m.*
crewman [kruːmən] (*pl.* **crewmen**) *s.* membro *m.* dell'equipaggio
crew-neck ['kruːnɛk] *agg.* (a) girocollo
crib [krɪb] *s.* **1** greppia *f.* **2** presepe *m.* **3** (*USA*) culla *f.*

to crib [krɪb] *v. tr.* (*fam.*) copiare (*i compiti*)
crick [krɪk] *s.* crampo *m.*
cricket (1) ['krɪkɪt] *s.* (*sport*) cricket *m. inv.*
cricket (2) ['krɪkɪt] *s.* grillo *m.*
crime [kraɪm] *s.* crimine *m.*, delitto *m.*
criminal ['krɪmɪnl] *agg. e s.* criminale *m. e f.*
crimson ['krɪmzn] *agg.* cremisi
to cringe [krɪndʒ] *v. intr.* **1** acquattarsi, farsi piccolo **2** umiliarsi, essere servile
crinkle ['krɪŋkl] *s.* crespa *f.*, grinza *f.*
to crinkle ['krɪŋkl] *v. tr. e intr.* increspare, incresparsi
cripple ['krɪpl] *s.* zoppo *m.*, mutilato *m.*
to cripple ['krɪpl] *v. tr.* azzoppare, menomare
crisis ['kraɪsɪs] (*pl.* **crises**) *s.* crisi *f.*
crisp [krɪsp] *agg.* **1** croccante **2** fresco, frizzante
crisscross ['krɪskrəs] *agg.* incrociato
criterion [kraɪ'tɪɜːrɪən] (*pl.* **criteria**) *s.* criterio *m.*
critic ['krɪtɪk] *s.* critico *m.*
critical ['krɪtɪk(ə)l] *agg.* critico
criticism ['krɪtɪsɪz(ə)m] *s.* critica *f.*
criticizable ['krɪtɪsaɪzəbl] *agg.* criticabile
to criticize ['krɪtɪsaɪz] *v. tr.* criticare, fare la critica
to croak [krɒʊk] *v. intr.* gracchiare, gracidare
crochet ['krɒʊʃeɪ] *s.* uncinetto *m.*
crockery ['krəkərɪ] *s.* terraglie *f. pl.*, vasellame *m.*
crocodile ['krəkədaɪl] *s.* coccodrillo *m.*
crook [krʊk] *s.* **1** uncino *m.*, gancio *m.* **2** bastone *m.* **3** (*pop.*) truffatore *m.*
to crook [krʊk] *v. tr.* piegare, curvare
crooked ['krʊkɪd] *agg.* **1** storto **2** disonesto
crop [krəp] *s.* **1** raccolto *m.*, messe *f.* **2** (*di uccello*) gozzo *m.* **3** frustino *m.* **4** (*di capelli*) rapata *f.*
to crop [krəp] *v. tr.* **1** spuntare, tosare **2** coltivare ♦ **to c. up** spuntare, presentarsi
croquette [krɒ(ʊ)'kɛt] *s.* crocchetta *f.*
cross [krəs] **A** *agg.* **1** trasversale, obliquo **2** seccato, di cattivo umore **3** opposto, contrario **B** *s.* **1** croce *f.* **2** contrarietà *f.* **3** (*biol.*) incrocio *m.*
to cross [krəs] **A** *v. tr.* **1** attraversare, intersecare **2** incrociare **3** ostacolare **4** sbarrare **B** *v. intr.* **1** incrociarsi **2** compiere una traversata ♦ **to c. off/out** cancellare; **to c. over** attraversare
crossbar ['krəsbaːʳ] *s.* asticella *f.*
crossbow ['krəsbɒʊ] *s.* balestra *f.*
crossbreed ['krəsbriːd] *s.* incrocio *m.* (di razze)
cross-country [ˌkrəs'kʌntrɪ] *agg.* campestre
cross-eyed ['krəsaɪd] *agg.* strabico
crossfire ['krəsˌfaɪəʳ] *s.* fuoco *m.* incrociato
crossing ['krəsɪŋ] *s.* **1** attraversamento *m.*, incrocio *m.* **2** traversata *f.* ♦ **level c.** passaggio a livello
cross-purposes [ˌkrəs'pɜːpəsɪz] *s. pl.* scopi *m. pl.* contrastanti ♦ **to be at c.** fraintendersi
cross-reference [ˌkrəs'rɛf(ə)rəns] *s.* rinvio *m.*, rimando *m.*
crossroad ['krəsrɒʊd] *s.* **1** traversa *f.* **2** crocevia *m. inv.*, crocicchio *m.*
cross-section ['krəsˌsɛkʃ(ə)n] *s.* **1** sezione *f.* trasversale **2** gruppo *m.* rappresentativo
crosswalk ['krəswɜːk] *s.* (*USA*) attraversamento *m.* pedonale
crosswise ['krəswaɪz] *avv.* attraverso
crossword ['krəswɜːd] *s.* cruciverba *m. inv.*
crotchet ['krətʃɪt] *s.* **1** gancio *m.* **2** mania *f.* **3** (*mus.*) semiminima *f.*
to crouch [kraʊtʃ] *v. intr.* rannicchiarsi
crouton ['kruːtən] *s.* crostino *m.*
crow (1) [krɒʊ] *s.* corvo *m.*, cornacchia *f.*
crow (2) [krɒʊ] *s.* canto *m.* del gallo
crowd [kraʊd] *s.* calca *f.*, folla *f.*, moltitudine *f.*
to crowd [kraʊd] *v. intr.* affollarsi, accalcarsi
crowded ['kraʊdɪd] *agg.* affollato
crowding ['kraʊdɪŋ] *s.* affollamento *m.*
crown [kraʊn] *s.* **1** corona *f.* **2** calotta *f.* ♦ **c. cap** tappo a corona
to crown [kraʊn] *v. tr.* incoronare
crucial ['kruːʃjəl] *agg.* cruciale, decisivo
cruciate ['kruːʃɪeɪt] *agg.* (*bot.*) cruciforme
crucifix ['kruːsɪfɪks] *s.* crocifisso *m.*
crucifixion [ˌkruːsɪ'fɪkʃ(ə)n] *s.* crocifissione *f.*
cruciform ['kruːsɪfɜːm] *agg.* cruciforme
crude [kruːd] **A** *agg.* **1** grezzo **2** rozzo, grossolano **B** *s.* (petrolio) greggio *m.*
cruel [krʊəl] *agg.* crudele
cruelty ['krʊəltɪ] *s.* crudeltà *f.*
cruise [kruːz] *s.* crociera *f.*
cruiser ['kruːzəʳ] *s.* incrociatore *m.*
crumb [krʌm] *s.* **1** briciola *f.* **2** mollica *f.*
to crumb [krʌm] *v. tr.* **1** sbriciolare **2** impanare

to **crumble** ['krʌmbl] *v. tr. e intr.* sbriciolare, sbriciolarsi
to **crumple** ['krʌmpl] *v. tr.* stropicciare
crunch [krʌntʃ] *s.* **1** lo sgranocchiare **2** scricchiolio *m.* **3** (*fam.*) momento *m.* cruciale
to **crunch** [krʌn(t)ʃ] *v. tr.* sgranocchiare
crusade [kruː'seɪd] *s.* crociata *f.*
crush [krʌʃ] *s.* **1** calca *f.*, folla *f.* **2** (*fam.*) cotta *f.*
to **crush** [krʌʃ] *v. tr.* **1** schiacciare **2** stroncare, annientare
crust [krʌst] *s.* crosta *f.*
crustacean [krʌs'teɪʃjən] *s.* crostaceo *m.*
crutch [krʌtʃ] *s.* **1** gruccia *f.*, stampella *f.* **2** biforcazione *f.*
crux [krʌks] *s.* punto *m.* cruciale
cry [kraɪ] *s.* **1** grido *m.* **2** (*di animale*) verso *m.* **3** lamento *m.*, pianto *m.*
to **cry** [kraɪ] *v. tr. e intr.* **1** gridare **2** piangere ♦ **to c. down** denigrare; **to c. for** chiedere a gran voce; **to c. off** tirarsi indietro
crying ['kraɪɪŋ] *s.* pianto *m.*
crypt [krɪpt] *s.* cripta *f.*
cryptic ['krɪptɪk] *agg.* criptico
crystal ['krɪstl] *s.* cristallo *m.* ♦ **c. clear** limpido, cristallino
crystalline ['krɪstəlaɪn] *agg.* cristallino
to **crystallize** ['krɪstəlaɪz] *v. tr.* cristallizzare
cub [kəb] *s.* cucciolo *m.*
cube [kjuːb] *s.* cubo *m.*
cubic ['kjuːbɪk] *agg.* cubico
cubism ['kjuːbɪz(ə)m] *s.* cubismo *m.*
cubital ['kjuːbɪtl] *agg.* (*anat.*) cubitale
cuckoo ['kʊkuː] *s.* cuculo *m.* ♦ **c. clock** orologio a cucù
cucumber ['kjuːkəmbəʳ] *s.* cetriolo *m.*
to **cuddle** ['kʌdl] *v. tr.* abbracciare, coccolare ♦ **to c. up** raggomitolarsi
cudgel ['kʌdʒ(ə)l] *s.* randello *m.*
cue (1) [kjuː] *s.* **1** (*teatro, mus.*) battuta *f.* d'entrata, attacco *m.* **2** imbeccata *f.*
cue (2) [kjuː] *s.* (*biliardo*) stecca *f.*
cuff (1) [kʌf] *s.* **1** polsino *m.* **2** risvolto *m.* **3** *al pl.* manette *f. pl.* ♦ **c. links** gemelli (*per polsino*)
cuff (2) [kʌf] *s.* schiaffo *m.*
to **cuff** [kʌf] *v. tr.* schiaffeggiare
culinary ['kʌlɪnərɪ] *agg.* culinario
to **cull** [kʌl] *v. tr.* scegliere, selezionare
to **culminate** ['kʌlmɪneɪt] *v. intr.* culminare
culmination [ˌkʌlmɪ'neɪʃ(ə)n] *s.* culmine *m.*
culprit ['kʌlprɪt] *s.* colpevole *m. e f.*
cult [kʌlt] *s.* culto *m.*
cultivable ['kʌltɪvəbl] *agg.* coltivabile
to **cultivate** ['kʌltɪveɪt] *v. tr.* coltivare
cultivated ['kʌltɪveɪtɪd] *agg.* **1** coltivato **2** colto
cultivation [ˌkʌltɪ'veɪʃ(ə)n] *s.* coltura *f.*
cultural ['kʌltʃ(ə)r(ə)l] *agg.* culturale
culture ['kʌltʃəʳ] *s.* **1** cultura *f.*, istruzione *f.* **2** civiltà *f.* **3** coltura *f.*, coltivazione *f.*
cumbersome ['kʌmbəsəm] *agg.* ingombrante
cumulus ['kjuːmjʊləs] *s.* (*meteor.*) cumulo *m.*
cuneiform ['kjuːnɪɪfɜːm] *agg.* cuneiforme
cunning ['kʌnɪŋ] **A** *agg.* astuto, furbo **B** *s.* astuzia *f.*, furberia *f.*
cup [kʌp] *s.* **1** tazza *f.*, tazzina *f.* **2** coppa *f.* ♦ **paper c.** bicchiere di carta
cupboard ['kʌbəd] *s.* armadio *m.*
curable ['kjʊərəbl] *agg.* curabile
curate ['kjʊərɪt] *s.* curato *m.*, cappellano *m.*
curator [kjʊə'reɪtəʳ] *s.* (*di museo, biblioteca*) direttore *m.*, sovrintendente *m. e f.*
curb [kɜːb] *s.* freno *m.*, ostacolo *m.*
cure [kjʊəʳ] *s.* cura *f.*, rimedio *m.*
to **cure** [kjʊəʳ] **A** *v. tr.* **1** guarire, curare **2** (*un materiale*) trattare **3** (*un alimento*) affumicare, salare **B** *v. intr.* (*di alimento*) conservarsi
curfew ['kɜːfjuː] *s.* coprifuoco *m.*
curia ['kjʊərɪə] *s.* curia *f.*
curio ['kjʊ(ə)rɪəʊ] *s.* curiosità *f.*, oggetto *m.* da collezione
curiosity [ˌkjʊərɪ'ɔsɪtɪ] *s.* curiosità *f.*
curious ['kjʊərɪəs] *agg.* curioso
curl [kɜːl] *s.* riccio *m.*, ricciolo *m.*
to **curl** [kɜːl] *v. tr. e intr.* arricciare, arricciarsi ♦ **to c. up** raggomitolarsi, accartocciarsi
curler ['kɜːləʳ] *s.* bigodino *m.*
curly ['kɜːlɪ] *agg.* **1** ricciuto **2** increspato
currant ['kʌr(ə)nt] *s.* **1** ribes *m.* **2** uva *f.* sultanina
currency ['kʌr(ə)nsɪ] *s.* **1** valuta *f.*, moneta *f.* **2** circolazione *f.*, diffusione *f.*
current ['kʌr(ə)nt] **A** *agg.* corrente, attuale **B** *s.* corrente *f.*
currently ['kʌr(ə)ntlɪ] *avv.* attualmente
curriculum [kə'rɪkjʊləm] *s.* curriculum *m.*
curry ['kʌrɪ] *s.* curry *m. inv.*
to **curry** ['kʌrɪ] *v. tr.* **1** strigliare **2** (*pelli*) conciare **3** adulare
curse [kɜːs] *s.* **1** maledizione *f.* **2** impre-

cazione *f.*, bestemmia *f.*
to **curse** [kə(ː)s] **A** *v. tr.* maledire **B** *v. intr.* imprecare, bestemmiare
cursed ['kɜːsɪd] *agg.* maledetto
cursor ['kɜːsəʳ] *s.* cursore *m.*
curt [kɜːt] *agg.* brusco, secco, conciso
to **curtail** [kɜː'teɪl] *v. tr.* **1** accorciare, abbreviare **2** ridurre, limitare
curtain ['kɜːt(ə)n] *s.* **1** tenda *f.* **2** (*teatro*) sipario *m.* ♦ **behind the c.** dietro le quinte
curts(e)y ['kɜːtsɪ] *s.* inchino *m.*, riverenza *f.*
curve [kɜːv] *s.* curva *f.*
to **curve** [kɜːv] *v. tr. e intr.* curvare, curvarsi
curvilinear [ˌkɜːvɪ'lɪnɪəʳ] *agg.* curvilineo
cushion ['kʊʃ(ə)n] *s.* cuscino *m.*
to **cushion** ['kʊʃ(ə)n] *v. tr.* **1** imbottire **2** smorzare, attutire
custard ['kʌstəd] *s.* crema *f.* pasticciera
custodian [kʌs'tɒʊdjən] *s.* custode *m.*
custody ['kʌstədɪ] *s.* **1** custodia *f.*, sorveglianza *f.* **2** detenzione *f.*
custom ['kʌstəm] *s.* **1** costume *m.*, abitudine *f.*, usanza *f.* **2** *al pl.* dogana *f.* **3** clientela *f.* ♦ **c.-made** su ordinazione, su misura; **customs officer** doganiere
customary ['kʌstəm(ə)rɪ] *agg.* consueto, usuale
customer ['kʌstəməʳ] *s.* cliente *m. e f.*
customized ['kəstəmaɪzd] *agg.* fuori serie, su misura
cut [kʌt] *s.* **1** taglio *m.* **2** riduzione *f.*
to **cut** [kʌt] (*pass. e p. p.* **cut**) **A** *v. tr.* **1** tagliare **2** incidere **3** ridurre **B** *v. intr.* tagliare, tagliarsi ♦ **to c. a tooth** mettere un dente; **to c. back** ridurre; **to c. down** abbattere, ridurre; **to c. in** interloquire; **to c. off** troncare, recidere; **to c. out** ritagliare; **to c. up** tagliare a pezzetti
cutaneous [kjʊ(ː)'teɪnjəs] *agg.* cutaneo
cute [kjuːt] *agg.* (*fam.*) carino
cutis ['kjuːtɪs] *s.* cute *f.*
cutlery ['kʌtlərɪ] *s.* posate *f. pl.*
cutlet ['kʌtlɪt] *s.* costoletta *f.*
cutoff ['kʌtəf] *s.* **1** limite *m.* estremo **2** (*USA*) scorciatoia *f.* **3** (*mecc.*) otturatore *m.* **4** (*elettr.*) apertura *f.* di circuito
cut-out ['kʌtaʊt] *s.* **1** (*di giornale*) ritaglio *m.* **2** (*elettr.*) interruttore *m.*
cut-price ['kʌtpraɪs] *agg.* a prezzo ridotto
cutthroat ['kʌtθrɒʊt] *s.* assassino *m.*
cutting ['kʌtɪŋ] **A** *agg.* **1** tagliente **2** sferzante **B** *s.* **1** taglio *m.* **2** ritaglio *m.* **3** (*bot.*) talea *f.* **4** (*cine.*) montaggio *m.*
cuttlefish ['kʌtlfɪʃ] *s.* seppia *f.*
cyanide ['saɪənaɪd] *s.* cianuro *m.*
cycle ['saɪkl] *s.* **1** ciclo *m.* **2** bicicletta *f.* ♦ **c. track** velodromo
cyclic ['sɪklɪk] *agg.* ciclico
cycling ['saɪklɪŋ] *s.* ciclismo *m.*
cyclist ['saɪklɪst] *s.* ciclista *m. e f.*
cyclopean [saɪ'klɒʊpjən] *agg.* ciclopico
cylinder ['sɪlɪndəʳ] *s.* **1** cilindro *m.* **2** bombola *f.*
cylindrical [ˌsɪ'lɪndrɪk(ə)l] *agg.* cilindrico
cynical ['sɪnɪkl] *agg.* cinico
cynicism ['sɪnɪsɪz(ə)m] *s.* cinismo *m.*
cypress ['saɪprɪs] *s.* cipresso *m.*
cyst [sɪst] *s.* cisti *f.*
cystitis [sɪs'taɪtɪs] *s.* cistite *f.*
czar [zaːʳ] *s.* zar *m. inv.*
Czech [tʃɛk] *agg. e s.* ceco *m.*

D

to **dab** [dæb] *v. tr.* **1** picchiettare, tamponare **2** applicare, spalmare
to **dabble** ['dæbl] **A** *v. tr.* schizzare, bagnare **B** *v. intr.* sguazzare ♦ **to d. in/at** occuparsi da dilettante di (q.c.)
dabbler ['dæbləʳ] *s.* dilettante *m. e f.*
dad [dæd] *s.* (*fam.*) papà *m.*
Dadaism ['dɑdəɪz(ə)m] *s.* dadaismo *m.*
daddy ['dædɪ] *s.* (*fam.*) papà *m.*
daffodil ['dæfədɪl] *s.* giunchiglia *f.*
daft [dɑːft] *agg.* (*fam.*) sciocco
dagger ['dægəʳ] *s.* pugnale *m.*
daily ['deɪlɪ] **A** *agg.* giornaliero, quotidiano **B** *s.* quotidiano *m.* **C** *avv.* giornalmente, quotidianamente
daintiness ['deɪntɪnɪs] *s.* delicatezza *f.*, raffinatezza *f.*
dainty ['deɪntɪ] *agg.* **1** delicato, fine **2** prelibato
dairy ['dɛərɪ] *s.* **1** caseificio *m.* **2** latteria *f.* ♦ **d. products** latticini
dais ['deɪɪs] *s.* predella *f.*, palco *m.*
daisy ['deɪzɪ] *s.* margherita *f.*
dale [deɪl] *s.* vallata *f.*
dam [dæm] *s.* diga *f.*
to **dam** [dæm] *v. tr.* sbarrare, arginare
damage ['dæmɪdʒ] *s.* **1** avaria *f.*, danno *m.*, guasto *m.* **2** *al pl.* danni *m. pl.*, risarcimento *m.* ♦ **claim for damages** richiesta di risarcimento
to **damage** ['dæmɪdʒ] *v. tr.* danneggiare, lesionare
damask ['dæməsk] *s.* damasco *m.*
damn [dæm] *inter.* maledizione!
to **damn** [dæm] *v. tr.* **1** dannare, condannare **2** maledire, imprecare **3** rovinare
damned [dæmd] *agg.* **1** dannato **2** (*pop.*) maledetto
damp [dæmp] **A** *agg.* umido, bagnato **B** *s.* umidità *f.*, umido *m.*
to **damp** [dæmp] *v. tr.* **1** inumidire, bagnare **2** soffocare, estinguere **3** deprimere
to **dampen** ['dæmp(ə)n] *v. tr.* inumidire
damper ['dæmpəʳ] *s.* **1** freno *m.* **2** (*autom.*) ammortizzatore *m.*
damson ['dæmz(ə)n] *s.* susino *m.* selvatico
dance [dɑːns] *s.* ballo *m.*, danza *f.* ♦ **d. hall** sala da ballo
to **dance** [dɑːns] *v. tr. e intr.* ballare, danzare
dancer ['dɑːnsəʳ] *s.* ballerino *m.*, ballerina *f.*
dancing ['dɑːnsɪŋ] *s.* la danza *f.*, il ballo *m.* ♦ **d. school** scuola di danza
dandelion ['dændɪlaɪən] *s.* (*bot.*) tarassaco *m.*, dente *m.* di leone
dandruff ['dændrəf] *s.* forfora *f.*
dandy ['dændɪ] *agg.* elegante, affettato
Dane [deɪn] *s.* danese *m. e f.*
danger ['deɪn(d)ʒəʳ] *s.* pericolo *m.*
dangerous ['deɪn(d)ʒrəs] *agg.* pericoloso
to **dangle** ['dæŋgl] **A** *v. intr.* penzolare, dondolare **B** *v. tr.* **1** far penzolare, far dondolare **2** far balenare
Danish ['deɪnɪʃ] **A** *agg.* danese **B** *s.* (*lingua*) danese *m.*
dapper ['dæpəʳ] *agg.* azzimato
dapple ['dæpl] *agg.* maculato, pezzato
dare [dɛəʳ] *s.* sfida *f.*
to **dare** [dɛəʳ] (*pass.* **dared**, **durst**, *p. p.* **dared**) **A** *v. intr.* osare **B** *v. tr.* **1** sfidare **2** atterrire ♦ **I d. say** suppongo; **to d. sb. to do st.** sfidare qc. a fare q.c.
daredevil ['dɛə,dɛvl] **A** *agg.* audace, temerario **B** *s.* scavezzacollo *m.*
daring ['dɛərɪŋ] **A** *agg.* ardito, audace **B** *s.* audacia *f.*
dark [dɑːk] **A** *agg.* **1** buio, scuro **2** (*di colore*) cupo **3** (*fig.*) nero, tetro, triste **B** *s.* buio *m.*, oscurità *f.* ♦ **to get d.** oscurare, farsi notte
to **darken** ['dɑːk(ə)n] **A** *v. tr.* oscurare, offuscare **B** *v. intr.* **1** oscurarsi, offuscarsi **2** imbrunire
darkness [dɑːknɪs] *s.* buio *m.*, oscurità *f.*
darling ['dɑːlɪŋ] **A** *agg.* caro, diletto **B** *s.* caro *m.*, tesoro *m.*
to **darn** [dɑːn] *v. tr.* rammendare
darnel ['dɑːnl] *s.* loglio *m.*
darning ['dɑːnɪŋ] *s.* rammendo *m.*
dart [dɑːt] *s.* **1** freccetta *f.* **2** (*letter.*) dardo *m.* **3** pungiglione *m.* **4** pince *f. inv.*
to **dart** [dɑːt] **A** *v. tr.* scagliare **B** *v. intr.* **1** dardeggiare, saettare **2** scagliarsi in avanti
dash [dæʃ] *s.* **1** balzo *m.*, scatto *m.* **2** slancio *m.*, impeto *m.* **3** tonfo *m.*, urto *m.* **4** piccola quantità *f.*, goccia *f.* **5** trattino *m.*, lineetta *f.*
to **dash** [dæʃ] **A** *v. tr.* **1** gettare, lanciare,

sbattere **2** infrangere **3** cospargere, spruzzare **B** *v. intr.* **1** precipitarsi, scagliarsi **2** cozzare, urtare ♦ **to d. off** scappare via
dashboard ['dæʃbɜːd] *s.* cruscotto *m.*
dashing ['dæʃɪŋ] *agg.* **1** impetuoso, focoso **2** vivace, vistoso
data ['deɪtə] *s. pl.* dati *m. pl.* ♦ **d. bank** banca dati; **d. processing** elaborazione di dati
date (1) [deɪt] *s.* **1** data *f.* **2** scadenza *f.* **3** appuntamento *m.*, impegno *m.* ♦ **at long/short d.** a lunga/breve scadenza; **to d.** fino a oggi; **up to d.** aggiornato
date (2) [deɪt] *s.* dattero *m.*
to date [deɪt] **A** *v. tr.* **1** datare, mettere la data **2** attribuire la data, far risalire a **3** (*USA*, *fam.*) frequentare **B** *v. intr.* datare, risalire a
dated ['deɪtɪd] *agg.* datato, sorpassato
daub [dɜːb] *s.* (*fam.*) sgorbio *m.*
to daub [dɜːb] *v. tr.* impiastricciare, imbrattare
daughter ['dɜːtəʳ] *s.* figlia *f.* ♦ **d.-in-law** nuora
to daunt [dɜːnt] *v. tr.* **1** intimidire **2** scoraggiare
to dawdle ['dɜːdl] *v. intr.* gingillarsi
dawn [dɜːn] *s.* **1** alba *f.* **2** (*fig.*) principio *m.*
to dawn [dɜːn] *v. intr.* **1** albeggiare **2** apparire ♦ **to d. on** venire in mente, rendersi conto di
day [deɪ] *s.* **1** giorno *m.*, giornata *f.* **2** tempo *m.*, epoca *f.* ♦ **by d.** di giorno; **d. by d.** giorno per giorno; **d. return** biglietto di andata e ritorno in giornata; **d. time** diurno; **d.-to-d.** quotidiano; **every other d.** un giorno sì e uno no; **the d. before yesterday** l'altro ieri; **the d. after tomorrow** dopodomani
daybreak ['deɪbreɪk] *s.* alba *f.*
to daydream ['deɪdriːm] *v. intr.* sognare a occhi aperti
daylight ['deɪlaɪt] *s.* luce *f.* del giorno
daze [deɪz] *s.* stupore *m.*, stordimento *m.* ♦ **to be in a d.** essere sbalordito
to daze [deɪz] *v. tr.* stordire
to dazzle ['dæzl] *v. tr.* abbagliare
dead [dɛd] *agg.* **1** morto **2** fuori uso **3** completo, perfetto **4** spento, insensibile ♦ **d. and gone** morto e sepolto; **d. end** vicolo cieco; **d. heat** (*in gara*) arrivo alla pari; **d. letter** lettera giacente; **d.-shot** tiratore scelto; **d. wood** ramo secco; **to come to a d. stop** fermarsi di colpo
to deaden ['dɛdn] *v. tr.* **1** attutire, smorzare **2** insonorizzare
deadline ['dɛdlaɪn] *s.* scadenza *f.*
deadlock ['dɛdlək] *s.* punto *m.* morto
deadly ['dɛdlɪ] *agg.* micidiale, letale
deadpan ['dɛdpæn] *agg.* (*fam.*) impassibile
deaf [dɛf] *agg.* sordo ♦ **d.-and-dumb** sordomuto
deafness ['dɛfnɪs] *s.* sordità *f.*
deal (1) [diːl] *s.* quantità *f.* ♦ **a great d. of** un bel po' di
deal (2) [diːl] *s.* **1** accordo *m.*, affare *m.* **2** trattamento *m.* **3** (*giocando a carte*) mano *f.*
to deal [diːl] (*pass. e p. p.* **dealt**) **A** *v. tr.* **1** distribuire, fornire **2** dare le carte **B** *v. intr.* fare affari ♦ **to d. in** commerciare in; **to d. with** trattare con, fare affari con, trattare di
dealer ['diːləʳ] *s.* commerciante *m. e f.*, distributore *m.*
dealing ['diːlɪŋ] *s.* **1** *al pl.* rapporti *m. pl.* **2** commercio *m.* **3** distribuzione *f.*
dealt [dɛlt] *pass. e p. p. di* **to deal**
deambulatory [dɪ'æmbjʊlətərɪ] *s.* deambulatorio *m.*
dean [diːn] *s.* **1** (*relig.*) decano *m.* **2** (*di facoltà universitaria*) preside *m. e f.*
dear [dɪəʳ] *agg.* **1** caro, amato **2** caro, costoso
dearly ['dɪəlɪ] *avv.* **1** caramente **2** ardentemente, intensamente **3** a caro prezzo
death [dɛθ] *s.* morte *f.* ♦ **d. duty** tassa di successione; **d. rate** indice di mortalità; **d. toll** vittime
to debar [dɪ'baːʳ] *v. tr.* escludere, impedire, privare di ♦ **to d. sb. from doing st.** impedire a qc. di fare q.c.
to debase [dɪ'beɪs] *v. tr.* **1** avvilire, degradare **2** adulterare **3** deprezzare
debatable [dɪ'beɪtəbl] *agg.* discutibile
debate [dɪ'beɪt] *s.* dibattito *m.*, discussione *f.*
to debate [dɪ'beɪt] *v. tr. e intr.* **1** dibattere, discutere **2** considerare, pensare
debauched [dɪ'bɜːtʃt] *agg.* dissoluto
debauchery [dɪ'bɜːtʃ(ə)rɪ] *s.* dissolutezza *f.*, pervertimento *m.*
debit ['dɛbɪt] *s.* (*comm.*) debito *m.*, addebito *m.*
to debit ['dɛbɪt] *v. tr.* (*comm.*) addebitare
debris ['dɛbriː] *s. inv.* detriti *m. pl.*, macerie *f. pl.*

debt [dɛt] *s.* debito *m.* ♦ **to be in d. to** essere indebitato con; **to get out of d.** sdebitarsi
debtor ['dɛtəʳ] *s.* debitore *m.*
to debug [dɪ'bʌg] *v. tr.* **1** mettere a punto **2** (*inf.*) eliminare errori
to debunk [ˌdiː'bʌŋk] *v. tr.* (*fam.*) ridimensionare
debut ['deɪbuː] *s.* debutto *m.*
decade ['dɛkeɪd] *s.* decade *f.*, decennio *m.*
decadence ['dɛkəd(ə)ns] *s.* decadenza *f.*
decadent ['dɛkədənt] *agg.* decadente
decadentism ['dɛkədəntɪz(ə)m] *s.* decadentismo *m.*
to decaffeinate [diː'kæfɪˌneɪt] *v. tr.* decaffeinare
decalogue ['dɛkələg] decalogo *m.*
to decant [dɪ'kænt] *v. tr.* travasare
decanter [dɪ'kæntəʳ] *s.* caraffa *f.*
to decapitate [dɪ'kæpɪteɪt] *v. tr.* decapitare
decay [dɪ'keɪ] *s.* **1** decadenza *f.*, degrado *m.* **2** disfacimento *m.*, putrefazione *f.*
to decay [dɪ'keɪ] *v. intr.* **1** andare in rovina, crollare **2** decadere, deperire **3** marcire, imputridire
to decease [dɪ'siːs] *v. intr.* decedere
deceased [dɪ'siːst] *s.* defunto *m.*
deceit [dɪ'siːt] *s.* **1** inganno *m.* **2** falsità *f.*
deceitful [dɪ'siːtf(ʊ)l] *agg.* ingannevole, perfido
to deceive [dɪ'siːv] *v. tr.* **1** ingannare, raggirare **2** deludere
deceleration [diːˌsɛlə'reɪʃ(ə)n] *s.* decelerazione *f.*, rallentamento *m.*
December [dɪ'sɛmbəʳ] *s.* dicembre *m.*
decency ['diːsnsɪ] *s.* **1** decenza *f.*, pudore *m.* **2** decoro *m.*
decennium [dɪ'sɛnɪəm] *s.* decennio *m.*
decent ['diːs(ə)nt] *agg.* **1** decente, dignitoso **2** discreto, soddisfacente **3** (*fam.*) simpatico, carino
decentralization [diːˌsɛntrəlaɪ'zeɪʃ(ə)n] *s.* decentramento *m.*
deception [dɪ'sɛpʃ(ə)n] *s.* inganno *m.*
deceptive [dɪ'sɛptɪv] *agg.* ingannevole
to decide [dɪ'saɪd] **A** *v. tr.* **1** decidere, risolvere **2** indurre **B** *v. intr.* prendere una decisione, decidersi ♦ **to d. on** decidere su; **to d. (not) to do st.** decidere di (non) fare q.c.
decided [dɪ'saɪdɪd] *agg.* **1** deciso, risoluto **2** indubbio
deciduous [dɪ'sɪdjʊəs] *agg.* deciduo
decilitre ['dɛsɪˌliːtəʳ] *s.* decilitro *m.*
decimal ['dɛsɪm(ə)l] *agg.* decimale
to decimate ['dɛsɪmeɪt] *v. tr.* decimare
to decipher [dɪ'saɪfəʳ] *v. tr.* decifrare
decision [dɪ'sɪʒ(ə)n] *s.* decisione *f.*
decisive [dɪ'saɪsɪv] *agg.* **1** decisivo **2** deciso, risoluto
deck [dɛk] *s.* **1** (*naut.*) ponte *m.*, coperta *f.* **2** (*di autobus*) piano *m.* **3** (*fam.*) mazzo *m.* di carte ♦ **d. house** tuga
to deck [dɛk] *v. tr.* adornare
deckchair ['dɛktʃɛəʳ] *s.* sedia *f.* a sdraio
to declaim [dɪ'kleɪm] *v. tr.* declamare
declaration [ˌdɛklə'reɪʃ(ə)n] *s.* dichiarazione *f.*
to declare [dɪ'klɛəʳ] *v. tr.* dichiarare, proclamare
decline [dɪ'klaɪn] *s.* declino *m.*, decadenza *f.*
to decline [dɪ'klaɪn] **A** *v. tr.* declinare, rifiutare, evitare **B** *v. intr.* declinare, diminuire, deperire
decoction [dɪ'kɔkʃ(ə)n] *s.* decotto *m.*
to decode [ˌdiː'kɒʊd] *v. tr.* decifrare, decodificare
decolorization [diːˌkʌləraɪ'zeɪʃ(ə)n] *s.* decolorazione *f.*
decomposable [ˌdɪ(ː)kəm'pɒʊzəbl] *agg.* scomponibile
to decompose [ˌdiːkəm'pɒʊz] *v. tr.* decomporre, scomporre
decomposition [ˌdiːkɔmpə'zɪʃ(ə)n] *s.* decomposizione *f.*, scomposizione *f.*
to decongest [ˌdiːkən'dʒɛst] *v. tr.* decongestionare
decor ['deɪkɜːʳ] *s.* **1** arredamento *m.* **2** decorazione *f.*
to decorate ['dɛkəreɪt] *v. tr.* **1** decorare **2** imbiancare **3** arredare
decoration [ˌdɛkə'reɪʃ(ə)n] *s.* **1** decorazione *f.*, ornamento *m.* **2** onorificenza *f.*
decorative ['dɛk(ə)rətɪv] *agg.* decorativo
decorator ['dɛkəreɪtəʳ] *s.* decoratore *m.*
decoy [dɪ'kɔɪ] *s.* esca *f.*, richiamo *m.*
decrease ['diːkriːs] *s.* diminuzione *f.*
to decrease [diː'kriːs] *v. tr. e intr.* diminuire
decree [dɪ'kriː] *s.* decreto *m.*, sentenza *f.*
to decree [dɪ'kriː] *v. tr.* decretare
decrepit [dɪ'krɛpɪt] *agg.* decrepito
to dedicate ['dɛdɪkeɪt] *v. tr.* dedicare
dedication [ˌdɛdɪ'keɪʃ(ə)n] *s.* **1** dedica *f.* **2** dedizione *f.*
to deduce [dɪ'djuːs] *v. tr.* dedurre, desumere
deducible [dɪ'djuːsəbl] *agg.* deducibile
to deduct [dɪ'dʌkt] *v. tr.* dedurre, detrarre

deductible [dɪ'dʌktəbl] *agg.* deducibile
deduction [dɪ'dʌkʃ(ə)n] *s.* deduzione *f.*, detrazione *f.*
deed [diːd] *s.* **1** atto *m.*, azione *f.* **2** (*dir*) atto *m.* (legale)
to deem [diːm] *v. tr.* credere, ritenere
deep [diːp] **A** *agg.* **1** fondo, profondo **2** largo **3** (*di suono*) grave, (*di colore*) intenso **B** *avv.* in profondità
to deepen ['diːp(ə)n] **A** *v. tr.* **1** approfondire **2** rendere più cupo, rendere più intenso **B** *v. intr.* **1** approfondirsi **2** incupirsi, farsi più intenso, farsi più grave
deep-freeze [ˌdiːp'friːz] *s.* congelatore *m.*, freezer *m. inv.*
to deep-freeze [ˌdiːp'friːz] *v. tr.* surgelare
deep-sea [ˌdiːp'sɪ] **A** *agg.* abissale **B** *s.* alto mare *m.*
deep-seated [ˌdiːp'siːtɪd] *agg.* inveterato, radicato
deer [dɪə[r]] *s.* cervo *m.*, daino *m.*, capriolo *m.*
deerskin ['dɪəˌskɪn] *s.* pelle *f.* di daino
to deface [dɪ'feɪs] *v. tr.* deturpare, sfregiare
defacement [dɪ'feɪsmənt] *s.* deturpazione *f.*, sfregio *m.*
defamation [ˌdɛfə'meɪʃ(ə)n] *s.* diffamazione *f.*
default [dɪ'fɜːlt] *s.* **1** difetto *m.*, mancanza *f.* **2** inadempienza *f.* **3** (*dir*) contumacia *f.* **4** (*sport*) abbandono *m.*
defeat [dɪ'fiːt] *s.* sconfitta *f.*, insuccesso *m.*
to defeat [dɪ'fiːt] *v. tr.* **1** sconfiggere **2** far fallire
defeatist [dɪ'fiːtɪst] disfattista *m. e f.*
defect [dɪ'fɛkt] *s.* difetto *m.*, imperfezione *f.*
to defect [dɪ'fɛkt] *v. intr.* disertare
defection [dɪ'fɛkʃ(ə)n] *s.* defezione *f.*, diserzione *f.*
defective [dɪ'fɛktɪv] *agg.* difettoso
defence [dɪ'fɛns] (*USA* **defense**) *s.* difesa *f.* ♦ **self d.** autodifesa
to defend [dɪ'fɛnd] *v. tr.* difendere
defendant [dɪ'fɛndənt] *s.* imputato *m.*
defender [dɪ'fɛndə[r]] *s.* difensore *s.*
defensive [dɪ'fɛnsɪv] **A** *agg.* **1** difensivo **2** diffidente **B** *s.* difensiva *f.*
to defer [dɪ'fɜː[r]] *v. tr.* differire, prorogare
deferential [ˌdɛfə'rɛnʃ(ə)l] *agg.* deferente, rispettoso
defiance [dɪ'faɪəns] *s.* sfida *f.* ♦ **in d. of** a dispetto di
defiant [dɪ'faɪənt] *agg.* provocatorio, insolente
deficiency [dɪ'fɪʃ(ə)nsɪ] *s.* **1** deficienza *f.*, difetto *m.*, mancanza *f.*, carenza *f.* **2** (*comm.*) disavanzo *m.*
deficient [dɪ'fɪʃ(ə)nt] *agg.* deficiente, difettoso, insufficiente
deficit ['dɛfɪsɪt] *s.* deficit *m. inv.*
to defile [dɪ'faɪl] *v. tr.* **1** contaminare, lordare **2** profanare
to define [dɪ'faɪn] *v. tr.* definire, determinare
definite ['dɛfɪnɪt] *agg.* **1** definito, preciso **2** sicuro, determinato **3** (*gramm.*) determinativo
definitely ['dɛfɪnɪtlɪ] *avv.* senza dubbio
definition [ˌdɛfɪ'nɪʃ(ə)n] *s.* definizione *f.*
definitive [dɪ'fɪnɪtɪv] *agg.* definitivo, decisivo
deflagration [ˌdɛflə'greɪʃ(ə)n] *s.* deflagrazione *f.*
to deflate [diː'fleɪt] *v. tr.* **1** sgonfiare **2** (*econ.*) deflazionare
to deflect [dɪ'flɛkt] *v. intr.* deviare, deflettere
to deforest [diː'fərɪst] *v. tr.* disboscare
to deform [dɪ'fɜːm] *v. tr.* deformare
deformation [ˌdiːfɜː'meɪʃ(ə)n] *s.* deformazione *f.*
deformed [dɪ'fɜːmd] *agg.* deforme
deformity [dɪ'fɜːmɪtɪ] *s.* deformità *f.*
to defraud [dɪ'frɜːd] *v. tr.* defraudare
to defrost [diː'frəst] *v. tr.* **1** sgelare, scongelare **2** sbrinare
defroster [diː'frəstə[r]] *s.* sbrinatore *m.*
deft [dɛft] *agg.* abile, destro
defunct [dɪ'fʌŋkt] *agg.* **1** defunto **2** liquidato
to defuse [diː'fjuːz] *v. tr.* disinnescare
to defy [dɪ'faɪ] *v. tr.* **1** sfidare **2** resistere a ♦ **to d. solution** essere insolubile
degenerate [dɪ'dʒɛn(ə)rət] *agg. e s.* degenerato *m.*
to degenerate [dɪ'dʒɛnəreɪt] *v. intr.* degenerare
degeneration [dɪˌdʒɛnə'reɪʃ(ə)] *s.* degenerazione *f.*
to degrade [dɪ'greɪd] *v. tr.* degradare, avvilire
degrading [dɪ'greɪdɪŋ] *agg.* degradante
to degrease [diː'griːs] *v. tr.* sgrassare
degree [dɪ'griː] *s.* **1** grado *m.* **2** livello *m.*, condizione *f.* **3** laurea *f.* ♦ **by degrees** gradatamente; **honorary d.** laurea ad honorem; **to take one's d.** laurearsi
to dehydrate [diː'haɪdreɪt] *v. tr.* disidratare
dehydration [ˌdiːhaɪ'dreɪʃ(ə)n] *s.* disidratazione *f.*

to deign [deɪn] **A** *v. intr.* degnarsi **B** *v. tr.* degnarsi di dare, concedere
deism ['diːɪz(ə)m] *s.* deismo *m.*
deity ['diːɪtɪ] *s.* divinità *f.*
to deject [dɪ'dʒɛkt] *v. tr.* abbattere, deprimere
dejection [dɪ'dʒɛkʃ(ə)n] *s.* **1** depressione *f.*, abbattimento *m.* **2** deiezione *f.*
delation [dɪ'leɪʃ(ə)n] *s.* delazione *f.*
delay [dɪ'leɪ] *s.* **1** ritardo *m.*, indugio *m.* **2** dilazione *f.*
to delay [dɪ'leɪ] **A** *v. tr.* ritardare, rimandare, prorogare **B** *v. intr.* tardare, indugiare
delectable [dɪ'lɛktəbl] *agg.* delizioso
to delegate ['dɛlɪgeɪt] *v. tr.* delegare
delegation [ˌdɛlɪ'geɪʃ(ə)n] *s.* **1** delega *f.* **2** delegazione *f.*
to delete [dɪ'liːt] *v. tr.* **1** cancellare **2** annullare
deleterious [ˌdɛlɪ'tɪərɪəs] *agg.* deleterio
deletion [dɪ'liːʃ(ə)n] *s.* cancellazione *f.*, soppressione *f.*
deliberate [dɪ'lɪbərɪt] *agg.* **1** deliberato, intenzionale **2** cauto, prudente
to deliberate [dɪ'lɪbəreɪt] **A** *v. tr.* deliberare **B** *v. intr.* **1** deliberare **2** riflettere, ponderare
delicacy ['dɛlɪkəsɪ] *s.* **1** delicatezza *f.* **2** manicaretto *m.*
delicate ['dɛlɪkɪt] *agg.* delicato
delicatessen [ˌdɛlɪkə'tɛsn] *s.* negozio *m.* di gastronomia, salumeria *f.*
delicious [dɪ'lɪʃəs] *agg.* delizioso, squisito
delight [dɪ'laɪt] *s.* **1** delizia *f.*, diletto *m.* **2** gioia *f.* ♦ **to take d. in doing st.** provare piacere nel fare q.c.
to delight [dɪ'laɪt] **A** *v. tr.* deliziare, rallegrare **B** *v. intr.* rallegrarsi, compiacersi
delighted [dɪ'laɪtɪd] *agg.* **1** ammirato **2** lietissimo, molto felice
delightful [dɪ'laɪtf(ʊ)l] *agg.* delizioso
to delimit [diː'lɪmɪt] *v. tr.* delimitare
delimitation [dɪˌlɪmɪ'teɪʃ(ə)n] *s.* delimitazione *f.*
delinquent [dɪ'lɪŋkwənt] *s.* delinquente *m. e f.*, malfattore *m.*
delirious [dɪ'lɪrɪəs] *agg.* delirante
delirium [dɪ'lɪrɪəm] *s.* delirio *m.*
to deliver [dɪ'lɪvər] **A** *v. tr.* **1** consegnare, recapitare, distribuire **2** far partorire **3** pronunciare **B** *v. intr.* **1** fare consegne a domicilio **2** partorire
delivery [dɪ'lɪv(ə)rɪ] *s.* **1** consegna *f.*, distribuzione *f.* **2** parto *m.* **3** dizione *f.* ♦ **cash on d.** pagamento alla consegna; **home d.** consegna a domicilio; **d. room** sala parto
delta ['dɛltə] *s.* delta *m. inv.*
to delude [dɪ'luːd] *v. tr.* illudere, ingannare
deluge ['dɛljuːdʒ] *s.* diluvio *m.*
delusion [dɪ'luːʒ(ə)n] *s.* illusione *f.*
to delve [dɛlv] *v. tr. e intr.* fare ricerche, scavare, rivangare
demagogy ['dɛməgəgɪ] *s.* demagogia *f.*
demand [dɪ'maːnd] *s.* **1** domanda *f.*, richiesta *f.* **2** esigenza *f.* **3** rivendicazione *f.*
to demand [dɪ'maːnd] *v. tr.* **1** domandare, richiedere **2** esigere **3** rivendicare
demanding [dɪ'maːndɪŋ] *agg.* **1** impegnativo, gravoso **2** (*di persona*) esigente
to demean [dɪ'miːn] *v. tr.* avvilire ♦ **to d. oneself** umiliarsi, avvilirsi
demented [dɪ'mɛntɪd] *agg.* demente
dementia [dɪ'mɛnʃɪə] *s.* (*med.*) demenza *f.*
demise [dɪ'maɪz] *s.* **1** decesso *m.* **2** (*dir.*) trasferimento *m.*
democracy [dɪ'məkrəsɪ] *s.* democrazia *f.*
democratic [ˌdɛmə'krætɪk] *agg.* democratico
demographic [ˌdɛːmə'græfɪk] *agg.* demografico
demography [dɪ'məgrəfɪ] *s.* demografia *f.*
to demolish [dɪ'məlɪʃ] *v. tr.* demolire
demolition [ˌdɛmə'lɪʃ(ə)n] *s.* demolizione *f.*
demon ['diːmən] *s.* demone *m.*
demonstrable [dɪ'mənstrəbl] *agg.* dimostrabile
to demonstrate ['dɛmənstreɪt] **A** *v. tr.* **1** dimostrare, spiegare **2** mostrare **B** *v. intr.* manifestare
demonstration [ˌdɛmən'streɪʃ(ə)n] *s.* **1** dimostrazione *f.* **2** manifestazione *f.*
demonstrator ['dɛmənˌstreɪtər] *s.* **1** dimostratore *m.* **2** dimostrante *m. e f.*
to demoralize [dɪ'mərɛlaɪz] *v. tr.* demoralizzare, scoraggiare
to demote [dɪ(ː)'mɒʊt] *v. tr.* retrocedere (*di grado*)
to demount [dɪ(ː)'maʊnt] *v. tr.* (*mecc.*) smontare
demur [dɪ'mɜːr] *s.* **1** esitazione *f.* **2** (*dir.*) obiezione *f.*
demure [dɪ'mjʊər] *agg.* contegnoso, schivo
demystification [diːˌmɪstɪfɪ'keɪʃ(ə)n] *s.* demistificazione *f.*
den [dɛn] *s.* **1** tana *f.* **2** covo *m.*, rifugio *m.*

to **denature** [di:'neɪtʃəʳ] *v. tr.* (*chim.*) denaturare

denial [dɪ'naɪ(ə)l] *s.* **1** rifiuto *m.*, diniego *m.* **2** smentita *f.*

to **denigrate** ['dɛnɪgreɪt] *v. tr.* denigrare

denomination [dɪˌnəmɪ'neɪʃ(ə)n] *s.* **1** denominazione *f.* **2** (*econ.*) valore *m.* nominale, (*di banconote*) taglio *m.* **3** (*relig.*) setta *f.*, confessione *f.*

to **denote** [dɪ'nɒʊt] *v. tr.* denotare

to **denounce** [dɪ'naʊns] *v. tr.* denunciare

dense [dɛns] *agg.* **1** denso, fitto, spesso **2** ottuso

density ['dɛns(ɪ)tɪ] *s.* densità *f.*

dent [dɛnt] *s.* **1** ammaccatura *f.* **2** (*tecnol.*) tacca *f.*

dental ['dɛntl] *agg.* dentale

dentist ['dɛntɪst] *s.* dentista *m. e f.*

denture ['dɛn(t)ʃəʳ] *s.* dentiera *f.*

denunciation [dɪˌnʌnsɪ'eɪʃ(ə)n] *s.* denuncia *f.*

to **deny** [dɪ'naɪ] *v. tr.* **1** negare, smentire **2** rinnegare **3** rifiutare ♦ **to d. oneself st.** privarsi di q.c.

deodorant [di:'ɒʊdərənt] *agg. e s.* deodorante *m.*

to **depart** [dɪ'pa:t] *v. intr.* **1** partire, allontanarsi **2** venir meno a, derogare

department [dɪ'pa:tmənt] *s.* **1** dipartimento *m.*, reparto *m.* **2** ministero *m.* ♦ **d. store** grande magazzino

departure [dɪ'pa:tʃəʳ] *s.* **1** partenza *f.* **2** allontanamento *m.*, deviazione *f.* **3** tendenza *f.*, direzione *f.* ♦ **time of d.** ora di partenza

to **depend** [dɪ'pɛnd] *v. intr.* **1** dipendere **2** essere a carico **3** fare assegnamento su ♦ **depending on** a seconda; **to d. on** dipendere da; **d. on it!** non c'è dubbio!

dependable [dɪ'pɛndəbl] *agg.* fidato, affidabile

dependent [dɪ'pɛndənt] *agg.* dipendente ♦ **to be d. on** essere a carico di

to **depict** [dɪ'pɪkt] *v. tr.* dipingere, rappresentare

depilation [ˌdɛpɪ'leɪʃ(ə)n] *s.* depilazione *f.*

depilatory [dɛ'pɪlət(ə)rɪ] *agg.* depilatorio

to **deplete** [dɪ'pli:t] *v. tr.* esaurire, vuotare

deplorable [dɪ'plɜ:rəbl] *agg.* deplorevole

to **deploy** [dɪ'plɔɪ] *v. tr.* (*mil.*) schierare, dispiegare

depollution [ˌdi:pə'lu:ʃ(ə)n] *s.* disinquinamento *m.*

depopulation [di:ˌpəpjʊ'leɪʃ(ə)n] *s.* spopolamento *m.*

to **deport** [dɪ'pɜ:t] *v. tr.* deportare, esiliare

deportment [dɪ'pɜ:tmənt] *s.* **1** portamento *m.* **2** comportamento *m.*, condotta *f.*

to **depose** [dɪ'pɒʊz] *v. tr.* **1** deporre, destituire **2** (*dir.*) deporre, testimoniare

deposit [dɪ'pəzɪt] *s.* **1** deposito *m.* **2** acconto *m.*, caparra *f.*, cauzione *f.* **3** giacimento *m.*, sedimento *m.*

to **deposit** [dɪ'pəzɪt] *v. tr.* **1** depositare **2** versare come acconto

depot ['dɛpɒʊ] *s.* **1** deposito *m.*, magazzino *m.* **2** (*USA*) rimessa *f.* (di autobus), stazione *f.* ferroviaria

depravity [dɪ'prævɪtɪ] *s.* depravazione *f.*

deprecable ['dɛprɪkəbl] *agg.* deprecabile

to **depreciate** [dɪ'pri:ʃɪeɪt] *v. tr. e intr.* **1** svalutare **2** ammortizzare

depreciation [dɪˌpri:ʃɪ'eɪʃ(ə)n] *s.* **1** svalutazione *f.*, deprezzamento *m.* **2** ammortamento *m.*

to **depress** [dɪ'prɛs] *v. tr.* **1** deprimere, rattristare **2** abbassare, premere **3** (*comm.*) indebolire, ridurre

depressant [dɪ'prɛsənt] *agg. e s.* sedativo *m.*

depressed [dɪ'prɛst] *agg.* **1** depresso, abbattuto **2** (*econ.*) depresso, in crisi

depressing [dɪ'prɛsɪŋ] *agg.* deprimente

depression [dɪ'prɛʃ(ə)n] *s.* depressione *f.*

deprivation [ˌdɛprɪ'veɪʃ(ə)n] *s.* privazione *f.*

to **deprive** [dɪ'praɪv] *v. tr.* privare

deprived [dɪ'praɪvd] *agg.* deprivato, svantaggiato

depth [dɛpθ] *s.* **1** profondità *f.* **2** fondo *m.*, fondale *m.* **3** (*di colore*) intensità *f.*, (*di suono*) altezza *f.* **4** *al pl.* abisso *m.* ♦ **d. finder** profondimetro; **in the depths of** nel profondo di

to **depurate** ['dɛpjʊreɪt] *v. tr.* depurare

depurator ['dɛpjʊreɪtəʳ] *s.* depuratore *m.*

to **deputize** ['dɛpjʊtaɪz] *v. intr.* fare le veci di

deputy ['dɛpjʊtɪ] *s.* **1** deputato *m.*, delegato *m.* **2** sostituto *m.*, vice *m. inv.* ♦ **by d.** per procura

to **derail** [dɪ'reɪl] *v. intr.* deragliare

derailment [dɪ(:)'reɪlmənt] *s.* deragliamento *m.*

to **derange** [dɪ'reɪn(d)ʒ] *v. tr.* sconvolgere, turbare, guastare

deranged [dɪ'reɪn(d)ʒd] *agg.* squilibrato ♦ **to become d.** diventare pazzo

deratization [dɪ(ː),rætaɪ'zeɪʃ(ə)n] *s.* derattizzazione *f.*
derby ['daːbɪ] *s.* **1** (*sport*) derby *m. inv.* **2** (*USA*) bombetta *f.*
deregulation [diː,rɛgjʊ'leɪʃ(ə)n] *s.* deregolamentazione *f.*, liberalizzazione *f.*
derelict ['dɛrɪlɪkt] *agg.* derelitto, abbandonato
to deride [dɪ'raɪd] *v. tr.* deridere
derisive [dɪ'raɪsɪv] *agg.* **1** derisorio **2** irrisorio
derivation [,dɛrɪ'veɪʃ(ə)n] *s.* derivazione *f.*
to derive [dɪ'raɪv] *v. tr. e intr.* derivare
dermatitis [,dɜːmə'taɪtɪs] *s.* dermatite *f.*
dermatologist [,dɜːmə'tələdʒɪst] *s.* dermatologo *m.*
derogation [,dɛrə'geɪʃ(ə)n] *s.* **1** deroga *f.* **2** detrimento *m.*
derogatory [dɪ'rəgət(ə)rɪ] *agg.* sprezzante, spregiativo
derv [dɜːv] *s.* gasolio *m.*
desalter [diː'sɜːltəʳ] *s.* dissalatore *m.*
to descend [dɪ'sɛnd] *v. tr. e intr.* scendere, discendere
descendant [dɪ'sɛndənt] *s.* discendente *m. e f.*
descent [dɪ'sɛnt] *s.* **1** discesa *f.* **2** discendenza *f.*, lignaggio *m.*
to describe [dɪs'kraɪb] *v. tr.* descrivere
description [dɪs'krɪpʃ(ə)n] *s.* **1** descrizione *f.* **2** (*fam.*) genere *m.*, sorta *f.*
descriptive [dɪs'krɪptɪv] *agg.* descrittivo
to desecrate ['dɛsɪkreɪt] *v. tr.* **1** sconsacrare **2** profanare
desert ['dɛzət] *agg. e s.* deserto *m.*
to desert [dɪ'zɜːt] **A** *v. tr.* abbandonare **B** *v. intr.* (*mil.*) disertare
deserted [dɪ'zɜːtɪd] *agg.* **1** deserto **2** abbandonato
deserter [dɪ'zɜːtə] *s.* disertore *m.*
desertion [dɪ'zɜːʃ(ə)nʳ] *s.* **1** diserzione *f.*, defezione *f.* **2** (*dir*) abbandono *m.*
deserts [dɪ'zɜːts] *s. pl.* meriti *m. pl.* ♦ **to get one's d.** avere quel che ci si merita
to deserve [dɪ'zɜːv] *v. tr.* meritare
deserving [dɪ'zɜːvɪŋ] *agg.* meritevole
design [dɪ'zaɪn] *s.* **1** disegno *m.*, motivo *m.* **2** piano *m.*, progetto *m.* **3** design *m. inv.*, progettazione *f.* **4** proposito *m.*, intento *m.*, mira *f.*
to design [dɪ'zaɪn] *v. tr.* **1** progettare, ideare **2** disegnare, fare il progetto di
to designate ['dɛzɪgneɪt] *v. tr.* designare, nominare
designer [dɪ'zaɪnəʳ] *s.* designer *m. inv.*, progettista *m. e f.*
desinence ['dɛsɪnəns] *s.* desinenza *f.*
desirable [dɪ'zaɪərəbl] *agg.* desiderabile
desire [dɪ'zaɪəʳ] *s.* desiderio *m.*
to desire [dɪ'zaɪəʳ] *v. tr.* desiderare
to desist [dɪ'zɪst] *v. intr.* desistere
desk [dɛsk] *s.* **1** scrivania *f.* **2** cattedra *f.* **3** banco *m.*, cassa *f.*
desolate ['dɛsəlɪt] *agg.* desolato
desolation [,dɛsə'leɪʃ(ə)n] *s.* desolazione *f.*
despair [dɪs'pɛəʳ] *s.* disperazione *f.*
to despair [dɪs'pɛəʳ] *v. intr.* disperare, disperarsi
desperate ['dɛsp(ə)rɪt] *agg.* disperato
desperation [,dɛspə'reɪʃ(ə)n] *s.* disperazione *f.*
despicable ['dɛspɪkəbl] *agg.* disprezzabile, spregevole
to despise [dɪs'paɪz] *v. tr.* disprezzare
despite [dɪs'paɪt] *prep.* malgrado, a dispetto di
to despond [dɪs'pənd] *v. intr.* abbattersi, perdersi d'animo
despondent [dɪs'pəndənt] *agg.* scoraggiato, abbattuto
despotic [dɛs'pətɪk] *agg.* dispotico
dessert [dɪ'zɜːt] *s.* dessert *m. inv.*
destination [,dɛstɪ'neɪʃ(ə)n] *s.* destinazione *f.*, meta *f.*
to destine ['dɛstɪn] **A** *v. tr.* destinare **B** *v. intr.* avere come destinazione
destiny ['dɛstɪnɪ] *s.* destino *m.*, sorte *f.*
destitute ['dɛstɪtjuːt] *agg.* **1** indigente, bisognoso **2** destituito, privo
to destroy [dɪs'trəɪ] *v. tr.* distruggere
destroyer [dɪs'trəɪəʳ] *s.* (*mil.*) cacciatorpediniere *m.*
destruction [dɪs'trʌkʃ(ə)n] *s.* distruzione *f.*
to detach [dɪ'tætʃ] *v. tr.* **1** staccare, separare **2** (*mil.*) distaccare
detachable [dɪ'tætʃəbl] *agg.* staccabile
detached [dɪ'tætʃt] *agg.* **1** distaccato, disinteressato **2** separato, isolato ♦ **d. house** casa unifamiliare
detachment [dɪ'tætʃmənt] *s.* **1** distacco *m.* **2** (*mil.*) distaccamento *m.*
detail ['diːteɪl] *s.* dettaglio *m.*, particolare *m.* ♦ **in d.** dettagliatamente
to detail ['diːteɪl] *v. tr.* esporre dettagliatamente

detailed ['di:teɪld] *agg.* dettagliato, particolareggiato
to detain [dɪ'teɪn] *v. tr.* trattenere, detenere
to detect [dɪ'tɛkt] *v. tr.* **1** scoprire **2** individuare, percepire, discernere **3** (*fis.*) rivelare
detection [dɪ'tɛkʃ(ə)n] *s.* **1** scoperta *f.* **2** investigazione *f.* **3** (*fis.*) rivelazione *f.*
detective [dɪ'tɛktɪv] *s.* investigatore *m.*
detector [dɪ'tɛktəʳ] *s.* **1** scopritore *m.* **2** (*fis.*) rivelatore *m.* ♦ **lie d.** macchina della verità
detention [dɪ'tɛnʃ(ə)n] *s.* detenzione *f.*
to deter [dɪ'tɜːʳ] *v. tr.* dissuadere, trattenere
detergent [dɪ'tɜːdʒ(ə)nt] *agg. e s.* detergente *m.*
to deteriorate [dɪ'tɪərɪəreɪt] *v. tr. e intr.* deteriorare, deteriorarsi
to determine [dɪ'tɜːmɪn] *v. tr.* **1** determinare, definire **2** decidere, risolvere **3** (*dir.*) porre termine
determined [dɪ'tɜːmɪnd] *agg.* **1** fissato, stabilito **2** risoluto, determinato
detersive [dɪ'tɜːsɪv] *s.* detersivo *m.*
to detest [dɪ'tɛst] *v. tr.* detestare
detestable [dɪ'tɛstəbl] *agg.* detestabile, odioso
detour ['diːtʊəʳ] *s.* deviazione *f.*
detoxication [diːˌtəksɪ'keɪʃ(ə)n] *s.* disintossicazione *f.*
to detract [dɪ'trækt] **A** *v. tr.* detrarre **B** *v. intr.* diminuire
detraction [dɪ'trækʃ(ə)n] *s.* **1** detrazione *f.* **2** diffamazione *f.*
devaluation [ˌdiːvæljʊ'eɪʃ(ə)n] *s.* svalutazione *f.*
to devalue [diː'væljuː] *v. tr.* svalutare
to devastate ['dɛvəsteɪt] *v. tr.* devastare, rovinare
devastating ['dɛvəsteɪtɪŋ] *agg.* **1** devastante, rovinoso **2** sconvolgente
to develop [dɪ'vɛləp] **A** *v. intr.* svilupparsi, evolversi, trasformarsi **B** *v. tr.* **1** sviluppare **2** potenziare, valorizzare **3** generare ♦ **developing countries** paesi in via di sviluppo
developer [dɪ'vɛləpəʳ] *s.* **1** (*fot.*) sviluppatore *m.* **2** costruttore *m.* edile, società *f.* immobiliare
development [dɪ'vɛləpmənt] *s.* **1** sviluppo *m.* **2** valorizzazione *f.*
to deviate ['diːvɪeɪt] *v. intr.* deviare
deviation [ˌdiːvɪ'eɪʃ(ə)n] *s.* deviazione *f.*
device [dɪ'vaɪs] *s.* **1** congegno *m.*, dispositivo *m.* **2** espediente *m.*, stratagemma *m.*
devil ['dɛvl] *s.* diavolo *m.*
devilish ['dɛvlɪʃ] *agg.* diabolico, infernale
devious ['diːvjəs] *agg.* **1** tortuoso **2** ambiguo, subdolo
to devise [dɪ'vaɪz] *v. tr.* **1** escogitare **2** (*dir.*) lasciare per testamento
devoid [dɪ'vɔɪd] *agg.* destituito, privo
to devote [dɪ'vɒʊt] *v. tr.* dedicare, consacrare
devotion [dɪ'vɒʊʃ(ə)n] *s.* devozione *f.*, dedizione *f.*
to devour [dɪ'vaʊəʳ] *v. tr.* divorare
devout [dɪ'vaʊt] *agg.* **1** devoto **2** fervente, leale
dew [djuː] *s.* rugiada *f.*
dexterity [dɛks'tɛrɪtɪ] *s.* destrezza *f.*
dexterous ['dɛkst(ə)rəs] *agg.* destro, abile
diabetes [ˌdaɪə'biːtiːz] *s.* diabete *m.*
diabetic [ˌdaɪə'bɛtɪk] *agg. e s.* diabetico *m.*
diabolical [ˌdaɪə'bəlɪk(ə)l] *agg.* diabolico
diadem ['daɪədɛm] *s.* diadema *m.*
to diagnose ['daɪəgnɒʊz] *v. tr.* diagnosticare
diagnosis [ˌdaɪəg'nɒʊsɪs] *s.* diagnosi *f.*
diagonal [daɪ'ægənl] *agg. e s.* diagonale *f.*
diagram ['daɪəgræm] *s.* diagramma *m.*, schema *m.*
dial ['daɪ(ə)l] *s.* **1** (*di strumento, orologio*) quadrante *m.* **2** (*di telefono*) disco *m.* combinatore
to dial ['daɪ(ə)l] *v. tr.* **1** comporre (*un numero telefonico*), chiamare al telefono **2** sintonizzarsi su (*una stazione*)
dialect ['daɪəlɛkt] *s.* dialetto *m.*
dialectal [ˌdaɪə'lɛktl] *agg.* dialettale
dialectic [ˌdaɪə'lɛktɪk] **A** *agg.* dialettico **B** *s.* dialettica *f.*
dialling ['daɪ(ə)lɪŋ] *s.* selezione *f.* (telefonica) ♦ **d. code** (*USA* **dial code**) prefisso telefonico; **d. tone** (*USA* **dial tone**) segnale di linea libera; **direct d.** teleselezione
dialogue ['daɪələg] (*USA* **dialog**) *s.* dialogo *m.*
dialysis [daɪ'ælɪsɪs] *s.* dialisi *f.*
diameter [daɪ'æmɪtəʳ] *s.* diametro *m.*
diamond ['daɪəmənd] *s.* **1** diamante *m.* **2** rombo *m.* **3** *al pl.* (*carte da gioco*) quadri *m. pl.*
diaper ['daɪəpəʳ] *s.* (*USA*) pannolino *m.*
diarrh(o)ea [ˌdaɪə'rɪə] *s.* diarrea *f.*
diary ['daɪərɪ] *s.* **1** diario *m.* **2** agenda *f.*
dice [daɪs] *s. inv.* dado *m.*, gioco *m.* dei dadi

to dice [daɪs] **A** *v. tr.* tagliare a cubetti **B** *v. intr.* giocare a dadi ♦ **to d. away** perdere ai dadi
to dictate [dɪk'teɪt] *v. tr.* dettare
dictation [dɪk'teɪʃ(ə)n] *s.* dettato *m.*
dictator [dɪk'teɪtəʳ] *s.* dittatore *m.*
dictatorship [dɪk'teɪtəʃɪp] *s.* dittatura *f.*
diction ['dɪkʃ(ə)n] *s.* dizione *f.*
dictionary ['dɪkʃ(ə)nrɪ] *s.* dizionario *m.*, vocabolario *m.*
did [dɪd] *pass. di* **to do**
didactic [dɪ'dæktɪk] *agg.* didattico
didactics [dɪ'dæktɪks] *s. pl.* (*v. al sing.*) didattica *f.*
die [daɪ] *s.* **1** dado *m.* **2** stampo *m.*
to die [daɪ] *v. intr.* morire ♦ **to d. away** smorzarsi; **to d. down** affievolirsi, appassire; **to d. out** estinguersi; **to be dying to do st.** morire dalla voglia di fare q.c.
diesel ['di:z(ə)l] *s.* diesel *m. inv.* ♦ **d. engine** motore diesel; **d. oil** gasolio
diet ['daɪət] *s.* dieta *f.*, alimentazione *f.* ♦ **to be on d.** essere a dieta
to diet ['daɪət] *v. intr.* essere a dieta
dietetic [ˌdaɪə'tɛtɪk] *agg.* dietetico
dietician [ˌdaɪə'tɪʃ(ə)n] *s.* dietologo *m.*
to differ ['dɪfəʳ] *v. intr.* **1** differire, essere diverso **2** dissentire
difference ['dɪfr(ə)ns] *s.* **1** differenza *f.* **2** divergenza *f.*, dissapore *m.*
different ['dɪfr(ə)nt] *agg.* differente, diverso
differential [ˌdɪfə'rɛnʃ(ə)l] *agg. e s.* differenziale *m.*
to differentiate [ˌdɪfə'rɛnʃɪeɪt] *v. tr.* **1** differenziare **2** distinguere
difficult ['dɪfɪk(ə)lt] *agg.* difficile
difficulty ['dɪfɪk(ə)ltɪ] *s.* difficoltà *f.*
diffident ['dɪfɪd(ə)nt] *agg.* timido, sfiduciato
diffuse [dɪ'fju:s] *agg.* **1** diffuso **2** prolisso
to diffuse [dɪ'fju:z] *v. tr.* diffondere
diffused [dɪ'fju:zd] *agg.* diffuso
diffusion [dɪ'fju:ʒ(ə)n] *s.* **1** (*fis.*) diffusione *f.* **2** prolissità *f.*
dig [dɪg] *s.* **1** scavo *m.*, sterro *m.* **2** (*pop.*) spintone *m.* **3** (*fig.*) frecciata *f.* **4** *al pl.* (*fam.*) camera *f.* ammobiliata
to dig [dɪg] (*pass. e p. p.* **dug**) **A** *v. tr.* **1** scavare **2** (*pop.*) dare uno spintone **B** *v. intr.* **1** scavare, zappare **2** (*fam.*) sgobbare ♦ **to d. in** affondare; **to d. out** scovare, scoprire
digest ['daɪdʒɛst] *s.* riassunto *m.*
to digest [daɪ'dʒɛst] *v. tr.* **1** digerire, assimilare **2** riassumere
digester [dɪ'dʒɛstəʳ] *s.* digestivo *m.*
digestible [dɪ'dʒɛstəbl] *agg.* digeribile
digestion [dɪ'dʒɛstʃ(ə)n] *s.* digestione *f.*
digestive [dɪ'dʒɛstɪv] **A** *agg.* **1** digestivo **2** digerente **B** *s.* digestivo *m.*
digger ['dɪgəʳ] *s.* **1** scavatrice *f.* **2** zappatore *m.*, sterratore *m.* ♦ **gold d.** cercatore d'oro
digit ['dɪdʒɪt] *s.* **1** numero *m.*, cifra *f.* **2** dito *m.*
digital ['dɪdʒɪtl] *agg.* digitale
dignified ['dɪgnɪfaɪd] *agg.* dignitoso
dignitary ['dɪgnɪt(ə)rɪ] *s.* dignitario *m.*
dignity ['dɪgnɪtɪ] *s.* dignità *f.*, decoro *m.*
to digress [daɪ'grɛs] *v. intr.* fare una digressione, divagare ♦ **to d. from** allontanarsi da
digression [daɪ'grɛʃ(ə)n] *s.* digressione *f.*
dike [daɪk] (o **dyke**) *s.* argine *m.*, diga *f.*
dilapidated [dɪ'læpɪdeɪtɪd] *agg.* decrepito, cadente
dilatation [ˌdaɪlə'teɪʃ(ə)n] *s.* dilatazione *f.*
to dilate [daɪ'leɪt] *v. tr. e intr.* dilatare, dilatarsi
dilemma [dɪ'lɛmə] *s.* dilemma *m.*
dilettante [ˌdɪlɪ'tæntɪ] *s.* dilettante *m. e f.*
diligence ['dɪlɪdʒ(ə)ns] *s.* diligenza *f.*
diligent ['dɪlɪdʒ(ə)nt] *agg.* diligente
to dilute [daɪ'lju:t] *v. tr.* **1** diluire **2** (*fig.*) attenuare
dim [dɪm] *agg.* **1** debole, fioco **2** incerto, indistinto **3** (*fam.*) ottuso
to dim [dɪm] *v. tr.* offuscare, oscurare
dimension [dɪ'mɛnʃ(ə)n] *s.* dimensione *f.*
to diminish [dɪ'mɪnɪʃ] *v. tr. e intr.* diminuire
diminutive [dɪ'mɪnjʊtɪv] **A** *agg.* (*fam.*) minuscolo **B** *s.* diminutivo *m.*
dimmer ['dɪməʳ] *s.* (*autom.*) commutatore *m.* delle luci
din [dɪn] *s.* fracasso *m.*
to din [dɪn] *v. tr.* assordare
to dine [daɪn] *v. intr.* cenare, pranzare ♦ **to d. in/out** cenare a casa/fuori
diner ['daɪnəʳ] *s.* **1** commensale *m.*, (*di ristorante*) cliente *m. e f.* **2** (*USA*) tavola *f.* calda
dinghy ['dɪŋgɪ] *s.* (*naut.*) canotto *m.*
dingy ['dɪn(d)ʒɪ] *agg.* **1** nerastro, grigio **2** sporco, squallido
dining-car ['daɪnɪŋka:ʳ] *s.* carrozza *f.* ristorante
dining-room ['daɪnɪŋrʊm] *s.* sala *f.* da pranzo

dinner ['dɪnəʳ] *s.* cena *f.*, pasto *m.* (*principale*) ♦ **d. jacket** smoking; **d. set** servizio da tavola; **to ask sb. to d.** invitare qc. a cena; **to be at d.** essere a tavola; **to have d.** cenare
dinosaur ['daɪnəsɜːʳ] *s.* dinosauro *m.*
dint [dɪnt] *s.* **1** tacca *f.*, segno *m.* **2** (*arc.*) forza *f.* ♦ **by d. of** a forza di
diocese ['daɪəsɪs] *s.* diocesi *f.*
dioptre [daɪ'ɔptəʳ] (*USA* **diopter**) *s.* diottria *f.*
dip [dɪp] *s.* **1** immersione *f.*, tuffo *m.* **2** inclinazione *f.*, avvallamento *m.* **3** flessione *f.* **4** (*cuc.*) salsa *f.*
to **dip** [dɪp] **A** *v. tr.* **1** immergere, tuffare **2** abbassare **B** *v. intr.* **1** immergersi, bagnarsi **2** abbassarsi **3** scendere ♦ **to d. into** attingere
diploma [dɪ'plɒʊmə] *s.* diploma *m.*
diplomacy [dɪ'plɒʊməsɪ] *s.* diplomazia *f.*
diplomat ['dɪpləmæt] *s.* diplomatico *m.*
diplomatic [ˌdɪplə'mætɪk] *agg.* diplomatico
dipper ['dɪpəʳ] *s.* mestolo *m.*
dipstick ['dɪpstɪk] *s.* asta *f.* di livello
dipswitch ['dɪpswɪtʒ] *s.* (*autom.*) commutatore *m.* delle luci
dire [daɪəʳ] *agg.* atroce, terribile
direct [dɪ'rɛkt] **A** *agg.* **1** diretto, immediato **2** franco, esplicito **B** *avv.* direttamente
to **direct** [dɪ'rɛkt] *v. tr.* **1** indirizzare, inviare **2** rivolgere **3** indicare (*la strada*) **4** dirigere, ordinare
direction [dɪ'rɛkʃ(ə)n] *s.* **1** direzione *f.*, senso *m.* **2** istruzione *f.*, indicazione *f.* **3** regia *f.*, direzione *f.*
directional [dɪ'rɛkʃənl] *agg.* direzionale
directly [dɪ'rɛktlɪ] *avv.* **1** direttamente **2** immediatamente
director [dɪ'rɛktəʳ] *s.* **1** direttore *m.*, dirigente *m. e f.* **2** amministratore *m.* **3** regista *m. e f.* ♦ **board of directors** consiglio di amministrazione
directory [dɪ'rɛkt(ə)rɪ] *s.* elenco *m.* ♦ **telephone d.** elenco telefonico
dirt [dɜːt] *s.* **1** sporcizia *f.*, immondizia *f.* **2** terra *f.* ♦ **d.-cheap** da due soldi; **d. road** strada sterrata
dirty ['dɜːtɪ] *agg.* **1** sporco, sudicio **2** (*del tempo*) brutto, orribile **3** grossolano, sconcio
to **dirty** ['dɜːtɪ] *v. tr. e intr.* sporcare, sporcarsi
disability [ˌdɪsə'bɪlɪtɪ] *s.* **1** incapacità *f.* **2** invalidità *f.*
disabled [dɪs'eɪbld] *agg. e s.* disabile *m. e f.*, invalido *m.*
disadvantage [ˌdɪsəd'vaːntɪdʒ] *s.* svantaggio *m.*
disadvantegeous [ˌdɪsædvaːn'teɪdʒəs] *agg.* svantaggioso
disaffected [ˌdɪsə'fɛktɪd] *agg.* disaffezionato, maldisposto, ostile
to **disagree** [ˌdɪsə'griː] *v. tr.* **1** dissentire **2** discordare, non coincidere **3** non confarsi
disagreeable [ˌdɪsə'grɪəbl] *agg.* sgradevole, antipatico
disagreement [ˌdɪsə'griːmənt] *s.* **1** disaccordo *m.*, discordia *f.* **2** discordanza *f.*
to **disallow** [ˌdɪsə'laʊ] *v. tr.* respingere, rifiutare
to **disappear** [ˌdɪsə'pɪəʳ] *v. intr.* scomparire, svanire
disappearance [ˌdɪsə'pɪər(ə)ns] *s.* sparizione *f.*, scomparsa *f.*
to **disappoint** [ˌdɪsə'pɔɪnt] *v. tr.* deludere
disappointed [ˌdɪsə'pɔɪntɪd] *agg.* deluso, insoddisfatto
disappointment [ˌdɪsə'pɔɪntmənt] *s.* delusione *f.*, disappunto *m.*
disapproval [ˌdɪsə'pruːv(ə)l] *s.* disapprovazione *f.*
to **disapprove** [ˌdɪsə'pruːv] *v. tr.* disapprovare ♦ **to d. of** trovare da ridire su
to **disarm** [dɪs'aːm] *v. tr.* disarmare
disarmament [dɪs'aːməmənt] *s.* disarmo *m.*
disarray [ˌdɪsə'reɪ] *s.* disordine *m.*, scompiglio *m.*
to **disassemble** [ˌdɪsə'sɛmbl] *v. tr.* smontare
disassembly [ˌdɪsə'sɛmblɪ] *s.* smontaggio *m.*
disaster [dɪ'zaːstəʳ] *s.* disastro *m.*, sciagura *f.*
disastrous [dɪ'zaːstrəs] *agg.* disastroso
to **disband** [dɪs'bænd] *v. tr.* disperdere, sciogliere, congedare
disbandment [dɪs'bændmənt] *s.* **1** sbandamento *m.*, dispersione *f.* **2** congedo *m.*
disbelief [ˌdɪsbɪ'liːf] *s.* incredulità *f.*
to **disbelieve** [ˌdɪsbɪ'liːv] *v. tr. e intr.* non credere
disbursement [dɪs'bɜːsmənt] *s.* esborso *m.*, pagamento *m.*
disc [dɪsk] *s.* disco *m.*
discard ['dɪskaːd] *s.* scarto *m.*
to **discard** [dɪs'kaːd] *v. tr.* **1** scartare **2** ab-

bandonare
to discern [dɪ'sɜːn] *v. tr.* discernere, distinguere
discerning [dɪ'sɜːnɪŋ] *agg.* perspicace, oculato
discharge [dɪs'tʃaːdʒ] *s.* **1** scarico *m.* **2** (*elettr., arma da fuoco*) scarica *f.* **3** congedo *m.*, licenziamento *m.* **4** (*dir*) assoluzione *f.*, liberazione *f.* **5** (*med.*) emissione *f.*, suppurazione *f.* **6** (*di debito*) pagamento *m.* **7** adempimento *m.*
to discharge [dɪs'tʃaːdʒ] *v. tr.* **1** scaricare **2** congedare, licenziare **3** emettere **4** (*dir*) liberare, assolvere **5** (*un debito*) saldare **6** (*un dovere*) compiere
disciple [dɪ'saɪpl] *s.* discepolo *m.*
discipline ['dɪsɪplɪn] *s.* disciplina *f.*
to discipline ['dɪsɪplɪn] *v. tr.* **1** disciplinare **2** punire
to disclaim [dɪs'kleɪm] *v. tr.* **1** (*dir*) rinunciare **2** disconoscere, rinnegare **3** negare
to disclose [dɪs'klɒʊz] *v. tr.* **1** scoprire, svelare **2** rivelare
disclosure [dɪs'klɒʊʒəʳ] *s.* rivelazione *f.*, scoperta *f.*
disco ['dɪskɒʊ] *s.* discoteca *f.*
to discolour [dɪs'kʌləʳ] (*USA* **to discolor**) *v. tr. e intr.* scolorire, scolorirsi
discomfort [dɪs'kʌmfət] *s.* **1** disagio *m.* **2** scomodità *f.*
to discomfort [dɪs'kʌmfət] *v. tr.* mettere a disagio
to disconcert [ˌdɪskən'sɜːt] *v. tr.* **1** sconcertare, turbare **2** sconvolgere
to disconnect [ˌdɪskə'nɛkt] *v. tr.* **1** sconnettere, staccare **2** interrompere un collegamento
disconnected [ˌdɪskə'nɛktɪd] *agg.* **1** sconnesso **2** disinserito, scollegato
disconsolate [dɪs'kɒns(ə)lɪt] *agg.* sconsolato, sconfortato
discontent [ˌdɪskən'tɛnt] *s.* scontentezza *f.*, scontento *m.*
to discontinue [ˌdɪskən'tɪnjuː] *v. tr. e intr.* cessare, interrompere, interrompersi
discontinuous [ˌdɪskən'tɪnjʊəs] *agg.* discontinuo, intermittente
discord ['dɪskɜːd] *s.* **1** discordia *f.*, contrasto *m.* **2** (*mus.*) dissonanza *f.*
discordant [dɪs'kɜːd(ə)nt] *agg.* discordante
discotheque ['dɪskətɛk] *s.* discoteca *f.*
discount ['dɪskaʊnt] *s.* sconto *m.*, ribasso *m.*, riduzione *f.*
to discount ['dɪskaʊnt] *v. tr.* **1** scontare **2** tenere in poco conto, non dar credito a
discountable [dɪs'kaʊntəbl] *agg.* scontabile
to discourage [dɪs'kʌrɪdʒ] *v. tr.* **1** scoraggiare **2** dissuadere
discouragement [dɪs'kʌrɪdʒmənt] *s.* **1** scoraggiamento *m.*, sconforto *m.* **2** disapprovazione *f.*
discourteous [dɪs'kɜːtjəs] *agg.* scortese
to discover [dɪs'kʌvəʳ] *v. tr.* scoprire
discoverer [dɪs'kʌvərəʳ] *s.* scopritore *m.*
discovery [dɪs'kʌv(ə)rɪ] *s.* scoperta *f.*
discredit [dɪs'krɛdɪt] *s.* **1** discredito *m.* **2** dubbio *m.*
to discredit [dɪs'krɛdɪt] *v. tr.* **1** discreditare **2** mettere in dubbio
discreet [dɪs'kriːt] *agg.* discreto, riservato
discrepancy [dɪs'krɛp(ə)nsɪ] *s.* discrepanza *f.*, divario *m.*
discretion [dɪs'krɛʃ(ə)n] *s.* **1** discrezione *f.*, discernimento *m.* **2** riservatezza *f.*
to discriminate [dɪs'krɪmɪneɪt] **A** *v. tr.* discriminare, distinguere **B** *v. intr.* fare discriminazioni
discriminating [dɪs'krɪmɪneɪtɪŋ] *agg.* **1** acuto, perspicace **2** distintivo
discrimination [dɪsˌkrɪmɪ'neɪʃ(ə)n] *s.* **1** discernimento *m.* **2** discriminazione *f.*
discus ['dɪskəs] *s.* (*sport*) disco *m.*
to discuss [dɪs'kʌs] *v. tr.* discutere
discussion [dɪs'kʌʃ(ə)n] *s.* discussione *f.*
disdain [dɪs'deɪn] *s.* sdegno *m.*, disprezzo *m.*
disease [dɪ'ziːz] *s.* malattia *f.*
diseased [dɪ'ziːzd] *agg.* malato
to disembark [ˌdɪsɪm'baːk] *v. tr. e intr.* sbarcare
to disengage [ˌdɪsɪn'geɪdʒ] *v. tr.* **1** districare, liberare **2** (*mecc.*) disinnestare
to disentangle [ˌdɪsɪn'tæŋgl] *v. tr.* sbrogliare, districare
to disfigure [dɪs'fɪgəʳ] *v. tr.* sfigurare, deturpare
disgrace [dɪs'greɪs] *s.* **1** disonore *m.*, vergogna *f.* **2** disgrazia *f.* sfavore *m.*
to disgrace [dɪs'greɪs] *v. tr.* **1** disonorare **2** discreditare, far cadere in disgrazia
disgraceful [dɪs'greɪsf(ʊ)l] *agg.* disonorevole, vergognoso
disgruntled [dɪs'grʌntld] *agg.* scontento, di cattivo umore
disguise [dɪs'gaɪz] *s.* travestimento *m.*
to disguise [dɪs'gaɪz] *v. tr.* **1** mascherare,

travestire **2** dissimulare
disgust [dɪs'gʌst] *s.* disgusto *m.*, schifo *m.*, nausea *f.*
to disgust [dɪs'gʌst] *v. tr.* disgustare, nauseare
disgusting [dɪs'gʌstɪŋ] *agg.* disgustoso, nauseante
dish [dɪʃ] *s.* **1** piatto *m.* **2** pietanza *f.*
to dish [dɪʃ] *v. tr.* scodellare, servire ♦ **to d. up** servire, presentare
dishcloth ['dɪʃkləθ] *s.* strofinaccio *m.*
to dishearten [dɪs'hɑːtn] *v. tr.* scoraggiare, sconfortare
disheartening [dɪs'hɑːtnɪŋ] *agg.* sconsolante
to dishevel [dɪ'ʃɛv(ə)l] *v. tr.* scompigliare
dishevelled [dɪ'ʃɛv(ə)ld] *agg.* arruffato, scarmigliato
dishonest [dɪs'ənɪst] *agg.* disonesto
dishonour [dɪs'ənə^r] (*USA* **dishonor**) *s.* disonore *m.*
to dishonour [dɪs'ənə^r] (*USA* **to dishonor**) *v. tr.* **1** disonorare **2** venir meno a **3** (*comm.*) rifiutare di pagare, far andare in protesto
dishtowel ['ɪʃtaʊəl] *s.* strofinaccio *m.*
dishwasher ['dɪʃˌwəʃə^r] *s.* lavastoviglie *f.*
disillusion [ˌdɪsɪ'luːʒ(ə)n] *s.* disillusione *f.*
to disillusion [ˌdɪsɪ'luːʒ(ə)n] *v. tr.* disilludere, disingannare
disincentive [ˌdɪsɪn'sɛntɪv] *s.* disincentivo *m.*
to disinfect [ˌdɪsɪn'fɛkt] *v. tr.* disinfettare
disinfectant [ˌdɪsɪn'fɛktənt] *agg. e s.* disinfettante *m.*
to disinfest [ˌdɪsɪn'fɛst] *v. tr.* disinfestare
disinhibited [ˌdɪsɪn'hɪbɪtɪd] *agg.* disinibito
to disintegrate [dɪs'ɪntɪgreɪt] *v. tr. e intr.* disintegrare, disintegrarsi
disinterested [dɪs'ɪntrɪstɪd] *agg.* **1** disinteressato **2** imparziale
to disjoint [dɪs'dʒəɪnt] *v. tr.* disgiungere, smembrare
disjointed [dɪs'dʒəɪntɪd] *agg.* **1** disgiunto, smembrato **2** sconnesso
disk [dɪsk] *s.* disco *m.*
diskette [dɪs'kɛt] *s.* dischetto *m.*, disco *m.*
dislike [dɪs'laɪk] *s.* avversione *f.*, antipatia *f.*
to dislike [dɪs'laɪk] *v. tr.* **1** non piacere **2** provare avversione per
to dislocate ['dɪsləkeɪt] *v. tr.* slogare, lussare
dislocation [ˌdɪslə'keɪʃ(ə)n] *s.* slogatura *f.*, lussazione *f.*
to dislodge [dɪs'lədʒ] *v. tr.* **1** sloggiare **2** rimuovere
disloyal [dɪs'ləɪəl] *agg.* sleale
dismal ['dɪzm(ə)l] *agg.* lugubre, tetro
to dismantle [dɪs'mæntl] *v. tr.* smontare, smantellare
dismay [dɪs'meɪ] *s.* sgomento *m.*
to dismay [dɪs'meɪ] *v. tr.* sgomentare, costernare
to dismiss [dɪs'mɪs] *v. tr.* **1** congedare, licenziare, destituire **2** abbandonare, scartare **3** (*dir*) respingere
to dismount [dɪs'maʊnt] *v. intr.* smontare, scendere
disobedient [ˌdɪsə'biːdjənt] *agg.* disobbediente
to disobey [ˌdɪsə'beɪ] *v. intr.* disubbidire
disorder [dɪs'ɜːdə^r] *s.* **1** disordine *m.*, confusione *f.* **2** tumulto *m.* **3** (*med.*) disturbo *m.*
disorderly [dɪs'ɜːdəlɪ] *agg.* **1** disordinato **2** tumultuoso
disorganization [dɪsˌɜːgənaɪ'zeɪʃ(ə)n] *s.* disorganizzazione *f.*
disorientation [dɪsˌərɪən'teɪʃ(ə)n] *s.* disorientamento *m.*
disparaging [dɪs'pærɪdʒɪŋ] *agg.* spregiativo, sprezzante
disparate ['dɪspərət] *agg.* disparato
dispassionate [dɪs'pæʃnɪt] *agg.* spassionato, imparziale
dispatch [dɪs'pætʃ] *s.* **1** invio *m.*, spedizione *f.* **2** messaggio *m.*
to dispatch [dɪs'pætʃ] *v. tr.* **1** spedire, inviare **2** espletare, sbrigare
to dispel [dɪs'pɛl] *v. tr.* disperdere, scacciare
to dispense [dɪs'pɛns] *v. tr.* **1** dispensare, distribuire **2** esentare **3** amministrare **4** somministrare ♦ **to d. with** fare a meno di
dispenser [dɪs'pɛnsə^r] *s.* distributore *m.*
to disperse [dɪs'pɜːs] *v. tr. e intr.* disperdere, disperdersi
dispersion [dɪs'pɜːʃ(ə)n] *s.* dispersione *f.*
to dispirit [dɪ'spɪrɪt] *v. tr.*, scoraggiare
dispirited [dɪ'spɪrɪtɪd] *agg.* scoraggiato, abbattuto
to displace [dɪs'pleɪs] *v. tr.* **1** spostare **2** sostituire, rimpiazzare **3** (*naut.*) dislocare
displacement [dɪs'pleɪsmənt] *s.* (*naut.*) dislocamento *m.*

display [dɪ'spleɪ] *s.* **1** mostra *f.*, esibizione *f.* **2** manifestazione *f.* **3** schermo *m.*, display *m. inv.*
to display [dɪ'spleɪ] *v. tr.* **1** esporre, mostrare **2** manifestare
to displease [dɪs'pliːz] *v. tr.* scontentare, dispiacere a ♦ **to be displeased with** essere scontento di
displeasure [dɪs'plɛʒəʳ] *s.* dispiacere *m.*, malcontento *m.*
disposable [dɪs'pɒʊzəbl] *agg.* **1** disponibile **2** monouso, usa e getta
disposal [dɪs'pɒʊz(ə)l] *s.* **1** disposizione *f.* **2** eliminazione *f.*, smaltimento *m.* **3** (*comm.*) cessione *f.*
to dispose [dɪs'pɒʊz] *v. tr. e intr.* disporre ♦ **to d. of** disfarsi di, risolvere
disposed [dɪs'pɒʊzd] *agg.* disposto, incline ♦ **to be d. to** essere portato a
disposition [ˌdɪspə'zɪʃ(ə)n] *s.* **1** disposizione *f.* **2** inclinazione *f.*, attitudine *f.* **3** prescrizione *f.*
disproportion [ˌdɪsprə'pɜːʃ(ə)n] *s.* sproporzione *f.*
disproportionate [ˌdɪsprə'pɜːʃnɪt] *agg.* sproporzionato
to disprove [dɪs'pruːv] *v. tr.* confutare
dispute [dɪs'pjuːt] *s.* disputa *f.*, vertenza *f.*, controversia *f.*
to dispute [dɪs'pjuːt] *v. intr.* disputare, discutere
disqualification [dɪsˌkwəlɪfɪ'keɪʃ(ə)n] *s.* squalifica *f.*
to disqualify [dɪs'kwəlɪfaɪ] *v. tr.* **1** squalificare, escludere **2** interdire
disquiet [dɪs'kwaɪət] **A** *agg.* inquieto **B** *s.* inquietudine *f.*, ansia *f.*
to disregard [ˌdɪsrɪ'gaːd] *v. tr.* trascurare, non badare a
disrepair [ˌdɪsrɪ'pɛəʳ] *s.* sfacelo *m.*, rovina *f.*
disreputable [dɪs'rɛpjʊtəbl] *agg.* sconveniente, disonorevole
disrepute [ˌdɪsrɪ'pjuːt] *s.* discredito *m.*
disrespect [ˌdɪsrɪs'pɛkt] *s.* irriverenza *f.*
disrespectful [ˌdɪsrɪs'pɛktf(ʊ)l] *agg.* irriverente
to disrupt [dɪsr'ʌpt] **1** disgregare **2** disturbare
dissatisfaction [dɪ(s)ˌsætɪs'fækʃ(ə)n] *s.* insoddisfazione *f.*, scontentezza *f.*
to dissatisfy [dɪ(s)'sætɪsfaɪ] *v. tr.* scontentare
to dissect [dɪ'sɛkt] *v. tr.* **1** sezionare, dissezionare **2** sviscerare
to disseminate [dɪ'sɛmɪneɪt] *v. tr.* disseminare
dissent [dɪ'sɛnt] *s.* dissenso *m.*
to dissent [dɪ'sɛnt] *v. intr.* dissentire
dissertation [ˌdɪsə(ː)'teɪʃ(ə)n] *s.* dissertazione *f.*
disservice [dɪs'sɜːvɪs] *s.* cattivo servizio *m.*, danno *m.*
dissident ['dɪsɪd(ə)nt] *agg.* dissidente
dissimilar [dɪ'sɪmɪləʳ] *agg.* dissimile
dissimilarity [ˌdɪsɪmɪ'lærɪtɪ] *s.* difformità *f.*, diversità *f.*
to dissimulate [dɪ'sɪmjʊleɪt] *v. tr.* dissimulare
to dissipate ['dɪsɪpeɪt] *v. tr.* dissipare, disperdere
to dissociate [dɪ'sɒʊʃɪeɪt] *v. tr. e intr.* dissociare, dissociarsi
dissolute ['dɪsəluːt] *agg.* dissoluto
dissolution [ˌdɪsə'luːʃ(ə)n] *s.* dissoluzione *f.*, scioglimento *m.*
to dissolve [dɪ'zəlv] **A** *v. tr.* **1** dissolvere, sciogliere **2** annullare **B** *v. intr.* **1** dissolversi, sciogliersi **2** disperdersi **3** svanire
dissonant ['dɪsənənt] *agg.* dissonante
to dissuade [dɪ'sweɪd] *v. tr.* dissuadere, distogliere
distance ['dɪst(ə)ns] *s.* distanza *f.*
distant ['dɪst(ə)nt] *agg.* **1** distante, lontano **2** riservato
distaste [dɪs'teɪst] *s.* avversione *f.*, disgusto *m.*
distasteful [dɪs'teɪstf(ʊ)l] *agg.* repellente, sgradevole
distension [dɪs'tɛnʃ(ə)n] *s.* (*med.*) dilatazione *f.*, gonfiore *m.*
to distil(l) [dɪs'tɪl] *v. tr.* distillare
distillate ['dɪstɪlɪt] *s.* distillato *m.*
distillery [dɪs'tɪlərɪ] *s.* distilleria *f.*
distinct [dɪs'tɪŋ(k)t] *agg.* **1** distinto, definito **2** separato, diverso
distinction [dɪs'tɪŋ(k)ʃ(ə)n] *s.* **1** distinzione *f.* **2** caratteristica *f.* **3** onorificenza *f.*
distinctive [dɪs'tɪŋ(k)tɪv] *agg.* distintivo
to distinguish [dɪs'tɪŋgwɪʃ] *v. tr.* **1** distinguere, discernere **2** caratterizzare
distinguished [dɪs'tɪŋgwɪʃt] *agg.* **1** distinto, raffinato **2** famoso, illustre
distinguishing [dɪ'stɪŋgwɪʃɪŋ] *agg.* distinto, peculiare
to distort [dɪs'tɜːt] *v. tr.* **1** distorcere **2** travisare
distortion [dɪs'tɜːʃ(ə)n] *s.* **1** distorsione *f.*

2 deformazione *f.*
to distract [dɪs'trækt] *v. tr.* distrarre
distraction [dɪs'trækʃ(ə)n] *s.* **1** distrazione *f.* **2** diversivo *m.*
to distrain [dɪs'treɪn] *v. tr.* pignorare
distraught [dɪs'trɜːt] *agg.* sconvolto, turbato
distress [dɪs'trɛs] *s.* **1** pena *f.*, angoscia *f.* **2** pericolo *m.* ♦ **d. signal** segnale di soccorso
to distress [dɪs'trɛs] *v. tr.* affliggere, angustiare
distressing [dɪ'strɛsɪŋ] *agg.* doloroso, penoso
to distribute [dɪs'trɪbjʊ(ː)t] *v. tr.* distribuire, assegnare
distribution [ˌdɪstrɪ'bjuːʃ(ə)n] *s.* distribuzione *f.*
distributor [dɪs'trɪbjʊtəʳ] *s.* **1** distributore *m.* **2** spinterogeno *m.*
district ['dɪstrɪkt] *s.* **1** distretto *m.*, circondario *m.* **2** regione *f.*, territorio *m.*
distrust [dɪs'trʌst] *s.* diffidenza *f.*, sospetto *m.*
to distrust [dɪs'trʌst] *v. tr.* diffidare di, non avere fiducia in
to disturb [dɪs'tɜːb] *v. tr.* disturbare
disturbance [dɪs'tɜːb(ə)ns] *s.* **1** disordine *m.*, confusione *f.* **2** disturbo *m.* **3** perturbazione *f.*
disturbed [dɪs'tɜːbd] *agg.* disturbato, turbato
disuse [dɪs'juːs] *s.* disuso *m.*
ditch [dɪtʃ] *s.* fossato *m.*, canale *m.*
to ditch [dɪtʃ] *v. tr.* **1** scavare, prosciugare **2** (*fam.*) piantare in asso
dither ['dɪðəʳ] *v. intr.* **1** tremare **2** oscillare, vacillare
ditto ['dɪtɒʊ] *s.* idem *pron. e avv.*
diuretic [ˌdaɪjʊə'rɛtɪk] *agg. e s.* diuretico *m.*
divan [dɪ'væn] *s.* divano *m.*
dive [daɪv] *s.* **1** tuffo *m.* **2** immersione *f.* **3** (*aer.*) picchiata *f.*
to dive [daɪv] *v. intr.* **1** tuffarsi **2** immergersi **3** (*aer.*) lanciarsi in picchiata ♦ **to d. in** farsi avanti
diver ['daɪvəʳ] *s.* **1** tuffatore *m.* **2** palombaro *m.*, sommozzatore *m.*
to diverge [daɪ'vɜːdʒ] *v. intr.* divergere
diverse [daɪ'vɜːs] *agg.* diverso
diversion [daɪ'vɜːʃ(ə)n] *s.* **1** diversione *f.*, deviazione *f.* **2** passatempo *m.*
diversity [daɪ'vɜːsɪtɪ] *s.* diversità *f.*
to divert [daɪ'vɜːt] *v. tr.* deviare
to divide [dɪ'vaɪd] **A** *v. tr.* **1** dividere, separare **2** ripartire **B** *v. intr.* **1** dividersi, separarsi **2** divergere
dividend ['dɪvɪdɛnd] *s.* dividendo *m.*
divine [dɪ'vaɪn] *agg.* divino
diving ['daɪvɪŋ] *s.* **1** tuffo *m.* **2** immersione *f.* **3** (*aer.*) picchiata *f.* ♦ **d. board** trampolino; **d. suit** scafandro
divinity [dɪ'vɪnɪtɪ] *s.* **1** divinità *f.* **2** teologia *f.*
divisible [dɪ'vɪzəbl] *agg.* divisibile
division [dɪ'vɪʒ(ə)n] *s.* **1** divisione *f.* **2** suddivisione *f.*, ripartizione *f.* **3** sezione *f.*
divorce [dɪ'vɜːs] *s.* divorzio *m.*
to divorce [dɪ'vɜːs] *v. intr.* divorziare
divorcee [dɪˌvɜː'siː] *s.* divorziato *m.*
to divulge [daɪ'vʌldʒ] *v. tr.* divulgare
dizzy ['dɪzɪ] *agg.* **1** vertiginoso **2** che ha le vertigini
do [duː] *s.* **1** ciò che si deve fare **2** (*fam.*) truffa *f.* **3** (*fam.*) festa *f.*
to do [duː, dʊ, də] (*pass.* **did**, *p. p.* **done**) **A** *v. ausiliare* **1** (*nella forma interr.*) (ES: **do you understand?** capisci?) **2** (*nella forma neg.*) (ES: **I don't understand** non capisco) **3** (*enf.*) (ES: **I did see him** l'ho visto davvero) **4** (*in sostituzione di un altro v.*) (ES: **who took my book? I did** chi ha preso il mio libro? io) **B** *v. tr.* **1** fare, compiere, eseguire, portare a termine **2** causare, procurare **3** visitare **4** ingannare, imbrogliare **C** *v. intr.* **1** comportarsi, agire **2** finire, smettere **3** stare, passarsela **4** bastare, andar bene ♦ **to do away with** abolire, sopprimere; **to do by st.** trattare qc., comportarsi con qc.; **to do for** arrangiarsi, fare le faccende, rovinare; **to do out** riordinare; **to do out of** portare via; **to do up** rinnovare, incartare; **to do with** aver bisogno di, avere a che fare con, andar bene
dock (1) [dɔk] *s.* **1** bacino *m.* **2** *al pl.* zona *f.* portuale
dock (2) [dɔk] *s.* banco *m.* degli imputati
to dock [dɔk] *v. intr.* entrare in bacino, attraccare
docking ['dɔkɪŋ] *s.* attracco *m.*
dockyard ['dɔkjaːd] *s.* arsenale *m.*, cantiere *m.* navale
doctor ['dɔktəʳ] *s.* dottore *m.*, medico *m.*
to doctor ['dɔktəʳ] *v. tr.* **1** curare, medicare **2** aggiustare **3** adulterare, falsificare **4** conferire una laurea a

doctrine ['dəktrɪn] *s.* dottrina *f.*
document ['dəkjʊmənt] *s.* documento *m.*
to **document** ['dəkjʊmɛnt] *v. tr.* documentare
documentary [ˌdəkjʊ'mɛnt(ə)rɪ] *s.* documentario *m.*
dodge [dədʒ] *s.* **1** balzo *m.* **2** espediente *m.*, trucco *m.*
to **dodge** [dədʒ] *v. tr.* **1** schivare, scansare **2** abbindolare
dodgem ['dədʒəm] *s.* autoscontro *m.*
doe [dɒʊ] *s.* femmina *f.* di cervo, daino, lepre, coniglio
dog [dəg] *s.* cane *m.* ♦ **d. catcher** accalappiacani; **d. collar** collare; **d. days** canicola; **d.-fancier** allevatore di cani
dogged ['dəgɪd] *agg.* ostinato, tenace
dogma ['dəgmə] *s.* dogma *m.*
dogmatic [dəg'mætɪk] *agg.* dogmatico
doings ['duːɪŋz] *s. pl.* fatti *m. pl.* azioni *f. pl.*
do-it-yourself ['duːɪtjɜːˌsɛlf] *s.* bricolage *m. inv.*, fai-da-te *m. inv.*
doldrums ['dəldrəmz] *s. pl.* **1** zona *f.* delle calme equatoriali **2** (*fig.*) depressione *f.* ♦ **to be in the d.** essere depresso
dole [dɒʊl] *s.* sussidio *m.* di disoccupazione
doleful ['dɒʊlf(ʊ)l] *agg.* triste
doll [dəl] *s.* bambola *f.*
dollar ['dələʳ] *s.* dollaro *m.*
to **doll up** [dəlˌʌp] *v. tr. e intr.* (*fam.*) agghindare, agghindarsi
dolly ['dəlɪ] *s.* **1** bambola *f.* **2** piattaforma *f.*, carrello *m.* ♦ **d. shot** (*cine.*) carrellata
dolphin ['dəlfɪn] *s.* delfino *m.*
doltish ['dɒʊltɪʃ] *agg.* sciocco
domain [də'meɪn] *s.* dominio *m.*
dome [dɒʊm] *s.* cupola *f.*
domestic [də'mɛstɪk] *agg.* **1** domestico, casalingo **2** nazionale
to **domesticate** [də'mɛstɪkeɪt] *v. tr.* addomesticare
domicile ['dəmɪsaɪl] *s.* domicilio *m.*
dominant ['dəmɪnənt] *agg.* dominante
to **dominate** ['dəmɪneɪt] *v. tr. e intr.* dominare
domination [ˌdəmɪ'neɪʃ(ə)n] *s.* dominazione *f.*
dominator ['dəmɪneɪtəʳ] *s.* dominatore *m.*
domineering [ˌdəmɪ'nɪərɪŋ] *agg.* dispotico
dominion [də'mɪnjən] *s.* **1** dominio *m.*, autorità *f.* **2** (*paese*) dominion *m. inv.*
dominoes ['dəmɪnɒʊz] *s. pl.* (gioco del) domino *m.*
to **donate** [dɒ(ʊ)'neɪt] *v. tr.* donare, elargire
donation [dɒ(ʊ)'neɪʃ(ə)n] *s.* donazione *f.*, elargizione *f.*
done [dʌn] **A** *p. p. di* **to do** **B** *agg.* **1** fatto, finito **2** giusto **3** cotto ♦ **well d.** ben cotto
donjon ['dən(d)ʒ(ə)n] *s.* torrione *m.*
donkey ['dəŋkɪ] *s.* asino *m.*
donor ['dɒʊnəʳ] *s.* donatore *m.* ♦ **blood d.** donatore di sangue
to **doodle** ['duːdl] *v. intr.* (*fam.*) scarabocchiare
door [dɜːʳ] *s.* **1** porta *f.* **2** sportello *m.* ♦ **d.-to-d.** porta a porta
doorbell ['dɜːbɛl] *s.* campanello *m.*
doorkeeper ['dɜːˌkiːpəʳ] *s.* portiere *m.*
doormat ['dɜːmæt] *s.* zerbino *m.*
doorway ['dɜːweɪ] *s.* vano *m.* della porta
dope [dɒʊp] *s.* (*fam.*) droga *f.*
to **dope** [dɒʊp] *v. tr.* drogare, somministrare stupefacenti
doping ['dɒʊpɪŋ] *s.* (*sport*) doping *m. inv.*
dopy ['dɒʊpɪ] *agg.* inebetito (*da alcol, stupefacenti*)
Doric ['dərɪk] *agg.* dorico
dormant ['dɜːmənt] *agg.* **1** inattivo **2** in letargo
dormitory ['dɜːmɪtrɪ] *s.* **1** dormitorio *m.* **2** (*USA*) casa *f.* per studenti
dormouse ['dɜːmaʊs] (*pl.* **dormice**) *s.* ghiro *m.*
dosage ['dɒʊsɪdʒ] *s.* dosaggio *m.*, posologia *f.*
dose [dɒʊs] *s.* dose *f.*
to **dose** [dɒʊs] *v. tr.* **1** somministrare **2** mescolare
dosshouse ['dəshaʊs] *s.* dormitorio *m.* pubblico
dot [dət] *s.* punto *m.*
to **dot** [dət] *v. tr.* punteggiare
to **dote** [dɒʊt] *v. intr.* essere rimbambito ♦ **to d. on sb. one** amare qc. alla follia
double ['dʌbl] **A** *agg.* doppio, duplice **B** *avv.* doppio, doppiamente, in due **C** *s.* **1** doppio *m.* **2** controfigura *f.* ♦ **d. bed** letto matrimoniale
to **double** ['dʌbl] **A** *v. tr.* **1** raddoppiare **2** piegare in due **3** (*naut.*) doppiare **B** *v. intr.* raddoppiare ♦ **to d. up with** dividere la stanza con
double-bass [ˌdʌbl'beɪs] *s.* contrabbasso *m.*
double-breasted [ˌdʌbl'brɛstɪd] *agg.* (a) doppio petto

double-cross [ˌdʌbl'krəs] *s.* doppio gioco *m.*
double-decker [ˌdʌbl'dɛkəʳ] *s.* autobus *m. inv.* a due piani
doublet ['dʌblɪt] *s.* doppione *m.*
doubling ['dʌblɪŋ] *s.* raddoppio *m.*
doubly ['dʌblɪ] *avv.* doppiamente
doubt [daʊt] *s.* dubbio *m.*
to doubt [daʊt] **A** *v. tr.* dubitare di **B** *v. intr.* dubitare
doubtful ['daʊtf(ʊ)l] *agg.* **1** incerto, dubbio **2** dubbioso
doubtless ['daʊtlɪs] *avv.* indubbiamente
dough [dɒʊ] *s.* **1** impasto *m.*, pasta *f.* per pane **2** *al pl.* (*fam.*) quattrini *m. pl.*
to douse [daʊs] *v. tr.* **1** immergere in acqua **2** gettare acqua su **3** (*fam.*) spegnere
dove [dʌv] *s.* colomba *f.*, colombo *m.*
dovetail ['dʌvteɪl] *s.* (*tecnol.*) incastro *m.* a coda di rondine
dowdy ['daʊdɪ] *agg.* sciatto, trasandato
down (1) [daʊn] *s.* collina *f.*
down (2) [daʊn] *s.* piuma *f.*, piumino *m.*
down (3) [daʊn] **A** *avv.* giù, in basso, di sotto **B** *agg.* **1** diretto verso il basso, inferiore, discendente **2** abbattuto, depresso **3** fuori uso
down-and-out [ˌdaʊnənd'aʊt] *agg.* **1** squattrinato **2** malandato, malconcio
down-at-heel [ˌdaʊnət'hiːl] *agg.* scalcagnato, scalcinato
downcast ['daʊnkaːst] *agg.* abbattuto, depresso
downfall ['daʊnfɜːl] *s.* **1** caduta *f.*, crollo *m.* **2** (*di pioggia*) rovescio *m.*
to downgrade ['daʊngreɪd] *v. tr.* degradare, retrocedere
downhill [ˌdaʊn'hɪl] **A** *agg. e avv.* in discesa, in pendio **B** *s.* **1** (*sport*) discesa *f.* **2** declino *m.* ♦ **to go d.** andare declinando, peggiorare
downhiller [ˌdaʊn'hɪləʳ] *s.* discesista *m. e f.*
downpour ['daʊnpɜːʳ] *s.* acquazzone *m.*
downright ['daʊnraɪt] **A** *agg.* **1** schietto, sincero **2** assoluto **B** *avv.* assolutamente, del tutto
downstairs [ˌdaʊn'stɛəz] *avv.* giù, disotto, al piano inferiore
downtown [ˌdaʊn'taʊn] *s.* centro *m.* (di città)
downward ['daʊnwəd] *agg. e avv.* verso il basso
downwind [ˌdaʊn'wɪnd] *avv.* sottovento
dowry ['daʊərɪ] *s.* dote *f.*
doze [dɒʊz] *s.* pisolino *m.*
to doze [dɒʊz] *v. intr.* sonnecchiare ♦ **to d. off** appisolarsi
dozen ['dʌzn] *s.* dozzina *f.*
drab [dræb] *agg.* **1** grigiastro **2** scialbo, incolore
draft [draːft] (anche **draught**) *s.* **1** tiro *m.*, trazione *f.* **2** schema *m.*, abbozzo *m.* **3** (*tip.*) bozza *f.* **4** (*USA*, *mil.*) leva *f.* **5** (*naut.*) immersione *f.*, pescaggio *m.* **6** (*comm.*) tratta *f.*
to draft [draːft] *v. tr.* **1** tirare **2** abbozzare **3** (*USA*) arruolare
draftsman ['draːftsmən] (*pl.* **draftsmen**) *s.* disegnatore *m.*
drag [dræg] *s.* **1** draga *f.* **2** rete *f.* a strascico **3** (*fis.*) resistenza *f.* **4** impedimento *m.*, ostacolo *m.* **5** seccatura *f.* ♦ **a man in d.** un uomo travestito da donna
to drag [dræg] *v. tr.* **1** trascinare, tirare **2** pescare a strascico ♦ **to d. on** protrarsi, andare avanti; **to d. out** tirare fuori a forza
dragon ['dræg(ə)n] *s.* drago *m.*
dragonfly ['dræg(ə)nflaɪ] *s.* libellula *f.*
drain [dreɪn] *s.* **1** tubo *m.* di scarico, fogna *f.* **2** (*fig.*) salasso *m.* **3** (*fam.*) goccio *m.*
to drain [dreɪn] *v. tr.* **1** far scolare **2** prosciugare **3** (*fig.*) dissanguare
drainage ['dreɪnɪdʒ] *s.* **1** scolo *m.*, scarico *m.*, fognatura *f.* **2** drenaggio *m.*
drama ['draːmə] *s.* dramma *m.*
dramatic [drə'mætɪk] *agg.* **1** drammatico **2** sensazionale
dramatist ['dræmətɪst] *s.* drammaturgo *m.*
dramatization [ˌdræmətaɪ'zeɪʃ(ə)n] *s.* drammatizzazione *f.*
to dramatize ['dræmətaɪz] *v. tr.* **1** drammatizzare **2** adattare alla rappresentazione
drank [dræŋk] *pass. di* **to drink**
to drape [dreɪp] *v. tr.* drappeggiare
draper ['dreɪpəʳ] *s.* negoziante *m. e f.* di tessuti
drapery ['dreɪpərɪ] *s.* **1** tessuti *m. pl.*, tendaggi *m. pl.* **2** drappeggio *m.* ♦ **d. store** negozio di tessuti
drastic ['dræstɪk] *agg.* energico
draught [draːft] *s.* → **draft** ♦ **d. beer** birra alla spina
draughtboard [draːftbɜːd] *s.* scacchiera *f.*
draughts [draːfts] *s. pl.* (gioco della) dama *f.*
draw [drɜː] *s.* **1** tiro *m.*, strattone *m.* **2** estrazione *f.*, sorteggio *m.* **3** pareggio *m.*
to draw [drɜː] (*pass.* **drew**, *p. p.* **drawn**) **A**

v. tr. **1** tirare, tendere, trascinare **2** attirare **3** estrarre, prelevare, spillare **4** tracciare, disegnare **5** (*naut.*) (*di imbarcazione*) pescare **B** *v. intr.* **1** avanzare **2** (*di camino*) tirare **3** disegnare **4** (*sport*) pareggiare ♦ **to d. away/back** tirarsi indietro; **to d. on** incitare; **to d. up** avvicinarsi, accostare, redigere

drawback ['drɜːbæk] *s.* inconveniente *m.*, svantaggio *m.*

drawbridge ['drɜːbrɪdʒ] *s.* ponte *m.* levatoio

drawer [drɜːʳ] *s.* cassetto *m.*

drawing ['drɜːɪŋ] *s.* disegno *m.* ♦ **d. board** tavolo da disegno; **d. room** salotto

to drawl [drɜːl] *v. intr.* strascicare le parole

drawn [drɜːn] *p. p. di* **to draw**

dread [drɛd] *s.* paura *f.*, timore *m.*

to dread [drɛd] *v. tr.* temere

dreadful ['drɛdf(ʊ)l] *agg.* terribile, spaventoso

dream [driːm] *s.* sogno *m.*

to dream [driːm] (*pass. e p. p.* **dreamt, dreamed**) *v. tr. e intr.* sognare

dreamy ['driːmɪ] *agg.* **1** sognante **2** vago

dreary ['drɪərɪ] *agg.* tetro

dredge [drɛdʒ] *s.* draga *f.*

to dredge [drɛdʒ] *v. tr.* dragare

dress [drɛs] *s.* **1** abito *m.*, vestito *m.* (*da donna*) **2** abbigliamento *m.* ♦ **d. hanger** gruccia

to dress [drɛs] **A** *v. tr.* **1** vestire, abbigliare **2** allestire, preparare, adornare **3** (*cuc.*) condire, guarnire **4** medicare **B** *v. intr.* vestirsi, abbigliarsi

dresser ['drɛsəʳ] *s.* **1** credenza *f.* **2** (*USA*) cassettone *m.* **3** (*teatro, cine.*) costumista *m. e f.*

dressing ['drɛsɪŋ] *s.* **1** abbigliamento *m.* **2** allestimento *m.* **3** (*cuc.*) condimento *m.* **4** medicazione *f.*, bendaggio *m.* ♦ **d. gown** vestaglia; **d. room** spogliatoio; **d. table** toilette; **d.-up** travestimento; **salad d.** condimento per insalata

dressmaker ['drɛsˌmeɪkəʳ] *s.* sarta *f.*, sarto *m.*

dressy ['drɛsɪ] *agg.* elegante

drew [druː] *pass. di* **to draw**

to dribble ['drɪbl] *v. intr.* **1** sgocciolare **2** sbavare **3** (*sport*) dribblare

dried [draɪd] *agg.* secco ♦ **d. milk** latte in polvere

drier ['draɪəʳ] → **dryer**

drift [drɪft] *s.* **1** moto *m.*, corso *m.* spostamento *m.* **2** tendenza *f.* **3** cumulo *m.*, ammasso *m.*, mucchietto *m.* **4** deriva *f.* **5** turbine *m.*, raffica *f.* **6** senso *m.*, significato *m.*

to drift [drɪft] *v. intr.* **1** essere trasportato, andare alla deriva **2** ammucchiarsi

drill [drɪl] *s.* **1** trapano *m.* **2** esercitazione *f.*

to drill [drɪl] *v. tr.* **1** trapanare, trivellare **2** addestrare, esercitare

drink [drɪŋk] *s.* **1** bevanda *f.* **2** bevuta *f.*, sorso *m.*

to drink [drɪŋk] (*pass.* **drank**, *p. p.* **drunk**) *v. tr. e intr.* bere

drinkable ['drɪŋkəbl] *agg.* bevibile, potabile

drinker ['drɪŋkəʳ] *s.* bevitore *m.*

drip [drɪp] *s.* **1** gocciolamento *m.* **2** (*arch.*) gocciolatoio *m.* **3** fleboclisi *f.*

to drip [drɪp] *v. tr. e intr.* gocciolare

drip-dry [ˌdrɪp'draɪ] *agg.* da non stirare

drive [draɪv] *s.* **1** giro *m.* in automobile **2** strada *f.* d'accesso **3** spinta *f.*, impulso *m.* **4** (*autom.*) trazione *f.* **5** (*autom.*) guida *f.* **6** (*inf.*) drive *m. inv.* ♦ **four-wheel d.** quattro ruote motrici; **left-hand/right-hand d.** guida a sinistra/destra

to drive [draɪv] (*pass.* **drove**, *p. p.* **driven**) **A** *v. tr.* **1** (*un veicolo*) guidare **2** azionare, far funzionare **3** conficcare **4** spingere **B** *v. intr.* **1** guidare **2** andare in automobile **3** avanzare ♦ **to d. away** scacciare; **to d. back** respingere; **to d. off** partire, portare via (*su un'automobile*)

driver ['draɪvəʳ] *s.* conducente *m.*, guidatore *m.* ♦ **d.'s license** (*USA*) patente di guida; **screw d.** cacciavite

driving ['draɪvɪŋ] *s.* guida *f.* ♦ **d. mirror** specchietto retrovisore; **d. school** scuola guida

to drizzle ['drɪzl] *v. intr.* piovigginare

droll [drɒʊl] *agg.* buffo

dromedary ['drʌməd(ə)rɪ] *s.* dromedario *m.*

drone [drɒʊn] *s.* **1** fuco *m.* **2** (*fam.*) fannullone *m.* **3** ronzio *m.*

to drool [druːl] *v. intr.* sbavare

to droop [druːp] *v. intr.* afflosciarsi, ripiegarsi

drop [drəp] *s.* **1** goccia *f.* **2** pasticca *f.* **3** sorso *m.* **4** caduta *f.*, diminuzione *f.* **5** dislivello *m.*

to drop [drəp] **A** *v. intr.* **1** cadere **2** diminuire **3** abbassarsi **B** *v. tr.* **1** far cadere **2** abbassare **3** (*da un veicolo*) far scendere

4 omettere, sopprimere ♦ **to d. in** far visita; **to d. off** diminuire, addormentarsi; **to d. out** ritirarsi
dropper ['drəpəʳ] *s.* contagocce *m. inv.*
droppings ['drəpɪŋz] *s. pl.* sterco *m.*
drought [draʊt] *s.* siccità *f.*
drove [drɒʊv] *pass. di* **to drive**
to drown [draʊn] **A** *v. tr.* **1** affogare, annegare **2** soffocare, offuscare **B** *v. intr.* affogare, annegare
drowsiness ['draʊzɪnɪs] *s.* sonnolenza *f.*
drowsy ['draʊzɪ] *agg.* sonnolento
drudge [drʌdʒ] *s.* sgobbone *m.*
to drudge [drʌdʒ] *v. intr.* sgobbare
drug [drʌg] *s.* **1** farmaco *m.* **2** droga *f.* ♦ **d. addict** tossicodipendente; **hard d.** droga pesante
drugstore ['drʌgstɜːʳ] *s.* drugstore *m. inv.*
drum [drʌm] *s.* **1** tamburo *m.*, *al pl.* batteria *f.* **2** bidone *m.* ♦ **ear d.** timpano
to drum [drʌm] *v. intr.* **1** suonare il tamburo **2** tamburellare
drunk [drʌŋk] **A** *p. p. di* **to drink** **B** *agg.* ubriaco ♦ **dead d.** ubriaco fradicio; **to get d.** sbronzarsi
drunkenness ['drʌŋk(ə)nnɪs] *s.* ubriachezza *f.*
dry [draɪ] *agg.* asciutto, arido, secco ♦ **d. cleaning** lavaggio a secco; **d. cleaner's** tintoria; **d. goods** (*USA*) tessuti
to dry [draɪ] *v. tr. e intr.* asciugare, seccare ♦ **to d. up** prosciugarsi
dryer ['draɪəʳ] *s.* **1** essiccatore *m.* **2** asciugacapelli *m.*
drying ['draɪɪŋ] *s.* asciugatura *f.*
dryness ['draɪnɪs] *s.* siccità *f.*
dual ['djuːəl] *agg.* doppio, duplice
dualism ['djʊ(ː)əlɪz(ə)m] *s.* dualismo *m.*
to dub [dʌb] *v. tr.* (*cine.*) doppiare
dubber ['dʌbəʳ] *s.* doppiatore *m.*
dubbing ['dʌbɪŋ] *s.* doppiaggio *m.*
dubious ['djuːbjəs] *agg.* **1** dubbio **2** dubbioso, incerto
duchess ['dʌtʃɪs] *s.* duchessa *f.*
duchy ['dʌtʃɪ] *s.* ducato *m.*
duck [dʌk] *s.* anatra *f.*
to duck [dʌk] **A** *v. tr.* **1** tuffare, immergere rapidamente **2** piegare **B** *v. intr.* **1** tuffare la testa **2** piegare la testa
duct [dʌkt] *s.* condotto *m.*, canale *m.*
ductile ['dʌktaɪl] *agg.* duttile
dud [dʌd] **A** *s.* **1** cosa *f.* che non funziona, bidone *m.* (*fam.*) **2** (*di persona*) incapace *m. e f.* **B** *agg.* falso ♦ **d. cheque** assegno a vuoto
due [djuː] **A** *agg.* **1** dovuto, da pagarsi **2** doveroso, adatto, adeguato **B** *avv.* (esattamente) in direzione **C** *s.* **1** il dovuto *m.* **2** *al pl.* tasse *f. pl.*, diritti *m. pl.* ♦ **d. to** a causa di; **to be d. to do** dover fare; **to be d. to** essere causato da
duel ['djʊ(ː)əl] *s.* duello *m.*
duet [djʊ(ː)'ɛt] *s.* (*mus.*) duetto *m.*
duffel ['dʌf(ə)l] *s.* tessuto *m.* pesante ♦ **d. bag** sacca da viaggio; **d. coat** montgomery
dug [dʌg] *pass. e p. p. di* **to dig**
duke [djuːk] *s.* duca *m.*
dukedom ['djuːkdəm] *s.* ducato *m.*
dull [dʌl] *agg.* **1** tardo, ottuso, lento **2** sordo, soffocato **3** depresso **4** monotono **5** smorto, fosco, scuro
to dull [dʌl] *v. tr.* **1** intorpidire **2** smussare **3** attenuare, smorzare
duly ['djuːlɪ] *avv.* **1** debitamente **2** puntualmente
dumb [dʌm] *agg.* **1** muto **2** (*fam.*) stupido
to dumbfound [dʌm'faʊnd] *v. tr.* stupire, stordire
dummy ['dʌmɪ] **A** *agg.* **1** muto **2** falso, fittizio **B** *s.* **1** manichino *m.* **2** prestanome *m.* **3** tettarella *f.* **4** (*tip.*) menabò *m.*
dump [dʌmp] *s.* **1** discarica *f.* **2** mucchio *m.*, ammasso *m.* **3** vendita *f.* sottocosto **4** tonfo *m.*
to dump [dʌmp] **A** *v. tr.* **1** scaricare **2** abbandonare **3** vendere sottocosto **B** *v. intr.* **1** scaricare rifiuti **2** vendere sottocosto
dumpy [dʌmpɪ] *agg.* tarchiato
dunce [dʌns] *s.* (*fam.*) somaro *m.*, ignorante *m. e f.*
dune [djuːn] *s.* duna *f.*
dung [dʌŋ] *s.* letame *m.*
dungarees [ˌdʌŋgə'riːz] *s. pl.* tuta *f.* da lavoro
dungeon ['dʌn(d)ʒən] *s.* segreta *f.*, prigione *f.*
duo ['djʊ(ː)ɒʊ] *s.* duo *m. inv.*, duetto *m.*
dupe [djuːp] *s.* gonzo *m.*, zimbello *m.*
to dupe [djuːp] *v. tr.* ingannare, abbindolare
duplex ['djuːplɛks] **A** *agg.* duplice, doppio **B** *s.* **1** (*USA*) casa *f.* bifamiliare **2** (*USA*) appartamento *m.* su due livelli
to duplicate ['djuːplɪkeɪt] *v. tr.* duplicare
duplication [ˌdjuːplɪ'keɪʃ(ə)n] *s.* duplicazione *f.*, raddoppio *m.*
durable ['djʊərəbl] *agg.* durevole
duration [djʊ(ə)'reɪʃ(ə)n] *s.* durata *f.*

duress [djʊə'rɛs] *s.* costrizione *f.*
during ['djʊərɪŋ] *prep.* durante
dusk [dʌsk] *s.* crepuscolo *m.*
dust [dʌst] *s.* **1** polvere *f.*, pulviscolo *m.* **2** polline *m.* **3** spazzatura *f.*
to dust [dʌst] *v. tr.* **1** spolverare **2** cospargere
dustbin ['dʌs(t)bɪn] *s.* pattumiera *f.*
duster ['dʌstəʳ] *s.* straccio *m.* per la polvere
dustman ['dʌs(t)mən] (*pl.* **dustmen**) *s.* netturbino *m.*
dustpan ['dʌs(t)pæn] *s.* paletta *f.* (*per la spazzatura*)
dusty ['dʌstɪ] *agg.* polveroso
Dutch [dʌtʃ] *agg.* olandese ♦ **to go d.** pagare alla romana
Dutchman ['dʌtʃmən] (*pl.* **Dutchmen**) *s.* olandese *m.*
Dutchwoman ['dʌtʃ,wʊmən] (*pl.* **Dutchwomen**) *s.* olandese *f.*
dutiful ['dju:tɪf(ʊ)l] *agg.* rispettoso, deferente
duty ['dju:tɪ] *s.* **1** dovere *m.* **2** compito *m.*, incarico *m.* **3** servizio *m.* **4** dazio *m.*, imposta *f.* ♦ **d.-free** esente da dazio; **harbour duties** diritti portuali; **to be on/off d.** essere in servizio/fuori servizio
dwarf [dwɜ:f] *s.* nano *m.*, gnomo *m.*
to dwell [dwɛl] (*pass. e p. p.* **dwelt**, **dwelled**) *v. intr.* (*letter.*) dimorare, risiedere
dwelling ['dwɛlɪŋ] *s.* dimora *f.*
to dwindle ['dwɪndl] *v. intr.* diminuire, rimpicciolire
dye [daɪ] *s.* colorante *m.*, tinta *f.* ♦ **hair d.** tintura per capelli
to dye [daɪ] *v. tr.* tingere
dyeing ['daɪɪŋ] *s.* tintura *f.*
dyer ['daɪəʳ] *s.* tintore *m.*
dying ['daɪɪŋ] *agg.* morente, moribondo
dyke [daɪk] *s.* → **dike**
dynamic [daɪ'næmɪk] *agg.* dinamico
dynamics [daɪ'næmɪks] *s. pl.* (*v. al sing.*) dinamica *f.*
dynamism ['daɪnəmɪz(ə)n] *s.* dinamismo *m.*
dynamite ['daɪnəmaɪt] *s.* dinamite *f.*
dynamo ['daɪnəmoʊ] *s.* dinamo *f. inv.*
dynasty ['dɪnəstɪ] *s.* dinastia *f.*
dysentery ['dɪsntrɪ] *s.* dissenteria *f.*
dystrophy ['dɪstrəfɪ] *s.* distrofia *f.*

E

each [iːtʃ] **A** *agg.* ciascuno, ogni **B** *pron.* ognuno, ciascuno ♦ **e. other** l'un l'altro
eager ['iːgəʳ] *agg.* **1** appassionato, entusiasta **2** desideroso, avido ♦ **to be e. to do st.** essere impaziente di fare q.c.
eagle ['iːgl] *s.* aquila *f.*
ear (1) [ɪəʳ] *s.* orecchio *m.*
ear (2) [ɪəʳ] *s.* (*bot.*) spiga *f.*, pannocchia *f.*
earache ['ɪəreɪk] *s.* mal *m.* d'orecchio
eardrum ['ɪədrʌm] *s.* (*anat.*) timpano *m.*
earl [ɜːl] *s.* conte *m.*
early ['ɜːlɪ] **A** *agg.* **1** mattiniero, mattutino **2** primo, della prima parte, iniziale **3** precoce, prematuro, primaticcio **4** (*nel tempo*) prossimo **5** remoto, antico **B** *avv.* **1** presto, di buon'ora **2** al principio ♦ **to be e.** essere in anticipo; **to get up e.** alzarsi presto
to earmark ['ɪəmaːk] *v. tr.* **1** marchiare **2** contrassegnare **3** destinare
to earn [ɜːn] *v. tr.* **1** guadagnare **2** ottenere, meritare ♦ **to e. one's living** mantenersi
earnest ['ɜːnɪst] *agg.* **1** serio, zelante **2** ardente, pressante ♦ **in e.** sul serio
earnings ['ɜːnɪŋz] *s. pl.* guadagno *m.*, stipendio *m.*
earphone ['ɪəfɒʊn] *s.* auricolare *m.*
earring ['ɪərɪŋ] *s.* orecchino *m.*
earshot ['ɪəʃət] *s.* portata *f.* d'orecchio
earth [ɜːθ] *s.* **1** terra *f.*, globo *m.* terrestre **2** suolo *m.*, terreno *m.* **3** covo *m.*, tana *f.* **4** (*elettr*) terra *f.*, massa *f.*
earthenware ['ɜːθənwɛəʳ] *s.* terraglia *f.*, terracotta *f.*
earthly ['ɜːθlɪ] *agg.* **1** terrestre **2** (*fam.*) concepibile
earthquake ['ɜːθkweɪk] *s.* terremoto *m.*
earthy ['ɜːθɪ] *agg.* **1** terroso **2** grossolano
ease [iːz] *s.* **1** agio *m.*, comodo *m.*, comodità *f.* **2** sollievo *m.* ♦ **to take one's e.** mettersi a proprio agio
to ease [iːz] *v. tr.* **1** alleviare, calmare **2** alleggerire, liberare **3** attenuare ♦ **to e. off** rallentare, diminuire
easel ['iːzl] *s.* cavalletto *m.*
easily ['iːzɪlɪ] *avv.* **1** facilmente **2** comodamente
east [iːst] **A** *s.* est *m. inv.* **B** *agg.* orientale
Easter ['iːstəʳ] *s.* Pasqua *f.* ♦ **E. Monday** pasquetta; **E. holidays** vacanze pasquali
easterly ['iːstəlɪ] **A** *agg.* dall'est, orientale **B** *avv.* verso est
eastern ['iːstən] *agg.* orientale
easy ['iːzɪ] **A** *agg.* **1** facile **2** comodo, agiato **3** tranquillo **4** disinvolto **B** *avv.* **1** facilmente **2** comodamente, con calma ♦ **e. chair** poltrona; **take it e.!** calma!; **to make e.** facilitare
easygoing ['iːzɪˌgɒʊɪŋ] *agg.* accomodante, compiacente
to eat [iːt] (*pass.* **ate**, *p. p.* **eaten**) **A** *v. tr.* **1** mangiare **2** corrodere, consumare **B** *v. intr.* mangiare, consumare i pasti ♦ **to e. into** corrodere, intaccare; **to e. up** divorare, rodere
eatable ['iːtəbl] *agg.* commestibile, mangiabile
eaten ['iːtn] *p. p. di* **to eat**
eaves [iːvz] *s. pl.* gronda *f.*, cornicione *m.*
to eavesdrop ['iːvzdrəp] *v. intr.* **1** origliare **2** (*comunicazioni*) intercettare
ebb [ɛb] *s.* riflusso *m.* ♦ **e. tide** bassa marea
to ebb [ɛb] *v. intr.* **1** (*di marea*) rifluire **2** decadere, scemare
ebony ['ɛbənɪ] *s.* ebano *m.*
ebullition [ˌɛbə'lɪʃ(ə)n] *s.* ebollizione *f.*
eccentric [ɪk'sɛntrɪk] *agg.* eccentrico
ecchymosis [ˌɛkɪ'mɒʊsɪs] *s.* ecchimosi *f.*
ecclesiastic [ɪˌkliːzɪ'æstɪk] *agg. e s.* ecclesiastico *m.*
echo ['ɛkɒʊ] *s.* eco *m. e f.* ♦ **e. sounder** ecoscandaglio
to echo ['ɛkɒʊ] *v. tr. e intr.* echeggiare
eclectic [ɛk'lɛktɪk] *agg.* eclettico
eclecticism [ɛk'lɛktɪsɪz(ə)m] *s.* eclettismo *m.*
eclipse [ɪ'klɪps] *s.* eclissi *f.*
to eclipse [ɪ'klɪps] *v. tr.* eclissare
ecliptic [ɪ'klɪptɪk] *agg.* eclittico
ecological [ˌiːkə'lədʒɪk(ə)l] *agg.* ecologico
ecology [iː'kələdʒɪ] *s.* ecologia *f.*
economic [ˌiːkə'nəmɪk] *agg.* economico
economical [ˌiːkə'nəmɪk(ə)l] *agg.* **1** economico, parsimonioso **2** che fa risparmiare
economics [ˌiːkə'nəmɪks] *s. pl.* (*v. al sing.*) economia *f.*, scienze *f. pl.* economiche

economist [iː'kɒnəmɪst] *s.* economista *m. e f.*
to economize [iː'kɒnəmaɪz] *v. intr.* economizzare, risparmiare
economy [ɪ'kɒnəmɪ] *s.* **1** economia *f.*, sistema *m.* economico **2** risparmio *m.* ♦ **e. size** formato risparmio
ecosystem ['iːkɒʊˌsɪstəm] *s.* ecosistema *m.*
ecstasy ['ɛkstəsɪ] *s.* estasi *f.*
eczema ['ɛksɪmə] *s.* eczema *m.*
eddy ['ɛdɪ] *s.* gorgo *m.*, vortice *m.*
edge [ɛdʒ] *s.* **1** bordo *m.*, estremità *f.*, orlo *m.* **2** spigolo *m.* **3** taglio *m.*, filo *m.*
to edge [ɛdʒ] **A** *v. tr.* **1** bordare **2** affilare, arrotare **B** *v. intr.* muoversi lentamente ♦ **to e. away** allontanarsi
edgeways ['ɛdʒweɪz] *avv.* di taglio, di traverso
edgy ['ɛdʒɪ] *agg.* **1** affilato, tagliente **2** irritabile
edible ['ɛdɪbl] *agg.* commestibile
edict ['iːdɪkt] *s.* editto *m.*
to edit ['ɛdɪt] *v. tr.* **1** (*una pubblicazione, una trasmissione*) curare **2** (*un giornale*) dirigere **3** correggere, rivedere ♦ **edited by** a cura di
editing ['ɛdɪtɪŋ] *s.* **1** redazione *f.* **2** (*di giornale e sim.*) direzione *f.*
edition [ɪ'dɪʃ(ə)n] *s.* edizione *f.*
editor ['ɛdɪtəʳ] *s.* **1** curatore *m.* **2** (*di giornale*) direttore *m.*, redattore *m.*
editorial [ˌɛdɪ'tɜːrɪəl] **A** *agg.* editoriale, redazionale **B** *s.* editoriale *m.*
to educate ['ɛdjʊ(ː)keɪt] *v. tr.* istruire, educare
education [ˌɛdjʊ(ː)'keɪʃ(ə)n] *s.* educazione *f.*, istruzione *f.*
educational [ˌɛdjʊ(ː)'keɪʃənl] *agg.* educativo
eel [iːl] *s.* anguilla *f.*
eerie ['ɪərɪ] *agg.* **1** fantastico, soprannaturale **2** che fa rabbrividire
effect [ɪ'fɛkt] *s.* **1** effetto *m.*, conseguenza *f.* **2** senso *m.*, tenore *m.* ♦ **in e.** effettivamente; **of no e.** senza risultato; **to take e.** entrare in vigore
to effect [ɪ'fɛkt] *v. tr.* **1** effettuare, compiere **2** causare, determinare
effective [ɪ'fɛktɪv] *agg.* **1** efficace **2** effettivo, reale **3** che fa effetto **4** (*USA*) vigente, operante
effectively [ɪ'fɛktɪvlɪ] *avv.* **1** efficacemente **2** effettivamente
effectiveness [ɪ'fɛktɪvnɪs] *s.* efficacia *f.*
effeminate [ɪ'fɛmɪneɪt] *agg.* effeminato
efficiency [ɪ'fɪʃ(ə)nsɪ] *s.* efficienza *f.*, rendimento *m.*
efficient [ɪ'fɪʃənt] *agg.* efficiente
effigy ['ɛfɪdʒɪ] *s.* effigie *f.*
effluvium [ɛ'fluːvjəm] *s.* effluvio *m.*
effort ['ɛfət] *s.* sforzo *m.*, fatica *f.*
effrontery [ɛ'frʌntərɪ] *s.* sfrontatezza *f.*
effusion [ɪ'fjuːʒ(ə)n] *s.* effusione *f.*
effusive [ɪ'fjuːsɪv] *agg.* espansivo
egg [ɛg] *s.* uovo *m.* ♦ **e. plant** melanzana; **e. cup** portauovo; **fried/hard-boiled/soft-boiled e.** uovo fritto/sodo/alla coque; **scrambled eggs** uova strapazzate
to egg [ɛg] *v. tr.* **to e. on** incitare
ego ['ɛgɒʊ] *s.* (*psic.*) Ego *m. inv.*, Io *m. inv.*
egocentric [ˌɛgɒ(ʊ)'sɛntrɪk] *agg.* egocentrico
egoist ['ɛgɒ(ʊ)ɪst] *s.* egoista *m. e f.*
Egyptian [ɪ'dʒɪpʃ(ə)n] *agg.* egiziano, egizio
Egyptology [ˌiːdʒɪp'tɒlədʒɪ] *s.* egittologia *f.*
eiderdown ['aɪdɛəˌdaʊn] *s.* **1** piumino *m.* (d'oca) **2** piumino *m.*, trapunta *f.*
eight [eɪt] *agg. num. card. e s.* otto *m. inv.*
eighteen [eɪ'tiːn] *agg. num. card. e s.* diciotto *m. inv.*
eighth [eɪtθ] *agg. num. ord.* ottavo
eighty ['eɪtɪ] *agg. num. card. e s.* ottanta *m. inv.*
either ['aɪðəʳ] **A** *agg. e pron.* **1** l'uno o l'altro, l'uno e l'altro, entrambi **2** (*in frasi neg.*) né l'uno né l'altro, nessuno dei due **B** *avv.* (*in frasi neg.*) neanche, nemmeno, neppure **C** *cong.* o ♦ **e. ... or** o ... o
to eject [ɪ(ː)'dʒɛkt] *v. tr.* espellere, gettare fuori, emettere
to eke [iːk] *v. tr.* **to e. out** integrare, arrotondare
to elaborate [ɪ'læbəreɪt] **A** *v. tr.* elaborare **B** *v. intr.* sviluppare un concetto, fornire particolari
to elapse [ɪ'læps] *v. intr.* (*del tempo*) trascorrere
elastic [ɪ'læstɪk] *agg. e s.* elastico *m.*
elasticity [ˌiːlæs'tɪsɪtɪ] *s.* elasticità *f.*
elated [ɪ'leɪtɪd] *agg.* esultante, euforico
elbow ['ɛlbɒʊ] *s.* gomito *m.*
elder (1) ['ɛldəʳ] **A** *agg.* (*comp. di* **old**) (*di età tra due*) maggiore, più vecchio **B** *s.* (*di età tra due*) il maggiore *m.*, anziano *m.*
elder (2) ['ɛldəʳ] *s.* sambuco *m.*

elderly ['ɛldəlɪ] *agg.* anziano, attempato
eldest ['ɛldɪst] *agg.* (*sup. di* **old**) (*tra fratelli*) il maggiore
elect [ɪ'lɛkt] *agg.* eletto, designato
to elect [ɪ'lɛkt] *v. tr.* **1** eleggere **2** decidere, scegliere
election [ɪ'lɛkʃ(ə)n] *s.* elezione *f.*
electioneering [ɪˌlɛkʃə'nɪərɪŋ] *s.* propaganda *f.* elettorale
elector [ɪ'lɛktəʳ] *s.* elettore *m.*
electoral [ɪ'lɛkt(ə)r(ə)l] *agg.* elettorale
electorate [ɪ'lɛkt(ə)rɪt] *s.* elettorato *m.*
electric [ɪ'lɛktrɪk] *agg.* elettrico
electrical [ɪ'lɛktrɪk(ə)l] *agg.* elettrico
electrician [ɪlɛk'trɪʃ(ə)n] *s.* elettricista *m.*
electricity [ɪlɛk'trɪsɪtɪ] *s.* elettricità *f.*
to electrify [ɪ'lɛktrɪfaɪ] *v. tr.* **1** elettrificare **2** elettrizzare
electrocardiogram [ɪˌlɛktrɒ(ʊ)'kaːdjɒʊgræm] *s.* elettrocardiogramma *m.*
to electrocute [ɪ'lɛktrəkjuːt] *v. tr.* fulminare
electrocution [ɪˌlɛktrə'kjuːʃ(ə)n] *s.* elettrocuzione *f.*, folgorazione *f.*
electroencephalogram [ɪˌlɛktrɒ(ʊ)ɛn'sɛfələgræm] *s.* elettroencefalogramma *m.*
electromagnetic [ɪˌlɛktrɒ(ʊ)mæg'nɛtɪk] *agg.* elettromagnetico
electronic [ɪlɛk'trənɪk] *agg.* elettronico
electronics [ɪlɛk'trənɪks] *s. pl.* (*v. al sing.*) elettronica *f.*
electrotechnician [ɪˌlɛktrɒ(ʊ)tɛk'nɪʃ(ə)n] *s.* elettrotecnico *m.*
elegance ['ɛlɪgəns] *s.* eleganza *f.*
elegant ['ɛlɪgənt] *agg.* elegante, raffinato
elegiac [ˌɛlɪ'dʒaɪək] *agg.* elegiaco
element ['ɛlɪmənt] *s.* elemento *m.*
elemental [ˌɛlɪ'mənt(ə)l] *agg.* **1** elementare **2** fondamentale, essenziale
elementary [ˌɛlɪ'mɛnt(ə)rɪ] *agg.* elementare, rudimentale
elephant ['ɛlɪfənt] *s.* elefante *m.*
to elevate ['ɛlɪveɪt] *v. tr.* elevare, innalzare
elevated ['ɛlɪveɪtɪd] *agg.* elevato
elevation [ˌɛlɪ'veɪʃ(ə)n] *s.* elevazione *f.*
elevator ['ɛlɪveɪtəʳ] *s.* **1** (*USA*) ascensore *m.* **2** elevatore *m.*, montacarichi *m. inv.*
eleven [ɪ'lɛvn] *agg. num. card. e s.* undici *m. inv.*
eleventh [ɪ'lɛvɛnθ] *agg. num. ord.* undicesimo
elf [ɛlf] *s.* elfo *m.*
to elicit [ɪ'lɪsɪt] *v. tr.* **1** provocare, suscitare **2** cavar fuori
eligible ['ɛlɪdʒəbl] *agg.* eleggibile, idoneo, che ha i requisiti per
to eliminate [ɪ'lɪmɪneɪt] *v. tr.* eliminare
elitist [eɪ'liːtɪst] *agg.* elitario
Elizabethan [ɪˌlɪzə'biːθ(ə)n] *agg.* elisabettiano
elk [ɛlk] *s.* alce *m.*
ellipse [ɪ'lɪps] *s.* ellisse *f.*
elliptic [ɪ'lɪptɪk] *agg.* ellittico
elm [ɛlm] *s.* olmo *m.*
to elongate ['iːləŋgeɪt] *v. tr. e intr.* allungare, allungarsi
to elope [ɪ'lɒʊp] *v. intr.* scappare (*con un amante*)
elopement [ɪ'lɒʊpmənt] *s.* fuga *f.* (*con un amante*)
eloquent ['ɛləkw(ə)nt] *agg.* eloquente
else [ɛls] **A** *agg. pred. e avv.* altro **B** *cong.* oppure, altrimenti ♦ **everybody e.** tutti gli altri; **everything e.** tutto il resto; **nothing e.** nient'altro; **what e.?** che altro?
elsewhere [ˌɛls'wɛəʳ] *avv.* altrove
to elucidate [ɪ'luːsɪdeɪt] *v. tr.* delucidare
elucidation [ɪˌluːsɪ'deɪʃ(ə)n] *s.* delucidazione *f.*
to elude [ɪ'luːd] *v. tr.* eludere, schivare
elusive [ɪ'luːsɪv] *agg.* elusivo
emaciated [ɪ'meɪʃɪeɪtɪd] *agg.* emaciato
to emanate ['ɛməneɪt] *v. intr.* emanare, provenire
to emancipate [ɪ'mænsɪpeɪt] *v. tr.* emancipare
emancipation [ɪˌmænsɪ'peɪʃ(ə)n] *s.* emancipazione *f.*
to embalm [ɪm'baːm] *v. tr.* imbalsamare
embankment [ɪm'bæŋkmənt] *s.* argine *m.*, terrapieno *m.*
embargo [ɛm'baːgɒʊ] *s.* embargo *m. inv.*
to embark [ɪm'baːk] *v. tr. e intr.* imbarcare, imbarcarsi ♦ **to e. on** intraprendere, imbarcarsi in
embarkation [ˌɛmbaː'keɪʃ(ə)n] *s.* imbarco *m.*
to embarrass [ɪm'bærəs] *v. tr.* imbarazzare
embarrassing [ɪm'bærəsɪŋ] *agg.* imbarazzante
embarrassment [ɪm'bærəsmənt] *s.* imbarazzo *m.*, disagio *m.*
embassy ['ɛmbəsɪ] *s.* ambasciata *f.*
to embed [ɪm'bɛd] *v. tr.* incassare, incastrare
to embellish [ɪm'bɛlɪʃ] *v. tr.* abbellire

ember ['ɛmbəʳ] *s.* **1** tizzone *m.* **2** *al pl.* brace *f.*
to **embezzle** [ɪm'bɛzl] *v. tr.* impossessarsi (indebitamente)
to **embitter** [ɪm'bɪtəʳ] *v. tr.* amareggiare, inasprire
emblematic(al) [ˌɛmblə'mætɪk(l)] *agg.* emblematico
to **embody** [ɪm'bɒdɪ] *v. tr.* **1** incarnare **2** incorporare
embolism ['ɛmbəlɪz(ə)m] *s.* embolia *f.*
embolus ['ɛmbələs] *s.* embolo *m.*
to **emboss** [ɪm'bɒs] *v. tr.* **1** lavorare a sbalzo **2** stampare in rilievo
embossed [ɪm'bɒst] *agg.* **1** sbalzato **2** stampato in rilievo
embrace [ɪm'breɪs] *s.* **1** abbraccio *m.*, stretta *f.* **2** amplesso *m.*
to **embrace** [ɪm'breɪs] *v. tr.* **1** abbracciare, stringere **2** dedicarsi a
to **embroider** [ɪm'brɔɪdəʳ] *v. tr.* ricamare
embroidery [ɪm'brɔɪd(ə)rɪ] *s.* ricamo *m.*
embryo ['ɛmbrɪɒʊ] *s.* embrione *m.*
emerald ['ɛmər(ə)ld] *s.* smeraldo *m.*
to **emerge** [ɪ'mɜːdʒ] *v. intr.* emergere
emergency [ɪ'mɜːdʒ(ə)nsɪ] *s.* emergenza *f.* ♦ **e. cord** segnale di allarme; **e. exit** uscita di sicurezza
emergent [ɪ'mɜːdʒənt] *agg.* emergente
emersion [ɪ(ː)'mɜːs(ə)n] *s.* emersione *f.*
emery ['ɛmərɪ] *s.* smeriglio *m.* ♦ **e. board** limetta per unghie
emigrant ['ɛmɪgrənt] *agg. e s.* emigrante *m. e f.*
to **emigrate** ['ɛmɪgreɪt] *v. intr.* emigrare
emigration [ˌɛmɪ'greɪʃ(ə)n] *s.* emigrazione *f.*
eminent ['ɛmɪnənt] *agg.* eminente
emir [ɛ'mɪəʳ] *s.* emiro *m.*
emirate [ɛ'mɪərɪt] *s.* emirato *m.*
emission [ɪ'mɪʃ(ə)n] *s.* emissione *f.*
to **emit** [ɪ'mɪt] *v. tr.* emettere
emitter [ɪ'mɪtəʳ] *s.* emettitore *m.*
emotion [ɪ'mɒʊʃ(ə)n] *s.* emozione *f.*
emotional [ɪ'mɒʊʃ(ə)nl] *agg.* **1** emotivo **2** emozionante, commovente
emperor ['ɛmpərəʳ] *s.* imperatore *m.*
emphasis ['ɛmfəsɪs] (*pl.* **emphases**) *s.* **1** accentuazione *f.*, rilievo *m.*, evidenza *f.* **2** enfasi *f.*
to **emphasize** ['ɛmfəsaɪz] *v. tr.* **1** accentuare, dare rilievo, mettere in evidenza **2** pronunciare con enfasi, enfatizzare
emphatic [ɪm'fætɪk] *agg.* **1** accentuato, enfatico **2** chiaro, netto
emphysema [ˌɛmfɪ'siːmə] *s.* enfisema *m.*
empire ['ɛmpaɪəʳ] *s.* impero *m.*
empiric [ɛm'pɪrɪk] *agg.* empirico
to **employ** [ɪm'plɔɪ] *v. tr.* **1** impiegare, assumere **2** adoperare
employee [ˌɛmplɔɪ'iː] *s.* impiegato *m.*, dipendente *m. e f.*
employer [ɪm'plɔɪəʳ] *s.* datore *m.* di lavoro, principale *m.*
employment [ɪm'plɔɪmənt] *s.* impiego *m.*, occupazione *f.*
to **empower** [ɪm'paʊəʳ] *v. tr.* autorizzare
empty ['ɛm(p)tɪ] *agg.* **1** vuoto **2** vano, vacuo ♦ **e.-handed** a mani vuote
to **empty** ['ɛm(p)tɪ] *v. tr.* vuotare
to **emulate** ['ɛmjʊleɪt] *v. tr.* emulare
emulator ['ɛmjʊˌleɪtəʳ] *s.* emulo *m.*
emulsion [ɪ'mʌlʃ(ə)n] *s.* emulsione *f.*
to **enable** [ɪ'neɪbl] *v. tr.* permettere, rendere capace di, mettere in grado di
to **enact** [ɪ'nækt] *v. tr.* **1** (*dir.*) decretare, promulgare **2** (*teatro*) recitare, rappresentare
enamel [ɪ'næm(ə)l] *s.* **1** smalto *m.* **2** pittura *f.* a smalto
enamelling [ɪ'næməlɪŋ] *s.* smaltatura *f.*
to **encase** [ɪn'keɪs] *v. tr.* **1** racchiudere **2** rivestire, ricoprire
to **enchain** [ɪn'tʃeɪn] *v. tr.* incatenare
to **enchant** [ɪn'tʃaːnt] *v. tr.* incantare, affascinare
enchanting [ɪn'tʃɑ(ː)ntɪŋ] *agg.* incantevole, affascinante
enchantment [ɪn'tʃɑ(ː)ntmənt] *s.* incanto *m.*, incantesimo *m.*
to **encircle** [ɪn'sɜːkl] *v. tr.* circondare
to **enclose** [ɪn'klɒʊz] *v. tr.* **1** chiudere, circondare, avvolgere **2** allegare, accludere
enclosure [ɪn'klɒʊʒəʳ] *s.* **1** recinto *m.*, recinzione *f.* **2** allegato *m.*
to **encompass** [ɪn'kʌmpəs] *v. tr.* **1** attorniare, circondare, racchiudere **2** compiere
encore ['ɔŋkɜːʳ] *s. e inter.* (*teatro*) bis *m. inv.*
encounter [ɪn'kaʊntəʳ] *s.* **1** incontro *m.* **2** scontro *m.*
to **encounter** [ɪn'kaʊntəʳ] *v. tr.* **1** incontrare **2** affrontare
to **encourage** [ɪn'kʌrɪdʒ] *v. tr.* incoraggiare
encouragement [ɪn'kʌrɪdʒmənt] *s.* incoraggiamento *m.*
to **encroach** [ɪn'krɒʊtʃ] *v. intr.* **to e. (up)on** intaccare, ledere, abusare, usurpare
encrustation [ˌɪnkrʌs'teɪʃ(ə)n] *s.* incro-

stazione *f.*
to encumber [ɪn'kʌmbəʳ] *v. tr.* **1** ingombrare, intralciare, impedire **2** gravare
encyclopaedia [ɛnˌsaɪklɒ(ʊ)'piːdjə] *s.* enciclopedia *f.*
end [ɛnd] *s.* **1** fine *f.*, estremità *f.*, limite *m.* **2** fine *f.*, termine *m.*, conclusione *f.* **3** (*fig.*) morte *f.*, distruzione *f.* **4** fine *m.*, scopo *m.*, mira *f.*, finalità *f.* **5** residuo *m.*, avanzo *m.* ♦ **at the e.** infine; **in the e.** in fondo; **on e.** di seguito, (*di oggetto*) diritto
to end [ɛnd] *v. tr. e intr.* finire, terminare, concludere ♦ **to e. up** concludersi
to endanger [ɪn'deɪn(d)ʒəʳ] *v. tr.* mettere in pericolo
endearing [ɪn'dɪərɪŋ] *agg.* affettuoso, avvincente
endeavour [ɪn'dɛvəʳ] (*USA* **endeavor**) *s.* sforzo *m.*, tentativo *m.*
to endeavour [ɪn'dɛvəʳ] (*USA* **to endeavor**) *v. tr.* cercare, sforzarsi, tentare di
endemic [ɛn'dɛmɪk] *agg.* endemico
ending ['ɛndɪŋ] *s.* **1** fine *f.*, finale *m.* **2** (*gramm.*) desinenza *f.*
endive ['ɛndaɪv] *s.* indivia *f.*
endless ['ɛndlɪs] *agg.* **1** infinito, senza fine **2** interminabile
endocrinologist [ˌɛndɒ(ʊ)krɪ'nələdʒɪst] *s.* endocrinologo *m.*
endocrinology [ˌɛndɒ(ʊ)krɪ'nələdʒɪ] *s.* endocrinologia *f.*
to endorse [ɪn'dɜːs] *v. tr.* **1** (*assegno, cambiale*) girare **2** approvare
endorsement [ɪn'də(ː)smənt] *s.* **1** (*di assegno, cambiale*) girata *f.* **2** approvazione *f.*, appoggio *m.*
to endow [ɪn'daʊ] *v. tr.* dotare, assegnare, fornire
endowment [ɪn'daʊmənt] *s.* **1** dotazione *f.*, assegnazione *f.* **2** (*fig.*) dote *f.*
endurable [ɪn'djʊərəbl] *agg.* sopportabile
endurance [ɪn'djʊər(ə)ns] *s.* **1** resistenza *f.*, sopportazione *f.* **2** (*mecc.*) durata *f.*
to endure [ɪn'djʊəʳ] *v. intr.* sopportare, tollerare, resistere
enemy ['ɛnɪmɪ] *s.* nemico *m.*
energetic [ˌɛnə'dʒɛtɪk] *agg.* energetico
energy ['ɛnədʒɪ] *s.* energia *f.*
to enforce [ɪn'fɜːs] *v. tr.* **1** imporre, far valere **2** (*dir*) applicare, mettere in vigore
to engage [ɪn'geɪdʒ] **A** *v. tr.* **1** ingaggiare, assumere **2** impegnare, impegnarsi **3** attirare **4** (*mecc.*) ingranare, innestare **B** *v. intr.* **1** (*mil.*) attaccare **2** (*mecc.*) innestarsi, ingranare ♦ **to e. in** dedicarsi a
engaged [ɪn'geɪdʒd] *agg.* **1** impegnato **2** fidanzato **3** occupato, riservato
engagement [ɪn'geɪdʒmənt] *s.* **1** impegno *m.*, appuntamento *m.* **2** fidanzamento *m.* **3** assunzione *f.*, reclutamento *m.* ♦ **e. ring** anello di fidanzamento
engaging [ɪn'geɪdʒɪŋ] *agg.* attraente, affascinante
engine ['ɛn(d)ʒɪn] *s.* **1** motore *m.*, macchina *f.* **2** (*ferr.*) locomotiva *f.*
engineer [ˌɛn(d)ʒɪ'nɪəʳ] *s.* **1** ingegnere *m.* **2** tecnico *m.* **3** (*ferr.*) macchinista *m.*
engineering [ˌɛn(d)ʒɪ'nɪərɪŋ] *s.* ingegneria *f.*
English ['ɪŋglɪʃ] *agg. e s.* inglese *m.* (*lingua*)
Englishman ['ɪŋglɪʃmən] (*pl.* **Englishmen**) *s.* inglese *m.*
Englishwoman ['ɪnglɪʃˌwʊmən] (*pl.* **Englishwomen**) *s.* inglese *f.*
to engrave [ɪn'greɪv] *v. tr.* incidere
engraver [ɪn'greɪvəʳ] *agg.* incisore
engraving [ɪn'greɪvɪŋ] *s.* incisione *f.*
to enhance [ɪn'haːns] *v. tr.* aumentare, accrescere, intensificare
enhancement [ɪn'haːnsmənt] *s.* aumento *m.*, accrescimento *m.*, rinforzo *m.*
enigma [ɪ'nɪgmə] *s.* enigma *m.*
enigmatic [ˌɛnɪg'mætɪk] *agg.* enigmatico
to enjoy [ɪn'dʒəɪ] *v. tr.* godere, gustare, provar piacere di ♦ **e. your meal!** buon appetito!; **to e. oneself doing st.** divertirsi a fare q.c.
enjoyable [ɪn'dʒəɪəbl] *agg.* gradevole, piacevole
enjoyment [ɪn'dʒəɪmənt] *s.* gioia *f.*, piacere *m.*, godimento *m.*
to enlarge [ɪn'laːdʒ] *v. tr.* **1** allargare, ampliare **2** (*fot.*) ingrandire ♦ **to e. on** dilungarsi su
enlargement [ɪn'laːdʒmənt] *s.* **1** allargamento *m.*, ampliamento *m.* **2** (*fot.*) ingrandimento *m.*
to enlighten [ɪn'laɪtn] *v. tr.* **1** illuminare **2** chiarire
to enlist [ɪn'lɪst] **A** *v. tr.* **1** (*mil.*) arruolare **2** procurarsi **B** *v. intr.* **1** (*mil.*) arruolarsi **2** aderire, dare il proprio appoggio a
enmity ['ɛnmɪtɪ] *s.* inimicizia *f.*, ostilità *f.*
enormous [ɪ'nɜːməs] *agg.* enorme
enough [ɪ'nʌʃ] **A** *agg.* sufficiente, bastante **B** *avv.* abbastanza, sufficientemente ♦ **that's e.!** basta!; **to be e.** bastare
to enounce [ɪ(ː)'naʊns] *v. tr.* enunciare

to **enrage** [ɪn'reɪdʒ] *v. tr.* irritare, far infuriare
enraged [ɪn'reɪdʒd] *agg.* furibondo
to **enrich** [ɪn'rɪtʃ] *v. tr.* arricchire
to **enrol(l)** [ɪn'rɒʊl] **A** *v. tr.* **1** arruolare, ingaggiare, iscrivere **2** registrare **B** *v. intr.* arruolarsi, iscriversi
enrol(l)ment [ɪn'rɒʊlmənt] *s.* **1** iscrizione *f.*, arruolamento *m.* **2** registrazione *f.*
ensemble [ən'səmbl] *s.* complesso *m.*
ensign ['ɛnsaɪn] *s.* insegna *f.*, bandiera *f.*
to **ensue** [ɪn'sjuː] *v. intr.* conseguire, derivare
to **ensure** [ɪn'ʃʊəʳ] *v. tr.* assicurare, garantire
to **entail** [ɪn'teɪl] *v. tr.* comportare, implicare
to **entangle** [ɪn'tæŋgl] *v. tr.* impigliare, intrappolare
to **enter** ['ɛntəʳ] **A** *v. tr.* **1** entrare in, penetrare in **2** entrare a far parte di **3** iscrivere, partecipare **4** (*comm.*) registrare **B** *v. intr.* **1** entrare **2** iscriversi ♦ **to e. into** iniziare, avviare, entrare in, far parte di
enterprise ['ɛntəpraɪz] *s.* **1** impresa *f.*, avventura *f.* **2** iniziativa *f.* **3** impresa *f.*, azienda *f.*
to **entertain** [ˌɛntə'teɪn] **A** *v. tr.* **1** ricevere, ospitare **2** intrattenere, divertire **3** avere (in mente), nutrire **4** prendere in considerazione **B** *v. intr.* ricevere, dare ricevimenti
entertainer [ˌɛntə'teɪnəʳ] *s.* intrattenitore *m.*, showman *m. inv.*
entertaining [ˌɛntə'teɪnɪŋ] *agg.* divertente
entertainment [ˌɛntə'teɪnmənt] *s.* **1** divertimento *m.* **2** spettacolo *m.* **3** ricevimento *m.*
to **enthral(l)** [ɪn'θrɜːl] *v. tr.* affascinare, incantare
enthusiasm [ɪn'θjuːzɪæz(ə)m] *s.* entusiasmo *m.*
enthusiast [ɪn'θjuːzɪæst] *s.* entusiasta *m. e f.*, appassionato *m.*
enthusiastic [ɪnˌθjuːzɪ'æstɪk] *agg.* entusiasta
enthusiastically [ɪnˌθjuːzɪ'æstɪk(ə)lɪ] *avv.* entusiasticamente
to **entice** [ɪn'taɪs] *v. tr.* sedurre, adescare, allettare
enticement [ɪn'taɪsmənt] *s.* adescamento *m.*, allettamento *m.*
entire [ɪn'taɪəʳ] *agg.* intero, completo
entirely [ɪn'taɪəlɪ] *avv.* interamente, completamente
entirety [ɪn'taɪətɪ] *s.* interezza *f.*, complesso *m.*
to **entitle** [ɪn'taɪtl] *v. tr.* **1** (*un libro*) intitolare **2** concedere un titolo, riconoscere un diritto ♦ **to be entitled to** avere diritto a
entrails ['ɛntreɪlz] *s. pl.* interiora *f. pl.*
entrance ['ɛntr(ə)ns] *s.* **1** entrata *f.*, accesso *m.*, ingresso *m.* **2** ammissione *f.* ♦ **e. fee** tassa d'iscrizione, biglietto d'ingresso; **free e.** ingresso libero; **main/side e.** entrata principale/laterale; **no e.** vietato l'ingresso
entrant ['ɛntr(ə)nt] *s.* **1** partecipante *m. e f.*, concorrente *m. e f.* **2** debuttante *m. e f.*
to **entreat** [ɪn'triːt] *v. tr.* implorare, supplicare
entrenched [ɪn'trɛntʃt] *agg.* trincerato
entrepreneur [ˌəntrəprə'nɜːʳ] *s.* **1** imprenditore *m.* **2** (*teatro*) impresario *m.*
to **entrust** [ɪn'trʌst] *v. tr.* affidare, consegnare
entry ['ɛntrɪ] *s.* **1** entrata *f.*, accesso *m.*, ingresso *m.* **2** iscrizione *f.* **3** (*di dizionario*) voce *f.* **4** (*comm.*) registrazione *f.*, annotazione *f.* ♦ **no e.** vietato l'accesso
to **enumerate** [ɪ'njuːməreɪt] *v. tr.* enumerare
enuresis [ˌɛnjʊə'rɪ(ː)sɪs] *s.* enuresi *f.*
to **envelop** [ɪn'vɛləp] *v. tr.* avvolgere, avviluppare
envelope ['ɛnvɪlɒʊp] *s.* **1** busta *f.* **2** involucro *m.*
envious ['ɛnvɪəs] *agg.* invidioso
environment [ɪn'vaɪər(ə)nmənt] *s.* **1** ambiente *m.*, condizioni *f. pl.* ambientali **2** territorio *m.* circostante
environmental [ɪnˌvaɪərən'mɛnt(ə)l] *agg.* ambientale
to **envisage** [ɪn'vɪzɪdʒ] *v. tr.* immaginare
envoy ['ɛnvəɪ] *s.* inviato *m.*, delegato *m.*
envy ['ɛnvɪ] *s.* invidia *f.*
to **envy** ['ɛnvɪ] *v. tr.* invidiare ♦ **to e. sb. st.** invidiare q.c. a qc.
ephebic [ɛ'fiːbɪk] *agg.* efebico
ephemeral [ɪ'fɛmər(ə)l] *agg.* effimero
ephemeris [ɪ'fɛm(ə)rɪs] (*pl.* **ephemerides**) *s.* effemeride *f.*
epic ['ɛpɪk] **A** *agg.* epico **B** *s.* poema *m.* epico, epopea *f.*
epicentre ['ɛpɪsɛntəʳ] (*USA* **epicenter**) *s.* epicentro *m.*
Epicureanism [ˌɛpɪkjʊə'rɪ(ː)ənɪz(ə)m] *s.* epicureismo *m.*
epidemic [ˌɛpɪ'dɛmɪk] **A** *agg.* epidemico **B** *s.* epidemia *f.*

epidermic [ˌɛpɪ'dɜːmɪk] *agg.* epidermico
epigraph ['ɛpɪgraːf] *s.* epigrafe *f.*
epigraphy ['ɛpɪgrəfɪ] *s.* epigrafia *f.*
epilepsy ['ɛpɪlɛpsɪ] *s.* epilessia *f.*
epilogue ['ɛpɪləg] *s.* epilogo *m.*
Epiphany [ɪ'pɪfənɪ] *s.* epifania *f.*
episcopal [ɪ'pɪskəp(ə)l] *agg.* episcopale, vescovile
episode ['ɛpɪsɒʊd] *s.* episodio *m.*
epistaxis [ˌɛpɪ'stæksɪs] *s.* epistassi *f.*
epistle [ɪ'pɪsl] *s.* epistola *f.*
epitaph ['ɛpɪtaːf] *s.* epitaffio *m.*
epithet ['ɛpɪθɛt] *s.* epiteto *m.*
epitome [ɪ'pɪtəmɪ] *s.* **1** epitome *f.*, compendio *m.* **2** personificazione *f.*, quintessenza *f.*
to epitomize [ɪ'pɪtəmaɪz] *v. tr.* **1** epitomare, compendiare **2** personificare, incarnare
epoch ['iːpək] *s.* epoca *f.*
eponym ['ɛpɒ(ʊ)nɪm] *s.* eponimo *m.*
eponymous [ɪ'pənɪməs] *agg.* eponimo
equable ['ɛkwəbl] *agg.* **1** uniforme **2** equilibrato, sereno
equal ['iːkw(ə)l] *agg.* **1** uguale, pari **2** calmo, fermo
to equal ['iːkw(ə)l] *v. tr.* uguagliare, equivalere
equality [ɪ(ː)'kwəlɪtɪ] *s.* uguaglianza *f.*, parità *f.*
to equalize ['iːkwəlaɪz] *v. tr.* **1** uguagliare, equiparare **2** pareggiare
equally ['ɪ(ː)kwəlɪ] *avv.* **1** ugualmente **2** allo stesso modo
equation [ɪ'kweɪʃ(ə)n] *s.* equazione *f.*
equator [ɪ'kweɪtəʳ] *s.* equatore *m.*
equatorial [ˌɛkwə'tɜːrɪəl] *agg.* equatoriale
equestrian [ɪ'kwɛstrɪən] *agg.* equestre
equidistant [ˌiːkwɪ'dɪst(ə)nt] *agg.* equidistante
equilibrium [ˌiːkwɪ'lɪbrɪəm] *s.* equilibrio *m.*
equine ['iːkwaɪn] *agg. e s.* equino *m.*
equinox ['iːkwɪnəks] *s.* equinozio *m.*
to equip [ɪ'kwɪp] *v. tr.* equipaggiare, allestire, attrezzare ♦ **to be equipped with** essere fornito di
equipment [ɪ'kwɪpmənt] *s.* equipaggiamento *m.*, attrezzatura *f.*
equitable ['ɛkwɪtəbl] *agg.* equo, giusto
equity ['ɛkwɪtɪ] *s.* **1** equità *f.* **2** (*econ.*) azione *f.* ordinaria
equivalent [ɪ'kwɪvələnt] *agg. e s.* equivalente *m.*
equivocal [ɪ'kwɪvək(ə)l] *agg.* equivoco
era ['ɪərə] *s.* era *f.*
to eradicate [ɪ'rædɪkeɪt] *v. tr.* sradicare
to erase [ɪ'reɪz] *v. tr.* cancellare
eraser [ɪ'reɪzəʳ] *s.* gomma *f.* (*per cancellare*)
erect [ɪ'rɛkt] *agg.* eretto
to erect [ɪ'rɛkt] *v. tr.* erigere
erection [ɪ'rɛkʃ(ə)n] *s.* erezione *f.*
to erode [ɪ'rɒʊd] *v. tr.* erodere, corrodere
erosion [ɪ'rɒʊʒ(ə)n] *s.* erosione *f.*
erotic [ɪ'rətɪk] *agg.* erotico
erotism ['ɪrətɪz(ə)m] *s.* erotismo *m.*
to err [ɜːʳ] *v. intr.* **1** errare, sbagliare **2** vagabondare
errand ['ɛr(ə)nd] *s.* commissione *f.* ♦ **e. boy** fattorino
erratic [ɪ'rætɪk] *agg.* **1** irregolare, incostante **2** eccentrico **3** (*geol.*) erratico
error [ɛrəʳ] *s.* **1** errore *m.*, sbaglio *m.* **2** colpa *f.*
to erupt [ɪ'rʌpt] **A** *v. intr.* **1** eruttare, entrare in eruzione **2** scoppiare **B** *v. tr.* eruttare
eruption [ɪ'rʌpʃ(ə)n] *s.* **1** eruzione *f.* **2** scoppio *m.*
erythema [ˌɛrɪ'θiːmə] *s.* eritema *m.*
to escalate ['ɛskəˌleɪt] *v. tr. e intr.* intensificare, aumentare
escalation [ˌɛskə'leɪʃ(ə)n] *s.* escalation *f. inv.*, intensificazione *f.*
escalator ['ɛskəleɪtəʳ] *s.* scala *f.* mobile
escalope ['ɛskələp] *s.* scaloppina *f.*
escapade [ˌɛskə'peɪd] *s.* scappatella *f.*
escape [ɪs'keɪp] *s.* **1** fuga *f.*, evasione *f.* **2** scampo *m.* **3** scarico *m.*, scappamento *m.*
to escape [ɪs'keɪp] *v. intr.* **1** fuggire, sfuggire, evadere **2** scamparla **3** fuoriuscire
escapism [ɪs'keɪpɪz(ə)m] *s.* evasione *f.* (dalla realtà)
escarpment [ɪs'kaːpmənt] *s.* scarpata *f.*
eschatological [ˌɛskətə'lədʒɪk(ə)l] *agg.* escatologico
escort ['ɛskɜːt] *s.* **1** scorta *f.* **2** accompagnatore *m.*, cavaliere *m.*
to escort [ɪs'kɜːt] *v. tr.* scortare, accompagnare
Eskimo ['ɛskɪmɒʊ] *agg. e s.* eschimese *m. e f.*
esoteric [ˌɛsɒʊ'tɛrɪk] *agg.* esoterico
especial [ɪs'pɛʃ(ə)l] *agg.* speciale, particolare
espionage [ˌɛspɪə'naːʒ] *s.* spionaggio *m.*
esplanade [ˌɛsplə'neɪd] *s.* passeggiata *f.*, spianata *f.*

essay ['ɛseɪ] *s.* **1** saggio *m.*, prova *f.*, tentativo *m.* **2** saggio *m.* (*libro*), composizione *f.* (*scolastica*)
essayist ['ɛseɪɪst] *s.* saggista *m. e f.*
essence ['ɛsns] *s.* essenza *f.*
essential [ɪ'sɛnʃ(ə)l] *agg.* essenziale
essentially [ɪ'sɛnʃ(ə)lɪ] *avv.* essenzialmente
to establish [ɪs'tæblɪʃ] **A** *v. tr.* **1** stabilire, costituire, fondare, impiantare **2** insediare, nominare **3** stabilire, dimostrare **B** *v. intr.* installarsi
established [ɪ'stæblɪʃt] *agg.* **1** istituito, fondato **2** provato, dimostrato **3** affermato, stabilito
establishment [ɪs'tæblɪʃmənt] *s.* **1** istituzione *f.*, fondazione *f.* **2** azienda *f.*, impresa *f.* **3** establishment *m. inv.*, classe *f.* dirigente
estate [ɪs'teɪt] *s.* **1** proprietà *f.*, tenuta *f.* **2** patrimonio *m.*, beni *m. pl.* **3** stato *m.*, condizione *f.* ♦ **e. agency** agenzia immobiliare; **real e.** beni immobili
esteem [ɪs'tiːm] *s.* stima *f.*
to esteem [ɪs'tiːm] *v. tr.* stimare
estimate ['ɛstɪmeɪt] *s.* **1** stima *f.*, valutazione *f.* **2** (*comm.*) preventivo *m.*
to estimate ['ɛstɪmeɪt] *v. tr.* **1** stimare, valutare **2** preventivare
estimation [ˌɛstɪ'meɪʃ(ə)n] *s.* **1** stima *f.*, apprezzamento *m.* **2** opinione *f.*
estimator ['ɛstɪmeɪtəʳ] *s.* (*comm.*) estimatore *m.*
to estrange [ɪs'treɪn(d)ʒ] *v. tr.* alienare, allontanare
estuary ['ɛstjʊərɪ] *s.* estuario *m.*
etching ['ɛtʃɪŋ] *s.* acquaforte *f.*
eternal [ɪ(ː)'tɜːnl] *agg.* eterno
eternity [ɪ(ː)'tɜːnɪtɪ] *s.* eternità *f.*
ether ['iːθəʳ] *s.* etere *m.*
ethereal [ɪ(ː)'θɪərɪəl] *agg.* etereo
ethical ['ɛθɪkl] *agg.* etico
ethics ['ɛθɪks] *s. pl.* (*v. al sing.*) etica *f.*
ethnic ['ɛθnɪk] *agg.* etnico
ethnology [ɛθ'nɔlədʒɪ] *s.* etnologia *f.*
etiquette [ɛtɪ'kɛt] *s.* etichetta *f.*, cerimoniale *m.*
Etruscan [ɪ'trʌskən] *agg. e s.* etrusco *m.*
etymology [ˌɛtɪ'mɔlədʒɪ] *s.* etimologia *f.*
euphemism ['juːfɪmɪz(ə)m] *s.* eufemismo *m.*
euphemistic [ˌjuːfɪ'mɪstɪk] *agg.* eufemistico
euphoria [jʊ(ː)'fɜːrɪə] *s.* euforia *f.*
European [ˌjʊərə'pɪ(ː)ən] *agg. e s.* europeo *m.*
Europeanism [ˌjʊərə'pɪ(ː)ənɪz(ə)m] *s.* europeismo *m.*
euthanasia [ˌjuːθə'neɪzjə] *s.* eutanasia *f.*
to evacuate [ɪ'vækjʊeɪt] *v. tr. e intr.* evacuare
to evade [ɪ'veɪd] *v. tr.* evitare, eludere
to evaluate [ɪ'væljʊeɪt] *v. tr.* valutare
evaluation [ɪˌvæljʊ'eɪʃ(ə)n] *s.* valutazione *f.*
evangelical [ˌiːvæn'dʒɛlɪk(ə)l] *agg.* evangelico
to evaporate [ɪ'væpəreɪt] *v. intr.* evaporare
evaporation [ɪˌvæpə'reɪʃ(ə)n] *s.* evaporazione *f.*
evasion [ɪ'veɪʒ(ə)n] *s.* **1** evasione *f.* **2** pretesto *m.*, scappatoia *f.* ♦ **tax e.** evasione fiscale
evasive [ɪ'veɪsɪv] *agg.* evasivo
eve [iːv] *s.* vigilia *f.*
even ['iːv(ə)n] **A** *agg.* **1** uguale, piano, uniforme **2** costante, regolare **3** pari, equo **4** (*mat.*) pari **B** *avv.* perfino, addirittura ♦ **e. if** anche se; **e. more** ancora di più; **e. so** ciò nonostante; **e. then** anche allora; **not e.** neppure
to even ['iːv(ə)n] *v. tr.* **1** appianare, livellare **2** uguagliare ♦ **to e. out** distribuire; **to e. up** pareggiare
evening ['iːvnɪŋ] *s.* sera *f.*, serata *f.* ♦ **last e.** ieri sera
event [ɪ'vɛnt] *s.* **1** caso *m.*, eventualità *f.* **2** avvenimento *m.*, fatto *m.* **3** (*sport*) prova *f.* ♦ **at all events** in ogni caso; **in the e.** di fatto; **in the e. of** in caso di
eventful [ɪ'vɛntfʊl] *agg.* pieno d'eventi, movimentato
eventual [ɪ'vɛntjʊəl] *agg.* finale, conclusivo
eventuality [ɪˌvɛntjʊ'ælɪtɪ] *s.* eventualità *f.*, evenienza *f.*
eventually [ɪ'vɛntjʊəlɪ] *avv.* infine, col tempo
ever ['ɛvəʳ] *avv.* **1** (*in frasi neg. e interr.*) mai **2** sempre ♦ **as e.** come sempre; **e. after** da allora; **e. since** sin da (quando), da allora in poi; **for e.** per sempre; **hardly e.** quasi sempre
evergreen ['ɛvəgriːn] *agg.* sempreverde
everlasting [ˌɛvə'laːstɪŋ] *agg.* perenne, eterno
every ['ɛvrɪ] *agg.* ogni, ciascuno ♦ **e. bit** tutto, del tutto; **e. day** tutti i giorni; **e. one** ciascuno, ognuno; **e. other day** un

giorno sì e uno no; **e. time** ogni volta; **in e. way** in tutto e per tutto
everybody ['ɛvrɪbədɪ] *pron. indef.* ciascuno, ognuno, tutti
everyday ['ɛvrɪdeɪ] *agg.* giornaliero, quotidiano, comune
everyone ['ɛvrɪwʌn] *pron. indef.* ciascuno, ognuno, tutti
everything ['ɛvrɪθɪŋ] *pron. indef.* tutto, ogni cosa
everywhere ['ɛvrɪwɛəʳ] *avv.* dovunque
to evict [ɪ(ː)'vɪkt] *v. tr.* sfrattare
eviction [ɪ(ː)'vɪkʃ(ə)n] *s.* sfratto *m.*
evidence ['ɛvɪd(ə)ns] *s.* **1** prova *f.*, dimostrazione *f.* **2** evidenza *f.* ♦ **to be called in e.** (*dir*) essere chiamato a testimoniare
evident ['ɛvɪd(ə)nt] *agg.* evidente
evil ['iːvl] **A** *agg.* **1** cattivo, malvagio **2** spiacevole **B** *s.* **1** male *m.*, malvagità *f.* **2** danno *m.*
evocative [ɪ'vəkətɪv] *agg.* suggestivo
to evoke [ɪ'vɒʊk] *v. tr.* **1** evocare **2** suscitare
evolution [ˌiːvə'luːʃ(ə)n] *s.* evoluzione *f.*
evolutive ['ɛvəlʊ(ː)tɪv] *agg.* evolutivo
to evolve [ɪ'vəlv] **A** *v. tr.* evolvere, sviluppare **B** *v. intr.* evolversi, svilupparsi
ewe [juː] *s.* pecora *f.* femmina
to exacerbate [ɛks'æsə(ː)beɪt] *v. tr.* esacerbare, inasprire
exact [ɪg'zækt] *agg.* esatto
to exact [ɪg'zækt] *v. tr.* **1** esigere, estorcere **2** pretendere, richiedere
exacting [ɪg'zæktɪŋ] *agg.* **1** esigente **2** impegnativo
exactly [ɪg'zæktlɪ] *avv.* esattamente, precisamente, proprio così
to exaggerate [ɪg'zædʒəreɪt] *v. tr. e intr.* esagerare
exaggeration [ɪgˌzædʒə'reɪʃ(ə)n] *s.* esagerazione *f.*
to exalt [ɪg'zɜːlt] *v. tr.* **1** innalzare, elevare **2** esaltare
exam [ɪg'zæm] *s.* esame *m.*
examination [ɪgˌzæmɪ'neɪʃ(ə)n] *s.* **1** esame *m.* **2** ispezione *f.*, verifica *f.* **3** (*med.*) controllo *m.*, visita *f.*
to examine [ɪg'zæmɪn] *v. tr.* **1** esaminare, controllare **2** interrogare **3** (*med.*) visitare
example [ɪg'zaːmpl] *s.* esempio *m.* ♦ **for e.** ad esempio
to exasperate [ɪg'zaːsp(ə)reɪt] *v. tr.* **1** esasperare **2** peggiorare, aggravare
exasperation [ɪgˌzaːspə'reɪʃ(ə)n] *s.* **1** esasperazione *f.* **2** peggioramento *m.*, aggravamento *m.*
to excavate ['ɛkskəveɪt] *v. tr.* scavare
excavation [ˌɛkskə'veɪʃ(ə)n] *s.* scavo *m.*
excavator ['ɛkskəveɪtəʳ] *s.* scavatrice *f.*
to exceed [ɪk'siːd] **A** *v. tr.* eccedere, oltrepassare, superare **B** *v. intr.* eccedere, esagerare
to excel [ɪk'sɛl] **A** *v. intr.* eccellere, primeggiare **B** *v. tr.* essere superiore a
excellent ['ɛksələnt] *agg.* eccellente, ottimo
except [ɪk'sɛpt] *prep.* eccetto, escluso, fuorché ♦ **e. for** fatta eccezione per; **e. that** salvo che; **e. when** tranne quando
exception [ɪk'sɛpʃ(ə)n] *s.* **1** eccezione *f.* **2** obiezione *f.*
exceptional [ɪk'sɛpʃənl] *agg.* eccezionale
excerpt ['ɛksɜːpt] *s.* estratto *m.*, passo *m.* scelto
excess [ɪk'sɛs] **A** *s.* **1** eccesso *m.*, abuso *m.* **2** eccedenza *f.* **B** *agg.* eccedente, in eccesso ♦ **e. fare** supplemento di tariffa
excessive [ɪk'sɛsɪv] *agg.* eccessivo
exchange [ɪks'tʃeɪn(d)ʒ] *s.* **1** scambio *m.* **2** (*econ.*) cambio *m.* **3** Borsa *f.*, mercato *m.* **4** (*tel.*) centralino *m.* ♦ **e. rate** tasso di cambio; **Stock E.** Borsa valori
to exchange [ɪks'tʃeɪn(d)ʒ] *v. tr.* **1** cambiare, scambiare, permutare **2** (*valuta*) cambiare
excise [ɛk'saɪz] *s.* dazio *m.*, imposta *f.*
excitable [ɪk'saɪtəbl] *agg.* eccitabile
to excite [ɪk'saɪt] *v. tr.* **1** eccitare, animare **2** suscitare
exciting [ɪk'saɪtɪŋ] *agg.* eccitante, emozionante, stimolante
to exclaim [ɪks'kleɪm] *v. tr. e intr.* esclamare
exclamation [ˌɛksklə'meɪʃ(ə)n] *s.* esclamazione *f.*, grido *m.* ♦ **e. mark** punto esclamativo
to exclude [ɪks'kluːd] *v. tr.* escludere
exclusion [ɪks'kluːʒ(ə)n] *s.* esclusione *f.*
exclusive [ɪks'kluːsɪv] *agg.* esclusivo ♦ **e. of** a esclusione di, escluso
to excommunicate [ˌɛkskə'mjuːnɪkeɪt] *v. tr.* scomunicare
excommunication ['ɛkskəˌmjuːnɪ'keɪʃ(ə)n] *s.* scomunica *f.*
to excoriate [ɛks'kɜːrɪeɪt] *v. tr.* escoriare, scorticare
excoriation [ɛksˌkɜːrɪ'eɪʃ(ə)n] *s.* escoriazione *f.*
excruciating [ɪks'krʊ(ː)ʃɪeɪtɪŋ] *agg.* stra-

ziante, atroce
to **exculpate** ['ɛkskʌlpeɪt] *v. tr.* discolpare, scagionare
excursion [ɪks'kɜːʃ(ə)n] *s.* escursione *f.*, gita *f.*
excursionist [ɪks'kɜːʃnɪst] *s.* escursionista *m. e f.*, gitante *m. e f.*
excuse [ɪks'kjuːs] *s.* **1** scusa *f.*, giustificazione *f.* **2** pretesto *m.*
to **excuse** [ɪks'kjuːz] *v. tr.* **1** scusare, perdonare **2** giustificare **3** dispensare ♦ **e. me!** (mi) scusi!
to **execute** ['ɛksɪkjuːt] *v. tr.* **1** giustiziare **2** eseguire, mettere in atto **3** interpretare
execution [ˌɛksɪ'kjuːʃ(ə)n] *s.* **1** esecuzione *f.* capitale **2** esecuzione *f.*
executioner [ˌɛksɪ'kjuːʃnəʳ] *s.* boia *m.*
executive [ɪg'zɛkjʊtɪv] **A** *agg.* **1** esecutivo **2** direttivo **B** *s.* **1** (potere) esecutivo *m.* **2** dirigente *m. e f.*, funzionario *m.*
exedra [ɛk'sɪ(ː)drə] *s.* esedra *f.*
exemplary [ɪg'zɛmplərɪ] *agg.* esemplare
exemplification [ɪgˌzɛmplɪfɪ'keɪʃ(ə)n] *s.* esemplificazione *f.*
to **exemplify** [ɪg'zɛmplɪfaɪ] *v. tr.* esemplificare
exempt [ɪg'zɛm(p)t] *agg.* esente, dispensato
to **exempt** [ɪg'zɛm(p)t] *v. tr.* esentare, dispensare
exemption [ɪg'zɛm(p)ʃ(ə)n] *s.* esenzione *f.*, dispensa *f.*
exercise ['ɛksəsaɪz] *s.* **1** esercizio *m.*, pratica *f.* **2** moto *m.*, esercizio *m.* fisico **3** esercizio *m.*, compito *m.*, esercitazione *f.* ♦ **e. book** quaderno
to **exercise** ['ɛksəsaɪz] **A** *v. tr.* **1** esercitare, praticare **2** allenare **3** preoccupare **B** *v. intr.* esercitarsi, allenarsi
to **exert** [ɪg'zɜːt] *v. tr.* impiegare, esercitare
exertion [ɪg'zɜːʃ(ə)n] *s.* **1** esercizio *m.*, impiego *m.* **2** sforzo *m.*
exhalation [ˌɛks(h)ə'leɪʃ(ə)n] *s.* esalazione *f.*
to **exhale** [ɛks'heɪl] **A** *v. tr.* esalare, emanare **B** *v. intr.* evaporare
exhaust [ɪg'zɜːst] *s.* scarico *m.*, scappamento *m.* ♦ **e. pipe** tubo di scarico
to **exhaust** [ɪg'zɜːst] *v. tr.* **1** esaurire **2** vuotare **3** aspirare **4** scaricare
exhausted [ɪg'zə(ː)stɪd] *agg.* esausto, esaurito
exhaustion [ɪg'zɜːstʃ(ə)n] *s.* **1** esaurimento *m.* **2** spossatezza *f.*
exhaustive [ɪg'zɜːstɪv] *agg.* esauriente
to **exhibit** [ɪg'zɪbɪt] *v. tr.* esibire
exhibition [ˌɛksɪ'bɪʃ(ə)n] *s.* esposizione *f.*, mostra *f.*
exhilaration [ɪgˌzɪlə'reɪʃ(ə)n] *s.* euforia *f.*
to **exhort** [ɪg'zɜːt] *v. tr.* esortare
exhortation [ˌɛgzɜː'teɪʃ(ə)n] *s.* esortazione *f.*
to **exhume** [ɛks'hjuːm] *v. tr.* esumare
exiguous [ɛg'zɪgjʊəs] *agg.* esiguo
exile ['ɛksaɪl] *s.* **1** esilio *m.* **2** esule *m. e f.*, esiliato *m.*
to **exile** ['ɛksaɪl] *v. tr.* esiliare
to **exist** [ɪg'zɪst] *v. intr.* esistere
existence [ɪg'zɪst(ə)ns] *s.* esistenza *f.*
existing [ɪg'zɪstɪŋ] *agg.* esistente
exit ['ɛksɪt] *s.* uscita *f.* ♦ **emergency e.** uscita di sicurezza
exodus ['ɛksədəs] *s.* esodo *m.*
to **exonerate** [ɪg'zɒnəreɪt] *v. tr.* **1** esonerare **2** discolpare
exorbitant [ɪg'zɜːbɪtənt] *agg.* esorbitante
to **exorcize** ['ɛksɜːsaɪz] *v. tr.* esorcizzare
exotic [ɛg'zɒtɪk] *agg.* esotico
to **expand** [ɪks'pænd] **A** *v. tr.* **1** espandere, dilatare **2** estendere, ingrandire **B** *v. intr.* **1** espandersi, dilatarsi **2** ingrandirsi, ampliarsi
expanse [ɪks'pæns] *s.* **1** distesa *f.*, estensione *f.* **2** espansione *f.*
expansion [ɪks'pænʃ(ə)n] *s.* **1** espansione *f.*, dilatazione *f.* **2** sviluppo *m.*, crescita *f.*
expansive [ɪks'pænsɪv] *agg.* **1** espansibile, dilatabile **2** (*di persona*) espansivo
to **expatriate** [ɛks'pætrɪeɪt] *v. intr.* espatriare
to **expect** [ɪks'pɛkt] *v. tr.* **1** aspettare, aspettarsi, prevedere **2** esigere, pretendere **3** supporre
expectancy [ɪks'pɛkt(ə)nsɪ] *s.* aspettativa *f.*, attesa *f.*
expectant [ɪks'pɛkt(ə)nt] *agg.* speranzoso, in attesa ♦ **e. mother** gestante
expectation [ˌɛkspɛk'teɪʃ(ə)n] *s.* aspettativa *f.*, attesa *f.*
expedience [ɪks'piːdjəns] *s.* **1** opportunità *f.*, convenienza *f.* **2** opportunismo *m.*
expedient [ɪks'piːdjənt] **A** *agg.* conveniente, opportuno **B** *s.* espediente *m.*, ripiego *m.*
expedition [ˌɛkspɪ'dɪʃ(ə)n] *s.* spedizione *f.*
expeditious [ˌɛkspɪ'dɪʃəs] *agg.* sbrigativo

to expel [ɪks'pɛl] *v. tr.* **1** espellere, scacciare **2** emettere
to expend [ɪks'pɛnd] *v. tr.* **1** spendere, impiegare **2** consumare
expendable [ɪks'pɛndəbl] *agg.* **1** spendibile **2** sacrificabile
expenditure [ɪks'pɛndɪtʃəʳ] *s.* **1** dispendio *m.*, consumo *m.* **2** spesa *f.*
expense [ɪks'pɛns] *s.* **1** spesa *f.*, costo *m.* **2** *al pl.* spese *f. pl.*, indennità *f.*
expensive [ɪks'pɛnsɪv] *agg.* costoso, caro
experience [ɪks'pɪərɪəns] *s.* esperienza *f.*
to experience [ɪks'pɪərɪəns] *v. tr.* esperimentare, provare
experiment [ɪks'pɛrɪmənt] *s.* esperimento *m.*, prova *f.*
to experiment [ɪks'pɛrɪmɛnt] *v. intr.* sperimentare, fare esperimenti
experimental [ɛksˌpɛrɪ'mɛntl] *agg.* sperimentale
expert ['ɛkspɜːt] **A** *agg.* esperto, competente **B** *s.* esperto *m.*, perito *m.*
expertise [ˌɛkspə(ː)'tɪ(ː)z] *s.* **1** abilità *f.*, competenza *f.* **2** (*arte*) perizia *f.*
to expiate ['ɛkspɪeɪt] *v. tr.* espiare
expiration [ˌɛkspɪ'reɪʃ(ə)n] *s.* **1** espirazione *f.* **2** scadenza *f.*
to expire [ɪks'paɪəʳ] **A** *v. intr.* **1** scadere, finire **2** morire, svanire **B** *v. tr.* espirare
expiry [ɪks'paɪərɪ] *s.* scadenza *f.*, termine *m.*
to explain [ɪks'pleɪn] *v. tr.* spiegare, chiarire
explanation [ˌɛksplə'neɪʃ(ə)n] *s.* spiegazione *f.*
explanatory [ɪks'plænət(ə)rɪ] *agg.* esplicativo
explicative [ɛks'plɪkətɪv] *agg.* esplicativo
explicit [ɪks'plɪsɪt] *agg.* esplicito
to explode [ɪks'plɒʊd] **A** *v. tr.* **1** far esplodere **2** screditare, smontare **B** *v. intr.* esplodere, scoppiare
exploit ['ɛksplɔɪt] *s.* impresa *f.*, prodezza *f.*
to exploit [ɪks'plɔɪt] *v. tr.* sfruttare
exploitation [ˌɛksplɔɪ'teɪʃ(ə)n] *s.* sfruttamento *m.*
exploiter [ɪks'plɔɪtəʳ] *s.* sfruttatore *m.*
exploration [ˌɛksplɜː'reɪʃ(ə)n] *s.* esplorazione *f.*
to explore [ɪks'plɜːʳ] *v. tr.* **1** esplorare **2** analizzare
explorer [ɪks'plɜːrəʳ] *s.* esploratore *m.*
explosion [ɪks'plɒʊʒ(ə)n] *s.* esplosione *f.*, scoppio *m.*
explosive [ɪks'plɒʊsɪv] *agg. e s.* esplosivo *m.*
exponent [ɛks'pɒʊnənt] *s.* esponente *m. e f.*
export ['ɛkspɜːt] *s.* **1** esportazione *f.* **2** prodotto *m.* d'esportazione
to export [ɛks'pɜːt] *v. tr.* esportare
exporter [ɛks'pə(ː)təʳ] *s.* esportatore *m.*
to expose [ɪks'pɒʊz] *v. tr.* **1** esporre **2** svelare, smascherare
exposition [ˌɛkspə'zɪʃ(ə)n] *s.* **1** esposizione *f.* **2** spiegazione *f.*
exposure [ɪks'pɒʊʒəʳ] *s.* **1** esposizione *f.* **2** mostra *f.* **3** (*fot.*) (tempo di) esposizione *f.* ♦ **e. meter** esposimetro
to expound [ɪks'paʊnd] *v. tr.* esporre, spiegare
express [ɪks'prɛs] **A** *agg.* **1** chiaro, esplicito **2** espresso, rapido **3** esatto, fedele **B** *s.* **1** (*corrispondenza*) espresso *m.* **2** (treno) espresso *m.*
to express [ɪks'prɛs] *v. tr.* **1** esprimere **2** mandare per espresso
expression [ɪks'prɛʃ(ə)n] *s.* espressione *f.*
expressionism [ɪks'prɛʃnɪz(ə)m] *s.* espressionismo *m.*
expressive [ɪks'prɛsɪv] *agg.* espressivo, significativo
expressly [ɪks'prɛslɪ] *avv.* espressamente
expressway [ɪks'prɛsweɪ] *s.* (*USA*) autostrada *f.*
expropriation [ɛksˌprɒʊprɪ'eɪʃ(ə)n] *s.* esproprio *m.*, espropriazione *f.*
expulsion [ɪks'pʌlʃ(ə)n] *s.* espulsione *f.*
exquisite ['ɛkskwɪzɪt] *agg.* squisito
extemporary [ɪks'tɛmp(ə)rərɪ] *agg.* estemporaneo
to extend [ɪks'tɛnd] **A** *v. tr.* **1** estendere, allargare, ampliare **2** prorogare, protrarre, prolungare **3** offrire, porgere **B** *v. intr.* **1** estendersi, allungarsi **2** protrarsi
extension [ɪks'tɛnʃ(ə)n] *s.* **1** estensione *f.*, prolungamento *m.*, ampliamento *m.* **2** proroga *f.* **3** (*di edificio*) prolunga *f.*, ampliamento *m.* **4** (*tel.*) interno *m.*
extensive [ɪks'tɛnsɪv] *agg.* **1** esteso, vasto **2** estensivo
extent [ɪks'tɛnt] *s.* **1** estensione *f.*, ampiezza *f.* **2** limite *m.*, grado *m.*
to extenuate [ɛks'tɛnjʊeɪt] *v. tr.* attenuare
exterior [ɛks'tɪərɪəʳ] **A** *agg.* esterno, esteriore **B** *s.* **1** esterno *m.* **2** esteriorità *f.*
to exterminate [ɛks'tɜːmɪneɪt] *v. tr.* sterminare, distruggere
extermination [ɛksˌtɜːmɪ'neɪʃ(ə)n] *s.* sterminio *m.*, distruzione *f.*

external [ɛks'tɜːnl] *agg.* **1** esterno, esteriore **2** estero **3** superficiale
extinct [ɪks'tɪŋkt] *agg.* estinto
extinction [ɪks'tɪŋkʃ(ə)n] *s.* estinzione *f.*
to **extinguish** [ɪks'tɪŋgwɪʃ] *v. tr.* estinguere, spegnere
extinguisher [ɪks'tɪŋgʊɪʃəʳ] *s.* estintore *m.*
to **extirpate** ['ɛkstɜːpeɪt] *v. tr.* estirpare
to **extort** [ɪks'tɜːt] *v. tr.* estorcere
extortionate [ɪks'tɜːʃnɪt] *agg.* esorbitante
extra ['ɛkstrə] **A** *agg.* aggiuntivo, supplementare **B** *avv.* extra, in più
extract ['ɛkstrækt] *s.* **1** estratto *m.* **2** citazione *f.*
to **extract** [ɪks'trækt] *v. tr.* estrarre
extractable [ɪks'træktəbl] *agg.* estraibile
extraction [ɪks'trækʃ(ə)n] *s.* estrazione *f.*
extradition [ˌɛkstrə'dɪʃ(ə)n] *s.* estradizione *f.*
extrados [ɛks'treɪdəs] *s.* estradosso *m.*
extramarital [ˌɛkstrə'mærɪtl] *agg.* extraconiugale
extramural [ˌɛkstrə'mjʊər(ə)l] *agg.* fuori dell'università
extraneous [ɛks'treɪnjəs] *agg.* estraneo
extraordinary [ɪks'trɜːd(ə)n(ə)rɪ] *agg.* straordinario, eccezionale
extraterrestrial [ˌɛkstrətɪ'rɛstrɪəl] *agg.* extraterrestre
extravagance [ɪks'trævɪgəns] *s.* **1** stravaganza *f.* **2** prodigalità *f.*
extravagant [ɪks'trævɪgənt] *agg.* **1** stravagante **2** prodigo
extreme [ɪks'triːm] **A** *agg.* **1** estremo, ultimo **2** eccezionale **B** *s.* estremo *m.*, estremità *f.*
extremist [ɪks'triːmɪst] *s.* estremista *m. e f.*
extremity [ɪks'trɛmɪtɪ] *s.* estremità *f.*
to **extricate** ['ɛkstrɪkeɪt] *v. tr.* districare, sbrogliare
extrinsic [ɛks'trɪnsɪk] *agg.* estrinseco
extrovert [ˌɛkstrɒ(ʊ)'vɜːt] *agg. e s.* estroverso *m.*
extroverted [ˌɛkstrɒ(ʊ)'vɜːtɪd] *agg.* estroverso
exuberant [ɪg'zjuːb(ə)r(ə)nt] *agg.* esuberante
to **exude** [ɪg'zjuːd] *v. tr. e intr.* essudare, trasudare
to **exult** [ɪg'zʌlt] *v. intr.* esultare
eye [aɪ] *s.* **1** occhio *m.*, sguardo *m.* **2** (*bot.*) gemma *f.* **3** occhiello *m.*, cruna *f.* ♦ **e. ball** bulbo oculare; **e.-opener** fatto rivelatore; **e. socket** orbita; **e. shadow** ombretto; **e. witness** testimone oculare
eyebrow ['aɪbraʊ] *s.* sopracciglio *m.*
eyelash ['aɪlæʃ] *s.* ciglio *m.*
eyelid ['aɪlɪd] *s.* palpebra *f.*
eyesight ['aɪsaɪt] *s.* vista *f.*

F

fable ['feɪbl] *s.* **1** favola *f.* **2** mito *m.*, leggenda *f.*
fabric ['fæbrɪk] *s.* **1** tessuto *m.*, stoffa *f.* **2** (*fig.*) struttura *f.*
to fabricate ['fæbrɪkeɪt] *v. tr.* **1** architettare, falsificare **2** fabbricare
fabrication [ˌfæbrɪ'keɪʃ(ə)n] *s.* **1** invenzione *f.* **2** falsificazione *f.*, contraffazione *f.*
fabulous ['fæbjʊləs] *agg.* favoloso
façade [fə'sɑːd] *s.* facciata *f.*
face [feɪs] *s.* **1** faccia *f.*, volto *m.* **2** facciata *f.*, fronte *m.* ♦ **f. down** a faccia in giù; **f. mask** maschera di bellezza; **f. powder** cipria; **f. to f.** faccia a faccia; **in the f. of** di fronte a, a dispetto di; **on the f. of it** a prima vista
to face [feɪs] *v. tr.* **1** fronteggiare, essere di fronte a, essere volto a **2** affrontare, tener testa a **3** ricoprire ♦ **to f. out** tener duro, far fronte
facet [fæsɪt] *s.* sfaccettatura *f.*
facetious [fə'siːʃəs] *agg.* faceto
facial ['feɪʃ(ə)l] *agg.* facciale
facile ['fæsaɪl] *agg.* **1** facile **2** svelto, abile **3** superficiale
facilitation [fəˌsɪlɪ'teɪʃ(ə)n] *s.* facilitazione *f.*, agevolazione *f.*
facility [fə'sɪlɪtɪ] *s.* **1** facilitazione *f.*, agevolazione *f.* **2** *al pl.* attrezzature *f. pl.*, mezzi *m. pl.*, servizi *m. pl.*
facing ['feɪsɪŋ] **A** *agg.* prospiciente **B** *s.* **1** rivestimento *m.* **2** risvolto *m.*
facsimile [fæk'sɪmɪlɪ] *s.* facsimile *m. inv.*
fact [fækt] *s.* **1** fatto *m.*, avvenimento *m.* **2** realtà *f.*
factious ['fækʃəs] *agg.* fazioso
factor ['fæktəʳ] *s.* fattore *m.*, coefficiente *m.*
factoring ['fæktərɪŋ] *s.* factoring *m. inv.*
factory ['fækt(ə)rɪ] *s.* fabbrica *f.*, stabilimento *m.*, manifattura *f.*
factual ['fæktjʊəl] *agg.* effettivo, reale
faculty ['fæk(ə)ltɪ] *s.* facoltà *f.*
fad [fæd] capriccio *m.*, mania *f.*
fade [feɪd] *s.* (*cine.*) dissolvenza *f.*
to fade [feɪd] **A** *v. intr.* **1** avvizzire, appassire **2** scolorire, sbiadire **3** svanire **B** *v. tr.* **1** far appassire **2** scolorire ♦ **to f. in** rinforzarsi, aumentare di intensità; **to f. out** affievolirsi, dissolversi
fading ['feɪdɪŋ] *s.* **1** appassimento *m.* **2** (*cine.*) dissolvenza *f.* **3** (*fig.*) tramonto *m.*
faeces ['fiːsiːz] *s. pl.* feci *f. pl.*
fag (1) [fæg] *s.* (*fam.*) faticata *f.*, sgobbata *f.*
fag (2) [fæg] *s.* (*pop.*) sigaretta *f.*, cicca *f.*
faience [faɪ'ɑː(n)s] *s.* ceramica *f.*, porcellana *f.*
fail [feɪl] *s.* fallo *m.*, insuccesso *m.* ♦ **without f.** senza fallo, certamente
to fail [feɪl] **A** *v. intr.* **1** fallire, non riuscire **2** mancare, venir meno **3** essere respinto, essere bocciato **B** *v. tr.* **1** bocciare, respingere **2** non superare
failing ['feɪlɪŋ] **A** *agg.* debole, scarso **B** *s.* **1** debolezza *f.*, difetto *m.* **2** mancanza *f.* **C** *prep.* in mancanza di
failure ['feɪljəʳ] *s.* **1** fallimento *m.*, insuccesso *m.* **2** mancanza *f.*, difetto *m.* **3** (*mecc.*) guasto *m.*
faint [feɪnt] **A** *agg.* **1** debole, esile, pallido **2** languido, fiacco **3** timido **4** vago **B** *s.* svenimento *m.*
to faint [feɪnt] *v. intr.* svenire ♦ **to feel f.** sentirsi svenire
fair (1) [fɛəʳ] **A** *agg.* **1** giusto, leale, onesto **2** discreto, sufficiente **3** biondo, chiaro **4** sereno, propizio, favorevole **5** gentile, affabile **B** *avv.* **1** giustamente **2** correttamente, onestamente **3** in bella copia
fair (2) [fɛəʳ] *s.* fiera *f.* ♦ **trade f.** fiera campionaria
fairly ['fɛəlɪ] *avv.* **1** discretamente, abbastanza **2** equamente, onestamente
fairness ['fɛənɪs] *s.* **1** bellezza *f.* **2** equità *f.*, imparzialità *f.*
fair play [ˌfɛə'pleɪ] *s.* fair play *m. inv.*, correttezza *f.*
fairy ['fɛərɪ] **A** *agg.* fatato, magico **B** *s.* fata *f.* ♦ **f. tale** fiaba
faith [feɪθ] *s.* **1** fede *f.*, fiducia *f.* **2** lealtà *f.*
faithful ['feɪθf(ʊ)l] *agg.* **1** fedele, leale **2** accurato
faithfully ['feɪθf(ʊ)lɪ] *avv.* **1** fedelmente, lealmente **2** accuratamente ♦ **yours f.** distinti saluti
faithfulness ['feɪθf(ʊ)lnɪs] *s.* **1** fedeltà *f.*, lealtà *f.* **2** esattezza *f.*
fake [feɪk] **A** *s.* **1** impostore *m.* **2** falsifi-

cazione *f.*, falso *m.* **B** *agg.* falso
to fake [feɪk] *v. tr.* **1** falsificare, contraffare **2** fingere
fakir ['fɑːkɪəʳ] *s.* fachiro *m.*
falcon ['fɜːlkən] *s.* falco *m.*, falcone *m.*
fall [fɜːl] *s.* **1** caduta *f.*, crollo *m.* **2** discesa *f.*, pendio *m.* **3** *spec. al pl.* cascata *f.* **4** ribasso *m.*, diminuzione *f.* **5** (*USA*) autunno *m.* ♦ **f. off** contrazione
to fall [fɜːl] (*pass.* **fell**, *p. p.* **fallen**) *v. intr.* **1** cadere, precipitare **2** diminuire **3** suddividersi **4** riversarsi, sfociare ♦ **to f. asleep** addormentarsi; **to f. back** indietreggiare, ritirarsi; **to f. back on** ripiegare su, ricorrere a; **to f. down** crollare; **to f. for** prendere una cotta per; **to f. ill** ammalarsi; **to f. in** crollare; **to f. in love** innamorarsi; **to f. off** cadere, diminuire; **to f. on** gettarsi su; **to f. out** cadere, litigare; **to f. through** fallire
fallacy ['fæləsɪ] *s.* errore *m.*, credenza *f.* errata
fallen ['fɜːl(ə)n] *p. p. di* **to fall**
falling ['fɜːlɪŋ] **A** *agg.* cadente **B** *s.* **1** caduta *f.* **2** decadimento *m.*, abbassamento *m.*
fallout ['fɜːl,aʊt] *s.* ricaduta *f.* radioattiva
fallow ['fælɒʊ] *agg.* incolto
false [fɜːls] **A** *agg.* **1** falso, falsificato, posticcio **2** errato, sbagliato **3** illusorio **B** *avv.* falsamente, slealmente
falsification [,fɜːlsɪfɪ'keɪʃ(ə)n] *s.* falsificazione *f.*
falsifier ['fɜːlsɪfaɪəʳ] *s.* falsario *m.*
to falsify ['fɜːlsɪfaɪ] *v. tr.* falsificare, truccare
to falter ['fɜːltəʳ] *v. intr.* **1** barcollare, esitare **2** balbettare
fame [feɪm] *s.* fama *f.*, rinomanza *f.*
familiar [fə'mɪljəʳ] *agg.* **1** familiare **2** consueto, comune ♦ **to be f. with** conoscere bene
to familiarize [fə'mɪljəraɪz] *v. tr.* rendere familiare ♦ **to f. oneself** familiarizzarsi
family ['fæmɪlɪ] **A** *s.* **1** famiglia *f.* **2** gruppo *m.* **B** *agg. attr.* familiare ♦ **f. name** cognome
famine ['fæmɪn] *s.* carestia *f.*
to famish ['fæmɪʃ] **A** *v. tr.* affamare **B** *v. intr.* morire di fame
famous ['feɪməs] *agg.* famoso
fan (1) [fæn] *s.* **1** ventaglio *m.* **2** ventilatore *m.*, ventola *f.*
fan (2) [fæn] *s.* fan *m. e f. inv.*, ammiratore *m.*
to fan [fæn] **A** *v. tr.* sventolare, fare vento **B** *v. intr.* aprirsi a ventaglio
fanatic [fə'nætɪk] *agg.* fanatico, tifoso
fanaticism [fə'nætɪsɪz(ə)m] *s.* fanatismo *m.*
fanciful ['fænsɪf(ʊ)l] *agg.* fantastico, fantasioso, immaginario
fancy ['fænsɪ] **A** *s.* **1** immaginazione *f.*, fantasia *f.* **2** capriccio *m.* **3** inclinazione *f.* **B** *agg. attr.* **1** di fantasia **2** speciale **3** stravagante, elaborato ♦ **f. dress** costume in maschera
to fancy ['fænsɪ] **A** *v. tr.* **1** immaginare, pensare **2** gradire, aver voglia di **B** *v. intr.* fantasticare
fang [fæŋ] *s.* **1** zanna *f.* **2** (*spec. di serpente*) dente *m.*
fantastic [fæn'tæstɪk] *agg.* fantastico
fantasy ['fæntəsɪ] *s.* **1** fantasia *f.*, immaginazione *f.* **2** fantasticheria *f.*
far [fɑːʳ] (*comp.* **farther**, **further**, *sup. rel.* **farthest**, **furthest**) **A** *agg.* lontano **B** *avv.* **1** lontano **2** assai, di gran lunga ♦ **as f. as** per quanto riguarda, fino a; **by f.** di gran lunga; **f. from** lontano da; **f. reaching** di vasta portata; **f. seeing** lungimirante; **how f.?** quanto lontano?, fino a dove?; **so f.** finora; **the Far East** l'Estremo Oriente
faraway ['fɑːrəweɪ] *agg.* **1** lontano, distante **2** assente
farce [fɑːs] *s.* farsa *f.*
farcical ['fɑːsɪk(ə)l] *agg.* farsesco
fare [fɛəʳ] *s.* **1** (*mezzo di trasporto, taxi*) prezzo *m.* della corsa, tariffa *f.* **2** passeggero *m.* **3** cibo *m.*, vitto *m.*
farewell [,fɛə'wɛl] **A** *s.* commiato *m.*, addio *m.* **B** *inter.* addio!
farinaceous [,færɪ'neɪʃəs] *agg.* farinaceo
farm [fɑːm] *s.* **1** podere *m.* **2** fattoria *f.* **3** allevamento *m.* ♦ **f. holidays** agriturismo
to farm [fɑːm] *v. tr.* **1** coltivare **2** allevare
farmer ['fɑːməʳ] *s.* **1** agricoltore *m.*, contadino *m.* **2** allevatore *m.*
farmhand ['fɑːm,hænd] *s.* bracciante *m.*
farmhouse ['fɑːmhaʊs] *s.* fattoria *f.*
farming ['fɑːmɪŋ] *s.* agricoltura *f.*, coltivazione *f.*
farrier ['færɪəʳ] *s.* maniscalco *m.*
farther ['fɑːðəʳ] (*comp. di* **far**) **A** *agg.* **1** più lontano, più distante **2** addizionale **B** *avv.* **1** oltre, più lontano **2** in più
farthest ['fɑːðɪst] (*sup. rel. di* **far**) **A** *agg.* il più lontano, più distante **B** *avv.* il più lontano possibile

to fascinate ['fæsɪneɪt] *v. tr.* affascinare
fascinating ['fæsɪneɪtɪŋ] *agg.* affascinante
fascination [ˌfæsɪ'neɪʃ(ə)n] *s.* fascino *m.*
Fascism ['fæʃɪz(ə)m] *s.* fascismo *m.*
fashion ['fæʃ(ə)n] *s.* **1** foggia *f.*, maniera *f.* **2** moda *f.* ♦ **in f.** alla moda; **out of f.** fuori moda
fashionable ['fæʃ(ə)nəbl] *agg.* alla moda
fast (1) [fa:st] **A** *agg.* **1** veloce, rapido **2** fisso, solido **B** *avv.* **1** velocemente, in fretta **2** saldamente, fermamente
fast (2) [fa:st] *s.* digiuno *m.*
to fast [fa:st] *v. intr.* digiunare
to fasten ['fa:sn] **A** *v. tr.* **1** attaccare, fissare **2** allacciare **B** *v. intr.* chiudersi, allacciarsi
fastening ['fa:snɪŋ] *s.* chiusura *f.*
fastidious [fæs'tɪdɪəs] *agg.* meticoloso
fat [fæt] **A** *agg.* **1** grasso, untuoso **2** adiposo, grosso **3** pingue, fertile **B** *s.* grasso *m.*
fatal ['feɪtl] *agg.* **1** fatidico, fatale **2** disastroso
fatalist ['feɪt(ə)lɪst] *s.* fatalista *m. e f.*
fatality [fə'tælɪtɪ] *s.* **1** fatalità *f.* **2** morte *f.* violenta
fate [feɪt] *s.* fato *m.*, sorte *f.*
fateful ['feɪtf(ʊ)l] *agg.* fatale, fatidico
father ['fa:ðə^r] *s.* padre *m.* ♦ **f.-in-law** suocero
fatherhood ['fa:ðəhʊd] *s.* paternità *f.*
fatherly ['fa:ðəlɪ] *agg.* paterno
fathom ['fæðəm] *s.* braccio *m.* (*misura*)
fatigue [fə'ti:g] *s.* fatica *f.*, stanchezza *f.*
to fatten ['fætn] *v. tr. e intr.* ingrassare
fatty ['fætɪ] **A** *agg.* grasso, untuoso **B** *s.* (*fam.*) grassone *m.*, ciccione *m.*
fatuous ['fætjʊəs] *agg.* fatuo
faucet ['fɜ:sɪt] *s.* (*USA*) rubinetto *m.*
fault [fɜ:lt] *s.* **1** difetto *m.* **2** colpa *f.* **3** mancanza *f.*, errore *m.* **4** (*sport*) fallo *m.* **5** (*geol.*) faglia *f.*
faultless ['fɜ:ltlɪs] *agg.* inappuntabile
faulty ['fɜ:ltɪ] *agg.* **1** difettoso **2** scorretto
faun [fɜ:n] *s.* fauno *m.*
fauna ['fɜ:nə] *s.* fauna *f.*
favour ['feɪvə^r] (*USA* **favor**) *s.* **1** favore *m.*, benevolenza *f.* **2** cortesia *f.* ♦ **to be in f. of** essere favorevole a
to favour ['feɪvə^r] (*USA* **favor**) *v. tr.* favorire, proteggere
favourable ['feɪv(ə)rəbl] *agg.* favorevole, vantaggioso
favourite ['feɪv(ə)rɪt] *agg. e s.* favorito *m.*
favouritism ['feɪv(ə)rɪtɪz(ə)m] *s.* favoritismo *m.*
fawn [fɜ:n] *s.* daino *m.*, cerbiatto *m.*
fax [fæks] *s.* fax *m. inv.*
to fax [fæks] *v. tr.* trasmettere via fax
fear [fɪə^r] *s.* timore *m.*, spavento *m.*, paura *f.*
to fear [fɪə^r] *v. tr.* temere
fearful ['fɪəf(ʊ)l] *agg.* **1** spaventoso **2** pauroso **3** spaventato
fearless ['fɪəlɪs] *agg.* intrepido
feasible ['fi:zəbl] *agg.* fattibile
feast [fi:st] *s.* **1** festa *f.* **2** banchetto *m.*
to feast [fi:st] *v. intr.* banchettare
feat [fi:t] *s.* prodezza *f.*, atto *m.*
feather ['fɛðə^r] *s.* penna *f.*, piuma *f.*
feature ['fi:tʃə^r] *s.* **1** sembianza *f.* **2** caratteristica *f.*, aspetto *m.* **3** (*TV, stampa*) numero *m.*, servizio *m.* principale ♦ **f. film** lungometraggio
to feature ['fi:tʃə^r] *v. tr.* **1** rappresentare **2** avere come protagonista
February ['fɛbrʊərɪ] *s.* febbraio *m.*
to fecundate ['fi:kəndeɪt] *v. tr.* fecondare
fed [fɛd] *pass. e p. p. di* **to feed** ♦ **f. up** (*fam.*) stufo
federal ['fɛdərəl] *agg.* federale
federation [ˌfɛdə'reɪʃ(ə)n] *s.* federazione *f.*
fee [fi:] *s.* **1** tassa *f.* **2** compenso *m.*, onorario *m.* ♦ **school fees** tasse scolastiche
feeble ['fi:bl] *agg.* debole, fragile
to feed [fi:d] (*pass. e p. p.* **fed**) *v. tr.* **1** cibare, nutrire **2** imboccare **3** (*mecc.*) alimentare ♦ **to f. oneself** nutrirsi
feedback ['fi:dbæk] *s.* retroazione *f.*, feedback *m. inv.*
feeding ['fi:dɪŋ] **A** *agg.* **1** nutriente **2** di alimentazione **B** *s.* nutrizione *f.*, alimentazione *f.* ♦ **f. bottle** biberon
feel [fi:l] *s.* **1** tatto *m.*, tocco *m.* **2** sensibilità *f.* **3** (*fig.*) atmosfera *f.*
to feel [fi:l] (*pass. e p. p.* **felt**) **A** *v. tr.* **1** sentire, toccare, palpare **2** percepire, provare **3** ritenere **B** *v. intr.* **1** sentire, sentirsi **2** sembrare (al tatto) **3** (*impers.*) sembrare ♦ **to f. as if** avere l'impressione che; **to f. blue** essere di cattivo umore; **to f. hungry** aver fame; **to f. like** aver voglia di; **to f. up to st.** sentirsi in grado di fare q.c.
feeler ['fi:lə^r] *s.* **1** (*zool.*) antenna *f.* **2** sonda *f.*
feeling ['fi:lɪŋ] *s.* sensazione *f.*, impressione *f.*
feet [fi:t] *pl. di* **foot**

to feign [feɪn] *v. tr.* fingere, dissimulare
feline ['fiːlaɪn] *agg. e s.* felino *m.*
fell [fɛl] *pass. di* **to fall**
to fell [fɛl] *v. tr.* abbattere, atterrare
fellow ['fɛlɒ(ʊ)] *s.* **1** individuo *m.*, tipo *m.* **2** compagno *m.* **3** (*di associazione, accademia*) membro *m.* ♦ **f. citizen** concittadino; **f. countryman** connazionale
fellowship ['fɛlɒ(ʊ)ʃɪp] *s.* **1** compagnia *f.*, amicizia *f.* **2** associazione *f.* **3** (*università*) borsa *f.* di studio
felony ['fɛlənɪ] *s.* (*dir.*) crimine *m.*
felt (1) [fɛlt] *s.* feltro *m.*
felt (2) [fɛlt] *pass. e p. p. di* **to feel**
female ['fiːmeɪl] **A** *agg.* femminile **B** *s.* femmina *f.*
feminine ['fɛmɪnɪn] *agg.* femminile, femmineo
femur ['fiːməʳ] *s.* femore *m.*
fen [fɛn] *s.* palude *f.*
fence [fɛns] *s.* **1** palizzata *f.*, recinto *m.*, staccionata *f.* **2** scherma *f.*
to fence [fɛns] **A** *v. tr.* recingere **B** *v. intr.* tirare di scherma
fencing ['fɛnsɪŋ] *s.* scherma *f.*
to fend [fɛnd] *v. tr. e intr.* difendere, difendersi ♦ **to f. off** schivare
fender ['fɛndəʳ] *s.* **1** parafuoco *m.* **2** (*naut.*) parabordo *m.* **3** (*USA*) paraurti *m. inv.*
fennel ['fɛnl] *s.* finocchio *m.*
ferment ['fɜːmɛnt] *s.* **1** fermento *m.* **2** fermentazione *f.*
to ferment [fə(ː)'mɛnt] **A** *v. tr.* **1** far fermentare **2** fomentare **B** *v. intr.* **1** fermentare **2** essere in fermento
fermentation [ˌfɜːmɛn'teɪʃ(ə)n] *s.* fermentazione *f.*
fern [fɜːn] *s.* felce *f.*
ferocious [fə'rɒʊʃəs] *agg.* feroce
ferret ['fɛrɪt] *s.* furetto *m.*
to ferret ['fɛrɪt] *v. tr.* indagare ♦ **to f. out** scovare
ferrule ['fɛruːl] *s.* puntale *m.*
ferry ['fɛrɪ] *s.* traghetto *m.*
to ferry ['fɛrɪ] *v. tr.* traghettare
fertile ['fɜːtaɪl] *agg.* fertile
fertilizer ['fɜːtɪlaɪzəʳ] *s.* fertilizzante *m.*
to fester ['fɛstəʳ] *v. intr.* **1** suppurare **2** guastarsi
festival ['fɛstəv(ə)l] *s.* festa *f.*, festival *m. inv.*
festive ['fɛstɪv] *agg.* festivo
festivity [fɛs'tɪvɪtɪ] *s.* **1** festività *f.* **2** *al pl.* festeggiamenti *m. pl.*
to festoon [fɛs'tuːn] *v. intr.* ornare di festoni
to fetch [fɛtʃ] *v. tr.* **1** portare, andare a prendere **2** rendere, raggiungere (*un certo prezzo*)
fetching ['fɛtʃɪŋ] *agg.* (*fam.*) attraente
fetish ['fɛːtɪʃ] *s.* feticcio *m.*
fetishism ['fɛːtɪʃɪz(ə)m] *s.* feticismo *m.*
fetus ['fiːtəs] *s.* → **foetus**
feud [fjuːd] *s.* **1** contesa *f.* **2** feudo *m.*
feudal ['fjuːdl] *agg.* feudale
feudalism ['fjuːdəlɪz(ə)m] *s.* feudalesimo *m.*
fever ['fiːvəʳ] *s.* febbre *f.* ♦ **hay f.** febbre da fieno
feverish ['fiːv(ə)rɪʃ] *agg.* **1** febbricitante **2** febbrile
few [fjuː] **A** *agg.* **1** pochi **2 a f.** alcuni, qualche **B** *pron.* **1** pochi **2 a f.** alcuni ♦ **a good f.** un buon numero; **not a f.** non pochi
fiancé [fɪ'aː(n)seɪ] *s.* fidanzato *m.*
fiancée [fɪ'aː(n)seɪ] *s.* fidanzata *f.*
fib [fɪb] *s.* (*fam.*) bugia *f.*
fibre ['faɪbəʳ] (*USA* **fiber**) *s.* fibra *f.* ♦ **f.-glass** fibra di vetro
fibula ['fɪbjʊlə] *s.* **1** (*anat.*) perone *m.* **2** (*archeol.*) fibula *f.*
fickle ['fɪkl] *agg.* incostante, mutevole
fiction ['fɪkʃ(ə)n] *s.* **1** narrativa *f.* **2** finzione *f.*
fictitious [fɪk'tɪʃəs] *agg.* fittizio, immaginario
fiddle ['fɪdl] *s.* **1** violino *m.* **2** (*fam.*) truffa *f.*
to fiddle ['fɪdl] **A** *v. intr.* **1** (*fam.*) suonare il violino **2** gingillarsi **B** *v. tr.* (*fam.*) falsificare, contraffare
fiddler ['fɪdləʳ] *s.* violinista *m. e f.*
fidelity [fɪ'dɛlɪtɪ] *s.* fedeltà *f.*
to fidget ['fɪdʒɪt] **A** *v. intr.* agitarsi, dimenarsi **B** *v. tr.* infastidire
fief [fiːf] *s.* feudo *m.*
field [fiːld] *s.* **1** campo *m.*, terreno *m.* **2** settore *m.*
fieldwork ['fiːldwɜːk] *s.* ricerca *f.* sul campo
fiend [fiːnd] *s.* demonio *m.*
fierce [fɪəs] *agg.* **1** feroce, violento **2** intenso
fiery ['faɪərɪ] *agg.* ardente, infocato
fifteen [fɪf'tiːn] *agg. e s.* quindici *m. inv.*
fifteenth [fɪf'tiːnθ] *agg. e s.* quindicesimo *m.*

fifth [fɪfθ] *agg. e s.* quinto *m.*, la quinta parte *f.*
fiftieth ['fɪftɪɪθ] *agg. e s.* cinquantesimo *m.*
fifty ['fɪftɪ] *agg. e s.* cinquanta *m. inv.* ♦ **f.-f.** a metà
fig [fɪg] *s.* fico *m.*
fight [faɪt] *s.* **1** combattimento *m.* **2** zuffa *f.*, rissa *f.*
to fight [faɪt] (*pass. e p. p.* **fought**) **A** *v. intr.* **1** combattere, lottare **2** fare a pugni, azzuffarsi **B** *v. tr.* combattere, opporsi a
fighter ['faɪtəʳ] *s.* **1** combattente *m. e f.* **2** aereo *m.* da caccia
figment ['fɪgmənt] *s.* finzione *f.*
figurative ['fɪgjʊrətɪv] *agg.* **1** figurato **2** figurativo
figure ['fɪgəʳ] *s.* **1** figura *f.*, immagine *f.* **2** figura *f.*, personaggio *m.* **3** cifra *f.*, numero *m.*
to figure ['fɪgəʳ] **A** *v. tr.* **1** raffigurare **2** immaginare **B** *v. intr.* spiccare, figurare ♦ **to f. out** calcolare, capire
to filch [fɪltʃ] *v. tr.* rubacchiare
file (1) [faɪl] *s.* **1** archivio *m.*, schedario *m.* **2** (*inf.*) file *m. inv.*
file (2) [faɪl] *s.* lima *f.* ♦ **f. dust** limatura
file (3) [faɪl] *s.* fila *f.*
to file (1) [faɪl] *v. tr.* archiviare, schedare
to file (2) [faɪl] *v. tr.* limare
to file (3) [faɪl] *v. intr.* marciare in fila
filibustering ['fɪlɪbʌstərɪn] *s.* (*USA*) ostruzionismo *m.*
filiform ['fɪlɪfɜːm] *agg.* filiforme
filigree ['fɪlɪgriː] *s.* filigrana *f.*
fill [fɪl] *s.* **1** sazietà *f.*, sufficienza *f.* **2** (*autom.*) pieno *m.*
to fill [fɪl] **A** *v. tr.* **1** riempire, colmare **2** (*un dovere, una mansione*) adempiere, compiere **B** *v. intr.* riempirsi ♦ **to f. in** compilare (un modulo); **to f. up** (*autom.*) fare il pieno
fillet ['fɪlɪt] *s.* **1** nastro *m.* **2** (*cuc.*) filetto *m.*
filling ['fɪlɪŋ] *s.* **1** riempimento *m.* **2** otturazione *f.* **3** ripieno *m.* **4** compilazione *f.* ♦ **f. station** stazione di servizio
film [fɪlm] *s.* **1** pellicola *f.*, membrana *f.* **2** (*fot.*) pellicola *f.* **3** (*cine.*) film *m. inv.*
to film [fɪlm] *v. tr.* filmare
filter ['fɪltəʳ] *s.* filtro *m.*
to filter ['fɪltəʳ] *v. tr. e intr.* filtrare
filth [fɪlθ] *s.* porcheria *f.*, sporcizia *f.*
filthiness ['fɪlθɪnɪs] *s.* sporcizia *f.*
filthy ['fɪlθɪ] *agg.* lurido, sporco
fin [fɪn] *s.* pinna *f.*
final ['faɪnl] **A** *agg.* **1** finale, ultimo **2** definitivo, conclusivo **B** *s.* **1** finale *f.* **2** *al pl.* esami *m. pl.* finali
finalist ['faɪnəlɪst] *s.* finalista *m. e f.*
finalize ['faɪnəlaɪz] *v. tr.* **1** concludere, ultimare **2** definire
finally ['faɪnəlɪ] *avv.* infine, finalmente
finance [faɪ'næns] *s.* finanza *f.*
financial [faɪ'nænʃ(ə)l] *agg.* finanziario
financier [faɪ'nænsɪəʳ] *s.* **1** finanziere *m.* **2** finanziatore *m.*
financing [faɪ'nænsɪŋ] *s.* finanziamento *m.*
find [faɪnd] *s.* scoperta *f.*, trovata *f.*, ritrovamento *m.*
to find [faɪnd] (*pass. e p. p.* **found**) *v. tr.* **1** trovare, ritrovare, rinvenire **2** pensare, considerare **3** provare **4** (*dir.*) giudicare ♦ **all found** tutto compreso; **to f. out** scoprire, cogliere in fallo
finding ['faɪndɪŋ] *s.* **1** ritrovamento *m.*, scoperta *f.* **2** (*dir.*) verdetto *m.*, sentenza *f.* **3** *al pl.* conclusioni *f. pl.*
fine (1) [faɪn] **A** *agg.* **1** bello, bravo, eccellente **2** fine, sottile **3** raffinato, pregiato **B** *avv.* **1** bene, benissimo **2** a piccoli pezzi ♦ **f. arts** belle arti; **to be f.** (*di persona*) star bene, (*di tempo*) far bello
fine (2) [faɪn] *s.* multa *f.*, contravvenzione *f.*
to fine [faɪn] *v. tr.* multare
finger ['fɪŋgəʳ] *s.* dito *m.* ♦ **little f.** mignolo; **ring f.** anulare
to finger ['fɪŋgəʳ] *v. tr.* palpare, toccare
fingernail ['fɪŋgəneɪl] *s.* unghia *f.* (*della mano*)
fingerprint ['fɪŋgəˌprɪnt] *s.* impronta *f.* digitale
fingertip ['fɪŋgətɪp] *s.* punta *f.* del dito
finicky ['fɪnɪkɪ] *agg.* esigente, pignolo
finish ['fɪnɪʃ] *s.* **1** fine *f.*, finale *m.* **2** finitura *f.*
to finish ['fɪnɪʃ] **A** *v. tr.* finire, rifinire **B** *v. intr.* cessare, terminare ♦ **to f. off** compiere, uccidere
finishing ['fɪnɪʃɪŋ] *agg.* conclusivo ♦ **f. line** traguardo; **f. touch** ritocco
finite ['faɪnaɪt] *agg.* **1** circoscritto **2** (*mat., gramm.*) finito
Finlander ['fɪnləndəʳ] *s.* finlandese *m. e f.*
Finn [fɪn] *s.* finlandese *m. e f.*
Finnish ['fɪnɪʃ] **A** *agg.* finlandese **B** *s.* (*lingua*) finlandese *m.*
fiord [fjɜːd] *s.* fiordo *m.*
fir [fɜːʳ] *s.* abete *m.*
fire ['faɪəʳ] *s.* **1** fuoco *m.* **2** incendio *m.* **3**

sparo *m.*, tiro *m.* ♦ **f. engine** autopompa; **f. extinguisher** estintore; **f. station** caserma dei pompieri; **on f.** in fiamme
to fire ['faɪəʳ] *v. tr.* **1** sparare **2** infiammare
firearm ['faɪərɑːm] *s.* arma *f.* da fuoco
fireguard ['faɪəgɑːd] *s.* parafuoco *m.*
fireman ['faɪəmən] (*pl.* **firemen**) *s.* pompiere *m.*
fireplace ['faɪəpleɪs] *s.* caminetto *m.*, camino *m.*
fireproof ['faɪəpruːf] *agg.* ignifugo
firewood ['faɪəwʊd] *s.* legna *f.* da ardere
fireworks ['faɪəwɜːks] *s. pl.* fuochi *m. pl.* d'artificio
firm (1) [fɜːm] *agg.* fermo, saldo, solido
firm (2) [fɜːm] *s.* azienda *f.*, ditta *f.* ♦ **f. name** ragione sociale
firmament ['fɜːməmənt] *s.* firmamento *m.*
first [fɜːst] **A** *agg. num. ord.* primo **B** *avv.* **1** per primo, innanzi tutto, prima **2** per la prima volta ♦ **at f.** dapprima; **f. aid** pronto soccorso; **f. born** primogenito; **f. class** prima classe, prima qualità; **f. floor** pianterreno; **f. fruits** primizie; **f.-hand** di prima mano; **f. lady** (*USA*) consorte del Presidente; **f. mate** (*naut.*) primo ufficiale; **f. name** (*USA*) nome di battesimo; **f. night** (*teatro*) prima; **f. rate** eccellente
fiscal ['fɪsk(ə)l] *agg.* fiscale
fish [fɪʃ] *s.* pesce *m.* ♦ **f. farm** vivaio
to fish [fɪʃ] *v. tr. e intr.* pescare
fishbone ['fɪʃbɒʊn] *s.* lisca *f.*
fisherman ['fɪʃəmən] *s.* (*pl.* **fishermen**) pescatore *m.*
fishhook ['fɪʃhʊk] *s.* amo *m.*
fishing ['fɪʃɪŋ] *s.* pesca *f.* ♦ **f. boat** peschereccio; **f. net** rete da pesca; **f. rod** canna da pesca
fishline ['fɪʃlaɪn] *s.* lenza *f.*
fishmonger ['fɪʃˌmʌŋgəʳ] *s.* pescivendolo *m.*
fissure ['fɪʃəʳ] *s.* fessura *f.*
fist [fɪst] *s.* pugno *m.*
fistful ['fɪstfəl] *s.* manciata *f.*
fit (1) [fɪt] **A** *agg.* **1** adatto, conveniente **2** in forma, sano **3** pronto **B** *s.* **1** adattamento *m.* **2** misura *f.*, taglia *f.*
fit (2) [fɪt] *s.* (*med.*) attacco *m.*, accesso *m.*
to fit [fɪt] **A** *v. tr.* **1** adattarsi a **2** adattare, adeguare **3** preparare, munire **4** (*un vestito*) provare **B** *v. intr.* **1** calzare, andare bene **2** adattarsi ♦ **to f. in** infilare, inserirsi; **to f. in with** accordarsi; **to f. out** fornire di; **to f. up** installare
fitchew ['fɪtʃuː] *s.* puzzola *f.*
fitful ['fɪtf(ʊ)l] *agg.* irregolare, incostante
fitment ['fɪtmənt] *s.* arredo *m.*
fitness ['fɪtnɪs] *s.* **1** idoneità *f.* **2** buona salute *f.*, forma *f.* fisica
fitted ['fɪtɪd] *agg.* **1** adatto **2** attrezzato **3** aderente **4** su misura ♦ **f. carpet** moquette
fitter ['fɪtəʳ] *s.* (*mecc.*) aggiustatore *m.*
fitting ['fɪtɪŋ] **A** *agg.* adatto, conveniente **B** *s.* **1** prova *f.* **2** misura *f.* **3** *al pl.* attrezzatura *f.*, equipaggiamento *m.*, accessori *m. pl.* ♦ **f. out** (*naut.*) allestimento, armamento; **f. room** camerino
five [faɪv] *agg. e s.* cinque *m. inv.*
fix [fɪks] *s.* (*fam.*) pasticcio *m.*
to fix [fɪks] *v. tr.* **1** fissare, attaccare **2** stabilire **3** sistemare ♦ **to f. up** sistemare, aggiustare
fixation [fɪk'seɪʃ(ə)n] *s.* fissazione *f.*
fixed [fɪkst] *agg.* fisso
fixing ['fɪksɪŋ] *s.* **1** (*fot.*) fissaggio *m.* **2** (*fin.*) quotazione *f.* ufficiale
fixture ['fɪkstʃəʳ] *s.* **1** apparecchiatura *f.* **2** installazioni *f. pl.* fisse, impianto *m.*
fizz [fɪz] *s.* **1** sibilo *m.* **2** effervescenza *f.* **3** bevanda *f.* effervescente
to fizz [fɪz] *v. intr.* frizzare, spumeggiare
to fizzle ['fɪzl] *v. intr.* spumeggiare ♦ **to f. out** finire in nulla
fizzy ['fɪzɪ] *agg.* effervescente, frizzante
to flabbergast ['flæbəgɑːst] *v. tr.* sbalordire
flabby ['flæbɪ] *agg.* flaccido, molle
flag (1) [flæg] *s.* bandiera *f.*, insegna *f.*
flag (2) [flæg] *s.* pietra *f.* da lastrico
to flag (1) [flæg] *v. tr.* imbandierare ♦ **to f. down** fare segno di fermarsi (*a un taxi*)
to flag (2) [flæg] *v. tr.* lastricare
flagellation [ˌflædʒə'leɪʃ(ə)n] *s.* flagellazione *f.*
flageolet [ˌflædʒə'lɛt] *s.* zufolo *m.*
flagon ['flægən] *s.* **1** caraffa *f.* **2** fiasco *m.*, bottiglione *m.*
flagship ['flægʃɪp] *s.* nave *f.* ammiraglia
flair [flɛəʳ] *s.* fiuto *m.*, intuito *m.*
flak [flæk] *s.* **1** fuoco *m.* contraereo **2** (*fam.*) opposizione *f.*
flake [fleɪk] *s.* **1** fiocco *m.* **2** scaglia *f.* ♦ **snow f.** fiocco di neve
to flake [fleɪk] *v. intr.* sfaldarsi
flame [fleɪm] *s.* fiamma *f.*
flamingo [flə'mɪŋgɒʊ] *s.* fenicottero *m.*
flammable ['flæməbl] *agg.* infiammabile

flan [flæn] *s.* flan *m. inv.*
flank [flæŋk] *s.* fianco *m.*, fiancata *f.*
to flank [flæŋk] *v. tr.* fiancheggiare
flannel ['flænl] *s.* flanella *f.*
flap [flæp] *s.* **1** falda *f.*, risvolto *m.*, ribalta *f.* **2** (*aer.*) ipersostentatore *m.*
to flap [flæp] **A** *v. tr.* agitare, battere **B** *v. intr.* sbattere
flare [flɛəʳ] *s.* **1** fiammata *f.* **2** svasatura *f.*
to flare [flɛəʳ] *v. intr.* **1** sfolgorare **2** allargarsi ♦ **to f. up** prendere fuoco
flash [flæʃ] *s.* **1** bagliore *m.*, lampo *m.* **2** (*fot.*) flash *m. inv.* **3** notizia *f.* lampo
to flash [flæʃ] **A** *v. intr.* lampeggiare, scintillare **B** *v. tr.* **1** proiettare, far balenare **2** trasmettere
flashback ['flæʃbæk] *s.* flashback *m. inv.*
flashy ['flæʃɪ] *agg.* sgargiante
flask ['flaːsk] *s.* fiasco *m.*, fiaschetta *f.*
flat [flæt] **A** *agg.* **1** piano, pianeggiante **2** netto **3** (*di pneumatico*) sgonfio **4** (*elettr.*) scarico **B** *s.* **1** appartamento *m.* **2** pianura *f.* **3** (*mus.*) bemolle *m. inv.*
to flatten ['flætn] **A** *v. tr.* **1** appiattire, spianare **2** abbattere, deprimere **B** *v. intr.* **1** appiattirsi, spianarsi **2** abbattersi, deprimersi
to flatter ['flætəʳ] *v. tr.* lusingare
flattering ['flætərɪŋ] *agg.* lusinghiero
flavour ['fleɪvəʳ] (*USA* **flavor**) *s.* aroma *m.*, gusto *m.*
to flavour ['fleɪvəʳ] (*USA* **to flavor**) *v. tr.* aromatizzare, insaporire, condire
flavouring ['fleɪvərɪŋ] *s.* condimento *m.*, essenza *f.*
flavourless ['fleɪvəlɪs] *agg.* insapore
flaw [flɔː] *s.* imperfezione *f.*, difetto *m.*
flax [flæks] *s.* lino *m.*
flaxen ['flæks(ə)n] *agg.* **1** di lino **2** biondo chiaro
flea [fliː] *s.* pulce *f.* ♦ **f. market** mercatino delle pulci
fleck [flɛk] *s.* macchiolina *f.*
fled [flɛd] *pass. e p. p. di* **to flee**
to flee [fliː] (*pass. e p. p.* **fled**) **A** *v. intr.* fuggire, scappare **B** *v. tr.* scappare da
fleece [fliːs] *s.* vello *m.*
to fleece [fliːs] *v. tr.* tosare
fleet [fliːt] *s.* flotta *f.*
fleeting ['fliːtɪŋ] *agg.* fugace
Fleming ['flɛmɪŋ] *s.* fiammingo *m.*
Flemish ['flɛmɪʃ] *agg. e s.* fiammingo *m.*
flesh [flɛʃ] *s.* **1** carne *f.* **2** polpa *f.*
flew [fluː] *pass. di* **to fly**
flex [flɛks] *s.* (*elettr.*) cordone *m.*
to flex [flɛks] *v. tr.* contrarre, flettere
flexibility [ˌflɛksə'bɪlɪtɪ] *s.* flessibilità *f.*, elasticità *f.*
flexible ['flɛxsəbl] *agg.* flessibile
flexuous ['flɛksjʊəs] *agg.* flessuoso
flick [flɪk] *s.* **1** colpo *m.* secco **2** buffetto *m.* **3** scarto *m.*
to flick [flɪk] **A** *v. tr.* **1** colpire leggermente **2** far schioccare **B** *v. intr.* muoversi a scatti ♦ **to f. through** (*un libro*) sfogliare
to flicker ['flɪkəʳ] *v. intr.* **1** tremolare **2** battere le ali
flight [flaɪt] *s.* **1** volo *m.* **2** stormo *m.* **3** traiettoria *f.* **4** fuga *f.*
flimsy ['flɪmzɪ] *agg.* fragile
to flinch [flɪntʃ] *v. intr.* ritirarsi, tirarsi indietro
to fling [flɪŋ] (*pass. e p. p.* **flung**) *v. tr.* gettare, scagliare
flint [flɪnt] *s.* **1** selce *f.* **2** (*di accendino*) pietrina *f.*
to flip [flɪp] **A** *v. intr.* dare un colpetto **B** *v. tr.* **1** (*una moneta*) lanciare **2** far scattare
flippant ['flɪpənt] *agg.* impertinente
flipper ['flɪpəʳ] *s.* pinna *f.*
flirt [flɜːt] *s.* (*di ragazza*) civetta *f.*
to flirt [flɜːt] *v. intr.* civettare, flirtare
to flit [flɪt] *v. intr.* svolazzare, volteggiare
float [flɒʊt] *s.* galleggiante *m.*
to float [flɒʊt] *v. intr.* **1** galleggiare **2** fluttuare
floating ['flɒʊtɪŋ] *agg.* **1** galleggiante **2** fluttuante **3** mobile
flock (1) [flək] *s.* batuffolo *m.*
flock (2) [flək] *s.* **1** gregge *m.*, stormo *m.* **2** stuolo *m.*
to flog [fləg] *v. tr.* frustare
flogging ['fləgɪŋ] *s.* fustigazione *f.*
flood [flʌd] *s.* **1** alluvione *f.*, diluvio *m.* **2** piena *f.* **3** marea *f.*
to flood [flʌd] **A** *v. tr.* allagare, inondare **B** *v. intr.* **1** (*di marea*) salire **2** straripare ♦ **to f. in** riversarsi in
flooding [flʌdɪŋ] *agg.* (*di carburatore*) ingolfato
floodlight ['flʌdlaɪt] *s.* riflettore *m.*
floor [flɜːʳ] *s.* **1** pavimento *m.* **2** piano *m.* **3** fondo *m.* ♦ **ground f.** pianterreno
to floor [flɜːʳ] *v. tr.* pavimentare
flooring ['flɜːrɪŋ] *s.* pavimentazione *f.*
flop [fləp] *s.* **1** tonfo *m.* **2** (*fam.*) fiasco *m.*, insuccesso *m.*
to flop [fləp] *v. intr.* **1** cadere pesantemente **2** fallire

floppy ['flɔpɪ] *agg.* floscio ♦ **f. disk** floppy disk
flora ['flɜːrə] *s.* flora *f.*
floral ['flɜːr(ə)l] *agg.* floreale
floriculture ['flɜːrɪˌkʌltʃəʳ] *s.* floricoltura *f.*
florid ['flɔrɪd] *agg.* **1** florido **2** fiorito
florist ['flɔrɪst] *s.* fioraio *m.*
flotilla [flɒ(ʊ)'tɪlə] *s.* flottiglia *f.*
flounce [flaʊns] *s.* **1** balzo *m.*, scatto *m.* **2** balza *f.*
to flounder ['flaʊndəʳ] *v. intr.* agitarsi, dibattersi
flour ['flaʊəʳ] *s.* farina *f.*
to flourish ['flʌrɪʃ] *v. intr.* fiorire, prosperare
flourishing ['flʌrɪʃɪŋ] *agg.* prosperoso
flout [flaʊt] *s.* burla *f.*
to flout [flaʊt] *v. tr.* schernire, disprezzare
flow [flɒʊ] *s.* **1** flusso *m.*, corrente *f.* **2** portata *f.* ♦ **f. chart** schema di flusso
to flow [flɒʊ] *v. intr.* **1** fluire, scorrere **2** circolare **3** ricadere, scendere ♦ **to f. in** affluire; **to f. out** defluire
flower ['flaʊəʳ] *s.* fiore *m.* ♦ **f. bed** aiuola; **f. box** fioriera
to flower ['flaʊəʳ] *v. intr.* fiorire
flowering ['flaʊərɪŋ] *s.* fioritura *f.*
flowing ['flɒʊɪŋ] *agg.* fluido, scorrevole
flown [flɒʊn] *p. p. di* **to fly**
flu [fluː] *s.* influenza *f.*
to fluctuate ['flʌktjʊeɪt] *v. intr.* fluttuare, oscillare
fluctuating ['flʌktʃʊətɪŋ] *agg.* fluttuante, oscillante
fluctuation [ˌflʌktjʊ'eɪʃ(ə)n] *s.* fluttuazione *f.*, oscillazione *f.*
fluency ['fluːənsɪ] *s.* scorrevolezza *f.*, scioltezza *f.*, facilità *f.* (di parola)
fluent ['fluːənt] *agg.* scorrevole, fluente ♦ **to speak f. English** parlare inglese correntemente
fluff [flʌf] *s.* lanugine *f.*, peluria *f.*
fluid ['fluːɪd] *agg. e s.* fluido *m.*
fluke [fluːk] *s.* colpo *m.* di fortuna
flung [flʌŋ] *pass. e p. p. di* **to fling**
fluorescent [flʊə'rɛsənt] *agg.* fluorescente
fluorine ['flʊəriːn] *s.* fluoro *m.*
flurry ['flʌrɪ] *s.* **1** raffica *f.* **2** (*di neve*) tempesta *f.* **3** (*di pioggia*) scroscio *m.*
flush [flʌʃ] **A** *agg.* **1** abbondante, ben fornito **2** prodigo **B** *s.* **1** getto *m.* **2** afflusso *m.* **3** rossore *m.* **4** rigoglio *m.*, vigore *m.*
to flush [flʌʃ] **A** *v. intr.* **1** scorrere **2** arrossire **B** *v. tr.* sciacquare, lavare (con un getto d'acqua) ♦ **to f. the toilet** tirare lo sciacquone
to fluster ['flʌstəʳ] *v. tr.* agitare, sconvolgere
flute [fluːt] *s.* **1** flauto *m.* **2** (*arch.*) scanalatura *f.*
flutter ['flʌtəʳ] *s.* **1** (*di ali*) battito *m.* **2** agitazione *f.* **3** vibrazione *f.*
to flutter ['flʌtəʳ] **A** *v. intr.* **1** battere le ali **2** fluttuare, ondeggiare, sventolare **3** agitarsi, tremare **B** *v. tr.* **1** battere **2** sventolare **3** scompigliare
flux [flʌks] *s.* **1** flusso *m.* **2** mutamento *m.* continuo
fly (1) [flaɪ] *s.* mosca *f.*
fly (2) [flaɪ] *s.* **1** volo *m.* **2** lembo *m.*, risvolto *m.* ♦ **f. leaf** risguardo, risvolto
to fly [flaɪ] (*pass.* **flew**, *p. p.* **flown**) **A** *v. intr.* **1** volare, andare in aereo **2** sventolare **3** fuggire **B** *v. tr.* **1** (*un aereo*) pilotare **2** (*in aereo*) trasportare **3** agitare **4** fuggire da ♦ **to f. across** trasvolare; **to f. off** decollare, fuggire
flying ['flaɪɪŋ] *agg.* **1** volante **2** ondeggiante **3** di volo, di aviazione **4** rapido **5** frettoloso ♦ **f. saucer** disco volante
flyover ['flaɪˌɒʊvəʳ] *s.* cavalcavia *m. inv.*
foal [fɒʊl] *s.* puledro *m.*
foam [fɒʊm] *s.* schiuma *f.* ♦ **f. rubber** gommapiuma
foamy ['fɒʊmɪ] *agg.* schiumoso
to fob [fɔb] *v. tr.* imbrogliare ♦ **to f. st. off on sb.** rifilare q.c. a qc.
focus ['fɒʊkəs] *s.* **1** (*fot.*) fuoco *m.* **2** focolaio *m.*, centro *m.* ♦ **in f.** a fuoco; **out of f.** sfocato
to focus ['fɒʊkəs] *v. tr.* **1** mettere a fuoco **2** far convergere ♦ **to f. on** fissare lo sguardo su
fodder ['fɔdəʳ] *s.* foraggio *m.*, mangime *m.*
foe [fɒʊ] *s.* nemico *m.*
foetus ['fiːtəs] (*USA* **fetus**) *s.* feto *m.*
fog [fɔg] *s.* nebbia *f.* ♦ **f. horn** corno da nebbia; **f. lamp** faro antinebbia
foggy ['fɔgɪ] *agg.* nebbioso
foil (1) [fɔɪl] *s.* lamina *f.*, (*di stagnola*) foglio *m.*
foil (2) [fɔɪl] *s.* (*sport*) fioretto *m.*
to foil (1) [fɔɪl] *v. tr.* **1** rivestire con lamina metallica **2** far risaltare
to foil (2) [fɔɪl] *v. tr.* **1** (*tracce*) confondere **2** frustrare
fold (1) [fɒʊld] *s.* **1** piega *f.* **2** battente *m.*
fold (2) [fɒʊld] *s.* **1** ovile *m.* **2** gregge *m.*

to fold [fɒʊld] **A** *v. tr.* **1** piegare **2** avvolgere **3** stringere **B** *v. intr.* piegarsi, chiudersi
folder ['fɒʊldəʳ] *s.* cartelletta *f.*
folding ['fəʊldɪŋ] *agg.* pieghevole
foliage ['fɒʊlɪɪdʒ] *s.* fogliame *m.*
folk [fɒʊk] **A** *s.* **1** gente *f.*, popolo *m.* **2** persone *f. pl.* **B** *agg.* popolare, folcloristico ♦ **one's folks** i parenti, i familiari
folklore ['fɒʊklɜːʳ] *s.* folclore *m.*
to follow ['fəlɒʊ] **A** *v. tr.* **1** seguire **2** derivare da **B** *v. intr.* **1** seguire, venir dopo **2** derivare, conseguire ♦ **to f. on** perseverare; **to f. up** fare seguito a
follower ['fəlɒʊəʳ] *s.* seguace *m. e f.*, discepolo *m.*
following ['fəlɒʊɪŋ] **A** *agg.* seguente, successivo **B** *s.* seguito *m.*
folly ['fəlɪ] *s.* follia *f.*, sciocchezza *f.*
fond [fənd] *agg.* affezionato, appassionato ♦ **to be f. of** piacere, voler bene a
to fondle ['fəndl] *v. tr.* vezzeggiare, accarezzare
font (1) [fənt] *s.* **1** fonte *m.* battesimale **2** acquasantiera *f.*
font (2) [fənt] *s.* (*tip.*) font *m. inv.*
food [fuːd] *s.* cibo *m.*, nutrimento *m.*, vitto *m.* ♦ **f. grinder** tritatutto; **sea f.** frutti di mare
foodstuffs ['fuːdstʌfs] *s. pl.* generi *m. pl.* alimentari, cibarie *f. pl.*
fool [fuːl] *s.* sciocco *m.*, stupido *m.*
to fool [fuːl] **A** *v. tr.* ingannare **B** *v. intr.* fare lo sciocco
foolhardy ['fuːl,haːdɪ] *agg.* avventato
foolish ['fuːlɪʃ] *agg.* sciocco, balordo
foolishness ['fuːlɪʃnɪs] *s.* stupidità *f.*
foolproof ['fuːlpruːf] *agg.* **1** sicurissimo, di semplice funzionamento **2** infallibile
foot [fʊt] (*pl.* **feet**) *s.* **1** piede *m.* **2** zampa *f.* **3** (*arch.*) zoccolo *m.* ♦ **on f.** a piedi
football ['fʊtbɜːl] *s.* **1** (*sport*) calcio *m.* **2** pallone *m.*
footballer ['fʊtbɜːləʳ] *s.* calciatore *m.*
footboard ['fʊtbɜːd] *s.* pedana *f.*
footbridge ['fʊtbrɪdʒ] *s.* passerella *f.*
foothold ['fʊthɒʊld] *s.* appiglio *m.*, punto *m.* di appoggio
footing ['fʊtɪŋ] *s.* posizione *f.*, appoggio *m.* ♦ **to lose one's f.** mettere un piede in fallo
footlights ['fʊtlaɪts] *s. pl.* luci *f. pl.* della ribalta
footman ['fʊtmən] (*pl.* **footmen**) *s.* valletto *m.*
footnote ['fʊtnɒʊt] *s.* nota *f.* a piè pagina
footpath ['fʊtpaːθ] *s.* sentiero *m.*
footprint ['fʊtprɪnt] *s.* orma *f.*
footstep ['fʊtstɛp] *s.* **1** passo *m.* **2** orma *f.*
footwear ['fʊtwɛəʳ] *s.* calzature *f. pl.*
fop [fəp] *s.* vanesio *m.*
foppish ['fəpɪʃ] *agg.* vanesio
for [fɜːʳ, fəʳ] **A** *prep.* **1** (*scopo*) per, al fine di (ES: **to dress for lunch** vestirsi per il pranzo) **2** (*causa*) per, a causa di (ES: **he was convicted for driving without licence** fu condannato per aver guidato senza patente) **3** (*tempo*) per, durante, da (ES: **I drove for hours** guidai per ore) **4** (*direzione*) per (ES: **the bus for Oxford** l'autobus per Oxford) **5** (*termine*) per (ES: **what can I do for you?** cosa posso fare per lei?) **6** (*prezzo*) per (ES: **I got it for five pounds** l'ho avuto per cinque sterline) **7** al posto di, per conto di (ES: **he spoke for us** parlò per conto nostro) **8** per quanto riguarda, come, in rapporto a (ES: **it's very expensive for a second-hand car** è molto cara per una macchina di seconda mano) **9** malgrado (ES: **for all you say** nonostante ciò che dici) **10** (*idiom.*) (ES: **it's necessary for me to go to the doctor** è necessario che vada dal medico) **B** *cong.* dal momento che, poiché
forage ['fərɪdʒ] *s.* foraggio *m.*
foray ['fəreɪ] *s.* incursione *f.*
forbade [fə'beɪd] (o **forbad** [fə'bæd]) *pass. di* **to forbid**
to forbid [fə'bɪd] (*pass.* **forbad(e)**, *p. p.* **forbidden**) *v. tr.* proibire, vietare
forbidden [fə'bɪdn] *p. p. di* **to forbid**
forbidding [fə'bɪdɪŋ] *agg.* ostile, minaccioso
force [fɜːs] *s.* forza *f.* ♦ **in f.** in gran numero, in vigore
to force [fɜːs] *v. tr.* forzare, costringere ♦ **to f. in** far entrare, conficcare; **to f. on** imporre a; **to f. out** spingere fuori; **to f. up** far salire
forced [fɜːst] *agg.* forzato, costretto
forcedly ['fɜːsɪdlɪ] *avv.* forzatamente
to force-feed ['fɜːsfiːd] (*pass. e p. p.* **force-fed**) *v. tr.* alimentare artificialmente
forceful ['fɜːsf(ʊ)l] *agg.* forte, vigoroso
forceps ['fɜːsɛps] *s. inv.* forcipe *m.*
forcibly ['fɜːsɪblɪ] *avv.* con forza
ford [fɜːd] *s.* guado *m.*
to ford [fɜːd] *v. tr.* guadare

fore [fɜːʳ] *agg.* **1** anteriore **2** (*naut.*) di prua
forearm ['fɜːraːm] *s.* avambraccio *m.*
to forebode [fɜː'bɒʊd] *v. tr.* presagire
forecast ['fɜːkaːst] *s.* previsione *f.*
to forecast ['fɜːkaːst] (*pass. e p. p.* **forecast, forecasted**) *v. tr.* prevedere
forefather ['fɜːˌfaːðəʳ] *s.* antenato *m.*, progenitore *m.*
forefinger ['fɜːˌfɪŋgəʳ] *s.* (dito) indice *m.*
forefront ['fɜːˌfrʌnt] *s.* **1** parte *f.* anteriore **2** avanguardia *f.*
foregone [fɜː'gɜːn] *agg.* previsto, scontato
foreground ['fɜːgraʊnd] *s.* primo piano *m.*
forehead ['fərɪd] *s.* fronte *f.*
foreign ['fərɪn] *agg.* **1** straniero, estero **2** estraneo ♦ **f. office** ministero degli esteri
foreigner ['fərɪnəʳ] *s.* straniero *m.*
foreman ['fɜːmən] (*pl.* **foremen**) *s.* caposquadra *m.*
foremost ['fɜːmɒʊst] **A** *agg.* principale, eminente **B** *avv.* **1** in prima fila **2** anzitutto ♦ **first and f.** per prima cosa
forename ['fɜːneɪm] *s.* nome *m.* (di battesimo)
forensic [fə'rɛnsɪk] *agg.* forense
forerunner ['fɜːˌrʌnəʳ] *s.* precursore *m.*
to foresee [fɜː'siː] (*pass.* **foresaw**, *p. p.* **foreseen**) *v. tr.* presagire, prevedere
to foreshadow [fɜː'ʃædɒʊ] *v. tr.* prefigurare
foreshortening [fɜː'ʃɜːt(ə)nɪŋ] *s.* (*arte*) scorcio *m.*
foresight ['fɜːsaɪt] *s.* **1** preveggenza *f.* **2** previdenza *f.*, lungimiranza *f.*
forest ['fərɪst] *s.* foresta *f.*
to forestall [fɜː'stɜːl] *v. tr.* prevenire
to foretaste ['fɜːˌteɪst] *v. tr.* pregustare
to foretell [fɜː'tɛl] (*pass. e p. p.* **foretold**) *v. tr.* predire
foretold [fɜː'tɒʊld] *pass. e p. p. di* **to foretell**
forever [fə'rɛvəʳ] *avv.* sempre, per sempre
to forewarn [fɜː'wɜːn] *v. tr.* preavvisare
foreword ['fɜːwɜːd] *s.* prefazione *f.*
forfeit ['fɜːfɪt] *s.* **1** perdita *f.* **2** penale *f.*, penalità *f.* **3** (*nel gioco*) penitenza *f.*
forgave [fə'geɪv] *pass. di* **to forgive**
to forge [fɜːdʒ] *v. tr.* **1** falsificare **2** forgiare ♦ **to f. ahead** avanzare con decisione, tirare avanti
forger ['fɜːdʒəʳ] *s.* falsario *m.*
forgery ['fɜːdʒ(ə)rɪ] *s.* **1** falsificazione *f.* **2** falso *m.*
to forget [fə'gɛt] (*pass.* **forgot**, *p. p.* **forgotten**) *v. tr. e intr.* dimenticare
forgetful [fə'gɛtf(ʊ)l] *agg.* immemore, dimentico
forgetfulness [fə'gɛtf(ʊ)lnɪs] *s.* dimenticanza *f.*
forget-me-not [fə'gɛtmɪnət] *s.* nontiscordardimé *m. inv.*
forgivable [fə'gɪvəbl] *agg.* perdonabile
to forgive [fə'gɪv] (*pass.* **forgave**, *p. p.* **forgiven**) *v. tr. e intr.* perdonare
forgiven [fə'gɪvn] *p. p. di* **to forgive**
forgiveness [fə'gɪvnɪs] *s.* perdono *m.*
to forgo [fɜː'gɒʊ] (*pass.* **forwent**, *p. p.* **forgone**) *v. tr.* astenersi da, rinunciare a
forgot [fə'gət] *pass. di* **to forget**
forgotten [fə'gətn] *p. p. di* **to forget**
fork [fɜːk] *s.* **1** forchetta *f.* **2** forca *f.*, forcone *m.* **3** bivio *m.*, biforcazione *f.*
to fork [fɜːk] *v. intr.* biforcarsi ♦ **to f. out** sborsare
forlorn [fə'lɜːn] *agg.* **1** abbandonato, trascurato **2** misero **3** vano
form [fɜːm] *s.* **1** forma *f.* **2** modulo *m.*, scheda *f.* **3** classe *f.* ♦ **bad f.** maleducazione
to form [fɜːm] **A** *v. tr.* formare, comporre, costituire **B** *v. intr.* **1** formarsi, costituirsi **2** ordinarsi, disporsi
formal ['fɜːm(ə)l] *agg.* **1** formale **2** simmetrico, regolare ♦ **f. dress** abito da cerimonia
formalism ['fɜːməlɪz(ə)m] *s.* formalismo *m.*
formality [fɜː'mælɪtɪ] *s.* formalità *f.*
format ['fɜːmæt] *s.* formato *m.*
formation [fɜː'meɪʃ(ə)n] *s.* formazione *f.*
formative [fɜː'mətɪv] *agg.* formativo
former ['fɜːməʳ] *agg.* **1** anteriore, precedente **2** passato, ex ♦ **the f. ... the latter** quello ... questo, (*di un elenco*) il primo ... l'ultimo
formerly ['fɜːməlɪ] *avv.* già, in passato
formidable ['fɜːm(ɪ)dəbl] *agg.* formidabile
formula ['fɜːmjʊlə] *s.* formula *f.*
formulary ['fɜːmjʊlərɪ] *s.* formulario *m.*
fornix ['fɜːnɪks] *s.* fornice *m.*
to forsake [fə'seɪk] (*pass.* **forsook**, *p. p.* **forsaken**) *v. tr.* abbandonare
forsaken [fə'seɪk(ə)n] *p. p. di* **to forsake**
forsook [fə'sʊk] *pass. di* **to forsake**
fort [fɜːt] *s.* forte *m.*
forth [fɜːθ] *avv.* avanti ♦ **and so f.** e così via
forthcoming [fɜːθ'kʌmɪŋ] *agg.* **1** prossi-

mo, venturo **2** disponibile **3** aperto, schietto
fortieth ['fɜːtɪɪθ] *agg. e s.* quarantesimo *m.*
fortification [ˌfɜːtɪfɪ'keɪʃ(ə)n] *s.* fortificazione *f.*, rafforzamento *m.*
to fortify ['fɜːtɪfaɪ] *v. tr.* fortificare
fortnight ['fɜːtnaɪt] *s.* due settimane *f. pl.*
fortnightly ['fɜːtˌnaɪtlɪ] *agg.* quindicinale
fortress ['fɜːtrɪs] *s.* rocca *f.*
fortuitous [fɜː'tjʊ(ː)ɪtəs] *agg.* fortuito
fortunate ['fɜːtʃnɪt] *agg.* **1** fortunato **2** fausto
fortune ['fɜːtʃ(ə)n] *s.* fortuna *f.*, sorte *f.* ♦ **f. teller** indovino
forty ['fɜːtɪ] *agg. num. card. e s.* quaranta *m. inv.*
forum ['fɜːrəm] *s.* foro *m.*
forward ['fɜːwəd] *agg.* **1** in avanti **2** in anticipo, precoce **3** sollecito **4** insolente
to forward ['fɜːwəd] *v. tr.* **1** promuovere, appoggiare **2** inoltrare, inviare
forwarder ['fɜːwədəʳ] *s.* spedizioniere *m.*
forwarding ['fɜːwədɪŋ] *s.* (*comm.*) invio *m.*, spedizione *f.*
forward(s) ['fɜːwəd(z)] *avv.* avanti, in avanti ♦ **to go f.** progredire; **to look f. to** attendere con ansia
fossil ['fəsɪl] *s. e agg.* fossile *m.*
to fossilize ['fəsɪlaɪz] *v. intr.* fossilizzarsi
foster ['fəstəʳ] **A** *s.* **1** tutela *f.* **2** nutrimento *m.* **B** *agg.* adottivo ♦ **f. child** figlio adottivo; **f. parent** genitore adottivo
to foster ['fəstəʳ] *v. tr.* **1** allevare, nutrire **2** favorire
fought [fɜːt] *pass. e p. p. di* **to fight**
foul [faʊl] **A** *agg.* **1** brutto, cattivo, schifoso **2** scorretto, disonesto **3** osceno **B** *s.* (*sport*) fallo *m.*
found [faʊnd] *pass. e p. p. di* **to find**
to found (1) [faʊnd] *v. tr.* fondare, istituire
to found (2) [faʊnd] *v. tr.* fondere
foundation [faʊn'deɪʃ(ə)n] *s.* fondazione *f.*
founder ['faʊndəʳ] *s.* fondatore *m.*
founding ['faʊndɪŋ] **A** *agg.* fondatore **B** *s.* **1** fondazione *f.* **2** fondatore *m.*
foundry ['faʊndrɪ] *s.* fonderia *f.*
fountain ['faʊntɪn] *s.* fontana *f.* ♦ **f. pen** stilografica
four [fɜːʳ] *agg. num. card. e s.* quattro *m. inv.*
fourteen [ˌfɜː'tiːn] *agg. num. card. e s.* quattordici *m. inv.*
fourteenth [ˌfɜː'tiːnθ] *agg. num. ord. e s.* quattordicesimo *m.*
fourth [fɜːθ] *agg. num. ord. e s.* quarto *m.*
fowl [faʊl] *s.* **1** pollame *m.* **2** volatile *m.*
fox [fəks] *s.* volpe *f.*
to fox [fəks] *v. tr.* (*fam.*) ingannare
fraction ['frækʃ(ə)n] *s.* frazione *f.*
to fractionize ['frækʃ(ə)naɪz] *v. tr.* frazionare
fracture ['fræktʃəʳ] *s.* frattura *f.*
fragile ['frædʒaɪl] *agg.* fragile
fragment ['frægmənt] *s.* frammento *m.*
fragmentary ['frægmənt(ə)rɪ] *agg.* frammentario
fragrant ['freɪgrənt] *agg.* fragrante, odoroso
frail [freɪl] *agg.* fragile, debole
frame [freɪm] *s.* **1** intelaiatura *f.*, armatura *f.* **2** cornice *f.* **3** struttura *f.* **4** ossatura *f.*, corpo *m.* **5** montatura *f.* ♦ **f. of mind** stato d'animo
to frame [freɪm] *v. tr.* **1** formare, formulare **2** incorniciare, inquadrare
framework ['freɪmwɜːk] *s.* **1** intelaiatura *f.* **2** struttura *f.*
franchise ['fræn(t)ʃaɪz] *s.* franchigia *f.*
Francophone ['fræŋkɒ(ʊ)fɒʊn] *agg.* francofono
frank [fræŋk] *agg.* franco, aperto
to frank [fræŋk] *v. tr.* (*corrispondenza*) affrancare
frantic ['fræntɪk] *agg.* frenetico
fraternity [frə'tɜːnɪtɪ] *s.* **1** fraternità *f.*, fratellanza *f.* **2** confraternita *f.*
to fraternize ['frætənaɪz] *v. intr.* fraternizzare
fraud [frɜːd] *s.* **1** frode *f.* **2** imbroglione *m.*
fraudulent ['frɜːdjʊlənt] *agg.* fraudolento
fraught [frɜːt] *agg.* carico, denso, gravido
fray [freɪ] *s.* mischia *f.*, baruffa *f.*
to fray [freɪ] **A** *v. tr.* logorare, consumare **B** *v. intr.* consumarsi, logorarsi
freak [friːk] *s.* **1** bizzarria *f.* **2** fenomeno *m.*, mostro *m.*
freckle ['frɛkl] *s.* lentiggine *f.*
free [friː] **A** *agg.* **1** libero **2** indipendente **3** esente, gratuito **4** abbondante **5** sciolto **B** *avv.* **1** gratis, gratuitamente **2** liberamente ♦ **admission f.** entrata libera
to free [friː] *v. tr.* **1** liberare **2** esentare
freedom ['friːdəm] *s.* libertà *f.*
freelance ['friːˌlaːns] *agg.* indipendente
freely ['friːlɪ] *avv.* liberamente
to freeze [friːz] (*pass.* **froze**, *p. p.* **frozen**) *v. tr. e intr.* congelare
freezer ['friːzəʳ] *s.* congelatore *m.*

freezing ['fri:zɪŋ] *agg.* ghiacciato ♦ **f.-point** punto di congelamento
freight [freɪt] *s.* **1** trasporto *m.* **2** carico *m.* **3** noleggio *m.*
freighter ['freɪtəʳ] **1** *s.* nave *f.* da carico, aereo *m.* da trasporto **2** noleggiatore *m.*
French [frɛn(t)ʃ] *agg. e s.* francese *m.* (*lingua*) ♦ **F. bean** fagiolino; **F. fries** (*USA*) patate fritte
Frenchman ['frɛn(t)ʃmən] (*pl.* **Frenchmen**) *s.* francese *m.*
Frenchwoman ['frɛn(t)ʃˌwʊmən] (*pl.* **Frenchwomen**) *s.* francese *f.*
frenzied ['frɛnzɪd] *agg.* frenetico
frenzy ['frɛnzɪ] *s.* frenesia *f.*
frequency ['fri:kwənsɪ] *s.* frequenza *f.*
frequent ['fri:kwənt] *agg.* frequente
to **frequent** [frɪ'kwənt] *v. tr.* frequentare, praticare
frequently ['fri:kwəntlɪ] *avv.* frequentemente
fresco ['frɛskɒʊ] *s.* affresco *m.*
fresh [frɛʃ] *agg.* **1** fresco, recente, nuovo **2** sfacciato
to **freshen** ['frɛʃn] *v. tr. e intr.* rinfrescare, rinfrescarsi
freshly ['frɛʃlɪ] *agg.* di fresco, di recente, appena
freshness ['frɛʃnɪs] *s.* freschezza *f.*
freshwater ['frɛʃˌwɜ:təʳ] *agg.* d'acqua dolce
to **fret** [frɛt] **A** *v. tr.* **1** consumare **2** affliggere, agitare **B** *v. intr.* **1** consumarsi **2** affliggersi, irritarsi
friable ['fraɪəbl] *agg.* friabile
friar ['fraɪəʳ] *s.* frate *m.*
friction ['frɪkʃ(ə)n] *s.* frizione *f.*
Friday ['fraɪdɪ] *s.* venerdì *m.*
fridge [frɪdʒ] *s.* frigorifero *m.*
fried [fraɪd] *p. p. di* **to fry** fritto
friend [frɛnd] *s.* amico *m.*
friendly ['frɛndlɪ] *agg.* amico, amichevole
friendship ['frɛn(d)ʃɪp] *s.* amicizia *f.*
frieze [fri:z] *s.* fregio *m.*
fright [fraɪt] *s.* paura *f.*, spavento *m.* ♦ **to take f. at st.** spaventarsi di q.c.
to **frighten** ['fraɪtn] *v. tr.* impaurire, spaventare, atterrire
frightful ['fraɪtf(ʊ)l] *agg.* spaventoso, tremendo
frigid ['frɪdʒɪd] *agg.* **1** glaciale **2** frigido
frill [frɪl] *s.* gala *f.*, trina *f.*
fringe [frɪn(d)ʒ] *s.* **1** frangia *f.* **2** margine *m.*
frippery ['frɪpərɪ] *s.* fronzolo *m.*
frisk [frɪsk] *v. tr.* **1** agitare **2** perquisire
frisky ['frɪskɪ] *agg.* vivace
fritter ['frɪtəʳ] *s.* frittella *f.*
frivolous ['frɪvələs] *agg.* frivolo
frizzy ['frɪzɪ] *agg.* crespo
fro [frɒʊ] *avv.* **to and f.** avanti e indietro
frock [frɔk] *s.* **1** vestito *m.* **2** tonaca *f.*
frog [frɔg] *s.* rana *f.*
frogman ['frɔgmən] *s.* sommozzatore *m.*
to **frolic** ['frɔlɪk] *v. intr.* **1** sgambettare **2** folleggiare
from [frɔm, frəm] *prep.* **1** (*provenienza*) da (ES: **a letter from my mother** una lettera da mia madre) **2** (*causa*) per, a causa di (ES: **to speak from experience** parlare per esperienza) **3** (*tempo e luogo*) da (ES: **from May to August** da maggio ad agosto, **how far is it from Rome to Naples?** quanto c'è da Roma a Napoli?)
front [frʌnt] **A** *agg. attr.* anteriore, frontale **B** *s.* **1** fronte *f.*, facciata *f.*, parte *f.* anteriore **2** fronte *m.* ♦ **f. page** prima pagina; **in f. of** di fronte a; **sea f.** lungomare
frontage ['frʌntɪdʒ] *s.* facciata *f.*
frontal ['frʌntl] *agg.* frontale
frontier ['frʌntjəʳ] *s.* frontiera *f.*
frontispiece ['frʌntɪspi:s] *s.* frontespizio *m.*
fronton ['frʌntən] *s.* frontone *m.*
frost [frɔst] *s.* **1** gelo *m.* **2** brina *f.*
frostbite [frɔs(t)baɪt] *s.* congelamento *m.*
froth [frɔθ] *s.* schiuma *f.*, spuma *f.*
frothy ['frɔθɪ] *agg.* schiumoso, spumoso
to **frown** [fraʊn] *v. intr.* aggrottare le ciglia
froze ['frɒʊz] *pass. di* **to freeze**
frozen ['frɒʊzn] **A** *p. p. di* **to freeze** **B** *agg.* **1** gelato, ghiacciato **2** congelato
frugal ['fru:g(ə)l] *agg.* frugale
fruit [fru:t] *s.* frutto *m.*, frutta *f.* ♦ **f. salad** macedonia
fruiterer ['fru:tərəʳ] *s.* fruttivendolo *m.*
fruitful ['fru:tf(ʊ)l] *agg.* fecondo, fertile
fruition [fru:'ɪʃ(ə)n] *s.* **1** fruizione *f.*, godimento *m.* **2** realizzazione *f.*
to **frustrate** [frʌs'treɪt] *v. tr.* frustrare, deludere
frustration [frʌs'treɪʃ(ə)n] *s.* frustrazione *f.*
fry [fraɪ] *s.* frittura *f.*, fritto *m.*
to **fry** [fraɪ] *v. tr.* friggere
frying ['fraɪɪŋ] *s.* frittura *f.* ♦ **f. pan** padella
fuel [fjʊəl] *s.* combustibile *m.* ♦ **f. tank** serbatoio della benzina

fugitive ['fjuːdʒɪtɪv] *agg. e s.* fuggiasco *m.*, profugo *m.*
fulcrum ['fʌlkrəm] *s.* fulcro *m.*
to fulfil [fʊl'fɪl] *v. tr.* **1** compiere, adempiere **2** esaudire, appagare
fulfilment [fʊl'fɪlm(ə)nt] *s.* **1** adempimento *m.*, esecuzione *f.* **2** appagamento *m.*
full [fʊl] **A** *agg.* **1** pieno, completo **2** intero **3** ampio, abbondante **B** *avv.* completamente, interamente ♦ **at f. speed** a tutta velocità; **f. age** maggiore età; **f. size** a grandezza naturale; **f. stop** punto (*segno ortografico*); **f.-time** a tempo pieno; **f. up** sazio; **in f.** completamente
fully [fʊlɪ] *avv.* interamente, del tutto
fulminant ['fʌlmɪnənt] *agg.* fulminante
fulsome ['fʊlsəm] *agg.* esagerato, eccessivo
to fumble ['fʌmbl] *v. intr.* **1** armeggiare **2** brancolare
fume [fjuːm] *s.* fumo *m.*, esalazione *f.*
to fume [fjuːm] *v. intr.* **1** fumare, esalare vapore **2** essere furioso
fumigator ['fjuːmɪgeɪtəʳ] *s.* zampirone *m.*
fun [fʌn] *s.* divertimento *m.* ♦ **f. fair** luna park; **to have f.** divertirsi; **to make f. of sb.** prendersi gioco di qc.
function ['fʌŋkʃ(ə)n] *s.* funzione *f.*
functional ['fʌŋkʃənl] *agg.* funzionale
functionalism ['fʌŋkʃ(ə)nəlɪz(ə)m] *s.* funzionalismo *m.*
functionality [ˌfʌŋkʃə'nælɪtɪ] *s.* funzionalità *f.*
functionary ['fʌŋ(k)ʃnərɪ] *s.* funzionario *m.*
fund [fʌnd] *s.* **1** fondo *m.*, cassa *f.* **2** *al pl.* capitali *m. pl.*
fundamental [ˌfʌndə'mentl] *agg.* fondamentale, basilare
funeral ['fjuːn(ə)r(ə)l] **A** *agg.* funebre, funerario **B** *s.* funerale *m.*
funerary ['fjuːnərərɪ] *agg.* funerario
funereal [fjʊ(ː)'nɪərɪəl] *agg.* funereo
fungicide ['fʌndʒɪsaɪd] *s.* fungicida *m.*
fungus ['fʌŋgəs] *s.* fungo *m.*
funicular [fjʊ(ː)'nɪkjʊləʳ] *s.* funicolare *f.*
funk [fʌŋk] *s.* (*fam.*) paura *f.*, fifa *f.*
funnel ['fʌnl] *s.* **1** imbuto *m.* **2** ciminiera *f.*
funny ['fʌnɪ] *agg.* **1** buffo, divertente **2** strano
fur [fɜːʳ] *s.* pelo *m.*, pelliccia *f.*
furious ['fjʊərɪəs] *agg.* furioso
furlough ['fɜːlɒʊ] *s:* (*mil.*) licenza *f.*
furnace ['fɜːnɪs] *s.* fornace *f.*
to furnish ['fɜːnɪʃ] *v. tr.* **1** ammobiliare **2** fornire
furnishing ['fɜːnɪʃɪŋ] *s.* arredamento *m.*
furnishings ['fɜːnɪʃɪŋz] *s. pl.* mobili *m. pl.*, arredamento *m.*
furniture ['fɜːnɪtʃəʳ] *s.* arredamento *m.*
furrier ['fʌrɪəʳ] *s.* pellicciaio *m.*
furrow ['fʌrɒʊ] *s.* solco *m.*
further ['fɜːðəʳ] (*comp. di* **far**) **A** *agg.* **1** ulteriore **2** più lontano, altro **B** *avv.* **1** oltre **2** ulteriormente
furthermore [ˌfɜːðə'mɔːʳ] *avv.* per di più, inoltre
furthest ['fɜːðɪst] (*sup. rel. di* **far**) **A** *agg.* il più lontano, remoto **B** *avv.* più lontano
fury ['fjʊərɪ] *s.* furia *f.*
fuse [fjuːz] *s.* **1** fusibile *m.* **2** miccia *f.*
to fuse [fjuːz] *v. tr. e intr.* fondere, fondersi
fuselage [fjuːzɪlaːʒ] *s.* fusoliera *f.*
fusible ['fjuːzəbl] *agg.* fusibile
fusion ['fjuːz(ə)n] *s.* fusione *f.*
fuss [fʌs] *s.* **1** confusione *f.*, trambusto *m.* **2** smancerie *f. pl.*
to fuss [fʌs] *v. intr.* agitarsi
fussiness ['fʌsɪnɪs] *s.* agitazione *f.*
fussy ['fʌsɪ] *agg.* **1** agitato **2** puntiglioso, esigente
fustian ['fʌstɪən] *s.* fustagno *m.*
futility [fjʊ(ː)'tɪlɪtɪ] *s.* futilità *f.*
future ['fjuːtʃəʳ] *agg. e s.* futuro *m.* ♦ **in f., for the f.** in futuro, d'ora innanzi
futurism ['fjuːtʃərɪz(ə)m] *s.* futurismo *m.*
futuristic ['fjuːtʃərɪstɪk] *agg.* **1** avveniristico **2** (*arte*) futuristico
fuzzy ['fʌzɪ] *agg.* **1** crespo **2** (*fot.*) sfocato, indistinto

G

gab [gæb] *s.* (*fam.*) chiacchiera *f.*, parlantina *f.*
to gabble ['gæbl] *v. tr. e intr.* borbottare, farfugliare
gable ['geɪbl] *s.* (*arch.*) timpano *m.*
gadfly ['gædflaɪ] *s.* **1** (*zool.*) tafano *m.* **2** seccatore *m.*
gadget ['gædʒɪt] *s.* aggeggio *m.*, congegno *m.*, dispositivo *m.*
Gaelic ['geɪlɪk] *agg. e s.* gaelico *m.* (*lingua*)
gaff [gæf] *s.* fiocina *f.*, arpione *m.*
gag [gæg] *s.* **1** bavaglio *m.* **2** facezia *f.*, battuta *f.*
to gag [gæg] **A** *v. tr.* imbavagliare **B** *v. intr.* improvvisare battute
gaiety ['geɪətɪ] *s.* allegria *f.*, gaiezza *f.*
gaily ['geɪlɪ] *avv.* gaiamente, allegramente
gain [geɪn] *s.* **1** guadagno *m.*, profitto *m.* **2** miglioramento *m.*, aumento *m.*
to gain [geɪn] **A** *v. tr.* guadagnare, conseguire, ottenere **B** *v. intr.* **1** guadagnarci **2** progredire, aumentare, migliorare **3** (*di orologio*) andare avanti ♦ **to g. on** guadagnare terreno su
gait [geɪt] *s.* andatura *f.*
galaxy ['gæləksɪ] *s.* galassia *f.*
gale [geɪl] *s.* **1** burrasca *f.*, vento *m.* forte **2** (*di risa*) scoppio *m.*
gall [gɔːl] *s.* bile *f.*, fiele *m.* ♦ **g. bladder** cistifellea; **g.-stone** calcolo biliare
gallant ['gælənt] *agg.* **1** coraggioso, valoroso **2** galante **3** sfarzoso
galleon ['gælɪən] *s.* galeone *m.*
gallery ['gælərɪ] *s.* **1** galleria *f.* **2** loggione *m.*
galley ['gælɪ] *s.* **1** galea *f.* **2** (*naut.*) cucina *f.*
gallicism ['gælɪsɪz(ə)m] *s.* gallicismo *m.*
gallon ['gælən] *s.* gallone *m.*
gallop ['gæləp] *s.* galoppo *m.*
to gallop ['gæləp] *v. intr.* galoppare
gallows ['gælɒuz] *s. pl.* forca *f.*, patibolo *m.*
galore [gə'lɜːʳ] *avv.* in abbondanza, a iosa
to galvanize ['gælvənaɪz] *v. tr.* galvanizzare
gamble ['gæmbl] *s.* azzardo *m.*, rischio *m.*
to gamble ['gæmbl] *v. intr.* giocare d'azzardo ♦ **to g. on** giocare su
gambler ['gæmbləʳ] *s.* giocatore *m.* d'azzardo
gambling ['gæmblɪŋ] *s.* gioco *m.* d'azzardo
game [geɪm] **A** *s.* **1** gioco *m.* **2** partita *f.*, mano *f.* **3** tranello *m.*, scherzo *m.* **4** selvaggina *f.* **B** *agg.* pronto ♦ **big g.** selvaggina grossa; **g.-licence** licenza di caccia
gamekeeper ['geɪmˌkiːpəʳ] *s.* guardacaccia *m. inv.*
gammon ['gæmən] *s.* **1** prosciutto *m.* affumicato **2** quarto *m.* di maiale
gamut ['gæmət] *s.* gamma *f.*
gang [gæŋ] *s.* banda *f.*, squadra *f.*
gangrene ['gæŋgriːn] *s.* cancrena *f.*
gangster ['gæŋstəʳ] *s.* gangster *m.*, bandito *m.*
gangway ['gæŋweɪ] *s.* passerella *f.*
gap [gæp] *s.* **1** apertura *f.*, varco *m.* **2** divario *m.*, lacuna *f.*
to gape [geɪp] *v. intr.* **1** spalancare la bocca, restare a bocca aperta **2** aprirsi
garage ['gæraːʒ] *s.* garage *m. inv.*, autorimessa *f.*
garbage ['gaːbɪdʒ] *s.* immondizia *f.*, rifiuti *m. pl.* ♦ **g. can** pattumiera
to garble ['gaːbl] *v. tr.* alterare, confondere
garden ['gaːdn] *s.* **1** giardino *m.* **2** orto *m.* ♦ **g. centre** vivaio; **roof g.** giardino pensile
gardener ['gaːdnəʳ] *s.* giardiniere *m.*
gardenia [gaː'diːnjə] *s.* gardenia *f.*
gardening ['gaːdnɪŋ] *s.* giardinaggio *m.*
gargle ['gaːgl] *s.* gargarismo *m.*
garish ['gɛərɪʃ] *agg.* sgargiante, vistoso
garland ['gaːlənd] *s.* ghirlanda *f.*
garlic ['gaːlɪk] *s.* aglio *m.*
garment ['gaːmənt] *s.* indumento *m.*
garnish ['gaːnɪʃ] *s.* guarnizione *f.*
to garnish ['gaːnɪʃ] *v. tr.* guarnire
garrison ['gærɪsn] *s.* guarnigione *f.*
garrulous ['gærʊləs] *agg.* garrulo, loquace
garter ['gaːtəʳ] *s.* giarrettiera *f.* ♦ **g. belt** reggicalze
gas [gæs] *s.* **1** gas *m. inv.* **2** (*USA*) benzina *f.* ♦ **g. mask** maschera antigas; **g. meter** contatore del gas; **g. ring** fornello; **g. station** (*USA*) distributore di benzina
gash [gæʃ] *s.* sfregio *m.*
to gash [gæʃ] *v. tr.* sfregiare

gasket ['gæskɪt] *s.* (*mecc.*) guarnizione *f.*
gasoline ['gæsəliːn] *s.* benzina *f.*
gasp [gaːsp] *s.* respiro *m.* affannoso
to gasp [gaːsp] *v. intr.* **1** boccheggiare, ansimare **2** restare senza fiato ♦ **to g. out** dire a fatica, dire ansimando
gassy ['gæsɪ] *agg.* gassoso
gastric ['gæstrɪk] *agg.* gastrico
gastritis [gæs'traɪtɪs] *s.* gastrite *f.*
gastroenteric [ˌgæstrɒ(ʊ)en'tɛrɪk] *agg.* gastroenterico
gastronomic [ˌgæstrə'nəmɪk] *agg.* gastronomico
gastronomy [gæs'trənəmɪ] *s.* gastronomia *f.*
gate [geɪt] *s.* **1** cancello *m.*, porta *f.* **2** (*aer*) uscita *f.*
to gatecrash ['geɪtkræʃ] *v. intr.* (*fam.*) partecipare senza invito
gateway ['geɪtˌweɪ] *s.* **1** entrata *f.*, ingresso *m.* **2** porta *f.*
to gather ['gæðəʳ] **A** *v. tr.* **1** raccogliere, radunare **2** assumere, prendere **3** increspare **B** *v. intr.* **1** raccogliersi, radunarsi **2** aumentare, gonfiarsi
gathering ['gæðərɪŋ] *s.* raduno *m.*
gauche [gɒʊʃ] *agg.* goffo, maldestro
gaudy ['gɜːdɪ] *agg.* sgargiante
gauge [geɪdʒ] *s.* **1** calibro *m.*, manometro *m.*, misuratore *m.* **2** (*ferr.*) scartamento *m.*
gaunt [gɜːnt] *agg.* **1** scarno, macilento **2** desolato, arido
gauntlet ['gɜːntlɪt] *s.* guanto *m.* di sfida
gauze [gɜːz] *s.* garza *f.*
gave [geɪv] *pass. di* **to give**
gay [geɪ] **A** *agg.* allegro, vivace **B** *s.* omosessuale *m. e f.*
gaze [geɪz] *s.* sguardo *m.* fisso
to gaze [geɪz] *v. intr.* guardare fissamente ♦ **to g. at/on** fissare
gazebo [gə'ziːbɒʊ] *s.* gazebo *m. inv.*
gazelle [gə'zəl] *s.* gazzella *f.*
gazette [gə'zɛt] *s.* gazzetta *f.*
gazetteer [ˌgæzɪ'tɪəʳ] *s.* dizionario *m.* geografico
gear [gɪəʳ] *s.* **1** meccanismo *m.*, ingranaggio *m.* **2** arnesi *m. pl.*, equipaggiamento *m.* **3** (*autom.*) cambio *m.* ♦ **g. box** scatola del cambio; **in g.** con la marcia ingranata
geese [giːs] *pl. di* **goose**
gel [dʒɛl] *s.* gelatina *f.*, gel *m. inv.*
gelatin(e) [ˌdʒɛlə'tɪ(ː)n] *s.* gelatina *f.*
gem [dʒɛm] *s.* gemma *f.*, pietra *f.* preziosa
gender ['dʒɛndəʳ] *s.* (*gramm.*) genere *m.*
genealogy [ˌdʒiːnɪ'ælədʒɪ] *s.* genealogia *f.*
general ['dʒɛn(ə)r(ə)l] **A** *agg.* **1** generale, comune **2** generico **B** *s.* generale *m.* ♦ **g. delivery** fermo posta; **in g.** in genere
generality [ˌdʒɛnə'rælɪtɪ] *s.* generalità *f.*
to generalize ['dʒɛn(ə)rɛlaɪz] *v. tr.* generalizzare
generally ['dʒɛn(ə)r(ə)lɪ] *avv.* generalmente
to generate ['dʒɛnəreɪt] *v. tr.* generare
generation [ˌdʒɛnə'reɪʃ(ə)n] *s.* generazione *f.*
generational [ˌdʒɛnə'reɪʃ(ə)n(ə)l] *agg.* generazionale
generator ['dʒɛnəreɪtəʳ] *s.* generatore *m.*
generic [dʒɪ'nɛrɪk] *agg.* generico
generosity [ˌdʒɛnə'rəsɪtɪ] *s.* generosità *f.*
generous ['dʒɛn(ə)rəs] *agg.* **1** generoso **2** abbondante
genesis ['dʒɛnɪsɪs] *s.* genesi *f.*
genetic [dʒɪ'nɛtɪk] *agg.* genetico
genetics [dʒɪ'nɛtɪks] *s. pl.* (*v. al sing.*) genetica *f.*
genial ['dʒiːnjəl] *agg.* **1** cordiale, socievole **2** benigno, mite
genie ['dʒiːnɪ] *s.* genio *m.*
genitalia [ˌdʒɛnɪ'teɪljə] *s. pl.* genitali *m. pl.*
genitals ['dʒɛnɪtlz] *s. pl.* genitali *m. pl.*
genius ['dʒiːnjəs] *s.* genio *m.*
genteel [dʒɛn'tiːl] *agg.* garbato
gentle ['dʒɛntl] *agg.* **1** gentile, garbato **2** delicato, lieve
gentleman ['dʒɛntlmən] (*pl.* **gentlemen**) *s.* signore *m.*, gentiluomo *m.*
gently ['dʒɛntlɪ] *avv.* delicatamente, dolcemente
gentry ['dʒɛntrɪ] *s.* piccola nobiltà *f.*
genuine ['dʒɛnjʊɪn] *agg.* genuino, autentico
genuineness ['dʒɛnjʊɪnnɪs] *s.* genuinità *f.*, autenticità *f.*
genus ['dʒːnəs] *s.* genere *m.*
geographic [dʒɪə'græfɪk] *agg.* geografico
geography [dʒɪ'əgrəfɪ] *s.* geografia *f.*
geology [dʒɪ'ələdʒɪ] *s.* geologia *f.*
geometric(al) [dʒɪə'mɛtrɪk((ə)l)] *agg.* geometrico
geometry [dʒɪ'əmɪtrɪ] *s.* geometria *f.*
geophysics [ˌdʒiːɒ(ʊ)'fɪzɪks] *s. pl.* (*v. al sing.*) geofisica *f.*
geopolitics [ˌdʒiːɒ(ʊ)'pəlɪtɪks] *s. pl.* (*v. al sing.*) geopolitica *f.*
georgic ['dʒɜːdʒɪk] *agg.* georgico

geothermal [ˌdʒiːɒ(ʊ)'θɜːm(ə)l] *agg.* geotermico
geranium [dʒɪ'reɪŋjəm] *s.* geranio *m.*
geriatric [ˌdʒɛrɪ'ætrɪk] *agg.* geriatrico
geriatrics [ˌdʒɛrɪ'ætrɪks] *s. pl.* (*v. al sing.*) geriatria *f.*
germ [dʒɜːm] *s.* germe *m.*
German ['dʒɜːmən] *agg.* tedesco ♦ **G. measles** rosolia
to germinate ['dʒɜːmɪneɪt] *v. intr.* germogliare
gestation [dʒɛs'teɪʃ(ə)n] *s.* gestazione *f.*
gesture ['dʒɛstʃəʳ] *s.* gesto *m.*, atto *m.*
to get [gɛt] (*pass.* **got**, *p. p.* **got**, *USA* **gotten**) **A** *v. tr.* **1** prendere **2** ottenere, procurarsi **3** afferrare, capire, cogliere **4** convincere, persuadere **5** mettere **6** portare, mandare, condurre **B** *v. intr.* **1** diventare, farsi **2** andare, arrivare **3** mettersi **4** (*nella costruzione passiva*) essere, venire (ES: **my father got dismissed last week** mio padre è stato licenziato la settimana scorsa) ♦ **to g. about** circolare, diffondersi; **to g. along** andare d'accordo; **to g. away** scappare; **to g. back** riavere; **to g. down** scendere; **to g. off** scendere **to g. on** salire; **to g. over** superare; **to g. out** uscire; **to g. up** alzarsi, salire; **to have got** avere, dovere
getaway ['gɛtəweɪ] *s.* fuga *f.*
ghastly ['gaːstlɪ] *agg.* **1** orribile, spaventoso **2** spettrale
gherkin ['gɜːkɪn] *s.* cetriolino *m.*
ghetto ['gɛtɒʊ] *s.* ghetto *m.*
ghost [gɒʊst] *s.* fantasma *m.*, spirito *m.* ♦ **g. writer** scrittore per conto di altri
giant ['dʒaɪənt] *agg. e s.* gigante *m.*
gibberish ['gɪbərɪʃ] *s.* borbottio *m.*
giblets ['dʒɪblɪts] *s. pl.* frattaglie *f. pl.*
giddiness ['gɪdɪnɪs] *s.* capogiro *m.*, vertigini *f. pl.*
giddy ['gɪdɪ] *agg.* stordito ♦ **to be g.** avere le vertigini
gift [gɪft] *s.* **1** dono *m.*, regalo *m.* **2** pregio *m.*, dote *f.*
gifted ['gɪftɪd] *agg.* dotato
gigantic [dʒaɪ'gæntɪk] *agg.* gigantesco
gigantism ['dʒaɪgænˌtɪz(ə)m] *s.* gigantismo *m.*
to giggle ['gɪgl] *v. intr.* sghignazzare, ridere scioccamente
gills [gɪlz] *s. pl.* (*zool.*) branchie *f. pl.*
gilt [gɪlt] **A** *agg.* dorato **B** *s.* doratura *f.*
gimmick ['gɪmɪk] *s.* (*fam.*) **1** trovata *f.*, trucco *m.* **2** aggeggio *m.*
gin [dʒɪn] *s.* gin *m. inv.*
ginger ['dʒɪn(d)ʒəʳ] *s.* zenzero *m.*
gingerly ['dʒɪn(d)ʒəlɪ] *avv.* cautamente, con circospezione *m.*
gipsy ['dʒɪpsɪ] *s.* gitano *m.*, zingaro *m.*
giraffe [dʒɪ'raːf] *s.* giraffa *f.*
to gird [gɜːd] (*pass. e p. p.* **girded**, **girt**) *v. tr.* cingere
girder ['gɜːdəʳ] *s.* trave *f.*
girdle ['gɜːdl] *s.* guaina *f.*, busto *m.*
girl [gɜːl] *s.* **1** ragazza *f.*, signorina *f.* **2** figlia *f.* **3** fidanzata *f.*
girlfriend ['gɜːlfrɛnd] *s.* ragazza *f.*, fidanzata *f.*
girlish ['gɜːlɪʃ] *agg.* da ragazza
giro ['dʒaɪrɒʊ] *s.* giroconto *m.*, postagiro *m.*
girt [gɜːt] *pass. e p. p. di* **to gird**
girth [gɜːθ] *s.* giro *m.*, circonferenza *f.*
gist [dʒɪst] *s.* essenza *f.*
to give [gɪv] (*pass.* **gave**, *p. p.* **given**) **A** *v. tr.* **1** dare, fornire **2** regalare **3** eseguire, rappresentare **4** dare come risultato **5** causare **B** *v. intr.* **1** cedere, piegarsi, addolcirsi **2** dare su, guardare su ♦ **to g. back** rendere; **to g. in** cedere; **to g. up** consegnare, rinunciare
giver ['gɪvəʳ] *s.* donatore *m.*
glacial ['gleɪsjəl] *agg.* glaciale
glacier ['glæsjəʳ] *s.* ghiacciaio *m.*
glad [glæd] *agg.* **1** felice, lieto **2** grato
glade [gleɪd] *s.* radura *f.*
gladly ['glædlɪ] *avv.* volentieri, con piacere
glamorous ['glæmərəs] *agg.* attraente, affascinante
glamour ['glæməʳ] *s.* fascino *m.*, seduzione *f.*, incanto *m.*
glance [glaːns] *s.* occhiata *f.*, sguardo *m.*
to glance [glaːns] *v. tr.* **1** guardare brevemente **2** far rimbalzare, deviare ♦ **to g. at** gettare uno sguardo su
gland [glænd] *s.* ghiandola *f.*
glare [glɛəʳ] *s.* **1** bagliore *m.*, riverbero *m.*, luce *f.* abbagliante **2** sguardo *m.* furioso
to glare [glɛəʳ] *v. intr.* sfolgorare ♦ **to g. at** guardare di traverso
glaring ['glɛərɪŋ] *agg.* **1** abbagliante **2** torvo **3** evidente, madornale
glass [glaːs] *s.* **1** vetro *m.* **2** bicchiere *m.* **3** *al pl.* occhiali *m. pl.* ♦ **sun-glasses** occhiali da sole
glasshouse ['glaːshaʊs] *s.* serra *f.*
glassware ['glaːswɛəʳ] *s.* cristalleria *f.*
glassworks ['glaːswɜːks] *s. pl.* (*v. al sing.*)

vetreria *f.*
glaze [gleɪz] *s.* **1** smalto *m.* **2** (*cuc.*) glassa *f.*
to glaze [gleɪz] *v. tr.* **1** fornire di vetri **2** smaltare **3** (*cuc.*) glassare
glazier ['gleɪzjəʳ] *s.* vetraio *m.*
gleam [gliːm] *v. intr.* brillare, luccicare
to glean [gliːn] *v. tr. e intr.* spigolare, racimolare
glee [gliː] *s.* gioia *f.*
glib [glɪb] *agg.* **1** loquace **2** scorrevole
glide [glaɪd] *s.* **1** scivolata *f.* **2** planata *f.*
to glide [glaɪd] *v. intr.* **1** scivolare **2** fluire **3** planare
glider ['glaɪdəʳ] *s.* aliante *m.*
gliding ['glaɪdɪŋ] *s.* volo *m.* a vela
glimmer ['glɪməʳ] *s.* barlume *m.*
glimpse [glɪm(p)s] *s.* **1** occhiata *f.* di sfuggita **2** apparizione *f.*
to glint [glɪnt] *v. intr.* brillare, luccicare
to glisten ['glɪsn] *v. intr.* brillare, luccicare
to glitter ['glɪtəʳ] *v. intr.* brillare, luccicare
to gloat [glɒʊt] *v. intr.* gongolare
global ['glɒʊbl] *agg.* globale
globe [glɒʊb] *s.* **1** globo *m.*, sfera *f.* **2** mappamondo *m.*
gloom [gluːm] *s.* **1** oscurità *f.* **2** tristezza *f.*
gloomy ['gluːmɪ] *agg.* **1** oscuro, cupo, lugubre **2** tetro, triste
glorious ['glɜːrɪəs] *agg.* **1** glorioso **2** magnifico
glory ['glɜːrɪ] *s.* **1** gloria *f.* **2** splendore *m.*
gloss (1) [gləs] *s.* **1** lucentezza *f.*, lustro *m.* **2** vernice *f.*, smalto *m.*
gloss (2) [gləs] *s.* glossa *f.*, chiosa *f.*
to gloss (1) [gləs] *v. tr.* lucidare, lustrare ♦ **to g. over** scivolare su, dissimulare
to gloss (2) [gləs] *v. tr.* glossare, chiosare
glossary ['gləsərɪ] *s.* glossario *m.*
glossy ['gləsɪ] *agg.* lucente, lucido
glottology [glə'tələdʒɪ] *s.* glottologia *f.*
glove [glʌv] *s.* guanto *m.*
to glow [glɒʊ] *v. intr.* ardere, fiammeggiare
to glower ['glaʊəʳ] *v. intr.* guardare in cagnesco
glucose ['gluːkɒʊs] *s.* glucosio *m.*
glue [gluː] *s.* colla *f.*
to glue [gluː] *v. tr.* incollare
glum [glʌm] *agg.* depresso, abbattuto
glut [glʌt] *s.* eccesso *m.*, saturazione *f.*
to glut [glʌt] *v. tr.* saziare, saturare
gluteus [gluː'tiːəs] *s.* gluteo *m.*
glutton ['glʌtn] *s.* ghiottone
gluttonous ['glʌtnəs] *agg.* ghiotto
glyc(a)emia [glaɪ'siːmɪə] *s.* glicemia *f.*
glycerin(e) [ˌglɪsə'rɪ(ː)n] *s.* glicerina *f.*
gnarled [naːld] *agg.* (*di legno*) nodoso
gnat [næt] *s.* moscerino *m.*, zanzara *f.*
to gnaw [nɜː] *v. tr. e intr.* rosicchiare
gnome [nɒʊm] *s.* gnomo *m.*
to go [gɒʊ] (*pass.* **went**, *p. p.* **gone**) *v. intr.* **1** andare, andarsene, viaggiare **2** (*seguito da agg.*) diventare (ES: **to go mad** diventare matto, impazzire) **3** andare, svolgersi **4** funzionare **5** (*seguito da participio pres.*) andare a (ES: **to go swimming** andare a fare una nuotata) ♦ **let's go!** andiamo!; **to be going to** (*seguito da inf.*) stare per, essere sul punto di; **to go away** andar via; **to go back** ritornare; **to go in** entrare; **to go on** continuare; **to go out** uscire; **to go through** esaminare, subire
to goad [gɒʊd] *v. tr.* incitare, spronare
go-ahead ['gɒ(ʊ)əhɛd] **A** *agg.* intraprendente, audace **B** *s.* via *m.*, permesso *m.* di agire
goal [gɒʊl] *s.* **1** meta *f.*, scopo *m.* **2** (*sport*) goal *m. inv.*, rete *f.*
goalkeeper ['gɒʊlˌkɪ(ː)pəʳ] *s.* (*sport*) portiere *m.*
goat [gɒʊt] *s.* capra *f.* ♦ **the G.** Capricorno
to gobble ['gəbl] *v. tr.* ingoiare, trangugiare
go-between ['gɒʊbɪˌtwiːn] *s.* intermediario *m.*
goblet ['gəblɪt] *s.* calice *m.*
goblin ['gəblɪn] *s.* gnomo *m.*
God [øəd] *s.* Dio *m.*
godchild ['gədtʃaɪld] (*pl.* **godchildren**) *s.* figlioccio *m.*
goddaughter ['gədˌdɜːtəʳ] *s.* figlioccia *f.*
goddess ['gədɪs] *s.* dea *f.*
godfather ['gədˌfaːðəʳ] *s.* padrino *m.*
god-forsaken ['gədfəˌseɪkn] *agg.* desolato, abbandonato
godhead ['gədhɛd] *s.* divinità *f.*
godmother ['gədˌmʌðəʳ] *s.* madrina *f.*
godson ['gədsʌn] *s.* figlioccio *m.*
goggles ['gəglz] *s. pl.* occhiali *m. pl.* di protezione
going ['gɒʊɪŋ] **A** *agg.* **1** corrente, in vigore **2** efficiente **3** di moda **4** disponibile **B** *s.* **1** andata *f.* **2** andatura *f.* **3** (*di strada, terreno*) stato *m.*, condizione *f.* ♦ **coming and g.** andirivieni; **g.-down** discesa
gold [gɒʊld] **A** *s.* oro *m.* **B** *agg.* aureo ♦ **fine g.** oro zecchino; **g.-mine** miniera; **g. plated** placcato in oro
golden ['gɒʊld(ə)n] *agg.* **1** dorato, d'oro

2 biondo
goldsmith ['gɒʊldsmɪθ] *s.* orafo *m.*
golf [gɔlf] *s.* (*sport*) golf *m. inv.* ♦ **g. club** circolo del golf, mazza da golf; **g. course** campo da golf
golfer ['gɔlfəʳ] *s.* giocatore *m.* di golf
gone [gɔn] **A** *p. p. di* **to go** **B** *agg.* **1** andato, finito **2** debole, sfinito
gong [gɔŋ] *s.* gong *m. inv.*
good [gʊd] (*comp.* **better**, *sup. rel.* **best**) **A** *agg.* **1** buono, bravo, bello **2** piacevole, felice **B** *s.* **1** bene *m.*, beneficio *m.* **2** *al pl.* beni *m. pl.*, merce *f.* ♦ **as g. as** praticamente, come; **for g.** per sempre; **g. evening** buonasera; **G. Friday** Venerdì santo; **g. looking** prestante, bello; **g. morning** buongiorno; **g. night** buonanotte; **goods train** treno merci; **to be g. at** essere bravo in
goodbye [gʊ(d)'baɪ] *inter.* addio, arrivederci
goodness ['gʊdnɪs] *s.* bontà *f.*, cortesia *f.* ♦ **my g.!** accidenti!
goodwill [ˌgʊd'wɪl] *s.* benevolenza *f.*, amicizia *f.*
goose [guːs] (*pl.* **geese**) *s.* oca *f.*
gooseberry ['gʊzb(ə)rɪ] *s.* uva *f.* spina
gooseflesh ['guːsflɛʃ] *s.* pelle *f.* d'oca
to gore [gɜːʳ] *v. tr.* incornare
gorge [gɜːdʒ] *s.* gola *f.*
to gorge [gɜːdʒ] *v. tr. e intr.* rimpinzare, rimpinzarsi
gorgeous ['gɜːdʒəs] *agg.* fastoso, magnifico
gorilla [gə'rɪlə] *s.* gorilla *m. inv.*
gorse [gɜːs] *s.* ginestrone *m.*
gory ['gɔrɪ] *agg.* insanguinato, sanguinoso
gosh [gɔʃ] *inter.* perbacco!
gospel ['gɔsp(ə)l] *s.* vangelo *m.*
gossip ['gɔsɪp] *s.* **1** chiacchiera *f.*, pettegolezzo *m.* **2** pettegolo *m.*
to gossip ['gɔsɪp] *v. intr.* **1** chiacchierare **2** pettegolare
gossipy ['gɔsɪpɪ] *agg.* pettegolo
got [gɔt] *pass. e p. p. di* **to get**
Gothic ['gɔθɪk] *agg.* gotico
gotten ['gɔtn] *p. p. di* **to get** (*USA*)
gouache [gʊ'aːʃ] *s.* (*arte*) guazzo *m.*
gourmet ['gʊəmeɪ] *s.* buongustaio *m.*
gout [gaʊt] *s.* (*med.*) gotta *f.*
to govern ['gʌv(ə)n] *v. tr.* **1** governare, dirigere **2** controllare
government ['gʌvnmənt] *s.* governo *m.*, amministrazione *f.*
governor ['gʌvənəʳ] *s.* governatore *m.*, amministratore *m.*
gown [gaʊn] *s.* **1** toga *f.* **2** veste *f.* lunga
to grab [græb] *v. tr.* afferrare, agguantare ♦ **to g. at** tentare di afferrare
grace [greɪs] *s.* grazia *f.*
to grace [greɪs] *v. tr.* **1** abbellire **2** onorare
graceful ['greɪsf(ʊ)l] *agg.* leggiadro, elegante
gracious ['greɪʃəs] *agg.* **1** grazioso, benevolo **2** misericordioso
gradation [grə'deɪʃ(ə)n] *s.* gradazione *f.*
grade [greɪd] *s.* **1** grado *m.* **2** categoria *f.*, qualità *f.* **3** (*USA*) classe *f.*, anno *m.* (di scuola) **4** (*USA*) voto *m.* (scolastico) ♦ **g. school** scuola elementare
to grade [greɪd] *v. tr.* classificare
gradient ['greɪdjənt] *s.* **1** pendenza *f.*, inclinazione *f.* **2** gradiente *m.*
gradual ['grædjʊəl] *agg.* graduale
gradually ['grædjʊəlɪ] *avv.* gradualmente
graduate ['grædjʊət] *s.* **1** laureato *m.* **2** (*USA*) diplomato *m.*
to graduate ['grædjʊeɪt] *v. intr.* **1** laurearsi **2** (*USA*) diplomarsi
graduation [ˌgrædjʊ'eɪʃ(ə)n] *s.* **1** laurea *f.* **2** (*USA*) diploma *m.* **3** graduazione *f.* **4** scala *f.* graduata
graffito [graː'fiːtɒʊ] (*pl.* **graffiti**) *s.* graffito *m.*
graft (1) [graːft] *s.* **1** (*bot.*) innesto *m.* **2** (*med.*) trapianto *m.*
graft (2) [graːft] *s.* corruzione *f.*, peculato *m.*
to graft (1) [graːft] *v. tr.* **1** (*bot.*) innestare **2** (*med.*) trapiantare
to graft (2) [graːft] *v. tr.* guadagnare con mezzi illeciti
grain [greɪn] *s.* **1** grano *m.*, granello *m.* **2** grana *f.*, (*del legno*) venatura *f.*
grained [greɪnd] *agg.* granulato
gram (1) [græm] *s.* grammo *m.*
gram (2) [græm] *s.* cece *m.*
grammar ['græməʳ] *s.* grammatica *f.* ♦ **g. school** liceo
grammatical [grə'mætɪk(ə)l] *agg.* grammaticale
granary ['grænərɪ] *s.* granaio *m.*
grand [grænd] *agg.* **1** grandioso, imponente **2** grande, importante **3** complessivo ♦ **g. piano** pianoforte a coda
grandchild ['græn(d)tʃaɪld] (*pl.* **grandchildren**) *s.* nipote *m. e f.* (*di nonni*)
granddaughter ['grænˌdɜːtəʳ] *s.* nipote *f.*

(*di nonni*)
grandeur ['grænd(d)ʒəʳ] *s.* grandiosità *f.*
grandfather ['græn(d),fa:ðəʳ] *s.* nonno *m.*
grandma ['grænma:] *s.* (*fam.*) nonna *f.*
grandmother ['græn,mʌðəʳ] *s.* nonna *f.*
grandpa ['grænpa:] *s.* (*fam.*) nonno *m.*
grandparent ['græn(d),pɛər(ə)nt] *s.* nonno *m.*, nonna *f.*
grandson ['græn(d)sʌn] *s.* nipote *m.* (*di nonni*)
granite ['grænɪt] *s.* granito *m.*
granny ['grænɪ] *s.* (*fam.*) nonna *f.*
grant [gra:nt] *s.* **1** concessione *f.*, assegnazione *f.* **2** sussidio *m.*, sovvenzione *f.* **3** borsa *f.* di studio
to grant [gra:nt] *v. tr.* **1** accordare, concedere **2** accogliere, esaudire **3** attribuire ♦ **to take st. for granted** dare q.c. per scontato
granular ['grænjʊləʳ] *agg.* granuloso, granulare
granulation [,grænjʊ'leɪʃ(ə)n] *s.* granulazione *f.*
granule ['grænju:l] *s.* granello *m.*
grape [greɪp] *s.* **1** acino *m.* **2** *al pl.* uva *f.*
grapefruit ['greɪpfru:t] *s.* pompelmo *m.*
graph [græf] *s.* grafico *m.*, diagramma *m.*
graphic ['græfɪk] *agg.* grafico
graphically ['græfɪkəlɪ] *avv.* graficamente
graphics ['græfɪks] *s. pl.* (*v. al sing.*) grafica *f.*
to grapple ['græpl] *v. tr.* afferrare, agganciare ♦ **to g. with** lottare con, essere alle prese con
grasp [gra:sp] *s.* **1** presa *f.*, stretta *f.* **2** padronanza *f.*, controllo *m.* **3** comprensione *f.*
to grasp [gra:sp] *v. tr.* **1** afferrare, stringere **2** comprendere ♦ **to g. at** cercare di afferrare
grass [gra:s] *s.* erba *f.*
grasshopper ['gra:s,hɔpəʳ] *s.* cavalletta *f.*
grassland ['gra:slænd] *s.* prateria *f.*
grate [greɪt] *s.* grata *f.*
to grate [greɪt] **A** *v. tr.* grattugiare **B** *v. intr.* cigolare, stridere
grateful ['greɪtf(ʊ)l] *agg.* grato
gratefully ['greɪtf(ʊ)lɪ] *avv.* con gratitudine
grater ['greɪtəʳ] *s.* grattugia *f.*
to gratify ['grætɪfaɪ] *v. tr.* gratificare, compiacere
grating (1) ['greɪtɪŋ] *s.* griglia *f.*, grata *f.*
grating (2) ['greɪtɪŋ] **A** *agg.* stridulo **B** *s.* stridore *m.*
gratis ['greɪtɪs] *avv.* gratis
gratitude ['grætɪtju:d] *s.* gratitudine *f.*
gratuity [grə'tju:ɪtɪ] *s.* mancia *f.*, gratifica *f.*
grave (1) [greɪv] *s.* tomba *f.*
grave (2) [greɪv] *agg.* grave, serio
gravel ['græv(ə)l] *s.* ghiaia *f.*
gravelly ['grævəlɪ] *agg.* ghiaioso
gravestone ['greɪvstɒʊn] *s.* pietra *f.* tombale
graveyard ['greɪv,ja:d] *s.* cimitero *m.*
gravity ['grævɪtɪ] *s.* **1** gravità *f.*, peso *m.* **2** serietà *f.*, solennità *f.*
gravy ['greɪvɪ] *s.* sugo *m.* (*di carne*) ♦ **g. boat** salsiera
gray [greɪ] *agg.* (*USA*) → **grey**
graze [greɪz] *s.* escoriazione *f.*
to graze (1) [greɪz] *v. tr.* **1** sfiorare **2** scalfire, escoriare, graffiare
to graze (2) [greɪz] *v. intr.* pascolare
grazing ['greɪzɪŋ] *s.* pascolo *m.* ♦ **g. land** terreno da pascolo
grease [gri:s] *s.* **1** grasso *m.* **2** brillantina *f.* ♦ **g.-proof paper** carta oleata
to grease [gri:z] *v. tr.* ungere, ingrassare, lubrificare
greasing ['gri:sɪŋ] *s.* ingrassaggio *m.*
greasy ['gri:sɪ] *agg.* untuoso, grasso
great [greɪt] *agg.* **1** grande, grosso **2** grandioso **3** insigne, celebre
greatly ['greɪtlɪ] *avv.* molto, grandemente
greatness ['greɪtnɪs] *s.* grandezza *f.*
grecism ['gri:sɪz(ə)m] *s.* grecismo *m.*
greediness ['gri:dɪnɪs] *s.* **1** avidità *f.* **2** golosità *f.*
greedy ['gri:dɪ] *agg.* **1** avido **2** goloso
Greek [gri:k] *agg. e s.* greco *m.*
green [gri:n] **A** *agg.* **1** verde **2** giovane, fresco **3** inesperto **B** *s.* **1** verde *m.* **2** prato **3** *al pl.* verdura *f.*
greengrocer ['gri:n,grɒʊsəʳ] *s.* fruttivendolo *m.*
greenhouse ['gri:nhaʊs] *s.* serra *f.*
greenish ['gri:nɪʃ] *agg.* verdastro
to greet [gri:t] *v. tr.* salutare
greeting ['gri:tɪŋ] *s.* **1** saluto *m.* **2** *al pl.* auguri *m. pl.*
gregarious [grɪ'gɛərɪəs] *agg.* **1** gregario **2** socievole
gremlin ['grɛmlɪn] *s.* folletto *m.*
grenade [grɪ'neɪd] *s.* (*mil.*) granata *f.*
grew [gru:] *pass. di* **to grow**
grey [greɪ] (*USA* **gray**) *agg.* grigio ♦ **g.-haired** brizzolato

greyhound ['greɪhaʊnd] *s.* levriero *m.*
grid [grɪd] *s.* **1** grata *f.*, griglia *f.* **2** reticolo *m.*, rete *f.*
grief [gri:f] *s.* afflizione *f.*, dolore *m.*
grievance ['gri:v(ə)ns] *s.* lagnanza *f.*, reclamo *m.*
to grieve [gri:v] **A** *v. tr.* addolorare, affliggere **B** *v. intr.* addolorarsi, affliggersi ♦ **to g. at/for sb.** rattristarsi per qc.
grievous ['gri:vəs] *agg.* doloroso, atroce ♦ **g. bodily harm** grave danno fisico, aggressione
griffin ['grɪfɪn] *s.* grifone *m.*
grill [grɪl] *s.* **1** griglia *f.*, grata *f.* **2** grigliata *f.*
to grill [grɪl] *v. tr.* cuocere alla griglia
grille [grɪl] *s.* grata *f.*, griglia *f.*
grilled [grɪld] *agg.* alla griglia
grim [grɪm] *agg.* **1** orribile, sinistro **2** spietato, feroce, risoluto **3** sgradevole, repellente
grimace [grɪ'meɪs] *s.* smorfia *f.*
grime [graɪm] *s.* sporcizia *f.*
grin [grɪn] *s.* **1** sogghigno *m.* **2** sorriso *m.*
grind [graɪnd] *s.* **1** cigolio *m.* **2** (*fam.*) sgobbata *f.*
to grind [graɪnd] (*pass. e p. p.* **ground**) *v. tr.* **1** macinare, frantumare **2** arrotare, affilare **3** smerigliare
grinder ['graɪndə^r] *s.* **1** arrotino *m.* **2** macina *f.*, macinino *m.* **3** (*dente*) molare *m.*
grinding ['graɪndɪŋ] *s.* macinazione *f.*
grip [grɪp] *s.* **1** stretta *f.*, presa *f.* **2** impugnatura *f.* **3** (*USA*) borsa *f.* da viaggio
to grip [grɪp] *v. tr.* **1** stringere, impugnare **2** avvincere
grisly ['grɪzlɪ] *agg.* orrendo, macabro
gristle ['grɪsl] *s.* cartilagine *f.*
grit [grɪt] *s.* **1** ghiaia *f.*, pietrisco *m.* **2** coraggio *m.*
grizzled ['grɪzld] *agg.* brizzolato
groan [grɒʊn] *s.* gemito *m.*
to groan [grɒʊn] *v. intr.* gemere
grocer ['grɒʊsə^r] *s.* droghiere *m.*
grocery ['grɒʊsərɪ] *s.* drogheria *f.*
groggy ['grəgɪ] *agg.* barcollante, intontito
groin [grəɪn] *s.* inguine *m.*
groom [gru:m] *s.* **1** stalliere *m.* **2** sposo *m.*
groove [gru:v] *s.* scanalatura *f.*, incavo *m.*
to grope [grɒʊp] *v. intr.* brancolare, andare a tentoni ♦ **to g. for st.** cercare q.c. a tentoni
gross [grɒʊs] *agg.* **1** grossolano, volgare **2** grasso **3** complessivo, lordo
grotesque [grɒ(ʊ)'tɛsk] *agg.* grottesco
grotto ['grətɒʊ] *s.* grotta *f.*
grotty ['grətɪ] *agg.* orrendo
ground (1) [graʊnd] **A** *pass. e p. p. di* **to grind** **B** *agg.* **1** macinato **2** levigato **3** arrotato
ground (2) [graʊnd] **A** *agg.* **1** terrestre, di terra **2** del suolo **3** di base **B** *s.* **1** terreno *m.*, terra *f.* **2** campo *m.* **3** (*di mare, lago*) fondo *m.* **4** sfondo *m.* **5** motivo *m.*, ragione *f.* **6** (*elettr.*) massa *f.*, terra *f.* **7** *al pl.* sedimenti *m. pl.*, fondi *m. pl.* ♦ **g. floor** pianterreno
to ground [graʊnd] *v. intr.* **1** fondarsi, basarsi **2** (*naut.*) incagliarsi
grounding ['graʊndɪŋ] *s.* **1** basi *f. pl.*, fondamento *m.* **2** messa *f.* a terra
groundless ['graʊndlɪs] *agg.* infondato
groundwork ['graʊnd,wɜ:k] *s.* fondamento *m.*
group [gru:p] *s.* gruppo *m.*
to group [gru:p] **A** *v. tr.* raggruppare, radunare **B** *v. intr.* raggrupparsi, radunarsi
grouper ['gru:pə^r] *s.* cernia *f.*
grouse [graʊs] *s.* gallo *m.* cedrone
grove [grɒʊv] *s.* boschetto *m.*
to grovel ['grəvl] *v. intr.* **1** strisciare per terra **2** umiliarsi
to grow [grɒʊ] (*pass.* **grew**, *p. p.* **grown**) **A** *v. intr.* **1** crescere, aumentare **2** diventare **B** *v. tr.* coltivare ♦ **to g. old** invecchiare; **to g. rich** arricchire; **to g. up** diventare adulto, crescere
grower ['grɒʊə^r] *s.* coltivatore *m.*
to growl [graʊl] *v. intr.* ringhiare, grugnire
grown [grɒʊn] *p. p. di* **to grow**
growth [grɒʊθ] *s.* **1** crescita *f.*, sviluppo *m.* **2** produzione *f.* **3** escrescenza *f.*
grub [grʌb] *s.* **1** larva *f.* **2** (*fam.*) cibo *m.*
grubby ['grʌbɪ] *agg.* sporco
grudge [grʌdʒ] *s.* rancore *m.*
gruelling ['grʊəlɪŋ] *agg.* faticoso
gruesome ['gru:səm] *agg.* orribile
gruff [grʌf] *agg.* **1** rude, aspro **2** roco
to grumble ['grʌmbl] *v. intr.* lamentarsi, brontolare
grumpy ['grʌmpɪ] *agg.* scontroso
to grunt [grʌnt] *v. intr.* grugnire, borbottare
guarantee [,gær(ə)n'tɪ] *s.* garanzia *f.*
to guarantee [,gær(ə)n'tɪ] *v. tr.* garantire
guaranty ['gær(ə)ntɪ] *s.* garanzia *f.*
guard [ga:d] *s.* **1** guardia *f.*, custodia *f.* **2** guardiano *m.* **3** capotreno *m.*
to guard [ga:d] **A** *v. tr.* sorvegliare, proteg-

gere **B** *v. intr.* stare in guardia ♦ **to g. against st.** guardarsi da q.c.
guardian ['gaːdjən] *s.* **1** guardiano *m.*, custode *m.* **2** tutore *m.*
Guelph [gwɛlf] *s.* guelfo *m.*
guerilla [gə'rɪlə] *s.* guerriglia *f.*
guess [gɛs] *s.* congettura *f.* ♦ **to take a g.** provare a indovinare
to guess [gɛs] *v. tr. e intr.* indovinare, azzeccare
guest [gɛst] *s.* **1** ospite *m. e f.*, invitato *m.* **2** (*d'albergo*) cliente *m. e f.* ♦ **g.-house** pensione; **g.-room** stanza degli ospiti
to guffaw [gʌ'fɜː] *v. intr.* sghignazzare
guidance ['gaɪdəns] *s.* guida *f.*
guide [gaɪd] *s.* **1** guida *f.*, cicerone *m.* **2** guida *f.*, manuale *m.*
to guide [gaɪd] *v. tr.* guidare
guideline ['gaɪdlaɪn] *s.* direttiva *f.*, orientamento *m.*
guild [gɪld] *s.* corporazione *f.*, gilda *f.*
guile [gaɪl] *s.* astuzia *f.*
guillotine [ˌgɪlə'tiːn] *s.* ghigliottina *f.*
guilt [gɪlt] *s.* colpa *f.*, colpevolezza *f.*
guilty ['gɪltɪ] *agg.* colpevole
guinea-pig ['gɪnɪpɪg] *s.* cavia *f.*, porcellino *m.* d'India
guise [gaɪz] *s.* **1** sembianza *f.* **2** maschera *f.*
guitar [gɪ'taːʳ] *s.* chitarra *f.*
guitarist [gɪ'taːrɪst] *s.* chitarrista *m. e f.*
gulf [gʌlf] *s.* **1** golfo *m.* **2** abisso *m.*
gull [gʌl] *s.* gabbiano *m.*
gullet ['gʌlɪt] *s.* gola *f.*
gully ['gʌlɪ] *s.* **1** burrone *m.*, gola *f.* **2** calanco *m.* **3** canale *m.*
gulp [gʌlp] *s.* sorso *m.*, boccone *m.*
to gulp [gʌlp] **A** *v. intr.* deglutire **B** *v. tr.* inghiottire, tracannare
gum [gʌm] *s.* **1** gomma *f.* **2** colla *f.* **3** caramella *f.* gommosa **4** gengiva *f.*
gumption ['gʌm(p)ʃ(ə)n] *s.* buon senso *m.*
gun [gʌn] *s.* fucile *m.*, pistola *f.*, arma *f.* da fuoco, cannone *m.*
gunman ['gʌnmən] (*pl.* **gunmen**) *s.* bandito *m.*
gunpoint ['gʌnˌpɔɪnt] *s.* mira *f.* ♦ **at g.** sotto tiro
gunpowder ['gʌnˌpaʊdəʳ] *s.* polvere *f.* da sparo
gunshot ['gʌnʃət] *s.* sparo *m.*
to gurgle ['gɜːgl] *v. intr.* gorgogliare
guru ['gʊruː] *s.* guru *m. inv.*
gush [gʌʃ] *s.* zampillo *m.*
to gush [gʌʃ] *v. intr.* **1** sgorgare **2** entusiasmarsi
gushing ['gʌʃɪŋ] *agg.* zampillante
gust [gʌst] *s.* raffica *f.*
gusto ['gʌstɒʊ] *s.* **1** godimento *m.*, piacere *m.* **2** gusto *m.*, sapore *m.*
gut [gʌt] *s.* budello *m.*, *al pl.* budella *f. pl.*
gutter ['gʌtəʳ] *s.* **1** grondaia *f.* **2** cunetta *f.*
guttural ['gʌt(ə)r(ə)l] *agg.* gutturale
guy [gaɪ] *s.* (*USA, fam.*) individuo *m.*, tipo *m.*
to guzzle ['gʌzl] *v. intr.* gozzovigliare
gym [dʒɪm] *s.* **1** palestra *f.* **2** ginnastica *f.*
gymnasium [dʒɪm'neɪzjəm] *s.* palestra *f.*
gymnastics [dʒɪm'næstɪks] *s. pl.* (*v. al sing.*) ginnastica *f.*
gyn(a)ecologist [ˌgaɪnɪ'kɔlədʒɪst] *s.* ginecologo *m.*
to gyrate [ˌdʒaɪ'reɪt] *v. intr.* girare, turbinare
gyroscope ['dʒaɪərəskɒʊp] *s.* giroscopio *m.*

H

haberdasher ['hæbədæʃəʳ] *s.* merciaio *m.*
haberdashery ['hæbədæʃərɪ] *s.* merceria *f.*
habit ['hæbɪt] *s.* **1** abitudine *f.* **2** temperamento *m.* **3** abito *m.*, tonaca *f.*
habitual [hə'bɪtjʊəl] *agg.* **1** abituale **2** inveterato
hack (1) [hæk] *s.* **1** spacco *m.*, fenditura *f.* **2** ferita *f.* **3** piccone *m.*
hack (2) [hæk] *s.* **1** scribacchino *m.* **2** ronzino *m.*
to hack [hæk] *v. tr.* fare a pezzi
hackneyed ['hæknɪd] *agg.* trito, banale
had [hæd, həd, əd] *pass. e p. p. di* **to have**
h(a)emorrhage ['hɛmərɪdʒ] *s.* emorragia *f.*
h(a)emostatic [ˌhiːmɒ(ʊ)'stætɪk] *agg. e s.* emostatico *m.*
haggard ['hægəd] *agg.* smunto, sparuto
to haggle ['hægl] *v. intr.* **1** mercanteggiare **2** cavillare
hagiography [ˌhægɪ'əgrəfɪ] *s.* agiografia *f.*
hail (1) [heɪl] *s.* **1** grandine *f.* **2** gragnuola *f.*
hail (2) [heɪl] *inter.* salve, salute
to hail (1) [heɪl] **A** *v. intr.* grandinare **B** *v. tr.* scagliare, lanciare
to hail (2) [heɪl] *v. tr.* **1** chiamare, salutare **2** fare un cenno *(per fermare)*
hailstone ['heɪlˌstɒʊn] *s.* chicco *m.* di grandine
hailstorm ['heɪlˌstɜːm] *s.* grandinata *f.*
hair [hɛəʳ] *s.* **1** capelli *m. pl.*, chioma *f.* **2** capello *m.* **3** *(di animale)* pelo *m.*, mantello *m.* ♦ **h.-raising** orripilante; **h.-splitting** pedanteria
hairbrush ['hɛəbrʌʃ] *s.* spazzola *f.* (per capelli)
haircut ['hɛəkət] *s.* taglio *m.* di capelli
hairdo ['hɛəduː] *s.* pettinatura *f.*
hairdresser ['hɛəˌdrɛsəʳ] *s.* parrucchiere *m.*
hairdryer ['hɛəˌdraɪəʳ] *s.* asciugacapelli *m. inv.*
hairgrip ['hɛəgrɪp] *s.* molletta *f.*
hairless ['hɛəlɪs] *agg.* calvo, glabro
hairpin ['hɛəpɪn] *s.* molletta *f.* ♦ **h. bend** tornante
hairstyle ['hɛəstaɪl] *s.* acconciatura *f.*
hairy ['hɛərɪ] *agg.* **1** peloso, irsuto **2** *(fam.)* pericoloso
hake [heɪk] *s.* nasello *m.*
half [haːf] *(pl.* **halves)** **A** *agg.* mezzo **B** *s.* **1** metà *f.*, mezzo *m.* **2** *(sport)* tempo *m.* **C** *avv.* mezzo, a metà ♦ **h.-and-h.** metà e metà, a metà; **h. an hour** mezz'ora; **h. brother** fratellastro; **h.-mast** mezz'asta; **h. moon** mezzaluna; **not h.** molto, veramente; **h.-price** metà prezzo; **h. time** *(sport)* intervallo; **two and a h.** due e mezzo
half-baked [ˌhaːf'beɪkt] *agg.* **1** cotto a metà **2** *(fig.)* immaturo
half-hearted [ˌhaːf'haːtɪd] *agg.* apatico, tiepido
halfway [ˌhaːf'weɪ] *agg. e avv.* a metà strada
halibut ['hælɪbət] *s.* ippoglosso *m.*
hall [hɜːl] *s.* **1** sala *f.*, salone *m.* **2** vestibolo *m.* **3** palazzo *m.*, villa *f.*
hallmark ['hɜːlˌmaːk] *s.* **1** marchio *m.* di garanzia **2** *(fig.)* caratteristica *f.*
hallo [hə'lɒʊ] *inter.* **1** ciao, salve **2** *(al telefono)* pronto
hallucination [həˌluːsɪ'neɪʃ(ə)n] *s.* allucinazione *f.*
hallway ['hɜːlweɪ] *s.* *(USA)* corridoio *m.*, vestibolo *m.*
halo ['heɪlɒʊ] *s.* aureola *f.*
halt [hɜːlt] **A** *s.* sosta *f.*, fermata *f.* **B** *inter.* alt!
to halt [hɜːlt] **A** *v. tr.* **1** fermare **2** *(mil.)* far fare tappa a **B** *v. intr.* fermarsi
to halve [haːv] *v. tr.* dimezzare, fare a metà di
halves [haːvz] *pl. di* **half**
halyard ['hæljəd] *s.* *(naut.)* drizza *f.*
ham (1) [hæm] *s.* prosciutto *m.*
ham (2) [hæm] *s.* *(fam.)* radioamatore *m.*
hamburger ['hæmbɜːgəʳ] *s.* hamburger *m. inv.*
hamlet ['hæmlɪt] *s.* borgo *m.*
hammer ['hæməʳ] *s.* **1** martello *m.* **2** maglio *m.* **3** martelletto *m.* ♦ **h. drill** martello pneumatico
to hammer ['hæməʳ] *v. tr. e intr.* martellare, battere
hammering ['hæmərɪŋ] *s.* martellamento *m.*

hammock ['hæmək] *s.* amaca *f.*
hamper ['hæmpər] *s.* cesta *f.*, paniere *m.*
to hamper ['hæmpər] *v. tr.* impedire, ostacolare
hamster ['hæmstər] *s.* criceto *m.*
hand [hænd] *s.* **1** mano *f.* **2** manovale *m.*, operaio *m.* **3** (*di orologio*) lancetta *f.* **4** grafia *f.*, firma *f.* **5** (*nel gioco delle carte*) mano *f.* **6** (*di banane*) casco *m.* ♦ **at h.** a portata di mano; **by h.** a mano; **h. luggage** bagaglio a mano; **in h.** a disposizione, sotto controllo
to hand [hænd] *v. tr.* dare, porgere ♦ **to h. back** restituire; **to h. out** distribuire; **to h. over** consegnare, trasmettere
handbag ['hæn(d)bæg] *s.* borsetta *f.*
handball ['hæn(d)bɜːl] *s.* pallamano *f.*
handbook ['hæn(d)bʊk] *s.* manuale *m.*
handbrake ['hæn(d)breɪk] *s.* freno *m.* a mano
handcart ['hæn(d)kaːt] *s.* carretto *m.*
handcuffs ['hæn(d)kʌfs] *s. pl.* manette *f. pl.*
handful ['hæn(d)fʊl] *s.* manciata *f.*
handhold ['hændhɒʊld] *s.* appiglio *m.*
handicap ['hændɪkæp] *s.* **1** (*med.*) handicap *m. inv.* **2** ostacolo *m.*, svantaggio *m.* **3** (*sport*) handicap *m. inv.*
to handicap ['hændɪkæp] *v. tr.* **1** ostacolare **2** (*sport*) dare un handicap
handicraft ['hændɪkraːft] *s.* **1** artigianato *m.*, lavoro *m.* artigianale **2** abilità *f.* manuale
handiwork ['hændɪwɜːk] *s.* **1** lavoro *m.* manuale **2** operato *m.*
handkerchief ['hæŋkətʃɪf] *s.* fazzoletto *m.*
handle ['hændl] *s.* **1** manico *m.*, maniglia *f.*, impugnatura *f.* **2** (*fig.*) appiglio *m.*, pretesto *m.*
to handle ['hændl] *v. tr.* **1** maneggiare, manipolare **2** trattare, occuparsi di ♦ **h. with care** maneggiare con cura
handlebar ['hændlbaːr] *s. spec. al pl.* manubrio *m.* (di bicicletta)
handling ['hændlɪŋ] *s.* trattamento *m.*
handmade [ˌhæn(d)'meɪd] *agg.* fatto a mano
handout ['hændaʊt] *s.* **1** sussidio *m.*, elemosina *f.* **2** volantino *m.* **3** dichiarazione *f.* (per la stampa)
handrail ['hændˌreɪl] *s.* corrimano *m.*
handshake ['hændʃeɪk] *s.* stretta *f.* di mano
handsome ['hænsəm] *agg.* **1** bello, prestante **2** generoso **3** considerevole
handwork ['hændwɜːk] *s.* → **handiwork**
handwriting ['hændˌraɪtɪŋ] *s.* scrittura *f.*, grafia *f.*
handy ['hændɪ] *agg.* **1** abile **2** maneggevole, manovrabile **3** comodo, utile **4** vicino, sottomano
handyman ['hændɪmæn] (*pl.* **handymen**) *s.* tuttofare *m. inv.*
to hang [hæŋ] (*pass. e p. p.* **to hung**) **A** *v. tr.* **1** appendere, sospendere **2** impiccare **B** *v. intr.* pendere, penzolare ♦ **to h. about** ciondolare, perdere tempo; **to h. on** aggrapparsi, aspettare; **to h. up** riattaccare (il telefono)
hangar ['hæŋər] *s.* hangar *m. inv.*
hanger ['hæŋər] *s.* **1** gruccia *f.* **2** gancio *m.* ♦ **h.-on** scroccone
hang-glider ['hæŋˌglaɪdər] *s.* deltaplano *m.*
hanging ['hæŋɪŋ] **A** *agg.* sospeso, pendente **B** *s.* impiccagione *f.*
hangover ['hæŋˌɒʊvər] *s.* postumi *m. pl.* di sbornia
hang-up ['hæŋʌp] *s.* **1** (*fam.*) problema *m.* **2** (*inf.*) sospensione *f.*
hank [hæŋk] *s.* matassa *f.*
to hanker ['hæŋkər] *v. intr.* desiderare ardentemente
hanky ['hæŋkɪ] *s.* fazzoletto *m.*
haphazard [ˌhæp'hæzəd] **A** *agg.* casuale, fortuito **B** *avv.* a casaccio
to happen ['hæp(ə)n] *v. intr.* **1** accadere, succedere **2** (*costruzione pers.*) capitare, accadere (ES: **I happened to loose my way home** mi capitò di perdere la strada di casa) ♦ **as it happens** guarda caso, precisamente
happening ['hæpənɪn] *s.* avvenimento *m.*
happy ['hæpɪ] *agg.* felice, contento
happy-go-lucky ['hæpɪgɒ(ʊ)ˌlʌkɪ] *agg.* spensierato
harangue [hə'ræŋ] *s.* arringa *f.*
to harangue [hə'ræŋ] *v. tr.* arringare
to harass ['hærəs] *v. tr.* molestare
harassment ['hærəsmənt] *s.* molestia *f.*
harbour ['haːbər] (*USA* **harbor**) *s.* porto *m.* ♦ **h.-master** capitano del porto; **h. office** capitaneria
to harbour ['haːbər] (*USA* **to harbor**) *v. tr.* accogliere, ospitare
hard [haːd] **A** *agg.* **1** duro **2** severo, spietato **3** difficile, gravoso **4** accanito **5** (*di*

bevanda) forte, (*di droga*) pesante **B** *avv.* **1** energicamente, con forza **2** duramente, con difficoltà ♦ **h. disk** disco rigido; **h. luck** sfortuna; **h. of hearing** duro d'orecchi; **to be h. on sb.** trattare qc. duramente; **to drink h.** bere molto; **to follow h. on sb.** seguire qc. da vicino; **to look h. at sb.** guardare fisso qc.
hardback ['ha:dˌbæk] *s.* libro *m.* rilegato
hardcover ['ha:dkʌvəʳ] *agg.* rilegato
hardheaded [ˌha:d'hɛdɪd] *agg.* pratico, realista
hardly ['ha:dlɪ] *avv.* **1** appena, a malapena **2** quasi ♦ **h. ever** quasi mai
hardness ['ha:dnɪs] *s.* durezza *f.*
hardship ['ha:dʃɪp] *s.* privazione *f.*, stento *m.*
hard-up [ˌha:d'ʌp] *agg.* (*fam.*) **1** al verde **2** bisognoso di
hardware ['ha:dwɛəʳ] *s.* **1** ferramenta *f.* **2** attrezzi *m. pl.* **3** (*mil.*) armamenti *m. pl.* **4** (*inf.*) hardware *m. inv.*
hardwearing ['ha:dwɛərɪŋ] *agg.* resistente
hardy ['ha:dɪ] *agg.* robusto, resistente
hare [hɛəʳ] *s.* lepre *f.*
hare-brained ['hɛəʳbreɪnd] *agg.* scervellato
harm [ha:m] *s.* danno *m.*
to harm [ha:m] *v. tr.* nuocere a, danneggiare
harmful ['ha:mf(ʊ)l] *agg.* nocivo
harmless ['ha:mlɪs] *agg.* innocuo, inoffensivo
harmonica [ha:'mɔnɪkə] *s.* armonica *f.*
harmonious [ha:'mɒʊnjəs] *agg.* armonioso, melodioso
harmony ['ha:m(ə)nɪ] *s.* armonia *f.*, accordo *m.*
harness ['ha:nɪs] *s.* **1** finimenti *m. pl.* **2** imbracatura *f.*
to harness ['ha:nɪs] *v. tr.* **1** mettere i finimenti **2** imbrigliare
harp [ha:p] *s.* arpa *f.*
to harp [ha:p] *v. intr.* suonare l'arpa ♦ **to h. on** insistere noiosamente
harpoon [ha:'pu:n] *s.* arpione *m.*, fiocina *f.*, rampone *m.*
harquebus ['ha:kwɪbəs] *s.* archibugio *m.*
harrowing ['hærɒʊɪŋ] *agg.* straziante
harsh [ha:ʃ] *agg.* **1** aspro, ruvido **2** duro, severo **3** stridente, stridulo **4** (*di clima*) rigido
hart [ha:t] *s.* cervo *m.* maschio
harvest ['ha:vɪst] *s.* mietitura *f.*, raccolto *m.*, vendemmia *f.*
to harvest ['ha:vɪst] *v. tr.* mietere, fare il raccolto, vendemmiare
has [hæz, həz, əz] *3ª sing. pres. di* **to have**
to hash [hæʃ] *v. tr.* **1** tritare, sminuzzare **2** pasticciare
hashish ['hæʃi:ʃ] *s.* hascisc *m. inv.*
hassle ['hæsl] *s.* (*fam.*) **1** problema *m.* **2** scocciatura *f.*
haste [heɪst] *s.* fretta *f.*, premura *f.*
to hasten ['heɪsn] **A** *v. tr.* affrettare, sollecitare **B** *v. intr.* affrettarsi, precipitarsi
hasty ['heɪstɪ] *agg.* **1** frettoloso, affrettato **2** sconsiderato
hat [hæt] *s.* cappello *m.* ♦ **top h.** cilindro
hatch [hætʃ] *s.* **1** portello *m.* **2** (*naut.*) boccaporto *m.*
hatchet [hætʃɪt] *s.* accetta *f.*
hate [heɪt] *s.* odio *m.*
to hate [heɪt] *v. tr.* odiare, detestare
hateful ['heɪtf(ʊ)l] *agg.* odioso
hatred ['heɪtrɪd] *s.* odio *m.*
haughty ['hɜ:tɪ] *agg.* arrogante, superbo
haul [hɜ:l] *s.* **1** tiro *m.* **2** raccolta *f.*, retata *f.* **3** bottino *m.*
to haul [hɜ:l] *v. tr.* **1** tirare, trainare **2** trasportare
haulage ['hɜ:lɪdʒ] *s.* trasporto *m.*
haulier ['hɜ:ljəʳ] *s.* autotrasportatore *m.*
haunch [hɜ:n(t)ʃ] *s.* **1** anca *f.*, fianco *m.* **2** (*in macelleria*) coscia *f.*
to haunt [hɜ:nt] *v. tr.* **1** frequentare, bazzicare **2** (*di fantasmi*) infestare **3** perseguitare
to have [hæv, həv, əv] (*pass. e p. p.* **had**) *v. tr.* **1** (*ausiliare*) avere, essere (ES: **have you seen it?** l'hai visto?, **she has already been here** è già stata qui) **2** avere **3** possedere, ottenere, ricevere **4** prendere, mangiare, bere **5** fare, compiere **6 to h. to** (*seguito da inf.*) dovere (ES: **I h. to stay at home tonight** devo stare in casa questa sera)
haven ['heɪvn] *s.* **1** porto *m.* **2** rifugio *m.* ♦ **tax h.** paradiso fiscale
haversack ['hævəsæk] *s.* bisaccia *f.*
havoc ['hævək] *s.* rovina *f.*, distruzione *f.*
hawk [hɜ:k] *s.* falco *m.*
hay [heɪ] *s.* fieno *m.* ♦ **h. fever** febbre da fieno
hayloft ['heɪˌlɔft] *s.* fienile *m.*
haystack ['heɪˌstæk] *s.* pagliaio *m.*
haywire ['heɪwaɪəʳ] *agg.* confuso ♦ **to go h.** impazzire
hazard ['hæzəd] *s.* **1** azzardo *m.*, rischio *m.*, pericolo *m.* **2** caso *m.*, sorte *f.*

to hazard ['hæzəd] *v. tr.* **1** azzardare **2** rischiare
hazardous ['hæzədəs] *agg.* rischioso, pericoloso
haze [heɪz] *s.* **1** foschia *f.* **2** confusione *f.* mentale
hazel ['heɪzl] *s.* nocciolo *m.*
hazelnut ['heɪzlnʌt] *s.* nocciola *f.*
hazy ['heɪzɪ] *agg.* **1** nebbioso **2** confuso
he [hɪ(ː)] *pron. pers. 3ª m. sing.* egli, lui
head [hɛd] **A** *s.* **1** testa *f.* **2** capo *m.* **B** *agg.* principale centrale ♦ **h. office** sede centrale
to head [hɛd] *v. tr.* **1** dirigere, capeggiare **2** intestare, intitolare **3** affrontare ♦ **to h. for** dirigersi; **to h. off** precedere
headache ['hɛdeɪk] *s.* cefalea *f.*, mal *m.* di testa
headdress ['hɛddrɛs] *s.* **1** copricapo *m.* **2** acconciatura *f.*
headfirst [ˌhɛd'fɜːst] *avv.* a capofitto
heading ['hɛdɪŋ] *s.* intestazione *f.*, titolo *m.*
headland ['hɛdlənd] *s.* promontorio *m.*
headlight ['hɛdlaɪt] *s.* faro *m.*, fanale *m.*
headline ['hɛdlaɪn] *s.* titolo *m.*
headlong ['hɛdlɔŋ] *avv.* **1** a capofitto **2** precipitosamente
headmaster [ˌhɛd'maːstəʳ] *s.* direttore *m.* di scuola
head-on [ˌhɛd'ɔn] *agg.* frontale
headphones ['hɛdfɒʊnz] *s. pl.* auricolare *m.*, cuffia *f.*
headquarters ['hɛdˌkwɜːtəz] *s. pl.* **1** quartier *m.* generale **2** sede *f.* centrale
headrest ['hɛdrɛst] *s.* poggiatesta *m. inv.*
headscarf ['hɛdskaːf] *s.* foulard *m. inv.*
headstrong ['hɛdstrəŋ] *agg.* caparbio, ostinato
headway ['hɛdweɪ] *s.* **1** abbrivio *m.* **2** (*fig.*) progresso *m.*
heady ['hɛdɪ] *s.* eccitante
to heal [hiːl] **A** *v. tr.* curare **B** *v. intr.* guarire, rimarginarsi
healing ['hiːlɪŋ] *s.* guarigione *f.*
health [hɛlθ] *s.* salute *f.* ♦ **h. farm** clinica della salute; **h. food** cibo naturale; **public h. office** ufficio d'igiene
healthy ['hɛlθɪ] *agg.* **1** sano **2** salubre
heap [hiːp] *s.* cumulo *m.*, mucchio *m.*
to heap [hiːp] *v. tr.* **1** accumulare, ammassare **2** riempire di
to hear [hɪəʳ] (*pass. e p. p.* **heard**) **A** *v. tr.* **1** sentire, udire **2** venire a sapere **3** ascoltare **B** *v. intr.* sentire ♦ **to h. about/of** sentir parlare di
heard [hɜːd] *pass. e p. p. di* **to hear**
hearing ['hɪərɪŋ] *s.* **1** udito *m.* **2** udienza *f.* ♦ **h. aid** apparecchio acustico
hearsay ['hɪəseɪ] *s.* diceria *f.* ♦ **by h.** per sentito dire
heart [haːt] *s.* **1** cuore *m.* **2** (*fig.*) centro *m.*, nucleo *m.* **3** *al pl.* (*carte da gioco*) cuori *m. pl.* ♦ **by h.** a memoria; **h. attack** attacco di cuore; **h. broken** desolato; **to be out of h.** essere scoraggiato; **to take h.** farsi coraggio; **to take st. to h.** prendere q.c. a cuore
heartbeat ['haːtˌbiːt] *s.* battito *m.* del cuore
heartbreak ['haːtˌbreɪk] *s.* crepacuore *m. inv.*
heartbreaking ['haːtˌbreɪkɪŋ] *agg.* straziante
heartbroken ['haːtˌbrɒʊk(ə)n] *agg.* straziato, affranto
heartburn ['haːtˌbɜːn] *s.* bruciore *m.* di stomaco
heartfelt ['haːtfɛlt] *agg.* sincero
hearth [haːθ] *s.* focolare *m.*
heartily ['haːtɪlɪ] *avv.* **1** cordialmente, di cuore **2** vigorosamente **3** assai, abbondantemente
heartless ['haːtlɪs] *agg.* insensibile, crudele
hearty ['haːtɪ] *agg.* **1** cordiale, caloroso **2** robusto, vigoroso
heat [hiːt] *s.* **1** caldo *m.*, calore *m.* **2** foga *f.*, impeto *m.* **3** fuoco *m.*, fiamma *f.* **4** (*sport*) batteria *f.*
to heat [hiːt] *v. tr.* scaldare, riscaldare
heated ['hiːtɪd] *agg.* **1** riscaldato **2** (*fig.*) appassionato, animato
heater ['hiːtəʳ] *s.* calorifero *m.*, stufa *f.*, impianto *m.* di riscaldamento
heath [hiːθ] *s.* **1** brughiera *f.* **2** erica *f.*
heathen ['hiːð(ə)n] *agg. e s.* pagano *m.*
heathenism ['hiːðənɪz(ə)m] *s.* paganesimo *m.*
heather ['hɛðəʳ] *s.* erica *f.*
heating ['hiːtɪŋ] *s.* riscaldamento *m.* ♦ **central h.** riscaldamento centrale
heatstroke ['hiːtstrɒʊk] *s.* colpo *m.* di calore
to heave [hiːv] (*pass. e p. p.* **heaved, hove**) **A** *v. tr.* **1** sollevare, alzare **2** gettare, lanciare, tirare **3** emettere **B** *v. intr.* **1** sollevarsi, alzarsi **2** ansimare
heaven ['hɛvn] *s.* cielo *m.*, paradiso *m.*
heavenly ['hɛvnlɪ] *agg.* celeste, divino

heavily ['hɛvɪlɪ] *avv.* **1** pesantemente **2** assai, molto **3** duramente, fortemente
heaviness ['hɛvɪnɪs] *s.* pesantezza *f.*
heavy ['hɛvɪ] *agg.* **1** pesante, gravoso **2** grande, forte, violento **3** triste, grave **4** plumbeo
Hebraic [hɪ(ː)'breɪɪk] *agg.* ebraico
Hebrew ['hiːbruː] *agg. e s.* ebreo *m.*
hecatomb ['hɛkətɒʊm] *s.* ecatombe *f.*
hectare ['hɛktaːʳ] *s.* ettaro *m.*
hectic ['hɛktɪk] *agg.* febbrile, agitato
hedge [hɛdʒ] *s.* **1** siepe *f.* **2** barriera *f.*
hedgehog ['hɛdʒhəg] *s.* (*zool.*) riccio *m.*
hedonism ['hiːdənɪz(ə)m] *s.* edonismo *m.*
heed [hiːd] *s.* attenzione *f.*, cura *f.* ♦ **to give h. to** dare ascolto a
to heed [hiːd] *v. tr.* fare attenzione a
heedless ['hiːdlɪs] *agg.* sbadato, disattento
heel (1) [hiːl] *s.* **1** calcagno *m.*, tallone *m.* **2** tacco *m.*
heel (2) [hiːl] *s.* (*naut.*) sbandamento *m.*
to heel [hiːl] *v. intr.* (*naut.*) sbandare
hefty ['hɛftɪ] *agg.* (*fam.*) forte, robusto
hegemony [hɪ(ː)'gɛmənɪ] *s.* egemonia *f.*
heifer ['hɛfəʳ] *s.* giovenca *f.*
height [haɪt] *s.* **1** altezza *f.* **2** altitudine *f.* **3** cima *f.*, apice *m.*
to heighten ['haɪtn] **A** *v. tr.* accrescere, innalzare **B** *v. intr.* aumentare, innalzarsi
heir [ɛəʳ] *s.* erede *m.*
heiress ['ɛərɪs] *s.* erede *f.*
heirloom ['ɛəluːm] *s.* **1** (*dir.*) bene *m.* spettante all'erede **2** oggetto *m.* di famiglia
held [hɛld] *pass. e p. p. di* **to hold**
helicopter ['hɛlɪkəptəʳ] *s.* elicottero *m.*
heliotherapy [ˌhiːlɪʊ(ʊ)'θɛrəpɪ] *s.* elioterapia *f.*
heliport ['hɛlɪpɜːt] *s.* eliporto *m.*
helium ['hiːljəm] *s.* elio *m.*
hell [hɛl] *s.* inferno *m.*
Hellenic [hɛ'liːnɪk] *agg.* ellenico
Hellenistic [ˌhɛlɪ'nɪstɪk] *agg.* ellenistico
hellish ['hɛlɪʃ] *agg.* infernale
hello [hɛ'lɒʊ] *inter.* **1** salve, ciao **2** (*al telefono*) pronto
helm [hɛlm] *s.* timone *m.*
helmet ['hɛlmɪt] *s.* **1** elmetto *m.* **2** casco *m.*
help [hɛlp] *s.* **1** aiuto *m.*, assistenza *f.* **2** rimedio *m.* **3** persona *f.* di servizio
to help [hɛlp] *v. tr.* **1** aiutare, assistere, soccorrere **2** contribuire a, favorire **3** (*a tavola*) servire, passare **4** (*preceduto da 'can', 'could'*) fare a meno di, evitare ♦ **I can't h. laughing** non posso fare a meno di ridere; **it can't be helped** non c'è niente da fare; **to h. oneself to** servirsi di
helper ['hɛlpəʳ] *s.* aiutante *m. e f.*
helpful ['hɛlpf(ʊ)l] *agg.* **1** servizievole **2** utile, vantaggioso
helping ['hɛlpɪŋ] *s.* (*di cibo*) porzione *f.*
helpless ['hɛlplɪs] *agg.* **1** indifeso **2** debole, impotente
hem [hɛm] *s.* orlo *m.*, bordo *m.*
to hem [hɛm] *v. tr.* orlare ♦ **to h. in** circondare
hemisphere ['hɛmɪsfɪəʳ] *s.* emisfero *m.*
hemp [hɛmp] *s.* canapa *f.*
hen [hɛn] *s.* **1** gallina *f.* **2** (*di volatili*) femmina *f.* ♦ **h. house** pollaio
hence [hɛns] *avv.* **1** da questo momento, di qui a **2** quindi, perciò ♦ **a h. week** fra una settimana
henceforth [ˌhɛns'fɜːθ] *avv.* d'ora innanzi
henchman ['hɛn(t)ʃmən] (*pl.* **henchmen**) *s.* accolito *m.*
henpecked ['hɛnpɛkt] *agg.* bistrattato dalla moglie
hepatic [hɪ'pætɪk] *agg.* epatico
hepatitis [ˌhɛpə'taɪtɪs] *s.* epatite *f.*
her [hɛːʳ, (h)əʳ] **A** *pron. pers. 3ª sing. f.* (*compl.*) lei, la, a lei, le **B** *agg. poss.* (*riferito a possessore f.*) suo, sua, suoi, sue
heraldic [hɛ'rældɪk] *agg.* araldico
heraldry ['hɛr(ə)ldrɪ] *s.* araldica *f.*
herb [hɜːb] *s.* erba *f.*
herbaceous [hɜː'beɪʃəs] *agg.* erbaceo
herbarium [hɜː'bɛərɪəm] *s.* erbario *m.*
herbicide ['hɜːbɪˌsaɪd] *s.* erbicida *m.*
herbivorous [hɜː'bɪvərəs] *agg.* erbivoro
herd [hɜːd] *s.* **1** mandria *f.*, gregge *m.* **2** moltitudine *f.*
here [hɪəʳ] *avv.* **1** qua, qui **2** ecco ♦ **h.!** (*rispondendo a un appello*) presente!; **h. and now** una volta per tutte; **h. I am** eccomi; **h. he is** eccolo qui; **near h.** qua vicino; **up h.** quassù
hereafter [ˌhɪər'aːftəʳ] *avv.* in avvenire
hereby [ˌhɪə'baɪ] *avv.* con ciò, con la presente
hereditary [hɪ'rɛdɪt(ə)rɪ] *agg.* ereditario
heredity [hɪ'rɛdɪtɪ] *s.* eredità *f.*
herein [ˌhɪər'ɪn] *avv.* (*comm.*) qui accluso
heresy ['hɛrəsɪ] *s.* eresia *f.*
heretic [hɛ'rətɪk] *agg. e s.* eretico *m.*
heretical [hɪ'rɛtɪk(ə)l] *agg.* eretico
herewith [ˌhɪə'wɪð] *avv.* qui accluso

heritage ['hɛrɪtɪdʒ] *s.* **1** eredità *f.* **2** retaggio *m.*
hermaphrodite [hɜː'mæfrədaɪt] *agg. e s.* ermafrodito *m.*
hermetic [hɜː'mɛtɪk] *agg.* ermetico
hermit ['hɜːmɪt] *s.* eremita *m.*
hermitage ['hɜːmɪtɪdʒ] *s.* eremo *m.*
hernia ['hɜːnjə] *s.* ernia *f.*
hero ['hɪərɒʊ] *s.* eroe *m.*
heroic [hɪ'rɒ(ʊ)ɪk] *agg.* eroico
heroin ['hɛrɒ(ʊ)ɪn] *s.* (*chim.*) eroina *f.*
heroine ['hɛrɒ(ʊ)ɪn] *s.* eroina *f.*
heron ['hɛr(ə)n] *s.* airone *m.*
herring ['hɛrɪŋ] *s.* aringa *f.*
hers [hɜːz] *pron. poss. 3ª sing.* (*riferito a possessore f.*) suo, sua, suoi, sue
herself [hɜː'sɛlf] **A** *pron. 3ª sing. f.* **1** (*rifl.*) se stessa, si **2** (*enf.*) ella stessa, lei stessa **B** *s.* ella stessa, lei ♦ **she is not h. today** oggi non sembra nemmeno lei
hesitant ['hɛzɪt(ə)nt] *agg.* esitante
to hesitate ['hɛzɪteɪt] *v. intr.* esitare
hesitation [ˌhɛzɪ'teɪʃ(ə)n] *s.* esitazione *f.*
heterodox ['hɛt(ə)rədɔks] *agg.* eterodosso
heterogeneous [ˌhɛtərɒ(ʊ)'dʒiːnjəs] *agg.* eterogeneo
heterosexual [ˌhɛtərɒ(ʊ)'sɛksjʊəl] *agg.* eterosessuale
heuristic [hjʊ(ə)'rɪstɪk] *agg.* euristico
to hew [hjuː] (*pass.* **hewed**, *p. p.* **hewed**, **hewn**) *v. tr.* tagliare, spaccare, fendere ♦ **to h. out** sbozzare, scavare
hexagonal [hɛk'sægənl] *agg.* esagonale
heyday ['heɪdeɪ] *s.* apice *m.*, apogeo *m.*
hi [haɪ] *inter.* ciao!
hiatus [haɪ'eɪtəs] *s.* **1** iato *m.* **2** lacuna *f.*
to hibernate ['haɪbɜːneɪt] *v. intr.* **1** ibernare **2** svernare
hiccup ['hɪkʌp] (o **hiccough**) *s.* singhiozzo *m.*
to hiccup ['hɪkʌp] (o **to hiccough**) *v. intr.* avere il singhiozzo
hid [hɪd] *pass. e p. p. di* **to hide**
hidden ['hɪdn] **A** *p. p. di* **to hide** **B** *agg.* **1** nascosto, segreto **2** ignoto
hide (1) [haɪd] *s.* pellame *m.*
hide (2) [haɪd] *s.* nascondiglio *m.*
to hide [haɪd] (*pass.* **hid**, *p. p.* **hid**, **hidden**) **A** *v. tr.* nascondere **B** *v. intr.* nascondersi ♦ **to h. st. from sb.** nascondere q.c. a qc.
hideaway ['haɪdəˌweɪ] *s.* nascondiglio *m.*
hideous ['hɪdɪəs] *agg.* ripugnante, orribile
hiding (1) ['haɪdɪŋ] *s.* occultamento *m.* ♦ **h.-place** nascondiglio; **to be in h.** tenersi nascosto
hiding (2) ['haɪdɪŋ] *s.* (*fam.*) bastonatura *f.*
hierarchic [ˌhaɪə'rɑːkɪk] *agg.* gerarchico
hierarchy ['haɪərɑːkɪ] *s.* gerarchia *f.*
hieratic [ˌhaɪə'rætɪk] *agg.* ieratico
hieroglyph ['haɪərəglɪf] *s.* geroglifico *m.*
high [haɪ] **A** *agg.* **1** alto, elevato **2** forte, intenso, acuto **3** caro, costoso **4** avanzato, inoltrato **B** *avv.* **1** alto, in alto **2** fortemente ♦ **h. class** di prim'ordine; **h. court** corte suprema; **h. school** scuola secondaria; **h. season** alta stagione; **h. street** strada principale; **h. relief** altorilievo
highbrow ['haɪˌbraʊ] *s.* (*fam.*) intellettuale *m. e f.*, (*spreg.*) intellettualoide *m. e f.*
high-handed [ˌhaɪ'hændɪd] *agg.* prepotente
highlight ['haɪlaɪt] *s.* momento *m.* culminante
to highlight ['haɪlaɪt] *v. tr.* mettere in luce
highly ['haɪlɪ] *avv.* estremamente, molto, assai ♦ **h.-strung** nervoso
highness ['haɪnɪs] *s.* altezza *f.*, elevatezza *f.* ♦ **His Royal H.** Sua Altezza Reale
high-pitched [ˌhaɪ'pɪtʃt] *agg.* **1** (*di suono*) acuto **2** (*di tetto*) spiovente
high-tech [ˌhaɪ'tɛk] **A** *s.* alta tecnologia *f.* **B** *agg.* tecnologicamente avanzato
highway ['haɪweɪ] *s.* strada *f.* di grande comunicazione ♦ **h. code** codice della strada
to hijack ['haɪˌdʒæk^r] *v. tr.* dirottare
hijacker ['haɪˌdʒækə^r] *s.* dirottatore *m.*
hijacking ['haɪˌdʒækɪŋ] *s.* dirottamento *m.*
hike [haɪk] *s.* escursione *f.* (*a piedi*)
to hike [haɪk] *v. intr.* fare un'escursione (*a piedi*)
hiker ['haɪkə^r] *s.* escursionista *m. e f.*
hilarious [hɪ'lɛərɪəs] *agg.* allegro, divertente
hill [hɪl] *s.* **1** colle *m.*, collina *f.* **2** pendio *m.*
hillock ['hɪlək] *s.* poggio *m.*
hillside ['hɪlˌsaɪd] *s.* pendio *m.*
hilly ['hɪlɪ] *agg.* collinoso
hilt [hɪlt] *s.* elsa *f.*
him [hɪm, ɪm] *pron. pers. 3ª sing. m.* (*compl.*) lui, lo, gli
himself [hɪm'sɛlf] **A** *pron. 3ª sing. m.* **1** (*rifl.*) se stesso, si **2** (*enf.*) egli stesso, proprio lui **B** *s.* se stesso, lui, sé ♦ **(all) by h.** da solo; **he is not h. today** oggi non è proprio in sé
hind [haɪnd] *agg.* posteriore
to hinder ['hɪndə^r] *v. tr.* **1** impedire **2** in-

ceppare, ostacolare
hindrance ['hɪndr(ə)ns] *s.* impaccio *m.*, ostacolo *m.*, impedimento *m.*
hindsight ['haɪndsaɪt] *s.* il senno *m.* di poi
Hindu ['hɪndʊ] *agg. e s.* indù *m. e f.*
hinge [hɪn(d)ʒ] *s.* cardine *m.*, cerniera *f.*
to hinge [hɪn(d)ʒ] *v. intr.* girare sui cardini ♦ **to h. on/upon** dipendere da
hint [hɪnt] *s.* **1** cenno *m.*, traccia *f.*, allusione *f.* **2** piccola quantità *f.* **3** consiglio *m.*, suggerimento *m.*
to hint [hɪnt] **A** *v. tr.* accennare, suggerire **B** *v. intr.* fare insinuazioni, dare suggerimenti ♦ **to h. at st.** insinuare q.c.
hinterland ['hɪntəlænd] *s.* hinterland *m. inv.*, retroterra *m. inv.*
hip [hɪp] *s.* anca *f.*
hippo ['hɪpɒʊ] *s.* ippopotamo *m.*
hippocampus [ˌhɪpɒ(ʊ)'kæmpəs] *s.* ippocampo *m.*
hippodrome ['hɪpədrɒʊm] *s.* ippodromo *m.*
hippopotamus [ˌhɪpə'pətəməs] *s.* ippopotamo *m.*
hire ['haɪəʳ] *s.* **1** noleggio *m.*, affitto *m.* **2** salario *m.* ♦ **h. purchase** acquisto (o vendita) rateale
to hire ['haɪəʳ] *v. tr.* **1** noleggiare, affittare **2** assumere, dare lavoro a
his [hɪz, ɪz] *agg. e pron. poss. 3ª sing.* (*riferito a possessore m.*) suo, sua, suoi, sue
Hispanic [hɪs'pænɪk] *agg.* ispanico
hiss [hɪs] *s.* sibilo *m.*, fischio *m.*
to hiss [hɪs] *v. intr.* sibilare, fischiare
historian [hɪs'tɜːrɪ(ə)n] *s.* storico *m.*
historic(al) [hɪs'tərɪk((ə)l)] *agg.* storico
historiography [hɪsˌtɜːrɪ'əgrəfɪ] *s.* storiografia *f.*
history ['hɪst(ə)rɪ] *s.* storia *f.*
histrion ['hɪstrɪən] *s.* istrione *m.*
hit [hɪt] *s.* **1** colpo *m.*, urto *m.* **2** successo *m.*
to hit [hɪt] (*pass. e p. p.* **hit**) **A** *v. tr.* **1** battere, colpire, picchiare **2** incontrare, trovare **3** raggiungere **B** *v. intr.* urtare, entrare in collisione ♦ **to h. it off with sb.** andare d'accordo con qc.; **to h. on** trovare per caso, scoprire
hitch [hɪtʃ] *s.* **1** strattoni *m.*, sobbalzo *m.* **2** intoppo *m.*, difficoltà *f.*
to hitch [hɪtʃ] **A** *v. tr.* **1** muovere a strattoni **2** attaccare **B** *v. intr.* **1** muoversi a sbalzi **2** attaccarsi **3** (*pop.*) fare l'autostop ♦ **to h. up** sollevare, tirare su
to hitchhike ['hɪtʃhaɪk] *v. intr.* fare l'autostop
hitchhiker ['hɪtʃˌhaɪkəʳ] *s.* autostoppista *m. e f.*
hitchhiking ['hɪtʃˌhaɪkɪŋ] *s.* autostop *m. inv.*
hitherto [ˌhɪðə'tuː] *avv.* finora
hive [haɪv] *s.* alveare *m.*
to hive [haɪv] *v. intr.* **1** entrare nell'alveare **2** vivere in comunità ♦ **to h. off** separare, sciamare
hoard [hɜːd] *s.* **1** gruzzolo *m.* **2** *al pl.* scorte *f. pl*
to hoard [hɜːd] *v. tr.* accumulare, ammassare, accaparrare
hoarding ['hɜːdɪŋ] *s.* **1** staccionata *f.* **2** tabellone *m.* pubblicitario
hoarfrost ['hɜːˌfrəst] *s.* brina *f.*
hoarse [hɜːs] *agg.* rauco
hoarseness ['hɜːsnɪs] *s.* raucedine *f.*
hoax [hɒʊks] *s.* beffa *f.*, truffa *f.*
hob [həb] *s.* piastra *f.* (di fornello)
to hobble ['həbl] *v. intr.* zoppicare
hobby ['həbɪ] *s.* hobby *m. inv.*, passatempo *m.*
hobbyhorse ['həbɪhɜːs] **1** cavalluccio *m.* di legno **2** (*fig.*) cavallo *m.* di battaglia, chiodo *m.* fisso
hobo ['hɒʊbɒʊ] *s.* (*USA*, *pop.*) vagabondo *m.*
hockey ['həkɪ] *s.* hockey *m. inv.* ♦ **ice h.** hockey su ghiaccio
hoe [hɒʊ] *s.* zappa *f.*
to hoe [hɒʊ] *v. tr.* zappare
hog [həg] *s.* maiale *m.*
to hog [həg] *v. tr.* (*fam.*) arraffare
hoist [həɪst] *s.* paranco *m.*
to hoist [həɪst] *v. tr.* issare, sollevare
hold (1) [hɒʊld] *s.* **1** presa *f.* **2** ascendente *m.*, influenza *f.* **3** sostegno *m.* ♦ **on h.** (*al telefono*) in linea; **to catch h. over** afferrare; **to have an h. over** avere il controllo su
hold (2) [hɒʊld] *s.* (*naut.*) stiva *f.*
to hold [hɒʊld] (*pass. e p. p.* **held**) **A** *v. tr.* **1** tenere, mantenere **2** contenere **3** possedere, detenere, occupare **4** trattenere, fermare **5** ritenere, pensare **B** *v. intr.* **1** durare, continuare, persistere **2** essere valido ♦ **to h. back** trattenere, tener nascosto; **to h. down** tener giù, trattenere; **to h. off** tenere a distanza; **to h. on** aspettare, (*al telefono*) rimanere in linea, restare aggrappato a; **to h. out** resistere, offrire; **to h. up** bloccare, rapinare

holdall ['hɒʊldɜːl] *s.* sacca *f.* da viaggio
holder ['hɒʊldəʳ] *s.* **1** detentore *m.*, titolare *m. e f.* **2** contenitore *m.*
holding ['hɒʊldɪŋ] *s.* **1** possesso *m.* **2** tenuta *f.*, proprietà *f.* **3** patrimonio *m.*, dotazione *f.* **4** *al pl.* (*econ.*) azioni *f. pl.*, pacchetto *m.* azionario ♦ **h. company** holding, società finanziaria
holdup ['hɒʊldʌp] *s.* **1** rapina *f.* a mano armata **2** (*nel traffico*) intoppo *m.*, ingorgo *m.*
hole [hɒʊl] *s.* **1** buco *m.*, foro *m.*, apertura *f.* **2** tana *f.* **3** (*golf*) buca *f.*
to hole [hɒʊl] *v. tr.* bucare, forare
holiday ['hɔlədeɪ] *s.* **1** festività *f.*, giorno *m.* festivo **2** vacanza *f.* ♦ **h. camp** villaggio turistico; **h. resort** luogo di villeggiatura
holidaymaker ['hɔlədeɪˌmeɪkəʳ] *s.* villeggiante *m. e f.*
holiness ['hɒʊlɪnɪs] *s.* santità *f.*
hollow ['hɔlɒʊ] **A** *agg.* **1** cavo, incavato, vuoto **2** (*di suono*) cupo, sordo **3** vacuo, vano **B** *s.* **1** cavità *f.*, buca *f.* **2** valletta *f.*
to hollow ['hɔlɒʊ] *v. tr.* incavare, scavare
holly ['hɔlɪ] *s.* agrifoglio *m.*
holocaust ['hɔləkɜːst] *s.* olocausto *m.*
holster ['hɒʊlstəʳ] *s.* fondina *f.*
holy ['hɒʊlɪ] *agg.* sacro, santo
homage ['hɔmɪdʒ] *s.* omaggio *m.* ♦ **to pay h. to** rendere omaggio a
home [hɒʊm] **A** *s.* **1** casa *f.*, dimora *f.*, abitazione *f.* **2** patria *f.* **3** asilo *m.*, ricovero *m.* **4** (*sport*) meta *f.*, traguardo *m.*, porta *f.* **B** *agg. attr.* **1** casalingo, domestico, familiare **2** nazionale ♦ **h. address** domicilio; **h. cooking** cucina casalinga; **h. fire** focolare domestico; **h. life** vita familiare; **h. of rest** casa di riposo
homeland ['hɒʊmlænd] *s.* patria *f.*
homeless ['hɒʊmlɪs] *agg.* senzatetto
homely ['hɒʊmlɪ] *agg.* **1** semplice, modesto **2** casalingo
homemade [ˌhɒʊm'meɪd] *agg.* fatto in casa
homesick ['hɒʊmsɪk] *agg.* nostalgico ♦ **to be h.** avere la nostalgia
homesickness ['hɒʊmsɪknɪs] *s.* nostalgia *f.*
homestead ['hɒʊmstɛd] *s.* fattoria *f.*
hometown ['hɒʊmtaʊn] *s.* luogo *m.* di nascita
homeward ['hɒʊmwəd] **A** *avv.* verso casa **B** *agg.* di ritorno
homework ['hɒʊmwɜːk] *s.* compiti *m. pl.* a casa
homicide ['hɔmɪsaɪd] *s.* **1** omicidio *m.* **2** omicida *m. e f.*
hom(o)eopathic [ˌhɒʊmɪɒ(ʊ)'pæθɪk] *agg.* omeopatico
hom(o)eopathy [ˌhɒʊmɪ'ɔpəθɪ] *s.* omeopatia *f.*
homogeneity [ˌhɔmɒ(ʊ)dʒɛ'niːtɪ] *s.* omogeneità *f.*
homogeneous [ˌhɔmɒ(ʊ)'dʒiːnjəs] *agg.* omogeneo
homogenized [hɒ(ʊ)'mədʒənaɪzd] *agg.* omogeneizzato
to homologate [hə'mələgeɪt] *v. tr.* omologare
homology [hə'mələdʒɪ] *s.* omologia *f.*
homonym ['hɔmənɪm] *s.* omonimo *m.*
homonymous [hə'mənɪməs] *agg.* omonimo
homosexual [ˌhɒʊmɒ(ʊ)'sɛksjʊəl] *agg.* omosessuale
honest ['ənɪst] *agg.* **1** onesto, sincero, leale **2** semplice, genuino
honestly ['ənɪstlɪ] *avv.* onestamente, sinceramente
honesty ['ənɪstɪ] *s.* onestà *f.*
honey ['hʌnɪ] *s.* **1** miele *m.* **2** (*fam.*) dolcezza *f.*, tesoro *m.* ♦ **h.-bee** ape domestica
honeycomb ['hʌnɪkɒʊm] *s.* favo *m.*, nido *m.* d'ape
honeyed ['hʌnɪd] *agg.* **1** dolce **2** mellifluo
honeymoon ['hʌnɪmuːn] *s.* luna *f.* di miele
honeysuckle ['hʌnɪˌsʌkl] *s.* caprifoglio *m.*
to honk [həŋk] *v. intr.* **1** starnazzare **2** suonare il clacson
honorary ['ən(ə)rərɪ] *agg.* onorario
honour ['ənəʳ] (*USA* **honor**) *s.* **1** onore *m.* **2** *al pl.* onorificenza *f.*
honourable ['ən(ə)rəbl] *agg.* onorevole
hood [hʊd] *s.* **1** cappuccio *m.* **2** cappa *f.* **3** capote *f. inv.* **4** (*USA*) cofano *m.*
hoodlum ['hʊdl(ə)m] *s.* (*pop.*) teppista *m.*
to hoodwink ['hʊdwɪŋk] *v. tr.* ingannare
hoof [huːf] *s.* (*zool.*) zoccolo *m.*
hook [hʊk] *s.* **1** gancio *m.* **2** amo *m.*
to hook [hʊk] *v. tr.* **1** agganciare **2** prendere all'amo
hooligan ['huːlɪgən] *s.* teppista *m. e f.*
hoop (1) [huːp] *s.* urlo *m.*, grido *m.*
hoop (2) [huːp] *s.* cerchio *m.*, cerchione *m.*
hoopoe ['huːpuː] *s.* upupa *f.*
hooray [hʊ'reɪ] *inter.* urrà!

hoot [huːt] *s.* **1** (*di civetta*) grido *m.* **2** fischio *m.* **3** colpo *m.* di clacson
to hoot [huːt] *v. intr.* **1** gridare, urlare **2** fischiare **3** suonare il clacson ♦ **to h. at sb.** fischiare qc.
hop (1) [hɔp] *s.* salto *m.*
hop (2) [hɔp] *s.* luppolo *m.*
to hop [hɔp] *v. intr.* saltare, saltellare
hope [hɒʊp] *s.* speranza *f.*
to hope [hɒʊp] *v. tr. e intr.* sperare ♦ **I h. so/not** spero di sì/di no
hopeful ['hɒʊpf(ʊ)l] *agg.* **1** pieno di speranza **2** promettente
hopeless ['hɒʊplɪs] *agg.* disperato, senza speranza
horde [hɜːd] *s.* orda *f.*
horizon [hə'raɪzn] *s.* orizzonte *m.*
horizontal [ˌhərɪ'zəntl] *agg.* orizzontale
hormone ['hɜːmɒʊn] *s.* ormone *m.*
horn [hɜːn] *s.* **1** corno *m.* **2** clacson *m. inv.*
horned ['hɜːnd] *agg.* cornuto
hornet ['hɜːnɪt] *s.* calabrone *m.*
horoscope ['hərəskɒʊp] *s.* oroscopo *m.*
horrendous [hə'rɛndəs] *agg.* orrendo
horrible ['hərəbl] *agg.* orribile
horrid ['hərɪd] *agg.* orrido
horror ['hərəʳ] *s.* orrore *m.*
horse [hɜːs] *s.* cavallo *m.* ♦ **h. racing** ippica
horseback ['hɜːsbæk] *s.* dorso *m.* di cavallo ♦ **on h.** a cavallo
horse-chestnut [ˌhɜːs'tʃɛs(t)nʌt] *s.* ippocastano *m.*
horse-fly ['hɜːsflaɪ] *s.* tafano *m.*
horseman ['hɜːsmən] (*pl.* **horsemen**) *s.* cavallerizzo *m.*
horsepower ['hɜːsˌpaʊəʳ] *s.* cavallo *m.* (vapore)
horseradish ['hɜːsˌrædɪʃ] *s.* rafano *m.*
horseshoe ['hɜːsˌʃuː] *s.* ferro *m.* di cavallo
horsewoman ['hɜːsˌwʊmən] (*pl.* **horsewomen**) *s.* amazzone *f.*
horticulture ['hɜːtɪkʌltʃəʳ] *s.* orticoltura *f.*
hose [hɒʊz] *s.* **1** tubo *m.*, manichetta *f.* **2** calze *f. pl.*
hosiery ['hɒʊʒərɪ] *s.* maglieria *f.*
hospice ['həspɪs] *s.* ospizio *m.*
hospitable ['həspɪt(ə)bl] *agg.* ospitale
hospital ['həspɪtl] *s.* ospedale *m.*
hospitality [ˌhəspɪ'tælɪtɪ] *s.* ospitalità *f.*
to hospitalize ['həspɪtəlaɪz] *v. tr.* ospedalizzare, ricoverare in ospedale
host (1) [hɒʊst] **A** *agg.* ospite, che ospita **B** *s.* ospite *m.*, padrone *m.* di casa
host (2) [hɒʊst] *s.* schiera *f.*, moltitudine *f.*
hostage ['həstɪdʒ] *s.* ostaggio *m.*
hostel ['həst(ə)l] *s.* ostello *m.*
hostess ['hɒʊstɪs] *s.* **1** ospite *f.*, padrona *f.* di casa **2** hostess *f. inv.*, assistente *f.*
hostile ['həstaɪl] *agg.* ostile, nemico
hostility [həs'tɪlɪtɪ] *s.* ostilità *f.*
hot [hət] *agg.* **1** caldo, rovente, bollente **2** piccante, forte **3** violento, ardente, focoso **4** ancora caldo, fresco, recente ♦ **h. air** aria fritta; **h. pepper** peperoncino; **h. news** notizie fresche; **h. tempered** collerico; **to be h.** (*di persona*) aver caldo, (*di cosa*) essere caldo, (*del tempo*) far caldo
hotbed ['hətbɛd] *s.* focolaio *m.*
hotchpotch ['hətʃpətʃ] *s.* **1** stufato *m.* **2** guazzabuglio *m.*
hotel [hɒ(ʊ)'tɛl] *s.* albergo *m.* ♦ **h. keeper** albergatore
hot-headed [ˌhət'hɛdɪd] *agg.* focoso, impetuoso
hotplate ['hətpleɪt] *s.* piastra *f.* (di fornello elettrico)
hound [haʊnd] *s.* (*zool.*) segugio *m.*
to hound [haʊnd] *v. tr.* **1** cacciare con i cani **2** (*fig.*) perseguitare
hour ['aʊəʳ] *s.* **1** ora *f.* **2** *al pl.* orario *m.* ♦ **an h. ago** un'ora fa; **at 9 on the h.** alle 9 in punto; **half an h.** mezz'ora; **peak hours** ore di punta
hourly ['aʊəlɪ] **A** *agg.* **1** orario **2** continuo **B** *avv.* **1** ogni ora **2** d'ora in ora, da un momento all'altro **3** continuamente
house [haʊs] *s.* **1** casa *f.*, abitazione *f.*, dimora *f.* **2** (*pol.*) camera *f.* **3** teatro *m.*, pubblico *m.*, spettacolo *m.* **4** casata *f.*, dinastia *f.* **5** albergo *m.*, pensione *f.* **6** ditta *f.* ♦ **full h.** (*teatro*) tutto esaurito
houseboat ['haʊsbɒʊt] *s.* houseboat *f. inv.*, casa *f.* galleggiante
housebound ['haʊsbaʊnd] *agg.* costretto a stare in casa
housebreaker ['haʊsˌbreɪkəʳ] *s.* scassinatore *m.*
housecoat ['haʊsˌkɒʊt] *s.* vestaglia *f.*
housekeeper ['haʊsˌkiːpəʳ] *s.* **1** governante *f.* **2** donna *f.* di casa
housekeeping ['haʊsˌkiːpɪŋ] *s.* governo *m.* della casa
housemaid ['haʊsˌmeɪd] *s.* domestica *f.*
housewife ['haʊswaɪf] (*pl.* **housewives**) *s.* casalinga *f.*
housework ['haʊswɜːk] *s.* lavori *m. pl.* di

casa
housing ['haʊzɪŋ] *s.* **1** alloggio *m.*, abitazione *f.* **2** rifugio *m.*
hovel ['hɒv(ə)l] *s.* baracca *f.*
to hover ['hɒvəʳ] *v. intr.* librarsi, stare sospeso
hovercraft ['hɒvəˌkrɑːft] *s.* hovercraft *m. inv.*
how [haʊ] *avv.* **1** (*in frasi interr. ed escl.*) come, in che modo **2** quanto **3** in qualunque modo ♦ **h. about** che ne diresti di, a proposito di; **h.'s that?** come mai?; **h. far is?** quanto dista?; **h. long** quanto tempo; **h. much** quanto; **h. many** quanti; **h. often** quante volte; **h. old are you?** quanti anni hai?
however [haʊ'ɛvəʳ] **A** *avv.* comunque, per quanto **B** *cong.* comunque, tuttavia
howl [haʊl] *s.* urlo *m.*, ululato *m.*
to howl [haʊl] *v. intr.* urlare, ululare
hub [hʌb] *s.* **1** (*di ruota*) mozzo *m.* **2** (*fig.*) centro *m.*
hubbub ['hʌbʌb] *s.* confusione *f.*, fracasso *m.*
hubcap ['hʌbkæp] *s.* (*mecc.*) coprimozzo *m.*
huddle ['hʌdl] *s.* calca *f.*, folla *f.*
to huddle ['hʌdl] **A** *v. tr.* ammucchiare (alla rinfusa) **B** *v. intr.* accalcarsi, affollarsi
hue (1) [hjuː] *s.* tinta *f.*
hue (2) [hjuː] *s.* grido *m.* ♦ **h. and cry** clamore
huff [hʌf] *s.* stizza *f.* ♦ **to be in a h.** essere di cattivo umore
to hug [hʌg] *v. tr.* abbracciare, stringere
huge [hjuːdʒ] *agg.* enorme, immenso
hull [hʌl] *s.* **1** guscio *m.* **2** (*naut.*) scafo *m.*
hullo [hə'lɒʊ] → **hello**
hum [hʌm] *s.* ronzio *m.*, mormorio *m.*
to hum [hʌm] **A** *v. intr.* **1** ronzare, mormorare **2** canticchiare **B** *v. tr.* **1** canticchiare **2** borbottare
human ['hjuːmən] **A** *agg.* umano **B** *s.* essere *m.* umano
humane [hjʊ(ː)'meɪn] *agg.* umano, umanitario
humanism ['hjuːmənɪz(ə)m] *s.* umanesimo *m.*
humanist ['hjuːmənɪst] *s.* umanista *m. e f.*
humanitarian [hjʊ(ː)ˌmænɪ'tɛərɪən] *agg.* umanitario
humanity [hjʊ(ː)'mænɪtɪ] *s.* umanità *f.*
humble ['hʌmbl] *agg.* umile, modesto
to humble ['hʌmbl] *v. tr.* umiliare, avvilire
humbug ['hʌmbʌg] *s.* falsità *f.*, fandonia *f.*
humdrum ['hʌmdrʌm] *agg.* monotono, noioso
humerus ['hjuːmərəs] *s.* omero *m.*
humid ['hjuːmɪd] *agg.* umido
humidifier [hjʊ(ː)'mɪdɪfaɪəʳ] *s.* umidificatore *m.*
to humidify [hjʊ(ː)'mɪdɪfaɪ] *v. tr.* umidificare
humidity [hjʊ(ː)'mɪdɪtɪ] *s.* umidità *f.*
to humiliate [hjʊ(ː)'mɪlɪeɪt] *v. tr.* umiliare
humiliating [hjʊ(ː)'mɪlɪeɪtɪŋ] *agg.* umiliante
humiliation [hjʊ(ː)ˌmɪlɪ'eɪʃ(ə)n] *s.* umiliazione *f.*
humility [hjʊ(ː)'mɪlɪtɪ] *s.* umiltà *f.*
humor ['hjuːməʳ] *s.* → **humour**
humorist ['hjuːmərɪst] *s.* umorista *m. e f.*
humorous ['hjuːm(ə)r(ə)s] *agg.* **1** umoristico, divertente **2** arguto, spiritoso
humour ['hjuːməʳ] (*USA* **humor**) *s.* **1** umore *m.*, disposizione *f.* d'animo **2** umorismo *m.*, senso *m.* dell'umorismo ♦ **to be out of h.** essere di cattivo umore
hump [hʌmp] *s.* **1** gobba *f.* **2** collinetta *f.* **3** (*pop.*) malinconia *f.*, malumore *m.*
humpbacked ['hʌmpbækt] *agg.* con gobba ♦ **h. bridge** ponte a schiena d'asino
hunch [hʌn(t)ʃ] *s.* **1** gobba *f.*, gibbosità *f.* **2** (*pop.*) sospetto *m.*, impressione *f.*
hunchbacked ['hʌn(t)ʃbækt] *agg.* gobbo, gibboso
hundred ['hʌndrəd] *agg. num. card. e s.* cento *m. inv.* ♦ **by hundreds** a centinaia
hundredth ['hʌndrədθ] *agg. num. ord. e s.* centesimo *m.*
hung [hʌŋ] *pass. e p. p. di* **to hang**
Hungarian [hʌŋ'gɛərɪən] *agg. e s.* ungherese *m. e f.*
hunger ['hʌŋgəʳ] *s.* fame *f.* ♦ **h. strike** sciopero della fame
to hunger ['hʌŋgəʳ] *v. intr.* desiderare ardentemente
hungry ['hʌŋgrɪ] *agg.* **1** affamato **2** avido, bramoso ♦ **to be h.** aver fame
hunk [hʌŋk] *s.* (*fam.*) pezzo *m.*
hunt [hʌnt] *s.* caccia *f.*
to hunt [hʌnt] **A** *v. tr.* **1** cacciare **2** perlustrare, battere **B** *v. intr.* **1** andare a caccia **2** cercare ♦ **to h. out** scovare
hunter ['hʌntəʳ] *s.* cacciatore *m.*
hunting ['hʌntɪŋ] *s.* caccia *f.*
hurdle ['hɜːdl] *s.* **1** graticcio *m.*, barriera *f.* **2** (*sport*) ostacolo *m.*

to hurl [hɜːl] *v. tr.* lanciare, scagliare
hurrah [hʊ'rɑː] *inter.* evviva!
hurricane ['hʌrɪkən] *s.* uragano *m.*
hurried ['hʌrɪd] *agg.* frettoloso, affrettato
hurry ['hʌrɪ] *s.* fretta *f.*, premura *f.* ♦ **to be in a h.** aver fretta
to hurry ['hʌrɪ] **A** *v. tr.* **1** affrettare, sollecitare **2** spedire in fretta **B** *v. intr.* affrettarsi, sbrigarsi
hurt [hɜːt] *s.* **1** ferita *f.* **2** danno *m.*, offesa *f.*
to hurt [hɜːt] (*pass. e p. p.* **hurt**) **A** *v. tr.* **1** ferire, far male **2** offendere **3** danneggiare **B** *v. intr.* far male ♦ **to h. oneself** ferirsi, farsi male
hurtful ['hɜːtf(ʊ)l] *agg.* **1** nocivo, dannoso **2** offensivo
to hurtle ['hɜːtl] *v. intr.* sfrecciare, precipitarsi
husband ['hʌzbənd] *s.* marito *m.*
hush [hʌʃ] *s.* silenzio *m.*, quiete *f.*
to hush [hʌʃ] **A** *v. tr.* zittire, calmare **B** *v. intr.* far silenzio, tacere ♦ **to h. up** mettere a tacere
husk [hʌsk] *s.* buccia *f.*, guscio *m.*
husky ['hʌskɪ] *agg.* rauco, fioco
Husky ['hʌskɪ] *s.* eschimese *m. e f.*
to hustle ['hʌsl] **A** *v. tr.* **1** far fretta, incalzare **2** spingere, spintonare **B** *v. intr.* **1** affrettarsi **2** spingere
hut [hʌt] *s.* capanna *f.*, baracca *f.*
hutch [hʌtʃ] *s.* gabbia *f.*
hyacinth ['haɪəsɪnθ] *s.* giacinto *m.*
hybrid ['haɪbrɪd] *agg. e s.* ibrido *m.*
hydrant ['haɪdr(ə)nt] *s.* idrante *m.*
hydraulic [haɪ'drɜːlɪk] *agg.* idraulico
hydraulics [haɪ'drɜːlɪks] *s. pl.* (*v. al sing.*) idraulica *f.*
hydrobiology [ˌhaɪdrɒ(ʊ)baɪ'ələdʒɪ] *s.* idrobiologia *f.*
hydrocarbon [ˌhaɪdrɒ(ʊ):'kaːbən] *s.* idrocarburo *m.*
hydrofoil ['haɪdrəfəɪl] *s.* aliscafo *m.*
hydrogen ['haɪdrədʒ(ə)n] *s.* idrogeno *m.*
hydrography [haɪ'drəgrəfɪ] *s.* idrografia *f.*
hydrophobia [ˌhaɪdrə'fɒʊbjə] *s.* idrofobia *f.*
hydrostatic [ˌhaɪdrɒ(ʊ)'stætɪk] *agg.* idrostatico
hydrothermal [ˌhaɪdrɒ(ʊ)'θɜːm(ə)l] *agg.* idrotermale
hyena [haɪ'iːnə] *s.* iena *f.*
hygiene ['haɪdʒiːn] *s.* igiene *f.*
hygienic [haɪ'dʒiːnɪk] *agg.* igienico
hygrometer [haɪ'grəmɪtəʳ] *s.* igrometro *m.*
hymn [hɪm] *s.* inno *m.*
hype [haɪp] *s.* **1** lancio *m.* pubblicitario **2** montatura *f.* giornalistica
hypercritical [ˌhaɪpə'krɪtɪk(ə)l] *agg.* ipercritico
hypermarket ['haɪpəˌmaːkɪt] *s.* ipermercato *m.*
hypermetropia [ˌhaɪpə(ː)mɪ'trɒʊpɪə] *s.* ipermetropia *f.*
hypertension [ˌhaɪpə'tɛnʃ(ə)n] *s.* ipertensione *f.*
hyphen ['haɪf(ə)n] *s.* trattino *m.*
to hyphenate ['haɪfəneɪt] *v. tr.* unire (o dividere) parole con il trattino
hypnotism ['hɪpnətɪz(ə)m] *s.* ipnotismo *m.*
to hypnotize ['hɪpnətaɪz] *v. tr.* ipnotizzare
hypocrisy [hɪ'pəkrəsɪ] *s.* ipocrisia *f.*
hypocrite ['hɪpəkrɪt] *s.* ipocrita *m. e f.*
hypocritical [ˌhɪpə'krɪtɪk(ə)l] *agg.* ipocrita
hypogeum [ˌhaɪpə'dʒiːəm] *s.* ipogeo *m.*
hypothesis [haɪ'pəθɪsɪs] (*pl.* **hypotheses**) *s.* ipotesi *f.*
hypothetic(al) [ˌhaɪpɒ(ʊ)'θɛtɪk((ə)l)] *agg.* ipotetico
hysteria [hɪs'tɪərɪə] *s.* isterismo *m.*
hysteric(al) [hɪs'tɛrɪk((ə)l)] *agg.* isterico
hysterics [hɪs'tɛrɪks] *s. pl.* crisi *f.* isterica

I

I [aɪ] *pron. pers. 1ª sing.* io
ice [aɪs] *s.* **1** ghiaccio *m.* **2** gelo *m.* ♦ **i. cream** gelato; **i. crusher** tritaghiaccio; **i. cube** cubetto di ghiaccio; **i. lolly** ghiacciolo; **i. pack** banchisa; **i. rink** pista da pattinaggio
to ice [aɪs] **A** *v. tr.* **1** ghiacciare, congelare **2** (*cuc.*) glassare **B** *v. intr.* ghiacciare ♦ **to i. over/up** coprirsi di ghiaccio
iceberg ['aɪsbɜːg] *s.* iceberg *m. inv.*
icebox ['aɪsbəks] *s.* **1** ghiacciaia *f.* **2** (*USA*) frigorifero *m.*
Icelander ['aɪsləndəʳ] *s.* islandese *m. e f.*
Icelandic [aɪs'lændɪk] *agg.* islandese
ice-skating ['aɪsˌskeɪtɪŋ] *s.* pattinaggio *m.* su ghiaccio
ichthyic ['ɪkθɪɪk] *agg.* ittico
ichthyology [ˌɪkθɪ'ələdʒɪ] *s.* ittiologia *f.*
icicle ['aɪsɪkl] *s.* ghiacciolo *m.*
icing ['aɪsɪŋ] **A** *agg.* glassato **B** *s.* glassa *f.* ♦ **i. sugar** zucchero a velo
icon ['aɪkən] *s.* icona *f.*
iconoclast [aɪ'kənəklæst] *agg.* iconoclasta
iconographic [aɪˌkənə'græfɪk] *agg.* iconografico
iconography [ˌaɪkə'nəgrəfɪ] *s.* iconografia *f.*
icy ['aɪsɪ] *agg.* gelato, gelido
idea [aɪ'dɪə] *s.* idea *f.*
ideal [aɪ'dɪəl] *agg. e s.* ideale *m.*
idealism [aɪ'dɪəlɪz(ə)m] *s.* idealismo *m.*
to idealize [aɪ'dɪəlaɪz] *v. tr.* idealizzare
ideation [ˌaɪdɪ'eɪʃ(ə)n] *s.* ideazione *f.*
identical [aɪ'dɛntɪk(ə)l] *agg.* identico
identifiable [aɪˌdɛntɪ'faɪəbl] *agg.* identificabile
identification [aɪˌdɛntɪfɪ'keɪʃ(ə)n] *s.* **1** identificazione *f.*, riconoscimento *m.* **2** documento *m.* d'identità
to identify [aɪ'dɛntɪfaɪ] *v. tr.* identificare
identikit [aɪ'dɛntɪkɪt] *s.* identikit *m. inv.*
identity [aɪ'dɛntɪtɪ] *s.* identità *f.* ♦ **i. card** documento d'identità
ideogram ['ɪdɪɒ(ʊ)græm] *s.* ideogramma *m.*
ideological [ˌaɪdɪə'lədʒɪk(ə)l] *agg.* ideologico
ideology [ˌaɪdɪ'ələdʒɪ] *s.* ideologia *f.*
idiocy ['ɪdɪəsɪ] *s.* idiozia *f.*
idiom ['ɪdɪəm] *s.* **1** idioma *m.* **2** espressione *f.* idiomatica
idiosyncrasy [ˌɪdɪə'sɪŋkrəsɪ] *s.* idiosincrasia *f.*
idiot ['ɪdɪət] *s.* idiota *m.*
idiotic [ˌɪdɪ'ətɪk] *agg.* idiota
idle ['aɪdl] *agg.* **1** pigro, ozioso, sfaccendato **2** inutile, vano
to idle ['aɪdl] *v. intr.* **1** oziare **2** (*di motore*) girare al minimo ♦ **to i. away** sprecare
idleness ['aɪdlnɪs] *s.* **1** pigrizia *f.*, ozio *m.* **2** inutilità *f.*
idol ['aɪdl] *s.* idolo *m.*
idolatry [aɪ'dələtrɪ] *s.* idolatria *f.*
to idolize ['aɪdəlaɪz] *v. tr.* idolatrare
idyllic [aɪ'dɪlɪk] *agg.* idilliaco
if [ɪf] *cong.* se, posto che, nel caso che, qualora, anche se ♦ **if anyting** se mai; **if I were you** se fossi in te; **if not** altrimenti; **if so** in tal caso
to ignite [ɪg'naɪt] *v. tr.* infiammare, dare fuoco
ignition [ɪg'nɪʃ(ə)n] *s.* accensione *f.* ♦ **i. key** (*autom.*) chiave dell'accensione
ignoble [ɪg'nɒʊbl] *agg.* ignobile
ignorance ['ɪgn(ə)r(ə)ns] *s.* ignoranza *f.*
ignorant ['ɪgn(ə)r(ə)nt] *agg.* ignorante ♦ **to be i. of** ignorare
to ignore [ɪg'nɜːʳ] *v. tr.* ignorare, trascurare
ilex ['aɪlɛks] *s.* leccio *m.*
ill [ɪl] **A** *agg.* (*comp.* **worse**, *sup. rel.* **worst**) **1** malato **2** cattivo, dannoso, nocivo **3** sfavorevole, avverso **B** *s.* **1** male *m.* **2** malattia *f.* **3** *al pl.* avversità *f.* **C** *avv.* **1** male, malamente **2** a mala pena, a stento ♦ **i. at ease** a disagio; **to fall i.** ammalarsi; **to feel i.** sentirsi male; **to speak i. of sb.** parlar male di qc.
ill-advised [ˌɪləd'vaɪzd] *agg.* sconsiderato
illation [ɪ'leɪʃ(ə)n] *s.* illazione *f.*
ill-bred [ˌɪl'brɛd] *agg.* maleducato
illegal [ɪ'liːg(ə)l] *agg.* illegale
illegality [ˌɪlɪ(ː)'gælɪtɪ] *s.* illegalità *f.*
illegible [ɪ'lɛdʒəbl] *agg.* illeggibile
illegitimate [ˌɪlɪ'dʒɪtɪmɪt] *agg.* illegittimo
ill-fated [ˌɪl'feɪtɪd] *agg.* sfortunato
illicit [ɪ'lɪsɪt] *agg.* illecito
illiterate [ɪ'lɪt(ə)rɪt] *agg. e s.* **1** analfabeta

m. e f. **2** ignorante *m. e f.*
ill-mannered [ˌɪl'mænəd] *agg.* maleducato
illness ['ɪlnɪs] *s.* malattia *f.*
illogical [ɪ'lədʒɪk(ə)l] *agg.* illogico
ill-timed [ˌɪl'taɪmd] *agg.* inopportuno
to **ill-treat** [ˌɪl'triːt] *v. tr.* maltrattare
to **illuminate** [ɪ'ljuːmɪneɪt] *v. tr.* **1** illuminare, rischiarare **2** miniare
illumination [ɪˌljuːmɪ'neɪʃ(ə)n] *s.* **1** illuminazione *f.* **2** miniatura *f.*
illusion [ɪ'luːʒ(ə)n] *s.* illusione *f.*
to **illustrate** ['ɪləstreɪt] *v. tr.* illustrare
illustration [ˌɪləs'treɪʃ(ə)n] *s.* illustrazione *f.*
image ['ɪmɪdʒ] *s.* immagine *f.*
imagery ['ɪmɪdʒ(ə)rɪ] *s.* **1** immagini *f. pl.* **2** linguaggio *m.* figurato
imaginary [ɪ'mædʒɪn(ə)rɪ] *agg.* immaginario
imagination [ɪˌmædʒɪ'neɪʃ(ə)n] *s.* immaginazione *f.*
imaginative [ɪ'mædʒ(ɪ)nətɪv] *agg.* fantasioso
to **imagine** [ɪ'mædʒɪn] **A** *v. tr.* **1** immaginare **2** supporre, credere **B** *v. intr.* fantasticare
imbalance [ɪm'bæləns] *s.* squilibrio *m.*
imbecile ['ɪmbɪsaɪl] *agg.* imbecille
to **imbue** [ɪm'bjuː] *v. tr.* impregnare, permeare
to **imitate** ['ɪmɪteɪt] *v. tr.* imitare
imitation [ˌɪmɪ'teɪʃ(ə)n] *s.* imitazione *f.*
imitator ['ɪmɪteɪtəʳ] *s.* imitatore *m.*
immaculate [ɪ'mækjʊlɪt] *agg.* **1** immacolato **2** impeccabile
immanent ['ɪmənənt] *agg.* immanente
immaterial [ˌɪmə'tɪərɪəl] *agg.* **1** indifferente, irrilevante **2** immateriale
immature [ˌɪmə'tjʊəʳ] *agg.* immaturo
immeasurable [ɪ'mɛʒ(ə)rəbl] *agg.* incommensurabile
immediate [ɪ'miːdjət] *agg.* immediato
immediately [ɪ'miːdjətlɪ] *avv.* immediatamente, subito
immemorial [ˌɪmɪ'mɜːrɪəl] *agg.* immemorabile
immense [ɪ'mɛns] *agg.* immenso
immensity [ɪ'mɛnsɪtɪ] *s.* immensità *f.*
to **immerse** [ɪ'mɜːs] *v. tr.* immergere
immersion [ɪ'mɜːʃ(ə)n] *s.* immersione *f.*
immigrant ['ɪmɪgr(ə)nt] *agg. e s.* immigrante *m. e f.*
to **immigrate** ['ɪmɪgreɪt] *v. intr.* immigrare
immigration [ˌɪmɪ'greɪʃ(ə)n] *s.* immigrazione *f.*
imminent ['ɪmɪnənt] *agg.* imminente
to **immobilize** [ɪ'mɒʊbɪlaɪz] *v. tr.* immobilizzare
immoderate [ɪ'məd(ə)rɪt] *agg.* smodato
immodest [ɪ'mədɪst] *agg.* immodesto, impudico
immoral [ɪ'mər(ə)l] *agg.* immorale
immortal [ɪ'mɜːtl] *agg. e s.* immortale *m. e f.*
immortality [ˌɪmɜː'tælɪtɪ] *s.* immortalità *f.*
to **immortalize** [ɪ'mɜːtəlaɪz] *v. tr.* immortalare
immovable [ɪ'muːvəbl] *agg.* **1** immobile, immutabile **2** impassibile ♦ **i. estate** beni immobili
immune [ɪ'mjuːn] *agg.* immune
immunity [ɪ'mjuːnɪtɪ] *s.* immunità *f.*
to **immunize** ['ɪmjʊ(ː)naɪz] *v. tr.* immunizzare
immutable [ɪ'mjuːtəbl] *agg.* immutabile
imp [ɪmp] *s.* diavoletto *m.*, folletto *m.*
impact ['ɪmpækt] *s.* impatto *m.*
to **impair** [ɪm'pɛəʳ] *v. tr.* **1** indebolire **2** danneggiare
impairment [ɪm'pɛəmənt] *s.* **1** indebolimento *m.* **2** danneggiamento *m.*, menomazione *f.*
to **impale** [ɪm'peɪl] *v. tr.* **1** impalare **2** immobilizzare (*con lo sguardo*)
impalpable [ɪm'pælpəbl] *agg.* impalpabile
to **impart** [ɪm'paːt] *v. tr.* **1** impartire **2** comunicare, rivelare **3** distribuire
impartial [ɪm'paːʃ(ə)l] *agg.* imparziale
impartiality [ɪmˌpaːʃɪ'ælɪtɪ] *s.* imparzialità *f.*
impassable [ɪm'paɪsəbl] *agg.* invalicabile, impraticabile
impasse [æm'paːs] *s.* impasse *f. inv.*
impassioned [ɪm'pæʃ(ə)nd] *agg.* appassionato
impassive [ɪm'pæsɪv] *agg.* impassibile
impatience [ɪm'peɪʃ(ə)ns] *s.* **1** impazienza *f.* **2** intolleranza *f.*
impatient [ɪm'peɪʃ(ə)nt] *agg.* **1** impaziente **2** intollerante
impeccable [ɪm'pɛkəbl] *agg.* impeccabile
to **impede** [ɪm'piːd] *v. tr.* impedire, ostacolare
impediment [ɪm'pɛdɪmənt] *s.* impedimento *m.*, ostacolo *m.*
impeller [ɪm'pɛləʳ] *s.* (*mecc.*) girante *f.*
impending [ɪm'pɛndɪŋ] *agg.* incombente, imminente

impenetrable [ɪm'pɛnɪtrəbl] *agg.* impenetrabile
imperative [ɪm'pɛrətɪv] **A** *agg.* **1** imperativo, imperioso, perentorio **2** (*gramm.*) imperativo **B** *s.* **1** imperativo *m.*, obbligo *m.* **2** (*gramm.*) imperativo *m.*
imperceptible [ˌɪmpə'sɛptəbl] *agg.* impercettibile
imperfect [ɪm'pɜːfɪkt] **A** *agg.* **1** imperfetto, difettoso **2** (*gramm.*) imperfetto **B** *s.* (*gramm.*) imperfetto *m.*
imperfection [ˌɪmpə'fɛkʃ(ə)n] *s.* imperfezione *f.*
imperial [ɪm'pɪərɪəl] *agg.* imperiale
imperialism [ɪm'pɪərɪəlɪz(ə)m] *s.* imperialismo *m.*
impersonal [ɪm'pɜːsən(ə)l] *agg.* impersonale
to impersonate [ɪm'pɜːsəneɪt] *v. tr.* **1** impersonare **2** spacciarsi per
impertinent [ɪm'pɜːtɪnənt] *agg.* impertinente
imperturbable [ˌɪmpə(ː)'tɜːbəbl] *agg.* imperturbabile
impervious [ɪm'pɜːvjəs] *agg.* **1** impervio, inaccessibile **2** insensibile
impetuosity [ɪmˌpɛtjʊ'əsɪtɪ] *s.* impetuosità *f.*
impetuous [ɪm'pɛtjʊəs] *agg.* impetuoso
impetus ['ɪmpɪtəs] *s.* impeto *m.*, impulso *m.*
to impinge [ɪm'pɪn(d)ʒ] *v. intr.* **1** urtare contro **2** contrastare **3** violare
implacable [ɪm'plækəbl] *agg.* implacabile
implement ['ɪmplɪmənt] *s.* arnese *m.*, utensile *m.*, attrezzo *m.*
to implement ['ɪmplɪmənt] *v. tr.* realizzare, compiere
to implicate ['ɪmplɪkeɪt] *v. tr.* implicare
implication [ˌɪmplɪ'keɪʃ(ə)n] *s.* **1** implicazione *f.*, coinvolgimento *m.* **2** insinuazione *f.*
implicit [ɪm'plɪsɪt] *agg.* **1** implicito **2** completo, assoluto
implied [ɪm'plaɪd] *agg.* implicito
impluvium [ɪm'pluːvjəm] *s.* impluvio *m.*
to imply [ɪm'plaɪ] *v. tr.* **1** implicare, sottintendere **2** comportare
impolite [ˌɪmpə'laɪt] *agg.* scortese
import ['ɪmpɜːt] *s.* importazione *f.*
to import [ɪm'pɜːt] *v. tr.* importare
importance [ɪm'pɜːt(ə)ns] *s.* importanza *f.*
important [ɪm'pɜːtənt] *agg.* importante
importation [ˌɪmpɜː'teɪʃ(ə)n] *s.* importazione *f.*
importer [ɪm'pɜːtəʳ] *s.* importatore *m.*
to importune [ɪm'pɜːtjuːn] *v. tr.* importunare
to impose [ɪm'pɒʊz] *v. tr.* imporre ♦ **to i. on** approfittare di
imposing [ɪm'pɒʊzɪŋ] *agg.* imponente
imposition [ˌɪmpə'zɪʃ(ə)n] *s.* imposizione *f.*
impossibility [ɪmˌpəsə'bɪlɪtɪ] *s.* impossibilità *f.*
impossible [ɪm'pəsəbl] *agg.* impossibile
imposture [ɪm'pəstʃəʳ] *s.* impostura *f.*
impotent ['ɪmpətənt] *agg.* impotente
to impound [ɪm'paʊnd] *v. tr.* confiscare, sequestrare
to impoverish [ɪm'pəv(ə)rɪʃ] *v. tr.* **1** impoverire **2** indebolire
impracticable [ɪm'præktɪkəbl] *agg.* **1** impraticabile **2** inattuabile
impractical [ɪm'præktɪkl] *agg.* non pratico
imprecation [ˌɪmprɪ'keɪʃ(ə)n] *s.* imprecazione *f.*
impregnable [ɪm'prɛgnəbl] *agg.* **1** inespugnabile **2** (*fig.*) incrollabile
to impregnate ['ɪmprɛgneɪt] *v. tr.* impregnare
to impress [ɪm'prɛs] *v. tr.* **1** imprimere **2** impressionare
impression [ɪm'prɛʃ(ə)n] *s.* **1** impressione *f.*, impronta *f.* **2** stampa *f.*, tiratura *f.* **3** (*fig.*) impressione *f.*, effetto *m.*
impressionism [ɪm'prɛʃnɪz(ə)m] *s.* impressionismo *m.*
impressive [ɪm'prɛsɪv] *agg.* **1** impressionante **2** toccante **3** solenne, di effetto
imprint ['ɪmprɪnt] *s.* **1** impronta *f.*, impressione *f.* **2** sigla *f.* editoriale
to imprison [ɪm'prɪzn] *v. tr.* imprigionare
imprisonment [ɪm'prɪznmənt] *s.* prigionia *f.*, reclusione *f.*
improbable [ɪm'prəbəbl] *agg.* improbabile
improper [ɪm'prəpəʳ] *agg.* **1** improprio **2** scorretto, sbagliato **3** sconveniente
to improve [ɪm'pruːv] **A** *v. tr.* **1** migliorare, perfezionare **2** profittare di, fare buon uso di **B** *v. intr.* perfezionarsi, migliorare
improvement [ɪm'pruːvmənt] *s.* miglioramento *m.*, perfezionamento *m.*, progresso *m.*
to improvise ['ɪmprəvaɪz] *v. tr. e intr.* improvvisare
imprudence [ɪm'pruːd(ə)ns] *s.* impruden-

za *f.*, leggerezza *f.*
imprudent [ɪm'pruːdənt] *agg.* imprudente
impudence ['ɪmpjʊd(ə)ns] *s.* impudenza *f.*, sfacciataggine *f.*
impudent ['ɪmpjʊdənt] *agg.* impudente, sfacciato
impulse ['ɪmpʌls] *s.* impulso *m.*
impulsive [ɪm'pʌlsɪv] *agg.* impulsivo
impure [ɪm'pjʊəʳ] *agg.* impuro
impurity [ɪm'pjʊərɪtɪ] *s.* impurità *f.*
in [ɪn] **A** *prep.* **1** (*stato in luogo, posizione, condizione*) in, a, dentro (ES: **in Milan** a Milano, **in the light** alla luce) **2** (*tempo*) in, entro, durante, fra, di (ES: **in Spring** in primavera, **in the evening**, di sera) **3** (*limitazione, misura, modo*) in, di, su (ES: **Italy is rich in monuments** l'Italia è ricca di monumenti, **one in a million** uno su un milione) **4** (*seguito da un gerundio*) nell'atto di, in, *idiom.* (ES: **in driving home** nel tornare a casa, tornando a casa in macchina) **B** *avv.* dentro, in casa
inability [ɪnə'bɪlɪtɪ] *s.* inabilità *f.*, incapacità *f.*
inaccessible [ˌɪnæk'sɛsəbl] *agg.* inaccessibile
inaccuracy [ɪn'ækjʊrəsɪ] *s.* imprecisione *f.*, inesattezza *f.*
inaccurate [ɪn'ækjʊrɪt] *agg.* impreciso, inesatto
inactive [ɪn'æktɪv] *agg.* inattivo
inactivity [ˌɪnæk'tɪvɪtɪ] *s.* inattività *f.*, inerzia *f.*
inadequate [ɪn'ædɪkwɪt] *agg.* inadeguato
inadmissible [ˌɪnəd'mɪsəbl] *agg.* inammissibile
inadvertence [ˌɪnəd'vɜːt(ə)ns] *s.* sbadataggine *f.*, disattenzione *f.*
inadvertently [ˌɪnəd'vɜːt(ə)ntlɪ] *avv.* inavvertitamente
inadvisable [ɪnəd'vaɪzəbl] *agg.* sconsigliabile
inalienable [ɪn'eɪljənəbl] *agg.* inalienabile
inane [ɪ'neɪn] *agg.* vacuo, insensato
inanimate [ɪn'ænɪmɪt] *agg.* inanimato
inappropriate [ˌɪnə'prɒʊprɪɪt] *agg.* non appropriato, inadeguato
inapt [ɪn'æpt] *agg.* **1** improprio, inadatto **2** incapace
inarticulate [ˌɪnɑː'tɪkjʊlɪt] *agg.* **1** inarticolato **2** che si esprime con difficoltà
inasmuch [ˌɪnəz'mʌtʃ] *avv.* in quanto ♦ **i. as** visto che
inattentive [ˌɪnə'tɛntɪv] *agg.* disattento
inaudible [ɪn'ɜːdəbl] *agg.* impercettibile
inaugural [ɪ'nɜːgjʊr(ə)l] *agg.* inaugurale
to inaugurate [ɪ'nɜːgjʊreɪt] *v. tr.* inaugurare
inauguration [ɪˌnɜːgjʊ'reɪʃ(ə)n] *s.* inaugurazione *f.*
inauspicious [ˌɪnɜːs'pɪʃəs] *agg.* nefasto
inboard ['ɪnˌbɜːd] *agg. e avv.* entrobordo
inborn [ˌɪn'bɜːn] *agg.* innato
inbred [ˌɪn'brɛd] *agg.* innato
incalculable [ɪn'kælkjʊləbl] *agg.* incalcolabile
incapable [ɪn'keɪpəbl] *agg.* incapace
to incapacitate [ˌɪnkə'pæsɪteɪt] *v. tr.* **1** rendere incapace **2** (*dir.*) dichiarare incapace
to incarnate ['ɪnkaːneɪt] *v. tr.* incarnare
incense ['ɪnsɛns] *s.* incenso *m.*
to incense ['ɪnsɛns] *v. tr.* **1** incensare **2** esasperare, provocare
incentive [ɪn'sɛntɪv] *s.* incentivo *m.*
incessant [ɪn'sɛsnt] *agg.* incessante
incest ['ɪnsɛst] *s.* incesto *m.*
inch [ɪn(t)ʃ] *s.* pollice *m.* (*misura*)
to inch [ɪn(t)ʃ] *v. tr.* muovere gradatamente ♦ **to i. forward** avanzare poco alla volta
incidence ['ɪnsɪdəns] *s.* incidenza *f.*
incident ['ɪnsɪdənt] **A** *agg.* **1** inerente **2** incidente **B** *s.* incidente *m.*, caso *m.*
incidental [ˌɪnsɪ'dɛntl] *agg.* **1** incidentale **2** casuale, accidentale
incidentally [ˌɪnsɪ'dɛntlɪ] *avv.* incidentalmente
incision [ɪn'sɪʒ(ə)n] *s.* incisione *f.*
incisive [ɪn'saɪsɪv] *agg.* incisivo
incisor [ɪn'saɪzəʳ] *s.* incisivo *m.*
to incite [ɪn'saɪt] *v. tr.* incitare
incivility [ˌɪnsɪ'vɪlɪtɪ] *s.* inciviltà *f.*
inclinable [ɪn'klaɪnəbl] *agg.* inclinabile
inclination [ˌɪnklɪ'neɪʃ(ə)n] *s.* inclinazione *f.*, disposizione *f.*
incline [ɪn'klaɪn] *s.* pendenza *f.*
to incline [ɪn'klaɪn] **A** *v. tr.* inclinare **B** *v. intr.* tendere, propendere
to include [ɪn'kluːd] *v. tr.* includere, comprendere
inclusive [ɪn'kluːsɪv] *agg.* **1** inclusivo, comprendente **2** complessivo
incoherent [ˌɪnkɒ(ʊ)'hɪərənt] *agg.* incoerente
income ['ɪnkʌm] *s.* reddito *m.*, entrata *f.* ♦ **i. tax** imposta sul reddito
incoming ['ɪnˌkʌmɪŋ] *agg.* **1** entrante, subentrante **2** in arrivo **3** (*di marea*) mon-

tante
incomparable [ɪn'kəmp(ə)rəbl] *agg.* incomparabile
incompetent [ɪn'kəmpɪt(ə)nt] *agg.* incompetente, incapace
incomplete [ˌɪnkəm'pliːt] *agg.* incompleto
incomprehensible [ɪnˌkəmprɪ'hɛnsəbl] *agg.* incomprensibile
inconceivable [ˌɪnkən'siːvəbl] *agg.* inconcepibile
inconclusive [ˌɪnkən'kluːsɪv] *agg.* inconcludente
incongruous [ɪn'kəŋgrʊəs] *agg.* incongruente
inconsequent [ɪn'kənsɪkwənt] *agg.* incongruente, illogico
inconsiderate [ˌɪnkən'sɪd(ə)rɪt] *agg.* sconsiderato, avventato
inconsistency [ˌɪnkən'sɪst(ə)nsɪ] *s.* incoerenza *f.*
inconsistent [ˌɪnkən'sɪstənt] *agg.* incoerente
inconspicuous [ˌɪnkən'spɪkjʊəs] *agg.* non appariscente
inconstant [ɪn'kənstənt] *agg.* incostante
inconvenience [ˌɪnkən'viːnjəns] *s.* disturbo *m.*, disagio *m.*
to inconvenience [ˌɪnkən'viːnjəns] *v. tr.* disturbare
inconvenient [ˌɪnkən'viːnjənt] *agg.* fastidioso, scomodo
to incorporate [ɪn'kɜːpəreɪt] **A** *v. tr.* **1** incorporare **2** includere, comprendere **B** *v. intr.* incorporarsi, fondersi
incorrect [ˌɪnkə'rɛkt] *agg.* scorretto
incorrectness [ˌɪnkə'rɛktnɪs] *s.* scorrettezza *f.*
incorruptible [ˌɪnkə'rʌptəbl] *agg.* incorruttibile
increase ['ɪnkriːs] *s.* aumento *m.*, incremento *m.*
to increase [ɪn'kriːs] **A** *v. tr.* accrescere, aumentare **B** *v. intr.* crescere, ingrandirsi
increasing [ɪn'kriːsɪŋ] *agg.* crescente
incredible [ɪn'krɛdəbl] *agg.* incredibile
incredulous [ɪn'krɛdjʊləs] *agg.* incredulo
increment ['ɪnkrɪmənt] *s.* incremento *m.*
to incriminate [ɪn'krɪmɪneɪt] *v. tr.* incriminare
incubator ['ɪnkjʊbeɪtəʳ] *s.* incubatrice *f.*
to inculcate ['ɪnkʌlkeɪt] *v. tr.* inculcare
incumbent [ɪn'kʌmbənt] *agg.* incombente
incunabulum [ˌɪnkjʊ(ː)'næbjʊləm] *s.* incunabolo *m.*
to incur [ɪn'kɜːʳ] *v. tr.* **1** incorrere in **2** esporsi a **3** attirarsi
incurable [ɪn'kjʊərəbl] *agg.* incurabile
indebted [ɪn'dɛtɪd] *agg.* **1** indebitato **2** obbligato
indecent [ɪn'diːs(ə)nt] *agg.* indecente
indecipherable [ˌɪndɪ'saɪf(ə)rəbl] *agg.* indecifrabile
indecision [ˌɪndɪ'sɪʒ(ə)n] *s.* indecisione *f.*
indecisive [ˌɪndɪ'saɪsɪv] *agg.* **1** indeciso **2** non decisivo
indeed [ɪn'diːd] **A** *avv.* realmente, infatti, in verità **B** *inter.* davvero ♦ **no i.!** no davvero!; **yes i.!** certamente!
indefatigable [ˌɪndɪ'fætɪgəbl] *agg.* instancabile
indefinable [ˌɪndɪ'faɪnəbl] *agg.* indefinibile
indefinite [ɪn'dɛfɪnɪt] *agg.* indefinito
indefinitely [ɪn'dɛf(ə)nɪtlɪ] *avv.* indefinitamente
indelible [ɪn'dɛlɪbl] *agg.* indelebile
indemnification [ɪnˌdɛmnɪfɪ'keɪʃ(ə)n] *s.* indennizzo *m.*
to indemnify [ɪn'dɛmnɪfaɪ] *v. tr.* indennizzare
indemnity [ɪn'dɛmnɪtɪ] *s.* **1** indennità *f.* **2** assicurazione *f.*
to indent [ɪn'dɛnt] **A** *v. tr.* dentellare, frastagliare **B** *v. intr.* essere frastagliato
independence [ˌɪndɪ'pɛndəns] *s.* indipendenza *f.*
independent [ˌɪndɪ'pɛndənt] *agg.* indipendente
indestructible [ˌɪndɪs'trʌktəbl] *agg.* indistruttibile
indeterminate [ˌɪndɪ'tɜːmɪnɪt] *agg.* indeterminato
indeterminateness [ˌɪndɪ'tɜːmɪnɪtnɪs] *s.* indeterminatezza *f.*
index ['ɪndɛks] *s.* **1** indice *m.* **2** elenco *m.*, catalogo *m.* ♦ **i. finger** (dito) indice
Indian ['ɪndjən] *agg. e s.* indiano *m.*
to indicate ['ɪndɪkeɪt] *v. tr.* indicare, mostrare
indication [ˌɪndɪ'keɪʃ(ə)n] *s.* indicazione *f.*
indicative [ɪn'dɪkətɪv] *agg.* indicativo
indicator ['ɪndɪkeɪtəʳ] *s.* **1** indicatore *m.* **2** (*autom.*) freccia *f.*
indictment [ɪn'daɪtmənt] *s.* (*dir.*) accusa *f.*
indifference [ɪn'dɪfr(ə)ns] *s.* indifferenza *f.*
indifferent [ɪn'dɪfr(ə)nt] *agg.* **1** indiffe-

rente **2** neutrale **3** mediocre
indigenous [ɪn'dɪdʒɪnəs] *agg.* indigeno
indigestible [ˌɪndɪ'dʒɛstəbl] *agg.* indigesto
indigestion [ˌɪndɪ'dʒɛstʃ(ə)n] *s.* indigestione *f.*
indignant [ɪn'dɪgnənt] *agg.* indignato
indignity [ɪn'dɪgnɪtɪ] *s.* trattamento *m.* indegno, oltraggio *m.*
indirect [ˌɪndɪ'rɛkt] *agg.* indiretto
indiscreet [ˌɪndɪs'kriːt] *agg.* indiscreto
indiscriminate [ˌɪndɪs'krɪmɪnɪt] *agg.* indiscriminato
indispensable [ˌɪndɪs'pɛnsəbl] *agg.* indispensabile
indisposition [ˌɪndɪspə'zɪʃ(ə)n] *s.* indisposizione *f.*
indisputable [ˌɪndɪs'pjuːtəbl] *agg.* indiscutibile
indissoluble [ˌɪndɪ'sɔljʊbl] *agg.* indissolubile
indistinct [ˌɪndɪs'tɪŋkt] *agg.* indistinto
individual [ˌɪndɪ'vɪdjʊəl] **A** *agg.* **1** individuale **2** particolare **B** *s.* individuo *m.*
individualism [ˌɪndɪ'vɪdjʊəlɪz(ə)m] *s.* individualismo *m.*
individualist [ˌɪndɪ'vɪdjʊəlɪst] *agg. e s.* individualista *m. e f.*
to individualize [ˌɪndɪ'vɪdjʊəlaɪz] *v. tr.* individuare
individually [ˌɪndɪ'vɪdjʊəlɪ] *avv.* individualmente
indivisible [ˌɪndɪ'vɪzəbl] *agg.* indivisibile
indoctrination [ɪnˌdɔktrɪ'neɪʃ(ə)n] *s.* indottrinamento *m.*
Indo-European ['ɪndɒ(ʊ)ˌjʊərə'piːən] *agg.* indoeuropeo
indolent ['ɪndələnt] *agg.* indolente
indoor ['ɪndɔːʳ] *agg.* interno, al coperto ♦ **i. plant** pianta da appartamento
indoors [ˌɪn'dɔːz] *avv.* in casa, all'interno, al coperto ♦ **to go i.** entrare in casa
to induce [ɪn'djuːs] *v. tr.* **1** indurre, persuadere **2** provocare
inducement [ɪn'djuːsmənt] *s.* incentivo *m.*, stimolo *m.*
to indulge [ɪn'dʌldʒ] **A** *v. tr.* **1** assecondare, compiacere **2** appagare, soddisfare **B** *v. intr.* concedersi, permettersi
indulgence [ɪn'dʌldʒ(ə)ns] *s.* **1** indulgenza *f.*, compiacenza *f.* **2** appagamento *m.*
indulgent [ɪn'dʌldʒənt] *agg.* indulgente
industrial [ɪn'dʌstrɪəl] *agg.* industriale ♦ **i. action** agitazione sindacale; **i. estate/park** zona industriale
industrialization [ɪnˌdʌstrɪəlaɪ'zeɪʃ(ə)n] *s.* industrializzazione *f.*
industrious [ɪn'dʌstrɪəs] *agg.* industrioso, operoso
industry ['ɪndəstrɪ] *s.* **1** industria *f.* **2** industriosità *f.*, operosità *f.*
inebriate [ɪ'niːbrɪɪt] *agg. e s.* ubriaco *m.*
inedible [ɪn'ɛdɪbl] *agg.* immangiabile
ineffective [ˌɪnɪ'fɛktɪv] *agg.* **1** inefficace **2** incapace, inefficiente
inefficiency [ˌɪnɪ'fɪʃ(ə)nsɪ] *s.* inefficienza *f.*
inefficient [ˌɪnɪ'fɪʃ(ə)nt] *agg.* inefficiente, inefficace
ineluctable [ˌɪnɪ'lʌktəbl] *agg.* ineluttabile
inept [ɪ'nɛpt] *agg.* inetto
inequality [ˌɪnɪ(ː)'kwɔlɪtɪ] *s.* **1** ineguaglianza *f.* **2** irregolarità *f.*
inertia [ɪ'nɜːʃjə] *s.* inerzia *f.*
inescapable [ˌɪnɪs'keɪpəbl] *agg.* inevitabile
inessential [ˌɪnɪ'sɛnʃ(ə)l] *agg.* non essenziale
inevitable [ɪn'ɛvɪtəbl] *agg.* inevitabile
inexact [ˌɪnɪg'zækt] *agg.* inesatto
inexactitude [ˌɪnɪg'zæktɪtjuːd] *s.* inesattezza *f.*
inexcusable [ˌɪnɪks'kjuːzəbl] *agg.* imperdonabile
inexhaustible [ˌɪnɪg'zɔːstəbl] *agg.* inesauribile
inexistent [ˌɪnɪg'zɪstənt] *agg.* inesistente
inexpensive [ˌɪnɪks'pɛnsɪv] *agg.* economico, a buon mercato
inexperience [ˌɪnɪks'pɪərɪəns] *s.* inesperienza *f.*
inexperienced [ˌɪnɪks'pɪərɪənst] *agg.* inesperto
inexpert [ɪn'ɛkspɜːt] *agg.* inesperto
inexplicable [ɪn'ɛksplɪkəbl] *agg.* inesplicabile
inexpugnable [ˌɪnɪks'pʌgnəbl] *agg.* inespugnabile
infallible [ɪn'fæləbl] *agg.* infallibile
infamous ['ɪnfəməs] *agg.* infame
infancy ['ɪnfənsɪ] *s.* infanzia *f.*
infant ['ɪnfənt] **A** *agg.* infantile **B** *s.* infante *m. e f.*, neonato *m.*
infantile ['ɪnfəntaɪl] *agg.* infantile
infantry ['ɪnf(ə)ntrɪ] *s.* fanteria *f.*
infarct [ɪn'faːkt] *s.* infarto *m.*
infatuated [ɪn'fætjʊeɪtɪd] *agg.* infatuato

infatuation [ɪnˌfætjʊ'eɪʃ(ə)n] *s.* infatuazione *f.*
to infect [ɪn'fɛkt] *v. tr.* infettare, contagiare
infected [ɪn'fɛktɪd] *agg.* infetto
infection [ɪn'fɛkʃ(ə)n] *s.* infezione *f.*
infectious [ɪn'fɛkʃəs] *agg.* infettivo, contagioso
to infer [ɪn'fɜːʳ] *v. tr.* **1** inferire, dedurre **2** insinuare
inference ['ɪnf(ə)r(ə)ns] *s.* inferenza *f.*, deduzione *f.*
inferior [ɪn'fɪərɪəʳ] **A** *agg.* **1** inferiore, subordinato **2** scadente **B** *s.* inferiore *m. e f.*, subalterno *m.*
inferiority [ɪnˌfɪərɪ'ərɪtɪ] *s.* inferiorità *f.*
infernal [ɪn'fɜːnl] *agg.* infernale
infertile [ɪn'fɜːtaɪl] *agg.* infecondo, sterile
to infest [ɪn'fɛst] *v. tr.* infestare
infighting ['ɪnˌfaɪtɪŋ] *s.* **1** lotta *f.* corpo a corpo **2** lotta *f.* intestina
to infiltrate ['ɪnfɪltreɪt] **A** *v. tr.* **1** infiltrarsi in **2** infiltrare **B** *v. intr.* infiltrarsi, insinuarsi
infinite ['ɪnfɪnɪt] *agg. e s.* infinito *m.*
infinitesimal [ˌɪnfɪnɪ'tɛsɪm(ə)l] *agg.* infinitesimale
infinitive [ɪn'fɪnɪtɪv] *agg. e s.* (*gramm.*) infinito *m.*
infinity [ɪn'fɪnɪtɪ] *s.* **1** infinità *f.* **2** (*mat.*) infinito *m.*
infirmary [ɪn'fɜːmərɪ] *s.* infermeria *f.*
infirmity [ɪn'fɜːmɪtɪ] *s.* **1** infermità *f.* **2** debolezza *f.*
to inflame [ɪn'fleɪm] *v. tr. e intr.* infiammare, infiammarsi
inflammable [ɪn'flæməbl] *agg.* infiammabile
inflammation [ˌɪnflə'meɪʃ(ə)n] *s.* infiammazione *f.*
inflatable [ɪn'fleɪtəbl] *agg.* gonfiabile
to inflate [ɪn'fleɪt] *v. tr. e intr.* gonfiare, gonfiarsi
inflated [ɪn'fleɪtɪd] *agg.* gonfio
inflation [ɪn'fleɪʃ(ə)n] *s.* inflazione *f.*
inflationary [ɪn'fleɪʃ(ə)n(ə)rɪ] *agg.* inflazionistico
inflexible [ɪn'flɛksəbl] *agg.* inflessibile
to inflict [ɪn'flɪkt] *v. tr.* infliggere
influence ['ɪnflʊəns] *s.* influenza *f.*, influsso *m.*
to influence ['ɪnflʊəns] *v. tr.* influenzare, influire su
influential [ˌɪnflʊ'ɛnʃ(ə)l] *agg.* influente
influenza [ˌɪnflʊ'ɛnzə] *s.* (*med.*) influenza *f.*
influx ['ɪnflʌks] *s.* afflusso *m.*, affluenza *f.*
to inform [ɪn'fɔːm] **A** *v. tr.* informare, far sapere, avvertire **B** *v. intr.* dare informazioni
informal [ɪn'fɔːml] *agg.* informale
informally [ɪn'fɔːməlɪ] *avv.* senza formalità
informant [ɪn'fɔːmənt] *s.* informatore *m.*
informatics [ˌɪnfə'mætɪks] *s. pl.* (*v. al sing.*) informatica *f.*
information [ˌɪnfə'meɪʃ(ə)n] *s.* informazioni *f. pl.*
informative [ɪn'fɔːmətɪv] *agg.* informativo
informer [ɪn'fɔːməʳ] *s.* informatore *m.*
to infringe [ɪn'frɪn(d)ʒ] *v. tr.* infrangere, contravvenire a
infringement [ɪn'frɪn(d)ʒmənt] *s.* infrazione *f.*, trasgressione *f.*
to infuriate [ɪn'fjʊərɪeɪt] *v. tr.* far infuriare
to infuse [ɪn'fjuːz] *v. tr.* infondere
infusion [ɪn'fjuːʒ(ə)n] *s.* infusione *f.*
ingenious [ɪn'dʒiːnjəs] *agg.* **1** ingegnoso **2** geniale
ingenuity [ˌɪn(d)ʒɪ'njuːɪtɪ] *s.* ingegnosità *f.*
ingenuous [ɪn'dʒɛnjʊəs] *agg.* **1** ingenuo, semplice **2** sincero
ingenuousness [ɪn'dʒɛnjʊəsnɪs] *s.* ingenuità *f.*
to ingest [ɪn'dʒɛst] *v. tr.* ingerire
ingot ['ɪŋgət] *s.* lingotto *m.*
ingrained [ɪn'greɪnd] *agg.* radicato, inveterato
to ingratiate [ɪn'greɪʃɪeɪt] *v. tr.* ingraziare ♦ **to i. oneself with sb.** ingraziarsi qc.
ingratitude [ɪn'grætɪtjuːd] *s.* ingratitudine *f.*
ingredient [ɪn'griːdjənt] *s.* ingrediente *m.*
to inhabit [ɪn'hæbɪt] *v. tr.* abitare
inhabitant [ɪn'hæbɪtənt] *s.* abitante *m. e f.*
to inhale [ɪn'heɪl] *v. tr.* inalare, aspirare
inherent [ɪn'hɪər(ə)nt] *agg.* inerente, intrinseco
to inherit [ɪn'hɛrɪt] *v. tr. e intr.* ereditare
inheritance [ɪn'hɛrɪtəns] *s.* eredità *f.*
to inhibit [ɪn'hɪbɪt] *v. tr.* **1** inibire, reprimere **2** impedire
inhibition [ˌɪn(h)ɪ'bɪʃ(ə)n] *s.* **1** inibizione *f.* **2** divieto *m.*
inhospitable [ɪn'həspɪtəbl] *agg.* inospitale
inhuman [ɪn'hjuːmən] *agg.* inumano
inimitable [ɪ'nɪmɪtəbl] *agg.* inimitabile

initial [ɪ'nɪʃ(ə)l] **A** *agg.* iniziale **B** *s.* iniziale *f.*, sigla *f.*
to initial [ɪ'nɪʃ(ə)l] *v. tr.* siglare
initiate [ɪ'nɪʃɪɪt] *agg. e s.* iniziato *m.*
to initiate [ɪ'nɪʃɪeɪt] *v. tr.* **1** avviare, dare inizio **2** (*una persona*) iniziare
initiative [ɪ'nɪʃɪətɪv] *s.* iniziativa *f.*
initiator [ɪ'nɪʃɪeɪtəʳ] *agg.* iniziatore
to inject [ɪn'dʒɛkt] *v. tr.* iniettare
injection [ɪn'dʒɛkʃ(ə)n] *s.* iniezione *f.*
injector [ɪn'dʒɛktəʳ] *s.* iniettore *m.*
injunction [ɪn'dʒʌŋ(k)ʃ(ə)n] *s.* ingiunzione *f.*
to injure ['ɪn(d)ʒəʳ] *v. tr.* **1** ferire **2** danneggiare
injury ['ɪn(d)ʒərɪ] *s.* **1** ferita *f.*, lesione *f.* **2** danno *m.*
injustice [ɪn'dʒʌstɪs] *s.* ingiustizia *f.*
ink [ɪŋk] *s.* inchiostro *m.*
inkling ['ɪŋklɪŋ] *s.* sentore *m.*, sospetto *m.*
inland ['ɪnlənd] **A** *s.* entroterra *m. inv.* **B** *agg.* interno **C** *avv.* all'interno, nell'entroterra
inlay ['ɪnleɪ] *s.* intarsio *m.*
inlet ['ɪnlɛt] *s.* **1** insenatura *f.* **2** (*mecc.*) immissione *f.*
inmate ['ɪnmeɪt] *s.* **1** degente *m. e f.* **2** carcerato *m.*
inn [ɪn] *s.* locanda *f.*, taverna *f.*
innate ['ɪ'neɪt] *agg.* innato
inner ['ɪnəʳ] *agg.* **1** interno, interiore **2** segreto, intimo ♦ **i. city** centro (di grande città); **i. tube** camera d'aria
innkeeper ['ɪn,kiːpəʳ] *s.* locandiere *m.*
innocence ['ɪnəsəns] *s.* innocenza *f.*
innocent ['ɪnəsənt] *agg.* innocente
innocuous [ɪ'nəkjʊəs] *agg.* innocuo
innovator ['ɪnɒ(ʊ)veɪtəʳ] *s.* innovatore *m.*
innuendo [,ɪnjʊ(ː)'ɛndɒʊ] (*pl.* **innuendo(e)s**) *s.* insinuazione *f.*
innumerable [ɪ'njuːm(ə)rəbl] *agg.* innumerevole
inoffensive [,ɪnə'fɛnsɪv] *agg.* inoffensivo
inopportune [ɪn'əpətjuːn] *agg.* inopportuno
inordinate [ɪ'nɜːdɪnɪt] *agg.* smodato, eccessivo
inorganic [,ɪnɜː'gænɪk] *agg.* inorganico
in-patient ['ɪn,peɪʃ(ə)nt] *s.* degente *m. e f.*
input ['ɪnpʊt] *s.* **1** introduzione *f.*, immissione *f.*, input *m. inv.* **2** (*mecc.*) energia *f.* assorbita **3** (*inf.*) input *m. inv.*, ingresso *m.*
inquest ['ɪnkwɛst] *s.* inchiesta *f.*
to inquire [ɪn'kwaɪəʳ] **A** *v. tr.* chiedere, domandare **B** *v. intr.* indagare, investigare ♦ **to i. about/for** informarsi su; **to i. into** investigare su; **to i. of** informarsi da
inquiry [ɪn'kwaɪərɪ] *s.* **1** domanda *f.* **2** indagine *f.* ♦ **i. office** ufficio informazioni
inquisition [,ɪnkwɪ'zɪʃ(ə)n] *s.* investigazione *f.*
inquisitive [ɪn'kwɪzɪtɪv] *agg.* curioso, indiscreto
inroad ['ɪnrɒʊd] *s.* **1** (*mil.*) incursione *f.* **2** intromissione *f.* ♦ **to make inroads on st.** danneggiare q.c., intaccare q.c.
insane [ɪn'seɪn] *agg.* insano, pazzo
insanity [ɪn'sænɪtɪ] *s.* insania *f.*, pazzia *f.*
insatiable [ɪn'seɪʃjəbl] *agg.* insaziabile
to inscribe [ɪn'skraɪb] *v. tr.* **1** incidere, scolpire **2** (*mat.*) iscrivere **3** dedicare
inscription [ɪn'skrɪpʃ(ə)n] *s.* **1** iscrizione *f.* **2** dedica *f.*
inscrutable [ɪn'skruːtəbl] *agg.* imperscrutabile
insect ['ɪnsɛkt] *s.* insetto *m.*
insecticide [ɪn'sɛktɪsaɪd] *s.* insetticida *m.*
insecure [,ɪnsɪ'kjʊəʳ] *agg.* insicuro, malsicuro
insecurity [,ɪnsɪ'kjʊərɪtɪ] *s.* insicurezza *f.*
insemination [ɪn,sɛmɪ'neɪʃ(ə)n] *s.* inseminazione *f.*
insensibility [ɪn,sɛnsə'bɪlɪtɪ] *s.* **1** insensibilità *f.* **2** incoscienza *f.* ♦ **in a state of i.** privo di sensi
insensible [ɪn'sɛnsəbl] *agg.* **1** insensibile **2** privo di sensi **3** inconsapevole
insensitive [ɪn'sɛnsɪtɪv] *agg.* insensibile
inseparable [ɪn'sɛp(ə)rəbl] *agg.* inseparabile
to insert [ɪn'sɜːt] *v. tr.* inserire
insertion [ɪn'sɜːʃ(ə)n] *s.* inserzione *f.*
inshore [,ɪn'ʃɜːʳ] **A** *agg.* costiero **B** *avv.* verso la costa
inside ['ɪnsaɪd] **A** *agg.* interno, interiore **B** *s.* interno *m.*, parte *f.* interna **C** *avv.* dentro, interiormente **D** *prep.* **1** dentro, all'interno di **2** entro
insidious [ɪn'sɪdɪəs] *agg.* insidioso
insight ['ɪnsaɪt] *s.* acume *m.*, intuito *m.*
insignificant [,ɪnsɪg'nɪfɪkənt] *agg.* insignificante
insincere [,ɪnsɪn'sɪəʳ] *agg.* insincero
to insinuate [ɪn'sɪnjʊeɪt] **A** *v. tr.* **1** insinuare **2** introdurre **B** *v. intr.* fare insinuazioni ♦ **to i. oneself** insinuarsi
insipid [ɪn'sɪpɪd] *agg.* insipido
to insist [ɪn'sɪst] **A** *v. intr.* insistere **B** *v. tr.* sostenere, asserire

insistent [ɪn'sɪst(ə)nt] *agg.* insistente
insolation [ˌɪnsɒ(ʊ)'leɪʃ(ə)n] *s.* insolazione *f.*
insole ['ɪnsɒʊl] *s.* soletta *f.*
insolence ['ɪns(ə)ləns] *s.* insolenza *f.*
insolent ['ɪns(ə)lənt] *agg.* insolente
insoluble [ɪn'səljʊbl] *agg.* insolubile
insolvent [ɪn'səlv(ə)nt] *agg.* insolvente
insomnia [ɪn'səmnɪə] *s.* insonnia *f.*
to **inspect** [ɪn'spɛkt] *v. tr.* ispezionare, controllare
inspection [ɪn'spɛkʃ(ə)n] *s.* ispezione *f.*, controllo *m.*
inspector [ɪn'spɛktəʳ] *s.* ispettore *m.*
inspiration [ˌɪnspə'reɪʃ(ə)n] *s.* **1** (*med.*) inspirazione *f.* **2** ispirazione *f.*
to **inspire** [ɪn'spaɪəʳ] *v. tr.* **1** (*med.*) inspirare **2** ispirare, infondere, suscitare
inspirer [ɪn'spaɪərəʳ] *s.* ispiratore *m.*
to **install** [ɪn'stɜːl] *v. tr.* **1** insediare **2** installare
installation [ˌɪnstə'leɪʃ(ə)n] *s.* **1** insediamento *m.*, investitura *f.* **2** installazione *f.*
instalment [ɪn'stɜːlmənt] (*USA* **installment**) *s.* **1** rata *f.* **2** puntata *f.*, parte *f.*, fascicolo *m.* **3** acconto *m.* ♦ **to pay by instalments** pagare a rate
instance ['ɪnstəns] *s.* **1** esempio *m.* **2** caso *m.* ♦ **for i.** per esempio; **in the first i.** in primo luogo
instant ['ɪnstənt] **A** *agg.* **1** urgente **2** immediato, istantaneo **3** corrente **B** *s.* istante *m.*
instantaneous [ˌɪnst(ə)n'teɪnjəs] *agg.* istantaneo
instantly ['ɪnstəntlɪ] *avv.* istantaneamente
instead [ɪn'stɛd] *avv.* invece
instep ['ɪnˌstɛp] *s.* collo *m.* del piede
to **instil** [ɪn'stɪl] *v. tr.* instillare, infondere
instinct ['ɪnstɪŋkt] *s.* istinto *m.*
instinctive [ɪn'stɪŋktɪv] *agg.* istintivo
institute ['ɪnstɪtjuːt] *s.* istituto *m.*
to **institute** ['ɪnstɪtjuːt] *v. tr.* **1** istituire **2** iniziare **3** intentare
institution [ˌɪnstɪ'tjuːʃ(ə)n] *s.* istituzione *f.*
institutional [ˌɪnstɪ'tjuːʃənl] *agg.* istituzionale
to **instruct** [ɪn'strʌkt] *v. tr.* **1** istruire, insegnare **2** dare istruzioni, incaricare **3** informare ♦ **to i. sb. to do st.** dare ordini a qc. di fare q.c.
instruction [ɪn'strʌkʃ(ə)n] *s.* **1** insegnamento *m.* **2** istruzione *f.*
instructive [ɪn'strʌktɪv] *agg.* istruttivo
instructor [ɪn'strʌktəʳ] *s.* istruttore *m.*
instrument ['ɪnstrəmənt] *s.* strumento *m.*, apparecchio *m.*
instrumental [ˌɪnstrə'mɛnt(ə)l] *agg.* **1** attivo, utile **2** strumentale
instrumentalist [ˌɪnstrə'mɛnt(ə)lɪst] *s.* (*mus.*) strumentista *m. e f.*
insubstantial [ˌɪnsəb'stænʃ(ə)l] *agg.* **1** incorporeo **2** inconsistente
insufficient [ˌɪnsə'fɪʃ(ə)nt] *agg.* insufficiente, inadeguato
insular ['ɪnsjʊləʳ] *agg.* **1** insulare **2** gretto, di vedute ristrette
to **insulate** ['ɪnsjʊleɪt] *v. tr.* isolare
insulated ['ɪnsjʊleɪtɪd] *agg.* isolato
insulating ['ɪnsjʊleɪtɪŋ] *agg.* isolante ♦ **i. tape** nastro isolante
insulation [ˌɪnsjʊ'leɪʃ(ə)n] *s.* isolamento *m.*
insulin ['ɪnsjʊlɪn] *s.* insulina *f.*
insult ['ɪnsʌlt] *s.* insulto *m.*, offesa *f.*
to **insult** [ɪn'sʌlt] *v. tr.* insultare, offendere
insulting [ɪn'sʌltɪŋ] *agg.* ingiurioso, offensivo
insuperable [ɪn'sjuːp(ə)rəbl] *agg.* insuperabile
insurance [ɪn'ʃʊər(ə)ns] *s.* assicurazione *f.* ♦ **i. policy** polizza di assicurazione; **life i.** assicurazione sulla vita
to **insure** [ɪn'ʃʊəʳ] *v. tr.* assicurare
insurrection [ˌɪnsə'rɛkʃ(ə)n] *s.* insurrezione *f.*, sommossa *f.*
intact [ɪn'tækt] *agg.* intatto
intake ['ɪnteɪk] *s.* **1** (*d'acqua, ecc.*) presa *f.*, immissione *f.* **2** quantità *f.* immessa **3** *al pl.* reclute *f. pl.*, nuovi assunti *m. pl.*
integral ['ɪntɪgr(ə)l] *agg.* **1** integrale **2** integrante
to **integrate** ['ɪntɪgreɪt] *v. tr.* **1** unire, incorporare **2** integrare
integrity [ɪn'tɛgrɪtɪ] *s.* integrità *f.*
intellectual [ˌɪntɪ'lɛktjʊəl] *agg. e s.* intellettuale *m. e f.*
intellectualism [ˌɪntɪ'lɛktjʊəlɪz(ə)m] *s.* intellettualismo *m.*
intelligence [ɪn'tɛlɪdʒ(ə)ns] *s.* **1** intelligenza *f.* **2** informazioni *f. pl.*, notizie *f. pl.*
intelligent [ɪn'tɛlɪdʒ(ə)nt] *agg.* intelligente
intelligible [ɪn'tɛlɪdʒəbl] *agg.* intelligibile
to **intend** [ɪn'tɛnd] *v. tr.* **1** intendere, avere intenzione di **2** significare **3** destinare ♦ **to i. to do st.** avere intenzione di fare q.c.

intended [ɪn'tɛndɪd] *agg.* **1** intenzionale, premeditato **2** designato
intense [ɪn'tɛns] *agg.* intenso
to intensify [ɪn'tɛnsɪfaɪ] *v. tr.* intensificare
intensity [ɪn'tɛnsɪtɪ] *s.* intensità *f.*
intensive [ɪn'tɛnsɪv] *agg.* intensivo, intenso ♦ **i. care unit** reparto di terapia intensiva
intent [ɪn'tɛnt] **A** *agg.* **1** intento **2** deciso **B** *s.* intento *m.*, intenzione *f.*, scopo *m.* ♦ **to all intents and purposes** a tutti gli effetti; **to be i. to do st.** essere deciso a fare q.c.
intention [ɪn'tɛnʃ(ə)n] *s.* intenzione *f.*, proposito *m.*
intentional [ɪn'tɛnʃənl] *agg.* intenzionale
to inter [ɪn'tɜːʳ] *v. tr.* sotterrare
to interact [ˌɪntər'ækt] *v. intr.* interagire
interaction [ˌɪntər'ækʃ(ə)n] *s.* interazione *f.*
to intercept [ˌɪntə(ː)'sɛpt] *v. tr.* intercettare
intercession [ˌɪntə'sɛʃ(ə)n] *s.* intercessione *f.*
interchange ['ɪntə(ː)ˌtʃeɪn(d)ʒ] *s.* **1** scambio *m.* **2** avvicendamento *m.* **3** svincolo *m.* (autostradale)
interchangeable [ˌɪntə(ː)'tʃeɪn(d)ʒəbl] *agg.* intercambiabile
intercolumn [ˌɪntə'kələm] *s.* intercolunnio *m.*
intercom ['ɪntəkəm] *s.* interfono *m.*
intercontinental [ˌɪntəˌkəntɪ'nɛntl] *agg.* intercontinentale
intercourse ['ɪntə(ː)kɜːs] *s.* rapporto *m.*
interdisciplinary [ˌɪntə'dɪsɪplɪnərɪ] *agg.* interdisciplinare
interest ['ɪntrɪst] *s.* interesse *m.*
to interest ['ɪntrɪst] *v. tr.* interessare
interested ['ɪntrɪstɪd] *agg.* interessato
interesting ['ɪntrɪstɪŋ] *agg.* interessante
interface ['ɪntəˌfeɪs] *s.* interfaccia *f.*
to interfere [ˌɪntə'fɪəʳ] *v. intr.* interferire, intromettersi ♦ **to i. with** toccare, manomettere
interference [ˌɪntə'fɪər(ə)ns] *s.* interferenza *f.*, ingerenza *f.*
interior [ɪn'tɪərɪəʳ] **A** *agg.* interiore, interno **B** *s.* **1** interno *m.* **2** entroterra *m.* ♦ **i. decoration** arredamento
to interlace [ˌɪntə(ː)'leɪs] *v. tr. e intr.* allacciare, allacciarsi
to interlock [ˌɪntə(ː)'lək] **A** *v. tr.* congiungere, unire, collegare **B** *v. intr.* **1** unirsi, congiungersi **2** essere collegato
interlocutor [ˌɪntə(ː)'ləkjʊtəʳ] *s.* interlocutore *m.*
interloper ['ɪntə(ː)ˌlɒʊpəʳ] *s.* intruso *m.*
interlude ['ɪntə(ː)luːd] *s.* interludio *m.*, intermezzo *m.*
intermediate [ˌɪntə(ː)'miːdjət] *agg.* intermedio
intermezzo [ˌɪntə(ː)'mɛtsɒʊ] *s.* intermezzo *m.*
interminable [ɪn'tɜːmɪnəbl] *agg.* interminabile
intermission [ˌɪntə(ː)'mɪʃ(ə)n] *s.* interruzione *f.*, pausa *f.*
intermittent [ˌɪntə'mɪt(ə)nt] *agg.* intermittente
intern ['ɪntɜːn] *s.* (medico) interno *m.*
to intern [ɪn'tɜːn] *v. tr.* internare
internal [ɪn'tɜːnl] *agg.* interno, interiore
international [ˌɪntə(ː)'næʃənl] *agg.* internazionale
interphone ['ɪntəfɒʊn] *s.* citofono *m.*
interplay ['ɪntə(ː)ˌpleɪ] *s.* interazione *f.*
to interpolate [ɪn'tɜːpɒ(ʊ)leɪt] *v. tr.* interpolare
to interpose [ˌɪntə(ː)'pɒʊz] **A** *v. tr.* interporre, frapporre **B** *v. intr.* **1** interporsi, intromettersi **2** interferire
to interpret [ɪn'tɜːprɪt] **A** *v. tr.* interpretare **B** *v. intr.* fare da interprete
interpretation [ɪnˌtɜːprɪ'teɪʃ(ə)n] *s.* interpretazione *f.*
interpreter [ɪn'tɜːprɪtəʳ] *s.* interprete *m. e f.*
to interrelate [ˌɪntərɪ'leɪt] *v. tr.* porre in relazione, collegare
to interrogate [ɪn'tɛrəgeɪt] *v. tr.* interrogare
interrogation [ɪnˌtɛrə'geɪʃ(ə)n] *s.* interrogazione *f.*, interrogatorio *m.*
interrogative [ˌɪntə'rəgətɪv] *agg.* interrogativo
to interrupt [ˌɪntə'rʌpt] *v. tr.* interrompere
interruption [ˌɪntə'rʌpʃ(ə)n] *s.* interruzione *f.*
intersection [ˌɪntə(ː)'sɛkʃ(ə)n] *s.* **1** intersezione *f.* **2** incrocio *m.*
to intersperse [ˌɪntə(ː)'spɜːs] *v. tr.* cospargere
interstice [ɪn'tɜːstɪs] *s.* interstizio *m.*
to intertwine [ˌɪntə(ː)'twaɪn] **A** *v. tr.* intrecciare, attorcigliare **B** *v. intr.* intrecciarsi, attorcigliarsi
intertwinement [ˌɪntə(ː)'twaɪnmənt] *s.* intreccio *m.*
interurban [ˌɪntər'ɜːbən] *agg.* interurbano
interval ['ɪntəv(ə)l] *s.* intervallo *m.*

to **intervene** [ˌɪntə(ː)'viːn] *v. intr.* **1** intervenire **2** accadere **3** intercorrere
intervention [ˌɪntə(ː)'vɛnʃ(ə)n] *s.* intervento *m.*
interview ['ɪntəvjuː] *s.* **1** intervista *f.* **2** colloquio *m.*, udienza *f.*
to **interview** ['ɪntəvjuː] *v. tr.* **1** intervistare **2** sottoporre a un colloquio
intestinal [ɪn'tɛstɪnl] *agg.* intestinale
intestine [ɪn'tɛstɪn] *s.* intestino *m.*
intimacy ['ɪntɪməsɪ] *s.* intimità *f.*
intimate ['ɪntɪmɪt] *agg.* **1** intimo, interiore **2** profondo, completo
to **intimate** ['ɪntɪmeɪt] *v. tr.* **1** accennare, suggerire **2** (*dir.*) intimare, notificare
into ['ɪntʊ, 'ɪntə] *prep.* in, dentro
intolerable [ɪn'təl(ə)rəbl] *agg.* intollerabile
intolerance [ɪn'tələr(ə)ns] *s.* intolleranza *f.*
intolerant [ɪn'tələrənt] *agg.* intollerante
intoxication [ɪnˌtəksɪ'keɪʃ(ə)n] *s.* **1** intossicazione *f.* **2** ebbrezza *f.*
intractable [ɪn'træktəbl] *agg.* intrattabile
intrados [ɪn'treɪdəs] *s.* intradosso *m.*
intransigent [ɪn'trænsɪdʒ(ə)nt] *agg. e s.* intransigente *m.*
intransitive [ɪn'trænsɪtɪv] *agg. e s.* intransitivo *m.*
intravenous [ˌɪntrə'viːnəs] *agg.* endovenoso
intricate ['ɪntrɪkɪt] *agg.* intricato, complicato
intrigue [ɪn'triːg] *s.* intrigo *m.*
to **intrigue** [ɪn'triːg] *v. tr.* **1** ottenere con intrighi **2** affascinare, interessare
intriguing [ɪn'triːgɪŋ] *agg.* **1** intrigante **2** affascinante
intrinsic(al) [ɪn'trɪnsɪk((ə)l)] *agg.* intrinseco
to **introduce** [ˌɪntrə'djuːs] *v. tr.* **1** introdurre **2** presentare
introduction [ˌɪntrə'dʌkʃ(ə)n] *s.* **1** introduzione *f.* **2** presentazione *f.*
introductory [ˌɪntrə'dʌkt(ə)rɪ] *agg.* introduttivo, preliminare
introspective [ˌɪntrɒ(ʊ)'spɛktɪv] *agg.* introspettivo
introvert ['ɪntrɒ(ʊ)vɜːt] *agg.* introverso
to **intrude** [ɪn'truːd] **A** *v. intr.* intromettersi **B** *v. tr.* imporre
intruder [ɪn'truːdəʳ] *s.* intruso *m.*
intrusion [ɪn'truːʒ(ə)n] *s.* intrusione *f.*
intrusive [ɪn'truːsɪv] *agg.* importuno
intuition [ˌɪntjʊ(ː)'ɪʃ(ə)n] *s.* intuizione *f.*
intuitive [ɪn'tjʊ(ː)ɪtɪv] *agg.* intuitivo
to **inundate** ['ɪnʌndeɪt] *v. tr.* inondare
inundation [ˌɪnʌn'deɪʃ(ə)n] *s.* inondazione *f.*
inurement [ɪ'njʊəmənt] *s.* assuefazione *f.*, abitudine *f.*
to **invade** [ɪn'veɪd] *v. tr.* invadere
invader [ɪn'veɪdəʳ] *s.* invasore *m.*
invalid ['ɪnvəliːd] **A** *agg.* **1** invalido, infermo **2** non valido, nullo **B** *s.* invalido *m.*
invalidity [ˌɪnvə'lɪdɪtɪ] *s.* invalidità *f.*
invaluable [ɪn'væljʊəbl] *agg.* inestimabile
invariable [ɪn'vɛərɪəbl] *agg.* invariabile
invasion [ɪn'veɪʒ(ə)n] *s.* invasione *f.*
to **invent** [ɪn'vɛnt] *v. tr.* inventare
invention [ɪn'vɛnʃ(ə)n] *s.* invenzione *f.*
inventiveness [ɪn'vɛntɪvnɪs] *s.* inventiva *f.*
inventor [ɪn'vɛntəʳ] *s.* inventore *m.*
inventory ['ɪnvəntrɪ] *s.* inventario *m.*
inversion [ɪn'vɜːʃ(ə)n] *s.* inversione *f.*
to **invert** [ɪn'vɜːt] *v. tr.* **1** invertire **2** capovolgere
invertebrate [ɪn'vɜːtɪbrɪt] *agg. e s.* invertebrato *m.*
to **invest** [ɪn'vɛst] *v. tr. e intr.* investire
to **investigate** [ɪn'vɛstɪgeɪt] *v. tr. e intr.* investigare
investigation [ɪnˌvɛstɪ'geɪʃ(ə)n] *s.* indagine *f.*, investigazione *f.*
investment [ɪn'vɛs(t)mənt] *s.* investimento *m.*
investor [ɪn'vɛstəʳ] *s.* (*fin.*) investitore *m.*
invidious [ɪn'vɪdɪəs] *agg.* odioso, spiacevole
invigilation [ɪnˌvɪdʒɪ'leɪʃ(ə)n] *s.* sorveglianza *f.*
to **invigorate** [ɪn'vɪgəreɪt] *v. tr.* rinvigorire, rinforzare
invincible [ɪn'vɪnsəbl] *agg.* invincibile
invisible [ɪn'vɪzəbl] *agg.* invisibile
invitation [ˌɪnvɪ'teɪʃ(ə)n] *s.* invito *m.* ♦ **i. card** biglietto d'invito
to **invite** [ɪn'vaɪt] *v. tr.* **1** invitare **2** sollecitare, stimolare
inviting [ɪn'vaɪtɪŋ] *agg.* invitante, attraente
invoice ['ɪnvəɪs] *s.* fattura *f.*
to **invoice** ['ɪnvəɪs] *v. tr.* fatturare
involuntary [ɪn'vələnt(ə)rɪ] *agg.* involontario
involution [ˌɪnvə'luːʃ(ə)n] *s.* involuzione *f.*
to **involve** [ɪn'vəlv] *v. tr.* **1** coinvolgere **2** comportare, richiedere **3** complicare

involved [ɪn'vɔlvd] *agg.* **1** coinvolto **2** complicato
inward ['ɪnwəd] *agg.* interno, interiore
inwards ['ɪnwədz] *avv.* **1** verso l'interno **2** in entrata
iodine ['aɪədiːn] *s.* iodio *m.*
Ionian [aɪ'ɒʊnjən] *agg.* (*geogr.*) Ionico
ionic [aɪ'ənɪk] *agg.* ionico
Iranian [ɪ'reɪnjən] *agg. e s.* iraniano *m.*
Iraqi [ɪ'raːkɪ] *agg. e s.* iracheno *m.*
irascible [ɪ'ræsɪbl] *agg.* irascibile
irate [aɪ'reɪt] *agg.* irato
iris ['aɪərɪs] *s.* **1** (*meteor., anat.*) iride *m.* **2** (*bot.*) iris *m.*
Irish ['aɪərɪʃ] *agg. e s.* irlandese *m.* (*lingua*)
Irishman ['aɪərɪʃmən] (*pl.* **Irishmen**) *s.* irlandese *m.*
Irishwoman ['aɪərɪʃˌwʊmən] (*pl.* **Irishwomen**) *s.* irlandese *f.*
to irk [ɜːk] *v. tr.* affliggere, infastidire
irksome ['ɜːksəm] *agg.* fastidioso, seccante
iron ['aɪən] **A** *s.* **1** ferro *m.* **2** ferro *m.* (da stiro) **B** *agg. attr.* **1** di ferro **2** relativo al ferro ♦ **steam i.** ferro a vapore
to iron ['aɪən] *v. tr.* stirare ♦ **to i. out** appianare, risolvere
ironic(al) [aɪ'rənɪk((ə)l)] *agg.* ironico
ironing ['aɪənɪŋ] **A** *s.* stiratura *f.* **B** *agg.* da stiro ♦ **i. board** asse da stiro
ironmongery ['aɪənˌmʌŋg(ə)rɪ] *s.* negozio *m.* di ferramenta
irony ['aɪərənɪ] *s.* ironia *f.*
irrational [ɪ'ræʃənl] **A** *agg.* irrazionale **B** *s.* numero *m.* irrazionale
irredentism [ˌɪrɪ'dɛntɪz(ə)m] *s.* irredentismo *m.*
irregular [ɪ'rɛgjʊlə^r] *agg.* irregolare
irrelevant [ɪ'rɛlɪvənt] *agg.* non pertinente
irremediable [ˌɪrɪ'miːdjəbl] *agg.* irrimediabile
irreparable [ɪ'rɛp(ə)rəbl] *agg.* irreparabile
irreplaceable [ˌɪrɪ'pleɪsəbl] *agg.* insostituibile
irrepressible [ˌɪrɪ'prɛsəbl] *agg.* irrefrenabile
irresistible [ˌɪrɪ'zɪstəbl] *agg.* irresistibile
irrespective [ˌɪrɪs'pɛktɪv] *agg.* noncurante
irrespirable [ɪ'rɛspɪrəbl] *agg.* irrespirabile
irresponsible [ˌɪrɪs'pənsəbl] *agg.* irresponsabile
to irrigate ['ɪrɪgeɪt] *v. tr.* irrigare
irrigation [ˌɪrɪ'geɪʃ(ə)n] *s.* irrigazione *f.*
irritable ['ɪrɪtəbl] *agg.* irritabile
to irritate ['ɪrɪteɪt] *v. tr.* irritare
irritating ['ɪrɪteɪtɪŋ] *agg.* irritante
irritation [ˌɪrɪ'teɪʃ(ə)n] *s.* irritazione *f.*
irruption [ɪ'rʌpʃ(ə)n] *s.* irruzione *f.*
Islamic [ɪz'læmɪk] *agg.* islamico
island ['aɪlənd] *s.* isola *f.*
islander ['aɪləndə^r] *s.* isolano *m.*
isle [aɪl] *s.* isola *f.*
islet ['aɪlɪt] *s.* isolotto *m.*
isobar ['aɪsɒ(ʊ)baː^r] *s.* isobara *f.*
isobath ['aɪsɒ(ʊ)bæθ] *s.* isobata *f.*
to isolate ['aɪsəleɪt] *v. tr.* isolare
isolated ['aɪsəleɪtɪd] *agg.* isolato
isolation [ˌaɪsə'leɪʃ(ə)n] *s.* isolamento *m.*
Israeli [ɪz'reɪlɪ] *agg. e s.* israeliano *m.*
Israelite ['ɪzrɪəlaɪt] *agg. e s.* israelita *m. e f.*
issue ['ɪʃjuː] *s.* **1** questione *f.*, problema *m.* **2** emissione *f.* **3** pubblicazione *f.*, edizione *f.* **4** uscita *f.*, sbocco *m.*, fuoriuscita *f.*
to issue ['ɪʃjuː] **A** *v. tr.* **1** emettere **2** pubblicare **3** rilasciare **B** *v. intr.* scaturire, venir fuori ♦ **to i. in** concludersi; **to i. tickets** rilasciare biglietti
isthmus ['ɪsməs] *s.* istmo *m.*
it [ɪt] *pron. neutro 3ª sing.* **1** (*sogg.*) esso, essa, ciò (*spesso sottinteso*) (ES: **at what time does it leave?** a che ora parte?) **2** (*compl.*) lo, la, ciò, gli, le, ne, ci, sé (ES: **I don't like it** non mi piace) **3** (*sogg. di v. impers.*) *idiom.* (ES: **it is snowing** sta nevicando, **it is midday** è mezzogiorno) **4** (*prolettico*) *idiom.* (ES: **it is obvious that ...** è ovvio che ...)
Italian [ɪ'tæljən] *agg. e s.* italiano *m.*
Italic [ɪ'tælɪk] *agg.* **1** italico **2** corsivo
italics [ɪ'tælɪks] *s. pl.* corsivo *m.*
itch [ɪtʃ] *s.* **1** prurito *m.* **2** (*fig.*) voglia *f.*
to itch [ɪtʃ] *v. intr.* **1** prudere, sentire prurito **2** (*fig.*) aver voglia
item ['aɪtəm] *s.* **1** articolo *m.*, capo *m.* **2** elemento *m.* **3** notizia *f.*
to itemize ['aɪtəmaɪz] *v. tr.* specificare, esporre in dettaglio
iterative ['ɪtərətɪv] *agg.* iterativo
itinerant [ɪ'tɪn(ə)rənt] *agg.* ambulante
itinerary [aɪ'tɪn(ə)rərɪ] *s.* itinerario *m.*
its [ɪts] *agg. poss.* (*possessore neutro*) suo, sua, suoi, sue
itself [ɪt'sɛlf] *pron. 3ª sing. neutro* **1** (*rifl.*) si, sé, se stesso, se stessa **2** (*enf.*) stesso, stessa, in persona
ivory ['aɪv(ə)rɪ] *s.* avorio *m.*
ivy ['aɪvɪ] *s.* edera *f.*

J

jab [dʒæb] *s.* **1** stilettata *f.*, stoccata *f.* **2** colpetto *m.* **3** (*fam.*) iniezione *f.*
to jab [dʒæb] *v. tr.* **1** conficcare **2** colpire
jack [dʒæk] *s.* **1** (*fam.*) tipo *m.*, amico *m.* **2** boccino *m.* **3** (*mecc.*) cric *m.* **4** (*carte da gioco*) fante *m.*
jackal ['dʒækɜːl] *s.* sciacallo *m.*
jackass ['dʒækæs] *s.* asino *m.*
jackdaw ['dʒækdɜː] *s.* taccola *f.*
jacket ['dʒækɪt] *s.* **1** giacca *f.*, giubbotto *m.* **2** rivestimento *m.* **3** copertina *f.*, sovraccoperta *f.* ♦ **blue j.** marinaio; **dinner j.** smoking; **life j.** giubbotto di salvataggio
jackknife ['dʒæknaɪf] *s.* coltello *m.* a serramanico
Jacobin ['dʒækəbɪn] *agg. e s.* giacobino *m.*
jade [dʒeɪd] *s.* giada *f.*
jaded ['dʒəɪdɪd] *agg.* **1** stanco, affaticato **2** logoro
jag [dʒæg] *s.* sporgenza *f.* appuntita, dente *m.* di sega
jagged ['dʒægɪd] *agg.* frastagliato, dentellato
jail [dʒeɪl] *s.* prigione *f.*
to jail [dʒeɪl] *v. tr.* imprigionare
jailer ['dʒeɪləʳ] *s.* carceriere *m.*, secondino *m.*
jam (1) [dʒæm] *s.* **1** compressione *f.* **2** blocco *m.*, inceppamento *m.* **3** (*nel traffico*) ingorgo *m.* **4** (*fam.*) pasticcio *m.*
jam (2) [dʒæm] *s.* confettura *f.*, marmellata *f.*
to jam [dʒæm] **A** *v. tr.* **1** comprimere, schiacciare **2** bloccare, inceppare **3** (*una trasmissione*) disturbare con interferenze **B** *v. intr.* bloccarsi, incepparsi
Jamaican [dʒ(ə)'meɪkən] *agg. e s.* giamaicano *m.*
jamb [dʒæm] *s.* stipite *m.*
to jangle ['dʒæŋgl] *v. intr.* **1** stridere **2** risuonare
janitor ['dʒænɪtəʳ] *s.* custode *m. e f.*
January ['dʒænjʊərɪ] *s.* gennaio *m.*
Japanese [ˌdʒæpə'niːz] *agg. e s.* giapponese *m. e f.*
jar (1) [dʒaːʳ] *s.* barattolo *m.*, vasetto *m.*
jar (2) [dʒaːʳ] *s.* **1** stridore *m.*, vibrazione *f.* **2** colpo *m.*, urto *m.* **3** litigio *m.*
to jar [dʒaːʳ] *v. intr.* **1** stridere, vibrare **2** discordare **3** litigare
jargon ['dʒaːgən] *s.* gergo *m.*
jasmin(e) ['dʒæsmɪn] *s.* gelsomino *m.*
jasper ['dʒæspəʳ] *s.* diaspro *m.*
jaundice ['dʒɜːndɪs] *s.* (*med.*) itterizia *f.*
jaunt [dʒɜːnt] *s.* gita *f.*, passeggiata *f.*
jaunty ['dʒɜːntɪ] *agg.* vivace, disinvolto
javelin ['dʒævlɪn] *s.* giavellotto *m.*
jaw [dʒɜː] *s.* mascella *f.*
jay [dʒeɪ] *s.* **1** (*zool.*) ghiandaia *f.* **2** (*fam.*) chiacchierone *m.*
jazz [dʒæz] *s.* jazz *m. inv.*
jealous ['dʒɛləs] *agg.* geloso, invidioso
jealousy ['dʒɛləsɪ] *s.* gelosia *f.*, invidia *f.*
jeans [dʒiːnz] *s. pl.* jeans *m. pl.*
jeer [dʒɪəʳ] *s.* beffa *f.*
to jeer [dʒɪəʳ] *v. intr.* prendersi gioco
jelly ['dʒɛlɪ] *s.* gelatina *f.*
jellyfish ['dʒɛlɪfɪʃ] *s.* medusa *f.*
jeopardy ['dʒɛpədɪ] *s.* pericolo *m.*, rischio *m.*, repentaglio *m.*
jerk [dʒɜːk] *s.* **1** sobbalzo *m.* **2** strattone *m.* **3** (*fam.*) stupido *m.*
to jerk [dʒɜːk] **A** *v. tr.* dare una spinta, dare un colpo **B** *v. intr.* sobbalzare
jerry can ['dʒɛrɪkæn] *s.* tanica *f.*
jersey ['dʒɜːzɪ] *s.* **1** maglia *f.* **2** jersey *m. inv.*
jest [dʒɛst] *s.* **1** scherzo *m.* **2** canzonatura *f.*
to jest [dʒɛst] *v. intr.* **1** scherzare **2** farsi beffe
jester ['dʒɛstəʳ] *s.* **1** giullare *m.* **2** buffone *m.*
Jesuit ['dʒɛzjʊɪt] **A** *s.* gesuita *m.* **B** *agg.* gesuitico
jet [dʒɛt] *s.* **1** getto *m.*, zampillo *m.* **2** jet *m. inv.*, aviogetto *m.* **3** ugello *m.*
jet-black [ˌdʒɛt'blæk] *agg.* nero lucente
to jettison ['dʒɛtɪsn] *v. tr.* **1** gettare a mare **2** scaricare in volo **3** disfarsi di
jetty ['dʒɛtɪ] *s.* gettata *f.*, molo *m.*
Jew [dʒuː] *s.* ebreo *m.*
jewel ['dʒuːəl] *s.* **1** gioiello *m.* **2** gemma *f.*
jeweller ['dʒuːələʳ] *s.* gioielliere *m.*
jewel(le)ry ['dʒuːəlrɪ] *s.* **1** gioielleria *f.* **2** gioielli *m. pl.*
Jewess ['dʒuːɪs] *s.* ebrea *f.*
Jewish ['dʒuːɪʃ] *agg.* ebraico

jib [dʒɪb] *s.* (*naut.*) fiocco *m.*
jibe [dʒɪb] *s.* beffa *f.*
jiffy ['dʒɪfɪ] *s.* (*fam.*) attimo *m.* ♦ **in a j.** in un attimo
jigsaw ['dʒɪgsɜː] *s.* **1** sega *f.* per traforo **2** puzzle *m. inv.*
to jilt [dʒɪlt] *v. tr.* piantare (*un innamorato*)
jingle ['dʒɪŋgl] *s.* **1** tintinnio *m.* **2** cantilena *f.* **3** canzonetta *f.* pubblicitaria
to jingle ['dʒɪŋgl] *v. intr.* tintinnare
jinx [dʒɪŋks] *s.* **1** iettatura *f.* **2** iettatore *m.*
jitters ['dʒɪtəz] *s. pl.* (*pop.*) nervosismo *m.* ♦ **to have the j.** avere i nervi a fior di pelle, essere agitato
job [dʒəb] *s.* **1** lavoro *m.*, impiego *m.*, occupazione *f.* **2** mansione *f.*, compito *m.* **3** (*fam.*) faccenda *f.* ♦ **j. center** ufficio di collocamento
jobless ['dʒəblɪs] *agg.* disoccupato
jockey ['dʒəkɪ] *s.* fantino *m.*
jocular ['dʒəkjʊləʳ] *agg.* giocoso, gioviale
to jog [dʒəg] **A** *v. tr.* **1** spingere, urtare **2** scuotere, sballottare **B** *v. intr.* **1** avanzare a scatti **2** avanzare, avviarsi **3** fare jogging
jogging ['dʒəgɪŋ] *s.* jogging *m. inv.*
to join [dʒəɪn] **A** *v. tr.* **1** unire, collegare **2** partecipare a **3** raggiungere **B** *v. intr.* **1** unirsi, congiungersi, confluire **2** essere contiguo ♦ **to j. in** prendere parte a; **to j. up** arruolarsi
joiner ['dʒəɪnəʳ] *s.* falegname *m.*
joint [dʒəɪnt] **A** *agg.* unito, congiunto **B** *s.* **1** giunzione *f.* **2** (*mecc.*) giunto *m.* **3** articolazione *f.*, giuntura *f.* **4** (*cuc.*) arrosto *m.* **5** (*pop.*) bettola *f.* ♦ **out of j.** sconnesso
to joint [dʒəɪnt] *v. tr.* **1** congiungere, unire **2** (*mecc.*) connettere
joist ['dʒəɪst] *s.* trave *f.*
joke [dʒɒʊk] *s.* **1** scherzo *m.* **2** barzelletta *f.* ♦ **in j.** per scherzo; **no j.** senza scherzi; **to play a j. on sb.** fare uno scherzo a qc.
to joke [dʒɒʊk] **A** *v. intr.* scherzare **B** *v. tr.* canzonare
joker ['dʒɒʊkəʳ] *s.* jolly *m. inv.*
jolly ['dʒəlɪ] **A** *agg.* gioviale, allegro **B** *avv.* **1** molto **2** certamente, proprio
jolt [dʒɒʊlt] *s.* sobbalzo *m.*
to jolt [dʒɒʊlt] **A** *v. tr.* scuotere **B** *v. intr.* sobbalzare
to jostle ['dʒəsl] *v. tr.* **1** spingere, colpire a gomitate **2** (*pop.*) borseggiare
jostler ['dʒəsləʳ] *s.* (*pop.*) borsaiolo *m.*
jot [dʒət] *s.* inezia *f.* ♦ **I don't care a j.** non me ne importa nulla
to jot [dʒət] *v. tr.* annotare in fretta
journal ['dʒɜːnl] *s.* **1** giornale *m.*, rivista *f.* **2** diario *m.*
journalism ['dʒɜːnəlɪz(ə)m] *s.* giornalismo *m.*
journalist ['dʒɜːnəlɪst] *s.* giornalista *m. e f.*
journey ['dʒɜːnɪ] *s.* viaggio *m.*, tragitto *m.* ♦ **the j. out/home** il viaggio d'andata/di ritorno
jovial ['dʒɒʊvjəl] *agg.* gioviale
joy [dʒəɪ] *s.* gioia *f.*
joyful ['dʒəɪf(ʊ)l] *agg.* felice, allegro
jubilant ['dʒuːbɪlənt] *agg.* giubilante
jubilee ['dʒuːbɪliː] *s.* **1** giubileo *m.* **2** anniversario *m.*
judge [dʒʌdʒ] *s.* giudice *m. e f.*
to judge [dʒʌdʒ] *v. tr. e intr.* giudicare
judgment ['dʒʌdʒmənt] *s.* giudizio *m.*
judicial [dʒʊ(ː)'dɪʃ(ə)l] *agg.* giudiziario
judiciary [dʒʊ(ː)'dɪʃɪərɪ] **A** *agg.* giudiziario **B** *s.* magistratura *f.*
judo ['dʒuːdɒʊ] *s.* judo *m. inv.*
jug [dʒʌg] *s.* brocca *f.*
juggle ['dʒʌgl] *s.* gioco *m.* di prestigio
juggler ['dʒʌgləʳ] *s.* giocoliere *m.*
juice [dʒuːs] *s.* succo *m.*
juicy ['dʒuːsɪ] *agg.* **1** succoso **2** interessante
July [dʒʊ(ː)'laɪ] *s.* luglio *m.*
jumble ['dʒʌmbl] *s.* miscuglio *m.*
to jumble ['dʒʌmbl] *v. tr. e intr.* mescolare, mescolarsi
jumbo ['dʒʌmbɒʊ] *s.* jumbo *m. inv.*
jump [dʒʌmp] *s.* salto *m.*, balzo *m.*
to jump [dʒʌmp] **A** *v. intr.* **1** saltare, balzare **2** trasalire **3** (*di prezzo, merce*) rincarare, avere un'impennata **B** *v. tr.* **1** saltare, scavalcare **2** far salire ♦ **to j. at** cogliere al volo; **to j. off** saltare giù
jumper (1) ['dʒʌmpəʳ] *s.* **1** maglione *m.* **2** (*USA*) grembiule *m.*
jumper (2) ['dʒʌmpəʳ] *s.* (*elettr.*) jumper *m. inv.*, cavallotto *m.*
jumpy ['dʒʌmpɪ] *agg.* nervoso, agitato
junction ['dʒʌŋ(k)ʃ(ə)n] *s.* **1** congiunzione *f.* **2** (*ferr., strada*) raccordo *m.* **3** (*elettr.*) giunzione *f.*
June [dʒuːn] *s.* giugno *m.*
jungle ['dʒʌŋgl] *s.* giungla *f.*
junior ['dʒuːnjəʳ] *agg.* **1** inferiore **2** junior, il giovane, (*tra fratelli*) minore
juniper ['dʒuːnɪpəʳ] *s.* ginepro *m.*

junk [dʒʌŋk] *s.* **1** cianfrusaglie *f. pl.* **2** rottame *m.*
junkie ['dʒʌŋkɪ] *s.* (*pop.*) drogato *m.*
junoesque [ˌdʒuːnɒ(ʊ)'ɛsk] *agg.* giunonico
juridical [dʒʊə'rɪdɪk(ə)l] *agg.* giuridico
jurisdictional [ˌdʒʊərɪs'dɪkʃənl] *agg.* giurisdizionale
jurisprudence ['dʒʊərɪsˌpruːdəns] *s.* giurisprudenza *f.*
jurist ['dʒʊərɪst] *s.* giurista *m. e f.*
juror ['dʒʊərəʳ] *s.* giurato *m.*
jury ['dʒʊərɪ] *s.* giuria *f.*
just [dʒʌst] **A** *agg.* **1** giusto, onesto **2** legittimo, fondato **3** adeguato, meritato **B** *avv.* **1** appena **2** proprio **3** soltanto, semplicemente **4** esattamente, precisamente **5** a malapena ♦ **j. about** quasi; **j. after** subito dopo; **j. a minute** un minuto; **j. in case** caso mai; **j. now** poco fa, in questo momento; **j. over** poco più; **j. so** proprio così; **j. then** proprio allora
justice ['dʒʌstɪs] *s.* giustizia *f.*
justifiable ['dʒʌstɪfaɪəbl] *agg.* giustificabile
justification [ˌdʒʌstɪfɪ'keɪʃ(ə)n] *s.* giustificazione *f.*
to **justify** ['dʒʌstɪfaɪ] *v. tr.* **1** giustificare, scusare **2** motivare
jut [dʒʌt] *s.* sporgenza *f.*
to **jut** [dʒʌt] *v. intr.* sporgere, aggettare
jute [dʒuːt] *s.* iuta *f.*
juvenile ['dʒuːvɪnaɪl] **A** *agg.* **1** giovanile **2** immaturo **3** minorile **B** *s.* **1** giovane *m. e f.* **2** minorenne *m. e f.*
to **juxtapose** ['dʒʌkstəpɒʊz] *v. tr.* giustapporre
juxtaposition [ˌdʒʌkstəpə'zɪʃ(ə)n] *s.* giustapposizione *f.*

K

kaki ['kɑ(ː)kɪ] *s.* cachi *m. inv.*
kale [keɪl] *s.* ravizzone *m.*
kaleidoscope [kə'laɪdəskɒʊp] *s.* caleidoscopio *m.*
kangaroo [ˌkæŋgə'ruː] *s.* canguro *m.*
kaolin ['kɛ(ɪ)əlɪn] *s.* caolino *m.*
karate [kə'raːtɪ] *s.* karatè *m. inv.*
kayak ['kaɪæk] *s.* kayak *m. inv.*
keel [kiːl] *s.* (*naut.*) chiglia *f.* ♦ **on an even k.** in equilibrio
keen [kiːn] *agg.* **1** appassionato **2** forte, intenso **3** acuto, sottile, penetrante **4** aguzzo, affilato, tagliente ♦ **to be k. of st.** essere appassionato di q.c.
keep [kiːp] *s.* **1** mantenimento *m.*, sostentamento *m.* **2** torrione *m.*, fortezza *f.* ♦ **for keeps** per sempre
to keep [kiːp] (*pass. e p. p.* **kept**) **A** *v. tr.* **1** tenere, conservare **2** mantenere, sostentare, amministrare **3** trattenere, impedire **4** osservare, rispettare, attenersi a **B** *v. intr.* **1** mantenersi, restare **2** continuare, durare, perseverare ♦ **to k. away** stare lontano; **to k. from** sottrarre, trattenersi da; **to k. in** stare in casa; **to k. off** stare lontano, evitare; **to k. on** tenere, continuare; **to k. out** tenere fuori; **to k. up** mantenere
keeper ['kiːpəʳ] *s.* guardiano *m.*
keeping ['kiːpɪŋ] *s.* **1** guardia *f.*, sorveglianza *f.* **2** accordo *m.* **3** conservazione *f.* ♦ **to be in k. with** essere in armonia con; **to be out of k. with** essere in disaccordo con
keepsake ['kiːpseɪk] *s.* (oggetto) ricordo *m.*
kennel ['kɛnl] *s.* canile *m.*
kept [kɛpt] *pass. e p. p. di* **to keep**
kerb [kɜːb] *s.* orlo *m.* del marciapiede
kernel ['kɜːnl] *s.* **1** nocciolo *m.*, gheriglio *m.* **2** (*fis.*) nucleo *m.*
kerosene ['kɛrəsiːn] *s.* cherosene *m.*
ketch [kɛtʃ] *s.* (*naut.*) ketch *m. inv.*
kettle ['kɛtl] *s.* bollitore *m.*
kettledrum ['kɛtldrʌm] *s.* (*mus.*) timpano *m.*
key(1) [kiː] **A** *s.* **1** chiave *f.* **2** tasto *m.*, pulsante *m.* **3** tono *m.* **B** *agg. attr.* chiave, importante
key(2) [kiː] *s.* isoletta *f.*
to key [kiː] *v. tr.* **1** (*mecc.*) collegare con una chiavetta **2** (*mus.*) accordare **3** adattare ♦ **to k. in** (*inf.*) digitare; **to k. up** eccitare, stimolare
keyboard ['kiːbɜːd] *s.* tastiera *f.*
keyhole ['kiːhɒʊl] *s.* buco *m.* della serratura
keynote ['kiːnɒʊt] *s.* (*mus.*) nota *f.* fondamentale
keystone ['kiːstɒʊn] *s.* chiave *f.* di volta
kick [kɪk] *s.* **1** calcio *m.*, pedata *f.* **2** (*fam.*) divertimento *m.*, gusto *m.* **3** (*fam.*) energia *f.*, forza *f.* ♦ **corner k.** calcio d'angolo; **penalty k.** calcio di rigore
to kick [kɪk] **A** *v. tr.* **1** dare calci a, spingere a calci **2** (*fam.*) liberarsi di **B** *v. intr.* **1** tirare calci **2** recalcitrare ♦ **to k. off** dare il calcio d'inizio; **to k. sb. out** buttare fuori qc. a calci
kid [kɪd] *s.* **1** capretto *m.* **2** (*fam.*) bambino *m.*, ragazzo *m.*
to kid [kɪd] *v. tr.* (*fam.*) prendere in giro
to kidnap ['kɪdnæp] *v. tr.* rapire
kidnapper ['kɪdˌnæpəʳ] *s.* rapitore *m.*
kidnapping ['kɪdˌnæpɪŋ] *s.* rapimento *m.*
kidney ['kɪdnɪ] *s.* **1** rene *m.* **2** rognone *m.* ♦ **k. machine** rene artificiale
kill [kɪl] *s.* **1** uccisione *f.* **2** cacciagione *f.*, preda *f.*
to kill [kɪl] *v. tr.* **1** uccidere, ammazzare **2** distruggere, rovinare **3** respingere
killer ['kɪləʳ] *s.* killer *m. inv.*, sicario *m.*
killing ['kɪlɪŋ] **A** *agg.* **1** mortale **2** faticoso, massacrante **3** (*fam.*) attraente **B** *s.* **1** assassinio *m.*, uccisione *f.* **2** forte guadagno *m.*, bel colpo *m.*
killjoy ['kɪldʒɔɪ] *s.* guastafeste *m. e f.*
kiln [kɪln] *s.* fornace *f.*
kilogram ['kɪləgræm] *s.* chilogrammo *m.*
kilometre ['kɪləˌmiːtəʳ] (*USA* **kilometer**) *s.* chilometro *m.*
kilometric [ˌkɪlɒ(ʊ)'mɛtrɪk] *agg.* chilometrico
kilt [kɪlt] *s.* kilt *m. inv.*
kin [kɪn] *s. inv.* parente *m. e f.*, congiunto *m.*
kind [kaɪnd] **A** *agg.* gentile, cortese **B** *s.* **1** genere *m.*, razza *f.* **2** tipo *m.*, varietà *f.*, categoria *f.* ♦ **a k. of** una specie di; **k. of** quasi; **to pay in k.** pagare in natura
kindergarten ['kɪndəˌgaːtn] *s.* asilo *m.*

kind-hearted [ˌkaɪnd'hɑːtɪd] *agg.* di animo gentile
to **kindle** ['kɪndl] **A** *v. tr.* **1** accendere, infiammare **2** suscitare **B** *v. intr.* prender fuoco, infiammarsi
kindly ['kaɪndlɪ] **A** *agg.* **1** gentile, benevolo **2** piacevole, favorevole **B** *avv.* **1** gentilmente, per favore **2** benevolmente **3** volentieri
kindness ['kaɪndnɪs] *s.* gentilezza *f.*, cortesia *f.*
kindred ['kɪndrɪd] **A** *agg.* **1** imparentato **2** affine **B** *s.* **1** (*v. al pl.*) parenti *m. pl.* **2** parentela *f.*
kinetic [kaɪ'nɛtɪk] *agg.* cinetico
king [kɪŋ] *s.* re *m. inv.*
kingdom ['kɪŋdəm] *s.* regno *m.*
kingfisher ['kɪŋˌfɪʃəʳ] *s.* martin pescatore *m.*
king-size(d) ['kɪŋsaɪz(d)] *agg.* di taglia superiore al normale
kinky ['kɪŋkɪ] *agg.* **1** ingarbugliato **2** (*fam.*) eccentrico
kinship ['kɪnʃɪp] *s.* **1** parentela *f.* **2** affinità *f.*
kinsman ['kɪnzmən] (*pl.* **kinsmen**) *s.* consanguineo *m.*
kiosk [kɪ'əsk] *s.* chiosco *m.*, edicola *f.*
kiss [kɪs] *s.* bacio *m.*
to **kiss** [kɪs] *v. tr. e intr.* baciare, baciarsi
kit [kɪt] *s.* **1** equipaggiamento *m.*, corredo *m.* **2** attrezzi *m. pl.*
kitchen ['kɪtʃɪn] *s.* cucina *f.* ♦ **k. garden** orto
kite [kaɪt] *s.* **1** nibbio *m.* **2** aquilone *m.*
kith [kɪθ] *s.* amici *m. pl.* ♦ **k. and kin** amici e parenti
kitten ['kɪtn] *s.* gattino *m.*
knack [næk] *s.* abilità *f.*, destrezza *f.* ♦ **to have a k. for st.** essere tagliato per q.c.
knapsack ['næpsæk] *s.* zaino *m.*
to **knead** [niːd] *v. tr.* impastare
kneading ['niːdɪŋ] *s.* impastatura *f.* ♦ **k. trough** madia
knee [niː] *s.* ginocchio *m.*
kneecap ['niːˌkæp] *s.* rotula *f.*
to **kneel** [niːl] (*pass. e p. p.* **knelt**) *v. intr.* inginocchiarsi
knew [njuː] *pass. di* **to know**
knickers ['nɪkəz] *s. pl.* mutandine *f. pl.*
knickknack ['nɪknæk] *s.* gingillo *m.*, soprammobile *m.*
knife [naɪf] (*pl.* **knives**) *s.* coltello *m.*
to **knife** [naɪf] *v. tr.* **1** accoltellare, pugnalare **2** tagliare
knight [naɪt] *s.* **1** cavaliere *m.* **2** (*scacchi*) cavallo *m.*
to **knit** [nɪt] (*pass. e p. p.* **knit, knitted**) **A** *v. tr.* **1** lavorare a maglia **2** (*fronte, ciglia*) corrugare, aggrottare **3** saldare, unire **B** *v. intr.* **1** sferruzzare **2** saldarsi, unirsi
knitting ['nɪtɪŋ] *s.* lavoro *m.* a maglia ♦ **k. machine** macchina per maglieria; **k. needle** ferro da calza
knitwear ['nɪtwɛəʳ] *s.* maglieria *f.*
knives ['naɪvz] *pl. di* **knife**
knob [nəb] *s.* **1** protuberanza *f.*, (*di legno*) nodo *m.* **2** manopola *f.*, pomello *m.*
knock [nək] *s.* botta *f.*, colpo *m.*, percossa *f.*, bussata *f.*
to **knock** [nək] **A** *v. tr.* **1** picchiare, battere **2** (*fam.*) criticare **B** *v. intr.* battere, bussare ♦ **to k. about** girovagare, bazzicare; **to k. at the door** bussare alla porta; **to k. down** abbattere; **to k. in** conficcare; **to k. off** buttare giù, abbassare, rubare; **to k. out** mettere k.o.
knocker ['nəkəʳ] *s.* battente *m.*
knockout ['nəkˌaʊt] **A** *agg.* che mette fuori combattimento **B** *s.* knockout *m. inv.*
knoll [nɒʊl] *s.* poggio *m.*
knot [nət] *s.* **1** nodo *m.* **2** (*fig.*) legame *m.*, vincolo *m.* **3** (*fig.*) difficoltà *f.*, problema *m.* **4** capannello *m.*, mucchio *m.*
to **knot** [nət] *v. tr.* annodare
knotty ['nətɪ] *agg.* **1** nodoso **2** intricato
to **know** [nɒʊ] (*pass.* **knew**, *p. p.* **known**) *v. tr.* **1** conoscere, sapere **2** riconoscere, distinguere ♦ **to k. about** essere a conoscenza di; **you never k.** non si sa mai
know-all ['nɒʊɜːl] *s.* saccente *m. e f.*
know-how ['nɒʊhaʊ] *s.* **1** abilità *f.* tecnica **2** know-how *m. inv.*
knowing ['nɒ(ʊ)ɪŋ] *agg.* **1** informato **2** intelligente, abile **3** d'intesa
knowledge ['nəlɪdʒ] *s.* **1** conoscenza *f.* **2** sapere *m.*, scienza *f.*
knowledgeable ['nəlɪdʒəbl] *agg.* bene informato
known [nɒʊn] **A** *p. p. di* **to know** **B** *agg.* noto, conosciuto
knuckle ['nʌkl] *s.* nocca *f.*
koala [kɒ(ʊ)'ɑːlə] *s.* koala *m. inv.*
kudos ['kjuːdəs] *s.* (*fam.*) fama *f.*
Kurdish ['kɜːdɪʃ] *agg.* curdo

L

lab [læb] *s.* (*fam.*) laboratorio *m.*
label ['leɪbl] *s.* etichetta *f.*, cartellino *m.*
to label ['leɪbl] *v. tr.* **1** contrassegnare, etichettare **2** classificare
laboratory [lə'bɔrət(ə)rɪ] *s.* laboratorio *m.*
labour ['leɪbəʳ] (*USA* **labor**) *s.* **1** lavoro *m.* **2** manodopera *f.* **3** doglie *f. pl.*, travaglio *m.* ♦ **hard l.** lavori forzati; **L. party** partito laburista
to labour ['leɪbəʳ] (*USA* **to labor**) *v. intr.* **1** lavorare, faticare **2** avere le doglie
laboured ['leɪbəd] *agg.* **1** affannoso, affaticato **2** elaborato
labourer ['leɪbərəʳ] *s.* manovale *m.*
labyrinth ['læbərɪnθ] *s.* labirinto *m.*
lace [leɪs] *s.* **1** pizzo *m.* **2** laccio *m.*, stringa *f.*
to lace [leɪs] *v. tr.* **1** allacciare **2** ornare di pizzi **3** (*una bevanda*) correggere ♦ **to l. up one's shoes** allacciarsi le scarpe
laceration [ˌlæsə'reɪʃ(ə)n] *s.* lacerazione *f.*
lack [læk] *s.* mancanza *f.*, insufficienza *f.*
to lack [læk] *v. tr.* **1** mancare di **2** aver bisogno di ♦ **to be lacking in st.** essere privo di q.c.
lackadaisical [ˌlækə'deɪzɪk(ə)l] *agg.* apatico, noncurante
lackey ['lækɪ] *s.* lacchè *m.*
laconic [lə'kɔnɪk] *agg.* laconico
lacquer ['lækəʳ] *s.* lacca *f.*
to lacquer ['lækəʳ] *v. tr.* laccare
lactose ['læktɒʊs] *s.* lattosio *m.*
lad [læd] *s.* ragazzo *m.*, giovanotto *m.*
ladder ['lædəʳ] *s.* **1** scala *f.* (*a pioli*) **2** (*di calze*) smagliatura *f.* ♦ **double l.** scala a libro
to lade [leɪd] (*p. p.* **laden**) *v. tr.* caricare
ladle ['leɪdl] *s.* mestolo *m.*
lady ['leɪdɪ] *s.* signora *f.* ♦ **l.-in-waiting** dama di corte; **Our L.** la Madonna
ladybird ['leɪdɪbɜːd] *s.* coccinella *f.*
ladylike ['leɪdɪlaɪk] *agg.* adatto a una signora, signorile
lag (1) [læg] *s.* ritardo *m.*, intervallo *m.*
lag (2) [læg] *s.* **1** doga *f.* **2** rivestimento *m.* (isolante)
to lag (1) [læg] *v. intr.* ritardare, ristagnare
to lag (2) [læg] *v. tr.* rivestire (con materiale isolante)
lager ['lɑːgəʳ] *s.* birra *f.* chiara
lagoon [lə'guːn] *s.* laguna *f.*
laicism ['leɪɪsɪz(ə)m] *s.* laicismo *m.*
laid [leɪd] *pass. e p. p. di* **to lay**
lain [leɪn] *p. p. di* **to lie**
lair [lɛəʳ] *s.* covo *m.*, tana *f.*
lake (1) [leɪk] *s.* lago *m.*
lake (2) [leɪk] *s.* lacca *f.*
to lam [læm] *v. tr.* (*fam.*) bastonare, colpire
lamb [læm] *s.* agnello *m.* ♦ **l. chop** costata d'agnello
lame [leɪm] *agg.* **1** zoppo, storpio **2** zoppicante
lament [lə'mɛnt] *s.* lamento *m.*
to lament [lə'mɛnt] *v. tr. e intr.* lamentare, lamentarsi
lamina ['læmɪnə] (*pl.* **laminae**) *s.* lamina *f.*
to laminate ['læmɪneɪt] *v. tr.* laminare
lamp [læmp] *s.* lampada *f.*, lampadina *f.*, lampione *m.* ♦ **l. post** lampione; **l. shade** paralume
lampoon [læm'puːn] *s.* libello *m.* satirico
lance [lɑːns] *s.* lancia *f.*
lancer ['lɑːnsəʳ] *s.* lanciere *m.*
lancet ['lɑːnsɪt] *s.* bisturi *m.* ♦ **l. window** finestra ogivale
lancinating ['lɑːnsɪneɪtɪŋ] *agg.* lancinante
land [lænd] *s.* **1** terra *f.* **2** suolo *m.*, terreno *m.* **3** paese *m.*, contrada *f.* **4** proprietà *f.* ♦ **l. agent** agente immobiliare; **l. tax** imposta fondiaria
to land [lænd] **A** *v. intr.* **1** sbarcare, approdare, atterrare **2** cadere **B** *v. tr.* **1** far approdare, far atterrare **2** sbarcare, scaricare **3** procurarsi **4** (*un colpo*) assestare ♦ **to l. up** finire
landed ['lændɪd] *agg.* fondiario
landing ['lændɪŋ] *s.* **1** approdo *m.*, sbarco *m.*, atterraggio *m.* **2** pianerottolo *m.* ♦ **l. gear** carrello di atterraggio; **l. strip** pista di atterraggio
landlady ['læn(d)ˌleɪdɪ] *s.* **1** padrona *f.* di casa **2** affittacamere *f. inv.*
landlord ['læn(d)lɔːd] *s.* **1** padrone *m.* di casa **2** affittacamere *m. inv.*
landmark ['læn(d)mɑːk] *s.* **1** punto *m.* di riferimento **2** pietra *f.* miliare
landowner ['lændˌɒʊnəʳ] *s.* proprietario *m.* terriero

landscape ['lændskeɪp] *s.* paesaggio *m.*, panorama *m.*
landslide ['læn(d)slaɪd] *s.* frana *f.*
landslip ['læn(d)slɪp] *s.* smottamento *m.*
lane [leɪn] *s.* **1** sentiero *m.*, viottolo *m.*, vicolo *m.* **2** corsia *f.*
language ['læŋgwɪdʒ] *s.* lingua *f.*, linguaggio *m.* ♦ **bad l.** linguaggio volgare; **l. laboratory** laboratorio linguistico
languid ['læŋgwɪd] *agg.* languido
languor ['læŋgəʳ] *s.* languore *m.*
lank [læŋk] *agg.* **1** smilzo, magro **2** (*di capelli*) liscio
lantern ['læntən] *s.* lanterna *f.*
lap (1) [læp] *s.* **1** lembo *m.*, falda *f.* **2** grembo *m.* **3** (*di circuito*) giro *m.* **4** tappa *f.*
lap (2) [læp] *s.* **1** leccata *f.* **2** sciabordio *m.*
to **lap (1)** [læp] *v. tr.* **1** piegare, avvolgere **2** coccolare **3** doppiare, dare giri di distacco
to **lap (2)** [læp] *v. tr. e intr.* **1** leccare, lappare **2** sciabordare ♦ **to l. up** bearsi di
lapel [lə'pɛl] *s.* risvolto *m.*
lapidary ['læpɪdərɪ] *agg.* lapidario
to **lapidate** ['læpɪdeɪt] *v. tr.* lapidare
Laplander ['læplændəʳ] *s.* lappone *m. e f.*
Lappish ['læpɪʃ] *agg. e s.* lappone *m.* (*lingua*)
lapse [læps] *s.* **1** errore *m.*, mancanza *f.*, scorrettezza *f.* **2** lasso *m.*, intervallo *m.* **3** (*dir.*) estinzione *f.* ♦ **l. of memory** vuoto di memoria; **l. of time** lasso di tempo
to **lapse** [læps] *v. intr.* **1** cadere, scivolare **2** passare, trascorrere **3** mancare, venir meno **4** estinguersi, cessare, scadere
larceny ['lɑːsɪnɪ] *s.* (*dir.*) furto *m.*
larch [lɑːtʃ] *s.* larice *m.*
lard [lɑːd] *s.* lardo *m.*
larder ['lɑːdəʳ] *s.* dispensa *f.*
large [lɑːdʒ] *agg.* grande, grosso, ampio, vasto ♦ **at l.** in generale, nell'insieme, in libertà; **l.-scale** su larga scala
large-hearted [ˌlɑːdʒ'hɑːtɪd] *agg.* generoso
largely ['lɑːdʒlɪ] *avv.* largamente, in gran parte
largeness ['lɑːdʒnɪs] *s.* larghezza *f.*, ampiezza *f.*, grandezza *f.*
largess(e) [lɑː'dʒɛs] *s.* liberalità *f.*
lark (1) [lɑːk] *s.* allodola *f.*
lark (2) [lɑːk] *s.* scherzo *m.*, beffa *f.*
larval ['lɑːv(ə)l] *agg.* larvale
laryngitis [ˌlærɪn'dʒaɪtɪs] *s.* laringite *f.*
larynx ['lærɪŋks] *s.* laringe *f.*
laser ['leɪzəʳ] *s.* laser *m. inv.*
lash [læʃ] *s.* **1** sferza *f.* **2** sferzata *f.*, frustata *f.* **3** (*dell'occhio*) ciglio *m.*
to **lash** [læʃ] *v. tr.* **1** sferzare, frustare **2** agitare **3** battere violentemente, frangersi su **4** legare ♦ **to l. out at** assalire, attaccare
lass [læs] *s.* ragazza *f.*
last [lɑːst] (*sup. rel. di* **late**) **A** *agg.* **1** ultimo **2** scorso, più recente **3** finale, definitivo **B** *avv.* **1** per ultimo, ultimo **2** ultimamente **C** *s.* termine *m.* ♦ **at l.** alla fine; **l. but one** penultimo; **l. name** cognome; **l. week** la settimana scorsa
to **last** [lɑːst] *v. intr.* durare, resistere
lasting ['lɑːstɪŋ] *agg.* duraturo, durevole
lastly ['lɑːstlɪ] *avv.* da ultimo, per finire
latch [lætʃ] *s.* chiavistello *m.*
late [leɪt] (*comp.* **later**, **latter**, *sup.* **latest**, **last**) **A** *agg.* **1** tardi, in ritardo **2** tardo, inoltrato **3** tardivo **4** precedente, defunto **B** *avv.* **1** tardi, in ritardo **2** recentemente ♦ **as l. as** fino a; **of l.** da poco; **to be l.** essere in ritardo
latecomer ['leɪtˌkʌməʳ] *s.* ritardatario *m.*
lately ['leɪtlɪ] *avv.* recentemente
latent ['leɪt(ə)nt] *agg.* latente
later ['leɪtəʳ] (*comp. di* **late**) **A** *agg.* posteriore, ulteriore **B** *avv.* più tardi, dopo ♦ **l. on** poi; **see you l.!** a più tardi!
lateral ['læt(ə)r(ə)l] *agg.* laterale
latest ['leɪtɪst] (*sup. rel. di* **late**) *agg.* ultimo, recentissimo ♦ **at the l.** al più tardi
lathe [leɪð] *s.* tornio *m.*
lather ['lɑːðəʳ] *s.* schiuma *f.*
lathery ['lɑːðərɪ] *agg.* schiumoso
Latin ['lætɪn] *agg. e s.* latino *m.*
Latinism ['lætɪnɪz(ə)m] *s.* latinismo *m.*
Latinist ['lætɪnɪst] *s.* latinista *m. e f.*
Latinity [lə'tɪnɪtɪ] *s.* latinità *f.*
latitude ['lætɪtjuːd] *s.* latitudine *f.*
latter ['lætəʳ] (*comp. di* **late**) **A** *agg.* posteriore, secondo, (quest')ultimo **B** *pron.* il secondo, l'ultimo (*di due*)
lattice ['lætɪs] *s.* grata *f.*, traliccio *m.*, reticolo *m.*
laudable ['lɔːdəbl] *agg.* lodevole
laugh [lɑːf] *s.* **1** riso *m.*, risata *f.* **2** divertimento *m.*, spasso *m.*
to **laugh** [lɑːf] **A** *v. intr.* ridere **B** *v. tr.* deridere ♦ **to l. at** ridere di
laughable ['lɑːfəbl] *agg.* ridicolo
laughing ['lɑːfɪŋ] **A** *agg.* ridente, allegro **B** *s.* riso *m.*, risata *f.*
laughingstock ['lɑːfɪŋstək] *s.* zimbello *m.*

laughter ['lɑːftəʳ] *s.* risata *f.*
launch (1) [lɔːn(t)ʃ] *s.* **1** varo *m.* **2** lancio *m.*
launch (2) [lɔːn(t)ʃ] *s.* lancia *f.*, scialuppa *f.*
to launch [lɔːn(t)f] **A** *v. tr.* **1** varare **2** lanciare **B** *v. intr.* **1** lanciarsi **2** scendere in mare ♦ **to l. into** lanciarsi in
launching [lɔːn(t)ʃɪŋ] *s.* **1** lancio *m.* **2** varo *m.*
to launder ['lɔːndəʳ] *v. tr.* lavare e stirare
launderette [ˌlɔːndə'rɛt] *s.* lavanderia *f.* automatica
laundry ['lɔːndrɪ] *s.* **1** lavanderia *f.* **2** bucato *m.*
laurel ['lɔr(ə)l] *s.* alloro *m.*
lava ['lɑːvə] *s.* lava *f.*
lavage ['lævɪdʒ] *s.* (*med.*) lavaggio *m.* ♦ **gastric l.** lavanda gastrica
lavatory ['lævət(ə)rɪ] *s.* gabinetto *m.*
lavender ['lævɪndəʳ] *s.* lavanda *f.*
lavish ['lævɪʃ] *agg.* **1** generoso **2** eccessivo **3** sontuoso, sfarzoso
to lavish ['lævɪʃ] *v. tr.* prodigare, profondere
law [lɔː] *s.* **1** legge *f.* **2** diritto *m.*, giurisprudenza *f.* **3** giustizia *f.* ♦ **l. court** tribunale
law-abiding ['lɔːəˌbaɪdɪŋ] *agg.* rispettoso della legge
lawful ['lɔːf(ʊ)l] *agg.* lecito, legale
lawgiver ['lɔːˌgɪvəʳ] *s.* legislatore *m.*
lawless ['lɔːlɪs] *agg.* **1** senza legge **2** illegale
lawn [lɔːn] *s.* prato *m.* ♦ **l.-mower** tosaerba
lawsuit ['lɔːsjuːt] *s.* causa *f.*, processo *m.*
lawyer ['lɔːjəʳ] *s.* avvocato *m.*
lax [læks] *agg.* **1** molle, rilassato **2** negligente, trascurato
laxative ['læksətɪv] *agg. e s.* lassativo *m.*
lay (1) [leɪ] *agg.* **1** laico, secolare **2** profano
lay (2) [leɪ] *s.* disposizione *f.*, configurazione *f.*
to lay [leɪ] (*pass. e p. p.* **laid**) *v. tr.* **1** posare, collocare **2** (*uova*) deporre **3** disporre, preparare, ordire **4** abbattere **5** progettare, elaborare **6** sottoporre **7** ricoprire, rivestire **8** scommettere ♦ **to l. aside/by** mettere da parte; **to l. down** deporre, esporre, stabilire; **to l. off** riposare, licenziare; **to l. on** fornire, organizzare; **to l. out** preparare, distendere, tracciare, spendere; **to l. up** fare scorta di
layabout ['leɪəbaʊt] *s.* sfaccendato *m.*
lay-by ['leɪbaɪ] *s.* piazzuola *f.* (*di sosta*)
layer ['lɛ(ɪ)əʳ] *s.* strato *m.*
layman ['leɪmən] (*pl.* **laymen**) *s.* **1** laico *m.* **2** profano *m.*
layout ['leɪaʊt] *s.* **1** disposizione *f.* **2** tracciato *m.*, progetto *m.*, bozzetto *m.* **3** impaginazione *f.*
to laze [leɪz] *v. intr.* oziare
laziness ['leɪzɪnɪs] *s.* pigrizia *f.*
lazy ['leɪzɪ] *agg.* pigro
lead (1) [lɛd] *s.* **1** piombo *m.* **2** (*per matita*) mina *f.*
lead (2) [liːd] *s.* **1** comando *m.*, guida *f.*, posizione *f.* di testa **2** vantaggio *m.* **3** guinzaglio *m.* **4** traccia *f.*, indizio *m.* **5** (*teatro*) parte *f.* principale **6** filo *m.* elettrico ♦ **to be in the l.** essere in testa, essere all'avanguardia
to lead [liːd] (*pass. e p. p.* **led**) **A** *v. tr.* **1** condurre, guidare **2** indurre a **B** *v. intr.* **1** condurre, portare **2** essere in testa ♦ **to l. away** condurre via; **to l. back** ricondurre; **to l. off** cominciare; **to l. on** trascinare; **to l. up to** portare a
leaden ['lɛdn] *agg.* plumbeo
leader ['liːdəʳ] *s.* **1** leader *m. inv.*, capo *m.*, direttore *m.* **2** articolo *m.* di fondo
leadership ['liːdəʃɪp] *s.* guida *f.*, direzione *f.*, comando *m.*
leading ['liːdɪŋ] *agg.* principale, primo ♦ **l. man/lady** primo attore/prima attrice
leaf [liːf] (*pl.* **leaves**) *s.* **1** foglia *f.*, fogliame *m.* **2** foglio *m.* ♦ **to come into l.** mettere le foglie
leaflet ['liːflɪt] *s.* volantino *m.*
league [liːg] *s.* **1** lega *f.*, associazione *f.* **2** (*sport*) federazione *f.* ♦ **to be in l. with sb.** essere in combutta con qc.
leak [liːk] *s.* **1** falla *f.*, fessura *f.* **2** fuoriuscita *f.*, fuga *f.*
to leak [liːk] **A** *v. intr.* **1** perdere, fare acqua **2** (*di liquido*) fuoriuscire **3** trapelare **B** *v. tr.* **1** (*liquido*) perdere **2** far trapelare
lean (1) [liːn] *s.* inclinazione *f.*, pendenza *f.*
lean (2) [liːn] *agg.* **1** magro **2** snello, agile **3** scarno
to lean [liːn] (*pass. e p. p.* **leaned**, **leant**) *v. intr.* **1** pendere, inclinarsi **2** appoggiarsi ♦ **to l. on** dipendere da; **to l. out** sporgersi; **to l. towards** tendere a
leaning ['liːnɪŋ] **A** *agg.* pendente **B** *s.* propensione *f.*
leanness ['liːnnɪs] *s.* magrezza *f.*
leant [lɛnt] *pass. e p. p. di* **to lean**
leap [liːp] *s.* **1** salto *m.*, balzo *m.* **2** cambiamento *m.* ♦ **l. year** anno bisestile
to leap [liːp] (*pass. e p. p.* **leapt**, **leaped**) **A**

v. intr. saltare, balzare, lanciarsi **B** *v. tr.* **1** saltare **2** far saltare ♦ **to l. up** balzare in piedi, sobbalzare
to learn [lɜːn] (*pass. e p. p.* **learned, learnt**) **A** *v. tr.* imparare, studiare **B** *v. intr.* **1** imparare, istruirsi **2** venire a sapere
learned ['lɜːnɪd] *agg.* colto, istruito
learner ['lɜːnəʳ] *s.* allievo *m.*, apprendista *m. e f.*
learning ['lɜːnɪŋ] *s.* **1** cultura *f.* **2** apprendimento *m.*
learnt [lɜːnt] *pass. e p. p. di* **to learn**
lease [liːs] *s.* contratto *m.* d'affitto
to lease [liːs] *v. tr.* affittare
leash [liːʃ] *s.* guinzaglio *m.*
least [liːst] (*sup. di* **little**) **A** *agg.* il minimo, il più piccolo **B** *avv.* il meno (di tutti), minimamente ♦ **at l.** almeno; **l. of all** tanto meno; **not in the l.** per nulla; **to say the l.** a dir poco
leather ['lɛðəʳ] *s.* cuoio *m.*, pelle *f.* ♦ **l. goods shop** pelletteria; **shammy l.** pelle di camoscio
leatherwear ['lɛðəwɛəʳ] *s.* pelletteria *f.*
leave [liːv] *s.* **1** permesso *m.*, autorizzazione *f.* **2** congedo *m.*
to leave [liːv] (*pass. e p. p.* **left**) **A** *v. tr.* **1** lasciare, abbandonare **2** partire da, andarsene da **3** consegnare, affidare **B** *v. intr.* partire, andarsene, uscire ♦ **to l. behind** dimenticare; **to l. off** smettere; **to l. out** tralasciare; **to be left** rimanere, avanzare
leaves [liːvz] *pl. di* **leaf**
leaving ['liːvɪŋ] *s.* **1** partenza *f.* **2** avanzi *m. pl.*
lecherous ['lɛtʃ(ə)rəs] *agg.* lascivo
lecture ['lɛktʃəʳ] *s.* **1** conferenza *f.*, lezione *f.* **2** predica *f.*
to lecture ['lɛktʃəʳ] **A** *v. tr.* **1** tenere una conferenza a, fare lezione a **2** fare una predica a **B** *v. intr.* tenere una conferenza, fare lezione
lecturer ['lɛktʃ(ə)rəʳ] *s.* conferenziere *m.*, docente *m. e f.*
led [lɛd] *pass. e p. p. di* **to lead**
ledge [lɛdʒ] *s.* **1** sporgenza *f.*, ripiano *m.* **2** (*di montagna*) cornice *f.* ♦ **window l.** davanzale
ledger ['lɛdʒəʳ] *s.* **1** libro *m.* mastro **2** pietra *f.* tombale
lee [liː] **A** *agg.* sottovento **B** *s.* **1** (lato) sottovento *m.* **2** ridosso *m.*
leech [liːtʃ] *s.* sanguisuga *f.*
leek [liːk] *s.* porro *m.*
to leer [lɪəʳ] *v. intr.* **1** guardare di traverso **2** dare occhiate maliziose
lees [liːz] *s.* sedimento *m.*, feccia *f.*
leeward ['liːwəd] *agg. e avv.* sottovento
leeway ['liːweɪ] *s.* **1** scarroccio *m.*, deriva *f.* **2** (*fig.*) margine *m.*
left (1) [lɛft] **A** *agg.* **1** sinistro **2** di sinistra **B** *s.* sinistra *f.* **C** *avv.* a sinistra
left (2) [lɛft] *pass. e p. p. di* **to leave**
left-hand ['lɛfthænd] *agg.* di sinistra, a sinistra
left-handed [ˌlɛft'hændɪd] *agg.* mancino
leftovers ['lɛftɒʊvəz] *s. pl.* avanzi *m. pl.*
leg [lɛg] *s.* **1** gamba *f.* **2** zampa *f.* **3** cosciotto *m.* **4** (*di viaggio*) tappa *f.*
legacy ['lɛgəsɪ] *s.* legato *m.*, eredità *f.*
legal ['liːg(ə)l] *agg.* legale
to legalize ['liːgəlaɪz] *v. tr.* legalizzare
legend ['lɛdʒ(ə)nd] *s.* leggenda *f.*
legendary ['lɛdʒ(ə)nd(ə)rɪ] *agg.* leggendario
legion ['liːdʒ(ə)n] *s.* legione *f.*
legislation [ˌlɛdʒɪs'leɪʃ(ə)n] *s.* legislazione *f.*
legislative ['lɛdʒɪslətɪv] *agg.* legislativo
legislature ['lɛdʒɪsleɪtʃəʳ] *s.* corpo *m.* legislativo
legitimate [lɪ'dʒɪtɪmɪt] *agg.* legittimo
to legitimate [lɪ'dʒɪtɪmeɪt] *v. tr.* legittimare
legroom ['lɛgˌruːm] *s.* spazio *m.* per le gambe
legume ['lɛgjʊ(ː)m] *s.* legume *m.*
leisure ['lɛʒəʳ] **1** *s.* tempo *m.* libero **2** agio *m.*, ozio *m.*
leisurely ['lɛʒəlɪ] *avv.* con comodo
lemon ['lɛmən] *s.* limone *m.*
lemonade [ˌlɛmə'neɪd] *s.* limonata *f.*
to lend [lɛnd] (*pass. e p. p.* **lent**) **A** *v. tr.* prestare **B** *v. intr.* concedere prestiti ♦ **lending library** biblioteca circolante; **to l. oneself to st.** prestarsi a q.c.
length [lɛŋθ] *s.* **1** lunghezza *f.* **2** durata *f.* **3** pezzo *m.*, tratto *m.* ♦ **at l.** per esteso, alla fine; **l. and breadth** in lungo e in largo
to lengthen ['lɛŋθ(ə)n] *v. tr. e intr.* allungare, allungarsi
lengthways ['lɛŋθweɪz] *avv.* per il lungo
lengthy ['lɛŋθɪ] *agg.* lungo, prolisso
leniency ['liːnjənsɪ] *s.* mitezza *f.*
lenient ['liːnjənt] *agg.* indulgente, mite
lenitive ['lɛnɪtɪv] *agg.* lenitivo
lens [lɛnz] *s.* **1** lente *f.* **2** (*fot.*) obiettivo *m.* ♦ **contact l.** lente a contatto

lent [lɛnt] *pass. e p. p. di* **to lend**
Lent [lɛnt] *s.* quaresima *f.*
lentil ['lɛntɪl] *s.* lenticchia *f.*
leopard ['lɛpəd] *s.* leopardo *m.*
leotard ['liːətaːd] *s.* calzamaglia *f.*
leper ['lɛpəʳ] *agg.* lebbroso
leprosy ['lɛprəsɪ] *s.* lebbra *f.*
lesbian ['lɛzbɪən] *agg.* lesbico
lesion ['liːʒ(ə)n] *s.* lesione *f.*
less [lɛs] (*comp. di* **little**) **A** *agg.* meno, minore **B** *avv.* meno, di meno **C** *s.* meno *m.* **D** *prep.* meno ♦ **l. and l.** sempre meno; **more or l.** più o meno; **none the l.** nondimeno
to lessen ['lɛsn] *v. tr. e intr.* diminuire
lesser ['lɛsəʳ] *agg.* minore
lesson ['lɛsn] *s.* lezione *f.* ♦ **to teach sb. a l.** dare una lezione a qc.
lest [lɛst] *cong.* per paura che
let [lɛt] *s.* affitto *m.*
to let [lɛt] (*pass. e p. p.* **let**) *v. tr.* **1** lasciare, permettere, autorizzare **2** affittare **3** (*forma l'imperativo*) (ES: **let's go** andiamo, **l. it be** sia pure) ♦ **to l.** (*nei cartelli*) si affitta; **to l. down** abbassare, allungare, scontentare, sgonfiare; **to l. in** lasciar entrare, ammettere; **to l. off** scaricare, lasciar andare, far uscire; **to l. on** far salire, rivelare; **to l. out** emettere, far uscire; **to l. up** rallentare, allentare
lethal ['liːθ(ə)l] *agg.* letale
lethargy ['lɛθədʒɪ] *s.* letargo *m.*
letter ['lɛtəʳ] *s.* lettera *f.* ♦ **capital/small l.** lettera maiuscola/minuscola; **l. box** buca delle lettere; **l. paper** carta da lettere; **registered l.** raccomandata
lettuce ['lɛtɪs] *s.* lattuga *f.*
let-up ['lɛtˌʌp] *s.* diminuzione *f.*
leuk(a)emia [ljuː'kiːmɪə] *s.* leucemia *f.*
level ['lɛvl] **A** *agg.* **1** livellato, piano **2** a livello, pari **3** equilibrato, regolare **B** *s.* **1** livello *m.* **2** superficie *f.* piana ♦ **l. crossing** passaggio a livello; **to be on a l. with sb.** essere sullo stesso piano di qc.
to level ['lɛvl] *v. tr.* livellare, pareggiare, uguagliare ♦ **to l. off** livellarsi
level-headed [ˌlɛvl'hɛdɪd] *agg.* equilibrato
lever ['liːvəʳ] *s.* leva *f.*
leverage ['liːv(ə)rɪdʒ] *s.* **1** azione *f.* di una leva **2** leveraggio *m.* **3** influenza *f.*, autorità *f.*
levity ['lɛvɪtɪ] *s.* frivolezza *f.*
levy ['lɛvɪ] *s.* **1** (*mil.*) leva *f.* **2** imposta *f.*
to levy ['lɛvɪ] *v. tr.* **1** (*mil.*) arruolare **2** tassare
lewd [luːd] *agg.* osceno
lexical ['lɛksɪk(ə)l] *agg.* lessicale
lexicon ['lɛksɪkən] *s.* lessico *m.*
liability [ˌlaɪə'bɪlɪtɪ] *s.* **1** (*dir.*) responsabilità *f.* **2** svantaggio *m.*, inconveniente *m.* **3** *al pl.* (*fin.*) passivo *m.*, debiti *m. pl.*
liable ['laɪəbl] *agg.* **1** (*dir.*) responsabile **2** soggetto, passibile
to liaise [lɪ'eɪz] *v. intr.* fare da collegamento
liaison [lɪ(ː)'eɪzən] *s.* **1** legame *m.*, relazione *f.* **2** collegamento *m.*
liar ['laɪəʳ] *s.* bugiardo *m.*
libel ['laɪb(ə)l] *s.* **1** libello *m.* **2** calunnia *f.*, diffamazione *f.*
to libel ['laɪb(ə)l] *v. tr.* diffamare
liberal ['lɪb(ə)r(ə)l] *agg.* generoso, liberale
liberalism ['lɪb(ə)rəlɪz(ə)m] *s.* liberalismo *m.*
liberalization [ˌlɪb(ə)rəlaɪ'zeɪʃ(ə)n] *s.* liberalizzazione *f.*
to liberate ['lɪbəreɪt] *v. tr.* liberare
libertine ['lɪbətiːn] *agg. e s.* libertino *m.*
liberty ['lɪbətɪ] *s.* libertà *f.*
librarian [laɪ'brɛərɪən] *s.* bibliotecario *m.*
library ['laɪbrərɪ] *s.* biblioteca *f.*
librettist [lɪ'brɛtɪst] *s.* librettista *m. e f.*
libretto [lɪ'brɛtɒʊ] *s.* (*mus.*) libretto *m.*
licence ['laɪs(ə)ns] (*USA* **licence**) *s.* licenza *f.*, autorizzazione *f.*, patente *f.* ♦ **driving l.** patente di guida
licentious [laɪ'sɛnʃəs] *agg.* licenzioso
licit ['lɪsɪt] *agg.* lecito
lick [lɪk] *s.* **1** leccata *f.* **2** piccola quantità *f.*
to lick [lɪk] *v. tr.* leccare
licorice ['lɪkərɪs] *s.* → **liquorice**
lid [lɪd] *s.* coperchio *m.*, copertura *f.*
lie (1) [laɪ] *s.* **1** bugia *f.* **2** falsa credenza *f.*
lie (2) [laɪ] *s.* posizione *f.*, disposizione *f.*, configurazione *f.*
to lie (1) [laɪ] (*pass. e p. p.* **lied**, *p. pres.* **lying**) *v. intr.* mentire, ingannare
to lie (2) [laɪ] (*pass.* **lay**, *p. p.* **lain**, *p. pr.* **lying**) *v. intr.* **1** giacere, star disteso, rimanere **2** trovarsi, essere posto **3** (*dir.*) essere ammissibile ♦ **to l. about** essere sparso qua e là, oziare; **to l. down** coricarsi, sdraiarsi; **to l. up** stare nascosto
lieu [ljuː] *s.* luogo *m.* ♦ **in l. of** in luogo di
lieutenant [lɛf'tɛnənt] *s.* tenente *m.*
life [laɪf] (*pl.* **lives**) *s.* vita *f.* ♦ **l. annuity** vitalizio; **l. insurance** assicurazione sulla vita; **l. preserver** (giubbotto) salvagente;

l. sentence ergastolo; **still l.** natura morta
lifebelt ['laɪfbɛlt] *s.* salvagente *m.*
lifeboat ['laɪfbɒʊt] *s.* battello *m.* di salvataggio
lifeguard ['laɪfgaːd] *s.* bagnino *m.*
lifeless ['laɪflɪs] *agg.* esanime, senza vita
lifelike ['laɪflaɪk] *agg.* realistico
lifelong ['laɪfləŋ] *agg.* che dura tutta una vita
lifesize ['laɪfsaɪz] *agg.* a grandezza naturale
lifespan ['laɪfspæn] *s.* durata *f.* (media) della vita
lifestyle ['laɪfstaɪl] *s.* stile *m.* di vita
lifetime ['laɪftaɪm] *s.* (durata della) vita *f.*
lift [lɪft] *s.* **1** ascensore *m.* **2** (*aer.*) portanza *f.* **3** (*su veicolo*) passaggio *m.*
to lift [lɪft] *v. tr.* **1** sollevare, alzare **2** plagiare, contraffare **3** abolire **4** (*pop.*) rubare ♦ **to l. off** decollare
light (1) [laɪt] **A** *agg.* chiaro, luminoso **B** *s.* **1** luce *f.*, bagliore *m.* **2** lume *m.*, lampada *f.*, faro *m.* **3** *al pl.* semaforo *m.* **4** (*per accendere*) fuoco *m.* ♦ **l. pen** penna ottica; **l. year** anno luce; **parking lights** luci di posizione
light (2) [laɪt] **A** *agg.* **1** leggero, lieve **2** piacevole, divertente **3** moderato **4** agile, svelto **B** *avv.* leggermente, facilmente
to light [laɪt] (*pass. e p. p.* **lighted, lit**) *v. tr.* **1** accendere **2** illuminare ♦ **have you got a l.?** ha da accendere?; **l. bulb** lampadina; **to l. up** illuminare, (*sigaretta e sim.*) accendere
to lighten (1) ['laɪtn] *v. tr. e intr.* illuminare, illuminarsi
to lighten (2) ['laɪtn] *v. tr.* **1** alleggerire **2** mitigare
lighter ['laɪtəʳ] *s.* accendino *m.*
light-headed [ˌlaɪt'hɛdɪd] *agg.* **1** stordito **2** sventato
light-hearted [ˌlaɪt'haːtɪd] *agg.* allegro
lighthouse ['laɪthaʊs] *s.* faro *m.*
lighting ['laɪtɪŋ] *s.* illuminazione *f.*
lightness (1) ['laɪtnɪs] *s.* **1** luminosità *f.* **2** illuminazione *f.*
lightness (2) ['laɪtnɪs] *s.* **1** leggerezza *f.* **2** agilità *f.*
lightning ['laɪtnɪŋ] *s.* lampo *m.*, fulmine *m.* ♦ **l. conductor** (*USA* **l. rod**) parafulmine
like [laɪk] **A** *agg.* simile, somigliante, uguale, stesso **B** *s.* (l')uguale *m.* **C** *prep.* come, alla maniera di, tipico di **D** *avv.* come dire, per così dire **E** *cong.* come, come se ♦ **l. as not** forse; **l. enough** probabilmente; **to be l.** assomigliare
to like [laɪk] *v. tr.* (*costruzione pers.*) **1** piacere, gradire, amare, aver voglia di **2** volere ♦ **as you l.** come vuoi; **to l. best** preferire; **would you l. some coffee?** vuoi del caffè?
likelihood ['laɪklɪhʊd] *s.* probabilità *f.*, verosimiglianza *f.*
likely ['laɪklɪ] **A** *agg.* probabile, verosimile **B** *avv.* probabilmente, verosimilmente
likeness ['laɪknɪs] *s.* somiglianza *f.*
likewise ['laɪkwaɪz] *avv.* similmente, allo stesso modo ♦ **to do l.** fare altrettanto
liking ['laɪkɪŋ] *s.* simpatia *f.*, predilezione *f.*, gradimento *m.*
lilac ['laɪlək] **A** *agg.* lilla **B** *s.* lillà *m.*
lily ['lɪlɪ] *s.* giglio *m.* ♦ **l. of the valley** mughetto
limb [lɪm] *s.* membro *m.*, arto *m.*
limber ['lɪmbəʳ] *agg.* agile, flessibile
to limber ['lɪmbəʳ] *v. tr.* rendere agile, rendere flessibile ♦ **to l. up** scaldarsi i muscoli
lime (1) [laɪm] *s.* tiglio *m.*
lime (2) [laɪm] *s.* lime *m. inv.*, limetta *f.*
lime (3) [laɪm] *s.* calce *f.*
limelight ['laɪmlaɪt] *s.* (luci della) ribalta *f.*
limestone ['laɪmstɒʊn] *s.* calcare *m.*
limit ['lɪmɪt] *s.* limite *m.*
to limit ['lɪmɪt] *v. tr.* limitare
limitation [ˌlɪmɪ'teɪʃ(ə)n] *s.* limitazione *f.*
limited ['lɪmɪtɪd] *agg.* limitato, ristretto ♦ **l. company** società a responsabilità limitata
limousine ['lɪmʊ(ː)ziːn] *s.* limousine *f. inv.*
limp (1) [lɪmp] *s.* andatura *f.* zoppicante ♦ **to have a l.** zoppicare
limp (2) [lɪmp] *agg.* **1** floscio, flaccido **2** fiacco
to limp [lɪmp] *v. intr.* zoppicare
limpet ['lɪmpɪt] *s.* patella *f.*
limpid ['lɪmpɪd] *agg.* limpido
line [laɪn] *s.* **1** linea *f.* **2** riga *f.*, fila *f.* **3** fune *f.* **4** lenza *f.* **5** (linea di) confine *m.* **6** ruga *f.*, solco *m.* **7** verso *m.* ♦ **finishing l.** linea del traguardo; **in l. with** d'accordo con, allineato con; **new l.** (*dettando*) a capo; **shipping l.** compagnia di navigazione; **the L.** l'equatore
to line (1) [laɪn] *v. tr.* **1** delineare, segnare **2** fiancheggiare ♦ **to l. up** allinearsi, mettersi in fila
to line (2) [laɪn] *v. tr.* foderare, rivestire

linear ['lɪnɪəʳ] *agg.* lineare
linearity [ˌlɪnɪ'ærɪtɪ] *s.* linearità *f.*
linen ['lɪnɪn] *s.* **1** tela *f.* di lino **2** biancheria *f.* ♦ **table l.** biancheria da tavola
liner ['laɪnəʳ] *s.* **1** nave *f.* di linea **2** aereo *m.* di linea
linesman ['laɪnzmən] (*pl.* **linesmen**) *s.* segnalinee *m. inv.*
line-up ['laɪnʌp] *s.* **1** allineamento *m.*, schieramento *m.* **2** (*sport*) formazione *f.* di gioco
to linger ['lɪŋgəʳ] *v. intr.* **1** attardarsi **2** permanere
lingo ['lɪŋgɒʊ] (*pl.* **lingoes**) *s.* gergo *m.*, linguaggio *m.*
linguistic [lɪŋ'gwɪstɪk] *agg.* linguistico
linguistics [lɪŋ'gwɪstɪks] *s. pl.* (*v. al sing.*) linguistica *f.*
lining ['laɪnɪŋ] *s.* **1** fodera *f.*, rivestimento *m.* **2** (*autom.*) pastiglia *f.*
link [lɪŋk] *s.* **1** (*di catena*) anello *m.* **2** collegamento *m.*, legame *m.*
to link [lɪŋk] *v. tr.* collegare, unire, congiungere
linoleum [lɪ'nɒʊljəm] *s.* linoleum *m. inv.*
lint [lɪnt] *s.* garza *f.*
lintel ['lɪntl] *s.* architrave *m.*
lion ['laɪən] *s.* leone *m.*
lioness ['laɪənɪs] *s.* leonessa *f.*
lip [lɪp] *s.* **1** labbro *m.* **2** orlo *m.* ♦ **l. service** adesione formale
lipid ['lɪpɪd] *s.* lipide *m.*
lipsalve ['lɪpsaːv] *s.* pomata *f.* per labbra
lipstick ['lɪpstɪk] *s.* rossetto *m.*
to liquefy ['lɪkwɪfaɪ] *v. tr. e intr.* liquefare, liquefarsi
liqueur [lɪ'kjʊəʳ] *s.* liquore *m.*
liquid ['lɪkwɪd] *agg. e s.* liquido *m.*
to liquidate ['lɪkwɪdeɪt] *v. tr.* liquidare
liquidation [ˌlɪkwɪ'deɪʃ(ə)n] *s.* liquidazione *f.*
liquidity [lɪ'kwɪdɪtɪ] *s.* liquidità *f.*
liquor ['lɪkəʳ] *s.* liquore *m.*
liquorice ['lɪkərɪs] (*USA* **licorice**) *s.* liquirizia *f.*
to lisp [lɪsp] *v. intr.* parlare con pronuncia blesa
list [lɪst] *s.* **1** lista *f.*, elenco *m.*, catalogo *m.* **2** listino *m.* ♦ **l. price** prezzo di listino; **mailing l.** indirizzario; **price l.** listino prezzi; **waiting l.** lista d'attesa
to list [lɪst] *v. tr.* **1** elencare, catalogare **2** mettere in listino
to listen ['lɪsn] *v. intr.* ascoltare ♦ **to l. in** ascoltare un programma; **to l. to sb.** ascoltare qc.
listener ['lɪsnəʳ] *s.* ascoltatore *m.*
listless ['lɪstlɪs] *agg.* disattento, sbadato
lit [lɪt] *pass. e p. p. di* **to light**
litany ['lɪtənɪ] *s.* litania *f.*
liter ['liːtəʳ] → **litre**
literacy ['lɪt(ə)rəsɪ] *s.* alfabetizzazione *f.*
literal ['lɪt(ə)r(ə)l] *agg.* letterale
literally ['lɪt(ə)rəlɪ] *avv.* letteralmente
literary ['lɪt(ə)rərɪ] *agg.* letterario
literate ['lɪtərɪt] *agg.* **1** che sa leggere e scrivere **2** colto, istruito
literature ['lɪt(ə)rɪtʃəʳ] *s.* letteratura *f.*
lithe [laɪð] *agg.* agile
lithograph ['lɪθəgraːf] *s.* litografia *f.* (*riproduzione*)
lithography [lɪ'θəgrəfɪ] *s.* litografia *f.* (*arte*)
litigation [ˌlɪtɪ'geɪʃ(ə)n] *s.* (*dir.*) causa *f.*, vertenza *f.*
litre ['liːtəʳ] (*USA* **liter**) *s.* litro *m.*
litter ['lɪtəʳ] *s.* **1** rifiuti *m. pl.* **2** confusione *f.* **3** nidiata *f.* ♦ **l. bin** cestino per i rifiuti
little ['lɪtl] (*comp.* **less, lesser** *sup.* **least**) **A** *agg.* **1** piccolo **2** corto, breve **3** poco **B** *pron. indef. e s.* poco *m.* **C** *avv.* **1** poco **2** (*con art. indeterm.*) piuttosto, alquanto ♦ **a l.** un po' (di); **as l. as possible** il meno possibile; **l. by l.** poco a poco; **l. or nothing** poco o nulla
liturgic(al) [lɪ'tɜːdʒɪk((ə)l)] *agg.* liturgico
liturgy ['lɪtədʒɪ] *s.* liturgia *f.*
live [laɪv] *agg.* **1** vivo **2** (*elettr.*) sotto tensione **3** (*di arma*) carico, (*di proiettile*) inesploso **4** dal vivo, in diretta
to live [lɪv] **A** *v. intr.* **1** vivere **2** abitare, stare **B** *v. tr.* vivere ♦ **to l. down** far dimenticare; **to l. on st.** vivere di q.c.; **to l. up to** essere all'altezza di
livelihood ['laɪvlɪhʊd] *s.* mezzi *m. pl.* di sussistenza
liveliness ['laɪvlɪnɪs] *s.* vivacità *f.*
lively ['laɪvlɪ] *agg.* vivace, animato
to liven ['laɪvn] *v. tr. e intr.* animare, animarsi
liver ['lɪvəʳ] *s.* fegato *m.*
livery (1) ['lɪvərɪ] *s.* livrea *f.*
livery (2) ['lɪvərɪ] *agg.* **1** malato di fegato **2** irritabile
lives [laɪvz] *pl. di* **life**
livestock ['laɪvstək] *s.* bestiame *m.*
livid ['lɪvɪd] *agg.* livido, paonazzo
living ['lɪvɪŋ] **A** *agg.* **1** vivente, vivo **2** profondo, forte **3** di vita **B** *s.* mezzi *m. pl.*

di sussistenza, vita *f.* ♦ **l. conditions** condizioni di vita; **l. standard** tenore di vita; **to earn a l.** guadagnarsi da vivere
living-room ['lɪvɪŋrʊm] *s.* stanza *f.* di soggiorno
lizard ['lɪzəd] *s.* lucertola *f.*
load [lɒʊd] *s.* carico *m.*, peso *m.* ♦ **a l. of** un sacco di
to load [lɒʊd] *v. tr.* **1** caricare **2** appesantire, opprimere, gravare
loaded ['lɒʊdɪd] *agg.* **1** carico, caricato **2** insidioso **3** (*fam.*) ricco
loaf [lɒʊf] (*pl.* **loaves**) *s.* pagnotta *f.*
to loaf [lɒʊf] *v. intr.* bighellonare
loan [lɒʊn] *s.* prestito *m.*
to loan [lɒʊn] *v. tr.* prestare
loath [lɒʊθ] *agg.* restio, riluttante
to loathe [lɒʊð] *v. tr.* detestare, odiare
loaves [lɒʊvz] *pl. di* **loaf**
lobby ['ləbɪ] *s.* **1** atrio *m.*, ridotto *m.*, vestibolo *m.* **2** lobby *f. inv.*, gruppo *m.* di pressione
lobster ['ləbstəʳ] *s.* aragosta *f.*
local ['lɒʊk(ə)l] *agg.* locale
locality [lɒ(ʊ)'kælɪtɪ] *s.* (*USA*) luogo *m.*, vicinanze *f. pl.*
to localize ['lɒʊkəlaɪz] *v. tr.* localizzare
to locate [lɒ(ʊ)'keɪt] *v. tr.* **1** individuare, localizzare **2** situare
location [lɒ(ʊ)'keɪʃ(ə)n] *s.* **1** ubicazione *f.* **2** localizzazione *f.* **3** (*cine.*) (set) esterno *m.*
lock (1) [lək] *s.* **1** serratura *f.* **2** chiusa *f.* **3** (*mecc.*) blocco *m.*
lock (2) [lək] *s.* ciocca *f.*, ricciolo *m.*
to lock [lək] *v. tr.* **1** chiudere (a chiave), serrare **2** mettere sotto chiave **3** bloccare ♦ **to l. in** rinchiudere; **to l. out** chiudere fuori; **to l. up** imprigionare
locker ['ləkəʳ] *s.* armadietto *m.*
locket ['ləkɪt] *s.* medaglione *m.*
locksmith ['lək,smɪθ] *s.* fabbro ferraio *m.*
lockup ['ləkʌp] *s.* (*fam.*) guardina *f.*
locomotive [,lɒʊkə'mɒʊtɪv] *s.* locomotiva *f.*
locust ['lɒʊkəst] *s.* locusta *f.*
lodge [lədʒ] *s.* **1** casetta *f.* **2** portineria *f.* **3** padiglione *m.* di caccia **4** loggia *f.* (massonica) **5** tana *f.*
to lodge [lədʒ] *v. tr.* **1** alloggiare, ospitare **2** assestare, piantare **3** (*dir.*) presentare
lodger ['lədʒəʳ] *s.* pensionante *m. e f.*
lodging ['lədʒɪŋ] *s.* **1** alloggio *m.* **2** *al pl.* appartamento *m.* in affitto, camera *f.* in affitto ♦ **board and l.** vitto e alloggio
loft [ləft] *s.* **1** soffitta *f.*, attico *m.* **2** loft *m. inv.*
lofty ['ləftɪ] *agg.* **1** alto, elevato **2** altero
log [ləg] *s.* **1** tronco *m.*, ceppo *m.* **2** (*naut.*) solcometro *m.* **3** (*naut.*) giornale *m.* di bordo, log *m. inv.*
logbook [ləgbʊk] *s.* **1** (*naut.*) giornale *m.* di bordo, log *m. inv.* **2** (*autom.*) libretto *m.* di circolazione
loggerhead ['ləgəhɛd] *agg.* zuccone, testa di legno ♦ **to be at loggerheads with sb.** essere ai ferri corti con qc.
loggia ['lədʒɪə] *s.* (*arch.*) loggia *f.*
logic ['lədʒɪk] *s.* logica *f.*
logical ['lədʒɪk(ə)l] *agg.* logico
logically ['lədʒɪk(ə)lɪ] *avv.* logicamente
lollipop ['ləlɪpəp] *s.* lecca-lecca *m. inv.*
Londoner ['lʌndənəʳ] *s.* londinese *m. e f.*
lone [lɒʊn] *agg.* solitario
loneliness ['lɒʊnlɪnɪs] *s.* solitudine *f.*
lonely ['lɒʊnlɪ] *agg.* **1** solo, solitario **2** isolato, poco frequentato
long [ləŋ] **A** *agg.* lungo **B** *avv.* a lungo, (per) molto (tempo) ♦ **as l. as** per tutto il tempo che, finché, se; **at l. last** finalmente; **before l.** tra poco; **how l.?** da quanto tempo?, per quanto tempo?; **l. after** molto dopo; **l. ago** molto tempo fa; **l. before** molto tempo prima; **no longer** non più
to long [ləŋ] *v. intr.* desiderare, avere molta voglia di
long-distance [,ləŋ'dɪst(ə)ns] *agg.* che copre una lunga distanza ♦ **l. call** telefonata interurbana
long-haired [,ləŋ'hɛəd] *agg.* dai capelli lunghi
longing ['ləŋɪŋ] *s.* voglia *f.*
longitude ['lən(d)ʒɪtju:d] *s.* longitudine *f.*
longitudinal [,lən(d)ʒɪ'tju:dɪnl] *agg.* longitudinale
long-life ['ləŋlaɪf] *agg.* di lunga durata
long-lived ['ləŋlɪvd] *agg.* durevole
long-range [,ləŋ'reɪn(d)ʒ] *agg.* a lungo raggio
long-sighted [,ləŋ'saɪtɪd] *agg.* presbite
long-standing [,ləŋ'stændɪŋ] *agg.* di vecchia data
long-suffering [,ləŋ'sʌf(ə)rɪŋ] *agg.* paziente, tollerante
longways ['ləŋweɪz] *avv.* per il lungo
long-winded [,ləŋ'wɪndɪd] *agg.* prolisso
loo [lu:] *s.* (*fam.*) gabinetto *m.*

look [lʊk] *s.* **1** sguardo *m.*, occhiata *f.* **2** aspetto *m.* **3** look *m. inv.*, stile *m.*
to look [lʊk] **A** *v. tr.* guardare **B** *v. intr.* **1** guardare, dare un'occhiata a **2** parere, sembrare **3** (*di edificio*) dare su, essere esposto a ♦ **to l. after** curare, curarsi di; **to l. (a)round** guardarsi intorno, dare un'-occhiata; **to l. at** guardare, osservare; **to l. back** guardare indietro, ricordare; **to l. down on** guardare dall'alto in basso; **to l. for** cercare; **to l. forward to** non vedere l'ora di; **to l. in** fare una visitina; **to l. like** assomigliare; **to l. on** considerare; **to l. out** stare in guardia, scovare; **to l. up** alzare lo sguardo; **to l. up to** guardare con rispetto
lookout ['lʊkˌaʊt] *s.* **1** guardia *f.*, vigilanza *f.* **2** posto *m.* di osservazione
loom [luːm] *s.* telaio *m.*
to loom [luːm] *v. intr.* profilarsi, apparire in lontananza
loony ['luːnɪ] *agg.* (*fam.*) pazzo
loop [luːp] *s.* **1** cappio *m.* **2** anello *m.*, occhiello *m.* **3** ansa *f.* **4** (*inf.*) ciclo *m.*
loophole ['luːphɒʊl] *s.* **1** feritoia *f.* **2** scappatoia *f.*
loose [luːs] **A** *agg.* **1** sciolto, slegato **2** (*di vestito*) largo, ampio **3** sciolto, non confezionato **4** vago **B** *s.* libertà *f.*, libero sfogo *m.* ♦ **l. cash/change** spiccioli; **l. end** questione insoluta; **to be at a l. end** non saper che fare
to loose [luːs] *v. tr.* **1** sciogliere, slacciare **2** liberare
to loosen ['luːsn] *v. tr.* **1** sciogliere, slacciare, allentare **2** mitigare ♦ **to l. up** rilassarsi
loot [luːt] *s.* refurtiva *f.*, bottino *m.*
to loot [luːt] *v. tr.* saccheggiare
to lop (1) [lɔp] *v. tr.* tagliare, potare
to lop (2) [lɔp] *v. intr.* pendere, penzolare
lop-sided [ˌlɔp'saɪdɪd] *agg.* sbilenco, asimmetrico
loquacious [lɒ(ʊ)'kweɪʃəs] *agg.* loquace
lord [lɜːd] *s.* **1** signore *m.*, capo *m.*, padrone *m.* **2** lord *m.* ♦ **The L.** il Signore
lore [lɜːʳ] *s.* tradizioni *f. pl.*
lorry ['lɔrɪ] *s.* camion *m. inv.* ♦ **l. driver** camionista
to lose [luːz] (*pass. e p. p.* **lost**) **A** *v. tr.* **1** perdere, smarrire **2** sprecare, sciupare **3** far perdere, sciupare **4** (*di orologio*) rimanere indietro **B** *v. intr.* **1** perdere **2** essere sconfitto **3** (*di orologio*) ritardare ♦ **to l. oneself** perdersi, smarrirsi
loser ['luːzəʳ] *s.* perdente *m. e f.*
loss [lɔs] *s.* **1** perdita *f.* **2** danno *m.*, svantaggio *m.* ♦ **to be at a l.** essere in perdita, essere perplesso
lost [lɔst] **A** *pass. e p. p. di* **to lose** **B** *agg.* smarrito, perduto ♦ **l. property (office)** (ufficio) oggetti smarriti; **to be l.** essere perduto
lot [lɔt] *s.* **1** gran quantità *f.*, mucchio *m.* **2** lotto *m.*, appezzamento *m.* **3** (*comm.*) lotto *m.*, partita *f.* **4** sorte *f.* ♦ **a l. of/lots of** un mucchio di; **the l.** tutto
lotion ['lɒʊʃ(ə)n] *s.* lozione *f.*
lottery ['lɔtərɪ] *s.* lotteria *f.*
lotting ['lɔtɪŋ] *s.* lottizzazione *f.*
loud [laʊd] **A** *agg.* **1** forte, alto **2** sgargiante, vistoso **B** *avv.* forte, ad alta voce
loud-hailer [ˌlaʊd'heɪləʳ] *s.* megafono *m.*
loud-speaker [ˌlaʊd'spiːkəʳ] *s.* altoparlante *m.*
lounge [laʊn(d)ʒ] *s.* salone *m.*, salotto *m.*, sala *f.* (d'albergo)
to lounge [laʊn(d)ʒ] *v. intr.* **1** bighellonare **2** poltrire
lounger ['laʊn(d)ʒəʳ] *s.* fannullone *m.*
louse [laʊs] (*pl.* **lice**) *s.* pidocchio *m.*
lousy ['laʊzɪ] *agg.* **1** pidocchioso **2** schifoso
lout [laʊt] *s.* villano *m.*
lovable ['lʌvəbl] *agg.* amabile, carino
love [lʌv] *s.* amore *m.* ♦ **l. affair** relazione (amorosa); **l. life** vita sentimentale; **to fall in l. with sb.** innamorarsi di qc.; **to make l.** fare l'amore
to love [lʌv] *v. tr.* **1** amare, voler bene **2** provar piacere in ♦ **I l. travelling** mi piace viaggiare
lovely ['lʌvlɪ] *agg.* bello, piacevole, attraente
lover ['lʌvəʳ] *s.* **1** innamorato *m.*, amante *m. e f.* **2** appassionato *m.*
loving ['lʌvɪŋ] *agg.* **1** affettuoso, affezionato **2** d'amore
low [lɒʊ] **A** *agg.* **1** basso **2** profondo **3** umile **4** abietto, volgare **5** scarso, povero di **B** *avv.* **1** in basso, giù **2** a voce bassa ♦ **l. beam headlights** anabbaglianti; **l. fat** a basso contenuto di grassi; **l. season** bassa stagione
to lower ['lɒ(ʊ)əʳ] *v. tr.* **1** abbassare **2** calare, far scendere **3** umiliare
lowland ['lɒʊlənd] *s.* bassopiano *m.*, pianura *f.*
lowly ['lɒʊlɪ] **A** *agg.* umile, modesto **B** *avv.*

umilmente, modestamente
loyal ['lɔɪ(ə)l] *agg.* leale
loyalty ['lɔɪ(ə)ltɪ] *s.* lealtà *f.*
lozenge ['lɔzɪn(d)ʒ] *s.* **1** losanga *f.* **2** pasticca *f.*
lubricant ['lu:brɪkənt] *s.* lubrificante *m.*
to lubricate ['lu:brɪkeɪt] *v. tr.* lubrificare
lubrication [ˌlu:brɪ'keɪʃ(ə)n] *s.* lubrificazione *f.*
lucid ['lu:sɪd] *agg.* lucido
lucidity [lu:'sɪdɪtɪ] *s.* lucidità *f.*
luck [lʌk] *s.* **1** sorte *f.*, destino *m.* **2** fortuna *f.* ♦ **bad l.** sfortuna; **good l.!** buona fortuna!
lucky ['lʌkɪ] *agg.* fortunato
lucre ['lu:kəʳ] *s.* lucro *m.*
ludicrous ['lu:dɪkrəs] *agg.* ridicolo
to luff [lʌf] *v. intr.* (*naut.*) orzare
to lug [lʌg] *v. tr.* tirare, trascinare
luggage ['lʌgɪdʒ] *s.* bagaglio *m.* ♦ **hand l.** bagaglio a mano; **left l. office** deposito bagagli
lukewarm ['lu:kwɜ:m] *agg.* tiepido
lull [lʌl] *s.* momento *m.* di quiete, stasi *f.*
to lull [lʌl] *v. tr.* **1** cullare **2** calmare
lullaby ['lʌləbaɪ] *s.* ninnananna *f.*
lumbago [lʌm'beɪgɒʊ] *s.* lombaggine *f.*
lumber ['lʌmbəʳ] *s.* **1** (*USA*) legname *m.* **2** cianfrusaglie *f. pl.* ♦ **l. room** ripostiglio
lumberjack ['lʌmbəˌdʒæk] *s.* **1** taglialegna *m. inv.* **2** (*USA*) commerciante *m. e f.* in legname
luminosity [ˌlu:mɪ'nɔsɪtɪ] *s.* luminosità *f.*
luminous ['lu:mɪnəs] *agg.* luminoso
lump [lʌmp] *s.* **1** grumo *m.*, zolletta *f.* **2** gonfiore *m.*, protuberanza *f.*
to lump [lʌmp] **A** *v. tr.* ammucchiare, mettere insieme **B** *v. intr.* raggrumarsi
lunacy ['lu:nəsɪ] *s.* demenza *f.*
lunar ['lu:nəʳ] *agg.* lunare
lunatic ['lu:nətɪk] *agg. e s.* pazzo *m.*
lunch [lʌn(t)ʃ] *s.* pranzo *m.* ♦ **l. time** ora di pranzo; **to have l.** pranzare
to lunch [lʌn(t)ʃ] *v. intr.* pranzare
luncheon ['lʌn(t)ʃ(ə)n] *s.* pranzo *m.*
lunette [lu:'nɛt] *s.* lunetta *f.*
lung [lʌŋ] *s.* polmone *m.*
to lunge [lʌndʒ] *v. intr.* balzare in avanti
to lurch [lɜ:tʃ] *v. intr.* **1** (*naut.*) rollare, beccheggiare **2** barcollare
lure [ljʊəʳ] *s.* esca *f.*, richiamo *m.*
to lure [ljʊəʳ] *v. tr.* adescare, allettare
lurid ['ljʊərɪd] *agg.* **1** fosco, livido **2** impressionante, sensazionale
to lurk [lɜ:k] *v. intr.* appostarsi, stare in agguato
luscious ['lʌʃəs] *agg.* delizioso, succulento
lush [lʌʃ] *agg.* lussureggiante
lust [lʌst] *s.* **1** lussuria *f.* **2** brama *f.*, avidità *f.*
to lust [lʌst] *v. intr.* **to l. after/for** bramare, desiderare
lustful ['lʌstf(ʊ)l] *agg.* lussurioso
lustre ['lʌstəʳ] *s.* lustro *m.*
lusty ['lʌstɪ] *agg.* vigoroso
lute [lu:t] *s.* liuto *m.*
Lutheranism ['lu:θ(ə)r(ə)nɪz(ə)m] *s.* luteranesimo *m.*
lutist ['lu:tɪst] *s.* liutaio *m.*
luxuriant [lʌg'zjʊərɪənt] *agg.* lussureggiante, rigoglioso
luxurious [lʌg'zjʊərɪəs] *agg.* lussuoso
luxury ['lʌkʃ(ə)rɪ] *s.* lusso *m.*
lycée ['li:seɪ] *s.* liceo *m.*
lying (1) ['laɪɪŋ] *agg.* bugiardo
lying (2) ['laɪɪŋ] *agg.* giacente
lymph [lɪmf] *s.* linfa *f.*
to lynch [lɪntʃ] *v. tr.* linciare
lynching ['lɪn(t)ʃɪŋ] *s.* linciaggio *m.*
lyre ['laɪəʳ] *s.* (*mus.*) lira *f.*
lyric ['lɪrɪk] **A** *agg.* lirico **B** *s.* **1** lirica *f.* **2** *al pl.* (*di canzone*) testo *m.*
lyricism ['lɪrɪsɪz(ə)m] *s.* lirismo *m.*

M

ma [maː] *s.* (*fam.*) mamma *f.*
mac [mæk] *s.* (*fam.*) → **mackintosh**
macabre [mə'kaːbr] *agg.* macabro
macaroni [ˌmækə'rɒʊnɪ] *s.* pasta *f.*, maccheroni *m. pl.*
to macerate ['mæsəreɪt] *v. tr.* macerare
machination [ˌmækɪ'neɪʃ(ə)n] *s.* macchinazione *f.*, complotto *m.*
machine [mə'ʃiːn] *s.* macchina *f.* ♦ **answering m.** segreteria telefonica; **m. shop** officina meccanica
to machine [mə'ʃiːn] *v. tr.* **1** fare (a macchina) **2** stampare
machinegun [mə'ʃiːngʌn] *s.* mitragliatrice *f.*
machinery [mə'ʃiːnərɪ] *s.* **1** macchinario *m.* **2** meccanismo *m.* **3** (*fig.*) macchina *f.*, organizzazione *f.*
mackerel ['mækr(ə)l] *s.* sgombro *m.* ♦ **m. sky** cielo a pecorelle
mackintosh ['mækɪntəʃ] *s.* impermeabile *m.*
macrobiotic [ˌmækrɒʊbaɪ'ətɪk] *agg.* macrobiotico
macroscopic [ˌmækrɒ(ʊ)'skəpɪk] *agg.* macroscopico
mad [mæd] *agg.* **1** folle, matto **2** furioso, arrabbiato **3** maniaco, entusiasta ♦ **to be m. about** andar matto per
to mad [mæd] *v. intr.* ammattire
madam ['mædəm] *s.* signora *f.* (*al vocativo senza nome proprio*)
to madden ['mædn] **A** *v. tr.* far impazzire **B** *v. intr.* impazzire
made [meɪd] **A** *pass. e p. p. di* **to make** **B** *agg.* **1** fatto, fabbricato **2** adatto ♦ **m.-to-measure** fatto su misura; **m.-up** truccato, alterato
madhouse ['mædhaʊs] *s.* manicomio *m.*
madly ['mædlɪ] *avv.* follemente
madman ['mædmən] (*pl.* **madmen**) *s.* pazzo *m.*
madness ['mædnɪs] *s.* follia *f.*, pazzia *f.*
madrigal ['mædrɪg(ə)l] *s.* madrigale *m.*
maecenas [mɪ(ː)'siːnæs] *s.* mecenate *m. e f.*
magazine [ˌmægə'ziːn] *s.* **1** periodico *m.*, rivista *f.* **2** (*di arma*) caricatore *m.* **3** (*mil.*) magazzino *m.*
maggot ['mægət] *s.* verme *m.*, larva *f.*
maggoty ['mægətɪ] *agg.* bacato
magic ['mædʒɪk] **A** *s.* magia *f.* **B** *agg.* magico
magical ['mædʒɪk(ə)l] *agg.* magico
magician [mə'dʒɪʃ(ə)n] *s.* mago *m.*
magistrate ['mædʒɪstrɪt] *s.* magistrato *m.*, giudice *m.*
magnanimous [mæg'nænɪməs] *agg.* magnanimo
magnate ['mægneɪt] *s.* magnate *m.*
magnet ['mægnɪt] *s.* magnete *m.*
magnetic [mæg'nɛtɪk] *agg.* magnetico
magnetism ['mægnɪtɪz(ə)m] *s.* magnetismo *m.*
magnificence [mæg'nɪfɪsns] *s.* grandiosità *f.*, sfarzo *m.*
magnificent [mæg'nɪfɪs(ə)nt] *agg.* magnifico, superbo
to magnify ['mægnɪfaɪ] *v. tr.* ingrandire ♦ **magnifying glass** lente d'ingrandimento
magnitude ['mægnɪtjuːd] *s.* **1** importanza *f.* **2** (*astr.*) magnitudine *f.*
magnolia [mæg'nɒʊljə] *s.* magnolia *f.*
magpie ['mægpaɪ] *s.* gazza *f.*
mahogany [mə'həgənɪ] *s.* mogano *m.*
maid [meɪd] *s.* cameriera *f.*, donna *f.* di servizio
maiden ['meɪdn] **A** *s.* **1** (*letter.*) fanciulla *f.* **2** zitella *f.* **B** *agg.* **1** virginale **2** nubile **3** primo, inaugurale, da esordiente ♦ **m. name** cognome da ragazza
maidenhair ['meɪdnˌhɛəʳ] *s.* capelvenere *m.*
maidenhood ['meɪdnhʊd] *s.* (*di ragazza*) fanciullezza *f.*, verginità *f.*
mail [meɪl] *s.* posta *f.* ♦ **by air m.** per posta aerea; **m. order** ordinazione per corrispondenza
to mail [meɪl] *v. tr.* **1** mandare per posta **2** imbucare
mailbox ['meɪlbəks] *s.* (*USA*) cassetta *f.* delle lettere
mailing ['meɪlɪŋ] *s.* mailing *m. inv.* ♦ **m. list** indirizzario
mailman ['meɪlmæn] (*pl.* **mailmen**) *s.* postino *m.*
to maim [meɪm] *v. tr.* mutilare, menomare

main [meɪn] **A** *agg.* principale **B** *s.* **1** conduttura *f.* principale **2** *al pl.* (*elettr*) rete *f.* d'alimentazione ♦ **in the m.** nel complesso; **m. road** strada maestra; **m. street** (*USA*) strada principale
mainframe ['meɪnfreɪm] *s.* (*inf.*) mainframe *m. inv.*
mainland ['meɪnlənd] **A** *agg.* continentale **B** *s.* terraferma *f.*, continente *m.*
mainly ['meɪnlɪ] *avv.* **1** principalmente **2** nel complesso
mainsail ['meɪnseɪl] *s.* (*naut.*) randa *f.*
mainstream ['meɪnˌstriːm] **A** *agg.* tradizionale **B** *s.* corrente *f.* principale
to maintain [meɪn'teɪn] *v. tr.* **1** mantenere, conservare **2** sostentare **3** curare la manutenzione di, mantenere in efficienza **4** affermare
maintenance ['meɪntɪnəns] *s.* **1** mantenimento *m.* **2** sostentamento *m.* **3** (*dir*) alimenti *m. pl.* **4** manutenzione *f.*
maize [meɪz] *s.* granturco *m.*, mais *m.*
majestic [mə'dʒɛstɪk] *agg.* maestoso
majesty ['mædʒɪstɪ] *s.* maestà *f.* ♦ **His/Her M.** Sua Maestà
majolica [mə'jəlɪkə] *s.* maiolica *f.*
major ['meɪdʒəʳ] **A** *agg.* maggiore, principale **B** *s.* **1** maggiorenne *m. e f.* **2** (*mil.*) maggiore *m.*
majority [mə'dʒərɪtɪ] *s.* maggioranza *f.*
make [meɪk] *s.* **1** fattura *f.*, forma *f.* **2** fabbricazione *f.*, marca *f.*
to make [meɪk] (*pass. e p. p.* **made**) *v. tr.* **1** fare, creare, costruire, comporre, preparare **2** far diventare **3** compiere, commettere **4** calcolare, assommare a, guadagnare **5** diventare ♦ **to m. away** allontanarsi in fretta; **to m. for** dirigersi; **to m. of** capire; **to m. off** svignarsela; **to m. oneself understood** farsi capire; **to m. out** compilare, dichiarare, cavarsela; **to m. st. do** far bastare q.c.; **to m. up** riconciliarsi, truccare, truccarsi, inventare, fare, confezionare
make-believe ['meɪkbɪˌliːv] *s.* finzione *f.*
maker ['meɪkəʳ] *s.* creatore *m.*, fabbricante *m.*
makeshift ['meɪkʃɪft] **A** *agg.* improvvisato, di fortuna **B** *s.* ripiego *m.*
make-up ['meɪkʌp] *s.* **1** trucco *m.* **2** composizione *f.*, formazione *f.* **3** disposizione *f.*, temperamento *m.*
making ['meɪkɪŋ] *s.* **1** fattura *f.*, confezione *f.* **2** sviluppo *m.*, formazione *f.* **3** *al pl.* occorrente *m.*, qualità *f. pl.* necessarie ♦ **in the m.** in via di formazione
maladjusted [ˌmælə'dʒʌstɪd] *agg.* disadattato
malaise [mæ'leɪz] *s.* malessere *m.*
malaria [mə'lɛərɪə] *s.* malaria *f.*
male [meɪl] **A** *agg.* maschile, maschio **B** *s.* maschio *m.* ♦ **m. chauvinist** maschilista; **m. nurse** infermiere
malediction [ˌmælɪ'dɪkʃ(ə)n] *s.* maledizione *f.*
malefic [mə'lɛfɪk] *agg.* malefico
malevolent [mə'lɛvələnt] *agg.* malevolo
malformation ['mælfɜː'meɪʃ(ə)n] *s.* (*med.*) malformazione *f.*
malfunction [mæl'fʌŋkʃ(ə)n] *s.* malfunzionamento *m.*
malice ['mælɪs] *s.* **1** malizia *f.* **2** malevolenza *f.*, astio *m.* **3** (*dir.*) dolo *m.*
malicious [mə'lɪʃəs] *agg.* **1** maligno, malizioso **2** (*dir*) doloso
malign [mə'laɪn] *agg.* maligno
to malign [mə'laɪn] *v. tr.* malignare su, diffamare
malignant [mə'lɪgnənt] *agg.* maligno
malignity [mə'lɪgnɪtɪ] *s.* malignità *f.*
mall [mɜːl] *s.* **1** viale *m.* **2** centro *m.* commerciale
malleable ['mælɪəbl] *agg.* malleabile
malleolus [mə'liːɒ(ʊ)ləs] *s.* malleolo *m.*
mallet ['mælɪt] *s.* maglio *m.*, mazza *f.*
mallow ['mælɒʊ] *s.* malva *f.*
malnutrition [ˌmælnjʊ(ː)'trɪʃ(ə)n] *s.* malnutrizione *f.*, denutrizione *f.*
malpractice [ˌmæl'præktɪs] *s.* azione *f.* illecita
malt [mɜːlt] *s.* malto *m.*
to maltreat [mæl'triːt] *v. tr.* maltrattare
mammal ['mæm(ə)l] *s.* mammifero *m.*
mammalian [mæ'meɪljɛn] *agg. e s.* mammifero *m.*
mammoth ['mæməθ] **A** *s.* mammut *m. inv.* **B** *agg.* mastodontico
man [mæn] (*pl.* **men**) *s.* **1** uomo *m.* **2** domestico *m.*, operaio *m.*, soldato *m.*, giocatore *m.* **3** marito *m.*, amante *m.* **4** (*gioco della dama*) pedina *f.* ♦ **m.-made** artificiale
to manage ['mænɪdʒ] **A** *v. tr.* **1** amministrare, gestire **2** saper trattare **3** maneggiare, manovrare **B** *v. intr.* riuscire, cavarsela
manageable ['mænɪdʒəbl] *agg.* **1** maneggevole **2** trattabile **3** agevole

management ['mænɪdʒmənt] *s.* **1** amministrazione *f.*, direzione *f.*, gestione *f.* **2** (*v. al pl.*) i dirigenti *m. pl.*, la direzione *f.*
manager ['mænɪdʒəʳ] *s.* **1** direttore *m.*, gestore *m.*, dirigente *m. e f.* **2** impresario *m.*, manager *m. inv.* ♦ **general m.** direttore generale
manageress ['mænɪdʒərɛs] *s.* direttrice *f.*
managerial [ˌmænə'dʒɪərɪəl] *agg.* direttivo, manageriale
managing ['mænɪdʒɪŋ] *agg.* dirigente, direttivo ♦ **m. director** amministratore *m.* delegato
mandarin ['mændərɪn] *s.* mandarino *m.*
mandatory ['mændət(ə)rɪ] **A** *agg.* obbligatorio **B** *s.* mandatario *m.*
mandible ['mændɪbl] *s.* mandibola *f.*
mandolin(e) [ˌmændə'liːn] *s.* mandolino *m.*
mandrel ['mændr(ə)l] *s.* mandrino *m.*
mane [meɪn] *s.* criniera *f.*
manège [mæ'neɪʒ] *s.* maneggio *m.*
maneuver [mə'nuːvəʳ] → **manoeuvre**
manful ['mænf(ʊ)l] *agg.* valoroso
manger ['meɪn(d)ʒəʳ] *s.* mangiatoia *f.*
to mangle ['mæŋgl] *v. tr.* straziare, mutilare
mango ['mæŋgɒʊ] *s.* mango *m.*
mangrove ['mæŋgrɒʊv] *s.* mangrovia *f.*
to manhandle ['mænˌhændl] *v. tr.* **1** manovrare **2** (*fam.*) maltrattare
manhole ['mænhɒʊl] *s.* botola *f.* ♦ **m. cover** tombino
manhood ['mænhʊd] *s.* virilità *f.*
manhunt ['mænhʌnt] *s.* caccia *f.* all'uomo
mania ['meɪnjə] *s.* mania *f.*
maniac ['meɪnɪæk] *agg.* maniaco
manicure ['mænɪkjʊəʳ] *s.* manicure *f. inv.* ♦ **m. set** necessaire da unghie
manifest ['mənɪfɛst] *agg.* manifesto, palese
to manifest ['mænɪfɛst] **A** *v. tr.* manifestare, mostrare **B** *v. intr.* manifestarsi, apparire
manifestation [ˌmænɪfɛs'teɪʃ(ə)n] *s.* manifestazione *f.*
manifesto [ˌmænɪ'fɛstɒʊ] *s.* manifesto *m.* (*ideologico, politico*)
manifold ['mænɪfɒʊld] *agg.* molteplice, vario
to manipulate [mə'nɪpjʊleɪt] *v. tr.* manipolare
manipulation [məˌnɪpjʊ'leɪʃ(ə)n] *s.* manipolazione *f.*
mankind [mæn'kaɪnd] *s.* genere *m.* umano
manliness ['mænlɪnɪs] *s.* virilità *f.*
manly ['mænlɪ] *agg.* maschio, virile
manna ['mænə] *s.* manna *f.*
manner ['mænəʳ] *s.* **1** modo *m.*, maniera *f.* **2** contegno *m.* **3** *al pl.* usanze *f. pl.* **4** specie *f.*, tipo *m.*, sorta *f.* ♦ **good/bad manners** belle/cattive maniere
mannerism ['mænərɪz(ə)m] *s.* **1** affettazione *f.* **2** manierismo *m.*
manoeuvre [mə'nuːvəʳ] (*USA* **maneuvre**) *s.* manovra *f.*
to manoeuvre [mə'nuːvəʳ] (*USA* **to maneuvre**) *v. tr. e intr.* manovrare
manometer [mə'nəmɪtəʳ] *s.* manometro *m.*
manor ['mænəʳ] *s.* proprietà *f.* terriera, feudo *m.* ♦ **m.-house** maniero, residenza di campagna
manpower ['mænˌpaʊəʳ] *s.* manodopera *f.*
mansard ['mænsaːd] *s.* mansarda *f.*
mansion ['mænʃ(ə)n] *s.* palazzo *m.*, dimora *f.* ♦ **m.-house** castello, residenza di campagna
manslaughter ['mænˌslɜːtəʳ] *s.* (*dir.*) omicidio *m.* colposo
mantelpiece ['mæntlˌpiːs] *s.* mensola *f.* del caminetto
mantle ['mæntl] *s.* mantello *m.*, manto *m.*
manual ['mænjʊəl] *agg. e s.* manuale *m.* ♦ **m. dexterity** abilità manuale
manufacture [ˌmænjʊ'fæktʃəʳ] *s.* manifattura *f.*, lavorazione *f.*, fabbricazione *f.*
to manufacture [ˌmænjʊ'fæktʃəʳ] *v. tr.* fabbricare, confezionare, produrre
manufacturer [ˌmænjʊ'fæktʃərəʳ] *s.* fabbricante *m.*, industriale *m.*
manufacturing [ˌmænjʊ'fæktʃərɪŋ] **A** *agg.* **1** manifatturiero **2** industriale **B** *s.* manifattura *f.*, produzione *f.*
manumission [ˌmænjʊ'mɪʃ(ə)n] *s.* (*stor.*) manomissione *f.*
manure [mə'njʊəʳ] *s.* concime *m.*, letame *m.*
to manure [mə'njʊəʳ] *v. tr.* concimare
manuscript ['mænjʊskrɪpt] *s.* manoscritto *m.*
many ['mɛnɪ] (*comp.* **more**, *sup.* **most**) **A** *agg.* molti, numerosi, un gran numero di **B** *pron.* molti **C** *s.* molti *m. pl.* molte persone *f. pl.* ♦ **a great m.** moltissimi; **as m.** altrettanti; **how m.?** quanti?; **m. sided** multiforme; **too m.** troppi
map [mæp] *s.* carta *f.* geografica, mappa *f.*
to map [mæp] *v. tr.* rilevare una carta, mappa

♦ **to m. out** progettare
maple ['meɪpl] *s.* acero *m.*
to mar [maːʳ] *v. tr.* danneggiare, guastare
marathon ['mærəθ(ə)n] *s.* maratona *f.*
to maraud [mə'rɜːd] *v. tr.* rubare, saccheggiare
marauder [mə'rɜːdəʳ] *s.* predone *m.*, predatore *m.*
marble ['maːbl] *s.* **1** marmo *m.* **2** bilia *f.* ♦ **m.-cutter** marmista; **m.-paper** carta marmorizzata
March [maːtʃ] *s.* marzo *m.*
march [maːtʃ] *s.* marcia *f.*
to march [maːtʃ] *v. intr.* marciare
mare [mɛəʳ] *s.* cavalla *f.*, giumenta *f.*
margarine [ˌmaːdʒə'riːn] *s.* margarina *f.*
margin ['maːdʒɪn] *s.* margine *m.*
marginal ['maːdʒɪn(ə)l] *agg.* marginale
to marginalize ['maːdʃɪnəlaɪz] *v. tr.* emarginare
marigold ['mærɪgɒʊld] *s.* calendola *f.*
marina [mə'riːnə] *s.* porticciolo *m.* turistico, marina *m. inv.*
marine [mə'riːn] **A** *agg.* **1** marino, marittimo **2** navale **B** *s.* **1** marina *f.* **2** (*mil.*) marine *m.*
mariner ['mærɪnəʳ] *s.* marinaio *m.*
marital [mə'raɪtl] *agg.* maritale, coniugale
maritime ['mærɪtaɪm] *agg.* marittimo
marjoram ['maːdʒ(ə)rəm] *s.* maggiorana *f.*
mark (1) [maːk] *s.* **1** segno *m.*, impronta *f.* **2** marca *f.*, marchio *m.* **3** voto *m.* **4** segno *m.* di interpunzione **5** (*sulla pelle*) macchia *f.*, voglia *f.* **6** bersaglio *m.* ♦ **exclamation m.** punto esclamativo; **question m.** punto interrogativo; **quotation marks** virgolette
mark (2) [maːk] *s.* (*moneta*) marco *m.*
to mark [maːk] *v. tr.* **1** segnare, marcare **2** contraddistinguere **3** dare un voto a ♦ **to m. down** (*prezzo*) ribassare; **to m. out** tracciare, delimitare
marked [maːkt] *agg.* **1** contrassegnato, marcato **2** considerevole, notevole
marker ['maːkəʳ] *s.* **1** segnapunti *m.* **2** segnalibro *m.* **3** segnale *m.*
market ['maːkɪt] *s.* mercato *m.* ♦ **m. place** (piazza del) mercato; **m. price** prezzo di mercato; **m. research** ricerca di mercato; **to play the m.** giocare in Borsa
marketable ['maːkɪtəbl] *agg.* vendibile
marketing ['maːkɪtɪŋ] *s.* **1** commercializzazione *f.* **2** marketing *m. inv.*
marksman ['maːksmən] (*pl.* **marksmen**) *s.* tiratore *m.* scelto
marmalade ['maːməleɪd] *s.* marmellata *f.* di agrumi
marmot ['maːmət] *s.* marmotta *f.*
maroon [mə'ruːn] *agg. e s.* marrone *m.* rossiccio
marquee [maː'kiː] *s.* tendone *m.*
marquess ['maːkwɪs] *s.* marchese *m.*
marquis ['maːkwɪs] *s.* marchese *m.*
marriage ['mærɪdʒ] *s.* matrimonio *m.* ♦ **m. licence** licenza di matrimonio; **to take in m.** prendere per marito (o per moglie)
married ['mærɪd] *agg.* **1** sposato **2** coniugale ♦ **to get m.** sposarsi
marrow ['mærɒʊ] *s.* **1** (*anat.*) midollo *m.* **2** (*bot.*) zucca *f.* ♦ **m. squash** zucchino
marrowbone ['mærɒ(ʊ)bɒʊn] *s.* ossobuco *m.*
to marry ['mærɪ] *v. tr.* sposare, sposarsi ♦ **to m. again** risposarsi
marsh [maːʃ] *s.* acquitrino *m.*, palude *f.*
marshal ['maːʃ(ə)l] *s.* **1** maresciallo *m.* **2** cerimoniere *m.*
to marshal ['maːʃ(ə)l] *v. tr.* ordinare, schierare
marshy ['maːʃɪ] *agg.* paludoso
martial ['maːʃ(ə)l] *agg.* marziale ♦ **m. court** corte marziale; **m. law** legge marziale
Martian ['maːʃjən] *agg. e s.* marziano *m.*
martyr ['maːtəʳ] *s.* martire *m. e f.*
martyrdom ['maːtədəm] *s.* martirio *m.*
marvel ['maːv(ə)l] *s.* meraviglia *f.*
to marvel ['maːv(ə)l] *v. intr.* meravigliarsi, stupirsi
marvellous ['maːvɪləs] *agg.* meraviglioso, stupendo
Marxism ['maːksɪz(ə)m] *s.* marxismo *m.*
Marxist ['maːksɪst] *agg. e s.* marxista *m. e f.*
marzipan [ˌmaːzɪ'pæn] *s.* marzapane *m.*
mascara [mæs'kaːrə] *s.* mascara *m. inv.*
mascot ['mæskət] *s.* mascotte *f. inv.*
masculine ['maːskjʊlɪn] *agg.* maschile, mascolino
mash [mæʃ] *s.* **1** poltiglia *f.*, pastone *m.* **2** purè *m. inv.*
to mash [mæʃ] *v. tr.* **1** schiacciare **2** macerare ♦ **mashed potatoes** purè di patate
masher ['mæʃəʳ] *s.* passaverdure *m.*
mask [maːsk] *s.* maschera *f.*
to mask [maːsk] *v. tr.* **1** mascherare **2** nascondere

masochism ['mæsəkɪz(ə)m] *s.* masochismo *m.*
mason ['meɪsn] *s.* **1** muratore *m.* **2** massone *m.*
masonry ['meɪs(ə)nrɪ] *s.* **1** muratura *m.* **2** massoneria *f.*
masquerade [ˌmæskə'reɪd] *s.* **1** finzione *f.* **2** mascherata *f.*, ballo *m.* in maschera
to **masquerade** [ˌmæskə'reɪd] *v. intr.* **1** mascherarsi **2** fingersi, farsi passare per
mass (1) [mæs] **A** *s.* **1** massa *f.*, quantità *f.* **2** folla *f.*, moltitudine *f.* **3** ammasso *m.* **4** (*fis.*) massa *f.* **B** *agg.* di massa ♦ **m. media** mezzi di comunicazione di massa
mass (2) [mæs] *s.* messa *f.* ♦ **to attend m.** andare a messa; **m. book** messale
to **mass** [mæs] *v. tr. e intr.* ammassare, ammassarsi
massacre ['mæsəkəʳ] *s.* massacro *m.*
massage ['mæsaːʒ] *s.* massaggio *m.*
to **massage** ['mæsaːʒ] *v. tr.* massaggiare
masseur [mæ'səʳ] *s.* massaggiatore *m.*
massif ['mæsiːf] *s.* (*geogr.*) massiccio *m.*
massive ['mæsɪv] *agg.* **1** massiccio, imponente **2** massivo, potente
mass-production ['mæsprəˌdʌkʃ(ə)n] *s.* produzione *f.* in serie
mast [maːst] *s.* (*naut.*) albero *m.*
master ['maːstəʳ] **A** *s.* **1** padrone *m.*, datore *m.* di lavoro **2** maestro *m.* **3** insegnante *m.*, professore *m.* **4** capo *m.*, direttore *m.* **5** originale *m.* (*da riprodurre*) **6** (*titolo accademico*) master *m. inv.* **B** *agg.* **1** padrone **2** principale **3** generale
to **master** ['maːstəʳ] *v. tr.* **1** approfondire, conoscere a fondo **2** dominare
masterly ['maːstəlɪ] *agg.* magistrale
mastermind ['maːstəmaɪnd] *s.* mente *f.* direttiva
masterpiece ['maːstəpiːs] *s.* capolavoro *m.*
mastery ['maːst(ə)rɪ] *s.* **1** dominio *m.*, padronanza *f.* **2** perizia *f.*, abilità *f.*
mastic ['mæstɪk] *s.* mastice *m.*
to **masticate** ['mæstɪkeɪt] *v. tr.* masticare
mastodontic [ˌmæstə'dəntɪk] *agg.* mastodontico
mat (1) [mæt] *s.* **1** stuoia *f.*, zerbino *m.* **2** sottopiatto *m.* **3** groviglio *m.*
mat (2) [mæt] *agg.* opaco
match (1) [mætʃ] *s.* **1** incontro *m.*, partita *f.* **2** compagno *m.*, (l')uguale *m.* **3** matrimonio *m.*, partito *m.* **4** coppia *f.*
match (2) [mætʃ] *s.* fiammifero *m.*
to **match** [mætʃ] **A** *v. tr.* **1** pareggiare, uguagliare **2** armonizzare, accompagnare **3** confrontare **4** accoppiare, unire in matrimonio **B** *v. intr.* **1** armonizzare, accordarsi, essere compatibile **2** competere, confrontarsi **3** combaciare
matching ['mætʃɪŋ] *agg.* ben assortito
mate [meɪt] *s.* **1** compagno *m.*, amico *m.* **2** coniuge *m. e f.* **3** aiutante *m. e f.* **4** (*naut.*) ufficiale *m.* in seconda
to **mate** [meɪt] *v. tr. e intr.* accoppiare, accoppiarsi
material [mə'tɪərɪəl] **A** *agg.* materiale **B** *s.* **1** materiale *m.*, sostanza *f.* **2** stoffa *f.* **3** *al pl.* occorrente *m.*, accessori *m. pl.*
materialism [mə'tɪərɪəlɪz(ə)m] *s.* materialismo *m.*
maternal [mə'tɜːnl] *agg.* materno
maternity [mə'tɜːnɪtɪ] *s.* maternità *f.* ♦ **m. leave** congedo per maternità
mathematic(al) [ˌməθɪ'mætɪk((ə)l)] *agg.* matematico
mathematics [ˌmæθɪ'mætɪks] *s. pl.* (*v. al sing.*) matematica *f.*
maths [mæθs] (*USA* **math**) *s. pl.* (*v. al sing.*) (*fam.*) matematica *f.*
matriarchal [ˌmeɪtrɪ'aːk(ə)l] *agg.* matriarcale
matriarchy ['meɪtrɪɑ(ː)kɪ] *s.* matriarcato *m.*
to **matriculate** [mə'trɪkjʊleɪt] *v. intr.* iscriversi all'università
matriculation [məˌtrɪkjʊ'leɪʃ(ə)n] *s.* immatricolazione *f.*, iscrizione *f.* (all'università)
matrimonial [ˌmætrɪ'mɒʊnjəl] *agg.* matrimoniale
matrimony ['mætrɪm(ə)nɪ] *s.* matrimonio *m.*
matrix ['meɪtrɪks] *s.* matrice *f.*
matron ['meɪtr(ə)n] *s.* **1** matrona *f.* **2** capo infermiera *f.*, governante *f.*
matted ['mætɪd] *agg.* ingarbugliato
matter ['mætəʳ] *s.* **1** affare *m.*, argomento *m.*, faccenda *f.* **2** importanza *f.* **3** materia *f.*, sostanza *f.*, contenuto *m.* ♦ **as a m. of fact** in verità; **no m.** non importa; **what is the m.?** cosa c'è?
to **matter** ['mætəʳ] *v. intr.* interessare
matter-of-fact [ˌmæt(ə)rəv'fækt] *agg.* prosaico, realistico
mattock ['mætək] *s.* zappa *f.*
mattress ['mætrɪs] *s.* materasso *m.*
maturation [ˌmætjʊə'reɪʃ(ə)n] *s.* matura-

zione *f.*
mature [mə'tjʊəʳ] *agg.* maturo
to mature [mə'tjʊəʳ] **A** *v. tr.* **1** far maturare, far stagionare **2** completare **B** *v. intr.* **1** maturare **2** completarsi **3** (*fin.*) maturare, scadere
maturity [mə'tjʊərɪtɪ] *s.* maturità *f.*
to maul [mɜːl] *v. tr.* **1** battere **2** bistrattare
mausoleum [ˌmɜːsə'lɪəm] *s.* mausoleo *m.*
mauve [mɒʊv] *agg. e s.* (color) malva *m.*
maxim ['mæksɪm] *s.* massima *f.*
maximalism ['mæksɪməlɪz(ə)m] *s.* massimalismo *m.*
maximum ['mæksɪməm] *agg. e s.* massimo *m.*
may [meɪ] (*congiuntivo pass. e condiz.* **might**) *v. difett.* **1** (*permesso*) potere, essere permesso, essere lecito (ES: **m. I speak?** posso parlare?) **2** (*possibilità, probabilità*) potere, essere possibile, essere probabile (ES: **it m. be true** può essere vero, **it might be very important** potrebbe essere molto importante) **3** (*augurio, speranza, richiesta, rimprovero, ecc.*) potere (ES: **m. you live in peace!** che tu possa vivere in pace!)
May [meɪ] *s.* maggio *m.* ♦ **M. Day** il primo maggio
maybe ['meɪbiː] *avv.* forse, probabilmente, può darsi che
mayhem ['meɪhɛm] *s.* confusione *f.*
mayonnaise [ˌmeɪə'neɪz] *s.* maionese *f.*
mayor [mɛəʳ] *s.* sindaco *m.*
maze [meɪz] *s.* dedalo *m.*, labirinto *m.* ♦ **to be in a m.** essere confuso
me [miː, mɪ] *pron. pers. 1ª sing.* (*compl.*) me, mi ♦ **it's me** sono io
meadow ['mɛdɒʊ] *s.* prato *m.*
meagre ['miːgəʳ] (*USA* **meager**) *agg.* magro, smunto
meal (1) [miːl] *s.* farina *f.*
meal (2) [miːl] *s.* pasto *m.* ♦ **m. ticket** buono pasto
mealtime ['miːltaɪm] *s.* ora *f.* dei pasti
mean (1) [miːn] *agg.* **1** gretto, meschino, avaro **2** sgarbato **3** miserabile, mediocre, spregevole
mean (2) [miːn] **A** *agg.* medio, intermedio **B** *s.* **1** mezzo *m.*, media *f.* **2** mezzo *m.*, strumento *m.*, maniera *f.* **3** *al pl.* mezzi *m.* economici, risorse *f. pl.* ♦ **by all means** con ogni mezzo; **by means of** per mezzo di
to mean [miːn] (*pass. e p. p.* **meant**) **A** *v. tr.* **1** significare, intendere **2** comportare, implicare **3** proporsi di, avere intenzione di **4** destinare, assegnare **B** *v. intr.* **1** voler dire, pensare **2** avere intenzione
meander [mɪ'ændəʳ] *s.* meandro *m.*
meaning ['miːnɪŋ] *s.* **1** significato *m.*, senso *m.* **2** pensiero *m.* **3** proposito *m.*
meaningful ['miːnɪŋfʊl] *agg.* significativo
meaningless ['miːnɪŋlɪs] *agg.* insignificante, senza senso
meant [mɛnt] *pass. e p. p. di* **to mean**
meantime ['miːnˌtaɪm] *avv.* intanto, nel frattempo ♦ **in the m.** nel frattempo
meanwhile [ˌmiːn'waɪl] *avv.* intanto, nel frattempo
measles ['miːzlz] *s. pl.* (*v. al sing.*) morbillo *m.*
measly ['miːzlɪ] *agg.* (*fam.*) miserabile, meschino
measurable ['məz(ə)rəbl] *agg.* misurabile
measure ['mɛʒəʳ] *s.* **1** misura *f.* **2** provvedimento *m.*
to measure ['məʒəʳ] *v. tr. e intr.* misurare ♦ **to m. out** dosare
measurement ['mɛʒəmənt] *s.* **1** misurazione *f.* **2** misura *f.*, dimensione *f.*
meat [miːt] *s.* carne *f.* ♦ **m. ball** polpetta; **m. grinder** tritacarne; **m. skewer** spiedino di carne
mechanic [mɪ'kænɪk] *s.* meccanico *m.*
mechanical [mɪ'kænɪk(ə)l] *agg.* meccanico
mechanics [mɪ'kænɪks] *s. pl.* (*v. al sing.*) meccanica *f.*
mechanism ['mɛkənɪz(ə)m] *s.* meccanismo *m.*
mechanization [ˌmɛkənaɪ'zeɪʃ(ə)n] *s.* meccanizzazione *f.*
medal ['mɛdl] *s.* medaglia *f.*
medallion [mɪ'dæljən] *s.* medaglione *m.*
to meddle ['mɛdl] *v. intr.* immischiarsi, interferire
media ['miːdjə] *s. pl.* mezzi *m.* di comunicazione di massa, media *m. pl.*
median ['miːdjən] *agg.* medio, mediano ♦ **m. strip** (*USA*) spartitraffico
to mediate ['miːdɪeɪt] *v. tr. e intr.* mediare
mediator ['miːdɪeɪtəʳ] *s.* mediatore *m.*
medical ['mɛdɪk(ə)l] **A** *agg.* medico, sanitario **B** *s.* visita *f.* medica
medicament [mɛ'dɪkəmənt] *s.* medicamento *m.*, farmaco *m.*
to medicate ['mɛdɪkeɪt] *v. tr.* medicare, curare
medicinal [mɛ'dɪsɪnl] *agg.* medicinale

medicine ['mɛdɪs(ɪ)n] *s.* medicina *f.*
medieval [ˌmɛdɪ'iːv(ə)l] *agg.* medievale
mediocre ['miːdɪɒʊkəʳ] *agg.* mediocre
mediocrity [ˌmiːdɪ'əkrɪtɪ] *s.* mediocrità *f.*
to meditate ['mɛdɪteɪt] *v. tr. e intr.* meditare
meditation [ˌmɛdɪ'teɪʃ(ə)n] *s.* meditazione *f.*
Mediterranean [ˌmɛdɪtə'reɪnjən] *agg.* mediterraneo
medium ['miːdjəm] **A** *agg.* medio **B** *s.* **1** mezzo *m.*, strumento *m.* **2** ambiente *m.*, elemento *m.* ♦ **m.-wave** a onde medie
medlar ['mɛdləʳ] *s.* nespola *f.*
medley ['mɛdlɪ] *s.* mescolanza *f.*
medusa [mɪ'djuːzə] *s.* medusa *f.*
meek [miːk] *agg.* docile, mite
to meet [miːt] (*pass. e p. p.* **met**) **A** *v. tr.* **1** incontrare, andare incontro, incrociare **2** conoscere, fare la conoscenza di **3** soddisfare, corrispondere, far fronte **4** affrontare **B** *v. intr.* **1** incontrarsi, riunirsi **2** conoscersi, far conoscenza ♦ **to m. up with** imbattersi in; **to m. with** incontrare
meeting ['miːtɪŋ] *s.* **1** riunione *f.*, convegno *m.*, meeting *m. inv.* **2** incontro *m.*
megalithic [ˌmɛgə'lɪθɪk] *agg.* megalitico
megalomaniac [ˌmɛgəlɒ(ʊ)'meɪnɪæk] *agg. e s.* megalomane *m. e f.*
megaphone ['mɛgəfɒʊn] *s.* megafono *m.*
melancholic [ˌmɛlən'kəlɪk] *agg.* malinconico
melancholy ['mɛlənkəlɪ] **A** *s.* malinconia *f.* **B** *agg.* malinconico
mellow ['mɛlɒʊ] *agg.* **1** maturo, succoso **2** fertile, ricco **3** comprensivo, pacato **4** pastoso, (*di luce, suono, ecc.*) caldo
melodious [mɪ'lɒʊdjəs] *agg.* melodioso
melodramatic [ˌmɛlɒ(ʊ)drə'mætɪk] *agg.* melodrammatico
melody ['mɛlədɪ] *s.* melodia *f.*
melon ['mɛlən] *s.* melone *m.*
to melt [mɛlt] *v. tr. e intr.* fondere, liquefare, sciogliere
melting ['mɛltɪŋ] **A** *agg.* **1** fondente **2** struggente **B** *s.* fusione *f.* ♦ **m. pot** crogiolo
member ['mɛmbəʳ] *s.* **1** membro *m.*, socio *m.* **2** elemento *m.*
membership ['mɛmbəʃɪp] *s.* **1** l'insieme *m.* dei soci **2** condizione *f.* di socio
membrane ['mɛmbreɪn] *s.* membrana *f.*
memo ['mɛmɒʊ] → **memorandum**
memorable ['mɛmərəbl] *agg.* memorabile
memorandum [ˌmɛmə'rændəm] *s.* promemoria *m. inv.*, appunto *m.*, comunicazione *f.* di servizio
memorial [mɪ'mɜːrɪəl] **A** *agg.* commemorativo **B** *s.* **1** monumento *m.* commemorativo **2** *al pl.* memoriale *m.* ♦ **m. tablet** lapide
memory ['mɛmərɪ] *s.* memoria *f.*
men [mɛn] *pl. di* **man**
menace ['mɛnəs] *s.* minaccia *f.*
to menace ['mɛnəs] *v. tr.* minacciare
menacing ['mɛnəsɪŋ] *agg.* minaccioso
to mend [mɛnd] **A** *v. tr.* aggiustare, rammendare, rattoppare **B** *v. intr.* correggersi, aggiustarsi
mendable ['mɛndəbl] *agg.* aggiustabile, riparabile
mending ['mɛndɪŋ] *s.* riparazione *f.*, rammendo *m.*
menial ['miːnjəl] *agg.* servile, umile
meningitis [ˌmɛnɪn'dʒaɪtɪs] *s.* meningite *f.*
meniscus [mɪ'nɪskəs] *s.* menisco *m.*
menopause ['mɛnɒ(ʊ)pɜːz] *s.* menopausa *f.*
menses ['mɛnsiːz] *s. pl.* mestruazioni *f. pl.*
menstruation [ˌmɛnstrʊ'eɪʃ(ə)n] *s.* mestruazione *f.*
mental ['mɛntl] *agg.* mentale ♦ **m. hospital** manicomio
mentality [mɛn'tælɪtɪ] *s.* mente *f.*, mentalità *f.*
menthol ['mɛnθəl] *s.* mentolo *m.*
mention ['mɛnʃ(ə)n] *s.* menzione *f.*, citazione *f.*
to mention ['mɛnʃ(ə)n] *v. tr.* nominare, menzionare, citare ♦ **above mentioned** sopracitato; **don't m. it!** non c'è di che!
menu ['mɛnjʊ] *s.* menu *m. inv.*
mercantile ['mɜːk(ə)ntaɪl] *agg.* mercantile
mercantilism ['mɛːkəntɪlɪz(ə)m] *s.* mercantilismo *m.*
mercenary ['mɜːsɪn(ə)rɪ] *agg. e s.* mercenario *m.*
merchandise ['mɜːtʃ(ə)ndaɪz] *s.* merce *f.*
merchant ['mɜːtʃ(ə)nt] **A** *s.* mercante *m.*, commerciante *m. e f.* **B** *agg.* mercantile ♦ **m. bank** banca d'affari; **m. navy** marina mercantile
merciful ['mɜːsɪf(ʊ)l] *agg.* misericordioso, clemente, pietoso
merciless ['mɜːsɪlɪs] *agg.* spietato, crudele
mercury ['mɜːkjʊrɪ] *s.* mercurio *m.*
mercy ['mɜːsɪ] *s.* misericordia *f.*, pietà *f.*
mere [mɪəʳ] *agg.* mero, puro, semplice

merely ['mɪəlɪ] *avv.* semplicemente, soltanto, appena
to merge [mɜːdʒ] **A** *v. tr.* fondere, incorporare **B** *v. intr.* fondersi, incorporarsi, essere assorbito
merger ['mɜːdʒəʳ] *s.* fusione *f.*
meridian [mə'rɪdɪən] *s.* meridiano *m.*
meringue [mə'ræŋ] *s.* meringa *f.*
merit ['mɛrɪt] *s.* merito *m.*, pregio *m.*
to merit ['mɛrɪt] *v. tr.* meritare
merlon ['mɜːlən] *s.* (*arch.*) merlo *m.*
mermaid ['mɜːmeɪd] *s.* (*mitol.*) sirena *f.*
merry ['mɛrɪ] *agg.* allegro, giocoso ♦ **m. go-round** giostra; **m. Christmas!** buon Natale!
mesh [mɛʃ] *s.* **1** (*di rete*) maglia *f.* **2** (*mecc.*) presa *f.* ♦ **in m.** inserito; **out of m.** disinserito
mess [mɛs] *s.* **1** confusione *f.*, scompiglio *m.* **2** pasticcio *m.* **3** (*mil.*) mensa *f.*, rancio *m.* ♦ **to make a m. of st.** rovinare qualcosa; **to get oneself in a m.** mettersi nei guai
to mess [mɛs] *v. intr.* **1** mangiare in mensa **2** (*fam.*) perdere tempo ♦ **to m. about** far baccano; **to m. around** bighellonare; **to m. up** mettere in disordine, mandare a monte
message ['mɛsɪdʒ] *s.* messaggio *m.*
messenger ['mɛsɪndʒəʳ] *s.* messaggero *m.*
messy ['mɛsɪ] *agg.* disordinato, caotico
met [mɛt] *pass. e p. p. di* **to meet**
metal ['mɛtl] *s.* metallo *m.*
metallic [mɪ'tælɪk] *agg.* metallico
metallurgic(al) [ˌmɛtə'lɜːdʒɪk((ə)l)] *agg.* metallurgico
metamorphism [ˌmɛtə'mɔːfɪz(ə)m] *s.* metamorfismo *m.*
metamorphosis [ˌmɛtə'mɔːfəsɪs] *s.* metamorfosi *f.*
metaphor ['mɛtəfəʳ] *s.* metafora *f.*
metaphoric(al) [ˌmɛtə'fɔrɪk((ə)l)] *agg.* metaforico
metaphysical [ˌmɛtə'fɪzɪk(ə)l] *agg.* metafisico
métayage ['mɛ(ɪ)təjaːʒ] *s.* mezzadria *f.*
to mete [miːt] *v. tr.* (*letter.*) misurare ♦ **to m. out** assegnare, infliggere
meteor ['miːtjəʳ] *s.* meteora *f.*
meteorologic(al) [ˌmiːtjərə'lɔdʒɪk((ə)l)] *agg.* meteorologico
meteorology [ˌmiːtjə'rɔlədʒɪ] *s.* meteorologia *f.*
meter ['miːtəʳ] *s.* **1** misuratore *m.*, contatore *m.* **2** (*fam.*) tassametro *m.* **3** (*USA*) → **metre** ♦ **parking m.** parchimetro
methane ['mɛθeɪn] *s.* metano *m.*
method ['mɛθəd] *s.* metodo *m.*
methodic(al) [mɪ'θɔdɪk((ə)l)] *agg.* metodico
methodist ['mɛθədɪst] *agg. e s.* metodista *m. e f.*
methodological [ˌmɛθədə'lɔdʒɪk(ə)l] *agg.* metodologico
meths [mɛθs] *s.* (*abbr. di* **methylated spirits**) alcol *m.* denaturato
meticulous [mɪ'tɪkjʊləs] *agg.* meticoloso
metope ['mɛtɒʊp] *s.* metopa *f.*
metre ['miːtəʳ] (*USA* **meter**) *s.* metro *m.* ♦ **cubic m.** metro cubo; **square m.** metro quadrato
metric ['mɛtrɪk] *agg.* metrico
metrical ['mɛtrɪk(ə)l] *agg.* metrico
metropolitan [ˌmɛtrə'pɔlɪt(ə)n] **A** *agg.* metropolitano **B** *s.* metropolita *m.*
mettle ['mɛtl] *s.* **1** coraggio *m.* **2** carattere *m.*, temperamento *m.*
to mew [mjuː] *v. intr.* miagolare
Mexican ['mɔksɪkən] *agg. e s.* messicano *m.*
mezzanine ['mɛzəniːn] *s.* mezzanino *m.*, ammezzato *m.*
to miaow [miː'aʊ] *v. intr.* miagolare
mice [maɪs] *pl. di* **mouse**
microbe ['maɪkrɒʊb] *s.* microbo *m.*
microchip ['maɪkrɒʊtʃɪp] *s.* microchip *m. inv.*
microcosm ['maɪkrɒ(ʊ)kɔz(ə)m] *s.* microcosmo *m.*
microfilm ['maɪkrɒ(ʊ)fɪlm] *s.* microfilm *m. inv.*
microorganism [ˌmaɪkrɒ(ʊ)'ɜːgənɪz(ə)m] *s.* microrganismo *m.*
microphone ['maɪkrəfɒʊn] *s.* microfono *m.*
microscope ['maɪkrəskɒʊp] *s.* microscopio *m.*
microwave ['maɪkrɒ(ʊ)weɪv] *s.* microonda *f.* ♦ **m. oven** forno a microonde
mid [mɪd] *agg.* medio, di mezzo ♦ **m. August holiday** ferragosto; **in m. winter** nel cuore dell'inverno
midday ['mɪddeɪ] *s.* mezzogiorno *m.*
middle [mɪdl] **A** *agg.* medio, di mezzo **B** *s.* mezzo *m.*, centro *m.* ♦ **m. age** mezza età; **Middle Ages** medioevo; **m. class** borghesia; **m. name** secondo nome; **m.-**

of-the-road moderato; **m. school** scuola media inferiore
middleman ['mɪdlmæn] (*pl.* **middlemen**) *s.* mediatore *m.*, intermediario *m.*
middling ['mɪdlɪŋ] *agg.* **1** medio **2** mediocre
midge [mɪdʒ] *s.* moscerino *m.*
midget ['mɪdʒɪt] **A** *agg.* minuscolo **B** *s.* nano *m.*
midnight ['mɪdnaɪt] *s.* mezzanotte *f.*
midriff ['mɪdrɪf] *s.* (*anat.*) diaframma *m.*
midst [mɪdst] *s.* (*letter.*) mezzo *m.*, centro *m.*
midsummer ['mɪd,sʌmə^r] *s.* mezza estate *f.*
midway [,mɪd'weɪ] *agg. e avv.* a metà strada
midwife ['mɪdwaɪf] (*pl.* **midwives**) *s.* levatrice *f.*, ostetrica *f.*
might [maɪt] *s.* potenza *f.*, forza *f.*
mighty ['maɪtɪ] **A** *agg.* poderoso, forte **B** *avv.* estremamente
migraine ['mi:greɪn] *s.* emicrania *f.*
migrant ['maɪgr(ə)nt] *agg.* migratore, emigrante
to migrate [maɪ'greɪt] *v. intr.* migrare, emigrare
migratory ['maɪgrət(ə)rɪ] *agg.* migratorio, migratore
mike [maɪk] *s.* (*fam.*) microfono *m.*
mild [maɪld] *agg.* **1** mite, dolce **2** leggero
mildew ['mɪldju:] *s.* muffa *f.*
mile [maɪl] *s.* miglio *m.* ♦ **nautical m.** miglio marino
mileage ['maɪlɪdʒ] *s.* distanza *f.* in miglia
mileometer [maɪ'lɒmɪtə^r] *s.* contamiglia *m.*
milestone ['maɪl,stəʊn] *s.* pietra *f.* miliare
militant ['mɪlɪtənt] *agg. e s.* militante *m. e f.*
military ['mɪlɪt(ə)rɪ] *s.* militare *m.*
to militate ['mɪlɪteɪt] *v. intr.* militare ♦ **to m. against st.** opporsi a q.c.
milk [mɪlk] *s.* latte *m.* ♦ **curdled m.** latte cagliato; **powdered m.** latte in polvere; **skimmed m.** latte scremato
to milk [mɪlk] **A** *v. tr.* mungere **B** *v. intr.* produrre latte
mill [mɪl] *s.* **1** mulino *m.* **2** fabbrica *f.*, opificio *m.* **3** macinino *m.* **4** (*mecc.*) fresa *f.*
to mill [mɪl] *v. tr.* **1** macinare, frantumare **2** (*mecc.*) fresare
milled [mɪld] *agg.* **1** macinato **2** (*mecc.*) fresato **3** (*di moneta*) zigrinato
millenary [mɪ'lɛnərɪ] **A** *agg.* millenario **B** *s.* millennio *m.*
millennium [mɪ'lɛnɪəm] *s.* millennio *m.*
miller ['mɪlə^r] *s.* **1** mugnaio *m.* **2** (*mecc.*) fresatrice *f.*
millesimal [mɪ'lɛsɪm(ə)l] *agg. e s.* millesimo *m.*
millet ['mɪlɪt] *s.* (*bot.*) miglio *m.*
milliard ['mɪlja:d] *s.* miliardo *m.*
millimetre ['mɪlɪ,mi:tə^r] *s.* millimetro *m.*
millinery ['mɪlɪn(ə)rɪ] *s.* modisteria *f.*
million ['mɪljən] *s.* milione *m.*
millionaire [,mɪljə'nɛə^r] *agg. e s.* milionario *m.*
millstone ['mɪl,stəʊn] *s.* macina *f.*
mime [maɪm] *s.* mimo *m.*
to mime [maɪm] *v. tr.* mimare
mimetic [mɪ'mɛtɪk] *agg.* mimetico
mimic ['mɪmɪk] **A** *agg.* **1** imitativo, mimetico **2** simulato **B** *s.* imitatore *m.*
to mimic ['mɪmɪk] *v. tr.* **1** mimare **2** imitare, simulare
minaret [,mɪnə'rɛt] *s.* minareto *m.*
mince [mɪns] *s.* carne *f.* tritata
to mince [mɪns] **A** *v. tr.* tritare, sminuzzare **B** *v. intr.* **1** parlare con affettazione **2** camminare a passettini
mincer ['mɪnsə^r] *s.* tritacarne *m. inv.*
mind [maɪnd] *s.* **1** mente *f.*, intelligenza *f.* **2** pensiero *m.* **3** opinione *f.*, parere *m.* **4** spirito *m.*, animo *m.* **5** memoria *f.* ♦ **to have in m.** avere in mente; **to lose one's m.** perdere la testa; **to make up one's m.** decidersi; **to my m.** secondo me
to mind [maɪnd] *v. tr.* **1** badare a, occuparsi di **2** fare attenzione a **3** dispiacere, rincrescere ♦ **if you don't m.** se non le spiace; **m. the step!** attenzione al gradino!
minder ['maɪndə^r] *s.* (*fam.*) guardia *f.* del corpo ♦ **child-m.** bambinaia
mindful ['maɪn(d)f(ʊ)l] *agg.* attento, memore
mindless ['maɪndlɪs] *agg.* **1** irragionevole **2** stupido **3** noncurante
mine (1) [maɪn] *pron. poss. 1ª sing.* il mio, la mia, i miei, le mie
mine (2) [maɪn] *s.* **1** miniera *f.* **2** mina *f.*
to mine [maɪn] *v. tr.* **1** estrarre, scavare **2** minare
minefield ['maɪn,fi:ld] *s.* campo *m.* minato
miner ['maɪnə^r] *s.* minatore *m.*
mineral ['mɪn(ə)r(ə)l] *agg. e s.* minerale *m.*
mineralogy [,mɪnə'rælədʒɪ] *s.* mineralogia *f.*
to mingle ['mɪŋgl] *v. tr. e intr.* mescolare, mescolarsi

miniature ['mɪnjətʃəʳ] **A** *s.* miniatura *f.* **B** *agg.* in miniatura, in scala ridotta
miniaturist ['mɪnjətjʊərɪst] *s.* miniaturista *m. e f.*
minim ['mɪnɪm] *s.* (*mus.*) minima *f.*
minimize ['mɪnɪmaɪz] *v. tr.* minimizzare
minimum ['mɪnɪməm] *agg. e s.* minimo *m.*
mining ['maɪnɪŋ] *s.* estrazione *f.*, attività *f.* mineraria
miniskirt ['mɪnɪˌskɜːt] *s.* minigonna *f.*
minister ['mɪnɪstəʳ] *s.* ministro *m.*
to minister ['mɪnɪstəʳ] *v. intr.* **1** portare aiuto, provvedere **2** officiare
ministerial [ˌmɪnɪs'tɪərɪəl] *agg.* ministeriale
ministry ['mɪnɪstrɪ] *s.* ministero *m.*
mink ['mɪŋk] *s.* visone *m.*
minnow ['mɪnɒʊ] *s.* pesciolino *m.* d'acqua dolce
minor ['maɪnəʳ] **A** *agg.* minore, meno importante **B** *s.* minorenne *m. e f.*
minority [maɪ'nərɪtɪ] *s.* **1** minoranza *f.* **2** minorità *f.*
minster ['mɪnstəʳ] *s.* chiesa *f.* abbaziale
minstrel ['mɪnstr(ə)l] *s.* menestrello *m.*
mint (1) [mɪnt] *s.* menta *f.*
mint (2) [mɪnt] *s.* zecca *f.*
to mint [mɪnt] *v. tr.* coniare
minuet [ˌmɪnjʊ'ɛt] *s.* minuetto *m.*
minus ['maɪnəs] **A** *agg.* **1** meno **2** negativo **B** *s.* meno *m.* **C** *prep.* meno
minute ['mɪnɪt] **A** *agg.* **1** minuto, minuscolo **2** minuzioso **B** *s.* **1** minuto *m.* **2** minuta *f.*, appunto *m.* **3** *al pl.* verbale *m.*
to minute ['mɪnɪt] *v. tr.* **1** verbalizzare **2** cronometrare
miracle ['mɪrəkl] *s.* miracolo *m.*
miraculous [mɪ'rækjʊləs] *agg.* miracoloso
mirage ['mɪraːʒ] *s.* miraggio *m.*
mire ['maɪəʳ] *s.* melma *f.*
mirror ['mɪrəʳ] *s.* specchio *m.*
to mirror ['mɪrəʳ] *v. tr.* rispecchiare
mirth [mɜːθ] *s.* allegria *f.*, gioia *f.*
miry ['maɪərɪ] *agg.* melmoso
misadventure [ˌmɪsəd'vɛntʃəʳ] *s.* disavventura *f.*, incidente *m.*
misanthrope ['mɪz(ə)nθrɒʊp] *s.* misantropo *m.*
misanthropic(al) [ˌmɪzən'θrəpɪk((ə)l)] *agg.* misantropico
to misapply [ˌmɪsə'plaɪ] *v. tr.* usare erroneamente
misapprehension [ˌmɪsæprɪ'hɛnʃ(ə)n] *s.* malinteso *m.*, equivoco *m.*
to misappropriate [ˌmɪsə'prɒʊprɪeɪt] *v. tr.* appropriarsi indebitamente di
misbecoming [ˌmɪsbɪ'kʌmɪŋ] *agg.* inadatto, sconveniente
to misbehave [ˌmɪsbɪ'heɪv] *v. intr.* comportarsi male
misbeliever [ˌmɪsbɪ'liːvəʳ] *s.* miscredente *m. e f.*
miscarriage ['mɪskærɪdʒ] *s.* **1** aborto *m.* **2** fallimento *m.* **3** (*di corrispondenza*) disguido *m.*, smarrimento *m.*
to miscarry [mɪs'kærɪ] *v. intr.* **1** abortire **2** fallire **3** (*di corrispondenza*) smarrirsi
miscellaneous [ˌmɪsɪ'leɪnjəs] *agg.* misto, eterogeneo
miscellany [mɪ'sɛlənɪ] *s.* miscellanea *f.*
mischance [mɪs'tʃaːns] *s.* disgrazia *f.*, sfortuna *f.*
mischief ['mɪstʃɪf] *s.* **1** danno *m.* **2** malizia *f.* **3** birichinata *f.*
misconception [ˌmɪskən'sɛpʃ(ə)n] *s.* idea *f.* sbagliata
misconduct [mɪs'kəndʌkt] *s.* **1** cattiva condotta *f.* **2** cattiva amministrazione *f.*
misdeed [ˌmɪs'diːd] *s.* misfatto *m.*
misdemeanour [ˌmɪsdɪ'miːnəʳ] *s.* infrazione *f.*
miser ['maɪzəʳ] *s.* tirchio *m.*
miserable ['mɪz(ə)r(ə)bl] *agg.* **1** infelice, avvilito **2** deprimente, spiacevole **3** miserabile, misero ♦ **to feel m.** sentirsi depresso
miserly ['maɪzəlɪ] *agg.* taccagno
misery ['mɪzərɪ] *s.* **1** sofferenza *f.*, infelicità *f.* **2** miseria *f.*
to misfire [ˌmɪs'faɪəʳ] *s.* **1** (*di arma*) far cilecca **2** (*autom.*) perdere colpi **3** (*fam.*) fallire
misfit ['mɪsfɪt] *s.* disadattato *m.*
misfortune [mɪs'fɜːtʃən] *s.* sfortuna *f.*, disgrazia *f.*
misgiving [mɪs'gɪvɪŋ] *s.* timore *m.*, apprensione *f.*
misgovernment [ˌmɪs'gʌvənmənt] *s.* malgoverno *m.*
misguided [ˌmɪs'gaɪdɪd] *agg.* malaccorto, fuorviato
to mishandle [ˌmɪs'hændl] *v. tr.* maltrattare
mishap ['mɪshæp] *s.* contrattempo *m.*, disavventura *f.*
to misinterpret [ˌmɪsɪn'tɜːprɪt] *v. tr.* interpretare male, travisare
to misjudge [ˌmɪs'dʒʌdʒ] *v. tr.* giudicare

male
to mislay [mɪs'leɪ] (*pass. e p. p.* **mislaid**) *v. tr.* non trovare più
to mislead [mɪs'li:d] (*pass. e p. p.* **misled**) *v. tr.* **1** fuorviare, trarre in inganno **2** traviare
misleading [mɪs'li:dɪŋ] *agg.* ingannevole
to mismanage [ˌmɪs'mænɪdʒ] *v. tr.* amministrare male
misnomer [ˌmɪs'nɒʊməʳ] *s.* nome *m.* sbagliato, definizione *f.* non appropriata
misogynist [maɪ'sədʒɪnɪst] *s.* misogino *m.*
to misplace [ˌmɪs'pleɪs] *v. tr.* collocare fuori posto
misprint ['mɪsˌprɪnt] *s.* errore *m.* di stampa, refuso *m.*
miss (1) [mɪs] *s.* signorina *f.* (*davanti al nome*)
miss (2) [mɪs] *s.* colpo *m.* mancato
to miss [mɪs] **A** *v. tr.* **1** fallire, sbagliare, non colpire **2** lasciarsi sfuggire, mancare a, far tardi a **3** tralasciare **4** sentire la mancanza, notare l'assenza **B** *v. intr.* **1** fallire, sbagliare il colpo **2** mancare ♦ **to m. the train** perdere il treno
missal ['mɪs(ə)l] *s.* messale *m.*
misshapen [ˌmɪs'ʃeɪp(ə)n] *agg.* deforme, sformato
missile ['mɪsaɪl] *s.* missile *m.*
missing ['mɪsɪŋ] *agg.* **1** smarrito, mancante **2** disperso, scomparso
mission ['mɪʃ(ə)n] *s.* missione *f.*
missionary ['mɪʃənərɪ] *s.* missionario *m.*
to misspend [ˌmɪs'spɛnd] (*pass. e p. p.* **misspent**) *v. tr.* dissipare, sprecare
mist [mɪst] *s.* **1** foschia *f.* **2** appannamento *m.*
to mist [mɪst] *v. tr. e intr.* annebbiare, annebbiarsi
mistake [mɪs'teɪk] *s.* errore *m.*, sbaglio *m.* ♦ **to make a m.** sbagliare
to mistake [mɪs'teɪk] (*pass.* **mistook**, *p. p.* **mistaken**) *v. tr.* **1** fraintendere, equivocare **2** sbagliare **3** confondere
mistaken [mɪs'teɪk(ə)n] **A** *p. p. di* **to mistake** **B** *agg.* **1** in errore **2** erroneo ♦ **to be m.** sbagliarsi
mister ['mɪstəʳ] *s.* signore (*davanti a nome proprio abbr. in* **Mr**)
mistletoe ['mɪsltɒʊ] *s.* vischio *m.*
mistook [mɪs'tʊk] *pass. di* **to mistake**
mistress ['mɪstrɪs, mɪsɪz] *s.* **1** padrona *f.*, signora *f.* **2** insegnante *f.* **3** mantenuta *f.* **4** signora (*davanti a nome proprio abbr. in* **Mrs**)
mistrust [ˌmɪs'trʌst] *s.* sfiducia *f.*, diffidenza *f.*
to mistrust [ˌmɪs'trʌst] *v. tr.* diffidare di
misty ['mɪstɪ] *agg.* nebbioso
to misunderstand [ˌmɪsʌndə'stænd] (*pass. e p. p.* **misunderstood**) *v. tr.* **1** equivocare, fraintendere **2** non capire
misunderstanding [ˌmɪsʌndə'stændɪŋ] *s.* **1** equivoco *m.*, malinteso *m.* **2** disaccordo *m.*, incomprensione *f.*
misunderstood [ˌmɪsʌndə'stʊd] **A** *pass. e p. p. di* **to misunderstand** **B** *agg.* **1** malinterpretato, frainteso **2** incompreso
to misuse [ˌmɪs'ju:z] *v. tr.* fare cattivo uso di
mite (1) [maɪt] *s.* **1** obolo *m.* **2** oggetto *m.* minuscolo **3** bimbo *m.*
mite (2) [maɪt] *s.* acaro *m.*
to mitigate ['mɪtɪgeɪt] *v. tr.* mitigare
mitre ['maɪtəʳ] *s.* mitra *f.*
mitt(en) [mɪt(n)] *s.* manopola *f.* (*guanto*), guantone *m.*
mix [mɪks] *s.* mescolanza *f.*
to mix [mɪks] *v. tr. e intr.* mescolare, mescolarsi ♦ **to m. up** mescolare, confondere, implicare
mixed [mɪkst] *agg.* misto ♦ **m. up** implicato, confuso; **to get m. up** confondersi
mixer ['mɪksəʳ] *s.* **1** frullatore *m.*, miscelatore *m.* **2** (*fam.*) persona *f.* socievole
mixture ['mɪkstʃəʳ] *s.* mescolanza *f.*, miscela *f.*
mix-up ['mɪksʌp] *s.* (*fam.*) confusione *f.*
mnemonic [ni:'mənɪk] *agg.* mnemonico
moan [mɒʊn] *s.* gemito *m.*, lamento *m.*
to moan [mɒʊn] *v. intr.* gemere, lamentarsi
moat [mɒʊt] *s.* fossato *m.*
mob [məb] *s.* **1** folla *f.*, calca *f.* **2** massa *f.*, popolo *m.*
mobile ['mɒʊbaɪl] *agg.* **1** mobile **2** instabile
mobility [mɒ(ʊ)'bɪlɪtɪ] *s.* mobilità *f.*
mobilization [ˌmɒʊbɪlaɪ'zeɪʃ(ə)n] *s.* mobilitazione *f.*
moccassin ['məkəsɪn] *s.* mocassino *m.*
mock [mək] *agg.* **1** finto **2** scherzoso
to mock [mək] *v. tr.* **1** deridere, burlarsi di **2** imitare
mockery ['məkərɪ] *s.* **1** scherno *m.*, derisione *f.* **2** beffa *f.*
mock-up ['məkʌp] *s.* (*tecnol.*) modello *m.*
modality [mɒ(ʊ)'dælɪtɪ] *s.* modalità *f.*

mode [mɒʊd] *s.* modo *m.*
model ['mədl] **A** *agg.* **1** modello, esemplare **2** in scala ridotta **B** *s.* **1** modello *m.* **2** modella *f.*, modello *m.*
to model ['mədl] **A** *v. tr.* modellare, plasmare **B** *v. intr.* fare la modella/il modello
modem ['məʊdɛm] *s.* modem *m. inv.*
moderate ['məd(ə)rɪt] *agg.* moderato, modico, discreto
to moderate ['mədəreɪt] *v. tr. e intr.* moderare, moderarsi
moderation [ˌmədə'rɛʃ(ə)n] *s.* moderazione *f.*
modern ['mədən] *agg.* moderno
modernism ['mədənɪz(ə)m] *s.* modernismo *m.*
modernity [mə'dɜːnɪtɪ] *s.* modernità *f.*
to modernize ['mədənaɪz] *v. tr.* modernizzare
modest ['mədɪst] *agg.* modesto
modesty ['mədəstɪ] *s.* modestia *f.*
modicum ['mədɪkəm] *s.* piccola quantità *f.*, briciola *f.*
modifiable ['mədɪfaɪəbl] *agg.* modificabile
modification [ˌmədɪfɪ'keɪʃ(ə)n] *s.* modifica *f.*, modificazione *f.*
to modify ['mədɪfaɪ] *v. tr.* modificare
modular ['mədjʊlə^r] *agg.* componibile, modulare
module ['mədjʊl] *s.* modulo *m.*
Mohammedan [mɒ(ʊ)'hæmɪdən] *agg. e s.* maomettano *m.*
moist [məɪst] *agg.* umido
to moisten ['məɪsn] *v. tr. e intr.* inumidire, inumidirsi
moisture ['məɪstʃə[r]] *s.* umidità *f.*
to moisturize ['məɪstʃəraɪz] *v. tr.* inumidire, (*la pelle*) idratare
moisturizing ['məɪstʃəraɪzɪŋ] *agg.* idratante
molar ['mɒʊlə[r]] *agg. e s.* molare *m.*
mold [mɒʊld] (*USA*) → **mould**
mole (1) [mɒʊl] *s.* neo *m.*
mole (2) [mɒʊl] *s.* talpa *f.*
mole (3) [mɒʊl] *s.* molo *m.*
molecule ['məlɪkjuːl] *s.* molecola *f.*
to molest [mɒ(ʊ)'lɛst] *v. tr.* molestare
to mollycoddle ['məlɪˌkədl] *v. tr.* coccolare
molten ['mɒʊlt(ə)n] *agg.* fuso
mom [məm] *s.* (*USA, fam.*) mamma *f.*
moment ['mɒʊmənt] *s.* **1** momento *m.* **2** importanza *f.* ♦ **at the m.** momentaneamente
momentary ['mɒʊmənt(ə)rɪ] *agg.* momentaneo
momentous [mɒ(ʊ)'mɛntəs] *agg.* molto importante
monachism ['mənəkɪz(ə)m] *s.* monachesimo *m.*
monarchic(al) [mə'naːkɪk((ə)l)] *agg.* monarchico
monarchy ['mənəkɪ] *s.* monarchia *f.*
monastery ['mənəst(ə)rɪ] *s.* monastero *m.*
monastic [mə'næstɪk] *agg.* monastico
Monday ['mʌndɪ] *s.* lunedì *m.*
monetary ['mʌnɪt(ə)rɪ] *agg.* monetario
money ['mʌnɪ] *s.* **1** denaro *m.*, soldi *m. pl.* **2** (*fin.*) moneta *f.*, valuta *f.* ♦ **for m.** in contanti; **m. box** salvadanaio; **m. changer** cambiavalute; **m. order** vaglia
mongrel ['mʌŋgr(ə)l] *s.* (cane) bastardo *m.*
monitor ['mənɪtə[r]] *s.* **1** dispositivo *m.* di controllo **2** monitor *m. inv.*
to monitor ['mənɪtə[r]] *v. tr.* controllare
monk [mʌŋk] *s.* monaco *m.*
monkey ['mʌŋkɪ] *s.* scimmia *f.* ♦ **m. business** imbrogli, scherzi; **m. nut** arachide
to monkey ['mʌŋkɪ] *v. tr.* scimmiottare
monochrome ['mənəkrɒʊm] *agg.* monocromatico
monogamy [mə'nəgəmɪ] *s.* monogamia *f.*
monograph ['mənəgraːf] *s.* monografia *f.*
monolithic [ˌmənɒ(ʊ)'lɪθɪk] *agg.* monolitico
monologue ['mənələg] *s.* monologo *m.*
monomaniac [ˌmənɒ(ʊ)'meɪnjæk] *agg.* monomaniaco
monopoly [mə'nəpəlɪ] *s.* monopolio *m.*
monosyllable ['mənəˌsɪləbl] *s.* monosillabo *m.*
monotheism ['mənɒ(ʊ)θiːˌɪz(ə)m] *s.* monoteismo *m.*
monotone ['mənətɒʊn] **A** *agg.* monotono **B** *s.* monotonia *f.* tono *m.* uniforme
monotonous [mə'nət(ə)nəs] *agg.* monotono, uniforme
monotony [mə'nət(ə)nɪ] *s.* monotonia *f.*
monsoon [mən'suːn] *s.* monsone *m.* ♦ **dry m.** monsone invernale; **wet m.** monsone estivo
monster ['mənstə[r]] **A** *s.* mostro *m.* **B** *agg. attr.* colossale
monstrous ['mənstrəs] *agg.* mostruoso
month [mʌnθ] *s.* mese *m.*
monthly ['mʌnθlɪ] **A** *agg. e s.* mensile *m.* **B** *avv.* mensilmente

monument ['mənjʊmənt] *s.* monumento *m.* (*anche funebre*)
monumental [ˌmənjʊ'mɛntl] *agg.* monumentale
to moo [mu:] *v. intr.* muggire
mood [mu:d] *s.* umore *m.*, stato *m.* d'animo
moody ['mu:dɪ] *agg.* **1** di malumore **2** lunatico
moon [mu:n] *s.* luna *f.*
moonlight ['mu:nlaɪ] *s.* chiaro *m.* di luna
moor [mʊəʳ] *s.* brughiera *f.*
to moor [mʊəʳ] *v. tr. e intr.* ormeggiare
mooring ['mʊərɪŋ] *s.* ormeggio *m.*
moose [mu:s] *s.* alce *m.* americano
mop [məp] *s.* **1** spazzolone *m.* (per pavimenti) **2** (*fam.*) zazzera *f.*
to mop [məp] *v. tr.* **1** pulire, lavare **2** asciugare, detergere ♦ **to m. up** asciugare, prosciugare
to mope [mɒʊp] *v. intr.* essere depresso, essere imbronciato
moped ['mɒʊpɛd] *s.* motorino *m.*
moquette [mə'kɛt] *s.* moquette *f. inv.*
moraine [mə'reɪn] *s.* morena *f.*
moral ['mər(ə)l] **A** *agg.* **1** morale **2** onesto, virtuoso **B** *s.* **1** morale *f.* **2** *al pl.* moralità *f.*
morale [mə'ra:l] *s.* morale *m.*, stato *m.* d'animo
moralism ['mər(ə)lɪz(ə)m] *s.* moralismo *m.*
moralist ['mərəlɪst] *s.* moralista *m. e f.*
morality [mə'rælɪtɪ] *s.* moralità *f.*
to moralize ['mərəlaɪz] *v. tr.* moralizzare
morally ['mər(ə)lɪ] *avv.* moralmente
morass [mə'ræs] *s.* acquitrino *m.*, palude *f.*
moray ['mɜ:reɪ] *s.* murena *f.*
morbid ['mɜ:bɪd] *agg.* morboso
more [mɜ:ʳ] (*comp. di* **much, many**) **A** *agg.* più, di più, una maggior quantità di **B** *avv.* **1** maggiormente, più, di più **2** ancora **3** (*forma il comp. di agg. e avv.*) più (ES: **m. beautiful** più bello) **C** *pron. indef. e s.* più *m.*, una quantità *f.* maggiore ♦ **m. or less** pressappoco; **once m.** ancora una volta; **no m.** non più
moreover [mɜ:'rɒʊvəʳ] *avv.* inoltre, peraltro
morgue [mɜ:g] *s.* obitorio *m.*
moribund ['mərɪbʌnd] *agg. e s.* moribondo *m.*
morning ['mɜ:nɪŋ] *s.* mattino *m.* ♦ **in the m.** di mattina; **good m.** buon giorno; **m. performance** (*teatro*) spettacolo pomeridiano; **this m.** stamattina
Moroccan [mə'rəkən] *agg. e s.* marocchino *m.*
moron ['mɜ:rən] *s.* ritardato *m.* mentale
morose [mə'rɒʊs] *agg.* imbronciato, cupo
morphological [ˌmɜ:fə'lədʒɪk(ə)l] *agg.* morfologico
morphology [mɜ:'fələdʒɪ] *s.* morfologia *f.*
morsel ['mɜ:s(ə)l] *s.* boccone *m.*
mortal ['mɜ:tl] *agg. e s.* mortale *m.*
mortality [mɜ:'tælɪtɪ] *s.* mortalità *f.*
mortar ['mɜ:təʳ] *s.* mortaio *m.*
mortgage ['mɜ:gɪdʒ] *s.* ipoteca *f.* ♦ **m. loan** prestito ipotecario
to mortgage ['mɜ:gɪdʒ] *v. tr.* ipotecare
mortification [ˌmɜ:tɪfɪ'keɪʃ(ə)n] *s.* mortificazione *f.*
to mortify ['mɜ:tɪfaɪ] *v. tr.* mortificare
mortuary ['mɜ:tjʊərɪ] *s.* obitorio *m.*, camera *f.* mortuaria
mosaic [mə'zeɪɪk] *s.* mosaico *m.*
Moslem ['məzlɛm] *agg. e s.* musulmano *m.*
mosque [məsk] *s.* moschea *f.*
mosquito [məs'ki:tɒʊ] *s.* zanzara *f.* ♦ **m. net** zanzariera
moss [məs] *s.* muschio *m.*
most [mɒʊst] (*sup. di* **much, many**) **A** *agg.* il più, la più, i più, le più, la maggior parte di **B** *avv.* **1** (*forma il sup. di agg. e avv.*) (ES: **the m. beautiful woman** la donna più bella) **2** estremamente **3** di più, maggiormente **C** *pron. indef. e s.* il massimo *m.*, la maggior parte *f.* ♦ **at (the) m.** tutt'al più, al massimo
mostly ['mɒʊstlɪ] *avv.* soprattutto
motel [mɒʊ'tɛl] *s.* motel *m. inv.*
moth [məθ] *s.* **1** tarma *f.* **2** farfalla *f.* notturna
mother ['mʌðəʳ] **A** *s.* madre *f.*, mamma *f.* **B** *agg.* materno, madre ♦ **m.-in-law** suocera; **m.-of-pearl** madreperla; **m. to-be** futura mamma; **m. tongue** madrelingua
motherhood ['mʌðəhʊd] *s.* maternità *f.*
motherland ['mʌðəlænd] *s.* madrepatria *f.*
motherly ['mʌðəlɪ] *agg.* materno
motif [mɒ(ʊ)'ti:f] *s.* motivo *m.*, tema *m.*
motion ['mɒʊʃ(ə)n] *s.* **1** movimento *m.*, moto *m.* **2** gesto *m.*, atto *m.* **3** mozione *f.* ♦ **m. picture** pellicola cinematografica, film
to motion ['mɒʊʃ(ə)n] *v. tr.* fare cenno a
motionless ['mɒʊʃ(ə)nlɪs] *agg.* immobile
to motivate ['mɒʊtɪveɪt] *v. tr.* motivare

motive ['mɒʊtɪv] *s.* motivo *m.*, movente *m.*
motocross ['mɒʊtəˌkrəs] *s.* motocross *m. inv.*
motor ['mɒʊtəʳ] **A** *s.* motore *m.* **B** *agg.* **1** a motore, motoristico, automobilistico **2** motorio ♦ **m. home** camper; **m. power** forza motrice; **m. scooter** motorino; **m. sled** motoslitta
motorbike ['mɒʊtəˌbaɪk] *s.* motocicletta *f.*
motorboat ['mɒʊtəbɒʊt] *s.* barca *f.* a motore, motoscafo *m.*
motorcycle ['mɒʊtəˌsaɪkl] *s.* motocicletta *f.*
motorist ['mɒʊtərɪst] *s.* automobilista *m. e f.*
motorway ['mɒʊtəweɪ] *s.* autostrada *f.*, superstrada *f.* ♦ **toll m.** autostrada a pedaggio
to mottle ['mətl] *v. tr.* screziare, chiazzare
motto ['mətɒʊ] *s.* motto *m.*, massima *f.*
mould (1) [mɒʊld] (*USA* **mold**) *s.* stampo *m.*, forma *f.*
mould (2) [mɒʊld] *s.* muffa *f.*
to mould [mɒʊld] (*USA* **to mold**) *v. tr.* forgiare, modellare
moulding ['mɒʊldɪŋ] *s.* **1** (*arch.*) cornice *f.*, modanatura *f.* **2** modellatura *f.* **3** formatura *f.*
mouldy ['mɒʊldɪ] *agg.* ammuffito
moult [mɒʊlt] *s.* muda *f.*
mound [maʊnd] *s.* **1** tumulo *m.* **2** cumulo *m.*
mount [maʊnt] *s.* monte *m.* (*davanti al nome*)
to mount [maʊnt] **A** *v. tr.* **1** salire su, ascendere a **2** montare, incastonare **3** mettere in scena **4** (*zootecnia*) montare **B** *v. intr.* **1** montare, salire **2** montare a cavallo ♦ **to m. up** aumentare
mountain ['maʊntɪn] **A** *s.* montagna *f.* **B** *agg. attr.* **1** montuoso **2** montano, di montagna ♦ **m. climber** alpinista; **m. pass** valico
mountaineer [ˌmaʊntɪ'nɪəʳ] *s.* alpinista *m. e f.*
mountaineering [ˌmaʊntɪ'nɪərɪŋ] *s.* alpinismo *m.*
mountainous ['maʊntɪnəs] *agg.* montagnoso
mountainside ['maʊntɪnˌsaɪd] *s.* versante *m.* (di montagna)
mountebank ['maʊntɪbæŋk] *s.* ciarlatano *m.*
mounting ['maʊntɪŋ] **A** *agg.* crescente **B** *s.* **1** montatura *f.*, montaggio *m.* **2** allestimento *m.* **3** salita *f.*, ascensione *f.*
to mourn [mɜːn] **A** *v. tr.* lamentare, piangere **B** *v. intr.* portare il lutto
mourner ['mɜːnəʳ] *s.* chi è in lutto
mournful ['mɜːnf(ʊ)l] *agg.* funebre, luttuoso
mourning ['mɜːnɪŋ] *s.* lutto *m.*
mouse [maʊs] *s.* **1** (*pl.* **mice**) topo *m.* **2** (*inf.*) (*pl.* **mouses**) mouse *m. inv.*
mousetrap ['maʊsˌtræp] *s.* trappola *f.* per topi
mousse [muːs] *s.* mousse *f. inv.*
moustache [məs'taːʃ] *s.* baffi *m. pl.*
mouth [maʊθ] *s.* **1** bocca *f.* **2** imboccatura *f.*, apertura *f.* **3** foce *f.*
mouthful ['maʊθfʊl] *s.* boccone *m.*
mouthorgan ['maʊθˌɜːgən] *s.* armonica *f.* a bocca
mouthpiece ['maʊθpiːs] *s.* **1** bocchino *m.*, boccaglio *m.*, imboccatura *f.* **2** portavoce *m. inv.*
mouthwash ['maʊθˌwəʃ] *s.* collutorio *m.*
movable ['muːvəbl] *agg.* mobile
move [muːv] *s.* **1** movimento *m.* **2** mossa *f.* **3** trasloco *m.*
to move [muːv] **A** *v. tr.* **1** muovere, spostare **2** commuovere **3** proporre, chiedere **B** *v. intr.* **1** muoversi, spostarsi **2** traslocare **3** (*al gioco*) fare una mossa ♦ **to m. about/around** spostarsi, muoversi in continuazione; **to m. along** spostarsi in avanti; **to m. away** traslocare; **to m. in** andare ad abitare; **to m. out** sgombrare; **to m. over** spostarsi; **to m. up** fare carriera, aumentare
movement ['muːvmənt] *s.* movimento *m.*, gesto *m.*
movie ['muːvɪ] *s.* **1** film *m. inv.* **2** *al pl.* cinema *m.*
moving ['muːvɪŋ] **A** *agg.* **1** commovente **2** mobile, in movimento **B** *s.* trasloco *m.*
to mow [mɒʊ] (*pass.* **mowed**, *p. p.* **mown**) *v. tr.* falciare, mietere
mower ['mɒʊəʳ] *s.* falciatrice *f.*
much [mʌtʃ] (*comp.* **more**, *sup.* **most**, *pl.* **many**) **A** *agg.* molto **B** *avv.* **1** molto, assai **2** più o meno **C** *pron. indef. e s.* molto *m.*, gran parte *f.* ♦ **as m. as** tanto quanto; **how m.** quanto; **not so m. ... as** non tanto ... quanto; **so m.** (così) tanto; **too m.** troppo
muck [mʌk] *s.* **1** letame *m.* **2** (*fam.*) porcheria *f.*
to muck [mʌk] *v. tr.* **1** concimare **2** insoz-

zare ♦ **to m. about/around** fare il cretino, perdere tempo; **to m. up** guastare, rovinare
mucous ['mju:kəs] *agg.* mucoso ♦ **m. membrane** (membrana) mucosa
mud [mʌd] *s.* fango *m.*, melma *f.*
to mud [mʌd] *v. tr.* infangare
muddle ['mʌdl] *s.* confusione *f.*, scompiglio *m.*
to muddle ['mʌdl] *v. tr.* confondere, scompigliare
muddler ['mʌdləʳ] *agg. e s.* confusionario *m.*
muddy ['mʌdɪ] *agg.* limaccioso, torbido, fangoso
mudguard ['mʌdgaːd] *s.* parafango *m.*
to muffle ['mʌfl] *v. tr.* **1** avvolgere, imbacuccare **2** attutire, smorzare
muffler ['mʌfləʳ] *s.* **1** sciarpa *f.* **2** (*USA*) marmitta *f.*, silenziatore *m.*
mug [mʌg] *s.* **1** boccale *m.*, tazzone *m.* **2** (*pop.*) muso *m.*, ceffo *m.* **3** (*fam.*) babbeo *m.*
to mug [mʌg] *v. tr.* **1** aggredire, rapinare **2** (*fam.*) sgobbare
mugging ['mʌgɪŋ] *s.* aggressione *f.*, rapina *f.*
muggy ['mʌgɪ] *agg.* afoso, opprimente
mulberry ['mʌlb(ə)rɪ] *s.* **1** gelso *m.* **2** mora *f.* (di gelso)
mule [mju:l] *s.* mulo *m.* ♦ **m. track** mulattiera
to mull [mʌl] *v. tr.* non riuscire in ♦ **to m. over st.** rimuginare q.c.
mullet ['mʌlɪt] *s.* **1** triglia *f.* **2** muggine *m.*
multiannual [,mʌltɪ'ænjʊəl] *agg.* poliennale
multicolour ['mʌltɪ,kʌləʳ] *agg.* multicolore
multiform ['mʌltɪfɜːm] *agg.* multiforme
multimillionaire [,mʌltɪmɪljə'nɛəʳ] *agg. e s.* multimilionario *m.*
multinational [,mʌltɪ'næʃənl] *agg. e s.* multinazionale *f.*
multiple ['mʌltɪpl] **A** *agg.* multiplo, molteplice **B** *s.* multiplo *m.*
multiplication [,mʌltɪplɪ'keɪʃ(ə)n] *s.* moltiplicazione *f.*
to multiply ['mʌltɪplaɪ] *v. tr. e intr.* moltiplicare, moltiplicarsi
multistorey ['mʌltɪstɜːrɪ] *agg. attr.* a più piani
multitude ['mʌltɪtju:d] *s.* moltitudine *f.*
mum (1) [mʌm] *agg.* (*fam.*) zitto ♦ **to keep m.** tacere
mum (2) [mʌm] *s.* (*fam.*) mamma *f.*
to mumble ['mʌmbl] *v. tr. e intr.* borbottare
mummy (1) ['mʌmɪ] *s.* mummia *f.*
mummy (2) ['mʌmɪ] *s.* (*fam.*) mamma *f.*
mumps [mʌmps] *s.* parotite *f.*, orecchioni *m. pl.*
to munch [mʌn(t)ʃ] *v. tr.* sgranocchiare
mundane ['mʌndeɪn] *agg.* **1** mondano **2** banale
municipal [mjʊ(ː)'nɪsɪp(ə)l] *agg.* municipale
municipality [mjʊ(ː),nɪsɪ'pælɪtɪ] *s.* municipio *m.*
munificence [mjʊ(ː)'nɪfɪsns] *s.* munificenza *f.*
munition [mjʊ(ː)'nɪʃ(ə)n] *s.* **1** fortificazione *f.* **2** munizioni *f. pl.*
mural ['mjʊər(ə)l] *s.* murale *m.*
murder ['mɜːdəʳ] *s.* assassinio *m.*
to murder ['mɜːdəʳ] *v. tr.* assassinare
murderer ['mɜːdərəʳ] *s.* assassino *m.*, omicida *m. e f.*
murderous ['mɜːd(ə)rəs] *agg.* omicida
murky ['mɜːkɪ] *agg.* oscuro, tenebroso
murmur ['mɜːməʳ] *s.* **1** mormorio *m.*, sussurro *m.* **2** (*med.*) soffio *m.*
to murmur ['mɜːməʳ] *v. tr. e intr.* mormorare
muscle ['mʌsl] *s.* **1** muscolo *m.* **2** (*fig.*) forza *f.*
to muscle ['mʌsl] *v. intr.* penetrare a forza, farsi largo ♦ **to m. in** intromettersi
muscular ['mʌskjʊləʳ] *agg.* **1** muscolare **2** muscoloso
muse [mju:z] *s.* **1** meditazione *f.* **2** musa *f.*
to muse [mju:z] *v. tr. e intr.* meditare, rimuginare
museum [mjʊ(ː)'zɪəm] *s.* museo *m.*
mushroom ['mʌʃru:m] *s.* fungo *m.*
to mushroom ['mʌʃru:m] *v. intr.* **1** raccogliere funghi **2** crescere come funghi
music ['mju:zɪk] *s.* musica *f.* ♦ **m. box** carillon; **m. stand** leggio
musical ['mju:zɪk(ə)l] **A** *agg.* **1** musicale **2** appassionato di musica **B** *s.* musical *m. inv.*, commedia *f.* musicale
musicassette ['mju:zɪkæ,sɛt] *s.* musicassetta *f.*
musician [mjʊ(ː)'zɪʃ(ə)n] *s.* musicista *m. e f.* ♦ **street m.** suonatore ambulante
musk [mʌsk] *s.* (*in profumeria*) muschio *m.*
Muslim ['mʊslɪm] *agg. e s.* musulmano *m.*
muslin ['mʌzlɪn] *s.* mussola *f.*
mussel ['mʌsl] *s.* cozza *f.*, mitilo *m.*

Mussulman ['mʌslmən] *agg. e s.* musulmano *m.*
must (1) [mʌst, məst] **A** *v. difett.* **1** (*dovere, obbligo*) dovere (ES: **you m. pay taxes** devi pagare le tasse) **2** (*probabilità, supposizione*) dovere (ES: **he m. be crazy** deve essere pazzo) **B** *s.* ciò di cui non si può fare a meno, dovere *m.*, must *m. inv.*
must (2) [mʌst] *s.* mosto *m.*
mustard ['mʌstəd] *s.* senape *f.*
muster ['mʌstəʳ] *s.* **1** (*mil.*) adunata *f.* **2** riunione *f.*
to muster ['mʌstəʳ] **A** *v. tr.* (*mil.*) radunare, chiamare a raccolta **B** *v. intr.* radunarsi
musty ['mʌstɪ] *agg.* ammuffito, stantio
mute [mjuːt] *agg. e s.* muto *m.*
muted ['mjuːtɪd] *agg.* (*di suono*) smorzato
mutilation [ˌmjuːtɪ'leɪʃ(ə)n] *s.* mutilazione *f.*
mutineer [ˌmjuːtɪ'nɪəʳ] *s.* ammutinato *m.*
mutinous ['mjuːtɪnəs] *agg.* ammutinato, ribelle, sovversivo
mutiny ['mjuːtɪnɪ] *s.* ammutinamento *m.*, rivolta *f.*
to mutiny ['mjuːtɪnɪ] *v. intr.* ammutinarsi, ribellarsi
mutism ['mjuːtɪz(ə)m] *s.* mutismo *m.*
to mutter ['mʌtəʳ] *v. tr. e intr.* borbottare
mutton ['mʌtn] *s.* carne *f.* di montone
mutual ['mjuːtʃʊəl] *agg.* mutuo, reciproco
muzzle ['mʌzl] *s.* **1** muso *m.* **2** museruola *f.* **3** (*di arma da fuoco*) bocca *f.*
to muzzle ['mʌzl] *v. tr.* **1** mettere la museruola a **2** (*fig.*) imbavagliare
my [maɪ] **A** *agg. poss. 1ª sing.* mio, mia, miei, mie **B** *inter.* perbacco, accipicchia
Mycenaean [maɪ'sɪnːən] *agg.* miceneo
myopic [maɪ'əpɪk] *agg.* miope
myriad ['mɪrɪəd] *s.* miriade *f.*
myself [maɪ'sɛlf] *pron. 1ª sing.* **1** (*rifl.*) mi, me, me stesso, me stessa **2** (*enf.*) io stesso, proprio io
mysterious [mɪs'tɪərɪəs] *agg.* misterioso
mystery ['mɪst(ə)rɪ] *s.* mistero *m.*
mystical ['mɪstɪk(ə)l] *agg.* mistico
mysticism ['mɪstɪsɪz(ə)m] *s.* misticismo *m.*
mystifier ['mɪstɪfaɪəʳ] *s.* mistificatore *m.*
to mystify ['mɪstɪfaɪ] *v. tr.* **1** mistificare, imbrogliare **2** confondere
mystique [mɪs'tiːk] *s.* **1** mistica *f.* **2** fascino *m.*
myth [mɪθ] *s.* mito *m.*
mythical ['mɪθɪk(ə)l] *agg.* mitico
to mythicize ['mɪθɪsaɪz] *v. tr.* mitizzare
mythologic(al) [ˌmɪθə'lədʒɪk((ə)l)] *agg.* mitologico
mythology [mɪ'θələdʒɪ] *s.* mitologia *f.*
mythomaniac [ˌmɪθə'meɪnɪæk] *agg. e s.* mitomane *m. e f.*

N

to nab [næb] *v. tr.* (*pop.*) agguantare
nabob ['neɪbəb] *s.* nababbo *m.*
nacelle [nə'sɛl] *s.* carlinga *f.*
to nag [næg] *v. tr. e intr.* brontolare, infastidire
nagging ['nægɪŋ] **A** *agg.* insistente, fastidioso **B** *s.* rimprovero *m.*
naiad ['naɪæd] *s.* naiade *f.*
nail [neɪl] *s.* **1** unghia *f.*, artiglio *m.* **2** chiodo *m.* ♦ **n. brush** spazzolino da unghie; **n. polish** smalto da unghie; **n. file** limetta
to nail [neɪl] *v. tr.* **1** inchiodare **2** (*fam.*) acchiappare
naïve [nɑː'iːv] *agg.* ingenuo, naïf
naïvety [nɑː'iːvtɪ] *s.* ingenuità *f.*
naked ['neɪkɪd] *agg.* nudo
name [neɪm] *s.* nome *m.* ♦ **Christian n.** (*USA* **first n.**) nome di battesimo; **family n.** cognome; **full n.** nome e cognome; **my n. is ...** mi chiamo ...; **n. day** onomastico; **pen n.** pseudonimo; **what's your n. ?** come ti chiami?
to name [neɪm] *v. tr.* **1** chiamare, dare un nome a **2** designare, nominare **3** fissare
namely ['neɪmlɪ] *cong.* ossia, cioè
namesake ['neɪm,seɪk] *s.* omonimo *m.*
nanny ['nænɪ] *s.* (*fam.*) bambinaia *f.*
nap (1) [næp] *s.* pisolino *m.*, siesta *f.* ♦ **to take a n.** schiacciare un pisolino
nap (2) [næp] *s.* peluria *f.*
to nap [næp] *v. intr.* sonnecchiare
nape [neɪp] *s.* nuca *f.*
napkin ['næpkɪn] *s.* **1** tovagliolo *m.* **2** pannolino *m.*
nappy ['næpɪ] *s.* pannolino *m.*
narcissist [nɑː'sɪsɪst] *s.* narcisista *m. e f.*
narcissus [nɑː'sɪsəs] (*pl.* **narcissi**) *s.* narciso *m.*
narcotic [nɑː'kɔtɪk] *agg. e s.* narcotico *m.*
to narrate [næ'reɪt] *v. tr.* narrare
narration [næ'reɪʃ(ə)n] *s.* narrazione *f.*
narrative ['nærətɪv] **A** *agg.* narrativo **B** *s.* narrazione *f.*
narrator [næ'reɪtəʳ] *s.* narratore *m.*
narrow ['nærɒʊ] **A** *agg.* stretto, ristretto, limitato **B** *s.* stretto *m.*
to narrow ['nærɒʊ] **A** *v. tr.* **1** restringere **2** limitare **B** *v. intr.* stringersi
narrow-minded [,nærɒ(ʊ)'maɪndɪd] *agg.* gretto
narthex ['nɑːθɛks] *s.* (*arch.*) nartece *m.*
nasal ['neɪz(ə)l] *agg.* nasale
nasty ['nɑːstɪ] *agg.* **1** cattivo, sgradevole **2** brutto, pericoloso **3** osceno, schifoso ♦ **n. smell** puzza
natality [neɪ'tælɪtɪ] *s.* natalità *f.*
nation ['neɪʃ(ə)n] *s.* nazione *f.*
national ['næʃənl] **A** *agg.* nazionale **B** *s.* cittadino *m.*
nationalism ['næʃnəlɪz(ə)m] *s.* nazionalismo *m.*
nationality [,næʃə'nælɪtɪ] *s.* nazionalità *f.*
to nationalize ['næʃ(ə)nəlaɪz] *v. tr.* nazionalizzare
nationwide ['neɪʃ(ə)n,waɪd] **A** *agg.* diffuso in tutta la nazione, di carattere nazionale **B** *avv.* per tutta la nazione
native ['neɪtɪv] **A** *agg.* **1** nativo, natale **2** innato, naturale **3** indigeno, originario, locale **B** *s.* nativo *m.*, indigeno *m.* ♦ **n. land** patria; **n. language** lingua materna
nativity [nə'tɪvɪtɪ] *s.* natività *f.*
natural ['nætʃr(ə)l] *agg.* **1** naturale, secondo natura **2** normale, ovvio **3** genuino, schietto, spontaneo **4** innato, connaturato
naturalism ['nætʃrəlɪz(ə)m] *s.* naturalismo *m.*
naturalist ['nætʃrəlɪst] *s.* naturalista *m. e f.*
to naturalize ['nætʃrəlaɪz] *v. tr.* **1** naturalizzare **2** acclimatare
naturally ['nætʃrəlɪ] *avv.* naturalmente
nature ['neɪtʃəʳ] *s.* **1** natura *f.* **2** carattere *m.*
naturism ['neɪtʃərɪz(ə)m] *s.* naturismo *m*
naturist ['neɪtʃərɪst] *s.* naturista *m. e f.*
naught [nɜːt] *s.* nulla *m.*
naughtiness ['nɜːtɪnɪs] *s.* cattiveria *f.*
naughty ['nɜːtɪ] *agg.* **1** (*di bambino*) cattivo, disubbidiente **2** indecente
naumachia [nɜː'meɪkjə] *s.* naumachia *f.*
nausea ['nɜːsjə] *s.* nausea *f.*
to nauseate ['nɜːsɪeɪt] *v. tr.* nauseare
nauseating ['nɜːsɪeɪtɪŋ] *agg.* nauseante
nautic(al) ['nɜːtɪk((ə)l)] *agg.* nautico ♦ **n. mile** miglio marino; **n. almanac** effemeridi
naval ['neɪv(ə)l] *agg.* navale, marittimo
nave [neɪv] *s.* (*arch.*) navata *f.* centrale
navel ['neɪv(ə)l] *s.* ombelico *m.*

navigability [ˌnævɪgə'bɪlɪtɪ] *s.* navigabilità *f.*
navigable ['nævɪgəbl] *agg.* navigabile
to navigate ['nævɪgeɪt] **A** *v. intr.* navigare **B** *v. tr.* percorrere navigando, traversare
navigation [ˌnævɪ'geɪʃ(ə)n] *s.* navigazione *f.*
navigator ['nævɪgeɪtəʳ] *s.* navigatore *m.*, ufficiale *m.* di rotta
navy ['neɪvɪ] *s.* marina *f.* militare
Nazi ['na:tsɪ] *agg. e s.* nazista *m. e f.*
Nazism ['na:tsɪz(ə)m] *s.* nazismo *m.*
near [nɪəʳ] **A** *agg.* **1** vicino, prossimo **2** affine, stretto **3** avaro, tirchio **4** a sinistra **5** quasi **B** *avv.* **1** vicino, presso **2** quasi **C** *prep.* vicino a, presso a ♦ **n. friend** amico intimo; **n. miss** mancato per poco; **n. sighted** miope
to near [nɪəʳ] *v. tr. e intr.* avvicinare, avvicinarsi
nearby ['nɪəbaɪ] **A** *agg.* vicino **B** *avv.* accanto, nelle vicinanze
nearly ['nɪəlɪ] *avv.* quasi, per poco
nearside ['nɪəˌsaɪd] *agg. attr.* di sinistra
nearsight ['nɪəsaɪt] *s.* miopia *f.*
neat [ni:t] *agg.* **1** ordinato, pulito, lindo **2** ben fatto, ben proporzionato **3** acuto, conciso **4** puro, non diluito
nebula ['nɛbjʊlə] *s.* nebulosa *f.*
nebulous ['nɛbjʊləs] *agg.* nebuloso, vago, indistinto
necessarily ['nɛsɪs(ə)rɪlɪ] *avv.* necessariamente
necessary ['neɪsɪs(ə)rɪ] *agg.* necessario, inevitabile
necessity [nɪ'sɛs(ɪ)tɪ] *s.* necessità *f.* ♦ **of n.** necessariamente
neck [nɛk] *s.* **1** collo *m.* **2** colletto *m.* **3** istmo *m.*
to neck [nɛk] *v. intr.* (*fam.*) sbaciucchiarsi
necklace ['nɛklɪs] *s.* collana *f.*
necklet ['nɛklɪt] *s.* colletto *m.*
neckline ['nɛklaɪn] *s.* scollatura *f.*
necktie ['nɛktaɪ] *s.* (*USA*) cravatta *f.*
necrology [nɛ'krələdʒɪ] *s.* necrologio *m.*
necropolis [nɛ'krəpəlɪs] *s.* necropoli *f.*
nectar ['nɛktəʳ] *s.* nettare *m.*
need [ni:d] *s.* **1** necessità *f.*, bisogno *m.*, esigenza *f.* **2** indigenza *f.*
to need [ni:d] *v. tr.* (*costruzione pers.*) **1** aver bisogno, occorrere (ES: **I don't n. your help** non ho bisogno del tuo aiuto) **2** essere obbligato, dovere, occorrere (ES: **I n. not go there** non occorre che ci vada)
needle ['ni:dl] *s.* ago *m.*
to needle ['ni:dl] *v. tr.* **1** cucire **2** forare (con un ago) **3** punzecchiare
needless ['ni:dlɪs] *agg.* inutile, superfluo
needlework ['ni:dlwɜ:k] *s.* cucito *m.*, ricamo *m.*
needy ['ni:dɪ] *agg.* bisognoso, povero
negation [nɪ'geɪʃ(ə)n] *s.* negazione *f.*
negative ['nɛgətɪv] **A** *agg.* negativo **B** *s.* **1** negazione *f.* **2** qualità *f.* negativa **3** (*fot.*) negativa *f.* **C** *avv.* no
neglect [nɪ'glɛkt] *s.* trascuratezza *f.*, negligenza *f.*
to neglect [nɪ'glɛkt] *v. tr.* trascurare
negligence ['nɛglɪdʒ(ə)ns] *s.* negligenza *f.*
negligent ['nɛglɪdʒənt] *agg.* negligente
negligible ['nɛglɪdʒəbl] *agg.* trascurabile, insignificante
negotiable [nɪ'gɒʊʃɪəbl] *agg.* **1** negoziabile **2** (*di assegno*) trasferibile **3** transitabile
to negotiate [nɪ'gɒʊʃɪeɪt] **A** *v. tr.* **1** negoziare, trattare **2** (*banca*) trasferire **3** superare **B** *v. intr.* negoziare
negotiation [nɪˌgɒʊʃɪ'eɪʃ(ə)n] *s.* negoziato *m.*, trattativa *f.*
neigh [neɪ] *s.* nitrito *m.*
to neigh [neɪ] *v. intr.* nitrire
neighbour ['neɪbəʳ] (*USA* **neighbor**) *s.* vicino *m.*
to neighbour ['neɪbəʳ] (*USA* **to neighbor**) *v. tr. e intr.* confinare con
neighbourhood ['neɪbəhʊd] (*USA* **neighborhood**) *s.* **1** quartiere *m.* **2** vicinato *m.* **3** dintorni *m. pl.*, vicinanze *f. pl.*
neighbourly ['neɪbəlɪ] (*USA* **neighborly**) *agg.* cortese, cordiale
neither ['naɪðəʳ] **A** *agg. e pron.* né l'uno né l'altro, nessuno dei due **B** *avv.* né **C** *cong.* neppure, nemmeno ♦ **n. ... nor ...** né ... né ...
neoclassic(al) [ˌni:ɒʊ'klæsɪk((ə)l)] *agg.* neoclassico
neoclassicism [ˌni:ɒ(ʊ)'klæsɪsɪz(ə)m] *s.* neoclassicismo *m.*
Neolithic [ˌni:ɒ(ʊ)'lɪθɪk] *agg.* neolitico
neologism [ni:'ələdʒɪz(ə)m] *s.* neologismo *m.*
neon ['ni:ən] *s.* neon *m. inv.*
neophyte ['ni:ɒ(ʊ)faɪt] *s.* neofita *m. e f.*
neorealism [ˌni:ɒ(ʊ)'ri:əlɪz(ə)m] *s.* neorealismo *m.*
nephew ['nɛvjʊ(:)] *s.* nipote *m.* (*di zii*)

nepotism ['nɛpətɪz(ə)m] *s.* nepotismo *m.*
nervation [nə(ː)'veɪʃ(ə)n] *s.* (*bot.*) nervatura *f.*
nerve [nɜːv] *s.* **1** nervo *m.* **2** nerbo *m.*, forza *f.* **3** coraggio *m.*, sangue *m.* freddo **4** (*fam.*) impudenza *f.*, faccia *f.* tosta ♦ **to get on sb.'s nerves** dare sui nervi a qc.; **to have a fit of nerves** avere una crisi di nervi
nerve-racking ['nɜːvˌrækɪŋ] *agg.* esasperante
nervous ['nɜːvəs] *agg.* **1** nervoso **2** agitato, inquieto
nervousness ['nɜːvəsnɪs] *s.* nervosismo *m.*
nest [nɛst] *s.* **1** nido *m.* **2** covo *m.*, tana *f.* ♦ **n. egg** gruzzolo
to nest [nɛst] *v. intr.* **1** nidificare **2** annidarsi, inserirsi l'uno nell'altro
to nestle ['nɛsl] *v. intr.* accoccolarsi
net (1) [nɛt] *agg.* netto
net (2) [nɛt] *s.* rete *f.*
netting ['nɛtɪŋ] *s.* reticolato *m.*
nettle ['nɛtl] *s.* ortica *f.*
network ['nɛtwɜːk] *s.* **1** rete *f.* **2** network *m. inv.*
neuralgia [njʊə'rældʒə] *s.* nevralgia *f.*
neurologist [njʊə'rələdʒɪst] *s.* neurologo *m.*
neurosis [njʊə'rɒʊsɪs] *s.* nevrosi *f.*
neurotic [njʊə'rətɪk] *agg. e s.* nevrotico *m.*
neuter ['njuːtəʳ] *agg.* neutro
to neuter ['njuːtəʳ] *v. tr.* castrare
neutral ['njuːtr(ə)l] **A** *agg.* **1** neutrale **2** neutro **B** *s.* (*autom.*) folle *m.*
neutrality [njuː'trælɪtɪ] *s.* neutralità *f.*
to neutralize ['njuːtrəlaɪz] *v. tr.* neutralizzare
never ['nɛvəʳ] *avv.* mai ♦ **n. again** mai più; **n. ending** incessante; **n. mind** non importa, pazienza; **well, I n.!** ma guarda un po'!, chi l'avrebbe detto!; **you n. know** non si sa mai
nevertheless [ˌnɛvəð(ə)'lɛs] *cong.* tuttavia
new [njuː] **A** *agg.* nuovo, novello, recente **B** *avv.* appena, di recente ♦ **brand n.** nuovo di zecca; **n. year's day** capodanno
newborn ['njuːbɜːn] *agg.* appena nato, neonato
newcomer ['njuːkʌməʳ] *s.* nuovo venuto *m.*
newfangled ['njuːˌfæŋgld] *agg.* modernissimo
newly ['njuːlɪ] *avv.* di recente ♦ **n.-weds** sposi novelli
news [njuːz] *s. pl.* (*v. al sing.*) **1** notizie *f. pl.* **2** notiziario *m.*, telegiornale *m.*, radiogiornale *m.* ♦ **a piece of n.** una notizia; **crime n.** cronaca nera; **n. agency** agenzia di stampa; **society n.** cronaca mondana
newsagent ['njuːzˌeɪdʒ(ə)nt] *s.* giornalaio *m.*
newsletter ['njuːzlɛtəʳ] *s.* notiziario *m.*
newspaper ['njʊsˌpeɪpəʳ] *s.* giornale *m.*
newsprint ['njuːzprɪnt] *s.* carta *f.* da giornale
newsreader ['njuːzˌriːdəʳ] *s.* (*TV, radio*) commentatore *m.*
newsreel ['njuːzˌriː] *s.* cinegiornale *m.*
newsstand ['njʊzːstænd] *s.* edicola *f.*
next [nɛkst] **A** *agg.* **1** prossimo, vicino, contiguo **2** prossimo, venturo, futuro, seguente **B** *avv.* dopo, in seguito ♦ **n.-door** della porta accanto, vicino; **n. to** vicino a, presso; **n. week** la prossima settimana
nexus ['nɛksəs] *s.* nesso *m.*
nib [nɪb] *s.* pennino *m.*
nice [naɪs] *agg.* **1** piacevole, bello, simpatico, grazioso **2** buono, gustoso **3** accurato, minuzioso, scrupoloso
nicely ['naɪslɪ] *avv.* **1** esattamente, bene **2** piacevolmente
niche [nɪtʃ] *s.* nicchia *f.*
nick [nɪk] *s.* **1** tacca *f.*, intaglio *m.* **2** (*pop.*) prigione *f.* ♦ **in the n. of time** al momento opportuno
to nick [nɪk] *v. tr.* **1** intagliare, intaccare **2** (*pop.*) afferrare, cogliere **3** (*pop.*) arrestare **4** (*pop.*) rubare
nickname ['nɪkneɪm] *s.* soprannome *m.*
to nickname ['nɪkneɪm] *v. tr.* soprannominare
nicotine ['nɪkətiːn] *s.* nicotina *f.*
niece [niːs] *s. f.* nipote *f.* (*di zii*)
nigger ['nɪgəʳ] *s.* (*spreg.*) negro *m.*
to niggle ['nɪgl] *v. intr.* **1** fare il pignolo, cavillare **2** molestare
niggling ['nɪglɪŋ] *agg.* **1** pignolo, minuzioso **2** molesto **3** insignificante
nigh [naɪ] **A** *avv.* vicino, accanto **B** *prep.* vicino a
night [naɪt] *s.* notte *f.*, sera *f.*, serata *f.* ♦ **at n., by n.** di notte; **good n.** buona notte; **last n.** ieri sera; **n. gown** camicia da notte; **n. porter** portiere di notte; **n. school** scuola serale; **n. time** ore nottur-

ne
nightclub ['naɪtklʌb] *s.* night-club *m. inv.*, locale *m.* notturno
nightfall ['naɪtfɜːl] *s.* crepuscolo *m.*
nightie ['naɪtɪ] *s.* camicia *f.* da notte
nightingale ['naɪtɪŋgeɪl] *s.* usignolo *m.*
nightlife ['naɪtlaɪf] *s.* vita *f.* notturna
nightly ['naɪtlɪ] **A** *agg.* notturno, di notte, serale, di ogni sera **B** *avv.* di notte, ogni notte, ogni sera
nightmare ['naɪtmɛəʳ] *s.* incubo *m.*
nihilism ['naɪɪlɪz(ə)m] *s.* nichilismo *m.*
nil [nɪl] *s.* **1** niente *m.* **2** (*sport*) zero *m.* ♦ **n. all** zero a zero
nimble ['nɪmbl] *agg.* agile, lesto
nimbleness ['nɪmblnɪs] *s.* agilità *f.*
nine [naɪn] *agg. num. card. e s.* nove *m. inv.*
nineteen [ˌnaɪn'tiːn] *agg. num. card. e s.* diciannove *m. inv.*
nineteenth [ˌnaɪn'tiːnθ] *agg. num. ord. e s.* diciannovesimo *m.*
ninetieth ['naɪntɪɪθ] *agg. num. ord. e s.* novantesimo *m.*
ninety ['naɪntɪ] *agg. num. card. e s.* novanta *m. inv.*
ninth [naɪnθ] **A** *agg. num. ord.* nono **B** *s.* **1** nono *m.* **2** (*mus.*) nona *f.*
nip [nɪp] *s.* **1** pizzicotto *m.*, morso *m.* **2** stretta *f.*
to nip [nɪp] *s.* **A** *v. tr.* **1** pizzicare, mordere **2** rovinare, distruggere **B** *v. intr.* **1** dare pizzicotti, dare morsi **2** (*di freddo*) essere pungente, mordere **3** (*fam.*) muoversi velocemente ♦ **to n. off** filarsela
nipper ['nɪpəʳ] *s.* **1** *al pl.* pinze *f. pl.*, tenaglie *f. pl.* **2** *al pl.* chela *f.* **3** (*fam.*) ragazzo *m.*
nipple ['nɪpl] *s.* capezzolo *m.*
nitrogen ['naɪtrədʒən] *s.* azoto *m.*
no [nɒʊ] **A** *agg.* nessuno, nessuna **B** *s.* (*pl.* **noes**) no *m.*, rifiuto *m.*, negazione *f.* **C** *avv.* no, non ♦ **no one** nessuno; **no parking** divieto di parcheggio; **no smoking** vietato fumare
nobiliary [nɒ(ʊ)'bɪljərɪ] *agg.* nobiliare
nobility [nɒ(ʊ)'bɪlɪtɪ] *s.* nobiltà *f.*
noble ['nɒʊbl] *agg.* nobile
nobody ['nɒʊbədɪ] **A** *pron. indef.* nessuno **B** *s.* nullità *f.* ♦ **n. else** nessun altro
nocturnal [nək'tɜːnl] *agg.* notturno
nod [nəd] *s.* cenno *m.* (*del capo*)
to nod [nəd] *v. intr.* **1** annuire, accennare col capo **2** ciondolare il capo, sonnecchiare ♦ **to n. off** addormentarsi
noise [nəɪz] *s.* rumore *m.*, chiasso *m.*, schiamazzo *m.*
to noise [nəɪz] *v. tr.* divulgare
noisy ['nəɪzɪ] *agg.* rumoroso, chiassoso
nomad(e) ['nɒʊmæd] *agg. e s.* nomade *m. e f.*
nominal ['nəmɪnl] *agg.* nominale
nomination [ˌnəmɪ'neɪʃ(ə)n] *s.* incarico *m.*, nomina *f.*, designazione *f.*
nominative ['nəm(ɪ)nətɪv] *agg.* nominativo
nominee [ˌnəmɪ'niː] *s.* persona *f.* incaricata, candidato *m.*
non-acceptance [ˌnənək'sɛpt(ə)ns] *s.* (*comm.*) mancata accettazione *f.*
non-addicting [ˌnənə'dɪktɪŋ] *agg.* che non causa assuefazione
non-alcoholic [ˌnənˌælkə'həlɪk] *agg.* analcolico
nonchalance ['nənʃ(ə)ləns] *s.* noncuranza *f.*
non-compliance [ˌnənkəm'plaɪəns] *s.* (*dir.*) inadempienza *f.*
nonconformism [ˌnənkən'fɜːmɪz(ə)m] *s.* anticonformismo *m.*
non-denominational [ˌnəndɪˌnəmɪ'neɪʃən(ə)l] *agg.* aconfessionale
nondescript ['nəndɪˌskrɪpt] *agg.* non classificabile
non-drinker [ˌnən'drɪŋkəʳ] *s.* astemio *m.*
none [nʌn] **A** *pron. indef.* nessuno, nessuna, niente **B** *avv.* non, per niente, niente affatto
nonentity [nən'ɛntɪtɪ] *s.* **1** inesistenza *f.* **2** nullità *f.*
nonetheless [ˌnənðə'lɛs] *avv.* ciò nonostante
non-existent [ˌnənɪg'zɪst(ə)nt] *agg.* inesistente
nonplus [ˌnən'plʌs] *s.* imbarazzo *m.*, perplessità *f.*
to nonplus [ˌnən'plʌs] *v. tr.* imbarazzare, sconcertare
nonsense ['nəns(ə)ns] *s.* nonsenso *m.*, controsenso *m.*, sciocchezza *f.*
non-smoker [ˌnən'smɒʊkəʳ] *s.* non fumatore *m.*
non-stop [ˌnən'stəp] **A** *agg.* ininterrotto **B** *avv.* di continuo
non-violence [ˌnən'vaɪələns] *s.* nonviolenza *f.*
nook [nʊk] *s.* cantuccio *m.*, angolino *m.*
noon [nuːn] *s.* mezzogiorno *m.*
noose [nuːs] *s.* cappio *m.*, laccio *m.*
to noose [nuːs] *v. tr.* accalappiare
nor [nɜː, nəʳ] *cong.* né, neanche ♦ **neither ... n.** né ... né

Nordic ['nɜːdɪk] *agg. e s.* nordico *m.*
norm [nɜːm] *s.* norma *f.*
normal ['nɜːm(ə)l] *agg.* normale
normality [nɜː'mælɪtɪ] *s.* normalità *f.*
Norman ['nɜːmən] *agg. e s.* normanno *m.*
north [nɜːθ] **A** *agg.* del nord, settentrionale **B** *s.* nord *m.*, settentrione *m.* **C** *avv.* a nord, verso nord ♦ **the N. Star** la stella polare
northerly ['nɜːðəlɪ] **A** *agg.* settentrionale, del nord, dal nord **B** *avv.* verso nord, dal nord
northern ['nɜːð(ə)n] *agg.* settentrionale, nordico
Norwegian [nɜː'wiːdʒ(ə)n] *agg. e s.* norvegese *m. e f.*
nose [nɒʊz] *s.* **1** naso *m.* **2** (*fig.*) odorato *m.*, fiuto *m.* **3** parte *f.* anteriore, muso *m.*
to **nose** [nɒʊz] *v. tr. e intr.* **1** fiutare, annusare **2** farsi largo, avanzare con cautela ♦ **to n. about/around** ficcare il naso; **to n. out** scovare
nosedive ['nɒʊzdaɪv] *s.* (*aer.*) picchiata *f.*
nosey ['nɒʊzɪ] *agg.* **1** nasuto **2** (*fam.*) ficcanaso
nostalgia [nəs'tældʒɪə] *s.* nostalgia *f.*
nostalgic [nəs'tældʒɪk] *agg.* nostalgico
nostril ['nəstrɪl] *s.* narice *f.*
not [nət] *avv.* non, no ♦ **I hope n.** spero di no; **n. at all** niente affatto, (*in risposta a 'grazie'*) prego!; **n. even** neanche, neppure
notable ['nɒʊtəbl] **A** *agg.* notevole, importante **B** *s.* notabile *m.*
notary ['nɒʊtərɪ] *s.* notaio *m.*
notation [nɒ(ʊ)'teɪʃ(ə)n] *s.* notazione *f.*
notch [nətʃ] *s.* tacca *f.*, incisione *f.*
note [nɒʊt] *s.* **1** nota *f.*, annotazione *f.*, commento *m.* **2** (*mus.*) nota *f.* **3** comunicazione *f.* scritta, biglietto *m.* **4** tono *m.*, accento *m.* **5** (*fin.*) titolo *m.* **6** (*comm.*) bolla *f.* **7** banconota *f.*
to **note** [nɒʊt] *v. tr.* **1** notare, osservare, constatare **2** prender nota, registrare
notebook ['nɒʊtbʊk] *s.* taccuino *m.*
noted ['nɒʊtɪd] *agg.* **1** degno di nota **2** noto, illustre
notepaper ['nɒʊtpeɪpəʳ] *s.* carta *f.* da lettere
nothing ['nʌθɪŋ] **A** *pron. indef.* niente, nulla **B** *s.* **1** niente *m.*, cosa *f.* da nulla **2** (*mat.*) zero *m.*
notice ['nɒʊtɪs] *s.* **1** avviso *m.*, annuncio *m.*, cartello *m.* **2** preavviso *m.*, disdetta *f.* **3** attenzione *f.*, cura *f.* ♦ **n. board** tabellone
to **notice** ['nɒʊtɪs] *v. tr.* **1** notare, osservare **2** fare attenzione a, occuparsi di
noticeable ['nɒʊtɪsəbl] *agg.* **1** notevole **2** evidente
to **notify** ['nɒʊtɪfaɪ] *v. tr.* notificare
notion ['nɒʊʃ(ə)n] *s.* nozione *f.*, idea *f.*, concetto *m.*
notoriety [ˌnɒʊtə'raɪətɪ] *s.* notorietà *f.*
notorious [nɒ(ʊ)'tɜːrɪəs] *agg.* famigerato
notwithstanding [ˌnətwɪθ'stændɪŋ] **A** *prep.* nonostante **B** *avv.* tuttavia
nought [nɜːt] *s.* zero *m.*, nulla *m.*
noun [naʊn] *s.* nome *m.*, sostantivo *m.*
to **nourish** ['nʌrɪʃ] *v. tr.* nutrire
nourishing ['nʌrɪʃɪŋ] *agg.* nutriente
nourishment ['nʌrɪʃmənt] *s.* nutrimento *m.*, alimento *m.*
novel (1) ['nəv(ə)l] *s.* romanzo *m.*
novel (2) ['nəv(ə)l] *agg.* nuovo
novelist ['nəvəlɪst] *s.* romanziere *m.*
novelty ['nəv(ə)ltɪ] *s.* novità *f.*
November [nɒ(ʊ)'vɛmbəʳ] *s.* novembre *m.*
novice ['nəvɪs] *s.* **1** apprendista *m. e f.* **2** novizio *m.*
now [naʊ] **A** *avv.* **1** adesso, ora **2** subito, immediatamente **B** *cong.* ora che ♦ **by n.** ormai; **from n. on** d'ora in poi; **just n.** proprio ora
nowadays ['naʊədeɪz] *avv.* oggigiorno, al giorno d'oggi
nowhere ['nɒʊwɛəʳ] *avv.* da nessuna parte
noxious ['nəkʃəs] *agg.* nocivo
nozzle ['nəzl] *s.* becco *m.*, beccuccio *m.*, ugello *m.*
nth [ɛnθ] *agg.* (*fam.*) ennesimo
nuance [njʊ(ː)'aː(n)s] *s.* sfumatura *f.*
nuclear ['njuːklɪəʳ] *agg.* nucleare
nucleus ['njuːklɪəs] (*pl.* **nuclei**) *s.* nucleo *m.*
nude [njuːd] *agg. e s.* nudo *m.*
nudge [nʌdʒ] *s.* gomitata *f.*
to **nudge** [nʌdʒ] *v. tr.* dare una gomitata a
nudism ['njuːdɪz(ə)m] *s.* nudismo *m.*
nudist ['njuːdɪst] *s.* nudista *m. e f.*
nuisance ['njuːsns] *s.* noia *f.*, seccatura *f.*, fastidio *m.*
null [nʌl] *agg.* nullo
numb [nʌm] *agg.* intorpidito, intirizzito
number ['nʌmbəʳ] *s.* numero *m.*
to **number** ['nʌmbəʳ] *v. tr.* **1** numerare, contare **2** annoverare **3** ammontare a
numbering ['nʌmb(ə)rɪŋ] *s.* numerazio-

ne *f.*
numberplate ['nʌmbəˌpleɪt] *s.* (*autom.*) targa *f.*
numbness ['nʌmnɪs] *s.* torpore *m.*
numeral ['nju:m(ə)r(ə)l] **A** *agg.* numerale **B** *s.* numero *m.*, cifra *f.*
numeration [ˌnju:mə'reɪʃ(ə)n] *s.* numerazione *f.*
numeric(al) [njʊ(:)'mɛrɪk((ə)l)] *agg.* numerico
numerous ['nju:m(ə)rəs] *agg.* numeroso ♦ **a n. acquaintance** un largo giro di conoscenze
numismatics [ˌnju:mɪz'mætɪks] *s. pl.* (*v. al sing.*) numismatica *f.*
nun [nʌn] *s.* suora *f.* ♦ **cloistered n.** suora di clausura
nuptial ['nʌpʃ(ə)l] *agg.* nuziale
nurse [nɜ:s] *s.* **1** balia *f.*, bambinaia *f.* **2** infermiera *f.*, infermiere *m.*
to nurse [nɜ:s] *v. tr.* **1** curare, assistere **2** allattare **3** allevare ♦ **nursing home** casa di cura
nursery ['nɜ:srɪ] *s.* **1** stanza *f.* dei bambini **2** asilo *m.* **3** vivaio *m.* ♦ **n. school** scuola materna; **n. tale** fiaba
nut [nʌt] *s.* **1** noce *f.*, nocciola *f.* **2** (*fam.*) testa *f.* **3** (*fam.*) matto *m.* **4** (*mecc.*) dado *m.* ♦ **to go nuts** impazzire
nutcracker ['nʌtˌkrækəʳ] *s.* schiaccianoci *m. inv.*
nutmeg ['nʌtmɛg] *s.* noce *f.* moscata
nutritionist [njʊ(:)'trɪʃ(ə)nɪst] *s.* dietologo *m.*
nutritious [njʊ(:)'trɪʃəs] *agg.* nutriente
nutshell ['nʌtˌʃəl] *s.* guscio *m.* di noce ♦ **in a n.** in poche parole
nylon ['naɪlən] *s.* nailon *m. inv.*
nymph [nɪmf] *s.* ninfa *f.*
nymphaeum [nɪm'fi:əm] *s.* ninfeo *m.*

O

oak [ɒʊk] *s.* quercia *f.* ♦ **bay o.** rovere
oar [ɜːʳ] *s.* remo *m.*
oarsman ['ɜːzmən] (*pl.* **oarsmen**) *s.* rematore *m.*
oasis [ɒ(ʊ)'eɪsɪs] (*pl.* **oases**) *s.* oasi *f.*
oat [ɒʊt] *s.* avena *f.*
oath [ɒʊθ] *s.* **1** giuramento *m.* **2** imprecazione *f.*, bestemmia *f.*
oatmeal ['ɒʊtmiːl] *s.* farina *f.* d'avena
obedience [ə'biːdjəns] *s.* ubbidienza *f.*
obedient [ə'biːdjənt] *agg.* ubbidiente
obelisk ['əbɪlɪsk] *s.* obelisco *m.*
obese [ɒ(ʊ)'biːs] *agg.* obeso
obesity [ɒ(ʊ)'biːsɪtɪ] *s.* obesità *f.*
to obey [ə'beɪ] *v. tr. e intr.* ubbidire
obituary [ə'bɪtjʊərɪ] *s.* necrologio *m.*, necrologia *f.*
objeot ['əbdʒɪkt] *s.* **1** oggetto *m.*, cosa *f.* **2** argomento *m.* **3** scopo *m.*, fine *m.* **4** (*gramm.*) oggetto *m.* ♦ **o. glass** obiettivo; **o. lesson** dimostrazione pratica
to object [əb'dʒɛkt] **A** *v. tr.* obiettare **B** *v. intr.* fare obiezioni, opporsi, disapprovare ♦ **to o. to do st.** rifiutarsi di fare q.c.
to objectify [əb'dʒɛktɪfaɪ] *v. tr.* oggettivare
objection [əb'dʒɛkʃ(ə)n] *s.* obiezione *f.*
objectionable [əb'dʒɛkʃnəbl] *agg.* **1** riprovevole **2** sgradevole
objective [əb'kʒɛktɪv] **A** *agg.* obiettivo, oggettivo **B** *s.* **1** obiettivo *m.* **2** caso *m.* oggettivo
objectivity [ˌəbdʒɛk'tɪvɪtɪ] *s.* obiettività *f.*
obligation [ˌəblɪ'geɪʃ(ə)n] *s.* obbligo *m.*, dovere *m.*, impegno *m.*
obligatory [ə'blɪgət(ə)rɪ] *agg.* obbligatorio
to oblige [ə'blaɪdʒ] *v. tr.* **1** obbligare **2** fare un favore a ♦ **to be obliged to do st.** dover fare q.c.
oblique [ə'bliːk] *agg.* **1** obliquo, inclinato **2** asimmetrico **3** (*gramm.*) obliquo, indiretto
to obliterate [ə'blɪtəreɪt] *v. tr.* **1** distruggere, cancellare **2** dimenticare, rimuovere
oblivion [ə'blɪvɪən] *s.* oblio *m.*
oblivious [ə'blɪvɪəs] *agg.* **1** dimentico **2** ignaro, inconsapevole
oblong ['əbləŋ] *agg.* oblungo
obnoxious [əb'nəkʃəs] *agg.* odioso, sgradevole, ripugnante
obscene [əb'siːn] *agg.* osceno
obscenity [əb'siːnɪtɪ] *s.* oscenità *f.*
obscurantism [ˌəbskjʊə'ræntɪz(ə)m] *s.* oscurantismo *m.*
obscure [əb'skjʊəʳ] *agg.* oscuro
to obscure [əb'skjʊəʳ] *v. tr.* **1** oscurare **2** nascondere
obscurity [əb'skjʊərɪtɪ] *s.* oscurità *f.*
observance [əb'zɜːv(ə)ns] *s.* osservanza *f.*
observant [əb'zɜːv(ə)nt] *agg.* osservatore, perspicace
observation [ˌəbzə(ː)'veɪʃ(ə)n] *s.* osservazione *f.*
observatory [əb'zɜːvətrɪ] *s.* osservatorio *m.*
to observe [əb'zɜːv] **A** *v. tr.* **1** osservare, rispettare **2** onorare **3** notare **4** studiare attentamente **B** *v. intr.* osservare, commentare, fare osservazioni
observer [əb'zɜːvəʳ] *s.* osservatore *m.*
to obsess [əb'sɛs] *v. tr.* ossessionare
obsession [əb'sɛʃ(ə)n] *s.* ossessione *f.*, fissazione *f.*
obsessive [əb'sɛsɪv] *agg.* ossessivo
obsolescence [ˌəbsə'lɛsəns] *s.* obsolescenza *f.*
obsolete ['əbsəliːt] *agg.* obsoleto
obstacle ['əbstəkl] *s.* ostacolo *m.*
obstetrician [ˌəbstɛ'trɪʃ(ə)n] *s.* ostetrico *m.*
obstinacy ['əbstɪnəsɪ] *s.* ostinazione *f.*
obstinate ['əbstɪnɪt] *agg.* ostinato
to obstruct [əb'strʌkt] *v. tr.* **1** ostruire, otturare **2** impedire, ritardare
obstruction [əb'strʌkʃ(ə)n] *s.* **1** ostruzione *f.* **2** ostacolo *m.*, impedimento *m.*
obstructionism [əb'strʌkʃənɪz(ə)m] *s.* ostruzionismo *m.*
to obtain [əb'teɪn] **A** *v. tr.* ottenere, raggiungere, conseguire **B** *v. intr.* essere in vigore, persistere
obtainable [əb'teɪnəbl] *agg.* ottenibile, disponibile
obturator ['əbtjʊəˌreɪtəʳ] *s.* otturatore *m.*
obtuse [əb'tjuːs] *agg.* ottuso
to obviate ['əbvɪeɪt] *v. intr.* ovviare
obvious ['əbvɪəs] *agg.* ovvio, evidente
occasion [ə'keɪʒ(ə)n] *s.* **1** occasione *f.*,

opportunità *f.* **2** motivo *m.*, ragione *f.* **3** avvenimento *m.* ♦ **on o.** occasionalmente
occasional [ə'keɪʒənl] *agg.* occasionale
occidental [ˌɔksɪ'dɛntl] *agg. e s.* occidentale *m. e f.*
to occlude [ə'kluːd] *v. tr.* occludere, ostruire
occlusion [ə'kluːʒ(ə)n] *s.* occlusione *f.*
to occult [ə'kʌlt] *v. tr. e intr.* occultare, occultarsi
occultism ['ɔk(ə)ltɪz(ə)m] *s.* occultismo *m.*
occupation [ˌɔkjʊ'peɪʃ(ə)n] *s.* **1** occupazione *f.* **2** professione *f.*
occupational [ˌɔkjuː'peɪʃ(ə)nl] *agg.* professionale, occupazionale
to occupy ['ɔkjʊpaɪ] *v. tr.* occupare ♦ **to o. oneself with** occuparsi di
to occur [ə'kɜːʳ] *v. intr.* **1** accadere, succedere, capitare **2** venire in mente **3** ricorrere **4** esserci, trovarsi
occurrence [ə'kʌr(ə)ns] *s.* **1** evento *m.*, avvenimento *m.* **2** il verificarsi ♦ **a thing of frequent o.** una cosa che capita spesso
ocean ['ɒʊʃ(ə)n] *s.* oceano *m.*
oceangoing ['ɒʊʃ(ə)nˌgɒʊɪŋ] *agg.* d'alto mare
oceanic [ˌɒʊʃɪ'ænɪk] *agg.* oceanico
oceanography [ˌɒʊʃ(ə)'nɔgrəfɪ] *s.* oceanografia *f.*
ocelot ['ɒʊsɪlət] *s.* ocelot *m. inv.*
ochre ['ɒʊkəʳ] *s.* ocra *f.*
octagonal [ɔk'tægənl] *agg.* ottagonale
octave ['ɔktɪv] *s.* ottava *f.*
October [ɔk'tɒʊbəʳ] *s.* ottobre *m.*
octopus ['ɔktəpəs] *s.* polpo *m.*
ocular ['ɔkjʊləʳ] *agg.* oculare
oculist ['ɔkjʊlɪst] *s.* oculista *m. e f.*
odd [ɔd] *agg.* **1** dispari **2** scompagnato **3** occasionale, casuale **4** strano, bizzarro ♦ **o. jobs** lavoretti occasionali; **o.-job man** tuttofare; **one pound o.** una sterlina e rotti
oddity ['ɔdɪtɪ] *s.* stranezza *f.*, bizzarria *f.*
oddly ['ɔdlɪ] *avv.* stranamente
oddments ['ɔdmənts] *s. pl.* fondi *m. pl.* di magazzino, rimasugli *m. pl.*
odds [ɔdz] *s. pl.* **1** disparità *f.*, differenza *f.* **2** disaccordo *m.* **3** vantaggio *m.* **4** probabilità *f.* **5** (*di scommessa*) quotazione *f.* ♦ **o. and ends** cianfrusaglie; **to be at o. with** essere in disaccordo con
odometer [ɒ(ʊ)'dɔmɪtəʳ] *s.* (*USA*) contachilometri *m. inv.*
odontologist [ˌɔdɔn'tɔlədʒɪst] *s.* odontoiatra *m. e f.*
odour ['ɒʊdəʳ] (*USA* **odor**) *s.* odore *m.*, profumo *m.*
odourless ['ɒʊdəlɪs] *agg.* inodore
oecumenical [ˌiːkjuː'mɛnɪk(ə)l] *agg.* ecumenico
oedema [ɪ(ː)'diːmə] *s.* edema *m.*
oenological [ˌiːnɒ(ʊ)'lɔdʒɪk(ə)l] *agg.* enologico
oenology [iː'nɔlədʒɪ] *s.* enologia *f.*
of [əv, ɔv] *prep.* **1** (*specificazione, denominazione, materia, qualità, causa, ecc.*) di (ES: **the piece of wood** il pezzo di legno, **to die of a broken heart** morire di crepacuore, **a cup of tea** una tazza di tè) **2** da parte di (ES: **it was very kind of you to write a letter** è stato gentile da parte tua scrivere una lettera) ♦ **of course** certamente; **of late** di recente
off [ɜːf] **A** *avv.* **1** via, lontano, distante **2** (*di apparecchio*) non in funzione, spento **B** *prep.* **1** da, via da **2** in meno di **C** *agg.* **1** libero **2** laterale, secondario **3** non funzionante, spento, disinserito **4** (*di cibo*) guasto
offal ['ɔf(ə)l] *s.* **1** frattaglie *f. pl.* **2** avanzi *m. pl.*, rifiuti *m. pl.*
offence [ə'fɛns] (*USA* **offense**) *s.* **1** offesa *f.* **2** reato *m.* ♦ **to take o.** offendere
to offend [ə'fɛnd] **A** *v. tr.* offendere **B** *v. intr.* commettere reati
offender [ə'fɛndəʳ] *s.* colpevole *m. e f.*, delinquente *m. e f.*
offensive [ə'fɛnsɪv] **A** *agg.* **1** offensivo **2** ripugnante **B** *s.* (*mil.*) offensiva *f.*
offer ['ɔfəʳ] *s.* offerta *f.*
to offer ['ɔfəʳ] *v. tr. e intr.* offrire, offrirsi
offerer ['ɔfərəʳ] *s.* offerente *m. e f.*
offering ['ɔfərɪŋ] *s.* offerta *f.*
offhand [ˌɜːf'hænd] **A** *agg.* **1** improvvisato, estemporaneo **2** sbrigativo **B** *avv.* **1** lì per lì, su due piedi **2** senza cerimonie
office ['ɔfɪs] *s.* **1** ufficio *m.* **2** ministero *m.* **3** funzione *f.*, carica *f.* **4** servizio *m.* ♦ **o. boy** fattorino; **o. hours** orario d'ufficio; **o.-worker** impiegato; **post o.** ufficio postale; **tourist o.** ufficio turistico
officer ['ɔfɪsəʳ] *s.* **1** (*mil.*) ufficiale *m.* **2** funzionario *m.* **3** agente *m.* di polizia
official [ə'fɪʃ(ə)l] **A** *agg.* ufficiale **B** *s.* funzionario *m.*, pubblico ufficiale *m.*
officialdom [ə'fɪʃ(ə)ldəm] *s.* burocrazia *f.*
officious [ə'fɪʃəs] *agg.* **1** invadente, importuno **2** ufficioso

offing ['ɔfɪŋ] *s.* largo *m.*, mare *m.* aperto ♦ **in the o.** in vista
offset ['ɜːfsɛt] *s.* **1** germoglio *m.* **2** rampollo *m.* **3** deviazione *f.* **4** (*tip.*, *inf.*) offset *m. inv.*
to offset ['ɜːfsɛt] (*pass. e p. p.* **offset**) **A** *v. tr.* **1** controbilanciare **2** deviare **B** *v. intr.* germogliare
offshoot ['ɜːfʃuːt] *s.* germoglio *m.*
offshore ['ɜːfʃɜːʳ] *agg.* **1** offshore, di mare aperto **2** (*econ.*) all'estero
offside [ˌɜːf'saɪd] **A** *s.* **1** fuori gioco *m.* **2** parte *f.* destra **B** *avv. e agg.* **1** di fuori gioco, in fuori gioco **2** sulla parte destra
offspring ['ɜːfsprɪŋ] *s. inv.* **1** discendenza *f.*, prole *f.* **2** frutto *m.*
offstage [ˌɜːf'steɪdʒ] *agg. e avv.* fuori scena, dietro le quinte
off-the-rack [ˌɔfðə'ræk] *agg.* (*USA, fam.*) di serie
off-the-record [ˌɔfðə'rɛkɜːd] *agg.* ufficioso, da non verbalizzare
off-white [ˌɜːf'waɪt] *agg.* bianco sporco
often ['ɜːfn] *avv.* frequentemente, spesso ♦ **as o. as not** il più delle volte; **how o.?** quante volte?
ogive ['ɒʊdʒaɪv] *s.* ogiva *f.*
ogle ['ɒʊgl] *s.* occhiata *f.* languida, sguardo *m.* amoroso
to ogle ['ɒʊgl] **A** *v. tr.* vagheggiare **B** *v. intr.* ammiccare
oil [ɔɪl] *s.* **1** olio *m.* **2** petrolio *m.*, nafta *f.* ♦ **castor o.** olio di ricino; **in o.** sott'olio; **o. mill** frantoio; **o. tanker** petroliera; **o. well** pozzo petrolifero; **sun tan o.** olio solare
to oil [ɔɪl] *v. tr.* lubrificare, oliare
oilcan ['ɔɪlˌkæn] *s.* oliatore *m.* (*a mano*)
oiler ['ɔɪləʳ] *s.* oliatore *m.*
oilfield ['ɔɪlˌfiːld] *s.* giacimento *m.* petrolifero
oily ['ɔɪlɪ] *agg.* oleoso, unto
ointment ['ɔɪntmənt] *s.* unguento *m.*, pomata *f.*
OK, okay [ˌɒʊ'keɪ] *agg., avv. e inter.* bene, tutto bene
old [ɒʊld] *agg.* vecchio, antico ♦ **how o. are you?** quanti anni hai?; **o. age** vecchiaia; **o. fashions** moda antiquata; **o. fashioned** superato; **to be o. in** essere esperto in; **to grow o.** invecchiare
oleander [ˌɒʊlɪ'ændɛʳ] *s.* oleandro *m.*
olfaction [əl'fækʃən] *s.* olfatto *m.*
oligarchy ['əlɪgaːkɪ] *s.* oligarchia *f.*
olive ['əlɪv] *s.* oliva *f.*
Olympiad [ɒ(ʊ)'lɪmpɪæd] *s.* olimpiade *f.*
Olympic [ɒ(ʊ)'lɪmpɪk] *agg.* olimpico ♦ **O. games** olimpiadi
omelette ['əmlɪt] *s.* omelette *f. inv.*, frittata *f.*
omen ['ɒʊmən] *s.* presagio *m.*
ominous ['əmɪnəs] *agg.* di malaugurio
omission [ɒ(ʊ)'mɪʃ(ə)n] *s.* omissione *f.*
to omit [ɒ(ʊ)'mɪt] *v. tr.* omettere
omnipotent [əm'nɪpət(ə)nt] *agg.* onnipotente
omnipresent [ˌəmnɪ'prɛz(ə)nt] *agg.* onnipresente
omnivorous [əm'nɪv(ə)rəs] *agg.* onnivoro
on [ən] **A** *prep.* **1** (*posizione, luogo*) sopra, su, a (ES: **a teapot on the table** una teiera sul tavolo, **to get on the bus** salire sull'autobus) **2** (*argomento*) su, circa, di (ES: **a book on the President's life** un libro sulla vita del Presidente) **3** (*tempo*) di, in, a (ES: **on Saturdays** di sabato) **4** (*modo, mezzo, funzione, ecc.*) con, in, da, di (ES: **on strike** in sciopero, **on principle** per principio) **B** *avv.* **1** su, sopra, addosso **2** avanti, in avanti, in poi **3** in corso, in atto, (*di apparecchio*) in funzione ♦ **go on!** avanti!; **on board** a bordo; **on foot** a piedi; **to switch on** accendere
once [wʌns] **A** *avv.* una volta, un tempo **B** *cong.* una volta che ♦ **all at o.** improvvisamente; **at o.** subito; **for o.** per una volta; **o. or twice** una o due volte; **O. upon a time there was ...** C'era una volta ...
one [wʌn] **A** *agg. num. card. e s.* uno *m.* **B** *agg.* **1** (*indef.*) uno, un certo (ES: **one Mr Jones** un certo Mr Jones) **2** solo, unico, stesso (ES: **that's the one and only way to do it** questo è l'unico modo per farlo) **C** *pron.* **1** (*indef.*) uno, una, l'uno, l'una, qualcuno (ES: **one by one** a uno a uno; **any one of us** uno qualunque di noi) **2** (*dimostr.*) questo, quello (ES: **I don't like modern cars, I prefer old ones** non mi piacciono le automobili moderne, preferisco quelle antiche) ♦ **no one** nessuno; **one another** l'un l'altro; **one's** il proprio
one-man [ˌwʌn'mæn] *agg.* individuale
one-off [ˌwʌn'ɜːf] *s.* esemplare *m.* unico
onerous ['ənərəs] *agg.* oneroso
oneself [wʌn'sɛlf] *pron. rifl.* sé, se stesso ♦ **by o.** da solo
one-sided [ˌwʌn'saɪdɪd] *agg.* **1** unilatera-

le **2** impari
one-to-one [ˌwʌntə'wʌn] *agg.* **1** biunivoco **2** tra due persone
one-way [ˌwʌn'weɪ] *agg.* **1** a senso unico **2** di sola andata
ongoing ['ɔnˌgɒ(ʊ)ɪŋ] *agg.* in corso
onion ['ʌnjən] *s.* cipolla *f.*
only ['ɒʊnlɪ] **A** *agg.* solo, unico **B** *cong.* solo (che), ma **C** *avv.* solo, soltanto, unicamente ♦ **not o. ... but also** non solo ... ma anche; **o. if** solamente se; **o. just** a malapena; **o. too** fin troppo
onset ['ɔnsɛt] *s.* assalto *m.*
onshore ['ɔnʃɜːʳ] **A** *agg.* di terra verso terra **B** *avv.* a terra, verso terra ♦ **o. wind** vento di mare
onslaught ['ɔnslɜːt] *s.* assalto *m.*
onto ['ɔntʊ] (*anche* **on to**) *prep.* su, sopra
onus ['ɒʊnəs] *s.* onere *m.*
onward(s) ['ɔnwəd(z)] *avv.* avanti, in avanti, oltre
onyx ['ɔnɪks] *s.* onice *f.*
to ooze [uːz] *v. intr.* colare, filtrare, stillare
opal ['ɒʊp(ə)l] *s.* opale *m.*
opalescent [ˌɒʊpə'lɛs(ə)nt] *agg.* opalescente
opaque [ɒ(ʊ)'peɪk] *agg.* opaco
open ['ɒʊp(ə)n] *agg.* **1** aperto **2** dischiuso, sbocciato **3** (aperto al) pubblico, disponibile, vacante **4** incerto, insoluto **5** manifesto, evidente ♦ **o. day** giorno di apertura
to open ['ɒʊp(ə)n] **A** *v. tr.* **1** aprire **2** inaugurare **B** *v. intr.* **1** aprire, aprirsi **2** sbocciare **3** cominciare ♦ **to o. onto/into** aprirsi su; **to o. out** aprire, allargarsi; **to o. up** aprire (la porta), aprirsi
open-air [ˌɒʊp(ə)n'ɛəʳ] *agg.* all'aperto
opener ['ɒʊp(ə)nəʳ] *s.* (*nei composti*) che apre ♦ **bottle-o.** apribottiglie; **tin-o.** apriscatole
opening ['ɒʊp(ə)nɪŋ] **A** *agg.* d'inizio, d'apertura **B** *s.* **1** apertura *f.*, inaugurazione *f.*, esordio *m.* **2** varco *m.* **3** opportunità *f.*
openly ['ɒʊp(ə)nlɪ] *avv.* apertamente, francamente
open-minded [ˌɒʊpn'maɪndɪd] *agg.* di larghe vedute
opera ['ɔp(ə)rə] *s.* opera *f.* (lirica) ♦ **comic o.** opera buffa
to operate ['ɔpəreɪt] **A** *v. intr.* **1** operare, agire, avere effetto **2** funzionare **3** (*med.*) operare **B** *v. tr.* **1** produrre, provocare **2** far funzionare **3** (*med.*) operare **4** gestire
operatic [ˌɔpə'rætɪk] *agg.* operistico, lirico
operating ['ɔpəreɪtɪŋ] *agg.* operativo ♦ **o. theatre** sala operatoria
operation [ˌɔpə'reɪʃ(ə)n] *s.* **1** operazione *f.* **2** azione *f.*, effetto *m.* **3** funzionamento *m.*, funzione *f.* ♦ **to come into o.** entrare in vigore
operative ['ɔp(ə)rətɪv] *agg.* operativo, efficace
operator ['ɔpəreɪtəʳ] *s.* **1** operatore *m. e f.* **2** (*tel.*) centralinista *m. e f.*
operetta [ˌɔpə'rɛtə] *s.* operetta *f.*
ophthalmology [ˌɔfθæl'mələdʒɪ] *s.* oftalmologia *f.*
opinion [ə'pɪnjən] *s.* **1** opinione *f.*, parere *m.* **2** stima *f.* ♦ **in his/in my o.** secondo lui/secondo me; **o. poll** sondaggio d'opinione
opinionated [ə'pɪnjəneɪtɪd] *agg.* supponente, presuntuoso
opium ['ɒʊpjəm] *s.* oppio *m.*
opponent [ə'pɒʊnənt] *s.* avversario *m.*
opportune ['ɔpətjuːn] *agg.* opportuno, tempestivo
opportunism [ˌɔpə'tjuːnɪz(ə)m] *s.* opportunismo *m.*
opportunist [ˌɔpə'tjʊ(ː)nɪst] *s.* opportunista *m. e f.*
opportunity [ˌɔpə'tjuːnɪtɪ] *s.* opportunità *f.*, occasione *f.*
to oppose [ə'pɒʊz] **A** *v. tr.* **1** opporsi a, contrastare, osteggiare **2** opporre, contrapporre **B** opporsi
opposed [ə'pɒʊzd] *agg.* **1** contrario, avverso **2** opposto ♦ **as o. to** in confronto a, rispetto a, invece di
opposite ['ɔpəzɪt] **A** *agg.* **1** opposto, contrario **2** di fronte **B** *s.* opposto *m.*, contrario *m.* **C** *avv.* davanti, di fronte **D** *prep.* di fronte a
opposition [ˌɔpə'zɪʃ(ə)n] *s.* opposizione *f.*
to oppress [ə'prɛs] *v. tr.* opprimere
oppression [ə'prɛʃ(ə)n] *s.* oppressione *f.*
oppressive [ə'prɛsɪv] *agg.* **1** oppressivo **2** opprimente
oppressor [ə'prɛsəʳ] *s.* oppressore *m.*
to opt [ɔpt] *v. intr.* optare ♦ **to o. out** dissociarsi, distaccarsi
optic ['ɔptɪk] *agg.* ottico
optical ['ɔptɪk(ə)l] *agg.* ottico
optician [ɔp'tɪʃ(ə)n] *s.* ottico *m.*
optics ['ɔptɪks] *s. pl.* (*v. al sing.*) ottica *f.*
optimal ['ɔptɪməl] *agg.* ottimale
optimism ['ɔptɪmɪz(ə)m] *s.* ottimismo *m.*
optimist ['ɔptɪmɪst] *s.* ottimista *m. e f.*

optimistic [ˌɔptɪ'mɪstɪk] *agg.* ottimistico
to optimize ['ɔptɪmaɪz] **A** *v. tr.* ottimizzare **B** *v. intr.* essere ottimista
optimum ['ɔptɪmən] **A** *s.* optimum *m.* **B** *agg.* ottimale
option ['ɔpʃ(ə)n] *s.* scelta *f.*, opzione *f.*
optional ['ɔpʃənl] *agg.* opzionale, facoltativo
opulence ['ɔpjʊləns] *s.* opulenza *f.*
or [ɜːʳ, əʳ] *cong.* o, oppure ♦ **either ... or ...** o ... o ...; **or else** altrimenti
oracle ['ɔrəkl] *s.* oracolo *m.*
oral ['ɜːr(ə)l] *agg.* orale
orange ['ɔrɪn(d)ʒ] **A** *s.* arancia *f.* **B** *agg.* arancione, arancio ♦ **o. peel** scorza d'arancia
orangeade [ˌɔrɪn(d)ʒ'eɪd] *s.* aranciata *f.*
orator ['ɔrətəʳ] *s.* oratore *m.*
oratory ['ɔrət(ə)rɪ] *s.* **1** oratorio *m.* **2** oratoria *f.*
orbit ['ɜːbɪt] *s.* orbita *f.*
to orbit ['ɜːbɪt] **A** *v. intr.* orbitare **B** *v. tr.* orbitare intorno a
orchard ['ɜːtʃəd] *s.* frutteto *m.*
orchestra ['ɜːkɪstrə] *s.* orchestra *f.*
orchid ['ɜːkɪd] *s.* orchidea *f.*
to ordain [ɜː'deɪn] *v. tr.* **1** (*relig.*) ordinare **2** decretare
ordeal [ɜː'diːl] *s.* **1** (*stor.*) ordalia *f.* **2** prova *f.*
order ['ɜːdəʳ] *s.* **1** ordine *m.* **2** successione *f.* **3** ordinamento *m.* **4** (*comm.*) commessa *f.* ♦ **mail o.** ordine per corrispondenza; **out of o.** fuori servizio; **postal o.** vaglia postale; **telegraphic money o.** vaglia telegrafico
to order ['ɜːdəʳ] *v. tr.* **1** ordinare, disporre **2** (*comm.*) commissionare ♦ **to o. away** mandare via; **to o. out** espellere
orderly ['ɜːdəlɪ] **A** *agg.* **1** ordinato, metodico **2** disciplinato **B** *s.* **1** (*mil.*) attendente *m.* **2** inserviente *m.*
ordinal ['ɜːdɪnl] *agg.* ordinale
ordinance ['ɜːdɪnəns] *s.* ordinanza *f.*
ordinary ['ɜːdnrɪ] *agg.* **1** ordinario, comune **2** mediocre, dozzinale
ordination [ˌɜːdɪ'neɪʃ(ə)n] *s.* (*relig.*) ordinazione *f.*
ore [ɜːʳ] *s.* minerale *m.* ♦ **o. district** distretto minerario
organ ['ɜːgən] *s.* organo *m.*
organic [ɜː'gænɪk] *agg.* organico
organism ['ɜːgənɪz(ə)m] *s.* organismo *m.*
organization [ˌɜːgənaɪ'zeɪʃ(ə)n] *s.* organizzazione *f.*, organismo *m.*
to organize ['ɜːgənaɪz] *v. tr. e intr.* organizzare, organizzarsi
orgasm ['ɜːgæz(ə)m] *s.* orgasmo *m.*
orgy ['ɜːdʒɪ] *s.* orgia *f.*
orient ['ɜːrɪənt] *agg. e s.* oriente *m.*
to orient ['ɜːrɪˌənt] *v. tr.* orientare
Oriental [ˌɜːrɪ'ɛntl] *agg. e s.* orientale *m. e f.*
to orientate ['ɜːrɪɛnteɪt] *v. tr.* orientare
orientation [ˌɜːrɪɛn'teɪʃ(ə)n] *s.* orientamento *m.*
origin ['ɔrɪdʒɪn] *s.* **1** origine *f.*, principio *m.* **2** nascita *f.*
original [ə'rɪdʒənl] **A** *agg.* originale, originario **B** *s.* originale *m.*
originality [əˌrɪdʒɪ'nælɪtɪ] *s.* originalità *f.*
to originate [ə'rɪdʒɪneɪt] **A** *v. tr.* dare origine **B** *v. intr.* aver origine, nascere, provenire
ornament ['ɜːnəmənt] *s.* **1** ornamento *m.* **2** ninnolo *m.*
ornamental [ˌɜːnə'ment(ə)l] *agg.* ornamentale
ornate [ɜː'neɪt] *agg.* riccamente ornato
ornithology [ˌɜːnɪθələdʒɪ] *s.* ornitologia *f.*
orography [ə'rəgrəfɪ] *s.* orografia *f.*
orphan ['ɜːf(ə)n] *agg. e s.* orfano *m.*
orphanage ['ɜːfənɪdʒ] *s.* orfanotrofio *m.*
orthodox ['ɜːθədəks] *agg.* ortodosso
orthodoxy ['ɜːθədəksɪ] *s.* ortodossia *f.*
orthogonal [ɜː'θəgənl] *agg.* ortogonale
orthography [ə(ː)'θəgrəfɪ] *s.* ortografia *f.*
orthop(a)edist [ˌɜːθɒ(ʊ)'piːdɪst] *s.* ortopedico *m.*
orthop(a)edy [ˌɜːθɒ(ʊ)'piːdɪ] *s.* ortopedia *f.*
to oscillate ['əsɪleɪt] *v. intr.* oscillare
oscillation [ˌəsɪl'leɪʃ(ə)n] *s.* oscillazione *f.*
osseous ['əsɪəs] *agg.* osseo
ostensible [əs'tɛnsəbl] *agg.* apparente, simulato
ostensibly [əs'tɛnsəblɪ] *avv.* apparentemente
ostensory [əs'tɛnsərɪ] *s.* ostensorio *m.*
ostentation [ˌəstɛn'teɪʃ(ə)n] *s.* ostentazione *f.*, esibizione *f.*
ostentatious [ˌəstɛn'teɪʃəs] *agg.* ostentato
ostrich ['əstrɪtʃ] *s.* struzzo *m.*
other ['ʌðəʳ] **A** *agg.* altro, diverso **B** *pron. indef.* (l')altro, (l')altra **C** *avv.* altrimenti, diversamente ♦ **any o.** qualche altro; **every o.** ogni altro; **none o. than** proprio, non altri che; **o. people** altri; **o.'s,**

o. people's altrui; **o. than** tranne
otherwise ['ʌðəwaɪz] **A** *agg.* diverso **B** *avv.* diversamente, altrimenti **C** *cong.* altrimenti, in caso contrario
otitis [ɒ(ʊ)'taɪtɪs] *s.* otite *f.*
otter ['ɔtəʳ] *s.* lontra *f.*
Ottoman ['ɔtəmən] *agg. e s.* ottomano *m.*
ought [ɜːt] *v. difett.* (*consiglio, dovere, rimprovero, probabilità*) dovere ♦ **You o. to do it** dovresti farlo; **he o. to have phoned me** avrebbe dovuto telefonarmi
ounce [aʊns] *s.* oncia *f.*
our ['aʊəʳ] *agg. poss. 1ª pl.* nostro, nostra, nostri, nostre
ours ['aʊəz] *pron. poss. 1ª pl.* il nostro, la nostra, i nostri, le nostre
ourselves [ˌaʊə'sɛlvz] *pron. rifl. 1ª pl.* noi stessi
to oust [aʊst] *v. tr.* cacciare, espellere
out [aʊt] **A** *avv.* **1** fuori, all'aperto, in fuori **2** spento, disattivato **3** finito, compiuto **4** passato di moda, inaccettabile **B** *prep.* **o. of 1** fuori, fuori da, da **2** a causa di, per **3** senza **4** su (ES: **in one case o. of ten** in un caso su dieci) ♦ **all o.** a tutta velocità; **o. here** qui fuori; **o. there** laggiù
out-and-out ['aʊtəndaʊt] *agg.* completo, vero e proprio
outboard ['aʊtbɜːd] *agg. e avv.* fuoribordo
outbreak ['aʊtbreɪk] *s.* **1** scoppio *m.*, esplosione *f.* **2** eruzione *f.* **3** epidemia *f.* **4** sommossa *f.*
outburst ['aʊtbɜːst] *s.* esplosione *f.*, scoppio *m.*
outcast ['aʊtkaːst] *s.* emarginato *m.*, reietto *m.*
outcome ['aʊtkʌm] *s.* esito *m.*, risultato *m.*
outcry ['aʊtkraɪ] *s.* **1** protesta *f.*, scalpore *m.* **2** grido *m.*
outdated ['aʊtdeɪtɪd] *agg.* antiquato, sorpassato
to outdo [ˌaʊt'duː] (*pass.* **outdid**, *p. p.* **outdone**) *v. tr.* sorpassare, far meglio di
outdoor ['aʊtdɜːʳ] *agg.* esterno, all'aperto
outdoors [ˌaʊt'dɜːz] **A** *avv.* all'aperto, all'aria aperta **B** *s.* l'aperto *m.*, l'esterno *m.*
outer ['aʊtəʳ] *agg.* esteriore, esterno ♦ **o. space** spazio cosmico
outfit ['aʊtfɪt] *s.* **1** equipaggiamento *m.*, attrezzatura *f.* **2** tenuta *f.*
outgoing ['aʊtˌgɒʊɪŋ] **A** *agg.* **1** uscente, dimissionario **2** socievole, estroverso **B** *s.* **1** uscita *f.* **2** *al pl.* spese *f. pl.*
to outgrow [aʊt'grɒʊ] (*pass.* **outgrew**, *p. p.* **outgrown**) *v. tr.* **1** superare in statura **2** perdere, disfarsi di ♦ **to o. one's clothes** diventare troppo grande per i propri vestiti
outing ['aʊtɪŋ] *s.* gita *f.*, escursione *f.*
outlandish [aʊt'lændɪʃ] *agg.* **1** straniero, esotico **2** strano, bizzarro
outlaw ['aʊtlɜː] **A** *s.* fuorilegge *m. e f.*, criminale *m. e f.* **B** *agg.* illegale
to outlaw ['aʊtlɜː] *v. tr.* bandire, proscrivere
outlay ['aʊtleɪ] *s.* spesa *f.*
outlet ['aʊtlɛt] *s.* **1** sbocco *m.*, sfogo *m.* **2** punto *m.* di vendita **3** presa *f.* elettrica
outline ['aʊtlaɪn] *s.* **1** contorno *m.*, profilo *m.* **2** abbozzo *m.*, schema *m.*
to outline ['aʊtlaɪn] *v. tr.* **1** tracciare il contorno di **2** delineare, abbozzare
to outlive [aʊt'lɪv] *v. tr.* sopravvivere a
outlook ['aʊtlʊk] *s.* **1** vista *f.*, veduta *f.* **2** prospettiva *f.* **3** modo *m.* di vedere
outlying ['aʊtˌlaɪɪŋ] *agg.* **1** esterno **2** remoto
outmatch [aʊt'mætʃ] *v. tr.* sorpassare
outmoded [aʊt'mɒʊdɪd] *agg.* antiquato, passato di moda
to outnumber [aʊt'nʌmbəʳ] *v. tr.* superare in numero
out-of-date [ˌaʊtəv'deɪt] *agg.* **1** fuori moda **2** scaduto
out-of-the-way [ˌaʊtəvð(ə)'weɪ] *agg.* **1** fuori mano **2** fuori del comune
outpost ['aʊtpɒʊst] *s.* avamposto *m.*
output ['aʊtpʊt] *s.* **1** produzione *f.*, rendimento *m.* **2** (*inf.*) output *m. inv.*
outrage ['aʊtreɪdʒ] *s.* **1** oltraggio *m.*, offesa *f.* **2** indignazione *f.*
to outrage ['aʊtreɪdʒ] *s.* oltraggiare
outrageous [aʊt'reɪdʒəs] *agg.* **1** oltraggioso, atroce **2** eccessivo, esorbitante
outright [aʊt'raɪt] **A** *agg. attr.* **1** aperto, schietto, diretto **2** completo, integrale **3** immediato **B** *avv.* **1** apertamente, francamente **2** completamente **3** immediatamente, sul colpo
outside ['aʊtsaɪd] **A** *agg.* **1** esterno, esteriore **2** estremo, massimo **B** *s.* **1** esterno *m.*, parte *f.* esterna **2** apparenza *f.*, aspetto *m.* esteriore **C** *avv.* **1** fuori, all'aperto **2** all'esterno **D** *prep.* **1** fuori di, all'esterno di **2** al di fuori, al di là **3** all'infuori di, eccetto
outsider [aʊt'saɪdəʳ] *s.* outsider *m. inv.*
outsize ['aʊtˌsaɪz] *agg.* **1** molto grande **2** (*di abito*) di taglia forte
outskirts ['aʊtskɜːts] *s. pl.* periferia *f.*, sob-

borghi *m. pl.*

outspoken [aʊt'spɒʊk(ə)n] *agg.* esplicito, schietto

outstanding [aʊt'stændɪŋ] *agg.* **1** sporgente **2** notevole, rilevante **3** eccezionale **4** in arretrato, in sospeso, inevaso

outward ['aʊtwəd] **A** *agg.* **1** esterno **2** esteriore **3** d'andata **B** *s.* aspetto *m.* esteriore **C** *avv.* al di fuori, esternamente

to **outweigh** [aʊt'weɪ] *v. tr.* superare (*in peso o valore*)

to **outwit** [aʊt'wɪt] *v. tr.* superare in astuzia

ouzel ['uːzl] *s.* (*zool.*) merlo *m.*

oval ['ɒʊv(ə)l] *agg.* ovale

ovary ['ɒʊvərɪ] *s.* ovaia *f.*

oven ['ʌvn] *s.* forno *m.*

ovenware ['ʌv(ə)nwɛəʳ] *s.* stoviglie *f. pl.* da forno

over ['ɒʊvəʳ] **A** *agg.* terminato, finito **B** *avv.* **1** al di sopra, di sopra **2** completamente, da cima a fondo **3** di più, troppo, in eccesso **C** *prep.* **1** sopra, su, al di sopra di **2** nei confronti di, riguardo a **3** durante, per **4** più di, oltre, al di là di ♦ **o. again** più volte, di nuovo, ripetutamente; **o. tired** stanchissimo

overall ['ɒʊvərɜːl] **A** *agg.* complessivo **B** *avv.* complessivamente **C** *s.* tuta *f.* (*da lavoro*)

to **overawe** [ˌɒʊvər'ɜː] *v. tr.* intimidire

to **overbalance** [ˌɒʊvə'bæləns] **A** *v. tr.* **1** superare in peso **2** prevalere su **3** sbilanciare **B** *v. intr.* sbilanciarsi

overbearing [ˌɒʊvə'bɛərɪŋ] *agg.* **1** arrogante, imperioso **2** soverchiante

overboard ['ɒʊvəbɜːd] *avv.* fuori bordo

to **overburden** [ˌɒʊvə'bɜːdn] *v. tr.* sovraccaricare

overcast ['ɒʊvəˌkaːst] *agg.* nuvoloso, coperto

overcharge [ˌɒʊvə'tʃaːdʒ] *s.* **1** sovraccarico *m.* **2** sovrapprezzo *m.*

to **overcharge** [ˌɒʊvə'tʃaːdʒ] *v. tr.* **1** far pagare troppo caro **2** sovraccaricare

overcoat ['ɒʊvəkɒʊt] *s.* soprabito *m.*

to **overcome** [ˌɒʊvə'kʌm] (*pass.* **overcame**, *p. p.* **overcome**) *v. tr.* superare, sopraffare

overcooked [ˌɒʊvə'kʊkt] *agg.* troppo cotto

overcrowded [ˌɒʊvə'krɒʊdɪd] *agg.* sovraffollato

to **overdo** [ˌɒʊvə'duː] (*pass.* **overdid**, *p. p.* **overdone**) **A** *v. tr.* **1** eccedere in, esagerare **2** affaticare **3** far cuocere troppo **B** *v. intr.* esagerare

overdose ['ɒʊvədɒʊs] *s.* dose *f.* eccessiva, overdose *f. inv.*

overdraft ['ɒʊvədraːft] *s.* (*banca*) scoperto *m.*

overdue [ˌɒʊvə'djuː] *agg.* **1** (*comm.*) scaduto **2** in ritardo **3** atteso, in attesa

to **overestimate** [ˌɒʊvər'ɛstɪmeɪt] *v. tr.* sopravvalutare

to **overexpose** [ˌɒʊv(ə)rɪk'spɒʊz] *v. tr.* (*fot.*) sovraesporre

overflow ['ɒʊvəflɒʊ] *s.* **1** straripamento *m.* inondazione *f.* **2** eccedenza *f.* **3** (*inf.*) overflow *m. inv.*

to **overflow** [ˌɒʊvə'flɒʊ] *v. intr.* straripare, traboccare

overflowing [ˌɒʊvə'flɒʊɪŋ] **A** *agg.* **1** straripante, traboccante **2** sovrabbondante **B** *s.* straripamento *m.*, inondazione *f.*

overhang ['ɒʊvəhæŋ] *s.* **1** sporgenza *f.* **2** strapiombo *m.*

overhaul ['ɒʊvəhɜːl] *s.* revisione *f.*

to **overhaul** [ˌɒʊvə'hɜːl] *v. tr.* **1** revisionare, verificare **2** esaminare, rivedere **3** sorpassare, superare

overhead [ˌɒʊvə'hɛd] **A** *avv.* in alto, di sopra **B** *agg.* **1** alto, sopraelevato, aereo **2** globale, generale **C** *s. al pl.* spese *f. pl.* generali

to **overhear** [ˌɒʊvə'hɪəʳ] (*pass. e p. p.* **overheard**) *v. tr.* udire per caso

to **overheat** [ˌɒʊvə'hiːt] *v. tr. e intr.* surriscaldare

overjoyed [ˌɒʊvə'dʒɔɪd] *agg.* felicissimo

overland [ˌɒʊvə'lænd] *agg. e avv.* via terra

to **overlap** [ˌɒʊvə'læp] *v. intr.* sovrapporsi, coincidere

to **overlay** [ˌɒʊvə'leɪ] (*pass. e p. p.* **overlaid**) *v. tr.* **1** coprire, ricoprire **2** opprimere

overleaf [ˌɒʊvə'liːf] *avv.* sul retro, a tergo

to **overload** [ˌɒʊvə'lɒʊd] *v. tr.* sovraccaricare

to **overlook** [ˌɒʊvə'lʊk] *v. tr.* **1** guardare dall'alto, dominare **2** trascurare, non rilevare, lasciarsi sfuggire **3** tollerare **4** sorvegliare

overnight [ˌɒʊvə'naɪt] **A** *agg.* **1** che si svolge di notte **2** per una notte **3** immediato **B** *avv.* **1** di notte, per la notte **2** improvvisamente

overpass ['ɒʊvəˌpaːs] *s.* cavalcavia *m. inv.*

to **overpower** [ˌɒʊvə'paʊəʳ] *v. tr.* sopraffare, opprimere

overpowering [ˌɒʊvəˈpaʊərɪŋ] *agg.* **1** opprimente **2** irresistibile
to **overrate** [ˌɒʊvəˈreɪt] *v. tr.* sopravvalutare
to **override** [ˌɒʊvəˈraɪd] (*pass.* **overrode**, *p. p.* **overriden**) *v. tr.* **1** passare sopra, non tener conto di **2** annullare
to **overrule** [ˌɒʊvəˈruːl] *v. tr.* **1** annullare, revocare **2** dominare
to **overrun** [ˌɒʊvəˈrʌn] (*pass.* **overran**, *p. p.* **overrun**) **A** *v. tr.* **1** invadere, devastare, infestare **2** sommergere **3** oltrepassare, superare **B** *v. intr.* **1** traboccare, straripare **2** protrarsi
overseas [ˌɒʊvəˈsiː(z)] **A** *agg.* estero, d'oltremare **B** *avv.* all'estero, oltremare
to **overshadow** [ˌɒʊvəˈʃædɒʊ] *v. tr.* **1** ombreggiare, fare ombra su **2** (*fig.*) oscurare, eclissare
to **overshoot** [ˌɒʊvəˈʃuːt] (*pass. e p. p.* **overshot**) *v. tr.* **1** lanciare troppo alto, sparare al di là del bersaglio, mancare **2** andare oltre
oversight [ˈɒʊvəsaɪt] *s.* **1** disattenzione *f.*, svista *f.* **2** sorveglianza *f.*
to **oversleep** [ˌɒʊvəˈsliːp] *v. intr.* dormire troppo
to **overstate** [ˌɒʊvəˈsteɪt] *v. tr.* esagerare
to **overstep** [ˌɒʊvəˈstɛp] *v. tr.* oltrepassare
overt [ˈɒʊvɜːt] *agg.* chiaro, evidente
to **overtake** [ˌɒʊvəˈteɪk] (*pass.* **overtook**, *p. p.* **overtaken**) *v. tr.* **1** raggiungere, sorpassare **2** sorprendere
overtaking [ˌɒʊvəˈteɪkɪŋ] *s.* sorpasso *m.* ♦ **no o.** divieto di sorpasso
to **overthrow** [ˌɒʊvəˈθrɒʊ] (*pass.* **overthrew**, *p. p.* **overthrow**) *v. tr.* rovesciare, abbattere
overtime [ˈɒʊvətaɪm] *s.* **1** (lavoro) straordinario *m.* **2** (*sport*) tempo *m.* supplementare
overturn [ˌɒʊvəˈtɜːn] *s.* ribaltamento *m.*
to **overturn** [ˌɒʊvəˈtɜːn] **A** *v. tr.* capovolgere, rovesciare **B** *v. intr.* ribaltarsi, capottarsi
overweight [ˈɒʊvəweɪt] *agg.* in sovrappeso
to **overwhelm** [ˌɒʊvəˈwɛlm] *v. tr.* **1** distruggere, sopraffare **2** seppellire, sommergere
overwhelming [ˌɒʊvəˈwɛlmɪŋ] *agg.* opprimente, travolgente
to **overwork** [ˌɒʊvəˈwɜːk] *v. intr.* lavorare troppo
overwrought [ˌɒʊvəˈrɜːt] *agg.* **1** nervoso, agitato **2** ricercato
ovine [ˈɒʊvaɪn] *agg.* ovino
oviparous [ɒ(ʊ)ˈvɪpərəs] *s.* oviparo *m.*
ovoid [ˈɒʊvəɪd] *agg.* ovoidale
to **owe** [ɒʊ] **A** *v. tr.* dovere, essere debitore di **B** *v. intr.* essere indebitato ♦ **to o. sb. st.** dovere q.c. a qc.
owing [ˈɒ(ʊ)ɪŋ] *agg. attr.* dovuto ♦ **o. to** a causa di
owl [aʊl] *s.* gufo *m.*
own [ɒʊn] **A** *agg.* proprio **B** *s.* il proprio *m.*
to **own** [ɒʊn] *v. tr.* **1** possedere, avere **2** ammettere, riconoscere ♦ **to o. up** confessare
owner [ˈɒʊnəʳ] *s.* proprietario *m.*, padrone *m.*
ownership [ˈɒʊnəʃɪp] *s.* proprietà *f.*
ox [əks] (*pl.* **oxen**) *s.* bue *m.*
oxide [ˈəksaɪd] *s.* ossido *m.*
to **oxidize** [ˈəksɪdaɪz] *v. tr. e intr.* ossidare, ossidarsi
oxygen [ˈəksɪdʒ(ə)n] *s.* ossigeno *m.*
oyster [ˈəɪstəʳ] *s.* ostrica *f.*
ozone [ˈɒʊzɒʊn] *s.* ozono *m.*

P

pa [pɑː] *s.* (*fam.*) papà *m.*
pace [peɪs] *s.* **1** passo *m.* **2** andatura *f.*, ritmo *m.* **3** ambio *m.*
to pace [peɪs] **A** *v. intr.* andare al passo, camminare **B** *v. intr.* percorrere, misurare a passi
pacemaker ['peɪsˌmeɪkəʳ] *s.* **1** battistrada *m.* **2** (*med.*) pacemaker *m. inv.*
pacific [pə'sɪfɪk] *agg.* pacifico
pacification [ˌpæsɪfɪ'keɪʃ(ə)n] *s.* pacificazione *f.*
pacifism ['pæsɪfɪz(ə)m] *s.* pacifismo *m.*
to pacify ['pæsɪfaɪ] *v. tr.* pacificare
pack [pæk] *s.* **1** pacco *m.*, pacchetto *m.*, imballaggio *m.* **2** carico *m.*, soma *f.* **3** zaino *m.* **4** muta *f.*, branco *m.* **5** (*di carte da gioco*) mazzo *m.* **6** ammasso *m.*
to pack [pæk] **A** *v. tr.* **1** imballare, impacchettare **2** pigiare, pressare, stipare **B** *v. intr.* **1** fare i bagagli **2** stiparsi, accalcarsi ♦ **to p. in** smettere; **to p. off** mandar via; **to p. up** fare le valigie, smettere di lavorare, (*di motore*) spegnersi
package ['pækɪdʒ] *s.* **1** pacco *m.*, confezione *f.* **2** (*di proposte*) pacchetto *m.* ♦ **p. tour** viaggio organizzato
packet ['pækɪt] *s.* pacchetto *m.*
packing ['pækɪŋ] *s.* imballaggio *m.*
pact [pækt] *s.* patto *m.*
pad [pæd] *s.* **1** cuscinetto *m.*, imbottitura *f.* **2** tampone *m.* **3** blocco *m.* di carta **4** (*autom.*) pastiglia *f.* **5** piattaforma *f.*, (*di missile*) rampa *f.*
to pad [pæd] *v. tr.* **1** imbottire **2** (*fig.*) gonfiare
padding ['pædɪŋ] *s.* imbottitura *f.*
paddle ['pædl] *s.* **1** pagaia *f.* **2** spatola *f.* **3** (*naut.*) (*di elica, ruota*) pala *f.* **4** (*zool.*) pinna *f.* ♦ **p. steamer** battello a ruota
to paddle (1) ['pædl] *v. intr.* remare (con le pagaie)
to paddle (2) ['pædl] *v. intr.* sguazzare ♦ **paddling pool** piscina per bambini
paddock ['pædək] *s.* **1** (*per cavalli*) recinto *m.* **2** prato *m.* recintato
paddy ['pædɪ] *s.* riso *m.* (in erba) ♦ **p. field** risaia
padlock ['pædlək] *s.* lucchetto *m.*
p(a)ediatrics [ˌpiːdɪ'ætrɪks] *s. pl.* (*v. al sing.*) pediatria *f.*
p(a)ediatrist [ˌpiːdɪ'ætrɪst] *s.* pediatra *m. e f.*
pagan ['peɪgən] *agg. e s.* pagano *m.*
paganism ['peɪgənɪz(ə)m] *s.* paganesimo *m.*
page (1) [peɪdʒ] *s.* pagina *f.*
page (2) [peɪdʒ] *s.* **1** fattorino *m.* **2** paggio *m.*
pageant ['pædʒ(ə)nt] *s.* **1** parata *f.* storica **2** pompa *f.*, sfarzo *m.*
pagoda [pə'gɒʊdə] *s.* pagoda *f.*
paid [peɪd] *pass. e p. p. di* **to pay**
pail [peɪl] *s.* secchio *m.*
pain [peɪn] *s.* **1** dolore *m.*, male *m.* **2** pena *f.*, castigo *m.* **3** *al pl.* fatica *f.*, pena *f.* ♦ **p.-killer** antidolorifico
pained [peɪnd] *agg.* addolorato, afflitto
painful ['peɪnf(ʊ)l] *agg.* doloroso, penoso
painless ['peɪnlɪs] *agg.* indolore
paint [peɪnt] *s.* pittura *f.*, vernice *f.*, tinta *f.* ♦ **wet p.** vernice fresca
to paint [peɪnt] *v. tr. e intr.* dipingere, pitturare, verniciare
paintbrush ['peɪntbrʌʃ] *s.* pennello *m.*
painter ['peɪntəʳ] *s.* **1** pittore *m.* **2** decoratore *m.*, imbianchino *m.*
painting ['peɪntɪŋ] *s.* **1** pittura *f.*, verniciatura *f.* **2** dipinto *m.*, quadro *m.* **3** pittura *f.* (*arte*)
pair [pɛəʳ] *s.* **1** paio *m.* **2** coppia *f.* ♦ **in pairs** a coppie
Pakistani [ˌpɑːkɪs'tɑːnɪ] *agg. e s.* pachistano *m.*
pal [pæl] *s.* (*fam.*) amico *m.*, compagno *m.*
palace ['pælɪs] *s.* **1** palazzo *m.* **2** reggia *f.*
paladin ['pælədɪn] *s.* paladino *m.*
palaeography [ˌpælɪ'əgrəfɪ] *s.* paleografia *f.*
Palaeolithic [ˌpælɪɒ(ʊ)'lɪθɪk] *agg.* paleolitico
palafitte ['pæləfɪt] *s.* palafitta *f.*
palatable ['pælətəbl] *agg.* appetitoso, gustoso, gradevole
palate ['pælɪt] *s.* palato *m.*
palatial [pə'leɪʃ(ə)l] *agg.* sontuoso, lussuoso
palaver [pə'lɑːvəʳ] *s.* **1** colloquio *m.* **2** chiacchiere *f. pl.*

pale (1) [peɪl] *agg.* pallido, fioco, debole ♦ **p. ale** birra chiara
pale (2) [peɪl] *s.* **1** palo *m.*, picchetto *m.* **2** (*fig.*) limite *m.* **3** (*stor*) territorio *m.*
to pale [peɪl] *v. intr.* impallidire
Palestinian [ˌpælɪs'tɪnɪən] *agg. e s.* palestinese *m. e f.*
palette ['pælɪt] *s.* tavolozza *f.*
paling ['peɪlɪŋ] *s.* palizzata *f.*
pall [pɜːl] *s.* **1** drappo *m.* funebre **2** (*fig.*) cappa *f.*
pallet (1) ['pælɪt] *s.* giaciglio *m.*
pallet (2) ['pælɪt] *s.* **1** paletta *f.*, spatola *f.* **2** pallet *m. inv.*
palliative ['pælɪətɪv] *agg. e s.* palliativo *m.*
pallid ['pælɪd] *agg.* pallido, smunto
pallor ['pælə^r] *s.* pallore *m.*
palm (1) [paːm] *s.* (*bot.*) palma *f.* ♦ **date p.** palma da datteri
palm (2) [paːm] *s.* palmo *m.*
to palm [paːm] *v. tr.* **1** maneggiare **2** nascondere (in mano) ♦ **to p. st. off on sb.** affibbiare q.c. a qc.
palmiped ['pælmɪpɛd] *agg. e s.* palmipede *m.*
palmist ['paːmɪst] *s.* chiromante *m. e f.*
palpable ['pælpəbl] *agg.* palpabile, tangibile
to palpate ['pælpeɪt] *v. tr.* palpare
palpitation [ˌpælpɪ'teɪʃ(ə)n] *s.* palpitazione *f.*
paltry ['pɜːltrɪ] *agg.* meschino, ridicolo
to pamper ['pæmpə^r] *v. tr.* viziare, vezzeggiare
pamphlet ['pæmflɪt] *s.* opuscolo *m.*
pan [pæn] *s.* pentola *f.* ♦ **baking p.** teglia; **frying p.** padella
pancake ['pænkeɪk] *s.* frittella *f.*
pancreas ['pæŋkrɪəs] *s.* pancreas *m. inv.*
panda ['pændə] *s.* panda *m. inv.* ♦ **p. car** auto della polizia; **p. crossing** attraversamento pedonale con semaforo a controllo manuale
pandemonium [ˌpændɪ'mɒʊnjəm] *s.* pandemonio *m.*
to pander ['pændə^r] *v. intr.* fare il mezzano ♦ **to p. to** favorire, assecondare
pane [peɪn] *s.* **1** (lastra di) vetro *m.* **2** pannello *m.*
panegyric [ˌpænɪ'dʒɪrɪk] *s.* panegirico *m.*
panel ['pænl] *s.* **1** pannello *m.*, quadro *m.*, riquadro *m.* **2** lista *f.*, elenco *m.* **3** gruppo *m.* di esperti, commissione *f.*, giuria *f.* ♦ **p. doctor** medico della mutua
panelling ['pænlɪŋ] *s.* rivestimento *m.* a pannelli
pang [pæŋ] *s.* dolore *m.* acuto, fitta *f.* ♦ **pangs of hunger** morsi della fame
panic ['pænɪk] **A** *agg.* panico, dettato dal panico **B** *s.* **1** panico *m.*, terrore *m.* **2** (*fam.*) fretta *f.* **3** (*fam.*) spasso *m.* ♦ **p.-stricken** in preda al panico
to panic ['pænɪk] (*pass. e p. p.* **panicked**) **A** *v. tr.* **1** gettare il panico tra **2** (*fam.*) divertire (*il pubblico*) **B** *v. intr.* essere in preda al panico
panicky ['pænɪkɪ] *agg.* (*fam.*) in preda al panico
panicle ['pænɪkl] *s.* pannocchia *f.*
panning ['pænɪŋ] *s.* (*cine.*) panoramica *f.*
panorama [ˌpænə'raːmə] *s.* paesaggio *m.*
panoramic [ˌpænə'ræmɪk] *agg.* panoramico
pansy ['pænzɪ] *s.* viola *f.* del pensiero
pantagruelian [ˌpæntəgruː'ɛlɪən] *agg.* pantagruelico
pantheism ['pænθiːɪz(ə)m] *s.* panteismo *m.*
panther ['pænθə^r] *s.* pantera *f.*
panties ['pæntɪz] *s. pl.* mutandine *f. pl.* (*da bambino o da donna*)
pantihose ['pæntɪhɒʊz] *s.* (*USA*) collant *m. inv.*
pantomime ['pæntəmaɪm] *s.* pantomima *f.*
pantry ['pæntrɪ] *s.* dispensa *f.*
pants [pænts] *s. pl.* **1** mutande *f. pl.* **2** (*USA*) pantaloni *m. pl.*
pap [pæp] *s.* pappa *f.*
papa [pə'paː] *s.* (*fam.*) papà *m.*
papacy ['peɪpəsɪ] *s.* papato *m.*
papal ['peɪp(ə)l] *agg.* papale, pontificio
paper ['peɪpə^r] *s.* **1** carta *f.* **2** documento *m.* **3** prova *f.* scritta, composizione *f.* **4** saggio *m.*, relazione *f.* **5** giornale *m.* ♦ **heap of p.** scartoffia; **morning p.** giornale del mattino; **p. knife** tagliacarte; **p. mill** cartiera; **p. money** cartamoneta; **sheet of p.** foglio di carta; **toilet p.** carta igienica; **writing p.** carta da lettere
paperback ['peɪpəbæk] *s.* paperback *m. inv.*, libro *m.* in brossura
paperweight ['peɪpəweɪt] *s.* fermacarte *m. inv.*
paperwork ['peɪpəwɜːk] *s.* lavoro *m.* d'ufficio
papier maché [ˌpæpjeɪ'maːʃeɪ] *s.* cartapesta *f.*

papism ['peɪpɪz(ə)m] *s.* papismo *m.*
paprika ['pæprɪkə] *s.* paprica *f.*, pepe *m.* rosso
papyrus [pə'paɪərəs] *s.* papiro *m.*
par [paːʳ] *s.* parità *f.*, pari *f.* ♦ **on a p. with** alla pari con
parable ['pærəbl] *s.* parabola *f.* (*racconto*)
parabola [pə'ræbələ] *s.* (*geom.*) parabola *f.*
parachute ['pærəʃuːt] *s.* paracadute *m. inv.*
parade [pə'reɪd] *s.* **1** parata *f.*, mostra *f.* **2** sfilata *f.*, rivista *f.*
to parade [pə'reɪd] *v. tr.* **1** passare in rivista **2** ostentare
paradise ['pærədaɪs] *s.* paradiso *m.*
paradox ['pærədəks] *s.* paradosso *m.*
paradoxical [ˌpærə'dəksɪk(ə)l] *agg.* paradossale
paraffin ['pærəfɪ(ː)n] *s.* paraffina *f.*
paragon ['pærəgən] *s.* esemplare *m.*, modello *m.*
paragraph ['pærəgraːf] *s.* **1** paragrafo *m.* **2** capoverso *m.* **3** trafiletto *m.*
parallel ['pærəlɛl] **A** *agg.* parallelo **B** *s.* **1** (*geom.*) parallela *f.* **2** (*geogr.*) parallelo *m.*
parallelepiped [ˌpærəˌlɛlaɪ'pəpɛd] *s.* parallelepipedo *m.*
parallelism ['pærəlɛlɪz(ə)m] *s.* parallelismo *m.*
to paralyse ['pærəlaɪz] (*USA* **paralyze**) *v. tr.* paralizzare
paralysis [pə'rælɪsɪs] *s.* paralisi *f.*
parameter [pə'ræmɪtəʳ] *s.* parametro *m.*
paramount ['pærəmaʊnt] *agg.* supremo, primario
paranoia [ˌpærə'nəjə] *s.* paranoia *f.*
paranoid ['pærəˌnəɪd] **A** *agg.* paranoide **B** *s.* paranoico *m.*
parapet ['pærəpɪt] *s.* parapetto *m.*
paraphernalia [ˌpærəfə'neɪljə] *s. pl.* **1** attrezzi *m. pl.*, accessori *m. pl.* **2** oggetti *m. pl.* personali
paraphrase ['pærəfreɪz] *s.* parafrasi *f.*
parapsychology [ˌpærəsaɪ'kələdʒɪ] *s.* parapsicologia *f.*
parasite ['pærəsaɪt] *s.* parassita *m.*
parasol ['pærəˌsəl] *s.* parasole *m. inv.*
paratrooper ['pærəˌtruːpəʳ] *s.* (*mil.*) paracadutista *m.*
parcel ['paːsl] *s.* **1** pacco *m.*, pacchetto *m.* **2** (*comm.*) partita *f.* **3** lotto *m.*
to parcel ['paːsl] *v. tr.* impacchettare
to parch [paːtʃ] *v. tr.* **1** essiccare **2** inaridire
parching ['paːtʃɪŋ] *agg.* bruciante
parchment ['paːtʃmənt] *s.* pergamena *f.*
pardon ['paːdn] *s.* **1** perdono *m.*, scusa *f.* **2** (*dir.*) grazia *f.* ♦ **p.?** (*per invitare a ripetere*) prego?; **I beg your p.!** mi scusi!
to pardon ['paːdn] *v. tr.* **1** perdonare, scusare **2** (*dir.*) graziare
pardonable ['paːdnəbl] *agg.* perdonabile
parent ['pɛər(ə)nt] *s.* genitore *m.*
parenthesis [pə'rɛnθɪsɪs] (*pl.* **parentheses**) *s.* parentesi *f.*
paresis [pə'riːsɪs] *s.* paresi *f.*
parish ['pærɪʃ] *s.* **1** parrocchia *f.* **2** distretto *m.* rurale ♦ **p. priest** parroco
Parisian [pə'rɪzjən] *agg. e s.* parigino *m.*
parity ['pærɪtɪ] *s.* parità *f.*
park [paːk] *s.* parco *m.*
to park [paːk] *v. tr. e intr.* parcheggiare
parking ['paːkɪŋ] *s.* parcheggio *m.*, posteggio *m.* ♦ **no p.** divieto di sosta; **p. meter** parchimetro; **p. place** posto macchina
parlance ['paːləns] *s.* parlata *f.*, linguaggio *m.*
parliament ['paːləmənt] *s.* parlamento *m.*
parliamentary [ˌpaːlə'mɛnt(ə)rɪ] *agg.* parlamentare
parlour ['paːləʳ] (*USA* **parlor**) *s.* **1** salotto *m.* **2** parlatorio *m.* **3** (*USA*) salone *m.*, istituto *m.* ♦ **beauty p.** istituto di bellezza
parochial [pə'rɒʊkjəl] *agg.* **1** parrocchiale **2** (*spreg.*) provinciale
parochialism [pə'rɒʊkjəlɪz(ə)m] *s.* (*spreg.*) provincialismo *m.*
parody ['pærədɪ] *s.* parodia *f.*
parole [pə'rɒʊl] *s.* **1** parola *f.* d'onore **2** parola *f.* d'ordine
paroxysmal [ˌpærək'sɪzməl] *agg.* parossistico
parquet ['paːkeɪ] *s.* parquet *m. inv.*
parricide ['pærɪsaɪd] *s.* **1** parricidio *m.* **2** parricida *m. e f.*
parrot ['pærət] *s.* pappagallo *m.*
to parry ['pærɪ] *v. tr.* parare, schivare
parsimonious [ˌpaːsɪ'mɒʊnjəs] *agg.* parsimonioso
parsley ['paːslɪ] *s.* prezzemolo *m.*
parsnip ['paːsnɪp] *s.* pastinaca *f.*
parson ['paːsn] *s.* (*anglicano*) parroco *m.*, (*protestante*) pastore *m.*
part [paːt] **A** *agg.* parziale **B** *avv.* parzialmente **C** *s.* **1** parte *f.* **2** (*mecc.*) pezzo *m.* **3** dispensa *f.*, fascicolo *m.* **4** (*USA*) scriminatura *f.* ♦ **on my p.** da parte mia; **spare parts** pezzi di ricambio

to **part** [pa:t] **A** *v. tr.* dividere, separare **B** *v. intr.* **1** dividersi, divergere **2** separarsi ♦ **to p. with st.** rinunciare a q.c.

to **partake** [pa:'teɪk] (*pass.* **partook**, *p. p.* **partaken**) *v. intr.* prender parte

partial ['pa:ʃ(ə)l] *agg.* parziale

to **participate** [pa:'tɪsɪpeɪt] *v. intr.* partecipare

participation [pa:ˌtɪsɪ'peɪʃ(ə)n] *s.* partecipazione *f.*

participle ['pa:tsɪpl] *s.* participio *m.*

particle ['pa:tɪkl] *s.* particella *f.*

particular [pə'tɪkjʊləʳ] **A** *agg.* **1** particolare, speciale **2** preciso, accurato **3** esigente, meticoloso **B** *s.* **1** particolare *m.* **2** ragguaglio *m.*, informazione *f.*

particularity [pəˌtɪkjʊ'lærɪtɪ] *s.* particolarità *f.*

particularly [pə'tɪkjʊləlɪ] *avv.* in particolare

parting ['pa:tɪŋ] *s.* **1** distacco *m.*, partenza *f.*, separazione *f.* **2** scriminatura *f.* ♦ **p. visit** visita di congedo

partisan [ˌpa:tɪ'zæn] *agg. e s.* partigiano *m.*

partition [pa:'tɪʃ(ə)n] *s.* **1** partizione *f.*, divisione *f.* **2** tramezzo *m.*

partly ['pa:tlɪ] *avv.* parzialmente

partner ['pa:tnəʳ] *s.* socio *m.*, compagno *m.*, partner *m. e f. inv.*

partnership ['pa:tnəʃɪp] *s.* società *f.*, associazione *f.*

partridge ['pa:trɪdʒ] *s.* pernice *f.*

party ['pa:tɪ] *s.* **1** partito *m.*, fazione *f.* **2** gruppo *m.*, squadra *f.*, comitiva *f.* **3** festa *f.*, ricevimento *m.* **4** (*dir.*) parte *f.* (in causa) ♦ **p. dress** abito da sera

pass (1) [pa:s] *s.* passo *m.*, valico *m.*

pass (2) [pa:s] *s.* **1** passaggio *m.* **2** lasciapassare *m.*, permesso *m.* **3** biglietto *m.* gratuito **4** tessera *f.*, abbonamento *m.*

to **pass** [pa:s] **A** *v. tr.* **1** passare, oltrepassare, superare **2** dare, porgere **3** promuovere **4** trascorrere **B** *v. intr.* **1** passare, andare oltre **2** finire **3** trascorrere **4** accadere **5** essere promosso ♦ **to p. away** morire; **to p. by** passare vicino, trascurare; **to p. over** trascurare, lasciarsi sfuggire

passable ['pa:səbl] *agg.* **1** transitabile **2** passabile

passage ['pæsɪdʒ] *s.* **1** passaggio *m.*, varco *m.* **2** corridoio *m.* **3** tragitto *m.*, traversata *f.* **4** brano *m.*

passbook ['pa:sbʊk] *s.* libretto *m.* di risparmio

passenger ['pæsɪn(d)ʒəʳ] *s.* passeggero *m.*, viaggiatore *m.*

passer-by [ˌpa:sə'baɪ] (*pl.* **passers-by**) *s.* passante *m. e f.*

passing ['pa:sɪŋ] **A** *agg.* **1** passante, passeggero, di passaggio **2** casuale, incidentale **B** *s.* **1** passaggio *m.* **2** trapasso *m.*, morte *f.* ♦ **in p.** incidentalmente; **p. bell** campana a morto

passion ['pæʃ(ə)n] *s.* passione *f.*

passional ['pæʃənl] *agg.* passionale

passionate ['pæʃənɪt] *agg.* appassionato

passionflower ['pæʃ(ə)nˌflaʊəʳ] *s.* passiflora *f.*

passive ['pæsɪv] *agg.* passivo

Passover ['pa:sˌɒʊvəʳ] *s.* Pasqua *f.* ebraica

passport ['pa:spɔ:t] *s.* passaporto *m.*

password ['pa:sˌwɜ:d] *s.* parola *f.* d'ordine

past [pa:st] **A** *agg.* **1** passato, trascorso **2** (*gramm.*) passato **B** *s.* passato *m.* **C** *avv.* presso, accanto, oltre **D** *prep.* dopo, oltre ♦ **to go p.** passare

pasta ['pæstə] *s.* pasta *f.*, pastasciutta *f.*

paste [peɪst] *s.* **1** pasta *f.* **2** colla *f.* ♦ **tooth p.** dentifricio

pastel [pæs'tɛl] *s.* pastello *m.*

to **pasteurize** ['pæstəraɪz] *v. tr.* pastorizzare

pastille [pæs'ti:l] *s.* pastiglia *f.*

pastime ['pa:staɪm] *s.* passatempo *m.*

pastor ['pa:stəʳ] *s.* pastore *m.*

pastoral ['pa:st(ə)r(ə)l] *agg.* pastorale

pastry ['peɪstrɪ] *s.* **1** pasta *f.* (*per dolci*) **2** pasticcino *m.* ♦ **p. shop** pasticceria; **puff p.** pasta sfoglia

pasture ['pa:stʃəʳ] *s.* pascolo *m.*

pasty (1) ['peɪstɪ] *agg.* pastoso

pasty (2) ['pæstɪ] *s.* (*cuc.*) pasticcio *m.* di carne

to **pat** [pæt] **A** *v. tr.* dare un buffetto, accarezzare **B** *v. intr.* tamburellare

patch [pætʃ] *s.* **1** toppa *f.* **2** macchia *f.* **3** benda *f.*

to **patch** [pætʃ] *v. tr.* rattoppare, aggiustare ♦ **to p. up** appianare

patchwork ['pætʃwɜ:k] *s.* patchwork *m. inv.*

patchy ['pætʃɪ] *agg.* **1** rappezzato **2** chiazzato, a macchie **3** irregolare

paté ['pæteɪ] *s.* paté *m. inv.*

patent ['peɪt(ə)nt] **A** *agg.* **1** manifesto, palese **2** patentato, brevettato **3** (*fam.*) ingegnoso **B** *s.* brevetto *m.*

to **patent** ['peɪt(ə)nt] *v. tr.* brevettare

paternal [pə'tɜːnl] *agg.* paterno
paternalism [pə'tɜːn(ə)lɪz(ə)m] *s.* paternalismo *m.*
paternity [pə'tɜːnɪtɪ] *s.* paternità *f.*
path [paːθ] *s.* **1** sentiero *m.* **2** via *f.*, strada *f.* **3** traiettoria *f.* **4** (*inf.*) percorso *m.*, path *m. inv.*
pathetic [pə'θɛtɪk] *agg.* patetico
pathologic(al) [ˌpæθə'lɔdʒɪk((ə)l)] *agg.* patologico
pathology [pə'θɔlədʒɪ] *s.* patologia *f.*
pathos ['peɪθɔs] *s.* pathos *m.*
pathway ['paːθˌweɪ] *s.* sentiero *m.*
patience ['peɪʃ(ə)ns] *s.* **1** pazienza *f.* **2** (*con le carte*) solitario *m.*
patient ['peɪʃ(ə)nt] *agg. e s.* paziente *m. e f.*
patina ['pætɪnə] *s.* patina *f.*
patriarch ['peɪtrɪaːk] *s.* patriarca *m.*
patriarchate ['peɪtrɪaːkɪt] *s.* patriarcato *m.*
patrician [pə'trɪʃ(ə)n] *agg.* patrizio
patrimonial [ˌpætrɪ'mɒʊnjəl] *agg.* patrimoniale
patrimony ['pætrɪmənɪ] *s.* patrimonio *m.*
patriot ['pɔɪtrɪət] *s.* patriota *m. e f.*
patriotic [ˌpætrɪ'ɔtɪk] *agg.* patriottico
patriotism ['pætrɪətɪz(ə)m] *s.* patriottismo *m.*
patrol [pə'trɒʊl] *s.* **1** pattuglia *f.*, ronda *f.* **2** perlustrazione *f.*, pattugliamento *m.* ♦ **p. boat** vedetta della guardia costiera; **p. car** auto della polizia; **to be on p.** essere di pattuglia
patron ['peɪtr(ə)n] *s.* **1** patrono *m.*, protettore *m.*, mecenate *m.* **2** cliente *m. e f.* (abituale)
patronage ['pætrənɪdʒ] *s.* **1** patrocinio *m.*, mecenatismo *m.*, protezione *f.* **2** clientela *f.*
to patronize ['pætrənaɪz] *v. tr.* **1** patrocinare **2** trattare con condiscendenza **3** essere cliente abituale di
patronymic [ˌpætrə'nɪmɪk] *s.* patronimico *m.*
patter ['pætəʳ] *s.* picchiettio *m.*
to patter ['pætəʳ] *v. intr.* **1** picchiettare **2** sgambettare
pattern ['pætən] *s.* **1** modello *m.*, campione *m.* **2** motivo *m.*, disegno *m.*
paunch ['pɜːn(t)ʃ] *s.* pancione *m.*
pauper ['pɜːpəʳ] *s.* povero *m.*
pause [pɜːz] *s.* pausa *f.*, sosta *f.*, tregua *f.*
to pause [pɜːz] *v. intr.* fare una pausa
to pave [peɪv] *v. tr.* **1** (*una strada*) pavimentare, lastricare **2** (*fig.*) aprire la strada
pavement ['peɪvmənt] *s.* **1** selciato *m.* **2** marciapiede *m.*
pavilion [pə'vɪljən] *s.* padiglione *m.*
paving ['peɪvɪŋ] *s.* pavimentazione *f.*, selciato *m.*
paw [pɜː] *s.* zampa *f.*
pawn (1) [pɜːn] *s.* pegno *m.*, garanzia *f.*
pawn (2) [pɜːn] *s.* pedina *f.*, (*scacchi*) pedone *m.*
to pawn [pɜːn] *v. tr.* impegnare, dare in pegno
pay [peɪ] *s.* paga *f.*, compenso *m.* ♦ **p. packet** (*USA* **p. envelope**) busta paga
to pay [peɪ] (*pass. e p. p.* **paid**) **A** *v. tr.* **1** pagare, compensare **2** rendere, fruttare **3** fare, rendere **B** *v. intr.* **1** pagare **2** essere vantaggioso, convenire ♦ **to p. attention** prestare attenzione; **to p. back** ripagare; **to p. in** versare; **to p. off** saldare, liquidare; **to p. up** saldare
payable ['peɪəbl] *agg.* pagabile
payee [peɪ'iː] *s.* beneficiario *m.*
payment ['peɪmənt] *s.* pagamento *m.* ♦ **p. in full** saldo; **terms of p.** condizioni di pagamento
payroll ['peɪrɒʊl] *s.* libro *m.* paga
pea [piː] *s.* pisello *m.*
peace [piːs] *s.* pace *f.*
peaceful ['piːsf(ʊ)l] *agg.* pacifico, tranquillo
peach [piːtʃ] *s.* pesca *f.* (*frutto*)
peacock [piːkək] *s.* pavone *m.*
peak [piːk] **A** *s.* **1** vetta *f.*, picco *m.* **2** punta *f.* **3** visiera *f.* **4** massimo *m.* **B** *agg.* di punta, massimo ♦ **p. hours** ore di punta
peal [piːl] *s.* **1** scampanio *m.* **2** scoppio *m.*, scroscio *m.*
peanut ['piːnʌt] *s.* arachide *f.*
pear [pɛəʳ] *s.* pera *f.*
pearl [pɜːl] *s.* perla *f.*
pearly ['pɜːlɪ] *agg.* perlaceo
peasant ['pɛz(ə)nt] *s.* contadino *m.*
peat [piːt] *s.* torba *f.*
pebble ['pɛbl] *s.* ciottolo *m.*
peck [pɛk] *s.* **1** beccata *f.*, colpo *m.* di becco **2** (*fam.*) bacetto *m.*
to peck [pɛk] *v. tr. e intr.* beccare
peckish ['pɛkɪʃ] *s.* (*fam.*) languorino *m.*
peculiar [pɪ'kjuːlɪəʳ] *agg.* **1** peculiare **2** strano, insolito
peculiarity [pɪˌkjuːlɪ'ærɪtɪ] *s.* **1** peculiarità *f.* **2** stranezza *f.*
pedagogy ['pɛdəgəgɪ] *s.* pedagogia *f.*

pedal ['pɛdl] *s.* pedale *m.*
to **pedal** ['pɛdl] *v. intr.* pedalare
pedant ['pɛd(ə)nt] *s.* pedante *m. e f.*, pignolo *m.*
pedantic [pɪ'dæntɪk] *agg.* pedante
pedantry ['pɛd(ə)ntrɪ] *s.* pedanteria *f.*
to **peddle** ['pɛdl] **A** *v. intr.* fare il venditore ambulante **B** *v. tr.* **1** (*di ambulante*) vendere al minuto **2** (*droga*) spacciare
pedestal ['pɛdɪstl] *s.* piedistallo *m.*
pedestrian [pɪ'dɛstrɪən] **A** *agg.* **1** che va a piedi **2** pedestre **B** *s.* pedone *m.* ♦ **p. crossing** passaggio pedonale
pedicure ['pɛdɪkjʊəʳ] *s.* pedicure *m. e f. inv.*
pedigree ['pɛdɪgriː] *s.* **1** albero *m.* genealogico **2** lignaggio *m.* **3** pedigree *m. inv.*
pediment ['pɛdɪmənt] *s.* (*arch.*) frontone *m.*
pee [piː] *s.* (*fam.*) pipì *f.*
to **pee** [piː] *v. intr.* (*fam.*) fare pipì
to **peek** [piːk] *v. intr.* sbirciare
peel [piːl] *s.* buccia *f.*, scorza *f.*
to **peel** [piːl] **A** *v. tr.* pelare, sbucciare **B** *v. intr.* spellarsi, sbucciarsi, squamarsi
peep (1) [piːp] *s.* sbirciata *f.*
peep (2) [piːp] *s.* pigolio *m.*, squittio *m.*
to **peep (1)** [piːp] *v. intr.* **1** sbirciare, occhieggiare **2** fare capolino, spuntare ♦ **to p. at st.** guardare furtivamente q.c.
to **peep (2)** [piːp] *v. intr.* pigolare, squittire
peephole ['piːpˌhɒʊl] *s.* spioncino *m.*
peer [pɪəʳ] *s.* **1** pari *m.*, persona *f.* di pari rango **2** (*membro della Camera dei Lord*) Pari *m.*
to **peer** [pɪəʳ] *v. intr.* **1** far capolino, spuntare **2** scrutare
peerless ['pɪəlɪs] *agg.* impareggiabile
peeved [piːvd] *agg.* (*fam.*) irritato
peevish ['piːvɪʃ] *agg.* irritabile, permaloso
peg [pɛg] *s.* **1** piolo *m.*, picchetto *m.* **2** attaccapanni *m. inv.* **3** (*per bucato*) molletta *f.* **4** (*fig.*) appiglio *m.*, pretesto *m.*
pejorative [pɪ'dʒɜrətɪv] *agg.* peggiorativo
pelican ['pɛlɪkən] *s.* pellicano *m.* ♦ **p. crossing** attraversamento pedonale con semaforo a controllo manuale
pellet ['pɛlɪt] *s.* **1** pallina *f.* **2** pallottola *f.* **3** pillola *f.*
pelt (1) [pɛlt] *s.* pelle *f.* non conciata
pelt (2) [pɛlt] *s.* colpo *m.* (*di proiettile, sasso e sim.*) ♦ **at full p.** a tutta velocità
to **pelt** [pɛlt] **A** *v. tr.* colpire (*con proiettili, sassi e sim.*) **B** *v. intr.* scrosciare, piovere a dirotto
pelvis ['pɛlvɪs] *s.* pelvi *f.*, bacino *m.*
pen (1) [pɛn] *s.* penna *f.* ♦ **ballpoint p.** penna a sfera; **fountain p.** stilografica; **p. friend/p. pal** amico di penna; **p. name** pseudonimo; **quill p.** penna d'oca
pen (2) [pɛn] *s.* recinto *m.* (*per animali*)
penal ['piːnl] *agg.* penale
to **penalize** ['piːnəlaɪz] *v. tr.* penalizzare
penalty ['pɛn(ə)ltɪ] *s.* penalità *f.*, ammenda *f.*, punizione *f.* ♦ **p. kick** calcio di rigore
penance ['pɛnəns] *s.* penitenza *f.*
pence [pɛns] *pl. di* **penny**
pencil ['pɛnsl] *s.* matita *f.* ♦ **p. case** portamatite; **p. sharpener** temperamatite
pendant ['pɛndənt] *s.* pendente *m.*, ciondolo *m.*
pending ['pɛndɪŋ] **A** *agg.* **1** pendente, in sospeso **2** imminente **B** *prep.* **1** durante **2** fino a, in attesa di
pendular ['pɛndjʊləʳ] *agg.* pendolare
pendulum ['pɛndjʊləm] *s.* pendolo *m.*
to **penetrate** ['pɛnɪtreɪt] **A** *v. tr.* **1** penetrare **2** pervadere, permeare **3** comprendere **B** *v. intr.* **1** penetrare, introdursi **2** capire
penetration [ˌpɛnɪ'treɪʃ(ə)n] *s.* penetrazione *f.*
penguin ['pɛŋgwɪn] *s.* pinguino *m.*
penicillin [ˌpɛnɪ'sɪlɪn] *s.* penicillina *f.*
peninsula [pɪ'nɪnsjʊlə] *s.* penisola *f.*
peninsular [pɪ'nɪnsjʊləʳ] *agg.* peninsulare
penis ['piːnɪs] *s.* pene *m.*
penitence ['pɛnɪt(ə)ns] *s.* penitenza *f.*, pentimento *m.*
penitent ['pɛnɪt(ə)nt] *agg. e s.* penitente *m. e f.*
penitentiary [ˌpɛnɪ'tɛnʃərɪ] *s.* (*USA*) penitenziario *m.*
penknife ['pɛnnaɪf] *s.* temperino *m.*
pennant ['pɛnənt] *s.* **1** pennone *m.* **2** bandierina *f.*
penny ['pɛnɪ] *s.* (*pl.* **pennies** o **pence**) **1** un centesimo *m.* di sterlina **2** (*USA*) centesimo *m.*
pensile ['pɛnsaɪl] *agg.* pensile
pension ['pɛnʃ(ə)n] *s.* pensione *f.*
pensioner ['pɛnʃənəʳ] *s.* pensionato *m.*
pensive ['pɛnsɪv] *agg.* pensieroso
pentagon ['pɛntəgən] *s.* pentagono *m.*
pentagonal [pɛn'tægənl] *agg.* pentagonale
Pentecost ['pɛntɪkəst] *s.* pentecoste *f.*
penthouse ['pɛnthaʊs] *s.* attico *m.*
pent up ['pɛntˌʌp] *agg.* **1** rinchiuso **2** re-

presso
penultimate [pɪ'nʌltɪmɪt] *agg.* penultimo
penury ['pɛnjʊrɪ] *s.* penuria *f.*, miseria *f.*
peony ['pɪənɪ] *s.* peonia *f.*
people ['piːpl] *s.* **1** popolo *m.*, gente *f.* **2** (*pl. collettivo*) persone *f. pl.*, folla *f.* ♦ **a lot of p.** un mucchio di gente; **p. say** si dice
to people ['piːpl] *v. tr.* popolare
pep [pɛp] *s.* (*fam.*) energia *f.*, vigore *m.*
to pep [pɛp] *v. tr.* (*fam.*) **to p. up** stimolare, vivacizzare
peplos ['pəpləs] *s.* peplo *m.*
pepper ['pɛpəʳ] *s.* **1** pepe *m.* **2** peperone *m.* ♦ **p. mill** macinapepe; **red p.** peperoncino
to pepper ['pɛpəʳ] *v. tr.* **1** pepare **2** cospargere di **3** mitragliare, tempestare
peppermint ['pɛpəmɪnt] *s.* **1** menta *f.* piperita **2** caramella *f.* di menta
peppery ['pəpərɪ] *agg.* pepato
peppy ['pɛpɪ] *agg.* (*fam.*) energico, vigoroso
per [pə(ː)ʳ] *prep.* **1** per, per mezzo di, attraverso **2** per, ogni, a ♦ **p. capita** pro capite; **p. cent** per cento; **p. hour** all'ora
to perceive [pə'siːv] *v. tr.* **1** percepire **2** accorgersi
percent [pə'sɛnt] *agg. e s.* percentuale *f.*
percentage [pə'sɛntɪdʒ] *s.* percentuale *f.*
perceptible [pə'sɛptəbl] *agg.* percettibile
perception [pə'sɛpʃ(ə)n] *s.* percezione *f.*
perceptive [pə'sɛptɪv] *agg.* percettivo
perch (1) [pɜːtʃ] *s.* pertica *f.*, bastone *m.*
perch (2) [pɜːtʃ] *s.* pesce *m.* persico
to perch [pɜːtʃ] *v. intr.* appollaiarsi
to percolate ['pɜːkəleɪt] *v. tr. e intr.* filtrare
percolator ['pɜːkəleɪtəʳ] *s.* **1** filtro *m.* **2** macchinetta *f.* per il caffè
percussion [pɜː'kʌʃ(ə)n] *s.* percussione *f.*
peregrination [ˌpɛrɪgrɪ'neɪʃ(ə)n] *s.* peregrinazione *f.*
peremptory [pə'rɛm(p)t(ə)rɪ] *agg.* perentorio
perennial [pə'rɛnjəl] *agg.* perenne
perfect ['pɜːfɪkt] **A** *agg.* perfetto **B** *s.* (*gramm.*) perfetto *m.*
to perfect ['pɜːfɛkt] *v. tr.* perfezionare
perfection [pə'fɛkʃ(ə)n] *s.* **1** perfezione *f.* **2** perfezionamento *m.*
perfectionism [pə'fɛkʃ(ə)nɪz(ə)m] *s.* perfezionismo *m.*
perfectionist [pə'fɛkʃ(ə)nɪst] *s.* perfezionista *m. e f.*
perfidious [pɜː'fɪdɪəs] *agg.* perfido
to perforate [pɜːfəreɪt] *v. tr.* perforare
perforation [ˌpɜːfə'reɪʃ(ə)n] *s.* perforazione *f.*, traforo *m.*
to perform [pə'fɜːm] **A** *v. tr.* **1** eseguire, compiere **2** (*teatro*) recitare, rappresentare **B** *v. intr.* **1** funzionare, comportarsi **2** (*teatro*) esibirsi, interpretare una parte
performance [pə'fɜːməns] *s.* **1** esecuzione *f.*, rappresentazione *f.*, spettacolo *m.* **2** prestazione *f.*, rendimento *m.*
performer [pə'fɜːməʳ] *s.* **1** artista *m. e f.*, attore *m.*, interprete *m. e f.* **2** esecutore *m.*
perfume ['pɜːfjuːm] *s.* profumo *m.* ♦ **p. shop** profumeria
to perfume [pə'fjuːm] *v. tr.* profumare
perfunctory [pə'fʌŋ(k)tərɪ] *agg.* superficiale, trascurato
pergola ['pɜːgələ] *s.* pergola *f.*
perhaps [pə'hæps] *avv.* forse, probabilmente
peril ['pɛrɪl] *s.* pericolo *m.*
perimeter [pə'rɪmɪtəʳ] *s.* perimetro *m.*
perimetric(al) [ˌpɛrɪ'mɛtrɪk((ə)l)] *agg.* perimetrale
period ['pɪərɪəd] **A** *s.* **1** periodo *m.*, epoca *f.* **2** (*gramm.*) frase *f.*, periodo *m.* **3** (*segno ortografico*) punto *m.* **4** *al pl.* mestruazioni *f. pl.* **B** *agg.* d'epoca, caratteristico di un periodo
periodical [ˌpɪərɪ'ədɪk(ə)l] *agg.* periodico
periodicity [ˌpɪərɪə'dɪsɪtɪ] *s.* periodicità *f.*
peripheral [pə'rɪfərəl] **A** *agg.* **1** periferico **2** marginale **B** *s.* (*inf.*) (unità) periferica *f.*
periphrasis [pə'rɪfrəsɪs] *s.* perifrasi *f.*
periscope ['pɛrɪskɒʊp] *s.* periscopio *m.*
to perish ['pɛrɪʃ] *v. intr.* **1** perire, morire **2** deperire, deteriorarsi
perishable ['pɛrɪʃəbl] *agg.* deperibile, deteriorabile
peritonitis [ˌpərɪtə'naɪtɪs] *s.* peritonite *f.*
perjury ['pɜːdʒ(ə)rɪ] *s.* spergiuro *m.*
to perk up [ˌpɜːk'ʌp] *v. intr.* rianimarsi, riprendersi
perky ['pɜːkɪ] *agg.* **1** vivace, allegro **2** baldanzoso
perm [pɜːm] *s.* (*fam.*) permanente *f.*
permanent ['pɜːmənənt] *agg.* permanente, stabile ♦ **p. wave** permanente
permeable ['pɜːmjəbl] *agg.* permeabile
to permeate ['pɜːmɪeɪt] **A** *v. tr.* permeare **B** *v. intr.* diffondersi, penetrare
permissible [pə'mɪsəbl] *agg.* ammissibile

permission [pə'mɪʃ(ə)n] *s.* permesso *m.*
permissive [pə'mɪsɪv] *agg.* **1** permissivo, tollerante **2** lecito
permit ['pɜːmɪt] *s.* permesso *m.*, autorizzazione *f.*
to permit [pə'mɪt] *v. tr.* permettere, concedere
permutation [ˌpɜːmjuː'teɪʃ(ə)n] *s.* permuta *f.*
pernicious [pɜː'nɪʃəs] *agg.* pernicioso
perpendicular [ˌpɜːp(ə)n'dɪkjʊlə^r] *agg. e s.* perpendicolare *f.*
perpetual [pə'pətjʊəl] *agg.* perpetuo
to perplex [pə'plɛks] *v. tr.* **1** rendere perplesso **2** complicare
perplexed [pə'plɛkst] *agg.* **1** perplesso **2** complicato
perplexity [pə'plɛksɪtɪ] *s.* **1** perplessità *f.* **2** complicazione *f.*
to persecute ['pɜːsɪkjuːt] *v. tr.* perseguitare, molestare
persecution [ˌpɜːsɪ'kjuːʃ(ə)n] *s.* persecuzione *f.*
perseverance [ˌpɜːsɪ'vɪərəns] *s.* perseveranza *f.*
to persevere [ˌpɜːsɪ'vɪə^r] *v. intr.* perseverare ♦ **to p. in doing st.** insistere nel fare q.c.
Persian ['pɜːʃ(ə)n] *agg. e s.* persiano *m.*
to persist [pə'sɪst] *v. intr.* **1** persistere, continuare **2** ostinarsi
persistent [pə'sɪst(ə)nt] *agg.* persistente
person ['pɜːsn] *s.* persona *f.* ♦ **in p.** personalmente
personage ['pɜːsnɪdʒ] *s.* personaggio *m.*
personal ['pɜːsnl] *agg.* personale
personality [ˌpɜːsə'nælɪtɪ] *s.* **1** personalità *f.* **2** personaggio *m.* **3** *al pl.* osservazioni *f. pl.* di carattere personale
to personalize ['pɜːs(ə)nəlaɪz] *v. tr.* personalizzare
personification [pɜːˌsənɪfɪ'keɪʃ(ə)n] *s.* personificazione *f.*
to personify [pɜː'sənɪfaɪ] *v. tr.* personificare
personnel [ˌpɜːsə'nɛl] *s.* personale *m.*
perspective [pə'spɛktɪv] **A** *agg.* prospettico **B** *s.* prospettiva *f.*
perspicacity [ˌpɜːspɪ'kæsɪtɪ] *s.* perspicacia *f.*, sagacia *f.*
perspiration [ˌpɜːspə'reɪʃ(ə)n] *s.* sudore *m.*, sudorazione *f.*
to perspire [pə'spaɪə^r] *v. intr.* sudare
to persuade [pə'sweɪd] *v. tr.* persuadere
persuasion [pə'sweɪʒ(ə)n] *s.* persuasione *f.*, convincimento *m.*
persuasive [pə'sweɪzɪv] *agg.* persuasivo
pert [pɜːt] *agg.* impertinente
to pertain [pɜː'teɪn] *v. intr.* essere di pertinenza, spettare
pertinent ['pɜːtɪnənt] *agg.* pertinente, relativo
to perturb [pə'tɜːb] *v. tr.* turbare, sconvolgere
perturbation [ˌpɜːtɜː'beɪʃ(ə)n] *s.* perturbazione *f.*, turbamento *m.*
to peruse [pə'ruːz] *v. tr.* **1** leggere attentamente **2** esaminare
to pervade [pɜː'veɪd] *v. tr.* pervadere
pervasive [pɜː'veɪsɪv] *agg.* penetrante
perverse [pə'vɜːs] *agg.* perverso, iniquo
perversion [pə'vɜːʃ(ə)n] *s.* perversione *f.*
pervert ['pɜːvɜːt] *s.* pervertito *m.*
to pervert [pə'vɜːt] *v. tr.* pervertire, corrompere
pessimism ['pɛsɪmɪz(ə)m] *s.* pessimismo *m.*
pessimist ['pɛsɪmɪst] *s.* pessimista *m. e f.*
pessimistic [ˌpɛsɪ'mɪstɪk] *agg.* pessimistico
pest [pɛst] *s.* **1** insetto *m.* nocivo **2** pianta *f.* infestante **3** persona *f.* fastidiosa
to pester ['pɛstə^r] *v. tr.* seccare, importunare
pestiferous [pɛs'tɪf(ə)rəs] *agg.* pestifero
pestilence ['pɛstɪləns] *s.* pestilenza *f.*
pet [pɛt] *s.* **1** animale *m.* domestico **2** beniamino *m.* ♦ **p. name** vezzeggiativo
to pet [pɛt] **A** *v. tr.* **1** coccolare **2** (*fam.*) pomiciare con **B** *v. intr.* (*fam.*) pomiciare
petal ['pɛtl] *s.* petalo *m.*
petard [pə'taːd] *s.* petardo *m.*
to peter ['piːtə^r] *v. intr.* (*fam.*) **to p. out** esaurirsi, estinguersi
petition [pɪ'tɪʃən] *s.* **1** petizione *f.*, supplica *f.* **2** (*dir.*) ricorso *m.*
petrified ['pɛtrɪfaɪd] *agg.* **1** pietrificato **2** impietrito
to petrify ['pɛtrɪfaɪ] *v. intr.* **1** pietrificarsi **2** impietrirsi
petrol ['pɛtr(ə)l] *s.* benzina *f.* ♦ **p. station** stazione di servizio; **p. tank** serbatoio della benzina
petroleum [pɪ'trɒʊljəm] *s.* petrolio *m.* ♦ **crude p.** petrolio grezzo
petticoat ['pɛtɪkɒʊt] *s.* sottoveste *f.*
pettifogger ['pɛtɪfəgə^r] *s.* leguleio *m.*
petty ['pɛtɪ] *agg.* **1** piccolo, insignificante **2** meschino **3** subalterno, subordinato ♦

p. officer sottufficiale di marina
petulance ['pɛtjʊləns] *s.* petulanza *f.*
petulant ['pɛtjʊlənt] *agg.* petulante, irritabile
pew [pjuː] *s.* (*di chiesa*) panca *f.*
pewter ['pjuːtəʳ] *s.* peltro *m.*
phagocyte [fə'gɒʊsaɪt] *s.* (*biol.*) fagocita *m.*
phalanstery ['fælənst(ə)rɪ] *s.* falansterio *m.*
phalanx ['fælæŋks] *s.* falange *f.*
phallic ['fælɪk] *agg.* fallico
phallus ['fæləs] *s.* fallo *m.*
phantom ['fæntəm] *s.* fantasma *m.*
pharaonic [fɛə'rənɪk] *agg.* faraonico
pharmaceutic(al) [ˌfaːmə'sjuːtɪk((ə)l)] **A** *agg.* farmaceutico **B** *s.* farmaco *m.*
pharmacy ['faːməsɪ] *s.* farmacia *f.*
pharyngitis [ˌfærɪn'dʒaɪtɪs] *s.* faringite *f.*
pharynx ['færɪŋks] *s.* faringe *f.*
phase [feɪz] *s.* fase *f.* ♦ **p. displacement** (*elettr.*) sfasamento
pheasant ['fɛznt] *s.* fagiano *m.*
phenomena [fɪ'nəmɪnə] *pl. di* **phenomenon**
phenomenal [fɪ'nəmɪnl] *agg.* fenomenale
phenomenon [fɪ'nəmɪnən] (*pl.* **phenomena**) *s.* fenomeno *m.*
philanthropic(al) [ˌfɪlən'θrəpɪk((ə)l)] *agg.* filantropico
philanthropist [fɪ'lænθrəpɪst] *s.* filantropo *m.*
philanthropy [fɪ'lænθrəpɪ] *s.* filantropia *f.*
philatelic(al) [ˌfɪlə'tɛlɪk((ə)l)] *agg.* filatelico
philately [fɪ'lætəlɪ] *s.* filatelia *f.*
philharmonic [ˌfɪlaː'mənɪk] *agg. e s.* filarmonica *f.*
Philippine ['fɪlɪpiːn] *agg.* filippino
philology [fɪ'lələdʒɪ] *s.* filologia *f.*
philosopher [fɪ'ləsəfəʳ] *s.* filosofo *m.*
philosophic(al) [ˌfɪlə'səfɪk((ə)l)] *agg.* filosofico
philosophy [fɪ'ləsəfɪ] *s.* filosofia *f.*
phlebitis [flɪ'baɪtɪs] *s.* flebite *f.*
phleboclysis ['flɛbɒ(ʊ)ˌklaɪsɪs] *s.* fleboclisi *f.*
phlegm [flɛm] *s.* **1** (*med.*) muco *m.* **2** flemma *f.*, sangue *m.* freddo
phlegmatic [flɛg'mætɪk] *agg.* flemmatico
phlogosis [flə'gɒʊsɪs] *s.* flogosi *f.*
phobia ['fɒʊbjə] *s.* fobia *f.*
Phoenician [fɪ'nɪʃ(ɪ)ən] *agg. e s.* fenicio *m.*
phone [fɒʊn] *s.* telefono *m.* ♦ **p. book** elenco telefonico; **p. booth/box** cabina telefonica; **to be on the p.** essere al telefono
to phone [fɒʊn] *v. tr. e intr.* telefonare ♦ **to p. back** richiamare; **to p. in** comunicare per telefono; **to p. up** telefonare
phonetic [fɒ(ʊ)'nɛtɪk] *agg.* fonetico
phonetics [fɒ(ʊ)'nɛtɪks] *s. pl.* (*v. al sing.*) fonetica *f.*
phoney ['fɒʊnɪ] **A** *agg.* (*fam.*) falso, fasullo **B** *s.* **1** cosa *f.* falsa **2** impostore *m.*
phosphorescent [ˌfəsfə'rɛsənt] *agg.* fosforescente
phosphorus ['fəsfərəs] *s.* fosforo *m.*
photo ['fɒʊtɒʊ] *s.* fotografia *f.*
photocell ['fɒʊtəsɛl] *s.* fotocellula *f.*
photocopier ['fɒʊtɒ(ʊ)ˌkəpɪəʳ] *s.* fotocopiatrice *f.*
photocopy ['fɒʊtɒ(ʊ)ˌkəpɪ] *s.* fotocopia *f.*
to photocopy ['fɒʊtɒ(ʊ)ˌkəpɪ] *v. tr.* fotocopiare
photogenic [ˌfɒʊtɒ(ʊ)'dʒɛnɪk] *agg.* fotogenico
photograph ['fɒʊtəgraːf] *s.* fotografia *f.*
to photograph ['fɒʊtəgraːf] *v. tr.* fotografare
photographer [f(ə)'təgrəfəʳ] *s.* fotografo *m.*
photographic [ˌfɒʊtə'græfɪk] *agg.* fotografico
photography [fə'təgrəfɪ] *s.* fotografia *f.*
phrasal ['freɪz(ə)l] *agg.* di locuzione, di frase ♦ **p. verb** verbo fraseologico
phrase [freɪz] *s.* **1** locuzione *f.*, espressione *f.*, frase *f.* fatta **2** (*mus.*) frase *f.*
phraseological [ˌfreɪzɪə'lədʒɪk(ə)l] *agg.* fraseologico
physical ['fɪzɪk(ə)l] *agg.* fisico
physician [fɪ'zɪʃ(ə)n] *s.* medico *m.*
physics ['fɪzɪks] *s. pl.* (*v. al sing.*) fisica *f.*
physiognomist [ˌfɪzɪ'ənəmɪst] *s.* fisionomista *m. e f.*
physiological [ˌfɪzɪə'lədʒɪk(ə)l] *agg.* fisiologico
physiology [ˌfɪzɪ'ələdʒɪ] *s.* fisiologia *f.*
physiotherapist [ˌfɪzɪɒ(ʊ)'θɛrəpɪst] *s.* fisioterapista *m. e f.*
physiotherapy [ˌfɪzɪɒ(ʊ)'θɛrəpɪ] *s.* fisioterapia *f.*
physique [fɪ'ziːk] *s.* fisico *m.*, corporatura *f.*
pianist ['pɪənɪst] *s.* pianista *m. e f.*
piano ['pjænɒʊ] *s.* pianoforte *m.*
pick (1) [pɪk] *s.* **1** piccone *m.* **2** strumento

m. appuntito
pick (2) [pɪk] *s.* **1** scelta *f.* **2** parte *f.* migliore
to pick [pɪk] **A** *v. tr.* **1** cogliere, raccogliere **2** togliere **3** scegliere **4** pulire, ripulire **5** perforare, grattare, scavare **6** rubare, borseggiare **B** *v. intr.* **1** picconare **2** mangiucchiare, piluccare ♦ **to p. at** sbocconcellare; **to p. on** prendersela con; **to p. out** scegliere, riconoscere; **to p. up** raccogliere, dare un passaggio, passare a prendere, imparare, acquistare
picket ['pɪkɪt] *s.* **1** piolo *m.*, picchetto *m.* **2** (*di scioperanti*) picchetto *m.*
pickle ['pɪkl] *s.* **1** salamoia *f.* **2** sottaceti *m. pl.*
to pickle ['pɪkl] *v. tr.* mettere sotto aceto, conservare in salamoia
pickpocket ['pɪk,pəkɪt] *s.* borseggiatore *m.*
picnic ['pɪknɪk] *s.* picnic *m. inv.*
pictorial [pɪk'tɜːrɪəl] *agg.* **1** illustrato **2** pittorico
picture ['pɪktʃəʳ] *s.* **1** quadro *m.*, immagine *f.*, illustrazione *f.*, disegno *m.* **2** fotogramma *m.*, fotografia *f.* **3** ritratto *m.* **4** descrizione *f.* **5** situazione *f.*, quadro *m.* **6** film *m. inv.*, cinema *m.* ♦ **p. book** libro illustrato; **to be in the p.** essere informato
to picture ['pɪktʃəʳ] *v. tr.* **1** dipingere, ritrarre, raffigurare **2** immaginare ♦ **to p. to oneself** immaginarsi
picturesque [,pɪktʃə'rɛsk] *agg.* pittoresco
pie [paɪ] *s.* torta *f.*, pasticcio *m.* ♦ **apple p.** torta di mele; **p. chart** diagramma a torta
piece [piːs] *s.* **1** pezzo *m.* **2** moneta *f.* **3 a p. of** (*seguito da s.*) un, una ♦ **a p. of news** una notizia
to piece [piːs] *v. tr.* **1** unire, connettere **2** rappezzare ♦ **to p. together** mettere insieme
piecemeal ['piːsmiːl] **A** *agg.* frammentario **B** *avv.* pezzo per pezzo, un po' alla volta
piecework ['piːswɜːk] *s.* lavoro *m.* a cottimo
pier [pɪəʳ] *s.* **1** banchina *f.*, molo *m.* **2** (*di ponte*) pila *f.*
to pierce [pɪəs] *v. tr.* **1** forare, perforare **2** trafiggere ♦ **to p. through st.** penetrare attraverso q.c.
piercing ['pɪəsɪŋ] *agg.* penetrante, pungente
pig [pɪg] *s.* **1** maiale *m.*, porco *m.* **2** (*metall.*) pane *m.* ♦ **Guinea p.** porcellino d'India; **sucking p.** maialino da latte
pigeon ['pɪdʒɪn] *s.* piccione *m.* ♦ **carrier p.** piccione viaggiatore; **p. house** piccionaia
pigeonhole ['pɪdʒɪnhɒʊl] *s.* casella *f.*
piggery ['pɪgərɪ] *s.* porcile *m.*, allevamento *m.* di suini
piggy ['pɪgɪ] *s.* porcellino *m.*, maialino *m.* ♦ **p. bank** salvadanaio (*a forma di porcellino*)
pigheaded [,pɪg'hɛdɪd] *agg.* (*fam.*) caparbio
piglet ['pɪglɪt] *s.* porcellino *m.*, maialino *m.*
pigment ['pɪgmənt] *s.* pigmento *m.*
pigmentation [,pɪgmən'teɪʃ(ə)n] *s.* pigmentazione *f.*
pigpen ['pɪgpɛn] *s.* (*USA*) porcile *m.*
pigskin ['pɪgskɪn] *s.* (pelle di) cinghiale *m.*
pigsty ['pɪgstaɪ] *s.* porcile *m.*
pigtail ['pɪgteɪl] *s.* **1** codino *m.* di maiale **2** treccia *f.*
pike [paɪk] *s.* luccio *m.*
pilchard ['pɪltʃəd] *s.* sardina *f.*
pile (1) [paɪl] *s.* **1** pila *f.*, catasta *f.*, mucchio *m.* **2** (*fig.*) grande quantità *f.* **3** (*fis.*) pila *f.*
pile (2) [paɪl] *s.* palo *m.*, palafitta *f.*, pilone *m.*
pile (3) [paɪl] *s.* (*di tessuto*) pelo *m.*
to pile [paɪl] **A** *v. tr.* ammucchiare, accatastare **B** *v. intr.* ammucchiarsi, affollarsi ♦ **to p. on** esagerare, aumentare; **to p. up** accumularsi, (*di veicoli*) tamponarsi
piles [paɪlz] *s. pl.* emorroidi *f. pl.*
pileup ['paɪlʌp] *s.* (*fam.*) tamponamento *m.* a catena
to pilfer ['pɪlfəʳ] *v. tr. e intr.* rubacchiare
pilgrim ['pɪlgrɪm] *s.* pellegrino *f.*
pilgrimage ['pɪlgrɪmɪdʒ] *s.* pellegrinaggio *m.*
pill [pɪl] *s.* pillola *f.*
pillage ['pɪlɪdʒ] *s.* saccheggio *m.*
to pillage ['pɪlɪdʒ] *v. tr. e intr.* saccheggiare
pillager ['pɪlɪdʒəʳ] *s.* saccheggiatore *m.*
pillar ['pɪləʳ] *s.* pilastro *m.*, colonna *f.* ♦ **p. box** buca delle lettere
pillion ['pɪljən] *s.* sellino *m.* posteriore
to pillory ['pɪlərɪ] *v. tr.* mettere alla berlina
pillow ['pɪlɒʊ] *s.* guanciale *m.*, cuscino *m.* ♦ **p. case** federa
pilot ['paɪlət] **A** *s.* pilota *m.* **B** *agg.* pilota, sperimentale, di prova ♦ **p. book** portolano; **p. boat** pilotina
to pilot ['paɪlət] *v. tr.* pilotare
pimp [pɪmp] *s.* protettore *m.*, magnaccia *m.*

pimple ['pɪmpl] *s.* pustola *f.*, foruncolo *m.*
pin [pɪn] *s.* **1** spillo *m.* **2** perno *m.*, spinotto *m.*
to pin [pɪn] *v. tr.* puntare con spilli, fissare ♦ **to p. down** costringere; **to p. up** appendere con spilli
pinafore ['pɪnəfəʳ] *s.* grembiulino *m.*
pinball ['pɪnbɜːl] *s.* flipper *m. inv.*
pincers ['pɪnsəz] *s. pl.* pinze *f. pl.*, tenaglie *f. pl.*
pinch [pɪntʃ] *s.* **1** pizzico *m.*, pizzicotto *m.* **2** (*di sale, tabacco*) presa *f.* **3** stretta *f.*, morsa *f.*, angustia *f.*
to pinch [pɪntʃ] *v. tr.* **1** pizzicare, schiacciare **2** tormentare **3** lesinare **4** (*pop.*) rubare
pine [paɪn] *s.* pino *m.* ♦ **p. cone** pigna; **p. seed** pinolo; **p. wood** pineta
to pine [paɪn] *v. intr.* **1** struggersi, tormentarsi **2** anelare ♦ **to p. after st.** desiderare ardentemente q.c.; **to p. away** consumarsi dal dolore
pineapple ['paɪn,æpl] *s.* ananas *m. inv.*
ping [pɪŋ] *s.* sibilo *m.*
ping-pong ['pɪŋpəŋ] *s.* ping-pong *m. inv.*
pink [pɪŋk] **A** *agg.* rosa **B** *s.* **1** (color) rosa *m.* **2** garofano *m.*
pinnacle ['pɪnəkl] *s.* pinnacolo *m.*
to pinpoint ['pɪn,pəɪnt] *v. tr.* localizzare, indicare con esattezza
pint [paɪnt] *s.* pinta *f.*
pioneer [,paɪə'nɪəʳ] *s.* pioniere *m.*
pious ['paɪəs] *agg.* **1** pio, devoto **2** ipocrita
pip (1) [pɪp] *s.* (*di frutto*) seme *m.*
pip (2) [pɪp] *s.* (*pop.*) malessere *m.*
pipe [paɪp] *s.* **1** tubo *m.*, condotto *m.*, conduttura *f.* **2** (*dell'organo*) canna *f.* **3** piffero *m.*, *al pl.* cornamusa *f.* **4** pipa *f.* ♦ **exhaust p.** tubo di scappamento; **p. dream** sogno irrealizzabile
to pipe [paɪp] **A** *v. intr.* **1** suonare il piffero (o la cornamusa) **2** fischiare **3** parlare (o cantare) con voce acuta **B** *v. tr.* **1** convogliare con tubazioni **2** suonare (con il piffero, la cornamusa) **3** dire con voce acuta ♦ **to p. down** tacere
pipeline ['paɪp,laɪn] *s.* conduttura *f.* ♦ **oil p.** oleodotto
piper ['paɪpəʳ] *s.* pifferaio *m.*, zampognaro *m.*
piping ['paɪpɪŋ] **A** *s.* tubazioni *f. pl.* **B** *agg.* acuto, penetrante ♦ **p. hot** bollente
pique [piːk] *s.* ripicca *f.*, puntiglio *m.*
piracy ['paɪərəsɪ] *s.* pirateria *f.*
pirate ['paɪərɪt] *agg. e s.* pirata *m.*
pisciculture ['pɪsɪkʌltʃəʳ] *s.* piscicoltura *f.*
to piss [pɪs] *v. intr.* (*volg.*) pisciare
pissed [pɪst] *agg.* (*volg.*) sbronzo
pistachio [pɪs'taːʃɪɒʊ] *s.* pistacchio *m.*
pistol ['pɪstl] *s.* pistola *f.*
piston ['pɪstən] *s.* pistone *m.*
pit (1) [pɪt] *s.* **1** buca *f.*, fossa *f.* **2** cava *f.*, miniera *f.* **3** platea *f.*
pit (2) [pɪt] *s.* nocciolo *m.*, seme *m.*
to pit [pɪt] *v. tr.* **1** infossare **2** butterare **3** contrapporre ♦ **to p. against** aizzare contro, opporre
pitch (1) [pɪtʃ] *s.* **1** lancio *m.* **2** intonazione *f.*, tono *m.* **3** grado *m.*, punto *m.* **4** (*arch.*) altezza *f.* (*di arco*) **5** (*di elica*) passo *m.* **6** (*di carattere tipografico*) passo *m.*, pitch *m. inv.* **7** (*naut.*) beccheggio *m.* **8** campo *m.* da gioco
pitch (2) [pɪtʃ] *s.* pece *f.*
to pitch [pɪtʃ] **A** *v. tr.* **1** piantare, rizzare **2** lanciare **3** intonare, impostare **4** ingranare **5** pavimentare **B** *v. intr.* **1** accamparsi **2** cadere, stramazzare **3** (*naut.*) beccheggiare ♦ **pitched battle** battaglia campale; **to p. in** darci dentro
pitcher (1) ['pɪtʃəʳ] *s.* brocca *f.*
pitcher (2) ['pɪtʃəʳ] *s.* (*baseball*) lanciatore *m.*
pitchfork ['pɪtʃfɜːk] *s.* forcone *m.*
piteous ['pɪtɪəs] *agg.* pietoso, miserevole
pitfall ['pɪtfɜːl] *s.* trappola *f.*
pith [pɪθ] *s.* **1** midollo *m.* **2** (*bot.*) albedo *f.* **3** (*fig.*) essenza *f.*
pithy ['pɪθɪ] *agg.* **1** conciso **2** vigoroso
pitiful ['pɪtɪf(ʊ)l] *agg.* pietoso
pitiless ['pɪtɪlɪs] *agg.* spietato
pittance ['pɪt(ə)ns] *s.* paga *f.* (*esigua*)
pity ['pɪtɪ] *s.* **1** pietà *f.*, compassione *f.* **2** peccato *m.* ♦ **what a p.!** che peccato!
to pity ['pɪtɪ] *v. tr.* compatire
pivot ['pɪvət] *s.* cardine *m.*, perno *m.*
pixie ['pɪksɪ] *s.* fata *f.*, folletto *m.*
placard ['plækaːd] *s.* manifesto *m.*, cartellone *m.*
to placate [plə'keɪt] *v. tr.* placare
place [pleɪs] *s.* **1** località *f.*, luogo *m.*, posto *m.* **2** impiego *m.*, posizione *f.* **3** (*a sedere, a tavola*) posto *m.* **4** (*fam.*) casa *f.*, casa *f.* di campagna ♦ **in p. of** invece di; **in the first p.** in primo luogo; **out of p.** fuori posto, inopportuno; **p. card** segnaposto; **to take p.** accadere

to place [pleɪs] *v. tr.* **1** collocare, disporre, mettere **2** riconoscere, individuare **3** (*denaro*) investire ♦ **to be placed** piazzarsi; **to p. oneself** mettersi, porsi
placement ['pleɪsmənt] *s.* collocamento *m.*
placid ['plæsɪd] *agg.* placido
plagiarism ['pleɪdʒjərɪz(ə)m] *s.* plagio *m.*
to plagiarize ['pleɪdʒjəraɪz] *v. tr.* plagiare
plague [pleɪg] *s.* **1** peste *f.* **2** piaga *f.*, flagello *m.*
to plague [pleɪg] *v. tr.* affliggere, tormentare
plaice [pleɪs] *s.* passera *f.* di mare
plaid [plæd] *s.* plaid *m. inv.*
plain [pleɪn] **A** *agg.* **1** chiaro, evidente **2** semplice, liscio, non lavorato **3** facile **4** comune, ordinario **5** sincero, schietto **6** puro **B** *s.* pianura *f.* **C** *avv.* **1** chiaramente, francamente **2** semplicemente ♦ **p. chocolate** cioccolato fondente; **p.-clothes** in borghese; **p. cooking** cucina casalinga; **the p. truth** la pura verità
plaintiff ['pleɪntɪf] *s.* (*dir*) attore *m.*
plaintive ['pleɪntɪv] *agg.* lamentoso
plait [plæt] *s.* treccia *f.*
plan [plæn] *s.* **1** piano *m.*, progetto *m.* **2** pianta *f.*
to plan [plæn] **A** *v. tr.* **1** impostare, progettare, pianificare **2** fare il piano di **B** *v. intr.* fare progetti
plane (1) [pleɪn] **A** *agg.* piano **B** *s.* **1** piano *m.* **2** livello *m.* **3** aereo *m.*
plane (2) [pleɪn] *s.* platano *m.*
plane (3) [pleɪn] *s.* pialla *f.*
to plane (1) [pleɪn] *v. intr.* planare
to plane (2) [pleɪn] *v. tr.* piallare
planer ['pleɪnəʳ] *s.* piallatrice *f.*
planet ['plænɪt] *s.* pianeta *m.*
planimetry [plæ'nɪmɪtrɪ] *s.* planimetria *f.*
planisphere ['plænɪsfɪəʳ] *s.* planisfero *m.*
plank [plæŋk] *s.* asse *f.*, tavola *f.*
planner ['plænəʳ] *s.* progettista *m. e f.*
planning ['plænɪŋ] *s.* progettazione *f.*, pianificazione *f.* ♦ **p. permission** licenza edilizia
plant [plaːnt] *s.* **1** pianta *f.* **2** impianto *m.*, stabilimento *m.*
to plant [plaːnt] *v. tr.* **1** piantare **2** fissare, conficcare **3** collocare, mettere
plantation [plæn'teɪʃən] *s.* piantagione *f.*
plaque [plaːk] *s.* placca *f.*
plaster ['plaːstəʳ] *s.* **1** cerotto *m.* **2** gesso *m.*, intonaco *m.* **3** (*med.*) gesso *m.*
to plaster ['plaːstəʳ] *v. tr.* **1** intonacare **2** ingessare **3** ricoprire
plastered ['plaːstəd] *agg.* **1** ricoperto **2** ubriaco
plastic ['plæstɪk] **A** *agg.* plastico **B** *s.* plastica *f.* ♦ **p. surgery** chirurgia plastica
plasticity [plæs'tɪsɪtɪ] *s.* plasticità *f.*
to plasticize ['plæstɪsaɪz] *v. tr.* plastificare
plate [pleɪt] *s.* **1** piatto *m.* **2** posateria *f.*, vasellame *m.* (*di metallo prezioso*) **3** lamiera *f.*, lastra *f.*, lamina *f.* **4** (*autom.*) targa *f.* **5** (*tip.*) lastra *f.* **6** (*illustrazione*) tavola *f.* **7** (*premio per il vincitore*) coppa *f.* **8** dentiera *f.*
plateau ['plætɒʊ] *s.* altopiano *m.*
platform ['plætfɜːm] *s.* **1** piattaforma *f.* **2** palco *m.*, impalcatura *f.* **3** (*ferr*) marciapiede *m.* ♦ **p. roof** pensilina
platinum ['plætɪnəm] *s.* platino *m.*
platitude ['plætɪtjuːd] *s.* banalità *f.*
Platonic [plə'tənɪk] *agg.* platonico
platonically [plə'tənɪkəlɪ] *avv.* platonicamente
platoon [plə'tuːn] *s.* plotone *m.*
platter ['plætəʳ] *s.* piatto *m.* da portata
plausible ['plɜːzəbl] *agg.* plausibile
play [pleɪ] *s.* **1** gioco *m.* **2** partita *f.*, mossa *f.* **3** azione *f.*, attività *f.* **4** commedia *f.*, dramma *m.* **5** (*mus.*) esecuzione *f.* ♦ **fair p.** lealtà; **p. on words** gioco di parole
to play [pleɪ] *v. tr. e intr.* **1** giocare **2** suonare **3** recitare, interpretare **4** agire, comportarsi ♦ **to p. about** scherzare; **to p. down** minimizzare; **to p. off** disputare la bella; **to p. up** mettere in evidenza, tormentare
playbill ['pleɪbɪl] *s.* locandina *f.*
playboy ['pleɪbəɪ] *s.* playboy *m. inv.*
player ['pleɪəʳ] *s.* giocatore *m.*, suonatore *m.*
playful ['pleɪf(ʊ)l] *agg.* giocoso
playground ['pleɪgraʊnd] *s.* terreno *m.* di gioco, luogo *m.* di svago
playgroup ['pleɪˌgruːp] *s.* asilo *m.* infantile
playing-card ['pleɪɪŋkaːd] *s.* carta *f.* da gioco
playing-field ['pleɪɪŋfiːld] *s.* campo *m.* da gioco
playmate ['pleɪmeɪt] *s.* compagno *m.* di gioco
play-off ['pleɪɜːf] *s.* (*sport*) spareggio *m.*
playpen ['pleɪpɛn] *s.* box *m. inv.* (*per bambini*)
plaything ['pleɪˌθɪŋ] *s.* giocattolo *m.*
playtime ['pleɪˌtaɪm] *s.* ricreazione *f.*
playwright ['pleɪraɪt] *s.* commediografo

m., drammaturgo *m.*
plea [pliː] *s.* **1** richiesta *f.*, petizione *f.*, appello *m.* **2** (*dir.*) difesa *f.* **3** scusa *f.*
to plead [pliːd] *v. tr.* **1** (*dir.*) patrocinare **2** chiedere, supplicare **3** addurre a giustificazione
pleasant ['plɛznt] *agg.* piacevole, gradevole, ameno
please [pliːz] *inter.* per favore!, prego!
to please [pliːz] **A** *v. tr.* **1** piacere a, essere gradito a **2** volere, aver voglia di **B** *v. intr.* **1** piacere, volere **2** accontentare, soddisfare ♦ **p. yourself** fa' come vuoi
pleased [pliːzd] *agg.* contento, compiaciuto
pleasing ['pliːzɪŋ] *agg.* piacevole
pleasure ['pləʒəʳ] *s.* piacere *m.*, godimento *m.*, divertimento *m.* ♦ **to take p. in** compiacersi, divertirsi
pleat [pliːt] *s.* piega *f.*
plebs [plɛbz] *s.* (*stor.*) plebe *f.*
plectrum ['plɛktrəm] *s.* plettro *m.*
pledge [plɛdʒ] *s.* **1** pegno *m.* **2** promessa *f.*
to pledge [plɛdʒ] *v. tr.* **1** impegnare **2** promettere ♦ **to p. oneself to do st.** impegnarsi a fare q.c.
plentiful ['plɛntɪf(ʊ)l] *agg.* abbondante
plenty ['plɛntɪ] **A** *agg. pred.* abbondante, sufficiente **B** *s.* abbondanza *f.* **C** *avv.* abbondantemente, molto
pleonastic [ˌplɪə'næstɪk] *agg.* pleonastico
pleurisy ['plʊərɪsɪ] *s.* pleurite *f.*
pliable ['plaɪəbl] *agg.* pieghevole, flessibile
pliant ['plaɪənt] *agg.* pieghevole, flessibile
pliers ['plaɪəz] *s. pl.* pinze *f. pl.*
plight [plaɪt] s. condizione *f.* (*spec. avversa*)
plimsolls ['plɪms(ə)lz] *s. pl.* scarpe *f. pl.* da ginnastica
plinth [plɪnθ] *s.* (*arch.*) plinto *m.*, base *f.*
to plod [pləd] *v. intr.* **1** arrancare **2** sgobbare
plonk [pləŋk] *s.* tonfo *m.*, rumore *m.* sordo
plot [plət] *s.* **1** appezzamento *m.* di terreno **2** intreccio *m.*, trama *f.* **3** macchinazione *f.*, complotto *m.*
to plot [plət] *v. tr.* **1** rilevare, fare la pianta di **2** disegnare, tracciare **3** complottare, tramare
plotter ['plətəʳ] *s.* **1** cospiratore *m.* **2** (*inf.*) plotter *m. inv.*
plough [plaʊ] (*USA* **plow**) *s.* aratro *m.*
to plough [plaʊ] (*USA* **to plow**) **A** *v. tr.* arare, solcare **B** *v. intr.* **1** arare **2** farsi strada ♦ **to p. into** fendere, assalire, (*denaro*) investire; **to p. through** avanzare attraverso
ploy [pləɪ] *s.* stratagemma *m.*
pluck [plʌk] *s.* **1** strappo *m.* **2** *al pl.* frattaglie *f. pl.* **3** (*fig.*) coraggio *m.*, fegato *m.*
to pluck [plʌk] *v. tr.* **1** strappare, cogliere **2** tirare **3** (*strumento musicale*) pizzicare **4** spennare
plug [plʌg] *s.* **1** tappo *m.* **2** (*elettr.*) spina *f.* **3** (*mecc.*) candela *f.* **4** (*med.*) tampone *m.* **5** (*fam.*) annuncio *m.* pubblicitario
to plug [plʌg] *v. tr.* **1** tappare, tamponare **2** pubblicizzare **3** (*pop.*) colpire ♦ **to p. in** innestare (la spina)
plum [plʌm] *s.* **1** prugna *f.*, susina *f.* **2** (*fig.*) cosa *f.* eccellente
plumb [plʌm] **A** *s.* (filo a) piombo *m.*, piombino *m.* **B** *agg.* **1** a piombo **2** completo, assoluto **C** *avv.* **1** a piombo, verticalmente **2** esattamente
to plumb [plʌm] *v. tr.* **1** mettere a piombo **2** scandagliare **3** piombare
plumber ['plʌməʳ] *s.* idraulico *m.*
plumbing ['plʌmɪŋ] *s.* **1** piombatura *f.* **2** impianto *m.* idraulico, tubazioni *f. pl.*
plume [pluːm] *s.* penna *f.*, piuma *f.*
plummet ['plʌmɪt] *s.* **1** (filo) a piombo *m.* **2** scandaglio *m.*
to plummet ['plʌmɪt] *v. intr.* cadere a piombo, precipitare
plump (1) [plʌmp] *agg.* paffuto, grassottello
plump (2) [plʌmp] **A** *agg.* **1** diretto, netto **2** a piombo **B** *avv.* **1** di peso **2** verticalmente **3** chiaramente
to plump (1) [plʌmp] *v. tr. e intr.* gonfiare, gonfiarsi
to plump (2) [plʌmp] *v. intr.* piombare, cadere ♦ **to p. for** scegliere, preferire, votare per
plunder ['plʌndəʳ] *s.* saccheggio *m.*
to plunder ['plʌndəʳ] *v. tr. e intr.* saccheggiare
plunge [plʌn(d)ʒ] *s.* **1** tuffo *m.*, immersione *f.* **2** (*fam.*) speculazione *f.* avventata **3** (*econ.*) caduta *f.*, crollo *m.*
to plunge [plʌn(d)ʒ] **A** *v. tr.* tuffare, immergere **B** *v. intr.* **1** tuffarsi, immergersi **2** precipitarsi **3** scommettere, rischiare
plunger ['plʌn(d)ʒəʳ] *s.* **1** tuffatore *m.* **2** pistone *m.* **3** sturalavandini *m. inv.* **4** (*pop.*) speculatore *m.*
pluperfect [pluː'pɜːfɪkt] *agg. e s.* (*gramm.*) piucchepperfetto *m.*
plural ['plʊər(ə)l] *agg. e s.* plurale *m.*
pluralism ['plʊərəlɪz(ə)m] *s.* plurali-

smo *m.*
plurality [plʊə'rælɪtɪ] *s.* pluralità *f.*
pluriannual [ˌplʊərɪ'ænjʊəl] *agg.* pluriennale
plus [plʌs] **A** *agg.* **1** addizionale, in più **2** positivo **B** *s.* **1** (*mat.*) più *m.* **2** quantità *f.* in più, extra *m. inv.* **3** fattore *m.* positivo **C** *prep.* più
plush [plʌʃ] **A** *agg.* lussuoso, elegante **B** *s.* felpa *f.*
plutocracy [pluː'tɔkrəsɪ] *s.* plutocrazia *f.*
pluvial ['pluːvjəl] *agg.* pluviale
ply [plaɪ] *s.* **1** piega *f.* **2** capo *m.*, filo *m.*, trefolo *m.* **3** (*di legno, cartone*) strato *m.*
to ply [plaɪ] **A** *v. tr.* **1** maneggiare, adoperare **2** attendere a, esercitare **3** (*con offerte, domande*) importunare **4** rimpinzare **B** *v. intr.* **1** lavorare assiduamente **2** (*naut.*) fare servizio di linea
plywood ['plaɪwʊd] *s.* (legno) compensato *m.*
pneumatic [njuː'mætɪk] *agg. e s.* pneumatico *m.*
pneumonia [njʊ(ː)'mɒʊnjə] *s.* polmonite *f.*
to poach (1) [pɒʊtʃ] *v. tr.* cuocere in bianco ♦ **poached eggs** uova affogate
to poach (2) [pɒʊtʃ] *v. tr. e intr.* cacciare (o pescare) di frodo
pocket ['pɔkɪt] **A** *agg.* tascabile **B** *s.* **1** tasca *f.* **2** cavità *f.*, sacca *f.* ♦ **p. money** piccola somma (*corrisposta ai figli*)
to pocket ['pɔkɪt] *v. tr.* **1** intascare, appropriarsi di **2** sopportare **3** nascondere, soffocare
pocketbook ['pɔkɪtbʊk] *s.* **1** taccuino *m.* **2** (*USA*) portafoglio *m.*
pocketknife ['pɔkɪtnaɪf] *s.* temperino *m.*
pod [pɔd] *s.* baccello *m.*, guscio *m.*
podgy ['pɔdʒɪ] *agg.* tozzo, grassoccio
podiatrist [pə'daɪətrɪst] *s.* podologo *m.*
podium ['pɒʊdɪəm] *s.* podio *m.*
poem ['pɒ(ʊ)ɪm] *s.* poesia *f.*, poema *m.*
poet ['pɒ(ʊ)ɪt] *s.* poeta *m.*
poetic(al) [pɒ(ʊ)'ɛtɪk((ə)l)] *agg.* poetico
poetics [pɒ(ʊ)'ɛtɪks] *s. pl.* (*v. al sing.*) poetica *f.*
poetry ['pɒ(ʊ)ɪtrɪ] *s.* poesia *f.*
poignant ['pɔɪnjənt] *agg.* **1** acuto, intenso **2** mordace
point [pɔɪnt] *s.* **1** punto *m.* **2** motivo *m.*, scopo *m.*, senso *m.* **3** punta *f.*, estremità *f.* **4** (*geogr.*) punta *f.*, promontorio *m.* **5** *al pl.* (*ferr.*) scambio *m.* ♦ **at all points** sotto ogni aspetto; **p. of view** punto di vista
to point [pɔɪnt] *v. tr. e intr.* **1** indicare **2** appuntire, fare la punta a **3** puntare ♦ **to p. to/at** indicare, guardare su; **to p. out** far notare, segnalare; **to p. up** mettere in evidenza
point-blank [ˌpɔɪnt'blæŋk] **A** *agg.* **1** netto, preciso **2** a bruciapelo **B** *avv.* **1** nettamente, chiaro e tondo **2** a bruciapelo
pointed ['pɔɪntɪd] *agg.* **1** appuntito, aguzzo **2** (*fig.*) pungente, arguto **3** esplicito, intenzionale
pointer ['pɔɪntəʳ] *s.* **1** indice *m.*, lancetta *f.* **2** bacchetta *f.* **3** (*zool.*) pointer *m. inv.* **4** (*fam.*) suggerimento *m.*, indicazione *f.*
pointillism ['pwæntɪlɪz(ə)m] *s.* divisionismo *m.*
pointless ['pɔɪntˌlɪs] *agg.* **1** spuntato, smussato **2** inutile, vano
poise [pɔɪz] *s.* **1** equilibrio *m.*, stabilità *f.* **2** portamento *m.*
poison ['pɔɪzn] *s.* veleno *m.*
to poison ['pɔɪzn] *v. tr.* avvelenare
poisoning ['pɔɪznɪŋ] *s.* avvelenamento *m.*
poisonous ['pɔɪznəs] *agg.* velenoso
to poke [pɒʊk] **A** *v. tr.* **1** colpire, urtare, spingere **2** infilare, conficcare **3** sporgere **4** attizzare (il fuoco) **B** *v. intr.* **1** dare un colpo, pungolare **2** sporgere **3** curiosare, immischiarsi, intromettersi ♦ **to p. about** frugare
poker (1) ['pɒʊkəʳ] *s.* attizzatoio *m.*
poker (2) ['pɒʊkəʳ] *s.* (*gioco*) poker *m. inv.*
poky ['pɒʊkɪ] *agg.* angusto, misero
polar ['pɒʊləʳ] *agg.* polare
polarity [pɒ(ʊ)'lærɪtɪ] *s.* polarità *f.*
to polarize ['pɒʊləraɪz] *v. tr.* polarizzare
pole (1) [pɒʊl] *s.* asta *f.*, palo *m.*
pole (2) [pɒʊl] *s.* polo *m.*
Pole [pɒʊl] *s.* polacco *m.*
polecat ['pɒʊlkæt] *s.* puzzola *f.*
polemic [pə'lɛmɪk] **A** *agg.* polemico **B** *s.* polemica *f.*
police [pə'liːs] *s.* polizia *f.* ♦ **p. dog** cane poliziotto; **p. station** stazione di polizia
policeman [pə'liːsmən] (*pl.* **policemen**) *s.* poliziotto *m.*
policewoman [pə'liːsˌwʊmən] (*pl.* **policewomen**) donna *f.* poliziotto
policy (1) ['pɔlɪsɪ] *s.* politica *f.*, linea *f.* di condotta
policy (2) ['pɔlɪsɪ] *s.* polizza *f.*
Polish ['pɒʊlɪʃ] *agg. e s.* polacco *m.* (*lingua*)
polish ['pɔlɪʃ] *s.* **1** lucentezza *f.* **2** lucida-

tura *f.* **3** lucido *m.*, cera *f.*, smalto *m.*
to polish ['pəlɪʃ] *v. tr.* **1** lucidare, levigare **2** raffinare, ingentilire ♦ **to p. off** sbrigare, finire, mangiarsi
polished ['pəlɪʃt] *agg.* **1** lucido **2** raffinato
polite [pə'laɪt] *agg.* **1** cortese, garbato **2** raffinato, elegante
politeness [pə'laɪtnɪs] *s.* **1** cortesia *f.*, educazione *f.* **2** raffinatezza *f.*, eleganza *f.*
political [pə'lɪtɪk(ə)l] *agg.* politico
politics ['pəlɪtɪks] *s. pl.* (*v. al sing.*) politica *f.* ♦ **home p.** politica interna; **foreign p.** politica estera
poll [pɒʊl] *s.* **1** votazione *f.*, elezione *f.* **2** scrutinio *m.*, voti *m. pl.* **3** seggio *m.* elettorale **4** sondaggio *m.*
to poll [pɒʊl] *v. tr.* **1** ottenere (voti) **2** scrutinare **3** sondare (l'opinione)
pollen ['pəlɪn] *s.* polline *m.*
pollination [ˌpəlɪ'neɪʃ(ə)n] *s.* impollinazione *f.*
polling [ˌpɒʊlɪŋ] **A** *agg.* votante **B** *s.* votazione *f.* ♦ **p. day** giorno delle elezioni; **p. station** seggio elettorale
to pollute [pə'lu:t] *v. tr.* inquinare
pollution [pə'lu:ʃ(ə)n] *s.* inquinamento *m.*
polo ['pɒʊlɒʊ] *s.* (*sport*) polo *m.* ♦ **water p.** pallanuoto
polychromatic [ˌpəlɪkrɒ(ʊ)'mætɪk] *agg.* policromatico
polyclinic [ˌpəlɪ'klɪnɪk] *s.* policlinico *m.*
polyester ['pəlɪˌɛstə] *s.* poliestere *m.*
polygamist [pə'lɪgəmɪst] *s.* poligamo *m.*
polygamous [pə'lɪgəməs] *agg.* poligamo
polygamy [pə'lɪgəmɪ] *s.* poligamia *f.*
polyglot ['pəlɪglət] *agg. e s.* poliglotta *m. e f.*
polygon ['pəlɪgən] *s.* poligono *m.*
polygonal [pə'lɪgənl] *agg.* poligonale
polyhedral [ˌpəlɪ'hɛdrəl] *agg.* poliedrico
polymer ['pəlɪmə^r] *s.* polimero *m.*
polymorphous [ˌpəlɪ'mɜ:fəs] *agg.* polimorfo
polyp ['pəlɪp] *s.* polipo *m.*
polyphonic [ˌpəlɪ'fənɪk] *agg.* polifonico
polyptych ['pəlɪptɪk] *s.* polittico *m.*
polytechnic [ˌpəlɪ'tɛknɪk] *agg. e s.* politecnico *m.*
polytheism ['pəlɪθi:ɪz(ə)m] *s.* politeismo *m.*
polyvalent [ˌpəlɪ'veɪlənt] *agg.* polivalente
pomegranate ['pəmɪˌgrænɪt] *s.* melagrana *f.*
pomp [pəmp] *s.* pompa *f.*, sfarzo *m.*
pompom ['pəmpəm] *s.* pompon *m. inv.*
pompous ['pəmpəs] *agg.* pomposo
pond [pənd] *s.* stagno *m.*, laghetto *m.*
to ponder ['pəndə^r] **A** *v. tr.* ponderare, considerare **B** *v. intr.* meditare, riflettere
ponderous ['pənd(ə)rəs] *agg.* ponderoso, pesante
pong [pəŋ] *s.* (*fam.*) puzzo *m.*
pontiff ['pəntɪf] *s.* pontefice *m.*
pontifical [pən'tɪfɪk(ə)l] *agg.* pontificio
pontificate [pən'tɪfɪkɪt] *s.* pontificato *m.*
pony ['pɒʊnɪ] *s.* pony *m. inv.* ♦ **p. tail** (pettinatura a) coda di cavallo; **p. trekking** trekking a cavallo
poodle ['pu:dl] *s.* (cane) barbone *m.*
pool (1) [pu:l] *s.* **1** stagno *m.*, laghetto *m.* **2** pozza *f.* ♦ **swimming p.** piscina
pool (2) [pu:l] *s.* **1** (*nei giochi di carte*) piatto *m.* **2** biliardo *m.* **3** consorzio *m.*, pool *m. inv.* **4** *al pl.* totocalcio *m. inv.*
to pool [pu:l] *v. tr.* mettere in comune, consorziare, riunire
poor [pʊə^r] *agg.* **1** povero, misero **2** scarso, insufficiente **3** scadente ♦ **p. figure** figuraccia
poorly ['pʊəlɪ] **A** *avv.* malamente, scarsamente **B** *agg.* indisposto, malaticcio
pop (1) [pəp] *s.* **1** schiocco *m.*, botto *m.* **2** (*fam.*) bevanda *f.* gassata
pop (2) [pəp] *agg. e s.* (*mus.*) pop *m. inv.*
pop (3) [pəp] *s.* (*fam.*) papà *m.*
to pop [pəp] **A** *v. tr.* **1** far scoppiare, far schioccare **2** far fuoco con **3** (*granturco*) soffiare **4** ficcare **5** dare in pegno, impegnare **B** *v. intr.* **1** schioccare **2** scoppiare ♦ **to p. in** fare una capatina in; **to p. off** saltare via, andarsene in fretta; **to p. out** fare un salto fuori, fare capolino; **to p. up** balzar fuori, saltar su
popcorn ['pəpkɜ:n] *s.* popcorn *m. inv.*
pope [pɒʊp] *s.* papa *m.*
poplar ['pəplə^r] *s.* pioppo *m.*
popper ['pəpə^r] *s.* (bottone) automatico *m.*
poppy ['pəpɪ] *s.* papavero *m.*
populace ['pəpjʊləs] *s.* plebaglia *f.*
popular ['pəpjʊlə^r] *agg.* popolare
popularity [ˌpəpjʊ'lærɪtɪ] *s.* popolarità *f.*
to popularize ['pəpjʊləraɪz] *v. tr.* **1** rendere popolare **2** divulgare
to populate ['pəpjʊleɪt] *v. tr.* popolare
population [ˌpəpjʊ'leɪʃ(ə)n] *s.* popolazione *f.*
populism ['pəpjʊlɪz(ə)m] *s.* populismo *m.*

populous ['pɔpjuləs] *agg.* popoloso
porcelain ['pɜːslɪn] *s.* porcellana *f.*
porch [pɜːtʃ] *s.* **1** portico *m.* **2** (*USA*) veranda *f.*
porcupine ['pɜːkjupaɪn] *s.* porcospino *m.*
pore [pɜːʳ] *s.* poro *m.*
to **pore** [pɜːʳ] *v. intr.* **to p. over** esaminare attentamente, riflettere su
pork [pɜːk] *s.* (carne di) maiale *m.* ♦ **p. chop** braciola di maiale
pornographic [ˌpɜːnə'græfɪk] *agg.* pornografico
pornography [pɜː'nɔgrəfɪ] *s.* pornografia *f.*
porphyry ['pɜːfɪrɪ] *s.* porfido *m.*
porpoise ['pɜːpəs] *s.* **1** focena *f.* **2** (*pop.*) delfino *m.*
porridge ['pɔrɪdʒ] *s.* porridge *m. inv.*
port (1) [pɜːt] *s.* porto *m.* ♦ **p. of call** scalo
port (2) [pɜːt] *s.* (*naut.*) sinistra *f.*, fianco *m.* sinistro
port (3) [pɜːt] *s.* (*naut.*) portello *m.*
portable ['pɜːtəbl] *agg.* portatile
portal ['pɜːtl] *s.* portale *m.*
portent ['pɜːtɛnt] *s.* **1** presagio *m.* (negativo) **2** portento *m.*
portentous [pɜː'tɛntəs] *agg.* **1** funesto **2** prodigioso
porter (1) ['pɜːtəʳ] *s.* portiere *m.*, portinaio *m.*
porter (2) ['pɜːtəʳ] *s.* facchino *m.*, portabagagli *m. inv.*
portfolio [pɜːt'fɒuljɒu] *s.* **1** cartella *f.* **2** portfolio *m. inv.* **3** (*fin.*) portafoglio *m.* (di attività)
porthole ['pɜːthɒul] *s.* oblò *m.*
portico ['pɜːtɪkɒu] *s.* loggiato *m.*, portico *m.*
portion ['pɜːʃ(ə)n] *s.* porzione *f.*, quota *f.*
portly ['pɜːtlɪ] *agg.* corpulento
portrait ['pɜːtrɪt] *s.* ritratto *m.*
to **portray** [pɜː'treɪ] *v. tr.* **1** ritrarre, fare il ritratto di **2** descrivere
Portuguese [ˌpɜːtju'giːz] *agg. e s.* portoghese *m. e f.*
pose [pɒuz] *s.* posa *f.*
to **pose** [pɒuz] **A** *v. intr.* **1** posare, mettersi in posa **2** atteggiarsi a, spacciarsi per **B** *v. tr.* **1** mettere in posa **2** (*un quesito*) porre, sollevare
posh [pɔʃ] *agg.* (*fam.*) elegante
position [pə'zɪʃ(ə)n] *s.* posizione *f.*
to **position** [pə'zɪʃ(ə)n] *v. tr.* collocare, sistemare
positive ['pɔzɪtɪv] *agg.* **1** positivo **2** preciso, assoluto, esplicito **3** certo, sicuro, convinto
positivism ['pɔzɪtɪvɪz(ə)m] *s.* positivismo *m.*
posology [pɒ(u)'sɔlədʒɪ] *s.* posologia *f.*
to **possess** [pə'zɛs] *v. tr.* possedere, avere
possession [pə'zɛʃ(ə)n] *s.* possesso *m.*
possessive [pə'zɛsɪv] *agg.* possessivo
possibility [ˌpɔsə'bɪlɪtɪ] *s.* possibilità *f.*
possible ['pɔsəbl] *agg.* possibile
possibly ['pɔsɪblɪ] *avv.* **1** forse **2** in alcun modo
post (1) [pɒust] *s.* posta *f.* ♦ **p. office** ufficio postale
post (2) [pɒust] *s.* **1** palo *m.*, pilastro *m.* **2** (*sport*) traguardo *m.*
post (3) [pɒust] *s.* posto *m.*, postazione *f.*
to **post (1)** [pɒust] *v. tr.* imbucare, impostare ♦ **to p. up** informare, mettere al corrente
to **post (2)** [pɒust] *v. tr.* **1** affiggere **2** annunciare
postage ['pɒustɪdʒ] *s.* affrancatura *f.*
postal ['pɒust(ə)l] *agg.* postale ♦ **p. order** vaglia postale
postcard ['pɒus(t)kaːd] *s.* cartolina *f.*
postcode ['pɒus(t)ˌkɒud] *s.* codice *m.* postale
to **postdate** [ˌpɒust'deɪt] *v. tr.* postdatare
poster ['pɒustəʳ] *s.* poster *m. inv.*, manifesto *m.*
posterior [pɔs'tɪərɪəʳ] *agg.* posteriore
posterity [pɔs'tɛrɪtɪ] *s.* posterità *f.*
posthumous ['pɔstjuməs] *agg.* postumo
postman ['pɒus(t)mən] (*pl.* **postmen**) *s.* postino *m.*
postmark ['pɒus(t)maːk] *s.* timbro *m.* postale
post-modern [ˌpɒus(t)'mɔdən] *agg. e s.* postmoderno *m.*
postmortem [ˌpɒus(t)'mɜːtəm] **A** *agg.* post mortem **B** *s.* autopsia *f.*
to **postpone** [ˌpɒus(t)'pɒun] *v. tr.* posporre, posticipare
postponement [pɒus(t)'pɒunmənt] *s.* rinvio *m.*
postscript ['pɒusˌskrɪpt] *s.* poscritto *m.*
postulate ['pɔstjulɪlt] *s.* postulato *m.*
posture ['pɔstʃəʳ] *s.* posizione *f.*, atteggiamento *m.*
post-war [ˌpɒust'wɜːʳ] *agg.* postbellico
posy ['pɒuzɪ] *s.* mazzolino *m.* di fiori
pot [pɔt] *s.* **1** vaso *m.*, barattolo *m.* **2** pentola *f.* **3** teiera *f.*, caffettiera *f.* **4** (*fam.*)

premio *m.* **5** (*pop.*) marijuana *f.* ♦ **a big p.** (*fam.*) un pezzo grosso
potable ['pɒʊtəbl] *agg.* potabile
potato [p(ə)'teɪtɒʊ] (*pl.* **potatoes**) *s.* patata *f.*
potency ['pɒʊt(ə)nsɪ] *s.* efficacia *f.*
potent ['pɒʊt(ə)nt] *agg.* potente
potential [pə'tɛnʃ(ə)l] *agg. e s.* potenziale *m.*
to **potentiate** [pə'tɛnʃ(ɪ)eɪt] *v. tr.* potenziare
pot-herbs ['pəthɜːbz] *s. pl.* erbe *f. pl.* aromatiche
pothole ['pəthɒʊl] *s.* **1** buca *f.* **2** caverna *f.*
potholing ['pəthɒʊlɪŋ] *s.* (*fam.*) speleologia *f.*
potluck [ˌpət'lʌk] *s.* **1** pasto *m.* alla buona **2** sorte *f.* ♦ **to take p.** tentare la sorte
potroast ['pətrɒʊst] *s.* brasato *m.*
potted ['pətɪd] *agg.* **1** (*di pianta*) in vaso **2** (*di cibo*) conservato, inscatolato **3** (*fig.*) condensato, abbreviato
potter ['pətəʳ] *s.* vasaio *m.*
to **potter** ['pətəʳ] *v. intr.* lavoricchiare
pottery ['pətərɪ] *s.* **1** ceramica *f.*, ceramiche *f. pl.* **2** arte *f.* della ceramica **3** fabbrica *f.* di ceramiche
potty ['pətɪ] *agg.* **1** insignificante **2** pazzo, bizzarro
pouch [paʊtʃ] *s.* **1** borsa *f.*, sacchetto *m.* **2** marsupio *m.*
poultry ['pɒʊltrɪ] *s.* pollame *m.* ♦ **p. farming** pollicoltura
to **pounce** [paʊns] *v. intr.* balzare addosso, avventarsi
pound (1) [paʊnd] *s.* **1** libbra *f.* **2** sterlina *f.*
pound (2) [paʊnd] *s.* botta *f.*, martellata *f.*
to **pound** [paʊnd] *v. tr.* **1** triturare **2** colpire, battere
to **pour** [pɜːʳ] **A** *v. tr.* versare **B** *v. intr.* **1** riversarsi **2** (*anche* **to p. down**) piovere a dirotto ♦ **to p. in** affluire; **to p. out** riversarsi fuori
pout [paʊt] *s.* broncio *m.*
poverty ['pəvətɪ] *s.* miseria *f.*, povertà *f.* ♦ **p.-stricken** molto povero
powder ['paʊdəʳ] *s.* **1** polvere *f.* **2** cipria *f.* ♦ **bath p.** borotalco
to **powder** ['paʊdəʳ] **A** *v. tr.* **1** spolverizzare **2** ridurre in polvere **3** incipriare **B** *v. intr.* **1** polverizzarsi **2** incipriarsi ♦ **powdered milk** latte in polvere
power ['paʊəʳ] *s.* **1** potere *m.*, autorità *f.*, potenza *f.* facoltà *f.* **2** (*elettr.*) energia *f.*, forza *f.*, corrente *f.* **3** (*fam.*) quantità *f.*, mucchio *m.* ♦ **p. boat** barca a motore; **p. cut** interruzione di corrente; **p. point** presa di corrente; **p. station** centrale elettrica; **p. steering** servosterzo
powerful ['paʊəf(ʊ)l] *agg.* poderoso, potente
powerless ['paʊəlɪs] *agg.* impotente
practicable ['præktɪkəbl] *agg.* praticabile
practical ['præktɪk(ə)l] *agg.* pratico
practicality [ˌpræktɪ'kælɪtɪ] *s.* praticità *f.*
practically ['præktɪkəlɪ] *avv.* **1** praticamente **2** quasi
practice ['præktɪs] *s.* **1** pratica *f.* **2** abitudine *f.*, prassi *f.* **3** esercizio *m.* della professione **4** (*sport*) allenamento *m.* **5** clientela *f.* ♦ **out of p.** fuori esercizio; **to get p.** impratichirsi
to **practise** ['præktɪs] (*USA* **to practice**) **A** *v. tr.* **1** esercitarsi in, allenarsi in **2** professare, praticare **B** *v. intr.* esercitarsi, fare esercizi
practising ['præktɪsɪŋ] *agg.* praticante
practitioner [præk'tɪʃnəʳ] *s.* professionista *m. e f.* (*spec. medico*) ♦ **general p.** medico generico
praetor ['priːtəʳ] *s.* (*stor.*) pretore *m.*
pragmatic [præg'mætɪk] *agg.* pragmatico
prairie ['prɛərɪ] *s.* prateria *f.*
praise [preɪz] *s.* elogio *m.*, lode *f.*
to **praise** [preɪz] *v. tr.* elogiare, lodare
praiseworthy ['preɪzˌwɜːðɪ] *agg.* lodevole, encomiabile
pram (1) [præm] *s.* carrozzina *f.* (per bambini)
pram (2) [præm] *s.* (*naut.*) battellino *m.*
to **prance** [prɑːns] *v. intr.* **1** (*di cavallo*) impennarsi **2** camminare impettito
prank [præŋk] *s.* birichinata *f.*, burla *f.*
prawn [prɜːn] *s.* gamberetto *m.*
praxis ['præksɪs] *s.* prassi *f.*
to **pray** [preɪ] *v. tr. e intr.* pregare
prayer [prɛəʳ] *s.* preghiera *f.*
preach [priːtʃ] *s.* predica *f.*
to **preach** [priːtʃ] *v. tr. e intr.* predicare
preacher ['priːtʃəʳ] *s.* predicatore *m.*
preaching ['priːtʃɪŋ] *s.* predicazione *f.*
preamble [priː'æmbl] *s.* preambolo *m.*
precarious [prɪ'kɛərɪəs] *agg.* precario
precariousness [prɪ'kɛərɪəsnɪs] *s.* precarietà *f.*
precaution [prɪ'kɜːʃ(ə)n] *s.* precauzione *f.*
to **precede** [prɪ(ː)'siːd] *v. tr. e intr.* precedere

precedence ['prɛsiːd(ə)ns] *s.* precedenza *f.*, priorità *f.*
precedent [prɛ'siːd(ə)nt] *agg.* precedente
preceding [prɪ(ː)'siːdɪŋ] *agg.* precedente
precept ['priːsɛpt] *s.* precetto *m.*
precinct ['priːsɪŋ(k)t] *s.* **1** recinto *m.* **2** area *f.* delimitata **3** distretto *m.* **4** *al pl.* vicinanze *f. pl.* ♦ **pedestrian p.** zona pedonale
preciosity [ˌprɛʃɪ'əsɪtɪ] *s.* preziosismo *m.*
precious ['prɛʃəs] *agg.* prezioso
to **precipitate** [prɪ'sɪpɪteɪt] *v. tr. e intr.* precipitare
precipitation [prɪˌsɪpɪ'teɪʃ(ə)n] *s.* precipitazione *f.*
precipitous [prɪ'sɪpɪtəs] *agg.* precipitoso
precise [prɪ'saɪs] *agg.* preciso
precisely [prɪ'saɪslɪ] *avv.* precisamente
precision [prɪ'sɪʒ(ə)n] *s.* precisione *f.*
to **preclude** [prɪ'kluːd] *v. tr.* precludere
precocious [prɪ'kɒʊʃəs] *agg.* precoce
preconception [ˌpriːkən'sɛpʃ(ə)n] *s.* preconcetto *m.*
precondition [ˌpriːkən'dɪʃ(ə)n] *s.* requisito *m.* indispensabile
precursor [priː'kɜːsəʳ] *s.* precursore *m.*
predator ['prɛdətəʳ] *s.* predatore *m.*
predatory ['prɛdət(ə)rɪ] *agg.* predatore
to **predecease** [ˌpriːdɪ'siːs] *v. tr.* premorire
predecessor ['priːdɪsɛsəʳ] *s.* predecessore *m.*
to **predestinate** [priː'dɛstɪneɪt] *v. tr.* predestinare
predestination [priːˌdɛstɪ'neɪʃ(ə)n] *s.* predestinazione *f.*
to **predetermine** [ˌpriːdɪ'tɜːmɪn] *v. tr.* predeterminare
predicament [prɪ'dɪkəmənt] *s.* frangente *m.*, situazione *f.* (*spec. difficile*)
to **predict** [prɪ'dɪkt] *v. tr.* predire
predictable [prɪ'dɪktəbl] *agg.* prevedibile
prediction [prɪ'dɪkʃ(ə)n] *s.* predizione *f.*, profezia *f.*
to **predispose** [ˌpriːdɪs'pɒʊz] *v. tr.* predisporre
predominance [prɪ'dəmɪnəns] *s.* predominanza *f.*, prevalenza *f.*
predominant [prɪ'dəmɪnənt] *agg.* predominante, prevalente
to **predominate** [prɪ'dəmɪneɪt] *v. intr.* predominare, prevalere
pre-eminent [prɪ'ɛmɪnənt] *agg.* preminente
pre-empt [prɪ(ː)'ɛm(p)t] *v. tr.* **1** acquistare con diritto di prelazione **2** pregiudicare, mandare a vuoto **3** impadronirsi di
to **preen** [priːn] *v. tr.* (*di uccello*) lisciarsi col becco ♦ **to p. oneself** agghindarsi
to **pre-exist** [ˌpriːɪg'zɪst] *v. intr.* preesistere
pre-existent [ˌpriːɪg'zɪst(ə)nt] *agg.* preesistente
prefab ['priːfæb] *s.* (*fam.*) casa *f.* prefabbricata
preface ['prɛfɪs] *s.* prefazione *f.*
prefecture ['priːfɛktjʊəʳ] *s.* prefettura *f.*
to **prefer** [prɪ'fɜːʳ] *v. tr.* **1** preferire **2** (*dir.*) presentare, avanzare
preferable ['prɛf(ə)rəbl] *agg.* preferibile
preference ['prɛf(ə)r(ə)ns] *s.* preferenza *f.*
preferential [ˌprɛfə'rɛnʃ(ə)l] *agg.* preferenziale
to **prefigure** [priː'fɪgəʳ] *v. tr.* prefigurare
prefix ['priːfɪks] *s.* prefisso *m.*
to **prefix** [priː'fɪks] *v. tr.* **1** premettere **2** prefissare
pregnancy ['prɛgnənsɪ] *s.* **1** gestazione *f.*, gravidanza *f.* **2** pregnanza *f.*
pregnant ['prɛgnənt] *agg.* **1** incinta **2** pregnante
prehistoric [ˌpriː(h)ɪs'tərɪk] *agg.* preistorico
prehistory [priː'(h)ɪst(ə)rɪ] *s.* preistoria *f.*
prejudice ['prɛdʒʊdɪs] *s.* **1** pregiudizio *m.* **2** danno *m.*
prejudiced ['prɛdʒʊdɪst] *agg.* prevenuto ♦ **p. in favour of** ben disposto nei confronti di
prelate ['prɛlɪt] *s.* prelato *m.*
preliminary [prɪ'lɪm(ɪ)nərɪ] *agg. e s.* preliminare *m.*
prelude ['prɛljuːd] *s.* preludio *m.*
premarital [priː'mærɪt(ə)l] *agg.* prematrimoniale
premature [ˌprɛmə'tjʊəʳ] *agg.* prematuro
premeditation [prɪ(ː)ˌmɛdɪ'teɪʃ(ə)n] *s.* premeditazione *f.*
premier ['prɛmjəʳ] **A** *agg.* primo **B** *s.* premier *m. inv.*, primo ministro *m.*
première ['prɛmɪɛəʳ] *s.* (*teatro*) prima *f.*
premise ['prɛmɪs] *s.* **1** premessa *f.* **2** *al pl.* edificio *m.*, fabbricato *m.* ♦ **to be drunk on the premises** da bersi sul posto
to **premise** [prɪ'maɪz] *v. tr. e intr.* premettere
premium ['priːmjəm] *s.* premio *m.*
premonition [ˌpriːmə'nɪʃ(ə)n] *s.* premonizione *f.*
premonitory [prɪ'mənɪt(ə)rɪ] *agg.* premo-

nitore
preoccupation [pri:,əkjʊ'peɪʃ(ə)n] *s.* **1** preoccupazione *f.* **2** coinvolgimento *m.*
preoccupied [,pri:'əkjʊpaɪd] *agg.* preoccupato, assorto
prepaid [,pri:'peɪd] **A** *pass. e p. p. di* **to prepay B** *agg.* pagato in anticipo
preparation [,prɛpə'reɪʃ(ə)n] *s.* preparazione *f.*, preparativo *m.*
preparatory [prɪ'pærət(ə)rɪ] *agg.* preparatorio
to **prepare** [prɪ'pɛəʳ] *v. tr. e intr.* preparare, prepararsi
preponderant [prɪ'pənd(ə)r(ə)nt] *agg.* preponderante
preposition [,prɛpə'zɪʃ(ə)n] *s.* preposizione *f.*
preposterous [prɪ'pəst(ə)rəs] *agg.* **1** assurdo **2** ridicolo
Pre-Raphaelite [,pri:'ræfəlaɪt] *agg. e s.* preraffaellita *m. e f.*
prerequisite [pri:'rɛkwɪzɪt] **A** *agg.* necessario **B** *s.* requisito *m.* indispensabile
prerogative [prɪ'rəgətɪv] *s.* prerogativa *f.*
presage ['prɛsɪdʒ] *s.* presagio *m.*
to **presage** ['prɛsɪdʒ] *v. tr.* presagire
Presbyterian [,prɛzbɪ'tɪərɪən] *agg.* presbiteriano
presbytery ['prɛzbɪt(ə)rɪ] *s.* presbiterio *m.*
to **prescind** [prɪ'sɪnd] *v. intr.* prescindere
to **prescribe** [prɪs'kraɪb] *v. tr.* prescrivere
prescription [prɪs'krɪpʃ(ə)n] *s.* **1** prescrizione *f.* **2** (*med.*) ricetta *f.*
presence ['prɛzns] *s.* presenza *f.*
present (1) ['prɛznt] **A** *agg.* **1** presente **2** attuale, corrente **B** *s.* presente *m.* ♦ **at p.** momentaneamente; **to be p.** presenziare, assistere
present (2) ['prɛznt] *s.* presente *m.*, dono *m.*
to **present** [prɪ'zɛnt] *v. tr.* **1** presentare **2** regalare ♦ **to p. sb. with st.** regalare q.c. a qc.
presentable [prɪ'zɛntəbl] *agg.* presentabile
presentation [,prɛzɛn'teɪʃ(ə)n] *s.* **1** presentazione *f.* **2** rappresentazione *f.*
present-day [,prɛz(ə)nt'deɪ] *agg.* attuale
presenter [prɪ'zɛntəʳ] *s.* presentatore *m.*
presentiment [prɪ'zɛntɪmənt] *s.* presentimento *m.*
presently ['prɛzntlɪ] *avv.* **1** tra poco, a momenti **2** attualmente
preservation [,prɛsə(:)'veɪʃ(ə)n] *s.* preservazione *f.*, conservazione *f.*
preservative [prɪ'zɜ:vətɪv] *s.* conservante *m.*
preserve [prɪ'zɜ:v] *s.* **1** marmellata *f.*, conserva *f.* **2** (*di caccia, pesca*) riserva *f.*
to **preserve** [prɪ'zɜ:v] *v. tr.* **1** preservare, proteggere **2** mantenere, conservare **3** mettere in conserva
to **preside** [prɪ'zaɪd] *v. intr.* presiedere
presidency ['prɛzɪd(ə)nsɪ] *s.* presidenza *f.*
president ['prɛzɪd(ə)nt] *s.* presidente *m.*
presidential [,prɛzɪ'dɛnʃ(ə)l] *agg.* presidenziale
press [prɛs] *s.* **1** stampa *f.* **2** pressione *f.*, stretta *f.* **3** pressa *f.*, torchio *m.* ♦ **p. conference** conferenza stampa
to **press** [prɛs] **A** *v. tr.* **1** comprimere, premere, spremere **2** stringere, abbracciare **3** stirare **4** incalzare, insistere su **B** *v. intr.* **1** incalzare **2** affollarsi, premere ♦ **to p. on** continuare
pressing ['prɛsɪŋ] *agg.* urgente, incalzante
pressure ['prɛʃəʳ] *s.* pressione *f.* ♦ **blood p.** pressione sanguigna; **p. cooker** pentola a pressione; **p. gauge** manometro
to **pressure** ['prɛʃəʳ] *v. tr.* fare pressione su
to **pressurize** ['prɛʃəraɪz] *v. tr.* **1** fare pressione su **2** pressurizzare
prestige [prɛs'ti:ʒ] **A** *agg.* prestigioso **B** *s.* prestigio *m.*
prestigious [prɛs'tɪdʒəs] *agg.* prestigioso
presumable [prɪ'zju:məbl] *agg.* presumibile
to **presume** [prɪ'zju:m] *v. tr.* presumere
presumption [prɪ'zʌm(p)ʃ(ə)n] *s.* presunzione *f.*
presumptuous [prɪ'zʌm(p)tjʊəs] *agg.* presuntuoso
to **presuppose** [,pri:sə'pɒʊz] *v. tr.* presupporre
presupposition [,pri:sʌpə'zɪʃ(ə)n] *s.* presupposizione *f.*, presupposto *m.*
pretence [prɪ'tɛns] (*USA* **pretense**) *s.* **1** finzione *f.*, simulazione *f.* **2** pretesa *f.* **3** pretesto *m.* ♦ **to make a p. of** far finta di
to **pretend** [prɪ'tɛnd] **A** *v. tr.* **1** fingere, simulare **2** pretendere **B** *v. intr.* **1** fingere **2** aspirare a
pretender [prɪ'tɛndəʳ] *s.* **1** simulatore *m.* **2** pretendente *m. e f.*
pretension [prɪ'tɛnʃ(ə)n] *s.* **1** pretesa *f.* **2** presunzione *f.*

pretentious [prɪ'tɛnʃəs] *agg.* pretenzioso
pretext ['pri:tɛkst] *s.* pretesto *m.*
pretty ['prɪtɪ] **A** *agg.* **1** carino, grazioso, gradevole **2** acuto, intelligente **3** considerevole **B** *avv.* piuttosto, abbastanza
to prevail [prɪ'veɪl] *v. intr.* **1** prevalere, avere la meglio su **2** predominare, essere diffuso ♦ **to p. (up) on sb. to do st.** convincere qc. a fare q.c.
prevailing [prɪ'veɪlɪŋ] *agg.* prevalente, dominante
prevalence ['prɛvələns] *s.* prevalenza *f.*
prevalent ['prɛvələnt] *agg.* prevalente, comune
to prevaricate [prɪ'værɪkeɪt] *v. intr.* **1** tergiversare **2** equivocare
to prevent [prɪ'vɛnt] *v. tr.* **1** impedire, ostacolare **2** evitare ♦ **to p. oneself** trattenersi; **to p. sb. from doing st.** impedire a qc. di fare q.c.
prevention [prɪ'vɛnʃ(ə)n] *s.* prevenzione *f.*
preventive [prɪ'vɛntɪv] **A** *agg.* preventivo, profilattico **B** *s.* misura *f.* preventiva
preview ['pri:vju:] *s.* anteprima *f.*
previous ['pri:vjəs] *agg.* **1** precedente, anteriore **2** (*fam.*) precipitoso, prematuro ♦ **p. to** prima di
previously ['pri:vjəslɪ] *avv.* precedentemente, prima
prevision [prɪ(:)'vɪʒ(ə)n] *s.* previsione *f.*
pre-war [ˌpri:'wɔ:ʳ] *agg.* prebellico
prey [preɪ] *s.* preda *f.*
to prey [preɪ] *v. intr.* **1** (*di animale*) predare, cacciare **2** depredare, saccheggiare **3** tormentare
price [praɪs] *s.* prezzo *m.* ♦ **p. list** listino prezzi
to price [praɪs] *v. tr.* **1** fissare il prezzo di **2** stimare, valutare
priceless ['praɪslɪs] *agg.* inestimabile, d'incalcolabile valore
prick [prɪk] *s.* **1** punta *f.*, aculeo *m.* **2** puntura *f.*
to prick [prɪk] **A** *v. tr.* **1** pungere, punzecchiare **2** tormentare **3** rizzare, aguzzare **B** *v. intr.* formicolare, pizzicare
prickle ['prɪkl] *s.* **1** spina *f.*, pungiglione *m.* **2** pungolo *m.* **3** formicolio *m.*
prickly ['prɪklɪ] *agg.* **1** spinoso, pungente **2** (*fig.*) permaloso ♦ **p.-pear** fico d'India
pride [praɪd] *s.* **1** orgoglio *m.*, superbia *f.* **2** colmo *m.*, pienezza *f.*
priest [pri:st] *s.* prete *m.*, sacerdote *m.*
priesthood ['pri:sthʊd] *s.* sacerdozio *m.*
prig [prɪg] *s.* **1** presuntuoso *m.* **2** ladro *m.*
prim [prɪm] *agg.* affettato, cerimonioso
primal ['praɪm(ə)l] *agg.* **1** primario, principale **2** originale, primitivo
primarily ['praɪm(ə)rɪlɪ] *avv.* **1** principalmente, soprattutto **2** originalmente
primary ['praɪmərɪ] **A** *agg.* **1** primo, primario, originario **2** principale, fondamentale **3** elementare, di base **B** *s.* **1** fondamento *m.*, elemento *m.* principale **2** elezioni *f. pl.* primarie **3** scuola *f.* elementare
prime [praɪm] **A** *agg.* **1** primario, primo **2** di prima qualità **B** *s.* **1** principio *m.* **2** rigoglio *m.*, fiore *m.* **3** (minuto) primo *m.*
to prime [praɪm] *v. tr.* **1** innescare, caricare **2** mettere al corrente
primeval [praɪ'mi:v(ə)l] *agg.* primordiale, primitivo
primitive ['prɪmɪtɪv] *agg.* primitivo
primordial [praɪ'mɔ:djəl] *agg.* primordiale
primrose ['prɪmrɒʊz] *s.* primula *f.*
prince [prɪns] *s.* principe *m.* ♦ **p. Charming** il principe azzurro
princedom ['prɪnsdəm] *s.* principato *m.*
princess [prɪn'sɛs] *s.* principessa *f.*
principal ['prɪnsəp(ə)l] **A** *agg.* principale **B** *s.* **1** capo *m.*, direttore *m.*, preside *m. e f.* **2** (*econ.*) capitale *m.*
principality [ˌprɪnsɪ'pælɪtɪ] *s.* principato *m.*
principle ['prɪnsɪpl] *s.* principio *m.*, regola *f.*, norma *f.* ♦ **in p.** in linea di principio; **on p.** per principio
print [prɪnt] *s.* **1** impronta *f.*, segno *m.* **2** stampa *f.* **3** tessuto *m.* stampato ♦ **out of p.** (*di libro*) esaurito; **off-p.** estratto
to print [prɪnt] *v. tr.* **1** stampare **2** imprimere
printed ['prɪntɪd] *agg.* stampato, pubblicato ♦ **p. matter** stampe
printer ['prɪntəʳ] *s.* **1** tipografo *m.* **2** stampante *f.*
printing ['prɪntɪŋ] *s.* **1** stampa *f.* **2** tiratura *f.* **3** pubblicazione *f.*
printout ['prɪntˌaʊt] *s.* tabulato *m.*
prior ['praɪəʳ] **A** *agg.* **1** precedente, anteriore **2** prioritario **B** *s.* priore *m.*
priority [praɪ'ɔrɪtɪ] *s.* priorità *f.*
prism ['prɪz(ə)m] *s.* prisma *m.*
prison ['prɪzn] *s.* prigione *f.*
prisoner ['prɪznəʳ] *s.* prigioniero *m.*
pristine ['prɪstaɪn] *agg.* **1** originario **2** puro, incontaminato

privacy ['praɪvəsɪ] *s.* **1** intimità *f.*, vita *f.* privata, privacy *f. inv.* **2** riserbo *m.*
private ['praɪvɪt] **A** *agg.* **1** privato **2** personale, riservato **3** isolato, solitario **B** *s.* soldato *m.* semplice ♦ **in p.** privatamente; **p. eye/detective** investigatore privato; **p. parts** parti intime; **p. property** proprietà privata
privet ['prɪvɪt] *s.* ligustro *m.*
privilege ['prɪvɪlɪdʒ] *s.* privilegio *m.*
to privilege ['prɪvɪlɪdʒ] *v. tr.* privilegiare
privy ['prɪvɪ] *agg.* privato, segreto ♦ **to be p. to st.** essere a conoscenza di q.c.
prize [praɪz] **A** *s.* premio *m.* **B** *agg.* **1** premiato, da premio **2** dato come premio **3** a premi **4** (*fam.*) perfetto, classico ♦ **p. giving** premiazione
to prize (1) [praɪz] *v. tr.* stimare, valutare
to prize (2) [praɪz] *v. tr.* far leva su ♦ **to p. out** estorcere
pro [prɒʊ] *s.* (*fam.*) professionista *m. e f.*
probability [ˌprəbə'bɪlɪtɪ] *s.* probabilità *f.* ♦ **in all p.** con tutta probabilità
probable ['prəb(ə)bl] *agg.* probabile
probation [prə'beɪʃ(ə)n] *s.* **1** prova *f.*, esame *m.* **2** tirocinio *m.* **3** (*dir*) sospensione *f.* condizionale della pena
probe [prɒʊb] *s.* **1** sonda *f.* **2** (*fig.*) indagine *f.*
to probe [prɒʊb] *v. tr.* sondare
problem ['prəbləm] *s.* problema *m.*
problematic(al) [ˌprəblɪ'mætɪk((ə)l)] *agg.* problematico
procedural [prə'siːdʒər(ə)l] *agg.* procedurale
procedure [prə'siːdʒəʳ] *s.* procedura *f.*, procedimento *m.*
to proceed [prə'siːd] *v. intr.* **1** procedere, proseguire **2** agire **3** provenire
proceeding [prə'siːdɪŋ] *s.* **1** procedimento *m.* **2** *al pl.* riunione *f.* **3** *al pl.* (*di convegno*) atti *m. pl.*
proceeds ['prɒʊsiːdz] *s. pl.* ricavo *m.*, profitto *m.*
process ['prɒʊsɛs] *s.* **1** andamento *m.*, procedimento *m.* **2** processo *m.*, sviluppo *m.* **3** elaborazione *f.*
to process ['prɒʊsɛs] *v. tr.* **1** trattare, sottoporre a un processo **2** (*dir*) procedere contro **3** (*inf.*) elaborare
processing ['prɒʊsɛsɪŋ] *s.* **1** trattamento *m.*, lavorazione *f.* **2** (*inf.*) elaborazione *f.*
procession [prə'sɛʃ(ə)n] *s.* processione *f.*, corteo *m.*
to proclaim [prə'kleɪm] *v. tr.* proclamare
proclamation [ˌprəklə'meɪʃ(ə)n] *s.* proclamazione *f.*
to procreate ['prɒʊkrɪeɪt] *v. tr.* procreare, generare
to procure [prə'kjʊəʳ] *v. tr.* procurare, procacciare
to prod [prəd] *v. tr. e intr.* pungolare, incitare
prodigal ['prədɪgəl] **A** *agg.* prodigo **B** *s.* scialacquatore *m.*
prodigality [ˌprədɪ'gælɪtɪ] *s.* prodigalità *f.*, generosità *f.*
prodigious [prə'dɪdʒəs] *agg.* prodigioso
prodigy ['prədɪdʒɪ] *s.* prodigio *m.*, portento *m.*
produce ['prədjuːs] *s.* **1** prodotto *m.*, risultato *m.* **2** produzione *f.* agricola, materie *f. pl.* prime
to produce [prə'djuːs] *v. tr.* **1** produrre, fabbricare, generare **2** esibire, presentare
producer [prə'djuːsəʳ] *s.* produttore *m.*
product ['prədəkt] *s.* prodotto *m.*
production [prə'dʌkʃ(ə)n] *s.* produzione *f.*
productivity [ˌprədʌk'tɪvɪtɪ] *s.* produttività *f.*, rendimento *m.*
profane [prə'feɪn] *agg.* **1** profano **2** empio
to profess [prə'fɛs] **A** *v. tr.* **1** professare, dichiarare **2** pretendere di, fingere di **3** esercitare **B** *v. intr.* esercitare una professione
profession [prə'fɛʃ(ə)n] *s.* professione *f.*
professional [prə'fɛʃənl] **A** *agg.* professionale **B** *s.* professionista *m. e f.*
professionalism [prə'fɛʃnəlɪz(ə)m] *s.* professionismo *m.*
professor [prə'fɛsəʳ] *s.* professore *m.* (*universitario*)
proficiency [prə'fɪʃ(ə)nsɪ] *s.* abilità *m.*, competenza *f.*, conoscenza *f.*
profile ['prɒʊfaɪl] *s.* profilo *m.*
profit ['prəfɪt] *s.* profitto *m.*, beneficio *m.*, guadagno *m.*
to profit ['prəfɪt] **A** *v. tr.* giovare a **B** *v. intr.* beneficiare, approfittare
profitability [ˌprəfɪtə'bɪlɪtɪ] *s.* redditività *f.*
profitable ['prəfɪtəbl] *agg.* proficuo, redditizio
profound [prə'faʊnd] *agg.* **1** profondo **2** intenso **3** assoluto
profuse [prə'fjuːs] *agg.* **1** profuso, abbondante **2** prodigo
profusion [prə'fjuːʒ(ə)n] *s.* **1** profusione

f. **2** prodigalità *f.*
progenitor [prɒ(ʊ)'dʒɛnɪtəʳ] *s.* progenitore *m.*
prognosis [prəg'nɒʊsɪs] *s.* prognosi *f.*
prognostic [prəg'nəstɪk] *s.* pronostico *m.*
program ['prɒʊgræm] *s.* (*USA*) programma *m.*
to **program** ['prɒʊgræm] *v. tr.* (*USA*) programmare
programme ['prɒʊgræm] *s.* programma *m.*
programmer ['prɒʊgræməʳ] *s.* programmatore *m.*
programming ['prɒʊgræmɪŋ] *s.* programmazione *f.*
progress ['prɒʊgrɛs] *s.* **1** avanzamento *m.* **2** andamento *m.*, corso *m.* **3** progresso *m.*, sviluppo *m.* ♦ **works in p.** lavori in corso
to **progress** [prə'grɛs] *v. intr.* progredire, avanzare
progression [prɛə'grɛʃ(ə)n] *s.* progressione *f.*
progressive [prə'grɛsɪv] *agg.* **1** progressivo **2** progressista
to **prohibit** [prə'hɪbɪt] *v. tr.* proibire
prohibition [ˌprɒ(ʊ)ɪ'bɪʃ(ə)n] *s.* **1** proibizione *f.* **2** proibizionismo *m.*
prohibitive [prə'hɪbɪtɪv] *agg.* proibitivo
project ['prədʒɛkt] *s.* progetto *m.*, piano *m.*
to **project** [prə'dʒɛkt] **A** *v. tr.* **1** proiettare **2** progettare **B** *v. intr.* sporgere, aggettare
projectile [prə'dʒɛktaɪl] **A** *s.* proiettile *m.* **B** *agg.* **1** propulsivo **2** proiettabile
projection [prə'dʒɛkʃ(ə)n] *s.* **1** proiezione *f.* **2** aggetto *m.*, sporgenza *f.*
projector [prə'dʒəktəʳ] *s.* proiettore *m.*
proletarian [ˌprɒʊlɪ'tɛərɪən] *agg. e s.* proletario *m.*
to **proliferate** [prɒ(ʊ)'lɪfəreɪt] *v. intr.* proliferare
prolific [prə'lɪfɪk] *agg.* prolifico, fecondo
prolix ['prɒʊlɪks] *agg.* prolisso
prologue ['prɒʊləg] *s.* prologo *m.*
to **prolong** [prə'ləŋ] *v. tr.* prolungare
prolongation [ˌprɒʊləŋ'geɪʃ(ə)n] *s.* prolungamento *m.*
promenade [ˌprəmɪ'nɑːd] *s.* lungomare *m.*, passeggiata *f.*
prominence ['prəmɪnəns] *s.* **1** prominenza *f.*, sporgenza *f.* **2** importanza *f.*
prominent ['prəmɪnənt] *agg.* **1** prominente, sporgente **2** importante
promiscuity [ˌprəmɪs'kjʊ(ː)tɪ] *s.* promiscuità *f.*
promiscuous [prə'mɪskjʊəs] *agg.* **1** promiscuo, confuso **2** casuale
promise ['prəmɪs] *s.* promessa *f.*
to **promise** ['prəmɪs] *v. tr. e intr.* promettere ♦ **to p. oneself st.** ripromettersi q.c.
promising ['prəmɪsɪŋ] *agg.* promettente
to **promote** [prə'mɒʊt] *v. tr.* promuovere
promoter [prə'mɒʊtəʳ] *s.* promotore *m.*
promotion [prə'mɒʊʃ(ə)n] *s.* promozione *f.*
prompt [prəm(p)t] **A** *agg.* **1** pronto, sollecito **2** (*di pagamento*) in contanti, a pronti **B** *s.* **1** suggerimento *m.* **2** termine *m.* di pagamento **3** (*inf.*) prompt *m. inv.* **C** *avv.* in punto
to **prompt** [prəm(p)t] *v. tr.* **1** suggerire, consigliare **2** incitare
prompter ['prəm(p)təʳ] *s.* suggeritore *m.*
pronaos [prɒ(ʊ)'neɪəs] *s.* pronao *m.*
prone [prɒʊn] *agg.* **1** prono **2** disposto, incline
prong [prəŋ] *s.* **1** forca *f.* **2** rebbio *m.*
pronoun ['prɒʊnaʊn] *s.* pronome *m.*
to **pronounce** [prə'naʊns] **A** *v. tr.* **1** pronunciare **2** dichiarare **B** *v. intr.* pronunciarsi, dichiararsi
pronunciation [prəˌnʌnsɪ'eɪʃ(ə)n] *s.* pronuncia *f.*
proof [pruːf] **A** *s.* **1** prova *f.*, dimostrazione *f.* **2** (*tip.*) bozza *f.* **3** (*fot.*) provino *m.* **B** *agg.* (*nei composti*) a prova di, resistente a ♦ **bullet-p.** antiproiettile; **water-p.** impermeabile
prop [prəp] *s.* puntello *m.*, sostegno *m.*
to **prop** [prəp] *v. tr.* **1** appoggiare, puntellare **2** sostenere
propaganda [ˌprəpə'gændə] *s.* propaganda *f.*
to **propagate** ['prəpəgeɪt] *v. tr. e intr.* propagare, propagarsi
to **propel** [prə'pɛl] *v. tr.* muovere in avanti, spingere
propeller [prə'pɛləʳ] *s.* elica *f.*
proper ['prəpəʳ] *agg.* **1** proprio, particolare **2** appropriato, corretto **3** decoroso, rispettabile **4** propriamente detto, vero e proprio
properly ['prəpəlɪ] *avv.* **1** bene, opportunamente **2** convenientemente **3** propriamente
property ['prəpətɪ] *s.* **1** proprietà *f.* **2** beni *m.*, patrimonio *m.*
prophecy ['prəfɪsɪ] *s.* profezia *f.*
prophet ['prəfɪt] *s.* profeta *m.*
prophetic(al) [prə'fɛtɪk((ə)l)] *agg.* profe-

tico

prophylactic [ˌprəfɪ'læktɪk] *s.* preservativo *m.*

prophylaxis [ˌprəfɪ'læksɪs] *s.* profilassi *f.*

to propitiate [prə'pɪʃɪeɪt] *v. tr.* propiziare

propitious [prə'pɪʃəs] *agg.* propizio

proportion [prə'pɜːʃ(ə)n] *s.* proporzione *f.*

proportional [prə'pɜːʃənl] *agg.* proporzionale

proportionate [prə'pɜːʃnɪt] *agg.* proporzionato

proposal [prə'pɒʊz(ə)l] *s.* proposta *f.*

to propose [prə'pɒʊz] *v. tr. e intr.* **1** proporre, presentare **2** fare una proposta di matrimonio

proposition [ˌprəpə'zɪʃ(ə)n] *s.* **1** affermazione *f.* **2** proposizione *f.* **3** proposta *f.*

proprietor [prə'praɪətəʳ] *s.* proprietario *m.*, titolare *m. e f.*

propriety [prə'praɪətɪ] *s.* **1** convenienza *f.*, proprietà *f.*, correttezza *f.* **2** decoro *m.*, decenza *f.* **3** *al pl.* convenienze *f. pl.* sociali

propulsion [prə'pʌlʃ(ə)n] *s.* propulsione *f.*

propylaeum [ˌprəpɪ'liːəm] *s.* propileo *m.*

prose [prɒʊz] *s.* prosa *f.*

to prosecute ['prəsɪkjuːt] *v. tr.* **1** proseguire, portare avanti **2** (*dir.*) perseguire

prosecution [ˌprəsɪ'kjuːʃ(ə)n] *s.* **1** prosecuzione *f.* **2** (*dir.*) accusa *f.*, processo *m.*

prosecutor ['prəsɪkjuːtəʳ] *s.* **1** prosecutore *m.* **2** (*dir.*) accusatore *m.*, attore *m.*

prospect ['prəspɛkt] *s.* prospettiva *f.*

prospective [prəs'pɛktɪv] *agg.* **1** futuro, concernente il futuro **2** probabile, potenziale

prospectus [prəs'pɛktəs] *s.* prospetto *m.*, programma *m.*

to prosper ['prəspəʳ] *v. intr.* prosperare

prosperity [prəs'pɛrɪtɪ] *s.* prosperità *f.*

prosperous ['prəsp(ə)rəs] *agg.* prospero, favorevole

prosthesis ['prəsθɪsɪs] *s.* protesi *f.*

prostitute ['prəstɪtjuːt] *s.* prostituta *f.*

prostrate [prə'streɪt] *agg.* prostrato, abbattuto

prostyle ['prɒʊstaɪl] *s.* prostilo *m.*

protagonist [prɒ(ʊ)'tægənɪst] *s.* protagonista *m. e f.*

to protect [prə'tɛkt] *v. tr.* proteggere

protection [prə'tɛkʃ(ə)n] *s.* protezione *f.*, difesa *f.*, riparo *m.*

protectionism [prə'tɛkʃənɪz(ə)m] *s.* protezionismo *m.*

protective [prə'tɛktɪv] *agg.* protettivo

protein ['prɒʊtiːn] *s.* proteina *f.*

protest ['prɒʊtɛst] *s.* **1** protesta *f.* **2** protesto *m.*

to protest [prə'tɛst] **A** *v. tr.* **1** dichiarare **2** mandare in protesto **B** *v. intr.* **1** protestare, reclamare **2** fare una dichiarazione

Protestant ['prətɪst(ə)nt] *agg. e s.* protestante *m. e f.*

Protestantism ['prətɪst(ə)ntɪz(ə)m] *s.* protestantesimo *m.*

protester [prə'tɛstəʳ] *s.* dimostrante *m. e f.*

protocol ['prɒʊtəkəl] *s.* protocollo *m.*

protomartyr ['prɒʊtɒ(ʊ)ˌmaːtəʳ] *s.* protomartire *m.*

prototype ['prɒʊtətaɪp] *s.* prototipo *m.*

to protract [prə'trækt] *v. tr.* protrarre

to protrude [prə'truːd] *v. tr. e intr.* sporgere

protruding [prə'truːdɪŋ] *agg.* sporgente

protuberance [prə'tjuːb(ə)r(ə)ns] *s.* protuberanza *f.*

protuberant [prə'tjuːb(ə)r(ə)nt] *agg.* sporgente

proud [praʊd] *agg.* **1** orgoglioso, fiero **2** superbo

to prove [pruːv] **A** *v. tr.* **1** provare, dimostrare **2** mettere alla prova **3** verificare **B** *v. intr.* risultare, rivelarsi

provenance ['prəvɪnəns] *s.* provenienza *f.*, origine *f.*

Provençal [ˌprəvaː(n)'saːl] *agg. e s.* provenzale *m. e f.*

proverb ['prəvɜːb] *s.* proverbio *m.*

proverbial [prə'vɜːbjəl] *agg.* proverbiale

to provide [prə'vaɪd] **A** *v. tr.* provvedere, fornire, procurare **B** *v. intr.* **1** provvedere **2** premunirsi ♦ **to p. oneself with st.** fornirsi di q.c.

provided [prə'vaɪdɪd] (*spesso* **p. that**) *cong.* purché, sempre che, a condizione che

providence ['prəvɪd(ə)ns] *s.* **1** previdenza *f.* **2** provvidenza *f.*

provident ['prəvɪd(ə)nt] *agg.* previdente

providential [ˌprəvɪ'dɛnʃ(ə)l] *agg.* provvidenziale, opportuno

providing [prə'vaɪdɪŋ] *cong.* purché

province ['prəvɪns] *s.* provincia *f.*

provincial [prə'vɪnʃ(ə)l] *agg.* provinciale

provincialism [prə'vɪnʃəlɪz(ə)m] *s.* provincialismo *m.*

provision [prə'vɪʒ(ə)n] *s.* **1** provvedimento *m.*, preparativo *m.* **2** fornitura *f.* **3** *al pl.* provviste *f. pl.*, viveri *m. pl.* **4** riserva *f.* **5** (*dir.*) clausola *f.*

provisional [prə'vɪʒənl] *agg.* provvisorio
proviso [prə'vaɪzɒʊ] *s.* (*dir.*) condizione *f.*
provocation [ˌprəvə'keɪʃ(ə)n] *s.* provocazione *f.*
provocative [prə'vəkətɪv] *agg.* provocante, stimolante
to provoke [prə'vɒʊk] *v. tr.* **1** provocare **2** irritare
provoking [prə'vɒʊkɪŋ] *agg.* **1** provocante **2** irritante
prow [praʊ] *s.* prua *f.*
prowess ['praʊɪs] *s.* prodezza *f.*, abilità *f.*
to prowl [praʊl] *v. intr.* muoversi furtivamente ♦ **to p. about** vagare
prowler ['praʊlər] *s.* malintenzionato *m.*
proximity [prək'sɪmɪtɪ] *s.* prossimità *f.*, vicinanza *f.*
proxy ['prəksɪ] **A** *s.* **1** procuratore *m.* **2** procura *f.* **B** *agg.* per procura
prudence ['pruːd(ə)ns] *s.* prudenza *f.*
prudent ['pruːd(ə)nt] *agg.* prudente
prudish ['pruːdɪʃ] *s.* moralista *m. e f.*, puritano *m.*
prune [pruːn] *s.* prugna *f.* secca
to prune [pruːn] *v. tr.* potare
to pry [praɪ] *v. intr.* spiare, curiosare
psalm [saːm] *s.* salmo *m.*
pseudonym ['sjuːdənɪm] *s.* pseudonimo *m.*
psyche ['saɪkɪ] *s.* psiche *f.*
psychiatric(al) [ˌsaɪkɪ'ætrɪk((ə)l)] *agg.* psichiatrico
psychiatrist [saɪ'kaɪətrɪst] *s.* psichiatra *m. e f.*
psychic(al) ['saɪkɪk((ə)l)] *agg.* **1** psichico **2** medianico
psychoanalysis [ˌsaɪkɒ(ʊ)ə'næləsɪs] *s.* psicoanalisi *f.*
psychoanalyst [ˌsaɪkɒ(ʊ)'ænəlɪst] *s.* psicoanalista *m. e f.*
psychologic(al) [ˌsaɪkə'lədʒɪk((ə)l)] *agg.* psicologico
psychologist [saɪ'kələdʒɪst] *s.* psicologo *m.*
psychology [saɪ'kələdʒɪ] *s.* psicologia *f.*
psychopath ['saɪkɒ(ʊ)pæθ] *s.* psicopatico *m.*
psychosis [saɪ'kɒʊsɪs] *s.* psicosi *f.*
pub [pʌb] *s.* pub *m. inv.*
puberty ['pjuːbətɪ] *s.* pubertà *f.*
pubic ['pjuːbɪk] *agg.* pubico
public ['pʌblɪk] *agg. e s.* pubblico *m.* ♦ **p.-address system** impianto di amplificazione; **p. house** pub; **p. relations** relazioni pubbliche
publican ['pʌblɪkən] *s.* oste *m.*
publication [ˌpʌblɪ'keɪʃ(ə)n] *s.* pubblicazione *f.*
publicity [pʌb'lɪsɪtɪ] *s.* pubblicità *f.*
to publicize ['pʌblɪsaɪz] *v. tr.* pubblicizzare
to publish ['pʌblɪʃ] *v. tr.* pubblicare
publisher ['pʌblɪʃər] *s.* editore *m.*
publishing ['pʌblɪʃɪŋ] *s.* editoria *f.*
to pucker ['pʌkər] *v. tr.* corrugare, increspare
pudding ['pʊdɪŋ] *s.* budino *m.*
puddle ['pʌdl] *s.* pozzanghera *f.*
puff [pʌf] *s.* soffio *m.*, sbuffo *m.* ♦ **p. pastry** pasta sfoglia
to puff [pʌf] *v. intr.* soffiare, sbuffare ♦ **to p. out** gonfiare, spegnere con un soffio
puffy ['pʌfɪ] *agg.* **1** ansante **2** gonfio **3** paffuto
pull [pʊl] *s.* **1** strappo *m.*, tiro *m.* **2** boccata *f.*, sorso *m.* **3** maniglia *f.*, tirante *m.* **4** (*fig.*) influenza *f.*, ascendente *m.*
to pull [pʊl] **A** *v. tr.* **1** tirare, tendere **2** trascinare, trainare **3** estrarre, tirar fuori, cavare **4** attirare **B** *v. intr.* **1** tirare **2** lasciarsi tirare, trascinarsi ♦ **to p. about** maltrattare; **to p. apart** fare a pezzi; **to p. back** ritirarsi; **to p. down** abbassare, demolire; **to p. in** accostarsi, (*di treno*) entrare in stazione; **to p. off** togliere, togliersi, portare a segno; **to p. on** indossare; **to p. out** uscire, partire, staccare, ritirare; **to p. over** accostare; **to p. through** farcela; **to p. up** fermarsi, sradicare, strappare
pulley ['pʊlɪ] *s.* puleggia *f.*
pullover ['pʊlˌɒʊvər] *s.* pullover *m. inv.*
pulmonary ['pʌlmənərɪ] *agg.* polmonare
pulp [pʌlp] *s.* polpa *f.*
pulpit ['pʊlpɪt] *s.* pulpito *m.*
to pulsate [pʌl'seɪt] *v. intr.* pulsare
pulsation [pʌl'seɪʃ(ə)n] *s.* pulsazione *f.*
pulse (1) [pʌls] *s.* **1** (*med.*) polso *m.*, battito *m.* **2** impulso *m.*
pulse (2) [pʌls] *s.* legume *m.*
to pulverize ['pʌlvəraɪz] *v. tr. e intr.* polverizzare, polverizzarsi
to pummel ['pʌml] *v. tr.* prendere a pugni
pump [pʌmp] *s.* **1** pompa *f.* **2** distributore *m.* di benzina
to pump [pʌmp] *v. tr.* pompare ♦ **to p. up** gonfiare
pumpkin ['pʌm(p)kɪn] *s.* zucca *f.*
pun [pʌn] *s.* gioco *m.* di parole

punch (1) [pʌn(t)ʃ] *s.* pugno *m.*
punch (2) [pʌn(t)ʃ] *s.* **1** punzone *m.* **2** perforatrice *f.*
punch (3) [pʌn(t)ʃ] *s.* ponce *m. inv.*, punch *m. inv.*
to punch (1) [pʌn(t)ʃ] *v. tr.* dare un pugno a
to punch (2) [pʌn(t)ʃ] *v. tr.* punzonare, perforare
punch-up ['pʌn(t)ʃʌʊp] *s.* zuffa *f.*
punctual ['pʌŋ(k)tjʊəl] *agg.* puntuale
punctuality [ˌpʌŋ(k)tjʊ'ælɪtɪ] *s.* puntualità *f.*
to punctuate ['pʌŋ(k)tjʊeɪt] *v. tr.* punteggiare
punctuation [ˌpʌŋ(k)tjʊ'eɪʃ(ə)n] *s.* punteggiatura *f.*
puncture ['pʌŋktʃəʳ] *s.* **1** (*di pneumatico*) foratura *f.* **2** puntura *f.* ♦ **to get a p.** forare
pundit ['pʌndɪt] *s.* sapientone *m.*
pungent ['pʌndʒ(ə)nt] *agg.* pungente
to punish ['pʌnɪʃ] *v. tr.* punire, infliggere una punizione
punishment ['pʌnɪʃmənt] *s.* punizione *f.*
punk [pʌŋk] *agg. e s.* punk *m. inv.*
punt [pʌnt] *s.* barchino *m.*
punter ['pʌntəʳ] *s.* **1** scommettitore *m.* **2** (*pop.*) cliente *m. e f.*
puny ['pjuːnɪ] *agg.* gracile, sparuto
pup [pʌp] *s.* cucciolo *m.*
pupil (1) ['pjuːpl] *s.* allievo *m.*, scolaro *m.*
pupil (2) ['pjuːpl] *s.* pupilla *f.*
puppet ['pʌpɪt] *s.* burattino *m.*, fantoccio *m.*
puppeteer [ˌpʌpɪ'tɪəʳ] *s.* burattinaio *m.*
puppy ['pʌpɪ] *s.* cucciolo *m.*
purchase ['pɜːtʃəs] *s.* **1** acquisto *m.*, compera *f.* **2** (*spec. di immobili*) valore *m.* **3** paranco *m.*
to purchase ['pɜːtʃəs] *v. tr.* **1** acquistare, comprare **2** acquisire **3** sollevare (con paranco)
purchaser ['pɜːtʃəsəʳ] *s.* acquirente *m. e f.*, compratore *m.*
purchasing ['pɜːtʃəsɪŋ] *s.* acquisto *m.*
pure [pjʊəʳ] *agg.* puro
purée ['pjʊəreɪ] *s.* purè *m.*
purgative ['pɜːgətɪv] *agg. e s.* purgante *m.*
purgatory ['pɜːgət(ə)rɪ] *s.* purgatorio *m.*
purge [pɜːdʒ] *s.* **1** purga *f.*, purgante *m.* **2** epurazione *f.*
to purge [pɜːdʒ] *v. tr.* **1** purgare, purificare **2** epurare
purging ['pɜːdʒɪŋ] *s.* purga *f.*, purificazione *f.*
to purify ['pjʊərɪfaɪ] *v. tr.* purificare
purism ['pjʊərɪz(ə)m] *s.* purismo *m.*
Puritan ['pjʊərɪt(ə)n] *agg. e s.* puritano *m.*
Puritanism ['pjʊərɪt(ə)nɪz(ə)m] *s.* puritanesimo *m.*
purity ['pjʊərɪtɪ] *s.* purezza *f.*
to purloin [pɜː'lɔɪn] *v. tr.* trafugare
purple ['pɜːpl] **A** *agg.* purpureo, violaceo **B** *s.* (*colore*) porpora *m.*, viola *m.*
to purport ['pɜːpɜːt] *v. tr.* **1** significare **2** dare a intendere
purpose ['pɜːpəs] *s.* **1** scopo *m.*, fine *m.*, intenzione *f.* **2** effetto *m.*, risultato *m.* **3** proposito *m.*, fermezza *f.* ♦ **on p.** appositamente; **to no p.** invano
purposeful ['pɜːpəsf(ʊ)l] *agg.* **1** risoluto, determinato **2** intenzionale
purpura ['pɜːpjʊərə] *s.* porpora *f.*
to purr [pɜː] *v. intr.* fare le fusa
purse [pɜːs] *s.* **1** borsellino *m.* **2** borsa *f.*
purser ['pɜːsəʳ] *s.* commissario *m.* di bordo
pursuance [pə'sjuːəns] *s.* proseguimento *m.*
to pursue [pə'sjuː] *v. tr.* **1** inseguire **2** perseguire, aspirare a **3** proseguire, procedere
pursuit [pə'sjuːt] *s.* **1** inseguimento *m.*, ricerca *f.* **2** occupazione *f.* **3** passatempo *m.*
pus [pʌs] *s.* pus *m. inv.*
push [pʊʃ] *s.* **1** spinta *f.* **2** pressione *f.* **3** sforzo *m.* **4** energia *f.* ♦ **p.-button** pulsante
to push [pʊʃ] *v. tr.* **1** spingere, premere **2** fare pressione su **3** propagandare **4** (*pop.*) spacciare (droga) ♦ **to p. aside** scostare; **to p. back** respingere; **to p. forward** spingere innanzi, avanzare; **to p. in** intromettersi; **to p. off** andar via; **to p. out** buttar fuori; **to p. up** far salire
pushchair ['pʊʃtʃɛəʳ] *s.* passeggino *m.*
pusher ['pʊʃəʳ] *s.* spacciatore *m.*
pussycat ['pʊsɪkæt] *s.* micio *m.*
to put [pʊt] (*pass. e p. p.* **put**) **A** *v. tr.* **1** mettere, porre, collocare **2** apporre, applicare **3** esporre, presentare, esprimere **4** sottoporre **5** valutare, calcolare **6** piantare, conficcare **7** scommettere, puntare, investire **B** *v. intr.* (*naut.*) dirigersi, far rotta per ♦ **to p. away** mettere via, mettere da parte; **to p. back** riporre, posticipare, ritardare; **to p. by** risparmiare; **to p. down** posare, sopprimere, umiliare, annotare, attribuire; **to p. forward** proporre, sugge-

rire, anticipare; **to p. in** inserire, intromettersi, presentare domanda; **to p. off** rinviare, impedire, dissuadere; **to p. on** indossare, accendere, metter su, mettere in scena; **to p. out** metter fuori, trasmettere, pubblicare, produrre, spegnere, offendere, disturbare; **to p. through** portare a compimento, far approvare, mettere in comunicazione; **to p. up** alzare, aumentare, affiggere, costruire, ospitare; **to p. up with** sopportare

putrefaction [ˌpju:trɪ'fækʃ(ə)n] *s.* putrefazione *f.*, marciume *m.*

to putrefy ['pju:trɪfaɪ] *v. intr.* imputridire

putty ['pʌtɪ] *s.* stucco *m.*, mastice *m.*

to putty ['pʌtɪ] *v. tr.* stuccare

puzzle ['pʌzl] *s.* **1** rompicapo *m.*, enigma *m.* **2** confusione *f.* ♦ **crossword p.** parole incrociate

to puzzle ['pʌzl] **A** *v. tr.* confondere **B** *v. intr.* essere perplesso ♦ **to p. out** decifrare

puzzling ['pʌzlɪŋ] *agg.* sconcertante

pyjamas [pə'dʒa:məz] *s. pl.* pigiama *m.*

pylon ['paɪlən] *s.* pilone *m.*

pyramid ['pɪrəmɪd] *s.* piramide *f.*

pyramidal [pɪ'ræmɪdl] *agg.* piramidale

pyre ['paɪə^r] *s.* pira *f.*

pyromaniac [ˌpaɪrɒ(ʊ)'meɪnjæk] *s.* piromane *m. e f.*

pyrotechnic(al) [ˌpaɪrɒ(ʊ)'tɛknɪk((ə)l)] *agg.* pirotecnico

python ['paɪθ(ə)n] *s.* pitone *m.*

Q

quack [kwæk] *s.* ciarlatano *m.*
quadrangle ['kwəˌdræŋgl] *s.* **1** (*geom.*) quadrangolo *m.* **2** cortile *m.* quadrangolare interno
quadrangular [kwə'dræŋgjʊlər] *agg.* quadrangolare
quadrant ['kwədr(ə)nt] *s.* quadrante *m.*
quadrature ['kwədrətʃər] *s.* quadratura *f.*
quadrennial [kwə'drɛnjəl] *agg.* quadriennale
quadrilateral [ˌkwədrɪ'læt(ə)r(ə)l] *agg. e s.* quadrilatero *m.*
quadruped ['kwədrupɛd] *agg. e s.* quadrupede *m.*
quadruple ['kwədrʊpl] *agg. e s.* quadruplo *m.*
to **quadruple** ['kwədrʊpl] *v. tr. e intr.* quadruplicare, quadruplicarsi
quagmire ['kwægmaɪər] *s.* pantano *m.*
quail [kweɪl] *s.* quaglia *f.*
to **quail** [kweɪl] *v. intr.* sgomentarsi, avvilirsi
quaint [kweɪnt] *agg.* **1** pittoresco **2** bizzarro, curioso
quake [kweɪk] *s.* **1** scossa *f.*, tremito *m.* **2** (*fam.*) terremoto *m.*
to **quake** [kweɪk] *v. intr.* tremare
Quaker ['kweɪkər] *s.* quacchero *m.*
Quakeress ['kweɪkərɪs] *s.* quacchera *f.*
qualifiable ['kwəlɪfaɪəbl] *agg.* qualificabile
qualification [ˌkwəlɪfɪ'keɪʃ(ə)n] *s.* **1** qualificazione *f.* **2** requisito *m.*, qualifica *f.*, titolo *m.* **3** restrizione *f.*
qualified ['kwəlɪfaɪd] *agg.* **1** qualificato, adatto, competente **2** condizionato, limitato **3** abilitato
to **qualify** ['kwəlɪfaɪ] **A** *v. tr.* **1** qualificare, definire **2** abilitare, autorizzare **3** modificare, limitare **B** *v. intr.* qualificarsi, abilitarsi
qualitative ['kwəlɪtətɪv] *agg.* qualitativo
quality ['kwəlɪtɪ] *s.* qualità *f.*
qualm [kwɜːm] *s.* **1** rimorso *m.* **2** nausea *f.*
quandary ['kwəndərɪ] *s.* difficoltà *f.*, imbarazzo *m.*
quantic ['kwəntɪk] *agg.* quantico, quantistico
to **quantify** ['kwəntɪfaɪ] *v. tr.* quantificare
quantity ['kwəntɪtɪ] *s.* quantità *f.*, abbondanza *f.*, quantitativo *m.*
quantum ['kwəntəm] (*pl.* **quanta**) *s.* (*fis.*) quanto *m.*
quarantine ['kwər(ə)ntiːn] *s.* quarantena *f.*
quarrel ['kwər(ə)l] *s.* disputa *f.*, litigio *m.*
to **quarrel** ['kwər(ə)l] *v. intr.* bisticciare, litigare
quarrelsome ['kwər(ə)lsəm] *agg.* litigioso, rissoso
quarry (1) ['kwərɪ] *s.* **1** cava *f.* **2** (*fig.*) miniera *f.*, fonte *f.*
quarry (2) ['kwərɪ] *s.* preda *f.*
quart [kwɜːt] *s.* quarto *m.* di gallone
quarter ['kwɜːtər] *s.* **1** quarto *m.* **2** trimestre *m.* **3** (*USA*) quarto *m.* di dollaro **4** quartiere *m.*, rione *m.* **5** alloggio *m.*
to **quarter** ['kwɜːtər] *v. tr.* **1** dividere in quarti **2** squartare **3** alloggiare
quarterly ['kwɜːtəlɪ] **A** *agg.* trimestrale **B** *s.* pubblicazione *f.* trimestrale **C** *avv.* trimestralmente
quartet [kwɜː'tɛt] *s.* quartetto *m.* ♦ **string q.** quartetto d'archi
quartz [kwɜːts] *s.* quarzo *m.*
to **quash** [kwəʃ] *v. tr.* **1** (*dir.*) annullare **2** sottomettere
quatrain ['kwətreɪn] *s.* quartina *f.*
quatrefoil ['kætrəfəɪl] *s.* (*arch.*) quadrifoglio *m.*
quaver ['kweɪvər] **1** trillo *m.* **2** tremolio *m.* **3** (*mus.*) croma *f.*
quay [kiː] *s.* banchina *f.*, molo *m.*
queasy ['kwiːzɪ] *agg.* **1** nauseabondo **2** delicato di stomaco
queen [kwiːn] *s.* regina *f.*
queer [kwɪər] *agg.* **1** strano, bizzarro **2** dubbio **3** indisposto **4** (*fam.*) omosessuale
to **quell** [kwɛl] *v. tr.* **1** reprimere, domare **2** calmare
to **quench** [kwɛn(t)ʃ] *v. tr.* estinguere, spegnere ♦ **q. one's thirst** dissetarsi
querulous ['kwɛrʊləs] *agg.* querulo, lamentoso
query ['kwɪərɪ] *s.* domanda *f.*, quesito *m.*
to **query** ['kwɪərɪ] **A** *v. tr.* **1** interrogare, indagare su **2** mettere in dubbio **B** *v. intr.* fare domande

quest [kwɛst] *s.* cerca *f.*, ricerca *f.*
question ['kwɛstʃ(ə)n] *s.* **1** domanda *f.* **2** questione *f.*, problema *m.* ♦ **q. mark** punto interrogativo
to **question** ['kwɛstʃ(ə)n] *v. tr.* **1** interrogare **2** dubitare di
questionable ['kwɛstʃənəbl] *agg.* **1** dubbio, incerto **2** discutibile
questionnaire [ˌkwɛstɪə'nɛəʳ] *s.* questionario *m.*
queue [kjuː] *s.* **1** coda *f.* **2** fila *f.*
to **queue** [kjuː] *v. intr.* fare la coda ♦ **to q. up** mettersi in coda
to **quibble** ['kwɪbl] *v. intr.* cavillare
quick [kwɪk] **A** *agg.* **1** svelto, veloce **2** pronto, acuto **3** suscettibile **B** *avv.* rapidamente **C** *s.* **1** carne *f.* viva **2** punto *m.* vivo ♦ **to sting sb. to the q.** toccare qc. sul vivo
to **quicken** ['kwɪk(ə)n] *v. tr. e intr.* affrettare, affrettarsi
quickly ['kwɪklɪ] *avv.* in fretta, prontamente
quickness ['kwɪknɪs] *s.* sveltezza *f.*
quicksand ['kwɪksænd] *s.* sabbie *f. pl.* mobili
quicksilver ['kwɪkˌsɪlvəʳ] *s.* mercurio *m.*, argento *m.* vivo
quick-witted ['kwɪkˌwɪtɪd] *agg.* perspicace
quid [kwɪd] *s.* (*fam.*) sterlina *f.*
quiet ['kwaɪət] **A** *agg.* **1** quieto, tranquillo **2** modesto, semplice **3** segreto **B** *s.* quiete *f.*, tranquillità *f.* ♦ **on the q.** di nascosto
to **quiet** ['kwaɪət] *v. tr. e intr.* calmare, calmarsi
to **quieten** ['kwaɪətn] *v. tr. e intr.* calmare, calmarsi
quilt [kwɪlt] *s.* trapunta *f.*, piumino *m.*
quince [kwɪns] *s.* mela *f.* cotogna
quinine [kwɪ'niːn] *s.* chinino *m.*
quinquennal [kwɪŋ'kwɛnɪəl] *agg.* quinquennale
quintal ['kwɪntl] *s.* quintale *m.*
quintet [kwɪn'tɛt] *s.* quintetto *m.*
quintuple ['kwɪntjʊpl] *agg. e s.* quintuplo *m.*
to **quintuple** ['kwɪntjʊpl] *v. tr. e intr.* quintuplicare, quintuplicarsi
quip [kwɪp] *s.* frizzo *m.*
quirk [kwɜːk] *s.* **1** coincidenza *f.* **2** stranezza *f.*, ghiribizzo *m.*
to **quit** [kwɪt] (*pass. e p. p.* **quitted** o **quit**) **A** *v. tr.* **1** abbandonare **2** smettere, cessare **3** lasciar andare, mollare **B** *v. intr.* **1** andarsene **2** dimettersi **3** arrendersi
quite [kwaɪt] *avv.* **1** proprio, del tutto, completamente **2** abbastanza, piuttosto **3** esattamente ♦ **q. a bit, q. a lot** (*di quantità*) abbastanza; **q. a while** (*di tempo*) abbastanza; **q. right** giustissimo; **q. (so)** esatto, proprio così
quits [kwɪts] *avv.* pari, alla pari
quittance ['kwɪt(ə)ns] *s.* quietanza *f.*, ricevuta *f.*
quiver (1) ['kwɪvəʳ] *s.* faretra *f.*
quiver (2) ['kwɪvəʳ] *s.* tremito *m.*
to **quiver** ['kwɪvəʳ] *v. intr.* fremere, tremare
quiz [kwɪz] *s.* quiz *m. inv.*
quota ['kwɒʊtə] *s.* quota *f.*
quotation [kwɒ(ʊ)'teɪʃ(ə)n] *s.* **1** citazione *f.* **2** (*Borsa*) quotazione *f.* **3** preventivo *m.* ♦ **q. marks** virgolette
quote [kwɒʊt] *s.* **1** citazione *f.* **2** *al pl.* virgolette *f. pl.* **3** preventivo *m.*
to **quote** [kwɒʊt] *v. tr.* **1** citare, riportare **2** mettere fra virgolette **3** (*Borsa*) quotare
quotient ['kwɒʊʃ(ə)nt] *s.* quoziente *m.*

R

rabbi ['ræbaɪ] *s.* rabbino *m.*
rabbinic(al) [ræ'bɪnɪk((ə)l)] *agg.* rabbinico
rabbit ['ræbɪt] *s.* coniglio *m.*
rabble ['ræbl] *s.* (*spreg.*) folla *f.*, plebaglia *f.*
rabid ['ræbɪd] *agg.* **1** (*di animale*) rabbioso **2** furioso
rabies ['reɪbiːz] *s.* (*med.*) rabbia *f.*, idrofobia *f.*
raccoon [rə'kuːn] → **racoon**
race (1) [reɪs] *s.* **1** gara *f.*, corsa *f.*, competizione *f.* **2** (*di astro*) corso *m.* **3** (*geogr.*) corrente *f.*
race (2) [reɪs] *s.* **1** razza *f.* **2** categoria *f.*
to race [reɪs] **A** *v. intr.* **1** gareggiare, correre **2** andare a tutta velocità **3** (*di motore*) imballarsi **B** *v. tr.* **1** gareggiare con **2** far correre **3** far girare a vuoto
racecourse ['reɪskɜːs] *s.* ippodromo *m.*
racehorse ['reɪshɜːs] *s.* cavallo *m.* da corsa
racer ['reɪsəʳ] *s.* **1** cavallo *m.* da corsa **2** automobile *f.* (imbarcazione *f.*, aeroplano *m.* e sim.) da competizione
racetrack ['reɪstræk] *s.* (*sport*) pista *f.*
rachis ['reɪkɪs] *s.* rachide *m.*
rachitic [ræ'kɪtɪk] *agg.* rachitico
rachitis [ræ'kaɪtɪs] *s.* rachitismo *m.*
racial ['reɪʃəl] *agg.* razziale
racing ['reɪsɪŋ] **A** *agg.* da corsa **B** *s.* corsa *f.*
racism ['reɪsɪz(ə)m] *s.* razzismo *m.*
racist ['reɪsɪst] *agg. e s.* razzista *m. e f.*
rack (1) [ræk] *s.* **1** rastrelliera *f.* **2** cremagliera *f.* ♦ **luggage r.** portabagagli; **plate r.** scolapiatti; **r. rail** rotaia a cremagliera
rack (2) [ræk] *s.* (*strumento di tortura*) ruota *f.*
rack (3) [ræk] *s.* nuvolaglia *f.*
rack (4) [ræk] *s.* rovina *f.*
to rack [ræk] *v. tr.* **1** torturare **2** sforzare ♦ **to r. one's brains** scervellarsi
racket (1) ['rækɪt] *s.* **1** baccano *m.*, fracasso *m.* **2** racket *m. inv.* **3** (*fam.*) attività *f.*, occupazione *f.*
racket (2) ['rækɪt] *s.* racchetta *f.*
rackety ['rækɪtɪ] *agg.* chiassoso, rumoroso
racoon [rə'kuːn] *s.* procione *m.*
racy ['reɪsɪ] *agg.* **1** vivace, frizzante **2** salace
radar ['reɪdəʳ] *s.* radar *m. inv.*
radial ['reɪdjəl] *agg.* radiale
radiant ['reɪdjənt] *agg.* **1** raggiante **2** radiante
to radiate ['reɪdɪeɪt] **A** *v. intr.* diffondersi, irradiarsi **B** *v. tr.* emanare, irradiare
radiation [ˌreɪdɪ'eɪʃ(ə)n] *s.* radiazione *f.*
radiator ['reɪdɪeɪtəʳ] *s.* radiatore *m.*
radical ['rædɪk(ə)l] *agg. e s.* radicale *m. e f.*
radicalism ['rædɪkəlɪz(ə)m] *s.* radicalismo *m.*
radio ['reɪdɪɒʊ] **A** *agg.* radiofonico, (*nei composti*) radio- **B** *s.* radio *f.* ♦ **r. amateur** radioamatore
radioactive [ˌreɪdɪɒ(ʊ)'æktɪv] *agg.* radioattivo
radioactivity [ˌreɪdɪɒ(ʊ)æk'tɪvɪtɪ] *s.* radioattività *f.*
radiography [ˌreɪdɪ'əgrəfɪ] *s.* radiografia *f.*
radiologist [ˌreɪdɪ'ələdʒɪst] *s.* radiologo *m.*
radiology [ˌreɪdɪ'ələdʒɪ] *s.* radiologia *f.*
radiophone ['reɪdɪɒ(ʊ)fɒʊn] *s.* radiotelefono *m.*
radioscopy [ˌreɪdɪ'əskəpɪ] *s.* radioscopia *f.*
radish ['rædɪʃ] *s.* **1** ravanello *m.* **2** rafano *m.*
radium ['reɪdjəm] *s.* (*chim.*) radio *m.*
radius ['reɪdjəs] (*pl.* **radii**) *s.* **1** raggio *m.* **2** (*anat.*) radio *m.*
raffle ['ræfl] *s.* riffa *f.*, lotteria *f.*
raft [raːft] *s.* zattera *f.* ♦ **r. bridge** ponte galleggiante
rag [ræg] *s.* **1** straccio *m.*, brandello *m.* **2** frammento *m.* **3** *al pl.* abiti *m. pl.* vecchi **4** (*fam.*) giornalaccio *m.* ♦ **r. doll** bambola di stoffa
rage [reɪdʒ] *s.* **1** furia *f.*, rabbia *f.* **2** passione *f.*, mania *f.* ♦ **to be (all) the r.** furoreggiare
to rage [reɪdʒ] *v. intr.* **1** infuriarsi **2** imperversare, infierire
ragged ['rægɪd] *agg.* **1** lacero, cencioso **2** frastagliato, scabroso **3** irsuto, ispido **4** imperfetto, rozzo **5** aspro, stridente
raging ['reɪdʒɪŋ] **A** *agg.* infuriato **B** *s.* furia *f.*, furore *m.*
ragman ['rægmən] (*pl.* **ragmen**) *s.* stracci-

vendolo *m.*
raid [reɪd] *s.* incursione *f.*, irruzione *f.*
to raid [reɪd] *v. tr. e intr.* assalire, fare un'incursione
rail [reɪl] *s.* **1** sbarra *f.* **2** cancellata *f.*, inferriata *f.* **3** parapetto *m.*, ringhiera *f.*, (*naut.*) battagliola *f.* **4** rotaia *f.* ♦ **by r.** su rotaia, per ferrovia
railing ['reɪlɪŋ] *s.* **1** sbarra *f.* **2** *al pl.* cancellata *f.* **3** ringhiera *f.*, parapetto *m.*
railroad ['reɪlrɒʊd] *s.* (*USA*) ferrovia *f.*
railway ['reɪlweɪ] *s.* ferrovia *f.* ♦ **r. bridge** cavalcavia; **r. station** stazione ferroviaria; **r. track** binario
railwayman ['reɪlweɪmən] (*pl.* **railwaymen**) *s.* ferroviere *m.*
rain [reɪn] *s.* pioggia *f.* ♦ **in the r.** sotto la pioggia; **r. pipe** grondaia
to rain [reɪn] *v. intr. impers.* piovere ♦ **to r. down** riversarsi; **to r. off** sospendere per la pioggia; **to r. out** smettere di piovere
rainbow ['reɪnbɒʊ] *s.* arcobaleno *m.*
raincoat ['reɪnkɒʊt] *s.* impermeabile *m.*
rainfall ['reɪnfɜːl] *s.* **1** pioggia *f.*, precipitazione *f.* **2** piovosità *f.*, quantità *f.* di pioggia
rainless ['reɪnlɪs] *agg.* senza pioggia, secco
rainproof ['reɪnpruːf] *agg.* impermeabile
rainstorm ['reɪnstɜːm] *s.* temporale *m.*
rainwater ['reɪnwɜːtəʳ] *s.* acqua *f.* piovana
rainy ['reɪnɪ] *agg.* piovoso
raise [reɪz] *s.* aumento *m.*
to raise [reɪz] *v. tr.* **1** alzare, elevare, innalzare **2** sollevare, proporre, provocare **3** erigere **4** allevare, coltivare **5** (*denaro*) procurarsi, raccogliere **6** aumentare, far salire
raisin ['reɪzn] *s.* uva *f.* passa
raising ['reɪzɪŋ] *s.* **1** sollevamento *m.*, aumento *m.* **2** allevamento *m.* **3** educazione *f.* **4** sopralzo *m.*
rake [reɪk] *s.* rastrello *m.*
to rake [reɪk] *v. tr.* **1** rastrellare **2** raschiare, grattare **3** setacciare ♦ **to r. in** racimolare
rally ['rælɪ] *s.* **1** comizio *m.*, riunione *f.*, adunata *f.* **2** ripresa *f.*, recupero *m.* **3** (*sport*) rally *m. inv.* **4** (*nel tennis e sim.*) scambio *m.* di colpi
to rally ['rælɪ] **A** *v. tr.* **1** raccogliere, chiamare a raccolta, riunire **2** rianimare **B** *v. intr.* **1** raccogliersi, radunarsi **2** rianimarsi, riaversi ♦ **to r. round** venire in aiuto di, stringersi intorno a
ram [ræm] *s.* **1** montone *m.*, ariete *m.* **2** rostro *m.*
to ram [ræm] *v. tr.* **1** speronare **2** conficcare
ramble ['ræmbl] *s.* escursione *f.*
to ramble ['ræmbl] *v. intr.* **1** gironzolare **2** divagare
rambler ['ræmbləʳ] *s.* **1** escursionista *m. e f.* **2** rosa *f.* rampicante
rambling ['ræmblɪŋ] *agg.* **1** errante, girovago **2** incoerente, sconnesso **3** (*bot.*) rampicante **4** (*di edificio*) irregolare
ramification [ˌræmɪfɪ'keɪʃ(ə)n] *s.* diramazione *f.*
ramp [ræmp] *s.* rampa *f.*
to rampage [ræm'peɪdʒ] *v. intr.* scatenarsi
rampant ['ræmpənt] *agg.* dilagante
rampart ['ræmpaːt] *s.* bastione *m.*
ramshackle ['ræmˌʃækl] *agg.* decrepito, sgangherato
ran [ræn] *pass. di* **to run**
ranch [raːntʃ] *s.* ranch *m. inv.*
rancid ['rænsɪd] *agg.* rancido
rancour ['ræŋkəʳ] (*USA* **rancor**) *s.* rancore *m.*
random ['rændəm] *agg.* **1** casuale **2** irregolare
randy ['rændɪ] *agg.* (*fam.*) lascivo
rang [ræŋ] *pass. di* **to ring**
range [reɪn(d)ʒ] *s.* **1** (*di monti*) catena *f.*, fila *f.* **2** portata *f.*, gittata *f.* **3** raggio *m.* d'azione, gamma *f.*, campo *m.* **4** escursione *f.*, gradazione *f.*, variazione *f.*, intervallo *m.* **5** (*mus.*) estensione *f.* **6** (*di terreno*) distesa *f.* **7** cucina *f.* economica **8** poligono *m.* di tiro
to range [reɪn(d)ʒ] **A** *v. tr.* **1** disporre, allineare, schierare **2** classificare **3** percorrere, vagare per **B** *v. intr.* **1** oscillare, variare **2** estendersi **3** avere una portata di
ranger ['reɪn(d)ʒəʳ] *s.* **1** guardia *f.* forestale **2** poliziotto *m.* a cavallo
rank (1) [ræŋk] *s.* **1** fila *f.*, schiera *f.* **2** rango *m.*, grado *m.* **3** posteggio *m.* di taxi
rank (2) [ræŋk] *agg.* **1** rigoglioso, lussureggiante **2** rozzo **3** puzzolente, rancido **4** vero e proprio, bell'e buono
to rankle ['ræŋkl] *v. intr.* bruciare, far soffrire
to ransack ['rænsæk] *v. tr.* **1** frugare **2** saccheggiare, svaligiare
ransom ['rænsəm] *s.* riscatto *m.* ♦ **to hold sb. to r.** tenere in ostaggio qc. per ottenere il riscatto
to ransom ['rænsəm] *v. tr.* riscattare
to rant [rænt] *v. intr.* declamare
ranunculus [rə'nʌŋkjʊləs] *s.* ranunco-

lo *m.*
rap [ræp] *s.* **1** colpo *m.*, colpetto *m.* **2** rimprovero *m.*
to rap [ræp] *v. tr. e intr.* picchiare, bussare
rapacious [rə'peɪʃəs] *agg.* rapace
rape (1) [reɪp] *s.* **1** stupro *m.* **2** (*letter*) ratto *m.*
rape (2) [reɪp] *s.* **1** ravizzone *m.* **2** colza *f.*
to rape [reɪp] *v. tr.* stuprare, violentare
rapid ['ræpɪd] **A** *agg.* rapido **B** *s. al pl.* rapide *f. pl.*
rapidity [rə'pɪdɪtɪ] *s.* rapidità *f.*
rapist ['reɪpɪst] *s.* stupratore *m.*
rapture ['ræptʃər] *s.* rapimento *m.*, estasi *f.*
rare (1) [rɛər] *agg.* **1** raro, singolare **2** rarefatto
rare (2) [rɛər] *agg.* poco cotto, al sangue
rarely [rɛəlɪ] *avv.* **1** raramente **2** ottimamente
rareness ['rɛənɪs] *s.* rarità *f.*
rarity ['rɛərɪtɪ] *s.* rarità *f.*
rascal ['rɑːsk(ə)l] *s.* mascalzone *m.*
rash (1) [ræʃ] *agg.* imprudente, precipitoso
rash (2) [ræʃ] *s.* (*med.*) eruzione *f.*, esantema *m.*
rasher ['ræʃər] *s.* fetta *f.* di lardo (o prosciutto)
rashness ['ræʃnɪs] *s.* imprudenza *f.*
rasp [rɑːsp] *s.* raspa *f.*
to rasp [rɑːsp] *v. tr. e intr.* raspare
raspberry ['rɑːzb(ə)rɪ] *s.* lampone *m.*
rasping ['rɑːspɪŋ] *agg.* stridente
rat [ræt] *s.* ratto *m.*, topo *m.* ♦ **r. poison** topicida; **r. trap** trappola per topi
ratable ['reɪtəbl] *agg.* imponibile
rate [reɪt] *s.* **1** ammontare *m.*, indice *m.*, percentuale *f.* **2** velocità *f.*, ritmo *m.*, passo *m.* **3** tariffa *f.*, prezzo *m.* **4** (*fin.*) saggio *m.*, tasso *m.* **5** tassa *f.*, contributo *m.* ♦ **exchange r.** tasso di cambio
to rate [reɪt] *v. tr.* **1** valutare, stimare **2** giudicare, considerare **3** annoverare **4** tassare
rather ['rɑːðər] *avv.* **1** abbastanza, piuttosto **2** di preferenza, piuttosto che **3** (*fam.*) certamente, eccome ♦ **or r.** ovvero, o meglio
ratification [ˌrætɪfɪ'keɪʃ(ə)n] *s.* ratifica *f.*
to ratify ['rætɪfaɪ] *v. tr.* ratificare
rating ['reɪtɪŋ] *s.* **1** valutazione *f.*, qualifica *f.* **2** categoria *f.*, (*naut.*) rating *m. inv.* **3** (*fin.*) rating *m. inv.*
ratio ['reɪʃɪʊʊ] *s.* proporzione *f.*, rapporto *m.*
ration ['ræʃ(ə)n] *s.* razione *f.*
rational ['ræʃənl] *agg.* razionale
rationale [ræʃə'nɑːl] *s.* ragione *f.* fondamentale
rationalism ['ræʃnəlɪz(ə)m] *s.* razionalismo *m.*
rationalistic [ˌræʃnə'lɪstɪk] *agg.* razionalistico
to rationalize ['ræʃnəlaɪz] *v. tr.* razionalizzare
rattle ['rætl] *s.* **1** sonaglio *m.* **2** rumore *m.* secco **3** frastuono *m.* **4** chiacchiericcio *m.*
to rattle ['rætl] *v. intr.* sbatacchiare, tintinnare, picchiettare
rattlesnake ['rætlsneɪk] *s.* serpente *m.* a sonagli
raucous ['rɜːkəs] *agg.* rauco, cupo
ravage ['rævɪdʒ] *s.* **1** rovina *f.* **2** *al pl.* danni *m. pl.*
to ravage ['rævɪdʒ] *v. tr.* devastare
to rave [reɪv] *v. intr.* **1** delirare **2** andare in estasi **3** (*di mare*) infuriare
raven ['reɪvn] *s.* corvo *m.*
ravenous ['rævɪnəs] *agg.* famelico, ingordo
ravine [rə'viːn] *s.* burrone *m.*
raving ['reɪvɪŋ] **A** *agg.* **1** delirante, furioso **2** eccezionale **B** *s.* delirio *m.*
ravishing ['rævɪʃɪŋ] *agg.* affascinante, incantevole
raw [rɜː] *agg.* **1** crudo **2** greggio **3** inesperto **4** aperto, vivo **5** (*di clima*) freddo ♦ **r. deal** trattamento ingiusto; **r. materials** materie prime
ray [reɪ] *s.* raggio *m.*
to raze [reɪz] *v. tr.* radere al suolo, abbattere
razor ['reɪzər] *s.* rasoio *m.* ♦ **r. blade** lametta
re [riː] *prep.* in relazione a
reach [riːtʃ] *s.* **1** distanza *f.*, portata *f.* **2** possibilità *f.*, campo *m.* d'azione **3** tratto *m.* di fiume, braccio *m.* di mare
to reach [riːtʃ] **A** *v. tr.* **1** giungere a, raggiungere **2** allungare, porgere **3** stendere **4** toccare **B** *v. intr.* **1** estendersi, allungarsi **2** stendere il braccio, allungare la mano
to react [rɪ(ː)'ækt] *v. intr.* reagire
reaction [rɪ(ː)'ækʃ(ə)n] *s.* reazione *f.*
reactivity [ˌriːæk'tɪvɪtɪ] *s.* reattività *f.*
reactor [riː'æktər] *s.* reattore *m.*
to read [riːd] (*pass. e p. p.* **read**) *v. tr.* **1** leggere **2** (*di strumento*) segnare **3** interpretare, capire ♦ **to r. out** leggere a voce alta; **to r. through** leggere da cima a fondo; **to r. sb. a lesson** fare la predica

a qc.
readable ['riːdəbl] *agg.* leggibile
reader ['riːdəʳ] *s.* **1** lettore *m.* **2** libro *m.* di lettura
reading ['riːdɪŋ] *s.* **1** lettura *f.* **2** indicazione *f.* **3** interpretazione *f.*
to readjust [ˌriːə'dʒʌst] *v. tr.* riaggiustare
ready ['rɛdɪ] *agg.* **1** pronto, preparato **2** disposto **3** svelto ♦ **to get r.** prepararsi; **to make r.** preparare
ready-made [ˌrɛdɪ'meɪd] *agg.* confezionato, preconfezionato
to reaffirm [ˌriːə'fɜːm] *v. tr.* riaffermare
reagent [riː'eɪdʒənt] *s.* reagente *m.*
real [rɪəl] *agg.* **1** reale, effettivo **2** (*dir.*) immobile, immobiliare ♦ **r. estate** beni immobili
realism ['rɪəlɪz(ə)m] *s.* realismo *m.*
realist ['rɪəlɪst] *s.* realista *m. e f.*
realistic [rɪə'lɪstɪk] *agg.* realistico
reality [riː'ælɪtɪ] *s.* realtà *f.*
realization [ˌrɪəlaɪ'zeɪʃ(ə)n] *s.* **1** comprensione *f.*, percezione *f.* **2** realizzazione *f.* **3** (*econ.*) realizzo *m.*
to realize ['rɪəlaɪz] *v. tr.* **1** capire, accorgersi **2** realizzare, effettuare
really ['rɪəlɪ] *avv.* davvero, effettivamente, veramente, proprio
realm [rɛlm] *s.* (*letter.*) regno *m.*
realtor ['riːəltɜːʳ] *s.* (*USA*) agente *m. e f.* immobiliare
ream [riːm] *s.* risma *f.* (di carta)
to reap [riːp] *v. tr.* **1** mietere **2** raccogliere
to reappear [ˌriːə'pɪəʳ] *v. intr.* riapparire
reappointment [ˌriːə'pɔɪntmənt] *s.* **1** reintegrazione *f.* **2** rielezione *f.*
rear [rɪəʳ] **A** *agg.* posteriore **B** *s.* **1** parte *f.* posteriore, retro *m.* **2** retroguardia *f.* **3** (*fam.*) sedere *m.*
to rear ['rɪəʳ] **A** *v. tr.* **1** alzare, sollevare **2** crescere, allevare, coltivare **B** *v. intr.* innalzarsi ♦ **to r. up** impennarsi
to rearrange [ˌriːə'reɪn(d)ʒ] *v. tr.* riordinare
rearrangement [riːə'reɪn(d)ʒmənt] *s.* riordinamento *m.*
reason ['riːz(ə)n] *s.* **1** ragione *f.*, motivo *m.* **2** ragione *f.*, intelletto *m.*, raziocinio *m.*
to reason ['riːzn] **A** *v. intr.* ragionare **B** *v. tr.* **1** valutare, calcolare **2** convincere
reasonable ['riːznəbl] *agg.* ragionevole
reasoning ['riːznɪŋ] *s.* ragionamento *m.*
to reassure [ˌriːə'ʃʊəʳ] *v. tr.* rassicurare
rebate ['riːbeɪt] *s.* **1** rimborso *m.* **2** riduzione *f.*
to rebate [rɪ'beɪt] *v. tr.* **1** rimborsare **2** ridurre, ribassare
rebel ['rɛbl] *s.* ribelle *m.*
to rebel [rɪ'bɛl] *v. intr.* ribellarsi
rebellion [rɪ'bɛljən] *s.* ribellione *f.*
rebellious [rɪ'bɛljəs] *agg.* ribelle
rebound ['riːbaʊnd] *s.* rimbalzo *m.*
to rebound ['rɪbaʊnd] *v. intr.* rimbalzare, ripercuotersi
rebuff [rɪ'bʌf] *s.* rifiuto *m.*
to rebuild [ˌriː'bɪld] *v. tr.* ricostruire
rebuke [rɪ'bjuːk] *s.* rimprovero *m.*
to rebuke [rɪ'bjuːk] *v. tr.* rimproverare, sgridare
rebus ['riːbəs] *s.* rebus *m. inv.*
to rebut [rɪ'bʌt] *v. tr.* rifiutare
recall [rɪ'kɜːl] *s.* **1** richiamo *m.* **2** ricordo *m.*
to recall [rɪ'kɜːl] *v. tr.* **1** richiamare **2** rievocare, richiamare alla mente **3** ricordarsi **4** (*dir.*) revocare
to recant [rɪ'kænt] *v. tr.* **1** ritrattare **2** abiurare
to recapitulate [ˌriːkə'pɪtjʊleɪt] *v. tr. e intr.* ricapitolare
recapitulation [ˌriːkəˌpɪtjʊ'leɪʃ(ə)n] *s.* ricapitolazione *f.*, riepilogo *m.*
to recede [rɪ'siːd] *v. intr.* **1** ritirarsi, allontanarsi **2** calare, svanire
receipt [rɪ'siːt] *s.* **1** ricevimento *m.* **2** ricevuta *f.*, quietanza *f.* **3** *al pl.* entrate *f. pl.*
to receive [rɪ'siːv] *v. tr.* ricevere, accogliere
receiver [rɪ'siːvəʳ] *s.* **1** destinatario *m.* **2** (*del telefono*) ricevitore *m.* **3** apparecchio *m.* ricevente **4** ricettatore *m.* **5** (*dir.*) curatore *m.* fallimentare
recent ['riːsnt] *agg.* recente
reception [rɪ'sɛpʃ(ə)n] *s.* **1** ricevimento *m.* **2** ricezione *f.* **3** accoglienza *f.* **4** accettazione *f.*, reception *f. inv.*
receptive [rɪ'sɛptɪv] *agg.* ricettivo
recess [rɪ'sɛs] *s.* **1** intervallo *m.*, vacanza *f.* **2** rientranza *f.*, nicchia *f.* **3** recesso *m.*
recession [rɪ'sɛʃ(ə)n] *s.* **1** (*econ.*) recessione *f.* **2** ritiro *m.*, arretramento *m.*
recharge [riː'tʃaːdʒ] *s.* ricarica *f.*
to recharge [riː'tʃaːdʒ] *v. tr.* ricaricare
recidivism [rɪ'sɪdɪvɪz(ə)m] *s.* recidiva *f.*
recipe ['rɛsɪpɪ] *s.* ricetta *f.*
recipient [rɪ'sɪpɪənt] *s.* ricevente *m. e f.*, destinatario *m.*
reciprocal [rɪ'sɪprək(ə)l] *agg.* reciproco
recital [rɪ'saɪtl] *s.* recital *m. inv.*
recitation [ˌrɛsɪ'teɪʃ(ə)n] *s.* recitazione *f.*

to **recite** [rɪ'saɪt] *v. tr.* **1** recitare, declamare **2** enumerare
reckless ['rɛklɪs] *agg.* spericolato
to **reckon** ['rɛk(ə)n] *v. tr.* **1** calcolare, computare **2** considerare, stimare **3** (*fam.*) credere, supporre ♦ **to r. on** fare conto su; **to r. up** fare il totale di; **to r. with/without** fare i conti con/senza
reckoning ['rɛkənɪŋ] *s.* conto *m.*, calcolo *m.*
to **reclaim** [rɪ'kleɪm] *v. tr.* **1** reclamare, rivendicare **2** redimere, riabilitare **3** bonificare **4** ricuperare
reclamation [ˌrɛklə'meɪʃ(ə)n] *s.* **1** rivendicazione *f.* **2** ricupero *m.*, ritiro *m.* **3** bonifica *f.*
to **recline** [rɪ'klaɪn] **A** *v. tr.* reclinare **B** *v. intr.* appoggiarsi, adagiarsi
recognition [ˌrɛkəg'nɪʃ(ə)n] *s.* riconoscimento *m.*
recognizable ['rɛkəgnaɪzəbl] *agg.* riconoscibile
to **recognize** ['rɛkəgnaɪz] *v. tr.* **1** riconoscere, distinguere **2** ammettere **3** approvare, accogliere
recoil [rɪ'kɔɪl] *s.* **1** balzo *m.* indietro **2** (*mecc.*) contraccolpo *m.*, rinculo *m.*
to **recoil** [rɪ'kɔɪl] *v. intr.* **1** indietreggiare, retrocedere **2** rinculare
to **recollect (1)** [ˌriːkə'lɛkt] *v. tr.* raccogliere, radunare, rimettere insieme
to **recollect (2)** [ˌrɛkə'lɛkt] *v. tr. e intr.* ricordare, ricordarsi
recollection [ˌrɛkə'lɛkʃ(ə)n] *s.* ricordo *m.*
to **recommence** [ˌriːkə'mɛns] *v. tr. e intr.* ricominciare
to **recommend** [ˌrɛkə'mɛnd] *v. tr.* raccomandare, consigliare
recommendation [ˌrɛkəmɛn'deɪʃ(ə)n] *s.* raccomandazione *f.*
recompense ['rɛkəmpɛns] *s.* ricompensa *f.*, compenso *m.*
to **recompense** ['rɛkəmpɛns] *v. tr.* ricompensare
to **reconcile** ['rɛkənˌsaɪl] *v. tr.* riconciliare, conciliare ♦ **to r. oneself** rassegnarsi
reconciliation [ˌrɛkənsɪlɪ'eɪʃ(ə)n] *s.* **1** riconciliazione *f.* **2** conciliazione *f.*, composizione *f.*
to **recondition** [ˌriːkən'dɪʃ(ə)n] *v. tr.* ripristinare, revisionare
reconnaissance [rɪ'kɒnɪs(ə)ns] *s.* perlustrazione *f.*, ricognizione *f.*
to **reconnoitre** [ˌrɛkə'nɔɪtə^r^] *v. tr.* perlustrare
to **reconsider** [ˌriːkən'sɪdə^r^] *v. tr.* riconsiderare, riesaminare
to **reconstruct** [ˌrɪkəns'trʌkt] *v. tr.* ricostruire
record ['rɛkɜːd] *s.* **1** documento *m.*, registrazione *f.*, nota *f.*, verbale *m.*, testimonianza *f.* **2** *al pl.* atto *m.* pubblico, archivio *m.* **3** (*inf.*) record *m. inv.* **4** (*sport*) record *m. inv.*, primato *m.* **5** disco *m.* (fonografico) ♦ **r. holder** detentore di primato; **r. library** discoteca; **r. player** giradischi
to **record** [rɪ'kɜːd] *v. tr.* **1** registrare, prender nota di, verbalizzare **2** documentare, testimoniare **3** incidere, registrare
recorded [rɪ'kɜːdɪd] *agg.* registrato ♦ **r. delivery** raccomandata con ricevuta di ritorno
recorder [rɪ'kɜːdə^r^] *s.* registratore *m.*
recording [rɪ'kɜːdɪŋ] *s.* registrazione *f.*, incisione *f.*
to **recount (1)** [rɪ'kaʊnt] *v. tr.* raccontare dettagliatamente
to **recount (2)** [riː'kaʊnt] *v. tr.* contare di nuovo
to **recoup** [rɪ'kuːp] *v. tr.* **1** rimborsare, risarcire **2** ricuperare
recourse [rɪ'kɜːs] *s.* ricorso *m.*
to **recover** [riː'kʌvə^r^] **A** *v. tr.* riacquistare, ricuperare, ritrovare **B** *v. intr.* ristabilirsi, riprendersi, guarire
recovery [rɪ'kʌvərɪ] *s.* **1** ricupero *m.* **2** guarigione *f.*
recreation [ˌrɛkrɪ'eɪʃən] *s.* ricreazione *f.*, divertimento *m.*
recreational [ˌrɛkrɪ'eɪʃənl] *agg.* ricreativo
recreative ['rɛkrɪɛtɪv] *agg.* ricreativo
recrimination [rɛˌkrɪmɪ'neɪʃ(ə)n] *s.* recriminazione *f.*
recruit [rɪ'kruːt] *s.* **1** (*mil.*) recluta *f.* **2** principiante *m. e f.*, novellino *m.*
to **recruit** [rɪ'kruːt] *v. tr.* **1** (*mil.*) reclutare **2** assumere
rectangle ['rɛkˌtæŋgl] *s.* rettangolo *m.*
rectangular [rɛk'tæŋgjʊlə^r^] *agg.* rettangolare
rectification [ˌrɛktɪfɪ'keɪʃ(ə)n] *s.* rettifica *f.*
to **rectify** ['rɛktɪfaɪ] *v. tr.* rettificare
rectilinear [ˌrɛktɪ'lɪnɪə^r^] *agg.* rettilineo
rector ['rɛktə^r^] *s.* rettore *m.*
rectorate ['rɛktərət] *s.* rettorato *m.*
rectory ['rɛkt(ə)rɪ] *s.* canonica *f.*, presbiterio *m.*

to recuperate [rɪ'kjuːp(ə)reɪt] **A** *v. tr.* ricuperare, riguadagnare **B** *v. intr.* **1** ristabilirsi, riprendersi **2** rifarsi
to recur [rɪ'kɜːʳ] *v. intr.* **1** ritornare, ricorrere **2** riandare col pensiero, ritornare in mente
recurrence [rɪ'kʌr(ə)ns] *s.* ricorso *m.*, riapparizione *f.*, ricorrenza *f.*
recurrent [rɪ'kʌr(ə)nt] *agg.* ricorrente
to recuse [rɪ'kjuːz] *v. tr.* ricusare
to recycle [riː'saɪkl] *v. tr.* riciclare
red [rɛd] *agg. e s.* rosso *m.* ♦ **to be in the r.** essere in rosso
redcurrant [ˌrɛd'kʌrənt] *s.* ribes *m.* rosso
to redden ['rɛdn] **A** *v. intr.* arrossire **B** *v. tr.* **1** arrossare **2** far arrossire
reddish ['rɛdɪʃ] *agg.* rossiccio
to redeem [rɪ'diːm] *v. tr.* **1** riscattare **2** redimere, salvare **3** compensare
redeemer [rɪ'diːməʳ] *s.* redentore *m.*
redemption [rɪ'dɛm(p)ʃ(ə)n] *s.* **1** redenzione *f.* **2** (*fin.*) riscatto *m.*, rimborso *m.*
to redeploy [ˌriːdɪ'plɔɪ] *v. tr.* reimpiegare, riorganizzare
red-haired [ˌrɛd'hɛəd] *agg.* dai capelli rossi
red-handed [ˌrɛd'hændɪd] *agg.* con le mani nel sacco, in flagrante
redhead ['rɛdhɛd] *s.* persona *f.* dai capelli rossi
red-hot [ˌrɛd'hɔt] *agg.* **1** rovente **2** appassionato
to rediscover [ˌriːdɪs'kʌvəʳ] *v. tr.* riscoprire, ritrovare
to redo [riː'duː] (*pass.* **redid**, *p. p.* **redone**) *v. tr.* rifare
redolent ['rɛdɒʊlənt] *agg.* **1** fragrante **2** suggestivo
to redouble [rɪ'dʌbl] *v. tr. e intr.* raddoppiare
redress [rɪ'drɛs] *s.* riparazione *f.*, risarcimento *m.*
redskin ['rɛdˌskɪn] *s.* pellerossa *m. e f.*
red tape [ˌrɛd'teɪp] *s.* burocrazia *f.*
to reduce [rɪ'djuːs] *v. tr.* ridurre
reduction [rɪ'dʌkʃ(ə)n] *s.* riduzione *f.*
redundancy [rɪ'dʌndənsɪ] *s.* **1** sovrabbondanza *f.*, eccedenza *f.* **2** licenziamento *m.* (*per esuberanza di personale*) **3** ridondanza *f.*
redundant [rɪ'dʌndənt] *agg.* **1** eccedente, esuberante **2** ridondante ♦ **to be made r.** essere licenziato (*per esuberanza di personale*)
redwood ['rɛdwʊd] *s.* sequoia *f.*
reed [riːd] *s.* **1** canna *f.* **2** (*mus.*) ancia *f.* ♦ **r.-pipe** zampogna
reef (1) [riːf] *s.* scogliera *f.*, banco *m.* ♦ **barrier r.** barriera corallina
reef (2) [riːf] *s.* (*naut.*) terzarolo *m.*
to reek [riːk] *v. intr.* puzzare
reel [riːl] *s.* **1** rocchetto *m.*, bobina *f.* **2** (*pesca*) mulinello *m.* **3** (*cine.*) pizza *f.*
to reel (1) [riːl] *v. tr.* avvolgere, arrotolare ♦ **to r. in** tirare su (*col mulinello*); **to r. off** dipanare
to reel (2) [riːl] *v. intr.* **1** barcollare, vacillare **2** avere il capogiro **3** girare, turbinare
to re-elect [ˌriːɪ'lɛkt] *v. tr.* rieleggere
re-election [ˌriːɪ'lɛkʃ(ə)n] *s.* rielezione *f.*
to re-enter [riː'ɛntəʳ] *v. intr.* rientrare
ref [rɛf] *s.* (*fam.*) arbitro *m.*
refection [rɪ'fɛkʃ(ə)n] *s.* refezione *f.*
refectory [rɪ'fɛkt(ə)rɪ] *s.* refettorio *m.*
to refer [rɪ'fɜːʳ] **A** *v. tr.* **1** indirizzare, rinviare **2** inoltrare **B** *v. intr.* **1** riferirsi, riguardare, fare riferimento **2** ricorrere
referee [ˌrɛfə'riː] *s.* **1** arbitro *m.* **2** garante *m.*, referenza *f.*
to referee [ˌrɛfə'riː] *v. tr.* arbitrare
reference ['rɛfr(ə)ns] *s.* **1** riferimento *m.*, rapporto *m.*, relazione *f.* **2** allusione *f.*, accenno *m.* **3** consultazione *f.* **4** referenza *f.*, raccomandazione *f.*
referendum [ˌrɛfə'rɛndəm] *s.* referendum *m. inv.*
refill ['riːfɪl] *s.* **1** ricambio *m.*, ricarica *f.* **2** (*a tavola*) secondo giro *m.*
to refill [riː'fɪl] *v. tr.* riempire di nuovo, ricaricare
to refine [rɪ'faɪn] *v. tr.* raffinare
refined [rɪ'faɪnd] *agg.* raffinato
refinement [rɪ'faɪnmənt] *s.* **1** raffinazione *f.* **2** raffinatezza *f.*
refinery [rɪ'faɪnərɪ] *s.* raffineria *f.*
to reflect [rɪ'flɛkt] **A** *v. tr.* riflettere, rispecchiare **B** *v. intr.* **1** riflettersi **2** riflettere, meditare
reflection [rɪ'flɛkʃ(ə)n] *s.* **1** riflessione *f.*, riflesso *m.* **2** ripercussione *f.* **3** meditazione *f.*, considerazione *f.* **4** critica *f.*
reflex ['riːflɛks] *agg. e s.* riflesso *m.* ♦ **r. camera** macchina fotografica reflex
reflexive [rɪ'flɛksɪv] *agg.* riflessivo
reforestation [ˌriːfɔrɪs'teɪʃ(ə)n] *s.* rimboschimento *m.*
reform [rɪ'fɜːm] *s.* riforma *f.*
to reform [rɪ'fɜːm] *v. tr.* riformare
Reformation [ˌrɛfə'meɪʃ(ə)n] *s.* (*stor*) riforma *f.*

reformatory [rɪ'fɜːmət(ə)rɪ] *s.* riformatorio *m.*
refraction [rɪ'frækʃ(ə)n] *s.* rifrazione *f.*
refrain [rɪ'freɪn] *s.* ritornello *m.*
to refrain [rɪ'freɪn] *v. intr.* trattenersi, astenersi
to refresh [rɪ'frɛʃ] **A** *v. tr.* **1** rinfrescare, ristorare, rianimare **2** ricaricare, rifornire **B** *v. intr.* rinfrescarsi, ristorarsi, rianimarsi
refreshing [rɪ'frɛʃɪŋ] *agg.* rinfrescante, ristoratore
refreshment [rɪ'frɛʃmənt] *s.* **1** ristoro *m.* **2** rinfresco *m.*
to refrigerate [rɪ'frɪdʒəreɪt] *v. tr.* refrigerare
refrigerator [rɪ'frɪdʒəreɪtə[r]] *s.* **1** refrigerante *m.* **2** frigorifero *m.*
to refuel [riː'fjʊəl] **A** *v. tr.* rifornire (*carburante*) **B** *v. intr.* fare rifornimento
refuge ['rɛfjuːdʒ] *s.* rifugio *m.* ♦ **to take r.** rifugiarsi
refugee [ˌrɛfjuː'dʒiː] *s.* rifugiato *m.*, profugo *m.*
refund ['riːfʌnd] *s.* rimborso *m.*
to refund [riː'fʌnd] *v. tr.* rimborsare
to refurbish [ˌriː'fɜːbɪʃ] *v. tr.* rinnovare
refusal [rɪ'fjuːz(ə)l] *s.* **1** rifiuto *m.* **2** (*dir*) diritto *m.* di opzione
refuse [rɪ'fjuːs] **A** *agg.* di scarto **B** *s.* rifiuti *m. pl.*, immondizia *f.*
to refuse [rɪ'fjuːz] *v. tr. e intr.* rifiutare, rifiutarsi
to refute [rɪ'fjuːt] *v. tr.* confutare
to regain [rɪ'geɪn] *v. tr.* riguadagnare
regal ['riːg(ə)l] *agg.* regale, regio
regard [rɪ'gaːd] *s.* **1** riguardo *m.*, considerazione *f.* **2** stima *f.*, ammirazione *f.* **3** *al pl.* (*nelle formule di cortesia*) saluti *m. pl.* ♦ **in r. to** in merito a
to regard [rɪ'gaːd] *v. tr.* **1** considerare, giudicare **2** stimare **3** riguardare, concernere ♦ **as regards**, **regarding** per quanto riguarda
regardless [rɪ'gaːdlɪs] *agg.* incurante ♦ **r. of** a dispetto di
regatta [rɪ'gætə] *s.* regata *f.*
regency ['riːdʒ(ə)nsɪ] *s.* reggenza *f.*
to regenerate [rɪ'dʒɛnəreɪt] *v. tr. e intr.* rigenerare, rigenerarsi
regent ['riːdʒ(ə)nt] *s.* reggente *m. e f.*
regime [reɪ'ʒiːm] *s.* regime *m.*
regiment ['rɛdʒɪmənt] *s.* reggimento *m.*
region ['riːdʒ(ə)n] *s.* regione *f.*
regional ['riːdʒənl] *agg.* regionale
register ['rɛdʒɪstə[r]] *s.* **1** registro *m.* **2** lista *f.* elettorale
to register ['rɛdʒɪstə[r]] **A** *v. tr.* **1** registrare, iscrivere, immatricolare **2** (*corrispondenza*) raccomandare **3** (*di strumento*) segnare **B** *v. intr.* iscriversi, registrarsi
registered ['rɛdʒɪstəd] *agg.* registrato, immatricolato ♦ **r. letter** raccomandata; **r. trademark** marchio registrato
registration [ˌrɛdʒɪs'treɪʃ(ə)n] *s.* registrazione *f.*, iscrizione *f.* ♦ **r. number** numero di targa
registry ['rɛdʒɪstrɪ] *s.* **1** registrazione *f.* **2** ufficio *m.* di registrazione ♦ **r. office** anagrafe
regnant ['rɛgnənt] *agg.* regnante
regress ['riːgrɛs] *s.* regresso *m.*
regression [rɪ'grɛʃ(ə)n] *s.* regressione *f.*
regret [rɪ'grɛt] *s.* rimpianto *m.*, rincrescimento *m.*
to regret [rɪ'grɛt] *v. tr.* **1** rammaricarsi di **2** rimpiangere
regretfully [rɪ'grɛtf(ʊ)lɪ] *avv.* con rincrescimento, purtroppo
regrettable [rɪ'grɛtəbl] *agg.* spiacevole, deplorevole
regular ['rɛgjʊlə[r]] **A** *agg.* regolare **B** *s.* **1** soldato *m.* regolare **2** cliente *m. e f.* abituale
regularly ['rɛgjʊləlɪ] *avv.* regolarmente
to regulate ['rɛgjʊleɪt] *v. tr.* regolare
regulation [ˌrɛgjʊ'leɪʃ(ə)n] *s.* **1** regolazione *f.* **2** ordinamento *m.*, regolamento *m.*
to rehabilitate [ˌriːə'bɪlɪteɪt] *v. tr.* riabilitare
rehabilitation [ˌriːəˌbɪlɪ'teɪʃ(ə)n] *s.* riabilitazione *f.*
rehearsal [rɪ'hɜːs(ə)l] *s.* (*teatro*) prova *f.*
to rehearse [rɪ'hɜːs] *v. tr.* (*teatro*) provare, fare le prove di
reign [reɪn] *s.* regno *m.*
to reign [reɪn] *v. intr.* regnare
to reimburse [ˌriːɪm'bɜːs] *v. tr.* rimborsare
reimbursement [ˌriːɪm'bɜːsmənt] *s.* rimborso *m.*, risarcimento *m.*
rein [reɪn] *s.* briglia *f.*
reincarnation [ˌriːɪnkaː'neɪʃ(ə)n] *s.* reincarnazione *f.*
reindeer ['reɪndɪə[r]] *s.* renna *f.*
to reinforce [ˌriːɪn'fɔːs] *v. tr.* rinforzare
reinforcement [ˌriːɪn'fɔːsmənt] *s.* **1** rinforzo *m.*, rafforzamento *m.* **2** *al pl.* (*mil.*) rinforzi *m. pl.*
to reinstate [ˌriːɪn'steɪt] *v. tr.* ristabilire, reintegrare

to reiterate [riː'ɪtəreɪt] *v. tr.* reiterare
reject ['riːdʒɛkt] *s.* scarto *m.*
to reject [rɪ'dʒɛkt] *v. tr.* **1** rifiutare, respingere **2** scartare **3** (*med.*) rigettare
rejection [rɪ'dʒɛkʃ(ə)n] *s.* **1** scarto *m.*, rifiuto *m.* **2** (*med.*) rigetto *m.*
to rejoice [rɪ'dʒɔɪs] *v. intr.* rallegrarsi
to rejoin [riː'dʒɔɪn] *v. tr. e intr.* ricongiungere, ricongiungersi
to rejuvenate [rɪ'dʒuːvɪneɪt] *v. tr. e intr.* ringiovanire
relapse [rɪ'læps] *s.* ricaduta *f.*
to relapse [rɪ'læps] *v. intr.* **1** ricadere **2** (*med.*) avere una ricaduta
to relate [rɪ'leɪt] **A** *v. tr.* **1** riferire, raccontare **2** collegare, mettere in relazione **B** *v. intr.* **1** riferirsi a, concernere **2** andare d'accordo
related [rɪ'leɪtɪd] *agg.* **1** imparentato **2** connesso
relation [rɪ'leɪʃ(ə)n] *s.* **1** racconto *m.*, relazione *f.* **2** rapporto *m.* **3** parente *m. e f.*
relationship [rɪ'leɪʃ(ə)nʃɪp] *s.* **1** relazione *f.*, rapporto *m.* **2** parentela *f.*
relative ['rɛlətɪv] **A** *agg.* relativo **B** *s.* parente *m. e f.*
relativism ['rɛlətɪvɪz(ə)m] *s.* relativismo *m.*
relativity [ˌrɛlə'tɪvɪtɪ] *s.* relatività *f.*
to relax [rɪ'læks] **A** *v. tr.* **1** rilassare, distendere **2** allentare, mitigare **B** *v. intr.* **1** rilassarsi, riposarsi **2** attenuarsi
relaxation [ˌriːlæk'seɪʃ(ə)n] *s.* **1** rilassamento *m.* **2** riposo *m.*, svago *m.*, relax *m. inv.* **3** mitigazione *f.*
relay ['riːleɪ] *s.* **1** (corsa a) staffetta *f.* **2** (squadra di) turno *m.* **3** (*elettr.*) relè *m.*
to relay [rɪ'leɪ] *v. tr.* **1** fornire **2** trasmettere **3** riferire
release [rɪ'liːs] *s.* **1** rilascio *m.*, scarcerazione *f.* **2** quietanza *f.*, remissione *f.* **3** (*di film, disco*) distribuzione *f.* **4** (*inf.*) versione *f.* **5** (*mecc.*) rilascio *m.*, scatto *m.* **6** emissione *f.*
to release [rɪ'liːs] *v. tr.* **1** liberare, scarcerare **2** distribuire, diffondere **3** sganciare, sbloccare **4** emettere, scaricare ♦ **to r. on bail** rilasciare su cauzione
to relegate ['rɛlɪgeɪt] *v. tr.* relegare
to relent [rɪ'lɛnt] *v. intr.* placarsi, addolcirsi
relentless [rɪ'lɛntlɪs] *agg.* implacabile
relevant ['rɛlɪvənt] *agg.* relativo, pertinente, specifico
reliability [rɪˌlaɪə'bɪlɪtɪ] *s.* affidabilità *f.*
reliable [rɪ'laɪəbl] *agg.* affidabile, fidato
reliance [rɪ'laɪəns] *s.* fiducia *f.*
reliant [rɪ'laɪənt] *agg.* fiducioso
relic ['rɛlɪk] *s.* reliquia *f.*, resto *m.*
relief (1) [rɪ'liːf] *s.* **1** sollievo *m.* **2** aiuto *m.*, soccorso *m.* **3** cambio *m.*, sostituto *m.*
relief (2) [rɪ'liːf] *s.* rilievo *m.*
to relieve [rɪ'liːv] *v. tr.* **1** alleviare **2** soccorrere **3** alleggerire **4** dare il cambio, sostituire
reliever [rɪ'liːvəʳ] *s.* soccorritore *m.* ♦ **pain r.** farmaco antidolorifico
religion [rɪ'lɪdʒ(ə)n] *s.* religione *f.*
religious [rɪ'lɪdʒəs] *agg.* religioso
to relinquish [rɪ'lɪŋkwɪʃ] *v. tr.* abbandonare, rinunciare a
reliquary ['rɛlɪkwərɪ] *s.* reliquiario *m.*
relish ['rɛlɪʃ] *s.* **1** gusto *m.*, attrattiva *f.* **2** condimento *m.*, salsa *f.*
to relish ['rɛlɪʃ] *v. tr.* gustare, assaporare
to reload [ˌriː'lɒʊd] *v. tr.* ricaricare
to relocate [ˌriːləʊ'keɪt] *v. tr. e intr.* trasferire, trasferirsi
reluctance [rɪ'lʌktəns] *s.* riluttanza *f.*
reluctant [rɪ'lʌktənt] *agg.* riluttante, restio
to rely [rɪ'laɪ] *v. intr.* **1** fare affidamento, fidarsi **2** dipendere
to remain [rɪ'meɪn] *v. intr.* rimanere
remainder [rɪ'meɪndəʳ] *s.* **1** resto *m.*, residuo *m.* **2** persone *f. pl.* rimanenti **3** rimanenza *f.*
remains [rɪ'meɪnz] *s. pl.* rovine *f. pl.*, resti *m. pl.*
remake ['riːmeɪk] *s.* remake *m. inv.*
to remake [riː'meɪk] (*pass. e p. p.* **remade**) *v. tr.* rifare
remark [rɪ'maːk] *s.* osservazione *f.*, commento *m.*, nota *f.*
to remark [rɪ'maːk] *s.* osservare, rimarcare
remarkable [rɪ'maːkəbl] *agg.* notevole
to remarry [riː'mærɪ] *v. tr. e intr.* risposare, risposarsi
remedial [rɪ'miːdjəl] *agg.* **1** riparatore **2** (*med.*) correttivo
remedy ['rɛmɪdɪ] *s.* rimedio *m.*
to remedy ['rɛmɪdɪ] *v. intr.* rimediare
to remember [rɪ'mɛmbəʳ] *v. tr. e intr.* ricordare, ricordarsi
remembrance [rɪ'mɛmbr(ə)ns] *s.* ricordo *m.*, memoria *f.*
to remind [rɪ'maɪnd] *v. tr.* ricordare a, far ricordare
reminder [rɪ'maɪndəʳ] *s.* promemoria *m. inv.*

to reminisce [ˌrɛmɪ'nɪs] *v. intr.* abbandonarsi ai ricordi
reminiscence [ˌrɛmɪ'nɪsns] *s.* reminiscenza *f.*
reminiscent [ˌrɛmɪ'nɪsnt] *agg.* **1** che richiama alla mente **2** che si abbandona ai ricordi
remiss [rɪ'mɪs] *agg.* negligente
remission [rɪ'mɪʃ(ə)n] *s.* **1** remissione *f.* **2** diminuzione *f.*
to remit [rɪ'mɪt] *v. tr.* **1** rimettere, condonare **2** affidare **3** diminuire, ridurre **4** (*denaro*) rimettere, inviare **5** sospendere, differire, annullare
remittance [rɪ'mɪt(ə)ns] *s.* rimessa *f.*
remnant ['rɛmnənt] *s.* **1** avanzo *m.*, resto *m.* **2** scampolo *m.*
to remonstrate ['rɛmənstreɪt] *v. intr.* protestare, fare rimostranze
remorse [rɪ'mɜːs] *s.* rimorso *m.*
remorseless [rɪ'mɜːslɪs] *agg.* spietato, inesorabile
remote [rɪ'mɒʊt] *agg.* **1** remoto, lontano **2** estraneo, distaccato **3** comandato a distanza ♦ **r. control** telecomando
removable [rɪ'muːvəbl] *agg.* rimovibile
removal [rɪ'muːvəl] *s.* **1** rimozione *f.*, allontanamento *m.* **2** soppressione *f.*, destituzione *f.* **3** asportazione *f.* **4** trasferimento *m.*, trasloco *m.*
to remove [rɪ'muːv] *v. tr.* **1** rimuovere, togliere, spostare **2** destituire **3** sopprimere, eliminare **4** trasferire
to remunerate [rɪ'mjuːnəreɪt] *v. tr.* rimunerare
remuneration [rɪˌmjuːnə'reɪʃ(ə)n] *s.* rimunerazione *f.*
Renaissance [rə'neɪs(ə)ns] *s.* rinascimento *m.*
to rend [rɛnd] (*pass. e p. p.* **rent**) *v. tr.* spaccare, strappare
to render ['rɛndəʳ] *v. tr.* rendere
rendering ['rɛnd(ə)rɪŋ] *s.* **1** traduzione *f.* **2** interpretazione *f.*, esecuzione *f.*
renegade ['rɛnɪgeɪd] *s.* rinnegato *m.*
to renew [rɪ'njuː] *v. tr.* rinnovare, ripristinare
renewal [rɪ'njuːəl] *s.* **1** rinnovo *m.* **2** ripresa *f.*
rennet ['rɛnɪt] *s.* caglio *m.*
to renounce [rɪ'naʊns] *v. tr.* **1** rinunciare a **2** rinnegare
to renovate ['rɛnəveɪt] *v. tr.* rinnovare, ristrutturare
renovation [ˌrɛnə'veɪʃ(ə)n] *s.* rinnovamento *m.*, ristrutturazione *f.*
renown [rɪ'naʊn] *s.* rinomanza *f.*, fama *f.*
renowned [rɪ'naʊnd] *agg.* rinomato
rent (1) [rɛnt] *s.* affitto *m.*, nolo *m.*
rent (2) [rɛnt] **A** *pass. e p. p. di* **to rend** **B** *agg.* strappato **C** *s.* strappo *m.*
to rent [rɛnt] *v. tr.* affittare
rentable ['rɛntəbl] *agg.* affittabile
rental ['rɛntl] *s.* canone *m.* (di affitto), (prezzo del) noleggio *m.*
renunciation [rɪˌnʌnsɪ'eɪʃ(ə)n] *s.* rinuncia *f.*
to rep [rɛp] *v. intr.* (*fam.*) fare il rappresentante
to repaint [riː'peɪnt] *v. tr.* ridipingere, riverniciare
repair [rɪ'pɛəʳ] *s.* **1** riparazione *f.* **2** condizione *f.*, stato *m.*
to repair [rɪ'pɛəʳ] *v. tr.* riparare, aggiustare
repairable [rɪ'pɛərəbl] *agg.* riparabile
to repatriate [riː'pætrɪeɪt] *v. intr.* rimpatriare
repatriation [riːˌpætrɪ'eɪʃ(ə)n] *s.* rimpatrio *m.*
to repay [rɪ'peɪ] (*pass. e p. p.* **repaid**) *v. tr.* ripagare, restituire, risarcire
repayable [riː'pɛ(ɪ)əbl] *agg.* rimborsabile
repayment [rɪ'peɪmənt] *s.* rimborso *m.*, ricompensa *f.*
repeal [rɪ'piːl] *s.* abrogazione *f.*, revoca *f.*
to repeal [rɪ'piːl] *v. tr.* abrogare, revocare
repeat [rɪ'piːt] *s.* **1** ripetizione *f.* **2** replica *f.*
to repeat [rɪ'piːt] *v. tr.* ripetere
to repel [rɪ'pɛl] *v. tr.* **1** respingere **2** ripugnare a
repellent [rɪ'pɛlənt] **A** *agg.* repellente, ripugnante **B** *s.* sostanza *f.* repellente
to repent [rɪ'pɛnt] *v. tr. e intr.* pentirsi
repentance [rɪ'pɛntəns] *s.* pentimento *m.*
repertory ['rɛpət(ə)rɪ] *s.* repertorio *m.*
repetition [ˌrɛpɪ'tɪʃ(ə)n] *s.* ripetizione *f.*
repetitive [rɪ'pɛtɪtɪv] *agg.* ripetitivo
to replace [rɪ'pleɪs] *v. tr.* **1** rimpiazzare, sostituire **2** riporre
replaceable [rɪ'pleɪsəbl] *agg.* sostituibile
replacement [rɪ'pleɪsmənt] *s.* **1** sostituzione *f.*, rimpiazzo *m.* **2** sostituto *m.* **3** (pezzo di) ricambio *m.*
replay ['riːpleɪ] *s.* **1** (*sport*) partita *f.* ripetuta **2** (*TV*) replay *m. inv.*
to replenish [rɪ'plɛnɪʃ] *v. tr.* riempire, rifornire

replete [rɪ'pliːt] *agg.* **1** pieno, zeppo **2** satollo
replica ['rɛplɪkə] *s.* **1** (*di opera d'arte*) copia *f.*, riproduzione *f.* **2** duplicato *m.*
reply [rɪ'plaɪ] *s.* **1** risposta *f.* **2** (*dir*) replica *f.*
to reply [rɪ'plaɪ] *v. tr.* rispondere, replicare
to repopulate [ˌriː'pɔpjʊleɪt] *v. tr.* ripopolare
report [rɪ'pɜːt] *s.* **1** diceria *f.* **2** rapporto *m.*, relazione *f.*, resoconto *m.*, cronaca *f.* **3** reputazione *f.* **4** pagella *f.* **5** rimbombo *m.*, detonazione *f.*
to report [rɪ'pɜːt] **A** *v. tr.* riportare, riferire **B** *v. intr.* **1** fare rapporto **2** fare il cronista
reportedly [rɪ'pɜːtɪdlɪ] *avv.* a quel che si dice
reporter [rɪ'pɜːtəʳ] *s.* cronista *m. e f.*
reprehensible [ˌrɛprɪ'hɛnsəbl] *agg.* riprovevole
to represent [ˌrɛprɪ'zɛnt] *v. tr.* rappresentare
representation [ˌrɛprɪzɛn'teɪʃ(ə)n] *s.* **1** rappresentazione *f.* **2** rappresentanza *f.* **3** rimostranza *f.*
representative [ˌrɛprɪ'zɛntətɪv] **A** *agg.* rappresentativo **B** *s.* **1** esempio *m.* tipico **2** rappresentante *m. e f.*
to repress [rɪ'prɛs] *v. tr.* reprimere
repression [rɪ'prɛʃ(ə)n] *s.* repressione *f.*
reprieve [rɪ'priːv] *s.* **1** dilazione *f.* **2** sospensione *f.* (di condanna a morte)
reprimand ['rɛprɪmaːnd] *s.* rimprovero *m.*
to reprimand ['rɛprɪmaːnd] *v. tr.* rimproverare
reprint ['riːˌprɪnt] *s.* ristampa *f.*
to reprint [riː'prɪnt] *v. tr.* ristampare
reprisal [rɪ'praɪz(ə)l] *s.* rappresaglia *f.*
reproach [rɪ'prɒʊtʃ] *s.* **1** rimprovero *m.* **2** disonore *m.*, discredito *m.*
to reproach [rɪ'prɒʊtʃ] *v. tr.* rimproverare, rinfacciare
to reproduce [ˌriːprə'djuːs] *v. tr. e intr.* riprodurre, riprodursi
reproducible [ˌriːprə'djuːsəbl] *agg.* riproducibile
reproduction [ˌriːprə'dʌkʃ(ə)n] *s.* **1** riproduzione *f.*, generazione *f.* **2** copia *f.*
reproof [rɪ'pruːf] *s.* rimprovero *m.*, biasimo *m.*
to reprove [rɪ'pruːv] *v. tr.* rimproverare, biasimare
reptant ['rɛptənt] *agg.* **1** strisciante **2** rampicante
reptile ['rɛptaɪl] *s.* rettile *m.*
republic [rɪ'pʌblɪk] *s.* repubblica *f.*
republican [rɪ'pʌblɪkən] *agg.* repubblicano
to repudiate [rɪ'pjuːdɪeɪt] *v. tr.* **1** respingere, negare **2** rifiutare **3** ripudiare
repulse [rɪ'pʌls] *s.* **1** ripulsa *f.*, rifiuto *m.* **2** sconfitta *f.*, scacco *m.*
to repulse [rɪ'pʌls] *v. tr.* respingere
repulsive [rɪ'pʌlsɪv] *agg.* ripulsivo
reputable ['rɛpjʊtəbl] *agg.* rispettabile
reputation [ˌrɛpjuː'teɪʃ(ə)n] *s.* reputazione *f.*, fama *f.*
repute [rɪ'pjuːt] *s.* reputazione *f.*
to repute [rɪ'pjuːt] *v. tr.* reputare
request [rɪ'kwɛst] *s.* domanda *f.*, richiesta *f.* ♦ **r. stop** fermata a richiesta
to request [rɪ'kwɛst] *v. tr.* richiedere
to require [rɪ'kwaɪəʳ] *v. tr.* **1** richiedere, esigere **2** ordinare **3** aver bisogno di
required [rɪ'kwaɪəd] *agg.* richiesto, obbligatorio, occorrente
requirement [rɪ'kwaɪəmənt] *s.* **1** richiesta *f.*, esigenza *f.*, necessità *f.* **2** requisito *m.* **3** fabbisogno *m.*
requisite ['rɛkwɪzɪt] **A** *agg.* richiesto **B** *s.* requisito *m.*
requisition [ˌrɛkwɪ'zɪʃ(ə)n] *s.* **1** (*mil.*) requisizione *f.* **2** istanza *f.*
to requisition [ˌrɛkwɪ'zɪʃ(ə)n] *v. tr.* **1** (*mil.*) requisire **2** fare richiesta di
resale ['riːseɪl] *s.* rivendita *f.*
to rescind [rɪ'sɪnd] *v. tr.* rescindere
rescue ['rɛskjuː] *s.* salvataggio *m.*, soccorso *m.*
to rescue ['rɛskjuː] *v. tr.* salvare, liberare
rescuer ['rɛskjʊəʳ] *s.* soccorritore *m.*
research [rɪ'sɜːtʃ] *s.* ricerca *f.*, indagine *f.*
to research [rɪ'sɜːtʃ] *v. intr.* fare ricerche
researcher [rɪ'sɜːtʃəʳ] *s.* ricercatore *m.*
resemblance [rɪ'zɛmbləns] *s.* somiglianza *f.*
to resemble [rɪ'zɛmbl] *v. tr.* somigliare a
to resent [rɪ'zɛnt] *v. tr.* risentirsi di
resentful [rɪ'zɛntf(ʊ)l] *agg.* risentito, offeso
resentment [rɪ'zɛntmənt] *s.* risentimento *m.*
reservation [ˌrɛzə'veɪʃ(ə)n] *s.* **1** riserva *f.*, restrizione *f.* **2** prenotazione *f.* **3** scorta *f.*, provvista *f.*
reserve [rɪ'zɜːv] *s.* **1** riserva *f.* **2** riserbo *m.*
to reserve [rɪ'zɜːv] *v. tr.* **1** conservare, ri-

servare **2** prenotare **3** riservarsi
reserved [rɪ'zɜːvd] *agg.* riservato, prenotato
reservoir ['rɛzəvwaːʳ] *s.* **1** cisterna *f.*, serbatoio *m.* **2** giacimento *m.* petrolifero **3** (*fig.*) riserva *f.*
to **reset** [riː'sɛt] (*pass. e p. p.* **reset**) **1** rimettere a posto, risistemare **2** regolare **3** (*inf.*) eseguire un reset
to **reshuffle** [riː'ʃʌfl] *v. tr.* **1** rimescolare le carte **2** rimaneggiare, rimpastare
to **reside** [rɪ'zaɪd] *v. intr.* risiedere
residence ['rɛzɪd(ə)ns] *s.* **1** residenza *f.*, soggiorno *m.* **2** dimora *f.*
resident ['rɛzɪd(ə)nt] **A** *agg.* **1** residente, locale **2** interno **B** *s.* residente *m. e f.*
residential [ˌrɛzɪ'dɛnʃ(ə)l] *agg.* residenziale
residue ['rɛzɪdjuː] *s.* residuo *m.*
to **resign** [rɪ'zaɪn] **A** *v. tr.* **1** dimettersi da, abbandonare **2** consegnare, affidare **B** *v. intr.* dimettersi ♦ **to r. oneself** rassegnarsi
resignation [ˌrɛzɪg'neɪʃ(ə)n] *s.* **1** dimissioni *f. pl.* **2** rassegnazione *f.*
resigned [rɪ'zaɪnd] *agg.* rassegnato
resilience [rɪ'zɪlɪəns] *s.* **1** elasticità *f.* **2** capacità *f.* di ricupero
resilient [rɪ'zɪlɪənt] *agg.* **1** elastico, rimbalzante **2** che ha capacità di ricupero
resin ['rɛzɪn] *s.* resina *f.*
to **resist** [rɪ'zɪst] *v. intr.* resistere a, opporsi a
resistance [rɪ'zɪst(ə)ns] *s.* resistenza *f.*
to **resole** [riː'sɒʊl] *v. tr.* risuolare
resolution [ˌrɛzə'luːʃ(ə)n] *s.* **1** risolutezza *f.* **2** risoluzione *f.* **3** scomposizione *f.*
to **resolve** [rɪ'zəlv] *v. tr.* **1** risolvere **2** scomporre
resonance ['rɛzənəns] *s.* risonanza *f.*
resonant ['rɛzənənt] *agg.* risonante, sonoro
resort [rɪ'zɜːt] *s.* **1** luogo *m.* di soggiorno, stazione *f.* climatica **2** ricorso *m.* **3** risorsa *f.*
to **resort** [rɪ'zɜːt] *v. intr.* ricorrere
to **resound** [rɪ'zaʊnd] *v. intr.* risonare, echeggiare
resounding [rɪ'zaʊndɪŋ] *agg.* **1** risonante **2** clamoroso, strepitoso
resource [rɪ'sɜːs] *s.* risorsa *f.*
resourceful [rɪ'sɜːsf(ʊ)l] *agg.* pieno di risorse
respect [rɪ'spɛkt] *s.* rispetto *m.* ♦ **in r. of** riguardo a; **with r. to** in riferimento a
to **respect** [rɪ'spɛkt] *v. tr.* rispettare
respectability [rɪˌspɛktə'bɪlɪtɪ] *s.* rispettabilità *f.*
respectable [rɪ'spɛktəbl] *agg.* rispettabile
respectful [rɪ'spɛktf(ʊ)l] *agg.* rispettoso
respective [rɪ'spɛktɪv] *agg.* rispettivo
respiration [ˌrɛspə'reɪʃ(ə)n] *s.* respirazione *f.*
respite ['rɛspaɪt] *s.* pausa *f.*, tregua *f.*, respiro *m.*
resplendent [rɪ'splɛndənt] *agg.* risplendente
to **respond** [rɪ'spənd] *v. intr.* rispondere
response [rɪ'spəns] *s.* responso *m.*
responsibility [rɪˌspənsə'bɪlɪtɪ] *s.* responsabilità *f.*
responsible [rɪ'spənsəbl] *agg.* **1** responsabile **2** di responsabilità
responsive [rɪ'spənsɪv] *agg.* **1** di risposta **2** che reagisce
rest (1) [rɛst] *s.* **1** riposo *m.* **2** sosta *f.*, pausa *f.* **3** sostegno *m.*, appoggio *m.* **4** ricovero *m.*, alloggio *m.* ♦ **r. home** casa di riposo
rest (2) [rɛst] *s.* resto *m.*
to **rest (1)** [rɛst] **A** *v. tr.* **1** far riposare **2** appoggiare **B** *v. intr.* **1** riposarsi **2** appoggiarsi
to **rest (2)** [rɛst] *v. intr.* restare, rimanere, stare ♦ **to r. with** spettare a
to **restart** [riː'staːt] **A** *v. tr.* **1** ricominciare **2** rimettere in moto **B** *v. intr.* **1** ricominciare **2** ripartire
restaurant ['rɛst(ə)rəŋt] *s.* ristorante *m.*
restful ['rɛstf(ʊ)l] *agg.* riposante
restitution [ˌrɛstɪ'tjuːʃ(ə)n] *s.* restituzione *f.*
restive ['rɛstɪv] *agg.* **1** recalcitrante, restio **2** irrequieto
restless ['rɛstlɪs] *agg.* **1** irrequieto **2** incessante
to **restock** [riː'stək] *v. tr.* rifornire
restoration [ˌrɛstə'reɪʃ(ə)n] *s.* **1** restituzione *f.* **2** restauro *m.* **3** (*stor.*) restaurazione *f.*
to **restore** [rɪ'stɜːʳ] *v. tr.* **1** restituire **2** restaurare, ripristinare **3** reintegrare **4** ristorare
restorer [rɪ'stɜːrəʳ] *s.* restauratore *m.*
to **restrain** [rɪ'streɪn] *v. tr.* **1** contenere, reprimere, trattenere **2** imprigionare
restrained [rɪ'streɪnd] *agg.* riservato, controllato
restraint [rɪ'streɪnt] *s.* **1** limitazione *f.*, restrizione *f.* **2** riserbo *m.*, controllo *m.* **3**

detenzione *f.*
to **restrict** [rɪ'strɪkt] *v. tr.* restringere, limitare
restriction [rɪ'strɪkʃ(ə)n] *s.* restrizione *f.*, limitazione *f.*
restrictive [rɪ'strɪktɪv] *agg.* restrittivo
rest room ['rɛstrʊm] *s.* (*USA*) toilette *f. inv.*
to **restructure** [ˌriː'strʌktʃəʳ] *v. tr.* ristrutturare
result [rɪ'zʌlt] *s.* risultato *m.*
to **result** [rɪ'zʌlt] *v. intr.* **1** risultare, derivare **2** risolversi
to **resume** [rɪ'zjuːm] *v. tr.* riprendere, ricominciare
résumé ['rɛzjuːmeɪ] *s.* **1** riassunto *m.* **2** (*USA*) curriculum *m.*
resumption [rɪ'zʌm(p)ʃ(ə)n] *s.* ripresa *f.*
resurgence [rɪ'sɜːdʒ(ə)ns] *s.* rinascita *f.*
resurrection [ˌrɛzə'rɛkʃ(ə)n] *s.* resurrezione *f.*
to **resuscitate** [rɪ'sʌsɪteɪt] *v. tr. e intr.* (*med.*) rianimare, rianimarsi
resuscitation [rɪˌsʌsɪ'teɪʃ(ə)n] *s.* (*med.*) rianimazione *f.*
retail ['riːteɪl] **A** *s.* (vendita al) dettaglio *m.* **B** *agg.* al dettaglio
retailer [riː'teɪləʳ] *s.* dettagliante *m.*, rivenditore *m.*
to **retain** [rɪ'teɪn] *v. tr.* **1** trattenere, ritenere **2** conservare
to **retaliate** [rɪ'tælɪeɪt] *v. intr.* rivalersi, far rappresaglie
retaliation [rɪˌtælɪ'eɪʃ(ə)n] *s.* rappresaglia *f.*
to **retard** [rɪ'taːd] *v. tr. e intr.* ritardare
retardation [ˌriːtaː'deɪʃ(ə)n] *s.* ritardo *m.*
to **retch** [riːtʃ] *v. intr.* avere conati di vomito
reticence ['rɛtɪs(ə)ns] *s.* reticenza *f.*
retina ['rɛtɪnə] *s.* (*anat.*) retina *f.*
to **retire** [rɪ'taɪəʳ] *v. intr.* **1** ritirarsi **2** andare in pensione
retired [rɪ'taɪəd] *agg.* a riposo, pensionato
retirement [rɪ'taɪəmənt] *s.* **1** pensionamento *m.* **2** isolamento *m.*
retiring [rɪ'taɪərɪŋ] *agg.* **1** riservato **2** uscente, che si ritira
to **retort** [rɪ'tɜːt] *v. tr.* **1** ritorcere **2** ribattere
to **retrace** [rɪ'treɪs] *v. tr.* **1** rintracciare **2** ripercorrere ♦ **to r. one's steps** ritornare sui propri passi
to **retract** [rɪ'trækt] *v. tr.* **1** ritirare, tirare indietro **2** ritrattare
retractive [rɪ'træktɪv] *agg.* retrattile
to **retrain** [riː'treɪn] *v. tr.* riqualificare
retreat [rɪ'triːt] *s.* ritirata *f.*
to **retreat** [rɪ'triːt] *v. intr.* **1** ritirarsi **2** battere in ritirata
retribution [ˌrɛtrɪ'bjuːʃ(ə)n] *s.* **1** castigo *m.* **2** ricompensa *f.*
retrieval [rɪ'triːvl] *s.* **1** ricupero *m.*, ripristino *m.* **2** riparazione *f.*
to **retrieve** [rɪ'triːv] *v. tr.* **1** ricuperare **2** riparare, rimediare a **3** salvare **4** (*di cane da caccia*) riportare
retriever [rɪ'triːvəʳ] *s.* cane *m.* da riporto
retrograde ['rɛtrɒ(ʊ)greɪd] *agg.* retrogrado
retrospect ['rɛtrɒ(ʊ)spɛkt] *s.* esame *m.* retrospettivo
retrospective [ˌrɛtrɒ(ʊ)'spɛktɪv] **A** *agg.* **1** retrospettivo **2** retroattivo **B** *s.* retrospettiva *f.*
return [rɪ'tɜːn] *s.* **1** ritorno *m.* **2** resa *f.* **3** profitto *m.* **4** rapporto *m.*, rendiconto *m.* **5** (*di elezione*) risultato *m.* **6** (*sport*) rimando *m.*, risposta *f.* ♦ **by r. (of mail)** a giro di posta; **in r. for** in cambio di; **r. match** rivincita; **r. ticket** biglietto di andata e ritorno
to **return** [rɪ'tɜːn] **A** *v. intr.* **1** ritornare **2** replicare, ribattere **B** *v. tr.* **1** restituire, ridare **2** rimettere **3** ricambiare, contraccambiare **4** rendere, produrre **5** eleggere **6** (*sport*) rinviare
reunion [riː'juːnjən] *s.* riunione *f.*
to **reunite** [ˌriːjuː'naɪt] *v. tr.* riunire
rev [rɛv] *s. acrt. di* **revolution** (*fam.*) giro *m.* (*di motore*) ♦ **r. counter** contagiri
revaluation [riːˌvæljʊ'eɪʃ(ə)n] *s.* rivalutazione *f.*
to **revalue** [riː'væljʊ] *v. tr.* rivalutare
to **revamp** [riː'væmp] *v. tr.* rimodernare
to **reveal** [rɪ'viːl] *v. tr.* rivelare
to **revel** ['rɛvl] *v. intr.* divertirsi, far festa
revelation [ˌrɛvɪ'leɪʃ(ə)n] *s.* rivelazione *f.*
revelry ['rɛvlrɪ] *s.* baldoria *f.*
revenge [rɪ'vɛn(d)ʒ] *s.* **1** vendetta *f.* **2** rivincita *f.* ♦ **to give sb. his r.** dare la rivincita a qc.
to **revenge** [rɪ'vɛn(d)ʒ] *v. tr. e intr.* vendicare, vendicarsi
revenue ['rɛvɪnjuː] *s.* **1** reddito *m.* **2** fisco *m.*
to **reverberate** [rɪ'vɜːb(ə)reɪt] *v. tr. e intr.* **1** riverberare, riverberarsi **2** riecheggiare
reverberation [rɪˌvɜːbə'reɪʃ(ə)n] *s.* riverbero *m.*

to revere [rɪ'vɪəʳ] *v. tr.* venerare
reverence ['rɛv(ə)r(ə)ns] *s.* riverenza *f.*
reverend ['rɛv(ə)r(ə)nd] *agg.* reverendo
reversal [rɪ'vɜːs(ə)l] *s.* inversione *f.*, rovesciamento *m.*
reverse [rɪ'vɜːs] **A** *agg.* rovescio, inverso **B** *s.* **1** rovescio *m.*, inverso *m.* **2** (*di fortuna*) rovescio *m.* **3** (*autom.*) retromarcia *f.* ♦ **on the r.** a marcia indietro
to reverse [rɪ'vɜːs] **A** *v. tr.* **1** rovesciare, invertire **2** far andare in senso contrario **3** (*dir.*) revocare **B** *v. intr.* **1** funzionare in senso contrario **2** (*autom.*) fare retromarcia
reversibility [rɪˌvɜːsə'bɪlɪtɪ] *s.* reversibilità *f.*
reversible [rɪ'vɜːsəbl] *agg.* reversibile
to revert [rɪ'vɜːt] *v. intr.* ritornare
review [rɪ'vjuː] *s.* **1** rivista *f.*, parata *f.* **2** revisione *f.*, esame *m.*, analisi *f.* **3** rivista *f.*, periodico *m.* **4** recensione *f.*
to review [rɪ'vjuː] *v. tr.* **1** passare in rassegna **2** rivedere, riesaminare **3** recensire
reviewer [rɪ'vjʊəʳ] *s.* recensore *m.*
to revile [rɪ'vaɪl] *v. tr.* ingiuriare
revisal [rɪ'vaɪz(ə)l] *s.* revisione *f.*
to revise [rɪ'vaɪz] *v. tr.* **1** rivedere, correggere **2** modificare **3** (*la lezione*) ripassare
reviser [rɪ'vaɪzəʳ] *s.* revisore *m.*
revision [rɪ'vɪʒ(ə)n] *s.* revisione *f.*
revisionist [rɪ'vɪʒ(ə)nɪst] *s.* revisionista *m. e f.*
to revisit [riː'vɪzɪt] *v. tr.* rivisitare
to revitalize [riː'vaɪtəlaɪz] *v. tr.* rivitalizzare
revival [rɪ'vaɪv(ə)l] *s.* **1** revival *m. inv.*, ripresa *f.* **2** rinascita *f.*
to revive [rɪ'vaɪv] **A** *v. tr.* **1** rianimare, ravvivare **2** far rivivere **3** rimettere in uso **B** *v. intr.* **1** rianimarsi, riprendersi **2** rivivere, tornare in vita
revocation [ˌrɛvə'keɪʃ(ə)n] *s.* revoca *f.*
to revoke [rɪ'vɒʊk] *v. tr.* revocare
revolt [rɪ'vɒʊlt] *s.* rivolta *f.*, sommossa *f.*
to revolt [rɪ'vɒʊlt] **A** *v. intr.* **1** rivoltarsi, ribellarsi **2** provare disgusto **B** *v. tr.* disgustare
revolution [ˌrɛvə'luːʃ(ə)n] *s.* **1** rivoluzione *f.* **2** giro *m.*, rotazione *f.*
revolutionary [ˌrɛvə'luːʃnərɪ] *agg.* rivoluzionario
to revolve [rɪ'vəlv] *v. intr.* ruotare
revolver [rɪ'vəlvəʳ] *s.* rivoltella *f.*
revolving [rɪ'vəlvɪŋ] *agg.* girevole
revue [rɪ'vjuː] *s.* (*teatro*) rivista *f.*
reward [rɪ'wɜːd] *s.* **1** ricompensa *f.*, premio *m.* **2** taglia *f.*
to reward [rɪ'wɜːd] *v. tr.* ricompensare, premiare
rewarding [rɪ'wɜːdɪŋ] *agg.* gratificante
to rewind [riː'waɪnd] (*pass. e p. p.* **rewound**) *v. tr.* **1** (*un orologio*) ricaricare **2** (*una cassetta*) riavvolgere
to reword [riː'wɜːd] *v. tr.* esprimere con altre parole
to rewrite [riː'raɪt] *v. tr.* riscrivere
rhapsodist ['ræpsədɪst] *s.* rapsodo *m.*
rhapsody ['ræpsədy] *s.* rapsodia *f.*
rhetoric ['rɛtərɪk] *s.* retorica *f.*
rhetorical [rɪ'tərɪk(ə)l] *agg.* retorico
rheumatism ['ruːmətɪz(ə)m] *s.* reumatismo *m.*
rhinoceros [raɪ'nəs(ə)rəs] *s.* rinoceronte *m.*
rhododendron [ˌrɒʊdə'dɛndr(ə)n] *s.* rododendro *m.*
rhomboidal [rəm'bəɪdl] *agg.* romboidale
rhombus ['rəmbəs] *s.* rombo *m.*
rhubarb ['ruːbaːb] *s.* rabarbaro *m.*
rhyme [raɪm] *s.* rima *f.*
rhythm ['rɪð(ə)m] *s.* ritmo *m.*
rhythmic(al) ['rɪðmɪk((ə)l)] *agg.* ritmico
rib [rɪb] *s.* **1** costola *f.* **2** costoletta *f.* **3** nervatura *f.*
to rib [rɪb] *v. tr.* **1** rinforzare con nervature **2** scanalare **3** (*fam.*) prendere in giro
ribbon ['rɪbən] *s.* nastro *m.* ♦ **in ribbons** a brandelli
rice [raɪs] *s.* riso *m.* ♦ **r. field** risaia
rich [rɪtʃ] *agg.* ricco ♦ **r. in** ricco di
riches ['rɪtʃɪz] *s. pl.* ricchezze *f. pl.*
richly ['rɪtʃlɪ] *avv.* **1** riccamente **2** pienamente, abbondantemente
richness ['rɪtʃnɪs] *s.* ricchezza *f.*
rickets ['rɪkɪts] *s.* rachitismo *m.*
rickety ['rɪkɪtɪ] *agg.* **1** rachitico **2** traballante
rickshaw ['rɪkʃɜː] *s.* risciò *m.*
to rid [rɪd] (*pass.* **rid**, **ridded**, *p. p.* **rid**) *v. tr.* liberare, sbarazzare ♦ **to get r. of st.** sbarazzarsi di q.c.
ridden ['rɪdn] *p. p. di* **to ride**
riddle (1) ['rɪdl] *s.* indovinello *m.*, rompicapo *m.*, enigma *m.*
riddle (2) ['rɪdl] *s.* setaccio *m.*
to riddle (1) ['rɪdl] **A** *v. tr.* risolvere (*un enigma*) **B** *v. intr.* **1** parlare per enigmi **2** proporre indovinelli
to riddle (2) ['rɪdl] *v. tr.* **1** setacciare, va-

gliare **2** crivellare
ride [raɪd] *s.* **1** cavalcata *f.* **2** (*su un veicolo*) giro *m.*, corsa *f.* **3** tragitto *m.* **4** (*per cavalli*) pista *f.*, sentiero *m.*
to ride [raɪd] (*pass.* **rode**, *p. p.* **ridden**) **A** *v. intr.* **1** andare a cavallo, cavalcare **2** (*in bicicletta, moto, ecc.*) andare, (*su un veicolo*) viaggiare **3** (*di fantino*) pesare **4** (*naut.*) galleggiare, fluttuare **B** *v. tr.* **1** cavalcare, montare **2** percorrere **3** opprimere ♦ **to r. a bike** andare in bicicletta; **to r. at anchor** stare alla fonda
rider ['raɪdəʳ] *s.* **1** cavaliere *m.*, fantino *m.* **2** ciclista *m. e f.*, motociclista *m. e f.*, (*su un veicolo*) viaggiatore *m.*
ridge [rɪdʒ] *s.* **1** cresta *f.*, cima *f.*, colmo *m.* **2** catena *f.*, dorsale *f.*
ridicule ['rɪdɪkjuːl] *s.* ridicolo *m.*, derisione *f.*
to ridicule ['rɪdɪkjuːl] *v. tr.* ridicolizzare
ridiculous [rɪ'dɪkjʊləs] *agg.* ridicolo, assurdo
riding ['raɪdɪŋ] *s.* **1** cavalcata *f.* **2** equitazione *f.* **3** (*naut.*) ancoraggio *m.*
to rif [rɪf] *v. tr.* (*USA, pop.*) licenziare
rife [raɪf] *agg. pred.* **1** comune, diffuso **2** ricco, abbondante ♦ **to be r. with** abbondare di
riffraff ['rɪfræf] *s.* (*fam.*) canaglia *f.*, marmaglia *f.*
rifle ['raɪfl] *s.* **1** fucile *m.*, carabina *f.* **2** *al pl.* fucilieri *m. pl.* ♦ **r. range** poligono di tiro
to rifle ['raɪfl] **A** *v. tr.* saccheggiare, depredare, svaligiare **B** *v. intr.* frugare
rift [rɪft] *s.* **1** crepaccio *m.*, fenditura *f.* **2** (*fig.*) rottura *f.*, dissenso *m.* ♦ **r. valley** fossa tettonica
rig [rɪg] *s.* **1** (*naut.*) attrezzatura *f.* **2** tenuta *f.*, abbigliamento *m.* **3** impianto *m.*, installazione *f.* **4** piattaforma *f.* di trivellazione
to rig (1) [rɪg] *v. tr.* **1** (*naut.*) attrezzare **2** allestire, sistemare **3** vestire ♦ **to be rigged out as** vestirsi da; **to r. up** montare
to rig (2) [rɪg] *v. tr.* truccare, manipolare
rigging ['rɪgɪŋ] *s.* (*naut.*) attrezzatura *f.*, sartiame *m.*
right [raɪt] **A** *agg.* **1** giusto, retto, onesto **2** esatto, corretto **3** adatto, appropriato, conveniente **4** (*geom.*) retto **5** destro **6** sano, che sta bene **B** *s.* **1** (il) giusto *m.*, (il) bene *m.* **2** diritto *m.*, facoltà *f.* **3** destra *f.*, lato *m.* destro, mano *f.* destra **4** (*di tessuto*) diritto *m.* **C** *avv.* **1** bene, giustamente, esattamente **2** direttamente, dritto **3** a destra **4** subito, immediatamente **5** del tutto, completamente ♦ **on the r., to the r.** a destra; **r. of way** (*tra veicoli*) (diritto di) precedenza; **r. on** senza interruzione; **to be r.** avere ragione
right-about ['raɪtəbaʊt] *s.* dietrofront *m. inv.*
righteous ['raɪtʃəs] *agg.* retto, virtuoso
rightful ['raɪtf(ʊ)l] *agg.* **1** legittimo **2** giusto, equo
right-hand ['raɪthænd] *agg.* **1** destro **2** fatto con la destra **3** da usare con la destra ♦ **r.-h. man** braccio destro
rigid ['rɪdʒɪd] *agg.* rigido
rigidity [rɪ'dʒɪdɪtɪ] *s.* rigidità *f.*
rigmarole ['rɪgm(ə)rɒʊl] *s.* tiritera *f.*
rigorous ['rɪg(ə)rəs] *agg.* rigido, rigoroso
rigour ['rɪgəʳ] *s.* rigore *m.*
to rile [raɪl] *v. tr.* (*fam.*) irritare
rim [rɪm] *s.* **1** bordo *m.*, ciglio *m.* **2** (*autom.*) cerchione *m.*
rime [raɪm] *s.* brina *f.*
rind [raɪnd] *s.* **1** buccia *f.*, scorza *f.* **2** cotenna *f.*
ring (1) [rɪŋ] *s.* **1** anello *m.*, cerchio *m.*, alone *m.*, collare *m.* **2** recinto *m.*, pista *f.*, quadrato *m.*, ring *m.* ♦ **r. finger** anulare; **r. road** circonvallazione
ring (2) [rɪŋ] *s.* **1** squillo *m.*, scampanellata *f.* **2** (*fam.*) telefonata *f.*
to ring (1) [rɪŋ] *v. tr.* accerchiare, circondare, cingere
to ring (2) [rɪŋ] (*pass.* **rang**, *p. p.* **rung**) **A** *v. tr.* **1** suonare **2** telefonare **B** *v. intr.* **1** suonare, squillare **2** risuonare **3** telefonare ♦ **to r. around** fare un giro di telefonate; **to r. back** richiamare; **to r. in/up** telefonare; **to r. off** metter giù (il telefono)
ringing ['rɪŋɪŋ] **A** *agg.* sonoro **B** *s.* suono *m.*, scampanellio *m.*
ringleader ['rɪŋˌliːdəʳ] *s.* capobanda *m. inv.*
ringlet ['rɪŋlɪt] *s.* ricciolo *m.*
rink [rɪŋk] *s.* pista *f.* per pattinaggio
rinse [rɪns] *s.* risciacquo *m.*
to rinse [rɪns] *v. tr.* sciacquare
riot ['raɪət] *s.* **1** tumulto *m.*, sommossa *f.* **2** fracasso *m.*, frastuono *m.* **3** orgia *f.*, sfrenatezza *f.* **4** profusione *f.*
to riot ['raɪət] *v. intr.* **1** tumultuare, insorgere **2** gozzovigliare
riotous ['raɪətəs] *agg.* **1** sedizioso, tumultuante **2** dissoluto
rip [rɪp] *s.* strappo *m.*

to rip [rɪp] *v. tr.* strappare
ripe [raɪp] *agg.* **1** maturo **2** stagionato **3** (*fig.*) pronto
to ripen ['raɪp(ə)n] *v. tr. e intr.* **1** maturare **2** stagionare
ripeness ['raɪpnɪs] *s.* maturità *f.*
ripple ['rɪpl] *s.* **1** increspatura *f.*, ondulazione *f.* **2** mormorio *m.*
to ripple ['rɪpl] *v. intr.* **1** incresparsi, ondularsi **2** gorgogliare, mormorare
rise [raɪz] *s.* **1** altura *f.*, rialzo *m.* **2** salita *f.*, ascesa *f.* **3** aumento *m.*, crescita *f.*, rialzo *m.* **4** progresso *m.*, avanzamento *m.*, promozione *f.* **5** innalzamento *m.* di livello, altezza *f.* **6** origine *f.* ♦ **to give r. to** dare origine a
to rise [raɪz] (*pass.* **rose**, *p. p.* **risen**) *v. intr.* **1** alzarsi, sorgere, levarsi, spuntare **2** crescere, aumentare **3** ergersi **4** insorgere, sollevarsi, ribellarsi **5** provenire, aver origine
rising ['raɪzɪŋ] **A** *agg.* **1** sorgente, nascente **2** crescente **3** ascendente **4** promettente **B** *s.* **1** rivolta *f.*, sommossa *f.* **2** salita *f.*, ascesa *f.* **3** crescita *f.* **4** miglioramento *m.*
risk [rɪsk] *s.* rischio *m.* ♦ **at one's own r.** a proprio rischio e pericolo
to risk [rɪsk] *v. tr. e intr.* rischiare
risky ['rɪskɪ] *agg.* rischioso
risqué [ˌriːs'keɪ] *agg.* osé
rissole ['rɪsɒʊl] *s.* polpetta *f.*
rite [raɪt] *s.* rito *m.*
ritual ['rɪtjʊəl] *agg. e s.* rituale *m.*
rival ['raɪv(ə)l] *agg. e s.* rivale *m. e f.*
to rival ['raɪv(ə)l] *v. tr.* rivaleggiare con
rivalry ['raɪv(ə)lrɪ] *s.* rivalità *f.*, concorrenza *f.*
to rive [raɪv] (*pass.* **rived**, *p. p.* **riven**) *v. tr.* strappare, spezzare
river ['rɪvəʳ] *s.* fiume *m.* ♦ **down r.** a valle; **r.-bank** sponda; **r.-bed** alveo; **up r.** a monte
rivet ['rɪvɪt] *s.* rivetto *m.*
to rivet ['rɪvɪt] *v. tr.* **1** inchiodare, rivettare **2** (*fig.*) fissare
road [rɒʊd] *s.* **1** strada *f.*, via *f.* **2** cammino *m.*, percorso *m.* **3** (*naut.*) rada *f.* ♦ **main/side r.** strada principale/secondaria; **one-way r.** senso unico; **r. hog** pirata della strada; **r. map** carta stradale; **r. sign** segnale stradale; **uneven r.** strada dissestata
roadbed ['rɒʊdbɛd] *s.* massicciata *f.*
roadblock ['rɒʊdblək] *s.* blocco *m.* stradale
roadside ['rɒʊdsaɪd] *s.* bordo *m.* della strada
roadway ['rɒʊdweɪ] *s.* carreggiata *f.*
roadworthy ['rɒʊdˌwɜːðɪ] *agg.* (*autom.*) in grado di tenere la strada
to roam [rɒʊm] *v. intr.* vagare
roar [rɜːʳ] *s.* **1** ruggito *m.* **2** mugghio *m.*, rombo *m.*, urlo *m.* **3** scoppio *m.*, scroscio *m.*
to roar [rɜːʳ] *v. intr.* **1** ruggire **2** rumoreggiare, mugghiare, urlare
roast [rɒʊst] *agg. e s.* arrosto *m.*
to roast [rɒʊst] *v. tr.* **1** arrostire **2** tostare
to rob [rəb] *v. tr.* derubare, rapinare
robber ['rəbəʳ] *s.* ladro *m.*, rapinatore *m.*
robbery ['rəbərɪ] *s.* rapina *f.*
robe [rɒʊb] *s.* **1** toga *f.* **2** accappatoio *m.*
robin ['rəbɪn] *s.* pettirosso *m.*
robot ['rɒʊbət] *s.* robot *m. inv.*
robotics [rɒʊ'bətɪks] *s. pl.* (*v. al sing.*) robotica *f.*
robust [rə'bʌst] *agg.* robusto, forte
rock (1) [rək] *s.* **1** roccia *f.* **2** macigno *m.*, masso *m.* **3** scoglio *m.*, scogliera *f.* **4** rocca *f.*, rupe *f.* ♦ **on the rocks** con ghiaccio; **r.-bottom** fondo, punto più basso; **r. climber** rocciatore; **r. crystal** cristallo di rocca; **r. garden** giardino roccioso; **r. goat** stambecco
rock (2) [rək] *s.* **1** dondolio *m.*, oscillazione *f.* **2** (*mus.*) rock *m. inv.*
to rock [rək] **A** *v. tr.* **1** dondolare **2** scuotere **B** *v. intr.* dondolarsi, oscillare
rocket ['rəkɪt] *s.* razzo *m.*
rocking ['rəkɪŋ] *agg.* **1** a dondolo **2** oscillante ♦ **r. chair** sedia a dondolo; **r. horse** cavallo a dondolo
rocky (1) ['rəkɪ] *agg.* **1** roccioso, sassoso **2** duro come la roccia **3** saldo, irremovibile
rocky (2) ['rəkɪ] *agg.* malfermo, traballante
rococo [rə'kɒʊkɒʊ] *agg. e s.* rococò *m.*
rod [rəd] *s.* **1** verga *f.*, bacchetta *f.* **2** asta *f.*, barra *f.* **3** canna *f.* da pesca
rode [rɒʊd] *pass. di* **to ride**
rodent ['rɒʊd(ə)nt] *agg. e s.* roditore *m.*
rodeo [rɒ(ʊ)'deɪɒ(ʊ)] *s.* rodeo *m.*
roe (1) [rɒʊ] *s.* capriolo *m.*
roe (2) [rɒʊ] *s.* uova *f. pl.* di pesce
rogue [rɒʊg] *s.* furfante *m.*, imbroglione *m.*
role [rɒʊl] *s.* ruolo *m.*
roll [rɒʊl] *s.* **1** rotolo *m.*, rullo *m.*, rullino

m. **2** panino m. **3** ruolo m., registro m. **4** (*naut., aer.*) rollio m. **5** ondeggiamento m. **6** (*di tamburo*) rullo m. ♦ **r. call** appello
to roll [rɒʊl] **A** v. intr. **1** rotolare, rotolarsi **2** ruotare **3** arrotolarsi, avvolgersi **4** ondeggiare **5** (*di tamburo*) rullare **6** (*naut., aer.*) rollare **B** v. tr. **1** far rotolare **2** far ruotare, roteare **3** avvolgere, arrotolare **4** spianare (*con rullo e sim.*) ♦ **to r. down** srotolare; **to r. in** arrivare in gran quantità; **to r. over** rivoltare, rivoltarsi; **to r. up** arrotolare, arrivare
rolled ['rɒʊld] agg. **1** arrotolato **2** laminato
roller ['rɒʊləʳ] s. **1** rullo m., rotella f., cilindro m. **2** rullo m. compressore **3** onda f. lunga **4** bigodino m. ♦ **r. coaster** montagne russe; **r. skates** pattini a rotelle
rolling ['rɒʊlɪŋ] **A** agg. **1** rotolante **2** rotante, girevole **3** oscillante **4** ondulato **5** rimbombante **B** s. rotolamento m. ♦ **r. mill** laminatoio; **r. pin** matterello
Roman ['rɒʊmən] agg. e s. romano m. ♦ **R. numeral** numero romano
romance [rə'mæns] s. **1** (*letter.*) romanzo m. cavalleresco, racconto m. fantastico **2** avventura f. romanzesca **3** avventura f. sentimentale, idillio m. **4** (*mus.*) romanza f.
Romance [rə'mæns] agg. romanzo
Romanesque [ˌrɒʊmə'nɛsk] agg. romanico
romantic [rə'mæntɪk] agg. **1** romantico **2** romanzesco
Romanticism [rə'mæntɪsɪz(ə)m] s. romanticismo m.
romp [rəmp] s. gioco m. chiassoso
rompers ['rəmpəz] s. pl. pagliaccetto m.
rood [ruːd] s. croce f., crocifisso m.
roof [ruːf] s. tetto m., volta f. ♦ **r. garden** giardino pensile; **r. rack** portapacchi
to roof [ruːf] v. tr. coprire con un tetto
rook (1) [rʊk] s. **1** corvo m. **2** (*fam.*) truffatore m.
rook (2) [rʊk] s. (*scacchi*) torre f.
room [ruːm] s. **1** camera f., stanza f., locale m. **2** ambiente m., spazio m. **3** (*fig.*) possibilità f.
to room [ruːm] v. tr. e intr. (*USA*) alloggiare
roomy ['ruːmɪ] agg. spazioso
to roost [ruːst] v. intr. appollaiarsi
rooster ['ruːstəʳ] s. (*USA*) gallo m.
root [ruːt] s. radice f.
to root (1) [ruːt] v. intr. attecchire, radicarsi ♦ **to r. out/up** sradicare
to root (2) [ruːt] v. intr. **1** grufolare **2** frugare ♦ **to r. for** fare il tifo per
rope [rɒʊp] s. corda f., fune f., cima f. ♦ **r. ladder** scala di corda
to rope [rɒʊp] v. tr. legare con corde ♦ **to r. in/off** cintare con corde
rosary ['rɒʊzərɪ] s. rosario m.
rose (1) [rɒʊz] agg. e s. rosa f. ♦ **r. bud** bocciolo di rosa; **r. window** rosone
rose (2) [rɒʊz] pass. di **to rise**
rosemary ['rɒʊzm(ə)rɪ] s. rosmarino m.
rosette [rɒ(ʊ)'zɛt] s. rosetta f., coccarda f.
roster ['rəstəʳ] s. **1** elenco m., lista f. **2** ruolino m.
rostrum ['rəstrəm] s. rostro m.
rosy ['rɒʊzɪ] agg. roseo
rot [rət] s. **1** putrefazione f., marciume m. **2** rovina f. **3** (*fam.*) sciocchezze f. pl.
to rot [rət] v. intr. imputridire, marcire
rota ['rɒʊtə] s. tabella f. dei turni
rotary ['rɒʊtərɪ] agg. rotante, rotatorio
to rotate [rɒ(ʊ)'teɪt] v. tr. e intr. ruotare
rotation [rɒ(ʊ)'teɪʃ(ə)n] s. rotazione f.
rotor ['rɒʊtəʳ] s. girante f., rotore m.
rotten ['rətn] agg. **1** marcio, putrido **2** corrotto **3** sgradevole ♦ **to feel r.** sentirsi male
rotula ['rətjʊlə] s. rotula f.
rotundity [rɒ(ʊ)'tʌndɪtɪ] s. rotondità f.
rouge [ruːʒ] s. rossetto m.
rough [rʌf] **A** agg. **1** ruvido, irregolare, scabro **2** tempestoso, burrascoso, agitato **3** grezzo, greggio **4** rozzo, grossolano, sgarbato **5** approssimativo **6** disagevole, scomodo, difficile **7** aspro **B** s. **1** terreno m. accidentato **2** teppista m. e f. **C** avv. **1** rudemente **2** semplicemente ♦ **r. and ready** alla buona; **r. copy** brutta copia; **r. luck** sfortuna; **r. road** strada accidentata; **to have a r. time** passarsela male
roughage ['rʌfɪdʒ] s. crusca f. di cereali
roughcast ['rʌfkaːst] s. intonaco m. rustico
roulette [ruː'lɛt] s. roulette f. inv.
Roumanian [ruː'meɪnjən] agg. e s. romeno m.
round [raʊnd] **A** agg. **1** rotondo, circolare, rotondeggiante **2** completo, intero **3** (*di suono, voce*) pieno, sonoro **4** (*di stile*) fluente, scorrevole **B** avv. intorno, in giro **C** prep. intorno a, nelle vicinanze di, circa **D** s. **1** cerchio m., tondo m., sfera f. **2** giro m. **3** ciclo m., turno m., round m. inv. **4** colpo m., scarica f., proiettile m. ♦ **r. table**

tavola rotonda; **r.-the-clock** ventiquattr'ore su ventiquattro; **r. trip** viaggio di andata e ritorno
to round [raʊnd] **A** *v. tr.* **1** arrotondare **2** girare **3** accerchiare **B** *v. intr.* **1** arrotondarsi **2** girare, girarsi, voltarsi ♦ **to r. down** arrotondare (alla cifra inferiore); **to r. up** riunire, arrotondare (alla cifra superiore)
roundabout ['raʊndəbaʊt] **A** *agg.* indiretto **B** *s.* **1** rotatoria *f.* **2** giostra *f.*
roundish ['raʊndɪʃ] *agg.* tondeggiante
roundly ['raʊndlɪ] *avv.* **1** completamente **2** francamente, esplicitamente
roundness ['raʊndnɪs] *s.* rotondità *f.*
roundup ['raʊndʌp] *s.* **1** riunione *f.*, raccolta *f.* **2** retata *f.*
to rouse [raʊz] *v. tr.* **1** svegliare **2** (*selvaggina*) stanare **3** suscitare, provocare
rout [raʊt] *s.* rotta *f.*, disfatta *f.*
to rout [raʊt] *v. tr.* sconfiggere
route [ruːt] *s.* itinerario *m.*, percorso *m.*, rotta *f.*
routine [ruː'tiːn] *s.* **1** routine *f. inv.* **2** (*teatro*) numero *m.*
to rove [rɒʊv] *v. intr.* vagabondare
row (1) [rɒʊ] *s.* fila *f.*, riga *f.*
row (2) [raʊ] *s.* (*fam.*) **1** tafferuglio *m.*, zuffa *f.* **2** baccano *m.*
row (3) [rɒʊ] *s.* remata *f.*, vogata *f.*
to row (1) [rɒʊ] **A** *v. intr.* remare, vogare **B** *v. tr.* trasportare in barca a remi
to row (2) [raʊ] **A** *v. tr.* (*fam.*) sgridare **B** *v. intr.* litigare, azzuffarsi
rowboat ['rɒʊbɒʊt] *s.* barca *f.* a remi
rowdy ['raʊdɪ] *agg.* litigioso, turbolento
rower ['rɒ(ʊ)əʳ] *s.* rematore *m.*, vogatore *m.*
rowing ['rɒʊɪŋ] *s.* canottaggio *m.*
royal ['rɔɪ(ə)l] *agg.* reale
royalty ['rɔɪ(ə)ltɪ] *s.* **1** regalità *f.*, dignità *f.* regale **2** la famiglia *f.* reale **3** *al pl.* diritti *m. pl.* d'autore
rub [rʌb] *s.* **1** sfregamento *m.*, massaggio *m.* **2** (*del terreno*) asperità *f.* **3** difficoltà *f.*
to rub [rʌb] *v. tr.* **1** fregare, strofinare **2** lucidare ♦ **to r. in** far penetrare sfregando; **to r. off/out** cancellare, togliere sfregando
rubber ['rʌbəʳ] *s.* gomma *f.* ♦ **r. band** elastico; **r. dinghy/boat** gommone, canotto
rubbing ['rʌbɪŋ] *s.* sfregamento *m.*, frizione *f.*
rubbish ['rʌbɪʃ] *s.* **1** immondizia *f.*, spazzatura *f.* **2** macerie *f. pl.* **3** sciocchezze *f. pl.* ♦ **r. bin** pattumiera
rubble ['rʌbl] *s.* **1** macerie *f. pl.* **2** pietrisco *m.* **3** detrito *m.*
ruby ['ruːbɪ] *s.* rubino *m.*
ruck [rʌk] *s.* mucchio *m.*
rucksack [rʌksæk] *s.* zaino *m.*
rudder ['rʌdəʳ] *s.* timone *m.*
ruddy ['rʌdɪ] *agg.* **1** rubicondo **2** (*pop.*) dannato
rude [ruːd] *agg.* **1** maleducato, villano **2** primitivo, grezzo **3** volgare, osceno
rudeness ['ruːdnɪs] *s.* maleducazione *f.*
rudiment ['ruːdɪmənt] *s.* rudimento *m.*
rudimentary [ˌruːdɪ'mɛnt(ə)rɪ] *agg.* rudimentale
rueful ['ruːf(ʊ)l] *agg.* addolorato
ruffian ['rʌfjən] *s.* furfante *m.*
to ruffle ['rʌfl] **A** *v. tr.* **1** increspare **2** arruffare, scompigliare **3** agitare, turbare **B** *v. intr.* **1** incresparsi **2** arruffarsi **3** agitarsi, turbarsi
rug [rʌg] *s.* **1** coperta *f.* **2** tappeto *m.*, tappetino *m.*
rugby ['rʌgbɪ] *s.* rugby *m.*
rugged ['rʌgɪd] *agg.* **1** ruvido, aspro, irregolare **2** rozzo, rude **3** ispido, irsuto **4** duro, rigido
rugger ['rʌgəʳ] *s.* (*fam.*) rugby *m.*
rugosity [rʊ'gəsɪtɪ] *s.* (*bot.*) rugosità *f.*
ruin [rʊɪn] *s.* rovina *f.*
to ruin [rʊɪn] *v. tr.* rovinare
ruinous ['ruːɪnəs] *agg.* **1** rovinoso **2** in rovina
rule [ruːl] *s.* **1** regola *f.*, regolamento *m.*, norma *f.* **2** governo *m.*, dominazione *f.* **3** riga *f.* (da disegno)
to rule [ruːl] **A** *v. tr.* **1** governare, dominare **2** guidare, regolare **3** (*dir*) dichiarare **B** *v. intr.* **1** governare **2** predominare ♦ **to r. out** escludere
ruler ['ruːləʳ] *s.* **1** governante *m.*, sovrano *m.* **2** riga *f.* (da disegno)
ruling ['ruːlɪŋ] **A** *agg.* **1** dirigente, che governa **2** dominante **B** *s.* (*dir.*) decisione *f.*
rum [rʌm] *s.* rum *m. inv.*
rumble ['rʌmbl] *s.* rimbombo *m.*, rombo *m.*, borbottio *m.*
to rumble ['rʌmbl] *v. intr.* rimbombare, rumoreggiare
ruminant ['ruːmɪnənt] *agg. e s.* ruminante *m.*
to rummage ['rʌmɪdʒ] *v. tr. e intr.* frugare, perquisire
rummy ['rʌmɪ] *s.* ramino *m.*

rumour ['ru:mər] (*USA* **rumor**) *s.* diceria *f.*, voce *f.*
rump [rʌmp] *s.* (*di animale*) posteriore *m.*, groppa *f.* ♦ **r. steak** bistecca di scamone
rumpus ['rʌmpəs] *s.* (*fam.*) chiasso *m.*, cagnara *f.*
run [rʌn] *s.* **1** corsa *f.* tragitto *m.*, percorso *m.* **2** breve viaggio *m.*, giro *m.* **3** corso *m.*, andamento *m.*, direzione *f.* **4** serie *f.*, periodo *m.* **5** classe *f.*, categoria *f.* **6** adito *m.*, libero accesso *m.* **7** (*per animali*) recinto *m.* **8** (*sci*) pista *f.* **9** (*di libro*) tiratura *f.* ♦ **at a r.** di corsa; **in the long r.** a lungo andare; **in the short r.** a breve scadenza; **on the r.** in fuga
to run [rʌn] (*pass.* **ran**, *p. p.* **run**) **A** *v. intr.* **1** correre **2** fuggire **3** (*di veicoli*) passare, partire, fare servizio **4** andare, scorrere, estendersi **5** diventare **6** funzionare **7** essere in vigore, avere validità **8** presentarsi candidato **B** *v. tr.* **1** correre, far correre **2** dirigere, amministrare, gestire **3** far funzionare **4** seguire **5** passare, far scorrere ♦ **to r. about** correre qua e là; **to r. across** imbattersi in; **to r. along** andar via; **to r. away** fuggire; **to r. back** tornare indietro; **to r. down** scaricare, (*di batteria*) scaricarsi, (*con un'auto*) investire, indebolire; **to r. in** rodare; **to r. into** imbattersi, sbattere contro; **to r. off** scappare, duplicare; **to r. out** esaurirsi, scadere; **to r. over** traboccare, investire; **to r. through** dare una scorsa, sperperare; **to r. to** bastare per, tendere a; **to r. up** issare, mettere insieme, accumulare
runaway ['rʌnəweɪ] *s.* fuggiasco *m.*
rung (1) [rʌŋ] *p. p. di* **to ring**
rung (2) [rʌŋ] *s.* piolo *m.*
runner ['rʌnər] *s.* **1** corridore *m.* **2** fattorino *m.* **3** contrabbandiere *m.* **4** (*di slitta*) pattino *m.* **5** viticcio *m.* ♦ **r. bean** fagiolo rampicante; **r.-up** secondo classificato
running ['rʌnɪŋ] **A** *agg.* **1** in corsa, da corsa **2** corrente **3** continuo, consecutivo **4** funzionante **B** *s.* **1** corsa *f.* **2** marcia *f.*, funzionamento *m.* **3** gestione *f.*, direzione *f.* ♦ **r.-in** rodaggio
runny ['rʌnɪ] *agg.* **1** liquefatto **2** che cola
run-of-the-mill [ˌrʌnəvðə'mɪl] *agg.* ordinario, comune
run-up ['rʌnˌʌp] *s.* rincorsa *f.*
runway ['rʌnweɪ] *s.* (*aer.*) pista *f.*
rupture ['rʌptʃər] *s.* **1** rottura *f.* **2** (*med.*) ernia *f.*
rural ['rʊər(ə)l] *agg.* campestre, rurale
ruse [ru:z] *s.* stratagemma *m.*
rush (1) [rʌʃ] *s.* **1** assalto *m.*, corsa *f.* precipitosa **2** furia *f.*, fretta *f.* **3** afflusso *m.*
rush (2) [rʌʃ] *s.* giunco *m.*
to rush [rʌʃ] **A** *v. intr.* **1** precipitarsi **2** affrettarsi **B** *v. tr.* **1** spingere, far fretta **2** spedire velocemente **3** affrettare, accelerare, prendere d'assalto
Russian ['rʌʃ(ə)n] *agg. e s.* russo *m.*
rust [rʌst] *s.* ruggine *f.*
to rust [rʌst] *v. tr. e intr.* arrugginire, arrugginirsi
rustic ['rʌstɪk] *agg.* rustico
rustle ['rʌsl] *s.* fruscio *m.*
to rustle ['rʌsl] *v. intr.* frusciare, stormire
rustproof ['rʌstpru:f] *agg.* antiruggine, inossidabile
rusty (1) ['rʌstɪ] *agg.* arrugginito
rusty (2) ['rʌstɪ] *agg.* arrabbiato
rut (1) [rʌt] *s.* **1** solco *m.*, carreggiata *f.* **2** routine *f. inv.*
rut (2) [rʌt] *s.* (*di animali*) fregola *f.*
ruthless ['ru:θlɪs] *agg.* spietato
rye [raɪ] *s.* segale *f.*

S

sabbatical [sə'bætɪk(ə)l] *agg.* sabbatico
sable ['seɪbl] *s.* zibellino *m.*
sabotage ['sæbətaːʒ] *s.* sabotaggio *m.*
to sabotage ['sæbətaːʒ] *v. tr.* sabotare
sabre ['seɪbəʳ] *s.* sciabola *f.*
saccharin(e) ['sækərɪn] *s.* saccarina *f.*
saccharose ['sækərɒʊs] *s.* saccarosio *m.*
sachet ['sæʃeɪ] *s.* sacchetto *m.*, bustina *f.*
sack (1) [sæk] *s.* sacco *m.* ♦ **to get the s.** (*fam.*) essere licenziato
sack (2) [sæk] *s.* saccheggio *m.*
to sack (1) [sæk] *v. tr.* **1** insaccare **2** (*fam.*) licenziare ♦ **to s. out** andare a dormire
to sack (2) [sæk] *v. tr.* saccheggiare
sacker ['sækəʳ] *s.* saccheggiatore *m.*
sacking ['sækɪŋ] *s.* **1** tela *f.* da sacco **2** (*fam.*) licenziamento *m.*
sacrament ['sækrəmənt] *s.* sacramento *m.*
sacrarium [sə'krɛərɪəm] *s.* sacrario *m.*
sacred ['seɪkrɪd] *agg.* sacro
sacrifice ['sækrɪfaɪs] *s.* sacrificio *m.*
to sacrifice ['sækrɪfaɪs] *v. tr.* sacrificare
sacrilege ['sækrɪlɪdʒ] *s.* sacrilegio *m.*
sad [sæd] *agg.* **1** triste, addolorato **2** (*di colore*) spento **3** scadente
saddle ['sædl] *s.* sella *f.*
to saddle ['sædl] *v. tr.* **1** sellare **2** gravare
saddlebag ['sædl,bæg] *s.* **1** bisaccia *f.* **2** (*per bicicletta e sim.*) borsa *f.*
sadism ['seɪdɪz(ə)m] *s.* sadismo *m.*
sadist ['seɪdɪst] *s.* sadico *m.*
sadistic [sə'dɪstɪk] *agg.* sadico
sadness ['sædnɪs] *s.* tristezza *f.*
sadomasochism [,seɪdɒʊ'mæsəkɪz(ə)m] *s.* sadomasochismo *m.*
safari [sə'faːrɪ] *s.* safari *m. inv.*
safe [seɪf] **A** *agg.* **1** sicuro, al sicuro, protetto **2** salvo, illeso **3** cauto, prudente **B** *s.* cassaforte *f.* ♦ **s. and sound** sano e salvo; **s.-deposit box** cassetta di sicurezza; **s. room** camera blindata
safe-conduct [,seɪf'kʌndəkt] *s.* salvacondotto *m.*
safeguard ['seɪfgaːd] *s.* salvaguardia *f.*
to safeguard ['seɪfgaːd] *v. tr.* salvaguardare
safe-keeping [,seɪf'kiːpɪŋ] *s.* custodia *f.*
safety ['seɪftɪ] *s.* **1** salvezza *f.*, sicurezza *f.* **2** (*mecc.*) sicura *f.* ♦ **s. belt** cintura di sicurezza; **s. pin** spilla di sicurezza
saffron ['sæfr(ə)n] *s.* zafferano *m.*
to sag [sæg] *v. intr.* **1** incurvarsi, abbassarsi **2** diminuire, attenuarsi
saga ['saːgə] *s.* saga *f.*
sage (1) [seɪdʒ] *s.* salvia *f.*
sage (2) [seɪdʒ] *agg.* saggio
said [sɛd] *pass. e p. p. di* **to say**
sail [seɪl] *s.* vela *f.*, velatura *f.* ♦ **s. maker** velaio
to sail [seɪl] **A** *v. intr.* **1** navigare (*a vela*) **2** salpare **3** volare, sorvolare **B** *v. tr.* **1** (*una barca a vela*) condurre **2** percorrere navigando ♦ **to s. into sb.** inveire contro qc.
sailer ['seɪləʳ] *s.* veliero *m.*
sailing ['seɪlɪŋ] *s.* **1** navigazione *f.* **2** (*sport*) vela *f.* ♦ **s. boat** barca a vela
sailor ['seɪləʳ] *s.* marinaio *m.*, navigante *m.*
saint [seɪnt] *agg. e s.* santo *m.*
sake [seɪk] *s.* interesse *m.*, beneficio *m.*, vantaggio *m.* ♦ **for the s. of** per amor di
salad ['sæləd] *s.* insalata *f.* ♦ **s. bowl** insalatiera; **s. dressing** condimento per l'insalata
salami [sə'laːmɪ] *s.* salame *m.*
salary ['sælərɪ] *s.* stipendio *m.*
sale [seɪl] *s.* **1** vendita *f.* **2** liquidazione *f.*, svendita *f.*, saldo *m.* ♦ **for/on s.** in vendita; **sales** saldi
saleable ['seɪləbl] *agg.* vendibile
salesman ['seɪlzmən] (*pl.* **salesmen**) *s.* commesso *m.*, venditore *m.*
saleswoman ['seɪlz,wʊmən] (*pl.* **saleswomen**) commessa *f.*, venditrice *f.*
saline ['seɪlaɪn] *agg.* salino
saliva [sə'laɪvə] *s.* saliva *f.*
sallow ['sælɒʊ] *agg.* giallastro
salmi ['sælmɪ(ː)] *s.* salmì *m.*
salmon ['sæmən] *s.* salmone *m.* ♦ **s. trout** trota salmonata; **smoked s.** salmone affumicato
salmonellosis [,sælmənə'lɒʊsɪs] *s.* salmonellosi *f.*
salon [sæ'lən] *s.* **1** sala *f.* (da ricevimenti) **2** negozio *m.*, salone *m.* **3** (*letterario*) salotto *m.* ♦ **beauty s.** salone di bellezza
saloon [sə'luːn] *s.* **1** salone *m.*, sala *f.* **2** (*USA*) saloon *m. inv.* **3** (*autom.*) berlina *f.*
salt [sɜːlt] **A** *s.* sale *m.* **B** *agg. attr.* **1** salato

2 conservato sotto sale ♦ **s. lake** lago salato; **s. pit** salina
to salt [sɜːlt] *v. tr.* salare ♦ **to s. away** mettere sotto sale
saltcellar ['sɜːlt,sɛləʳ] *s.* saliera *f.*
saltless ['sɜːltlɪs] *agg.* insipido
saltwater ['sɜːlt,wətəʳ] *agg. attr.* d'acqua salata, di mare
salty ['sɜːltɪ] *agg.* salato
salubrious [sə'luːbrɪəs] *agg.* salubre, sano
salubrity [sə'luːbrɪtɪ] *s.* salubrità *f.*
salutary ['sæljʊt(ə)rɪ] *agg.* salutare
salutation [,sælju(ː)'teɪʃ(ə)n] *s.* saluto *m.*
salute [sə'luːt] *s.* saluto *m.*
to salute [sə'luːt] *v. tr.* **1** salutare **2** rendere gli onori
salvage ['sælvɪdʒ] *s.* **1** salvataggio *m.*, ricupero *m.* **2** merci *f. pl.* ricuperate
to salvage ['sælvɪdʒ] *v. tr.* salvare, ricuperare
salvation [sæl'veɪʃ(ə)n] *s.* salvezza *f.*
same [seɪm] **A** *agg.* stesso, medesimo **B** *pron.* lo stesso, la stessa cosa **C** *avv.* allo stesso modo ♦ **all the s.** lo stesso, ugualmente; **much the s.** quasi lo stesso; **s. here** anche da parte mia
sample ['saːmpl] *s.* campione *m.*, modello *m.*, esemplare *m.*
to sample ['saːmpl] *v. tr.* **1** assaggiare **2** campionare
sanatorium [,sænə'tɜːrɪəm] *s.* sanatorio *m.*
to sanctify ['sæŋ(k)tɪfaɪ] *v. tr.* santificare, consacrare
sanctimonious [,sæŋ(k)tɪ'mɒʊnjəs] *agg.* bigotto
sanction ['sæŋ(k)ʃ(ə)n] *s.* **1** autorizzazione *f.* **2** ratifica *f.* **3** sanzione *f.*
to sanction ['sæŋ(k)ʃ(ə)n] *v. tr.* **1** autorizzare **2** ratificare **3** sancire
sanctity ['sæŋ(k)tɪtɪ] *s.* santità *f.*
sanctuary ['sæŋ(k)tjʊərɪ] *s.* **1** santuario *m.* **2** rifugio *m.* **3** riserva *f.* naturale
sand [sænd] *s.* **1** sabbia *f.* **2** *al pl.* spiaggia *f.* ♦ **s. bath** sabbiatura; **s. glass** clessidra
to sand [sænd] *v. tr.* **1** coprire di sabbia **2** insabbiare **3** sabbiare, smerigliare
sandal ['sændl] *s.* sandalo *m.*
sandbar ['sæn(d)baːʳ] *s.* barra *f.* di sabbia
sandcastle ['sæn(d),kaːsl] *s.* castello *m.* di sabbia
sandpaper ['sæn(d),peɪpəʳ] *s.* carta *f.* vetrata
sandstone ['sæn(d)stɒʊn] *s.* arenaria *f.*
sandwich ['sænwɪdʒ] *s.* sandwich *m. inv.*, tramezzino *m.*
to sandwich ['sænwɪdʒ] *v. tr.* serrare, mettere in mezzo
sandy ['sændɪ] *agg.* **1** sabbioso **2** di color sabbia **3** (*di capelli*) biondo rossiccio
sane [seɪn] *agg.* **1** sano di mente **2** sensato
sang [sæŋ] *pass. di* **to sing**
sanitary ['sænɪt(ə)rɪ] *agg.* **1** sanitario **2** igienico ♦ **s. towel/napkin** assorbente igienico
sanitation [,sænɪ'teɪʃən] *s.* impianti *m. pl.* igienici, fognature *f. pl.*
sanity ['sænɪtɪ] *s.* **1** salute *f.* mentale **2** buon senso *m.*
sank [sæŋk] *pass. di* **to sink**
sap [sæp] *s.* linfa *f.*
to sap (1) [sæp] *v. tr.* essiccare (*legno*)
to sap (2) [sæp] **A** *v. intr.* scavare trincee **B** *v. tr.* **1** scavare, scalzare **2** fiaccare, indebolire
sapid ['sæpɪd] *agg.* sapido
sapling ['sæplɪŋ] *s.* alberello *m.*
to saponify [sə'pənɪfaɪ] *v. tr.* saponificare
sapphire ['sæfaɪəʳ] *s.* zaffiro *m.*
sarcasm ['saːkæz(ə)m] *s.* sarcasmo *m.*
sarcastic [saː'kæstɪk] *agg.* sarcastico
sarcophagus [saː'kəfəgəs] *s.* sarcofago *m.*
sardine [saː'diːn] *s.* sardina *f.*
Sardinian [saː'dɪnjən] *agg. e s.* sardo *m.*
sash (1) [sæʃ] *s.* fascia *f.*, sciarpa *f.*
sash (2) [sæʃ] *s.* (*di finestra*) telaio *m.* scorrevole ♦ **s. window** finestra a ghigliottina
sat [sæt] *pass. e p. p. di* **to sit**
satanic(al) [sə'tænɪk((ə)l)] *agg.* satanico
satchel ['sætʃ(ə)l] *s.* cartella *f.*
satellite ['sætəlaɪt] *s.* satellite *m.*
to satiate ['seɪʃɪeɪt] *v. tr.* saziare
satin ['sætɪn] *s.* raso *m.*
satire ['sætaɪəʳ] *s.* satira *f.*
satiric(al) [sə'tɪrɪk((ə)l)] *agg.* satirico
satisfaction [,sætɪs'fækʃ(ə)n] *s.* soddisfazione *f.*
satisfactory [,sætɪs'fækt(ə)rɪ] *agg.* soddisfacente, esauriente
to satisfy ['sætɪsfaɪ] *v. tr.* **1** soddisfare, appagare **2** convincere, persuadere **3** (*comm.*) pagare
satisfying ['sætɪsfaɪɪŋ] *agg.* soddisfacente
to saturate ['sætʃəreɪt] *v. tr.* **1** saturare **2** impregnare
saturation [,sætʃə'reɪʃ(ə)n] *s.* saturazione *f.*

Saturday ['sætədɪ] *s.* sabato *m.*
satyr ['sætəʳ] *s.* satiro *m.*
sauce [sɜːs] *s.* **1** salsa *f.*, sugo *m.* **2** (*fam.*) impertinenza *f.* ♦ **s.-boat** salsiera
saucepan ['sɜːspən] *s.* casseruola *f.*
saucer ['sɜːsəʳ] *s.* piattino *m.*
saucy ['sɜːsɪ] *agg.* (*fam.*) impertinente
Saudi ['saʊdɪ] *agg.* saudita
sauna ['sɜːnə] *s.* sauna *f.*
to **saunter** ['sɜːntəʳ] *v. intr.* gironzolare
sausage ['səsɪdʒ] *s.* **1** salsiccia *f.* **2** *al pl.* salumi *m. pl.*
savage ['sævɪdʒ] **A** *agg.* **1** selvaggio, primitivo **2** feroce, crudele **3** non coltivato **B** *s.* **1** selvaggio *m.* **2** individuo *m.* brutale
to **savage** ['sævɪdʒ] *v. tr.* assalire con violenza
savanna(h) [sə'vænə] *s.* savana *f.*
save [seɪv] **A** *prep.* eccetto, salvo, tranne **B** *s.* (*sport*) parata *f.*
to **save** [seɪv] **A** *v. tr.* **1** salvare, preservare **2** conservare, mettere da parte, risparmiare **3** (*inf.*) salvare, memorizzare **B** *v. intr.* **1** risparmiare **2** (*sport*) parare
saver ['seɪvəʳ] *s.* risparmiatore *m.*
saving ['seɪvɪŋ] **A** *agg.* **1** che salva **2** parsimonioso **3** economico **B** *s.* **1** salvezza *f.* **2** economia *f.*, *al pl.* risparmi *m. pl.* **C** *prep. e cong.* eccetto, tranne ♦ **savings bank** cassa di risparmio; **the s. grace** l'unica buona qualità
saviour ['seɪvjəʳ] (*USA* **savior**) *s.* salvatore *m.*
savour ['seɪvəʳ] (*USA* **savor**) *s.* sapore *m.*
to **savour** ['seɪvəʳ] (*USA* **to savor**) *v. tr.* gustare, assaporare ♦ **to s. of** sapere di
savoury ['seɪv(ə)rɪ] *agg.* saporito, appetitoso
savoy [sə'vɔɪ] *s.* verza *f.*
saw (1) [sɜː] *s.* sega *f.*
saw (2) [sɜː] *pass. di* **to say**
to **saw** [sɜː] (*pass.* **sawed**, *p. p.* **sawn, sawed**) *v. tr.* segare
sawdust ['sɜːdʌst] *s.* segatura *f.*
sawmill ['sɜːmɪl] *s.* segheria *f.*
sawn [sɜːn] *p. p. di* **to saw**
sax [sæks] *s.* sassofono *m.*
Saxon ['sæksən] *agg. e s.* sassone *m. e f.*
saxophone ['sæksəfɒʊn] *s.* sassofono *m.*
saxophonist [sæk'səfənɪst] *s.* sassofonista *m. e f.*
say [seɪ] *s.* detto *m.*, parola *f.*, voce *f.* ♦ **to have a s. in the matter** aver voce in capitolo; **to have one's s.** dire la propria
to **say** [seɪ] (*pass. e p. p.* **said**) *v. tr. e intr.* dire
saying ['seɪɪŋ] *s.* detto *m.*, proverbio *m.*
scab [skæb] *s.* **1** (*di ferita*) crosta *f.* **2** scabbia *f.*, rogna *f.* **3** (*fam.*) crumiro *m.*
scabrous ['skeɪbrəs] *agg.* scabroso
scaffold ['skæf(ə)ld] *s.* **1** impalcatura *f.*, ponteggio *m.* **2** patibolo *m.*
scald [skɜːld] *s.* scottatura *f.*
to **scald** [skɜːld] *v. tr.* scottare, ustionare
scalding ['skɜːldɪŋ] **A** *agg.* bollente **B** *s.* scottatura *f.*, ustione *f.*
scale (1) [skeɪl] *s.* **1** piatto *m.* di bilancia **2** *al pl.* bilancia *f.*
scale (2) [skeɪl] *s.* **1** scaglia *f.*, squama *f.* **2** incrostazione *f.*
scale (3) [skeɪl] *s.* **1** scala *f.*, gradazione *f.* **2** (*mus.*) scala *f.*
to **scale (1)** [skeɪl] *v. tr.* pesare, soppesare
to **scale (2)** [skeɪl] *v. tr.* **1** squamare **2** incrostare ♦ **to s. off** scrostarsi
to **scale (3)** [skeɪl] **A** *v. tr.* **1** scalare, arrampicarsi su **2** graduare **B** *v. intr.* arrampicarsi ♦ **to s. down/up** aumentare/diminuire progressivamente
scallion ['skæljən] *s.* scalogno *m.*
scallop ['skələp] *s.* **1** (*zool.*) pettine *m.* **2** conchiglia *f.* di pettine **3** dentellatura *f.*, smerlo *m.*
scalp [skælp] *s.* scalpo *m.*
scalpel ['skælp(ə)l] *s.* scalpello *m.*, bisturi *m.*
to **scan** [skæn] *v. tr.* **1** esaminare, scrutare **2** analizzare **3** scandire
scandal ['skændl] *s.* **1** scandalo *m.* **2** maldicenza *f.* ♦ **to talk s. about sb.** sparlare di qc.
to **scandalize** ['skændəlaɪz] *v. tr.* scandalizzare
scandalmonger ['skændlˌmʌŋgəʳ] *s.* seminatore *m.* di scandali
scandalous ['skændələs] *agg.* scandaloso
Scandinavian [ˌskændɪ'neɪvjən] *agg. e s.* scandinavo *m.*
scant [skænt] *agg.* scarso, insufficiente
scanty ['skæntɪ] *agg.* scarso, insufficiente
scapegoat ['skeɪpgɒʊt] *s.* capro *m.* espiatorio
scapula ['skæpjʊlə] *s.* scapola *f.*
scar [skaːʳ] *s.* cicatrice *f.*, sfregio *m.*
to **scar** [skaːʳ] *s.* sfregiare, deturpare
scarce [skɛəs] *agg.* **1** scarso **2** raro, introvabile ♦ **to make oneself s.** squagliarsela
scarcely ['skɛəslɪ] *avv.* appena, a malapena

scarcity ['skɛəsɪtɪ] *s.* **1** scarsezza *f.* **2** rarità *f.*
scare [skɛəʳ] *s.* terrore *m.*, spavento *m.*, allarme *m.*
to scare [skɛəʳ] *v. tr.* spaventare, atterrire
scarecrow ['skɛəkrɒʊ] *s.* spaventapasseri *m.*
scarf [skaːf] *s.* sciarpa *f.*, foulard *m. inv.*
to scarify ['skɛərɪfaɪ] *v. tr.* scarificare
scarlet ['skaːlɪt] *agg.* scarlatto ♦ **s. fever** scarlattina
scarred [skaːd] *agg.* sfregiato
scary ['skærɪ] *agg.* pauroso, terrificante
to scat [skæt] *v. intr.* (*fam.*) svignarsela
scathing ['skeɪðɪŋ] *agg.* aspro, pungente
to scatter ['skætəʳ] **A** *v. tr.* **1** spargere, cospargere **2** disperdere **B** *v. intr.* **1** spargersi, sparpagliarsi **2** disperdersi
scatterbrain ['skætəbreɪn] *s.* sbadato *m.*
to scavenge ['skævɪn(d)ʒ] *v. tr.* **1** pulire dai rifiuti **2** frugare tra i rifiuti **3** scovare
scenario [sɪ'naːrɪɒʊ] *s.* sceneggiatura *f.*
scene [siːn] *s.* scena *f.* ♦ **s. painter** scenografo
scenery ['siːnərɪ] *s.* **1** scena *f.*, scenario *m.* **2** veduta *f.*
scenic ['siːnɪk] agg. **1** scenico **2** panoramico, pittoresco
scenographer [sɪ'nəgrəfəʳ] *s.* scenografo *m.*
scenographic [ˌsiːnɒ(ʊ)'græfɪk] *agg.* scenografico
scenography [sɪ'nəgrəfɪ] *s.* scenografia *f.*
scent [sɛnt] *s.* **1** odore *m.*, profumo *m.* **2** (*miscela*) profumo *m.* **3** pista *f.*, scia *f.* **4** odorato *m.*
to scent [sɛnt] *v. tr.* **1** fiutare **2** (*fig.*) subodorare **3** profumare
sceptical ['skɛptɪk(ə)l] *agg.* scettico
scepticism ['skɛptɪsɪz(ə)m] *s.* scetticismo *m.*
sceptre ['sɛptəʳ] *s.* scettro *m.*
schedule ['ʃɛdjuːl] *s.* **1** tabella *f.*, elenco *m.*, distinta *f.* **2** programma *m.*, piano *m.*, orario *m.*
to schedule ['ʃɛdjuːl] *v. tr.* **1** elencare, includere in una lista **2** programmare ♦ **scheduled flight** volo di linea
schematic [skɪ'mætɪk] *agg.* schematico
scheme [skiːm] *s.* **1** schema *m.*, progetto *m.* **2** disposizione *f.*, sistema *m.* **3** intrigo *m.* **4** abbozzo *m.*
to scheme [skiːm] *v. tr. e intr.* **1** pianificare **2** complottare
scheming ['skiːmɪŋ] *agg.* intrigante
schism ['sɪz(ə)m] *s.* scisma *m.*
schizophrenia [ˌskɪtsɒ(ʊ)'friːnjə] *s.* schizofrenia *f.*
schizophrenic [ˌskɪtsɒ(ʊ)'frɛnɪk] *agg. e s.* schizofrenico *m.*
scholar ['skələʳ] *s.* **1** studioso *m.*, erudito *m.* **2** borsista *m. e f.*
scholarship ['skələʃɪp] *s.* **1** dottrina *f.* **2** borsa *f.* di studio
scholastic [skə'læstɪk] *agg.* **1** scolastico **2** accademico
school [skuːl] *s.* scuola *f.* ♦ **s. age** età scolare; **s.-days** giorni di scuola; **s.-friend** compagno di scuola
schoolboy ['skuːlbəɪ] *s.* scolaro *m.*
schoolgirl ['skuːlgɜːl] *s.* scolara *f.*
schoolroom ['skuːlrʊm] *s.* aula *f.*
schoolteacher ['skuːlˌtiːtʃəʳ] *s.* insegnante *m. e f.*
schooner ['skuːnəʳ] *s.* goletta *f.*
sciatica [saɪ'ætɪkə] *s.* sciatica *f.*
science ['saɪəns] *s.* scienza *f.* ♦ **s. fiction** fantascienza
scientific [ˌsaɪən'tɪfɪk] *agg.* scientifico
scientist ['saɪəntɪst] *s.* scienziato *m.*
scissors ['sɪzəz] *s. pl.* forbici *f. pl.*
sclerosis [sklɪə'rɒʊsɪs] *s.* sclerosi *f.*
scoff [skəf] *s.* beffa *f.*
to scoff (1) [skəf] *v. intr.* farsi beffe
to scoff (2) [skəf] *v. tr.* (*fam.*) ingozzarsi
to scold [skɒʊld] *v. tr.* rimproverare, sgridare
scolding ['skɒʊldɪŋ] *s.* rimprovero *m.*
scoliosis [ˌskəlɪ'ɒʊsɪs] *s.* scoliosi *f.*
scoop [skuːp] *s.* **1** cucchiaione *m.*, mestolo *m.*, paletta *f.* **2** cucchiaiata *f.*, mestolata *f.*, palettata *f.* **3** (*fam.*) colpo *m.* di fortuna **4** scoop *m. inv.*
to scoop [skuːp] *v. tr.* **1** (*con mestolo e sim.*) tirare su, raccogliere **2** cavare **3** battere con uno scoop
scooter ['skuːtəʳ] *s.* **1** monopattino *m.* **2** scooter *m. inv.*
scope [skɒʊp] *s.* **1** possibilità *f.*, opportunità *f.* **2** portata *f.*, ambito *m.*
scorch [skɜːtʃ] *s.* bruciatura *f.*, scottatura *f.*
to scorch [skɜːtʃ] *v. tr.* **1** bruciacchiare, scottare **2** inaridire, seccare
score [skɜːʳ] *s.* **1** linea *f.*, segno *m.*, tratto *m.* **2** punto *m.*, punteggio *m.*, votazione *f.* **3** (*mus.*) spartito *m.*, partitura *f.* **4** (*fam.*) colpo *m.* di fortuna **5** ventina *f.* **6** *al pl.* grande quantità *f.* **7** causa *f.*, motivo *m.* ♦

half a s. una decina; **on the s. of** a causa di; **scores of** un mucchio di; **to keep the s.** segnare i punti
to score [skɜːʳ] *v. tr.* **1** segnare, marcare **2** (*sport*) segnare, fare (un punto) **3** ottenere, riportare **4** (*mus.*) orchestrare ♦ **to s. out** cancellare; **to s. up** mettere in conto, registrare
scoreboard ['skɜːbɜːd] *s.* tabellone *m.* segnapunti
scorekeeper ['skɜːˌkiːpəʳ] *s.* segnapunti *m. inv.*
scoria ['skɜːrɪə] *s.* scoria *f.*
scorn [skɜːn] *s.* disprezzo *m.*
to scorn [skɜːn] *v. tr.* disprezzare
scornful [skɜːnf(ʊ)l] *agg.* sprezzante
Scorpio ['skɜːpɪɒʊ] *s.* (*astr*) Scorpione *m.*
scorpion ['skɜːpjən] *s.* scorpione *m.*
Scot [skət] *s.* scozzese *m. e f.*
Scotch [skətʃ] **A** *agg.* scozzese **B** *s.* **1 the S.** gli scozzesi *m. pl.* **2** scotch *m. inv.*, whisky *m. inv.* scozzese
to scotch (1) [skətʃ] *v. tr.* **1** colpire **2** mettere a tacere, rendere innocuo
to scotch (2) [skətʃ] *v. tr.* **1** bloccare (con una zeppa) **2** impedire, ostacolare
Scots [skəts] *agg.* scozzese
Scotsman ['skətsmən] (*pl.* **Scotsmen**) *s.* scozzese *m.*
Scottish ['skətɪʃ] *agg.* (*di cose*) scozzese
scoundrel ['skaʊndr(ə)l] *s.* mascalzone *m.*
to scour (1) ['skaʊəʳ] *v. tr.* **1** strofinare, lucidare **2** sgombrare
to scour (2) ['skaʊəʳ] *v. tr.* **1** percorrere **2** perlustrare
scourge [skɜːdʒ] *s.* **1** frusta *f.* **2** flagello *m.*
to scourge [skɜːdʒ] *v. tr.* **1** frustare **2** affliggere
scout [skaʊt] *s.* **1** esploratore *m.* **2** scout *m. inv.* **3** aereo *m.* (o nave *f.*) da ricognizione
to scout [skaʊt] *v. intr.* andare in esplorazione ♦ **to s. around for** andare in cerca di
scouting ['skaʊtɪŋ] *s.* **1** esplorazione *f.* **2** scoutismo *m.*
scowl [skaʊl] *s.* cipiglio *m.*, sguardo *m.* minaccioso
to scowl [skaʊl] *v. intr.* accigliarsi
to scrabble ['skræbl] *v. intr.* **1** raspare, grattare **2** frugare, rovistare
scraggy ['skrægɪ] *agg.* scheletrico
to scram [skræm] *v. intr.* (*pop.*) battersela
scramble ['skræmbl] *s.* **1** arrampicata *f.* **2** gara *f.*, mischia *f.*
to scramble ['skræmbl] **A** *v. intr.* **1** arrampicarsi **2** affrettarsi **3** accapigliarsi **B** *v. tr.* **1** mescolare **2** (*cuc.*) strapazzare ♦ **scrambled eggs** uova strapazzate
scrap (1) [skræp] *s.* **1** pezzo *m.*, frammento *m.* **2** avanzo *m.*, scarto *m.*, (*di giornale*) ritaglio *m.* **3** rottame *m.* ♦ **s. metal** ferraglia
scrap (2) [skræp] *s.* (*fam.*) bisticcio *m.*
to scrap (1) [skræp] *v. tr.* **1** smantellare, demolire **2** scartare
to scrap (2) [skræp] *v. intr.* (*fam.*) bisticciare
scrape [skreɪp] *s.* **1** graffio *m.*, scorticatura *f.* **2** raschiatura *f.* **3** stridore *m.* **4** (*fam.*) guaio *m.*, impiccio *m.*
to scrape [skreɪp] *v. tr.* **1** raschiare, grattare **2** scorticare **3** raggranellare ♦ **to s. along** tirare avanti; **to s. through** farcela a malapena **to s. together** raggranellare
scraper [skreɪpəʳ] *s.* raschietto *m.*
scrap-heap ['skræpˌhiːp] *s.* mucchio *m.* di rifiuti ♦ **on the s.** nel dimenticatoio
scraping ['skreɪpɪŋ] *s.* raschiatura *f.*, scrostatura *f.*
scrappy ['skræpɪ] *agg.* frammentario, sconnesso
scratch [skrætʃ] **A** *agg.* raffazzonato, raccogliticcio **B** *s.* **1** graffio *m.* **2** sgorbio *m.* **3** grattata *f.* **4** linea *f.* di partenza ♦ **to start from s.** cominciare da zero
to scratch [skrætʃ] *v. tr.* **1** graffiare **2** grattare
scrawl [skrɜːl] *s.* scarabocchio *m.*
to scrawl [skrɜːl] *v. tr. e intr.* scarabocchiare
scrawly ['skrɜːlɪ] *agg.* pieno di scarabocchi
scrawny ['skrɜːnɪ] *agg.* magro, ossuto
scream [skriːm] *s.* grido *m.*
to scream [skriːm] *v. tr. e intr.* gridare
to screech [skriːtʃ] *v. intr.* **1** gridare **2** stridere
screen [skriːn] *s.* **1** cortina *f.*, riparo *m.*, paravento *m.* **2** schermo *m.* **3** vaglio *m.* ♦ **wide s.** schermo panoramico
to screen [skriːn] *v. tr.* **1** riparare, proteggere **2** schermare **3** setacciare, selezionare **4** (*cine.*) proiettare
screening ['skriːnɪŋ] *s.* **1** schermatura *f.* **2** proiezione *f.* **3** selezione *f.* **4** (*med.*) controllo *m.* (*a scopo diagnostico*)
screenplay ['skriːnˌpleɪ] *s.* sceneggiatura *f.*
screenwriter ['skriːnˌraɪtəʳ] *s.* sceneggiatore *m.*

screw [skruː] *s.* **1** (*mecc.*) vite *f.* **2** giro *m.* (di vite) **3** elica *f.* ♦ **s. thread** filettatura
to screw [skruː] *v. tr.* **1** avvitare **2** torcere, accartocciare ♦ **to s. up** accartocciare, rovinare
screwdriver ['skruːˌdraɪvəʳ] *s.* cacciavite *m. inv.*
scribble ['skrɪbl] *s.* scarabocchio *m.*
to scribble ['skrɪbl] *v. tr. e intr.* scarabocchiare
script [skrɪpt] *s.* **1** testo *m.*, manoscritto *m.*, copione *m.* **2** esame *m.* scritto ♦ **s. writer** sceneggiatore
scripture ['skrɪptʃəʳ] *s.* (la Sacra) Scrittura *f.*
scroll [skrɒʊl] *s.* **1** (*di carta*) rotolo *m.* **2** (*arch.*) voluta *f.*
to scrounge ['skraʊn(d)ʒ] *v. tr.* scroccare
scrub (1) [skrʌb] *s.* boscaglia *f.*
scrub (2) [skrʌb] *s.* spazzolata *f.*, pulitura *f.*
to scrub [skrʌb] *v. tr.* **1** pulire sfregando **2** annullare
scruff [skrʌf] *s.* collottola *f.*
scruffy ['skrʌfɪ] *agg.* (*fam.*) trasandato
scrum(mage) ['skrʌm(ɪdʒ)] *s.* (*sport*) mischia *f.*
scruple ['skruːpl] *s.* scrupolo *m.*
scrupulous ['skruːpjʊləs] *agg.* scrupoloso
scrutiny ['skruːtɪnɪ] *s.* esame *m.* minuzioso
scuba ['skjuːbə] *s.* autorespiratore *m.*
to scuff [skʌf] *v. tr.* **1** (*i piedi*) strascicare **2** (*le scarpe*) consumare
scuffle ['skʌfl] *s.* mischia *f.*, tafferuglio *m.*
to scuffle ['skʌfl] *v. intr.* azzuffarsi
sculptor ['skʌlptəʳ] *s.* scultore *m.*
sculptural ['skʌlptʃ(ə)r(ə)l] *agg.* scultoreo
sculpture ['skʌlptʃəʳ] *s.* scultura *f.*
to sculpture ['skʌlptʃəʳ] *v. tr.* scolpire
scum [skʌm] *s.* **1** schiuma *f.* superficiale **2** (*fig.*) feccia *f.*
scurrilous ['skʌrɪləs] *agg.* scurrile
to scurry ['skʌrɪ] *v. intr.* correre velocemente
scurvy ['skɜːvɪ] *s.* scorbuto *m.*
to scuttle ['skʌtl] *v. intr.* correr via
scythe [saɪð] *s.* falce *f.*
sea [siː] *s.* mare *m.* ♦ **s. level** livello del mare; **s. mile** miglio marino; **s. quake** maremoto; **s. storm** mareggiata; **s. urchin** riccio di mare
seabird ['siːbɜːd] *s.* uccello *m.* marino
seaboard ['siːbɜːd] *s.* costa *f.*, litorale *m.*
seafood ['siːfuːd] *s.* frutti *m. pl.* di mare
seafront ['siːfrʌnt] *s.* lungomare *m.*
seagull ['siːgʌl] *s.* gabbiano *m.*
seahorse ['siːˌhɜːs] *s.* ippocampo *m.*
seal (1) [siːl] *s.* foca *f.*
seal (2) [siːl] *s.* sigillo *m.*
to seal [siːl] *v. tr.* sigillare ♦ **to s. in** chiudere dentro; **to s. off** isolare (*una zona*)
seam [siːm] *s.* **1** cucitura *f.*, giuntura *f.* **2** (*miner.*) filone *m.*, strato *m.*
seaman ['siːmən] (*pl.* **seamen**) *s.* marinaio *m.*
seamy ['siːmɪ] *agg.* **1** provvisto di cuciture **2** squallido
seaplane ['siːˌpleɪn] *s.* idrovolante *m.*
search [sɜːtʃ] *s.* **1** ricerca *f.* **2** perquisizione *f.* ♦ **s. warrant** mandato di perquisizione
to search [sɜːtʃ] **A** *v. tr.* **1** perquisire, perlustrare **2** frugare, rovistare **B** *v. intr.* andare in cerca di ♦ **to s. about/through** frugare; **to s. out** scovare
searching ['sɜːtʃɪŋ] **A** *agg.* **1** penetrante, scrutatore **2** approfondito, minuzioso **B** *s.* **1** esame *m.*, indagine *f.* **2** perlustrazione *f.*
searchlight ['sɜːtʃˌlaɪt] *s.* riflettore *m.*
seashore ['siːʃɜːʳ] *s.* spiaggia *f.*, lido *m.*
seasickness ['siːˌsɪknɪs] *s.* mal *m.* di mare
seaside ['siːˌsaɪd] *s.* spiaggia *f.*, lido *m.* ♦ **s. resort** stazione balneare; **to go to the s.** andare al mare
season ['siːzn] *s.* **1** stagione *f.* **2** epoca *f.*, tempo *m.* ♦ **high/low s.** alta/bassa stagione; **out of s.** fuori stagione; **s. ticket** abbonamento; **off s.** fuori stagione
to season ['siːzn] *v. tr.* **1** condire, insaporire **2** stagionare, far maturare
seasonal ['siːzənl] *agg.* stagionale
seasoned ['siːzənd] *agg.* **1** stagionato **2** condito **3** abituato, esperto
seasoning ['siːznɪŋ] *s.* **1** condimento *m.* **2** stagionatura *f.*
seat [siːt] *s.* **1** sedile *m.*, sedia *f.*, posto *m.* (a sedere) **2** seggio *m.* **3** didietro *m.*, fondo *m.* **4** sede *f.* ♦ **s. belt** cintura di sicurezza
to seat [siːt] *v. tr.* **1** far sedere **2** insediare, collocare **3** (*posti a sedere*) disporre di
seawards ['siːwədz] *avv.* verso il mare
seaweed ['siːwiːd] *s.* alga *f.* marina
sebaceous [sɪ'beɪʃəs] *agg.* sebaceo
secession [sɪ'sɛʃ(ə)n] *s.* secessione *f.*
secessionism [sɪ'sɛʃnɪz(ə)m] *s.* secessionismo *m.*
to seclude [sɪ'kluːd] *v. tr.* isolare, appartare
secluded [sɪ'kluːdɪd] *agg.* isolato, appartato

seclusion [sɪ'kluːʒ(ə)n] *s.* **1** isolamento *m.* **2** clausura *f.*
second ['sɛk(ə)nd] **A** *agg.* **1** secondo **2** secondario, inferiore **3** nuovo, altro **B** *s.* **1** secondo *m.* **2** (minuto) secondo *m.* **C** *avv.* secondariamente ♦ **s. born** secondogenito; **s.-class** di seconda classe, di qualità scadente; **s.-hand** usato, di seconda mano; **s.-rate** scadente; **s. thoughts** ripensamento
to second (1) ['sɛk(ə)nd] *v. tr.* assecondare, favorire
to second (2) ['sɛk(ə)nd] *v. tr.* distaccare (*ad altro incarico*)
secondary ['sɛk(ə)nd(ə)rɪ] *agg.* secondario
seconder [sɪ'k(ə)ndəʳ] *s.* sostenitore *m.*
secondly ['sɛk(ə)ndlɪ] *avv.* in secondo luogo
secrecy ['siːkrɪsɪ] *s.* segretezza *f.*
secret ['siːkrɪt] *agg. e s.* segreto *m.* ♦ **to keep a s.** mantenere un segreto
secretariat [ˌsɛkrə'tɛərɪət] *s.* segretariato *m.*
secretary ['sɛkrətrɪ] *s.* segretario *m.*, segretaria *f.*
to secrete [sɪ'kriːt] *v. tr.* secernere
secretion [sɪ'kriːʃ(ə)n] *s.* secrezione *f.*
secretive [sɪ'kriːtɪv] *agg.* riservato, segreto
sect [sɛkt] *s.* setta *f.*
sectarian [sɛk'tɛərɪən] *s.* settario *m.*
section ['sɛkʃ(ə)n] *s.* **1** sezione *f.*, porzione *f.*, parte *f.* **2** paragrafo *m.* **3** (*geom.*) sezione *f.*
sector ['sɛktəʳ] *s.* settore *m.*
secular ['sɛkjʊləʳ] *agg.* secolare, laico
secure [sɪ'kjuːəʳ] *agg.* **1** sicuro, certo **2** (*dir.*) garantito **3** saldo, ben fermato
to secure [sɪ'kjʊəʳ] *v. tr.* **1** assicurare, difendere **2** (*dir.*) garantire **3** assicurare, fissare **4** assicurarsi, ottenere, procurarsi
security [sɪ'kjʊərɪtɪ] *s.* **1** sicurezza *f.*, certezza *f.* **2** protezione *f.*, difesa *f.* **3** garanzia *f.*, cauzione *f.* ♦ **social s.** previdenza sociale
sedan [sɪ'dæn] *s.* **1** (*USA*) berlina *f.* **2** portantina *f.*
sedate [sɪ'deɪt] *agg.* calmo, posato
sedative ['sɛdətɪv] *agg. e s.* sedativo *m.*
sedentary ['sɛdnt(ə)rɪ] *agg.* sedentario
sediment ['sɛdɪmənt] *s.* sedimento *m.*
sedition [sɪ'dɪʃ(ə)n] *s.* sedizione *f.*
to seduce [sɪ'djuːs] *v. tr.* sedurre, corrompere
seducer [sɪ'djuːsəʳ] *s.* seduttore *m.*
seduction [sɪ'dʌkʃ(ə)n] *s.* seduzione *f.*
seductive [sɪ'dʌktɪv] *agg.* seducente
to see [siː] (*pass.* **saw**, *p. p.* **seen**) **A** *v. tr.* **1** vedere **2** capire, rendersi conto di **3** esaminare, osservare **4** visitare **5** accompagnare **B** *v. intr.* **1** vedere, vederci **2** capire, accorgersi **3** pensare **4** fare in modo ♦ **s. you (later)** ci vediamo (più tardi); **to s. about** occuparsi di: **to s. off** salutare (alla partenza); **to s. out** accompagnare alla porta; **to s. to** occuparsi di
seed [siːd] *s.* seme *m.*, semenza *f.*
seeding ['siːdɪŋ] *s.* semina *f.*
seedling ['siːdlɪŋ] *s.* piantina *f.*
to seek [siːk] (*pass. e p. p.* **sought**) *v. tr.* **1** cercare **2** chiedere **3** tentare di ♦ **to s. out** scovare
to seem [siːm] *v. intr.* sembrare, parere
seemingly ['siːmɪŋlɪ] *avv.* apparentemente
seen [siːn] *p. p. di* **to see**
to seep [siːp] *v. intr.* gocciolare, filtrare
seer ['siːəʳ] *s.* veggente *m. e f.*
seesaw ['siːˌsɜː] **A** *agg.* ondeggiante **B** *s.* altalena *f.*
to seethe [siːð] *v. intr.* ribollire
see-through ['siːθruː] *agg.* (*di indumento*) trasparente
segment ['sɛgmənt] *s.* segmento *m.*
to segregate ['sɛgrɪgeɪt] *v. tr.* segregare
segregation [ˌsɛgrɪ'geɪʃ(ə)n] *s.* segregazione *f.*
seismic(al) ['saɪzmɪk((ə)l)] *agg.* sismico
seismologist [saɪz'mələdʒɪst] *s.* sismologo *m.*
to seize [siːz] *v. tr.* **1** afferrare, impadronirsi di **2** (*dir.*) confiscare ♦ **to s. on** appigliarsi a; **to s. up** gripparsi, bloccarsi
seizure ['siːʒəʳ] *s.* **1** presa *f.*, conquista *f.*, cattura *f.* **2** (*dir.*) confisca *f.* **3** (*med.*) attacco *m.* **4** (*mecc.*) grippaggio *m.*
seldom ['sɛldəm] *avv.* raramente
select [sɪ'lɛkt] *agg.* scelto, selezionato
to select [sɪ'lɛkt] *v. tr.* scegliere, selezionare
selection [sɪ'lɛkʃ(ə)n] *s.* scelta *f.*, selezione *f.*
selective [sɪ'lɛktɪv] *agg.* selettivo
self (1) [sɛlf] (*pl.* **selves**) *s.* l'io *m.*, l'individuo *m.* ♦ **one's better s.** la parte migliore di sé
self (2) [sɛlf] *agg.* **1** della stessa sostanza **2** dello stesso colore
self- [sɛlf] *pref.* da sé, automatico, auto- ♦ **s.-acting** automatico; **s.-centred** ego-

centrico; **s.-confidence** fiducia in sé; **s.-consistent** coerente; **s.-control** autocontrollo; **s.-defence** autodifesa; **s.-employed** che lavora in proprio; **s.-explanatory** che si spiega da sé; **s.-government** autogoverno; **s.-interest** interesse personale; **s.-made** che si è fatto da sé; **s.-portrait** autoritratto; **s.-respect** amor proprio; **s.-sticking** autoadesivo; **s.-sufficient** autosufficiente; **s.-taught** autodidatta; **s.-willed** ostinato

to sell [sɛl] (*pass. e p. p.* **sold**) *v. tr.* vendere ♦ **to s. off** svendere; **to be sold out** essere esaurito

seller ['sɛləʳ] *s.* venditore *m.*

selling ['sɛlɪŋ] *s.* vendita *f.* ♦ **s. off** svendita

selves [sɛlvz] *pl. di* **self**

semaphore ['sɛməfɜːʳ] *s.* **1** sistema *m.* di segnalazione con bandierine **2** (*ferr.*) semaforo *m.*

semblance ['sɛmbləns] *s.* **1** apparenza *f.* **2** somiglianza *f.*

semen ['siːmən] s. sperma *m.*

semester [sɪ'mɛstəʳ] *s.* semestre *m.*

semiaxis [ˌsɛmɪ'æksɪs] *s.* semiasse *m.*

semicircle ['sɛmɪˌsɜːkəl] *s.* semicerchio *m.*

semicircular [ˌsɛmɪ'sɜːkjʊləʳ] *agg.* semicircolare

semicolon [ˌsɛmɪ'kɒʊlən] *s.* punto e virgola *m.*

semiconductor [ˌsɛmɪkən'dʌktəʳ] *s.* semiconduttore *m.*

semifinal [ˌsɛmɪ'faɪnl] *s.* semifinale *f.*

seminar ['sɛmɪnaːʳ] *s.* seminario *m.* (*di studio*)

seminarist ['sɛmɪnərɪst] *s.* (*relig.*) seminarista *m.*

seminary ['sɛmɪnərɪ] *s.* (*relig.*) seminario *m.*

semolina [ˌsɛmə'liːnə] *s.* semolino *m.*

senate ['sɛnɪt] *s.* senato *m.*

senator ['sɛnətəʳ] *s.* senatore *m.*

to send [sɛnd] (*pass. e p. p.* **sent**) *v. tr.* mandare, inviare, spedire ♦ **to s. away** scacciare; **to s. away for** ordinare per posta; **to s. back** restituire; **to s. for** mandare a chiamare; **to s. off** spedire; **to s. out** distribuire, far circolare; **to s. up** far salire, prendere in giro

sender ['sɛndəʳ] *s.* mittente *m. e f.*

send-off ['sɛndˌɜːf] *s.* festa *f.* di commiato

senile ['siːnaɪl] *agg.* senile

senility [sɪ'nɪlɪtɪ] *s.* senilità *f.*

senior ['siːnɪəʳ] *agg.* **1** più vecchio, più anziano **2** (*abbr* **sen.**, **sr.**) senior, padre, fratello maggiore

seniority [ˌsiːnɪ'ɔrɪtɪ] *s.* anzianità *f.*

sensation [sɛn'seɪʃ(ə)n] *s.* sensazione *f.*

sensational [sɛn'seɪʃənl] *agg.* sensazionale

sense [sɛns] *s.* **1** senso *m.* **2** sensazione *f.* **3** significato *m.* **4** opinione *f.* comune, buonsenso *m.*

sensibility [ˌsɛnsɪ'bɪlɪtɪ] *s.* sensibilità *f.*

sensible ['sɛnsəbl] *agg.* **1** sensato, ragionevole **2** sensibile, percepibile

sensitive ['sɛnsɪtɪv] *agg.* **1** sensibile **2** permaloso, suscettibile

sensual ['sɛnsjʊəl] *agg.* sensuale

sensuality [ˌsɛnsjʊ'ælɪtɪ] *s.* sensualità *f.*

sensuous ['sɛnsjʊəs] *agg.* sensuale, voluttuoso

sent [sɛnt] *pass. e p. p. di* **to send**

sentence ['sɛntəns] *s.* **1** sentenza *f.*, condanna *f.* **2** (*gramm.*) frase *f.*

to sentence ['sɛntəns] *v. tr.* pronunciare una sentenza, condannare

sentiment ['sɛntɪmənt] *s.* **1** sentimento *m.* **2** opinione *f.*

sentimental [ˌsɛntɪ'mɛntl] *agg.* sentimentale

sentry ['sɛntrɪ] *s.* sentinella *f.* ♦ **s. box** garitta

separate ['sɛprɪt] **A** *agg.* **1** separato, staccato **2** distinto **B** *s. al pl.* (*di abiti*) coordinati *m. pl.*

to separate ['sɛpəreɪt] *v. tr. e intr.* separare, separarsi

separation [ˌsɛpə'reɪʃ(ə)n] *s.* separazione *f.*

separator ['sɛpəreɪtəʳ] *s.* separatore *m.*

sepia ['siːpjə] *s.* nero *m.* di seppia

September [səp'tɛmbəʳ] *s.* settembre *m.*

septic ['sɛptɪk] *agg.* settico ♦ **to go s.** infettarsi

septic(a)emia [ˌsɛptɪ'siːmjə] *s.* setticemia *f.*

septum ['sɛptəm] *s.* setto *m.*

sepulchral [sɪ'pʌlkr(ə)l] *agg.* sepolcrale

sepulchre ['sɛp(ə)lkəʳ] *s.* sepolcro *m.*

sepulture ['sɛp(ə)ltʃəʳ] *s.* sepoltura *f.*

sequel ['siːkw(ə)l] *s.* **1** seguito *m.* **2** effetto *m.*

sequence ['siːkwəns] *s.* sequenza *f.*, successione *f.*, serie *f.*

to sequestrate [sɪ'kwɛstreɪt] *v. tr.* sequestrare

sequestration [ˌsiːkwɛs'treɪʃ(ə)n] *s.* sequestro *m.*

sequin ['siːkwɪn] *s.* lustrino *m.*

serene [sɪ'riːn] *agg.* sereno

serenity [sɪ'rɛnɪtɪ] *s.* serenità *f.*

sergeant ['saːdʒ(ə)nt] *s.* **1** sergente *m.* **2** (*di polizia*) brigadiere *m.*

serial ['sɪərɪəl] **A** *agg.* **1** seriale, in serie **2** a puntate, a fascicoli **B** *s.* **1** sceneggiato *m.*, serial *m. inv.* **2** romanzo *m.* a puntate

to **serialize** ['sɪərɪəlaɪz] *v. tr.* pubblicare (o trasmettere) a puntate

series ['sɪəriːz] *s. inv.* serie *f. inv.*

serious ['sɪərɪəs] *agg.* **1** serio **2** grave

seriousness ['sɪərɪəsnɪs] *s.* **1** serietà *f.* **2** gravità *f.*

sermon ['sɜːmən] *s.* sermone *m.*

to **sermonize** ['sɜːmənaɪz] *v. intr.* **1** predicare **2** fare la predica

serotherapy [ˌsɪərɒ(ʊ)'θɛrəpɪ] *s.* sieroterapia *f.*

serpent ['sɜːp(ə)nt] *s.* serpente *m.*

serpentine ['sɜːp(ə)ntaɪn] **A** *agg.* serpentino, serpeggiante **B** *s.* serpentina *f.*

serrate ['sɛrɪt] *agg.* dentellato, seghettato

serrated [sɛ'reɪtɪd] *agg.* → **serrate**

serum ['sɪərəm] *s.* siero *m.*

servant ['sɜːv(ə)nt] *s.* **1** domestico *m.*, cameriere *m.* **2** (*fig.*) servitore *m.* **3** impiegato *m.* ♦ **civil s.** dipendente pubblico

to **serve** [sɜːv] **A** *v. tr.* **1** servire, offrire **2** essere al servizio di **3** essere utile a **4** espiare, scontare **B** *v. intr.* **1** prestare servizio **2** servire, essere utile **3** (*sport*) servire ♦ **to s. out** distribuire, servire

service ['sɜːvɪs] *s.* **1** servizio *m.*, prestazione *f.* **2** favore *m.* **3** *al pl.* servizi *m. pl.* **4** assistenza *f.*, manutenzione *f.* **5** (*di posate*) servizio *m.* ♦ **s. charge** (*al ristorante*) servizio; **s. station** stazione di servizio

to **service** ['sɜːvɪs] *v. tr.* **1** revisionare **2** fornire

serviceable ['sɜːvɪsəbl] *agg.* **1** utile, pratico **2** resistente

serviette [ˌsɜːvɪ'ɛt] *s.* tovagliolo *m.*

servile ['sɜːvaɪl] *agg.* servile

servo-brake ['sɜːvəˌbreɪk] *s.* servofreno *m.*

servo-control ['sɜːvɒ(ʊ)kənˌtrɒʊl] *s.* servocomando *m.*

servo-mechanism ['sɜːvɒ(ʊ)ˌmɛkənɪz(ə)m] *s.* servomeccanismo *m.*

servomotor ['sɜːvɒ(ʊ)ˌmɒʊtə^r] *s.* servomotore *m.*

sesame ['sɛsəmɪ] *s.* sesamo *m.*

session ['sɛʃ(ə)n] *s.* **1** sessione *f.*, seduta *f.* **2** anno *m.* accademico

set [sɛt] **A** *agg.* **1** fisso, saldo, stabilito **2** posto, collocato **3** studiato, preparato **4** pronto **B** *s.* **1** complesso *m.*, insieme *m.*, assortimento *m.*, collezione *f.*, serie *f.*, (*di posate, biancheria, ecc.*) set *m. inv.* **2** (*di persone*) gruppo *m.* **3** (*radio, TV*) apparecchio *m.* **4** (*tennis*) set *m. inv.* **5** posizione *f.* **6** messa *f.* in piega **7** (*cine., teatro*) set *m. inv.*, scene *f. pl.* **8** tendenza *f.*, direzione *f.* **9** (*bot.*) pianticella *f.* **10** (*mat.*) insieme *m.*

to **set** [sɛt] (*pass. e p. p.* **set**) **A** *v. tr.* **1** mettere, porre, disporre, collocare **2** piantare, conficcare **3** regolare, registrare, mettere a punto, preparare **4** assegnare **5** fissare, stabilire **6** indurire, rendere solido **7** incastonare, montare **8** (*inf.*) impostare **B** *v. intr.* **1** tramontare **2** indurirsi, solidificarsi **3** volgersi, muoversi ♦ **to s. about** accingersi a; **to s. against** mettere contro; **to s. aside** mettere da parte, lasciare da parte; **to s. back** bloccare, ritardare, mettere indietro, (*fam.*) costare; **to s. in** incominciare; **to s. off** far scoppiare, far risaltare, partire; **to s. out** partire, disporre, esporre; **to s. up** installare, costituire, causare, fornire

setback ['sɛtˌbæk] *s.* **1** ostacolo *m.*, intoppo *m.* **2** (*med.*) ricaduta *f.*

set-down ['sɛtˌdaʊn] *s.* rimbrotto *m.*

settee [sɛ'tiː] *s.* divano *m.*

setting ['sɛtɪŋ] *s.* **1** collocazione *f.*, installazione *f.*, sistemazione *f.* **2** incastonatura *f.* **3** regolazione *f.*, messa *f.* a punto **4** messa *f.* in scena, ambientazione *f.* **5** tramonto *m.*

settle ['sɛtl] *s.* cassapanca *f.*

to **settle** ['sɛtl] **A** *v. tr.* **1** decidere, fissare, stabilire, risolvere, definire **2** pagare, saldare **3** sistemare, aggiustare **4** calmare **B** *v. intr.* **1** sistemarsi, accomodarsi **2** stabilirsi, insediarsi **3** calmarsi, ricomporsi **4** depositarsi, decantare, sedimentare **5** abbassarsi, assestarsi ♦ **to s. down** adagiarsi, calmarsi, stabilirsi, stabilizzarsi; **to s. in** sistemarsi; **to s. up** saldare (il conto)

settlement ['sɛtlmənt] *s.* **1** sistemazione *f.*, accordo *m.*, soluzione *f.* **2** saldo *m.*, liquidazione *f.* **3** insediamento *m.*, coloniz-

zazione *f.*, colonia *f.*
settler ['sɛtləʳ] *s.* **1** colonizzatore *m.* **2** (*fam.*) argomento *m.* decisivo
set-up ['sɛt,ʌp] *s.* **1** organizzazione *f.*, sistemazione *f.* **2** situazione *f.*
seven ['sɛvn] *agg. num. card. e s.* sette *m. inv.*
seventeen [,sɛvn'tiːn] *agg. num. card. e s.* diciassette *m. inv.*
seventeenth [,sɛvn'tiːnθ] *agg. num. ord. e s.* diciassettesimo *m.*
seventh ['sɛvnθ] *agg. num. ord. e s.* settimo *m.*
seventhieth ['sɛvntɪɪθ] *agg. num. ord. e s.* settantesimo *m.*
seventy ['sɛvntɪ] *agg. num. card. e s.* settanta *m. inv.*
several ['sɛvr(ə)l] *agg. e pron.* parecchi, diversi, alcuni
severance ['sɛv(ə)r(ə)ns] *s.* separazione *f.*, rottura *f.* ♦ **s. pay** liquidazione
severe [sɪ'vɪəʳ] *agg.* **1** severo, rigoroso **2** rigido, duro **3** acuto, violento **4** difficile, arduo
severity [sɪ'vɛrɪtɪ] *s.* **1** severità *f.*, rigore *m.* **2** gravità *f.* **3** difficoltà *f.*
to sew [sɒʊ] (*pass.* **sewed**, *p. p.* **sewn**) *v. tr.* cucire ♦ **to s. up** rammendare
sewage ['sjuːɪdʒ] *s.* acque *f. pl.* di scolo
sewer ['sjuːəʳ] *s.* fogna *f.*
sewing ['sɒ(ʊ)ɪŋ] *s.* **1** cucitura *f.* **2** cucito *m.* ♦ **s. machine** macchina per cucire
sewn ['sɒʊn] *p. p. di* **to sew**
sex [sɛks] **A** *s.* sesso *m.* **B** *agg.* sessuale ♦ **to have s. with** avere rapporti sessuali con
sexism ['sɛksɪz(ə)m] *s.* discriminazione *f.* sessuale
sexist ['sɛksɪst] *agg.* sessista
sexologist [,sɛk'ələdʒɪst] *s.* sessuologo *m.*
sexology [,sɛk'ələdʒɪ] *s.* sessuologia *f.*
sextant ['sɛkst(ə)nt] *s.* sestante *m.*
sexual ['sɛksjʊəl] *agg.* sessuale
sexuality [,sɛksjʊ'ælɪtɪ] *s.* sessualità *f.*
sexy ['sɛksɪ] *agg.* (*fam.*) sexy
shabby ['ʃæbɪ] *agg.* **1** malmesso, trasandato **2** meschino
shack [ʃæk] *s.* capanna *f.*
shackles ['ʃæklz] *s. pl.* ferri *m. pl.*, catene *f. pl.*
shade [ʃeɪd] *s.* **1** ombra *f.* **2** sfumatura *f.*
to shade [ʃeɪd] *v. tr.* ombreggiare
shading ['ʃeɪdɪŋ] *s.* **1** ombreggiatura *f.* **2** sfumatura *f.* **3** protezione *f.* (*dalla luce*)
shadow ['ʃædɒʊ] *s.* **1** ombra *f.* **2** spettro *m.* **3** segno *m.*, traccia *f.* **4** pedinatore *m.*
to shadow ['ʃædɒʊ] *v. tr.* **1** ombreggiare **2** oscurare **3** pedinare
shadowy ['ʃædɒ(ʊ)ɪ] *agg.* **1** ombroso, ombreggiato **2** indistinto **3** irreale
shady ['ʃeɪdɪ] *agg.* **1** ombroso, ombreggiato **2** equivoco, losco
shaft [ʃaːft] *s.* **1** asta *f.*, palo *m.*, stanga *f.* **2** freccia *f.*, strale *m.* **3** fusto *m.*, gambo *m.* **4** (*mecc.*) albero *m.* **5** (*miniera*) pozzo *m.*
shaggy ['ʃægɪ] *agg.* irsuto, ruvido
shake [ʃeɪk] *s.* **1** scossa *f.*, scossone *m.* **2** tremito *m.* **3** frappé *m. inv.*, frullato *m.*
to shake [ʃeɪk] (*pass.* **shook**, *p. p.* **shaken**) **A** *v. tr.* **1** agitare, scuotere **2** impressionare **3** (*fam.*) liberarsi di **B** *v. intr.* **1** scuotersi, agitarsi **2** barcollare, traballare ♦ **to s. down** ambientarsi, adattarsi; **to s. hands with sb.** stringere la mano a qc.; **to s. off** scuotersi di dosso, liberarsi di; **to s. up** scuotere
shaking ['ʃeɪkɪŋ] **A** *agg.* **1** che scuote, che agita **2** tremante, traballante **B** *s.* **1** scossone *m.* **2** tremore *m.*
shaky ['ʃeɪkɪ] *agg.* malfermo, traballante
shall [ʃæl, ʃəl] (*pass.* **should**) *v. difett.* **1** (*ausiliare per la formazione del futuro*) (ES: **we s. be in London tomorrow** saremo a Londra domani) **2** (*in frasi interr.*) dovere (ES: **s. I close the door?** devo chiudere la porta?)
shallop ['ʃæləp] *s.* scialuppa *f.*
shallow ['ʃælɒʊ] *agg.* **1** basso, poco profondo **2** (*fig.*) superficiale
sham [ʃæm] **A** *agg.* falso, simulato **B** *s.* **1** finzione *f.*, imitazione *f.* **2** impostore *m.*
shambles ['ʃæmblz] *s. pl.* **1** macello *m.*, carneficina *f.* **2** confusione *f.*
shame [ʃeɪm] *s.* vergogna *f.*
to shame [ʃeɪm] *v. tr.* **1** far vergognare **2** disonorare
shamefaced ['ʃeɪm,feɪst] *agg.* vergognoso, imbarazzato
shameful ['ʃeɪmf(ʊ)l] *agg.* vergognoso
shameless ['ʃeɪmlɪs] *agg.* svergognato
shammy ['ʃæmɪ] **A** *s.* pelle *f.* di daino **B** *agg.* scamosciato
shampoo [ʃæm'puː] *s.* shampoo *m. inv.*
shamrock ['ʃæmrək] *s.* trifoglio *m.*
shank [ʃæŋk] *s.* stinco *m.*
shanty ['ʃæntɪ] *s.* baracca *f.* ♦ **s. town** bidonville
shape [ʃeɪp] *s.* **1** forma *f.*, foggia *f.*, sagoma

f., modello *m.* **2** condizione *f.*, forma *f.* fisica ♦ **to be in s.** essere in forma; **to be out of s.** essere fuori forma
to shape [ʃeɪp] **A** *v. tr.* **1** formare, modellare, plasmare **2** adattare **B** *v. intr.* prendere forma, concretarsi ♦ **to s. up** procedere, darsi da fare
shaped [ʃeɪpt] *agg.* (*nei composti*) a forma di ♦ **leaf-s.** a forma di foglia
shapeless ['ʃeɪplɪs] *agg.* informe
shapely ['ʃeɪplɪ] *agg.* armonioso, ben proporzionato
share [ʃɛəʳ] *s.* **1** parte *f.*, porzione *f.*, quota *f.* **2** (*fin.*) azione *f.*
to share [ʃɛəʳ] **A** *v. tr.* **1** dividere, distribuire **2** condividere, avere in comune **B** *v. intr.* partecipare ♦ **to s. out** distribuire
sharecropping ['ʃɛəˌkrɔpɪŋ] *s.* mezzadria *f.*
shareholder ['ʃɛəˌhoʊldəʳ] *s.* azionista *m.* e *f.*
sharing ['ʃɛərɪŋ] *s.* **1** divisione *f.*, distribuzione *f.* **2** (*econ.*) partecipazione *f.*
shark [ʃaːk] *s.* squalo *m.*
sharp [ʃaːp] **A** *agg.* **1** affilato, acuminato, tagliente **2** (*fig.*) acuto, sveglio, pungente **3** netto, chiaro, marcato **4** secco, brusco, improvviso **5** scaltro, disonesto, privo di scrupoli **6** energico, forte **7** (*mus.*) diesis **B** *avv.* **1** esattamente, in punto **2** bruscamente
to sharpen ['ʃaːp(ə)n] *v. tr.* affilare, aguzzare, appuntire
sharp-eyed ['ʃaːpˌaɪd] *agg.* **1** dalla vista acuta **2** perspicace
to shatter ['ʃætəʳ] **A** *v. tr.* **1** frantumare, infrangere **2** rovinare **B** *v. intr.* frantumarsi, andare in pezzi
shave [ʃeɪv] *s.* rasatura *f.*
to shave [ʃeɪv] **A** *v. tr.* **1** radere, rasare, sbarbare **2** tagliare, affettare **3** pareggiare, lisciare, piallare **4** rasentare **5** ridurre leggermente **B** *v. intr.* radersi
shaver ['ʃeɪvəʳ] *s.* **1** rasoio *m.* (elettrico) **2** barbiere *m.*
shaving ['ʃeɪvɪŋ] *s.* rasatura *f.* ♦ **s. brush** pennello da barba; **s. foam** schiuma da barba
shawl [ʃɔːl] *s.* scialle *m.*
she [ʃiː] **A** *pron. pers. 3ª sing. f.* ella, lei **B** *s.* femmina *f.*
sheaf [ʃiːf] (*pl.* **sheaves**) *s.* **1** covone *m.* **2** fascio *m.*
to shear [ʃɪəʳ] (*pass.* **sheared**, *p. p.* **shorn**, **sheared**) *v. tr.* **1** tosare **2** tagliare, recidere
shears [ʃɪəʳz] *s.* cesoie *f. pl.*
sheath [ʃiːθ] *s.* guaina *f.*, fodero *m.*
sheaves [ʃiːvz] *pl. di* **sheaf**
shed [ʃɛd] *s.* capannone *m.*
to shed [ʃɛd] (*pass. e p. p.* **shed**) *v. tr.* **1** spargere, versare **2** perdere, lasciar cadere **3** diffondere, emanare
sheen [ʃiːn] *s.* lucentezza *f.*
sheep [ʃiːp] *s.* pecora *f.*
sheepdog ['ʃiːpdəg] *s.* cane *m.* da pastore
sheepfold ['ʃiːpfɒuld] *s.* ovile *m.*
sheepish ['ʃiːpɪʃ] *agg.* **1** imbarazzato, vergognoso **2** mite, timido
sheer [ʃɪəʳ] **A** *agg.* **1** puro, semplice **2** liscio, non diluito **3** perpendicolare, a picco **4** sottile, diafano **B** *avv.* **1** completamente, del tutto **2** a picco
sheet [ʃiːt] *s.* **1** lenzuolo *m.* **2** foglio *m.*, lamina *f.* **3** lamiera *f.*, lastra *f.* **4** (*naut.*) scotta *f.*
sheik(h) [ʃeɪk] *s.* sceicco *m.*
shelf [ʃɛlf] *s.* mensola *f.*, scaffale *m.*
shell [ʃɛl] *s.* **1** guscio *m.*, conchiglia *f.* **2** carcassa *f.*, ossatura *f.*, struttura *f.* **3** apparenza *f.* **4** schema *m.*, schizzo *m.* **5** proiettile *m.*, granata *f.*
to shell [ʃɛl] *v. tr.* **1** sgusciare, sgranare **2** bombardare
shellfish ['ʃɛlˌfɪʃ] *s.* mollusco *m.*, crostaceo *m.*
shelter ['ʃɛltəʳ] *s.* riparo *m.*, rifugio *m.*
to shelter ['ʃɛltəʳ] **A** *v. tr.* riparare, proteggere **B** *v. intr.* ripararsi, rifugiarsi
to shelve [ʃɛlv] *v. tr.* accantonare, rimandare
shepherd ['ʃɛpəd] *s.* pastore *m.*
to shepherd ['ʃɛpəd] *v. tr.* guidare, custodire
sheriff ['ʃɛrɪf] *s.* sceriffo *m.*
sherry ['ʃɛrɪ] *s.* sherry *m. inv.*
shield [ʃiːld] *s.* **1** scudo *m.* **2** riparo *m.*, protezione *f.*
to shield [ʃiːld] *v. tr.* **1** proteggere, riparare **2** schermare
shift [ʃɪft] *s.* **1** cambiamento *m.*, spostamento *m.*, avvicendamento *m.* **2** turno *m.* **3** espediente *m.* ♦ **s. work** lavoro a turni; **to make s.** ingegnarsi
to shift [ʃɪft] **A** *v. tr.* **1** spostare, trasferire, cambiare **2** rimuovere **B** *v. intr.* **1** spostarsi, trasferirsi, muoversi **2** ingegnarsi **3** (*autom.*) cambiare marcia
shiftless ['ʃɪftlɪs] *agg.* incapace, inefficiente

shifty ['ʃɪftɪ] *agg.* sfuggente, ambiguo
shilling ['ʃɪlɪŋ] *s.* scellino *m.*
to shilly-shally ['ʃɪlɪˌʃælɪ] *v. intr.* (*fam.*) esitare
to shimmer ['ʃɪmər] *v. intr.* brillare, luccicare
shin [ʃɪn] *s.* stinco *m.* ♦ **s.-bone** tibia
shine [ʃaɪn] *s.* **1** splendore *m.*, lucentezza *f.* **2** lucidata *f.*
to shine [ʃaɪn] (*pass. e p. p.* **shone**) **A** *v. intr.* brillare, risplendere **B** *v. tr.* **1** far luce su **2** (*pass. e p. p.* **shined**) lucidare, lustrare
shingle (1) ['ʃɪŋgl] *s.* ciottoli *m. pl.*
shingle (2) ['ʃɪŋgl] *s.* (*edil.*) scandola *f.*
shingles ['ʃɪŋglz] *s. pl.* (*v. al sing.*) (*med.*) herpes zoster *m. inv.*
shining ['ʃaɪnɪŋ] *agg.* fulgido, lucente
shiny ['ʃaɪnɪ] *agg.* brillante, lucente
ship [ʃɪp] *s.* nave *f.* ♦ **s.'s chandler** fornitore navale
to ship [ʃɪp] **A** *v. tr.* **1** imbarcare **2** trasportare, spedire **B** *v. intr.* imbarcarsi
shipbuilder ['ʃɪpˌbɪldər] *s.* costruttore *m.* navale
shipmaster ['ʃɪpˌmaːstər] *s.* capitano *m.*
shipment ['ʃɪpmənt] *s.* **1** carico *m.* **2** imbarco *m.*, spedizione *f.*
shipping ['ʃɪpɪŋ] *s.* **1** imbarco *m.*, spedizione *f.* **2** naviglio *m.*, navigazione *f.* ♦ **s. agent** spedizioniere marittimo
shipshape ['ʃɪpʃeɪp] **A** *agg.* ordinato **B** *avv.* in perfetto ordine
shipwreck ['ʃɪpˌrɛk] *s.* **1** naufragio *m.* **2** relitto *m.*
to shipwreck ['ʃɪpˌrɛk] **A** *v. intr.* naufragare **B** *v. tr.* far naufragare
shipyard ['ʃɪpjaːd] *s.* cantiere *m.* navale
shire ['ʃaɪər] *s.* contea *f.*
to shirk [ʃɜːk] *v. tr.* evitare, sottrarsi a
shirt [ʃɜːt] *s.* camicia *f.*, camicetta *f.*
shit [ʃɪt] *s.* (*volg.*) merda *f.*
shiver ['ʃɪvər] *s.* brivido *m.*
to shiver ['ʃɪvər] *v. intr.* rabbrividire
shivering ['ʃɪvərɪŋ] *agg.* tremante
shoal (1) [ʃɒʊl] *s.* bassofondo *m.*, secca *f.*
shoal (2) [ʃɒʊl] *s.* **1** (*di pesci*) banco *m.* **2** moltitudine *f.*
shock [ʃək] *s.* **1** colpo *m.*, collisione *f.* **2** scossa *f.* **3** (*med.*) collasso *m.*, shock *m. inv.* ♦ **s. absorber** ammortizzatore
to shock [ʃək] **A** *v. tr.* **1** colpire, scuotere **2** scandalizzare **B** *v. intr.* scontrarsi
shocking ['ʃəkɪŋ] *agg.* **1** vistoso **2** scioccante, scandaloso
shoe [ʃuː] *s.* **1** scarpa *f.* **2** ferro *m.* di cavallo ♦ **s. lace** stringa; **s. rack** scarpiera; **s. repairer** calzolaio
shoehorn ['ʃuːhɜːn] *s.* calzascarpe *m. inv.*
shoemaker ['ʃuːˌmeɪkər] *s.* calzolaio *m.*
shoeshine ['ʃuːʃaɪn] *s.* lustrascarpe *m. inv.*
shone [ʃən] *pass. e p. p. di* **to shine**
shoo [ʃuː] *inter.* sciò
shook [ʃʊk] *pass. di* **to shake**
shoot [ʃuːt] *s.* **1** germoglio *m.* **2** battuta *f.* di caccia
to shoot [ʃuːt] (*pass. e p. p.* **shot**) **A** *v. tr.* **1** sparare a **2** lanciare, gettare **3** filmare, riprendere **B** *v. intr.* **1** sparare, tirare **2** andare a caccia **3** (*cine.*) girare **4** passare velocemente, sfrecciare **5** germogliare ♦ **to s. at** mirare a; **to s. down** abbattere; **to s. up** balzare fuori, salire alle stelle
shooting ['ʃuːtɪŋ] *s.* **1** sparatoria *f.* **2** caccia *f.* ♦ **s. box** casino di caccia; **s. range** tiro a segno
shop [ʃəp] *s.* **1** bottega *f.*, negozio *m.* **2** officina *f.*, laboratorio *m.* ♦ **s. assistant** commesso, commessa; **s. lifter** taccheggiatore; **s. window** vetrina
to shop [ʃəp] *v. intr.* fare acquisti
shopkeeper ['ʃəpˌkiːpər] *s.* negoziante *m. e f.*
shopper ['ʃəpər] *s.* acquirente *m. e f.*
shopping ['ʃəpɪŋ] *s.* **1** compere *f. pl.*, acquisti *m. pl.*, shopping *m. inv.* **2** spesa *f.* ♦ **s. mall/centre** centro commerciale
shore (1) [ʃɜːr] *s.* riva *f.*, sponda *f.*, spiaggia *f.*, lido *m.* ♦ **off s.** al largo; **on s.** a terra
shore (2) [ʃɜːr] *s.* puntello *m.*
to shore [ʃɜːr] *v. tr.* puntellare
shorn [ʃɜːn] *p. p. di* **to shear**
short [ʃɜːt] **A** *agg.* **1** corto, breve **2** basso, piccolo **3** scarso, insufficiente **4** brusco, rude **5** friabile **6** (*metall.*) fragile **7** (*comm.*) a breve scadenza **8** (*fam.*) (*di liquore*) liscio **B** *s.* **1** (sillaba) breve *f.* **2** (*cine.*) cortometraggio *m.* **3** *al pl.* pantaloni *m. pl.* corti, shorts *m. pl.* **C** *avv.* **1** bruscamente, improvvisamente **2** brevemente ♦ **in s.** in breve; **s. cut** scorciatoia; **s. lived** momentaneo, caduco; **s. of** all'infuori di; **s. pastry** pasta frolla; **s. sighted** miope; **s. story** racconto; **s. tempered** irascibile; **s.-wave** a onde corte; **to fall s. st.** non raggiungere q.c., essere inadeguato a q.c.; **to run s. of** essere a corto di
shortage ['ʃɜːtɪdʒ] *s.* mancanza *f.*, scarsi-

tà *f.*
shortbread ['ʃɜːtbrɛd] *s.* biscotto *m.* di pasta frolla
short-circuit [ˌʃɜːt'sɜːkɪt] *s.* cortocircuito *m.*
shortcoming ['ʃɜːtkˌʌmɪŋ] *s.* **1** mancanza *f.*, deficienza *f.* **2** difetto *m.*
to shorten ['ʃɜːtn] *v. tr.* accorciare, ridurre
shortfall ['ʃɜːtfɜːl] *s.* **1** diminuzione *f.* **2** (*econ.*) deficit *m. inv.*
shorthand ['ʃɜːthænd] *s.* stenografia *f.*
shortly ['ʃɜːtlɪ] *avv.* **1** presto, in breve tempo **2** bruscamente
shot (1) [ʃət] *s.* **1** sparo *m.*, colpo *m.* **2** (*sport*) tiro *m.* **3** tiratore *m.* **4** pallottola *f.*, proiettile *m.* **5** (*atletica*) peso *m.* **6** (*fam.*) prova *f.*, tentativo *m.* **7** (*fam.*) foto *f.* **8** (*fam.*) (*di droga*) iniezione *f.* **9** (*fam.*) sorso *m.*, goccio *m.* ♦ **s. put** lancio del peso
shot (2) [ʃət] *pass. e p. p. di* **to shoot**
shotgun ['ʃətgʌn] *s.* fucile *m.* da caccia, schioppo *m.*
should [ʃʊd, ʃəd] (*pass. di* **shall**) *v. difett.* **1** (*ausiliare per la formazione del condizionale*) (ES: **I s. eat it if I were not on a diet** lo mangerei se non fossi a dieta) **2** (*indica suggerimento o probabilità*) dovere (ES: **you s. pay your debts** dovresti pagare i tuoi debiti, **if the weather s. get worse** se il tempo dovesse peggiorare) **3** (*ausiliare per la formazione del congiuntivo*) (ES: **it's wonderful that you s. come** è stupendo che tu venga)
shoulder ['ʃɒʊldəʳ] *s.* **1** spalla *f.* **2** (*di strada*) bordo *m.* ♦ **hard s.** corsia d'emergenza; **s. bag** borsa a tracolla; **s. blade** scapola; **s. strap** spallina
to shoulder ['ʃɒʊldəʳ] *v. tr.* **1** portare sulle spalle **2** addossarsi
shout [ʃaʊt] *s.* grido *m.*, urlo *m.*
to shout [ʃaʊt] *v. tr. e intr.* gridare, urlare ♦ **to s. sb. down** far tacere qc. gridando
shouting ['ʃaʊtɪŋ] *s.* grida *f. pl.*
shove [ʃʌv] *s.* spinta *f.*
to shove [ʃʌv] **A** *v. tr.* **1** spingere **2** (*fam.*) ficcare, mettere **3** respingere **B** *v. intr.* **1** farsi largo a spinte **2** spostarsi ♦ **to s. off** scostarsi da terra, andarsene
shovel ['ʃʌvl] *s.* pala *f.*, paletta *f.*
to shovel ['ʃʌvl] *v. tr.* spalare
show [ʃɒʊ] *s.* **1** mostra *f.*, esposizione *f.* **2** dimostrazione *f.*, manifestazione *f.* **3** apparenza *f.*, parvenza *f.* **4** spettacolo *m.* **5** (*fam.*) affare *m.*, faccenda *f.*
to show [ʃɒʊ] (*pass.* **showed**, *p. p.* **shown**) **A** *v. tr.* **1** mostrare, esporre, esibire **2** indicare, rappresentare **3** provare, rivelare **4** accompagnare **5** (*spettacoli, film*) programmare, dare **B** *v. intr.* apparire, vedersi ♦ **to s. in** introdurre; **to s. off** mettere in risalto, ostentare; **to s. oneself** mostrarsi; **to s. out** accompagnare all'uscita; **to s. up** mettere in luce, farsi vivo
showcase ['ʃɒʊkeɪs] *s.* bacheca *f.*
shower ['ʃaʊəʳ] *s.* **1** acquazzone *m.*, scroscio *m.* **2** (*fig.*) pioggia *f.*, scarica *f.*, nugolo *m.* **3** doccia *f.* ♦ **to take a s.** fare la doccia
to shower ['ʃaʊəʳ] **A** *v. tr.* **1** far cadere, versare **2** inondare di **B** *v. intr.* **1** diluviare **2** fare la doccia
showing ['ʃɒ(ʊ)ɪŋ] *s.* rappresentazione *f.*, spettacolo *m.*
shown [ʃɒʊn] *p. p. di* **to show**
showpiece ['ʃɒʊpiːs] *s.* **1** pezzo *m.* forte **2** oggetto *m.* da esposizione
showroom ['ʃɒʊruːm] *s.* sala *f.* da esposizione, showroom *m. inv.*
showy ['ʃɒ(ʊ)ɪ] *agg.* appariscente, vistoso
shrank [ʃræŋk] *pass. di* **to shrink**
shred [ʃrɛd] *s.* brandello *m.*, frammento *m.*
to shred [ʃrɛd] *v. tr.* lacerare, ridurre a brandelli
shrewd [ʃruːd] *agg.* accorto, sagace
shriek [ʃriːk] *s.* **1** grido *m.*, strillo *m.* **2** fischio *m.*
to shriek [ʃriːk] *v. intr.* gridare, strillare
shrill [ʃrɪl] *agg.* stridulo, acuto
shrimp [ʃrɪmp] *s.* gamberetto *m.*
shrine [ʃraɪn] *s.* **1** reliquiario *m.* **2** santuario *m.*
shrink [ʃrɪŋk] *s.* (*pop.*) psichiatra *m. e f.*
to shrink [ʃrɪŋk] (*pass.* **shrank**, *p. p.* **shrunk**) **A** *v. intr.* **1** restringersi, ritirarsi **2** indietreggiare, tirarsi indietro, rifuggire **B** *v. tr.* far restringere, accorciare ♦ **to s. into oneself** chiudersi in sé
shrinkage ['ʃrɪŋkɪdʒ] *s.* contrazione *f.*, restringimento *m.*
shrinkproof ['ʃrɪŋkpruːf] *agg.* irrestringibile
to shrivel ['ʃrɪvl] *v. intr.* raggrinzirsi
shroud [ʃraʊd] *s.* **1** sudario *m.* **2** (*fig.*) velo *m.* **3** (*naut.*) sartia *f.*
to shroud [ʃraʊd] *v. tr.* **1** avvolgere nel sudario **2** velare, nascondere
Shrove Tuesday [ˌʃrɒʊv'tjuːzdɪ] *s.* martedì *m.* grasso
shrub [ʃrʌb] *s.* arbusto *m.*

shrubbery ['ʃrʌbərɪ] *s.* **1** boschetto *m.* **2** arbusti *m. pl.*
to **shrug** [ʃrʌg] *v. intr.* scrollare le spalle ♦ **to s. off** passare sopra a
shrunk [ʃrʌŋk] *p. p. di* **to shrink**
shuck [ʃʌk] *s.* **1** guscio *m.*, baccello *m.* **2** conchiglia *f.*
shudder ['ʃʌdər] *s.* brivido *m.*
to **shudder** ['ʃʌdər] *v. intr.* rabbrividire
to **shuffle** ['ʃʌfl] *v. tr.* **1** rimescolare **2** trascinare, strascicare ♦ **to s. off** sottrarsi a
to **shun** [ʃʌn] *v. tr.* evitare, schivare
to **shunt** [ʃʌnt] *v. tr.* **1** deviare **2** smistare **3** accantonare
shunting ['ʃʌntɪŋ] *s.* **1** (*elettr.*) derivazione *f.* **2** smistamento *m.*
shut [ʃʌt] *agg.* chiuso
to **shut** [ʃʌt] (*pass. e p. p.* **shut**) *v. tr. e intr.* chiudere, chiudersi ♦ **to s. down** chiudere i battenti; **to s. off** chiudere, bloccare; **to s. out** escludere; **to s. up** serrare, rinchiudere, mettere a tacere; **s. up!** piantala!
shutter ['ʃʌtər] *s.* **1** persiana *f.*, saracinesca *f.* **2** (*fot.*) otturatore *m.*
shuttle ['ʃʌtl] *s.* navetta *f.*
shy [ʃaɪ] *agg.* **1** timido, pauroso **2** diffidente
shyness ['ʃaɪnɪs] *s.* timidezza *f.*
sibling ['sɪblɪŋ] *s. spec. al pl.* fratello *m.*, sorella *f.*
sick [sɪk] *agg.* **1** malato, indisposto **2** che ha la nausea **3** nauseante ♦ **to be s.** stare per vomitare; **to fall s.** ammalarsi; **to feel s.** avere la nausea
sickbay ['sɪkbeɪ] *s.* infermeria *f.*
to **sicken** ['sɪkn] **A** *v. tr.* **1** nauseare, disgustare **2** far ammalare **B** *v. intr.* **1** ammalarsi **2** sentire nausea, essere disgustato **3** annoiarsi
sickening ['sɪknɪŋ] *agg.* nauseabondo
sickle ['sɪkl] *s.* falce *f.*
sickly ['sɪklɪ] *agg.* **1** malaticcio **2** pallido **3** malsano, nauseabondo
sickness ['sɪknɪs] *s.* **1** malattia *f.* **2** nausea *f.*, vomito *m.*
side [saɪd] **A** *s.* **1** lato *m.*, fianco *m.*, fiancata *f.* **2** sponda *f.*, margine *m.* **3** parte *f.*, lato *m.* **4** partito *m.*, fazione *f.*, squadra *f.* **B** *agg.* **1** laterale **2** secondario ♦ **from s. to s.** da una parte all'altra; **on the other s.** d'altra parte; **s. by s.** fianco a fianco; **s. effect** effetto collaterale; **s. glance** sguardo in tralice
to **side** [saɪd] *v. intr.* parteggiare
sideboard ['saɪdbɜːd] *s.* credenza *f.*
sideboards ['saɪdbɜːdz] *s. pl.* basette *f. pl.*
sidecar ['saɪdkaː] *s.* sidecar *m. inv.*
sidelight ['saɪdlaɪt] *s.* (*autom.*) luce *f.* di posizione
sideline ['saɪdlaɪn] *s.* attività *f.* secondaria
sidelong ['saɪdləŋ] **A** *agg.* obliquo **B** *avv.* obliquamente
sideslip ['saɪdslɪp] *s.* slittamento *m.*, sbandata *f.*
to **sidestep** ['saɪdstɛp] *v. tr.* scansare
sidewalk ['saɪd,wɜːk] *s.* (*USA*) marciapiede *m.*
sideways ['saɪd,weɪz] *avv.* lateralmente, obliquamente
siding ['saɪdɪŋ] *s.* (*ferr.*) binario *m.* di raccordo
to **sidle** ['saɪdl] *v. intr.* muoversi furtivamente
siege [siːdʒ] *s.* assedio *m.*
sieve [sɪv] *s.* setaccio *m.*
to **sieve** [sɪv] *v. tr.* setacciare
to **sift** [sɪft] *v. tr.* **1** setacciare **2** vagliare
sigh [saɪ] *s.* sospiro *m.*
to **sigh** [saɪ] *v. intr.* sospirare
sight [saɪt] *s.* **1** vista *f.* **2** visione *f.*, veduta *f.* **3** mira *f.* **4** giudizio *m.*, opinione *f.* **5** *al pl.* cose *f. pl.* da vedere, curiosità *f. pl.*
to **sight** [saɪt] *v. tr.* **1** avvistare **2** traguardare **3** prendere la mira con, mirare a
sightseeing ['saɪt,siːɪŋ] *s.* giro *m.* turistico
sign [saɪn] *s.* **1** segno *m.*, cenno *m.*, gesto *m.* **2** indizio *m.*, traccia *f.* **3** insegna *f.*, segnale *m.* **4** (*mat., astr.*) segno *m.*
to **sign** [saɪn] *v. tr.* **1** firmare, sottoscrivere **2** arruolare, ingaggiare ♦ **to s. away/over** cedere (*una proprietà firmando un documento*); **to s. on** arruolarsi, sottoscrivere un impegno; **to s. up** arruolarsi, iscriversi
signal ['sɪgnl] *s.* segnale *m.* ♦ **warning s.** segnale d'allarme
to **signal** ['sɪgnl] *v. tr. e intr.* segnalare
signature ['sɪgnɪtʃər] *s.* firma *f.* ♦ **s. tune** sigla musicale
signboard ['saɪnbɜːd] *s.* cartello *m.*, insegna *f.*
signet ['sɪgnɪt] *s.* sigillo *m.*
significance [sɪg'nɪfɪkəns] *s.* **1** significato *m.* **2** importanza *f.*
significant [sɪg'nɪfɪkənt] *agg.* **1** significativo, espressivo **2** importante
to **signify** ['sɪgnɪfaɪ] **A** *v. tr.* **1** significare, voler dire **2** denotare **B** *v. intr.* **1** essere

significativo **2** avere importanza
signpost ['saɪn,pɒʊst] *s.* cartello *m.* indicatore
silence ['saɪləns] *s.* silenzio *m.*
to silence ['saɪləns] *v. tr.* far tacere
silencer ['saɪlənsəʳ] *s.* silenziatore *m.*
silent ['saɪlənt] *agg.* **1** silenzioso **2** muto
silhouette [ˌsɪlʊ(ː)'ɛt] *s.* silhouette *f. inv.*, sagoma *f.* ♦ **in s.** in controluce
silicon ['sɪlɪkən] *s.* silicio *m.*
silicone ['sɪlɪkɒʊn] *s.* silicone *m.*
silk [sɪlk] *s.* seta *f.*
silky ['sɪlkɪ] *agg.* **1** di seta, serico **2** morbido, lucente
sill [sɪl] *s.* soglia *f.*, davanzale *m.*
silly ['sɪlɪ] *agg. e s.* sciocco *m.*
silo ['saɪlɒʊ] (*pl.* **silos**) *s.* silo *m.*
silt [sɪlt] *s.* limo *m.*
silvan ['sɪlvən] *agg.* silvestre
silver ['sɪlvəʳ] **A** *s.* **1** argento *m.* **2** argenteria *f.* **B** *agg.* d'argento ♦ **s. fox** volpe argentata; **s. paper** carta stagnola; **s. wedding** nozze d'argento
to silver-plate ['sɪlvə,pleɪt] placcare d'argento
silverware ['sɪlvəwɛəʳ] *s.* argenteria *f.*
similar ['sɪmɪləʳ] *agg.* simile
similarity [ˌsɪmɪ'lærɪtɪ] *s.* somiglianza *f.*
simile ['sɪmɪlɪ] *s.* similitudine *f.*
similitude [sɪ'mɪlɪtjuːd] *s.* similitudine *f.*
to simmer ['sɪməʳ] *v. tr.* far bollire lentamente ♦ **to s. down** calmarsi
to simper ['sɪmpəʳ] *v. intr.* sorridere affettatamente
simple ['sɪmpl] *agg.* semplice
simplicity [sɪm'plɪsɪtɪ] *s.* semplicità *f.*
to simplify ['sɪmplɪfaɪ] *v. tr.* semplificare
simply ['sɪmplɪ] *avv.* semplicemente
to simulate ['sɪmjʊleɪt] *v. tr.* simulare
simulation [ˌsɪmjʊ'leɪʃ(ə)n] *s.* simulazione *f.*
simultaneous [ˌsɪm(ə)l'teɪnjəs] *agg.* simultaneo
sin [sɪn] *s.* peccato *m.*, colpa *f.*
to sin [sɪn] *v. intr.* peccare
since [sɪns] **A** *avv.* da allora **B** *prep.* da **C** *cong.* **1** da quando **2** poiché, giacché ♦ **ever s.** da allora in poi; **long s.** da tempo
sincere [sɪn'sɪəʳ] *agg.* sincero
sincerely [sɪn'sɪəlɪ] *avv.* sinceramente ♦ **yours s.** (*nelle lettere*) cordialmente vostro
sincerity [sɪn'sɛrɪtɪ] *s.* sincerità *f.*
sine [saɪn] *s.* (*mat.*) seno *m.*
sinew ['sɪnjuː] *s.* tendine *m.*
sinewy ['sɪnjuːɪ] *agg.* muscoloso
sinful ['sɪnf(ʊ)l] *agg.* peccaminoso
to sing [sɪŋ] (*pass.* **sang**, *p. p.* **sung**) *v. tr. e intr.* cantare
to singe ['sɪn(d)ʒ] *v. tr. e intr.* bruciacchiare, bruciacchiarsi
singer ['sɪŋəʳ] *s.* cantante *m. e f.*
singing ['sɪŋɪŋ] *s.* canto *m.*
single ['sɪŋgl] **A** *agg.* **1** singolo, semplice, individuale **2** celibe, nubile **3** sincero, leale **B** *s.* **1** singolo *m.* **2** single *m. e f. inv.* **3** (camera) singola *f.* **4** biglietto *m.* di sola andata ♦ **s. file** fila indiana
to single ['sɪŋgl] *v. tr.* scegliere ♦ **to s. out** selezionare
single-handed [ˌsɪŋgl'hændɪd] **A** *agg.* **1** con una mano sola **2** da solo **B** *avv.* da solo, senza aiuto
singly ['sɪŋglɪ] *avv.* singolarmente
singsong ['sɪŋˌsəŋ] *s.* cantilena *f.*
singular ['sɪŋgjʊləʳ] *agg. e s.* singolare *m.*
sinister ['sɪnɪstəʳ] *agg.* **1** sinistro, funesto **2** infame
sink [sɪŋk] *s.* lavandino *m.*
to sink [sɪŋk] (*pass.* **sank**, *p. p.* **sunk**) **A** *v. intr.* **1** affondare **2** sprofondare **3** abbassarsi, calare **4** cadere **5** penetrare, filtrare **6** incavarsi, infossarsi **B** *v. tr.* **1** affondare **2** abbassare, far calare **3** scavare, perforare, incassare **4** dimenticare **5** (*denaro*) investire ♦ **to s. in** penetrare, far presa
sinner ['sɪnəʳ] *s.* peccatore *m.*
sinus ['saɪnəs] *s.* (*anat.*) seno *m.*
sinusitis [ˌsaɪnə'saɪtɪs] *s.* sinusite *f.*
sip [sɪp] *s.* sorso *m.*
to sip [sɪp] *v. tr. e intr.* sorseggiare
siphon ['saɪf(ə)n] *s.* sifone *m.*
sir [sɜːʳ] *s.* **1** signore *m.* (*al vocativo*) **2** sir *m. inv.*
siren ['saɪərɪn] *s.* sirena *f.*
sirloin ['sɜːləɪn] *s.* lombo *m.* di manzo, controfiletto *m.*
sissy ['sɪsɪ] *s.* (*fam.*) donnicciola *f.*
sister ['sɪstəʳ] *s.* **1** sorella *f.* **2** suora *f.* **3** (infermiera) caposala *f.* ♦ **half s.** sorellastra; **s.-in-law** cognata
to sit [sɪt] (*pass. e p. p.* **sat**) *v. intr.* **1** sedere, stare seduto **2** essere in seduta **3** posare **4** (*di uccelli*) covare **5** (*di abiti*) cadere ♦ **to s. down** mettersi a sedere, accomodarsi; **to s. for** sostenere (un esame); **to s. in on** partecipare a; **to s. up** tirarsi su a sedere, stare alzato

site [saɪt] *s.* sito *m.*, luogo *m.*
sitting ['sɪtɪŋ] *s.* **1** seduta *f.* **2** sessione *f.*, udienza *f.* **3** turno *m.* ♦ **s. room** salotto
situated ['sɪtjʊeɪtɪd] *agg.* situato, posto
situation [ˌsɪtjʊ'eɪʃ(ə)n] *s.* **1** situazione *f.*, posizione *f.* **2** impiego *m.*
six [sɪks] *agg. num. card. e s.* sei *m. inv.*
sixteen [ˌsɪks'tiːn] *agg. num. card. e s.* sedici *m. inv.*
sixteenth [ˌsɪks'tiːnθ] *agg. num. ord. e s.* sedicesimo *m.*
sixth [sɪksθ] *agg. num. ord. e s.* sesto *m.*
sixtieth [sɪkstɪɪθ] *agg. num. ord. e s.* sessantesimo *m.*
sixty ['sɪkstɪ] *agg. num. card. e s.* sessanta *m. inv.*
sizable ['saɪzəbl] *agg.* considerevole
size (1) [saɪz] *s.* **1** dimensione *f.*, grandezza *f.* **2** misura *f.*, taglia *f.*, formato *m.*
size (2) [saɪz] *s.* colla *f.*, appretto *m.*
to size [saɪz] *s.* classificare secondo la misura ♦ **to s. up** valutare
skate (1) [skeɪt] *s.* pattino *m.*
skate (2) [skeɪt] *s.* (*zool.*) razza *f.*
to skate [skeɪt] *v. intr.* pattinare
skateboard ['skeɪtbɜːd] *s.* skateboard *m. inv.*
skater [skeɪtər] *s.* pattinatore *m.*
skating ['skeɪtɪŋ] *s.* pattinaggio *m.* ♦ **figure s.** pattinaggio artistico; **ice s.** pattinaggio su ghiaccio; **roller s.** pattinaggio a rotelle; **s. rink** pista da pattinaggio
skein [skeɪn] *s.* matassa *f.*
skeleton ['skɛlɪtn] **A** *s.* **1** scheletro *m.* **2** ossatura *f.* **3** schema *m.*, abbozzo *m.* **B** *agg.* ridotto (all'essenziale)
sketch [skɛtʃ] *s.* **1** schizzo *m.*, abbozzo *m.* **2** scenetta *f.*, sketch *m. inv.*
sketchy ['skɛtʃɪ] *agg.* abbozzato, approssimativo
skewer ['skjʊər] *s.* spiedo *m.*
ski [skiː] *s.* sci *m.* ♦ **s. boot** scarpone da sci; **s. jump** salto (con gli sci, dal trampolino); **s. lift** ski-lift, sciovia; **s. rack** portascì; **s. slope** pista da sci; **s. stick/pole** racchetta da sci; **water s.** sci nautico
to ski [skiː] *v. intr.* sciare
skid [skɪd] *s.* slittamento *m.*, slittata *f.*
to skid [skɪd] *v. intr.* scivolare, slittare
skier ['skiːər] *s.* sciatore *m.*
skiing ['skiːɪŋ] *s.* (*sport*) sci *m.*
skilful ['skɪlf(ʊ)l] *agg.* abile, destro
skill [skɪl] *s.* destrezza *f.*, maestria *f.*
skilled [skɪld] *agg.* esperto, qualificato
to skim [skɪm] *v. tr.* **1** schiumare, scremare **2** sfiorare **3** scorrere, sfogliare ♦ **skimmed milk** latte scremato
to skimp [skɪmp] **A** *v. tr.* economizzare **B** *v. intr.* **1** lesinare **2** fare economie
skimpy ['skɪmpɪ] *agg.* scarso, misero
skin [skɪn] *s.* **1** pelle *f.* **2** buccia *f.*, scorza *f.*
to skin [skɪn] *v. tr.* spellare, sbucciare
skin-deep [ˌskɪn'diːp] *agg.* superficiale
to skin-dive ['skɪndaɪv] *v. intr.* immergersi in apnea
skinny ['skɪnɪ] *agg.* macilento
skin-tight [ˌskɪn'taɪt] *agg.* aderente
skip [skɪp] *s.* **1** salto *m.* **2** omissione *f.*
to skip [skɪp] *v. tr. e intr.* saltare
skipper ['skɪpər] *s.* **1** (*naut.*) skipper *m. inv.*, comandante *m.* **2** (*sport*) capitano *m.*
skirmish ['skɜːmɪʃ] *s.* scaramuccia *f.*
skirt [skɜːt] *s.* **1** gonna *f.* **2** lembo *m.*, margine *m.*
to skirt [skɜːt] *v. tr.* costeggiare, fiancheggiare
skit [skɪt] *s.* parodia *f.*
skittish ['skɪtɪʃ] *agg.* **1** vivace, volubile **2** (*di cavallo*) ombroso
skittle ['skɪtl] *s.* birillo *m.*
to skive [skaɪv] *v. intr.* (*fam.*) fare il lavativo, gingillarsi
to skulk [skʌlk] *v. intr.* **1** muoversi furtivamente **2** nascondersi
skull [skʌl] *s.* cranio *m.*, teschio *m.*
skunk [skʌŋk] *s.* moffetta *f.*
sky [skaɪ] *s.* cielo *m.* ♦ **s. diving** paracadutismo
skylark ['skaɪlaːk] *s.* allodola *f.*
skylight ['skaɪlaɪt] *s.* lucernario *m.*
skyscraper ['skaɪˌskreɪpər] *s.* grattacielo *m.*
slab [slæb] *s.* **1** lastra *f.*, piastra *f.* **2** fetta *f.*
slack [slæk] **A** *agg.* **1** lento, allentato **2** pigro, indolente **3** fiacco **B** *s.* **1** rilassamento *m.* **2** periodo *m.* morto **3** *al pl.* pantaloni *m. pl.* **4** (*mecc.*) gioco *m.*
to slacken ['slæk(ə)n] **A** *v. tr.* **1** allentare, mollare **2** diminuire **B** *v. intr.* **1** rilassarsi, rallentare il ritmo **2** ridursi
slag [slæg] *s.* scoria *f.*
slain [sleɪn] *p. p. di* **to slay**
to slam [slæm] **A** *v. tr.* **1** sbattere, chiudere violentemente **2** scaraventare **3** (*fam.*) criticare **B** *v. intr.* (*di porta*) sbattere
slander ['slaːndər] *s.* calunnia *f.*, diffamazione *f.*

slang [slæŋ] *s.* gergo *m.*, slang *m. inv.*
slant [slaːnt] *s.* **1** inclinazione *f.*, pendenza *f.*, pendio *m.* **2** angolazione *f.*
to **slant** [slaːnt] **A** *v. intr.* **1** pendere, inclinarsi **2** propendere **B** *v. tr.* **1** deviare **2** presentare in maniera tendenziosa
slanting ['slaːntɪŋ] *agg.* obliquo, inclinato
slap [slæp] **A** *s.* ceffone *m.*, sberla *f.* **B** *avv.* **1** improvvisamente **2** in pieno ♦ **s.-bang** di colpo
to **slap** [slæp] *v. tr.* **1** schiaffeggiare **2** sbattere
slapdash ['slæpdæʃ] **A** *agg.* precipitoso, affrettato **B** *avv.* frettolosamente
slap-up ['slæpʌp] *agg.* (*fam.*) eccellente
slash [slæʃ] *s.* **1** taglio *m.*, squarcio *m.* **2** frustata *f.* **3** (*segno grafico*) barra *f.*
to **slash** [slæʃ] *v. tr.* **1** tagliare, squarciare **2** frustare **3** ridurre drasticamente **4** criticare, stroncare
slat [slæt] *s.* assicella *f.*, stecca *f.*
slate [sleɪt] *s.* **1** ardesia *f.* **2** tegola *f.* d'ardesia
to **slate** [sleɪt] *v. tr.* (*fam.*) **1** criticare, stroncare **2** rimproverare
slating ['sleɪtɪŋ] *s.* stroncatura *f.*
slaughter ['slɜːtəʳ] *s.* massacro *m.*, strage *f.* ♦ **s. house** mattatoio
to **slaughter** ['slɜːtəʳ] *v. tr.* massacrare, macellare
slave [sleɪv] *agg. e s.* schiavo *m.*
slavery ['sleɪvərɪ] *s.* schiavitù *f.*
Slavic ['slaːvɪk] *agg. e s.* slavo *m.*
slavish ['sleɪvɪʃ] *agg.* servile
to **slay** [sleɪ] (*pass.* **slew**, *p. p.* **slain**) *v. tr.* (*letter.*) ammazzare
sleazy ['sliːzɪ] *agg.* squallido
sled [slɛd] *s.* slitta *f.*
sledge [slɛdʒ] *s.* slitta *f.*
sledgehammer ['slɛdʒˌhæməʳ] *s.* mazza *f.*, maglio *m.*
sleek [sliːk] *agg.* **1** liscio, lucido **2** mellifluo **3** di lusso, elegante
sleep [sliːp] *s.* **1** sonno *m.* **2** dormita *f.* ♦ **sound s.** sonno profondo; **to go to s.** addormentarsi
to **sleep** [sliːp] (*pass. e p. p.* **slept**) *v. intr.* dormire ♦ **to s. in** dormire fino a tardi
sleeper ['sliːpəʳ] *s.* **1** dormiglione *m.* **2** (*ferr.*) traversina *f.* **3** (*ferr.*) vagone letto *m.*
sleepiness ['sliːpɪnɪs] *s.* sonnolenza *f.*
sleeping ['sliːpɪŋ] *agg.* addormentato ♦ **s. bag** sacco a pelo; **s. car** vagone letto; **s. draught/pill** sonnifero
sleepless ['sliːplɪs] *agg.* insonne
sleeplessness ['sliːplɪsnɪs] *s.* insonnia *f.*
sleepwalker ['sliːpˌwɜːkəʳ] *s.* sonnambulo *m.*
sleepy ['sliːpɪ] *agg.* assonnato ♦ **s. head** dormiglione
sleet [sliːt] *s.* nevischio *m.*
sleeve [sliːv] *s.* **1** manica *f.* **2** copertina *f.*, custodia *f.*
sleigh [sleɪ] *s.* slitta *f.*
sleight [slaɪt] *s.* abilità *f.* ♦ **s. of hand** gioco di prestigio
slender ['slɛndəʳ] *agg.* **1** esile, snello **2** scarso, tenue
slept [slɛpt] *pass. e p. p. di* **to sleep**
slew [sluː] *pass. di* **to slay**
slice [slaɪs] *s.* fetta *f.*, trancio *m.*
to **slice** [slaɪs] *v. tr.* affettare, tagliare
slick [slɪk] **A** *agg.* **1** liscio, sdrucciolevole **2** astuto **3** untuoso, viscido **B** *s.* **oil s.** chiazza *f.* di petrolio
slide [slaɪd] *s.* **1** scivolata *f.*, scivolone *m.* **2** scivolo *m.* **3** (*mecc.*) guida *f.*, cursore *m.* **4** (*per microscopio*) vetrino *m.* **5** diapositiva *f.* ♦ **s. fastener** chiusura lampo
to **slide** [slaɪd] (*pass. e p. p.* **slid**) *v. intr.* scivolare
sliding ['slaɪdɪŋ] *agg.* scorrevole, mobile ♦ **s. scale** scala mobile (*dei salari*)
slight [slaɪt] **A** *agg.* **1** esile, smilzo, minuto **2** leggero, lieve **3** insignificante **B** *s.* **1** affronto *m.*, mancanza *f.* di riguardo **2** trascuratezza *f.*
to **slight** [slaɪt] *v. tr.* **1** disprezzare **2** trascurare
slightly ['slaɪtlɪ] *avv.* **1** leggermente, un poco **2** scarsamente
slim [slɪm] *agg.* magro, snello
to **slim** [slɪm] *v. intr.* **1** dimagrire (*seguendo una dieta*) **2** fare la dieta
slime [slaɪm] *s.* limo *m.*, melma *f.*
slimming ['slɪmɪŋ] *agg.* dimagrante
slimy ['slaɪmɪ] *agg.* **1** fangoso **2** viscido
sling [slɪŋ] *s.* **1** fionda *f.* **2** imbracatura *f.* ♦ **baby s.** marsupio
to **sling** [slɪŋ] (*pass. e p. p.* **slung**) *v. tr.* **1** lanciare, scagliare **2** sospendere, imbracare **3** portare a tracolla
slip [slɪp] *s.* **1** scivolone *m.* **2** errore *m.*, svista *f.* **3** tagliando *m.*, scontrino *m.* **4** striscia *f.* **5** scivolo *m.*, imbarcadero *m.* **6** federa *f.* **7** sottoveste *f.* ♦ **s.-road** rampa di accesso (*a un'autostrada*)
to **slip** [slɪp] **A** *v. intr.* **1** scivolare **2** sgu-

sciare, sgattaiolare **3** decadere, peggiorare **B** *v. tr.*, **1** far scivolare, infilare **2** sciogliere, liberare **3** sottrarsi a ♦ **to let s.** lasciarsi scappare; **to s. away** svignarsela; **to s. up** sbagliare
slipper ['slɪpəʳ] *s.* pantofola *f.*
slippery ['slɪp(ə)rɪ] *agg.* scivoloso, sdrucciolevole, viscido
slipshod ['slɪpʃəd] *agg.* trasandato
slip-up ['slɪpʌp] *s.* (*fam.*) sbaglio *m.*
slipway ['slɪpweɪ] *s.* (*naut.*) scalo *m.*
slit [slɪt] *s.* fenditura *f.*, fessura *f.*, spacco *m.*
to slit [slɪt] (*pass. e p. p.* **slit**) *v. tr.* tagliare, fendere
to slither ['slɪðəʳ] *v. intr.* scivolare
sliver ['slɪvəʳ] *s.* scheggia *f.*, frammento *m.*
slob [sləb] *s.* (*pop.*) zoticone *m.*
to slog [sləg] *v. intr.* **1** colpire con violenza **2** sgobbare **3** procedere a fatica
slogan ['slɒʊgən] *s.* slogan *m. inv.*
to slop [sləp] **A** *v. tr.* **1** versare, rovesciare **2** schizzare **B** *v. intr.* **1** traboccare **2** sguazzare
slope [slɒʊp] *s.* **1** pendio *m.*, scarpata *f.* **2** inclinazione *f.*, pendenza *f.*
to slope [slɒʊp] *v. intr.* pendere, essere inclinato ♦ **to s. off** svignarsela
sloppy ['sləpɪ] *agg.* **1** fangoso, umido **2** trascurato, sciatto
slot [slət] *s.* **1** fessura *f.*, apertura *f.* **2** scanalatura *f.*
to slot [slət] *v. tr.* **1** (*in una fessura*) introdurre, inserire **2** scanalare
sloth [slɒʊtθ] *s.* pigrizia *f.*
to slouch [slaʊtʃ] *v. intr.* trascinarsi, ciondolare ♦ **to s. about** gironzolare
slow [slɒʊ] **A** *agg.* **1** lento **2** tardo, ottuso **3** monotono, noioso **4** indietro, in ritardo **B** *avv.* lentamente, piano ♦ **in s. motion** al rallentatore
to slow [slɒʊ] *v. tr. e intr.* rallentare
slowness ['slɒʊnɪs] *s.* lentezza *f.*
sludge [slʌdʒ] *s.* fango *m.*
slug (1) [slʌg] *s.* lumaca *f.*
slug (2) [slʌg] *s.* **1** pallottola *f.*, proiettile *m.* **2** gettone *m.*
sluggish ['slʌgɪʃ] *agg.* indolente, pigro
sluice [slu:s] *s.* chiusa *f.*
slum [slʌm] *s.* **1** catapecchia *f.* **2** *al pl.* bassifondi *m. pl.*
slumber ['slʌmbəʳ] *s.* sonno *m.*
slump [slʌmp] *s.* **1** crollo *m.*, caduta *f.* **2** (*econ.*) recessione *f.*
to slump [slʌmp] *v. intr.* crollare
slung [slʌŋ] *pass. e p. p. di* **to sling**
slur [slɜ:ʳ] *s.* **1** affronto *m.*, accusa *f.* **2** pronuncia *f.* indistinta **3** (*mus.*) legatura *f.*
to slurp [slɜ:p] *v. tr. e intr.* trangugiare
slush [slʌʃ] *s.* fanghiglia *f.* ♦ **s. fund** fondi neri
slut [slʌt] *s.* **1** sciattona *f.* **2** sgualdrina *f.*
sly [slaɪ] *agg.* furbo, scaltro
smack (1) [smæk] *s.* aroma *m.*, gusto *m.*
smack (2) [smæk] *s.* **1** schiaffo *m.* **2** (*di bacio, frusta*) schiocco *m.* **3** bacio *m.* con lo schiocco
to smack (1) [smæk] *v. intr.* sapere di
to smack (2) [smæk] *v. tr.* **1** schioccare **2** schiaffeggiare
small [smɜ:l] *agg.* piccolo ♦ **s. change** spiccioli; **s. hours** ore piccole; **s. talk** chiacchiere
smallpox ['smɜ:lpəks] *s.* vaiolo *m.*
smart [sma:t] *agg.* **1** elegante, alla moda **2** intelligente, sveglio **3** forte, acuto, aspro ♦ **the s. set** il bel mondo
to smart [sma:t] *v. intr.* **1** bruciare, far male **2** soffrire
to smarten up ['sma:tn ʌp] **A** *v. tr.* **1** abbellire **2** ravvivare **B** *v. intr.* farsi bello
smash [smæʃ] *s.* **1** scontro *m.*, collisione *f.* **2** tracollo *m.*, rovina *f.* **3** (*fam.*) grande successo *m.* **4** (*tennis*) smash *m. inv.*, schiacciata *f.*
to smash [smæʃ] **A** *v. tr.* **1** fracassare, schiantare **2** sconfiggere, stroncare **3** (*tennis*) schiacciare **B** *v. intr.* frantumarsi, schiantarsi
smashing ['smæʃɪŋ] *agg.* (*fam.*) formidabile
smash-up ['smæʃˌʌp] *s.* **1** scontro *m.*, incidente *m.* stradale **2** rovina *f.*
smattering ['smæt(ə)rɪŋ] *s.* infarinatura *f.* (*fig.*)
smell [smɛl] *s.* **1** odorato *m.* **2** odore *m.*
to smell [smɛl] (*pass. e p. p.* **smelt**) **A** *v. tr.* annusare, fiutare **B** *v. intr.* odorare, aver profumo, puzzare
smile [smaɪl] *s.* sorriso *m.*
to smile [smaɪl] *v. intr.* sorridere
smiling ['smaɪlɪŋ] *agg.* sorridente
smirk [smɜ:k] *s.* sorriso *m.* affettato
smith [smɪθ] *s.* fabbro *m.*
smithery ['smɪθərɪ] *s.* fucina *f.*
smock [smək] *s.* grembiule *m.*
smog [sməg] *s.* smog *m. inv.*
smoke [smɒʊk] *s.* fumo *m.*
to smoke [smɒʊk] **A** *v. tr.* **1** fumare **2**

affumicare **B** *v. intr.* fumare
smoker ['smɒʊkəʳ] *s.* **1** fumatore *m.* **2** scompartimento *m.* per fumatori
smoking ['smɒʊkɪŋ] *s.* fumo *m.* ♦ **no s.** vietato fumare
smoky ['smɒʊkɪ] *agg.* fumoso
smooth [smuːð] *agg.* **1** liscio, levigato **2** omogeneo, ben amalgamato **3** dolce, amabile **4** sdolcinato, mellifluo **5** facile
to smooth [smuːð] *v. tr.* **1** lisciare, levigare **2** appianare
smoothness ['smuːðnɪs] *s.* levigatezza *f.*
to smother ['smʌðəʳ] *v. tr.* soffocare, reprimere
to smoulder ['smɒʊldəʳ] (*USA* **to smolder**) *v. intr.* covare sotto la cenere
smudge [smʌdʒ] *s.* **1** macchia *f.*, sbavatura *f.* **2** (*USA*) fumo *m.* denso
to smudge [smʌdʒ] *v. tr.* macchiare, imbrattare
smug [smʌg] *agg.* compiaciuto
to smuggle ['smʌgl] *v. tr.* contrabbandare
smuggler ['smʌgləʳ] *s.* contrabbandiere *m.*
smuggling ['smʌglɪŋ] *s.* contrabbando *m.*
smut [smʌt] *s.* **1** fuliggine *f.* **2** (*fam.*) oscenità *f.*
snack [snæk] *s.* spuntino *m.*, snack *m. inv.*
snag [snæg] *s.* **1** protuberanza *f.* **2** impedimento *m.*, ostacolo *m.*
snail [sneɪl] *s.* lumaca *f.*, chiocciola *f.*
snake [sneɪk] *s.* serpente *m.*
snap [snæp] **A** *s.* **1** scatto *m.*, schiocco *m.*, schianto *m.* **2** fermaglio *m.* **3** (*fot.*) istantanea *f.* **B** *agg.* **1** improvviso **2** a scatto
to snap [snæp] **A** *v. tr.* **1** spezzare **2** schioccare, far scattare **3** addentare **4** fare una foto a **B** *v. intr.* **1** spezzarsi **2** scattare, schioccare **3** parlare in modo brusco ♦ **to s. at** addentare, afferrare; **to s. up** prendere al volo
snappy ['snæpɪ] *agg.* **1** brusco, aspro **2** brillante **3** alla moda ♦ **make it s.!** sbrigati!
snapshot ['snæpʃət] *s.* (*fot.*) istantanea *f.*
snare [snɛəʳ] *s.* tranello *m.*, trappola *f.*
to snarl [snaːl] *v. intr.* ringhiare
snarling ['snaːlɪŋ] *agg.* ringhioso
snatch [snætʃ] *s.* **1** strappo *m.*, strattone *m.* **2** (*pop.*) scippo *m.* **3** frammento *m.*
to snatch [snætʃ] *v. tr.* **1** afferrare, strappare **2** scippare, rubare
sneer [snɪəʳ] *s.* sogghigno *m.*
to sneer [snɪəʳ] *v. intr.* sogghignare
sneeze [sniːz] *s.* starnuto *m.*
to sneeze [sniːz] *v. intr.* starnutire
to sniff [snɪf] *v. tr. e intr.* annusare, fiutare, tirare su con il naso
to snigger ['snɪgəʳ] *v. intr.* ridacchiare
snip [snɪp] *s.* **1** forbiciata *f.* **2** ritaglio *m.*, pezzetto *m.* **3** scampolo *m.* **4** (*fam.*) affare *m.*, occasione *f.*
to snip [snɪp] *v. tr.* tagliare (*con forbici*)
snipe [snaɪp] *s.* beccaccino *m.*
sniper ['snaɪpəʳ] *s.* franco tiratore *m.*
snippet ['snɪpɪt] *s.* frammento *m.*
snivelling ['snɪvlɪŋ] *agg.* piagnucoloso
snob [snəb] *s.* snob *m. e f. inv.*
snobbery ['snəbərɪ] *s.* snobismo *m.*
snobbish ['snəbɪʃ] *agg.* snobistico, snob
to snoop [snuːp] *v. intr.* curiosare
snooty ['snuːtɪ] *agg.* borioso
snooze [snuːz] *s.* pisolino *m.*, dormitina *f.*
to snooze [snuːz] *v. intr.* sonnecchiare
to snore [snɜːʳ] *v. intr.* russare
snorkel ['snɜːk(ə)l] *s.* boccaglio *m.*
snort [snɜːt] *s.* sbuffo *m.*
to snort [snɜːt] *v. intr.* sbuffare
snout [snaʊt] *s.* muso *m.*, grugno *m.*
snow [snɒʊ] *s.* neve *f.*
to snow [snɒʊ] *v. intr.* nevicare
snowball ['snɒʊbɜːl] *s.* palla *f.* di neve
snowbound ['snɒʊbaʊnd] *agg.* bloccato dalla neve
snowdrift ['snɒʊdrɪft] *s.* cumulo *m.* di neve
snowdrop ['snɒʊdrəp] *s.* bucaneve *m.*
snowfall ['snɒʊfɜːl] *s.* nevicata *f.*
snowflake ['snɒʊfleɪk] *s.* fiocco *m.* di neve
snowman ['snɒʊmæn] (*pl.* **snowmen**) *s.* pupazzo *m.* di neve
snowplough ['snɒʊˌplaʊ] (*USA* **snowplow**) *s.* spazzaneve *m. inv.*
snowshoe ['snɒʊʃuː] *s.* racchetta *f.* da neve
snowslide ['snɒʊslaɪd] *s.* slavina *f.*
snowstorm ['snɒʊstɜːm] *s.* bufera *f.* di neve
snowy ['snɒ(ʊ)ɪ] *agg.* **1** nevoso **2** candido
snub (1) [snʌb] *s.* affronto *m.*
snub (2) [snʌb] *agg.* camuso
to snub [snʌb] *v. tr.* **1** rimproverare, umiliare **2** snobbare
snuff [snʌf] *s.* tabacco *m.* da fiuto
snug [snʌg] **1** comodo, accogliente **2** (*di abito*) aderente
to snuggle ['snʌgl] *v. intr.* rannicchiarsi
so [sɒʊ] **A** *avv.* **1** così, tanto, talmente **2** allora, così **3** molto **B** *cong.* perciò, così

♦ **and so on** e così via; **or s.** all'incirca; **so as** così da; **so much** (così) tanto; **so many** (così) tanti; **so far** finora; **so long** a presto!; **so what?** e allora?

to **soak** [sɒʊk] **A** *v. tr.* **1** immergere, mettere a bagno **2** (*fam.*) tartassare **B** *v. intr.* **1** inzupparsi **2** penetrare ♦ **to s. up** assorbire

soap [sɒʊp] *s.* sapone *m.* ♦ **s. dish** portasapone; **s. flakes** sapone in scaglie; **s. powder** detersivo in polvere

to **soap** [sɒʊp] *v. tr.* insaponare

soapy ['sɒʊpɪ] *agg.* insaponato, saponoso

to **soar** [sɜːʳ] *v. intr.* **1** alzarsi in volo **2** (*aer.*) veleggiare **3** elevarsi, svettare **4** aumentare vertiginosamente, salire alle stelle

sob [səb] *s.* singhiozzo *m.*

to **sob** [səb] *v. intr.* singhiozzare, piangere

sober ['sɒʊbəʳ] *agg.* **1** sobrio, non ubriaco **2** moderato, equilibrato

to **sober** ['sɒʊbəʳ] **A** *v. tr.* **1** calmare, moderare **2 to s. up** far passare la sbornia a **B** *v. intr.* **1** calmarsi, rinsavire **2 to s. up** smaltire la sbornia

so-called [ˌsɒʊ'kɜːld] *agg.* cosiddetto

soccer ['səkəʳ] *s.* (*sport*) calcio *m.*

sociable ['sɒʊʃɛbl] *agg.* socievole

social ['sɒʊʃəl] *agg.* **1** sociale **2** socievole ♦ **s. democracy** socialdemocrazia; **s. security** previdenza sociale; **s. worker** assistente sociale

socialism ['sɒʊʃəlɪz(ə)m] *s.* socialismo *m.*

socialist ['sɒʊʃəlɪst] *agg. e s.* socialista *m. e f.*

to **socialize** ['sɒʊʃəlaɪz] *v. tr. e intr.* socializzare

society [sə'saɪətɪ] *s.* società *f.*

sociologist [ˌsɒʊsɪ'əlɒdʒɪst] *s.* sociologo *m.*

sociology [ˌsɒʊsɪ'əlɒdʒɪ] *s.* sociologia *f.*

sock [sək] *s.* calza *f.* (*da uomo*), calzino *m.*

socket ['səkɪt] *s.* **1** cavità *f.*, incavo *m.* **2** presa *f.* di corrente **3** (*elettron.*) zoccolo *m.* ♦ **eye s.** orbita

sod (1) [səd] *s.* zolla *f.*

sod (2) [səd] *s.* canaglia *f.*

sodium ['sɒʊdjəm] *s.* sodio *m.*

sofa ['sɒʊfə] *s.* sofà *m.*

soft [səft] *agg.* **1** molle, morbido, tenero **2** leggero, delicato **3** sommesso, tenue **4** gentile, amabile **5** (*fam.*) facile **6** leggero, non alcolico ♦ **s. drink** bevanda non alcolica

to **soften** ['səfn] **A** *v. tr.* **1** ammorbidire **2** abbassare, mitigare, attenuare **B** *v. intr.* **1** ammorbidirsi **2** addolcirsi, intenerirsi **3** placarsi ♦ **to s. up** indebolire

softness ['səftnɪs] *s.* **1** mollezza *f.*, morbidezza *f.* **2** mitezza *f.*, dolcezza *f.* **3** stupidità *f.*

to **soft-soap** ['səftˌsɒʊp] *v. tr.* (*fam.*) adulare, lisciare

software ['səftwɛəʳ] *s.* software *m. inv.*

soggy ['səgɪ] *agg.* fradicio, inzuppato

soil (1) [səɪl] *s.* suolo *m.*, terreno *m.*

soil (2) [səɪl] *s.* **1** sporco *m.*, sudiciume *m.* **2** concime *m.*

to **soil** [səɪl] *v. tr.* imbrattare, sporcare

soiled [səɪld] *agg.* sporco, macchiato

solace ['sələs] *s.* conforto *m.*, consolazione *f.*

solar ['sɒʊləʳ] *agg.* solare

sold [sɒʊld] *pass. e p. p. di* **to sell** ♦ **s. out** (*di merce*) esaurito

to **solder** ['səldəʳ] *v. tr.* saldare

soldier ['sɒʊldʒəʳ] *s.* soldato *m.*

soldierly ['sɒʊldʒəlɪ] *agg.* militaresco

sole (1) [sɒʊl] *agg.* unico, singolo

sole (2) [sɒʊl] *s.* **1** suola *f.* **2** (*del piede*) pianta *f.* **3** base *f.*, fondo *m.*

sole (3) [sɒʊl] *s.* sogliola *f.*

to **sole** [sɒʊl] *v. tr.* risuolare

solely ['sɒʊllɪ] *avv.* solamente, unicamente

solemn ['sələm] *agg.* solenne

solemnity [sə'lɛmnɪtɪ] *s.* solennità *f.*

solfeggio [səl'fɛdʒɪɒʊ] *s.* solfeggio *m.*

to **solicit** [sə'lɪsɪt] *v. tr.* **1** sollecitare **2** adescare **3** istigare

solicitation [səˌlɪsɪ'teɪʃ(ə)n] *s.* **1** sollecitazione *f.* **2** adescamento *m.* **3** istigazione *f.*

solicitor [sə'lɪsɪtəʳ] *s.* procuratore *m.* legale

solicitous [sə'lɪsɪtəs] *agg.* premuroso

solid ['səlɪd] **A** *agg.* **1** solido **2** compatto, uniforme **3** pieno, massiccio **B** *s.* solido *m.*, sostanza *f.* solida

solidarity [ˌsəlɪ'dærɪtɪ] *s.* solidarietà *f.*

solidity [sə'lɪdɪtɪ] *s.* solidità *f.*

soliloquy [sə'lɪləkwɪ] *s.* monologo *m.*

solitaire [ˌsəlɪ'tɛəʳ] *s.* solitario *m.*

solitary ['səlɪt(ə)rɪ] *agg.* solitario ♦ **s. confinement** cella d'isolamento

solitude ['səlɪtjuːd] *s.* solitudine *f.*

to **solmizate** ['səlmɪzeɪt] *v. tr. e intr.* (*mus.*) solfeggiare

solo ['sɒʊlɒʊ] *s.* (*mus.*) assolo *m.*

soloist ['sɒʊlɒ(ʊ)ɪst] *s.* solista *m. e f.*

solstice ['sɔlstɪs] *s.* solstizio *m.*
soluble ['sɔljʊbl] *agg.* solubile
solution [sə'luːʃ(ə)n] *s.* soluzione *f.*
to solve [sɔlv] *v. tr.* risolvere
solvent ['sɔlv(ə)nt] **A** *agg.* **1** (*comm.*) solvibile **2** (*chim.*) solvente **B** *s.* solvente *m.*
sombre ['sɔmbəʳ] (*USA* **somber**) *agg.* **1** scuro **2** cupo, malinconico
some [sʌm, səm] **A** *agg.* **1** (*con valore partitivo*) del, dello, dei, della, delle, un po' di (ES: **would you like s. tea?** gradisci del tè?) **2** alcuni, alcune, qualche (ES: **s. years ago** alcuni anni fa) **3** un, una, un certo, una certa, qualche (ES: **s. time or other** una volta o l'altra) **B** *pron. indef.* alcuni, alcune, qualcuno, qualcuna, un po', ne (ES: **would you like s. biscuits? I already had s.** vuoi dei biscotti? ne ho già presi) **C** *avv.* **1** circa **2** (*fam.*) un po', piuttosto
somebody ['sʌmbədɪ] *pron. indef.* qualcuno
someday ['sʌmdeɪ] *avv.* un giorno o l'altro
somehow ['sʌmhaʊ] *avv.* in qualche modo, in un modo o nell'altro
someone ['sʌmwʌn] *pron. indef.* qualcuno
someplace ['sʌmpleɪs] *avv.* (*USA*) in qualche luogo
somersault ['sʌməsɜːlt] *s.* **1** capriola *f.* **2** salto *m.* mortale
something ['sʌmθɪŋ] *pron. indef.* qualcosa
sometime ['sʌmtaɪm] **A** *agg. attr.* di un tempo, precedente, ex, già **B** *avv.* un giorno o l'altro
sometimes ['sʌmtaɪmz] *avv.* qualche volta, talvolta
somewhat ['sʌmwət] *avv.* piuttosto, un po'
somewhere ['sʌmwɛəʳ] *avv.* in qualche parte ♦ **s. else** in qualche altra parte
son [sʌn] *s.* figlio *m.* ♦ **s.-in-law** genero
song [sɔŋ] *s.* canto *m.*, canzone *f.* ♦ **s.-bird** uccello canoro; **s-book** canzoniere
sonic ['sɔnɪk] *agg.* sonico
sonnet ['sɔnɪt] *s.* sonetto *m.*
sonneteer [ˌsɔnɪ'tɪəʳ] *s.* scrittore *m.* di sonetti
sonny ['sʌnɪ] *s.* (*fam.*) ragazzo *m.* mio, figlio *m.* mio
sonority [sə'nɔrɪtɪ] *s.* sonorità *f.*
sonorous [sə'nɔːrəs] *agg.* sonoro
soon [suːn] *avv.* **1** presto, fra breve, fra poco **2** piuttosto ♦ **as s. as (possible)** non appena (possibile); **sooner or later** prima o poi
soot [sʊt] *s.* fuliggine *f.*
to soothe [suːð] *v. tr.* consolare, calmare
to sophisticate [sə'fɪstɪkeɪt] *v. tr.* sofisticare, adulterare
sophisticated [sə'fɪstɪkeɪtɪd] *agg.* **1** sofisticato, raffinato **2** adulterato
soppy ['sɔpɪ] *agg.* (*fam.*) **1** fradicio **2** sentimentale
soprano [sə'prɑːnɒʊ] *s.* soprano *m.*
sorbet ['sɜːbət] *s.* sorbetto *m.*
sorcerer ['sɜːs(ə)rəʳ] *s.* stregone *m.*, mago *m.*
sorceress ['sɜːs(ə)rɪs] *s.* strega *f.*, maga *f.*
sorcery ['sɜːs(ə)rɪ] *s.* stregoneria *f.*
sordid ['sɜːdɪd] *agg.* sordido
sore [sɜːʳ] **A** *agg.* **1** dolorante, che fa male **2** addolorato **3** (*fam.*) irritato **B** *s.* piaga *f.*, infiammazione *f.* ♦ **to have a s. throat** avere mal di gola
sorely ['sɜːlɪ] *avv.* grandemente, molto
sorrow ['sɔrɒʊ] *s.* dolore *m.*, pena *f.*
sorrowful ['sɔrəf(ʊ)l] *agg.* **1** addolorato, afflitto **2** doloroso
sorry ['sɔrɪ] **A** *agg.* **1** spiacente, dolente **2** pentito, rammaricato **3** meschino, miserabile **B** *inter.* **1** scusi, scusate, scusa **2** prego?, come? ♦ **to be s.** dispiacersi
sort [sɜːt] *s.* **1** genere *m.*, qualità *f.*, tipo *m.* **2** ordinamento *m.* ♦ **a s. of** una specie di
to sort [sɜːt] *v. tr.* **1** classificare, selezionare, smistare **2** (*inf.*) ordinare
sorting ['sɜːtɪŋ] *s.* **1** classificazione *f.* **2** smistamento *m.* **3** (*inf.*) ordinamento *m.*
so-so ['sɒʊsɒʊ] *agg. e avv.* così così
sought [sɜːt] *pass. e p. p. di* **to seek**
soul [sɒʊl] *s.* anima *f.*
soulful [sɒʊlf(ʊ)l] *agg.* sentimentale
sound (1) [saʊnd] **A** *agg.* **1** sano, in buono stato **2** solido, valido, efficace **3** accurato **4** completo, totale, profondo **B** *avv.* profondamente
sound (2) [saʊnd] *s.* **1** suono *m.*, rumore *m.* **2** tono *m.* **3** audio *m. inv.* ♦ **s. effects** effetti sonori
sound (3) [saʊnd] *s.* scandaglio *m.*, sonda *f.*
sound (4) [saʊnd] *s.* braccio *m.* di mare, stretto *m.*
to sound (1) [saʊnd] **A** *v. intr.* **1** suonare, risuonare **2** sembrare **B** *v. tr.* **1** suonare, far risuonare **2** far risapere, proclamare **3** auscultare ♦ **to s. like** assomigliare a
to sound (2) [saʊnd] *v. tr.* scandagliare, sondare ♦ **to s. out** tastare il terreno su
sounding ['saʊndɪŋ] *s.* **1** scandaglio *m.* **2**

al pl. bassi fondali *m. pl.* **3** sondaggio *m.*
soundness ['saʊndnɪs] *s.* **1** vigore *m.*, buona condizione *f.* **2** solidità *f.*
soundproof ['saʊnd,prʊf] *agg.* insonorizzato
soundtrack ['saʊndtræk] *s.* colonna *f.* sonora
soup [suːp] *s.* minestra *f.*, zuppa *f.* ♦ **to be in the s.** trovarsi nei pasticci
sour ['saʊəʳ] *agg.* **1** acidulo, aspro **2** bisbetico, inacidito ♦ **s. orange** arancia amara
to sour ['saʊəʳ] *v. tr. e intr.* inacidire, inacidirsi
source [sɜːs] *s.* sorgente *f.*, fonte *f.*
soutane [suː'taːn] *s.* tonaca *f.*
south [saʊθ] **A** *s.* sud *m. inv.*, meridione *m.* **B** *agg.* del sud, meridionale **C** *avv.* a sud, da sud
southeast [,saʊθ'iːst] **A** *s.* sud-est *m. inv.* **B** *agg.* di sud-est, sud-orientale
southerly ['sʌðəlɪ] **A** *agg.* **1** meridionale **2** proveniente da sud **B** *avv.* verso sud, da sud
southern ['sʌðən] *agg.* meridionale
southwards ['saʊθwədz] *avv.* verso sud
southwest [,saʊθ'wɛst] **A** *s.* sud-ovest *m. inv.* **B** *agg.* di sud-ovest, sud-occidentale
souvenir ['suːvənɪəʳ] *s.* souvenir *m. inv.*
sovereign ['səvrɪn] *s.* sovrano *m.*, sovrana *f.*
soviet ['sɒʊvɪɛt] **A** *s.* soviet *m. inv.* **B** *agg.* sovietico
sow [sɒʊ] *s.* scrofa *f.*
to sow [sɒʊ] (*pass.* **sowed**, *p. p.* **sowed**, **sown**) *v. tr.* seminare
sowing ['sɒ(ʊ)ɪŋ] *s.* semina *f.*
sown [sɒʊn] *p. p. di* **to sow**
soya-bean ['səɪəbiːn] *s.* soia *f.*
spa [spaː] *s.* terme *f. pl.*
space [speɪs] **A** *s.* spazio *m.* **B** *agg.* spaziale
to space [speɪs] *v. tr.* spaziare, distanziare
space-bar ['speɪsbaːʳ] *s.* barra *f.* spaziatrice
spaceman ['speɪsmən] (*pl.* **spacemen**) *s.* astronauta *m.*
spaceship ['speɪsʃɪp] *s.* astronave *f.*
spacing ['speɪsɪŋ] *s.* spaziatura *f.*
spacious ['speɪʃəs] *agg.* spazioso
spade [speɪd] *s.* **1** vanga *f.* **2** (*carte da gioco*) picche *m. inv.*
to spade [speɪd] *v. tr.* vangare
span [spæn] *s.* **1** spanna *f.*, palmo *m.* **2** intervallo *m.*, durata *f.* **3** larghezza *f.*, apertura *f.* **4** (*aer.*) apertura *f.* alare **5** (*arch.*) campata *f.*
Spaniard ['spænjəd] *s.* spagnolo *m.*
Spanish ['spænɪʃ] *agg.* spagnolo
to spank [spæŋk] *v. tr.* sculacciare
spanking ['spæŋkɪŋ] *agg.* (*fam.*) magnifico, ottimo
spanner ['spænəʳ] *s.* (*mecc.*) chiave *f.*
spare [spɛəʳ] **A** *agg.* **1** di scorta, di ricambio **2** disponibile, libero, in più **3** scarno, sparuto **4** frugale, misero **B** *s.* (pezzo di) ricambio *m.* ♦ **s. time** tempo libero; **s. wheel** ruota di scorta
to spare [spɛəʳ] *v. tr.* **1** risparmiare, fare a meno di **2** dare, offrire, dedicare **3** evitare, risparmiarsi
spark [spaːk] *s.* scintilla *f.*
to spark [spaːk] *v. intr.* emettere scintille
sparking plug ['spaːkɪŋ plʌg] *s.* candela *f.* (d'accensione)
to sparkle ['spaːkl] *v. intr.* **1** scintillare **2** spumeggiare
sparkling ['spaːklɪŋ] *agg.* **1** scintillante **2** spumante, effervescente ♦ **s. water** acqua gassata; **s. wine** spumante
sparrow ['spærɒʊ] *s.* passero *m.*
sparse [spaːs] *agg.* sparso, rado
spasm ['spæz(ə)m] *s.* spasmo *m.*, accesso *m.*
spasmodic(al) [spæz'mədɪk((ə)l)] *agg.* spasmodico
spastic ['spæstɪk] *agg. e s.* spastico *m.*
spat [spæt] *pass. e p. p. di* **to spit**
spate [speɪt] *s.* **1** piena *f.* **2** grande quantità *f.*
spatter ['spætəʳ] *s.* schizzo *m.*
to spatter ['spætəʳ] *v. tr.* schizzare
spawn [spɜːn] *s.* uova *f. pl.* (*di pesci, molluschi*)
to speak [spiːk] (*pass.* **spoke**, *p. p.* **spoken**) **A** *v. intr.* parlare **B** *v. tr.* **1** dire, esprimere **2** (*una lingua*) parlare ♦ **to s. about** parlare di; **to s. up** parlare a voce alta, parlare chiaro
speaker ['spiːkəʳ] **1** oratore *m.* **2** speaker *m. inv.*, annunciatore *m.* **3** altoparlante *m.*
spear [spɪəʳ] *s.* **1** lancia *f.* **2** fiocina *f.*
to spear [spɪəʳ] *v. tr.* **1** colpire (con una lancia), trafiggere **2** fiocinare
spearhead ['spɪəhɛd] *s.* **1** punta *f.* di lancia **2** avanguardia *f.*
to spearhead ['spɪəhɛd] *v. tr.* essere alla testa di
special ['spɛʃ(ə)l] *agg.* speciale, particolare

specialist ['spɛʃəlɪst] *s.* specialista *m. e f.*
speciality [ˌspɛʃɪ'ælɪtɪ] *s.* specialità *f.*
specialization [ˌspɛʃəlaɪ'zeɪʃ(ə)n] *s.* specializzazione *f.*
to specialize ['spɛʃəlaɪz] *v. tr. e intr.* specializzare, specializzarsi
specialized ['spɛʃəlaɪzd] *agg.* specializzato
specially ['spɛʃəlɪ] *avv.* **1** specialmente **2** appositamente
species ['spiːʃiːz] *s.* specie *f. inv.*
specific [spɪ'sɪfɪk] *s.* specifico *m.*
to specify ['spɛsɪfaɪ] *v. tr.* specificare
specimen ['spɛsɪmɪn] *s.* esemplare *m.*, campione *m.*
speck [spɛk] *s.* **1** macchiolina *f.* **2** granello *m.*
to speckle ['spɛkl] *v. tr.* macchiettare, punteggiare
specs [spɛks] *s. pl.* (*fam.*) occhiali *m. pl.*
spectacle ['spɛktəkl] *s.* spettacolo *m.*
spectacular [spɛk'tækjʊlər] *agg.* spettacolare
spectator [spɛk'teɪtər] *s.* spettatore *m.*
spectre ['spɛktər] (*USA* **specter**) *s.* spettro *m.*
spectrum ['spɛktrəm] (*pl.* **spectra**) *s.* (*fis.*) spettro *m.*
specular ['spɛkjʊlər] *agg.* speculare
to speculate ['spɛkjʊleɪt] *v. intr.* **1** meditare, fare congetture **2** speculare
speculation [ˌspɛkjʊ'leɪʃ(ə)n] *s.* speculazione *f.*
speech [spiːtʃ] *s.* **1** linguaggio *m.*, parola *f.* **2** lingua *f.*, parlata *f.* **3** discorso *m.*
speechless ['spiːtʃlɪs] *agg.* **1** ammutolito, muto **2** inesprimibile
speed [spiːd] *s.* **1** velocità *f.*, rapidità *f.* **2** (*autom.*) marcia *f.* ♦ **s. limit** limite di velocità
to speed [spiːd] (*pass. e p. p.* **sped, speeded**) *v. intr.* **1** andare a tutta velocità **2** affrettarsi ♦ **to s. up** accelerare
speeding ['spiːdɪŋ] *s.* eccesso *m.* di velocità
speedometer [spɪ'dəmɪtər] *s.* tachimetro *m.*
speedway ['spiːdweɪ] *s.* **1** (*USA*) autostrada *f.* **2** (*per corse motociclistiche*) pista *f.*
speedy ['spiːdɪ] *agg.* veloce, rapido
spel(a)eologist [ˌspiːlɪ'ələdʒɪst] *s.* speleologo *m.*
spel(a)eology [ˌspiːlɪ'ələdʒɪ] *s.* speleologia *f.*
spell (1) [spɛl] *s.* incantesimo *m.*
spell (2) [spɛl] *s.* **1** turno *m.* di lavoro **2** periodo *m.*, intervallo *m.*
to spell [spɛl] (*pass. e p. p.* **spelt, spelled**) *v. tr.* **1** compitare **2** (*fam.*) significare
spellbound ['spɛlbaʊnd] *agg.* incantato
spelling ['spɛlɪŋ] *s.* **1** compitazione *f.* **2** ortografia *f.* ♦ **s. book** sillabario
spelt [spɛlt] *pass. e p. p. di* **to spell**
to spend [spɛnd] (*pass. e p. p.* **spent**) **A** *v. tr.* **1** spendere **2** dedicare **3** trascorrere, passare **B** *v. intr.* **1** spendere (denaro) **2** esaurirsi
spendthrift ['spɛn(d)θrɪft] *s.* spendaccione *m.*
spent [spɛnt] *pass. e p. p. di* **to spend**
sperm [spɜːm] *s.* sperma *m.*
to spew [spjuː] *v. tr. e intr.* vomitare
sphere [sfɪər] *s.* sfera *f.*
sphinx [sfɪŋks] *s.* sfinge *f.*
spice [spaɪs] *s.* **1** spezie *f. pl.*, droga *f.* **2** aroma *m.*, gusto *m.*
to spice [spaɪs] *v. tr.* aromatizzare
spick-and-span ['spɪkən'spæn] *agg.* lindo, splendente
spicy ['spaɪsɪ] *agg.* aromatico, piccante
spider ['spaɪdər] *s.* ragno *m.*
spike [spaɪk] *s.* punta *f.*, chiodo *m.*
to spill [spɪl] (*pass. e p. p.* **spilt, spilled**) **A** *v. tr.* **1** versare, rovesciare **2** far cadere **B** *v. intr.* versarsi, rovesciarsi ♦ **to s. over** traboccare
spin [spɪn] *s.* **1** rotazione *f.* **2** (*aer.*) avvitamento *m.* **3** (*fam.*) giretto *m.*
to spin [spɪn] (*pass.* **spun, span**, *p. p.* **spun**) **A** *v. tr.* **1** filare **2** far girare **B** *v. intr.* girare, ruotare ♦ **to s. out** prolungare
spinach ['spɪnɪdʒ] *s.* spinacio *m.*
spinal ['spaɪnl] *agg.* spinale ♦ **s. cord** midollo spinale
spindle ['spɪndl] *s.* **1** fuso *m.* **2** (*mecc.*) mandrino *m.*
spindly ['spɪndlɪ] *agg.* affusolato
spine [spaɪn] *s.* **1** spina *f.* **2** spina *f.* dorsale *f.* **3** (*di libro*) dorso *m.*
spinet [spɪ'nɛt] *s.* spinetta *f.*
spinning ['spɪnɪŋ] **A** *agg.* girevole **B** *s.* filatura *f.* ♦ **s. top** trottola
spinster ['spɪnstər] *s.* zitella *f.*
spiral ['spaɪər(ə)l] *s.* spirale *f.* ♦ **s. staircase** scala a chiocciola
spire ['spaɪər] *s.* guglia *f.*
spirit ['spɪrɪt] *s.* **1** spirito *m.* **2** *al pl.* liquori

m. pl.
spirited ['spɪrɪtɪd] *agg.* vivace, vigoroso
spirit-level ['spɪrɪt,lɛvl] *s.* livella *f.* a bolla
spiritual ['spɪrɪtjʊəl] **A** *agg.* spirituale **B** *s.* spiritual *m.*
spiritualism ['spɪrɪtjʊəlɪz(ə)m] *s.* **1** spiritualismo *m.* **2** spiritismo *m.*
spit (1) [spɪt] *s.* spiedo *m.*
spit (2) [spɪt] *s.* sputo *m.*, saliva *f.*
to spit [spɪt] (*pass. e p. p.* **spat**) *v. tr. e intr.* **1** sputare **2** spruzzare **3** scoppiettare
spite [spaɪt] *s.* dispetto *m.*, ripicca *f.* ♦ **in s. of** nonostante; **out of s.** per dispetto
to spite [spaɪt] *v. tr.* fare un dispetto a, contrariare
spittle ['spɪtl] *s.* sputo *m.*, saliva *f.*
splash [splæʃ] *s.* **1** schizzo *m.*, spruzzo *m.* **2** tonfo *m.* **3** macchia *f.* **4** colpo *m.*, sensazione *f.*
to splash [splæʃ] **A** *v. tr.* **1** schizzare, spruzzare **2** scialacquare **3** (*fam.*) dare (*una notizia*) con grande rilievo **B** *v. intr.* **1** schizzare **2** sguazzare
spleen [spli:n] *s.* **1** milza *f.* **2** malumore *m.* **3** malinconia *f.*
splendid ['splɛndɪd] *agg.* splendido
splendour ['splɛndəʳ] *s.* splendore *m.*
spline [splaɪn] *s.* linguetta *f.*
splinter ['splɪntəʳ] *s.* scheggia *f.*
to splinter ['splɪntəʳ] *v. tr. e intr.* scheggiare, scheggiarsi
split [splɪt] *s.* **1** fessura *f.*, crepa *f.* **2** rottura *f.*, scissione *f.*, divisione *f.*
to split [splɪt] (*pass. e p. p.* **split**) **A** *v. tr.* **1** fendere, spaccare **2** dividere, scindere **3** strappare, lacerare **B** *v. intr.* **1** fendersi, spaccarsi **2** dividersi, separarsi **3** strapparsi, lacerarsi ♦ **to s. up** dividersi, suddividere
splitting ['splɪtɪŋ] *s.* **1** spaccatura *f.* **2** suddivisione *f.*
to splutter ['splʌtəʳ] *v. tr. e intr.* farfugliare
spoil [spɔɪl] *s.* spoglie *f. pl.*, bottino *m.*
to spoil [spɔɪl] (*pass. e p. p.* **spoilt, spoiled**) **A** *v. tr.* **1** guastare, rovinare **2** viziare **B** *v. intr.* guastarsi, andare a male
spoilsport ['spɔɪl,spɜ:t] *s.* guastafeste *m. e f.*
spoilt [spɔɪlt] *pass. e p. p. di* **to spoil**
spoke (1) [spɒʊk] *s.* **1** (*di ruota*) raggio *m.* **2** (*di scala*) piolo *m.*
spoke (2) [spɒʊk] *pass. di* **to speak**
spoken [spɒʊk(ə)n] *p. p. di* **to speak**
spokesman ['spɒʊksmən] (*pl.* **spokesmen**) *s.* portavoce *m. inv.*
spokeswoman ['spɒʊks,wʊmən] (*pl.* **spokeswomen**) *s.* portavoce *f. inv.*
sponge [spʌn(d)ʒ] *s.* spugna *f.* ♦ **s. cake** pan di Spagna; **s. cloth** tessuto di spugna
to sponge [spʌn(d)ʒ] *v. tr.* **1** pulire con una spugna, passare una spugna su **2** (*fam.*) scroccare
sponsor ['spənsəʳ] *s.* **1** (*dir*) garante *m. e f.* **2** sponsor *m. inv.*
to sponsor ['spənsəʳ] *v. tr.* **1** garantire **2** sponsorizzare
sponsorship ['spənsəʃɪp] *s.* **1** garanzia *f.* **2** sponsorizzazione *f.*
spontaneity [,spəntə'ni:tɪ] *s.* spontaneità *f.*
spontaneous [spən'teɪnjəs] *agg.* spontaneo
spook [spu:k] *s.* (*fam.*) spettro *m.*
spooky ['spu:kɪ] *agg.* (*fam.*) sinistro, pauroso
spool [spu:l] *s.* bobina *f.*
spoon [spu:n] *s.* cucchiaio *m.*
spoonful ['spu:nf(ʊ)l] *s.* cucchiaiata *f.*
sporadic [spə'rædɪk] *agg.* sporadico
sport [spɜ:t] *s.* **1** sport *m. inv.* **2** *al pl.* gare *f. pl.* sportive **3** persona *f.* sportiva
sporting ['spɜ:tɪŋ] *agg.* sportivo
sports [spɜ:ts] *agg.* **1** sportivo, dello sport **2** (*di abbigliamento*) sportivo, casual
sportswear ['spɜ:tswɛəʳ] *s.* abbigliamento *m.* sportivo
spot [spət] *s.* **1** posto *m.*, punto *m.* **2** chiazza *f.*, macchia *f.*, pallino *m.* **3** brufolo *m.* **4** piccola quantità *f.*, goccio *m.* **5** spot *m. inv.*, annuncio *m.* pubblicitario ♦ **on the s.** sul posto, su due piedi
to spot [spət] *v. tr.* **1** macchiare, punteggiare **2** individuare, riconoscere
spotless ['spətlɪs] *agg.* immacolato
spotlight ['spət,laɪt] *s.* proiettore *m.*, riflettore *m.*
spotted ['spətɪd] *agg.* **1** chiazzato, maculato **2** a pallini
spouse [spaʊz] *s.* consorte *m. e f.*
spout [spaʊt] *s.* **1** beccuccio *m.* **2** tubo *m.* di scarico **3** getto *m.*, zampillo *m.*
to spout [spaʊt] *v. intr.* scaturire, zampillare
sprain [spreɪn] *s.* distorsione *f.*, slogatura *f.*
to sprain [spreɪn] *v. tr.* slogarsi
sprang [spræŋ] *pass. di* **to spring**
to sprawl [sprɜ:l] *v. intr.* **1** adagiarsi, distendersi **2** estendersi irregolarmente
spray (1) [spreɪ] *s.* ramoscello *m.*

spray (2) [spreɪ] *s.* **1** spruzzo *m.* **2** spray *m. inv.*
to spray [spreɪ] *v. tr.* spruzzare, vaporizzare
spread [sprɛd] *s.* **1** diffusione *f.*, propagazione *f.* **2** apertura *f.*, ampiezza *f.* **3** (*fam.*) banchetto *m.* **4** (*cuc.*) pasta *f.* (*da spalmare*)
to spread [sprɛd] (*pass. e p. p.* **spread**) **A** *v. tr.* **1** stendere, spiegare **2** spargere, diffondere, propagare **3** distribuire, dividere **4** spalmare **B** *v. intr.* **1** tendersi, estendersi **2** spargersi, diffondersi, propagarsi ♦ **to s. out** sparpagliarsi
spreadsheet ['sprɛdʃiːt] *s.* (*inf.*) foglio *m.* elettronico
spree [spriː] *s.* baldoria *f.*
sprightly ['spraɪtlɪ] *agg.* allegro, vivace
spring [sprɪŋ] *s.* **1** salto *m.*, balzo *m.* **2** sorgente *f.*, fonte *f.* **3** origine *f.*, motivo *m.* **4** primavera *f.* **5** molla *f.* ♦ **hot springs** sorgente termale; **s. board** trampolino; **s.-clean** pulizie di primavera; **s. water** acqua di sorgente
to spring [sprɪŋ] (*pass.* **sprang**, *p. p.* **sprung**) **A** *v. intr.* **1** saltare, balzare **2** derivare, provenire **3** sgorgare, zampillare **B** *v. tr.* **1** saltare **2** far scattare, azionare ♦ **to s. up** saltar su, spuntare
springtime ['sprɪŋ,taɪm] *s.* primavera *f.*
sprinkle ['sprɪŋkl] *s.* spruzzo *m.*
to sprinkle ['sprɪŋkl] *v. tr.* spruzzare
sprinkler ['sprɪŋkləʳ] *s.* spruzzatore *m.*
sprint [sprɪnt] *s.* scatto *m.*, volata *f.*, sprint *m. inv.*
to sprint [sprɪnt] *v. intr.* scattare
sprinter ['sprɪntəʳ] *s.* scattista *m. e f.*, velocista *m. e f.*
sprite [spraɪt] *s.* folletto *m.*
sprout [spraʊt] *s.* germoglio *m.* ♦ **Brussels sprouts** cavolini di Bruxelles
to sprout [spraʊt] *v. intr.* germogliare, spuntare
spruce (1) [spruːs] *agg.* azzimato
spruce (2) [spruːs] *s.* abete *m.* rosso
sprung [sprʌŋ] *p. p. di* **to spring**
spry [spraɪ] *agg.* attivo, energico
spun [spʌn] *pass. e p. p. di* **to spin**
spur [spɜːʳ] *s.* **1** sperone *m.* **2** pungolo *m.*, incentivo *m.*
to spur [spɜːʳ] *v. tr.* spronare, incitare
spurious ['spjʊərɪəs] *agg.* spurio
to spurn [spɜːn] *v. tr.* rifiutare, respingere
spurt [spɜːt] *s.* **1** getto *m.*, zampillo *m.* **2** scatto *m.*
to spurt [spɜːt] *v. intr.* **1** sprizzare, zampillare **2** scattare
spy [spaɪ] *s.* spia *f.*
to spy [spaɪ] **A** *v. intr.* fare la spia **B** *v. tr.* notare
spying ['spaɪɪŋ] *s.* spionaggio *m.*
squabble ['skwəbl] *s.* diverbio *m.*, litigio *m.*
to squabble ['skwəbl] *v. intr.* litigare
squad [skwəd] *s.* squadra *f.*, plotone *m.*
squadron ['skwədr(ə)n] *s.* squadrone *m.*, squadriglia *f.*
squalid ['skwəlɪd] *agg.* squallido
squall (1) [skwɜːl] *s.* grido *m.*
squall (2) [skwɜːl] *s.* bufera *f.*
squalor ['skwələʳ] *s.* squallore *m.*
to squander ['skwəndəʳ] *v. tr.* dilapidare, dissipare
square [skwɛəʳ] **A** *agg.* **1** quadrato, (*mat.*) al quadrato **2** tarchiato, tozzo **3** sistemato, in ordine **4** giusto, onesto **5** (*sport*) pari **6** (*fam.*) abbondante, sostanzioso **7** (*fam.*) antiquato, tradizionalista **B** *s.* **1** quadrato *m.* **2** piazza *f.* **3** squadra *f.* (da disegno) **4** casella *f.*, riquadro *m.* **C** *avv.* **1** ad angolo retto, a squadra **2** esattamente ♦ **s. root** radice quadrata
to square [skwɛəʳ] *v. tr.* **1** quadrare, squadrare **2** regolare, pareggiare **3** elevare al quadrato
squash [skwəʃ] *s.* **1** spremuta *f.* **2** (*sport*) squash *m. inv.*
to squash [skwəʃ] *v. tr.* schiacciare, spremere
squat [skwət] *agg.* **1** tozzo, tarchiato **2** accovacciato
to squat [skwət] *v. intr.* **1** accovacciarsi **2** occupare abusivamente
to squawk [skwɜːk] *v. intr.* emettere strida rauche
to squeak [skwiːk] *v. intr.* squittire, stridere
to squeal [skwiːl] *v. intr.* strillare
squeamish ['skwiːmɪʃ] *agg.* schifiltoso
squeeze [skwiːz] *s.* **1** compressione *f.*, stretta *f.* **2** calca *f.* **3** spremitura *f.*
to squeeze [skwiːz] *v. tr.* **1** spremere, comprimere **2** stringere **3** infilare **4** estorcere
to squelch [skwɛl(t)ʃ] **A** *v. tr.* **1** schiacciare **2** soffocare **B** *v. intr.* sguazzare, fare cic ciac
squid [skwɪd] *s.* calamaro *m.*
squiggle ['skwɪg(ə)l] *s.* ghirigoro *m.*
squint [skwɪnt] **A** *agg.* strabico **B** *s.* strabismo *m.*

squire ['skwaɪəʳ] *s.* gentiluomo *m.*
to **squirm** [skwɜːm] *v. intr.* **1** contorcersi **2** essere imbarazzato
squirrel ['skwɪr(ə)l] *s.* scoiattolo *m.*
squirt [skwɜːt] *s.* schizzo *m.*, zampillo *m.*
to **squirt** [skwɜːt] *v. tr.* schizzare
stab [stæb] *s.* **1** pugnalata *f.*, coltellata *f.* **2** fitta *f.* **3** tentativo *m.*
to **stab** [stæb] *v. tr.* pugnalare
stability [stə'bɪlɪtɪ] *s.* stabilità *f.*
stable ['steɪbl] *s.* scuderia *f.*, stalla *f.*
stack [stæk] *s.* **1** catasta *f.* **2** mucchio *m.*, grande quantità *f.*
to **stack** [stæk] *v. tr.* accatastare, ammucchiare, ammassare
stadium ['steɪdjəm] *s.* stadio *m.*
staff [stɑːf] *s.* personale *m.*, staff *m. inv.*
to **staff** [stɑːf] *v. tr.* fornire di personale
stag [stæg] *s.* cervo *m.*
stage [steɪdʒ] *s.* **1** palcoscenico *m.* **2** scena *f.*, teatro *m.* **3** stadio *m.*, fase *f.*, periodo *m.* **4** tappa *f.* **5** impalcatura *f.*
to **stagger** ['stægəʳ] **A** *v. intr.* barcollare **B** *v. tr.* **1** far barcollare **2** impressionare, sconcertare **3** scaglionare
staggering ['stæg(ə)rɪŋ] *agg.* **1** barcollante **2** sbalorditivo
stagnant ['stægnənt] *agg.* stagnante
to **stagnate** ['stægneɪt] *v. intr.* ristagnare
stagy ['steɪdʒɪ] *agg.* teatrale
staid [steɪd] *agg.* serio, contegnoso
stain [steɪn] *s.* **1** macchia *f.* **2** colorante *m.* ♦ **s. remover** smacchiatore
to **stain** [steɪn] *v. tr.* **1** macchiare, sporcare **2** colorare
stainless ['steɪnlɪs] *agg.* **1** immacolato **2** che non stinge **3** inossidabile ♦ **s. steel** acciaio inox
stair [stɛəʳ] *s.* **1** gradino *m.*, scalino *m.* **2** *al pl.* scala *f.*
staircase ['stɛəkeɪs] *s.* scala *f.*
stake [steɪk] *s.* **1** palo *m.*, piolo *m.* **2** puntata *f.*, scommessa *f.*
to **stake** [steɪk] *v. tr.* **1** recintare con pali **2** puntare, scommettere
stalactite ['stæləktaɪt] *s.* stalattite *f.*
stalagmite ['stæləgmaɪt] *s.* stalagmite *f.*
stale [steɪl] *agg.* **1** stantio, vecchio, raffermo **2** caduto in prescrizione
stalemate ['steɪl,meɪt] *s.* stallo *m.*, punto *m.* morto
stalk [stɜːk] *s.* gambo *m.*, stelo *m.*
stall [stɜːl] *s.* **1** stalla *f.*, box *m. inv.* **2** chiosco *m.*, edicola *f.*, bancarella *f.* **3** (*teatro*) poltrona *f.* (di platea)
to **stall** [stɜːl] *v. intr.* **1** impantanarsi **2** (*di motore*) spegnersi, bloccarsi **3** (*fam.*) tirare per le lunghe
stallion ['stæljən] *s.* stallone *m.*
stalwart ['stɜːlwət] *agg.* **1** forte, robusto **2** coraggioso
stamina ['stæmɪnə] *s.* vigore *m.*, capacità *f.* di resistenza
stammer ['stæməʳ] *s.* balbuzie *f.*
to **stammer** ['stæməʳ] *v. intr.* balbettare
stamp [stæmp] *s.* **1** bollo *m.*, francobollo *m.* **2** marchio *m.*, timbro *m.* **3** (*fig.*) impronta *f.*
to **stamp** [stæmp] **A** *v. tr.* **1** timbrare, marchiare, marcare **2** affrancare **3** caratterizzare **4** frantumare **B** *v. intr.* pestare i piedi
stamping ['stæmpɪŋ] *s.* affrancatura *f.*, stampigliatura *f.*
stand [stænd] *s.* **1** arresto *m.*, fermata *f.* **2** posto *m.*, posizione *f.* **3** palco *m.*, podio *m.*, tribuna *f.* **4** banco *m.*, bancarella *f.*, padiglione *m.* **5** (*di taxi*) posteggio *m.* **6** supporto *m.*, sostegno *m.*
to **stand** [stænd] (*pass. e p. p.* **stood**) **A** *v. intr.* **1** stare in piedi **2** stare, trovarsi **3** resistere, durare **4** ristagnare, depositarsi **B** *v. tr.* **1** mettere (*in piedi*), collocare **2** sopportare, resistere a **3** sostenere **4** sostenere le spese di ♦ **to s. by** stare vicino, tenersi pronto; **to s. down** ritirarsi; **to s. for** stare per, significare; **to s. in for sb.** fare da controfigura a qc.; **to s. out** distinguersi; **to s. up** alzarsi in piedi; **to s. up for sb.** prendere le parti di qc.; **to s. up to sb.** tener testa a qc.
standard ['stændəd] **A** *agg.* **1** standard, comune, regolare **2** di base, fondamentale **B** *s.* **1** stendardo *m.* **2** standard *m. inv.*, modello *m.*, norma *f.* **3** livello *m.*, tenore *m.* **4** base *f.*, sostegno *m.*
standardization [,stændədaɪ'zeɪʃ(ə)n] *s.* standardizzazione *f.*
to **standardize** ['stændədaɪz] *v. tr.* standardizzare, normalizzare, unificare
stand-by ['stæn(d)baɪ] scorta *f.*, riserva *f.*
stand-in ['stænd,ɪn] *s.* **1** sostituto *m.* **2** controfigura *f.*
standing ['stændɪŋ] **A** *agg.* **1** eretto, in piedi **2** fisso, stabile, permanente **3** fermo, inattivo **B** *s.* **1** posizione *f.*, condizione *f.* **2** durata *f.* ♦ **s. price** prezzo fisso; **s. room** posti in piedi
standoffish [,stænd'ɔfɪʃ] *agg.* riservato,

scostante
standpoint ['stændpɔɪnt] *s.* punto *m.* di vista
standstill ['stændstɪl] *s.* arresto *m.*, stasi *f.*, punto *m.* morto
stank [stæŋk] *pass. di* **to stink**
staple (1) ['steɪpl] *s.* **1** forcella *f.* **2** graffetta *f.*
staple (2) ['steɪpl] **A** *agg.* di base, di prima necessità **B** *s.* prodotto *m.* principale, alimento *m.* principale
to staple ['steɪpl] *v. tr.* graffettare
star [stɑːʳ] *s.* **1** stella *f.*, astro *m.* **2** stella *f.*, celebrità *f.*
to star [stɑːʳ] *v. intr.* **1** (*in un film*) essere il protagonista **2** avere come interpreti principali
starboard ['stɑːbəd] *s.* (*naut.*) dritta *f.*
starch [stɑːtʃ] *s.* amido *m.*
to starch [stɑːtʃ] *v. tr.* inamidare
stardom ['stɑːdəm] *s.* celebrità *f.*
stardust ['stɑːdʌst] *s.* polvere *f.* di stelle
stare [stɛəʳ] *s.* sguardo *m.* fisso
to stare [stɛəʳ] *v. tr.* fissare, guardare fisso
starfish ['stɑːfɪʃ] *s.* stella *f.* di mare
stark [stɑːk] *agg.* **1** desolato **2** assoluto, completo
starling ['stɑːlɪŋ] *s.* (*zool.*) storno *m.*
starry ['stɑːrɪ] *agg.* stellato
start [stɑːt] *s.* **1** inizio *m.*, avvio *m.*, partenza *f.* **2** balzo *m.*, sobbalzo *m.* **3** vantaggio *m.* **4** (*mecc.*) avviamento *m.*
to start [stɑːt] **A** *v. intr.* **1** balzare, sobbalzare **2** partire, avviarsi **3** cominciare, mettersi a **B** *v. tr.* **1** cominciare, avviare **2** mettere in moto ♦ **to s. doing st.** cominciare a fare q.c.
starter ['stɑːtəʳ] *s.* **1** iniziatore *m.* **2** (*sport*) partente *m.* **3** antipasto *m.* **4** motorino *m.* d'avviamento, starter *m. inv.*
starting ['stɑːtɪŋ] *s.* **1** inizio *m.* **2** avviamento *m.*
to startle ['stɑːtl] *v. tr.* far trasalire, spaventare
starvation [stɑː'veɪʃ(ə)n] *s.* inedia *f.*, fame *f.*
to starve [stɑːv] **A** *v. intr.* morire di fame **B** *v. tr.* far morire di fame
state [steɪt] **A** *s.* **1** stato *m.*, condizione *f.*, situazione *f.* **2** stato *m.*, nazione *f.* **B** *agg. attr.* **1** statale **2** di gala
to state [steɪt] *v. tr.* **1** dichiarare, affermare **2** stabilire
stately ['steɪtlɪ] *agg.* grandioso
statement ['steɪtmənt] *s.* **1** dichiarazione *f.* **2** rapporto *m.* ♦ **s. of account** estratto conto
statesman ['steɪtsmən] (*pl.* **statesmen**) *s.* statista *m.*
static ['stætɪk] **A** *agg.* statico **B** *s.* **1** scarica *f.* statica **2** *al pl.* (*v. al sing.*) statica *f.*
station ['steɪʃ(ə)n] *s.* stazione *f.* ♦ **s. master** capostazione
to station ['steɪʃ(ə)n] *v. tr.* collocare, appostare
stationary ['steɪʃn(ə)rɪ] *agg.* stazionario, fermo
stationer ['steɪʃnəʳ] *s.* cartolaio *m.*
stationery ['steɪʃn(ə)rɪ] *s.* cartoleria *f.*
statistics [stə'tɪstɪks] *s. pl.* (*v. al sing.*) statistica *f. sing.*
statue ['stætjuː] *s.* statua *f.*
status ['steɪtəs] *s.* **1** condizione *f.* sociale, posizione *f.* **2** stato *m.* giuridico
statute ['stætjuːt] *s.* legge *f.*, statuto *m.*
statutory ['stætjʊt(ə)rɪ] *agg.* prescritto dalla legge
staunch [stɔːn(t)ʃ] *agg.* **1** fedele, devoto **2** solido, resistente
stave [steɪv] *s.* **1** doga *f.* **2** pentagramma *m.* **3** strofa *f.*
to stave [steɪv] (*pass. e p. p.* **stove, staved**) **A** *v. tr.* **1** costruire con doghe **2** sfondare **B** *v. intr.* sfondarsi ♦ **to s. off** sfuggire a
stay (1) [steɪ] *s.* soggiorno *m.*, permanenza *f.*
stay (2) [steɪ] *s.* (*naut.*) strallo *m.*
to stay [steɪ] **A** *v. intr.* stare, rimanere, trattenersi, soggiornare **B** *v. tr.* **1** sopportare **2** differire ♦ **to s. in** stare in casa; **to s. on** trattenersi; **to s. up** stare alzato
stead [stɛd] *s.* **1** posto *m.*, vece *f.* **2** vantaggio *m.* ♦ **in my s.** in mia vece; **to stand sb. in good s.** tornare utile a qc.
steadfast ['stɛdfəst] *agg.* costante, risoluto
steadily ['stɛdɪlɪ] *avv.* **1** fermamente **2** costantemente
steady ['stɛdɪ] *agg.* **1** fermo, fisso, stabile **2** costante, regolare **3** serio, posato ♦ **(go) s.!** piano!, attenzione!
to steady ['stɛdɪ] **A** *v. tr.* consolidare, rinforzare **B** *v. intr.* consolidarsi, rafforzarsi
steak [steɪk] *s.* **1** bistecca *f.* **2** fetta *f.* ♦ **grilled s.** bistecca ai ferri; **rare/well-done s.** bistecca al sangue/ben cotta
to steal [stiːl] (*pass.* **stole**, *p. p.* **stolen**) **A** *v. tr.* rubare **B** *v. intr.* **1** rubare **2** muoversi furtivamente

stealth [stɛlθ] *s.* **by s.** di nascosto
stealthy ['stɛlθɪ] *agg.* furtivo
steam [sti:m] *s.* vapore *m.* ♦ **s.-engine** macchina a vapore
to steam [sti:m] **A** *v. tr.* **1** esporre al vapore, vaporizzare **2** cuocere a vapore **B** *v. intr.* **1** emettere vapore, fumare **2** funzionare a vapore
steamer ['sti:məʳ] *s.* battello *m.* a vapore
steamy ['sti:mɪ] *agg.* **1** coperto di vapore, appannato **2** che esala vapore
steel [sti:l] *s.* acciaio *m.*
steelworks ['sti:lwɜ:ks] *s. pl.* acciaieria *f.*
steep [sti:p] *agg.* **1** ripido, scosceso **2** (*fam.*) esorbitante, eccessivo
to steep [sti:p] *v. tr.* **1** bagnare, immergere, tuffare **2** impregnare
steeple ['sti:pl] *s.* **1** campanile *m.* **2** guglia *f.*
to steer [stɪəʳ] **A** *v. tr.* **1** guidare, governare, pilotare **2** dirigere, indirizzare **B** *v. intr.* **1** timonare **2** governare, manovrare **3** dirigersi
steering ['stɪərɪŋ] *s.* sterzo *m.* ♦ **s. look** bloccasterzo; **s. wheel** volante, ruota del timone
steersman ['stɪəzmən] (*pl.* **steersmen**) *s.* timoniere *m.*
stele ['sti:lɪ] *s.* stele *f.*
stem [stɛm] *s.* gambo *m.*, stelo *m.*
to stem (1) [stɛm] *v. tr.* arginare, frenare
to stem (2) [stɛm] *v. intr.* derivare, scaturire
stench [stɛn(t)ʃ] *s.* puzzo *m.*
stencil ['stɛnsl] *s.* stampino *m.*, matrice *f.*
stenography [stɛ'nɔgrəfɪ] *s.* stenografia *f.*
step [stɛp] *s.* **1** passo *m.*, andatura *f.* **2** orma *f.*, impronta *f.* **3** (*fig.*) provvedimento *m.*, misura *f.*, mossa *f.* **4** gradino *m.*, scalino *m.* **5** promozione *f.*, avanzamento *m.*
to step [stɛp] *v. intr.* **1** fare un passo, andare, venire **2** misurare a passi **3** mettere i piedi su ♦ **to s. down** discendere; **to s. off** scendere da; **to s. up** farsi avanti, aumentare
stepbrother ['stɛpˌbrʌðəʳ] *s.* fratellastro *m.*
stepdaughter ['stɛpˌdɔ:təʳ] *s.* figliastra *f.*
stepfather ['stɛpˌfa:ðəʳ] *s.* patrigno *m.*
stepladder ['stɛpˌlædəʳ] *s.* scaletta *f.*
stepmother ['stɛpˌmʌðəʳ] *s.* matrigna *f.*
stepsister ['stɛpˌsɪstəʳ] *s.* sorellastra *f.*
stepson ['stɛpˌsʌn] *s.* figliastro *m.*
sterile ['stɛraɪl] *agg.* sterile
sterility [stɛ'rɪlɪtɪ] *s.* sterilità *f.*
sterilization [ˌstɛrɪlaɪ'zeɪʃ(ə)n] *s.* sterilizzazione *f.*
to sterilize ['stɛrɪlaɪz] *v. tr.* sterilizzare
sterilizer ['stɛrɪlaɪzəʳ] *s.* sterilizzatore *m.*
sterling ['stɜ:lɪŋ] **A** *agg.* genuino, di buona lega **B** *s.* sterlina *f.*
stern (1) [stɜ:n] *agg.* severo, rigido
stern (2) [stɜ:n] *s.* poppa *f.*
stew [stju:] *s.* stufato *m.*
to stew [stju:] *v. tr. e intr.* stufare
steward [stjʊəd] *s.* **1** assistente *m.* di volo, steward *m. inv.* **2** (*mil.*) dispensiere *m.*
stick [stɪk] *s.* **1** bastone *m.*, bastoncino *m.*, bacchetta *f.* **2** barra *f.*, stecca *f.* **3** gambo *m.*
to stick [stɪk] (*pass. e p. p.* **stuck**) **A** *v. tr.* **1** conficcare, infilare **2** attaccare, incollare **3** (*fam.*) sopportare **B** *v. intr.* **1** conficcarsi **2** attaccarsi, appiccicarsi **3** incepparsi, bloccarsi ♦ **to s. out** sporgere; **to s. to** restare fedele a; **to s. up** attaccare, rapinare; **to s. up for** sostenere, difendere
sticker ['stɪkəʳ] *s.* cartellino *m.* adesivo, sticker *m. inv.*
sticking ['stɪkɪŋ] *agg.* appiccicoso, adesivo ♦ **s. plaster** cerotto
sticky ['stɪkɪ] *agg.* **1** appiccicoso, adesivo **2** (*fam.*) spiacevole
stiff [stɪf] **A** *agg.* **1** duro, rigido **2** indolenzito **3** freddo, austero **4** difficile, faticoso **5** (*di prezzo*) alto **6** (*di bevanda*) forte **B** *avv.* completamente ♦ **bored s.** annoiato a morte; **s. neck** torcicollo
to stiffen ['stɪfn] **A** *v. tr.* irrigidire, indurire **B** *v. intr.* **1** indurirsi, irrigidirsi **2** indolenzirsi
stiffening ['stɪfnɪŋ] *s.* irrigidimento *m.*
to stifle ['staɪfl] *v. tr. e intr.* soffocare
stifling ['staɪflɪŋ] *agg.* soffocante
to stigmatize ['stɪgmətaɪz] *v. tr.* stigmatizzare
stile [staɪl] *s.* scaletta *f.*
stiletto [stɪ'lɛtɒʊ] *s.* stiletto *m.*, punteruolo *m.* ♦ **s. heel** tacco a spillo
still (1) [stɪl] *agg.* **1** tranquillo, calmo **2** immobile, fermo ♦ **s. life** natura morta
still (2) [stɪl] *avv.* **1** ancora, tuttora **2** (*davanti a comp.*) anche, ancora **3** pure, tuttavia
stillborn ['stɪlbɔ:n] *agg.* **1** nato morto **2** fallito
stillness ['stɪlnɪs] *s.* tranquillità *f.*
stilt [stɪlt] *s.* trampolo *m.*, palo *m.*
to stimulate ['stɪmjʊleɪt] *v. tr.* incentivare,

stimolare
stimulus ['stɪmjʊləs] (*pl.* **stimuli**) *s.* stimolo *m.*
sting [stɪŋ] *s.* **1** pungiglione *m.*, aculeo *m.* **2** puntura *f.* **3** stimolo *m.*
to sting [stɪŋ] (*pass. e p. p.* **stung**) *v. tr.* **1** pungere **2** offendere, tormentare **3** incitare
stingy ['stɪndʒɪ] *agg.* avaro, taccagno
stink [stɪŋk] *s.* puzzo *m.*
to stink [stɪŋk] (*pass.* **stank**, **stunk**, *p. p.* **stunk**) *v. intr.* puzzare
stinking ['stɪŋkɪŋ] *agg.* **1** puzzolente, maleodorante **2** disgustoso
stint [stɪnt] *s.* **1** compito *m.*, lavoro *m.* **2** limite *m.*
to stint [stɪnt] *v. tr.* lesinare
to stipulate ['stɪpjʊleɪt] *v. tr.* stipulare, pattuire, convenire
stir [stɜːʳ] *s.* **1** rimescolata *f.* **2** confusione *f.*, trambusto *m.*
to stir [stɜːʳ] **A** *v. tr.* **1** agitare, mescolare **2** eccitare, incitare **B** *v. intr.* **1** agitarsi **2** alzarsi, essere attivo
stirrup ['stɪrəp] *s.* staffa *f.*
stitch [stɪtʃ] *s.* **1** punto *m.* **2** maglia *f.* **3** fitta *f.*
to stitch [stɪtʃ] *v. tr. e intr.* cucire
stoat [stɒʊt] *s.* ermellino *m.*
stock [stək] **A** *s.* **1** assortimento *m.*, riserva *f.*, scorta *f.*, stock *m. inv.* **2** (*fin.*) azione *f.*, titolo *m.* **3** ceppo *m.*, tronco *m.* **4** base *f.*, sostegno *m.* **5** bestiame *m.* **6** razza *f.*, schiatta *f.* **7** materia *f.* prima **8** brodo *m.* **B** *agg.* comune, usuale ♦ **out of s.** esaurito; **s. cube** dado da brodo; **s. exchange** borsa valori; **s. farm** allevamento; **s. market** mercato azionario; **to take s.** fare l'inventario
to stock [stək] **A** *v. tr.* **1** fornire, approvvigionare **2** tenere in magazzino **B** *v. intr.* germogliare ♦ **to s. up** fare provviste
stockbroker ['stəkˌbrɒʊkəʳ] *s.* agente *m.* di cambio
stocking ['stəkɪŋ] *s.* calza *f.*
stockist ['stəkɪst] *s.* grossista *m.*, fornitore *m.*
stockpile ['stəkpaɪl] *s.* scorta *f.*
stocktaking ['stəkteɪkɪŋ] *s.* inventario *m.*
stocky ['stəkɪ] *agg.* tarchiato
stodgy ['stədʒɪ] *agg.* **1** pesante, indigesto **2** noioso
to stoke [stɒʊk] *v. tr.* attizzare, alimentare
stole (1) [stɒʊl] *s.* stola *f.*
stole (2) [stɒʊl] *pass. di* **to steal**
stolen ['stɒʊl(ə)n] *p. p. di* **to steal**
stolid ['stəlɪd] *agg.* imperturbabile, flemmatico
stomach ['stʌmək] *s.* stomaco *m.*, pancia *f.* ♦ **s.-ache** mal di stomaco
to stomach ['stʌmək] *v. tr.* **1** digerire **2** tollerare
stone [stɒʊn] **A** *s.* **1** pietra *f.*, masso *m.*, sasso *m.*, ciottolo *m.* **2** nocciolo *m.* **3** (*med.*) calcolo *m.* **B** *avv.* completamente ♦ **S. Age** età della pietra; **s.-cold** gelido
to stone [stɒʊn] *v. tr.* **1** lapidare **2** pavimentare **3** snocciolare
stood [stʊd] *pass. e p. p. di* **to stand**
stool [stuːl] *s.* sgabello *m.*
stoop (1) [stuːp] *s.* curvatura *f.*, inclinazione *f.*
stoop (2) [stuːp] *s.* (*USA*) veranda *f.*
to stoop [stuːp] *v. intr.* **1** chinarsi, piegarsi **2** accondiscendere
stop [stəp] *s.* **1** arresto *m.*, fermata *f.*, sosta *f.* **2** segno *m.* di punteggiatura, punto *m.* **3** dispositivo *m.* di arresto ♦ **s. press** notizie dell'ultima ora
to stop [stəp] **A** *v. tr.* **1** arrestare, fermare **2** interrompere, bloccare **3** tamponare **B** *v. intr.* **1** fermarsi, smettere, cessare **2** fare una fermata, fermarsi ♦ **to s. off** fare una sosta; **to s. up** intasare, ostruire
stopover ['stəpˌɒʊvəʳ] *s.* fermata *f.*, scalo *m.*
stoppage ['stəpɪdʒ] *s.* **1** interruzione *f.*, sosta *f.* **2** ostruzione *f.*, intasamento *m.*
stopper [stəpəʳ] *s.* tappo *m.*, turacciolo *m.*
stopwatch ['stəpwətʃ] *s.* cronografo *m.*
storage ['stɜːrɪdʒ] *s.* **1** immagazzinamento *m.* **2** magazzino *m.* **3** (*di batteria*) carica *f.*
store [stɜːʳ] *s.* **1** scorta *f.*, provvista *f.* **2** deposito *m.*, magazzino *m.* **3** negozio *m.* **4** *al pl.* depositi *m. pl.* di magazzino ♦ **department s.** grande magazzino; **s. room** dispensa, ripostiglio
to store [stɜːʳ] *v. tr.* **1** immagazzinare, accumulare **2** fornire, provvedere **3** (*inf.*) memorizzare
storey ['stɜːrɪ] (*USA* **story**) *s.* (*di casa*) piano *m.*
stork [stɜːk] *s.* cicogna *f.*
storm [stɜːm] *s.* **1** tempesta *f.*, burrasca *f.*, uragano *m.* **2** assalto *m.*
to storm [stɜːm] **A** *v. intr.* **1** infuriare, scatenarsi **2** precipitarsi **B** *v. tr.* assalire

stormy ['stɜːmɪ] *agg.* tempestoso
story ['stɜːrɪ] *s.* storia *f.*, racconto *m.*, narrazione *f.* ♦ **s. teller** narratore
stout [staʊt] **A** *agg.* **1** forte, robusto **2** corpulento **3** coraggioso **B** *s.* birra *f.* scura
stove (1) [stɒʊv] *s.* stufa *f.*, fornello *m.*
stove (2) [stɒʊv] *pass. e p. p. di* **to stave**
to stow [stɒʊ] *v. tr.* mettere via, stivare ♦ **to s. away** fare il clandestino
strabismus [strə'bɪzməs] *s.* strabismo *m.*
to straddle ['strædl] *v. intr.* **1** stare a cavalcioni **2** esitare, essere titubante
to straggle ['strægl] *v. intr.* **1** disperdersi, sbandarsi **2** girovagare
straggly ['stræglɪ] *agg.* sparpagliato
straight [streɪt] **A** *agg.* **1** diritto, ritto, eretto **2** giusto, onesto **3** franco, leale **4** in ordine, a posto **5** puro, liscio **B** *avv.* **1** diritto, in linea retta **2** direttamente **3** francamente **4** onestamente ♦ **s. off** subito, senza esitazioni; **s. on** sempre dritto
to straightaway ['streɪtəweɪ] *avv.* immediatamente
to straighten ['streɪtn] *v. tr. e intr.* raddrizzare, raddrizzarsi ♦ **to s. out** mettere a posto
straightforward [ˌstreɪt'fɜːwəd] *agg.* **1** diritto **2** retto, onesto **3** semplice, chiaro
strain [streɪn] *s.* **1** sforzo *m.*, tensione *f.* **2** preoccupazione *f.* **3** (*med.*) strappo *m.* muscolare, distorsione *f.* **4** (*tecnol.*) sollecitazione *f.*
to strain [streɪn] *v. tr.* **1** tendere, sforzare **2** affaticare **3** distorcere **4** abusare di **5** filtrare, colare
strained [streɪnd] *agg.* **1** teso, difficile **2** sforzato **3** affaticato, indebolito
strainer ['streɪnəʳ] *s.* colino *m.*, filtro *m.*
strait [streɪt] *s.* **1** (*geogr.*) stretto *m.* **2** *al pl.* ristrettezze *f. pl.*, difficoltà *f. pl.*
straitjacket ['streɪtˌdʒækɪt] *s.* camicia *f.* di forza
strand [strænd] *s.* **1** filo *m.*, trefolo *m.* **2** (*di capelli*) ciocca *f.*
to strand [strænd] *v. intr.* arenarsi, incagliarsi
strange [streɪn(d)ʒ] *agg.* **1** strano, bizzarro **2** estraneo, sconosciuto **3** non abituato
stranger ['streɪn(d)ʒəʳ] *s.* sconosciuto *m.*
to strangle ['stræŋgl] *v. tr.* strangolare, strozzare
strap [stræp] *s.* **1** cinghia *f.*, cinturino *m.* **2** spallina *f.*, bretella *f.*
strapping ['stræpɪŋ] *agg.* robusto, ben piantato
strategic(al) [strə'tiːdʒɪk((ə)l)] *agg.* strategico
strategics [strə'tiːdʒɪks] *s. pl.* (*v. al sing.*) strategia *f.*
strategy ['strætɪdʒɪ] *s.* strategia *f.*
to stratify ['strætɪfaɪ] *v. tr. e intr.* stratificare, stratificarsi
stratosphere ['strætɒ(ʊ)sfɪəʳ] *s.* stratosfera *f.*
stratum ['straːtəm] (*pl.* **strata**) *s.* strato *m.*
straw [strɜː] *s.* **1** paglia *f.* **2** cannuccia *f.*
strawberry ['strɜːb(ə)rɪ] *s.* fragola *f.*
stray [streɪ] *agg.* **1** smarrito, randagio **2** casuale, fortuito **3** isolato, sparso
to stray [streɪ] *v. intr.* **1** vagare, vagabondare **2** deviare, divagare
streak [striːk] *s.* **1** striscia *f.*, riga *f.* **2** vena *f.*, filone *m.* **3** traccia *f.*, tocco *m.*
to streak [striːk] **A** *v. tr.* venare, screziare **B** *v. intr.* (*fam.*) andare come un lampo
stream [striːm] *s.* **1** corso *m.* d'acqua, ruscello *m.*, torrente *m.* **2** corrente *f.* **3** fiumana *f.*, flusso *m.*, fiotto *m.*
to stream [striːm] *v. intr.* **1** scorrere, fluire **2** fluttuare, ondeggiare
streamer ['striːməʳ] *s.* **1** stella *f.* filante **2** aurora *f.* boreale **3** (*naut.*) fiamma *f.* **4** (*USA*) titolone *m.* (*su giornale*)
streamlined ['striːmlaɪnd] *agg.* aerodinamico, affusolato
street [striːt] *s.* strada *f.*, via *f.* ♦ **s. lamp** lampione
streetcar ['striːtkaːʳ] *s.* tram *m.*
strength [strɛŋθ] *s.* forza *f.*, energia *f.*, potenza *f.*
to strengthen ['strɛŋθ(ə)n] *v. tr.* fortificare, potenziare, rinforzare
strenuous ['strɛnjʊəs] *agg.* **1** strenuo, energico, attivo **2** faticoso, arduo
stress [strɛs] *s.* **1** spinta *f.*, pressione *f.* **2** tensione *f.*, stress *m. inv.* **3** (*mecc.*) sforzo *m.*, sollecitazione *f.* **4** accento *m.*
to stress [strɛs] *v. tr.* **1** forzare **2** accentuare **3** accentare
stretch [strɛtʃ] *s.* **1** stiramento *m.*, allungamento *m.*, tensione *f.* **2** distesa *f.*, estensione *f.*
to stretch [strɛtʃ] **A** *v. tr.* **1** tendere, distendere, tirare, allungare **2** forzare **B** *v. intr.* stendersi, distendersi, allungarsi ♦ **to s. out** tendere, allungare
stretcher ['strɛtʃəʳ] *s.* barella *f.*
stretching ['strɛtʃɪŋ] *s.* stiramento *m.*, al-

lungamento *m.*
to strew [stru:] (*pass.* **strewed** *p. p.* **strewn, strewed**) *v. tr.* spargere, cospargere
stricken ['strɪk(ə)n] *agg.* colpito
strict [strɪkt] *agg.* **1** severo, rigoroso **2** stretto, preciso
strictness ['strɪk(t)nɪs] *s.* **1** severità *f.*, rigore *m.* **2** precisione *f.*
to stride [straɪd] (*pass.* **strode**, *p. p.* **stridden**) *v. intr.* camminare a gran passi
strife [straɪf] *s.* conflitto *m.*
strike [straɪk] *s.* **1** sciopero *m.* **2** (*mil.*) attacco *m.* **3** (*di giacimento*) scoperta *f.* **4** colpo *m.* di fortuna
to strike [straɪk] (*pass.* **struck**, *p. p.* **struck, stricken**) **A** *v. tr.* **1** battere, colpire **2** impressionare, trovare, scoprire **3** coniare **B** *v. intr.* **1** battere, urtare **2** battere le ore **3** penetrare, infiltrarsi **4** attecchire **5** scioperare ♦ **to s. at** colpire; **to s. down** abbattere; **to s. off** mozzare, cancellare, radiare; **to s. up** attaccare (a suonare)
striking ['straɪkɪŋ] *agg.* impressionante
string [strɪŋ] *s.* **1** stringa *f.*, legaccio *m.* **2** corda *f.*, spago *m.* **3** (*mus.*) corda *f.* **4** serie *f.*, sfilza *f.*, catena *f.* ♦ **s. bean** fagiolino
to string [strɪŋ] (*pass. e p. p.* **strung**) *v. tr.* **1** legare con corde **2** incordare **3** infilare ♦ **to s. out** disporre in fila; **to s. up** appendere
stringed [strɪŋd] *agg.* (*mus.*) a corda
stringent ['strɪn(d)ʒənt] *agg.* **1** rigoroso **2** impellente
strip [strɪp] *s.* striscia *f.* ♦ **s. cartoon** fumetto
to strip [strɪp] **A** *v. tr.* **1** strappare, togliere **2** denudare, spogliare **3** smontare, smantellare **B** *v. intr.* **1** spogliarsi, svestirsi **2** (*di vite*) spanarsi
stripe [straɪp] *s.* **1** striscia *f.* **2** gallone *m.*
striped [straɪpt] *agg.* **1** a strisce, a righe **2** gallonato
stripper ['strɪpəʳ] *s.* spogliarellista *m. e f.*
striptease ['strɪpˌti:z] *s.* spogliarello *m.*
to strive [straɪv] (*pass.* **strove**, *p. p.* **striven**) *v. intr.* sforzarsi, lottare
strode [strɒʊd] *pass. di* **to stride**
stroke [strɒʊk] *s.* **1** colpo *m.*, percossa *f.* **2** (*nuoto*) bracciata *f.*, (*canottaggio*) vogata *f.*, (*tennis*) battuta *f.* **3** tocco *m.*, tratto *m.* **4** (*med.*) colpo *m.* apoplettico
to stroke (1) [strɒʊk] *v. tr.* lisciare, accarezzare
to stroke (2) [strɒʊk] *v. intr.* vogare
stroll [strɒʊl] *s.* passeggiata *f.*
to stroll [strɒʊl] *v. intr.* passeggiare
stroller ['strɒʊləʳ] *s.* passeggino *m.*
strong [strɔŋ] *agg.* **1** forte, robusto **2** energico, vigoroso **3** efficace **4** considerevole ♦ **s. room** camera blindata
strongbox ['strɔŋbɔks] *s.* cassaforte *f.*
stronghold ['strɔŋhɒʊld] *s.* roccaforte *f.*
strongly ['strɔŋlɪ] *avv.* **1** molto, fortemente, vivamente **2** solidamente
strophe ['strɒʊfɪ] *s.* strofa *f.*
strove [strɒʊv] *pass. di* **to strive**
structural ['strʌktʃ(ə)r(ə)l] *agg.* strutturale
structuralism ['strʌktʃ(ə)r(ə)lɪz(ə)m] *s.* strutturalismo *m.*
structure ['strʌktʃəʳ] *s.* struttura *f.*
struggle ['strʌgl] *s.* lotta *f.*
to struggle ['strʌgl] *v. intr.* lottare, sforzarsi
to strum [strʌm] *v. tr. e intr.* strimpellare
strung [strʌŋ] *pass. e p. p. di* **to string**
strut [strʌt] *s.* puntone *m.*
to strut [strʌt] *v. intr.* incedere impettito, pavoneggiarsi
stub [stʌb] *s.* **1** troncone *m.*, ceppo *m.* **2** mozzicone *m.* **3** matrice *f.*, talloncino *m.*
to stub [stʌb] *v. tr.* **1** estirpare, sradicare **2** urtare ♦ **to s. out** (*sigaretta*) spegnere
stubble ['stʌbl] *s.* stoppia *f.*
stubborn ['stʌbən] *agg.* ostinato, testardo
stubbornness ['stʌbənnɪs] *s.* ostinazione *f.*, testardaggine *f.*
stucco ['stʌkɒʊ] *s.* stucco *m.*
stuck [stʌk] **A** *pass. e p. p. di* **to stick B** *agg.* **1** bloccato **2** incollato **3** (*fam.*) nei guai ♦ **s.-up** presuntuoso
stud (1) [stʌd] *s.* **1** bottoncino *m.* **2** borchia *f.* **3** perno *m.*
stud (2) [stʌd] *s.* **1** scuderia *f.* **2** stallone *m.*
student ['stju:d(ə)nt] *s.* **1** studente *m.* **2** studioso *m.*
studio ['stju:dɪɒʊ] (*pl.* **studios**) *s.* **1** (*d'artista*) studio *m.* **2** (*cine., TV*) teatro *m.* di posa, studio *m.* **3** monolocale *m.*
studious ['stju:djəs] *agg.* **1** studioso **2** studiato
study ['stʌdɪ] *s.* studio *m.*
to study ['stʌdɪ] **A** *v. tr.* **1** studiare **2** esaminare **B** *v. intr.* studiare
stuff [stʌf] *s.* **1** materiale *m.*, sostanza *f.* **2** cosa *f.*, roba *f.*
to stuff [stʌf] *v. tr.* **1** riempire, imbottire **2** (*cuc.*) farcire **3** impagliare, imbalsamare

4 rimpinzare
stuffing ['stʌfɪŋ] *s.* **1** imbottitura *f.* **2** (*cuc.*) ripieno *m.* ♦ **s. box** premistoppa
stuffy ['stʌfɪ] *agg.* **1** soffocante, senz'aria **2** ottuso
to **stumble** ['stʌmbl] *v. intr.* **1** inciampare **2** impappinarsi **3** fare un passo falso
stumbling-block ['stʌmblɪŋblɔk] *s.* ostacolo *m.*, impedimento *m.*
stump [stʌmp] *s.* **1** ceppo *m.* **2** moncone *m.* **3** matrice *f.*
to **stun** [stʌn] *v. tr.* **1** stordire **2** sbalordire
stung [stʌŋ] *pass. e p. p. di* **to sting**
stunk [stʌŋk] *pass. e p. p. di* **to stink**
stunning ['stʌnɪŋ] *agg.* **1** assordante **2** (*fam.*) stupendo
stunt [stʌnt] *s.* **1** acrobazia *f.* **2** bravata *f.*, esibizione *f.* **3** trovata *f.* pubblicitaria ♦ **s. man** cascatore
stunted ['stʌntɪd] *agg.* stentato, striminzito
to **stupefy** ['stju:pɪfaɪ] *v. tr.* **1** instupidire, stordire **2** stupefare
stupendous [stju:'pɛndəs] *agg.* stupendo
stupid ['stju:pɪd] *agg.* stupido, cretino
stupidity [stju:'pɪdɪtɪ] *s.* stupidità *f.*
sturdy ['stɜ:dɪ] *agg.* robusto, forte
stutter ['stʌtəʳ] *s.* balbuzie *f.*
to **stutter** ['stʌtəʳ] *v. intr.* balbettare
sty (1) [staɪ] *s.* porcile *m.*
sty (2) [staɪ] *s.* orzaiolo *m.*
style [staɪl] *s.* stile *m.*
stylish ['staɪlɪʃ] *agg.* elegante, alla moda
stylist ['staɪlɪst] *s.* stilista *m. e f.*
stylobate ['staɪləbeɪt] *s.* stilobate *m.*
stylus ['staɪləs] *s.* stilo *m.*
suave [swa:v] *agg.* soave
subaqueous [sʌb'eɪkwɪəs] *agg.* subacqueo
subconscious [sʌb'kɔnʃəs] *agg. e s.* subconscio *m.*
subcutaneous [ˌsʌbkju:'teɪnjəs] *agg.* sottocutaneo
to **subdivide** [ˌsʌbdɪ'vaɪd] *v. tr. e intr.* suddividere, suddividersi
to **subdue** [səb'dju:] *v. tr.* **1** sottomettere, dominare **2** attenuare
subject ['sʌbdʒɪkt] **A** *agg.* soggetto, sottoposto **B** *s.* **1** soggetto *m.*, argomento *m.*, materia *f.* **2** (*gramm.*) soggetto *m.* **3** cittadino *m.*, suddito *m.* **4** esemplare *m.*, soggetto *m.*
to **subject** [səb'dʒɛkt] *v. tr.* **1** assoggettare **2** esporre, sottoporre
subjective [sʌb'dʒɛktɪv] *agg.* soggettivo
subjunctive [səb'dʒʌŋ(k)tɪv] *agg. e s.* (*gramm.*) congiuntivo *m.*
to **sublet** [sʌb'lɛt] (*pass. e p. p.* **sublet**) *v. tr.* subaffittare
sublime [sə'blaɪm] *agg.* sublime, eccelso
submarine ['sʌbməri:n] **A** *agg.* sottomarino, subacqueo **B** *s.* sottomarino *m.*
to **submerge** [səb'mɜ:dʒ] *v. tr. e intr.* immergere, immergersi
submersion [səb'mɜ:ʃ(ə)n] *s.* immersione *f.*
submission [səb'mɪʃ(ə)n] *s.* **1** sottomissione *f.* **2** (*di domanda*) presentazione *f.*
to **submit** [səb'mɪt] **A** *v. tr.* sottoporre, presentare **B** *v. intr.* sottomettersi, arrendersi
subnormal [sʌb'nɜ:m(ə)l] *agg.* subnormale
subordinate [sə'bɜ:dɪnɪt] *agg. e s.* subordinato *m.*
to **subordinate** [sə'bɜ:dɪneɪt] *v. tr.* subordinare
subpoena [səb'pi:nə] *s.* (*dir*) citazione *f.* in giudizio
to **subscribe** [səb'skraɪb] **A** *v. tr.* **1** sottoscrivere, firmare **2** contribuire con **B** *v. intr.* **1** sottoscrivere **2** approvare, aderire **3** abbonarsi
subscriber [səb'skraɪbəʳ] *agg. e s.* abbonato *m.*
subscription [səb'skrɪpʃ(ə)n] *s.* **1** sottoscrizione *f.* **2** abbonamento *m.* ♦ **to discontinue a s.** disdire un abbonamento; **to take out a s.** abbonarsi
subsequent ['sʌbsɪkwənt] *agg.* successivo, seguente
to **subside** [səb'saɪd] *v. intr.* **1** calare, abbassarsi **2** calmarsi, placarsi **3** lasciarsi cadere
subsidence [səb'saɪd(ə)ns] *s.* abbassamento *m.*, cedimento *m.*
subsidiary [səb'sɪdjərɪ] **A** *agg.* sussidiario, ausiliario, accessorio **B** *s.* (società) consociata *f.*
to **subsidize** ['sʌbsɪdaɪz] *v. tr.* sovvenzionare
subsidy ['sʌbsɪdɪ] *s.* sussidio *m.*
subsistence [səb'sɪst(ə)ns] *s.* sussistenza *f.*, mantenimento *m.*
substance ['sʌbst(ə)ns] *s.* sostanza *f.*
substantial [səb'stænʃ(ə)l] *agg.* **1** sostanzioso, solido **2** sostanziale, notevole
substantive ['sʌbst(ə)ntɪv] *s.* sostantivo *m.*

substitute ['sʌbstɪtjuːt] *s.* **1** sostituto *m.*, delegato *m.* **2** surrogato *m.*
to substitute ['sʌbstɪtjuːt] *v. tr.* sostituire, rimpiazzare
substitution [ˌsʌbstɪ'tjuːʃ(ə)n] *s.* sostituzione *f.*
subterfuge ['sʌbtəfjuːdʒ] *s.* sotterfugio *m.*
subterranean [ˌsʌbtə'reɪnjən] *agg.* sotterraneo
to subtilize ['sʌtɪlaɪz] *v. tr. e intr.* sottilizzare
subtle ['sʌtl] *agg.* sottile
to subtract [səb'trækt] *v. tr.* sottrarre
subtraction [səb'trækʃ(ə)n] *s.* sottrazione *f.*
suburb ['sʌbɜːb] *s.* sobborgo *m.*, periferia *f.*
suburban [sə'bɜːb(ə)n] *agg.* suburbano, periferico
suburbia [sə'bɜːbɪə] *s.* sobborghi *m. pl.*
subvention [səb'vɛnʃ(ə)n] *s.* sovvenzione *f.*
subversive [sʌb'vɜːsɪv] *agg.* sovversivo
subway ['sʌbweɪ] *s.* **1** sottopassaggio *m.* **2** (*USA*) metropolitana *f.*
to succeed [sək'siːd] **A** *v. intr.* **1** riuscire, aver successo **2** succedere **B** *v. tr.* succedere a, subentrare a
succeeding [sək'siːdɪŋ] *agg.* successivo, seguente
success [sək'sɛs] *s.* successo *m.*
successful [sək'sɛsf(ʊ)l] *agg.* riuscito, di successo
succession [sək'sɛʃ(ə)n] *s.* successione *f.*
successive [sək'sɛsɪv] *agg.* successivo
successor [sək'sɛsəʳ] *s.* successore *m.*
to succumb [sə'kʌm] *v. intr.* soccombere
such [sʌtʃ, sətʃ] **A** *agg.* **1** tale, simile **2** così tanto **B** *pron.* tale, tali, questo, questa, questi, queste **C** *avv.* così, talmente, tanto ♦ **and s.** e così via, e simili; **as s.** come tale; **s. as** come, quale; **s. that** tale che
to suck [sʌk] *v. tr.* succhiare
sucker ['sʌkəʳ] *s.* **1** ventosa *f.* **2** (*fam.*) babbeo *m.*
to suckle ['sʌkl] *v. tr.* allattare
suction ['sʌkʃ(ə)n] *s.* **1** suzione *f.* **2** (*mecc.*) aspirazione *f.*
sudden ['sʌdn] *agg.* improvviso ♦ **all of a s.** improvvisamente
suds [sʌdz] *s. pl.* schiuma *f.* di sapone
to sue [sjuː] *v. tr.* querelare, citare in giudizio
suede [sweɪd] *s.* pelle *f.* scamosciata
suet [sjʊɪt] *s.* sugna *f.*
to suffer ['sʌfəʳ] **A** *v. tr.* **1** soffrire, patire **2** sopportare **B** *v. intr.* soffrire
sufferer ['sʌf(ə)rəʳ] *s.* sofferente *m. e f.*
suffering ['sʌf(ə)rɪŋ] *s.* sofferenza *f.*
to suffice [sə'faɪs] *v. tr. e intr.* bastare
sufficient [s(ə)'fɪʃ(ə)nt] *agg.* sufficiente, bastante
to suffocate ['sʌfəkeɪt] *v. tr. e intr.* soffocare
suffocation [ˌsʌfə'keɪʃ(ə)n] *s.* soffocamento *m.*
suffrage ['sʌfrɪdʒ] *s.* suffragio *m.*
to suffuse [sə'fjuːz] *v. tr.* soffondere
sugar ['ʃʊgəʳ] *s.* zucchero *m.* ♦ **cane s.** zucchero di canna; **lump s.** zucchero in zollette; **s. basin/bowl** zuccheriera; **s. beet** barbabietola da zucchero
to sugar ['ʃʊgəʳ] *v. tr.* zuccherare
sugared ['ʃʊgəd] *agg.* zuccherato
sugary ['ʃʊgərɪ] *agg.* **1** zuccherino **2** mellifluo
to suggest [sə'dʒɛst] *v. tr.* **1** suggerire, proporre **2** indicare, far pensare a **3** sostenere
suggestible [sə'dʒɛstəbl] *agg.* suggestionabile
suggestion [sə'dʒɛstʃ(ə)n] *s.* suggerimento *m.*
suggestive [sə'dʒɛstɪv] *agg.* **1** suggestivo, evocativo **2** indicativo **3** provocante, sconveniente
suicide ['sjʊɪsaɪd] *s.* **1** suicidio *m.* **2** suicida *m. e f.*
suit [sjuːt] *s.* **1** abito *m.* (*da uomo*), completo *m.* **2** (*di carte da gioco*) seme *m.* **3** (*dir*) causa *f.*
to suit [sjuːt] **A** *v. tr.* adattarsi a, soddisfare **B** *v. intr.* convenire, andare bene
suitable ['sjuːtəbl] *agg.* adatto, appropriato
suitcase ['sjuːtkeɪs] *s.* valigia *f.*
suite [swiːt] *s.* **1** appartamento *m.* **2** (*mus.*) suite *f.*
suitor ['sjuːtəʳ] *s.* pretendente *m. e f.*
to sulk [sʌlk] *v. intr.* essere imbronciato
sulky ['sʌlkɪ] *agg.* imbronciato
sullen ['sʌlən] *agg.* scontroso
to sully ['sʌlɪ] *v. tr.* macchiare, deturpare
sulphate ['sʌlfeɪt] *s.* solfato *m.*
sulphur ['sʌlfəʳ] *s.* zolfo *m.*
sultan ['sʌlt(ə)n] *s.* sultano *m.*
sultana [sʌl'tɑːnə] *s.* **1** sultana *f.* **2** uva *f.* sultanina
sultanate ['sʌltənɪt] *s.* sultanato *m.*
sultriness ['sʌltrɪnɪs] *s.* afa *f.*
sultry ['sʌltrɪ] *agg.* **1** afoso, soffocante **2** appassionato
sum [sʌm] *s.* **1** somma *f.*, addizione *f.* **2**

(*di denaro*) somma *f.*, quantità *f.*
to sum [sʌm] *v. tr. e intr.* sommare ♦ **to s. up** ricapitolare, riassumere
to summarize ['sʌməraɪz] *v. tr.* ricapitolare, riassumere
summary ['sʌmərɪ] *s.* compendio *m.*, riassunto *m.*
summer ['sʌmər] **A** *s.* estate *f.* **B** *agg.* estivo ♦ **s. house** casa di campagna, padiglione; **s. time** ora legale
summertime ['sʌmətaɪm] *s.* estate *f.*
summit ['sʌmɪt] *s.* **1** sommità *f.*, vertice *m.* **2** summit *m. inv.*, incontro *m.* al vertice
to summon ['sʌmən] *v. tr.* **1** citare in giudizio **2** convocare ♦ **to s. up** chiamare a raccolta
summons ['sʌmənz] *s.* citazione *f.*
sump [sʌmp] *s.* **1** pozzo *m.* nero **2** (*mecc.*) coppa *f.*
sumptuous ['sʌm(p)tjʊəs] *agg.* sontuoso
sun [sʌn] *s.* sole *m.*
to sunbathe ['sʌnbeɪð] *v. intr.* prendere il sole
sunburn ['sʌnbɜːn] *s.* scottatura *f.*
sunburnt ['sʌnbɜːnt] *agg.* scottato dal sole
Sunday ['sʌndɪ] *s.* domenica *f.*
sundial ['sʌndaɪ(ə)l] *s.* meridiana *f.*
sundown ['sʌndaʊn] *s.* tramonto *m.*
sundries ['sʌndrɪz] *s. pl.* **1** oggetti *m. pl.* vari, cianfrusaglie *f. pl.* **2** spese *f. pl.* varie
sundry ['sʌndrɪ] *agg.* diversi, vari
sunflower ['sʌnˌflaʊər] *s.* girasole *m.*
sung [sʌŋ] *p. p. di* **to sing**
sunk [sʌŋk] *p. p. di* **to sink**
sunlight ['sʌnlaɪt] *s.* luce *f.* del giorno
sunny ['sʌnɪ] *agg.* **1** soleggiato **2** allegro
sunrise ['sʌnraɪz] *s.* levata *f.* del sole
sunset ['sʌnsɛt] *s.* tramonto *m.*
sunshade ['sʌnˌʃeɪd] *s.* parasole *m. inv.*
sunshine ['sʌnˌʃaɪn] *s.* (luce del) sole *m.*
sunstroke ['sʌnˌstrɒʊk] *s.* insolazione *f.*
suntan ['sʌnˌtæn] *s.* abbronzatura *f.*
super ['sjuːpər] *agg.* (*fam.*) ottimo, eccellente, di prim'ordine
superannuation [ˌsjuːpəˌrænjʊ'eɪʃ(ə)n] *s.* collocamento *m.* a riposo, pensione *f.*
superb [sjuː'pɜːb] *agg.* superbo, magnifico
supercilious [ˌsjuːpə'sɪlɪəs] *agg.* altezzoso
superconductivity ['sjuːpəˌkəndʌk'tɪvɪtɪ] *s.* superconduttività *f.*
superficial [ˌsjuːpə'fɪʃ(ə)l] *agg.* superficiale
superfluous [sjʊ(ː)'pɜːflʊəs] *agg.* superfluo
superhuman [ˌsjuːpə'hjuːmən] *agg.* sovrumano
to superimpose [ˌsjuːp(ə)rɪm'pɒʊz] *v. tr.* sovrapporre
to superintend [ˌsjuːp(ə)rɪn'tɛnd] *v. tr. e intr.* soprintendere
superior [sjuː'pɪərɪər] *agg.* superiore
superiority [sjuːˌpɪərɪ'ərɪtɪ] *s.* superiorità *f.*
superlative [sjuː'pɜːlətɪv] *agg. e s.* superlativo *m.*
supermarket ['sjuːpəˌmaːkɪt] *s.* supermercato *m.*, supermarket *m. inv.*
supernatural [ˌsjuːpə'nætʃr(ə)l] *agg.* soprannaturale
superpower ['sjuːpəˌpaʊər] *s.* superpotenza *f.*
to supersede [ˌsjʊ(ː)pə'siːd] *v. tr.* soppiantare, rimpiazzare
superstition [ˌsjuːpə'stɪʃ(ə)n] *s.* superstizione *f.*
superstitious [ˌsjuːpə'stɪʃəs] *agg.* superstizioso
supertanker ['sjuːpəˌtænkər] *s.* superpetroliera *f.*
to supervene [ˌsjuːpə'viːn] *v. intr.* sopraggiungere
to supervise ['sjuːpəvaɪz] *v. tr.* sovrintendere, dirigere
supervision [ˌsjuːpə'vɪʒ(ə)n] *s.* supervisione *f.*
supervisor ['sjuːpəvaɪzər] *s.* sorvegliante *m. e f.*, supervisore *m.*
supine [sjuː'paɪn] *agg.* supino
supper ['sʌpər] *s.* cena *f.*
to supplant [sə'plaːnt] *v. tr.* soppiantare, scavalcare
supple ['sʌpl] *agg.* **1** flessibile **2** agile
supplement ['sʌplɪmənt] *s.* supplemento *m.*
to supplement ['sʌplɪˌmənt] *v. tr.* completare, integrare
supplementary [ˌsʌplɪ'mɛnt(ə)rɪ] *agg.* supplementare, integrativo
supplier [sə'plaɪər] *s.* fornitore *m.*
supply [sə'plaɪ] *s.* **1** rifornimento *m.*, provvista *f.*, scorta *f.* **2** (*econ.*) offerta *f.* **3** *al pl.* viveri *m. pl.* **4** *al pl.* sussidi *m. pl.*
to supply [sə'plaɪ] *v. tr.* **1** fornire, provvedere **2** soddisfare **3** supplire
support [sə'pɜːt] *s.* supporto *m.*, sostegno *m.*
to support [sə'pɜːt] *v. tr.* sostenere

supporter [sə'pɜːtəʳ] *s.* sostenitore *m.*, tifoso *m.*
to suppose [sə'pɒʊz] *v. tr.* supporre
supposedly [sə'pɒʊzɪdlɪ] *avv.* **1** presumibilmente **2** apparentemente
supposition [ˌsʌpə'zɪʃ(ə)n] *s.* supposizione *f.*
suppository [sə'pəzɪt(ə)rɪ] *s.* supposta *f.*
to suppress [sə'prɛs] *v. tr.* sopprimere
supremacy [sjʊ'prɛməsɪ] *s.* supremazia *f.*
supreme [sjʊ(ː)'priːm] *agg.* supremo
surcharge ['sɜːtʃaːdʒ] *s.* **1** sovraccarico *m.* **2** soprattassa *f.*, maggiorazione *f.* **3** sovrapprezzo *m.*
to surcharge [sɜː'tʃaːdʒ] *v. tr.* **1** sovraccaricare **2** applicare una sovrattassa, un sovrapprezzo a
sure [ʃʊəʳ] **A** *agg.* sicuro **B** *avv.* certamente, sicuramente, davvero
surely ['ʃʊɛlɪ] *avv.* certamente
surety ['ʃʊɛtɪ] *s.* (*dir*) garanzia *f.*
surf [sɜːf] *s.* **1** cresta *f.* dell'onda **2** *al pl.* frangenti *m. pl.*
to surf [sɜːf] *v. intr.* praticare il surf
surface ['sɜːfɪs] *s.* superficie *f.*
to surface ['sɜːfɪs] **A** *v. tr.* **1** far emergere **2** spianare, pavimentare **B** *v. intr.* venire alla superficie, emergere
surfboard ['sɜːfˌbɜːd] *s.* (tavola da) surf *m. inv.*
surfeit ['sɜːfɪt] *s.* **1** eccesso *m.* **2** sazietà *f.*
surfing ['sɜːfɪŋ] *s.* surf *m. inv.*
surge [sɜːdʒ] *s.* **1** ondata *f.* **2** slancio *m.*, impeto *m.*
to surge [sɜːdʒ] *v. intr.* ondeggiare, fluttuare, agitarsi
surgeon ['sɜːdʒ(ə)n] *s.* chirurgo *m.*
surgery ['sɜːdʒ(ə)rɪ] *s.* **1** chirurgia *f.* **2** ambulatorio *m.* ♦ **s. hours** orario delle visite
surgical ['sɜːdʒɪk(ə)l] *agg.* **1** chirurgico **2** ortopedico
surly ['sɜːlɪ] *agg.* burbero
surname ['sɜːneɪm] *s.* cognome *m.*
to surpass [sɜː'paːs] *v. tr.* superare
surplus ['sɜːpləs] **A** *agg.* eccedente **B** *s.* eccedenza *f.*, sovrappiù *m. inv.*, surplus *m. inv.* ♦ **s. value** plusvalore
surprise [sə'praɪz] *s.* sorpresa *f.*
to surprise [sə'praɪz] *v. tr.* sorprendere
surprising [sə'praɪzɪŋ] *agg.* sorprendente
surrealism [sə'rɪəlɪz(ə)m] *s.* surrealismo *m.*
surrealist [sə'rɪəlɪst] *s.* surrealista *m. e f.*
surrender [sə'rɛndəʳ] *s.* **1** resa *f.*, capitolazione *f.* **2** cessione *f.*
to surrender [sə'rɛndəʳ] **A** *v. tr.* **1** cedere, consegnare **2** rinunciare a **B** *v. intr.* arrendersi, capitolare
surreptitious [ˌsʌrəp'tɪʃəs] *agg.* **1** clandestino, furtivo **2** (*dir*) surrettizio
surrogate ['sʌrəgɪt] *s.* sostituto *m.*, surrogato *m.*
to surround [sə'raʊnd] *v. tr.* circondare
surrounding [sə'raʊndɪŋ] **A** *agg.* circostante **B** *s. al pl.* **1** dintorni *m. pl.* **2** condizioni *f. pl.* ambientali
surveillance [sɜː'veɪləns] *s.* sorveglianza *f.*
survey ['sɜːveɪ] *s.* **1** esame *m.*, indagine *f.*, rassegna *f.* **2** perizia *f.*, verifica *f.*, valutazione *f.* **3** rilevamento *m.*
to survey [sɜː'veɪ] *v. tr.* **1** osservare, esaminare **2** ispezionare, sorvegliare, visitare **3** valutare, fare la perizia di **4** rilevare
surveyor [sɜː'veɪəʳ] *s.* ispettore *m.*, sovraintendente *m.*
survival [sə'vaɪv(ə)l] *s.* **1** sopravvivenza *f.* **2** reliquia *f.*
to survive [sə'vaɪv] *v. tr. e intr.* sopravvivere (a)
survivor [sə'vaɪvəʳ] *s.* superstite *m. e f.*
susceptible [sə'sɛptəbl] *agg.* **1** sensibile **2** suscettibile
suspect [sʌs'pɛkt] **A** *agg.* sospetto **B** *s.* persona *f.* sospetta
to suspect ['səspɛkt] *v. tr. e intr.* sospettare
to suspend [səs'pɛnd] *v. tr.* **1** sospendere, appendere **2** differire
suspender [səs'pɛndəʳ] *s.* **1** giarrettiera *f.* **2** *al pl.* (*USA*) bretelle *f. pl.* ♦ **s. belt** reggicalze
suspense [səs'pɛns] *s.* suspense *f. inv.*
suspension [səs'pɛnʃ(ə)n] *s.* sospensione *f.*
suspicion [səs'pɪʃ(ə)n] *s.* sospetto *m.*
suspicious [səs'pɪʃəs] *agg.* **1** sospettoso **2** sospetto
to sustain [səs'teɪn] *v. tr.* **1** sostenere, sopportare, reggere **2** (*dir*) appoggiare, accogliere **3** confermare
sustenance ['sʌstɪnəns] *s.* sostentamento *m.*
sutler ['sʌtləʳ] *s.* vivandiere *m.*
suture ['suːtʃəʳ] *s.* sutura *f.*
to suture ['suːtʃəʳ] *v. tr.* suturare
swab [swəb] *s.* (*med.*) tampone *m.*
to swagger ['swægəʳ] *v. intr.* pavoneggiarsi

swallow (1) ['swəlɒʊ] *s.* rondine *f.*
swallow (2) ['swəlɒʊ] *s.* **1** deglutizione *f.* **2** boccone *m.*, sorso *m.*
to swallow ['swəlɒʊ] *v. tr. e intr.* deglutire, inghiottire
swam [swæm] *pass. di* **to swim**
swamp [swəmp] *s.* palude *f.*
to swamp [swəmp] *v. tr.* inondare
swampy ['swəmpɪ] *agg.* paludoso
swan [swən] *s.* cigno *m.*
to swap [swəp] *v. tr.* barattare, scambiare
swarm [swɜːm] *s.* sciame *m.*
to swarm [swɜːm] *v. intr.* **1** sciamare **2** brulicare
swarthy ['swɜːðɪ] *agg.* bruno, scuro
swastika ['swæstɪkə] *s.* svastica *f.*
to swat [swət] *v. tr.* colpire, schiacciare
swatch [swətʃ] *s.* campione *m.* (di stoffa)
to sway [sweɪ] **A** *v. tr.* **1** far oscillare, far ondeggiare **2** dominare, governare **3** influenzare **B** *v. intr.* oscillare, ondeggiare
to swear [swɛəʳ] (*pass.* **swore**, *p. p.* **sworn**) *v. tr. e intr.* **1** giurare **2** imprecare, bestemmiare
swearword ['swɛəwɜːd] *s.* parolaccia *f.*, imprecazione *f.*
sweat [swɛt] *s.* **1** sudore *m.* **2** sudata *f.*, faticata *f.*
to sweat [swɛt] **A** *v. intr.* **1** sudare **2** sgobbare **B** *v. tr.* **1** sudare, trasudare **2** bagnare **3** sfruttare
sweater ['swətəʳ] *s.* maglione *m.*
sweatshirt ['swətʃɜːt] *s.* felpa *f.*
sweaty ['swɛtɪ] *agg.* sudato
Swede [swiːd] *s.* svedese *m. e f.*
Swedish ['swiːdɪʃ] *agg.* svedese
sweep [swiːp] *s.* **1** scopata *f.*, spazzata *f.* **2** movimento *m.* ampio **3** ambito *m.*, portata *f.* **4** distesa *f.*, tratto *m.* **5** spazzacamino *m.*
to sweep [swiːp] (*pass. e p. p.* **swept**) **A** *v. tr.* **1** scopare, spazzare **2** percorrere, sfiorare **3** spaziare su **B** *v. intr.* **1** incedere maestosamente **2** estendersi ♦ **to s. away** spazzar via, eliminare
sweeping ['swiːpɪŋ] **A** *agg.* **1** ampio, vasto **2** completo, assoluto **3** impetuoso **B** *s. al pl.* rifiuti *m. pl.*
sweet [swiːt] **A** *agg.* **1** dolce **2** piacevole **3** profumato **4** (*fam.*) carino **B** *s.* **1** caramella *f.* **2** dolce *m.* **3** dolcezza *f.*
to sweeten ['swiːtn] *v. tr.* **1** zuccherare **2** addolcire
sweetener ['swiːt(ə)nəʳ] *s.* dolcificante *m.*
sweetheart ['swiːthaːt] *s.* innamorato *m.*
sweetish ['swiːtɪʃ] *agg.* dolciastro
sweetness ['swiːtnɪs] *s.* **1** dolcezza *f.* **2** aroma *f.*, fragranza *f.*
swell [swɛl] **A** *s.* **1** rigonfiamento *m.* **2** mare *m.* lungo **3** (*mus.*) crescendo *m.* **B** *agg.* **1** elegante **2** (*fam.*) magnifico
to swell [swɛl] (*pass.* **swelled**, *p. p.* **swollen**, **swelled**) **A** *v. intr.* **1** dilatarsi, gonfiarsi **2** aumentare, crescere **B** *v. tr.* **1** gonfiare, dilatare **2** aumentare
swelling ['swɛlɪŋ] *s.* gonfiore *m.*, rigonfiamento *m.*
sweltering ['swɛltɛrɪŋ] *agg.* soffocante
swept [swɛpt] *pass. e p. p. di* **to sweep**
to swerve [swɜːv] *v. intr.* deviare, sterzare
swift (1) [swɪft] *agg.* rapido, veloce
swift (2) [swɪft] *s.* rondone *m.*
swig [swɪg] *s.* sorsata *f.*
to swig [swɪg] *v. tr.* tracannare
swim [swɪm] *s.* nuotata *f.*
to swim [swɪm] (*pass.* **swam**, *p. p.* **swum**) **A** *v. intr.* **1** nuotare **2** essere inondato, essere coperto **3** vacillare, ondeggiare **B** *v. tr.* attraversare a nuoto
swimmer ['swɪməʳ] *s.* nuotatore *m.*
swimming ['swɪmɪŋ] *s.* nuoto *m.* ♦ **s. pool** piscina
swimsuit ['swɪmˌsjuːt] *s.* costume *m.* da bagno
swindle ['swɪndl] *s.* truffa *f.*, imbroglio *m.*
to swindle ['swɪndl] *v. tr.* truffare, raggirare
swine [swaɪn] *s. inv.* porco *m.*
swing [swɪŋ] *s.* **1** oscillazione *f.* **2** (*mus.*) ritmo *m.* **3** altalena *f.* **4** (*mus.*) swing *m. inv.* ♦ **in full s.** in piena attività
to swing [swɪŋ] (*pass. e p. p.* **swung**) **A** *v. tr.* **1** dondolare, far oscillare **2** agitare, roteare **B** *v. intr.* **1** dondolare, oscillare **2** ruotare, girare **3** girarsi, voltarsi
swingeing ['swɪn(d)ʒɪŋ] *agg.* (*fam.*) **1** violento, duro **2** enorme
swinging ['swɪŋɪŋ] **A** *s.* oscillazione *f.* **B** *agg.* **1** oscillante, orientabile **2** veloce **3** cadenzato, ritmico
to swipe [swaɪp] *v. tr.* (*fam.*) **1** colpire **2** rubare
to swirl [swɜːl] *v. intr.* turbinare
to swish [swɪʃ] *v. intr.* frusciare
Swiss [swɪs] *agg. e s. inv.* svizzero *m.*
switch [swɪtʃ] *s.* **1** frusta *f.* **2** cambiamento *m.* **3** interruttore *m.* **4** (*ferr.*) scambio *m.*
to switch [swɪtʃ] *v. tr.* **1** frustare **2** agitare **3** deviare, smistare **4** scambiare ♦ **to s.**

off spegnere; **to s. on** accendere
switchboard ['swɪtʃbɜːd] *s.* centralino *m.*
to swivel ['swɪvl] *v. intr.* ruotare, fare perno
swollen ['swɒʊl(ə)n] **A** *p. p. di* **to swell** **B** *agg.* gonfio
to swoon [swuːn] *v. intr.* svenire
to swoop [swuːp] *v. intr.* avventarsi, piombare ♦ **to s. up** afferrare al volo
sword [sɜːd] *s.* spada *f.*
swordfish ['sɜːdfɪʃ] *s.* pescespada *m.*
swore [swɜːʳ] *pass. di* **to swear**
sworn [swɜːn] *p. p. di* **to swear**
to swot [swət] *v. intr.* sgobbare
swum [swʌm] *p. p. di* **to swim**
swung [swʌŋ] *pass. e p. p. di* **to swing**
syllable ['sɪləbl] *s.* sillaba *f.*
symbiosis [ˌsɪmbɪ'ɒʊsɪs] *s.* simbiosi *f.*
symbol ['sɪmb(ə)l] *s.* simbolo *m.*
symbolic(al) [sɪm'bəlɪk((ə)l)] *agg.* simbolico
symbolist ['sɪmbəlɪst] *s.* simbolista *m. e f.*
symmetric(al) [sɪ'mɛtrɪk((ə)l)] *agg.* simmetrico
symmetry ['sɪmɪtrɪ] *s.* simmetria *f.*
sympathetic [ˌsɪmpə'θɛtɪk] *agg.* **1** comprensivo **2** congeniale **3** (*anat.*) simpatico
to sympathize ['sɪmpəθaɪz] *v. intr.* **1** mostrare comprensione **2** simpatizzare
sympathizer ['sɪmpəθaɪzəʳ] *s.* simpatizzante *m. e f.*
sympathy ['sɪmpəθɪ] *s.* **1** comprensione *f.*, partecipazione *f.* **2** simpatia *f.* **3** condoglianza *f.*
symphonic [sɪm'fənɪk] *agg.* sinfonico
symphony ['sɪmfənɪ] *s.* sinfonia *f.*
symptom ['sɪm(p)təm] *s.* sintomo *m.*
symptomatology [ˌsɪm(p)təmə'tələdʒɪ] *s.* sintomatologia *f.*
synagogue [ˌsɪnəgəg] *s.* sinagoga *f.*
synchrony ['sɪŋkrənɪ] *s.* sincronia *f.*
syndicalist ['sɪndɪkəlɪst] *s.* sindacalista *m. e f.*
syndicate ['sɪndɪkɪt] *s.* sindacato *m.*
syndrome ['sɪndrɒʊm] *s.* sindrome *f.*
synonym ['sɪnənɪm] *s.* sinonimo *m.*
synonymous [sɪ'nənɪməs] *agg.* sinonimo
synopsis [sɪ'nəpsɪs] *s.* sinossi *f.*
syntax ['sɪntæks] *s.* sintassi *f.*
synthesis ['sɪnθɪsɪs] (*pl.* **syntheses**) *s.* sintesi *f.*
synthetic(al) [sɪn'θɛtɪk((ə)l)] *agg.* sintetico
syphilis ['sɪfɪlɪs] *s.* sifilide *f.*
syringe ['sɪrɪn(d)ʒ] *s.* siringa *f.*
syrup ['sɪrəp] *s.* sciroppo *m.*
system ['sɪstɪm] *s.* **1** sistema *m.*, metodo *m.* **2** sistema *m.*, apparato *m.*, impianto *m.* **3** rete *f.* **4** organismo *m.*
systole [sɪstəlɪ] *s.* sistole *f.*

T

ta [tɑː] *inter.* (*infantile*) grazie
tab [tæb] *s.* **1** linguetta *f.* **2** etichetta *f.*
tabby ['tæbɪ] *agg.* tigrato, a strisce ♦ **t. cat** gatto soriano
tabernacle ['tæbə(ː)nækl] *s.* tabernacolo *m.*
table ['teɪbl] *s.* **1** tavolo *m.*, tavola *f.* **2** tavolata *f.* **3** tabella *f.*, elenco *m.* **4** tavoletta *f.*, lastra *f.* ♦ **t. of contents** indice; **to lay/to clear the t.** apparecchiare/sparecchiare la tavola
tablecloth ['teɪblkləθ] *s.* tovaglia *f.*
tablemat ['teɪbl,mæt] *s.* sottopiatto *m.*
tablespoon ['teɪbl,spuːn] *s.* cucchiaio *m.* da tavola
tablet ['tæblɪt] *s.* **1** compressa *f.*, pastiglia *f.* **2** targa *f.*, tavoletta *f.*
tabloid ['tæbləɪd] **A** *agg.* conciso, ridotto **B** *s.* **1** compressa *f.* **2** (giornale) tabloid *m. inv.*
taboo [tə'buː] *s.* tabù *m.*
to tabulate ['tæbjʊleɪt] *v. tr.* disporre in tabelle
tachycardia [,tækɪ'kɑːdɪəʳ] *s.* tachicardia *f.*
tacit ['tæsɪt] *agg.* tacito
taciturn ['tæsɪtɜːn] *agg.* taciturno
tack [tæk] *s.* **1** bulletta *f.*, chiodino *m.* **2** imbastitura *f.* **3** linea *f.* di condotta
to tack [tæk] **A** *v. tr.* **1** imbullettare, inchiodare **2** imbastire **B** *v. intr.* (*naut.*) bordeggiare
tackle ['tækl] *s.* **1** attrezzatura *f.* **2** paranco *m.*
to tackle ['tækl] *v. tr.* **1** affrontare **2** afferrare
tacky ['tækɪ] *agg.* appiccicaticcio
tact [tækt] *s.* tatto *m.*
tactful ['tæktf(ʊ)l] *agg.* pieno di tatto
tactical ['tæctɪk(ə)l] *agg.* tattico
tactics ['tæktɪks] *s. pl.* tattica *f.*
tactless [tæktlɪs] *agg.* che manca di tatto
tadpole ['tædpɒʊl] *s.* girino *m.*
taenia ['tiːnjə] *s.* tenia *f.*
tag [tæg] *s.* **1** cartellino *m.*, etichetta *f.* **2** appendice *f.*, estremità *f.* **3** puntale *m.* **4** frase *f.* fatta
to tag [tæg] *v. tr.* **1** contrassegnare (*con cartellino, etichetta*) **2** aggiungere **3** seguire da vicino ♦ **to t. along, t. behind** pedinare
tail [teɪl] *s.* coda *f.* ♦ **t. end** parte finale; **t. lamp** luce posteriore, fanalino
to tail [teɪl] *v. tr.* **1** essere in coda a **2** seguire, pedinare ♦ **to t. away/off** assottigliarsi, disperdersi; **to t. back** incolonnarsi
tailback ['teɪlbæk] *s.* (*di veicoli*) incolonnamento *m.*
tailcoat ['teɪl,kɒʊt] *s.* frac *m. inv.*
tailor ['teɪləʳ] *s.* sarto *m.* ♦ **t.-made** fatto su misura; **t.'s workshop** sartoria
tailoring ['teɪlərɪŋ] *s.* sartoria *f.*
to taint [teɪnt] *v. tr.* corrompere, guastare
to take [teɪk] (*pass.* **took**, *p. p.* **taken**) **A** *v. tr.* **1** prendere, afferrare, cogliere, conquistare **2** comprendere **3** condurre, portar via, accompagnare **4** fare **5** attirare, affascinare, colpire **6** impiegare, metterci, richiedere **7** (*cine.*, *TV*) riprendere, girare **8** contenere **B** *v. intr.* **1** far presa, attecchire **2** (*fam.*) essere fotogenico ♦ **t. it easy!** calma!; **to t. after** somigliare a; **to t. away** allontanare, rimuovere, asportare; **to t. back** riportare, ritirare; **to t. down** smantellare, registrare; **to t. in** accogliere, ospitare, comprendere, imbrogliare; **to t. off** decollare, staccare, togliere; **to t. on** imbarcare, assumere, sfidare; **to t. out** portare fuori, emettere, sottoscrivere; **to t. over** subentrare; **to t. part (in)** presenziare; **to t. to** darsi a; **to t. up** sollevare, iniziare, occupare
take-away ['teɪkəweɪ] *agg.* da asporto
take-off ['teɪk,ɜːf] *s.* decollo *m.*
take-over ['teɪk,ɒʊvəʳ] *s.* (*di società*) acquisizione *f.*
taking ['teɪkɪŋ] **A** *agg.* affascinante **B** *s.* **1** presa *f.* **2** *al pl.* incasso *m.*
talc [tælk] *s.* talco *m.*
talcum ['tælkəm] *s.* talco *m.* ♦ **t. powder** borotalco
tale [teɪl] *s.* racconto *m.*, novella *f.*
talent ['tælənt] *s.* talento *m.*
talisman ['tælɪzmən] *s.* talismano *m.*
talk [tɜːk] *s.* **1** colloquio *m.*, discorso *m.* **2** chiacchiere *f. pl.* **3** negoziato *m.*
to talk [tɜːk] *v. intr.* **1** parlare, conversare **2**

chiacchierare ♦ **to t. about** fare pettegolezzi su; **to t. out of** dissuadere da; **to t. to** rimproverare
tall [tɜːl] *agg.* **1** (*di statura*) alto **2** (*fam.*) incredibile
tally ['tælɪ] *s.* **1** cartellino *m.*, contrassegno *m.* **2** conteggio *m.*
to tally ['tælɪ] *v. intr.* corrispondere
talon ['tælən] *s.* artiglio *m.*
tamarind ['tæmərɪnd] *s.* tamarindo *m.*
tambour ['tæmbʊəʳ] *s.* (*arch.*) tamburo *m.*
tambourine [,tæmbə'riːn] *s.* tamburello *m.*
tame [teɪm] *agg.* **1** addomesticato **2** docile, mansueto **3** insulso, noioso
to tame [teɪm] *v. tr.* addomesticare, domare
tamer ['teɪməʳ] *s.* domatore *m.*
to tamper ['tæmpəʳ] *v. intr.* manomettere
tampon ['tæmpən] *s.* tampone *m.*
to tampon ['tæmpən] *v. tr.* tamponare
tamponage ['tæmpənɪdʒ] *s.* tamponamento *m.*
tan [tæn] **A** *agg.* marrone rossiccio **B** *s.* **1** abbronzatura *f.* **2** concia *f.*
to tan [tæn] **A** *v. tr.* **1** (*pelli*) conciare **2** abbronzare **B** *v. intr.* abbronzarsi
tandem ['tændəm] *s.* tandem *m. inv.*
tang [tæŋ] *s.* **1** sapore *m.* piccante **2** punta *f.*, traccia *f.*
tangent ['tæn(d)ʒ(ə)nt] *agg. e s.* tangente *f.*
tangerine [,tæn(d)ʒə'riːn] *s.* mandarino *m.*
tangle ['tæŋgl] *s.* groviglio *m.*, imbroglio *m.*
to tangle ['tæŋgl] *v. tr.* aggrovigliare, imbrogliare
tango ['tæŋgɒʊ] *s.* tango *m.*
tank [tæŋk] *s.* **1** serbatoio *m.*, bidone *m.* **2** carro *m.* armato
tanker ['tæŋkəʳ] *s.* **1** autobotte *f.* **2** petroliera *f.*
tanning ['tænɪŋ] *s.* **1** abbronzatura *f.* **2** concia *f.*
to tantalize ['tæntəlaɪz] *v. tr.* tormentare
tantalizing ['tæntəlaɪzɪŋ] *agg.* allettante
tantamount ['tæntəmaʊnt] *agg. pred.* equivalente
tantrum ['tæntrəm] *s.* (*fam.*) collera *f.*
tap (1) [tæp] *s.* **1** rubinetto *m.*, spina *f.* **2** presa *f.* ♦ **on t.** alla spina, a disposizione
tap (2) [tæp] *s.* colpetto *m.* ♦ **t. dance** tip tap
to tap (1) [tæp] *v. tr.* **1** spillare **2** incidere **3** (*tel.*) intercettare
to tap (2) [tæp] **A** *v. intr.* picchiettare, bussare **B** *v. intr.* battere leggermente
tape [teɪp] *s.* nastro *m.* ♦ **t. player** mangianastri; **t. recorder** registratore
to tape [teɪp] *v. tr.* **1** registrare (*su nastro magnetico*) **2** sigillare (*con nastro adesivo*)
taper ['teɪpəʳ] *s.* **1** candelina *f.*, lumicino *m.* **2** assottigliamento *m.*, rastremazione *f.*
tapestry ['tæpɪstrɪ] *s.* **1** arazzo *m.* **2** tappezzeria *f.*
tapeworm ['teɪp,wɜːm] *s.* tenia *f.*
tapir ['teɪpəʳ] *s.* tapiro *m.*
tar [taːʳ] *s.* catrame *m.*
tare [tɛəʳ] *s.* tara *f.*
target ['taːgɪt] *s.* **1** bersaglio *m.* **2** obiettivo *m.*
tariff ['tærɪf] *s.* tariffa *f.*
to tarnish ['taːnɪʃ] *v. tr.* **1** appannare, offuscare **2** macchiare
tarot ['tærɒʊ] *s.* tarocco *m.*
tarpaulin [taː'pɜːlɪn] *s.* telone *m.* impermeabile
tarragon ['tærəgən] *s.* dragoncello *m.*
tarsia ['taːsɪə] *s.* tarsia *f.*
tart (1) [taːt] *agg.* aspro, acido
tart (2) [taːt] *s.* torta *f.* (*di frutta*), crostata *f.*
tart (3) [taːt] *s.* (*fam.*) sgualdrina *f.*
tartan ['taːt(ə)n] *s.* tartan *m. inv.*
tartar ['taːtəʳ] *s.* tartaro *m.*
task [taːsk] *s.* compito *m.*, mansione *f.* ♦ **t. force** unità operativa, squadra speciale
tassel ['tæs(ə)l] *s.* nappa *f.*, pennacchio *m.*
taste [teɪst] *s.* **1** gusto *m.*, sapore *m.* **2** assaggio *m.* **3** propensione *f.*, inclinazione *f.* **4** buon gusto *m.*
to taste [teɪst] **A** *v. tr.* **1** sentire (il sapore di), assaggiare **2** gustare, provare **B** *v. intr.* sapere di, avere sapore
tasteful ['teɪstf(ʊ)l] *agg.* raffinato
tasteless ['teɪstlɪs] *agg.* insapore, insipido
tasting ['teɪstɪŋ] *s.* assaggio *m.*, degustazione *f.*
tasty ['teɪstɪ] *agg.* gustoso, saporito
tatter ['tætəʳ] *s.* straccio *m.*, brandello *m.*
tattle ['tætl] *s.* chiacchiere *f. pl.*
tattoo (1) [tə'tuː] *s.* tatuaggio *m.*
tattoo (2) [tə'tuː] *s.* **1** (*mil.*) ritirata *f.* **2** parata *f.* militare
to tattoo [tə'tuː] *v. tr.* tatuare
taught [tɜːt] *pass. e p. p. di* **to teach**
taunt [tɜːnt] *s.* scherno *m.*
tauromachy [tɜː'rəməkɪ] *s.* tauromachia *f.*

Taurus ['tɜːrəs] *s.* (*astr.*) toro *m.*
taut [tɜːt] *agg.* **1** teso, tirato **2** stiracchiato, conciso **3** pulito, in ordine
tavern ['tævən] *s.* taverna *f.*
tax [tæks] **A** *agg.* fiscale, di imposta **B** *s.* **1** tassa *f.* **2** peso *m.*, onere *m.* ♦ **income t.** imposta sul reddito; **inheritance t.** tassa di successione; **t. allowance** detrazione fiscale; **t. disc** bollo di circolazione; **t.-free** esentasse; **t. return** dichiarazione dei redditi; **t. stamp** bollo
to tax [tæks] *v. tr.* **1** tassare **2** mettere alla prova
taxable ['tæksəbl] *agg.* tassabile
taxation [tæk'seɪʃ(ə)n] *s.* tassazione *f.*
taxi ['tæksɪ] *s.* taxi *m. inv.* ♦ **t. driver** tassista; **t. rank** (*USA* **t. stand**) posteggio di taxi
taximeter ['tæksɪˌmiːtəʳ] *s.* tassametro *m.*
taxpayer ['tæksˌpeɪəʳ] *s.* contribuente *m. e f.*
tea [tiː] *s.* tè *m. inv.* ♦ **t. set** servizio da tè; **t. towel** strofinaccio
teabag ['tiːbæg] *s.* bustina *f.* di tè
to teach [tiːtʃ] (*pass. e p. p.* **taught**) *v. tr. e intr.* insegnare
teacher ['tiːtʃəʳ] *s.* insegnante *m. e f.*, docente *m. e f.*, professore *m.*, maestro *m.*
teaching ['tiːtʃɪŋ] *s.* insegnamento *m.*
teacup ['tiːkʌp] *s.* tazza *f.* da tè
teak [tiːk] *s.* tek *m.*
team [tiːm] *s.* squadra *f.*, team *m. inv.* ♦ **t. work** lavoro d'équipe
teapot ['tiːpət] *s.* teiera *f.*
tear (1) [tɪəʳ] *s.* lacrima *f.*
tear (2) [tɛəʳ] *s.* spacco *m.*, lacerazione *f.*
to tear [tɛəʳ] (*pass.* **tore**, *p. p.* **torn**) **A** *v. tr.* **1** lacerare, strappare **2** (*fig.*) dilaniare **B** *v. intr.* **1** lacerarsi, strapparsi **2** correre a gran velocità ♦ **to t. off** staccare; **to t. up** fare a pezzi
tearful ['tɪəf(ʊ)l] *agg.* lacrimoso, piangente
tearoom ['tiːruːm] *s.* sala *f.* da tè
to tease [tiːz] *v. tr.* canzonare, molestare, fare dispetti a
teaspoon ['tiːspuːn] *s.* cucchiaino *m.*
teatime ['tiːtaɪm] *s.* ora *f.* del tè
technical ['tɛknɪk(ə)l] *agg.* tecnico
technician [tɛk'nɪʃ(ə)n] *s.* tecnico *m.*
technique [tɛk'niːk] *s.* tecnica *f.*
technological [ˌtɛknə'lədʒɪkl] *agg.* tecnologico
technology [tɛk'nələdʒɪ] *s.* tecnologia *f.*
teddy bear ['tɛdɪˌbɛəʳ] *s.* orsacchiotto *m.* (*di peluche*)
tedious ['tiːdjəs] *agg.* noioso
to teem [tiːm] *v. intr.* **1** abbondare, brulicare **2** diluviare
teenage ['tiːnˌeɪdʒ] *agg.* di, per teen-ager
teen-ager ['tiːnˌeɪdʒəʳ] *s.* adolescente *m. e f.*
teens [tiːnz] *s. pl.* adolescenza *f.*
to teeter ['tiːtəʳ] *v. intr.* traballare
teeth [tiːθ] *pl. di* **tooth**
to teethe [tiːð] *v. intr.* mettere i denti
teething ['tiːðɪŋ] *s.* dentizione *f.* ♦ **t. ring** dentaruolo; **t. troubles** difficoltà iniziali
teetotal [tɪ'ːtɒʊtl] *agg. e s.* astemio *m.*
telecamera [ˌtɛlɪ'kæmərə] *s.* telecamera *f.*
telecontrol [ˌtɛlɪkən'trɒʊl] *s.* telecomando *m.*
telegram ['tɛlɪgræm] *s.* telegramma *m.*
telegraph ['tɛlɪgrɑːf] *s.* telegrafo *m.*
telematics [ˌtɛlɪ'mætɪks] *s. pl.* (*v. al sing.*) telematica *f.*
telepathy [tɪ'lɛpəθɪ] *s.* telepatia *f.*
telephone ['tɛlɪfɒʊn] *s.* telefono *m.* ♦ **t. book/directory** elenco telefonico; **t. booth** cabina telefonica; **t. exchange** centralino; **t. number** numero di telefono
to telephone ['tɛlɪfɒʊn] *v. tr. e intr.* telefonare
telescope ['tɛlɪskɒʊp] *s.* telescopio *m.*
television ['tɛlɪˌvɪʒ(ə)n] *s.* televisione *f.* ♦ **t. set** televisore
telex ['tɛlɛks] *s.* telex *m. inv.*, telescrivente *f.*
to tell [tɛl] (*pass. e p. p.* **told**) **A** *v. tr.* **1** dire, raccontare **2** rivelare, divulgare **3** distinguere, riconoscere **B** *v. intr.* avere effetto, farsi sentire ♦ **to t. off** rimproverare
teller ['tɛləʳ] *s.* (*banca*) cassiere *m.*
telling ['tɛlɪŋ] *agg.* espressivo
telly ['tɛlɪ] *s.* (*fam.*) televisione *f.*
temerity [tɪ'mɛrɪtɪ] *s.* temerarietà *f.*
temper ['tɛmpəʳ] *s.* **1** carattere *m.*, umore *m.* **2** malumore *m.*, collera *f.* **3** calma *f.*, sangue *m.* freddo
to temper ['tɛmpəʳ] *v. tr.* temperare, moderare
tempera ['tɛmpərə] *s.* tempera *f.*
temperament ['tɛmp(ə)rəmənt] *s.* temperamento *m.*
temperamental [ˌtɛmp(ə)rə'məntl] *agg.* **1** capriccioso, instabile **2** connaturato
temperate ['tɛmp(ə)rɪt] *agg.* temperato
temperature ['tɛmprɪtʃəʳ] *s.* **1** temperatura *f.* **2** febbre *f.*
tempest ['tɛmpɪst] *s.* tempesta *f.*

Templar ['tɛmpləʳ] *s.* templare *m.*
template ['tɛmplɪt] *s.* sagoma *f.*
temple (1) ['tɛmpl] *s.* tempio *m.*
temple (2) ['tɛmpl] *s.* tempia *f.*
temporary ['tɛmp(ə)rərɪ] *agg.* temporaneo, provvisorio
to **tempt** [tɛm(p)t] *v. tr.* tentare, allettare
temptation [tɛm(p)'teɪʃ(ə)n] *s.* tentazione *f.*
tempting ['tɛm(p)tɪŋ] *agg.* invitante, allettante
ten [tɛn] *agg. num. card. e s.* dieci *m. inv.*
tenacious [tɪ'neɪʃəs] *agg.* tenace
tenacity [tɪ'næsɪtɪ] *s.* tenacia *f.*
tenancy ['tɛnənsɪ] *s.* locazione *f.*, affitto *m.*
tenant ['tɛnənt] *s.* inquilino *m.*
tench [tɛnʃ] *s.* tinca *f.*
to **tend (1)** [tɛnd] *v. tr.* badare a
to **tend (2)** [tɛnd] *v. intr.* tendere
tendency ['tɛndənsɪ] *s.* tendenza *f.*
tendentious [tɛn'dɛnʃəs] *agg.* tendenzioso
tender (1) ['tɛndəʳ] *agg.* **1** tenero, molle, morbido **2** delicato
tender (2) ['tɛndəʳ] *s.* **1** guardiano *m.* **2** (*naut.*) tender *m. inv.*
tender (3) ['tɛndəʳ] *s.* **1** offerta *f.* **2** valuta *f.*, moneta *f.*
to **tender** ['tɛndəʳ] *v. tr.* offrire
tenderness ['tɛndənɪs] *s.* tenerezza *f.*
tendon ['tɛndən] *s.* tendine *m.*
tenement ['tɛnɪmənt] *s.* **1** appartamento *m.* **2** caseggiato *m.*
tenet ['tɛnɪt] *s.* principio *m.*, canone *m.*
tennis ['tɛnɪs] *s.* tennis *m. inv.*
tenor ['tɛnəʳ] *s.* (*mus.*) tenore *m.*
tenpin ['tɛnpɪn] *s.* (*USA*) birillo *m.*
tense (1) [tɛns] *agg.* teso, tirato
tense (2) [tɛns] *s.* (*gramm.*) tempo *m.*
tension ['tɛnʃ(ə)n] *s.* tensione *f.*
tent [tɛnt] *s.* tenda *f.*, tendone *m.* ♦ **t.-peg** picchetto per tenda
to **tent** [tɛnt] *v. intr.* attendarsi
tentative ['tɛntətɪv] *agg.* sperimentale, provvisorio
tenth [tɛnθ] *agg. num. ord. e s.* decimo *m.*
tenuous ['tɛnjʊəs] *agg.* tenue
tenure ['tɛnjʊəʳ] *s.* (*dir.*) possesso *m.*
tepid ['tɛpɪd] *agg.* tiepido
term [tɜːm] *s.* **1** termine *m.* **2** (*a scuola*) trimestre *m.* **3** (*dir.*) sessione *f.* **4** *al pl.* condizioni *f. pl.*
to **term** [tɜːm] *v. tr.* definire
terminal ['tɜːmɪnl] **A** *agg.* terminale, finale **B** *s.* **1** terminale *m.*, estremità *f.* **2** capolinea *m. inv.*, terminal *m. inv.* **3** (*elettr.*) morsetto *m.* **4** (*inf.*) terminale *m.*
to **terminate** ['tɜːmɪneɪt] *v. tr.* terminare, porre fine a
terminology [ˌtɜːmɪ'nɒlədʒɪ] *s.* terminologia *f.*
terminus ['tɜːmɪnəs] *s.* capolinea *m. inv.*
termite ['tɜːmaɪt] *s.* termite *f.*
terrace ['tɛrəs] *s.* **1** terrazzo *m.*, terrapieno *m.* **2** terrazza *f.* **3** case *f. pl.* a schiera
terracotta [ˌtɛrə'kɒtə] *s.* terracotta *f.*
terrain ['tɛreɪn] *s.* terreno *m.*
terrestrial [tɪ'rɛstrɪəl] *agg.* terrestre
terrible ['tɛrəbl] *agg.* terribile, tremendo
terrier ['tɛrɪəʳ] *s.* terrier *m. inv.*
terrific [tə'rɪfɪk] *agg.* **1** spaventoso **2** (*fam.*) fantastico, straordinario
to **terrify** ['tɛrɪfaɪ] *v. tr.* terrorizzare
territorial [ˌtɛrɪ'tɜːrɪəl] *agg.* territoriale
territory ['tɛrɪt(ə)rɪ] *s.* territorio *m.*
terror ['tɛrəʳ] *s.* **1** terrore *m.* **2** (*fam.*) (*di bambino*) peste *f.*
terrorism ['tɛrərɪz(ə)m] *s.* terrorismo *m.*
terrorist ['tɛrərɪst] *s.* terrorista *m. e f.*
terse [tɜːs] *agg.* conciso
tertiary ['tɜːʃərɪ] *s.* terziario *m.*
test [tɛst] *s.* esame *m.*, prova *f.*, test *m. inv.* ♦ **t. pilot** pilota collaudatore; **t. tube** provetta
to **test** [tɛst] *v. tr.* esaminare, analizzare, collaudare, sperimentare
testament ['tɛstəmənt] *s.* testamento *m.*
testator [tɛs'teɪtəʳ] *s.* testatore *m.*
testicle ['tɛstɪkl] *s.* testicolo *m.*
to **testify** ['tɛstɪfaɪ] *v. tr. e intr.* **1** testimoniare **2** dimostrare
testimony ['tɛstɪmənɪ] *s.* testimonianza *f.*
testis ['tɛstɪs] (*pl.* **testes**) *s.* testicolo *m.*
tetanus ['tɛtənəs] *s.* tetano *m.*
tether ['tɛðəʳ] *s.* **1** pastoia *f.*, catena *f.* **2** (*fig.*) campo *m.*, portata *f.*
text [tɛkst] *s.* testo *m.*
textbook ['tɛks(t)bʊk] *s.* manuale *m.*
textile ['tɛkstaɪl] *agg.* tessile
texture ['tɛkstʃəʳ] *s.* **1** trama *f.* **2** struttura *f.*
than [ðæn] *cong.* **1** (*comparativo*) che, di, di quello che (ES: **You are younger t. I am** sei più giovane di me) **2** (*dopo 'other, else, rather, sooner'*) che (ES: **no other t.** nient'altro che, **rather t.** piuttosto che) **3** (*correlativo di 'hardly, scarcely'*) quando, che (ES: **hardly was your mother gone t. you**

began crying tua madre era appena uscita che già iniziavi a piangere)
to thank [θæŋk] *v. tr.* ringraziare ♦ **t. you** grazie!
thankful ['θæŋkf(ʊ)l] *agg.* riconoscente
thankfulness ['θæŋkf(ʊ)lnɪs] *s.* riconoscenza *f.*
thanks [θæŋks] *s. pl.* ringraziamenti *m. pl.* ♦ **t. to** grazie a
that [ðæt] (*pl.* **those**) **A** *agg. dimostr.* quello, quella (ES: **t. pen** quella penna) **B** *pron. dimostr.* quello, quella, questo, questa, ciò (ES: **who's t.?** chi è quello?, **what's t.** cos'è quello?) **C** *pron. rel.* **1** che, il quale, la quale, i quali, le quali (ES: **the book t. I read** il libro che ho letto) **2** in cui, che (ES: **the day t. Kennedy was murdered** il giorno in cui Kennedy venne assassinato) **D** *cong.* che (ES: **it was so cold t. we decided to stay at home** faceva così freddo che decidemmo di stare a casa)
thatch [θætʃ] *s.* paglia *f.*
thaw [θɜː] *s.* disgelo *m.*
to thaw [θɜː] *v. tr.* sgelare, scongelare
the [ðiː] *art. determ.* il, lo, la, i, gli, le
theatre ['θɪətəʳ] (*USA* **theater**) *s.* teatro *m.*
theatrical [θɪ'ætrɪk(ə)l] *agg.* teatrale
theft [θɛft] *s.* furto *m.*
their [ðɛəʳ] *agg. poss.* il loro, la loro, i loro, le loro
theirs [ðɛəz] *pron. poss.* il loro, la loro, i loro, le loro
them [ðɛm, ðəm] *pron. pers. 3ª pl.* (*compl.*) li, le, loro
theme [θiːm] *s.* tema *m.* ♦ **t. park** parco divertimenti; **t. song** tema musicale
themselves [ðəm'sɛlvz] *pron. 3ª pl.* **1** (*rifl.*) se stessi, se stesse, sé, si **2** (*enf.*) essi stessi, esse stesse, proprio loro
then [ðɛn] **A** *avv.* **1** allora, a quel tempo **2** dopo, poi **3** allora, in tal caso **4** anche, poi **B** *cong.* dunque, allora ♦ **before t.** prima di allora; **by t.** a quel tempo, ormai; **now and t.** di tanto in tanto; **what t.?** e allora?
theologian [θɪə'lɒʊdʒjən] *s.* teologo *m.*
theology [θɪ'ələdʒɪ] *s.* teologia *f.*
theorem ['θɪərəm] *s.* teorema *m.*
theory ['θɪərɪ] *s.* teoria *f.*
therapeutic [ˌθɛrə'pjuːtɪk] *agg.* terapeutico
therapy ['θɛrəpɪ] *s.* terapia *f.*
there [ðɛəʳ] **A** *avv.* **1** là, lì (ES: **where is it? it is t.** dov'è? là) **2** ci, vi (ES: **t. is an apple on the table** c'è una mela sul tavolo) **B** *inter.* ecco!
thereabout(s) ['ðɛərəˌbaʊt(s)] *avv.* **1** nei pressi **2** all'incirca
thereafter [ˌðɛər'aːftəʳ] *avv.* da allora in poi, quindi
thereby [ˌðɛə'baɪ] *avv.* con ciò, per mezzo di ciò
therefore ['ðɛəfɜːʳ] *avv.* dunque, perciò, quindi
thermae ['θɜːmɪ] *s. pl.* (*archeol.*) terme *f.*
thermal ['θɜːm(ə)l] *agg.* termale
thermic ['θɜːmɪk] *agg.* termico
thermodynamics [ˌθɜːmɒ(ʊ)daɪ'næmɪks] *s. pl.* (*v. al sing.*) termodinamica *f.*
thermometer [θə'məmɪtəʳ] *s.* termometro *m.*
thermos ['θɜːməs] *s.* thermos *m. inv.*
thermostat ['θɜːmɒ(ʊ)stæt] *s.* termostato *m.*
thesaurus [θiː'sɜːrəs] *s.* dizionario *m.* dei sinonimi
these [ðiːz] *pl. di* **this**
thesis ['θiːsɪs] (*pl.* **theses**) *s.* tesi *f.*
they [ðeɪ] *pron. pers. 3ª pl.* essi, esse, loro ♦ **t. say** si dice
thick [θɪk] **A** *agg.* **1** spesso, denso, folto **2** ottuso **B** *s.* il folto *m.* **C** *avv.* **1** fittamente **2** a strati spessi
to thicken ['θɪk(ə)n] **A** *v. tr.* addensare, ispessire, infoltire **B** *v. intr.* **1** addensarsi, ispessirsi, infoltirsi **2** (*del tempo*) offuscarsi
thicket ['θɪkɪt] *s.* boscaglia *f.*
thickness ['θɪknɪs] *s.* **1** densità *f.* **2** spessore *m.*
thickset [ˌθɪk'sɛt] *agg.* **1** fitto, folto **2** tarchiato
thief [θiːf] *s.* ladro *m.*
thigh [θaɪ] *s.* coscia *f.* ♦ **t. bone** femore
thimble ['θɪmbl] *s.* ditale *m.*
thin [θɪn] *agg.* **1** sottile, fine **2** magro **3** rado, poco denso **4** diluito
to thin [θɪn] **A** *v. tr.* **1** assottigliare **2** diradare, sfoltire **3** diluire **B** *v. intr.* **1** assottigliarsi **2** diradarsi, sfoltirsi
thing [θɪŋ] *s.* cosa *f.*
to think [θɪŋk] (*pass. e p. p.* **thought**) *v. tr. e intr.* pensare ♦ **to t. about** pensare a; **to t. out** meditare su, escogitare; **to t. over** riflettere; **to t. up** trovare, inventare
thinker ['θɪŋkəʳ] *s.* pensatore *m.*
thinness ['θɪnnɪs] *s.* **1** finezza *f.* **2** ma-

grezza *f.*
third [θɜːd] **A** *agg. num. ord.* terzo **B** *s.* **1** terzo *m.* **2** (*mus.*) terza *f.* **3** (*autom.*) terza *f.* (marcia) ♦ **t.-rate** di terz'ordine, scadente
thirdly [θɜːdlɪ] *avv.* in terzo luogo
thirst [θɜːst] *s.* sete *f.*
thirsty ['θɜːstɪ] *agg.* assetato
thirteen [ˌθɜː'tiːn] *agg. num. card. e s.* tredici *m. inv.*
thirteenth [ˌθɜː'tiːnθ] *agg. num. ord. e s.* tredicesimo *m.*
thirtieth ['θɜːtɪɪθ] *agg. num. ord. e s.* trentesimo *m.*
thirty ['θɜːtɪ] *agg. num. card. e s.* trenta *m. inv.*
this [ðɪs] (*pl.* **these**) **A** *agg. dimostr.* questo, questa **B** *pron. dimostr.* questo, questa, costui, ciò **C** *avv.* (*fam.*) così ♦ **t. evening** stasera; **t. morning** stamattina; **t. night** stanotte; **t. time** stavolta
thistle ['θɪsl] *s.* cardo *m.*
thong [θɔŋ] *s.* cinghia *f.*
thorn [θɜːn] *s.* spina *f.*
thorough ['θʌrə] *agg.* **1** completo, minuzioso, profondo **2** bell'e buono, perfetto
thoroughbred ['θʌrəbrɛd] *s.* purosangue *m.*
thoroughfare ['θʌrəfɛəʳ] *s.* strada *f.* di transito ♦ **no t.** divieto di transito
thoroughly ['θʌrəlɪ] *avv.* completamente
those [ðɒʊz] *pl. di* **that**
though [ðɒʊ] **A** *cong.* sebbene, benché, malgrado **B** *avv.* comunque
thought (1) [θɜːt] *s.* pensiero *m.*
thought (2) [θɜːt] *pass. e p. p. di* **to think**
thoughtful ['θɜːtf(ʊ)l] *agg.* **1** pensieroso **2** sollecito, pieno di attenzioni
thoughtless ['θɜːtlɪs] *agg.* **1** sconsiderato **2** noncurante
thousand ['θaʊz(ə)nd] **A** *agg. num. card.* mille **B** *s.* migliaio *m.* ♦ **by thousands, by the t.** a migliaia; **t. millions** miliardo
to thrash [θræʃ] **A** *v. tr.* battere, percuotere **B** *v. intr.* muoversi ♦ **to t. about** dimenarsi; **to t. out** chiarire, definire
thread [θrɛd] *s.* **1** filo *m.* **2** filetto *m.*, filettatura *f.*
to thread [θrɛd] *v. tr.* **1** infilare **2** filettare
threadbare ['θrɛdbɛəʳ] *agg.* consumato, logoro
threat [θrɛt] *s.* minaccia *f.*
to threaten ['θrɛtn] *v. tr. e intr.* minacciare
threatening ['θrɛtnɪŋ] *agg.* minaccioso
three [θriː] *agg. num. card. e s.* tre *m. inv.*
three-dimensional [ˌθrɪdɪ'mɛnʃənl] *agg.* tridimensionale
threshing ['θrɛʃɪŋ] *s.* trebbiatura *f.* ♦ **t. floor** aia; **t. machine** trebbiatrice
threshold ['θrɛʃ(h)ɒʊld] *s.* soglia *f.*
threw [θruː] *pass. di* **to throw**
thrifty ['θrɪftɪ] *agg.* parsimonioso
thrill [θrɪl] *s.* brivido *m.*
to thrill [θrɪl] **A** *v. tr.* eccitare, commuovere **B** *v. intr.* fremere, rabbrividire, eccitarsi
thriller ['θrɪləʳ] *s.* thriller *m. inv.*
thrilling ['θrɪlɪŋ] *agg.* elettrizzante, eccitante, sensazionale
to thrive [θraɪv] (*pass.* **throve**, *p. p.* **thriven**) *v. intr.* **1** prosperare, aver fortuna **2** crescere rigogliosamente
throat [θrɒʊt] *s.* gola *f.*
throb [θrəb] *s.* **1** battito *m.*, pulsazione *f.* **2** fremito *m.*
to throb [θrəb] *v. intr.* **1** battere, pulsare **2** fremere
throes [θrɒʊz] *s. pl.* doglie *f. pl.*, spasimi *m. pl.*
thrombosis [θrəm'bɒʊsɪs] *s.* trombosi *f.*
throne [θrɒʊn] *s.* trono *m.*
throng [θrəŋ] *s.* folla *f.*, ressa *f.*
to throng [θrəŋ] *v. tr. e intr.* affollare, affollarsi
throttle ['θrətl] *s.* gola *f.* ♦ **t. valve** valvola a farfalla
to throttle ['θrətl] *v. tr.* strangolare
through (1) [θruː] **A** *avv.* **1** attraverso, da parte a parte **2** da cima a fondo **3** direttamente **B** *prep.* **1** (*moto per luogo*) attraverso, per **2** (*tempo*) durante, per la durata di, per **3** (*mezzo*) mediante, per mezzo di **4** (*causa*) a causa di, per
through (2) [θruː] *agg.* **1** finito, chiuso **2** diretto
throughout [θruː'aʊt] **A** *avv.* da parte a parte, dal principio alla fine, completamente **B** *prep.* in tutto, per tutto, durante tutto
throve [θrɒʊv] *pass. di* **to thrive**
throw [θrɒʊ] *s.* lancio *m.*, tiro *m.*
to throw [θrɒʊ] (*pass.* **threw**, *p. p.* **thrown**) *v. tr.* **1** buttare, lanciare, scagliare **2** abbattere, disarcionare **3** confondere, imbarazzare ♦ **to t. away** gettare via; **to t. off** togliersi, disfarsi di; **to t. out** buttar via, respingere; **to t. up** abbandonare, vomitare
thrush [θrʌʃ] *s.* tordo *m.*
thrust [θrʌst] *s.* spinta *f.*
to thrust [θrʌst] (*pass. e p. p.* **thrust**) **A** *v.*

tr. **1** spingere, ficcare **2** conficcare, piantare **B** *v. intr.* **1** ficcarsi, infilarsi, farsi largo **2** spingersi ♦ **to t. through** trafiggere
thud [θʌd] *s.* tonfo *m.*
thumb [θʌmb] *s.* pollice *m.*
to thumb [θʌmb] *v. tr.* **1** (*pagine*) sfogliare **2** lasciare ditate su **3** strimpellare ♦ **to t. a lift** fare l'autostop
thumbtack ['θʌmtæk] *s.* puntina *f.* da disegno
thump [θʌmp] *s.* **1** botta *f.*, colpo *m.* **2** tonfo *m.*
to thump [θʌmp] **A** *v. tr.* battere, picchiare **B** *v. intr.* **1** menare colpi **2** cadere con un tonfo
thunder ['θʌndəʳ] *s.* tuono *m.*
to thunder ['θʌndəʳ] *v. intr.* tuonare
thunderbolt ['θʌndə,bɒult] *s.* fulmine *m.*
thunderclap ['θʌndə,klæp] *s.* (rombo di) tuono *m.*
thunderstorm ['θʌndə,stɜːm] *s.* temporale *m.*
thundery ['θʌndərɪ] *agg.* tempestoso, temporalesco
Thursday ['θɜːzdɪ] *s.* giovedì *m.*
thus [ðʌs] *avv.* **1** così, pertanto, quindi **2** talmente
to thwart [θwɜːt] *v. tr.* ostacolare
thyme [taɪm] *s.* (*bot.*) timo *m.*
thymus ['θaɪməs] *s.* (*anat.*) timo *m.*
thyroid ['θaɪrəɪd] *s.* tiroide *f.*
tiara [tɪ'aːrə] *s.* tiara *f.*
tibia ['tɪbɪə] *s.* tibia *f.*
tick (1) [tɪk] *s.* (*zool.*) zecca *f.*
tick (2) [tɪk] *s.* **1** ticchettio *m.*, tic tac *m. inv.* **2** attimo *m.* **3** visto *m.*, segno *m.*
to tick [tɪk] **A** *v. intr.* **1** ticchettare, fare tic tac **2** funzionare **B** *v. tr.* segnare, spuntare ♦ **to t. off** sgridare; **to t. over** perdere colpi, tirare avanti
ticket ['tɪkɪt] *s.* **1** biglietto *m.*, tessera *f.* **2** scontrino *m.*, cartellino *m.* ♦ **one-way t.** biglietto di sola andata; **return t.** biglietto di andata e ritorno; **t. clerk** (*in stazione*) bigliettaio; **t. collector** (*in treno*) bigliettaio, (*sui mezzi pubblici*) controllore; **t. office** biglietteria; **t. window** sportello della biglietteria
to tickle ['tɪkl] *v. tr.* **1** solleticare **2** stuzzicare, stimolare
ticklish ['tɪklɪʃ] *agg.* **1** che soffre il solletico **2** delicato **3** permaloso, suscettibile
tidal ['taɪdl] *agg.* di marea
tiddlywinks ['tɪdlɪwɪŋks] *s.* gioco *m.* delle pulci
tide [taɪd] *s.* **1** marea *f.* **2** corso *m.*, corrente *f.* ♦ **high/low t.** alta/bassa marea
to tide [taɪd] *v. intr.* navigare con la marea ♦ **to t. over** aiutare a superare
tidy ['taɪdɪ] *agg.* ordinato, pulito
to tidy ['taɪdɪ] *v. tr.* riordinare ♦ **to t. out** sgombrare; **to t. up** riordinare
tie [taɪ] *s.* **1** laccio *m.*, stringa *f.* **2** cravatta *f.* **3** legame *m.*, vincolo *m.* **4** (*sport*) pareggio *m.*, spareggio *m.*
to tie [taɪ] **A** *v. tr.* **1** legare, annodare **2** pareggiare, uguagliare **B** *v. intr.* **1** essere allacciato **2** pareggiare ♦ **to t. down** legare, vincolare; **to t. up** legare, collegare, impegnare, vincolare
tier [tɪəʳ] *s.* fila *f.*, ordine *m.*, strato *m.*
tiger ['taɪgəʳ] *s.* tigre *f.*
tight [taɪt] **A** *agg.* **1** teso, tirato **2** stretto, aderente **3** fermo, saldo, ben fissato **4** ermetico, stagno **5** severo, fermo, difficile **6** scarso **7** avaro, tirchio **8** (*fam.*) sbronzo **B** *avv.* **1** strettamente **2** fermamente **3** completamente
to tighten ['taɪtn] *v. tr.* **1** stringere, serrare **2** tendere, tirare
tightfisted [,taɪt'fɪstɪd] *agg.* avaro, tirchio
tightly ['taɪtlɪ] *avv.* strettamente
tightrope ['taɪt,rɒup] *s.* fune *f.* (*di funambolo*)
tights [taɪts] *s. pl.* **1** collant *m. inv.* **2** calzamaglia *f.*
tile [taɪl] *s.* **1** piastrella *f.* **2** tegola *f.*
till (1) [tɪl] **A** *cong.* finché, fino a che non **B** *prep.* fino a ♦ **not t.** non prima di; **t. now** finora
till (2) [tɪl] *s.* cassa *f.* ♦ **cash t.** registratore di cassa
to till [tɪl] *v. tr.* coltivare, arare, dissodare
tiller ['tɪləʳ] *s.* (*naut.*) barra *f.* del timone
tilt (1) [tɪlt] *s.* copertone *m.*, telone *m.*
tilt (2) [tɪlt] *s.* **1** inclinazione *f.*, pendenza *f.* **2** (*stor.*) torneo *m.*, giostra *f.* ♦ **at full t.** a tutta forza
to tilt [tɪlt] **A** *v. intr.* **1** inclinarsi, piegarsi **2** (*stor.*) giostrare **B** *v. tr.* inclinare, piegare ♦ **to t. up** rovesciare
timbal ['tɪmb(ə)l] *s.* (*mus.*) timballo *m.*, timpano *m.*
timber ['tɪmbəʳ] *s.* legname *m.*
timbre ['tɪmbəʳ] *s.* (*di voce*) timbro *m.*
time [taɪm] *s.* **1** tempo *m.* **2** momento *m.*, ora *f.* **3** periodo *m.*, epoca *f.* **4** volta *f.* **5** orario *m.* ♦ **at any t.** in qualunque mo-

mento; **at no t.** mai; **at the same t.** contemporaneamente; **at times** talvolta; **from t. to t.** di tanto in tanto; **in good t.** per tempo; **next t.** la prossima volta; **t. table** orario; **on t.** puntuale; **opening t.** ora d'apertura; **t. bomb** bomba a orologeria; **t. off** periodo di permesso; **what t. is it?** che ora è?
to time [taɪm] *v. tr.* **1** fare al momento giusto **2** determinare i tempi, l'orario **3** sincronizzare **4** cronometrare
timeless ['taɪmlɪs] *agg.* senza tempo, eterno
timeliness ['taɪmlɪnɪs] *s.* tempestività *f.*
timely ['taɪmlɪ] *agg.* tempestivo
timer ['taɪməʳ] *s.* **1** cronometro *m.* **2** timer *m. inv.*
timid ['tɪmɪd] *agg.* timido, timoroso
timing ['taɪmɪŋ] *s.* **1** sincronizzazione *f.* **2** tempismo *m.*
tin [tɪn] *s.* **1** (*chim.*) stagno *m.* **2** latta *f.*, lamiera *f.* **3** lattina *f.*, barattolo *m.* ♦ **t. opener** apriscatole
tinfoil ['tɪnfɔɪl] *s.* stagnola *f.*
tinge [tɪn(d)ʒ] *s.* sfumatura *f.*, traccia *f.*
to tinge [tɪn(d)ʒ] *v. tr.* sfumare
to tingle ['tɪŋgl] *v. intr.* pizzicare, formicolare
to tinker ['tɪŋkəʳ] *v. tr.* rabberciare, rattoppare ♦ **to t. up** riparare alla meglio
to tinkle ['tɪŋkl] *v. intr.* tintinnare
tinned [tɪnd] *agg.* in scatola
tinning ['tɪnɪŋ] *s.* **1** stagnatura *f.* **2** inscatolamento *m.*
tint [tɪnt] *s.* colore *m.*, sfumatura *f.*
tiny ['taɪnɪ] *agg.* minuscolo, piccino
tip (1) [tɪp] *s.* punta *f.*, estremità *f.*
tip (2) [tɪp] *s.* **1** inclinazione *f.* **2** deposito *m.*, discarica *f.*
tip (3) [tɪp] *s.* colpetto *m.*, tocco *m.*
tip (4) [tɪp] *s.* **1** mancia *f.* **2** informazione *f.* riservata, soffiata *f.*
to tip (1) [tɪp] *v. tr.* versare, rovesciare, scaricare ♦ **to t. up** ribaltare
to tip (2) [tɪp] *v. tr.* colpire leggermente
to tip (3) [tɪp] *v. tr.* **1** dare la mancia a **2** avvertire, informare ♦ **to t. off** passare una soffiata
tipsy ['tɪpsɪ] *agg.* (*fam.*) brillo
tiptoe ['tɪptɒʊ] *avv.* **on t.** in punta di piedi
tiptop [,tɪp'tɔp] *agg.* (*fam.*) eccellente
tire [taɪəʳ] *s.* (*USA*) → **tyre**
to tire [taɪəʳ] *v. tr. e intr.* stancare, stancarsi
tired ['taɪəd] *agg.* **1** stanco **2** annoiato, infastidito ♦ **to get t.** affaticarsi
tiredness ['taɪədnɪs] *s.* stanchezza *f.*
tireless ['taɪəlɪs] *agg.* infaticabile
tiresome ['taɪəsəm] *agg.* noioso
tiring ['taɪərɪŋ] *agg.* faticoso
tissue ['tɪsjuː] *s.* **1** tessuto *m.* **2** fazzoletto *m.* di carta ♦ **t. paper** carta velina
titbit ['tɪtbɪt] *s.* golosità *f.*, leccornia *f.*
title ['taɪtl] *s.* titolo *m.* ♦ **t. deed** titolo di proprietà; **t. page** frontespizio
to titter ['tɪtəʳ] *v. intr.* ridacchiare
to (1) [tuː, tʊ, tə] *prep.* **1** (*termine, destinazione*) a, verso, per (ES: **I will send a letter to you** ti manderò una lettera) **2** (*moto a luogo*) in, a, verso (ES: **to go to school** andare a scuola) **3** (*confronto, relazione, preferenza*) a, in confronto a, per (ES: **three sets to one** tre set a uno)
to (2) [tuː, tʊ, tə] *particella preposta all'infinito* **1** (*idiom.*) (ES: **to be** essere, **I want to stay** voglio rimanere) **2** di, da, per, a (ES: **is there anything to do?** c'è qualcosa da fare?)
toad [tɒʊd] *s.* rospo *m.*
toadstool ['tɒʊdstuːl] *s.* fungo *m.* velenoso
toast (1) [tɒʊst] *s.* pane *m.* tostato
toast (2) [tɒʊst] *s.* brindisi *m.*
to toast (1) [tɒʊst] *v. tr.* abbrustolire, tostare
to toast (2) [tɒʊst] *v. intr.* brindare
toaster ['tɒʊstəʳ] *s.* tostapane *m. inv.*
tobacco [tə'bækɒʊ] *s.* tabacco *m.*
tobacconist [tə'bækənɪst] *s.* tabaccaio *m.* ♦ **t.'s shop** tabaccheria
today [tə'deɪ] *s. e avv.* oggi *m. inv.*
toddler ['tɔdləʳ] *s.* bambino *m.* ai primi passi
toe [tɒʊ] *s.* **1** (*del piede*) dito *m.* **2** punta *f.* ♦ **big t.** alluce; **little t.** mignolo
toenail ['tɒʊneɪl] *s.* (*del piede*) unghia *f.*
toffee ['tɔfɪ] *s.* caramella *f.*
toga ['tɒʊgə] *s.* toga *f.*
together [tə'gɛðəʳ] *avv.* **1** insieme **2** contemporaneamente **3** di seguito
toil [tɔɪl] *s.* fatica *f.*
to toil [tɔɪl] *v. intr.* affaticarsi
toilet ['tɔɪlɪt] *s.* **1** gabinetto *m.* **2** toeletta *f.* ♦ **t. case** necessaire; **t. paper** carta igienica; **t. roll** rotolo di carta igienica
token ['tɒ(ʊ)k(ə)n] *s.* **1** segno *m.*, simbolo *m.* **2** pegno *m.* **3** contrassegno *m.*, gettone *m.* **4** buono *m.*
told [tɒʊld] *pass. e p. p. di* **to tell**
tolerable ['tɔlərəbl] *agg.* **1** tollerabile **2**

passabile
tolerance ['tələr(ə)ns] *s.* tolleranza *f.*
tolerant ['tələr(ə)nt] *agg.* tollerante
to **tolerate** ['tələreɪt] *v. tr.* tollerare
toll (1) [tɒʊl] *s.* **1** pedaggio *m.* **2** tributo *m.*, costo *m.*
toll (2) [tɒʊl] *s.* rintocco *m.*
to **toll** [tɒʊl] *v. intr.* rintoccare
tomato [tə'maːtɒʊ] *s.* pomodoro *m.*
tomb [tuːm] *s.* tomba *f.*, sepolcro *m.*
tombola ['təmbələ] *s.* tombola *f.*
tomboy ['təmbəɪ] *s.* maschiaccio *m.*
tombstone ['tuːmˌstɒʊn] *s.* lapide *f.*
tomcat ['təmˌkæt] *s.* (*fam.*) micio *m.*
tome [tɒʊm] *s.* tomo *m.*
tomfoolery [ˌtəm'fuːlərɪ] *s.* scemenza *f.*
tomorrow [tə'mərɒ(ʊ)] *s. e avv.* domani *m. inv.* ♦ **the day after t.** dopodomani
ton [tʌn] *s.* tonnellata *f.*
tonality [tɒ(ʊ)'nælɪtɪ] *s.* tonalità *f.*
tone [tɒʊn] *s.* tono *m.*
to **tone** [tɒʊn] **A** *v. tr.* dare il tono a, intonare **B** *v. intr.* intonarsi ♦ **to t. down** attenuare; **to t. up** tonificare
tongs [təŋz] *s. pl.* pinze *f. pl.*
tongue [tʌŋ] *s.* lingua *f.* ♦ **t. twister** scioglilingua
tonic ['tənɪk] **A** *agg.* tonico, tonificante **B** *s.* **1** tonico *m.*, ricostituente *m.* **2** (*mus.*) tonica *f.* ♦ **t. water** acqua tonica
tonight [tə'naɪt] **A** *avv.* stasera, stanotte **B** *s.* questa sera *f.*, questa notte *f.*
tonnage ['tʌnɪdʒ] *s.* tonnellaggio *m.*
tonsil ['tənsl] *s.* tonsilla *f.*
tonsillitis [ˌtənsɪ'laɪtɪs] *s.* tonsillite *f.*
too [tuː] *avv.* **1** anche, pure **2** per di più, per giunta **3** troppo ♦ **t. bad** che peccato!; **t. many** troppi; **t. much** troppo
took [tʊk] *pass. di* **to take**
tool [tuːl] *s.* attrezzo *m.*, strumento *m.*, utensile *m.*
toolbox ['tuːlbəks] *s.* cassetta *f.* portautensili
toot [tuːt] *s.* colpo *m.* di clacson
tooth [tuːθ] (*pl.* **teeth**) *s.* dente *m.*
toothache ['tuːθˌeɪk] *s.* mal *m.* di denti
toothbrush ['tuːθbrʌʃ] *s.* spazzolino *m.* da denti
toothpaste ['tuːθpeɪst] *s.* dentifricio *m.*
toothpick ['tuːθpɪk] *s.* stuzzicadenti *m. inv.*
top (1) [təp] **A** *s.* **1** cima *f.*, vetta *f.*, sommità *f.* **2** parte *f.* superiore **3** tappo *m.*, coperchio *m.* **B** *agg. attr.* superiore, massimo, il più alto ♦ **t. floor** ultimo piano; **t. level** massimo livello
top (2) [təp] *s.* trottola *f.*
topaz ['tɒʊpæz] *s.* topazio *m.*
topic ['təpɪk] *s.* argomento *m.*, tema *m.*
topical ['təpɪk(ə)l] *agg.* d'attualità
topmost ['təpmɒʊst] *agg.* il più elevato
topography [tə'pəgrəfɪ] *s.* topografia *f.*
toponym ['təpənɪm] *s.* toponimo *m.*
to **topple** ['təpl] **A** *v. intr.* **1** crollare, cadere **2** traballare, vacillare **B** *v. tr.* far cadere, rovesciare
top-secret [ˌtəp'siːkrɪt] *agg.* segretissimo, top-secret
topsy-turvy [ˌtəpsɪ'tɜːvɪ] *avv. e agg.* sottosopra
torch [tɜːtʃ] *s.* **1** torcia *f.*, fiaccola *f.* **2** torcia *f.* elettrica, lampadina *f.* tascabile
tore [tɜːʳ] *pass. di* **to tear**
torment [tɜː'mɛnt] *s.* tormento *m.*
to **torment** [tə'mɛnt] *v. tr.* tormentare
torn [tɜːn] *p. p. di* **to tear**
tornado [tɜː'neɪdɒʊ] *s.* tornado *m. inv.*
torpedo [tɜː'piːdɒʊ] **1** (*zool.*) torpedine *f.* **2** siluro *m.*
torpor ['tɜːpəʳ] *s.* torpore *m.*
torrent ['tər(ə)nt] *s.* torrente *m.*
torrential [tə'rɛnʃ(ə)l] *agg.* torrenziale
torrid ['tərɪd] *agg.* torrido
torsion ['tɜːʃ(ə)n] *s.* torsione *f.*
tortoise ['tɜːtəs] *s.* testuggine *f.*
tortuous ['tɜːtjʊəs] *agg.* tortuoso
torture ['tɜːtʃəʳ] *s.* tortura *f.*
to **torture** ['tɜːtʃəʳ] *v. tr.* torturare
Tory ['tɜːrɪ] *agg. e s.* conservatore *m.*
to **toss** [təs] **A** *v. tr.* **1** gettare, lanciare **2** sballottare, scuotere **B** *v. intr.* **1** lanciare una moneta, fare a testa o croce **2** agitarsi ♦ **to t. off** tracannare
tot [tət] *s.* **1** (*fam.*) bambino *m.* **2** sorso *m.*, goccio *m.*
total ['tɒʊtl] *agg. e s.* totale *m.*
to **total** ['tɒʊtl] *v. tr.* sommare, ammontare a
totem ['tɒʊtəm] *s.* totem *m. inv.*
to **totter** ['tətəʳ] *v. intr.* barcollare, vacillare
tottery ['tətərɪ] *agg.* barcollante, vacillante
touch [tʌtʃ] *s.* **1** tocco *m.*, colpetto *m.* **2** tatto *m.* **3** contatto *m.*, relazione *f.* **4** tocco *m.*, modo *m.*, impronta *f.* **5** pizzico *m.*, piccola quantità *f.* ♦ **t. up** ritocco
to **touch** [tʌtʃ] **A** *v. tr.* **1** toccare **2** riguardare, concernere **3** raggiungere **4** essere in contatto con **5** commuovere **B** *v. intr.* toccarsi ♦ **to t. at a port** fare scalo in un

porto; **to t. down** atterrare; **to t. on** sfiorare; **to t. up** ritoccare
touch-and-go [ˌtʌtʃən'gɒʊ] *agg.* incerto, rischioso
touched [tʌtʃt] *agg.* **1** commosso **2** (*fam.*) tocco
touching ['tʌtʃɪŋ] *agg.* toccante
touchy ['tʌtʃɪ] *agg.* permaloso
tough [tʌf] *agg.* **1** duro, coriaceo **2** forte, robusto **3** difficile
to toughen ['tʌfn] *v. tr. e intr.* indurire, indurirsi
toughness ['tʌfnɪs] *s.* durezza *f.*
toupee ['tuːpeɪ] *s.* toupet *m. inv.*
tour [tʊəʳ] *s.* **1** giro *m.*, viaggio *m.*, escursione *f.* **2** tournée *f. inv.* ♦ **package t.** viaggio tutto compreso
to tour [tʊəʳ] *v. intr.* viaggiare, girare
touring ['tʊərɪŋ] **A** *agg.* turistico **B** *s.* turismo *m.*, escursionismo *m.*
tourism ['tʊərɪz(ə)m] *s.* turismo *m.*
tourist ['tʊərɪst] **A** *s.* turista *m. e f.* **B** *agg.* turistico ♦ **t. class** classe turistica
tournament ['tʊənəmənt] *s.* torneo *m.*
to tousle ['taʊzl] *v. tr.* scompigliare
to tout [taʊt] *v. intr.* **1** fare il procacciatore, cercare clienti **2** fare il bagarinaggio
tow [tɒʊ] *s.* rimorchio *m.* ♦ **t. truck** carro attrezzi
to tow [tɒʊ] *v. tr.* rimorchiare, trainare
toward(s) [tə'wɜːd(z)] *prep.* **1** verso, in direzione di **2** nei confronti di **3** verso, circa **4** in previsione di
towel ['taʊəl] *s.* asciugamano *m.* ♦ **t. rack/horse** portasciugamani
tower ['taʊəʳ] *s.* torre *f.* ♦ **t. block** palazzo a molti piani
towering ['taʊərɪŋ] *agg.* torreggiante, imponente
town [taʊn] *s.* **1** città *f.* **2** cittadinanza *f.* ♦ **t. council** consiglio comunale; **t. hall** municipio; **t. planning** urbanistica
toxic ['təksɪk] *agg.* tossico
toxin ['təksɪn] *s.* tossina *f.*
toy [təɪ] *s.* giocattolo *m.* ♦ **t. soldier** soldatino
to toy [təɪ] *v. intr.* giocherellare, trastullarsi
trace [treɪs] *s.* **1** traccia *f.*, orma *f.* **2** residuo *m.* **3** tracciato *m.*
to trace [treɪs] *v. tr.* **1** tracciare **2** seguire le tracce di **3** rintracciare
trachea [trə'kɪ(ː)ə] *s.* trachea *f.*
tracing ['treɪsɪŋ] *s.* tracciato *m.*
track [træk] *s.* **1** traccia *f.*, impronta *f.* **2** pista *f.*, sentiero *m.* **3** binario *m.*
to track [træk] *v. tr.* **1** inseguire **2** (*un sentiero*) percorrere, (*una pista*) seguire ♦ **to t. down** scovare; **to t. out** rintracciare
tracksuit ['træksuːt] *s.* tuta *f.* (sportiva)
tract (1) [trækt] *s.* tratto *m.*, distesa *f.*
tract (2) [trækt] *s.* trattatello *m.*, opuscolo *m.*
tractable ['træktəbl] *agg.* trattabile
traction ['trækʃ(ə)n] *s.* trazione *f.*
tractor ['træktəʳ] *s.* trattore *m.*
trade [treɪd] **A** *s.* **1** commercio *m.*, scambio *m.* **2** industria *f.*, settore *m.* **3** mestiere *m.*, occupazione *f.* **B** *agg.* commerciale ♦ **building t.** industria edilizia; **free t.** libero scambio; **t. mark** marchio registrato; **t. name** nome depositato; **t. union** sindacato; **t. winds** alisei
to trade [treɪd] **A** *v. tr.* **1** scambiare **2** commerciare **B** *v. intr.* trafficare, commerciare ♦ **to t. in** dar dentro (*l'usato*); **to t. off** controbilanciare
trader ['treɪdəʳ] *s.* commerciante *m. e f.*, mercante *m.*
tradition [trə'dɪʃ(ə)n] *s.* tradizione *f.*
traditional [trə'dɪʃənl] *agg.* tradizionale
traffic ['træfɪk] *s.* **1** traffico *m.* **2** circolazione *f.* ♦ **t. divider** spartitraffico; **t. jam** ingorgo stradale; **t. light** semaforo
tragedy ['trædʒɪdɪ] *s.* dramma *m.*, tragedia *f.*
tragic ['trædʒɪk] *agg.* tragico
tragicomic(al) [ˌtrædʒɪ'kəmɪk((ə)l)] *agg.* tragicomico
trail [treɪl] *s.* **1** traccia *f.*, orma *f.* **2** pista *f.* **3** scia *f.*
to trail [treɪl] **A** *v. tr.* **1** trascinare, tirarsi dietro **2** inseguire **B** *v. intr.* **1** strisciare **2** seguire le tracce **3** (*di pianta*) arrampicarsi
trailer ['treɪləʳ] *s.* **1** rimorchio *m.* **2** (*USA*) roulotte *f. inv.* **3** (*cine.*) trailer *m. inv.*
train [treɪn] *s.* **1** treno *m.* **2** strascico *m.*, coda *f.*, scia *f.* **3** corteo *m.* **4** serie *f.*, successione *f.* ♦ **express t.** rapido; **fast t.** direttissimo; **slow t.** accelerato; **through t.** diretto
to train [treɪn] **A** *v. tr.* **1** allenare, addestrare, formare **2** puntare, orientare **B** *v. intr.* esercitarsi, allenarsi
trained [treɪnd] *agg.* **1** esperto, qualificato **2** ammaestrato
trainee [treɪ'niː] *s.* apprendista *m. e f.*
trainer ['treɪnəʳ] *s.* **1** allenatore *m.*, istruttore *m.* **2** scarpa *f.* da ginnastica

training ['treɪnɪŋ] *s.* **1** allenamento *m.*, preparazione *f.*, formazione *f.* **2** apprendistato *m.*
to traipse [treɪps] *v. intr.* gironzolare
trait [treɪ] *s.* tratto *m.* saliente
traitor ['treɪtəʳ] *s.* traditore *m.*
trajectory [trə'dʒɛkt(ə)rɪ] *s.* traiettoria *f.*
tram [træm] *s.* tram *m. inv.*
tramp [træmp] *s.* **1** vagabondo *m.* **2** scarpinata *f.* **3** (*fam.*) sgualdrina *f.*
to tramp [træmp] *v. intr.* scarpinare, camminare pesantemente
to trample ['træmpl] *v. tr.* camminare su, calpestare
tranquil ['træŋkwɪl] *agg.* tranquillo
tranquillity [træŋ'kwɪlɪtɪ] *s.* tranquillità *f.*
tranquillizer ['træŋkwɪlaɪzəʳ] *s.* tranquillante *m.*, calmante *m.*
to transact [træn'zækt] *v. tr.* trattare
transaction [træn'zækʃ(ə)n] *s.* transazione *f.*
transatlantic [ˌtrænzət'læntɪk] *agg.* transatlantico
to transcribe [træns'kraɪb] *v. tr.* trascrivere
transcript ['trænskrɪpt] *s.* trascrizione *f.*
transcription [træns'krɪpʃ(ə)n] *s.* trascrizione *f.*
transept ['trænsɛpt] *s.* transetto *m.*
transfer ['trænsfɜːʳ] *s.* trasferimento *m.*
to transfer [træns'fɜːʳ] *v. tr.* trasferire
to transform [træns'fɜːm] *v. tr. e intr.* trasformare, trasformarsi
transformer [træns'fɜːməʳ] *s.* trasformatore *m.*
transfusion [træns'fjuːʒ(ə)n] *s.* trasfusione *f.*
transgression [træns'grɛʃ(ə)n] *s.* trasgressione *f.*
transiency ['trænzɪənsɪ] *s.* transitorietà *f.*
transient ['trænzɪənt] *agg.* transitorio
transistor [træn'sɪstəʳ] *s.* transistor *m. inv.*
transit ['trænsɪt] *s.* transito *m.*, passaggio *m.*
transitive ['trænsɪtɪv] *agg.* (*gramm.*) transitivo
transitory ['trænsɪt(ə)rɪ] *agg.* passeggero
to translate [træns'leɪt] *v. tr.* tradurre
translation [træns'leɪʃ(ə)n] *s.* traduzione *f.*
translator [træns'leɪtəʳ] *s.* traduttore *m.*
transliteration ['trænzlɪtə'reɪʃ(ə)n] *s.* traslitterazione *f.*
transmission [trænz'mɪʃ(ə)n] *s.* trasmissione *f.*
to transmit [trænz'mɪt] *v. tr.* trasmettere
transmitter [trænz'mɪtəʳ] *s.* trasmettitore *m.*
transparency [træns'pɛərənsɪ] *s.* **1** trasparenza *f.* **2** diapositiva *f.*
transparent [træns'pɛər(ə)nt] *agg.* trasparente
transpiration [ˌtrænspɪ'reɪʃ(ə)n] *s.* traspirazione *f.*
to transpire [træns'paɪəʳ] *v. intr.* **1** traspirare **2** trapelare **3** (*fam.*) accadere
transplant ['trænsplaːnt] *s.* trapianto *m.*
to transplant [træns'plaːnt] *v. tr.* trapiantare
transplantation [ˌtrænsplaːn'teɪʃ(ə)n] *s.* trapianto *m.*
transport ['trænspɜːt] *s.* **1** trasporto *m.* **2** mezzo *m.* di trasporto
to transport [træns'pɜːt] *v. tr.* trasportare
transportable [træns'pɜːtəbl] *agg.* trasportabile
transporter [træns'pɜːtəʳ] *s.* trasportatore *m.*
transsexual [træn'sɛkʃʊəl] *agg. e s.* transessuale *m. e f.*
transversal [trænz'vɜːs(ə)l] *agg.* trasversale
trap [træp] *s.* **1** trappola *f.* **2** tranello *m.* **3** calesse *m.*
to trap [træp] *v. tr.* prendere in trappola, intrappolare
trap-door ['træpdɜːʳ] *s.* botola *f.*
trapeze [trə'piːz] *s.* trapezio *m.*
trapezium [trə'piːzɪəm] *s.* (*geom.*) trapezio *m.*
trappings ['træpɪŋz] *s. pl.* **1** bardatura *f.* **2** ornamenti *m. pl.*
traps [træps] *s. pl.* (*fam.*) bagaglio *m.*
trapshooting ['træpˌʃuːtɪŋ] *s.* tiro *m.* al piattello
trash [træʃ] *s.* **1** ciarpame *m.*, robaccia *f.* **2** (*USA*) immondizie *f. pl.* **3** porcheria *f.* **4** sciocchezza *f.*
trauma ['trɜːmə] *s.* trauma *m.*
traumatic [trɜː'mætɪk] *agg.* traumatico
travel ['trævl] *s.* il viaggiare, viaggi *m. pl.* ♦ **t. agency** agenzia di viaggi
to travel ['trævl] **A** *v. intr.* viaggiare **B** *v. tr.* attraversare, percorrere
traveller ['trævləʳ] *s.* viaggiatore *m.* ♦ **t.'s cheque** travellers' chèque, assegno turistico
travelling ['trævlɪŋ] *agg.* **1** viaggiante **2** da viaggio, di viaggio

travertine ['trævə(ː)tɪn] *s.* travertino *m.*
travesty ['trævɪstɪ] *s.* parodia *f.*
to **trawl** [trɜːl] *v. tr. e intr.* pescare a strascico
tray [treɪ] *s.* **1** vassoio *m.* **2** bacinella *f.*
treacherous ['trɛtʃ(ə)rəs] *agg.* sleale, infido
treachery ['trɛtʃ(ə)rɪ] *s.* tradimento *m.*, slealtà *f.*
treacle ['triːkl] *s.* melassa *f.*
tread [trɛd] *s.* **1** passo *m.* **2** (*di scalino*) pedata *f.* **3** battistrada *m. inv.*
to **tread** [trɛd] (*pass.* **trod**, *p. p.* **trodden**) **A** *v. tr.* **1** calpestare **2** percorrere **B** *v. intr.* camminare, procedere
treason ['triːz(ə)n] *s.* tradimento *m.*
treasure ['trɛʒəʳ] *s.* tesoro *m.*
to **treasure** ['trɛʒəʳ] *v. tr.* **1** accumulare **2** custodire gelosamente
treasurer ['trɛʒ(ə)rəʳ] *s.* tesoriere *m.*
treat [triːt] *s.* trattenimento *m.*, festa *f.*
to **treat** [triːt] **A** *v. tr.* **1** trattare **2** curare **3** offrire, regalare **B** *v. intr.* **1** trattare, negoziare **2** trattare, discutere ♦ **to t. sb. to st.** offrire q.c. a qc.
treatable ['triːtəbl] *agg.* trattabile
treatise ['triːtɪz] *s.* trattato *m.*
treatment ['triːtmənt] *s.* trattamento *m.*, cura *f.*
treaty ['triːtɪ] *s.* trattato *m.*, accordo *m.*
treble [trɛbl] *agg. e s.* triplo *m.*
to **treble** [trɛbl] *v. tr. e intr.* triplicare, triplicarsi
tree [triː] *s.* albero *m.*, arbusto *m.*
trefoil ['trɛfɔɪl] *s.* trifoglio *m.*
trek [trɛk] *s.* **1** migrazione *f.*, spedizione *f.* **2** percorso *m.* accidentato **3** trekking *m. inv.*
to **trek** [trɛk] *v. intr.* **1** emigrare **2** fare escursioni, fare trekking
trellis ['trɛlɪs] *s.* traliccio *m.*
tremble ['trɛmbl] *s.* tremito *m.*
to **tremble** ['trɛmbl] *v. intr.* tremare
trembling ['trɛmblɪŋ] **A** *agg.* tremante **B** *s.* tremito *m.*
tremendous [trɪ'mɛndəs] *agg.* **1** formidabile, straordinario **2** tremendo, terribile
tremor ['trɛməʳ] *s.* **1** tremore *m.*, tremito *m.* **2** (*di terremoto*) scossa *f.*
trench [trɛn(t)ʃ] *s.* **1** fosso *m.* **2** trincea *f.*
trend [trɛnd] *s.* **1** direzione *f.* **2** andamento *m.*, orientamento *m.* **3** moda *f.*, tendenza *f.*
trendy ['trɛndɪ] *agg.* di moda
trepidation [ˌtrɛpɪ'deɪʃ(ə)n] *s.* trepidazione *f.*
to **trespass** ['trɛspəs] *v. intr.* **1** trasgredire **2** introdursi abusivamente
trestle ['trɛsl] *s.* **1** cavalletto *m.* **2** traliccio *m.*
trial ['traɪ(ə)l] *s.* **1** (*dir.*) giudizio *m.*, processo *m.* **2** esperimento *m.*, prova *f.* **3** collaudo *m.* **4** sofferenza *f.*, fastidio *m.*
triangle ['traɪæŋgl] *s.* triangolo *m.*
triangular [traɪ'æŋgjʊləʳ] *agg.* triangolare
triangulation [traɪˌæŋgjʊ'leɪʃ(ə)n] *s.* triangolazione *f.*
tribe [traɪb] *s.* tribù *f.*
tribunal [traɪ'bjuːnl] *s.* tribunale *m.*
tribune ['trɪbjuːn] *s.* tribuna *f.*
tributary ['trɪbjʊt(ə)rɪ] *agg. e s.* tributario *m.*, affluente *m.*
trice [traɪs] *s.* attimo *m.*
trichologist [trɪ'kɔlədʒɪst] *s.* tricologo *m.*
trichology [trɪ'kɔlədʒɪ] *s.* tricologia *f.*
trick [trɪk] *s.* **1** trucco *m.*, stratagemma *m.* **2** scherzo *m.*, raggiro *m.*, inganno *m.* **3** abitudine *f.* **4** (*nel gioco delle carte*) mano *f.*
to **trick** [trɪk] *v. tr.* ingannare, raggirare
trickery ['trɪkərɪ] *s.* inganno *m.*
to **trickle** ['trɪkl] *v. intr.* gocciolare
tricky ['trɪkɪ] *agg.* **1** scaltro **2** complicato
tricolour ['trɪkələʳ] *agg.* tricolore
tricycle ['traɪsɪkl] *s.* triciclo *m.*
tridimensional [ˌtraɪdɪ'mɛnʃənl] *agg.* tridimensionale
trifle ['traɪfl] *s.* inezia *f.*, sciocchezza *f.*
trifling ['traɪflɪŋ] *agg.* irrilevante
trigger ['trɪgəʳ] *s.* grilletto *m.*
triglyph ['traɪglɪf] *s.* triglifo *m.*
trill [trɪl] *s.* trillo *m.*
trim [trɪm] **A** *agg.* ordinato **B** *s.* **1** ordine *m.*, disposizione *f.* **2** assetto *m.* **3** taglio *m.*, spuntata *f.*
to **trim** [trɪm] *v. tr.* **1** ordinare **2** regolare **3** potare, spuntare **4** guarnire
trimming ['trɪmɪŋ] *s.* guarnizione *f.*
trinity ['trɪnɪtɪ] *s.* trinità *f.*
trinket ['trɪŋkɪt] *s.* gingillo *m.*, ciondolo *m.*
trio ['triːɒʊ] *s.* trio *m.*
trip [trɪp] *s.* **1** gita *f.*, viaggio *m.*, escursione *f.* **2** passo *m.* leggero **3** passo *m.* falso **4** sgambetto *m.*
to **trip** [trɪp] **A** *v. intr.* **1** inciampare **2** camminare con passo leggero **3** fare un passo falso **B** *v. tr.* **1** far inciampare **2** fare lo sgambetto
tripe [traɪp] *s.* **1** trippa *f.* **2** (*fam.*) sciocchezze *f. pl.*

triple ['trɪpl] *agg.* triplo
triplicate ['trɪplɪkɪt] **A** *agg.* triplo **B** *s.* triplice copia *f.*
to triplicate ['trɪplɪkeɪt] *v. tr.* triplicare
tripod ['traɪpəd] *s.* treppiedi *m. inv.*
triptych ['trɪptɪk] *s.* trittico *m.*
trite [traɪt] *agg.* trito, banale
triumph ['traɪəmf] *s.* trionfo *m.*
to triumph ['traɪəmf] *v. intr.* trionfare
triumphal [traɪ'ʌmf(ə)l] *agg.* trionfale
trivial ['trɪvɪəl] *agg.* insignificante, banale
trod [trəd] *pass. di* **to tread**
trodden ['trədn] *p. p. di* **to tread**
troglodyte ['trəglədaɪt] *s.* troglodita *m. e f.*
trolley ['trəlɪ] *s.* carrello *m.* ♦ **t. car** tram; **t.-bus** filobus
trombone [trəm'bɒʊn] *s.* trombone *m.*
troop [truːp] **1** truppa *f.*, gruppo *m.* **2** squadrone *m.* di cavalleria **3** *al pl* truppe *f. pl.*
to troop [truːp] **A** *v. intr.* adunarsi, ammassarsi, schierarsi **B** *v. tr.* adunare, schierare
trophy ['trɒʊfɪ] *s.* trofeo *m.*, cimelio *m.*
tropic ['trəpɪk] *s.* tropico *m.*
tropical ['trəpɪk(ə)l] *agg.* tropicale
trot [trət] *s.* trotto *m.*
to trot [trət] *v. intr.* trottare
trotter ['trətəʳ] *s.* trottatore *m.*
trouble ['trʌbl] *s.* **1** guaio *m.*, pasticcio *m.* **2** disturbo *m.*, seccatura *f.* **3** difficoltà *f.*, preoccupazione *f.*, pena *f.* **4** disgrazia *f.* **5** disturbo *m.*, malattia *f.* **6** (*tecnol.*) guasto *m.*, anomalia *f.* ♦ **to get out of t.** tirarsi fuori dai guai; **t. shooting** ricerca e riparazione dei guasti
to trouble ['trʌbl] **A** *v. tr.* **1** disturbare **2** affliggere **B** *v. intr.* **1** disturbarsi **2** preoccuparsi, affliggersi
troubled ['trʌbld] *agg.* agitato, preoccupato
troublesome ['trʌblsəm] *agg.* fastidioso
trousers ['traʊzəz] *s. pl.* pantaloni *m. pl.*
trout [traʊt] *s. inv.* trota *f.*
trowel ['traʊ(ə)l] *s.* cazzuola *f.*, paletta *f.*
truant ['truːənt] *agg. e s.* che (o chi) marina la scuola ♦ **to play t.** marinare
truce [truːs] *s.* tregua *f.*
truck (1) [trʌk] *s.* camion *m. inv.* ♦ **t. driver** camionista
truck (2) [trʌk] *s.* **1** scambio *m.* **2** rapporto *m.*, relazione *f.*
to trudge [trʌdʒ] *v. intr.* trascinarsi a fatica
true [truː] **A** *agg.* **1** vero, esatto **2** reale, autentico **3** preciso, accurato **4** puro, genuino **B** *avv.* esattamente, precisamente ♦ **t.-life** realistico
truffle ['trʌfl] *s.* tartufo *m.*
truly ['truːlɪ] *avv.* **1** veramente **2** sinceramente
trumpet ['trʌmpɪt] *s.* tromba *f.*
truncheon ['trʌn(t)ʃ(ə)n] *s.* sfollagente *m. inv.*
trunk [trʌŋk] *s.* **1** tronco *m.*, busto *m.* **2** (*d'albero*) tronco *m.* **3** proboscide *f.* **4** tratto *m.* **5** baule *m.* **6** calzoni *m. pl.* corti **7** (*USA, autom.*) bagagliaio *m.*
truss [trʌs] **1** travatura *f.* **2** fascio *m.* **3** (*med.*) cinto *m.* erniario
trust [trʌst] *s.* **1** fiducia *f.*, fede *f.* **2** credito *m.* **3** amministrazione *f.* fiduciaria **4** trust *m. inv.* **5** società *m.*
to trust [trʌst] **A** *v. tr.* **1** fidarsi di, aver fiducia in **2** sperare **3** far credito a **B** *v. intr.* **1** fidarsi, confidare **2** sperare **3** far credito
trustee [trʌs'tiː] *s.* **1** amministratore *m.* fiduciario, curatore *m.* **2** amministratore *m.*
trustful ['trʌstf(ʊ)l] *agg.* fiducioso
trustworthy ['trʌstˌwɜːðɪ] *agg.* fidato
truth [truːθ] *s.* verità *f.*
truthful ['truːθf(ʊ)l] *s.* **1** vero **2** sincero
try [traɪ] *s.* prova *f.*, tentativo *m.*
to try [traɪ] **A** *v. tr.* **1** provare, tentare **2** assaggiare **3** mettere alla prova **4** collaudare **5** (*dir.*) processare, giudicare **B** *v. intr.* provare, tentare ♦ **to t. for** cercare di ottenere; **to t. on** (*un vestito*) provare; **to t. out** collaudare
trying ['traɪɪŋ] *agg.* duro, difficile
tsar [zaːʳ] *s.* zar *m. inv.*
T-shirt ['tiːʃɜːt] *s.* maglietta *f.*, tee shirt *f. inv.*
tub [tʌb] *s.* tinozza *f.*
tuba ['tjuːbə] *s.* tuba *f.*
tubby ['tʌbɪ] *agg.* grasso, obeso
tube [tjuːb] *s.* **1** tubo *m.* **2** tubetto *m.*, provetta *f.* **3** (*fam., USA*) metropolitana *f.* ♦ **inner t.** camera d'aria
tuber ['tjuːbəʳ] *s.* tubero *m.*
tuberculosis [tjʊ(ː)ˌbɜːkjʊ'lɒʊsɪs] *s.* tubercolosi
tubular ['tjuːbjʊləʳ] *agg.* tubolare
tuck [tʌk] *s.* **1** piega *f.* **2** (*pop.*) dolci *m. pl.*, merendine *f. pl.*
to tuck [tʌk] *v. tr.* **1** piegare **2** riporre **3** mettere, infilare ♦ **to t. away** riporre, nascondere; **to t. in** rimboccare; **to t. into** ingozzarsi; **to t. up** rimboccare

Tuesday ['tju:zdɪ] *s.* martedì *m.* ♦ **Shrove T.** martedì grasso
tufa ['tju:fə] *s.* tufo *m.*
tuft [tʌft] *s.* ciuffo *m.*
tug [tʌg] *s.* **1** strappo *m.*, tirata *f.* **2** rimorchiatore *m.*
to **tug** [tʌg] *v. tr.* **1** tirare, strappare **2** rimorchiare ♦ **t.-of-war** tiro alla fune
tuition [tjʊ(:)'ɪʃ(ə)n] *s.* **1** istruzione *f.* **2** tassa *f.* scolastica
tulip ['tju:lɪp] *s.* tulipano *m.*
tumble ['tʌmbl] *s.* **1** capitombolo *m.* **2** crollo *m.*, caduta *f.*
to **tumble** ['tʌmbl] *v. intr.* **1** ruzzolare, cascare **2** agitarsi **3** gettarsi, precipitarsi ♦ **to t. down** essere in rovina
tumbler ['tʌmbləʳ] *s.* **1** acrobata *m. e f.* **2** bicchiere *m.* (*senza piede*)
tumefaction [ˌtju:mɪ'fækʃ(ə)n] *s.* tumefazione *f.*
tummy ['tʌmɪ] *s.* (*fam.*) pancia *f.*
tumour ['tju:məʳ] (*USA* **tumor**) *s.* tumore *m.*
tumulus ['tju:mjʊləs] *s.* tumulo *m.*
tun [tʌn] *s.* tino *m.*
tuna ['tju:nə] *s.* tonno *m.*
tundra ['tʌndrə] *s.* tundra *f.*
tune [tju:n] *s.* **1** tono *m.* **2** melodia *f.*, aria *f.* **3** (*radio, TV*) sintonia *f.*
to **tune** [tju:n] *v. tr.* **1** accordare **2** mettere a punto **3** sintonizzare ♦ **to t. in** sintonizzarsi; **to t. up** accordarsi, armonizzarsi
tuneful ['tju:nf(ʊ)l] *agg.* armonioso
tuner ['tju:nəʳ] *s.* **1** accordatore *m.* **2** sintetizzatore *m.*
tunic ['tju:nɪk] *s.* tunica *f.*
tunnel ['tʌnl] *s.* tunnel *m. inv.*, galleria *f.*
tunny ['tʌnɪ] *s.* tonno *m.*
turban ['tɜ:bən] *s.* turbante *m.*
turbine ['tɜ:bɪn] *s.* turbina *f.*
turbulence ['tɜ:bjʊləns] *s.* turbolenza *f.*
turbulent ['tɜ:bjʊlənt] *agg.* turbolento, agitato
tureen [tə'ri:n] *s.* zuppiera *f.*
turf [tɜ:f] *s.* zolla *f.*, tappeto *m.* erboso
Turk [tɜ:k] *s.* turco *m.*
turkey ['tɜ:kɪ] *s.* tacchino *m.*
Turkish ['tɜ:kɪʃ] *agg.* turco
turmoil ['tɜ:məɪl] *s.* tumulto *m.*, agitazione *f.*
turn [tɜ:n] *s.* **1** giro *m.* **2** curva *f.*, svolta *f.*, cambiamento *m.* di direzione **3** turno *m.* **4** attitudine *f.*, disposizione *f.* **5** numero *m.*, esibizione *f.* **6** (*fam.*) brutto colpo *m.*, accidente *m.* ♦ **in t.** a turno; **t.-off** svincolo; **t.-up** risvolto (dei pantaloni)
to **turn** [tɜ:n] **A** *v. tr.* **1** girare, curvare, voltare **2** rivolgere, dirigere **3** rovesciare **4** distogliere, sviare **5** cambiare, trasformare **B** *v. intr.* **1** girare, girarsi **2** dirigersi, rivolgersi **3** trasformarsi, diventare **4** andare a male ♦ **to t. about** fare dietrofront; **to t. against** rivoltarsi contro; **to t. away** girarsi, respingere; **to t. back** tornare indietro; **to t. down** abbassare, ripiegare; **to t. in** restituire, ripiegarsi, andare a letto; **to t. off** spegnere; **to t. on** accendere, eccitare; **to t. out** spegnere, mettere alla porta, rovesciare; **to t. over** girarsi, cappottare; **to t. up** saltar fuori, sopraggiungere, rialzare
turning ['tɜ:nɪŋ] **A** *agg.* girevole **B** *s.* **1** giro *m.* **2** curva *f.*, svolta *f.* **3** sterzata *f.*
turnip ['tɜ:nɪp] *s.* rapa *f.* ♦ **t. tops** cime di rapa
turnover ['tɜ:nˌɒʊvəʳ] *s.* **1** rovesciamento *m.* **2** giro *m.* d'affari **3** turnover *m. inv.*, ricambio *m.*
turnstile ['tɜ:nˌstaɪl] *s.* tornello *m.*
turntable ['tɜ:nˌteɪbl] *s.* (*di giradischi*) piatto *m.*
turpentine ['tɜ:p(ə)ntaɪn] *s.* trementina *f.*
turquoise ['tɜ:kwa:z] *s.* turchese *m.*
turret ['tʌrɪt] *s.* torretta *f.*
turtle ['tɜ:tl] *s.* tartaruga *f.*
tusk [tʌsk] *s.* zanna *f.*
tussle ['tʌsl] *s.* rissa *f.*
tutor ['tju:təʳ] *s.* **1** precettore *m.* **2** professore *m.*, assistente *m. e f.*
tutorial [tju:'tɜ:rɪəl] *s.* seminario *m.*
TV [ti:'vi:] *s.* TV *f.*, televisione *f.*
twang [twæŋ] *s.* **1** vibrazione *f.* **2** suono *m.* nasale
tweed [twi:d] *s.* tweed *m. inv.*
tweezers ['twi:zəz] *s. pl.* pinzette *f. pl.*
twelfth [twɛlfθ] *agg. num. ord. e s.* dodicesimo *m.*
twelve [twɛlv] *agg. num. card. e s.* dodici *m. inv.*
twentieth ['twɛntɪɪθ] *agg. num. ord. e s.* ventesimo *m.*
twenty ['twɛntɪ] *agg. num. card. e s.* venti *m. inv.*
twice [twaɪs] *avv.* due volte
to **twiddle** ['twɪdl] **A** *v. tr.* far girare **B** *v. intr.* giocherellare
twig [twɪg] *s.* ramoscello *m.*
to **twig** [twɪg] *v. tr.* capire, afferrare

twilight ['twaɪlaɪt] *s.* crepuscolo *m.*
twin [twɪn] *agg. e s.* gemello *m.* ♦ **t. birth** parto gemellare; **t. beds** letti gemelli
twine [twaɪn] *s.* **1** spago *m.* **2** garbuglio *m.*
to twine [twaɪn] *v. tr. e intr.* torcere, attorcigliarsi
twinge [twɪn(d)ʒ] *s.* **1** fitta *f.* **2** rimorso *m.*
to twinkle ['twɪŋkl] *v. intr.* brillare, scintillare
twinkling ['twɪŋklɪŋ] *s.* scintillio *m.*
twinning ['twɪnɪŋ] *s.* gemellaggio *m.*
twirl [twɜːl] *s.* giravolta *f.*
to twirl [twɜːl] *v. tr. e intr.* roteare
twist [twɪst] *s.* **1** torsione *f.*, storta *f.* **2** curva *f.*, tornante *m.* **3** spira *f.*, spirale *f.* **4** filo *m.* ritorto, treccia *f.* **5** variazione *f.*, cambiamento *m.* **6** colpo *m.* di scena
to twist [twɪst] **A** *v. tr.* **1** torcere, distorcere **2** intrecciare, attorcigliare **B** *v. intr.* **1** intrecciarsi, attorcigliarsi **2** torcersi **3** serpeggiare
twisted ['twɪstɪd] *agg.* **1** torto, ritorto **2** contorto
twit [twɪt] *s.* **1** presa *f.* in giro **2** (*fam.*) cretino *m.*
twitch [twɪtʃ] *s.* **1** contrazione *f.* **2** strattone *m.*
two [tuː] *agg. num. card. e s.* due *m. inv.*
twofold ['tuːfɒʊld] *agg.* doppio
twosome ['tuːsəm] **A** *agg.* per due, in coppia **B** *s.* coppia *f.*
two-way ['tuːweɪ] *agg.* a doppio senso
tycoon [taɪ'kuːn] *s.* magnate *m.*
tympanum ['tɪmpənəm] *s.* timpano *m.*
type [taɪp] *s.* **1** tipo *m.*, modello *m.*, esemplare *m.* **2** tipo *m.*, specie *f.*, genere *m.* **3** (*tip.*) carattere *m.*
to type [taɪp] *v. tr.* battere (*su tastiera*), dattilografare
typescript ['taɪpˌskrɪpt] *s.* dattiloscritto *m.*
typesetting ['taɪpˌsɛtɪŋ] *s.* composizione *f.* tipografica
typewriter ['taɪpˌraɪtə^r^] *s.* macchina *f.* per scrivere
typhoon [taɪ'fuːn] *s.* tifone *m.*
typhus ['taɪfəs] *s.* (*med.*) tifo *m.*
typical ['tɪpɪk(ə)l] *agg.* tipico
to typify ['tɪpɪfaɪ] *v. tr.* impersonare, simboleggiare
typing ['taɪpɪŋ] *s.* dattilografia *f.*
typist ['taɪpɪst] *s.* dattilografo *m.*
typographer [taɪ'pəgrəfə^r^] *s.* tipografo *m.*
typography [taɪ'pəgrəfɪ] *s.* tipografia *f.*
typology [taɪ'pələdʒɪ] *s.* tipologia *f.*
tyrant ['taɪər(ə)nt] *s.* tiranno *m.*
tyre ['taɪə^r^] (*USA* **tire**) *s.* pneumatico *m.*, gomma *f.* ♦ **flat t.** gomma a terra; **t. repairer** gommista; **t. rim** cerchione; **t. tread** battistrada

U

ubiquitous [jʊ(ː)'bɪkwɪtəs] *agg.* onnipresente
udder ['ʌdəʳ] *s.* (*zool.*) mammella *f.*
UFO ['juːfɒʊ] *s.* ufo *m. inv.*
ugh [ʊh] *inter.* puh!
ugly ['ʌglɪ] *agg.* **1** brutto, sgradevole **2** minaccioso
ulcer ['ʌlsəʳ] *s.* ulcera *f.*
ulna ['ʌlnə] *s.* ulna *f.*
ulterior [ʌl'tɪərɪəʳ] *agg.* **1** ulteriore, successivo **2** segreto, nascosto
ultimate ['ʌltɪmɪt] *agg.* **1** ultimo, estremo **2** definitivo **3** massimo, supremo
ultimately ['ʌltɪmɪtlɪ] *avv.* **1** in definitiva **2** fondamentalmente
ultrasound [ˌʌltrə'saʊnd] *s.* ultrasuono *m.*
ultraviolet [ˌʌltrə'vaɪəlɪt] *agg. e s.* ultravioletto *m.*
umbilical [ʌm'bɪlɪk(ə)l] *agg.* ombelicale ♦ **u. cord** cordone ombelicale
umbrella [ʌm'brɛlə] *s.* ombrello *m.* ♦ **u. stand** portaombrelli
umpire ['ʌmpaɪəʳ] *s.* arbitro *m.*
to umpire ['ʌmpaɪəʳ] *v. tr. e intr.* arbitrare
umpteen ['ʌm(p)tiːn] *agg.* (*fam.*) molti
umpteenth ['ʌm(p)tiːnθ] *agg.* (*fam.*) ennesimo
unable [ʌn'eɪbl] *agg.* incapace, impossibilitato, inadatto
unabridged [ˌʌnə'brɪdʒd] *agg.* (*di edizione*) non abbreviato, integrale
unacceptable [ˌʌnək'sɛptəbl] *agg.* inaccettabile
unaccompanied [ˌʌnə'kʌmp(ə)nɪd] *agg.* **1** solo, non accompagnato **2** (*mus.*) senza accompagnamento
unaccountable [ˌʌnə'kaʊntəbl] *agg.* **1** inesplicabile **2** irresponsabile
unaccustomed [ˌʌnə'kʌstəmd] *agg.* **1** insolito **2** non abituato
unacquainted [ˌʌnə'kweɪntɪd] *agg.* non pratico, non abituato
unaffected [ˌʌnə'fɛktɪd] *agg.* **1** spontaneo, sincero **2** non soggetto
unaided [ˌʌn'eɪdɪd] *agg.* senza aiuto
unalterable [ʌn'ɜːlt(ə)rəbl] *agg.* inalterabile
unanimity [ˌjuːnə'nɪmɪtɪ] *s.* unanimità *f.*
unanimous [juː'nænɪməs] *agg.* unanime
unanswerable [ʌn'aːns(ə)rəbl] *agg.* **1** incontestabile, irrefutabile **2** irresponsabile
unapproachable [ˌʌnə'prɒʊtʃəbl] *agg.* inavvicinabile
unapt [ʌn'æpt] *agg.* non adatto
to unarm [ʌn'aːm] *v. tr.* disarmare
unashamed [ˌʌnə'ʃeɪmd] *agg.* spudorato
unassuming [ˌʌnə'sjuːmɪŋ] *agg.* senza pretese
unattached [ˌʌnə'tætʃt] *agg.* **1** libero, indipendente **2** senza legami (sentimentali)
unattainable [ˌʌnə'teɪnəbl] *agg.* irraggiungibile
unattended [ˌʌnə'tɛndɪd] *agg.* incustodito
unattractive [ˌʌnə'træktɪv] *agg.* poco attraente
unauthorized [ʌn'ɜɪθəraɪzd] *agg.* non autorizzato
unavailable [ˌʌnə'veɪləbl] *agg.* non disponibile
unavoidable [ˌʌnə'vɔɪdəbl] *agg.* inevitabile
unaware [ˌʌnə'wɛəʳ] *agg.* ignaro
unawares [ˌʌnə'wɛəz] *avv.* **1** inavvertitamente, inconsapevolmente **2** di sorpresa
unbalanced [ʌn'bælənst] *agg.* squilibrato
unbearable [ʌn'bɛərəbl] *agg.* insopportabile
unbeatable [ʌn'biːtəbl] *agg.* imbattibile
unbelievable [ˌʌnbɪ'liːvəbl] *agg.* incredibile
to unbend [ʌn'bɛnd] (*pass. e p. p.* **unbent**) **A** *v. tr.* **1** raddrizzare **2** stendere, sciogliere **3** distendere, rilassare **B** *v. intr.* **1** raddrizzarsi **2** distendersi, rilassarsi
unbias(s)ed [ʌn'baɪəst] *agg.* imparziale
unborn [ʌn'bɜːn] *agg.* non ancora nato, futuro
unbreakable [ʌn'breɪkəbl] *agg.* infrangibile
unbroken [ʌn'brɒʊk(ə)n] *agg.* **1** intatto **2** ininterrotto **3** indomito
to unbutton [ʌn'bʌtn] *v. tr. e intr.* sbottonare, sbottonarsi
uncalled [ʌn'kɜːld] *agg.* non chiamato, non invitato ♦ **u. for** superfluo, fuori luogo
uncanny [ʌn'kænɪ] *agg.* misterioso
unceasing [ʌn'siːsɪŋ] *agg.* incessante
uncertain [ʌn'sɜːtn] *agg.* incerto

uncertainty [ʌn'sɜːt(ə)ntɪ] *s.* incertezza *f.*
to unchain [ʌn'tʃeɪn] *v. tr.* sciogliere
unchanged [ʌn'tʃeɪn(d)ʒd] *agg.* immutato
unchanging [ʌn'tʃeɪn(d)ʒɪŋ] *agg.* immutabile
unchecked [ʌn'tʃɛkt] *agg.* **1** sfrenato **2** non verificato
uncivil [ʌn'sɪvl] *agg.* incivile
uncle ['ʌŋkl] *s.* zio *m.*
unclean ['ʌŋkliːn] *agg.* immondo
unclear ['ʌŋklɪəʳ] *agg.* non chiaro, incerto
uncomfortable [ʌn'kʌmf(ə)təbl] *agg.* **1** scomodo **2** spiacevole
uncommon [ʌn'kəmən] *agg.* insolito
uncompromising [ʌn'kəmprəˌmaɪzɪŋ] *agg.* intransigente
unconcerned [ˌʌnkən'sɜːnd] *agg.* **1** indifferente **2** imparziale
unconditional [ˌʌnkən'dɪʃənl] *agg.* incondizionato
unconscious [ʌn'kənʃəs] **A** *agg.* **1** inconscio **2** incosciente **B** *s.* inconscio *m.*
unconstitutional [ˌʌnkənstɪ'tjuːʃənl] *agg.* anticostituzionale
uncontrollable [ˌʌnkən'trɒʊləbl] *agg.* incontrollabile
unconventional [ˌʌnkən'vɛnʃənl] *agg.* non convenzionale
uncouth [ʌn'kuːθ] *agg.* rozzo
to uncover [ʌn'kʌvəʳ] *v. tr.* **1** scoprire **2** svestire **3** rivelare
undamaged [ʌn'dæmɪdʒd] *agg.* non danneggiato
undated [ʌn'deɪtɪd] *agg.* non datato
undaunted [ʌn'dɜːntɪd] *agg.* imperterrito
undecided [ˌʌndɪ'saɪdɪd] *agg.* indeciso, incerto
undeniable [ˌʌndɪ'naɪəbl] *agg.* innegabile
under ['ʌndəʳ] **A** *prep.* **1** sotto **2** in, in corso di **3** meno di, per meno di **B** *avv.* sotto, al di sotto
underage [ˌʌndə'reɪdʒ] *agg.* minorenne
undercarriage ['ʌndəˌkærɪdʒ] *s.* carrello *m.* d'atterraggio
to undercharge [ˌʌndə'tʃaːdʒ] *v. tr.* far pagare meno
underclothing ['ʌndəˌklɒʊðɪŋ] *s.* biancheria *f.* intima
undercover [ˌʌndə'kʌvəʳ] *agg.* segreto
undercurrent ['ʌndəˌkʌrənt] *s.* **1** corrente *f.* sottomarina **2** tendenza *f.* occulta
to undercut ['ʌndəˌkʌt] (*pass. e p. p.* **undercut**) *v. tr.* **1** colpire dal basso **2** tagliare dal basso **3** vendere a prezzo inferiore
underdevelopment [ˌʌndədɪ'vɛləpmənt] *s.* sottosviluppo *m.*
underdone [ˌʌndə'dʌn] *agg.* poco cotto, al sangue
to underestimate [ˌʌndər'ɛstɪmeɪt] *v. tr.* sottovalutare
underfed [ˌʌndə'fɛd] *agg.* denutrito
to undergo [ˌʌndə'gɒʊ] (*pass.* **underwent**, *p. p.* **undergone**) *v. tr.* patire, subire
undergraduate [ˌʌndə'grædjʊɪt] *s.* studente *m.* universitario
underground [ˌʌndə'graʊnd] **A** *agg.* sotterraneo **B** *s.* **1** sottosuolo *m.* **2** metropolitana *f.* **3** movimento *m.* clandestino **C** *avv.* **1** sottoterra **2** segretamente, clandestinamente
undergrowth ['ʌndəgrɒʊθ] *s.* sottobosco *m.*
underhand ['ʌndəhænd] *agg.* nascosto, clandestino
to underlie [ˌʌndə'laɪ] (*pass.* **underlay**, *p. p.* **underlain**) **A** *v. tr.* **1** stare sotto a **2** essere alla base di **B** *v. intr.* essere sottostante
to underline [ˌʌndə'laɪn] *v. tr.* sottolineare, evidenziare
underlying [ˌʌndə'laɪɪŋ] *agg.* sottostante
to undermine [ˌʌndə'maɪn] *v. tr.* **1** minare **2** indebolire
underneath [ˌʌndə'niːθ] **A** *avv.* sotto, disotto **B** *prep.* sotto, al di sotto di **C** *agg. pred.* inferiore
underpaid ['ʌndəˌpeɪd] **A** *pass. e p. p. di* **to underpay** **B** *agg.* sottopagato
underpants ['ʌndəpænts] *s. pl.* mutande *f. pl.* (da uomo)
underpass ['ʌndəpaːs] *s.* sottopassaggio *m.*
to underrate [ˌʌndə'reɪt] *v. tr.* sottostimare
undershirt ['ʌndəʃɜːt] *s.* maglietta *f.* (intima)
underside ['ʌndəsaɪd] *s.* parte *f.* inferiore
underskirt [ˌʌndə'skɜːt] *s.* sottogonna *f.*
to understand [ˌʌndə'stænd] (*pass. e p. p.* **understood**) **A** *v. tr.* **1** capire, comprendere, intendere **2** venire a sapere, apprendere **3** interpretare **4** sottintendere **B** *v. intr.* **1** capire, rendersi conto **2** intendersi
understanding [ˌʌndə'stændɪŋ] **A** *agg.* comprensivo **B** *s.* **1** intelligenza *f.*, comprensione *f.* **2** accordo *m.*
to understate [ˌʌndə'steɪt] *v. tr.* sottovalutare, attenuare
understood [ˌʌndə'stʊd] **A** *pass. e p. p. di*

to understand **B** *agg.* sottinteso
understudy ['ʌndəˌstʌdɪ] *s.* sostituto *m.* (di attore)
to undertake [ˌʌndə'teɪk] (*pass.* **undertook**, *p. p.* **undertaken**) **A** *v. tr.* **1** intraprendere **2** assumersi l'impegno di **B** *v. intr.* garantire
undertaking [ˌʌndə'teɪkɪŋ] *s.* **1** impresa *f.* **2** impegno *m.*
undertone ['ʌndəˌtɒʊn] *s.* **1** tono *m.* sommesso **2** senso *m.* occulto
undertook [ˌʌndə'tʊk] *pass. di* **to undertake**
underwater [ˌʌndə'wɜːtəʳ] **A** *agg.* subacqueo **B** *avv.* sott'acqua
underwear ['ʌndəwɛəʳ] *s.* biancheria *f.* intima
underwood ['ʌndəwʊd] *s.* sottobosco *m.*
underworld ['ʌndəwɜːld] *s.* malavita *f.*
underwriting ['ʌndəˌraɪtɪŋ] *s.* sottoscrizione *f.*
undeserved [ˌʌndɪ'zɜːvd] *agg.* immeritato
undesirable [ˌʌndɪ'zaɪərəbl] *agg.* indesiderabile, sgradito
undid [ʌn'dɪd] *pass. di* **to undo**
undies ['ʌndɪz] *s. pl.* (*fam.*) biancheria *f.* intima (*da donna*)
undifferentiated [ʌnˌdɪfə'rɛnʃɪeɪtɪd] *agg.* indifferenziato
undisturbed [ˌʌndɪs'tɜːbd] *agg.* indisturbato
to undo [ʌn'duː] (*pass.* **undid**, *p. p.* **undone**) *v. tr.* **1** disfare, annullare **2** sciogliere, sbrogliare **3** rovinare
undoing [ʌn'duːɪŋ] *s.* rovina *f.*
undone [ʌn'dʌn] **A** *p. p. di* **to undo** **B** *agg.* **1** disfatto **2** incompiuto
undoubted [ʌn'daʊtɪd] *agg.* indubbio, sicuro
to undress [ʌn'drɛs] *v. intr.* denudarsi, spogliarsi
undue [ʌn'djuː] *agg.* **1** indebito **2** inadatto **3** eccessivo
undulating ['ʌndjʊleɪtɪŋ] *agg.* **1** ondulato **2** ondeggiante
undulation [ˌʌndjʊ'leɪʃ(ə)n] *s.* ondulazione *f.*
undulatory ['ʌndjʊlətərɪ] *agg.* **1** ondulato **2** ondulatorio
unduly [ˌʌn'djuːlɪ] *avv.* **1** eccessivamente **2** indebitamente
to unearth [ʌn'ɜːθ] *v. tr.* **1** dissotterrare **2** scoprire
unearthly [ʌn'ɜːθlɪ] *agg.* **1** non terreno, soprannaturale **2** sinistro, misterioso **3** impossibile, assurdo
uneasiness [ʌn'iːzɪnɪs] *s.* disagio *m.*, inquietudine *f.*
uneasy [ʌn'iːzɪ] *agg.* inquieto, preoccupato
uneatable [ʌn'iːtəbl] *agg.* immangiabile
uneconomic(al) [ˌʌniːkə'nəmɪk((ə)l)] *agg.* antieconomico
uneducated [ʌn'ɛdjʊkeɪtɪd] *agg.* ignorante, illetterato
unemployed [ˌʌnɪm'plɔɪd] *s.* disoccupato *m.*
unemployment [ˌʌnɪm'plɔɪmənt] *s.* disoccupazione *f.*
unending [ʌn'ɛndɪŋ] *agg.* senza fine
unequal [ʌn'iːkw(ə)l] *agg.* disuguale
unequalled [ʌn'iːkw(ə)ld] *agg.* incomparabile
unerring [ʌn'ɜːrɪŋ] *agg.* infallibile
uneven [ʌn'iːv(ə)n] *agg.* irregolare, ineguale
uneveness [ʌn'iːv(ə)nɪs] *s.* disuguaglianza *f.*
unexceptionable [ˌʌnɪk'sɛpʃnəbl] *agg.* ineccepibile
unexpected [ˌʌnɪks'pɛktɪd] *agg.* imprevisto, improvviso, inatteso
unexplored [ˌʌnɪks'plɜːd] *agg.* inesplorato
unfailing [ʌn'feɪlɪŋ] *agg.* **1** infallibile **2** immancabile **3** inesauribile
unfair [ʌn'fɛəʳ] *agg.* ingiusto, sleale
unfaithful [ʌn'feɪθf(ʊ)l] *agg.* infedele
unfamiliar [ˌʌnfə'mɪljəʳ] *agg.* poco familiare, sconosciuto
unfashionable [ʌn'fæʃnəbl] *agg.* fuori moda
to unfasten [ʌn'faːsn] *v. tr.* slegare, slacciare
unfavourable [ʌn'feɪv(ə)rəbl] (*USA* **unfavorable**) *agg.* sfavorevole
unfeeling [ʌn'fiːlɪŋ] *agg.* insensibile
unfinished [ʌn'fɪnɪʃt] *agg.* incompiuto
unfit [ʌn'fɪt] *agg.* **1** inadatto, incapace **2** inabile
to unfold [ʌn'fɒʊld] **A** *v. tr.* **1** schiudere, spiegare **2** rivelare **B** *v. intr.* **1** aprirsi, schiudersi **2** rivelarsi
unforeseen [ˌʌnfɜː'siːn] *agg.* imprevisto
unforgettable [ˌʌnfə'gɛtəbl] *agg.* indimenticabile
unforgivable [ˌʌnfə'gɪvəbl] *agg.* imperdonabile
unfortunate [ʌn'fɜːtʃ(ə)nɪt] *agg.* sfortu-

nato
unfounded [ʌn'faʊndɪd] *agg.* infondato
unfruitful [ʌn'fruːtf(ʊ)l] *agg.* infruttuoso
unfulfilled [ˌʌnfʊl'fɪld] *agg.* incompiuto, inappagato
ungainly [ʌn'geɪnlɪ] *agg.* goffo
ungodly [ʌn'gədlɪ] *agg.* assurdo, impossibile
ungrateful [ʌn'greɪtf(ʊ)l] *agg.* ingrato
ungratefulness [ʌn'greɪtf(ʊ)lnɪs] *s.* ingratitudine *f.*
unhappiness [ʌn'hæpɪnɪs] *s.* infelicità *f.*
unhappy [ʌn'hæpɪ] *agg.* infelice
unharmed [ʌn'haːmd] *agg.* illeso, incolume
unhealthy [ʌn'hɛlθɪ] *agg.* **1** malsano **2** malaticcio
unheard [ʌn'hɜːd] *agg.* inascoltato ♦ **u. off** inaudito, incredibile
to unhinge [ʌn'hɪn(d)ʒ] *v. tr.* scardinare
to unhook [ʌn'hʊk] *v. tr.* sganciare
unhurt [ʌn'hɜːt] *agg.* incolume
unification [ˌjuːnɪfɪ'keɪʃ(ə)n] *s.* unificazione *f.*
uniform ['juːnɪfɜːm] **A** *agg.* uniforme **B** *s.* uniforme *f.*, divisa *f.*
uniformity [ˌjuːnɪ'fɜːmɪtɪ] *s.* uniformità *f.*
to unify ['juːnɪfaɪ] *v. tr.* unificare
unimaginable [ˌʌnɪ'mædʒ(ɪ)nəbl] *agg.* inimmaginabile
uninhabitable [ˌʌnɪn'hæbɪtəbl] *agg.* inabitabile
uninhabited [ˌʌnɪn'hæbɪtɪd] *agg.* disabitato
uninjured [ʌn'ɪn(d)ʒəd] *agg.* illeso
unintelligible [ˌʌnɪn'tɛlɪdʒəbl] *agg.* incomprensibile
unintentional [ˌʌnɪn'tɛnʃ(ə)nl] *agg.* involontario
uninterrupted [ˌʌnɪntə'rʌptɪd] *agg.* ininterrotto, incessante
union ['juːnjən] *s.* **1** unione *f.* **2** associazione *f.*, lega *f.*, consorzio *m.* **3** sindacato *m.*
unique [juː'niːk] *agg.* unico
unit ['juːnɪt] *s.* **1** unità *f.* **2** complesso *m.*, gruppo *m.* **3** (*mil.*) reparto *m.*
to unite [juː'naɪt] *v. tr. e intr.* unire, unirsi
united [juː'naɪtɪd] *agg.* unito, congiunto
unity ['juːnɪtɪ] *s.* **1** unità *f.* **2** accordo *m.*
universal [ˌjuːnɪ'vɜːs(ə)l] *agg.* universale
universe ['juːnɪvɜːs] *s.* universo *m.*
university [ˌjuːnɪ'vɜːsɪtɪ] *s.* università *f.*
univocal [ˌjuːnɪ'vɒʊk(ə)l] *agg.* univoco
unjust [ʌn'dʒʌst] *agg.* ingiusto
unkempt [ʌn'kɛm(p)t] *agg.* scarmigliato
unkind [ʌn'kaɪnd] *agg.* **1** scortese **2** crudele
unkindness [ʌn'kaɪn(d)nɪs] *s.* **1** scortesia *f.* **2** crudeltà *f.*
unknown [ʌn'nɒʊn] **A** *agg.* sconosciuto **B** *s.* (*mat.*) incognita *f.*
to unlace [ʌn'leɪs] *v. tr.* slacciare
unlawful [ʌn'lɜːf(ʊ)l] *agg.* abusivo, illegale
to unleash [ʌn'liːʃ] *v. tr.* sguinzagliare
unless [ən'lɛs] *cong.* eccetto che, a meno che
unlike [ʌn'laɪk] **A** *agg. pred.* diverso **B** *prep.* diversamente da, a differenza di
unlikely [ʌn'laɪklɪ] *avv.* improbabile
unlimited [ʌn'lɪmɪtɪd] *agg.* illimitato
unlined [ʌn'laɪnd] *agg.* sfoderato
to unload [ʌn'lɒʊd] *v. tr.* **1** scaricare **2** disfarsi di
unloaded [ʌn'lɒʊdɪd] *agg.* scarico
unloading [ʌn'lɒʊdɪŋ] *s.* scarico *m.*
to unlock [ʌn'lək] *v. tr.* **1** aprire **2** rivelare
unlucky [ʌn'lʌkɪ] *agg.* **1** sfortunato **2** di cattivo augurio
to unmake [ʌn'meɪk] (*pass. e p. p.* **unmade**) *v. tr.* disfare
unmarried [ʌn'mærɪd] *agg.* non sposato
unmatched [ʌn'mætʃt] *agg.* **1** impareggiabile **2** scompagnato
unmistakable [ˌʌnmɪs'teɪkəbl] *agg.* inconfondibile
to unnail [ʌn'nəɪl] *v. tr.* schiodare
unnatural [ʌn'nætʃr(ə)l] *agg.* innaturale
unnecessary [ʌn'nɛsɪs(ə)rɪ] *agg.* non necessario, superfluo
unnoticed [ʌn'nɒʊtɪst] *agg.* inosservato
unobtainable [ˌʌnəb'teɪnəbl] *agg.* non ottenibile
unobtrusive [ˌʌnəb'truːsɪv] *agg.* discreto, riservato
unofficial [ˌʌnə'fɪʃ(ə)l] *agg.* non ufficiale
to unpack [ʌn'pæk] *v. tr.* **1** (*valigie*) disfare **2** sballare
unpaid [ʌn'peɪd] *agg.* non pagato
unpalatable [ʌn'pælətəbl] *agg.* sgradevole
unpleasant [ʌn'plɛznt] *agg.* antipatico, sgradevole
to unplug [ʌn'plʌg] *v. tr.* togliere la spina a, staccare
unpopular [ʌn'pəpjʊlə^r] *agg.* impopolare
unprecedented [ʌn'prɛsɪd(ə)ntɪd] *agg.* inaudito

unpredictable [ˌʌnprɪ'dɪktəbl] *agg.* imprevedibile
unprepared [ˌʌnprɪ'pɛəd] *agg.* impreparato
unprofessional [ˌʌnprə'fɛʃ(ə)nl] *agg.* poco professionale
unprotected [ˌʌnprə'tɛktɪd] *agg.* indifeso
unprovided [ˌʌnprə'vaɪdɪd] *agg.* sprovvisto
unpublished [ʌn'pʌblɪʃt] *agg.* inedito
unqualified [ʌn'kwɔlɪfaɪd] *agg.* **1** incompetente **2** non abilitato, non qualificato **3** assoluto, categorico
unquestionable [ʌn'kwɛstʃ(ə)nəbl] *agg.* indiscutibile
to unravel [ʌn'ræv(ə)l] *v. tr.* districare, sbrogliare
unreal [ʌn'rɪəl] *agg.* irreale
unrealistic [ˌʌnrɪə'lɪstɪk] *agg.* non realistico
unreality [ˌʌnrɪ'ælɪltɪ] *s.* irrealtà *f.*
unreasonable [ʌn'riːz(ə)nəbl] *agg.* irragionevole
unrelated [ˌʌnrɪ'leɪtɪd] *agg.* senza rapporti
unrelenting [ˌʌnrɪ'lɛntɪŋ] *agg.* inesorabile
unreliable [ˌʌnrɪ'laɪəbl] *agg.* inaffidabile, inattendibile
unremitting [ˌʌnrɪ'mɪtɪŋ] *agg.* incessante
unrest [ʌn'rɛst] *s.* agitazione *f.*
unrestricted [ˌʌnrɪs'trɪktɪd] *agg.* illimitato, senza limiti
unripe [ʌn'raɪp] *agg.* acerbo
to unrivet [ʌn'rɪvɪt] *v. tr.* schiodare
to unroll [ʌn'rɒʊl] *v. tr.* srotolare
unruly [ʌn'ruːlɪ] *agg.* indisciplinato
unsafe [ʌn'seɪf] *agg.* pericoloso, malsicuro
unsaid [ʌn'sɛd] *pass. e p. p. di* **to unsay**
unsaleable [ʌn'seɪləbl] *agg.* invendibile
unsatisfactory [ˌʌnsætɪs'fækt(ə)rɪ] *agg.* insoddisfacente
unsavoury [ʌn'seɪv(ə)rɪ] *agg.* **1** scipito **2** disgustoso
to unsay [ʌn'seɪ] (*pass. e p. p.* **unsaid**) *v. tr.* ritrattare, negare
unscathed [ʌn'skeɪðd] *agg.* illeso
to unscrew [ʌn'skruː] *v. tr.* svitare
unscrupulous [ʌn'skruːpjʊləs] *agg.* senza scrupoli
unseasoned [ʌn'siːznd] *agg.* scondito
unseizable [ʌn'siːzəbl] *agg.* inafferrabile
unselfish [ʌn'sɛlfɪʃ] *agg.* altruista
unsettled [ʌn'sɛtld] *agg.* **1** disordinato, sconvolto **2** indeciso, incerto **3** non saldato, non pagato
unshakable [ʌn'ʃeɪkəbl] *agg.* irremovibile
to unsheathe [ʌn'ʃiːð] *v. tr.* sfoderare
unsightly [ʌn'saɪtlɪ] *agg.* brutto, sgradevole
unskilfulness [ʌn'skɪlf(ʊ)lnɪs] *s.* imperizia *f.*
unskilled [ʌn'skɪld] *agg.* inesperto
unsound [ʌn'saʊnd] *agg.* malsano
unspeakable [ʌn'spiːkəbl] *agg.* indicibile
unstable [ʌn'steɪbl] *agg.* instabile
unsteady [ʌn'stɛdɪ] *agg.* malfermo
to unstick [ʌn'stɪk] (*pass. e p. p.* **unstuck**) *v. tr.* scollare, staccare
to unstitch [ʌn'stɪtʃ] *v. tr.* scucire
unsuccessful [ˌʌns(ə)k'sɛsf(ʊ)l] *agg.* fallito, sfortunato
unsuitable [ʌn'sjuːtəbl] *agg.* **1** inadatto **2** inopportuno
unsure [ʌn'ʃʊəʳ] *agg.* incerto
unsuspected [ˌʌnsəs'pɛktɪd] *agg.* insospettato
unsympathetic [ˌʌnsɪmpə'θɛtɪk] *agg.* antipatico
untapped [ʌn'tæpt] *agg.* non sfruttato
untenable [ʌn'tɛnəbl] *agg.* insostenibile
unthinkable [ʌn'θɪŋkəbl] *agg.* impensabile
untidiness [ʌn'taɪdɪnɪs] *s.* disordine *m.*
untidy [ʌn'taɪdɪ] *agg.* disordinato
to untie [ʌn'taɪ] *v. tr.* **1** slegare **2** risolvere
until [ən'tɪl] **A** *prep.* fino a, fino al momento di **B** *cong.* finché non, fino a quando
untimely [ʌn'taɪmlɪ] *agg.* inopportuno
untiring [ʌn'taɪərɪŋ] *agg.* instancabile
untold [ʌn'tɒʊld] *agg.* **1** taciuto **2** innumerevole
untoward [ʌn'tɒ(ʊ)əd] *agg.* **1** scomodo **2** sconveniente
untranslatable [ˌʌntræns'leɪtəbl] *agg.* intraducibile
unusable [ʌn'juːzəbl] *agg.* inutilizzabile
unused [ʌn'juːzd] *agg.* **1** non usato **2** non abituato
unusual [ʌn'juːʒʊəl] *agg.* inconsueto, insolito
to unveil [ʌn'veɪl] *v. tr.* svelare
unwanted [ʌn'wɔntɪd] *agg.* non desiderato
unwavering [ʌn'weɪv(ə)rɪŋ] *agg.* incrollabile
unwelcome [ʌn'wɛlkəm] *agg.* sgradito
unwell [ʌn'wɛl] *agg. pred.* indisposto
unwieldy [ʌn'wiːldɪ] *agg.* **1** ingombrante **2** impacciato
unwilling [ʌn'wɪlɪŋ] *agg.* riluttante, non di-

sposto

to unwind [ʌn'waɪnd] (*pass. e p. p.* **unwound**) **A** *v. tr.* sdipanare, srotolare **B** *v. intr.* **1** srotolarsi **2** rilassarsi

unwise [ʌn'waɪz] *agg.* malaccorto

unwitting [ʌn'wɪtɪŋ] *agg.* involontario

unworkable [ʌn'wɜːkəbl] *agg.* inattuabile

unworthy [ʌn'wɜːðɪ] *agg.* immeritevole, indegno

to unwrap [ʌn'ræp] *v. tr.* scartare, disfare

up [ʌp] **A** *avv.* **1** su, in alto **2** più avanti, oltre **3** completamente **B** *prep.* su, su per **C** *agg.* **1** alzato **2** finito, compiuto **3** ascendente ♦ **up against** di fronte a; **up here** quassù; **up there** lassù; **up to** fino a; **up to now** finora

upbringing ['ʌpˌbrɪŋɪŋ] *s.* allevamento *m.* (di bambini)

to update [ʌp'deɪt] *v. tr.* aggiornare

upgrade ['ʌpgreɪd] **A** *s.* salita *f.*, pendenza *f.* **B** *agg. e avv.* in salita

to upgrade [ˌʌp'greɪd] *v. tr.* **1** promuovere **2** incrementare

upheaval [ʌp'hiːv(ə)l] *s.* **1** sollevamento *m.* **2** agitazione *f.*

upheld [ʌp'hɛld] *pass. e p. p. di* **to uphold**

uphill [ˌʌp'hɪl] **A** *agg.* **1** in salita **2** faticoso **B** *s.* salita *f.* **C** *avv.* in salita

to uphold [ʌp'hɒʊld] (*pass. e p. p.* **upheld**) *v. tr.* sostenere, sorreggere

upkeep ['ʌpkiːp] *s.* manutenzione *f.*

upon [ə'pən] *prep.* sopra, su

upper ['ʌpər] **A** *agg.* superiore, più alto **B** *s.* **1** parte *f.* superiore **2** tomaia *f.* ♦ **u. case** maiuscolo

uppermost ['ʌpəmɒʊst] **A** *agg.* **1** il più alto **2** principale, predominante **B** *avv.* al di sopra, per prima cosa

upright ['ʌpˌraɪt] *agg.* **1** dritto, eretto, verticale **2** integro, onesto

uprising ['ʌpˌraɪzɪŋ] *s.* sollevazione *f.*

uproar ['ʌpˌrɜːr] *s.* pandemonio *m.*, tumulto *m.*

to uproot [ʌp'ruːt] *v. tr.* sradicare

upset [ʌp'sɛt] **A** *agg.* **1** capovolto **2** agitato, sconvolto **B** *s.* **1** capovolgimento *m.* **2** turbamento *m.*

to upset [ʌp'sɛt] (*pass. e p. p.* **upset**) **A** *v. tr.* **1** capovolgere **2** agitare, sconvolgere **B** *v. intr.* capovolgersi

upsetting [ʌp'sɛtɪŋ] *agg.* sconvolgente

upshot ['ʌpʃət] *s.* conclusione *f.*, risultato *m.*

upside ['ʌpsaɪd] *avv.* di sopra ♦ **u. down** sottosopra, alla rovescia

upstairs [ˌʌp'stɛəz] *avv.* al piano superiore

upstream [ˌʌp'striːm] *agg. e avv.* **1** a monte **2** contro corrente

uptake ['ʌpteɪk] *s.* comprensione *f.*, comprendonio *m.*

up-to-date [ˌʌptə'deɪt] *agg.* **1** aggiornato **2** alla moda

upturn ['ʌptɜːn] *s.* ripresa *f.*, rialzo *m.*

to upvalue [ʌp'væljuː] *v. tr.* sopravvalutare

upward ['ʌpwəd] **A** *agg.* ascendente **B** *avv.* **1** in su, in alto **2** oltre

uranium [jʊ'reɪnjəm] *s.* uranio *m.*

urban ['ɜːbən] *agg.* urbano, cittadino

urbane [ɜː'beɪn] *agg.* urbano, cortese

urbanist ['ɜːbɛnɪst] *s.* urbanista *m. e f.*

urbanization [ˌɜːbənaɪ'zeɪʃ(ə)n] *s.* urbanizzazione *f.*

urchin ['ɜːtʃɪn] *s.* **1** monello *m.* **2** riccio *m.*, porcospino *m.*

urea ['jʊərɪə] *s.* urea *f.*

urethra [jʊə'riːθrə] *s.* uretra *f.*

urge [ɜːdʒ] *s.* impulso *m.*, stimolo *m.*

to urge [ɜːdʒ] *v. tr.* **1** spingere, sollecitare **2** raccomandare **3** addurre

urgency ['ɜːdʒ(ə)nsɪ] *s.* **1** urgenza *f.* **2** insistenza *f.*

urgent ['ɜːdʒ(ə)nt] *agg.* **1** urgente **2** insistente

urine ['jʊɛrɪn] *s.* urina *f.*

urn [ɜːn] *s.* urna *f.*

urologist [jʊə'rələdʒɪst] *s.* urologo *m.*

urticaria [ˌɜːtɪ'kɛərɪə] *s.* orticaria *f.*

us [ʌs] *pron. pers. 1ª pl.* (*compl.*) noi, ci

usage ['juːzɪdʒ] *s.* **1** uso *m.*, applicazione *f.* **2** usanza *f.*

use [juːs] *s.* **1** uso *m.*, utilizzo *m.*, impiego *m.* **2** utilità *f.* **3** usanza *f.* ♦ **out of u.** fuori uso; **to be of u.** servire

to use [juːz] *v. tr.* usare, adoperare ♦ **to u. up** esaurire, consumare

used [juːzd] *agg.* usato

useful ['juːsf(ʊ)l] *agg.* utile

usefulness ['juːsf(ʊ)lnɪs] *s.* utilità *f.*

useless ['juːslɪs] *agg.* inutile

user ['juːzər] *s.* utente *m. e f.* ♦ **u.-friendly** di facile uso

usher ['ʌʃər] *s.* usciere *m.*

to usher ['ʌʃər] *v. tr.* fare strada a

usherette [ˌʌʃə'rɛt] *s.* (*cine.*) maschera *f.*

usual ['juːʒʊəl] *agg.* consueto, solito ♦ **as u.** come al solito

usually ['juːʒʊəlɪ] *avv.* abitualmente, solitamente

usufruct ['juːsjuːfrʌkt] *s.* usufrutto *m.*
utensil [juː'tɛnsl] *s.* utensile *m.*
uterus ['juːtərəs] *s.* utero *m.*
utility [juː'tɪlɪtɪ] *s.* **1** utilità *f.* **2** *al pl.* servizi *m. pl.* pubblici **3** (*inf.*) utility *f. inv.* ♦ **u. car** utilitaria
utilization [ˌjuːtɪlaɪ'zeɪʃ(ə)n] *s.* utilizzo *m.*
to utilize ['juːtɪlaɪz] *v. tr.* utilizzare
utmost ['ʌtmɒʊst] **A** *agg.* **1** estremo **2** massimo **B** *s.* limite *m.* estremo, massimo *m.* ♦ **to the u.** a oltranza; **to try one's u.** fare del proprio meglio
utopia [juː'tɒʊpjə] *s.* utopia *f.*
utopian [jʊ'ːtɒʊpjən] *s.* utopista *m. e f.*
utter ['ʌtəʳ] *agg.* completo, totale
to utter ['ʌtəʳ] *v. tr.* **1** emettere **2** pronunciare
utterly ['ʌtəlɪ] *avv.* completamente
U-turn ['juːtɜːn] *s.* inversione *f.* a U
uxoricide [ʌk'sɜːrɪsaɪd] *s.* uxoricida *m. e f.*

V

vacancy ['veɪk(ə)nsɪ] *s.* **1** vacanza *f.* (*l'essere vacante*) **2** posto *m.* libero ♦ **no vacancies** al completo
vacant ['veɪk(ə)nt] *agg.* **1** vacante, libero, disponibile **2** vacuo
to vacate [və'keɪt] *v. tr.* sgombrare
vacation [və'keɪʃ(ə)n] *s.* vacanza *f.*, ferie *f. pl.*
to vaccinate ['væksɪneɪt] *v. tr. e intr.* vaccinare, fare una vaccinazione
vaccination [ˌvæksɪ'neɪʃ(ə)n] *s.* vaccinazione *f.*
vaccine ['væksiːn] *s.* vaccino *m.*
vacuum ['vækjʊəm] *s.* vuoto *m.* ♦ **v. cleaner** aspirapolvere; **v.-packed** confezionato sotto vuoto
vagina [və'dʒaɪnə] *s.* vagina *f.*
vaginitis [ˌvædʒɪ'naɪtɪs] *s.* vaginite *f.*
vagrant ['veɪgr(ə)nt] *agg. e s.* vagabondo *m.*
vague [veɪg] *agg.* **1** vago, indistinto **2** incerto
vain [veɪn] *agg.* **1** vano, inutile **2** vanitoso
valediction [ˌvælɪ'dɪkʃ(ə)n] *s.* commiato *m.*
valentine ['væləntaɪn] *s.* biglietto *m.* di S. Valentino
valerian [və'lɪərɪən] *s.* valeriana *f.*
valet ['vælɪt] *s.* valletto *m.*, cameriere *m.* (personale)
valiancy ['væljənsɪ] *s.* valore *m.*
valiant ['væljənt] *agg.* valoroso
valid ['vælɪd] *agg.* valido, valevole
to validate ['vælɪdeɪt] *v. tr.* **1** convalidare, render valido **2** (*inf.*) abilitare
validity [və'lɪdɪtɪ] *s.* validità *f.*
valley ['vælɪ] *s.* vallata *f.*, valle *f.*
valour ['væləʳ] *s.* valore *m.*
valuable ['væljʊebl] **A** *agg.* pregevole, prezioso **B** *s. al pl.* oggetti *m. pl.* di valore
valuation [ˌvæljʊ'eɪʃ(ə)n] *s.* valutazione *f.*, stima *f.*
value ['væljuː] *s.* **1** valore *m.* **2** pregio *m.* ♦ **v.-added tax** imposta sul valore aggiunto
to value ['væljuː] *v. tr.* **1** valutare, stimare **2** apprezzare
valued ['væljuːd] *agg.* **1** valutato, stimato **2** apprezzato, pregiato
valve [vælv] *s.* valvola *f.*
vampire ['væmpaɪəʳ] *s.* vampiro *m.*
van [væn] *s.* **1** furgone *m.* **2** vagone *m.*
vandal ['vænd(ə)l] *s.* vandalo *m.*
vandalic [væn'dælɪk] *agg.* vandalico
vandalism ['vændælɪz(ə)m] *s.* vandalismo *m.*
vane [veɪn] *s.* **1** banderuola *f.* **2** aletta *f.*, paletta *f.*
vanguard ['vængaːd] *s.* avanguardia *f.*
vanilla [və'nɪlə] *s.* vaniglia *f.*
to vanish ['vænɪʃ] **A** *v. intr.* sparire, svanire **B** *v. tr.* far sparire
vanity ['vænɪtɪ] *s.* vanità *f.*
to vanquish ['væŋkwɪʃ] *v. tr.* debellare
vantage ['vaːntɪdʒ] *s.* vantaggio *m.*
vaporization [ˌveɪpəraɪ'zeɪʃ(ə)n] *s.* vaporizzazione *f.*
vaporizer ['veɪpəraɪzəʳ] *s.* vaporizzatore *m.*
vapour ['veɪpəʳ] (*USA* **vapor**) *s.* vapore *m.*
variable ['vɛərɪəbl] *agg.* variabile, mutevole
variance ['vɛərɪəns] *s.* **1** variazione *f.* **2** divergenza *f.*, disaccordo *m.* **3** varianza *f.*
variation [ˌvɛərɪ'eɪʃ(ə)n] *s.* variazione *f.*
varicella [ˌværɪ'sɛlə] *s.* varicella *f.*
varicose ['værɪkɒʊs] *agg.* varicoso
varied ['vɛərɪd] *agg.* vario, variato
variegated ['vɛərɪgeɪtɪd] *agg.* variegato
variety [və'raɪətɪ] *s.* varietà *f.*
various ['vɛərɪəs] *agg.* (*con s. pl.*) vari, diversi, parecchi
varix ['vɛərɪks] *s.* varice *f.*
varnish ['vaːnɪʃ] *s.* vernice *f.*
to varnish ['vaːnɪʃ] *v. tr.* verniciare
to vary ['vɛərɪ] **A** *v. tr.* variare, cambiare **B** *v. intr.* differire
vascular ['væskjʊləʳ] *agg.* vascolare
vase [vaːz] *s.* vaso *m.*
vasectomy [və'sɛktəmɪ] *s.* vasectomia *f.*
vaseline ['væsɪliːn] *s.* vaselina *f.*
vast [vaːst] *agg.* vasto
vat [væt] *s.* tino *m.*
vaudeville ['vɒʊdəvɪl] *s.* **1** vaudeville *m. inv.* **2** (*USA*) varietà *m.*
vault (1) [vɜːlt] *s.* **1** (*arch.*) volta *f.* **2** cripta *f.*, sotterraneo *m.* ♦ **barrel v.** volta a botte
vault (2) [vɜːlt] *s.* volteggio *m.* ♦ **pole v.** salto con l'asta

to vault [vɜːlt] *v. intr.* volteggiare, saltare
vaulting ['vɜːltɪŋ] **A** *agg.* che salta **B** *s.* volteggio *m.*
to vaunt [vɜːnt] *v. tr. e intr.* vantare, vantarsi
veal [viːl] *s.* (*cuc.*) vitello *m.*
vector ['vɛktəʳ] *s.* vettore *m.*
veer [vɪəʳ] *s.* virata *f.*
to veer [vɪəʳ] *v. intr.* virare
vegetable ['vɛdʒɪtəbl] **A** *agg.* vegetale **B** *s.* **1** vegetale *m.* **2** ortaggio *m.*, *al pl.* verdure *f. pl.*
vegetal ['vɛdʒɪtl] *agg.* vegetale, vegetativo
vegetarian [ˌvɛdʒɪ'tɛərɪən] *agg. e s.* vegetariano *m.*
vegetation [ˌvɛdʒɪ'teɪʃ(ə)n] *s.* vegetazione *f.*
vehemence ['viːɪməns] *s.* veemenza *f.*
vehement ['viːɪmənt] *agg.* veemente
vehicle ['viːɪkl] *s.* veicolo *m.*
veil [veɪl] *s.* velo *m.*
to veil [veɪl] *v. tr.* velare, coprire
vein [veɪn] *s.* **1** vena *f.* **2** venatura *f.*, nervatura *f.*
velocity [vɪ'lɔsɪtɪ] *s.* velocità *f.*
velvet ['vɛlvɪt] *s.* velluto *m.*
venal ['viːnl] *agg.* venale
vendor ['vɛndɜːʳ] *s.* venditore *m.*
veneer [vɪ'nɪəʳ] *s.* impiallacciatura *f.*
to venerate ['vɛnəreɪt] *v. tr.* venerare
venereal [vɪ'nɪərɪəl] *agg.* venereo
Venetian [vɪ'niːʃ(ə)n] *agg. e s.* veneziano *m.* ♦ **V. blind** (tenda alla) veneziana
vengeance ['vɛn(d)ʒəns] *s.* vendetta *f.* ♦ **with a v.** a tutta forza
venison ['vɛnzn] *s.* (*cuc.*) (carne di) cervo *m.*
venom ['vɛnəm] *s.* veleno *m.*
venomous ['vɛnəməs] *agg.* velenoso
vent [vɛnt] *s.* **1** foro *m.*, orifizio *m.*, apertura *f.* **2** sfogo *m.*
to vent [vɛnt] *v. tr.* **1** scaricare, svuotare **2** sfogare
to ventilate ['vɛntɪleɪt] *v. tr.* **1** ventilare **2** (*med.*) ossigenare
ventilation [ˌvɛntɪ'leɪʃ(ə)n] *s.* **1** ventilazione *f.*, aerazione *f.* **2** (*med.*) ossigenazione *f.*
ventilator ['vɛntɪleɪtəʳ] *s.* ventilatore *m.*
ventriloquist [vɛn'trɪləkwɪst] *s.* ventriloquo *m.*
venture ['vɛntʃəʳ] *s.* **1** avventura *f.*, impresa *f.* **2** (*econ.*) attività *f.* imprenditoriale
to venture ['vɛntʃəʳ] **A** *v. tr.* **1** rischiare, arrischiare **2** osare **B** *v. intr.* avventurarsi, arrischiarsi
venue ['vɛnjuː] *s.* **1** luogo *m.* di convegno **2** (*dir.*) sede *f.* di processo
veranda(h) [və'rændə] *s.* veranda *f.*
verb [vɜːb] *s.* verbo *m.*
verbal ['vɜːb(ə)l] *agg.* verbale
verbena [vɜː'biːnə] *s.* verbena *f.*
verdant ['vɜːd(ə)nt] *agg.* verdeggiante
verdict ['vɜːdɪkt] *s.* verdetto *m.*
verge [vɜːdʒ] *s.* **1** limite *m.*, orlo *m.*, margine *m.* **2** verga *f.* **3** (*arch.*) fusto *m.* ♦ **on the v. of** sul punto di
to verge [vɜːdʒ] *v. intr.* **1** declinare, tendere, volgere **2** confinare con
verifiable ['vɛrɪfaɪəbl] *agg.* verificabile
to verify ['vɛrɪfaɪ] *v. tr.* verificare
verisimilitude [ˌvɛrɪsɪ'mɪlɪtjuːd] *s.* verosimiglianza *f.*
verism ['vɪərɪz(ə)m] *s.* verismo *m.*
verist ['vɪərɪst] *s.* verista *m. e f.*
veritable ['vɛrɪtəbl] *agg.* vero, genuino
vermilion [və'mɪljən] *agg.* vermiglio
vermin ['vɜːmɪn] *s.* animali *m. pl.* nocivi, insetti *m. pl.* parassiti
vernacular [və'nækjʊləʳ] **A** *agg.* **1** vernacolo **2** indigeno, locale **B** *s.* vernacolo *m.*
verruca [vɛ'ruːkə] *s.* verruca *f.*
versant ['vɜːs(ə)nt] *s.* versante *m.*
versatile ['vɜːsətaɪl] *agg.* versatile
verse [vɜːs] *s.* verso *m.*, versetto *m.*
versed [vɜːst] *agg.* versato, pratico
to versify ['vɜːsɪfaɪ] *v. intr.* verseggiare
version ['vɜːʃ(ə)n] *s.* versione *f.*
versus ['vɜːsəs] *prep.* contro
vertebra ['vɜːtɪbrə] *s.* vertebra *f.*
vertebral ['vɜːtɪbr(ə)l] *agg.* vertebrale
vertebrate ['vɜːtɪbrɪt] *agg. e s.* vertebrato *m.*
vertex ['vɜːtɛks] *s.* (*geom.*) vertice *m.*
vertical ['vɜːtɪk(ə)l] *agg.* verticale
vertiginous [vɜː'tɪdʒɪnəs] *agg.* **1** vertiginoso **2** che soffre di vertigini
vertigo ['vɜːtɪgɒʊ] *s.* vertigine *f.*
vervain ['vɜːveɪn] *s.* verbena *f.*
verve [vɛəv] *s.* verve *f. inv.*, brio *m.*
very ['vɛrɪ] **A** *agg.* (*enf.*) proprio, esatto, assoluto, vero e proprio **B** *avv.* molto, assai
vesper ['vɛspəʳ] *s.* vespro *m.*
vessel ['vɛsl] *s.* **1** nave *f.*, vascello *m.* **2** recipiente *m.* **3** (*anat.*) vaso *m.*
vest [vɛst] *s.* **1** canottiera *f.* **2** (*USA*) panciotto *m.*, giubbotto *m.* **3** maglietta *f.* ♦ **life v.** giubbotto di salvataggio
vested ['vɛstɪd] *agg.* (*dir.*) acquisito

vestibule ['vɛstɪbjuːl] *s.* vestibolo *m.*
vestige ['vɛstɪdʒ] *s.* vestigio *m.*
vet [vɛt] *s.* (*fam.*) veterinario *m.*
veteran ['vɛt(ə)r(ə)n] **A** *agg.* veterano **B** *s.* veterano *m.*, reduce *m.*
veterinary ['vɛt(ə)rɪn(ə)rɪ] *agg.* veterinario ♦ **v. surgeon** (medico) veterinario
veto ['viːtɒʊ] *s.* veto *m.*
to veto ['viːtɒʊ] *v. tr.* mettere il veto a
to vex [vɛks] *v. tr.* **1** vessare, opprimere **2** irritare, contrariare
vexation [vɛk'seɪʃ(ə)n] *s.* **1** vessazione *f.* **2** fastidio *m.*, irritazione *f.*
via ['vaɪə] *prep.* per, attraverso, via
viable ['vaɪəbl] *agg.* **1** vitale **2** autosufficiente **3** praticabile, attuabile
viaduct ['vaɪədʌkt] *s.* viadotto *m.*
vibrant ['vaɪbr(ə)nt] *agg.* **1** vibrante **2** vivace
to vibrate [vaɪ'breɪt] *v. intr.* **1** vibrare **2** risuonare
vibration [vaɪ'breɪʃ(ə)n] *s.* vibrazione *f.*
vicar ['vɪkəʳ] *s.* **1** curato *m.* **2** vicario *m.*
vicarage ['vɪkərɪdʒ] *s.* canonica *f.*
vicarious [vaɪ'kɛərɪəs] *agg.* **1** vicario, sostituto **2** indiretto
vice (1) [vaɪs] *s.* **1** immoralità *f.* **2** vizio *m.* **3** difetto *m.*
vice (2) [vaɪs] *s.* (*mecc.*) morsa *f.*
vice (3) [vaɪs] **A** *s.* vice *m. e f.* **B** *prep.* al posto di
vice-president [ˌvaɪs'prɛzɪd(ə)nt] *s.* vicepresidente *m.*
viceroy ['vaɪsrɔɪ] *s.* viceré *m.*
vice versa [ˌvaɪsɪ'vɜːsɜː] *avv.* viceversa
vicinity [vɪ'sɪnɪtɪ] *s.* **1** vicinanza *f.* **2** vicinanze *f. pl.*, dintorni *m. pl.*
vicious ['vɪʃəs] *agg.* **1** cattivo, malvagio **2** pericoloso, feroce, ombroso **3** vizioso
vicissitude [vɪ'sɪsɪtjuːd] *s.* vicissitudine *f.*, vicenda *f.*
victim ['vɪktɪm] *s.* vittima *f.*
victor [vɪk'təʳ] *s.* vincitore *m.*
Victorian [vɪk'tɜːrɪən] *agg.* vittoriano
victorious [vɪk'tɜːrɪəs] *agg.* vittorioso
victory ['vɪkt(ə)rɪ] *s.* vittoria *f.*
victual ['vɪtl] *s.* vettovaglie *f. pl.*
vicugna o **vicuña** [vɪ'kjuːnə] *s.* vigogna *f.*
video ['vɪdɪɒʊ] **A** *agg.* video **B** *s.* **1** videoregistrazione *f.* **2** videocassetta *f.* **3** videoregistratore *m.* ♦ **v. game** videogioco
to vie [vaɪ] *v. intr.* gareggiare, competere
Vietnamese [ˌvjɛtnə'miːz] *agg. e s.* vietnamita *m. e f.*
view [vjuː] *s.* **1** vista *f.*, veduta *f.*, visione *f.* **2** vista *f.*, panorama *m.* **3** opinione *f.*, giudizio *m.* **4** intento *m.*, mira *f.*, scopo *m.* **5** rassegna *f.*, mostra *f.* ♦ **in my v.** secondo il mio punto di vista; **in v.** in vista; **in v. of** in considerazione di; **on v.** in mostra
to view [vjuː] *v. tr.* **1** guardare, osservare **2** esaminare, ispezionare **3** considerare
viewer ['vjuːəʳ] *s.* **1** spettatore *m.* **2** ispettore *m.*
viewfinder ['vjuːˌfaɪndəʳ] *s.* (*fot.*) mirino *m.*
viewpoint ['vjuːpɔɪnt] *s.* punto *m.* di vista
vigil ['vɪdʒɪl] *s.* veglia *f.*
vigilance ['vɪdʒɪləns] *s.* vigilanza *f.*
vigilant ['vɪdʒɪlənt] *agg.* vigile
vignette [vɪ'njɛt] *s.* vignetta *f.*
vigorous ['vɪg(ə)rəs] *agg.* vigoroso
vigour ['vɪgəʳ] *s.* vigore *m.*
vile [vaɪl] *agg.* **1** vile, abietto **2** (*fam.*) pessimo
villa ['vɪlə] *s.* villa *f.*
village ['vɪlɪdʒ] *s.* villaggio *m.*, paese *m.*, borgo *m.*
villain ['vɪlən] *s.* furfante *m.*, canaglia *f.*
to vindicate ['vɪndɪkeɪt] *v. tr.* **1** rivendicare **2** difendere, giustificare
vindictive [vɪn'dɪktɪv] *s.* vendicativo
vine [vaɪn] *s.* **1** (*bot.*) vite *f.*, vitigno *m.* **2** pianta *f.* rampicante
vinegar ['vɪnɪgəʳ] *s.* aceto *m.*
vineyard ['vɪnjəd] *s.* vigna *f.*, vigneto *m.*
vintage ['vɪntɪdʒ] **A** *s.* **1** vendemmia *f.* **2** annata *f.*, raccolto *m.* **B** *agg. attr.* d'annata, pregiato ♦ **v. car** auto d'epoca
vinyl ['vaɪnɪl] *s.* vinile *m.*
viola ['vaɪələ] *s.* (*mus.*, *bot.*) viola *f.*
to violate ['vaɪəleɪt] *v. tr.* **1** violare, infrangere **2** violentare
violence ['vaɪələns] *s.* violenza *f.*
violent ['vaɪələnt] *agg.* violento
violet ['vaɪəlɪt] *s.* violetta *f.*
violin [ˌvaɪə'lɪn] *s.* violino *m.*
violinist ['vaɪəlɪnɪst] *s.* violinista *m. e f.*
violoncellist [ˌvaɪələn'tʃɛlɪst] *s.* violoncellista *m. e f.*
violoncello [ˌvaɪələn'tʃɛlɒʊ] *s.* violoncello *m.*
viper ['vaɪpəʳ] *s.* vipera *f.*
viral ['vaɪrəl] *agg.* virale
virgin ['vɜːdʒɪn] *agg. e s.* vergine *f.*
virginity [vɛː'dʒnɪtɪ] *s.* verginità *f.*
Virgo ['vɜːgɒʊ] *s.* (*astr.*) vergine *f.*
virile [vɪ'raɪl] *agg.* virile
virility [vɪ'rɪlɪtɪ] *s.* virilità *f.*

virtual ['vɜːtjʊəl] *agg.* virtuale
virtue ['vɜːtjuː] *s.* **1** virtù *f.* **2** vantaggio *m.*, merito *m.*
virtuoso [ˌvɜːtjʊ'ɒʊzɒʊ] *s.* (*mus.*) virtuoso *m.*
virtuous ['vɜːtjʊəs] *agg.* virtuoso
virus ['vaɪrəs] *s.* virus *m.*
visa ['viːzə] *s.* visto *m.* ♦ **entry v.** visto d'ingresso
to visa ['viːzə] *v. tr.* vistare
viscid ['vɪsɪd] *agg.* viscido
viscount ['vaɪkaʊnt] *s.* visconte *m.*
viscountess ['vaɪkaʊntɪs] *s.* viscontessa *f.*
visibility [ˌvɪzɪ'bɪlɪtɪ] *s.* visibilità *f.* ♦ **poor v.** visibilità scarsa
visible ['vɪzəbl] *agg.* visibile
vision ['vɪʒ(ə)n] *s.* **1** vista *f.*, capacità *f.* visiva **2** visione *f.*
visionary ['vɪʒənərɪ] *agg. e s.* visionario *m.*
visit ['vɪzɪt] *s.* visita *f.*
to visit ['vɪzɪt] *v. tr.* visitare, fare visita a, andare a trovare
visitor ['vɪzɪtər] *s.* **1** visitatore *m.*, ospite *m. e f.* **2** ispettore *m.*
visor ['vaɪzər] *s.* visiera *f.*
vista ['vɪstə] *s.* **1** vista *f.*, veduta *f.*, prospettiva *f.* **2** ricordi *m. pl.*, memorie *f. pl.*
visual ['vɪzjʊəl] *agg.* visuale, visivo
to visualize ['vɪzjʊəlaɪz] *v. tr.* **1** immaginare **2** visualizzare
vital ['vaɪtl] *agg.* vitale
vitality [vaɪ'tælɪtɪ] *s.* vitalità *f.*
vitamin ['vɪtəmɪn] *s.* vitamina *f.*
vitreous ['vɪtrɪəs] *agg.* vitreo
to vitrify ['vɪtrɪfaɪ] *v. tr. e intr.* vetrificare, vetrificarsi
vivaclous [vɪ'veɪʃəs] *agg.* vivace
vivarium [vaɪ'vɛərɪəm] *s.* vivaio *m.* (di pesci)
vivid ['vɪvɪd] *agg.* vivido, vivo
vivisection [ˌvɪvɪ'sɛkʃ(ə)n] *s.* vivisezione *f.*
V-neck ['viːnɛk] *s.* scollatura *f.* a V
vocabulary [və'kæbjʊlərɪ] *s.* vocabolario *m.*
vocal ['vɒʊk(ə)l] *agg.* vocale
vocalic [vɒ(ʊ)'kælɪk] *agg.* vocalico
vocalization [ˌvɒʊkəlaɪ'zeɪʃ(ə)n] *s.* vocalizzazione *f.*
vocation [vɒ(ʊ)'keɪʃ(ə)n] *s.* **1** vocazione *f.* **2** professione *f.*
vocational [vɒ(ʊ)'keɪʃ(ə)nl] *agg.* professionale
vociferous [vɒ(ʊ)'sɪf(ə)rəs] *agg.* vociferante
vodka ['vədkə] *s.* vodka *f. inv.*
vogue [vɒʊg] *s.* voga *f.*, moda *f.*
voice [vəɪs] *s.* voce *f.*
to voice [vəɪs] *v. tr.* esprimere, dare voce a, farsi portavoce di
void [vəɪd] **A** *agg.* **1** vuoto **2** invalido, nullo **B** *s.* vuoto *m.*
volatile ['vələtaɪl] *agg.* **1** volatile **2** volubile
volcanic [vəl'kænɪk] *agg.* vulcanico
volcano [vəl'keɪnɒʊ] *s.* vulcano *m.*
volley ['vəlɪ] *s.* **1** raffica *f.*, scarica *f.* **2** (*sport*) colpo *m.* al volo, volée *f. inv.*
volleyball ['vəlɪbɜːl] *s.* pallavolo *f.*
volt [vɒʊlt] *s.* volt *m. inv.*
voltage ['vɒʊltɪdʒ] *s.* voltaggio *m.*
voluble ['vəljʊbl] *agg.* **1** loquace **2** (*bot.*) volubile
volume ['vəljʊm] *s.* volume *m.*
voluminous [və'ljuːmɪnəs] *agg.* voluminoso
voluntary ['vələnt(ə)rɪ] *agg.* volontario
volunteer [ˌvələn'tɪər] **A** *agg.* **1** volontario **2** (*bot.*) spontaneo **B** *s.* volontario *m.*
to volunteer [ˌvələn'tɪər] *v. intr.* **1** arruolarsi volontario **2** offrirsi volontariamente
voluptuous [və'lʌptjʊəs] *agg.* voluttuoso
volute [və'ljuːt] *s.* voluta *f.*
vomit ['vəmɪt] *s.* vomito *m.*
to vomit ['vəmɪt] *v. tr. e intr.* vomitare
vortex ['vɜːtɛks] *s.* vortice *m.*
vote [vɒʊt] *s.* voto *m.*
to vote [vɒʊt] *v. tr. e intr.* votare ♦ **to v. down** respingere (con votazione); **to v. in** eleggere; **to v. out** destituire (con votazione)
voter ['vɒʊtər] *s.* elettore *m.*
voting ['vɒʊtɪŋ] *s.* votazione *f.*
votive ['vɒʊtɪv] *agg.* votivo
to vouch [vaʊtʃ] *v. intr.* garantire
voucher ['vaʊtʃər] *s.* **1** (*dir.*) garante *m.* **2** documento *m.* giustificativo **3** buono *m.*, voucher *m. inv.*
vow [vaʊ] *s.* voto *m.*, promessa *f.* solenne
to vow [vaʊ] *v. tr.* **1** fare voto di, promettere solennemente **2** votare, consacrare
vowel ['vaʊ(ə)l] *s.* vocale *f.*
voyage [vəɪdʒ] *s.* viaggio *m.*, traversata *f.*
voyager ['vəɪədʒər] *s.* viaggiatore *m.*, passeggero *m.*
vulgar ['vʌlgər] *agg.* volgare
vulgarity [vʌl'gærɪtɪ] *s.* volgarità *f.*
vulnerable ['vʌln(ə)rəbl] *agg.* vulnerabile
vulture ['vʌltʃər] *s.* avvoltoio *m.*

W

wad [wɔd] *s.* **1** batuffolo *m.*, tampone *m.* **2** rotolo *m.*, fascio *m.*
to wad [wɔd] *v. tr.* **1** tamponare **2** foderare
to waddle ['wɔdl] *v. intr.* camminare ondeggiando
to wade [weɪd] **A** *v. intr.* **1** passare a guado **2** procedere a stento **B** *v. tr.* guadare
wader ['weɪdəʳ] *s.* **1** (*zool.*) trampoliere *m.* **2** *al pl.* stivaloni *m. pl.* impermeabili
wafer ['weɪfəʳ] *s.* cialda *f.*
to waffle ['wɔfl] *v. intr.* (*fam.*) cianciare, sbrodolare
to waft [wa:ft] **A** *v. tr.* spargere, diffondere **B** *v. intr.* spandersi, diffondersi
to wag [wæg] **A** *v. tr.* scuotere, agitare, dimenare **B** *v. intr.* scuotersi, agitarsi, dimenarsi
wage [weɪdʒ] *s.* paga *f.*, salario *m.*
to wage [weɪdʒ] *v. tr.* **1** intraprendere, condurre **2** retribuire ♦ **to w. war** muovere guerra
to waggle ['wægl] *v. tr.* (*fam.*) agitare, dimenare, scuotere
wag(g)on ['wægən] *s.* **1** carro *m.* **2** vagone *m.*
wail [weɪl] *s.* gemito *m.*, lamento *m.*
to wail [weɪl] *v. intr.* gemere, lamentarsi
waist [weɪst] *s.* **1** vita *f.*, cintola *f.* **2** strozzatura *f.*
waistcoat ['weɪskɒʊt] *s.* panciotto *m.*
waistline ['weɪstlaɪn] *s.* giro *m.* vita
wait [weɪt] *s.* **1** attesa *f.* **2** agguato *m.*, imboscata *f.*
to wait [weɪt] **A** *v. intr.* **1** aspettare **2** rimanere in sospeso **3** (*a tavola*) servire **B** *v. tr.* **1** aspettare **2** ritardare, rinviare ♦ **to w. and see** stare a vedere; **to w. behind** rimanere, fermarsi; **to w. for sb.** aspettare qc.; **to w. on** servire; **to w. up** rimanere alzato
waiter ['weɪtəʳ] *s.* cameriere *m.*
waiting ['weɪtɪŋ] *s.* **1** attesa *f.* **2** servizio *m.* ♦ **no w.** divieto di sosta; **w. list** lista di attesa; **w. room** sala d'aspetto
waitress ['weɪtrɪs] *s.* cameriera *f.*
to waive [weɪv] *v. tr.* rinunciare a
wake (1) [weɪk] *s.* **1** veglia *f.* **2** vigilia *f.*
wake (2) [weɪk] *s.* scia *f.*
to wake [weɪk] (*pass.* **woke**, **waked**, *p. p.* **waked, woke, woken**) **A** *v. intr.* **1** svegliarsi, destarsi **2** fare la veglia **B** *v. tr.* **1** svegliare **2** ridestare, rianimare **3** vegliare
to waken ['weɪk(ə)n] *v. tr. e intr.* svegliare, svegliarsi
walk [wɜ:k] *s.* **1** camminata *f.*, passeggiata *f.* **2** percorso *m.* **3** andatura *f.*, passo *m.* **4** sentiero *m.*, viale *m.*
to walk [wɜ:k] **A** *v. intr.* camminare, passeggiare **B** *v. tr.* **1** percorrere a piedi **2** far camminare **3** accompagnare ♦ **to w. away from** uscire incolume da, distanziare; **to w. in** entrare; **to w. out** uscire, scioperare, abbandonare per protesta; **to w. out on** piantare in asso; **to w. over** sconfiggere, sbaragliare; **to w. up** salire (a piedi)
walker ['wɜ:kəʳ] *s.* camminatore *m.*, pedone *m.*
walkie-talkie [,wɜ:kɪ'tɜ:kɪ] *s.* walkie-talkie *m. inv.*
walking ['wɜ:kɪŋ] **A** *agg.* **1** che cammina **2** da passeggio **3** a piedi **B** *s.* il camminare ♦ **w. stick** bastone da passeggio; **w. tour** escursione a piedi
walk-on ['wɜ:k,ən] *s.* (*cine., teatro*) comparsa *f.*, figurante *m.*
walkout ['wɜ:k,aʊt] *s.* (*fam.*) sciopero *m.*
walkway ['wɜ:kweɪ] *s.* passaggio *m.* pedonale
wall [wɜ:l] *s.* **1** muro *m.*, parete *f.* **2** *al pl.* mura *f. pl.*
to wall [wɜ:l] *v. tr.* cintare, cingere di mura
wallet ['wəlɪt] *s.* portafoglio *m.*
wallflower ['wɜ:l,flaʊəʳ] *s.* violacciocca *f.* ♦ **to be a w.** (*fam.*) fare da tappezzeria
wallop ['wələp] *s.* (*fam.*) bastonata *f.*, percossa *f.*
to wallop ['wələp] *s.* (*fam.*) percuotere
to wallow ['wəlɒʊ] *v. intr.* sguazzare, voltolarsi
wallpaper ['wɜ:l,peɪpəʳ] *s.* carta *f.* da parati
wally ['wəlɪ] *agg.* (*fam.*) scemo
walnut ['wɜ:lnət] *s.* noce *f. e m.*
walrus ['wɜ:lrəs] *s.* tricheco *m.*
waltz [wɜ:ls] *s.* valzer *m. inv.*
to waltz [wɜ:ls] *v. intr.* ballare il valzer
wan [wən] *agg.* pallido, esangue
wand [wənd] *s.* bacchetta *f.*

to wander ['wɒndəʳ] **A** *v. intr.* **1** vagare, girovagare **2** deviare, scostarsi **3** delirare **B** *v. tr.* vagare per
wandering ['wɒnd(ə)rɪŋ] **A** *agg.* **1** errante, nomade **2** tortuoso, serpeggiante **3** delirante **B** *s.* **1** vagabondaggio *m.*, peregrinazione *f.* **2** smarrimento *m.* **3** vaneggiamento *m.*
wane [weɪn] *s.* declino *m.*
to wane [weɪn] *v. intr.* calare, declinare
wangle ['wæŋgl] *s.* (*pop.*) imbroglio *m.*
to wangle ['wæŋgl] *v. tr.* (*pop.*) procurarsi con l'inganno
want [wɒnt] *s.* **1** bisogno *m.*, necessità *f.* **2** mancanza *f.*, scarsità *f.* **3** indigenza *f.*
to want [wɒnt] **A** *v. tr.* **1** volere, desiderare **2** aver bisogno di **3** ricercare **4** (*fam.*) dovere **B** *v. intr.* mancare ♦ **to w. for** esser privo di; **what do you w.?** cosa ti serve?, cosa vuoi?
wanted ['wɒntɪd] *agg.* **1** (*dir.*) ricercato **2** richiesto **3** (*negli annunci*) cercasi
wanting ['wɒntɪŋ] *agg.* mancante, carente
wanton ['wɒntən] *agg.* **1** sfrenato, sregolato **2** arbitrario, immotivato **3** licenzioso, scostumato
war [wɜːʳ] **A** *s.* guerra *f.* **B** *agg. attr.* bellico, di guerra ♦ **to be at w. with** essere in guerra con; **to wage w. upon** muovere guerra a
ward [wɔːd] *s.* **1** (*dir.*) tutela *f.*, custodia *f.* **2** (*dir.*) persona *f.* sotto tutela, pupillo *m.* **3** reparto *m.*, corsia *f.* **4** circoscrizione *f.*
warden ['wɔːdn] *s.* **1** guardiano *m.* **2** sovrintendente *m. e f.*, direttore *m.*
warder ['wɔːdəʳ] *s.* carceriere *m.*
wardrobe ['wɔːdrəʊb] *s.* guardaroba *m. inv.*
ware [wɛəʳ] *s.* articoli *m. pl.*, merce *f.*
warehouse ['wɛəhaʊs] *s.* magazzino *m.*
warfare ['wɔːfɛəʳ] *s.* guerra *f.*
warhead ['wɔːhɛd] *s.* (*mil.*) testata *f.*
warlike ['wɔːlaɪk] *agg.* bellico, guerriero
warm [wɔːm] *agg.* **1** caldo **2** caloroso, cordiale ♦ **to be w.** avere caldo, far caldo
to warm [wɔːm] **A** *v. tr.* **1** scaldare, riscaldare **2** animare **B** *v. intr.* **1** scaldarsi, riscaldarsi **2** animarsi
warm-blooded [ˌwɔːm'blʌdɪd] *agg.* a sangue caldo
warm-hearted [ˌwɔːm'hɑːtɪd] *agg.* affettuoso
warmonger ['wɔːˌmʌŋgəʳ] *s.* guerrafondaio *m.*
warmth [wɔːmθ] *s.* calore *m.*
to warn [wɔːn] *v. tr.* **1** avvertire, ammonire **2** (*dir.*) diffidare
warning ['wɔːnɪŋ] **A** *agg.* **1** di avvertimento **2** ammonitore **B** *s.* **1** avvertimento *m.*, preavviso *m.* **2** avviso *m.*, allarme *m.* **3** (*dir.*) diffida *f.* ♦ **w. light** spia luminosa
warp [wɔːp] *s.* **1** ordito *m.* **2** curvatura *f.*, deformazione *f.*
to warp [wɔːp] **A** *v. tr.* **1** curvare, distorcere, deformare **2** guastare **B** *v. intr.* **1** curvarsi, distorcersi, deformarsi **2** guastarsi
warrant ['wɒr(ə)nt] *s.* mandato *m.*, ordine *m.* ♦ **search w.** mandato di perquisizione
to warrant ['wɒr(ə)nt] *v. tr.* **1** garantire **2** autorizzare
warranty ['wɒr(ə)ntɪ] *s.* garanzia *f.*
warren ['wɒrɪn] *s.* conigliera *f.*
warrior ['wɒrɪəʳ] *s.* guerriero *m.*
warship ['wɔːʃɪp] *s.* nave *f.* da guerra
wart [wɔːt] *s.* verruca *f.*
wartime ['wɔːtaɪm] *s.* tempo *m.* di guerra
wary ['wɛərɪ] *agg.* cauto, diffidente
was [wəz, wɒz] *1ª e 3ª sing. pass. di* **to be**
wash [wɒʃ] *s.* **1** lavaggio *m.*, lavata *f.* **2** bucato *m.* **3** sciabordio *m.* **4** (*di nave*) scia *f.*
to wash [wɒʃ] **A** *v. tr.* **1** lavare **2** bagnare, spruzzare **B** *v. intr.* lavarsi ♦ **to w. away/off** togliere lavando; **to w. down** lavare con un getto d'acqua; **to w. up** lavare i piatti
washable ['wɒʃəbl] *agg.* lavabile
washbasin ['wɒʃˌbeɪsn] *s.* lavandino *m.*
washer ['wɒʃəʳ] *s.* (*mecc.*) rondella *f.*
washing ['wɒʃɪŋ] *s.* **1** lavaggio *m.* **2** bucato *m.* ♦ **w. machine** lavabiancheria; **w. powder** detersivo in polvere
washout [ˌwɒʃ'aʊt] *s.* (*fam.*) fiasco *m.*, fallimento *m.*
washroom ['wɒʃruːm] *s.* **1** gabinetto *m.* **2** lavanderia *f.*
wasp [wɒsp] *s.* vespa *f.*
wastage ['weɪstɪdʒ] *s.* **1** spreco *m.* **2** scarti *m. pl.* **3** diminuzione *f.*, calo *m.*
waste [weɪst] **A** *agg.* **1** deserto, incolto **2** di scarto, di rifiuto **3** di scarico, di scolo **B** *s.* **1** perdita *f.*, spreco *m.* **2** scarto *m.*, rifiuti *m. pl.*, scorie *f. pl.* **3** terreno *m.* incolto, deserto *m.* ♦ **radioactive w.** scorie radioattive; **w. pipes** tubazioni di scarico
to waste [weɪst] **A** *v. tr.* **1** sciupare, sprecare, dissipare **2** devastare, rovinare **B** *v.*

intr. consumarsi, logorarsi ♦ **to w. away** deperire
wasteful ['weɪstf(ʊ)l] *agg.* **1** sprecone **2** dispendioso **3** superfluo
wastepaper ['weɪstˌpeɪpəʳ] *s.* carta *f.* straccia ♦ **w. basket** cestino per la carta straccia
watch [wətʃ] *s.* **1** orologio *m.* (da polso) **2** guardia *f.*, ronda *f.*, sorveglianza *f.* **3** (*naut.*) turno *m.* di guardia, quarto *m.*
to **watch** [wətʃ] **A** *v. tr.* **1** osservare, guardare **2** sorvegliare, badare a, fare attenzione a **B** *v. intr.* **1** stare a guardare, osservare **2** stare in guardia, vigilare ♦ **to w. out** stare in guardia; **to w. over** vegliare su
watchdog ['wətʃdəg] *s.* cane *m.* da guardia
watchful ['wətʃf(ʊ)l] *agg.* vigile
watchmaker ['wətʃˌmeɪkəʳ] *s.* orologiaio *m.*
watchman ['wətʃmən] (*pl.* **watchmen**) *s.* sorvegliante *m.*, guardiano *m.*
watchstrap ['wətʃˌstræp] *s.* cinturino *m.* (dell'orologio)
water ['wɜːtəʳ] *s.* acqua *f.* ♦ **drinking w.** acqua potabile; **high/low w.** alta/bassa marea; **mineral w.** acqua minerale; **plane w.** (*USA*) acqua naturale; **running w.** acqua corrente; **shallow w.** bassofondo; **w. cannon** idrante; **w. gate** chiusa; **w. heater** scaldabagno; **w. lily** ninfea; **w. polo** pallanuoto; **w. skiing** sci nautico
to **water** ['wɜːtəʳ] **A** *v. tr.* **1** annaffiare, irrigare **2** annacquare **3** abbeverare **B** *v. intr.* **1** abbeverarsi **2** rifornirsi d'acqua **3** lacrimare ♦ **to w. down** allungare, diluire
watercolour ['wɜːtəˌkʌləʳ] *s.* acquerello *m.*
watercolourist ['wɜːtəˌkʌlərɪst] *s.* acquerellista *m. e f.*
waterfall ['wɜːtəfɜːl] *s.* cascata *f.*
watering ['wɜːtərɪŋ] *s.* **1** annaffiamento *m.*, irrigazione *f.* **2** diluizione *f.* **3** rifornimento *m.* d'acqua ♦ **w. can** annaffiatoio
waterline ['wɜːtəlaɪn] *s.* (*naut.*) linea *f.* di galleggiamento
to **waterlog** ['wɜːtərləg] *v. tr.* impregnare, imbevere
watermelon ['wɜːtəˌmɛlən] *s.* cocomero *m.*
waterproof ['wɜːtəpruːf] *agg.* impermeabile
watershed ['wɜːtəʃəd] *s.* spartiacque *m. inv.*
watertight ['wɜːtətaɪt] *agg.* stagno, a tenuta d'acqua
waterway ['wɜːtəweɪ] *s.* canale *m.*, via *f.* d'acqua
waterworks ['wɜːtəwɜːks] *s. pl.* acquedotto *m.*, impianto *m.* idrico
watery ['wɜːtərɪ] *agg.* **1** acquoso **2** lacrimoso **3** insipido **4** slavato
watt [wət] *s.* watt *m. inv.*
wave [weɪv] *s.* **1** onda *f.*, ondata *f.* **2** ondulazione *f.* **3** cenno *m.*, gesto *m.*
to **wave** [weɪv] **A** *v. tr.* **1** ondeggiare, sventolare **2** fare un cenno (con la mano) **3** essere ondulato **B** *v. tr.* **1** agitare, brandire, sventolare **2** fare segno di **3** ondulare
wavefront ['weɪvfrʌnt] *s.* fronte *m.* d'onda
wavelength ['weɪvlɛŋ(k)θ] *s.* lunghezza *f.* d'onda
to **waver** ['weɪvəʳ] *v. intr.* **1** oscillare, vacillare **2** esitare, tentennare
wavy ['weɪvɪ] *agg.* **1** ondulato **2** ondeggiante
wax [wæks] *s.* cera *f.*
to **wax (1)** [wæks] *v. tr.* dare la cera a
to **wax (2)** [wæks] *v. intr.* **1** (*della luna*) crescere **2** divenire, farsi
waxwork ['wæksˌwɜːk] *s.* **1** modello *m.* di cera, statua *f.* di cera **2** *al pl.* museo *m.* delle cere
way [weɪ] *s.* **1** via *f.*, strada *f.*, passaggio *m.*, percorso *m.*, cammino *m.* **2** maniera *f.*, modo *m.* **3** direzione *f.*, lato *m.* **4** abitudine *f.* **5** punto *m.* di vista, aspetto *m.* **6** condizione *f.*, stato *m.* ♦ **by the w.** a proposito, incidentalmente; **by w. of** via, passando per, a titolo di, invece di; **out of the w.** insolito, fuori mano; **in the wrong w.** in senso contrario; **w. in** entrata; **w. out** uscita
wayfarer ['weɪˌfɛərəʳ] *s.* viandante *m. e f.*
to **waylay** [weɪ'leɪ] (*pass. e p. p.* **waylaid**) *v. tr.* tendere un agguato a, attendere al varco
wayward ['weɪwəd] *agg.* **1** caparbio **2** capriccioso
wc [ˌdʌb(ə)ljuː'sɪ] *s.* gabinetto *m.*, wc *m. inv.*
we [wɪ(ː)] *pron. pers. 1ª pl.* noi
weak [wiːk] *agg.* **1** debole **2** diluito, leggero **3** tenue
to **weaken** ['wiːk(ə)n] *v. tr. e intr.* indebolire, indebolirsi
weakness ['wiːknɪs] *s.* **1** debolezza *f.* **2** lato *m.* debole
wealth [wɛlθ] *s.* **1** ricchezza *f.* **2** abbondanza *f.*

wealthy ['wɛlθɪ] *agg.* ricco
to wean [wiːn] *v. tr.* **1** svezzare **2** disabituare
weaning ['wiːnɪŋ] *s.* svezzamento *m.*
weapon ['wɛpən] *s.* arma *f.*
wear [wɛəʳ] *s.* **1** uso *m.* **2** consumo *m.*, logorio *m.* **3** durata *f.*, resistenza *f.* all'uso **4** abbigliamento *m.*
to wear [wɛəʳ] (*pass.* **wore**, *p. p.* **worn**) **A** *v. tr.* **1** indossare, portare **2** consumare **B** *v. intr.* **1** consumarsi, logorarsi **2** durare ♦ **to w. away** consumare, logorare; **to w. down** consumare, logorare, fiaccare; **to w. off** consumarsi, sparire lentamente; **to w. out** logorare, esaurire
weariness ['wɪərɪnɪs] *s.* stanchezza *f.*, fiacca *f.*
weary ['wɪərɪ] *agg.* **1** stanco **2** annoiato **3** stancante, estenuante
to weary ['wɪərɪ] *v. tr. e intr.* stancare, stancarsi
weasel ['wɪzl] *s.* donnola *f.*
weather ['wɛðəʳ] **A** *s.* tempo *m.* (atmosferico) **B** *agg. attr.* del tempo, meteorologico ♦ **bad/fine w.** tempo cattivo/buono; **w. forecast** previsioni del tempo
to weather ['wɛðəʳ] *v. tr.* **1** alterare, consumare **2** esporre all'aria **3** superare **4** (*naut.*) doppiare
weather-beaten ['wɛðə,biːtn] *agg.* esposto alle intemperie
weathercock ['wɛðəkək] *s.* banderuola *f.*
to weave [wiːv] (*pass.* **wove**, *p. p.* **woven**) *v. tr.* **1** tessere **2** intrecciare, ordire
weaver ['wiːvəʳ] *s.* tessitore *m.*
weaving ['wiːvɪŋ] *s.* tessitura *f.*
web [wɛb] *s.* **1** tela *f.*, trama *f.* **2** ragnatela *f.*
to wed [wɛd] (*pass. e p. p.* **wedded**) *v. tr. e intr.* sposare, sposarsi
wedding ['wɛdɪŋ] *s.* matrimonio *m.*, nozze *f. pl.* ♦ **w. dress** abito da sposa; **w. list** lista di nozze; **w. ring** fede
wedge [wɛdʒ] *s.* zeppa *f.*
Wednesday ['wɛnzdɪ] *s.* mercoledì *m.*
wee [wiː] *agg.* (*fam.*) minuscolo
weed [wiːd] *s.* erbaccia *f.*
weed-killer ['wiːd,kɪlə] *s.* diserbante *m.*
weedy ['wiːdɪ] *agg.* **1** coperto di erbacce **2** allampanato
week [wiːk] *s.* settimana *f.* ♦ **last w.** la settimana scorsa; **next w.** la settimana prossima; **today w.** fra otto giorni
weekday ['wiːkdeɪ] *s.* giorno *m.* feriale
weekend [,wiːk'ɛnd] *s.* weekend *m. inv.*, fine settimana *m. inv.*
weekly ['wiːklɪ] **A** *agg. e s.* settimanale *m.* **B** *avv.* settimanalmente
to weep [wiːp] (*pass. e p. p.* **wept**) *v. tr. e intr.* **1** piangere **2** stillare, trasudare
weeping ['wiːpɪŋ] **A** *agg.* **1** piangente **2** trasudante **B** *s.* pianto *m.* ♦ **w. willow** salice piangente
weft [wɛft] *s.* (*tess.*) trama *f.*
to weigh [weɪ] **A** *v. tr.* **1** pesare **2** soppesare, valutare **B** *v. intr.* **1** pesare **2** incidere, avere peso ♦ **to w. anchor** salpare; **to w. down** piegare; **to w. in** pesarsi; **to w. up** soppesare
weight [weɪt] *s.* peso *m.* ♦ **net/gross w.** peso netto/lordo; **to lose w.** dimagrire; **to put on w.** ingrassare; **w. lifting** sollevamento pesi
weighting [weɪtɪŋ] *s.* aggiunta *f.*, maggiorazione *f.*
weighty ['weɪtɪ] *agg.* pesante, gravoso
weir [wɪəʳ] *s.* chiusa *f.*, sbarramento *m.*
weird [wɪəd] *agg.* **1** soprannaturale, magico **2** strano
welcome ['wɛlkəm] **A** *agg.* gradito **B** *s.* benvenuto *m.*, accoglienza *f.* **C** *inter.* benvenuto ♦ **you're w.!** prego!
to welcome ['wɛlkəm] *v. tr.* **1** accogliere, dare il benvenuto **2** accettare, gradire
weld [wɛld] *s.* saldatura *f.*
to weld [wɛld] *v. tr. e intr.* saldare, saldarsi
welder ['wɛldəʳ] *s.* saldatore *m.*, saldatrice *f.*
welding ['wɛldɪŋ] *s.* saldatura *f.*
welfare ['wɛlfɛəʳ] *s.* **1** benessere *m.*, prosperità *f.* **2** sussidio *m.* ♦ **w. state** stato assistenziale; **w. work** assistenza sociale
well (1) [wɛl] *s.* **1** pozzo *m.* **2** fonte *f.*, sorgente *f.* **3** tromba *f.* delle scale
well (2) [wɛl] (*comp.* **better**, *sup.* **best**) **A** *avv.* bene **B** *agg.* **1** sano **2** opportuno, consigliabile **3** bello, buono **C** *inter.* dunque, ebbene, allora ♦ **as w.** anche; **as w. as** come pure; **very w.** ottimamente; **w. done!** ben fatto!, bravo!
well-advised [,wɛləd'vaɪzd] *agg.* saggio
well-behaved [,wɛlbɪ'heɪvd] *agg.* beneducato
well-being ['wɛl,biːɪŋ] *s.* benessere *m.*
well-dressed [,wɛl'drɛst] *agg.* ben vestito
well-heeled [,wɛl'hiːld] *agg.* (*fam.*) ricco
well-known [,wɛl'nɒʊn] *agg.* noto
well-meaning [,wɛl'miːnɪŋ] *agg.* ben intenzionato

well-nigh ['wɛlnaɪ] *avv.* quasi
well-off [ˌwɛl'ɜːf] *agg.* **1** benestante **2** ben fornito
well-read [ˌwɛl'rɛd] *agg.* colto
well-timed [ˌwɛl'taɪmd] *agg.* tempestivo
well-to-do [ˌwɛltə'duː] *agg.* (*fam.*) ricco
well-wisher [ˌwɛl'wɪʃəʳ] *s.* fautore *m.*
Welsh [wɛlʃ] *agg. e s.* gallese *m.*
went [wɛnt] *pass. di* **to go**
wept [wɛpt] *pass. e p. p. di* **to weep**
were [wɜːʳ, wəʳ] **1** *2ª sing. e 1ª, 2ª, 3ª pl. pass. di* **to be** **2** *congiuntivo pass. di* **to be**
west [wɛst] **A** *s.* ovest *m. inv.*, occidente *m.*, ponente *m.* **B** *agg.* occidentale **C** *avv.* verso ovest, da ovest
westerly ['wɛstəlɪ] *agg.* occidentale, da ovest
western ['wɛstən] **A** *agg.* occidentale, dell'ovest **B** *s.* western *m. inv.*
westwards ['wɛstwədz] **A** *agg.* occidentale **B** *avv.* verso occidente
wet [wɛt] **A** *agg.* **1** bagnato, umido, fradicio **2** piovoso **3** (*di vernice*) non asciutto, fresco **B** *s.* umidità *f.*, pioggia *f.* ♦ **w. blanket** (*fam.*) guastafeste; **w. dock** darsena; **w. suit** muta da sub
to wet [wɛt] (*pass. e p. p.* **wet, wetted**) *v. tr.* bagnare, inumidire, inzuppare
to whack [wæk] *v. tr.* battere, picchiare
whale [weɪl] *s.* balena *f.*
whaler ['weɪləʳ] *s.* **1** baleniere *m.* **2** baleniera *f.*
whaling ['weɪlɪŋ] *s.* caccia *f.* alla balena
wharf [wɜːf] *s.* pontile *m.*, banchina *f.*
what [wɔt] **A** *agg.* **1** (*interr.*) quale?, quali?, che? **2** (*rel.*) quello che, quella che, quelli che, quelle che **3** (*escl.*) che! **B** *pron.* **1** (*interr.*) che?, che cosa?, quale? **2** (*rel.*) ciò che **3** (*escl.*) quanto come! **C** *inter.* come! ♦ **w. for?** perché?; **w. a lot (of) ...** quanti ...!; **w. is more** peraltro
whatever [wɔt'ɛvəʳ] **A** *agg. indef.* **1** qualunque, qualsiasi **2** (*enf.*) alcuno, di sorta, affatto **B** *pron. indef.* qualunque cosa, qualsiasi cosa, ciò che, quello che
wheat [wiːt] *s.* frumento *m.*, grano *m.*
to wheedle ['wiːdl] *v. tr.* **1** adulare **2** ottenere con lusinghe
wheel [wiːl] *s.* **1** ruota *f.* **2** volante *m.*, ruota *f.* del timone ♦ **spare w.** ruota di scorta; **w. clamp** ceppo (*per auto in sosta vietata*)
to wheel [wiːl] **A** *v. tr.* **1** spingere, tirare **2** far girare, roteare **B** *v. intr.* **1** girare, ruotare, roteare **2** girarsi **3** fare un voltafaccia **4** (*fam.*) andare in bicicletta
wheelbarrow ['wiːlˌbærɒʊ] *s.* carriola *f.*
wheelchair ['wiːlˌtʃɛəʳ] *s.* sedia *f.* a rotelle
to wheeze [wiːz] *v. intr.* ansimare
when [wɛn] **A** *avv.* **1** (*interr.*) quando? **2** (*rel.*) in cui **B** *cong.* **1** quando, nel momento in cui **2** sebbene **3** quando, qualora
whenever [wɛn'ɛvəʳ] *avv. e cong.* **1** ogni qualvolta, ogni volta che, quando **2** una volta che, quando
where [wɛəʳ] **A** *avv.* **1** (*interr.*) dove? **2** dove, nel luogo in cui **B** *cong.* dove
whereabout(s) [ˌwɛərə'baʊt(s)] **A** *avv.* (*interr.*) dove?, da che parte? **B** *cong.* dove **C** *s.* luogo *m.*
whereas [wɛər'æz] *cong.* **1** dal momento che, siccome **2** (*avversativo*) mentre
whereby [wɛə'baɪ] *avv.* **1** (*interr.*) come?, in che modo? per mezzo di che cosa? **2** (*rel.*) con cui, per mezzo di cui, per cui
whereupon [ˌwɛərə'pɔn] *cong.* dopo di che, al che
wherever [wɛər'ɛvəʳ] **A** *avv.* **1** (*interr.*) dove (mai)? **2** in qualsiasi posto **B** *cong.* dovunque
wherewithal ['wɛəwɪðɜːl] *s.* l'occorrente *m.*, mezzi *m. pl.*
to whet [wɛt] *v. tr.* **1** affilare **2** aguzzare, stimolare
whether ['wɛðəʳ] *cong.* **1** (*dubitativo*) se **2** (*avversativo*) **w. ... or** o ... o
whey [weɪ] *s.* siero *m.* (del latte)
which [wɪtʃ] **A** *agg.* **1** (*interr.*) quale?, quali? **2** (*rel.*) il quale, la quale, i quali, le quali **B** *pron.* **1** (*interr.*) chi?, quale?, quali? **2** (*rel.*) il quale, la quale, i quali, le quali, che
whichever [wɪtʃ'ɛvəʳ] **A** *agg. indef.* qualunque, qualsiasi **B** *pron. indef.* chiunque, qualunque cosa
whiff [wɪf] *s.* **1** soffio *m.*, sbuffo *m.* **2** zaffata *f.*
while [waɪl] **A** *cong.* **1** mentre, intanto che **2** sebbene, quantunque **3** (*avversativo*) mentre **B** *s.* momento *m.*
to while [waɪl] *v. tr.* **to w. away** far passare piacevolmente (il tempo)
whim [wɪm] *s.* capriccio *m.*
whimper ['wɪmpəʳ] *s.* **1** piagnucolio *m.* **2** pigolio *m.*, uggiolio *m.*
to whimper ['wɪmpəʳ] *v. intr.* **1** piagnucolare **2** pigolare, uggiolare
whimsical ['wɪmzɪk(ə)l] *agg.* stravagante, capriccioso

whine [waɪn] *s.* **1** uggiolio *m.* **2** gemito *m.*, lamento *m.* **3** piagnucolio *m.*
to whine [waɪn] *v. intr.* **1** uggiolare **2** gemere, lamentarsi **3** piagnucolare
whinny ['wɪnɪ] *s.* nitrito *m.*
whip [wɪp] *s.* frusta *f.*
to whip [wɪp] *v. tr.* **1** frustare, battere **2** (*cuc.*) sbattere, montare, frullare ♦ **whipped cream** panna montata
whirl [wɜːl] *s.* **1** vortice *m.* **2** turbinio *m.* ♦ **w. wind** tromba d'aria
whirlpool ['wɜːlpuːl] *s.* vortice *m.*, mulinello *m.*
to whirr [wɜːʳ] *v. intr.* **1** ronzare **2** rombare
whisk [wɪsk] *s.* (*cuc.*) frusta *f.*, frullino *m.*
to whisk [wɪsk] *v. tr.* (*cuc.*) frullare, sbattere
whisker ['wɪskəʳ] *s.* **1** basetta *f.* **2** baffo *f.* di gatto
whisky ['wɪskɪ] (*USA*, *Irlanda* **whiskey**) *s.* whisky *m. inv.*
whisper ['wɪspəʳ] *s.* bisbiglio *m.*, sussurro *m.*
to whisper ['wɪspəʳ] *v. tr.* bisbigliare, sussurrare
whistle ['wɪsl] *s.* **1** fischio *m.* **2** fischietto *m.*
to whistle ['wɪsl] *v. tr. e intr.* fischiare
white [waɪt] *agg. e s.* bianco *m.* ♦ **w. coffee** caffellatte; **w. hot** incandescente
whiteness ['waɪtnɪs] *s.* **1** bianchezza *f.* **2** pallore *m.*
whitewash ['waɪtwɒʃ] *s.* (bianco di) calce *f.*
Whitsunday [ˌwɪt'sʌndɪ] *s.* pentecoste *f.*
to whittle ['wɪtl] *v. tr.* tagliuzzare ♦ **to w. away/down** ridurre
whizz [wɪz] *s.* **1** ronzio *m.* **2** (*fam.*) genio *m.*, mago *m.*
who [huː, hʊ] *pron. sogg.* **1** (*interr.*) chi? **2** (*rel.*) chi, che, il quale, la quale, i quali, le quali ♦ **w. knows** chissà
whoever [huː'ɛvəʳ] *pron.* **1** (*rel. indef.*) chiunque, chi **2** (*interr.*) chi mai?
whole [hɒʊl] **A** *agg.* **1** intero, tutto **2** integro, incolume **B** *s.* il complesso *m.*, l'insieme *m.*, il tutto *m.*
wholefood ['hɒʊlfuːd] *s.* cibo *m.* integrale
whole-hearted [ˌhɒʊl'haːtɪd] *agg.* cordiale, generoso
wholemeal ['hɒʊlmiːl] *agg.* integrale
wholesale ['hɒʊlseɪl] **A** *agg.* all'ingrosso **B** *s.* vendita *f.* all'ingrosso
wholesaler ['hɒʊlˌseɪləʳ] *s.* grossista *m.*
wholesome ['hɒʊlsəm] *agg.* salubre, salutare
wholly ['hɒʊllɪ] *avv.* completamente
whom [huːm] *pron. compl. ogg. e ind.* **1** (*interr.*) chi? **2** (*rel.*) che, il quale, la quale, i quali, le quali
whooping-cough ['huːpɪŋkəf] *s.* pertosse *f.*
whore [hɜːʳ] *s.* (*volg.*) puttana *f.*
whose [huːz] *pron.* **1** (*interr.*) di chi? **2** (*rel.*) di cui, del quale, della quale, dei quali, delle quali
why [waɪ] **A** *avv.* **1** (*interr.*) perché **2** (*rel.*) per cui **B** *cong.* perché, per quale ragione **C** *inter.* ma come! ma via!
wick [wɪk] *s.* stoppino *m.*
wicked ['wɪkɪd] *agg.* **1** cattivo **2** peccaminoso
wickedness ['wɪkɪdnɪs] *s.* cattiveria *f.*
wicker ['wɪkəʳ] **A** *s.* vimine *m.* **B** *agg.* di vimini
wide [waɪd] **A** *agg.* **1** ampio, largo **2** spalancato **3** lontano, fuori segno **B** *avv.* **1** largamente, in largo **2** completamente **3** fuori segno, a vuoto ♦ **w. angle** grandangolo
wide-awake [ˌwaɪdə'weɪk] *agg.* perfettamente sveglio
widely ['waɪdlɪ] *avv.* ampiamente, molto
to widen ['waɪdn] *v. tr. e intr.* allargare, allargarsi
widespread ['waɪdsprɛd] *agg.* diffuso
widget ['wɪdʒət] *s.* (*USA*) aggeggio *m.*
widow ['wɪdɒʊ] *s.* vedova *f.*
widower ['wɪdɒ(ʊ)əʳ] *s.* vedovo *m.*
width [wɪdθ] *s.* ampiezza *f.*, larghezza *f.*
to wield [wiːld] *v. tr.* **1** brandire **2** esercitare
wife [waɪf] *s.* moglie *f.*
wig [wɪg] *s.* parrucca *f.*
to wiggle ['wɪgl] *v. tr. e intr.* dimenare, dimenarsi
wild [waɪld] **A** *agg.* **1** feroce, selvaggio **2** selvatico **3** incolto **4** scompigliato, disordinato **5** agitato, tempestoso **6** furibondo, pazzo **7** sconclusionato **8** (*fam.*) strepitoso, eccellente **B** *s.* regione *f.* selvaggia **C** *avv.* senza freno, all'impazzata
wilderness ['wɪldənɪs] *s.* **1** deserto *m.* **2** regione *f.* selvaggia, riserva *f.* naturale
wildlife ['waɪldlaɪf] *s.* natura *f.*
wildly ['waɪldlɪ] *avv.* **1** selvaggiamente **2** violentemente **3** follemente
wilful ['wɪlf(ʊ)l] *agg.* **1** caparbio **2** premeditato
wilfulness ['wɪlf(ʊ)lnɪs] *s.* **1** caparbietà *f.*

2 premeditazione *f.*
will (1) [wɪl] *v. difett.* **1** (*ausiliare per la formazione del futuro semplice o volitivo*) (ES: **he w. be here by eight o'clock** sarà qui per le otto) **2** volere, desiderare (ES: **w. you have some more coffee?** vuoi dell'altro caffè?)
will (2) [wɪl] *s.* **1** volere *m.*, volontà *f.* **2** testamento *m.*
to will [wɪl] *v. tr.* **1** volere **2** costringere **3** lasciare (per testamento)
willing ['wɪlɪŋ] *agg.* volenteroso
willingly ['wɪlɪŋlɪ] *avv.* volentieri
willow ['wɪlɒʊ] *s.* salice *m.* ♦ **weeping w.** salice piangente
willpower ['wɪlpaʊəʳ] *s.* forza *f.* di volontà
willy-nilly [ˌwɪlɪ'nɪlɪ] *avv.* volente o nolente
to wilt [wɪlt] *v. intr.* appassire
wily ['waɪlɪ] *agg.* astuto
win [wɪn] *s.* vincita *f.*, vittoria *f.*
to win [wɪn] (*pass. e p. p.* **won**) *v. tr.* **1** vincere, battere **2** ottenere **3** persuadere ♦ **to w. out** trionfare; **to w. over** persuadere
winch [wɪntʃ] *s.* verricello *m.*
wind [wɪnd] *s.* **1** vento *m.* **2** respiro *m.*, fiato *m.* **3** sentore *m.* ♦ **w. instrument** strumento a fiato
to wind (1) [wɪnd] *v. tr.* **1** arieggiare **2** fiutare **3** sfiatare
to wind (2) [waɪnd] (*pass. e p. p.* **wound**) **A** *v. tr.* **1** avvolgere, attorcigliare **2** caricare, girare **B** *v. intr.* **1** serpeggiare **2** avvolgersi, attorcigliarsi ♦ **to w. up** avvolgere, arrotolare, (*orologio*) caricare, concludere
windfall ['wɪn(d)fɔːl] *s.* guadagno *m.* inatteso
winding ['waɪndɪŋ] **A** *agg.* **1** sinuoso, tortuoso **2** a chiocciola **B** *s.* **1** sinuosità *f.* **2** meandro *m.*
windmill ['wɪn(d)mɪl] *s.* **1** mulino *m.* a vento **2** mulinello *m.*, girandola *f.*
window ['wɪndɒʊ] *s.* **1** finestra *f.* **2** vetrina *f.* **3** sportello *m.* ♦ **w. pane** vetro (di finestra)
windowsill ['wɪndɒʊsɪl] *s.* davanzale *m.*
windpipe ['wɪn(d)paɪp] *s.* trachea *f.*
windscreen ['wɪn(d)ˌskriːn] *s.* parabrezza *m. inv.* ♦ **w. wiper** tergicristallo
windshield ['wɪndˌʃiːld] *s.* (*USA*) parabrezza *m. inv.*
windsurf ['wɪndsɜːf] *s.* windsurf *m. inv.*
windy ['wɪndɪ] *agg.* ventoso
wine [waɪn] *s.* vino *m.* ♦ **sparkling w.** spumante; **table w.** vino da pasto; **w. cellar** cantina
wing [wɪŋ] *s.* **1** ala *f.* **2** (*di porta*) battente *m.* **3** *al pl.* (*teatro*) quinte *f. pl.*
to wink [wɪŋk] *v. intr.* **1** ammiccare **2** lampeggiare
winner ['wɪnəʳ] *s.* vincitore *m.*
winning ['wɪnɪŋ] **A** *agg.* **1** vincente **2** avvincente **B** *s. solo pl.* vincite *f. pl.* (al gioco)
winter ['wɪntəʳ] **A** *s.* inverno *m.* **B** *agg. attr.* invernale
to winter ['wɪntəʳ] *v. intr.* svernare
wintry ['wɪntrɪ] *agg.* **1** invernale **2** freddo
to wipe [waɪp] *v. tr.* strofinare, asciugare, pulire ♦ **to w. off** cancellare; **to w. out** cancellare, estinguere, annullare; **to w. up** asciugare (con uno straccio)
wire ['waɪəʳ] *s.* **1** filo *m.* (metallico, elettrico), cavo *m.* **2** (*fam.*) telegramma *m.*
wireless ['waɪəlɪs] *agg. attr.* senza fili
wiring ['waɪərɪŋ] *s.* (*elettr*) impianto *m.*
wisdom ['wɪzdəm] *s.* saggezza *f.* ♦ **w. tooth** dente del giudizio
wise [waɪz] *agg.* previdente, saggio
wisecrack ['waɪzkræk] *s.* (*fam.*) spiritosaggine *f.*
wish [wɪʃ] *s.* **1** desiderio *m.* **2** augurio *m.* ♦ **best wishes** i migliori auguri
to wish [wɪʃ] *v. tr.* **1** desiderare **2** augurare
wishy-washy ['wɪʃɪˌwəʃɪ] *agg.* **1** brodoso, annacquato **2** insipido
wisp [wɪsp] *s.* ciuffo *m.*, fascio *m.*
wistaria [wɪs'tɛərɪə] *s.* glicine *m.*
wistful ['wɪstf(ʊ)l] *agg.* **1** desideroso **2** meditabondo
wit [wɪt] *s.* **1** brio *m.*, spirito *m.* **2** persona *f.* arguta
witch [wɪtʃ] *s.* strega *f.*
witchcraft ['wɪtʃkraːft] *s.* stregoneria *f.*
with [wɪð] *prep.* **1** (*compagnia*) con, insieme a **2** (*mezzo, modo*) con, per mezzo di **3** (*causa*) per, di, con, a causa di **4** riguardo a, quanto a
to withdraw [wɪð'drɔː] (*pass.* **withdrew**, *p. p.* **withdrawn**) **A** *v. tr.* **1** tirare indietro **2** ritirare, prelevare **3** ritrattare **B** *v. intr.* **1** ritirarsi, allontanarsi, indietreggiare **2** ritrattare
withdrawal [wɪð'drɔː(ə)l] *s.* **1** ritirata *f.*, ritiro *m.* **2** revoca *f.*, rinuncia *f.* **3** prelievo *m.* **4** ritrattazione *f.*
to wither ['wɪðəʳ] *v. intr.* appassire
to withhold [wɪð'hɒʊld] (*pass. e p. p.* **withheld**) *v. tr.* **1** trattenere, rifiutare **2** nascondere

within [wɪ'ðɪn] **A** *prep.* **1** dentro, entro, al di qua di **2** nel giro di **B** *avv.* **1** all'interno, dentro **2** in casa
without [wɪ'ðaʊt] *prep.* senza
to withstand [wɪð'stænd] (*pass. e p. p.* **withstood**) *v. tr.* resistere a
witness ['wɪtnɪs] *s.* testimone *m. e f.*
to witness ['wɪtnɪs] *v. tr. e intr.* testimoniare
witticism ['wɪtɪsɪz(ə)m] *s.* spiritosaggine *f.*
witty ['wɪtɪ] *agg.* spiritoso
wizard ['wɪzəd] *s.* mago *m.*
to wobble ['wəbl] *v. intr.* **1** oscillare, vacillare **2** esitare, titubare
woe [wɒʊ] *s.* **1** dolore *m.* **2** calamità *f.*
woke [wɒʊk] *pass. e p. p. di* **to wake**
woken [wɒʊk(ə)n] *pass. e p. p. di* **to wake**
wolf [wʊlf] *s.* lupo *m.*
woman ['wʊmən] (*pl.* **women**) *s.* donna *f.*
womanly ['wʊmənlɪ] *agg.* femminile
womb [wu:m] *s.* utero *m.*
won [wʌn] *pass. e p. p. di* **to win**
wonder ['wʌndəʳ] *s.* **1** meraviglia *f.*, prodigio *m.* **2** stupore *m.*
to wonder ['wʌndəʳ] *v. tr. e intr.* **1** meravigliarsi (di) **2** domandarsi
wonderful ['wʌndəf(ʊ)l] *agg.* meraviglioso
to woo [wu:] *v. tr.* sollecitare, cercare
wood [wʊd] *s.* **1** bosco *m.* **2** legna *f.*, legno *m.*, legname *m.* ♦ **w. carver** intagliatore
woodcock ['wʊdkək] *s.* beccaccia *f.*
woodcut ['wʊdkʌt] *s.* incisione *f.* (su legno)
wooded ['wʊdɪd] *agg.* boscoso
wooden ['wʊdn] *agg.* **1** di legno **2** rigido
woodman ['wʊdmən] (*pl.* **woodmen**) *s.* boscaiolo *m.*
woodpecker ['wʊd,pɛkəʳ] *s.* picchio *m.*
woodwind ['wʊdwɪnd] *s.* (*mus.*) legni *m. pl.*
woodworm ['wʊdwɜ:m] *s.* tarlo *m.*
woody ['wʊdɪ] *agg.* boscoso
wool [wʊl] *s.* lana *f.*
woollen ['wʊlən] (*USA* **woolen**) **A** *agg.* di lana **B** *s.* articolo *m.* di lana
word [wɜ:d] *s.* **1** parola *f.*, vocabolo *m.* **2** notizia *f.*, informazione *f.* **3** parola *f.* d'ordine **4** ordine *m.*, comando *m.* ♦ **w. processing** trattamento testi
to word [wɜ:d] *v. tr.* esprimere, formulare
wording ['wɜ:dɪŋ] *s.* **1** espressione *f.*, formulazione *f.* **2** dicitura *f.*
wore [wɜ:ʳ] *pass. di* **to wear**
work [wɜ:k] *s.* **1** lavoro *m.* **2** opera *f.* **3** *al pl.* (*v. al sing.*) officina *f.*, fabbrica *f.* **4** *al pl.* meccanismo *m.* ♦ **out of w.** disoccupato
to work [wɜ:k] **A** *v. intr.* **1** lavorare **2** funzionare, essere efficace **3** penetrare con difficoltà **4** contrarsi **B** *v. tr.* **1** lavorare, plasmare **2** far lavorare **3** far funzionare, manovrare, condurre **4** operare, causare, provocare **5** sfruttare ♦ **to w. in** introdurre; **to w. off** sbrigare, eliminare; **to w. out** elaborare, risolvere, calcolare, allenarsi; **to w. up** suscitare, elaborare, sviluppare
workable ['wɜ:kəbl] *agg.* **1** lavorabile, sfruttabile **2** realizzabile
workaday ['wɜ:kədeɪ] *agg.* **1** comune, ordinario **2** noioso
workaholic [,wɜ:kə'həlɪk] *s.* (*fam.*) maniaco *m.* del lavoro
worker ['wɜ:kəʳ] *s.* lavoratore *m.*, operaio *m.*
working ['wɜ:kɪŋ] **A** *agg.* **1** attivo, laborioso **2** funzionante **3** di lavoro, da lavoro **B** *s.* **1** lavoro *m.*, lavorazione *f.* **2** funzionamento *m.* **3** *al pl.* meccanismo *m.* ♦ **w. class** classe operaia; **w. day** giorno lavorativo; **w. order** efficienza
workman ['wɜ:kmən] (*pl.* **workmen**) *s.* operaio *m.*
workmanship ['wɜ:kmənʃɪp] *s.* **1** abilità *f.* tecnica **2** fattura *f.*, esecuzione *f.*
worksheet ['wɜ:kʃi:t] *s.* foglio *m.* di lavoro
workshop ['wɜ:kʃəp] *s.* laboratorio *m.*, officina *f.*
workstation ['wɜ:k,steɪʃn] *s.* (*inf.*) stazione *f.* di lavoro
world [wɜ:ld] **A** *s.* mondo *m.* **B** *agg. attr.* mondiale, del mondo
worldly ['wɜ:ldlɪ] *agg.* mondano, terreno
worldwide [,wɜ:ld'waɪd] **A** *agg.* mondiale, universale **B** *avv.* in tutto il mondo
worm [wɜ:m] *s.* verme *m.* ♦ **w. eaten** bacato, decrepito
worn [wɜ:n] **A** *p. p. di* **to wear** **B** *agg.* **1** consumato **2** indebolito ♦ **w. out** esausto
worried ['wʌrɪd] *agg.* preoccupato
worry ['wʌrɪ] *s.* **1** preoccupazione *f.*, inquietudine *f.* **2** fastidio *m.*, guaio *m.*
to worry ['wʌrɪ] **A** *v. tr.* **1** infastidire, seccare **2** preoccupare, affliggere **3** azzannare, dilaniare **B** *v. intr.* preoccuparsi, affliggersi
worrying ['wʌrɪɪŋ] *agg.* **1** inquietante, preoccupante **2** molesto
worse [wɜ:s] **A** *agg.* **1** (*comp. di* **bad**) peggio, peggiore **2** (*comp. di* **ill**) peggio, peg-

giorato **B** *s.* il peggio *m.* **C** *avv.* peggio ♦ **to get w.** peggiorare
to **worsen** ['wɜːsn] *v. tr. e intr.* peggiorare
worship ['wɜːʃɪp] *s.* **1** culto *m.*, venerazione *f.* **2** (*titolo*) eccellenza *f.*, eminenza *f.*
to **worship** ['wɜːʃɪp] *v. tr.* adorare, venerare
worst [wɜːst] **A** *agg.* (*sup. di* **bad**, **ill**) (il) peggiore **B** *s.* il peggio *m.* **C** *avv.* peggio, nel modo peggiore ♦ **at w.** al peggio
worth [wɜːθ] **A** *agg. pred.* **1** che vale, di valore, del valore di **2** degno, meritevole **B** *s.* valore *m.* ♦ **to be w.** meritare, valere
worthless ['wɜːθlɪs] *agg.* **1** di nessun valore **2** indegno, immeritevole
worthwile [ˌwɜːθ'waɪl] *agg.* utile, che vale la pena
worthy ['wɜːðɪ] **A** *agg.* **1** meritevole, degno **2** (*iron.*) rispettabile **B** *s.* notabile *m.*
would [wʊd, wəd] *v. difett.* **1** (*ausiliare per la formazione del condiz. pres. e pass.*) (ES: **I w. buy it, if I had enough money** lo comprerei, se avessi denaro a sufficienza) **2** volere, avere intenzione di (*passato e condizionale*) (ES: **I w. not stay** non volli rimanere, **w. you be so kind to give me a pen?** vorresti per favore darmi una penna?) **3** volere (*imperfetto cong.*) (ES: **I could do it, if I w.** potrei farlo se volessi) **4** (*idiom., indica consuetudine*) (ES: **he w. stare into the distance day after day** se ne stava a guardare lontano giorno dopo giorno)
wound (1) [wuːnd] *s.* ferita *f.*
wound (2) [waʊnd] *pass. e p. p. di* **to wind**
to **wound** [wuːnd] *v. tr.* ferire
wove [wɒʊv] *pass. di* **to weave**
woven ['wɒʊvn] *p. p. di* **to weave**
wrangle ['ræŋgl] *s.* litigio *m.*
wrap [ræp] *s.* scialle *m.*
to **wrap** [ræp] *v. tr.* **1** avvolgere, fasciare **2** impacchettare, incartare
wrapper ['ræpəʳ] *s.* involucro *m.*, copertina *f.*
wrapping ['ræpɪŋ] *s.* confezione *f.*, involucro *m.* ♦ **w. paper** carta da pacchi
wrath [rɜːθ] *s.* rabbia *f.*
wrathful ['rɜːθf(ʊ)l] *agg.* furibondo
to **wreak** [riːk] *v. tr.* **1** sfogare **2** provocare
wreath [riːθ] *s.* ghirlanda *f.*
wreck [rɛk] *s.* **1** naufragio *m.*, disastro *m.* **2** relitto *m.*
to **wreck** [rɛk] **A** *v. tr.* **1** far naufragare **2** rovinare, distruggere **B** *v. intr.* **1** naufragare **2** andare in pezzi
wreckage ['rɛkɪdʒ] *s.* relitti *m. pl.*, rottami *m. pl.*, macerie *f. pl.*
wren [rɛn] *s.* scricciolo *m.*
wrench [rɛn(t)ʃ] *s.* **1** strappo *m.*, torsione *f.* **2** (*med.*) strappo *m.* muscolare **3** (*USA*) (*mecc.*) chiave *f.*
to **wrench** [rɛn(t)ʃ] *v. tr.* strappare, torcere
wrestle ['rɛsl] *s.* (*sport*) lotta *f.*
to **wrestle** ['rɛsl] *v. intr.* (*sport*) lottare
wrestler ['rɛsləʳ] *s.* (*sport*) lottatore *m.*
wretched ['rɛtʃɪd] *agg.* **1** disgraziato, infelice **2** miserabile **3** orrendo, pessimo
to **wriggle** ['rɪgl] *v. intr.* **1** contorcersi, dimenarsi **2** essere evasivo
to **wring** [rɪŋ] (*pass. e p. p.* **wrung**) **A** *v. tr.* **1** torcere, strizzare **2** stringere con forza **3** estorcere **B** *v. intr.* contorcersi
wrinkle ['rɪŋkl] *s.* ruga *f.*, piega *f.*
to **wrinkle** ['rɪŋkl] *v. tr.* corrugare, raggrinzire
wrist [rɪst] *s.* polso *m.*
to **write** [raɪt] (*pass.* **wrote**, *p. p.* **written**) **A** *v. tr.* **1** scrivere **2** redigere, compilare **B** *v. intr.* **1** scrivere **2** fare lo scrittore ♦ **to w. down** prendere nota; **to w. in** inserire (in uno scritto); **to w. off** cancellare, annullare; **to w. out** trascrivere, compilare; **to w. up** riscrivere, recensire
writer ['raɪtəʳ] *s.* scrittore *m.*
to **writhe** [raɪð] *v. intr.* contorcersi
writing ['raɪtɪŋ] *s.* **1** scrittura *f.*, calligrafia *f.* **2** documento *m.* scritto, scritta *f.* **3** *al pl.* scritti *m. pl.* ♦ **w.-book** quaderno; **w. pad** blocco; **w. paper** carta da lettera
written ['rɪtn] *p. p. di* **to write**
wrong [rɔŋ] **A** *agg.* **1** sbagliato, scorretto **2** inopportuno, sconveniente **3** illegittimo **4** difettoso, guasto **B** *s.* **1** ingiustizia *f.*, torto *m.*, danno *m.* **2** male *m.* peccato *m.* **C** *avv.* **1** erroneamente, male **2** impropriamente ♦ **to be w.** ingannarsi, sbagliarsi
to **wrong** [rɔŋ] *v. tr.* far torto a
wrongful ['rɔŋf(ʊ)l] *agg.* **1** ingiusto, iniquo **2** illegittimo
wrongly ['rɔŋlɪ] *avv.* **1** male, erroneamente **2** a torto
wrote [rɒʊt] *pass. di* **to write**
wrought [rɜːt] *agg.* lavorato, battuto
wrung [rʌŋ] *pass. e p. p. di* **wring**
wry [raɪ] *agg.* storto, obliquo
wryneck ['raɪnɛk] *s.* torcicollo *m.*

X

xenon ['zɛnən] *s.* xeno *m.*
xenophobia [ˌzɛnə'fɒʊbjə] *s.* xenofobia *f.*
xerography [zɪ'rɒgrəfɪ] *s.* xerografia *f.*
Xmas ['krɪsməs] *s.* (*abbr fam. di* **Christmas**) Natale *m.*
X-ray ['ɛksˌreɪ] *s.* **1** raggi X *m. pl.* **2** radiografia *f.* ♦ **X- r. therapy** röntgenterapia *f.*
xylography [zaɪ'ləgrəfɪ] *s.* xilografia *f.*
xylophone ['zaɪləfɒʊn] *s.* xilofono *m.*

Y

yacht [jət] *s.* yacht *m. inv.*
yachting ['jətɪŋ] *s.* navigazione *f.* da diporto, yachting *m. inv.*
yank [jænk] *s.* (*fam.*) strattone *m.*
Yankee ['jæŋkɪ] *s.* (*fam.*) yankee *m. inv.*, americano *m.* (*degli USA*)
yard (1) [jaːd] *s.* iarda *f.*
yard (2) [jaːd] *s.* **1** cortile *m.*, recinto *m.* **2** (*ferr.*) scalo *m.* **3** cantiere *m.*
yarn [jaːn] *s.* **1** filo *m.*, filato *m.* **2** (*fig.*) racconto *m.*, storia *f.*
yawn [jɜːn] *s.* sbadiglio *m.*
to yawn [jɜːn] *v. intr.* sbadigliare
yeah [jɛə] *avv.* (*fam.*) sì
year [jɜːʳ, jɪəʳ] *s.* **1** anno *m.*, annata *f.* **2** *al pl.* anni *m. pl.*, età *f.* ♦ **leap y.** anno bisestile; **y. book** annuario; **y. by y.** ogni anno
yearly ['jɜːlɪ] **A** *agg.* annuale, annuo **B** *avv.* annualmente
to yearn [jɜːn] *v. intr.* agognare
yeast [jiːst] *s.* lievito *m.*
yell [jɛl] *s.* urlo *m.*
to yell [jɛl] *v. tr. e intr.* urlare
yellow ['jɛlɒʊ] *agg. e s.* giallo *m.*
yelp [jɛlp] *s.* guaito *m.*
to yelp [jɛlp] *v. intr.* guaire
yeoman ['jɒʊmən] (*pl.* **yeomen**) *s.* (*stor.*) piccolo proprietario *m.* terriero
yes [jɛs] **A** *avv.* **1** sì, certo **2** davvero?, ah sì? **B** *inter.* non solo, anzi **C** *s.* sì *m. inv.*, risposta *f.* affermativa
yesterday ['jɛstədɪ] *avv. e s.* ieri *m. inv.* ♦ **the day before y.** ieri l'altro
yet [jɛt] **A** *cong.* ma, però, tuttavia **B** *avv.* **1** ancora, finora, tuttora **2** ancora, già ♦ **as y.** finora; **just y.** proprio ora; **not y.** (e) neppure; **y. once** ancora una volta
yew [juː] *s.* (*bot.*) tasso *m.*
yield [jiːld] *s.* **1** prodotto *m.*, raccolto *m.* **2** produzione *f.*, rendimento *m.* **3** rendita *f.* **4** (*USA*) diritto *m.* di precedenza
to yield [jiːld] **A** *v. tr.* **1** produrre, fruttare, rendere **2** concedere, dare **B** *v. intr.* **1** fruttare **2** sottomettersi **3** (*USA*) dare la precedenza
yoghurt ['jəgɜːt] *s.* yogurt *m. inv.*
yoke [jɒʊk] *s.* giogo *m.*
to yoke [jɒʊk] *v. tr.* aggiogare
yolk [jɒʊk] *s.* tuorlo *m.*
yonder ['jəndəʳ] *avv.* lassù
you [jʊ(ː)] *pron. pers. 2ª sing. e pl.* **1** tu, te, ti, voi, ve, vi **2** (*con valore impers.*) se, si (ES: **y. never can be sure!** non si può mai essere sicuri!)
young [jʌŋ] **A** *agg.* giovane **B** *s. al pl.* **1** i giovani *m. pl.* **2** (*di animale*) i piccoli *m. pl.* ♦ **y. child** bimbo; **y. lady** signorina
youngster ['jʌŋstəʳ] *s.* giovincello *m.*
your [jɜːʳ] *agg. poss. 2ª sing. e pl.* **1** tuo, tua, tuoi, tue, vostro, vostra, vostri, vostre, Suo, Sua, Suoi, Sue, Loro **2** (*con valore indef.*) proprio
yours [jɜːz] *pron. poss. 2ª sing. e pl.* il tuo, la tua, i tuoi, le tue, il vostro, la vostra, i vostri, le vostre, il Suo, la Sua, i Suoi, le Sue, il Loro, la Loro, i Loro, le Loro

yourself [jɜː'sɛlf] (*pl.* **yourselves**) *pron. 2ª sing.* **1** (*rifl.*) ti, te, te stesso, si, se, Lei stesso, Lei stessa **2** (*enf.*) tu stesso, tu stessa, Lei stesso, Lei stessa (ES: **you have done it y.** lo hai fatto tu stesso)
youth [juːθ] *s.* **1** gioventù *f.*, giovinezza *f.* **2** i giovani *m. pl.* **3** giovane *m.* ♦ **y. hostel** ostello della gioventù
youthful ['juːθf(ʊ)l] *agg.* **1** giovane **2** giovanile
yummy ['jʌmɪ] *agg.* (*fam.*) delizioso
yuppie ['jʌpɪ] *s.* yuppie *m. e f. inv.*

Z

zany ['zeɪnɪ] **A** *s.* buffone *m.* **B** *agg.* buffonesco
to zap [zæp] **A** *v. tr.* (*fam.*) eliminare, cancellare **B** *v. intr.* sfrecciare
zeal [ziːl] *s.* zelo *m.*
zebra ['ziːbrə] *s.* zebra *f.* ♦ **z. crossing** passaggio pedonale, zebre
zebrine ['ziːbraɪn] *agg.* zebrato
zebu ['ziːbuː] *s.* zebù *m.*
zed [zɛd] *s.* zeta *f. inv.*
zee [ziː] *s.* (*USA*) zeta *f. inv.*
zero ['zɪərɒʊ] *s.* zero *m.*
to zero ['zɪərɒʊ] *v. tr.* azzerare
zest [zɛst] *s.* **1** aroma *m.*, gusto *m.* **2** (*di arancio, limone*) scorza *f.* **3** entusiasmo *m.*, interesse *m.*
zibeline ['zɪbəlɪn] *s.* zibellino *m.*
zigzag ['zɪgzæg] **A** *s.* zigzag *m. inv.* **B** *agg.* a zigzag
to zigzag ['zɪgzæg] *v. intr.* andare a zigzag, zigzagare
zinc [zɪŋk] *s.* zinco *m.*
zing [zɪŋ] *s.* (*fam.*) **1** sibilo *m.* **2** brio *m.*
Zionism ['zaɪənɪz(ə)m] *s.* sionismo *m.*
Zionist ['zaɪənɪst] *s.* sionista *m. e f.*
zip [zɪp] *s.* **1** (o **z. fastener**) cerniera *f.*, chiusura *f.* lampo **2** (*fam.*) fischio *m.*, sibilo *m.*
to zip [zɪp] **A** *v. tr.* **1** aprire (o chiudere) con una cerniera lampo **2** trasportare velocemente **B** *v. intr.* **1** aprire (o chiudere) una cerniera lampo **2** sfrecciare **3** fischiare, sibilare
zip code ['zɪp,kɒʊd] *s.* (*USA*) codice *m.* postale
zircon ['zɜːkən] *s.* zircone *m.*
zodiac ['zɒʊdɪæk] *s.* zodiaco *m.*
zodiacal [zɒ(ʊ)'daɪək(ə)l] *agg.* zodiacale
zombie ['zəmbɪ] *s.* zombie *m. inv.*
zone [zɒʊn] *s.* zona *f.*
zoo [zuː] *s.* zoo *m. inv.*
zoologist [zɒ(ʊ)'ələdʒɪst] *s.* zoologo *m.*
zoology [zɒ(ʊ)'ələdʒɪ] *s.* zoologia *f.*
zoom [zuːm] *s.* **1** rombo *m.* **2** (*cine.*, *TV*) zumata *f.* ♦ **z. lens** zoom
zootechnical [,zɒ(ʊ)ə'tɛknɪk(ə)l] *agg.* zootecnico
zootechnics [,zɒ(ʊ)ə'tɛknɪks] *s. pl.* (*v. al sing.*) zootecnia *f.*
zucchini [zuː'kiːnɪ] *s.* (*USA*) zucchino *m.*
zygoma [zaɪ'gɒʊmə] *s.* zigomo *m.*
zyme [zaɪm] *s.* enzima *m.*

ITALIANO-INGLESE
ITALIAN-ENGLISH

A

a o **ad** *prep.* **1** (*stato in luogo*) at, in (ES: **essere a casa** to be at home, **abitare a Londra** to live in London) **2** (*moto a luogo, direzione*) to, at, in (ES: **andare a teatro, a Londra** to go to the theatre, to London) **3** (*termine*) to (ES: **dai questo libro a Paolo** give this book to Paul) **4** (*tempo*) at, in (ES: **a mezzanotte** at midnight, **a maggio** in May) **5** (*mezzo*) by, in (ES: **scritto a mano** written by hand, **dipinto all'acquerello** painted in watercolours) **6** (*scopo, vantaggio, danno*) to, for (ES: **a proprio rischio** at one's own risk) **7** (*distributivo*) a, by, at (ES: **due volte al giorno** twice a day, **a uno a uno** one by one)
àbaco *s. m.* (*arch.*) abacus
abàte *s. m.* abbot
abbacchiàto *agg.* (*fam.*) depressed
abbagliànte *agg.* dazzling ♦ **luci abbaglianti** (*autom.*) high-beams, (*USA*) brights
abbagliàre *v. tr.* to dazzle
abbàglio *s. m.* blunder
abbaiàre *v. intr.* to bark
abbandonàre A *v. tr.* **1** to abandon, to desert, to leave, to forsake **2** (*rinunciare a*) to renounce, to give up **B** *v. rifl.* to let oneself go
abbandóno *s. m.* **1** abandonment **2** (*trascuratezza*) neglect
abbassaménto *s. m.* lowering
abbassàre A *v. tr.* **1** to lower **2** (*ridurre*) to reduce **3** (*far scendere*) to let down **B** *v. rifl.* **1** (*chinarsi*) to stoop **2** (*diminuire*) to lower **3** (*fig.*) to lower oneself **4** (*di vento, temperatura, ecc.*) to drop
abbastànza *avv.* **1** (*a sufficienza*) enough **2** (*alquanto*) quite, rather ♦ **averne a. di qc.** to have had enough of sb.
abbàttere A *v. tr.* **1** (*atterrare*) to knock down **2** (*demolire*) to demolish, to put down **B** *v. rifl.* **1** (*cadere*) to fall **2** (*scoraggiarsi*) to lose heart
abbazìa *s. f.* abbey
abbellìre *v. tr.* to embellish, to adorn
abbeveràre *v. tr.* to water
abbiènte *agg.* well-to-do
abbigliaménto *s. m.* clothes *pl.*, clothing ♦ **negozio d'a.** clothes shop
abbinàre *v. tr.* to couple, to combine
abboccàre *v. intr.* **1** to bite **2** (*fig.*) to rise to the bait
abboccàto *agg.* sweetish
abbonaménto *s. m.* **1** (*trasporti, teatro*) season ticket **2** (*a giornale*) subscription
abbonàrsi *v. rifl.* **1** (*trasporti, teatro*) to get a season ticket **2** (*giornale*) to subscribe, to take out a subscription
abbonàto *agg. e s. m.* **1** (*trasporti, teatro*) season ticket holder **2** (*giornale*) subscriber
abbondànte *agg.* abundant, plentiful
abbondànza *s. f.* abundance, plenty
abbottonàre *v. tr.* to button up
abbozzàre *v. tr.* to sketch, to outline
abbòzzo *s. m.* sketch, outline
abbracciàre A *v. tr.* **1** to embrace, to hug **2** (*comprendere*) to enclose, to include **B** *v. rifl. rec.* to embrace each other
abbràccio *s. m.* embrace, hug
abbreviàre *v. tr.* to shorten, to cut short, to abbreviate
abbreviazióne *s. f.* abbreviation
abbronzàre A *v. tr.* to tan **B** *v. rifl.* to get brown
abbronzatùra *s. f.* tan
abbrustolìre *v. tr.* (*pane*) to toast, (*caffè, carne*) to roast
abbuffàrsi *v. rifl.* to stuff oneself
abdicàre *v. intr.* to abdicate
abdicazióne *s. f.* abdication
aberrànte *agg.* aberrant
aberrazióne *s. f.* aberration
abéte *s. m.* fir
abiètto *agg.* despicable, base
àbile *agg.* **1** able, capable **2** (*idoneo*) fit
abilità *s. f.* ability, cleverness, skill
abilitàre *v. tr.* to qualify
abilitàto *agg.* qualified
abìsso *s. m.* abyss, gulf
abitàcolo *s. m.* cockpit, cabin
abitànte *s. m. e f.* inhabitant
abitàre A *v. intr.* to live, to reside **B** *v. tr.* to inhabit, to live in
abitazióne *s. f.* residence, house
àbito *s. m.* (*da uomo*) suit, (*da donna*) dress
abituàle *agg.* habitual, usual ♦ **cliente a.**

regular customer
abitualménte *avv.* usually, regularly
abituàre **A** *v. tr.* to accustom **B** *v. rifl.* to get used (to), to get accustomed (to), to accustom oneself (to)
abitùdine *s. f.* habit, custom ♦ **come d'a.** as usual
abolìre *v. tr.* to abolish, to suppress
abolizióne *s. f.* abolition, suppression
abolizionìsmo *s. m.* abolitionism
abominévole *agg.* abominable
aborìgeno *agg. e s. m.* aboriginal, native
aborrìre *v. tr.* to abhor
abortìre *v. intr.* to miscarry, (*volontariamente*) to abort
abòrto *s. m.* miscarriage, (*volontario*) abortion
abrasióne *s. f.* abrasion
abrogàre *v. tr.* to abrogate, to cancel, to repeal
abrogazióne *s. f.* abrogation, annulment, repeat
àbside *s. f.* (*arch.*) apse
abusàre *v. intr.* **1** to abuse, to misuse **2** (*approfittare*) to take advantage (of)
abusivaménte *avv.* illegally, unlawfully
abusìvo *agg.* abusive, unlawful, unauthorized
acàcia *s. f.* acacia
acànto *s. m.* acanthus
àcca *s. f.* aitch
accadèmia *s. f.* academy
accadèmico *agg.* academic
accadére *v. intr.* to happen, to occur
accalappiacàni *s. m.* dog-catcher
accalappiàre *v. tr.* to catch
accalcàrsi *v. intr. pron.* to crowd
accaldàrsi *v. intr. pron.* to grow hot
accaloràrsi *v. rifl.* to get heated
accampaménto *s. m.* camp
accampàre **A** *v. tr.* **1** to camp **2** (*fig.*) to advance **B** *v. rifl.* to camp
accaniménto *s. m.* **1** fury **2** (*ostinazione*) obstinacy
accanìrsi *v. intr. pron.* **1** to rage **2** (*ostinarsi*) to persist (in)
accanìto *agg.* **1** relentless, pitiless **2** (*ostinato*) obstinate, dogged ♦ **fumatore a.** inveterate smoker
accànto **A** *avv.* nearby **B** *agg.* next **C** *prep.* **a. a** near, by, next to, close to
accantonàre *v. tr.* to set aside
accaparràre *v. tr.* to corner, to buy up
accapigliarsi *v. rifl. rec.* to come to blows
accappatóio *s. m.* bathrobe
accarezzàre *v. tr.* to caress, to stroke
accartocciàre *v. tr.* to crumple up
accasàre **A** *v. tr.* to marry **B** *v. intr. pron.* to get married
accasciàre **A** *v. tr.* to prostrate **B** *v. intr. pron.* **1** to fall, to collapse **2** (*fig.*) to lose heart
accattóne *s. m.* beggar
accavallàre **A** *v. tr.* **1** (*incrociare*) to cross **2** (*sovrapporre*) to overlap **3** (*lavoro a maglia*) to cross over **B** *v. intr. pron.* to overlap, to pile up
accecàre **A** *v. tr.* to blind **B** *v. intr. pron. e rifl.* to become blind
accèdere *v. intr.* **1** to approach **2** (*entrare in*) to enter
acceleràre **A** *v. tr.* to speed up, to quicken **B** *v. intr.* to accelerate
acceleratóre *s. m.* accelerator
accelerazióne *s. f.* acceleration
accèndere *v. tr.* **1** to light **2** (*interruttore, radio, ecc.*) to switch on, to turn on
accendìno *s. m.* lighter
accendisìgaro *s. m.* lighter
accennàre **A** *v. intr.* **1** (*fare cenno*) to beckon, (*col capo*) to nod, to sign **2** (*alludere a*) to hint **3** (*dare segno di*) to show signs **B** *v. tr.* to outline
accénno *s. m.* **1** (*cenno*) sign, nod **2** (*allusione*) hint
accensióne *s. f.* **1** lighting **2** (*autom.*) ignition
accentàre *v. tr.* to accent, to accentuate
accènto *s. m.* accent, stress
accentràre *v. tr.* to centralize
accentuàre *v. tr.* to accentuate, to stress, to emphasize
accerchiàre *v. tr.* to encircle, to surround
accertàre *v. tr.* **1** to ascertain **2** (*verificare*) to control, to check
accéso *agg.* **1** alight (*pred.*), lit up **2** (*in funzione*) on **3** (*di colore*) bright
accessìbile *agg.* **1** accessible **2** (*persona*) approachable **3** (*prezzo*) reasonable
accèsso *s. m.* **1** access, admittance, entry **2** (*med.*) fit, attack, access
accessòrio **A** *agg.* accessory, secondary **B** *s. m.* accessory
accétta *s. f.* hatchet
accettàbile *agg.* acceptable
accettàre *v. tr.* to accept, to agree to
accettazióne *s. f.* **1** acceptance **2** (*ufficio*) reception
accezióne *s. f.* meaning

acchiappàre *v. tr.* to catch
acciàcco *s. m.* ailment
acciaierìa *s. f.* steelworks
acciàio *s. m.* steel ♦ **a. inossidabile** stainless steel
accidentàle *agg.* accidental
accidentàto *agg.* (*di strada, terreno*) uneven, bumpy
accidènte *s. m.* **1** accident **2** (*fam.*) (*colpo*) fit
accidènti *inter.* damn!
accigliàto *agg.* frowning
accìngersi *v. rifl.* to set about, to get ready
acciottolàto *s. m.* cobbled paving
acciuffàre *v. tr.* to seize, to catch
acciùga *s. f.* anchovy
acclamàre *v. tr.* to acclaim
acclimatàre **A** *v. tr.* to acclimatize **B** *v. rifl.* to become acclimatized, to get acclimatized
acclùdere *v. tr.* to enclose
acclùso *agg.* enclosed
accoccolàrsi *v. rifl.* to crouch
accogliènte *agg.* comfortable, cosy
accogliènza *s. f.* reception, welcome
accògliere *v. tr.* **1** (*ricevere*) to receive, to welcome **2** (*accettare*) to accept, to agree to **3** (*esaudire*) to grant
accollàto *agg.* high-necked
accoltellàre *v. tr.* to stab, to knife
accomiatàre **A** *v. tr.* to dismiss **B** *v. rifl.* to take leave (of)
accomodaménto *s. m.* agreement, settlement
accomodànte *agg.* obliging, accommodating
accomodàre **A** *v. tr.* **1** (*riparare*) to repair **2** (*sistemare*) to settle **B** *v. rifl.* **1** (*sedersi*) to sit down, to take a seat **2** (*entrare*) to come in ♦ **si accomodi!** take a seat!, come in!
accompagnaménto *s. m.* **1** (*seguito*) retinue **2** (*mus.*) accompaniment
accompagnàre *v. tr.* **1** to take to, to see to, (*in auto*) to drive **2** (*mus.*) to accompany
accompagnatóre *s. m.* companion ♦ **a. turistico** tourist guide
accomunàre *v. tr.* to join
acconciatùra *s. f.* hairstyle
accondiscéndere *v. intr.* to consent, to agree
acconsentìre *v. intr.* to consent, to assent
accontentàre **A** *v. tr.* to satisfy **B** *v. rifl.* to be satisfied (with), to be content (with)
accónto *s. m.* advance, part payment ♦ **in a.** in advance, on account
accoppiaménto *s. m.* **1** coupling, matching **2** (*mecc.*) connection **3** (*di animali*) mating
accoppiàre **A** *v. tr.* **1** to couple **2** (*unire*) to join **B** *v. rifl.* **1** (*accordarsi*) to match **2** (*di animali*) to mate
accorciàre **A** *v. tr.* to shorten **B** *v. intr. pron.* to shorten, to become shorten
accordàre **A** *v. tr.* **1** (*concedere*) to grant **2** (*gramm.*) to make agree **3** (*mus.*) to tune up **B** *v. rifl. rec.* to reach an agreement **C** *v. intr. pron.* (*armonizzarsi*) to match
accòrdo *s. m.* **1** (*intesa*) agreement, consent **2** (*patto*) arrangement, agreement **3** (*mus.*) chord ♦ **andare d'a. con qc.** to get on well with sb.; **essere d'a.** to agree
accòrgersi *v. intr. pron.* **1** (*notare*) to notice **2** (*rendersi conto*) to realize, to become aware (of)
accorgiménto *s. m.* **1** (*accortezza*) shrewdness **2** (*espediente*) trick, device
accórrere *v. intr.* to run, to rush
accòrto *agg.* shrewd
accostàre **A** *v. tr.* **1** to draw near **2** (*porta, finestra*) to set ajar **3** (*persone*) to approach **B** *v. rifl.* to go near
accovacciàrsi *v. rifl.* to crouch
accozzàglia *s. f.* rabble, jumble
accreditàre *v. tr.* **1** (*una somma*) to credit **2** (*una notizia*) to confirm **3** (*diplomazia*) to accredit
accréscere *v. tr. e intr. pron.* to increase
accrescitìvo *agg. e s. m.* (*gramm.*) augmentative
accucciàrsi *v. rifl.* to lie down
accudìre *v. tr. e intr.* to look after, to attend to
accumulàre *v. tr. e intr. pron.* to accumulate, to pile up
accumulatóre *s. m.* accumulator
accuratézza *s. f.* accuracy, care
accuràto *agg.* accurate, careful
accùsa *s. f.* accusation, charge
accusàre *v. tr.* to accuse, to charge ♦ **a. ricevuta** (*comm.*) to acknowledge receipt
accusatìvo *agg. e s. m.* (*gramm.*) accusative
accusàto *s. m.* (*dir.*) accused
accusatóre *s. m.* (*dir.*) accuser, prosecutor
acèfalo *agg.* acephalous
acèrbo *agg.* **1** unripe, green **2** (*aspro*) sour, sharp
àcero *s. m.* maple

acéto *s. m.* vinegar
àcido *agg. e s. m.* acid
acìdulo *agg.* acidulous
àcino *s. m.* grape
àcne *s. f.* acne
aconfessionàle *agg.* non-denominational, undenominational
àcqua *s. f.* water ♦ **a. dolce** fresh water; **a. minerale** mineral water; **a. piovana** rainwater; **a. potabile** drinking water; **sott'a.** underwater
acquafòrte *s. f.* etching
acquamarìna *s. f.* aquamarine
acquaràgia *s. f.* turpentine
acquàrio *s. m.* **1** aquarium **2** (*astr.*) Aquarius
acquasantièra *s. f.* stoup
acquàtico *agg.* aquatic
acquavìte *s. f.* brandy
acquazzóne *s. m.* downpour
acquedótto *s. m.* aqueduct, waterworks
àcqueo *agg.* aqueous
acquerellìsta *s. m. e f.* watercolourist
acquerèllo *s. m.* watercolour
acquirènte *s. m. e f.* purchaser, buyer, shopper
acquisìre *v. tr.* to acquire
acquisizióne *s. f.* acquisition
acquistàre *v. tr.* **1** (*comprare*) to buy, to purchase **2** (*ottenere*) to acquire, to gain, to obtain, to get
acquìsto *s. m.* **1** purchase, buy **2** (*acquisizione*) acquisition ♦ **andare a fare acquisti** to go shopping
acquitrìno *s. m.* bog, marsh, swamp
acquóso *agg.* watery
àcre *agg.* acrid, pungent
acrìlico *agg.* acrylic
acrìtico *agg.* uncritical
acròbata *s. m. e f.* acrobat
acrobazìa *s. f.* acrobatics *pl.*
acròpoli *s. f.* acropolis
acrotèrio *s. m.* acroterium
acuìre *v. tr.* to sharpen, to whet
acùleo *s. m.* **1** (*bot.*) aculeus, prickle **2** (*zool.*) aculeus, sting
acùme *s. m.* acumen, perspicacity
acùstica *s. f.* acoustics *pl.* (*v. al sing.*)
acùstico *agg.* acoustic ♦ **apparecchio a.** hearing aid
acùto **A** *agg.* **1** acute, sharp **2** (*intenso*) intense **3** (*perspicace*) sharp, subtle **4** (*mus.*) high **B** *s. m.* (*mus.*) high note
ad *prep.* → **a**
adagiàre **A** *v. tr.* to lay down **B** *v. rifl.* **1** to lie down **2** (*fig.*) to subside, to sink
adàgio (1) **A** *avv.* slowly **B** *s. m.* (*mus.*) adagio
adàgio (2) *s. m.* adage, proverb
adattaménto *s. m.* adaptation
adattàre **A** *v. tr.* to fit, to adapt, to adjust **B** *v. rifl.* to adapt oneself, to fit oneself **C** *v. intr. pron.* to suit, to be suitable
adàtto *agg.* fit, suited, suitable, right
addebitàre *v. tr.* to debit, to charge
addébito *s. m.* debit, charge
addensàre **A** *v. tr.* to thicken **B** *v. rifl.* **1** to thicken **2** (*ammassarsi*) to gather, to crowd
addentàre *v. tr.* to bite
addentràrsi *v. rifl.* to penetrate, to go into
addestraménto *s. m.* training
addestràre *v. tr. e rifl.* to train
addétto **A** *agg.* assigned (to) **B** *s. m.* **1** (*impiegato*) employee **2** (*mil., ambasciata*) attaché ♦ **a. stampa** press agent
addiàccio *s. m.* pen, (*mil.*) bivouac ♦ **dormire all'a.** to sleep in the open
addiètro *avv.* before, ago
addìo **A** *s. m.* **1** goodbye **2** (*letter.*) farewell **B** *inter.* goodbye, byebye
addirittùra *avv.* **1** (*direttamente*) directly, straight away **2** (*persino*) even **3** (*assolutamente*) absolutely
addìrsi *v. rifl.* to become, to suit
additàre *v. tr.* to point (at, out)
additìvo *agg. e s. m.* additive
addizionàre *v. tr.* to add (up), to sum (up)
addizióne *s. f.* addition
addobbàre *v. tr.* to adorn, to decorate
addòbbo *s. m.* decoration, ornament
addolcire **A** *v. tr.* **1** to sweeten **2** (*fig.*) to soften **B** *v. intr. pron.* to soften, to become milder
addoloràre **A** *v. tr.* to pain, to grieve **B** *v. intr. pron.* to grieve, to be sorry
addòme *s. m.* abdomen
addomesticàre *v. tr.* to domesticate, to tame
addomesticàto *agg.* tame
addominàle *agg.* abdominal
addormentàre **A** *v. tr.* **1** to send to sleep **2** (*anestetizzare*) to anaesthetize **3** (*intorpidire*) to deaden **B** *v. intr. pron.* to fall asleep
addormentàto *agg.* **1** sleeping, asleep (*pred.*) **2** (*assonnato*) sleepy **3** (*fig.*) slow
addossàre **A** *v. tr.* **1** (*appoggiare*) to lean **2** (*una colpa*) to charge with **B** *v. rifl.* **1** to

lean **2** (*prendere su di sé*) to take upon oneself
addòsso A *avv.* on **B** *prep.* **a. a 1** on **2** (*vicino*) close to ♦ **mettere le mani a. a qc.** to lay hands on sb.; **mettersi q.c. a.** to put st. on
addùrre *v. tr.* to adduce, to advance
adeguàre A *v. tr.* to conform, to adapt **B** *v. rifl.* to conform oneself
adémpiere *v. tr. e intr.* to fulfil, to accomplish, to carry out
adèpto *s. m.* initiate
aderènte *agg.* **1** adherent, sticking **2** (*di vestito*) tight, close-fitting
aderìre *v. intr.* **1** (*attaccarsi*) to adhere, to stick **2** (*acconsentire*) to assent, (*a un invito*) to accept, (*a una richiesta*) to comply with **3** (*associarsi*) to join
adescaménto *s. m.* enticement, allurement
adescàre *v. tr.* to entice, to allure
adesióne *s. f.* **1** adhesion, adherence **2** (*fig.*) assent, agreement
adesìvo *agg. e s. m.* adhesive
adèsso *avv.* now ♦ **per a.** right now; **proprio a.** just now
adiacènte *agg.* adjacent, adjoining
adibire *v. tr.* to use as, to assign
adiràrsi *v. intr. pron.* to get angry
àdito *s. m.* access, entrance
adocchiàre *v. tr.* to eye
adolescènte *s. m. e f.* adolescent, teenager
adolescènza *s. f.* adolescence, teens
adoperàre *v. tr.* to use, to employ
adoràre *v. tr.* to adore, to worship
adornàre *v. tr.* to adorn, to decorate
adottàre *v. tr.* to adopt
adottìvo *agg.* adoptive, adopted
adozióne *s. f.* adoption
adulàre *v. tr.* to flatter
adulazióne *s. f.* adulation, flattery
adulteràre *v. tr.* to adulterate
adultèrio *s. m.* adultery
adùlto A *agg.* adult, grown-up, (*bot., zool.*) fully-grown **B** *s. m.* grown-up
adunànza *s. f.* meeting, assembly
adunàre *v. tr. e intr. pron.* to assemble, to gather
adunàta *s. f.* assembly, (*mil.*) muster
adùnco *agg.* hooked
aeràre *v. tr.* to air, to ventilate
aerazióne *s. f.* aeration, ventilation
aèreo A *agg.* air, aerial **B** *s. m.* airplane, plane
aeròbica *s. f.* aerobics *pl.* (*v. al sing.*)
aeròbico *agg.* aerobic
aerodinàmica *s. f.* aerodynamics *pl.* (*v. al sing.*)
aerodinàmico *agg.* aerodynamic
aerofotografìa *s. f.* aerial photography
aeromodèllo *s. m.* model aircraft
aeronàutica *s. f.* aeronautics *pl.* (*v. al sing.*)
aeronàutico *agg.* aeronautic(al)
aeroplàno *s. m.* aircraft, aeroplane, plane, (*USA*) airplane
aeropòrto *s. m.* airport
aerosòl *s. m.* aerosol
aerospaziàle *agg.* aerospace
aerovìa *s. f.* airway
àfa *s. f.* sultriness
affàbile *agg.* affable
affaccendàrsi *v. rifl.* to busy oneself
affacciàrsi *v. rifl.* to appear
affamàto *agg.* hungry, starving
affannàrsi *v. intr. pron.* **1** to worry **2** (*darsi da fare*) to busy oneself
affànno *s. m.* **1** breathlessness **2** (*fig.*) worry, anxiety
affàre *s. m.* **1** affair, matter **2** (*comm.*) business, transaction, (*vantaggioso*) bargain **3** (*fam.*) (*aggeggio*) thing ♦ **concludere un a.** to strike a bargain; **fare affari** to do business; **viaggiare per affari** to travel on business
affascinànte *agg.* charming, fascinating
affascinàre *v. tr.* to charm, to fascinate
affaticàre A *v. tr.* to tire **B** *v. rifl.* to tire oneself, to get tired
affàtto *avv.* **1** quite, completely, entirely **2** (*in frasi neg.*) at all ♦ **niente a.** not at all
affermàre A *v. tr.* to assert, to affirm, to state **B** *v. rifl.* to impose oneself, to make a name for oneself
affermatìvo *agg.* affirmative
affermazióne *s. f.* **1** affirmation, assertion **2** (*successo*) achievement
afferràre *v. tr.* to seize, to grasp, to catch
affettàre (1) *v. tr.* (*tagliare a fette*) to slice
affettàre (2) *v. tr.* (*ostentare*) to affect
affettàto (1) *s. m.* (*salumi*) sliced salami
affettàto (2) *agg.* (*ostentato*) affected
affettìvo *agg.* affective
affètto *s. m.* affection, love
affettuosaménte *avv.* affectionately, lovingly
affettuóso *agg.* loving, affectionate, fond
affezionàrsi *v. rifl.* to grow fond (of)
affezionàto *agg.* affectionate, fond
affezióne *s. f.* affection, attachment ♦

prezzo d'a. fancy price
affiancàre *v. tr.* **1** to place side by side, to put beside **2** (*aiutare*) to help, to support
affiatàrsi *v. rifl* to get on well
affibbiàre *v. tr.* (*fam., fig.*) to saddle with, (*dare*) to give
affidàbile *agg.* reliable
affidaménto *s. m.* trust, confidence ♦ **fare a. su qc.** to rely (up) on sb.
affidàre A *v. tr.* **1** to entrust, to confide **2** (*dir.*) to grant **B** *v. rifl.* to rely (up) on
affievolìre A *v. tr.* to weaken **B** *v. intr. pron.* to weaken, to grow weak
affìggere *v. tr.* to post up, to stick up
affilàre *v. tr.* to sharpen
affilàto *agg.* **1** sharp **2** (*fig.*) thin
affiliàre A *v. tr.* to affiliate **B** *v. rifl.* to affiliate (with), to become a member (of)
affinàre *v. tr.* to improve, to refine
affinché *cong.* so that, in order that
affìne *agg.* similar, analogous
affinità *s. f.* affinity
affioràre *v. intr.* **1** to surface **2** (*fig.*) to emerge, to appear
affissióne *s. f.* bill-posting ♦ **divieto d'a.** post no bills
affittacàmere *s. m. e f. inv.* landlord *m.*, landlady *f.*
affittàre *v. tr.* **1** (*dare in affitto*) to let, to rent, to lease (out), (*a noleggio*) to hire (out) **2** (*prendere in affitto*) to rent, (*a noleggio*) to hire ♦ **affittasi** to rent
affìtto *s. m.* rent, (*contratto*) lease
affliggere A *v. tr.* to afflict, to distress **B** *v. rifl.* to grieve, to worry
afflizióne *s. f.* affliction, distress
afflosciàrsi *v. intr. pron.* to wilt, to sag
affluènte *s. m.* affluent, tributary
affluènza *s. f.* **1** flow **2** (*di persone*) crowd
affluìre *v. intr.* **1** to flow **2** (*di persone*) to crowd
afflùsso *s. m.* **1** flow **2** (*econ.*) inflow, influx
affogàre *v. tr. e intr.* to drown
affogàto *agg.* drowned ♦ **uova affogate** poached eggs
affollaménto *s. m.* crowding, over-crowding
affollàre *v. tr. e intr. pron.* to crowd
affollàto *agg.* crowded
affondàre *v. tr. e intr.* to sink
affrancàre A *v. tr.* **1** to free, to release **2** (*corrispondenza*) to stamp, to frank **B** *v. rifl.* to free oneself
affrancatùra *s. f.* (*posta*) stamping, postage
affrànto *agg.* **1** broken-hearted, disheartened **2** (*distrutto*) worn out
affrescàre *v. tr.* to fresco
affrésco *s. m.* fresco
affrettàre A *v. tr.* **1** to hasten, to hurry **2** (*anticipare*) to anticipate **B** *v. rifl.* to hurry, to make hasten ♦ **a. il passo** to quicken one's pace
affrontàre A *v. tr.* **1** to face, to confront **2** (*fig.*) to tackle, to deal with **B** *v. rifl. rec.* to come to blows
affrónto *s. m.* affront, insult
affumicàre *v. tr.* **1** (*riempire di fumo*) to fill with smoke **2** (*annerire di fumo*) to blacken with smoke **3** (*alimenti*) to smoke, to cure
affumicàto *agg.* (*di alimenti*) smoked, cured
affusolàto *agg.* tapered, tapering
àfono *agg.* voiceless, (*rauco*) hoarse
afóso *agg.* sultry
africàno *agg. e s. m.* African
afrodisìaco *agg. e s. m.* aphrodisiac
àfta *s. f.* aphtha
àgave *s. f.* agave
agènda *s. f.* diary
agènte *s. m.* agent ♦ **a. di cambio** stockbroker; **a. immobiliare** estate agent, realtor; **a. investigativo** detective; **a. di polizia** policeman
agenzìa *s. f.* **1** agency **2** (*succursale*) branch ♦ **a. di pubblicità** advertising agency; **a. di viaggi** travel agency/bureau; **a. immobiliare** estate agency
agevolàre *v. tr.* to facilitate
agevolazióne *s. f.* facilitation, facility
agévole *agg.* easy
agganciàre *v. tr.* **1** to hook **2** (*ferr.*) to couple
aggéggio *s. m.* gadget, device, contraption
aggettìvo *s. m.* adjective
agghiacciànte *agg.* chilling, dreadful
agghindàre *v. tr. e rifl.* to deck (oneself) out
aggiornaménto *s. m.* **1** updating **2** (*rinvio*) adjournment ♦ **corso di a.** refresher course
aggiornàre A *v. tr.* **1** to update, to bring up to date **2** (*rinviare*) to adjourn **B** *v. rifl.* to keep oneself up to date
aggiornàto *agg.* up-to-date
aggiràre A *v. tr.* **1** to go round, to avoid **2** (*mil.*) to outflank **B** *v. intr. pron.* **1** to wander about, to go about **2** (*approssi-*

marsi) to be around, to be about
aggiudicàre *v. tr.* **1** to award **2** (*asta*) to knock down **3** (*aggiudicarsi*) to win
aggiùngere **A** *v. tr.* to add **B** *v. intr. pron.* to join, to be added
aggiùnta *s. f.* addition
aggiustàre **A** *v. tr.* **1** (*riparare*) to mend, to repair, to fix **2** (*sistemare*) to adjust **B** *v. intr. pron.* to come out right **C** *v. rifl.* to make do
agglomeràto *s. m.* agglomerate
aggrappàrsi *v. rifl.* to cling
aggravàre **A** *v. tr.* to make worse, to worsen **B** *v. intr. pron.* to become worse
aggraziàto *agg.* graceful
aggredìre *v. tr.* to attack, to assault
aggregàre **A** *v. tr.* to aggregate **B** *v. rifl.* to join
aggressióne *s. f.* attack, assault
aggressività *s. f.* aggressiveness
aggressìvo *agg.* aggressive
aggressóre *s. m.* aggressor
aggrottàre *v. tr.* to wrinkle, (*le ciglia*) to frown
aggrovigliàre **A** *v. tr.* to tangle **B** *v. rifl.* to get entangled
agguantàre *v. tr.* to seize, to catch
agguàto *s. m.* ambush
agiàto *agg.* well-to-do
àgile *agg.* agile, nimble
agilità *s. f.* agility, nimbleness
àgio *s. m.* **1** comfort, ease **2** (*opportunità*) chance, time ♦ **sentirsi a proprio a.** to be at one's ease
agiografia *s. f.* hagiography
agìre *v. intr.* **1** to act **2** (*comportarsi*) to behave **3** (*influenzare*) to act, to influence **4** (*funzionare*) to work
agitàre **A** *v. tr.* **1** to agitate, to shake **2** (*fig.*) to upset **B** *v. intr. pron.* **1** to toss (about) **2** (*turbarsi*) to get excited, to become upset
agitazióne *s. f.* agitation, unrest
àglio *s. m.* garlic
agnèllo *s. m.* lamb
agnòstico *agg.* agnostic
àgo *s. m.* needle
agonìa *s. f.* death throes *pl.*, agony
agonìstico *agg.* agonistic, competitive
agonizzàre *v. intr.* to be in the throes of death
agopuntùra *s. f.* acupuncture
agósto *s. m.* August
agrària *s. f.* agriculture
agràrio *agg.* agricultural, agrarian
agrìcolo *agg.* agricultural
agricoltóre *s. m.* farmer
agricoltùra *s. f.* agriculture, farming
agrifòglio *s. m.* holly
agriturìsmo *s. m.* farm holidays *pl.*
àgro *agg.* **1** sour, bitter **2** (*fig.*) sharp
agrodólce *agg.* bitter-sweet, sweet-and-sour
agrùme *s. m.* citrus (fruit, tree)
aguzzàre *v. tr.* to sharpen
agùzzo *agg.* sharp
àia *s. f.* threshing-floor, farmyard
airóne *s. m.* heron
aiuòla *s. f.* flowerbed
aiutànte *s. m. e f.* assistant ♦ **a. di campo** aide-de-camp
aiutàre **A** *v. tr.* **1** to help, to assist, to aid **2** (*favorire*) to stimulate **B** *v. rifl.* to help oneself **C** *v. rifl. rec.* to help each other
aiùto *s. m.* **1** help, aid, assistance **2** (*persona*) helper, assistant ♦ **a.!** help!; **chiedere a.** to call for help
aizzàre *v. tr.* to incite
àla *s. f.* wing
alabàstro *s. m.* alabaster
alàno *s. m.* (*zool.*) Great Dane
alàre (1) *agg.* wing (*attr*)
alàre (2) *s. m.* firedog, andiron
àlba *s. f.* dawn
àlbatro *s. m.* albatross
albeggiàre *v. intr.* to dawn
albergatóre *s. m.* hotel keeper
alberghièro *agg.* hotel (*attr*)
albèrgo *s. m.* hotel
àlbero *s. m.* **1** tree **2** (*naut.*) mast **3** (*mecc.*) shaft
albicòcca *s. f.* apricot
àlbo *s. m.* roll, register
àlbum *s. m.* album ♦ **a. da disegno** sketchbook
albùme *s. m.* albumen
alcalìno *agg.* alkaline
àlce *s. m.* elk ♦ **a. americano** moose
alchimìa *s. f.* alchemy
àlcol *s. m.* alcohol
alcòlico **A** *agg.* alcoholic **B** *s. m.* alcoholic drink
alcolìsmo *s. m.* alcoholism
alcolizzato *agg. e s. m.* alcoholic
alcùno **A** *agg. indef.* **1** (*in frasi afferm. o interr. con risposta afferm.*) some, a few (ES: **alcuni anni fa** some years ago) **2** (*in frasi neg., interr., dubit.*) any, no (ES: **senza a. dubbio** without any doubt, **in garage non c'era alcuna macchina** no car was

in the garage) **B** *pron. indef.* **1** (*in frasi afferm. o interr. con risposta positiva*) some, a few, some people (ES: **alcuni pensano che pioverà** some people think that it will rain **2** (*in frasi neg., interr., dubit.*) (*persone*) anyone, anybody, no one, nobody (*cose*) any, none (ES: **non vidi a.** I didn't see anyone, I saw no one)
aldilà *s. m.* afterlife
alesàggio *s. m.* (*mecc.*) bore
alétta *s. f.* fin, flap
alettóne *s. m.* aileron
alfabèto *s. m.* alphabet
alfière *s. m.* **1** (*mil.*) ensign **2** (*fig.*) standard bearer **3** (*scacchi*) bishop
àlga *s. f.* alga, (*di mare*) seaweed
àlgebra *s. f.* algebra
aliànte *s. m.* glider
àlibi *s. m.* alibi
alìce *s. f.* anchovy
alienàre *v. tr.* to alienate
alienazióne *s. f.* alienation
alièno **A** *agg.* averse (to), opposed (to) **B** *s. m.* alien
alimentàre (1) *agg.* alimentary, food (*attr.*)
alimentàre (2) *v. tr.* to feed, to nourish
alimentazióne *s. f.* feeding
aliménto *s. m.* **1** food, nourishment **2** *al pl.* (*dir.*) alimony
alìquota *s. f.* **1** share, quote **2** (*tasse*) rate
aliscàfo *s. m.* hydrofoil
alisèi *s. m. pl.* trade winds, trades
àlito *s. m.* breath
allacciàre *v. tr.* **1** to lace (up), to tie, to fasten **2** (*abbottonare*) to button up
allagaménto *s. m.* flooding
allagàre *v. tr.* to flood, to inundate
allargàre **A** *v. tr.* **1** to widen, to enlarge **2** (*estendere*) to extend, to spread **3** (*un vestito*) to let out **B** *v. intr. pron.* **1** to become wide **2** (*estendersi*) to extend, to grow
allarmàre **A** *v. tr.* to alarm **B** *v. rifl.* to become alarmed, to worry
allàrme *s. m.* alarm
allarmìsmo *s. m.* alarmism
allattàre *v. tr.* to nurse, to suckle ♦ **a. al seno** to breast-feed, **a. artificialmente** to bottle-feed
alleànza *s. f.* alliance
alleàrsi *v. rifl.* to form an alliance
alleàto **A** *agg.* allied **B** *s. m.* ally
allegàre *v. tr.* to enclose, to append
allegàto *s. m.* enclosure
alleggerìre *v. tr.* to lighten, to relieve
allegorìa *s. f.* allegory
allegrìa *s. f.* mirth, cheerfulness
allégro *agg.* **1** cheerful, merry **2** (*di colore*) bright
allenaménto *s. m.* training
allenàre *v. tr. e rifl.* to train
allenatóre *s. m.* trainer, coach
allentàre **A** *v. tr.* to slacken, to loosen **B** *v. intr. pron.* to loosen, to become slack
allergìa *s. f.* allergy
allèrgico *agg.* allergic
allestìre *v. tr.* **1** to prepare **2** (*teatro*) to stage **3** (*naut.*) to fit out
allettàre *v. tr.* to attract, to tempt
allevaménto *s. m.* **1** (*di bambini*) upbringing **2** (*di animali*) breeding **3** (*luogo*) farm
allevàre *v. tr.* **1** (*bambini*) to bring up, to rear **2** (*animali*) to breed
alleviàre *v. tr.* to relieve, to alleviate
allibìre *v. intr.* to be astounded
allibratóre *s. m.* bookmaker
allietàre **A** *v. tr.* to cheer up, to gladden **B** *v. rifl.* to rejoice, to become cheerful
allièvo *s. m.* **1** pupil, student **2** (*mil.*) cadet
alligatóre *s. m.* alligator
allineàre **A** *v. tr.* to line up, to align **B** *v. rifl.* to fall into line (with)
allòcco *s. m.* **1** (*zool.*) tawny owl **2** (*fig.*) fool
allocuzióne *s. f.* allocution
allòdola *s. f.* skylark, meadow
alloggiàre **A** *v. tr.* to lodge, to put up **B** *v. intr.* to lodge, to live
allòggio *s. m.* **1** lodging, accomodation house **2** (*appartamento*) flat, apartment ♦ **vitto e a.** board and lodging
allontanaménto *s. m.* removal
allontanàre **A** *v. tr.* **1** to remove, to put away **2** (*mandare via*) to turn away, to send away **B** *v. intr. pron.* to go away, to go off, to depart
allóra *avv.* **1** (*in quel momento*) then **2** (*in quel tempo*) at that time, in those days **3** (*in tal caso*) then, in that case **4** (*quindi*) therefore, so ♦ **da a. in poi** from then on; **e a.?** so what?
allòro *s. m.* laurel
àlluce *s. m.* big toe
allucinànte *agg.* (*fig.*) incredible
allucinazióne *s. f.* hallucination
allùdere *v. intr.* to allude, to refer
allumìnio *s. m.* aluminium
allungàre **A** *v. tr.* **1** to lengthen, to prolong,

to extend **2** (*stendere*) to stretch out **3** (*porgere*) to pass **4** (*annacquare*) to water down **B** *v. intr. pron.* to lengthen
allusióne *s. f.* allusion
alluvionàle *agg.* alluvial
alluvióne *s. f.* flood, alluvion
alméno *avv.* at least
alpinìsmo *s. m.* alpinism, mountaineering
alpinista *s. m. e f.* alpinist, mountain-climber
alpìno *agg.* alpine ♦ **sci a.** downhill skiing
alquànto **A** *agg. indef.* **1** (*un po'*) some, a certain amount of **2** (*al pl.*) several, a few **B** *pron. indef.* **1** some, a certain amount **2** (*al pl.*) some, several, a few **C** *avv.* a little, rather, somewhat
alt *inter.* halt, stop
altaléna *s. f.* (*appesa*) swing, (*in bilico*) seesaw
altàre *s. m.* altar
alteràre **A** *v. tr.* **1** to alter, to change **2** (*falsificare*) to falsify, to forge **B** *v. rifl.* **1** to alter, to change **2** (*turbarsi*) to lose one's temper, to get angry **3** (*deteriorarsi*) to go bad, to go sour
altèrco *s. m.* wrangle, altercation
alternànza *s. f.* alternation
alternàre *v. tr. e intr. pron.* to alternate
alternatìva *s. f.* **1** (*scelta*) alternative **2** (*alternanza*) alternation
alternatìvo *agg.* alternative
alternàto *agg.* alternating, alternate(d)
alternatóre *s. m.* (*elettr.*) alternator
altèrno *agg.* alternate
altézza *s. f.* **1** height **2** (*statura*) height, stature **3** (*di stoffa*) width **4** (*profondità*) depth **5** (*di suono*) pitch **6** (*titolo*) Highness ♦ **essere all'a. di q.c.** to be up/equal to st.
altezzóso *agg.* haughty
altìccio *agg.* tipsy
altitùdine *s. f.* altitude, height
àlto **A** *agg.* **1** high **2** (*di statura*) tall **3** (*profondo*) deep **4** (*di stoffa*) wide **5** (*di suono*) high, loud **6** (*geogr.*) upper **7** (*fig.*) high, noble **B** *s. m.* top, height **C** *avv.* high, up
altoparlànte *s. m.* loudspeaker
altopiàno *s. m.* plateau, upland, tableland
altorilièvo *s. m.* alto-rilievo, high relief
altrettànto **A** *agg. indef.* as much (... as), (*pl.*) as many (... as); (*in frasi neg.*) so much (... as), (*pl.*) so many (... as) **B** *pron. indef.* **1** (*correlativo*) as much (... as), (*pl.*) as many (... as) **2** (*la stessa cosa*) the same **C** *avv.* **1** (*con agg. e avv.*) as (... as), (*in frasi neg.*) so (... as) **2** (*con verbi*) as much (as)
àltri *pron. indef. sing.* someone else, (*in frasi neg.*) anyone else
altriménti *avv. e cong.* otherwise
àltro **A** *agg. indef.* **1** other, (*un altro*) another, (*in più*) more, further (ES: **l'altra automobile** the other car, **un'altra automobile** another car, **vuoi altro caffè?** would you like more coffee?, **ho bisogno di altre notizie** I need further news) **2** (*con agg., avv. e pron. interr. o indef.*) else (ES: **qualcun a.** somebody else, **nessun a.** nobody else, **in nessun a. luogo** nowhere else) **3** (*diverso*) different (**questa è un'altra cosa** that's a different thing) **B** *pron. indef.* **1** (the) other, (*un altro*) another (one), (*in più*) more; (*pl.*) others, other people (ES: **una volta o l'altra** some time or other, **tutti gli altri sono già qui** all the others are already here) **2** (*altra cosa*) something else, (*in frasi neg. e interr.*) anything else (ES: **parliamo d'a.** let's talk of something else, **serve a.?** anything else?) **3** (*l'un l'altro*) one another, each other ♦ **l'a. ieri** the day before yesterday
altrónde, d' *avv.* on the other hand, however
altróve *avv.* somewhere else, elsewhere
altrùi *agg. poss. inv.* other's, other people's, someone else's
altruìsmo *s. m.* altruism, unselfishness
altruìsta *s. m. e f.* altruist
altùra *s. f.* **1** high ground **2** (*naut.*) high sea, deep sea
alùnno *s. m.* pupil
alveàre *s. m.* hive
àlveo *s. m.* river bed
alzàre **A** *v. tr.* **1** to lift up, to raise, (*sollevare*) to heave **2** (*il volume*) to turn up **3** (*costruire*) to build, to erect **B** *v. intr. pron.* **1** (*crescere, salire*) to raise **2** (*dal letto*) to get up **3** (*in piedi*) to stand up
amàbile *agg.* **1** lovable **2** (*di vino*) sweet
amàca *s. f.* hammock
amalgamàre *v. tr. e intr. pron.* to amalgamate
amànte **A** *agg.* fond, keen **B** *s. m. e f.* lover
amàre *v. tr.* **1** to love **2** (*piacere*) to be fond of, to like
amareggiàto *agg.* embittered
amarèna *s. f.* sour cherry
amarézza *s. f.* bitterness
amàro **A** *agg.* **1** bitter **2** (*senza zucchero*) without sugar, unsweetened **B** *s. m.* **1** (*sa-*

pore) bitter taste **2** (*liquore*) bitters *pl.*
ambascïàta *s. f.* embassy
ambasciatóre *s. m.* ambassador
ambedùe *agg. e pron.* both
ambientàle *agg.* environmental
ambientàre **A** *v. tr.* **1** to acclimatize **2** (*fig.*) to set **B** *v. rifl.* to get acclimatized, to settle down
ambiènte *s. m.* **1** environment, habitat **2** (*fig.*) environment, circle, milieu, setting **3** (*stanza*) room
ambiguità *s. f.* ambiguity
ambìguo *agg.* ambiguous
ambìre *v. tr. e intr.* to aspire (to), to long (for)
àmbito *s. m.* ambit
ambizióne *s. f.* ambition
ambizióso *agg.* ambitious
àmbo *agg.* both
àmbra *s. f.* amber ♦ **a. grigia** ambergris; **a. nera** jet
ambulànte *agg.* itinerant ♦ **venditore a.** pedlar
ambulànza *s. f.* ambulance
ambulatòrio *s. m.* surgery, (*di pronto soccorso*) first-aid station
amenità *s. f.* **1** pleasantness **2** (*facezia*) pleasantry, joke
amèno *agg.* **1** pleasant, agreeable **2** (*divertente*) funny
amenorrèa *s. f.* amenorrhea
americàno *agg. e s. m.* American
ametìsta *s. f.* amethyst
amiànto *s. m.* amiant(h)us
amichévole *agg.* friendly
amicìzia *s. f.* friendship
amìco **A** *agg.* friendly **B** *s. m.* friend
àmido *s. m.* starch
ammaccàre *v. tr.* to dent, (*di frutta*) to bruise
ammaccatùra *s. f.* dent, (*di frutta*) bruise
ammaestràre *v. tr.* to train
ammainàre *v. tr.* to furl, to strike
ammalàrsi *v. intr. pron.* to fall ill
ammalàto **A** *agg.* ill, sick, diseased **B** *s. m.* sick person
ammaliàre *v. tr.* to charm
ammànco *s. m.* shortage, deficit
ammanettàre *v. tr.* to handcuff
ammassàre **A** *v. tr.* to amass, to pile up **B** *v. intr. pron.* to crowd together, to gather together
ammattìre *v. intr.* to go mad
ammazzàre **A** *v. tr.* to kill, (*assassinare*) to murder **B** *v. rifl.* to kill oneself
ammènda *s. f.* **1** amends *pl.* **2** (*multa*) fine
amméttere *v. tr.* **1** (*accettare, introdurre*) to admit **2** (*riconoscere*) to admit, to concede, to acknowledge **3** (*supporre*) to suppose
ammezzàto *s. m.* mezzanine
ammiccàre *v. intr.* to wink
amministràre *v. tr.* **1** to manage, to direct, to run **2** (*dir., relig.*) to administer
amministratìvo *agg.* administrative
amministratóre *s. m.* manager, director ♦ **a. delegato** managing director
amministrazióne *s. f.* administration, management
ammiragliàto *s. m.* admiralty
ammiràglio *s. m.* admiral
ammiràre *v. tr.* to admire
ammiratóre *s. m.* admirer, fan
ammirazióne *s. f.* admiration
ammissìbile *agg.* admissible
ammissióne *s. f.* admission
ammobiliàre *v. tr.* to furnish
ammobiliàto *agg.* furnished
ammòllo *s. m.* soaking
ammonìaca *s. f.* ammonia
ammoniménto *s. m.* admonition, admonishment, (*avvertimento*) warming
ammonìre *v. tr.* to admonish, (*avvertire*) to warn
ammontàre (1) *v. intr.* to amount, to come to
ammontàre (2) *s. m.* amount, sum
ammorbidìre *v. tr.* to soften
ammortizzàre *v. tr.* **1** (*mecc.*) to dampen **2** (*econ.*) to amortize, to depreciate
ammortizzatóre *s. m.* (*mecc.*) shock absorber, damper
ammucchiàre *v. tr.* to pile up
ammuffìre *v. intr. e intr. pron.* to grow musty
ammuffìto *agg.* mouldy
ammutinaménto *s. m.* mutiny
ammutinàrsi *v. intr. pron.* to mutiny
ammutolìre *v. intr.* to be struck dump
amnesìa *s. f.* amnesia
amnistìa *s. f.* amnesty
àmo *s. m.* fish-hook
amoràle *agg.* amoral
amóre *s. m.* **1** love **2** (*persona amata*) beloved, love, darling **3** (*desiderio*) desire ♦ **a. proprio** self-respect
amorévole *agg.* loving
amòrfo *agg.* amorphous
amoróso *agg.* amorous
amperòmetro *s. m.* amperometer, ammeter
ampiézza *s. f.* **1** width, wideness **2** (*ab-*

bondanza) ampleness
àmpio *agg.* **1** wide, large, ample, spacious **2** (*abbondante*) abundant
amplèsso *s. m.* **1** embrace **2** (*rapporto sessuale*) sexual intercourse
ampliàre *v. tr.* to amplify, to extend
amplificàre *v. tr.* **1** to amplify **2** (*esagerare*) to magnify, to extol
amplificatóre *s. m.* amplifier
amputàre *v. tr.* to amputate
amulèto *s. m.* amulet
anabbagliànte **A** *agg.* dipped **B** *s. m.* low-beam headlight, dipped headlight
anacronìsmo *s. m.* anachronism
anacronìstico *agg.* anachronistic
anàgrafe *s. f.* registry office
anagràmma *s. m.* anagram
analcòlico **A** *agg.* non-alcoholic **B** *s. m.* soft drink
analfabèta *agg. e s. m. e f.* illiterate
analgèsico *agg. e s. m.* analgesic
anàlisi *s. f.* analysis, test
analìsta *s. m. e f.* analyst
analizzàre *v. tr.* to analyse
analogìa *s. f.* analogy
anàlogo *agg.* analogous
ànanas *s. m.* pineapple
anarchìa *s. f.* anarchy
anatomìa *s. f.* anatomy
ànatra *s. f.* duck
ànca *s. f.* hip
ancèlla *s. f.* maid
ànche *avv.* **1** (*pure*) also, too, as well **2** (*davanti a comp.*) even, still **3** (*persino*) even ♦ **a. se** even if
àncora (1) *s. f.* anchor
ancóra (2) *avv.* **1** still **2** (*in frasi neg.*) yet **3** (*di nuovo*) again **4** (*di più*) more
ancoràggio *s. m.* anchorage, berth
ancoràre *v. tr. e rifl.* to anchor
andaménto *s. m.* **1** (*tendenza*) trend **2** (*corso*) course, state
andàre **A** *v. intr.* **1** to go, (*a piedi*) to walk, (*in auto*) to drive **2** (*essere, stare di salute, procedere*) to be, to get on **3** (*funzionare*) to work, to run **4** (*piacere*) to like, to feel like **5** (*convenire, andar bene*) to suit, (*di misura*) to fit, (*armonizzare*) to match **6** (*essere di moda*) to be in (fashion) **7** (*in funzione dell'aus. 'essere'*) to be, to get (ES: **se non vado errato** if I'm not mistaken) **8** (*dover essere*) to have to be, must be (ES: **questa macchina va riparata** this car must be repaired) **B** *v. intr. pron.* to go (away)
andàta *s. f.* going ♦ **biglietto di a.** single/one-way ticket
andatùra *s. f.* **1** gait **2** (*velocità*) pace
andirivièni *s. m. inv.* coming and going
andróne *s. m.* entrance-hall
anèddoto *s. m.* anecdote
anelàre *v. intr.* to pant
anèllo *s. m.* **1** ring **2** (*di catena*) link
anemìa *s. f.* an(a)emia
anèmico *agg. e s. m.* an(a)emic
anemòmetro *s. m.* anemometer
anèmone *s. m.* anemone
anestesìa *s. f.* an(a)esthesia
anestètico *s. m.* an(a)esthetic
anestetizzàre *v. tr.* to an(a)esthetize
aneurìsma *s. m.* aneurism
anfetamìna *s. f.* amphetamine
anfìbio **A** *agg.* amphibious **B** *s. m.* amphibian
anfiteàtro *s. m.* amphitheatre
ànfora *s. f.* amphora
angèlico *agg.* angelic(al)
àngelo *s. m.* angel
angìna *s. f.* angina
anglicanésimo *s. m.* Anglicanism
anglicàno *agg. e s. m.* Anglican
anglicìsmo *s. m.* Anglicism
anglosàssone *agg. e s. m. e f.* Anglo-Saxon
angolàre *agg.* angular
angolazióne *s. f.* angle
àngolo *s. m.* **1** (*mat., fis.*) angle **2** corner
àngora *s. f.* angora
angòscia *s. f.* anguish, anxiety
anguìlla *s. f.* eel
angùria *s. f.* watermelon
angustiàre **A** *v. tr.* to torment **B** *v. rifl.* to worry
angùsto *agg.* narrow
ànice *s. m.* anise
ànima *s. f.* **1** soul **2** (*parte centrale*) core, centre
animàle *agg. e s. m.* animal
animàre **A** *v. tr.* to give life to, to animate **B** *v. intr. pron.* to become animated
animàto *agg.* **1** (*vivente*) animated, living **2** (*vivace*) animated, lively ♦ **cartoni animati** cartoons
animazióne *s. f.* animation ♦ **cinema d'a.** cartoon cinema
ànimo *s. m.* **1** (*mente*) mind **2** (*intenzione*) intention, thoughts *pl.* **3** (*coraggio*) courage, heart **4** (*indole*) disposition, character, nature

annacquàre *v. tr.* to water, to dilute
annaffiàre *v. tr.* to water
annaffiatóio *s. m.* watering can
annaspàre *v. intr.* to grope
annàta *s. f.* **1** year **2** (*raccolto*) vintage **3** (*di periodici*) volume
annebbiàre **A** *v. tr.* **1** to fog, to obscure **2** (*fig.*) to cloud **B** *v. intr. pron.* to become foggy, to grow dim
annegaménto *s. m.* drowning
annegàre *v. tr. e intr.* to drown
annerìre *v. tr. e intr. pron.* to blacken
annèttere *v. tr.* **1** to annex **2** (*accludere*) to enclose **3** (*attribuire*) to attach
annichilìre *v. tr.* to annihilate
annidàrsi *v. rifl.* **1** to nest **2** (*nascondersi*) to hide
annientàre *v. tr.* to annihilate, to destroy
anniversàrio *s. m.* anniversary
ànno *s. m.* year ♦ **l'a. prossimo** next year; **l'a. scorso** last year
annodàre *v. tr.* to knot, to tie (in knots)
annoiàre **A** *v. tr.* to annoy, to bore **B** *v. intr. pron.* to be bored, to get bored
annotàre *v. tr.* **1** (*postillare*) to annotate **2** (*prender nota*) to note
annotazióne *s. f.* annotation, note
annoveràre *v. tr.* to count, to number
annuàle *agg.* **1** annual, yearly **2** (*che dura un anno*) year's
annualménte *avv.* annually, yearly
annuàrio *s. m.* yearbook
annuìre *v. intr.* to nod
annullaménto *s. m.* annulment, cancellation
annullàre *v. tr.* to annul, to cancel
annunciàre *v. tr.* to announce
annunciatóre *s. m.* announcer
annùncio *s. m.* **1** announcement **2** (*pubblicitario*) advertisement, ad
ànnuo *agg.* annual, yearly
annusàre *v. tr.* to smell, to sniff
annuvolàrsi *v. intr. pron.* to cloud over, to get cloudy
àno *s. m.* anus
anomalìa *s. f.* anomaly
anòmalo *agg.* anomalous
anònimo *agg.* anonymous
anoressìa *s. f.* anorexia
anormàle *agg.* abnormal
ànsa *s. f.* **1** (*manico*) handle **2** (*di fiume*) bight, loop
ànsia *s. f.* anxiety
ansietà *s. f.* anxiety
ansimàre *v. intr.* to pant
ansiolìtico *s. m.* tranquillizer
ansióso *agg.* anxious
ànta *s. f.* shutter, (*di armadio*) door
antagonìsmo *s. m.* antagonism
antagonìsta *s. m. e f.* antagonist, opponent
antàrtico *agg.* antarctic
antecedènte *agg.* preceding, previous
antefàtto *s. m.* previous history
antenàto *s. m.* ancestor, forefather
anténna *s. f.* **1** (*radio, TV*) aerial **2** (*zool.*) antenna, feeler
anteprìma *s. f.* preview
anterióre *agg.* **1** (*che è davanti*) front **2** (*nel tempo*) former, preceding, previous
antiaèreo *agg.* anti-aircraft
antiallèrgico *s. m.* antiallergic
antiatòmico *agg.* anti-atomic
antibiòtico *s. m.* antibiotic
anticaménte *avv.* in ancient times, formerly
anticàmera *s. f.* anteroom, antechamber
antiohità *s. f.* **1** antiquity **2** (*oggetto*) antique
anticiclóne *s. m.* anticyclone
anticipàre **A** *v. tr.* **1** to anticipate **2** (*denaro*) to advance **3** (*notizie*) to disclose, to divulge **4** (*prevenire*) to anticipate, to forestall **B** *v. intr.* to come early, to be ahead of time
antìcipo *s. m.* anticipation, advance
anticlericàle *agg. e s. m. e f.* anticlerical
antìco *agg.* **1** ancient **2** (*vecchio*) old, antique
anticoncezionàle *agg. e s. m.* contraceptive
anticonformìsmo *s. m.* nonconformism
anticonformìsta *s. m. e f.* nonconformist
anticòrpo *s. m.* antibody
anticostituzionàle *agg.* anticonstitutional, unconstitutional
anticrittogàmico *s. m.* fungicide
antidolorìfico *agg. e s. m.* analgesic
antìdoto *s. m.* antidote
antiemorràgico *agg. e s. m.* antihemorrhagic
antiestètico *agg.* unaesthetic
antifascìsta *agg. e s. m. e f.* antifascist
antifecondatìvo *agg. e s. m.* contraceptive
antifùrto *agg. e s. m. inv.* antitheft
antigèlo *agg. e s. m. inv.* antifreeze, antifreezing
antìlope *s. f.* antelope
antincèndio *agg.* anti-fire
antinevràlgico *agg.* antineuralgic
antinfiammatòrio *agg. e s. m.* anti-inflam-

matory
antinfluenzàle *s. m.* anti-influenza, flu (*attr.*)
antioràrio *agg.* counterclockwise, anti-clockwise
antipàsto *s. m.* hors d'oeuvre, appetizer, starter
antipatìa *s. f.* antipathy, dislike
antipàtico *agg.* unpleasant, disagreeable
antiproièttile *agg.* bullet-proof
antiquariàto *s. m.* antique trade ♦ **mobili d'a.** antique furniture
antiquàrio A *agg.* antiquarian **B** *s. m.* antique dealer
antiquàto *agg.* antiquated
antiràbbico *agg.* antirabic
antireumàtico *agg. e s. m.* antirheumatic
antirùggine *agg. inv.* antirust, rustproof
antiscìvolo *agg.* anti-slip
antisemitìsmo *s. m.* anti-Semitism
antisèttico *agg.* antiseptic
antisìsmico *agg.* antiseismic
antistamìnico A *agg.* antihistaminic **B** *s. m.* antihistamine
antitetànico *agg.* antitetanus
antologìa *s. f.* anthology
antonomàsia *s. f.* antonomasia
antropologìa *s. f.* anthropology
antropològico *agg.* anthropological
antropòlogo *s. m.* anthropologist
antropomòrfo *agg.* anthropomorphous
anulàre A *agg.* ring-like **B** *s. m.* ring finger
ànzi *cong.* **1** (*al contrario*) on the contrary **2** (*rafforzativo*) rather **3** (*o meglio*) even better, or better still
anzianità *s. f.* seniority
anziàno A *agg.* **1** elderly, old **2** (*di grado*) senior **B** *s. m.* elderly person
anziché *cong.* **1** (*piuttosto che*) rather than **2** (*invece di*) instead of
anzitùtto *avv.* first of all
apatìa *s. f.* apathy
àpe *s. f.* bee
aperitìvo *s. m.* aperitif
apèrto *agg.* open ♦ **all'aria a.** in the open air
apertùra *s. f.* opening ♦ **orario d'a.** opening time
àpice *s. m.* apex
apicoltùra *s. f.* apiculture
apnèa *s. f.* apn(o)ea
apòcrifo *agg.* apocryphal
apòlide *agg. e s. m. e f.* stateless (person)
apologìa *s. f.* apology
apoplessìa *s. f.* apoplexy
apòstolo *s. m.* apostle
apòstrofo *s. m.* apostrophe
appagàre A *v. tr.* to satisfy, to fulfil **B** *v. rifl.* to be satisfied
appàlto *s. m.* contract
appannàre A *v. tr.* to mist, to tarnish **B** *v. intr. pron.* **1** to mist up **2** (*vista*) to grow dim
apparàto *s. m.* **1** (*tecnol.*) machinery, equipment **2** (*anat.*) apparatus, system
apparecchiàre *v. tr.* to prepare, (*la tavola*) to lay the table
apparécchio *s. m.* **1** apparatus, set **2** (*aeroplano*) aircraft
apparènte *agg.* apparent
apparenteménte *avv.* apparently
apparènza *s. f.* appearance
apparìre *v. intr.* **1** to appear **2** (*sembrare*) to seem, to look
appariscènte *agg.* striking
appartaménto *s. m.* flat, (*USA*) apartment
appartàrsi *v. rifl.* to withdraw, to keep apart
appartenére *v. intr.* to belong (to)
appassionàre A *v. tr.* to thrill, to move **B** *v. intr. pron.* to become fond of
appassionàto *agg.* **1** impassioned, passionate **2** (*amante*) keen (on)
appassìre *v. intr. e intr. pron.* to wither
appellàrsi *v. intr. pron.* to appeal
appèllo *s. m.* **1** (*dir.*) appeal **2** (*chiamata*) roll-call **3** (*invocazione*) call ♦ **fare l'a.** to call the roll
appéna A *avv.* **1** (*a stento*) hardly, scarcely **2** (*soltanto*) only **3** (*da poco tempo*) (only) just ♦ **B** *cong.* as soon as ♦ **a. ... che, a. ... quando** just ... when, no sooner ... than
appèndere *v. tr.* to hang
appendìce *s. f.* appendix ♦ **romanzo d'a.** serial
appendicìte *s. f.* appendicitis
appesantìre A *v. tr.* to make heavy **B** *v. intr. pron.* to grow stout
appetìto *s. m.* appetite
appetitóso *agg.* appetizing
appianàre A *v. tr.* (*fig.*) to smooth away **B** *v. intr. pron.* to be resolved
appiattìre *v. tr. e intr. pron.* to flatten
appiccicàre A *v. tr.* to stick **B** *v. intr.* to be sticky
appiccicóso *agg.* sticky, (*di persona*) clinging
appièno *avv.* fully, completely

appìglio *s. m.* **1** hold **2** (*fig.*) pretext
appisolàrsi *v. intr. pron.* to doze off
applaudìre *v. tr. e intr.* to applaud, to clap, to cheer
applàuso *s. m.* applause, cheers *pl.*
applicàre **A** *v. tr.* **1** to apply **2** (*dir*) to enforce **B** *v. rifl.* to apply oneself
applicazióne *s. f.* **1** application **2** (*dir*) enforcement
appoggiàre **A** *v. tr.* **1** to lean, to lay **2** (*sostenere*) to support **B** *v. rifl.* **1** to lean **2** (*fig.*) to rely
appoggiatèsta *s. m. inv.* headrest
appòggio *s. m.* support
appollaiàrsi *v. rifl.* to perch
appórre *v. tr.* to affix
appositaménte *avv.* expressly, on purpose
appòsito *agg.* **1** special **2** (*adatto*) proper
appòsta *avv.* **1** (*deliberatamente*) on purpose, intentionally **2** (*con uno scopo preciso*) specially, expressly
appostàre **A** *v. tr.* to lie in wait for **B** *v. rifl.* to lie in ambush, to lie in wait
apprèndere *v. tr.* **1** to learn **2** (*venire a sapere*) to hear
apprendìsta *s. m. e f.* apprentice
apprensióne *s. f.* apprehension, anxiety
apprensìvo *agg.* apprehensive, anxious
apprèsso *avv.* **1** (*vicino*) near, close **2** (*dietro*) behind **3** (*in seguito*) after, later, below
apprètto *s. m.* starch
apprezzàbile *agg.* appreciable
apprezzaménto *s. m.* **1** appreciation **2** (*giudizio*) opinion
apprezzàre *v. tr.* to appreciate
appròccio *s. m.* approach
approdàre *v. intr.* **1** (*naut.*) to dock, to land **2** (*riuscire*) to come to
appròdo *s. m.* landing, docking
approfittàre *v. intr. e intr. pron.* **1** to profit by, to take advantage of **2** (*abusare*) to impose on
approfondìre *v. tr.* **1** to deepen **2** (*fig.*) to study in deep
appropriàto *agg.* appropriate, suitable
approssimàrsi *v. rifl. e intr. pron.* to approach, to come near
approssimatìvo *agg.* **1** approximate, rough **2** (*impreciso*) imprecise, superficial
approvàre *v. tr.* to approve
approvazióne *s. f.* approval
approvvigionaménto *s. m.* **1** supplying **2** *al pl.* (*provviste*) provisions *pl.*, supplies *pl.*
appuntaménto *s. m.* appointment, date
appùnto (1) *s. m.* **1** note, record **2** (*osservazione*) remark
appùnto (2) *avv.* exactly, just
appuràre *v. tr.* **1** to ascertain **2** (*verificare*) to verify, to check
apribottìglie *s. m. inv.* bottle-opener
aprìle *s. m.* April
aprìre **A** *v. tr.* **1** to open **2** (*acqua, gas*) to turn on **3** (*cominciare*) to begin, to open **B** *v. intr. e intr. pron.* **1** to open **2** (*sbocciare*) to bloom
apriscàtole *s. m. inv.* tin-opener, can-opener
àptero *agg.* apterous
àquila *s. f.* eagle
aquilóne *s. m.* kite
àra (1) *s. f.* altar
àra (2) *s. f.* (*misura*) are
arabésco *s. m.* arabesque
aràbico *agg.* Arabic, Arabian
àrabo *agg. e s. m.* Arab, Arabian
aràchide *s. f.* peanut
aragósta *s. f.* lobster, crayfish
aràldica *s. f.* heraldry
aràldico *agg.* heraldic
arància *s. f.* orange
aranciàta *s. f.* orangeade
aràncio *s. m.* orange (tree)
arancióne *agg.* orange
aràre *v. tr.* to plough, (*USA*) to plow
aràtro *s. m.* plough, (*USA*) plow
aràzzo *s. m.* tapestry
arbitràre *v. tr.* **1** (*dir*) to arbitrate **2** (*sport*) to referee, to umpire
arbitràrio *agg.* arbitrary
arbìtrio *s. m.* **1** will **2** (*abuso*) abuse
àrbitro *s. m.* **1** (*dir*) arbitrator **2** (*sport*) referee, umpire
arbòreo *agg.* arboreal
arboricoltùra *s. f.* arboriculture
arbùsto *s. m.* shrub
àrca *s. f.* ark
arcàdico *agg.* Arcadian
arcàico *agg.* archaic
arcàngelo *s. m.* archangel
arcàno *agg.* arcane, mysterious
arcàta *s. f.* **1** arch **2** (*serie di archi*) arcade
archeologìa *s. f.* archaeology
archeològico *agg.* archaeologic
archeòlogo *s. m.* archaeologist
archètipo *s. m.* archetype
archétto *s. m.* (*mus.*) bow
archibùgio *s. m.* harquebus

architétto *s. m.* architect
architettònico *agg.* architectonic, architectural
architettùra *s. f.* architecture
architràve *s. m.* architrave
archìvio *s. m.* archives *pl.*, file
archivòlto *s. m.* archivolt
arcière *s. m.* archer, bowman
arcìgno *agg.* surly
arcipèlago *s. m.* archipelago
arcivéscovo *s. m.* archbishop
àrco *s. m.* **1** (*arch., anat.*) arch **2** (*arma, mus.*) bow **3** (*fis., geom.*) arc **4** (*fig.*) space
arcobaléno *s. m.* rainbow
ardènte *agg.* burning
àrdere *v. tr. e intr.* to burn
ardèsia *s. f.* slate
ardìre *v. intr.* to dare
ardóre *s. m.* ardour
àrduo *agg.* arduous
àrea *s. f.* area
aréna *s. f.* **1** (*sabbia*) sand **2** (*arch.*) arena
arenàrsi *v. intr. pron.* to strand
arenìle *s. m.* sandy shore
àrgano *s. m.* windlass, winch
argentàto *agg.* **1** (*color argento*) silvery, silver **2** (*rivestito d'argento*) silver-plated
argenterìa *s. f.* silverware
argènto *s. m.* silver
argìlla *s. f.* clay
àrgine *s. m.* bank, embankment, dyke
argoménto *s. m.* **1** (*tema*) subject, matter, topic **2** (*prova*) argument
arguìre *v. tr.* to deduce
argùto *agg.* quick-witted, witty
argùzia *s. f.* **1** wit **2** (*motto*) witty remark
ària *s. f.* **1** air **2** (*aspetto*) look, (*espressione*) expression **3** (*mus.*) tune, air, (*di opera*) aria ♦ **a. condizionata** air conditioned; **camera d'a.** inner tube; **darsi delle arie** to give oneself airs
àrido *agg.* dry, arid
arieggiàre *v. tr.* to air, to ventilate
arìete *s. m.* **1** ram **2** (*astr.*) Aries
arìnga *s. f.* herring
arióso *agg.* airy
aristocràtico **A** *agg.* aristocratic(al) **B** *s. m.* aristocrat
aristocrazìa *s. f.* aristocracy
aritmètica *s. f.* arithmetic
arlecchìno *agg. e s. m.* harlequin
àrma *s. f.* **1** arm, weapon **2** (*mil.*) force ♦ **porto d'armi** firearm licence
armàdio *s. m.* cupboard, wardrobe
armamentàrio *s. m.* instruments *pl.*
armaménto *s. m.* **1** armament, arming **2** (*naut.*) rigging, equipment
armàre **A** *v. tr.* **1** to arm **2** (*naut.*) to rig, to fit out **B** *v. rifl.* to arm oneself
armàta *s. f.* army
armatóre *s. m.* shipowner
armatùra *s. f.* **1** (*mil.*) armour **2** (*telaio*) framework
armeggiàre *v. intr.* **1** (*affaccendarsi*) to bustle, to fuss **2** (*intrigare*) to intrigue
armerìa *s. f.* armoury
armistìzio *s. m.* armistice
armonìa *s. f.* harmony
armònico *agg.* harmonic
armonióso *agg.* harmonious
armonizzàre *v. tr. e intr. pron.* to harmonize
arnése *s. m.* **1** (*attrezzo*) tool, implement **2** (*aggeggio*) gadget, contraption, thing
àrnia *s. f.* hive
aròma *s. m.* **1** aroma, fragrance **2** (*cuc.*) spice
aromàtico *agg.* aromatic
àrpa *s. f.* harp
arpìa *s. f.* harpy
arpióne *s. m.* harpoon
arrabbiàrsi *v. intr. pron.* to get angry
arrabbiàto *agg.* angry
arraffàre *v. tr.* to snatch
arrampicàrsi *v. intr. pron.* to scramble (up), to climb (up)
arrampicàta *s. f.* climb
arrancàre *v. intr.* to hobble, to trudge
arrangiàre **A** *v. tr.* to arrange **B** *v. intr. pron.* **1** to manage, to do the best one can **2** (*accordarsi*) to come to an agreement **3** (*accomodarsi*) to make oneself comfortable
arrecàre *v. tr.* **1** (*portare*) to bring **2** (*causare*) to cause
arredaménto *s. m.* **1** furnishing, fitting out, interior decoration **2** (*mobili*) furniture, furnishings *pl.*
arredàre *v. tr.* to furnish
arredatóre *s. m.* interior decorator
arrèdo *s. m.* furnishings *pl.*, furniture
arrèndersi *v. rifl.* **1** to surrender **2** (*fig.*) to give up
arrestàre **A** *v. tr.* **1** (*fermare*) to stop, to halt **2** (*trarre in arresto*) to arrest **B** *v. rifl.* to stop, to pause
arrèsto *s. m.* **1** (*fermata*) stop, halt, arrest **2** (*dir., mil.*) arrest

arretràre **A** *v. tr.* to withdraw **B** *v. intr.* to draw back
arretràto **A** *agg.* **1** behind, back, rear **2** (*sottosviluppato*) backward, underdeveloped **B** *s. m.* arrear ♦ **numero a.** back number
arricchìre **A** *v. tr.* to enrich **B** *v. rifl. e intr. pron.* to become rich, to grow rich
arricciàre **A** *v. tr.* to curl **B** *v. intr. pron.* to become curly ♦ **a. il naso** to turn up one's nose
arrìnga *s. f.* **1** harangue **2** (*dir*) pleading
arrivàre *v. intr.* **1** to arrive (at, in), to get (to), to reach, to come (to) **2** (*giungere a*) to go as far as, to go so far as, to be reduced to **3** (*riuscire*) to manage, to be able **4** (*avere successo*) to attain success **5** (*accadere*) to happen
arrivàto *agg.* successful
arrivedérci *inter.* goodbye, see you soon, see you later
arrivìsta *s. m. e f.* careerist, (*pop.*) go-getter
arrìvo *s. m.* **1** arrival **2** (*sport*) finish, finishing line
arrogànte *agg.* arrogant
arrossaménto *s. m.* reddening
arrossìre *v. intr.* to blush
arrostìre *v. tr.* to roast, (*su graticola*) to broil, to grill
arròsto *agg. e s. m.* roast
arrotàre *v. tr.* to sharpen
arrotolàre *v. tr.* to roll up
arrotondàre *v. tr.* **1** to round **2** (*fig.*) to round off
arrovellàrsi *v. rifl.* to strive, to work oneself up into a rage ♦ **a. il cervello** to rack one's brains
arrugginìre *v. tr., intr. e intr. pron.* to rust
arruolàre **A** *v. tr.* to recruit, to enlist **B** *v. rifl.* to join up, to enlist
arsenàle *s. m.* **1** (*naut.*) shipyard, dockyard **2** (*mil.*) arsenal
àrso *agg.* **1** (*bruciato*) burnt **2** (*riarso*) dry
arsùra *s. f.* **1** (*caldo*) scorching heat **2** (*sete*) burning thirst
àrte *s. f.* art ♦ **belle arti** fine arts
artefàtto *agg.* adulterated
artéfice *s. m.* artificer, maker
artèria *s. f.* artery
arterioscleròsi *s. f.* arteriosclerosis
arterióso *agg.* arterial
àrtico *agg.* arctic
articolàre (1) *agg.* articular
articolàre (2) **A** *v. tr.* **1** to articulate **2** (*proferire*) to utter **3** (*fig.*) to subdivide **B** *v. rifl.* **1** to articulate **2** (*fig.*) to be divided (into)
articolazióne *s. f.* articulation
artìcolo *s. m.* **1** (*gramm.*) article **2** (*di giornale*) article **3** (*comm.*) item, article
artificiàle *agg.* artificial
artificio *s. m.* artifice, device, stratagem ♦ **fuochi d'a.** fireworks
artigianàto *s. m.* handicraft, (*prodotti*) handicrafts
artigiàno *s. m.* artisan, craftsman
artiglierìa *s. f.* artillery
artìglio *s. m.* claw
artìsta *s. m. e f.* artist
artìstico *agg.* artistic
àrto *s. m.* **1** (*anat.*) limb **2** (*zool.*) arm
artrìte *s. f.* arthritis
artrósi *s. f.* arthrosis
arzìllo *agg.* lively, sprightly
ascèlla *s. f.* armpit
ascendènte **A** *agg.* ascendant, rising **B** *s. m.* **1** (*influenza*) ascendency, influence **2** (*astr*) ascendant **3** (*antenato*) ancestor
ascensióne *s. f.* ascension, ascent
ascensóre *s. m.* lift, (*USA*) elevator
ascésa *s. f.* ascent
ascèsso *s. m.* abscess
ascetìsmo *s. m.* asceticism
àscia *s. f.* axe
asciugacapélli *s. m. inv.* hairdryer
asciugamàno *s. m.* towel
asciugàre **A** *v. tr.* to dry, to wipe **B** *v. rifl.* to dry oneself, to wipe oneself **C** *v. intr. pron.* to dry up, to get dry
asciugatùra *s. f.* drying
asciùtto *agg.* **1** dry **2** (*fig.*) brusque, curt **3** (*magro*) thin
ascoltàre *v. tr.* **1** to listen to **2** (*dare retta*) to pay attention to
ascoltatóre *s. m.* listener, *pl.* audience
ascólto *s. m.* listening ♦ **stare in a.** to be listening
asfaltàre *v. tr.* to asphalt
asfàlto *s. m.* asphalt
asfissiàre **A** *v. tr.* **1** to asphyxiate, to suffocate **2** (*fig.*) to bore **B** *v. intr.* to suffocate
asiàtico *agg. e s. m.* Asiatic, Asian
asìlo *s. m.* **1** (*d'infanzia*) kindergarten, nursery school **2** (*rifugio*) shelter, asylum
asimmètrico *agg.* asymmetric
àsino *s. m.* ass, donkey
àsma *s. f. o m.* asthma
asmàtico *agg. e s. m.* asthmatic

àsola *s. f.* buttonhole
aspàrago *s. m.* asparagus, (*pop.*) sparrowgrass
aspettàre *v. tr.* **1** to wait for, to await, to expect, be looking forward **2** (*prevedere*) to expect ♦ **a. un bambino** to expect a baby
aspettatìva *s. f.* **1** (*attesa*) wait **2** (*speranza*) expectation, hope **3** (*congedo*) leave (of absence)
aspètto *s. m.* **1** appearance, look, aspect **2** (*punto di vista*) side, point of view
aspirànte **A** *agg.* **1** aspiring **2** (*mecc.*) sucking **B** *s. m.* aspirant, applicant, candidate
aspirapólvere *s. m. inv.* vacuum cleaner
aspiràre **A** *v. tr.* **1** to breathe in, to inhale **2** (*mecc.*) to suck **3** (*fon.*) to aspirate **B** *v. intr.* to aspire
aspiratóre *s. m.* aspirator
aspirìna *s. f.* aspirin
asportàre *v. tr.* to remove, to carry away, to take away
àspro *agg.* **1** sour, tart **2** (*fig.*) harsh, rough
assaggiàre *v. tr.* to taste, to try
assàggio *s. m.* **1** tasting **2** (*piccola quantità*) taste **3** (*campione*) sample
assài *avv.* **1** (*molto*) much, very **2** (*a sufficienza*) enough **3** (*in funzione di agg.*) a lot of, many
assalìre *v. tr.* to assail, to attack
assàlto *s. m.* assault, attack
assassinàre *v. tr.* to murder, to assassinate
assassìnio *s. m.* murder, assassination
assassìno **A** *agg.* murderous **B** *s. m.* murderer, assassin
àsse (1) *s. f.* board
àsse (2) *s. m.* **1** (*scient.*) axis **2** (*mecc.*) axle
assediàre *v. tr.* to besiege
assèdio *s. m.* siege
assegnàre *v. tr.* to assign, to allot, to award
asségno *s. m.* **1** (*banca*) cheque, (*USA*) check **2** (*contributo*) allowance ♦ **a. in bianco** blank cheque; **a. a vuoto** uncovered cheque
assemblèa *s. f.* assembly, meeting
assènso *s. m.* assent
assentàrsi *v. intr. pron.* to go away, to absent oneself
assènte **A** *agg.* absent **B** *s. m. e f.* absentee
assènza *s. f.* absence
assestàre **A** *v. tr.* **1** to arrange, to settle **2** (*un colpo*) to deal **B** *v. rifl.* to settle (down)
assetàto *agg.* thirsty
assètto *s. m.* **1** order, arrangement, disposition **2** (*naut., aer.*) trim
assicuràre **A** *v. tr.* **1** (*garantire, mettere al sicuro*) to assure, to secure, to ensure, to guarantee **2** (*fissare*) to fasten, to secure **3** (*fare un'assicurazione*) to insure **B** *v. rifl.* **1** (*accertarsi*) to make sure **2** (*legarsi*) to fasten oneself **3** (*fare un'assicurazione*) to insure oneself, to take out an insurance
assicurazióne *s. f.* **1** assurance **2** (*dir.*) insurance ♦ **a. sulla vita** life insurance; **a. contro l'incendio** fire insurance
assideraménto *s. m.* frostbite
assìduo *agg.* assiduous
assième *avv.* → **insieme**
assillàre *v. tr.* to pester, to bother
assistènte *s. m. e f.* assistant
assistènza *s. f.* **1** (*presenza*) presence, attendance **2** (*aiuto*) help, assistance, aid **3** (*comm.*) service **4** (*beneficenza*) welfare
assistere **A** *v. tr.* **1** to assist, to help **2** (*curare*) to treat, to look after **B** *v. intr.* to be present, to attend
àsso *s. m.* ace
associàre **A** *v. tr.* **1** to associate, to combine **2** (*fare socio*) to take into partnership **B** *v. rifl.* **1** to join **2** (*diventare membro*) to become a member **3** (*diventare socio*) to enter into partnership
associazióne *s. f.* association
assoggettàre *v. tr.* to subject, to subdue
assolàto *agg.* sunny
assoldàre *v. tr.* to recruit, to engage
assólo *s. m.* solo
assolutaménte *avv.* absolutely
assolùto *agg.* absolute
assoluzióne *s. f.* **1** (*dir.*) acquittal, discharge **2** (*relig.*) absolution
assòlvere *v. tr.* **1** (*dir.*) to acquit, to discharge **2** (*relig.*) to absolve **3** (*compiere*) to accomplish, to perform
assomigliàre **A** *v. intr.* to resemble, to be like **B** *v. rifl. rec.* to resemble each other, to be alike
assonnàto *agg.* sleepy
assopìrsi *v. intr. pron.* **1** to doze off **2** (*calmarsi*) to cool down
assorbènte *agg. e s. m.* absorbent ♦ **a. igienico** sanitary towel
assorbiménto *s. m.* absorption
assorbìre *v. tr.* to absorb
assordànte *agg.* deafening

assordàre *v. tr.* to deafen
assortiménto *s. m.* assortment
assortìto *agg.* **1** assorted **2** (*accoppiato*) matched
assòrto *agg.* absorbed, engrossed
assottigliàre A *v. tr.* **1** to thin, to make thin **2** (*ridurre*) to reduce, to diminish **B** *v. intr. pron.* **1** to grow thin **2** (*ridursi*) to diminish, to be reduced
assuefàre A *v. tr.* to accustom **B** *v. rifl.* to get accustomed, to accustom oneself, to get used
assuefazióne *s. f.* **1** habit, inurement **2** (*med.*) tolerance, (*dipendenza*) addiction
assùmere *v. tr.* **1** to assume, to put on **2** (*impegno, responsabilità*) to undertake, to taken upon oneself **3** (*in servizio*) to engage, to take on, to employ **4** (*ingerire*) to take, to consume
assurdità *s. f.* absurdity
assùrdo A *agg.* absurd **B** *s. m.* absurdity
àsta *s. f.* **1** pole **2** (*tecn.*) rod, bar **3** (*comm.*) auction ♦ **salto con l'a.** pole-jumping; **vendere all'a.** to auction
astèmio A *agg.* abstemious, teetotal **B** *s. m.* teetotaller
astenérsi *v. rifl.* to abstain, to refrain
asterìsco *s. m.* asterisk
àstice *s. m.* lobster
asticèlla *s. f.* little bar, (*per salto in alto*) crossbar
astigmàtico *agg.* astigmatic
astinènza *s. f.* abstinence
àstio *s. m.* rancour
astràgalo *s. m.* **1** (*anat., bot.*) astragalus **2** (*arch.*) astragal
astrattìsmo *s. m.* abstractionism
astrattìsta *s. m. e f.* abstractionist, abstract artist
astràtto *agg. e s. m.* abstract
astringènte *agg. e s. m.* astringent
àstro *s. m.* **1** star, celestial body **2** (*fig.*) star
astrofìsica *s. f.* astrophysics *pl.* (*v. al sing.*)
astrolàbio *s. m.* astrolabe
astrologìa *s. f.* astrology
astrològico *agg.* astrologic
astròlogo *s. m.* astrologer
astronàuta *s. m. e f.* astronaut
astronàutico *agg.* astronautical
astronàve *s. f.* spaceship
astronomìa *s. f.* astronomy
astronòmico *agg.* astronomical
astrònomo *s. m.* astronomer
astùccio *s. m.* case, box
astùto *agg.* astute, shrewd, cunning
astùzia *s. f.* **1** astuteness, shrewdness **2** (*azione*) trick, stratagem
atàvico *agg.* atavic
ateìsmo *s. m.* atheism
atenèo *s. m.* university
àteo A *agg.* atheistic **B** *s. m.* atheist
atìpico *agg.* atypic(al)
atlànte *s. m.* atlas
atlàntico *agg.* Atlantic
atlèta *s. m. e f.* athlete
atlètica *s. f.* athletics *pl.* (*v. al sing.*)
atlètico *agg.* athletic
atmosfèra *s. f.* atmosphere
atmosfèrico *agg.* atmospheric(al)
atòllo *s. m.* atoll
atòmico *agg.* atomic
àtomo *s. m.* atom
àtrio *s. m.* **1** entrance hall, lobby **2** (*anat.*) atrium
atróce *agg.* atrocious, terrible
attaccaménto *s. m.* attachment
attaccànte *s. m.* (*sport*) forward
attaccapànni *s. m.* (clothes) peg, hook, (*gruccia*) hanger
attaccàre A *v. tr.* **1** (*unire*) to attach, to fasten, to tie **2** (*appiccicare*) to stick, to glue **3** (*appendere*) to hang **4** (*assalire*) to attack, to assail **5** (*iniziare*) to begin, to start, (*iniziare a suonare*) to strike up **6** (*contagiare*) to infect, to pass on **B** *v. intr.* **1** (*aderire*) to stick **2** (*far presa*) to catch on **C** *v. rifl.* **1** (*appigliarsi*) to cling **2** (*affezionarsi*) to become attached
attàcco *s. m.* **1** (*mil.*) attack, assault **2** (*med.*) attack, fit **3** (*punto di unione*) junction, connection **4** (*avvio*) opening, beginning **5** (*fig.*) attack **6** (*per sci*) fastening, binding
atteggiaménto *s. m.* attitude, pose
attempàto *agg.* elderly
attendàrsi *v. intr. pron.* to camp
attèndere A *v. tr.* to wait for, to await **B** *v. intr.* **1** (*aspettare*) to wait **2** (*dedicarsi*) to attend
attendìbile *agg.* reliable
attenérsi *v. rifl.* to keep to
attentaménte *avv.* attentively, carefully
attentàre *v. intr.* to attempt, to make an attempt
attentàto *s. m.* attempt, outrage
attènto *agg.* attentive, careful ♦ **a.!** take care!, be careful!
attenuànte A *agg.* extenuating **B** *s. f.* ex-

tenuating circumstance
attenuàre *v. tr.* **1** to attenuate, to mitigate **2** (*diminuire la gravità di*) to extenuate
attenzióne *s. f.* **1** attention, care **2** *al pl.* (*premure*) kindness ♦ **a.!** take care!, be careful!; **fare a.** to take care, to be careful, to look out; **prestare a. a qc.** to pay attention to sb.
atterràggio *s. m.* landing ♦ **pista d'a.** landing strip
atterràre **A** *v. tr.* to knock down **B** *v. intr.* to land
atterrìre **A** *v. tr.* to terrify **B** *v. intr. pron.* to be terrified
attésa *s. f.* **1** wait, waiting **2** *al pl.* (*aspettativa*) expectation ♦ **lista d'a.** waiting list
attéso *agg.* **1** waited for, awaited **2** (*desiderato*) longed for
attestàto *s. m.* **1** certificate **2** (*prova*) proof, (*segno*) sign
àttico *s. m.* attic
attìguo *agg.* adjoining, adjacent, next (to)
attillàto *agg.* close-fitting, tight
àttimo *s. m.* moment
attinènte *agg.* relating, concerning
attìngere *v. tr.* **1** to draw **2** (*ricavare*) to get
attiràre *v. tr.* to attract, to draw
attitùdine *s. f.* aptitude
attivàre *v. tr.* to activate, to start up
attività *s. f.* **1** activity **2** (*lavoro*) occupation, job
attìvo **A** *agg.* active **B** *s. m.* **1** (*comm.*) assets *pl.* **2** (*gramm.*) active form
attizzàre *v. tr.* to poke
àtto *s. m.* **1** act, action, deed **2** (*atteggiamento*) attitude, (*gesto*) gesture, (*segno*) sign **3** (*teatro*) act **4** (*attestato*) certificate, document, (*dir.*) deed **5** *al pl.* (*di congresso, assemblea*) proceedings *pl.*, records *pl.* ♦ **all'a. del pagamento/della consegna** on payment/delivery; **a. di vendita** bill of sale; **mettere in a. q.c.** to carry out st.
attònito *agg.* astonished, amazed
attorcigliàre *v. tr. e rifl.* to twist, to twine
attóre *s. m.* actor
attórno **A** *avv.* about, around, round **B** *prep.* **a. a** about, around, round
attraccàre *v. tr. e intr.* to moore, to berth, to dock
attràcco *s. m.* mooring, berthing, docking
attraènte *agg.* attractive
attràrre *v. tr.* to attract
attrattìva *s. f.* attraction
attraversaménto *s. m.* crossing ♦ **a. pedonale** pedestrian crossing
attraversàre *v. tr.* to cross, to go through
attravèrso **A** *avv.* through **B** *prep.* **1** through, across **2** (*tempo*) over
attrazióne *s. f.* attraction
attrezzàre *v. tr.* **1** to equip, to fit out **2** (*naut.*) to rig
attrezzatùra *s. f.* **1** equipment, outfit **2** (*naut.*) rigging
attrézzo *s. m.* tool, implement
attribuìbile *agg.* attributable
attribuìre *v. tr.* **1** to attribute, to ascribe **2** (*assegnare*) to assign, to award
attribùto *s. m.* attribute
attrìce *s. f.* actress
attrìto *s. m.* friction
attuàle *agg.* **1** present, current **2** (*di attualità*) topical
attualità *s. f.* **1** topicality, up-to-dateness **2** *al pl.* (*fatti recenti*) current events *pl.*, up-to-date news
attualménte *avv.* at present
attuàre **A** *v. tr.* to carry out, to put into effect **B** *v. intr. pron.* to come true
attutìre **A** *v. tr.* to appease, to deaden **B** *v. intr. pron.* to become appeased, to calm down, to become deadened
audàce *agg.* **1** bold, audacious **2** (*arrischiato*) risky, rash **3** (*provocante*) daring, bold
audàcia *s. f.* audacity, daring, boldness
àudio *s. m. inv.* sound, audio
audiovisìvo *agg.* audiovisual
audizióne *s. f.* (*teatro*) audition
àuge *s. f.* height ♦ **essere in a.** to enjoy great favour
auguràre *v. tr.* to wish
augùrio *s. m.* **1** wish **2** (*presagio*) omen ♦ **i migliori auguri** best wishes
àula *s. f.* **1** hall, room **2** (*di tribunale*) courtroom **3** (*di scuola*) classroom
àulico *agg.* **1** aulic **2** (*solenne*) solemn, stately
aumentàre **A** *v. tr.* to increase, to raise, to augment **B** *v. intr.* to increase, to grow, to rise
auménto *s. m.* **1** increase, addition **2** (*rialzo*) rise
àureo *agg.* **1** (*d'oro*) gold (*attr.*) **2** (*dorato, fig.*) golden
aurèola *s. f.* halo
auricolàre **A** *agg.* auricular **B** *s. m.* ear-

phone
aurìga *s. m.* charioteer
auròra *s. f.* dawn ♦ **a. boreale** aurora borealis
ausiliàre *agg.* auxiliary
ausiliàrio *agg.* auxiliary
auspicàbile *agg.* desirable
auspìcio *s. m.* **1** auspice, omen **2** (*protezione*) patronage
austerità *s. f.* austerity
austéro *agg.* austere
australe *agg.* austral
australiàno *agg. e s. m.* Australian
austrìaco *agg. e s. m.* Austrian
autenticàre *v. tr.* to authenticate
autenticità *s. f.* authenticity
autèntico *agg.* authentic, genuine
autìsta *s. m. e f.* driver, (*privato*) chauffeur
àuto *abbr. di* → **automobile**
autoabbronzànte *agg.* self-tanning
autoadesìvo *agg.* self-adhesive
autobiografìa *s. f.* autobiography
autobiogràfico *agg.* autobiographic(al)
autoblìndo *s. m.* armoured car
autobótte *s. f.* tanker, tank lorry, (*USA*) tank truck
àutobus *s. m.* bus ♦ **a. a due piani** double-decker
autocàrro *s. m.* lorry, (*USA*) truck
autodidàtta *s. m. e f.* self-taught person, autodidact
autodifésa *s. f.* self-defence
autòdromo *s. m.* autodrome, circuit
autofilettànte *agg.* self-threading
autofurgóne *s. m.* van
autogòl *s. m. inv.* own-goal
autògrafo **A** *agg.* autographical **B** *s. m.* autograph
autogrill *s. m.* motorway restaurant
autogrù *s. f.* breakdown lorry, (*USA*) tow truck
autolìnea *s. f.* bus-line
autòma *s. m.* automaton
automàtico *agg.* automatic
automazióne *s. f.* automation
automèzzo *s. m.* motor vehicle
automòbile *s. f.* car
automobilìsta *s. m. e f.* (car) driver, motorist
automobilìstico *agg.* motor (*attr.*)
autonoléggio *s. m.* car hire, car rental
autonomìa *s. f.* **1** autonomy, self-government **2** (*fig.*) freedom, independence **3** (*aer., naut.*) range
autònomo *agg.* autonomous
autopilòta *s. m.* autopilot
autopsìa *s. f.* autopsy
autoràdio *s. f. inv.* car radio
autóre *s. m.* author
autorespiratóre *s. m.* aqualung, scuba
autorévole *agg.* authoritative
autoriméssa *s. f.* garage
autorità *s. f.* authority
autoritarìsmo *s. m.* authoritarianism
autoritràtto *s. m.* self-portrait
autorizzàre *v. tr.* to authorize
autorizzazióne *s. f.* **1** authorization, warrant **2** (*documento*) permit
autoscàtto *s. m.* self-timer
autoscuòla *s. f.* driving school
autostòp *s. m. inv.* hitchhiking ♦ **fare l'a.** to hitchhike
autostoppìsta *s. m. e f.* hitchhiker
autostràda *s. f.* motorway, (*USA*) speedway, expressway
autostradàle *agg.* motorway (*attr.*)
autosufficiènte *agg.* self-sufficient
autotrèno *s. m.* lorry with trailer, (*USA*) trailer truck
autoveìcolo *s. m.* motor vehicle
autovettùra *s. f.* motor car
autunnàle *agg.* autumnal
autùnno *s. m.* autumn, (*USA*) fall
avambràccio *s. m.* forearm
avampósto *s. m.* outpost
avanguàrdia *s. f.* vanguard, avant-garde
avànti *avv.* **1** (*di luogo*) forward, ahead, in front **2** (*di tempo*) before, forward, on ♦ **a.!** come in!; **a. e indietro** to and fro; **d'ora in a.** from now on
avantrèno *s. m.* forecarriage
avanzaménto *s. m.* **1** advancement, progress **2** (*promozione*) promotion
avanzàre **A** *v. tr.* to advance, to put forward, to present **B** *v. intr.* **1** to advance, to go forward **2** (*restare*) to be left
avanzàta *s. f.* advance
avànzo *s. m.* remainder, (*di cibo*) leftovers *pl.*
avarìa *s. f.* breakdown, damage, average
avàro *agg.* mean, miserly, stingy
avéna *s. f.* oats *pl.*
avére **A** *v. aus.* to have **B** *v. tr.* **1** (*possedere, tenere*) to have (got) **2** (*indossare*) to have on, to wear **3** (*ottenere, prendere, ricevere*) to get **4** (*provare, sentire*) to feel **5** **a. da** (*dovere*) to have to ♦ **a. fame/sete** to be hungry/thirsty; **quanti ne abbiamo oggi?** what's the date today?

aviazióne *s. f.* aviation, (*arma*) Air Force
avicoltùra *s. f.* aviculture
avidità *s. f.* avidity
àvido *agg.* avid
avifàuna *s. f.* avifauna
àvo *s. m.* **1** (*nonno*) grandfather **2** *al pl.* ancestors
avocàdo *s. m. inv.* avocado
avòrio *s. m.* ivory
avvallaménto *s. m.* sinking, subsidence
avvaloràre *v. tr.* to convalidate
avvampàre *v. intr.* to flare up
avvantaggiàre **A** *v. tr.* to favour, to benefit **B** *v. rifl.* to take advantage
avvelenaménto *s. m.* poisoning
avvelenàre *v. tr.* to poison
avvenènte *agg.* attractive, charming
avveniménto *s. m.* event
avvenìre (1) *s. m.* future
avvenìre (2) *v. intr.* to happen
avvenirìstico *agg.* futuristic
avventàrsi *v. rifl.* to rush, to throw oneself
avventàto *agg.* rash, reckless
avventìzio *agg.* **1** temporary, occasional **2** (*bot., dir.*) adventitious
avvènto *s. m.* advent, coming
avventùra *s. f.* **1** adventure **2** (*sentimentale*) affair, fling (*fam.*)
avventuràrsi *v. rifl.* to venture
avventurièro *s. m.* adventurer
avventuróso *agg.* adventurous
avveràrsi *v. intr. pron.* to come true
avvèrbio *s. m.* adverb
avversàrio **A** *agg.* opposing **B** *s. m.* opponent, adversary
avversióne *s. f.* aversion, dislike
avversità *s. f.* adversity
avvèrso *agg.* **1** (*contrario*) adverse, unfavourable, hostile **2** (*che sente avversione*) averse
avvertènza *s. f.* **1** (*attenzione, cura*) care, caution **2** (*avvertimento*) warning **3** *al pl.* instructions *pl.*, directions *pl.* **4** (*prefazione*) preface, foreword
avvertiménto *s. m.* warning
avvertìre *v. tr.* **1** (*avvisare*) to inform, to advise, to point out **2** (*ammonire*) to warn **3** (*percepire*) to feel
avvézzo *agg.* accustomed, used
avviaménto *s. m.* start, starting
avviàre **A** *v. tr.* **1** (*indirizzare*) to direct **2** (*iniziare*) to begin, to start up **3** (*metter in moto*) to start up **B** *v. intr. pron.* to set out
avvicendàre *v. tr. e rifl. rec.* to alternate
avvicinàre **A** *v. tr.* **1** to bring near **2** (*una persona*) to approach **B** *v. intr. pron.* to come near, to approach
avvilìre **A** *v. tr.* **1** (*scoraggiare*) to dishearten **2** (*degradare*) to degrade **B** *v. intr. pron.* **1** (*scoraggiarsi*) to lose heart, to be disheartened **2** (*degradarsi*) to degrade oneself
avvincènte *agg.* engaging, charming
avvìncere *v. tr.* to attract, to charm
avvìo *s. m.* start
avvisàre *v. tr.* to inform, to advise
avvìso *s. m.* **1** announcement, notice **2** (*avvertimento*) warning **3** (*opinione*) opinion
avvistàre *v. tr.* to sight
avvitàre *v. tr.* to screw
avvizzìre *v. intr.* to wither
avvocàto *s. m.* lawyer
avvòlgere *v. tr.* **1** to wrap up **2** (*arrotolare*) to wind, to roll up
avvoltóio *s. m.* vulture
azalèa *s. f.* azalea
azièndа *s. f.* firm, business, company, establishment ♦ **a. agricola** farm
azionàre *v. tr.* to operate, to set in motion, to drive
azióne *s. f.* **1** action, (*atto*) act **2** (*fin.*) share
azionìsta *s. m. e f.* shareholder
azòto *s. m.* azote
azzannàre *v. tr.* to snap
azzardàre **A** *v. tr.* to hazard, to risk **B** *v. intr. pron.* to dare, to risk
azzàrdo *s. m.* hazard, risk ♦ **gioco d'a.** game of chance
azzeccàre *v. tr.* **1** (*centrare*) to hit, to strike **2** (*indovinare*) to guess
azzeràre *v. tr.* to set to zero
azzoppàrsi *v. intr. pron.* to become lame
azzuffàrsi *v. rifl. e rifl. rec.* to come to blows
azzùrro *agg. e s. m.* blue

B

babbèo *s. m.* fool, simpleton
bàbbo *s. m.* father, dad, daddy
babbùccia *s. f.* slipper
babilonése *agg. e s. m. e f.* Babylonian
baby-sitter *s. f. e m.* baby-sitter ♦ **fare la/il b.-s.** to baby-sit
bacàto *agg.* **1** worm-eaten, maggoty **2** (*marcio*) rotten
bàcca *s. f.* berry
baccalà *s. m.* dried salted cod
baccàno *s. m.* row, clamour
baccèllo *s. m.* pod
bacchétta *s. f.* **1** stick, rod **2** (*di direttore d'orchestra*) baton ♦ **b. magica** magic wand
bacchettóne *s. m.* bigot
bachèca *s. f.* notice board
baciàre **A** *v. tr.* to kiss **B** *v. rifl. rec.* to kiss each other
bacìllo *s. m.* bacillus
bacinèlla *s. f.* basin
bacìno *s. m.* **1** basin **2** (*anat.*) pelvis **3** (*naut.*) dock **4** (*geol.*) field
bàcio *s. m.* kiss
bàco *s. m.* worm ♦ **b. da seta** silkworm
bacùcco *agg.* decrepit
badàre *v. intr.* **1** (*fare attenzione*) to be careful, to pay attention, to mind **2** (*prendersi cura*) to look after
badìa *s. f.* abbey
badìle *s. m.* shovel
bàffo *s. m.* **1** moustache **2** (*di animale*) whiskers *pl.*
bagagliàio *s. m.* **1** (*ferr.*) luggage van, (*USA*) baggage car **2** (*autom.*) boot, (*USA*) trunk
bagàglio *s. m.* luggage, (*USA*) baggage ♦ **b. a mano** hand-luggage; **deposito bagagli** left-luggage office, checkroom; **fare/disfare i bagagli** to pack/to unpack
bagarìno *s. m.* tout, (*USA*) scalper
baglióre *s. m.* flash, glare
bagnànte *s. m. e f.* bather
bagnàre **A** *v. tr.* **1** to wet, (*immergere*) to dip, (*inzuppare*) to soak, (*inumidire*) to moisten, to dampen, (*spruzzare*) to sprinkle **2** (*annaffiare*) to water **3** (*di fiume*) to flow through, (*di mare*) to wash **B** *v. rifl.* **1** to get wet **2** (*fare il bagno*) to bathe
bagnàto *agg.* wet
bagnìno *s. m.* bathing-attendant
bàgno *s. m.* **1** bath, (*in mare*) bathe **2** (*stanza*) bathroom, toilet ♦ **fare il b.** (*in vasca*) to take a bath, (*al mare*) to go swimming; **mettere a b.** to soak
bagnomarìa *s. m.* bain-marie
bagnoschiùma *s. m.* bubble bath
bàia *s. f.* bay
baionétta *s. f.* bayonet
balaùstra *s. f.* balustrade
balbettàre *v. tr. e intr.* to stammer, to stutter
balbuziènte *s. m. e f.* stammerer, stutterer
balconàta *s. f.* balcony
balcóne *s. m.* balcony
baldacchìno *s. m.* baldachin, canopy
baldànza *s. f.* self-confidence, boldness
baldòria *s. f.* merrymaking, good time
baléna *s. f.* whale ♦ **caccia alla b.** whaling
balenàre *v. intr.* **1** (*impers.*) to lighten **2** to flash
balenièra *s. f.* whaling ship, whaler
baléno *s. m.* lightning, flash ♦ **in un b.** in a flash
balèstra *s. f.* **1** crossbow **2** (*mecc.*) leaf spring
bàlia *s. f.* wet nurse
ballàre *v. tr. e intr.* to dance
ballàta *s. f.* ballad
ballerìna *s. f.* dancer, (*classica*) ballerina, ballet dancer
ballerìno *s. m.* dancer, (*classico*) ballet dancer
balletto *s. m.* ballet
bàllo *s. m.* **1** dance, dancing **2** (*festa*) ball ♦ **corpo di b.** corps de ballet; **essere in b.** to be involved in st.
ballottàggio *s. m.* second ballot
balneàre *agg.* bathing (*attr.*)
balòcco *s. m.* toy
balórdo *agg.* stupid, foolish
balsàmico *agg.* balsamic
bàlsamo *s. m.* balm, balsam
baluàrdo *s. m.* bulwark
bàlza *s. f.* **1** crag **2** (*di vestito*) frill
balzàre *v. intr.* to leap, to jump, to bounce
bàlzo *s. m.* leap, jump, bound
bambàgia *s. f.* cotton wool

bambìna *s. f.* child, baby-girl, little girl
bambinàia *s. f.* nursemaid
bambìno *s. m.* child, baby, little boy, kid
bàmbola *s. f.* doll
bambù *s. m.* bamboo
banàle *agg.* banal, commonplace, trivial
banàna *s. f.* banana
bànca *s. f.* bank ♦ **a mezzo b.** by banker; **b. dati** data bank; **conto in b.** bank account
bancarèlla *s. f.* stall
bancàrio **A** *agg.* banking, bank (*attr*) **B** *s. m.* bank clerk ♦ **assegno b.** cheque
bancarótta *s. f.* bankruptcy ♦ **fare b.** to go bankrupt
banchétto *s. m.* banquet
banchière *s. m.* banker
banchina *s. f.* **1** (*naut.*) quay, wharf, pier **2** (*ferr.*) platform **3** (*strada*) shoulder, verge
banchìsa *s. f.* ice pack
bànco *s. m.* **1** (*panca*) bench, (*di scuola*) desk, (*di chiesa*) pew **2** (*di negozio*) counter, (*di mercato*) stall, stand **3** (*da lavoro*) table, work bench **4** (*geogr.*) bank **5** (*banca*) bank ♦ **b. di corallo** coral reef; **b. di sabbia** sandbar
bàncomat *s. m. inv.* cash dispenser
banconòta *s. f.* banknote, (*USA*) bill
bànda (1) *s. f.* **1** (*di armati*) band, gang **2** (*di suonatori*) band
bànda (2) *s. f.* **1** (*striscia*) band, stripe **2** (*fis., elettr.*) band
banderuòla *s. f.* weathercock, vane
bandièra *s. f.* flag, banner
bandìre *v. tr.* **1** to proclaim, to advertise **2** (*esiliare*) to exile, to banish **3** (*metter da parte*) to dispense with
bandìto *s. m.* bandit, outlaw
banditóre *s. m.* **1** (*stor.*) (public) crier **2** (*asta*) auctioneer
bàndo *s. m.* **1** ban **2** (*esilio*) banishment **3** (*annuncio pubblico*) proclamation, announcement
bàndolo *s. m.* end of a skein
bar *s. m. inv.* bar
baràcca *s. f.* **1** hut, shed, hovel **2** (*oggetto*) junk
baraónda *s. f.* hubbub
baràre *v. intr.* to cheat
bàratro *s. m.* chasm
barattàre *v. tr.* to barter, to swap
baràtto *s. m.* barter
baràttolo *s. m.* jar, pot, (*di latta*) tin, can
bàrba *s. f.* **1** beard **2** (*fam.*) (*noia*) bore ♦ **b. e capelli** shave and haircut; **che b.!** what a bore!; **farsi la b.** to shave; **in b. a** in spite of
barbabiètola *s. f.* **1** beetroot **2** (*da zucchero*) sugar beet
barbacàne *s. m.* barbican
barbàrico *agg.* barbaric, barbarian
bàrbaro **A** *agg.* barbarous, barbaric **B** *s. m.* barbarian
barbecue *s. m. inv.* barbecue
barbière *s. m.* barber, (*negozio*) barber's shop
barbitùrico *s. m.* barbiturate
barbóne *s. m.* **1** (*barba*) long beard **2** (*vagabondo*) tramp **3** (*zool.*) poodle
barbóso *agg.* (*fam.*) boring
barbùto *agg.* bearded
bàrca *s. f.* boat ♦ **b. a motore** motor boat; **b. a remi** row boat; **b. a vela** sailing boat
barcaiòlo *s. m.* boatman
barcollàre *v. intr.* to stagger
barèlla *s. f.* stretcher
barìle *s. m.* barrel, cask
barìsta *s. m. e f.* barman *m.*, barmaid *f.*
barìtono *s. m.* baritone
barlùme *s. m.* glimmer, gleam
bàro *s. m.* cardsharper
baròcco *agg. e s. m.* Baroque
baròmetro *s. m.* barometer
baróne *s. m.* baron
baronéssa *s. f.* baroness
bàrra *s. f.* **1** bar **2** (*naut.*) helm, tiller **3** (*segno*) stroke
barricàre *v. tr. e rifl.* to barricade (oneself)
barricàta *s. f.* barricade
barrièra *s. f.* barrier
barùffa *s. f.* brawl, quarrel
barzellétta *s. f.* joke
basàre **A** *v. tr.* to base, to found **B** *v. rifl.* to base oneself, to be founded
bàsco **A** *agg.* Basque **B** *s. m.* **1** Basque **2** (*berretto*) beret
bàse **A** *s. f.* base, (*fig.*) basis **B** *agg.* basic, base (*attr*)
basétta *s. f.* sideburns *pl.*
basilàre *agg.* basic, fundamental
basìlica *s. f.* basilica
basìlico *s. m.* basil
bàsso **A** *agg.* **1** low **2** (*di statura*) short **3** (*di spessore*) thin **4** (*di acqua*) shallow **5** (*di suono*) low, soft **6** (*geogr.*) southern, lower **B** *s. m.* **1** lower part, bottom **2** (*mus.*) bass

bassofóndo *s. m.* shallow(s), shoal
bassopiàno *s. m.* lowland
bassorilièvo *s. m.* bas-relief, basso-rilievo
bàsta *inter.* (that's) enough!, that will do!
bastànte *agg.* sufficient, enough
bastàrdo *agg.* **1** bastard, illegitimate **2** (*bot., zool.*) underbred, crossbred
bastàre *v. intr.* **1** to be sufficient, to be enough, to suffice **2** (*durare*) to last
bastiménto *s. m.* vessel, ship
bastióne *s. m.* bastion, rampart
bàsto *s. m.* pack-saddle
bastonàre *v. tr.* to beat, to thrash
bastoncìno *s. m.* rod, small stick ♦ **b. da sci** ski pole
bastóne *s. m.* stick
batòsta *s. f.* blow
battage *s. m. inv.* campaign
battàglia *s. f.* battle, fight
battaglióne *s. m.* battalion
battèllo *s. m.* boat ♦ **b. a vapore** steamer; **b. di salvataggio** lifeboat
battènte *s. m.* (*di porta*) leaf, (*di finestra*) shutter
bàttere **A** *v. tr.* **1** to beat, to strike, to hit **2** (*sconfiggere*) to beat, to overcome **3** (*a macchina*) to type **4** (*moneta*) to mint **5** (*bandiera*) to fly **B** *v. intr.* **1** to beat, to knock **2** (*pulsare*) to beat **3** (*prostituirsi*) to walk the streets **C** *v. intr. pron.* to fight, (*in duello*) to duel
batterìa *s. f.* **1** battery **2** (*mus.*) drums *pl.*
battèrio *s. m.* bacterium
battesimàle *agg.* baptismal
battésimo *s. m.* baptism ♦ **nome di b.** Christian/first name
battezzàre *v. tr.* **1** to baptize, to christen **2** (*soprannominare*) to nickname
batticuòre *s. m.* heartthrob, palpitation
battimàni *s. m. inv.* (hand-)clapping, applause
battistèro *s. m.* baptistery
battistràda *s. m. inv.* **1** outrider **2** (*di pneumatico*) tread ♦ **b. liscio** smooth tread
battitappéto *s. m.* carpet cleaner
bàttito *s. m.* **1** beating **2** (*cardiaco*) heartbeat, pulsation **3** (*d'ali*) wingbeat
battùta *s. f.* **1** blow, beat, beating **2** (*di caccia*) hunting **3** (*tip.*) stroke, character **4** (*mus.*) beat, bar **5** (*teatro*) cue **6** (*frase spiritosa*) quip, witticism **7** (*tennis*) service **8** (*rastrellamento*) round-up
batùffolo *s. m.* flock
baùle *s. m.* **1** trunk **2** (*autom.*) boot, (*USA*) trunk
bàva *s. f.* slaver, dribble ♦ **b. di vento** breath
bavaglìno *s. m.* bib
bavàglio *s. m.* gag
bàvero *s. m.* collar
bazzècola *s. f.* trifle
bazzicàre *v. tr. e intr.* to frequent
beàto *agg.* **1** (*relig.*) blessed **2** happy, blissful ♦ **b. te!** lucky you!
beccàccia *s. f.* woodcock
beccaccìno *s. m.* snipe
beccàre **A** *v. tr.* **1** to peck **2** (*fam.*) (*buscare*) to catch, to get **B** *v. rifl. rec.* **1** to peck each other **2** (*litigare*) to squabble
beccheggiàre *v. intr.* to pitch
becchìno *s. m.* gravedigger, sexton
bécco *s. m.* **1** beak, bill **2** (*di bricco*) lip, spout
befàna *s. f.* **1** Befana, (*Epifania*) Epiphany **2** (*donna vecchia e brutta*) ugly old woman
bèffa *s. f.* **1** joke, cheat **2** (*scherno*) mockery
beffàrdo *agg.* mocking
beffàre **A** *v. tr.* to mock **B** *v. rifl.* to scoff at, to make fun of
bèga *s. f.* **1** quarrel, dispute **2** (*problema*) trouble, problem
begònia *s. f.* begonia
beige *agg. e s. m. inv.* beige
belàre *v. intr.* to bleat, to baa
bèlga *agg. e s. m. e f.* Belgian
bèlla *s. f.* **1** (*donna bella*) beauty, belle **2** (*fidanzata*) girlfriend **3** (*sport*) decider, (*a carte*) final game **4** (*bella copia*) fair copy
bellézza *s. f.* beauty, loveliness, good looks *pl.*, (*di uomo*) handsomeness
bèllico *agg.* war (*attr*)
bellicóso *agg.* warlike, combative
bèllo **A** *agg.* **1** beautiful, fine, lovely **2** (*di uomo*) handsome, good-looking **3** (*di tempo*) fine, nice, good **4** (*elegante*) smart **5** (*gentile*) fine, kind **6** (*piacevole*) nice, pleasant **B** *s. m.* **1** the beautiful, beauty **2** (*tempo*) fine weather **3** (*innamorato*) boyfriend
bélva *s. f.* wild beast
belvedére *s. m.* **1** (*arch.*) belvedere **2** (*luogo panoramico*) viewpoint
benché *cong.* although, though
bènda *s. f.* bandage
bendàggio *s. m.* bandaging, bandage
bendàre *v. tr.* **1** to bandage, to dress **2** (*gli occhi*) to blindfold
bène **A** *s. m.* **1** good **2** (*affetto*) fondness,

love **3** (*dono*) gift, blessing **4** *al pl.* goods *pl.*, property **B** *avv.* **1** well **2** (*per bene, completamente*) properly, thoroughly **3** (*rafforzativo*) very, really, quite
benedettìno *agg.* Benedictine
benedétto *agg.* blessed
benedìre *v. tr.* to bless
benedizióne *s. f.* blessing, benediction
beneducàto *agg.* well-mannered
benefattóre *s. m.* benefactor
beneficènza *s. f.* charity ♦ **istituto di b.** charitable institution; **spettacolo di b.** benefit performance
beneficiàre A *v. tr.* to benefit **B** *v. intr.* to profit, to benefit from, to take advantage of
beneficiàrio *s. m.* beneficiary
benefìcio *s. m.* benefit, advantage
benèfico *agg.* **1** beneficent, charitable **2** (*vantaggioso*) beneficial
benemerènza *s. f.* merit
benemèrito *agg.* meritorious
benèssere *s. m.* **1** wellbeing **2** (*prosperità*) welfare, affluence
benestànte *agg.* well-to-do
benestàre *s. m.* approval
benèvolo *agg.* benevolent, (*gentile*) kind
beniamìno *s. m.* pet
benìgno *agg.* benign
benintéso *avv.* of course
benìssimo *avv.* very well
bensì *cong.* but
benvenùto *agg., s. m. e inter.* welcome
benzìna *s. f.* petrol, (*USA*) gas, gasoline ♦ **fare b.** to get petrol/gas, to fill up
bére *v. tr.* to drink
berlìna (1) *s. f.* (*pena*) pillory
berlìna (2) *s. f.* **1** (*carrozza*) berlin **2** (*autom.*) saloon, limousine, (*USA*) sedan
bernòccolo *s. m.* **1** bump **2** (*fig.*) bent, flair
berrétto *s. m.* cap
bersagliàre *v. tr.* to bombard
bersàglio *s. m.* target, butt ♦ **tiro al b.** target-shooting
bestémmia *s. f.* **1** blasphemy, (*imprecazione*) curse **2** (*sproposito*) nonsense
bestemmiàre *v. intr.* to curse, to swear
béstia *s. f.* beast
bestiàle *agg.* **1** bestial, beastly **2** (*fam.*) terrible, incredible
bestiàme *s. m.* livestock, cattle
bestiàrio *s. m.* bestiary
béttola *s. f.* tavern
betùlla *s. f.* birch
bevànda *s. f.* drink, beverage
bevìbile *agg.* drinkable
bevitóre *s. m.* drinker
bevùta *s. f.* drink
biàda *s. f.* fodder
biancherìa *s. f.* linen ♦ **b. intima** underwear
biànco A *agg.* **1** white **2** (*non scritto*) blank **B** *s. m.* **1** white **2** (*uomo bianco*) white man ♦ **di punto in b.** all of a sudden; **in b.** (*non scritto*) blank, (*senza grassi*) plain, boiled
biasimàre *v. tr.* to blame, to reprove
biàsimo *s. m.* blame, reproof
Bìbbia *s. f.* Bible
biberòn *s. m. inv.* feeding bottle, (baby's) bottle
bìbita *s. f.* (soft) drink
bìblico *agg.* biblical
bibliòfilo *s. m.* bibliophile
bibliografìa *s. f.* bibliography
bibliotèca *s. f.* library
bibliotecàrio *s. m.* librarian
bicarbonàto *s. m.* bicarbonate
bicchière *s. m.* glass ♦ **b. di carta** paper cup
biciclétta *s. f.* bicycle, bike ♦ **andare in b.** to ride a bicycle, to cycle
bicìpite *s. m.* biceps
bicolóre *agg.* two-coloured, bicoloured
bidè *s. m.* bidet
bidèllo *s. m.* school caretaker
bidonàre *v. tr.* (*fam.*) to swindle, to cheat
bidóne *s. m.* **1** tank, drum, bin **2** (*fam.*) (*imbroglio*) swindle
biennàle *agg.* **1** (*che dura due anni*) two-year **2** (*ogni due anni*) biennial **3** (*bot.*) biennial
biènnio *s. m.* period of two years
bietola *s. f.* chard
bifocàle *agg.* bifocal
biforcàrsi *v. intr. pron.* to fork
biforcazióne *s. f.* fork
bigamìa *s. f.* bigamy
bìgamo *s. m.* bigamist
bighellonàre *v. intr.* to lounge about, to loiter, to loaf (about)
bigiotterìa *s. f.* trinkets *pl.*, costume jewellery
bigliettàio *s. m.* (*in stazione*) ticket clerk, (*in treno*) ticket collector, (*su autobus*) conductor
biglietterìa *s. f.* ticket office, booking office, (*teatro*) box office

bigliétto *s. m.* **1** (*breve scritto*) note **2** (*contrassegno*) ticket **3** (*cartoncino*) card **4** (*banconota*) note, (*USA*) bill ♦ **b. d'andata e ritorno** return ticket; **b. di sola andata** single ticket, one-way ticket; **b. da visita** (visiting) card
bignè *s. m. inv.* cream puff
bigodìno *s. m.* curler
bigòtto *s. m.* bigot
bilància *s. f.* **1** balance, scales *pl.* **2** (*astr.*) the Scales *pl.*, Libra
bilanciàre **A** *v. tr.* **1** to balance **2** (*soppesare*) to weigh (up) **B** *v. rifl. rec.* to balance out
bilàncio *s. m.* balance, budget
bile *s. f.* bile
biliàrdo *s. m.* billiards *pl.* (*v. al sing.*)
bilìngue *agg.* bilingual
bilinguìsmo *s. m.* bilingualism
bìmbo *s. m.* child, baby, kid
bimensìle *agg.* fortnightly
bimestràle *agg.* **1** two-monthly, bimonthly **2** (*che dura due mesi*) bimestrial, two-month
bimotóre *agg.* twin-engined
binàrio *s. m.* **1** (railway) track, line **2** (*marciapiede*) platform
binòcolo *s. m.* binoculars *pl.*
biochìmica *s. f.* biochemistry
biodegradàbile *agg.* biodegradable
biofìsica *s. f.* biophysics *pl.* (*v. al sing.*)
biografìa *s. f.* biography
biogràfico *agg.* biographical
biologìa *s. f.* biology
biològico *agg.* biological
biòlogo *s. m.* biologist
bióndo **A** *agg.* fair, blond (*f.* blonde), golden **B** *s. m.* blond colour, fair colour ♦ **b. cenere** ash-blond
biopsìa *s. f.* biopsy
birbànte *s. m.* rogue
birìllo *s. m.* skittle
bìro *s. f. inv.* biro, ballpoint pen
bìrra *s. f.* beer, ale ♦ **b. alla spina** draught beer; **b. chiara/scura** lager/stout
birrerìa *s. f.* beer house
bis *s. m. inv.* (*teatro*) encore
bisbètico *agg.* crabbed, shrewish
bisbigliàre *v. tr.* to whisper
bìsca *s. f.* gambling house
bìscia *s. f.* snake
biscòtto *s. m.* biscuit, (*USA*) cookie
bisessuàle *agg.* bisexual
bisestìle *agg.* bissextile ♦ **anno b.** leap year
bisettimanàle *agg.* twice-weekly
bislàcco *agg.* eccentric
bislùngo *agg.* oblong
bisnònna *s. f.* great-grandmother
bisnònno *s. m.* great-grandfather
bisognàre *v. intr. impers.* to be necessary, to have to, must
bisógno *s. m.* **1** need, necessity **2** (*mancanza*) lack ♦ **aver b. di q.c.** to need st.
bisognóso *agg.* needy, poor
bistécca *s. f.* steak ♦ **b. ai ferri** grilled steak; **b. al sangue** rare steak; **b. ben cotta** well-done steak
bistecchièra *s. f.* grill
bisticciàre *v. intr. e rifl. rec.* to quarrel, to bicker, to squabble
bistìccio *s. m.* **1** quarrel, bicker, squabble **2** (*di parole*) pun
bìsturi *s. m.* lancet, bistoury
bisùnto *agg.* greasy
bìtta *s. f.* bollard, bitt
bivàcco *s. m.* bivouac, camp
bìvio *s. m.* crossroads, fork
bizantìno *agg. e s. m.* Byzantine
bìzza *s. f.* tantrum
bizzàrro *agg.* strange, odd, bizarre
bizzèffe, a *loc. avv.* abundantly, in great quantity
blandìre *v. tr.* to blandish, to soothe
blàndo *agg.* bland, soft, gentle
blasfèmo *agg.* blasphemous
blasóne *s. m.* coat of arms
blateràre *v. tr. e intr.* to blether, to chatter
blèso *agg.* lisping
blindàto *agg.* armoured
bloccàre **A** *v. tr.* **1** to block **2** (*mecc.*) to lock, to stall **3** (*mil.*) to blockade **B** *v. intr. pron.* to jam, to stick **C** *v. rifl.* to stop, to get stuck
bloccastèrzo *s. m.* steering lock
blòcco (1) *s. m.* **1** (*atto di bloccare*) block, stoppage, halt **2** (*mil.*) blockade **3** (*econ.*) freeze ♦ **posto di b.** road block
blòcco (2) *s. m.* **1** (*pezzo*) block **2** (*comm.*) bulk, lump **3** (*di fogli*) pad
bloc-notes *s. m. inv.* notepad, notebook
blu *agg. e s. m.* (dark) blue
blùsa *s. f.* blouse
bòa (1) *s. m.* (*zool.*) boa
bòa (2) *s. f.* (*naut.*) buoy
boàto *s. m.* rumble
bòb *s. m.* (*sport*) bob(-sleighing)
bobìna *s. f.* spool, (*elettr.*) coil

bócca *s. f.* mouth
boccàccia *s. f.* grimace
boccàglio *s. m.* mouthpiece
boccàle *s. m.* jug, mug, (*di birra*) tankard
boccapòrto *s. m.* hatch
boccétta *s. f.* small bottle
boccheggiàre *v. intr.* to gasp
bocchettóne *s. m.* pipe union
bocchìno *s. m.* **1** (*per sigaretta*) cigarette holder **2** (*di pipa e strumenti musicali*) mouthpiece
bòccia *s. f.* bowl ♦ **giocare a bocce** to play bowls
bocciàre *v. tr.* **1** (*respingere*) to reject **2** (*agli esami*) to fail **3** (*a bocce*) to hit
boccìno *s. m.* jack
bocciòlo *s. m.* bud
boccóne *s. m.* mouthful, morsel, bite
boccóni *avv.* face downwards
bòga *s. f.* (*zool.*) boce
bòia *s. m.* executioner
boiàta *s. f.* rubbish
boicottàre *v. tr.* to boycott
bòlide *s. m.* bolide, fireball
bolìna *s. f.* close-hauling ♦ **navigare di b.** to sail close-hauled
bólla (1) *s. f.* bubble
bólla (2) *s. f.* (*comm.*) bill, note
bollàre *v. tr.* **1** to stamp **2** (*fig.*) to brand
bollènte *agg.* boiling, hot
bollétta *s. f.* bill, note ♦ **essere in b.** to be broke
bollettìno *s. m.* **1** (*comunicato*) report, bulletin **2** (*pubblicazione*) news, list, gazette **3** (*modulo*) note, bill, form ♦ **b. meteorologico** weather report
bollìre *v. tr. e intr.* to boil
bollìto *agg.* boiled
bollitóre *s. m.* kettle
bóllo *s. m.* **1** stamp **2** (*sigillo*) seal ♦ **b. di circolazione** road tax (stamp)
bòma *s. m.* boom
bómba *s. f.* bomb
bombardaménto *s. m.* bombing, bombardment
bombardàre *v. tr.* **1** to bomb **2** (*fis., fig.*) to bombard
bombardière *s. m.* bomber
bombétta *s. f.* bowler (hat)
bómbola *s. f.* bottle, bomb, cylinder
bombonièra *s. f.* bonbonnière, fancy sweet-box
bomprèsso *s. m.* bowsprit
bonàccia *s. f.* dead calm
bonàrio *agg.* kind
bonìfica *s. f.* reclamation, drainage
bonificàre *v. tr.* to reclaim
bonìfico *s. m.* (*banca*) money transfer
bontà *s. f.* **1** goodness, kindness **2** (*buona qualità*) excellence, good quality **3** (*di cibo*) tastiness
borbottàre *v. tr.* to mumble, to grumble, to mutter
bòrchia *s. f.* boss
bórdo *s. m.* **1** hem, border, edge **2** (*naut.*) board ♦ **a b.** aboard, on board
borgàta *s. f.* village
borghése **A** *agg.* **1** middle-class (*attr*), bourgeois **2** (*civile*) civilian **B** *s. m.* middle-class person ♦ **in b.** in civilian dress, in mufti
borghesìa *s. f.* bourgeoisie, middle class(es)
bórgo *s. m.* village
bòria *s. f.* arrogance, haughtiness
borotàlco *s. m.* talcum powder
borràccia *s. f.* water-bottle
bórsa *s. f.* **1** bag **2** (*Borsa valori*) (Stock) Exchange ♦ **b. da viaggio** travelling bag; **b. della spesa** shopping bag; **b. di studio** scholarship
borsaiòlo *s. m.* pickpocket
borsanéra *s. f.* black market
borseggiatóre *s. m.* pickpocket
borsellìno *s. m.* purse
borsétta *s. f.* handbag
boscàglia *s. f.* brush, scrub
boscaiòlo *s. m.* woodman
boschìvo *agg.* wooded, woody
bòsco *s. m.* wood
boscóso *agg.* woody, wooded
bòssolo *s. m.* (cartridge) case
botànica *s. f.* botany
botànico **A** *agg.* botanic(al) **B** *s. m.* botanist ♦ **orto b.** botanic garden
bòtola *s. f.* trapdoor
bòtta *s. f.* blow
bótte *s. f.* barrel, cask ♦ **volta a b.** barrel-vault
bottéga *s. f.* **1** (*negozio*) shop, store **2** (*laboratorio*) workshop, studio
bottegàio *s. m.* shopkeeper, storekeeper
botteghìno *s. m.* ticket office, (*teatro*) box office
bottìglia *s. f.* bottle ♦ **vino in b.** bottled wine
bottìno *s. m.* booty, loot
bòtto *s. m.* bang, shot ♦ **di b.** suddenly

bottóne *s. m.* button ♦ **b. automatico** press stud
bovìno **A** *agg.* bovine **B** *s. m. al pl.* cattle
box *s. m. inv.* **1** (*garage*) garage **2** (*per cavalli*) box **3** (*per auto da corsa*) pit **4** (*per bambini*) playpen
boxe *s. f.* boxing
bòzza *s. f.* draft, (*tip.*) proof
bozzèllo *s. m.* block
bozzétto *s. m.* sketch
bòzzolo *s. m.* cocoon
braccàre *v. tr.* to hunt (down)
braccétto, a *loc. avv.* arm in arm
braccìale *s. m.* armlet, bracelet
braccialétto *s. m.* bracelet
bracciànte *s. m.* (day-)labourer, worker ♦ **b. agricolo** farmhand
bracciàta *s. f.* **1** armful **2** (*nuoto*) stroke
bràccio *s. m.* **1** arm **2** *pl. f.* (*manodopera*) hands *pl.*, labourers *pl.* **3** (*di edificio*) wing **4** (*di fiume*) arm, (*di mare*) strait **5** (*di gru*) jib, (*di bilancia*) beam **6** (*misura*) fathom, ell
bracciòlo *s. m.* arm
bràcco *s. m.* hound
bracconièrе *s. m.* poacher
bràce *s. f.* embers *pl.* ♦ **cuocere alla b.** to barbecue
bracière *s. m.* brazier
braciòla *s. f.* chop
bradisìsmo *s. m.* bradyseism
bramàre *v. tr.* to desire, to long for
brànca *s. f.* branch
brànchia *s. f.* gill
brànco *s. m.* **1** (*mandria*) herd, (*di lupi*) pack, (*di pecore, uccelli*) flock **2** (*spreg.*) gang, pack
brancolàre *v. intr.* to grope
brànda *s. f.* camp bed
brandèllo *s. m.* shred
brandìre *v. tr.* to brandish
bràno *s. m.* piece, (*di testo*) passage
branzìno *s. m.* bass
brasàto *agg.* braised
brasiliàno *agg. e s. m.* Brazilian
bràvo *agg.* **1** (*abile*) clever, skilful, capable, fine, good **2** (*buono*) good ♦ **b.!** bravo!, well done!
bravùra *s. f.* cleverness, skill
bréccia *s. f.* breach, gap
bretèlla *s. f.* brace, (*USA*) suspender
brève *agg.* short, brief ♦ **in b.** briefly; **tra b.** shortly
brevettàre *v. tr.* to patent
brevétto *s. m.* **1** patent **2** (*di pilota*) pilot's licence
brézza *s. f.* breeze
brìcco *s. m.* pot, jug
briccóne *s. m.* rascal, rogue
brìciola *s. f.* crumb
brìciolo *s. m.* bit
brìga *s. f.* trouble
brigànte *s. m.* brigand, bandit
brigàre *v. intr.* to intrigue
brigàta *s. f.* **1** (*mil.*) brigade **2** (*compagnia*) party, company
brìglia *s. f.* bridle
brillànte **A** *agg.* bright, brilliant **B** *s. m.* brilliant
brillàre **A** *v. intr.* **1** to shine, to glitter, to twinkle, to sparkle **2** (*distinguersi*) to shine **B** *v. tr.* (*una mina*) to set off
brìllo *agg.* (*fam.*) tipsy, drunk
brìna *s. f.* frost, hoarfrost
brindàre *v. intr.* to toast, to drink a toast ♦ **b. alla salute di qc.** to drink sb.'s health
brìndisi *s. m.* toast ♦ **fare un b.** to drink a toast, to make a toast
brìo *s. m.* liveliness, (*fam.*) go
britànnico *agg.* British
brìvido *s. m.* shiver, shudder
brizzolàto *agg.* greying
bròcca *s. f.* pitcher, jug
broccàto *s. m.* brocade
bròccolo *s. m.* broccoli
bròdo *s. m.* broth
brodóso *agg.* watery, thin
bròglio *s. m.* fraud
bronchìte *s. f.* bronchitis
bróncio *s. m.* pout ♦ **tenere il b.** to sulk, to pout
brónco *s. m.* bronchus
broncopolmonìte *s. f.* bronchopneumonia
brontolàre *v. tr. e intr.* to grumble, to mutter
bronzìna *s. f.* bush, bushing
brónzo *s. m.* bronze
brucàre *v. tr.* to browse on, to nibble at
bruciacchiàre *v. tr.* to scorch
bruciapélo, a *loc. avv.* point-blank
bruciàre **A** *v. tr.* **1** to burn **2** (*incendiare*) to set fire to, to burn down **B** *v. intr.* **1** to burn, to blaze **2** (*causare bruciore*) to smart, to sting **3** (*scottare*) to be burning **C** *v. rifl.* to burn oneself **D** *v. intr. pron.* to burn out
bruciatóre *s. m.* burner
bruciatùra *s. f.* burning, burn
brucióre *s. m.* burning ♦ **b. di stomaco** heartburn

brùco *s. m.* caterpillar
brùfolo *s. m.* pimple
brughièra *s. f.* moor, heath
brulicàre *v. intr.* to swarm
brùllo *agg.* bare, bleak
brùma *s. f.* fog, mist
brùno *agg.* brown, dark
brùsco *agg.* **1** sharp, brusque **2** (*improvviso*) abrupt
brusìo *s. m.* buzz, buzzing
brutàle *agg.* brutal
brùto *agg. e s. m.* brute
bruttézza *s. f.* ugliness
brùtto A *agg.* **1** ugly, nasty **2** (*cattivo, sfavorevole, sgradevole*) bad, nasty, unpleasant **B** *s. m.* **1** ugliness **2** (*persona brutta*) ugly person ♦ **brutta copia** rough copy; **brutta figura** poor figure; **b. tempo** bad weather
bruttùra *s. f.* ugly thing
bùca *s. f.* hole, pit ♦ **b. delle lettere** letter box, (*USA*) mailbox
bucanéve *s. m.* snowdrop
bucàre A *v. tr.* **1** to hole **2** (*pneumatico*) to puncture **3** (*pungere*) to prick **B** *v. rifl. e intr. pron.* **1** to have a puncture **2** (*pungersi*) to prick oneself **3** (*drogarsi*) to shoot up
bucàto *s. m.* washing, laundry ♦ **fare il b.** to do the washing
bùccia *s. f.* **1** peel, rind, skin **2** (*di legumi*) pod, husk, (*USA*) shuck
bucherellàre *v. tr.* to riddle
bùco *s. m.* hole
bucòlico *agg.* bucolic
buddìsmo *s. m.* Buddhism
budèllo *s. m.* **1** bowel, gut **2** (*per corde*) (cat)gut **3** (*vicolo*) alley
budìno *s. m.* pudding
bùe *s. m.* **1** ox **2** (*cuc.*) beef
bùfalo *s. m.* buffalo
bufèra *s. f.* storm ♦ **b. di neve** blizzard; **b. di vento** windstorm, gale
bùffo *agg.* **1** funny, droll **2** (*teatro*) comic, buffo
buffonàta *s. f.* buffoonery, tomfoolery
buffóne *s. m.* buffoon, fool, joker
buggeràre *v. tr.* to trick, to cheat
bugìa (1) *s. f.* lie, fib
bugìa (2) *s. f.* (*per candela*) candleholder
bugiàrdo *agg.* lying
bugigàttolo *s. m.* poky little room, closet
bugnàto *s. m.* ashlar
bùio A *agg.* dark **B** *s. m.* darkness, dark
bùlbo *s. m.* **1** bulb **2** (*oculare*) eyeball
bùlgaro *agg. e s. m.* Bulgarian
bullóne *s. m.* bolt
bungalow *s. m. inv.* bungalow
bunker *s. m. inv.* bunker
buonanòtte *s. f. e inter.* good night
buonaséra *s. f. e inter.* good evening
buongiórno *s. m. e inter.* good morning
buongustàio *s. m.* gourmet
buongùsto *s. m.* good taste
buòno (1) A *agg.* **1** good, kind **2** (*di tempo*) fine, good **3** (*pregevole*) good, fine, first-rate **4** (*piacevole*) fine, nice, lovely **5** (*in esclamazioni*) good, happy, nice **B** *s. m.* **1** (the) good **2** (*persona buona*) good person
buòno (2) *s. m.* **1** (*tagliando*) voucher, coupon **2** (*fin.*) bill, bond
buonsènso *s. m.* common sense
buontempóne *s. m.* jovial person
burattinàio *s. m.* puppeteer
burattìno *s. m.* puppet
bùrbero *agg.* surly, gruff
bùrla *s. f.* joke, trick
burlàre A *v. tr.* to make a joke on, to play a trick on **B** *v. intr. pron.* to make fun of
burlésco *agg.* burlesque
burocràtico *agg.* bureaucratic
burocrazìa *s. f.* bureaucracy
burràsca *s. f.* storm, tempest, (*di vento*) gale
bùrro *s. m.* butter ♦ **b. di cacao** cacao butter
burróne *s. m.* ravine
bus *s. m. inv.* bus
buscàre *v. tr.* to get, to catch
bussàre *v. intr.* to knock, to tap
bùssola *s. f.* compass
bùsta *s. f.* **1** envelope **2** (*astuccio*) case
bustarèlla *s. f.* bribe
bùsto *s. m.* **1** bust **2** (*indumento*) corset
buttàre A *v. tr.* **1** (*lanciare*) to throw, to fling, to cast **2** (*gettare via*) to throw away, to waste **B** *v. intr.* (*di pianta*) to put out, to sprout **C** *v. rifl.* to throw oneself ♦ **b. giù** (*abbattere*) to knock down, to demolish, (*ingoiare*) to gulp down, to swallow, (*abbozzare*) to scribble, to rough out
bùzzo *s. m.* (*fam.*) potbelly
by-pass *s. m. inv.* bypass
bypassàre *v. tr.* to bypass

C

càbala *s. f.* cab(b)ala
cabalìstico *agg.* cab(b)alistic
cabìna *s. f.* **1** box, booth, hut **2** (*al mare*) bathing hut **3** (*naut.*) cabin **4** (*di ascensore, funivia*) cage ♦ **c. di pilotaggio** cockpit; **c. telefonica** telephone booth/box
cabinàto *s. m.* (cabin) cruiser
cabinovìa *s. f.* carway, cableway
cabotàggio *s. m.* coasting trade
cacào *s. m.* **1** (*bot.*) cacao **2** (*prodotto*) cocoa
càccia (1) *s. f.* hunting, hunt, (*con fucile*) shooting, (*inseguimento*) chase ♦ **c. alla volpe** fox hunting; **c. al tesoro** treasure hunt; **c. grossa** big game hunting; **licenza di c.** game licence; **riserva di c.** game preserve
càccia (2) *s. m.* (*aer.*) fighter
cacciabombardière *s. m.* (*aer.*) fighter-bomber
cacciagióne *s. f.* game
cacciàre A *v. tr.* **1** to hunt, to shoot **2** (*inseguire*) to chase **3** (*scacciare*) to drive away, to chase away, to throw out **4** (*fam.*) (*ficcare, mettere*) to thrust, to put, to stick **5** (*fam.*) (*emettere, tirare fuori*) to let out, to take out **B** *v. rifl.* **1** (*ficcarsi*) to plunge **2** (*andare a finire*) to get to
cacciatóre *s. m.* hunter
cacciavìte *s. m. inv.* screwdriver
cachemire *s. m. inv.* cashmire
càcio *s. m.* cheese
càctus *s. m. inv.* cactus
cadaùno *agg. e pron. indef.* each
cadàvere *s. m.* (dead) body, corpse
cadènte *agg.* **1** falling **2** (*di edificio*) crumbling, tumbledown **3** (*di persona*) decrepit ♦ **stella c.** shooting star
cadènza *s. f.* **1** cadence, rhythm **2** (*accento*) intonation
cadére *v. intr.* to fall, to drop
cadétto *agg. e s. m.* cadet (*attr.*)
cadùta *s. f.* **1** fall, falling, drop **2** (*perdita*) loss **3** (*comm.*) drop, fall **4** (*di aereo*) crash ♦ **c. massi** falling rocks
cadùto *agg.* fallen
caffè *s. m.* **1** coffee **2** (*bar*) coffe house/shop, café ♦ **c. ristretto** strong coffee; **c. lungo** weak coffee; **c. solubile** instant coffee
caffeìna *s. f.* caffeine
caffellàtte *s. m. inv.* white coffee
caffettièra *s. f.* coffeepot
cafóne *s. m.* boor
cagionàre *v. tr.* to cause
cagionévole *agg.* weak
cagliàre *v. intr. e rifl.* to curdle
càglio *s. m.* rennet
càgna *s. f.* bitch
cagnésco *agg.* surly ♦ **guardare qc. in c.** to scowl at sb.
càla *s. f.* (*geogr.*) creek, cove
calabróne *s. m.* hornet
calamàio *s. m.* inkpot
calamàro *s. m.* squid
calamita *s. f.* magnet
calamità *s. f.* calamity, disaster
calànco *s. m.* gully
calàre A *v. tr.* **1** to lower, to let down, to drop **2** (*a maglia*) to cast off **B** *v. intr.* **1** (*scendere*) to go down, to come down, to fall **2** (*tramontare*) to set **3** (*diminuire*) to fall, to ebb, to drop, (*di peso*) to lose weight **C** *v. rifl.* to let oneself down
càlca *s. f.* throng, crowd
calcàgno *s. m.* heel
calcàre (1) *s. m.* limestone
calcàre (2) *v. tr.* **1** (*calpestare*) to tread **2** (*premere*) to press down **3** (*sottolineare*) to emphasize
calcàreo *agg.* calcareous
càlce *s. f.* lime
calcestrùzzo *s. m.* concrete
calciàre *v. tr.* to kick
calciatóre *s. m.* footballer
calcìnaccio *s. m.* rubble
càlcio (1) *s. m.* (*chim.*) calcium
càlcio (2) *s. m.* **1** kick **2** (*sport*) football, soccer ♦ **c. d'angolo** corner; **c. di punizione** free kick; **c. di rigore** penalty; **partita di c.** football match
càlcio (3) *s. m.* (*di arma*) stock, butt
càlco *s. m.* **1** mould, cast **2** (*copia*) copy
calcolàre *v. tr.* **1** to calculate, to compute, to reckon **2** (*valutare*) to estimate, to calculate **3** (*includere nel calcolo*) to count in, to include

calcolatóre *s. m.* computer
calcolatrìce *s. f.* calculator
càlcolo *s. m.* **1** calculation, reckoning, computation, (*mat.*) calcolus **2** (*med.*) calculus, stone
caldàia *s. f.* boiler
caldaménte *avv.* warmly, heartily
caldarròsta *s. f.* roast chestnut
caldeggiàre *v. tr.* to support (warmly)
càldo A *agg.* **1** warm, hot **2** (*fig.*) warm, ardent, fervent **B** *s. m.* heat, hot weather
caleidoscòpio *s. m.* kaleidoscope
calendàrio *s. m.* calendar
càlibro *s. m.* **1** gauge, caliber, calibre **2** (*strumento*) callipers *pl.* **3** (*fig.*) caliber, calibre
càlice *s. m.* **1** goblet, calice **2** (*bot.*) calyx
calìgine *s. f.* haze
calligrafìa *s. f.* handwriting
calligràfico *agg.* calligraphic
callìsta *s. m. e f.* chiropodist
càllo *s. m.* corn, (*osseo*) callus
càlma *s. f.* calm
calmànte A *agg.* calming **B** *s. m.* sedative
calmàre A *v. tr.* **1** to calm (down), to appease **2** (*lenire*) to soothe **B** *v. intr. pron.* **1** to calm down **2** (*placarsi*) to abate
calmière *s. m.* ceiling price
càlmo *agg.* calm
càlo *s. m.* fall, drop, loss
calóre *s. m.* heat, warmth ♦ **colpo di c.** heatstroke
calorìa *s. f.* calorie
calòrico *agg.* caloric
calorìfero *s. m.* radiator
calorosaménte *avv.* warmly, heartily
caloróso *agg.* warm, hearty
calòtta *s. f.* cap
calpestàre *v. tr.* to trample on, to tread upon ♦ **è vietato c. l'erba** keep off the grass
calpestìo *s. m.* stamping
calùnnia *s. f.* slander
calùra *s. f.* great heat
calvàrio *s. m.* ordeal, trial
calvinìsmo *s. m.* Calvinism
calvinìsta *agg. e s. m. e f.* Calvinist
calvìzie *s. f. inv.* baldness
càlvo *agg.* bald
càlza *s. f.* **1** (*da donna*) stocking, (*da uomo*) sock **2** (*lavoro a maglia*) knitting
calzamàglia *s. f.* tights *pl.*, leotard
calzàre A *v. tr.* **1** (*mettere ai piedi*) to put on **2** (*indossare*) to wear **B** *v. intr.* to fit
calzascàrpe *s. m. inv.* shoehorn
calzatùra *s. f.* footwear ♦ **negozio di calzature** shoe shop
calzaturifìcio *s. m.* shoe factory
calzettóne *s. m.* knee sock
calzìno *s. m.* sock
calzolàio *s. m.* shoemaker, shoe repairer
calzolerìa *s. f.* shoemaker's shop, (*vendita*) shoe shop
calzoncìni *s. m. pl.* shorts *pl.*
calzóni *s. m. pl.* trousers *pl.*, (*USA*) pants *pl.*
camaleónte *s. m.* chameleon
cambiàle *s. f.* bill
cambiaménto *s. m.* change
cambiàre A *v. tr. e intr.* to change **B** *v. rifl.* to change (one's clothes)
cambiavalùte *s. m. e f. inv.* money-changer
càmbio *s. m.* **1** change, (*scambio*) exchange, (*modifica*) alteration **2** (*econ.*) exchange, change **3** (*autom.*) gear
cambùsa *s. f.* storeroom, galley
camèlia *s. f.* camelia
càmera *s. f.* **1** room **2** (*pol.*) Chamber, House **3** (*tecnol.*) chamber ♦ **c. a due letti** double room; **c. ammobiliata** furnished room; **c. da letto** bedroom; **c. d'aria** inner tube; **si affittano camere** rooms to let
cameràta (1) *s. f.* dormitory
cameràta (2) *s. m.* companion
camerièra *s. f.* (*al ristorante*) waitress, (*in albergo*) chambermaid, (*domestica*) (house)maid
camerière *s. m.* (*al ristorante*) waiter, (*domestico*) manservant
camerìno *s. m.* dressing room
càmice *s. m.* white coat
camicétta *s. f.* blouse, shirt
camìcia *s. f.* shirt ♦ **c. da notte** nightgown
caminétto *s. m.* fireplace
camìno *s. m.* **1** (*canna fumaria*) chimney **2** (*caminetto*) fireplace
càmion *s. m. inv.* lorry, (*USA*) truck ♦ **c. con rimorchio** lorry with trailer, (*USA*) trailer truck
camioncìno *s. m.* van, pick-up
camionìsta *s. m. e f.* lorry driver, (*USA*) truck driver
cammèllo *s. m.* camel
cammèo *s. m.* cameo
camminàre *v. intr.* **1** to walk, to go on foot **2** (*funzionare*) to work
camminàta *s. f.* **1** walk **2** (*andatura*) gait
cammìno *s. m.* **1** way, journey **2** (*itinerario*) route, path

camomìlla *s. f.* camomile
camòscio *s. m.* chamois ♦ **pelle di c.** shammy leather
campàgna *s. f.* **1** country, countryside **2** (*tenuta*) estate, property **3** (*mil.*) campaign **4** (*pubblicitaria*) campaign
campagnòlo *agg.* country (*attr.*)
campàle *agg.* field (*attr.*)
campàna *s. f.* bell
campanàrio *agg.* bell (*attr.*)
campanèllo *s. m.* bell
campanìle *s. m.* bell tower, belfry
campanilìsmo *s. m.* parochialism
campàre *v. intr.* to live
campàta *s. f.* span, bay
campeggiàre *v. intr.* **1** to camp **2** (*risaltare*) to stand out
campeggiatóre *s. m.* camper
campéggio *s. m.* **1** (*il campeggiare*) camping **2** (*luogo*) campsite
campèstre *agg.* rural, country (*attr.*)
campionàrio **A** *agg.* sample (*attr.*), trade (*attr.*) **B** *s. m.* (set of) samples *pl.* ♦ **c. di tessuti** pattern book
campionàto *s. m.* championship
campióne *agg. e s. m.* **1** (*sport*) champion **2** (*esemplare*) sample
càmpo *s. m.* **1** field **2** (*mil.*) camp **3** (*sport*) field, ground, pitch
camposànto *s. m.* cemetery
camuffàre **A** *v. tr.* to disguise **B** *v. rifl.* to disguise oneself, to dress as
camùso *agg.* snub
canadése *agg. e s. m. e f.* Canadian
canàglia *s. f.* scoundrel, rascal
canàle *s. m.* **1** canal **2** (*di mare*) channel **3** (*radio, TV*) channel **4** (*anat., biol.*) canal, duct
canalizzazióne *s. f.* canalization
cànapa *s. f.* hemp ♦ **c. indiana** cannabis
canarìno *s. m.* canary
canàsta *s. f.* canasta
cancellàre **A** *v. tr.* **1** to delete, (*con la gomma*) to erase, to rub out, (*con un frego*) to strike out, to cross out, (*con straccio, cancellino*) to wipe out **2** (*disdire, annullare*) to cancel **3** (*fig.*) to wipe out, to efface **B** *v. intr. pron.* to fade
cancellàta *s. f.* railing
cancellazióne *s. f.* cancellation, annulment
cancellerìa *s. f.* **1** (*pol.*) chancellery **2** (*articoli di cartoleria*) stationery
cancellière *s. m.* **1** (*pol.*) Chancellor **2** (*dir.*) registrar
cancèllo *s. m.* gate
cancerògeno *agg.* carcinogenic
cancrèna *s. f.* gangrene
càncro *s. m.* cancer
candéggio *s. m.* bleaching
candéla *s. f.* **1** candle **2** (*autom.*) sparking plug
candelàbro *s. m.* candelabrum
candelière *s. m.* candlestick, candelabrum
candidàto *s. m.* candidate
candidatùra *s. f.* candidature
càndido *agg.* **1** (snow-)white **2** (*innocente*) pure, innocent **3** (*sincero*) candid **4** (*ingenuo*) ingenuous
candìto *s. m.* candied fruit
càne *s. m.* dog
canèstro *s. m.* basket
cangiànte *agg.* changing
cangùro *s. m.* kangaroo
canìle *s. m.* kennels *pl.*
canìno *agg. e s. m.* canine
cànna *s. f.* **1** reed, canna **2** (*bastone*) stick, cane **3** (*da pesca*) rod **4** (*di fucile*) barrel **5** (*di organo*) pipe **6** (*di bicicletta*) crossbar ♦ **c. da zucchero** sugar cane; **c. fumaria** chimney flue
cannèlla *s. f.* cinnamon
cannéto *s. m.* cane thicket
cannibalìsmo *s. m.* cannibalism
cannocchiàle *s. m.* spyglass, telescope
cannóne *s. m.* gun
cannùccia *s. f.* straw
canòa *s. f.* canoe
cànone *s. m.* **1** (*regola*) canon, rule **2** (*somma da pagare*) rent, fee **3** (*mus., relig.*) canon
canònica *s. f.* vicarage
canònico **A** *agg.* canonical **B** *s. m.* canon
canòro *agg.* singing, song (*attr.*)
canottàggio *s. m.* rowing, boat racing
canottièra *s. f.* vest
canòtto *s. m.* dinghy, small boat, (*di gomma*) rubber boat
canovàccio *s. m.* **1** (*per piatti*) dish cloth **2** (*per ricamo*) canvas **3** (*trama*) plot **4** (*schema*) sketch
cantànte *s. m. e f.* singer
cantàre *v. tr. e intr.* **1** to sing **2** (*del gallo*) to crow **3** (*fam.*) (*tradire*) to squeal
cantàta *s. f.* (*mus.*) cantata
cantautóre *s. m.* song singer-writer
canticchiàre *v. tr. e intr.* to sing softly, to hum
cantière *s. m.* yard ♦ **c. navale** shipyard
cantilèna *s. f.* singsong

cantìna *s. f.* cellar
cànto *s. m.* **1** (*il cantare*) singing **2** (*canzone*) song, (*liturgico*) chant
cantonàta *s. f.* **1** corner **2** (*fig.*) blunder
cantóne *s. m.* **1** (*angolo*) corner **2** (*Svizzera*) canton
cantùccio *s. m.* nook
canzonàre *v. tr.* to make fun of, to tease
canzóne *s. f.* song
càos *s. m.* chaos
caòtico *agg.* chaotic
capàce *agg.* **1** able, capable **2** (*esperto*) skilful, clever **3** (*ampio*) large, spacious, capacious
capacità *s. f.* **1** (*abilità*) ability, capability, cleverness **2** (*capienza*) capacity **3** (*dir*) capacity **4** (*econ.*) power, capacity
capacitàre A *v. tr.* to persuade **B** *v. rifl.* to make out, to realize
capànna *s. f.* hut, cabin
capannèllo *s. m.* knot (of people)
capannóne *s. m.* shed
capàrbio *agg.* stubborn
capàrra *s. f.* deposit
capéllo *s. m.* hair
capezzàle *s. m.* bolster
capézzolo *s. m.* (*anat.*) nipple, (*zool.*) dug
capiènza *s. f.* capacity
capigliatùra *s. f.* hair
capillàre A *agg.* **1** capillary **2** (*fig.*) detailed **3** (*diffuso*) widespread, diffused **B** *s. m.* capillary (vessel)
capìre *v. tr.* to understand, to make out, to realize
capitàle (1) A *agg.* capital **B** *s. f.* capital (city)
capitàle (2) *s. m.* capital ♦ **c. azionario** share capital
capitalìsmo *s. m.* capitalism
capitalìsta *agg. e s. m. e f.* capitalist
capitanerìa *s. f.* harbour office
capitàno *s. m.* captain
capitàre *v. intr.* **1** (*accadere*) to happen, to occur **2** (*giungere*) to come, to turn up
capitèllo *s. m.* (*arch.*) capital
capitolàre *v. intr.* to capitulate
capìtolo *s. m.* chapter
capitómbolo *s. m.* tumble
càpo *s. m.* **1** (*testa*) head **2** (*estremità*) top, end, head **3** (*chi comanda*) chief, leader **4** (*geogr*) cape **5** (*di bestiame*) animal, head **6** (*di vestiario*) article ♦ **a c.** (*dettando*) new line; **da c.** over again
capodànno *s. m.* New Year's Day
capofamìglia *s. m. e f.* head of a family
capofitto, a *loc. avv.* headlong, headfirst
capogìro *s. m.* giddiness
capolavóro *s. m.* masterpiece
capolìnea *s. m.* terminus
capolìno *s. m.* peep ♦ **far c.** to peep (in, out)
capoluògo *s. m.* chief town
capoàle *s. m.* caporal
caposcuòla *s. m. e f.* leader of a movement
capostazióne *s. m. e f.* stationmaster
capostìpite *s. m. e f.* founder of a family, (*est.*) ancestor
capotrèno *s. m.* guard, (*USA*) conductor
capovòlgere A *v. tr.* **1** to turn upside down, to overturn **2** (*fig.*) to invert, to reverse **B** *v. intr. pron.* **1** to overturn, to capsize **2** to be reversed
càppa *s. f.* **1** (*mantello*) mantle, cloak **2** (*di camino*) cowl, (*di cucina*) hood **3** (*naut.*) cope
cappèlla (1) *s. f.* **1** chapel **2** (*mus.*) choir
cappèlla (2) *s. f.* (*di fungo*) cap
cappellàno *s. m.* chaplain
cappèllo *s. m.* hat ♦ **c. a cilindro** top hat
càppero *s. m.* caper
cappóne *s. m.* capon
cappottàre *v. intr.* to overturn
cappòtto *s. m.* (over) coat
cappuccìno (1) *s. m.* (*relig.*) Capuchin
cappuccìno (2) *s. m.* (*bevanda*) cappuccino
cappùccio *s. m.* hood, (*di penna*) cap
càpra *s. f.* goat
caprétto *s. m.* kid
caprìccio *s. m.* whim, caprice, fancy
capricciόso *agg.* whimsical, capricious, (*di bambino*) naughty
capricorno *s. m.* Capricorn
capriòla *s. f.* somersault
capriòlo *s. m.* roe (deer)
càpro *s. m.* he-goat ♦ **c. espiatorio** scapegoat
càpsula *s. f.* **1** capsule **2** (*di dente*) crown
captàre *v. tr.* **1** (*radio*) to pick up **2** (*attrarre*) to tap
carabìna *s. f.* rifle
caràffa *s. f.* carafe, decanter
caramèlla *s. f.* sweet, toffee, candy
caràto *s. m.* carat
caràttere *s. m.* **1** character, temper **2** (*caratteristica*) feature, characteristic **3** (*tip.*) type, character
caratterìstica *s. f.* characteristic, feature

caratterìstico *agg.* characteristic, typical
caratterizzàre *v. tr.* to characterize
carboidràto *s. m.* carbohydrate
carbóne *s. m.* coal
carbonizzàre *v. tr. e intr. pron.* **1** to carbonize, to char **2** (*bruciare*) to burn
carburànte *s. m.* fuel
carburatóre *s. m.* carburettor, (*USA*) carburetor ♦ **c. ingolfato** floodied carburettor
carcàssa *s. f.* **1** carcass **2** (*spreg.*) wreck
carceràrio *agg.* prison (*attr.*)
carceràto *s. m.* prisoner
càrcere *s. m.* jail, prison
carcerière *s. m.* jailor, warder
carciòfo *s. m.* artichoke
cardìaco *agg.* cardiac, heart (*attr.*) ♦ **attacco c.** heart attack; **insufficienza cardiaca** cardiac failure; **trapianto c.** heart transplant
cardinàle *agg. e s. m.* cardinal ♦ **punti cardinali** cardinal points
cardinalìzio *agg.* cardinal (*attr.*)
càrdine *s. m.* **1** hinge, pivot **2** (*fig.*) foundation
cardiocircolatòrio *agg.* cardiocirculatory
cardiologìa *s. f.* cardiology
cardiòlogo *s. m.* cardiologist
cardiopàtico *agg. e s. m.* cardiopath
càrdo *s. m.* thistle
carèna *s. f.* (*naut.*) hull
carènte *agg.* lacking
carènza *s. f.* **1** (*mancanza*) lack, want **2** (*scarsità*) scarcity, shortage
carestìa *s. f.* famine
carézza *s. f.* caress
cariàtide *s. f.* caryatid
cariàto *agg.* decayed
càrica *s. f.* **1** (*ufficio, dignità*) office, position **2** (*mil., elettr., di arma da fuoco*) charge **3** (*di orologio*) winding
caricàre *v. tr.* **1** to load up **2** (*di merce, passeggeri*) to take on, to load **3** (*riempire*) to fill **4** (*gravare*) to burden, to overload **5** (*mil., elettr.*) to charge **6** (*orologio*) to wind up
caricatùra *s. f.* caricature
càrico A *agg.* **1** loaded, laden **2** (*elettr.*) charged **3** (*riempito*) filled **B** *s. m.* **1** loading, lading **2** (*merce*) load, cargo, freight **3** (*fig.*) burden, weight ♦ **a c. di** charged to, at expense of; **essere a c. di qc.** to be dependent on sb.
càrie *s. f. inv.* decay, caries *pl.*
carìno *agg.* pretty, nice
carìsma *s. m.* charisma
carismàtico *agg.* charismatic
carità *s. f.* **1** charity **2** (*elemosina*) alms *pl.* **3** (*favore*) favour
carlinga *s. f.* nacelle
carnagióne *s. f.* complexion
càrne *s. f.* **1** flesh **2** (*alimento*) meat
carnéfice *s. m.* executioner
carneficìna *s. f.* slaughter, massacre
carnevàle *s. m.* carnival
carnìvoro *agg.* carnivorous
carnóso *agg.* plump
càro *agg.* **1** dear, charming **2** (*costoso*) expensive, dear
carógna *s. f.* **1** carrion **2** (*fig.*) swine
caròta *s. f.* carrot
carovàna *s. f.* caravan, convoy
carovìta *s. m.* high cost of living
carpentière *s. m.* carpenter
carpìre *v. tr.* to extort, to cheat, to do out of
carpóni *avv.* on all fours
carràbile *agg.* carriageable ♦ **passo c.** (*avviso*) keep clear
carreggiàta *s. f.* carriageway, roadway, track
carrellàta *s. f.* **1** (*cin., TV*) tracking shot, dolly shot **2** (*fig.*) roundup
carrèllo *s. m.* **1** trolley, truck **2** (*aer.*) undercarriage
carrétto *s. m.* handcart
carrièra *s. f.* career
carriòla *s. f.* wheelbarrow
càrro *s. m.* car, wagon ♦ **c. armato** tank
carròzza *s. f.* carriage, coach
carrozzèlla *s. f.* **1** (*di piazza*) cab **2** (*sedia a rotelle*) wheelchair
carrozzerìa *s. f.* **1** (*autom.*) bodywork, body **2** (*officina*) body shop
carrozzìna *s. f.* pram, (*USA*) baby carriage
carrùcola *s. f.* pulley
càrta *s. f.* **1** paper **2** (*documento*) card, paper, document **3** (*da gioco*) (playing) card **4** (*geografica*) map, chart **5** (*statuto*) charter ♦ **c. da lettere** writing paper; **c. di credito** credit card; **c. d'identità** identity card; **c. d'imbarco** boarding card; **c. igienica** toilet paper
cartàccia *s. f.* waste paper
cartàceo *agg.* paper (*attr.*)
cartamonéta *s. f.* paper money
cartapésta *s. f.* papier-mâché
cartéggio *s. m.* correspondence
cartèlla *s. f.* **1** (*di cartone*) folder, file, (*per*

disegni, foto) portfolio **2** (*valigetta*) briefcase, (*da scuola*) satchel **3** (*pagina*) page, sheet **4** (*fin.*) bond
cartellìno *s. m.* **1** label, tag, ticket **2** (*di presenza*) time card
cartèllo *s. m.* sign-board, sign, notice, (*pubblicitario*) poster, (*stradale*) road sign
cartellóne *s. m.* poster, board
càrter *s. m. inv.* **1** (*di bicicletta*) (chain-) guard **2** (*autom.*) case
cartièra *s. f.* paper mill
cartilàgine *s. f.* cartilage
cartìna *s. f.* **1** (*mappa*) map **2** (*per sigarette*) cigarette paper
cartòccio *s. m.* paper bag, cornet
cartografìa *s. f.* cartography
cartogràfico *agg.* cartographic
cartolàio *s. m.* stationer
cartolerìa *s. f.* stationery shop
cartolìna *s. f.* (post)card
cartomànte *s. m. e f.* fortune-teller
cartomanzìa *s. f.* cartomancy
cartóne *s. m.* **1** cardboard **2** (*scatola*) carton, box ♦ **cartoni animati** cartoons
cartùccia *s. f.* cartridge
càsa *s. f.* **1** house, (*la propria abitazione*) home, (*appartamento*) flat **2** (*famiglia*) house, family **3** (*comm.*) house, firm, company ♦ **c. colonica** farmhouse; **c. da gioco** gambling house; **c. di riposo** rest home; **seconda c.** holiday home
casàcca *s. f.* coat
casalìnga *s. f.* housewife
casalìngo *agg.* **1** (*di casa*) homely, domestic **2** (*che ama la casa*) home-loving **3** (*fatto in casa*) homemade **4** (*semplice*) plain, homely
casàto *s. m.* family, house
cascàre *v. intr.* to fall, to tumble
cascàta *s. f.* waterfall, cascade
cascìna *s. f.* dairy farm, farmhouse
càsco *s. m.* **1** helmet **2** (*di parrucchiere*) hair dryer **3** (*di banane*) bunch
caseggiàto *s. m.* block (of flats)
caseifìcio *s. m.* dairy
casèlla *s. f.* **1** (*di schedario*) pigeon-hole **2** (*riquadro*) square ♦ **c. postale** p. o. box
casèllo *s. m.* (*di autostrada*) tollbooth
casèrma *s. f.* barracks *pl.*
casìno *s. m.* **1** (*da caccia*) shooting lodge **2** (*bordello*) brothel **3** (*fam.*) (*chiasso*) row, mess
casinò *s. m. inv.* casino
càso *s. m.* **1** chance **2** (*fatto, vicenda*) case, event, affair **3** (*eventualità*) case ♦ **in c. contrario** otherwise; **in ogni c.** in any case; **per c.** by chance; **si dà il c. che ...** it so happens that ...
casolàre *s. m.* homestead, cottage
càspita *inter.* good heavens!
càssa *s. f.* **1** case, chest, box **2** (*negozio*) cash desk, cash, desk, counter **3** (*banca*) bank **4** (*bara*) coffin ♦ **c. continua** night safe; **registratore di c.** cash re-gister
cassafòrte *s. f.* safe, strongbox
cassapànca *s. f.* chest, settle
casseruòla *s. f.* saucepan
cassétta *s. f.* **1** box **2** (*mus.*) cassette ♦ **c. degli attrezzi** toolbox; **c. delle lettere** letterbox, (*USA*) mailbox; **film di c.** commercial film
cassétto *s. m.* drawer
cassière *s. m.* cashier
càsta *s. f.* caste
castàgna *s. f.* chestnut
castàgno *s. m.* chestnut
castàno *agg.* brown
castellàno *s. m.* lord of a castle
castèllo *s. m.* castle ♦ **letto a c.** bunk bed
castigàre *v. tr.* to punish
castigàto *agg.* chaste, decent
castìgo *s. m.* punishment
castità *s. f.* chastity
càsto *agg.* chaste, pure
castòro *s. m.* beaver
castràre *v. tr.* to castrate, to geld
casuàle *agg.* random, casual, fortuitous
casualménte *avv.* by chance, accidentally
cataclìsma *s. m.* cataclysm
catacómba *s. f.* catacomb
catalogàre *v. tr.* to catalogue
catàlogo *s. m.* catalogue, (*USA*) catalog
catamaràno *s. m.* catamaran
catapécchia *s. f.* hovel, slum
catarifrangènte *s. m.* reflector
catàrro *s. m.* catarrh
catàsta *s. f.* stack, pile
catàsto *s. m.* land register
catàstrofe *s. f.* catastrophe, disaster
catastròfico *agg.* catastrophic
catechìsmo *s. m.* catechism
categorìa *s. f.* category
categòrico *agg.* categorical
caténa *s. f.* chain
cateràtta *s. f.* cataract
catìno *s. m.* basin
catràme *s. m.* tar

càttedra *s. f.* **1** desk **2** (*posto di insegnante*) teaching post, (*all'università*) chair **3** (*seggio*) chair
cattedràle *s. f.* cathedral
cattedràtico *s. m.* professor
cattivèria *s. f.* **1** wickedness, spite, (*di bambino*) naughtiness **2** (*azione*) wicked action
cattività *s. f.* captivity
cattìvo *agg.* **1** bad **2** (*sgradevole*) nasty, bad **3** (*di tempo*) bad, (*di mare*) rough **4** (*malvagio*) wicked **5** (*di bambino*) naughty
cattolicésimo *s. m.* Catholicism
cattòlico *agg. e s. m.* Catholic
cattùra *s. f.* capture, (*arresto*) arrest
catturàre *v. tr.* to capture, to seize, to arrest
caucciù *s. m.* caoutchouc
càusa *s. f.* **1** cause **2** (*dir.*) suit, case ♦ **a c. di** because of, owing to; **c. civile** civil suit; **c. penale** criminal case; **far c. a qc.** to sue sb.
causàle **A** *agg.* causal **B** *s. f.* cause, reason
causàre *v. tr.* to cause, to bring about
càustico *agg.* caustic
cautèla *s. f.* caution
cautelàrsi *v. rifl.* to take precautions
càuto *agg.* cautious
cauzióne *s. f.* **1** security, deposit, caution (money) **2** (*dir.*) bail ♦ **essere liberato su c.** to be released on bail
càva *s. f.* quarry
cavalcàre *v. tr. e intr.* to ride
cavalcàta *s. f.* ride
cavalcavìa *s. m. inv.* flyover, overpass
cavalcióni, (a) *avv.* astride
cavalière *s. m.* **1** (*chi cavalca*) rider **2** (*stor.*) knight **3** (*mil.*) cavalryman **4** (*chi accompagna una donna*) escort, partner
cavallerésco *agg.* chivalrous
cavallerìa *s. f.* **1** (*mil.*) cavalry **2** (*stor.*) chivalry **3** (*comportamento*) chivalry, gallantry
cavallerìzzo *s. m.* horseman
cavallétta *s. f.* grasshopper
cavallétto *s. m.* trestle, (*per pittore*) easel, (*fot.*) tripod
cavàllo *s. m.* **1** horse **2** (*scacchi*) knight **3** (*cavallo vapore*) horsepower **4** (*di pantaloni*) crotch ♦ **andare a c.** to ride
cavallóne *s. m.* billow, (*frangente*) breaker
cavàre *v. tr.* **1** (*tirare fuori*) to take out, to draw, to pull out **2** (*togliere*) to take off, to remove **3** (*ricavare*) to get, to obtain **4** (*cavarsela*) to get off
cavatàppi *s. m.* corkscrew
càvea *s. f.* cavea
cavèrna *s. f.* cave, cavern
càvia *s. f.* guinea pig
caviàle *s. m.* caviar
cavìglia *s. f.* ankle
cavìllo *s. m.* cavil
cavità *s. f.* cavity, hollow, chamber
càvo (1) **A** *agg.* hollow **B** *s. m.* cavity, hollow ♦ **c. orale** buccal cavity
càvo (2) *s. m.* **1** (*elettr.*) cable **2** (*fune*) rope
cavolfióre *s. m.* cauliflower
cavolìni di Bruxelles *s. m. pl.* Brussels sprouts *pl.*
càvolo *s. m.* cabbage
cazzòtto *s. m.* punch
cazzuòla *s. f.* trowel
ce **A** *particella pron.* to us, us (ES: **perché non ce l'hai detto prima?** why didn't you tell us before?) **B** *avv.* there (ES: **quanti gatti ci sono? ce n'è uno** how many cats are there? there is one)
céce *s. m.* chickpea
cecità *s. f.* blindness
cèco *agg. e s. m.* Czech
cèdere **A** *v. tr.* **1** (*dare*) to give **2** (*trasferire*) to hand over, to transfer **3** (*vendere*) to sell **4** (*consegnare*) to surrender, (*con trattato*) to cede **B** *v. intr.* **1** (*arrendersi*) to surrender, to yield **2** (*sprofondare, rompersi*) to give way
cedévole *agg.* **1** yielding **2** (*di terreno*) soft
cèdola *s. f.* coupon
cédro *s. m.* **1** (*agrume*) citron **2** (*albero*) cedar
cèduo *agg.* **bosco c.** coppice
cefalèa *s. f.* cephalalgy, headache
cèffo *s. m.* (*spreg.*) mug
ceffóne *s. m.* slap, cuff
celàre **A** *v. tr.* to conceal, to hide **B** *v. rifl.* to hide oneself, to conceal oneself, to be hidden
celebèrrimo *agg.* very famous
celebrànte *s. m.* celebrant
celebràre *v. tr.* to celebrate
celebrazióne *s. f.* celebration
cèlebre *agg.* celebrated, famous, renowned
celebrità *s. f.* celebrity
cèlere *agg.* swift, quick
celèste **A** *agg.* **1** (*del cielo*) heavenly, celestial **2** (*colore*) light blue **B** *s. m.* light blue

cèlibe *agg.* single, unmarried
cèlla *s. f.* cell ♦ **c. frigorifera** cold store
cèllula *s. f.* cell
cellulàre *agg.* cellular
cellulìte *s. f.* **1** (*accumulo*) cellulite **2** (*infiammazione*) cellulitis
cèltico *agg. e s. m.* Celtic
cementàre *v. tr. e intr. pron.* to cement
ceménto *s. m.* cement
céna *s. f.* dinner, supper
cenàre *v. intr.* to have dinner/supper, to dine
céncio *s. m.* rag
cencióso *agg.* ragged
cénere *s. f.* ash(es)
cénno *s. m.* **1** sign, gesture, (*con il capo*) nod, (*con la mano*) wave **2** (*allusione*) hint, mention, allusion **3** (*breve notizia*) notice, note **4** *al pl.* (*breve trattato*) outline
censiménto *s. m.* census
censóre *s. m.* censor
censùra *s. f.* censorship
centàuro *s. m.* **1** (*mitol.*) centaur **2** (*motociclista*) motorcyclist
centenàrio **A** *agg.* **1** (*che ha cento anni*) hundred-year-old, (*di persona*) centennial **2** (*che ricorre ogni cento anni*) centenary **B** *s. m.* **1** (*anniversario*) centenary **2** (*persona*) centenarian
centesimàle *agg.* centesimal
centèsimo **A** *agg. num. ord.* hundredth **B** *s. m.* **1** (*la centesima parte*) (the, a) hundredth **2** (*moneta*) cent, penny
centìgrado *agg.* centigrade
centìmetro *s. m.* centimetre, (*USA*) centimeter
centinàio *s. m.* hundred ♦ **a centinaia** by hundreds
cènto *agg. num. card. e s. m.* (a, one) hundred
centràggio *s. m.* cent(e)ring
centràle **A** *agg.* central **B** *s. f.* plant, station
centralinìsta *s. m. e f.* operator
centralìno *s. m.* (*tel.*) exchange, (*di albergo*) switchboard
centralizzàre *v. tr.* to centralize
centràre *v. tr.* **1** (*colpire al centro*) to hit the centre of **2** (*mettere al centro, centrare*) to centre **3** (*fig.*) to grasp fully
centravànti *s. m. inv.* centre forward
centrìfuga *s. f.* **1** centrifuge **2** (*della lavatrice*) spin-dry
centrìfugo *agg.* centrifugal
centrìpeto *agg.* centripetal
cèntro *s. m.* centre, (*USA*) center
centrocàmpo *s. m.* centre field
céppo *s. m.* **1** (*d'albero*) stump, (*da ardere*) log **2** (*mecc.*) stock
céra (1) *s. f.* wax ♦ **c. vergine** beewax; **museo delle cere** waxworks
céra (2) *s. f.* (*aspetto*) air, look
ceràmica *s. f.* ceramics *pl.* (*v. al sing.*), pottery
ceramìsta *s. m. e f.* ceramist
cerbiàtto *s. m.* fawn
cérca *s. f.* search
cercàre **A** *v. tr.* **1** to look for, to search for, to seek **2** (*richiedere*) to ask for, to want **3** (*consultando*) to look up **B** *v. intr.* to try
cérchia *s. f.* circle
cérchio *s. m.* **1** circle, ring, round **2** (*di ruota*) rim **3** (*di botte*) hoop
cerchióne *s. m.* rim
cereàle *s. m.* cereal
cerimònia *s. f.* ceremony
cerìno *s. m.* (wax) match
cèrnia *s. f.* grouper
cernièra *s. f.* hinge ♦ **c. lampo** zip, zipper
cèrnita *s. f.* selection
céro *s. m.* candle
ceròtto *s. m.* plaster
certaménte *avv.* certainly, surely, of course
certézza *s. f.* certainty
certificàto *s. m.* certificate
cèrto (1) **A** *agg. indef.* **1** certain (ES: **un c. giorno** a certain day) **2** (*qualche, un po' di*) some (ES: **dopo un c. tempo** after some time) **3** (*di tale genere*) such (ES: **certe persone** such people) **B** *pron. indef. al pl.* some (people)
cèrto (2) **A** *agg.* certain, sure **B** *avv.* certainly, of course
certósa *s. f.* Chartreuse
cervellétto *s. m.* cerebellum
cervèllo *s. m.* **1** brain **2** (*fig.*) brain, mind ♦ **lambiccarsi il c.** to rack one's brains
cervicàle *agg.* cervical
cèrvo *s. m.* deer
cesellàre *v. tr.* **1** to chisel **2** (*fig.*) to polish
cesèllo *s. m.* chisel
cesóia *s. f.* shear
cespùglio *s. m.* bush
cessàre *v. tr. e intr.* to cease, to stop
cèsso *s. m.* (*fam.*) bog
césta *s. f.* basket
cestìno *s. m.* basket ♦ **c. per i rifiuti** litterbin, wastebasket
césto *s. m.* basket
cèto *s. m.* class
cetriolìno *s. m.* gherkin

cetriòlo *s. m.* cucumber
che (1) A *agg. interr.* **1** (*riferito a un numero indefinito di cose o persone*) what (ES: **c. città preferisci?** what town do you like best?) **2** (*riferito a un numero limitato di cose o persone*) which (ES: **c. città della Francia preferisci?** which French town do you like best?) **B** *pron. interr.* what (ES: **c. stai facendo?** what are you doing?)
che (2) A *agg. escl.* **1** (*quale*) what (ES: **c. festa noiosa!** what a boring party!) **2** (*come*) how (ES: **c. strano!** how strange!) **B** *pron. escl.* what (ES: **c. dici!** what are you saying!)
che (3) *pron. rel.* **1** (*sogg. riferito a persona*) who, that; (*sogg. riferito a cose o animali*) which, that (ES: **il ragazzo c. cadde dal tetto** the boy who fell off the roof, **l'albero c. cresce in giardino** the tree which grows in the garden) **2** (*ogg. riferito a persona*) whom, who, that; (*ogg. riferito a cose o animali*) which, that (*spesso sottinteso*) (ES: **il ragazzo che ho visto questa mattina** the boy (whom) I've seen this morning, **il libro c. vedi** the book (which) you see) **3** (*in cui, quando, con cui, per cui*) in which, on which, when (*spesso sottinteso*) (ES: **l'anno che andammo in Italia** the year (when) we went to Italy) **4** (*la qual cosa, il che*) which (ES: **mio fratello non può venire, il c. è un vero peccato** my brother cannot come, which is a real pity) **5** (*correl. di stesso, medesimo*) as, that
che (4) *pron. indef.* (*qualcosa*) something (ES: **c'è un c. di strano in quella casa** there's something strange about that house)
che (5) *cong.* **1** (*dichiarativa dopo i verbi che esprimono opinione, sentimento, ecc.*) that (*spesso sottinteso*) (ES: **mi dispiace c. tu non riesca a dormire** I'm sorry (that) you can't sleep) **2** (*dichiarativa dopo i verbi che esprimono volontà o comando o dopo loc. impers.*) *idiom.* (ES: **vorrei c. tu non venissi** I wish you wouldn't come) **3** (*consecutiva*) that (ES: **ti sei svegliato così tardi c. hai perso l'autobus** you woke up so late that you missed the bus) **4** (*finale*) that (*spesso sottinteso*) (ES: **bada c. non ti caschi** be careful (that) you don't drop it) **5** (*comparativa*) than (ES: **più c. mai** more than ever) **6** (*temporale*) when, since, for, after (ES: **arrivai c. tutto era già finito** everything was already over when I got there) **7** (*eccettuativa*) only, but (ES: **non fa altro c. dormire** he does nothing but sleep) **8** (*disgiuntiva*) whether (ES: **c. tu venga o no** whether you come or not)
chetichèlla, alla *loc. avv.* secretly ♦ **entrare/uscire alla c.** to slip in/away
chi (1) *pron. rel.* **1** (*colui, colei che*) who, the person (man, boy, ecc.) who; (*coloro che*) who, those who (ES: **non conosco c. ha scritto quel libro** I don't know who wrote that book) **2** (*chiunque*) whoever, anyone who (ES: **c. vuole entrare deve suonare due volte il campanello** anyone who wants to come in must ring the bell twice) **3** (*qualcuno che*) someone who, somebody who; (*in frasi neg.*) no one who, nobody who, anyone who, anybody who (ES: **c'è c. mi aiuterà** there's someone who will help me, **non trovo c. mi dia retta** I don't find anyone who pays attention to me) **4** (*chi ... chi*) some ... some, someone ... someone (ES: **c. viene, c. va** some come, some go)
chi (2) *pron. interr.* **1** (*sogg.*) who (ES: **c. è?** who is it?) **2** (*ogg. e compl. ind.*) whom, who (ES: **a c. scrivi?** who are you writing to?)
chiàcchiera *s. f.* **1** chatt, talk **2** (*pettegolezzo*) gossip, (*notizia infondata*) rumor
chiacchieràre *v. intr.* **1** to chat, to talk **2** (*pettegolare*) to gossip
chiacchieràta *s. f.* chat, talk
chiacchieróne *s. m.* **1** chatterer **2** (*pettegolo*) gossip
chiamàre A *v. tr.* **1** to call **2** (*al telefono*) to phone **3** (*dare nome*) to name **B** *v. intr. pron.* to be called ♦ **come ti chiami?** what is your name?
chiamàta *s. f.* call ♦ **c. alle armi** call-up
chiaraménte *avv.* clearly
chiarézza *s. f.* clearness, clarity
chiariménto *s. m.* explanation
chiarìre A *v. tr.* to clear up, to explain **B** *v. intr. pron.* to become clear
chiàro A *agg.* **1** clear **2** (*di colore*) light **3** (*luminoso*) bright **4** (*evidente*) clear, evident **B** *avv.* **1** clearly **2** (*con franchezza*) frankly
chiaroscùro *s. m.* chiaroscuro
chiaroveggènte *s. m. e f.* clairvoyant
chiàsso *s. m.* uproar, noise
chiassóso *agg.* **1** rowdy, noisy **2** (*fig.*)

gaudy
chiàve *s. f.* **1** key **2** (*mecc.*) spanner, (*USA*) wrench **3** (*mus.*) clef
chiavistèllo *s. m.* bolt
chiàzza *s. f.* spot, stain
chìcco *s. m.* (*di cereale*) grain, (*di caffè*) coffe-bean, (*d'uva*) grape
chièdere **A** *v. tr.* **1** (*per sapere*) to ask **2** (*per avere*) to ask for **3** (*come prezzo*) to charge **4** (*richiedere*) to demand, to require **B** *v. intr. pron.* to wonder
chiérico *s. m.* cleric
chièsa *s. f.* church
chìglia *s. f.* keel
chìlo *s. m.* kilo
chilogràmmo *s. m.* kilogram(me)
chilomètrico *agg.* kilometric
chilòmetro *s. m.* kilometre, (*USA*) kilometer
chìmica *s. f.* chemistry
chìmico **A** *agg.* chemical **B** *s. m.* chemist
chìna *s. f.* slope
chinàre **A** *v. tr.* to bend, to bow, to lower **B** *v. rifl.* to stoop, to bend down
chincaglierìa *s. f.* trinkets *pl.*, fancy goods *pl.*
chiòccia *s. f.* brooding hen
chiòcciola *s. f.* snail ♦ **scala a c.** winding staircase, spiral stairs
chiòdo *s. m.* **1** nail, (*da roccia*) piton, (*da scarpe*) hobnail **2** (*idea fissa*) fixed idea ♦ **c. di garofano** clove
chiòma *s. f.* **1** hair **2** (*di albero*) foliage
chiòsco *s. m.* kiosk, stall, stand
chiòstro *s. m.* cloister
chiromànte *s. m. e f.* chiromancer
chirurgìa *s. f.* surgery
chirùrgo *s. m.* surgeon
chissà *avv.* **1** I wonder **2** (*forse*) perhaps, maybe
chitàrra *s. f.* guitar
chitarrìsta *s. m. e f.* guitarist
chiùdere **A** *v. tr.* **1** to shut, to close **2** (*recingere*) to enclose **3** (*concludere*) to conclude, to end **4** (*rinchiudere*) to shut up **5** (*spegnere*) to turn off, to switch **B** *v. intr.* to close **C** *v. rifl. e intr. pron.* **1** to close **2** (*concentrarsi*) to withdraw
chiùnque **A** *pron. indef.* anyone, anybody (ES: **c. è capace di farlo** anybody can do it) **B** *pron. rel. indef.* **1** (*sogg.*) whoever, (*compl.*) who(m)ever, anyone, anybody (ES: **c. telefoni, digli che sono uscito** whoever calls, tell him I'm out; **c. tu conosca, ignoralo** ignore anyone you know) **2** (*seguito da part.*) whichever (ES: **c. di loro arrivi, fallo sedere** whichever of them comes, let him sit down)
chiùsa *s. f.* lock
chiùso *agg.* **1** closed, shut **2** (*racchiuso*) enclosed **3** (*di persona*) reserved, close
chiusùra *s. f.* **1** closing, shutting **2** (*fine*) end, close **3** (*allacciatura*) fastening **4** (*serratura*) lock ♦ **c. lampo** zip
ci (1) **A** *pron. pers. 1ª pl.* **1** (*compl. ogg.*) us, (*compl. di termine*) (to) us (ES: **non ci hanno chiamato** they didn't call us) **2** (*riflessivo*) ourselves (*spesso sottinteso*) (ES: **non ci siamo vestiti come dovremmo** we did't dress ourselves as we should) **3** (*reciproco*) each other, one another (ES: **ci vediamo ogni domenica** we see each other every Sunday) **B** *pron. dimostr.* this, that, it (ES: **non ci credo** I don't believe it)
ci (2) *avv.* **1** (*qui*) here, (*là*) there, (*per questo luogo*) through (ES: **ci vado sempre** I always go there) **2** (*con il v. essere*) there (ES: **c'è** there is, **ci sono** there are)
ciabàtta *s. f.* slipper
ciàlda *s. f.* wafer
ciambèlla *s. f.* **1** (*dolce*) bun, doughnut **2** (*salvagente*) life ring
cianfrusàglia *s. f.* junk, knick-knacks *pl.*
ciào *inter.* **1** (*incontrandosi*) hullo, (*USA*) hi **2** (*accomiatandosi*) bye-bye, so long, cheerio
ciarlatàno *s. m.* charlatan, quack
ciascùno **A** *agg. indef.* **1** (*ogni*) every **2** (*distributivo*) each **B** *pron. indef.* **1** (*ognuno*) everybody, everyone **2** (*distributivo*) each (one)
cibàre **A** *v. tr.* to feed, to nourish **B** *v. rifl.* to feed, to eat
cìbo *s. m.* food
cicàla *s. f.* cicada
cicalìno *s. m.* buzzer
cicatrìce *s. f.* scar
cìcca *s. f.* (*di sigaretta*) cigarette end
cìccia *s. f.* (*fam.*) flesh
ciceróne *s. m.* guide, cicerone
cìclico *agg.* cyclic
ciclìsmo *s. m.* cycling
ciclìsta *s. m. e f.* **1** cyclist **2** (*chi ripara biciclette*) bicycle repairer
cìclo *s. m.* cycle
ciclomotóre *s. m.* motor-bicycle, moped
ciclóne *s. m.* cyclone
ciclòpico *agg.* cyclopean

cicógna *s. f.* stork
cicòria *s. f.* chicory
cièco *agg.* blind ♦ **vicolo c.** blind alley
cièlo *s. m.* sky, (*letter*) heaven
cìfra *s. f.* **1** figure, digit, numeral, number **2** (*somma*) amount **3** (*monogramma*) cipher, monogram
cìglio *s. m.* **1** eyelashes *pl.* **2** (*bordo*) edge, brink, border ♦ **senza batter c.** without flinching
cìgno *s. m.* swan
cigolàre *v. intr.* to creak, to squeak
cigolìo *s. m.* creaking, squeaking
ciliègia *s. f.* cherry
cilindràta *s. f.* (piston) displacement ♦ **auto di grossa c.** high-powered car
cilìndrico *agg.* cylindrical
cilìndro *s. m.* cylinder
cìma *s. f.* **1** top, peak, summit **2** (*naut.*) line, rope **3** (*fig.*) genious
cimèlio *s. m.* relic, antique
cìmice *s. f.* bug
ciminièra *s. f.* chimney
cimiterlàle *agg.* cemeterial
cimitèro *s. m.* graveyard, cemetery, (*presso una chiesa*) churchyard
cimùrro *s. m.* distemper
cinàbro *s. m.* cinnabar
cincin *inter.* cheers
cineamatóre *s. m.* amateur film-maker
cìnema *s. m. inv.* cinema, films *pl.*
cinematogràfico *agg.* cinematographic, film (*attr.*)
cineprésa *s. f.* (cine) camera
cineràrio *agg.* cinerary
cinése *agg. e s. m. e f.* Chinese
cinètico *agg.* kinetic
cìngere *v. tr.* **1** to gird **2** (*circondare*) to encircle, to surround
cìnghia *s. f.* strap, belt
cinghiàle *s. m.* (wild) boar
cinguettàre *v. intr.* to chirp, to twitter
cinguettìo *s. m.* chirping, twittering
cìnico *agg.* cynical
cinìsmo *s. m.* cynicism
cinòfilo *s. m.* cynophilist
cinquànta *agg. num. card. e s. m. inv.* fifty
cinquantèsimo *agg. num. ord. e s. m.* fiftieth
cinquantìna *s. f.* about fifty
cìnque *agg. num. card. e s. m. inv.* five
cinquecentésco *agg.* sixteenth-century (*attr.*)
cinquecènto *agg. num. card. e s. m. inv.* five hundred
cintùra *s. f.* belt ♦ **c. di sicurezza** safety/seat belt
cinturìno *s. m.* strap
ciò *pron. dimostr.* this, that, it ♦ **c. che** what; **c. nonostante** in spite of this; **con tutto c.** for all that
ciòcca *s. f.* lock
cioccolàta *s. f.* chocolate ♦ **c. al latte/fondente** milk/plain chocolate
cioccolatìno *s. m.* chocolate
cioccolàto *s. m.* → **cioccolata**
cioè *avv.* **1** that is, i.e. (*id est*), namely **2** (*con valore di rettifica*) better, or rather ♦ **c.?** what do you mean?
ciondolàre *v. intr.* **1** to dangle **2** (*bighellonare*) to lounge about
cióndolo *s. m.* pendant
ciononostànte *avv.* nevertheless, in spite of this
ciòtola *s. f.* bowl
ciòttolo *s. m.* **1** pebble, cobble **2** (*per pavimentazione*) cobblestone
cipìglio *s. m.* scowl
cipólla *s. f.* onion
cìppo *s. m.* cippus
ciprèsso *s. m.* cypress
cìpria *s. f.* (face) powder
cìrca **A** *avv.* about, approximately **B** *prep.* with regard to, about, concerning
cìrco *s. m.* circus
circolànte *agg.* circulating ♦ **biblioteca c.** lending library; **moneta c.** currency
circolàre (1) **A** *agg.* circular **B** *s. f.* circular (letter)
circolàre (2) *v. intr.* to circulate
circolazióne *s. f.* **1** circulation **2** (*traffico*) traffic
cìrcolo *s. m.* **1** circle **2** (*associazione*) club
circoncisióne *s. f.* circumcision
circondàre **A** *v. tr.* to surround, to encircle **B** *v. rifl.* to surround oneself
circonferènza *s. f.* circumference
circonvallazióne *s. f.* ring road
circoscrìvere *v. tr.* to circumscribe
circoscrizióne *s. f.* district ♦ **c. elettorale** constituency
circospètto *agg.* circumspect, cautious
circostànte *agg.* surrounding
circostànza *s. f.* circumstance
circùito *s. m.* circuit
cistercènse *agg.* Cistercian
cistèrna *s. f.* cistern, tank ♦ **nave c.** tanker
cìsti *s. f.* cyst
citàre *v. tr.* **1** to cite, to mention **2** (*da un*

libro, da un discorso) to quote **3** (*dir*) to summon(s), (*fare causa*) to sue
citazióne *s. f.* **1** citation **2** (*da un libro, da un discorso*) quotation **3** (*dir*) summons
citòfono *s. m.* entry phone
città *s. f.* town, (*importante*) city
cittadèlla *s. f.* citadel
cittadinànza *s. f.* **1** nationality, citizenship **2** (*popolazione di città*) citizens *pl.*
cittadìno **A** *agg.* town (*attr*), city (*attr*) **B** *s. m.* citizen
ciùco *s. m.* ass, donkey
ciùffo *s. m.* tuft
civétta *s. f.* **1** (*zool.*) owl **2** (*fig.*) coquette ♦ **far la c.** to flirt
cìvico *agg.* civic
civìle *agg.* civil
civilizzazióne *s. f.* civilization
civiltà *s. f.* **1** civilization, culture **2** (*cortesia*) civility
clàcson *s. m. inv.* horn
clamóre *s. m.* outcry
clamoróso *agg.* clamorous
clandestìno *s. m.* clandestine
clarinétto *s. m.* clarinet
clàsse *s. f.* class
classicìsmo *s. m.* classicism
classicìsta *s. m. e f.* classicist
classicità *s. f.* classical antiquity
clàssico **A** *agg.* classic(al) **B** *s. m.* classic
classìfica *s. f.* classification, results *pl.*
classificàre **A** *v. tr.* to classify **B** *v. rifl.* to come
classìsta *agg.* class (*attr*)
clàusola *s. f.* clause
claustrofobìa *s. f.* claustrophobia
clausùra *s. f.* seclusion ♦ **suora di c.** cloistered nun
clàva *s. f.* club
clavicémbalo *s. m.* harpsichord
clavìcola *s. f.* clavicle
clemènte *agg.* **1** (*di persona*) clement, lenient, merciful **2** (*di tempo*) mild
clemènza *s. f.* **1** (*di persona*) clemency, leniency, mercifulness **2** (*di clima*) mildness **3** (*dir*) mercy
cleptòmane *agg. e s. m. e f.* kleptomaniac
clericàle *agg.* clerical
clèro *s. m.* clergy
clessìdra *s. f.* (*a sabbia*) sandglass, (*ad acqua*) clepsydra
cliènte *s. m. e f.* (*di negozio*) customer, (*di albergo*) guest, (*di professionista*) client
clìma *s. m.* climate
climàtico *agg.* climatic ♦ **stazione climatica** health resort
climatizzazióne *s. f.* air-conditioning
clìnica *s. f.* clinic
clìnico *agg.* clinical
clòro *s. m.* chlorine
clorofilla *s. f.* chlorophyl
club *s. m. inv.* club
coabitàre *v. intr.* to cohabit, to live together
coabitazióne *s. f.* cohabitation, house-sharing
coagulàre *v. intr. e intr. pron.* to coagulate
coalizióne *s. f.* coalition, alliance
coàtto *agg.* forced
coautóre *s. m.* coauthor
cocaìna *s. f.* cocaine
cocainòmane *s. m. e f.* cocaine addict
coccinèlla *s. f.* ladybird, ladybug
còccio *s. m.* **1** earthenware **2** (*frammento*) fragment (of pottery)
cocciùto *agg.* stubborn
còcco *s. m.* coconut
coccodrìllo *s. m.* crocodile
coccolàre *v. tr.* to cuddle
cocènte *agg.* burning, scorching
cocómero *s. m.* watermelon
cocùzzolo *s. m.* top, summit
códa *s. f.* **1** tail **2** (*fila*) queue, line ♦ **fare la c.** to queue up
codàrdo *s. m.* coward
codésto *agg. e pron. dimostr.* that
còdice *s. m.* **1** code **2** (*manoscritto*) codex
codìfica *s. f.* codification
coefficiènte *s. m.* coefficient, factor
coerènte *agg.* coherent, consistent
coerènza *s. f.* coherence, consistency
coesistènte *agg.* coexistent
coetàneo *agg. e s. m.* contemporary
coèvo *agg.* coeval, contemporary
còfano *s. m.* bonnet, (*USA*) hood
còglìere *v. tr.* **1** to pick, to gather **2** (*sorprendere*) to catch **3** (*colpire*) to hit, to get **4** (*capire*) to understand
cognàta *s. f.* sister-in-law
cognàto *s. m.* brother-in-law
cognizióne *s. f.* knowledge
cognóme *s. m.* surname, family name
coincidènza *s. f.* **1** coincidence **2** (*mezzi di trasporto*) connection
coincìdere *v. intr.* to coincide
coinvòlgere *v. tr.* to involve
colabròdo *s. m.* colander
colapàsta *s. m.* colander
colàre **A** *v. tr.* **1** (*filtrare*) to strain, to filter,

to drain **2** (*fondere*) to cast **B** *v. intr.* to drip ♦ **c. a picco** to sink
colàta *s. f.* **1** (*metall.*) casting **2** (*geol.*) flow
colazióne *s. f.* (*del mattino*) breakfast, (*di mezzogiorno*) lunch
colèi *pron. dimostr. f. sing.* she, the person (who)
colèra *s. m.* cholera
colesteròlo *s. m.* cholesterol
còlica *s. f.* colic
colìno *s. m.* strainer
còlla *s. f.* glue
collaboràre *v. intr.* to collaborate, to cooperate
collaboratóre *s. m.* collaborator
collaborazióne *s. f.* collaboration, cooperation, (*a giornale*) contribution
collàna *s. f.* **1** necklace **2** (*raccolta*) collection
collant *s. m. inv.* tights *pl.*
collàre *s. m.* collar
collàsso *s. m.* collapse, breakdown
collaudàre *v. tr.* to test, to try out
collàudo *s. m.* test
còlle *s. m.* hill
collèga *s. m. e f.* colleague
collegaménto *s. m.* connection, link
collegàre **A** *v. tr.* to connect, to join, to link **B** *v. rifl.* **1** to join, to link up **2** (*mettersi in collegamento*) to get in touch, to link up
collegiàta *s. f.* collegiate church
collègio *s. m.* **1** (*organo consultivo*) board **2** (*consesso*) college, **3** (*convitto*) boarding school **4** (*elettorale*) constituency
còllera *s. f.* anger, fury
collèrico *agg.* irascible, hot-tempered
collètta *s. f.* collection
collettivaménte *avv.* collectively
collettività *s. f.* collectivity, community
collettìvo *agg.* collective
collétto *s. m.* collar
collezionàre *v. tr.* to collect
collezióne *s. f.* collection
collezionìsta *s. m. e f.* collector
collimàre *v. intr.* to correspond
collìna *s. f.* hill
collinóso *agg.* hilly
collìrio *s. m.* eyewash
collisióne *s. f.* collision
còllo (1) *s. m.* **1** neck **2** (*colletto*) collar
còllo (2) *s. m.* (*pacco*) parcel, item
collocàre **A** *v. tr.* **1** to place, to put, to set **2** (*prodotti*) to sell **B** *v. rifl. e intr. pron.* **1** to place oneself **2** (*trovare lavoro*) to find employement
collòquio *s. m.* talk, meeting
collutòrio *s. m.* mouthwash
colmàre *v. tr.* **1** to fill up **2** (*fig.*) to fill, to load
cólmo **A** *agg.* full, brimful **B** *s. m.* **1** top, summit **2** (*fig.*) height, peak
colómba *s. f.* dove
colómbo *s. m.* pigeon
còlon *s. m.* colon
colònia *s. f.* **1** colony **2** (*di vacanze*) summer camp ♦ **c. penale** penal settlement
coloniàle *agg.* colonial ♦ **generi coloniali** groceries
colonialìsta *s. m. e f.* colonialist
colonizzàre *v. tr.* to colonize
colónna *s. f.* column ♦ **c. vertebrale** backbone
colonnàto *s. m.* colonnade
colonnèllo *s. m.* colonel
colorànte *s. m.* dye
coloràre *v. tr. e intr. pron.* to colour
coloràto *agg.* stained
colóre *s. m.* colour, (*USA*) color
colorìto **A** *agg.* **1** coloured, (*di viso*) rosy **2** (*fig.*) colourful **B** *s. m.* **1** (*carnagione*) complexion **2** (*fig.*) vivacity
colóro *pron. dimostr. m. e f. pl.* they, those people
colòsso *s. m.* colossus
cólpa *s. f.* **1** fault, wrong, (*peccato*) sin **2** (*colpevolezza*) guilt, guiltiness **3** (*responsabilità*) blame **4** (*dir*) negligence
colpévole **A** *agg.* guilty, culpable **B** *s. m. e f.* culprit, offender
colpìre *v. tr.* **1** to hit, to strike **2** (*con arma da fuoco*) to shoot **3** (*fig.*) to strike **4** (*danneggiare*) to damage
cólpo *s. m.* **1** blow, stroke **2** (*d'arma da fuoco*) shot **3** (*rumore*) bang **4** (*giornalistico*) scoop **5** (*rapina*) robbery ♦ **c. di sole** sunstroke; **c. di stato** coup d'état; **c. di telefono** ring; **c. di vento** gust; **far c.** to make a sensation
coltellàta *s. f.* stab
coltèllo *s. m.* knife
coltivàbile *agg.* cultivable
coltivàre *v. tr.* to cultivate, to till, to farm
coltivatóre *s. m.* tiller, farmer, grower
coltivazióne *s. f.* cultivation, growing, farming
cólto *agg.* cultured, well-educated

cóltre *s. f.* blanket
coltùra *s. f.* **1** cultivation, farming, growing **2** (*biol.*) culture
colùi *pron. dimostr. m. sing.* he, the man, the one
còma *s. m. inv.* coma
comandaménto *s. m.* (*relig.*) commandment
comandànte *s. m.* commander, master
comandàre **A** *v. tr.* **1** to order, to command **2** (*mil.*) to be in command of **3** (*mecc.*) to control, to drive **4** (*richiedere*) to demand, to require **B** *v. intr.* to be in charge, to be in command
comàndo *s. m.* **1** (*ordine*) order, command **2** (*autorità*) command **3** (*sede del comandante*) headquarters *pl.* **4** (*tecnol.*) control, drive **5** (*sport*) lead
combaciàre *v. intr.* to meet, to join, to correspond
combàttere *v. tr. e intr.* to fight, to combat
combattiménto *s. m.* fight, combat
combinàre **A** *v. tr.* **1** to combine, to match **2** (*organizzare, concludere*) to conclude, to arrange, to settle **3** (*fam.*) (*fare*) to do, to make **B** *v. intr.* to agree **C** *v. rifl. e intr. pron.* **1** (*accordarsi*) to agree **2** (*conciarsi*) to get oneself up **3** (*chim.*) to combine
combinazióne *s. f.* **1** combination **2** (*coincidenza*) chance, coincidence
combustìbile **A** *agg.* combustible **B** *s. m.* fuel
cóme **A** *avv.* **1** (*in frasi interr.*) how, (*quanto bene*) what ... like **2** (*in frasi escl.*) how **3** (*il modo in cui*) how, the way, (*nel modo in cui*) as **4** (*comp.*) as (so) ... as **5** (*in qualità di*) as **6** (*a somiglianza*) like **7** (*in correlazione con 'così, tanto'*) as, both ... and, as well as **B** *cong.* **1** (*non appena*) as, as soon as **2** (*dichiarativa*) that ♦ **c. se** as if, as though; **c. si dice in inglese ...?** what's the English for ...?
cométa *s. f.* comet
còmica *s. f.* (*cin.*) comedy
còmico **A** *agg.* **1** comical, funny **2** (*teatro*) comic **B** *s. m.* **1** (*comicità*) funniness, comicality **2** (*attore*) comic, comedian
comìgnolo *s. m.* chimney-pot
cominciàre *v. tr. e intr.* to begin, to start
comitàto *s. m.* committee, board
comitiva *s. f.* party, group
comìzio *s. m.* meeting
commèdia *s. f.* **1** comedy, play **2** (*fig.*) sham, pretence
commediògrafo *s. m.* playwright
commemoràre *v. tr.* to commemorate
commemorazióne *s. f.* commemoration
commensàle *s. m. e f.* table companion
commentàre *v. tr.* to comment on
commentatóre *s. m.* commentator
comménto *s. m.* comment, commentary
commerciàle *agg.* commercial, trade (*attr.*), business (*attr.*)
commercialìsta *s. m. e f.* business consultant
commerciànte *s. m. e f.* trader, dealer, (*negoziante*) shopkeeper
commerciàre *v. tr. e intr.* to trade (in)
commèrcio *s. m.* trade ♦ **c. all'ingrosso/al minuto** wholesale/retail trade; **fuori c.** not for sale, (*esaurito*) out of stock
comméssa *s. f.* **1** (*ordine*) order, job **2** (*venditrice*) shop assistant, shop-girl
commésso *s. m.* shop assistant, (*USA*) salesclerk ♦ **c. viaggiatore** salesman
commestìbile *agg.* eatable, edible
comméttere *v. tr.* to commit
commiàto *s. m.* leave-taking
comminàre *v. tr.* to comminate
commiseràre **A** *v. tr.* to commiserate, to pity **B** *v. rifl.* to feel sorry for oneself
commissariàto *s. m.* (*di polizia*) police station
commissàrio *s. m.* commissary
commissionàrio *agg.* commission (*attr.*)
commissióne *s. f.* **1** errand **2** (*incarico*) commission **3** (*compenso*) commission, fee **4** (*comitato*) committee, board, commission ♦ **fare commissioni** to go shopping
committènte *s. m. e f.* customer, buyer, client
commòsso *agg.* moved
commovènte *agg.* moving
commozióne *s. f.* emotion ♦ **c. cerebrale** concussion
commuòvere **A** *v. tr.* to move, to touch **B** *v. intr. pron.* to be moved
comò *s. m.* chest of drawers
comodìno *s. m.* bedside table
comodità *s. f.* **1** comfort **2** (*opportunità*) convenience
còmodo **A** *agg.* **1** (*confortevole*) comfortable **2** (*opportuno*) convenient **3** (*maneggevole*) handy **B** *s. m.* comfort, convenience
compaesàno *s. m.* fellow countryman

compàgine *s. f.* structure, team
compagnìa *s. f.* **1** company **2** (*gruppo di persone*) group, party, gathering **3** (*società*) company, (*USA*) corporation
compàgno *s. m.* companion, mate, (*fam.*) chum
comparàbile *agg.* comparable
comparàre *v. tr.* to compare
comparatìvo *agg. e s. m.* comparative
comparìre *v. intr.* to appear
compàrsa *s. f.* **1** appearance **2** (*teatro, cin.*) walk-on, extra
compartecipazióne *s. f.* **1** sharing **2** (*parte*) share
compartiménto *s. m.* compartment
compassàto *agg.* stiff
compassióne *s. f.* compassion, pity
compàsso *s. m.* compasses *pl.*
compatìbile *agg.* **1** (*conciliabile*) compatible **2** (*scusabile*) excusable
compatibilménte *avv.* compatibly
compatìre *v. tr.* **1** (*compiangere*) to pity, to be sorry for **2** (*scusare*) to forgive
compàtto *agg.* compact
compèndio *s. m.* outline, summary, digest
compensàre **A** *v. tr.* **1** (*controbilanciare*) to compensate for **2** (*supplire a*) to make up for, to compensate **3** (*ricompensare*) to reward **4** (*pagare*) to pay **5** (*risarcire*) to indemnify **B** *v. rifl. rec.* to compensate each other
compènso *s. m.* **1** compensation **2** (*retribuzione*) remuneration, payment **3** (*ricompensa*) reward
cómpera *s. f.* purchase, shopping
competènte *agg.* competent
competènza *s. f.* **1** competence **2** (*onorario*) fee
compètere *v. intr.* **1** (*gareggiare*) to compete **2** (*spettare*) to be due
competitività *s. f.* competitiveness
competitìvo *agg.* competitive
competizióne *s. f.* competition
compiacènte *agg.* obliging
compiacènza *s. f.* **1** courtesy, kindness **2** (*compiacimento*) pleasure, satisfaction
compiacére **A** *v. tr.* to please, to gratify **B** *v. intr. pron.* **1** to be pleased (with) **2** (*congratularsi*) to congratulate
compiàngere **A** *v. tr.* to pity, to be sorry for **B** *v. rifl.* to feel sorry for oneself
cómpiere **A** *v. tr.* **1** (*finire*) to finish, to complete **2** (*effettuare*) to do, to perform, to accomplish, to achieve, to carry out **3** (*adempiere*) to fulfil **4** (*gli anni*) to be **B** *v. intr. pron.* **1** to end **2** (*avverarsi*) to come true
compilàre *v. tr.* to compile
compilazióne *s. f.* compilation, (*di modulo*) filling in
compitàre *v. tr.* to spell out
cómpito (1) *s. m.* **1** task, duty, job **2** (*di scuola*) exercise, (*a casa*) homework
compito (2) *agg.* polite
compleànno *s. m.* birthday
complementàre *agg.* complementary
compleménto *s. m.* **1** complement **2** (*mil.*) reserve
complessàto *agg.* full of complexes
complessità *s. f.* complexity
complessìvo *agg.* total, overall (*attr*), comprehensive
complèsso **A** *agg.* complex **B** *s. m.* **1** (*totalità*) whole **2** (*serie*) combination, set **3** (*impresa*) group, plant **4** (*mus.*) ensemble, band **5** (*psic.*) complex
completàre *v. tr.* to complete
complèto **A** *agg.* **1** complete, full, whole **2** (*totale*) complete, absolute, total **3** (*pieno*) full up **B** *s. m.* **1** set, outfit **2** (*abbigliamento*) suit ♦ **al c.** full (up)
complicàre **A** *v. tr.* to complicate **B** *v. intr. pron.* to get complicated, to thicken
complicazióne *s. f.* complication
còmplice *s. m. e f.* accomplice, party
complimentàrsi *v. intr. pron.* to congratulate
compliménto *s. m.* **1** compliment **2** *al pl.* (*cortesia eccessiva*) ceremony **3** *al pl.* (*congratulazioni*) congratulations *pl.*
complòtto *s. m.* conspiracy
componènte **A** *agg.* component **B** *s. m. e f.* **1** (*persona*) member **2** (*cosa*) component
componìbile *agg.* modular
componiménto *s. m.* composition
compórre *v. tr.* **1** to compose, to make up, to arrange **2** (*musica*) to compose **3** (*conciliare*) to settle **4** (*tip.*) to set **5** (*numero telefonico*) to dial
comportaménto *s. m.* behaviour
comportàre **A** *v. tr.* to involve, to require **B** *v. intr. pron.* to behave, to act
compòsito *agg.* composite
compositóre *s. m.* composer
composizióne *s. f.* **1** composition **2** (*conciliazione*) settlement **3** (*tip.*) setting
compósta *s. f.* (*cuc.*) stewed fruit, compote
compostézza *s. f.* composure

compósto **A** *agg.* **1** compound **2** (*formato da*) made up of **3** (*ordinato*) tidy **4** (*calmo*) composed, calm **B** *s. m.* mixture, compound
compràre *v. tr.* **1** to buy, to purchase **2** (*corrompere*) to bribe
compratóre *s. m.* **1** buyer, purchaser **2** (*dir.*) vendee
comprèndere *v. tr.* **1** to comprise, to include **2** (*capire*) to understand, to realize
comprensìbile *agg.* understandable
comprensióne *s. f.* **1** comprehension, understanding **2** (*simpatia*) sympathy
comprensìvo *agg.* **1** inclusive, comprehensive **2** (*che prova comprensione*) sympathetic
compréso *agg.* **1** (*incluso*) included (*pred.*), inclusive **2** (*capito*) understood **3** (*assorto*) filled with
comprèssa *s. f.* tablet
compressióne *s. f.* compression
compressóre *s. m.* compressor
comprìmere *v. tr.* to compress
comprométtere *v. tr.* to compromise
comproprietà *s. f.* joint ownership
comproprietàrio *s. m.* joint owner
comprovàre *v. tr.* to prove
computàre *v. tr.* to calculate
computer *s. m. inv.* computer
computisterìa *s. f.* book-keeping
còmputo *s. m.* calculation
comunàle *agg.* **1** municipal, town (*attr.*) **2** (*stor.*) communal
comùne (1) **A** *agg.* **1** common **2** (*ordinario*) ordinary **B** *s. m.* common run ♦ **fuori del c.** unusual, uncommon
comùne (2) *s. m.* **1** municipality, town council **2** (*stor.*) commune
comuneménte *avv.* commonly, generally
comunicàre *v. tr. e intr.* to communicate
comunicàto *s. m.* announcement, bulletin ♦ **c. stampa** press release
comunicazióne *s. f.* **1** communication **2** (*tel.*) telephone call, line **3** (*comunicato*) announcement, (*messaggio*) message, (*relazione*) report
comunióne *s. f.* **1** communion **2** (*dir.*) community
comunìsmo *s. m.* communism
comunità *s. f.* community
comùnque **A** *avv.* **1** (*tuttavia*) but, all the same **2** (*in ogni caso*) however, anyhow, in any case **B** *cong.* however, whatever
cón *prep.* **1** (*compagnia, unione, comparazione, relazione*) with (ES: **sono c. lei** I'm with her, **paragonare un colore c. l'altro** to compare one colour with the other) **2** (*mezzo, strumento*) with, by (ES: **scrivere c. la matita** to write with a pencil; **andare c. l'autobus** to go by bus) **3** (*maniera*) with (ES: **trattare c. cura** to handle with care) **4** (*per indicare una caratteristica*) with (ES: **un uomo c. gli occhi azzurri** a man with blue eyes) **5** (*con valore temporale*) with, at, on, in (ES: **c. la sua partenza** on his departure) **6** (*verso*) to (ES: **essere scortese c. qc.** to be impolite to sb.) **7** (*contro*) against, with (ES: **scontrarsi c. la polizia** to clash with the police) **8** (*avversativo, concessivo*) with, for (ES: **c. tutti i suoi soldi, lo detesto** for all his money, I hate him) **9** (*consecutivo*) to (ES: **c. nostro profondo rammarico** to our great regret)
conàto *s. m.* **1** effort **2** (*di vomito*) retching
cónca *s. f.* basin
concatenazióne *s. f.* concatenation, link
còncavo *agg.* concave
concèdere *v. tr.* **1** to grant, to allow, to concede **2** (*permettere*) to allow **3** (*ammettere*) to admit
concentraménto *s. m.* concentration
concentràre **A** *v. tr.* to concentrate **B** *v. rifl.* **1** (*riunirsi*) to concentrate, to gather **2** (*fig.*) to concentrate
concentrazióne *s. f.* concentration
concèntrico *agg.* concentric
concepìbile *agg.* conceivable
concepiménto *s. m.* conception
concepìre *v. tr.* **1** (*generare, fig.*) to conceive **2** (*immaginare, escogitare*) to imagine, to contrive **3** (*nutrire*) to entertain **4** (*comprendere*) to understand
concèrnere *v. tr.* to concern, to regard
concertàre *v. tr.* **1** (*mus.*) to harmonize **2** (*fig.*) to plan, to arrange
concertìsta *s. m. e f.* concert player
concèrto *s. m.* concert, (*composizione*) concerto
concessionàrio *s. m.* concessionaire, agent ♦ **c. d'auto** car distributor
concessióne *s. f.* concession, (*autorizzazione*) franchise
concètto *s. m.* concept, conception, idea
concettuàle *agg.* conceptual
concezióne *s. f.* conception
conchìglia *s. f.* shell, conch

cóncia *s. f.* (*di pelli*) tanning, (*di tabacco*) curing
concïàre **A** *v. tr.* **1** (*trattare*) to treat, (*pelli*) to tan, (*tabacco*) to cure **2** (*maltrattare*) to ill-treat, to beat up **3** (*sporcare*) to dirty, to soil **B** *v. rifl.* **1** (*sporcarsi*) to get dirty **2** (*vestirsi*) to get oneself up
concilïàre *v. tr.* **1** to reconcile, to conciliate **2** (*favorire*) to induce ♦ **c. una contravvenzione** to settle a fine
concìlio *s. m.* council
concìme *s. m.* manure, dung
concisióne *s. f.* concision
concìso *agg.* concise
concitàto *agg.* excited
concittadìno *s. m.* fellow citizen
conclùdere **A** *v. tr.* **1** to conclude, to end, to finish **2** (*dedurre*) to conclude, to infer **3** (*combinare*) to do **B** *v. intr. pron.* to end up, to conclude
conclusióne *s. f.* conclusion
conclusìvo *agg.* conclusive
concomitànte *agg.* concomitant
concordànza *s. f.* **1** concordance, agreement **2** (*gramm.*) concord
concordàre **A** *v. tr.* **1** to agree, to arrange **2** (*mettere d'accordo*) to reconcile **3** (*gramm.*) to make agree **B** *v. intr.* to agree
concordàto *s. m.* **1** (*dir.*) composition, arrangement **2** (*relig.*) concordat
concòrde *agg.* in agreement
concorrènte *s. m. e f.* **1** (*comm., sport*) competitor **2** (*candidato*) candidate, applicant
concorrènza *s. f.* competition
concórrere *v. intr.* **1** (*contribuire*) to contribute, to concur **2** (*partecipare*) to share in, to take part in **3** (*competere*) to compete
concórso *s. m.* **1** (*competizione*) competition, contest **2** (*partecipazione*) contribution **3** (*assistenza*) assistance, aid **4** (*dir.*) complicity
concretézza *s. f.* concreteness
concrèto *agg.* concrete
concussióne *s. f.* extortion
condànna *s. f.* **1** condemnation, (*dir.*) conviction **2** (*pena*) punishment
condannàre *v. tr.* **1** (*dir.*) to convict, to sentence **2** (*est.*) to condemn
condannàto *agg. e s. m.* convict
condènsa *s. f.* condensate
condensàre *v. tr. e intr. pron.* to condense
condensazióne *s. f.* condensation, condensing
condiménto *s. m.* **1** flavouring, seasoning, (*per insalata*) dressing **2** (*sostanza*) condiment, dressing, sauce
condìre *v. tr.* to flavour, to season, (*insalata*) to dress
condiscendènza *s. f.* **1** (*degnazione*) condescension **2** (*remissività*) compliance
condivìdere *v. tr.* to share
condizionàle *agg.* conditional
condizionaménto *s. m.* conditioning
condizionàre *v. tr.* to condition
condizionatóre *s. m.* (air-)conditioner
condizióne *s. f.* condition
condoglïànza *s. f.* condolence
condomìnio *s. m.* joint ownership, (*edificio*) condominium
condonàre *v. tr.* to remit, to condone, to forgive
condóno *s. m.* remission, pardon
condótta *s. f.* **1** (*comportamento*) conduct, behaviour **2** (*conduzione*) conduct, direction **3** (*tubazione*) pipe
condottièro *s. m.* leader
condótto *s. m.* duct, pipe
conducènte *s. m.* driver
condùrre *v. tr.* **A** **1** (*guidare*) to lead, to conduct, (*veicolo*) to drive **2** (*accompagnare*) to take, to bring **3** (*gestire*) to manage **4** (*effettuare*) to carry out, to conduct **B** *v. intr.* to conduct
conduttùra *s. f.* piping ♦ **c. dell'acqua** water mains
confàrsi *v. intr. pron.* to suit, to fit, to become
confederazióne *s. f.* confederation
conferènza *s. f.* **1** lecture **2** (*riunione*) conference ♦ **c. stampa** press conference
conferenzière *s. m.* lecturer
conferire **A** *v. tr.* to confer, to give, to award **B** *v. intr.* to confer with
confèrma *s. f.* confirmation
confermàre **A** *v. tr.* to confirm **B** *v. rifl.* to prove oneself
confessàre *v. tr.* to confess
confessionàle *agg. e s. m.* confessional
confessióne *s. f.* confession
confessóre *s. m.* confessor
confetterìa *s. f.* confectionery, (*negozio*) sweet shop
confètto *s. m.* **1** sugared almond **2** (*med.*) pill
confettùra *s. f.* jam
confezionàre *v. tr.* **1** to make up, to manufacture **2** (*pacco*) to pack, to wrap up

confezióne *s. f.* **1** (*di abiti*) manufacture, tailoring, dressmaking **2** *al pl.* (*abiti*) clothes **3** (*imballaggio*) wrapping, packing **4** (*pacco*) package ♦ **c. regalo** gift wrapping
conficcàre **A** *v. tr.* to hammer **B** *v. rifl.* to stick
confidàre **A** *v. tr.* to confide **B** *v. intr.* to confide, to trust, to rely on **C** *v. rifl.* to confide in
confidènte *s. m. e f.* **1** (*amico*) confidant *m.*, confidante *f.* **2** (*informatore*) informer
confidènza *s. f.* **1** confidence, trust **2** (*cosa confidata*) confidence, secret **3** (*familiarità*) intimacy
confidenziàle *agg.* **1** confidential **2** (*cordiale*) friendly
configuràre **A** *v. tr.* to shape **B** *v. intr. pron.* to take shape, to assume a form
confinànte *agg.* neighbouring (*attr.*), bordering
confinàre **A** *v. tr.* to confine **B** *v. intr.* to border on, to adjoin
confìne *s. m.* border, boundary
confino *s. m.* internment
confìsca *s. f.* confiscation
confiscàre *v. tr.* to confiscate
conflìtto *s. m.* conflict
confluènza *s. f.* confluence
confluìre *v. intr.* **1** to flow, to meet **2** (*fig.*) to converge
confóndere **A** *v. tr.* **1** (*mescolare*) to confuse, to mix up **2** (*scambiare*) to mistake **3** (*disorientare*) to confuse, to embarrass **B** *v. rifl. e intr. pron.* **1** to get mixed up, to become confuse **2** (*mescolarsi*) to mix, to merge
conformàre **A** *v. tr.* to conform, to adapt **B** *v. rifl.* to conform, to comply with
conformeménte *avv.* according to
conformìsmo *s. m.* conformism
conformìsta *agg. e s. m. e f.* conformist
confortàre **A** *v. tr.* **1** (*consolare*) to comfort, to console **2** (*incoraggiare*) to encourage **3** (*sostenere*) to support **B** *v. rifl.* to take comfort
confortévole *agg.* **1** (*che conforta*) comforting **2** (*comodo*) comfortable
confòrto *s. m.* **1** comfort, consolation **2** (*incoraggiamento*) encouragement **3** (*sostegno*) support
confrontàre *v. tr.* to compare, to confront
confrónto *s. m.* comparison ♦ **in c. a** in comparison with
confusionàrio **A** *agg.* muddling **B** *s. m.* muddler
confusióne *s. f.* **1** muddle, confusion, mess **2** (*rumore*) row, noise **3** (*imbarazzo*) confusion, embarrassment
confùso *agg.* confused
confutàre *v. tr.* to refute
congedàre **A** *v. tr.* **1** to take leave of, to dismiss **2** (*mil.*) to discharge **B** *v. rifl.* **1** to take one's leave of **2** (*mil.*) to be discharged
congèdo *s. m.* **1** leave **2** (*mil.*) discharge
congegnàre *v. tr.* to contrive
congégno *s. m.* device, gear
congelàre *v. tr. e intr. pron.* to freeze
congelatóre *s. m.* freezer
congestióne *s. f.* congestion
congettùra *s. f.* conjecture
congetturàre *v. tr.* to conjecture
congiùngere **A** *v. tr.* **1** to join **2** (*collegare*) to connect, to join up **B** *v. rifl. e rifl. rec.* to join
congiuntivìte *s. f.* conjunctivitis
congiuntivo *agg. e s. m.* (*gramm.*) subjunctive
congiùnto *s. m.* relative
congiuntùra *s. f.* **1** (*giuntura*) joint **2** (*circostanza*) circumstance, situation **3** (*econ.*) conjuncture, situation, (*tendenza*) trend
congiunzióne *s. f.* **1** connection **2** (*gramm.*) conjunction
congiùra *s. f.* conspiracy
congiuràre *v. intr.* to conspire
conglobàre *v. tr.* to combine, to consolidate
congratulàrsi *v. intr. pron.* to congratulate
congratulazióni *s. f. pl.* congratulations *pl.*
congregazióne *s. f.* congregation
congrèsso *s. m.* congress
congruènza *s. f.* congruency
conguàglio *s. m.* balance, adjustment
coniàre *v. tr.* to coin
cònico *agg.* conic(al)
conìfera *s. f.* conifer
conìglio *s. m.* rabbit
coniugàre *v. tr.* **1** to conjugate **2** (*fig.*) to combine
coniugàto *agg.* married
coniugazióne *s. f.* conjugation
còniuge *s. m.* consort
connaturàto *agg.* ingrained
connazionàle *s. m. e f.* compatriot
connessióne *s. f.* connection
connèttere **A** *v. tr.* to connect, to link **B** *v.*

intr. to think straight **C** *v. intr. pron.* to be connected
connivènte *agg.* conniving
connotàto *s. m. spec. al pl.* description
còno *s. m.* cone ♦ **c. gelato** ice-cream cone
conoscènte *s. m. e f.* acquaintance
conoscènza *s. f.* **1** (*sapere*) knowledge **2** (*il conoscere una persona e la persona conosciuta*) acquaintance **3** (*coscienza*) consciousness
conóscere A *v. tr.* **1** to know **2** (*incontrare*) to meet **3** (*fare esperienza*) to experience **4** (*riconoscere*) to recognize **B** *v. rifl. rec.* **1** to know each other **2** (*fare conoscenza*) to meet
conoscitóre *s. m.* connoisseur
conosciùto *agg.* well-known, famous
conquìsta *s. f.* conquest
conquistàre *v. tr.* **1** to conquer **2** (*fig.*) to win **3** (*sedurre*) to conquer
consacràre A *v. tr.* to consecrate **B** *v. rifl.* to devote oneself
consanguìneo A *agg.* consanguineous, akin (*pred.*) **B** *s. m.* kinsman
consapévole *agg.* conscious, aware (*pred.*)
consapevolézza *s. f.* consciousness, awareness
cònscio *agg.* conscious, aware (*pred.*)
consecutìvo *agg.* **1** consecutive, in a row **2** (*seguente*) following **3** (*gramm.*) consecutive
conségna *s. f.* **1** delivery **2** (*custodia*) consignment **3** (*mil.*) orders *pl.* ♦ **c. a domicilio** home delivery; **pagamento alla c.** cash on delivery
consegnàre *v. tr.* to deliver, to hand over, to consign
conseguènte *agg.* consequent
conseguènza *s. f.* consequence
conseguìre A *v. tr.* to reach, to achieve **B** *v. intr.* to result
consènso *s. m.* consent
consensuàle *agg.* consensual
consentìre A *v. intr.* **1** (*essere d'accordo*) to agree **2** (*acconsentire*) to consent, to assent **B** *v. tr.* to allow
consèrva *s. f.* preserve ♦ **c. di pomodoro** tomato purée
conservànte *s. m.* preservative
conservàre A *v. tr.* to keep, to preserve **B** *v. intr. pron.* to keep, to remain
conservatóre *agg. e s. m.* conservative
conservatòrio *s. m.* conservatoire, (*USA*) conservatory
conservazióne *s. f.* conservation, preservation
consideràre A *v. tr.* **1** to consider, to think of **2** (*stimare*) to think higly of **B** *v. rifl.* to consider oneself
considerazióne *s. f.* **1** consideration **2** (*stima*) regard, respect
consideréVole *agg.* considerable
consigliàbile *agg.* advisable
consigliàre A *v. tr.* to advise, to counsel **B** *v. intr. pron.* to ask advice, to consult
consiglière *s. m.* **1** adviser, counsellor **2** (*membro di consiglio*) councillor
consiglio *s. m.* **1** advice, counsel **2** (*organo collegiale*) council, board
consistènte *agg.* substantial, solid
consistènza *s. f.* **1** concistency, solidity **2** (*fondatezza*) foundation, validity
consistere *v. intr.* to consist
consociàto *agg. e s. m.* associate
consolàre A *v. tr.* to console, to soothe, to comfort **B** *v. rifl.* **1** to take comfort **2** (*rallegrarsi*) to cheer up
consolàto *s. m.* consulate
consolazióne *s. f.* **1** consolation, comfort **2** (*gioia*) joy
cònsole *s. m.* consul
consolidàre *v. tr. e intr. pron.* to consolidate
consonànte *agg. e s. f.* consonant
cònsono *agg.* consonant, in accordance with
consòrte *s. m. e f.* consort
consorterìa *s. f.* faction, clique
consòrzio *s. m.* association, (*d'imprese*) syndicate
constàre A *v. intr.* (*essere composto*) to consist, to be made up **B** *v. intr. impers.* (*risultare*) to appear, to be proved
constatàre *v. tr.* **1** to ascertain **2** (*notare*) to note, to observe
constatazióne *s. f.* **1** ascertainment **2** (*osservazione*) observation
consuèto *agg.* usual, customary
consuetùdine *s. f.* custom
consulènte *agg. e s. m. e f.* consultant
consulènza *s. f.* advice
consultàre A *v. tr.* to consult **B** *v. intr. pron.* to confer, to consult **C** *v. rifl. rec.* to consult together, to confer
consultazióne *s. f.* consultation
consultìvo *agg.* advisory
consumàre A *v. tr.* **1** to consume, to use up, (*vestiti*) to wear **2** (*dissipare*) to waste **3** (*usare*) to consume, to use **4** (*mangiare*)

to eat, (*bere*) to drink **5** (*compiere*) to commit, to consumate **B** *v. intr. pron.* to consume, to wear out
consumatóre *s. m.* consumer
consumazióne *s. f.* **1** consumption **2** (*al bar*) order **3** (*compimento*) consummation
consùmo *s. m.* consumption
consuntivo A *agg.* final **B** *s. m.* final balance, survey
contàbile *s. m. e f.* book-keeper, accountant
contabilità *s. f.* book-keeping, accounting
contachilòmetri *s. m.* mileometer, (*USA*) odometer
contadìno A *agg.* rural, country (*attr.*) **B** *s. m.* farmer
contagiàre A *v. tr.* to infect **B** *v. intr. pron.* to get infected
contàgio *s. m.* contagion, infection
contagióso *agg.* contagious, infectious
contagìri *s. m. inv.* rev(olution) counter
contagócce *s. m. inv.* dropper
contaminàre *v. tr.* to contaminate
contaminazióne *s. f.* contamination
contànte *agg. e s. m.* cash
contàre A *v. tr.* **1** to count **2** (*annoverare*) to have **3** (*fam.*) (*raccontare*) to tell **B** *v. intr.* **1** (*sperare*) to expect **2** (*fare assegnamento*) to count, to depend **3** (*valere*) to mean
contatóre *s. m.* meter, counter
contattàre *v. tr.* to contact
contàtto *s. m.* contact
cónte *s. m.* count, earl
contèa *s. f.* (*titolo*) earldom, (*territorio*) county, -shire
conteggiàre *v. tr.* **1** to calculate **2** (*far pagare*) to charge, to put on the bill
contéggio *s. m.* count
contégno *s. m.* **1** (*comportamento*) behaviour **2** (*atteggiamento controllato*) self-control
contemplàre *v. tr.* **1** to admire, to contemplate **2** (*prevedere*) to provide for
contemplatìvo *agg.* contemplative
contemporaneaménte *avv.* at the same time
contemporàneo *agg. e s. m.* contemporary
contèndere A *v. tr.* to contend for, to contest **B** *v. intr.* to quarrel, to contest **C** *v. rifl. rec.* to contend for
contenére A *v. tr.* **1** to contain, to hold **2** (*frenare*) to contain, to control **B** *v. rifl.* to contain oneself
contenitóre *s. m.* container
contentàre A *v. tr.* to satisfy, to please **B** *v. intr. pron.* to be content, to be pleased
contentézza *s. f.* contentment, satisfaction, joy
contènto *agg.* pleased, happy
contenùto *s. m.* **1** contents *pl.* **2** (*argomento*) content, subject
contésa *s. f.* **1** contest, contention **2** (*gara*) competition
contéssa *s. f.* countess
contestàre *v. tr.* **1** (*negare*) to contest, to deny **2** (*notificare*) to notify **3** (*opporsi a*) to contest, to challenge, to dispute
contestazióne *s. f.* **1** dispute, controversy **2** (*notifica*) notification **3** (*protesta*) protest
contèsto *s. m.* context
contiguo *agg.* contiguous, adjoining
continentàle *agg.* continental
continènte *s. m.* continent
continènza *s. f.* continence
contingènte A *agg.* contingent **B** *s. m.* **1** (*mil.*) contingent **2** (*econ.*) quota, share
contingènza *s. f.* **1** (*circostanza*) circumstance **2** (*indennità di c.*) cost-of-living allowance
continuaménte *avv.* **1** (*ininterrottamente*) continuously, non-stop **2** (*frequentemente*) continually
continuàre *v. tr. e intr.* to go on, to continue, to keep on
continuazióne *s. f.* continuation ♦ **in c.** over and over again
contìnuo *agg.* **1** continuous, non-stop **2** (*frequente*) continual
cónto *s. m.* **1** (*calcolo*) calculation **2** (*econ., banca*) account **3** (*al ristorante*) bill **4** (*considerazione*) esteem, regard ♦ **fare c. di** to imagine, (*proporsi*) to intend; **fare c. su q.c./qc.** to rely on st./sb.; **per c. mio** as for me; **rendersi conto di q.c.** to realize st.
contòrcere *v. tr. e rifl.* to twist
contorciménto *s. m.* twisting
contornàre A *v. tr.* **1** to surround **2** to border **B** *v. rifl.* to surround oneself
contórno *s. m.* **1** contour, outline, edge **2** (*cuc.*) vegetables *pl.*
contòrto *agg.* twisted
contrabbandàre *v. tr.* to smuggle
contrabbandière *s. m.* smuggler
contrabbàndo *s. m.* smuggling
contrabbàsso *s. m.* double bass
contraccambiàre *v. tr.* to return, to repay

contraccettìvo *agg. e s. m.* contraceptive
contraccólpo *s. m.* **1** rebound, recoil **2** (*fig.*) reaction, consequence
contraddìre **A** *v. tr. e intr.* to contradict **B** *v. rifl.* to contradict oneself
contraddistinguere **A** *v. tr.* to mark **B** *v. intr. pron.* to stand out, to be characterised by
contraddittòrio **A** *agg.* contradictory **B** *s. m.* (*dir.*) cross-examination
contraddizióne *s. f.* contradiction
contraèreo *agg.* anti-aircraft
contraffàre *v. tr.* **1** (*simulare*) to counterfeit, to imitate, to simulate **2** (*falsificare*) to counterfeit, to falsify, to forge
contraffazióne *s. f.* **1** counterfeit **2** (*falsificazione*) forgery
contrappéso *s. m.* counterbalance
contrappórre **A** *v. tr.* to oppose, to counter **B** *v. rifl.* to oppose, to set oneself against
contrapposizióne *s. f.* contrast, opposition, contraposition
contrariaménte *avv.* **1** (*in modo contrario*) contrarily, contrary to **2** (*al contrario*) on the contrary
contrariàre *v. tr.* **1** to oppose **2** (*irritare*) to vex, to irritate
contrarietà *s. f.* **1** (*opposizione*) contrariety, opposition, aversion **2** (*avversità*) misfortune, trouble, problem
contràrio **A** *agg.* **1** contrary, opposite **2** (*sfavorevole*) unfavourable **3** (*riluttante*) unwilling **B** *s. m.* contrary, opposite ♦ **al c.** on the contrary, (*a ritroso*) backwards, (*a rovescio*) inside out
contràrre **A** *v. tr.* to contract **B** *v. intr. pron.* **1** to contract **2** (*ridursi*) to fall
contrassegnàre *v. tr.* to mark
contrasségno (1) *s. m.* mark
contrasségno (2) *avv.* cash on delivery
contrastàre **A** *v. tr.* to oppose, to resist **B** *v. intr.* to be in contrast, to contrast
contràsto *s. m.* contrast
contrattaccàre *v. tr. e intr.* to counterattack
contrattàcco *s. m.* counterattack
contrattàre *v. tr.* to bargain over, to negotiate
contrattèmpo *s. m.* mishap, hitch
contràtto *s. m.* agreement, contract
contrattuàle *agg.* contractual
contravvenzióne *s. f.* **1** infringement, violation **2** (*multa*) fine
contrazióne *s. f.* contraction
contribuènte *s. m. e f.* taxpayer
contribuìre *v. intr.* to contribute
contribùto *s. m.* **1** contribution **2** (*sovvenzione*) grant
cóntro **A** *prep.* **1** against **2** (*dir., sport*) versus **B** *avv.* against ♦ **il pro e il c.** the pros and cons
controbàttere *v. tr.* to refute, to rebut
controffensìva *s. f.* counter-offensive
controfigùra *s. f.* double
controindicazióne *s. f.* contraindication
controllàre **A** *v. tr.* to check, to control **B** *v. rifl.* to control oneself
contròllo *s. m.* control
controllóre *s. m.* **1** controller **2** (*mezzi di trasporto*) ticket collector
controlùce *s. f.* backlight
contromàno *avv.* in the wrong direction
contromàrca *s. f.* check, token
contropàrte *s. f.* counterpart
contropiède *s. m.* counterattack
controproducènte *agg.* counterproductive
contrórdine *s. m.* counterorder, countermand
controrifórma *s. f.* Counter-Reformation
controsènso *s. m.* countersense, nonsense
controspionàggio *s. m.* counter-espionage
controvalóre *s. m.* equivalent, (*banca*) exchange value
controvèrsia *s. f.* controversy
controvèrso *agg.* controversial
controvòglia *avv.* unwillingly
contumàcia *s. f.* (*dir.*) contumacy, default
contusióne *s. f.* bruise
contùso *agg.* bruised
convalescènte *agg. e s. m. e f.* convalescent
convalescènza *s. f.* convalescence
convalidàre *v. tr.* **1** to validate, to confirm **2** (*rafforzare*) to corroborate
convégno *s. m.* meeting, congress
convenévoli *s. m. pl.* compliments *pl.*, regards *pl.*
conveniènte *agg.* **1** (*adatto*) convenient, suitable **2** (*di prezzo*) good, (*di articolo*) cheap
conveniènza *s. f.* **1** convenience, suitability **2** (*vantaggio*) advantage, gain **3** (*di prezzo*) cheapness
convenìre *v. intr.* **1** (*impers.*) to be better, to suit **2** (*concordare*) to agree **3** (*essere vantaggioso*) to be worth
convènto *s. m.* convent
convenzionàle *agg.* **1** agreed, prearranged **2** (*tradizionale*) conventional

convenzióne *s. f.* convention
convergènza *s. f.* **1** convergence **2** (*fig.*) meeting
convèrgere *v. intr.* to converge
conversàre *v. intr.* to talk
conversazióne *s. f.* conversation, talk
conversióne *s. f.* conversion
convertìre **A** *v. tr.* to convert **B** *v. rifl. e intr. pron.* to be converted
convèsso *agg.* convex
convezióne *s. f.* convection
convìncere **A** *v. tr.* to convince **B** *v. rifl.* to convince oneself
convìnto *agg.* convinced
convinzióne *s. f.* conviction
convìtto *s. m.* boarding school
convivènte *s. m. e f.* cohabitant
convìvere *v. intr.* to cohabit, to live together
convocàre *v. tr.* to call, to convene
convocazióne *s. f.* convocation
convogliàre *v. tr.* **1** (*trasportare*) to carry **2** (*indirizzare*) to direct
convòglio *s. m.* **1** convoy **2** (*ferr.*) train
convulsióne *s. f.* fit, convulsion
convùlso *agg.* **1** convulsive **2** (*frenetico*) feverish
cooperàre *v. intr.* to cooperate, to collaborate
cooperatìva *s. f.* cooperative
cooperazióne *s. f.* cooperation
coordinaménto *s. m.* coordination
coordinàre *v. tr.* to coordinate
coordinàta *s. f.* coordinate
coordinatóre *s. m.* coordinator
copèrchio *s. m.* cover, lid, cap
copèrta *s. f.* **1** blanket, cover, rug **2** (*naut.*) deck
copertìna *s. f.* cover, (*USA*) jacket
copèrto (1) *agg.* **1** covered **2** (*del cielo*) overcast **3** (*vestito*) clothed **4** (*nascosto*) hidden
copèrto (2) *s. m.* **1** (*posto a tavola*) place, cover **2** (*prezzo*) cover charge
copertóne *s. m.* (*autom.*) tyre
copertùra *s. f.* cover, covering
còpia *s. f.* copy
copiàre *v. tr.* to copy
copióne (1) *s. m.* (*cin., teatro*) script
copióne (2) *s. m.* (*fam.*) copycat
copisterìa *s. f.* typing office
còppa *s. f.* cup ♦ **c. dell'olio** oil sump
còppia *s. f.* couple, pair
coprifuòco *s. m.* curfew
coprilètto *s. m. inv.* bedcover
coprìre **A** *v. tr.* **1** to cover **2** (*occupare*) to hold **B** *v. rifl.* to cover oneself, to wrap up **C** *v. intr. pron.* **1** to be covered **2** (*rannuvolarsi*) to become overcast
coràggio *s. m.* **1** courage, bravery **2** (*impudenza*) nerve, cheek ♦ **c.!** come on!, cheer up!
coraggióso *agg.* courageous, brave
coràle *agg.* choral
corallìno *agg.* coral
coràllo *s. m.* coral ♦ **banco di c.** coral reef
Coràno *s. m.* Koran
coràzza *s. f.* **1** (*mil.*) armour, (*stor.*) cuirass **2** (*zool.*) carapace, armour
corazzàta *s. f.* battleship
corazzàto *agg.* armoured
còrda *s. f.* **1** rope, cord **2** (*mus.*) string **3** (*anat.*) cord ♦ **c. vocale** vocal cord; **tagliare la c.** (*fig.*) to slip away
cordiàle *agg.* **1** cordial, warm **2** (*profondo*) hearty ♦ **cordiali saluti** best wishes
cordialità *s. f.* cordiality
cordialménte *avv.* **1** cordially, warmly **2** (*profondamente*) heartily
cordòglio *s. m.* grief, condolence
cordóne *s. m.* **1** cord, string **2** (*fig.*) cordon
coreografìa *s. f.* choreography
coriàceo *agg.* tough, coriaceous
coriàndolo *s. m.* **1** (*bot.*) coriander **2** *al pl.* confetti
coricàre **A** *v. tr.* **1** to lay down **2** (*mettere a letto*) to put to bed **B** *v. rifl.* **1** to lie down **2** (*andare a letto*) to go to bed
corìnzio *agg.* Corinthian
corìsta *s. m. e f.* chorister
cormoràno *s. m.* cormorant
cornàcchia *s. f.* crow
cornamùsa *s. f.* bagpipes *pl.*
còrnea *s. f.* cornea
cornétta *s. f.* **1** (*mus.*) cornet **2** (*tel.*) receiver
cornìce *s. f.* **1** frame **2** (*arch.*) cornice **3** (*scenario*) setting
cornicióne *s. m.* cornice, moulding
còrno *s. m.* horn
cornucòpia *s. f.* cornucopia
còro *s. m.* chorus, choir
coròlla *s. f.* corolla
coróna *s. f.* **1** crown **2** (*di fiori*) wreath
coronàre *v. tr.* **1** to crown **2** (*circondare*) to surround **3** (*realizzare*) to realize, to crown
còrpo *s. m.* **1** body **2** (*organismo*) corps, staff

corporàle *agg.* corporal
corporatùra *s. f.* build
corporazióne *s. f.* **1** corporation **2** (*stor*) guild
corpulènto *agg.* stout
corpùscolo *s. m.* corpuscle
corredàre *v. tr.* **1** to equip, to furnish **2** (*accompagnare*) to attach, to enclose
corredìno *s. m.* layette
corrèdo *s. m.* **1** equipment, kit, set **2** (*di sposa*) trousseau
corrèggere **A** *v. tr.* to correct **B** *v. rifl.* to correct oneself
correlazióne *s. f.* correlation
corrènte **A** *agg.* **1** (*che scorre*) running, flowing **2** (*scorrevole*) fluent, smooth **3** (*attuale*) current, present **4** (*di moneta*) current **5** (*comune*) common, current **6** (*ordinario*) common, ordinary **B** *s. f.* **1** current **2** (*flusso*) stream, flow
correntemènte *avv.* **1** fluently **2** (*comunemente*) currently
córrere **A** *v. intr.* **1** to run **2** (*precipitarsi*) to rush **3** (*di veicolo*) to speed along **4** (*gareggiare*) to race **5** (*circolare*) to go round, to circulate **B** *v. tr.* **1** (*sport*) to run, to take part in **2** (*affrontare*) to run
corrètto *agg.* **1** correct, right **2** (*onesto*) honest **3** (*educato*) polite **4** (*di caffè*) laced
correzióne *s. f.* correction
corridóio *s. m.* passage, corridor
corridóre *s. m.* runner, (*sport*) racer
corrièra *s. f.* coach
corrière *s. m.* **1** courier, messenger **2** (*chi trasporta merci*) carrier
corrimàno *s. m.* handrail
corrispettìvo **A** *agg.* corresponding **B** *s. m.* consideration, compensation
corrispondènte **A** *agg.* corresponding **B** *s. m. e f.* correspondent
corrispondénza *s. f.* correspondence
corrispóndere **A** *v. tr.* **1** (*pagare*) to pay **2** (*ricambiare*) to return **B** *v. intr.* **1** to correspond **2** (*coincidere*) to coincide **3** (*essere equivalente*) to be equivalent of
corroboràre *v. tr.* to corroborate
corródere *v. tr. e intr. pron.* to corrode
corrómpere **A** *v. tr.* to corrupt, (*con denaro*) to bribe **B** *v. intr. pron. e rifl.* **1** to become corrupted **2** (*putrefarsi*) to rot, to taint, to putrefy
corrosióne *s. f.* corrosion
corrosìvo *agg.* corrosive
corrótto *agg.* corrupt
corrugàre *v. tr. e intr. pron.* to wrinkle, to corrugate
corruzióne *s. f.* corruption, (*con denaro*) bribery
córsa *s. f.* **1** run **2** (*gara*) race **3** (*di mezzo di trasporto*) trip, journey **4** (*mecc.*) stroke
corsìa *s. f.* **1** (*sport, strada*) lane **2** (*ospedale*) ward
corsìvo *s. m.* **1** (*scrittura*) cursive **2** (*tip.*) italics *pl.*
córso *s. m.* **1** course **2** (*econ.*) course, (*prezzo*) rate, (*circolazione*) circulation **3** (*di fiume*) flow
córte *s. f.* court
cortéccia *s. f.* bark
corteggiàre *v. tr.* to court
cortèo *s. m.* procession
cortése *agg.* kind, polite, courteous
cortesìa *s. f.* **1** kindness, courtesy, politeness **2** (*favore*) favour
cortigiàno **A** *agg.* court (*attr*) **B** *s. m.* courtier
cortìle *s. m.* courtyard
cortìna *s. f.* curtain
cortisóne *s. m.* cortisone
córto *agg.* short
cortocircùito *s. m.* short circuit
còrvo *s. m.* raven, crow
còsa *s. f.* **1** thing **2** (*faccenda*) matter **3** (*che cosa*) what ♦ **qualche/una c.** anything, something
còscia *s. f.* thigh, (*di animale*) leg
coscïènte *agg.* conscious (*pred.*)
coscïènza *s. f.* **1** conscience **2** (*consapevolezza*) awareness **3** (*responsabilità*) consciousness **4** (*conoscenza*) consciousness
coscienzióso *agg.* conscientious, scrupulous
cosciòtto *s. m.* leg
così **A** *avv.* **1** (*in questo modo*) like this, this way **2** (*in quel modo*) like that, that way **3** (*in tal modo*) so, thus **4** (*come segue*) as follows **5** (*tanto*) so, such as **6** (*altrettanto*) so, the same **B** *cong.* **1** (*perciò*) so, (*dunque*) then **C** *agg. pred.* (*tale, siffatto*) such, like that ♦ **c. ... come** as ... as; **c. ... da/che** so ... that, so ... as
cosicché *cong.* **1** (*in modo che*) so that **2** (*perciò*) so
cosiddétto *agg.* so-called
cosmètico *agg. e s. m.* cosmetic
còsmico *agg.* cosmic

còsmo *s. m.* cosmos
cosmopolìta *agg.* cosmopolitan
còso *s. m.* (*fam.*) thing, thingummy
cospàrgere *v. tr.* to strew, to scatter, (*liquido*) to sprinkle
cospètto *s. m.* presence
cospìcuo *agg.* conspicuous
cospiràre *v. intr.* to conspire
cospiratóre *s. m.* conspirator
cospirazióne *s. f.* conspiracy
còsta *s. f.* **1** coast, coastline, (*litorale*) shore **2** (*anat.*) rib **3** (*di libro*) back
costànte *agg. e s. f.* constant
costàre *v. tr. e intr.* to cost ♦ **c. caro** to be expensive; **quanto costa?** how much does it cost?
costàta *s. f.* chop
costeggiàre *v. tr.* **1** (*naut.*) to coast, to hug the coast, to sail along **2** (*a terra*) to skirt
costèi *pron. dimostr. f. sing.* (*sogg.*) she, (*compl.*) her, (*spreg.*) this/that woman
costellazióne *s. f.* constellation
costernazióne *s. f.* consternation, dismay
costièro *agg.* coastal
costipazióne *s. f.* **1** constipation **2** (*raffreddore*) (bad) cold
costituìre **A** *v. tr.* **1** (*fondare*) to constitute, to set up **2** (*formare, comporre*) to constitute, to form, to make up **3** (*rappresentare*) to be **B** *v. rifl.* **1** (*dir*) to give oneself up **2** (*nominarsi*) to constitute oneself **3** (*formarsi*) to become, to set oneself up
costituzionàle *agg.* constitutional
costituzióne *s. f.* **1** (*di stato*) constitution **2** (*il costituire*) establishment, setting up
còsto *s. m.* cost, (*prezzo*) price, (*spesa*) expence
còstola *s. f.* rib
costolétta *s. f.* cutlet
costóro *pron. dimostr. m. e f. pl.* (*sogg.*) they, (*compl.*) them, (*spreg.*) these/those people
costóso *agg.* dear, expensive
costrìngere *v. tr.* to force, to compel
costrizióne *s. f.* constraint, compulsion
costruìre *v. tr.* to build, to construct
costruzióne *s. f.* **1** construction, building **2** (*edificio*) building
costùi *pron. dimostr. m. sing.* (*sogg.*) he, (*compl.*) him, (*spreg.*) this/that man
costùme *s. m.* **1** (*usanza*) custom, usage, habit **2** (*vestito*) costume **3** (*da bagno*) bathing costume, bathing suit
coténna *s. f.* pigskin, (*del lardo*) rind
cotógna *s. f.* quince
cotolétta *s. f.* cutlet, chop
cotóne *s. m.* cotton
còtta *s. f.* (*fam.*) crush
còttimo *s. m.* piecework ♦ **lavorare a c.** to do piecework
cottùra *s. f.* cooking, (*al forno*) baking
covàre **A** *v. tr.* **1** to brood, to hatch **2** (*fig.*) to brood over, to nurse **B** *v. intr.* to smoulder
cóvo *s. m.* den
covóne *s. m.* sheaf
còzza *s. f.* mussel
cozzàre *v. intr.* **1** to butt, to crash into, to bang against, (*di veicolo*) to collide **2** (*fig.*) to collide, to clash
crac *s. m. inv.* (*fig.*) crash, collapse
cràmpo *s. m.* cramp
crànico *agg.* cranial
crànio *s. m.* skull, cranium
cratère *s. m.* crater
cravàtta *s. f.* tie
creàre **A** *v. tr.* **1** to create **2** (*causare*) to produce, to cause **3** (*costituire*) to form, to set up **B** *v. intr. pron.* to be created
creatività *s. f.* creativity
creàto *s. m.* creation
creatóre **A** *agg.* creating **B** *s. m.* creator
creatùra *s. f.* creature
creazióne *s. f.* creation
credènte *s. m. e f.* believer
credènza (1) *s. f.* belief
credènza (2) *s. f.* (*mobile*) sideboard, (*in cucina*) dresser
credenziàli *s. f. pl.* credentials *pl.*
crédere **A** *v. intr.* to believe **B** *v. tr.* **1** (*credere vero*) to believe **2** (*pensare*) to think, to suppose **C** *v. rifl.* to consider oneself
credìbile *agg.* credible, believable
crédito *s. m.* **1** credit **2** (*reputazione*) esteem, reputation
creditóre *agg. e s. m.* creditor
crèdo *s. m.* creed
crèma *s. f.* cream
cremàre *v. tr.* to cremate
cremazióne *s. f.* cremation
crèmisi *agg. e s. m.* crimson
cremóso *agg.* creamy
crèn *s. m.* horseradish
crèpa *s. f.* **1** crack, crevice **2** (*fig.*) rift
crepàccio *s. m.* cleft, (*di giacciaio*) crevasse
crepacuòre *s. m.* heartbreak
crepàre **A** *v. intr.* (*fam.*) **1** (*scoppiare*) to die of, to burst **2** (*morire*) to snuff it **B** *v.*

intr. pron. to crack
crepitàre *v. intr.* to crackle, to pop
crepuscolàre *agg.* twilight (*attr*), crepuscular
crepùscolo *s. m.* twilight
crescèndo *s. m.* crescendo
créscere **A** *v. intr.* **1** to grow (up) **2** (*aumentare*) to increase, to rise **B** *v. tr.* (*allevare*) to bring up
créscita *s. f.* growth, increase, rise
crèsima *s. f.* confirmation
créspo *agg.* curly, frizzy
crésta *s. f.* crest
créta *s. f.* clay
cretinàta *s. f.* silly thing
cretìno *agg. e s. m.* stupid
cric *s. m.* jack
crìcca *s. f.* gang
criminàle *agg. e s. m. e f.* criminal
crìmine *s. m.* crime
crinàle *s. m.* ridge
crìne *s. m.* horsehair
crinièra *s. f.* mane
crìpta *s. f.* crypt
crìptico *agg.* cryptic
crisantèmo *s. m.* chrysanthemum
crìsi *s. f.* **1** crisis **2** (*med.*) attack, fit
cristallerìa *s. f.* crystalware, glassware
cristallìno *agg. e s. m.* crystalline
cristallizzàre *v. intr. e intr. pron.* to crystallize
cristàllo *s. m.* crystal
cristianésimo *s. m.* Christianity
cristianità *s. f.* Christendom
cristiàno *agg. e s. m.* Christian
critèrio *s. m.* **1** criterion, standard, principle **2** (*buon senso*) common sense
critica *s. f.* **1** criticism **2** (*saggio critico*) critical essay, (*recensione*) review **3** (*insieme dei critici*) critics *pl.*
criticàbile *agg.* criticizable
criticàre *v. tr.* to criticize
crìtico **A** *agg.* **1** critical **2** (*di crisi*) crucial **B** *s. m.* critic, reviewer
crivellàre *v. tr.* to riddle
crivèllo *s. m.* riddle
croccànte *agg.* crisp
crocchétta *s. f.* croquette
cróce *s. f.* cross
crocevìa *s. m. inv.* crossroads
crociàta *s. f.* crusade
crocìcchio *s. m.* crossroads
crocièra *s. f.* cruise
crocifìggere *v. tr.* to crucify
crocifissióne *s. f.* crucifixion
crocifìsso *s. m.* crucifix
crogiolàrsi *v. rifl.* to bask
crogiòlo *s. m.* melting pot
crollàre *v. intr.* **1** to collapse **2** (*lasciarsi cadere*) to flop down, to slump
cròllo *s. m.* **1** collapse **2** (*fig.*) downfall, ruin **3** (*econ.*) collapse, fall, drop
cromàtico *agg.* chromatic
cromatùra *s. f.* chromium-plating
cròmo *s. m.* chromium
cromosòma *s. m.* chromosome
cronaca *s. f.* **1** chronicle **2** (*di giornale*) news **3** (*resoconto*) description, (*radio, TV*) commentary ♦ **c. mondana** society news; **c. nera** crime news
crònico *agg.* chronic
cronìsta *s. m. e f.* **1** (*stor*) chronicler **2** (*di giornale*) reporter
cronistòria *s. f.* chronicle
cronologìa *s. f.* chronology
cronològico *agg.* chronologic
cronometràre *v. tr.* to time
cronòmetro *s. m.* chronometer, timer
cròsta *s. f.* crust ♦ **c. di formaggio** cheese rind
crostàceo *agg. e s. m.* crustacean
crostàta *s. f.* tart
crostìno *s. m.* crouton
crucciàre **A** *v. tr.* to trouble, to worry **B** *v. intr. pron.* to worry
crùccio *s. m.* worry
crucifórme *agg.* **1** cruciform **2** (*bot.*) cruciate
crucivèrba *s. m. inv.* crossword puzzle
crudèle *agg.* cruel
crudeltà *s. f.* cruelty
crùdo *agg.* **1** raw, (*poco cotto*) underdone **2** (*aspro*) harsh, crude
crumìro *s. m.* blackleg, scab
crùsca *s. f.* bran
cruscòtto *s. m.* (*autom.*) dashboard, (*aer.*) instrument panel
cùbico *agg.* cubic
cubìsmo *s. m.* cubism
cùbo **A** *agg.* cubic **B** *s. m.* cube
cuccàgna *s. f.* good time ♦ **albero della c.** greasy pole
cuccétta *s. f.* berth
cucchiaiàta *s. f.* spoonful
cucchiaìno *s. m.* teaspoon
cucchiàio *s. m.* spoon
cùccia *s. f.* dog's bed
cùcciolo *s. m.* cub, (*di cane, di foca*) pup
cucìna *s. f.* **1** kitchen **2** (*il cucinare*) cook-

ing **3** (*apparecchio*) stove, cooker ♦ **c. casalinga** homecooking; **c. vegetariana** vegetarian food
cucinàre *v. tr.* to cook
cucìre *v. tr.* to sew, to stitch
cucitùra *s. f.* seam
cucù *s. m.* cuckoo
cùculo *s. m.* cuckoo
cucùzzolo *s. m.* → **cocuzzolo**
cùffia *s. f.* **1** cap, bonnet **2** (*auricolare*) headphones *pl.*
cugìno *s. m.* cousin
cui *pron. rel. m. e f. sing. e pl.* **1** (*compl. ind.*) who(m) (*persone*), which (*cose e animali*) (*spesso sottinteso*) (ES: **la persona c. scrissi** the person to whom I wrote) **2** (*possessivo*) whose (*persone*), of which, whose (*cose e animali*) (ES: **la persona di c. ho scritto l'indirizzo** the person whose address I wrote) ♦ **in c.** (*dove*) where, (*quando*) when
culinàrio *agg.* culinary
cùlla *s. f.* cradle
cullàre *v. tr.* to rock, to cradle
culminàre *v. intr.* to culminate
cùlmine *s. m.* top
cùlto *s. m.* **1** cult, worship **2** (*religione*) religion
cultùra *s. f.* culture
culturàle *agg.* cultural
cumulatìvo *agg.* cumulative, inclusive
cùmulo *s. m.* **1** heap, pile **2** (*meteor.*) cumulus
cuneifórme *agg.* cuneiform
cùneo *s. m.* wedge
cunìcolo *s. m.* tunnel
cuòcere *v. tr. e intr.* to cook, (*alla griglia*) to grill, (*al forno*) to bake, to roast
cuòco *s. m.* cook
cuòio *s. m.* leather ♦ **articoli di c.** leather goods; **c. capelluto** scalp; **c. conciato** dressed leather
cuòre *s. m.* heart
cupidìgia *s. f.* cupidity, greed
cùpo *agg.* **1** dark, obscure **2** (*suono, colore*) deep **3** (*triste*) gloomy
cùpola *s. f.* dome
cùra *s. f.* **1** care **2** (*med.*) treatment ♦ **a c. di** (*libro*) edited by; **casa di c.** nursing home
curàbile *agg.* curable
curàre **A** *v. tr.* **1** to take care of, to look after of **2** (*med.*) to treat, to cure **3** (*fare in modo*) to make sure **4** (*un libro*) to edit **B** *v. rifl.* to take care of oneself, to follow a treatment
curàto *s. m.* curate
curatóre *s. m.* **1** (*dir.*) curator **2** (*di libro*) editor
cùria *s. f.* curia
curiosàre *v. intr.* to pry, to wander
curiosità *s. f.* curiosity
curióso *agg.* curious
cursóre *s. m.* cursor
cùrva *s. f.* curve, bend
curvàre **A** *v. tr., intr. e intr. pron.* to bend, to curve **B** *v. rifl.* to bend down
curvilìneo *agg.* curvilinear
cuscinétto *s. m.* **1** pad **2** (*mecc.*) bearing ♦ **c. a sfere** ball bearing
cuscìno *s. m.* cushion, (*guanciale*) pillow
cùspide *s. f.* cusp
custòde *s. m. e f.* **1** keeper, custodian **2** (*portiere*) doorkeeper
custòdia *s. f.* **1** custody, care **2** (*astuccio*) case
custodìre *v. tr.* **1** (*conservare*) to keep, to preserve **2** (*aver cura*) to take care of, to look after
cutàneo *agg.* cutaneous, skin (*attr.*)
cùte *s. f.* cutis, skin
cutìcola *s. f.* cuticle

D

da *prep.* **1** (*moto da luogo, provenienza, separazione*) from (ES: **arrivo da Londra** I'm coming from London, **separarsi da qc.** to part from sb.) **2** (*lontananza*) (away) from (ES: **essere assente da scuola** to be away from school) **3** (*moto a luogo*) to (ES: **sono andato da mia madre** I've been to my mother's) **4** (*stato in luogo*) at (ES: **dove sei? sono dal panettiere** where are you? I'm at the baker's) **5** (*moto per luogo*) through (ES: **entrare dalla finestra** to go in through the window) **6** (*agente, causa efficiente*) by (ES: **il granaio fu distrutto da un incendio** the barn was destroyed by a fire) **7** (*causa*) for, with (ES: **sta piangendo dal dolore** he's crying for pain, **tremare dal freddo** to shiver with cold) **8** (*durata nel tempo*) for (ES: **aspetto da un mese** I've been waiting for a month) **9** (*decorrenza*) (*riferito al pass.*) since, (*riferito al pres. e fut.*) (as) from (ES: **aspetto dal mese scorso** I've been waiting since last month, **da oggi in poi** from today onwards) **10** (*modo*) like (ES: **comportarsi da uomo** to behave like a man) **11** (*condizione*) as (ES: **da bambino** as a child) **12** (*uso, scopo*) *forme aggettivali* (ES: **occhiali da sole** sun glasses, **rete da pesca** fishing net) ♦ **non avere niente da fare** to have nothing to do; **tanto da** (*consec.*) so much as (to), (*a sufficienza*) enough (to); **un francobollo da 1000 lire** a 1000-lira stamp

dabbène *agg.* respectable, honest

daccàpo *avv.* **1** (*di nuovo*) over again **2** (*dall'inizio*) from the beginning

dadaìsmo *s. m.* Dadaism

dàdo *s. m.* **1** die (*pl.* dice) **2** (*mecc.*) nut **3** (*da brodo*) cube

daffàre *s. m.* work

dài *inter.* come on!

dàino *s. m.* fallow deer

daltònico *agg.* colour-blind

d'altrónde *avv.* on the other hand

dàma *s. f.* **1** lady **2** (*nel ballo*) partner **3** (*gioco*) draughts *pl.*, (*USA*) checkers *pl.*

damàsco *s. m.* damask

damigèlla *s. f.* bridesmaid

damigiàna *s. f.* demijohn

danése **A** *agg.* Danish **B** *s. m. e f.* Dane **C** *s. m.* (*lingua*) Danish

dannàre **A** *v. tr.* **1** to damn **2** (*far dannare*) to drive mad **B** *v. rifl.* **1** to be damned **2** (*affannarsi*) to strive hard

dannazióne *s. f.* damnation

danneggiàre *v. tr.* **1** to damage **2** (*sciupare*) to spoil **3** (*menomare*) to injure **4** (*nuocere*) to harm

dànno *s. m.* damage, harm, injury

dannóso *agg.* harmful

dànza *s. f.* dance, (*il danzare*) dancing

danzàre *v. tr. e intr.* to dance

danzatóre *s. m.* dancer

dappertùtto *avv.* everywhere

dapprìma *avv.* at first

dàrdo *s. m.* dart

dàre (1) **A** *v. tr.* **1** to give **2** (*porgere*) to pass **3** (*concedere*) to grant, to give **4** (*rappresentare*) to put on **5** (*produrre*) to yield, to bear **B** *v. intr.* **1** (*colpire, urtare*) to hit, to bump **2** (*di porta, finestra*) to look on to, to lead into **C** *v. rifl.* to devote oneself

dàre (2) *s. m.* debit

dàrsena *s. f.* wet dock

dàta *s. f.* date

datàre *v. tr. e intr.* to date

dàto (1) *agg.* given, stated ♦ **d. che** since, as

dàto (2) *s. m.* datum

dàttero *s. m.* date

dattilografàre *v. tr.* to type

dattilògrafo *s. m.* typist

davànti **A** *avv.* in front **B** *agg. e s. m.* front (*attr*) **C** *prep.* **d. a** **1** in front of, opposite **2** (*prima di*) before

davanzàle *s. m.* windowsill

davvéro *avv.* really, indeed

dàzio *s. m.* duty ♦ **esente da d.** duty free

dèa *s. f.* goddess

deambulatòrio *s. m.* (*arch.*) ambulatory

debellàre *v. tr.* to wipe out

debilitàre *v. tr. e intr. pron.* to weaken

débito (1) *s. m.* **1** debt **2** (*comm.*) debit

débito (2) *agg.* due, proper

debitóre *agg. e s. m.* debtor (*attr*)

débole **A** *agg.* weak, faint, feeble **B** *s. m.* **1** (*punto debole*) weak point **2** (*inclina-*

zione) weakness
debolézza *s. f.* weakness
debuttàre *v. intr.* to make one's début
debùtto *s. m.* début
dècade *s. f.* (*dieci anni*) decade, ten years *pl.*, (*dieci giorni*) ten days *pl.*
decadènte *agg.* decadent
decadentìsmo *s. m.* decadentism
decadènza *s. f.* **1** decay, decline **2** (*letter.*) decadence **3** (*dir.*) loss
decadére *v. intr.* to decay, to decline
decadùto *agg.* impoverished
decaffeinàto *agg.* decaffeinated
decàlogo *s. m.* **1** (*relig.*) decalogue **2** (*est.*) handbook
decàno *s. m.* doyen, dean
decapitàre *v. tr.* to behead, to decapitate
decappottàbile *agg. e s. f.* convertible
decedùto *agg.* deceased, dead
decelerazióne *s. f.* deceleration
decennàle *agg. e s. m.* decennial
decènnio *s. m.* decade, decennium
decènte *agg.* **1** (*decoroso*) decent, proper, decorous **2** (*accettabile*) acceptable, reasonable
decentraménto *s. m.* decentralization
decènza *s. f.* decency
decèsso *s. m.* death
decìdere **A** *v. tr. e intr.* to decide **B** *v. intr. pron.* to make up one's mind
decìduo *agg.* deciduous
decifràre *v. tr.* to decipher, to decode
decìlitro *s. m.* decilitre, (*USA*) deciliter
decimàle *agg. e s. m.* decimal
decimàre *v. tr.* to decimate
dècimo *agg. num. ord. e s. m.* tenth
decìna *s. f.* **1** (*dieci*) ten, half-a-score **2** (*circa dieci*) about ten
decisaménte *avv.* **1** decidedly, definitely **2** (*risolutamente*) resolutely
decisióne *s. f.* decision
decisionìsta *s. m. e f.* decision-maker
decisìvo *agg.* decisive, conclusive
decìso *agg.* **1** decided, firm, resolute **2** (*definito*) definite
declamàre *v. tr. e intr.* to declaim
declassàre *v. tr.* to declass, to degrade
declinàre **A** *v. tr.* (*gramm.*) to decline **B** *v. intr.* **1** (*tramontare*) to set **2** (*venir meno*) to decline, to wane **3** (*degradare*) to slope down
declinazióne *s. f.* **1** (*gramm.*) declension **2** (*fis.*) declination
declìno *s. m.* decline
declìvio *s. m.* slope
decodificàre *v. tr.* to decode
decollàre *v. intr.* to take off
decòllo *s. m.* take-off
decoloràre *v. tr.* to decolorate, to bleach
decolorazióne *s. f.* decoloration, bleaching
decompórre **A** *v. tr.* **1** to decompose **2** (*chim.*) to dissociate **B** *v. intr. pron.* **1** to decompose **2** (*putrefarsi*) to rot, to decay
decomposizióne *s. f.* decomposition
decongestionàre *v. tr.* to decongest
decontaminàre *v. tr.* to decontaminate
decoràre *v. tr.* to decorate
decoratìvo *agg.* decorative
decoratóre *s. m.* decorator
decorazióne *s. f.* decoration
decòro *s. m.* **1** (*dignità*) decorum, dignity **2** (*lustro*) honour **3** (*ornamento*) décor
decoróso *agg.* decorous
decórrere *v. intr.* **1** (*trascorrere*) to elapse **2** (*avere inizio*) to start, to run, (*avere effetto*) to become effective ♦ **a d. da** starting from
decòtto *s. m.* decoction
decrèpito *agg.* decrepit
decrescènte *agg.* decreasing
decréscere *v. intr.* to decrease, to diminish
decretàre *v. tr.* **1** to decree **2** (*tributare*) to confer
decréto *s. m.* decree
decurtàre *v. tr.* to curtail, to reduce
dèdalo *s. m.* maze
dèdica *s. f.* dedication
dedicàre **A** *v. tr.* **1** to dedicate **2** (*intitolare alla memoria*) to name after **B** *v. rifl.* to devote oneself
dèdito *agg.* **1** devoted, dedicated **2** (*a vizio*) addicted
deducìbile *agg.* **1** deducible **2** (*defalcabile*) deductible
dedùrre *v. tr.* **1** to deduce **2** (*defalcare*) to deduct
deduzióne *s. f.* deduction
defalcàre *v. tr.* to deduct
deferìre *v. tr.* to refer
defezióne *s. f.* defection, desertion
deficiènte **A** *agg.* **1** (*insufficiente*) insufficient **2** (*med.*) mentally deficient **B** *s. m. e f.* **1** mentally deficient person **2** (*stupido*) stupid
dèficit *s. m. inv.* deficit
deficitàrio *agg.* **1** showing a deficit **2** (*fig.*) insufficient
definìre *v. tr.* **1** to define **2** (*determinare*)

to determine, to fix **3** (*risolvere*) to settle
definitivaménte *avv.* definitively
definitìvo *agg.* definitive, final
definizióne *s. f.* **1** definition **2** (*risoluzione*) settlement
deflagrazióne *s. f.* deflagration
deflèttere *v. intr.* **1** to deflect, to deviate **2** (*cedere*) to yield
deflettóre *s. m.* deflector
defluìre *v. intr.* to flow
deflùsso *s. m.* downflow, (*di marea*) ebb
deformàre **A** *v. tr.* **1** to deform **2** (*alterare*) to distort, to warp **B** *v. intr. pron.* to get deformed, to lose one's shape
deformazióne *s. f.* deformation
defórme *agg.* deformed
deformità *s. f.* **1** deformity **2** (*med.*) deformation
defraudàre *v. tr.* to defraud, to cheat
defùnto **A** *agg.* dead, late (*attr*) **B** *s. m.* dead, deceased
degeneràre *v. intr.* to degenerate
degenerazióne *s. f.* degeneration
degènere *agg.* degenerate
degènte *s. m. e f.* patient
deglutìre *v. tr.* to swallow
degnàre **A** *v. tr.* to think worthy **B** *v. intr. pron.* do deign, to condescend
dégno *agg.* worthy
degradànte *agg.* degrading
degradàre **A** *v. tr.* **1** to demote **2** (*fig.*) to degrade **B** *v. rifl.* to degrade oneself **C** *v. intr. pron.* to deteriorate
degràdo *s. m.* decay, deterioration
degustàre *v. tr.* to taste
degustazióne *s. f.* tasting
delatóre *s. m.* informer
delazióne *s. f.* delation
dèlega *s. f.* **1** delegation **2** (*procura*) proxy
delegàre *v. tr.* to delegate
delegazióne *s. f.* delegation
deletèrio *agg.* deleterious, harmful
delfìno *s. m.* dolphin
deliberàre *v. tr.* **1** to deliberate **2** (*decidere*) to decide
deliberataménte *avv.* deliberately
delicataménte *avv.* gently
delicatézza *s. f.* **1** delicacy **2** (*cura*) care
delicàto *agg.* delicate
delimitàre *v. tr.* to delimit
delimitazióne *s. f.* delimitation
delineàre **A** *v. tr.* to outline **B** *v. intr. pron.* to loom, to take shape
delinquènte *agg. s. m. e f.* **1** criminal, delinquent **2** (*fig., fam.*) rogue
delinquènza *s. f.* delinquency, criminality
deliràre *v. intr.* to rave
delìrio *s. m.* delirium, raving
delìtto *s. m.* **1** crime **2** (*omicidio*) murder
delìzia *s. f.* delight
delizióso *agg.* delightful, (*di sapore, odore*) delicious
dèlta *s. m. inv.* delta
deltaplàno *s. m.* hang-glider
delucidazióne *s. f.* elucidation
delùdere *v. tr.* to disappoint
delusióne *s. f.* disappointment
demagogìa *s. f.* demagogy
demagògico *agg.* demagogic(al)
demaniàle *agg.* State (*attr*)
demànio *s. m.* State property
demènte **A** *agg.* **1** (*med.*) demented **2** (*est.*) insane, mad **B** *s. m. e f.* **1** (*med.*) dement **2** (*est.*) lunatic
demènza *s. f.* **1** (*med.*) dementia **2** (*est.*) insanity
demenziàle *agg.* **1** (*med.*) demential **2** (*est.*) crazy
demistificazióne *s. f.* demystification
democràtico **A** *agg.* democratic **B** *s. m.* democrat
democrazìa *s. f.* democracy
demografìa *s. f.* demography
demogràfico *agg.* demographic
demolìre *v. tr.* to demolish
demolizióne *s. f.* demolition
dèmone *s. m.* **1** d(a)emon **2** (*diavolo*) devil
demònio *s. m.* devil, demon
demonizzàre *v. tr.* to demonize
demoralizzàre **A** *v. tr.* to demoralize **B** *v. intr. pron.* to lose heart
demotivàre **A** *v. tr.* to demotivate **B** *v. intr. pron.* to become demotivated
denàro *s. m.* **1** money **2** *al pl.* (*carte da gioco*) diamonds *pl.*
denatalità *s. f.* fall in the birthrate
denaturàto *agg.* denatured
denigràre *v. tr.* to denigrate, to run down
denominàre **A** *v. tr.* to name, to call **B** *v. intr. pron.* to be named
denominazióne *s. f.* denomination, name
denotàre *v. tr.* to denote, to indicate
densità *s. f.* density, thickness
dènso *agg.* **1** dense, thick **2** (*pieno di*) full
dentàle *agg.* dental
dènte *s. m.* tooth ♦ **al d.** slightly underdone; **d. cariato** decayed tooth; **spazzolino**

da denti tooth-brush
dentellàto *agg.* indented
dentièra *s. f.* denture, false teeth *pl.*
dentifrìcio *s. m.* toothpaste
dentìsta *s. m. e f.* dentist
déntro A *avv.* **1** in, inside **2** (*interiormente*) inwardly **B** *prep.* **1** in, inside **2** (*entro*) within **3** (*con v. di moto*) into ♦ **d. casa** indoors; **qui d.** inside here
denudàre A *v. tr.* to strip, to denude **B** *v. rifl.* to strip (off), to undress
denùncia *s. f.* **1** accusation, complaint **2** (*dichiarazione*) declaration, report
denunciàre *v. tr.* **1** (*dir.*) to denounce **2** (*manifestare*) to denote, to reveal **3** (*dichiarare*) to declare
denutrìto *agg.* underfed
denutrizióne *s. f.* malnutrition
deodorànte *agg. e s. m.* deodorant
depennàre *v. tr.* to cross out, to strike out
deperìbile *agg.* perishable
deperìre *v. intr.* **1** to waste away, to decline **2** (*di pianta*) to wither **3** (*di cose*) to perish, to decay
depilàre *v. tr.* to depilate
depilatòrio *agg.* depilatory
depilazióne *s. f.* depilation
dépliant *s. m. inv.* brochure, leaflet
deploràre *v. tr.* to deplore
deplorévole *agg.* deplorable
depórre A *v. tr.* **1** to lay (down), to put down **2** (*da una carica*) to remove, to depose **3** (*depositare*) to deposit **4** (*rinunciare*) to give up, to renounce **B** *v. intr.* (*dir.*) to depose, to give evidence
deportàre *v. tr.* to deport
depositàre A *v. tr.* **1** to deposit **2** (*metter giù*) to put down **3** (*immagazzinare*) to store **4** (*un marchio*) to register **B** *v. intr. pron.* to settle, to deposit
depòsito *s. m.* **1** deposit **2** (*magazzino*) warehouse, (*mil.*) depot ♦ **d. bagagli** left-luggage (office), checkroom
deposizióne *s. f.* **1** deposition **2** (*da una carica*) removal
depravàto *agg.* depraved
depravazióne *s. f.* depravity
deprecàbile *agg.* deprecable, disgraceful
deprecàre *v. tr.* to deprecate
depredàre *v. tr.* to plunder, to pillage
depressióne *s. f.* depression
deprèsso *agg.* depressed
deprezzaménto *s. m.* depreciation
deprezzàre *v. tr.* to depreciate
deprìmere A *v. tr.* to depress **B** *v. intr. pron.* to get depressed, to lose heart
depuràre *v. tr.* to depurate
depuratóre *s. m.* depurator
deputàto *s. m.* deputy
deragliaménto *s. m.* derailment
deragliàre *v. intr.* to go off the rails ♦ **far d.** to derail
derattizzazióne *s. f.* deratization
derìdere *v. tr.* to deride, to mock
derisióne *s. f.* derision
deriva *s. f.* **1** drift **2** (*superficie*) keel
derivàre A *v. intr.* **1** (*provenire*) to derive, to come, to originate from **2** (*scaturire*) to rise **3** (*andare alla deriva*) to drift **B** *v. tr.* **1** to derive **2** (*fiume, canale*) to divert
derivazióne *s. f.* **1** derivation **2** (*elettr.*) shunt
dermatìte *s. f.* dermatitis
dermatologìa *s. f.* dermatology
dermatòlogo *s. m.* dermatologist
dèroga *s. f.* derogation
derràta *s. f.* **1** *al pl.* victuals *pl.*, foodstuffs *pl.* **2** (*merci*) goods *pl.*, commodity
derubàre *v. tr.* to steal, to rob
descrittìvo *agg.* descriptive
descrìvere *v. tr.* to describe
descrizióne *s. f.* description
desèrtico *agg.* desert (*attr.*), waste
desèrto A *agg.* **1** desert (*attr.*) **2** (*abbandonato*) deserted, (*vuoto*) empty **B** *s. m.* **1** desert **2** (*fig.*) wilderness, wasteland
desideràre *v. tr.* **1** to want, to desire, to wish **2** (*richiedere*) to want **3** (*sessualmente*) to desire
desidèrio *s. m.* wish, desire
desideróso *agg.* longing for
design *s. m. inv.* design
designàre *v. tr.* to designate
desinènza *s. f.* (*gramm.*) ending
desìstere *v. intr.* to desist, to give up
desolànte *agg.* distressing
desolàto *agg.* **1** desolate, **2** (*sconsolato*) disconsolate, sorrowful **3** (*spiacente*) sorry
desolazióne *s. f.* desolation
dessert *s. m. inv.* dessert
destàre *v. tr. e intr. pron.* to wake (up), to awake
destinàre *v. tr.* **1** to destine **2** (*assegnare*) to assign **3** (*nominare*) to appoint **4** (*stabilire*) to fix **5** (*riservare, dedicare*) to intend, to devote
destinatàrio *s. m.* receiver, (*di lettera*) ad-

dressee
destinazióne *s. f.* destination
destìno *s. m.* destiny
destituìre *v. tr.* to dismiss
destituìto *agg.* **1** (*rimosso*) dismissed **2** (*privo*) devoid, destitute
dèsto *agg.* awake
dèstra *s. f.* **1** (*mano*) right hand **2** (*parte*) right (side) **3** (*pol.*) Right ♦ **a d.** on the right
destreggiàrsi *v. intr. pron.* to manage
destrézza *s. f.* skill, dexterity
dèstro **A** *agg.* **1** right, right-hand (*attr*) **2** (*abile*) clever **B** *s. m.* chance
desùmere *v. tr.* to infer, to deduce
detenére *v. tr.* **1** to hold **2** (*dir*) to possess, to detain
detenùto *s. m.* prisoner, convict
detenzióne *s. f.* **1** (*possesso*) possession **2** (*imprigionamento*) detention, imprisonment
detergènte *agg. e s. m.* detergent
deterioràbile *agg.* perishable
deterioràre **A** *v. tr.* to deteriorate, to damage **B** *v. intr. pron.* to deteriorate, to go bad
determinàre *v. tr.* **1** to determine **2** (*causare*) to produce
determinàto *agg.* **1** (*definito*) determinate, definite **2** (*particolare*) certain **3** (*deciso*) resolute, determined
detersìvo *s. m.* detergent
detestàre *v. tr.* to detest, to hate
detraìbile *agg.* deductible
detràrre *v. tr. e intr.* to deduct, to detract
detrazióne *s. f.* deduction ♦ **d. fiscale** tax allowance
detrìto *s. m.* debris, rubble
dettagliànte *s. m. e f.* retailer
dettagliataménte *avv.* in detail
dettàglio *s. m.* **1** detail, particular **2** (*comm.*) retail
dettàre *v. tr.* to dictate
dettàto *s. m.* dictation
détto **A** *agg.* **1** (*chiamato*) called, named, (*soprannominato*) nicknamed **2** (*sopraddetto*) said, aforesaid **B** *s. m.* saying
deturpàre *v. tr.* to disfigure, to sully
devastàre *v. tr.* to devastate, to ravage
deviàre **A** *v. intr.* to deviate, to swerve **B** *v. tr.* to divert
deviazióne *s. f.* **1** deviation, deflection **2** (*stradale*) detour
devòlvere *v. tr.* to devolve, to assign
devòto *agg.* **1** (*relig.*) devotional, pious **2** (*affezionato*) devoted, sincere
devozióne *s. f.* devotion
di *prep.* **1** (*specificazione, denominazione, abbondanza, privazione, quantità, ecc.*) of (ES: **il senso dell'umorismo** a sense of humour, **la città di Oxford** the city of Oxford, **un chilo di pane** a kilo of bread) **2** (*possesso*) of, *genitivo sassone* (ES: **la coda del cane** the dog's tail) **3** (*partitivo*) some, any (ES: **vuoi ancora del caffè?** would you like any more coffee?) **4** (*appartenenza*) by (ES: **una poesia di Leopardi** a poem by Leopardi) **5** (*condizione, qualità*) at, in, by (ES: **conoscere di nome** to know by name) **6** (*argomento*) about, of (ES: **so molte cose di lui** I know a lot about him) **7** (*dopo un comp.*) than, (*dopo un sup.*) of, in (ES: **meglio di te** better than you, **il fiume più lungo del mondo** the longest river in the world) **8** (*materia, età, valore, misura*) of (*spesso idiom.*) (ES: **un tavolo di legno** a wooden table, **un conto di dieci sterline** a ten-pound bill) **9** (*causa*) of, for, with (ES: **tremare di paura** to tremble with fear, **piangere di dolore** to be crying for pain) **10** (*mezzo, strumento*) with, on (ES: **ungere di burro** to grease with butter) **11** (*moto da luogo, allontanamento, separazione, origine, provenienza*) from, out of (ES: **uscire di casa** to get out from home) **12** (*tempo*) in, at, on (ES: **di sera** in the evening, **di domenica** on Sundays) **13** (*con v. all'inf.*) *idiom.* (ES: **credo di essere proprio stanco** I think I'm really tired) **14** (*con altra prep.*) *idiom.* (ES: **dopo di te** after you)
diabète *s. m.* diabetes
diabètico *agg. e s. m.* diabetic
diàcono *s. m.* deacon
diadèma *s. m.* diadem
diaframma *s. m.* **1** diaphragm **2** (*fig.*) screen
diàgnosi *s. f.* diagnosis
diagnosticàre *v. tr.* to diagnose
diagonàle *agg.* diagonal
diagràmma *s. m.* diagram, chart
dialettàle *agg.* dialectal
dialèttico *agg.* dialectic(al)
dialètto *s. m.* dialect
diàlisi *s. f.* dialysis
dialogàre *v. intr.* to converse, to talk together
diàlogo *s. m.* dialogue
diamànte *s. m.* diamond
diametralménte *avv.* diametrically

diàmetro *s. m.* diameter
diàmine *inter.* good heavens!
diapositìva *s. f.* slide
diàrio *s. m.* diary, journal ♦ **d. di bordo** log
diarrèa *s. f.* diarr(ho)ea
diàvolo *s. m.* devil
dibàttere **A** *v. tr.* to debate, to discuss **B** *v. rifl.* to struggle
dibàttito *s. m.* **1** debate, discussion **2** (*disputa*) controversy
dicastèro *s. m.* ministry
dicèmbre *s. m.* December
dicerìa *s. f.* rumour, gossip
dichiaràre **A** *v. tr.* to declare, (*affermare*) to state **B** *v. rifl.* to declare oneself
dichiarazióne *s. f.* declaration, statement
diciannòve *agg. num. card. e s. m. inv.* nineteen
diciassètte *agg. num. card. e s. m. inv.* seventeen
diciòtto *agg. num. card. e s. m. inv.* eighteen
didascalìa *s. f.* caption, legend
didascàlico *agg.* didactic
didàttica *s. f.* didactics *pl.* (*v. al sing.*)
dièci *agg. num. card. e s. m. inv.* ten
diesel *agg. e s. m. inv.* diesel
dièta *s. f.* diet ♦ **essere a d.** to be on a diet
dietètico *agg.* dietetic
dietòlogo *s. m.* dietician
diètro **A** *avv.* behind, at the back **B** *prep.* behind, after **C** *agg. e s. m.* back (*attr.*) ♦ **d. l'angolo** round the corner
dietrofrónt *s. m.* about-turn
difàtti *cong.* in fact, as a matter of fact
difèndere **A** *v. tr.* **1** to defend **2** (*sostenere*) to maintain, to support **B** *v. rifl.* **1** to defend oneself **2** (*cavarsela*) to manage
difensìvo *agg.* defensive
difensóre *s. m.* **1** defender **2** (*sostenitore*) supporter, advocate
diféesa *s. f.* defence
difettàre *v. intr.* **1** (*avere difetti*) to be defective **2** (*mancare di*) to be wanting, to be lacking
difettìvo *agg.* defective
difètto *s. m.* **1** (*fisico*) defect, (*morale*) fault, (*imperfezione*) blemish **2** (*colpa*) fault **3** (*deficienza*) deficiency, (*mancanza*) lack
difettóso *agg.* defective, faulty
diffamàre *v. tr.* to defame, to slander
diffamazióne *s. f.* defamation, slander, (*a mezzo stampa*) libel
differènte *agg.* different
differenteménte *avv.* differently
differènza *s. f.* difference
differenziàle *agg. e s. m.* differential
differenziàre **A** *v. tr.* to differentiate **B** *v. rifl. e intr. pron.* to be different
differìre **A** *v. intr.* to differ **B** *v. tr.* to delay, to postpone
diffìcile **A** *agg.* **1** difficult, hard **2** (*incontentabile*) difficult to please **3** (*improbabile*) unlikely **B** *s. m.* difficulty
difficoltà *s. f.* **1** difficulty **2** (*obiezione*) objection
diffìda *s. f.* warning
diffidàre **A** *v. intr.* to distrust, to mistrust **B** *v. tr.* to warn
diffidènte *agg.* **1** distrustful, mistrustful **2** (*sospettoso*) suspicious
diffidènza *s. f.* **1** distrust, mistrust **2** (*sospetto*) suspicion
diffóndere **A** *v. tr.* to spread, to diffuse **B** *v. intr. pron.* **1** to spread **2** (*dilungarsi*) to dwell
difformità *s. f.* difference, dissimilarity
diffusaménte *avv.* diffusely
diffusióne *s. f.* **1** diffusion, spread **2** (*di giornale*) circulation
difterìte *s. f.* diphtheria
dìga *s. f.* **1** dam, dike **2** (*portuale*) breakwater
digerènte *agg.* digestive
digerìbile *agg.* digestible
digerìre *v. tr.* to digest
digestióne *s. f.* digestion
digestìvo *agg. e s. m.* digestive
digitàle *agg.* digital
digitàre *v. tr.* to type in
digiunàre *v. intr.* to fast
digiùno **A** *agg.* fasting **B** *s. m.* fast
dignità *s. f.* dignity
dignitóso *agg.* **1** dignified **2** (*decoroso*) decent, respectable
digressióne *s. f.* digression
digrignàre *v. tr.* to gnash
dilagàre *v. intr.* **1** to flood, to overflow **2** (*diffondersi*) to spread, to increase
dilaniàre *v. tr.* to tear (to pieces)
dilapidàre *v. tr.* to squander, to waste
dilatàre *v. tr. e intr. pron.* to dilate, to widen, to expand
dilatazióne *s. f.* dilatation, expansion
dilazionàre *v. tr.* to delay, to defer
dilazióne *s. f.* delay, extension
dileguàre **A** *v. tr.* to disperse **B** *v. intr. e intr. pron.* to vanish, to disappear, to fade away

dilèmma *s. m.* dilemma
dilettànte *agg. e s. m. e f.* amateur
dilettantésco *agg.* amateurish
dilettàre **A** *v. tr.* to delight, to give pleasure to **B** *v. intr. pron.* **1** to delight, to enjoy **2** (*occuparsi per diletto*) to dabble
dilètto *s. m.* pleasure, delight
diligènte *agg.* diligent, careful
diligènza (1) *s. f.* diligence, care
diligènza (2) *s. f.* (*carrozza*) stage-coach
diluìre *v. tr.* to dilute, (*con acqua*) to water
dilungàrsi *v. intr. pron.* to dwell, to talk at length
diluviàre *v. intr.* to pour
dilùvio *s. m.* deluge
dimagrànte *agg.* slimming (*attr*)
dimagrìre **A** *v. tr.* **1** to make thin **2** (*smagrire*) to slim **B** *v. intr.* to grow thin, to lose weight, to slim
dimenàre **A** *v. tr.* to wag, to wave **B** *v. rifl.* to fidget, to toss about
dimensióne *s. f.* dimension, (*grandezza*) size
dimenticànza *s. f.* **1** forgetfulness **2** (*svista*) oversight, (*inavvertenza*) inadvertence
dimenticàre **A** *v. tr.* **1** to forget **2** (*perdonare*) to forgive **3** (*lasciare in un posto*) to leave **B** *v. intr. pron.* to forget
dimésso *agg.* modest, (*trascurato*) shabby
dimestichézza *s. f.* familiarity
diméttere **A** *v. tr.* **1** to discharge **2** (*da una carica*) to dismiss, to remove **B** *v. rifl.* to resign
dimezzàre **A** *v. tr.* to halve **B** *v. intr. pron.* to be halved
diminuìre **A** *v. tr.* to diminish, to lessen, to reduce **B** *v. intr.* to decrease, to fall, to go down, to drop
diminutìvo *agg. e s. m.* diminutive
diminuzióne *s. f.* decrease, reduction
dimissióni *s. f. pl.* resignation ♦ **dare le d.** to resign
dimòra *s. f.* abode, home, residence
dimoràre *v. intr.* to reside, to live
dimostràbile *agg.* demonstrable
dimostràre **A** *v. tr.* **1** (*mostrare*) to show, (*età*) to look **2** (*provare*) to demonstrate, to prove, to show **B** *v. intr.* to protest, to demonstrate **C** *v. rifl.* to show oneself, to prove
dimostrazióne *s. f.* demonstration
dinàmica *s. f.* dynamics *pl.* (*v. al sing.*)
dinàmico *agg.* dynamic
dinamìsmo *s. m.* dynamism
dinamìte *s. f.* dynamite
dìnamo *s. f. inv.* dynamo
dinànzi → **davanti**
dinastìa *s. f.* dynasty
diniègo *s. m.* denial
dinoccolàto *agg.* slouching
dinosàuro *s. m.* dinosaur
dintórni *s. m. pl.* neighbourhood
dìo *s. m.* god
diòcesi *s. f.* diocese
diottrìa *s. f.* diopter
dipanàre *v. tr.* **1** to wind into a ball **2** (*districare*) to disentangle
dipartiménto *s. m.* department
dipendènte **A** *agg.* dependent, subordinate **B** *s. m. e f.* employee, subordinate
dipendènza *s. f.* dependence ♦ **essere alle dipendenze di qc.** to be employed by sb.
dipèndere *v. intr.* **1** to depend (on) **2** (*derivare*) to come from, to be due to, to derive **3** (*essere alle dipendenze*) to be under the authority (of)
dipìngere *v. tr.* to paint
dipinto *s. m.* painting
diplòma *s. m.* diploma, certificate
diplomàre **A** *v. tr.* to award a diploma to **B** *v. intr. pron.* to get a diploma
diplomàtico **A** *agg.* diplomatic **B** *s. m.* diplomat
diplomazìa *s. f.* **1** diplomacy **2** (*carriera*) diplomatic service
dipòrto *s. m.* recreation, pleasure
diradàre **A** *v. tr.* **1** to thin out **2** (*ridurre*) to reduce, to cut down **B** *v. intr. pron.* **1** to thin away, to clear away **2** (*ridursi*) to become less frequent
diramàre **A** *v. tr.* to issue, to diffuse **B** *v. intr. pron.* to branch out, (*di strada*) to branch off
diramazióne *s. f.* branch, ramification
dìre **A** *v. tr.* **1** to say, (*raccontare, riferire*) to tell **2** (*significare*) to mean **3** (*dimostrare*) to show **4** (*pensare*) to think, to say **B** *v. rifl.* to profess
direttaménte *avv.* directly, straight
dirètto **A** *agg.* **1** bound, going to **2** (*indirizzato*) addressed to **3** (*immediato*) direct, immediate **4** (*condotto*) conducted, run **5** (*gramm.*) direct **B** *s. m.* **1** (*ferr.*) through train **2** (*boxe*) straight right (*destro*), straight left (*sinistro*) **C** *avv.* direct, directly

direttóre *s. m.* **1** director, manager **2** (*d'orchestra*) conductor **3** (*di giornale*) editor in chief **4** (*di prigione*) governor **5** (*di scuola*) headmaster
direzionàle *agg.* **1** (*che dirige*) executive **2** (*che indica direzione*) directional
direzióne *s. f.* **1** (*verso*) direction, course **2** (*guida*) direction, guidance, management, leadership **3** (*sede*) head office, administrative department
dirigènte **A** *agg.* managing **B** *s. m. e f.* manager, executive, (*pol.*) leader
dirìgere **A** *v. tr.* **1** (*volgere*) to direct, to turn **2** (*rivolgere*) to address, to direct **3** (*amministrare*) to manage, to run **4** (*un'orchestra*) to conduct **B** *v. rifl.* to head for, to make for
dirigìbile *s. m.* dirigible
dirimpètto **A** *avv.* opposite **B** *prep.* **d. a** opposite to
diritto (1) **A** *agg.* **1** straight **2** (*eretto*) upright, erect **B** *s. m.* **1** right side **2** (*di moneta*) obverse **3** (*lavoro a maglia*) plain **C** *avv.* straight, directly ♦ **vada sempre d.** go straight on
diritto (2) *s. m.* **1** (*facoltà*) right **2** (*legge*) law **3** (*tributo*) due, duty, fee ♦ **diritti d'autore** royalties; **d. civile/penale** civil/criminal law; **d. di voto** right to vote
diroccàto *agg.* crumbling, in ruins
dirottaménto *s. m.* **1** diversion **2** (*di aereo*) hijacking, skyjacking
dirottàre **A** *v. tr.* **1** to divert **2** (*un aereo*) to hijack, to skyjack **B** *v. intr.* to change course
dirottatóre *s. m.* hijacker, skyjacker
dirótto *agg.* abundant, (*di pianto*) unrestrained ♦ **piovere a d.** to pour down
dirùpo *s. m.* crag
disabitàto *agg.* uninhabited, (*abbandonato*) deserted
disabituàre **A** *v. tr.* to disaccustom **B** *v. rifl.* to lose the habit (of)
disaccòrdo *s. m.* disagreement
disadattàto *agg.* maladjusted
disadàtto *agg.* unfit, unsuitable
disadórno *agg.* unadorned, (*semplice*) plain
disagévole *agg.* uncomfortable
disagiàto *agg.* **1** (*scomodo*) uncomfortable **2** (*povero*) poor, needy
disàgio *s. m.* **1** uneasiness, uncomfortableness **2** (*disturbo*) inconvenience, trouble **3** *al pl.* discomforts *pl.*, hardship ♦ **sentirsi a d.** to feel uneasy
disàmina *s. f.* examination
disapprovàre *v. tr.* to disapprove of, to deprecate
disapprovazióne *s. f.* disapproval
disappùnto *s. m.* disappointment
disarmàre *v. tr.* **1** to disarm **2** (*smantellare*) to dismantle **3** (*naut.*) to lay up
disarmònico *agg.* discordant
disastràto *agg.* devastated, badly hit
disàstro *s. m.* **1** disaster, damage **2** (*fiasco*) failure
disastróso *agg.* disastrous, deadful
disattènto *agg.* inattentive, careless
disattenzióne *s. f.* **1** inattention, carelessness **2** (*svista*) oversight
disavànzo *s. m.* deficit
disavventùra *s. f.* mishap, misadventure
disboscàre *v. tr.* to deforest
disbrìgo *s. m.* dispatching
discàpito *s. m.* detriment
discàrica *s. f.* dump
discendènte **A** *agg.* descending **B** *s. m. e f.* descendant
discéndere **A** *v. intr.* **1** to go down, to come down, to descend **2** (*declinare*) to descend, to slope down **3** (*di prezzi, temperatura*) to fall, to drop **4** (*trarre origine*) to descend, to come from **B** *v. tr.* to go down, to come down
discépolo *s. m.* disciple
discèrnere *v. tr.* **1** to discern **2** (*distinguere*) to distinguish
discésa *s. f.* **1** (*movimento*) descent **2** (*pendio*) slope, declivity **3** (*caduta*) fall, drop ♦ **strada in d.** downhill road
discesista *s. m. e f.* (*sci*) downhill racer
dischiùdere **A** *v. tr.* to open **B** *v. intr. pron.* to open out
disciògliere **A** *v. tr.* **1** (*slegare*) to unbind **2** (*sciogliere*) to dissolve **3** (*liquefare*) to melt **B** *v. intr. pron.* **1** (*slegarsi*) to loosen **2** (*sciogliersi*) to dissolve **3** (*liquefarsi*) to melt
disciplìna *s. f.* discipline
dìsco *s. m.* **1** disk, disc **2** (*mus.*) record, disc **3** (*sport*) discus
discolpàre *v. tr.* to clear, to excuse
discontìnuo *agg.* discontinuous
discordànte *agg.* discordant
discordàre *v. intr.* **1** to disagree, to dissent **2** (*essere differente*) to differ **3** (*di suoni*) to be discordant, (*di colori*) to clash
discòrdia *s. f.* discord, disagreement
discórrere *v. intr.* to talk

discorsìvo *agg.* conversational
discórso *s. m.* **1** speech **2** (*conversazione*) talk, conversation
discotèca *s. f.* **1** record library **2** (*locale*) disco(thèque)
discrepànza *s. f.* discrepancy
discretaménte *avv.* **1** (*con discrezione*) discreetly **2** (*a sufficienza*) quite well, fairly **3** (*piuttosto*) rather
discréto *agg.* **1** (*che ha discrezione*) discreet **2** (*abbastanza buono*) fair, fairly good **3** (*moderato*) moderate
discrezióne *s. f.* **1** (*riservatezza*) discretion **2** (*arbitrio*) judgement, discretion
discriminàre *v. tr.* to discriminate
discriminazióne *s. f.* discrimination
discussióne *s. f.* **1** discussion, debate **2** (*litigio*) argument
discùtere **A** *v. tr.* **1** to discuss, to debate **2** (*obiettare*) to question **B** *v. intr.* **1** to discuss **2** (*obiettare*) to argue
disdegnàre *v. tr.* to disdain
disdétta *s. f.* **1** (*dir.*) notice, cancellation **2** (*sfortuna*) bad luck
disdìre *v. tr.* to cancel, to call off
disegnàre *v. tr.* **1** to draw **2** (*progettare*) to design, to plan **3** (*fig.*) to outline
disegnatóre *s. m.* draftsman, (*progettista*) designer, (*illustratore*) illustrator
diségno *s. m.* **1** drawing **2** (*progetto*) design, plan **3** (*motivo*) pattern
diserbànte *s. m.* herbicide
disertàre *v. intr.* to desert
disertóre *s. m.* deserter
disfaciménto *s. m.* decay, break-up
disfàre **A** *v. tr.* **1** to undo, (*distruggere*) to destroy **2** (*un meccanismo*) to take down **3** (*slegare*) to untie, unfasten **4** (*sciogliere*) to melt **5** (*sconfiggere*) to defeat **B** *v. intr. pron.* **1** to break up **2** (*sciogliersi*) to melt **C** *v. rifl.* (*liberarsi di q.c.*) to get rid of ♦ **d. le valigie** to unpack
disfàtta *s. f.* defeat, overthrow
disfunzióne *s. f.* **1** (*med.*) disorder, trouble **2** (*malfunzionamento*) malfunction
disgèlo *s. m.* thaw
disgràzia *s. f.* **1** (*sventura*) misfortune, bad luck **2** (*sfavore*) disgrace, disfavour **3** (*incidente*) accident
disgraziataménte *avv.* unfortunately
disgraziàto **A** *agg.* **1** (*sfortunato*) unfortunate, unlucky **2** (*infelice*) miserable **B** *s. m.* **1** wretch **2** (*sciagurato*) rascal
disgregàre *v. tr. e intr. pron.* to disgregate, to break up
disguido *s. m.* **1** mistake, error **2** (*postale*) miscarriage
disgustàre **A** *v. tr.* to disgust, to sicken **B** *v. intr. pron.* to become disgusted
disgùsto *s. m.* **1** disgust **2** (*avversione*) dislike, aversion
disgustóso *agg.* disgusting
disidratàre *v. tr.* to dehydrate
disidratazióne *s. f.* dehydration
disillùdere **A** *v. tr.* to disillusion, to disenchant, to disappoint **B** *v. rifl.* to be disenchanted
disimparàre *v. tr.* to forget
disimpegnàre **A** *v. tr.* **1** (*un oggetto*) to get out of pawn, to redeem **2** (*liberare da un impegno*) to release, to disengage **3** (*assolvere*) to carry out **B** *v. intr. pron.* **1** to release oneself **2** (*cavarsela*) to manage
disincagliàre *v. tr.* to refloat, to get afloat
disincantàto *agg.* disenchanted
disinfestàre *v. tr.* to disinfest
disinfettànte *s. m.* disinfectant
disinfettàre *v. tr.* to disinfect
disinibìto *agg.* uninhibited
disinnescàre *v. tr.* to defuse
disinquinàre *v. tr.* to depollute
disintegràre *v. tr. e intr. pron.* to disintegrate
disinteressàrsi *v. intr. pron.* to lose one's interest (in)
disinterèsse *s. m.* **1** disinterestedness, unselfishness **2** (*indifferenza*) indifference
disintossicazióne *s. f.* detoxication
disinvòlto *agg.* self-assured, confident
disinvoltùra *s. f.* **1** self-assurance, ease **2** (*superficialità*) carelessness
dislessìa *s. f.* dyslexia
dislivèllo *s. m.* **1** difference in level/height **2** (*inclinazione*) slope **3** (*ineguaglianza*) difference, inequality
dislocaménto *s. m.* **1** (*naut.*) displacement **2** (*mil.*) deployment **3** (*distribuzione*) distribution
dislocàre *v. tr.* **1** (*naut.*) to displace **2** (*collocare*) to place
dismisùra *s. f.* excess
disoccupàto *agg. e s. m.* unemployed
disoccupazióne *s. f.* unemployment
disonestà *s. f.* dishonesty
disonèsto *agg.* dishonest
disonóre *s. m.* dishonour, disgrace
disópra **A** *avv.* upstairs **B** *s. m.* top **C** *prep.* **(al) d. di** over, above
disordinàto *agg.* **1** untidy, muddled **2**

(*sregolato*) intemperate, irregular
disórdine *s. m.* **1** disorder, untidiness, mess **2** (*sregolatezza*) intemperance **3** *al pl.* (*tumulti*) riot
disorganizzazióne *s. f.* disorganization
disorientaménto *s. m.* **1** disorientation **2** (*fig.*) confusion
disorientàre **A** *v. tr.* **1** to disorientate **2** (*fig.*) to bewilder, to disconcert **B** *v. intr. pron.* to get confused
disótto **A** *avv.* downstairs **B** *s. m.* underside **C** *prep.* **(al) d. di** under, below
dispàccio *s. m.* dispatch
disparàto *agg.* disparate
dìspari *agg.* **1** odd **2** (*diseguale*) unequal
disparità *s. f.* difference, inequality
dispàrte, in *loc. avv.* aside, apart
dispendióso *agg.* expensive, costly
dispènsa *s. f.* **1** pantry, larder **2** (*pubblicazione periodica*) instalment **3** (*dir*) exemption **4** (*relig.*) dispensation
dispensàre *v. tr.* **1** (*distribuire*) to dispense, to distribute **2** (*esentare*) to exempt
disperàre **A** *v. intr.* to despair, to give up hope **B** *v. intr. pron.* to despair, to be desperate
disperazióne *s. f.* despair
dispèrdere **A** *v. tr.* **1** to disperse, to scatter **2** (*dissipare*) *v. intr. pron.* to waste, to dissipate **B** *v. rifl. e intr. pron.* to disperse
dispersióne *s. f.* dispersion
dispèrso *s. m.* missing person
dispètto *s. m.* **1** spite **2** (*stizza*) vexation, annoyance ♦ **fare dispetti** to tease
dispettóso *agg.* spiteful
dispiacére (1) **A** *v. intr.* **1** to dislike, not to like (*costruzione pers.*) **2** (*essere spiacente*) to be sorry **3** (*nelle frasi di cortesia*) to mind **B** *v. intr. pron.* to be sorry
dispiacére (2) *s. m.* **1** regret, sorrow **2** (*dolore*) grief **3** (*preoccupazione*) trouble
displùvio *s. m.* **1** ridge **2** (*edil.*) hip
disponìbile *agg.* **1** available, disposable **2** (*libero*) vacant, free, available **3** (*disposto*) helpful
dispórre **A** *v. tr.* **1** to arrange, to set out, to dispose **2** (*preparare*) to prepare, to make arrangements **3** (*deliberare*) to order **B** *v. intr.* to have at one's disposal, to dispose, to have **C** *v. rifl.* **1** (*collocarsi*) to place oneself **2** (*prepararsi*) to prepare, to get ready
dispositìvo *s. m.* device
disposizióne *s. f.* **1** disposal **2** (*collocamento*) disposition, arrangement **3** (*ordine*) order, instruction **4** (*inclinazione*) bent
dispòtico *agg.* despotic
dispregiatìvo *agg.* **1** disparaging **2** (*gramm.*) pejorative
disprezzàre *v. tr.* to despise
disprèzzo *s. m.* contempt
dìsputa *s. f.* **1** dispute, discussion **2** (*lite*) quarrel
disputàre **A** *v. intr.* **1** to discuss, to dispute **2** (*gareggiare*) to contend **B** *v. tr.* **1** to dispute, to contend **2** (*sport*) to play
dissalatóre *s. m.* desalter
dissanguaménto *s. m.* bleeding
disseccàre *v. tr. e intr. pron.* to dry up, to wither
disseminàre *v. tr.* **1** to scatter, to disseminate **2** (*fig.*) to spread
dissènso *s. m.* dissent, disagreement
dissenterìa *s. f.* dysentery
dissentìre *v. intr.* to dissent, to disagree
dissertazióne *s. f.* dissertation
dissservìzio *s. m.* inefficiency
dissestàre *v. tr.* to upset, to ruin
dissèsto *s. m.* **1** instability **2** (*econ.*) financial trouble
dissetànte *agg.* refreshing, thirst-quenching
dissetàre **A** *v. tr.* to quench thirst **B** *v. rifl.* to quench one's thirst
dissidènte *agg. e s. m. e f.* dissident
dissìdio *s. m.* disagreement
dissìmile *agg.* unlike, dissimilar
dissimulàre *v. tr.* to dissimulate, to dissemble
dissipàre *v. tr.* **1** (*disperdere*) to dispel **2** (*scialacquare*) to dissipate, to waste, to squander
dissociàre **A** *v. tr.* to dissociate **B** *v. rifl.* to dissociate oneself
dissodàre *v. tr.* to break up, to till
dissolùto *agg.* dissolute, debauched
dissolvènza *s. f.* fading
dissòlvere **A** *v. tr.* **1** to dissolve **2** (*disperdere*) to dissipate **B** *v. intr. pron.* **1** to dissolve **2** (*svanire*) to fade away
dissonànte *agg.* dissonant
dissuadére *v. tr.* to dissuade
distaccàre **A** *v. tr.* **1** to detach, to separate **2** (*trasferire*) to detach, to detail **3** (*sport*) to leave behind **B** *v. intr. pron.* to come off, to break off
distàcco *s. m.* **1** detachment **2** (*partenza*)

separation, parting **3** (*indifferenza*) detachment, indifference **4** (*sport*) lead
distànte *agg.* distant, faraway (*attr.*)
distànza *s. f.* distance
distanziàre *v. tr.* **1** to space out **2** (*lasciare indietro*) to outdistance, to leave behind
distàre *v. intr.* to be distant, to be ... away
distèndere **A** *v. tr.* **1** to spread, to stretch (out) **2** (*porre*) to lay **3** (*rilassare*) to relax **B** *v. rifl. e intr. pron.* **1** to spread, to stretch (out) **2** (*sdraiarsi*) to lie down **3** (*rilassarsi*) to relax
distensióne *s. f.* **1** stretching **2** (*rilassamento*) relaxation **3** (*pol.*) détente
distésa *s. f.* expanse, stretch
distillàre *v. tr.* to distil(l)
distillàto *s. m.* distillate
distillerìa *s. f.* distillery
distìnguere **A** *v. tr.* **1** to distinguish **2** (*contrassegnare*) to mark **B** *v. intr. pron.* to distinguish oneself
distìnta *s. f.* list, note
distintìvo **A** *agg.* distinctive **B** *s. m.* badge
distìnto *agg.* **1** distinct **2** (*raffinato*) distinguished ♦ **distinti saluti** best regards
distinzióne *s. f.* distinction
distògliere *v. tr.* **1** (*dissuadere*) to dissuade **2** (*distrarre*) to divert, to distract **3** (*allontanare*) to remove
distòrcere **A** *v. tr.* to distort, to twist **B** *v. intr. pron.* to be sprained
distorsióne *s. f.* **1** distortion **2** (*med.*) sprain
distràrre **A** *v. tr.* **1** to distract **2** (*divertire*) to entertain, to amuse **3** (*dir.*) to misappropriate **B** *v. rifl.* **1** to divert one's attention **2** (*divertirsi*) to amuse oneself
distrattaménte *avv.* absent-mindedly
distràtto *agg.* absent-minded, inattentive
distrazióne *s. f.* **1** absent-mindedness **2** (*disattenzione*) inattention, carelessness **3** (*divertimento*) recreation, amusement **4** (*dir.*) misappropriation
distrétto *s. m.* district
distribuìre *v. tr.* to distribute
distributóre *s. m.* distributor, dispenser ♦ **d. di benzina** petrol pump, (*USA*) gasoline pump
distribuzióne *s. f.* distribution
districàre **A** *v. tr.* to disentangle **B** *v. rifl.* to disentangle oneself
distrùggere *v. tr.* **1** to destroy **2** (*fig.*) to shatter
distruzióne *s. f.* destruction
disturbàre **A** *v. tr.* **1** to disturb, to trouble **2** (*sconvolgere*) to upset **B** *v. rifl.* to trouble (oneself), to bother
distùrbo *s. m.* **1** trouble, inconvenience **2** (*med.*) trouble, illness **3** (*radio*) noise
disubbidiènte *agg.* disobedient
disubbidìre *v. intr.* to disobey
disuguagliànza *s. f.* inequality
disuguàle *agg.* **1** (*differente*) different **2** (*irregolare*) uneven
disumàno *agg.* inhuman
disùso *s. m.* disuse
ditàle *s. m.* thimble
ditàta *s. f.* fingerprint
dìto *s. m.* finger, (*del piede*) toe
dìtta *s. f.* firm, business
dittatóre *s. m.* dictator
dittatùra *s. f.* dictatorship
dittòngo *s. m.* diphthong
diurètico *agg. e s. m.* diuretic
diùrno *agg.* day (*attr.*), day-time (*attr.*)
divagàre *v. intr.* to stray, to digress
divampàre *v. intr.* to flare up
divàno *s. m.* sofa, divan
divaricàre *v. tr. e intr. pron.* to open wide
divàrio *s. m.* discrepancy, gap
divenìre → **diventare**
diventàre *v. intr.* **1** to become **2** (*farsi*) to grow (into), to turn (into), to get
divèrbio *s. m.* altercation, squabble
divèrgere *v. intr.* to diverge
diversaménte *avv.* differently, otherwise
diversificàre **A** *v. tr.* to diversify **B** *v. intr. pron.* to differ
diversità *s. f.* diversity, difference
diversìvo *s. m.* diversion, distraction
divèrso (1) **A** *agg. indef. spec. al pl.* several **B** *pron. indef. al pl.* several people
divèrso (2) *agg.* different
divertènte *agg.* amusing, funny
divertiménto *s. m.* amusement, fun
divertìre **A** *v. tr.* to amuse, to entertain **B** *v. rifl.* to amuse oneself, to have fun, to enjoy oneself
dividèndo *s. m.* dividend
divìdere **A** *v. tr.* **1** to divide, to split **2** (*condividere*) to share **3** (*separare*) to part **B** *v. rifl.* to part **C** *v. rifl. rec.* to separate
divièto *s. m.* prohibition ♦ **d. d'accesso** no entry; **d. di sosta** no parking
divincolàrsi *v. rifl.* to wriggle
divinità *s. f.* divinity
divìno *agg.* divine
divìsa (1) *s. f.* uniform

divìsa (2) *s. f.* (*valuta*) currency
divisìbile *agg.* divisible
divisióne *s. f.* division
divisionìsmo *s. m.* pointillism
divìso *agg.* **1** divided **2** (*separato*) separated **3** (*condiviso*) shared
dìvo *s. m.* star
divoràre *v. tr.* to devour, to eat up
divorziàre *v. intr.* to divorce
divorziàto *s. m.* divorcee
divòrzio *s. m.* divorce
divulgàre **A** *v. tr.* to spread, to divulge **B** *v. intr. pron.* to spread
divulgatìvo *agg.* popular
dizionàrio *s. m.* dictionary
dóccia *s. f.* shower ♦ **fare la d.** to take a shower
docènte **A** *agg.* teaching **B** *s. m. e f.* teacher
docènza *s. f.* teaching
dòcile *agg.* docile
documentàbile *agg.* documentable
documentàre **A** *v. tr.* to document **B** *v. rifl.* to gather information
documentàrio *s. m.* documentary
documénto *s. m.* document, paper, record
dódici *agg. num. card. e s. m. inv.* twelve
dogàna *s. f.* customs *pl.* ♦ **dichiarazione per la d.** customs declaration; **pagare la d.** to pay duty
doganière *s. m.* customs officer
dòglie *s. f. pl.* labour
dògma *s. m.* dogma
dogmàtico *agg.* dogmatic
dólce **A** *agg.* **1** sweet **2** (*mite*) mild **3** (*tenero*) soft **B** *s. m.* **1** (*sapore*) sweetness **2** (*cibo*) sweet **3** (*torta*) cake
dolcézza *s. f.* **1** sweetness **2** (*gentilezza*) kindness **3** (*di clima*) mildness **4** (*di suono, colore*) softness
dolciàstro *agg.* sweetish
dolcificànte *s. m.* sweetener
dolciùme *s. m.* sweet(meat)
dolènte *agg.* **1** sorrowful **2** (*che fa male*) aching
dolère *v. intr. e intr. pron.* **1** to ache **2** (*rincrescere*) to be sorry
dòllaro *s. m.* dollar
dòlo *s. m.* (*dir.*) malice, fraud
dolorànte *agg.* aching
dolóre *s. m.* **1** pain, ache **2** (*morale*) sorrow, grief
doloróso *agg.* **1** painful, sore **2** (*che procura dolore morale*) sorrowful, sad
dolóso *agg.* fraudulent ♦ **incendio d.** arson
domànda *s. f.* **1** question (*richiesta*) request, (*scritta*) application **2** (*econ.*) demand
domandàre **A** *v. tr.* **1** (*per sapere*) to ask, (*per avere*) to ask for **2** (*esigere*) to demand **B** *v. intr.* to inquire, to ask
domàni *avv. e s. m.* tomorrow
domàre *v. tr.* to tame
domatóre *s. m.* tamer
domattìna *avv.* tomorrow morning
doménica *s. f.* Sunday
domèstico **A** *agg.* domestic, home (*attr.*) **B** *s. m.* servant, domestic
domicìlio *s. m.* domicile ♦ **consegna a d.** home delivery
dominànte *agg. e s. f.* dominant
dominàre **A** *v. tr.* **1** to dominate, to rule **2** (*frenare*) to control **3** (*sovrastare*) to overlook, to dominate **B** *v. intr.* **1** to rule **2** (*prevalere*) to predominate **C** *v. rifl.* to control oneself
dominatóre *s. m.* ruler
dominazióne *s. f.* domination, rule
domìnio *s. m.* **1** domination, rule **2** (*territorio*) dominion **3** (*proprietà*) property **4** (*settore*) domain
donàre **A** *v. tr.* to give (as a present) **B** *v. intr.* (*addirsi*) to suit
donatóre *s. m.* donor, giver ♦ **d. di sangue** blood donor
dondolàre **A** *v. tr. e intr.* to swing, to rock **B** *v. rifl.* to swing, to rock oneself
dóndolo *s. m.* swing ♦ **a d.** rocking
dònna *s. f.* **1** woman **2** (*domestica*) maid **3** (*carte da gioco*) queen ♦ **d. di casa** housewife
dònnola *s. f.* weasel
dóno *s. m.* **1** gift, present **2** (*disposizione*) gift, talent
dópo **A** *avv.* **1** (*tempo*) after, afterwards, (*poi*) then, (*più tardi*) later, (*successivamente*) next **2** (*luogo*) after, next **B** *prep.* **1** (*tempo*) after, (*a partire da*) since **2** (*luogo*) after, (*oltre*) past, (*dietro*) behind **C** *cong.* after **D** *agg.* next, after
dopobàrba *s. m. inv.* aftershave
dopodomàni *avv.* the day after tomorrow
dopoguèrra *s. m. inv.* postwar period
dopoprànzo *s. m.* afternoon
doposcì *s. m.* après-ski
dopotùtto *avv.* after all
doppiàggio *s. m.* dubbing
doppiàre *v. tr.* **1** to double **2** (*sport*) to lap

3 (*cin.*) to dub
doppiatóre *s. m.* dubber
dóppio **A** *agg.* **1** double **2** (*mecc.*) dual **B** *s. m.* **1** double, twice the amount **2** (*tennis*) doubles *pl.* **C** *avv.* double ♦ **d. gioco** double-cross
doppióne *s. m.* duplicate
doppiopètto *agg.* double-breasted
doràto *agg.* gilt, (*color d'oro*) golden
dòrico *agg.* Doric
dormicchiàre *v. intr.* to doze
dormiglióne *s. m.* sleepy-head
dormìre *v. intr. e tr.* to sleep ♦ **andare a d.** to go to bed
dormìta *s. f.* sleep
dormitòrio *s. m.* dormitory
dormivéglia *s. m.* drowsiness
dorsàle **A** *agg.* dorsal **B** *s. f.* ridge ♦ **spina d.** backbone
dòrso *s. m.* back
dosàggio *s. m.* dosage
dosàre *v. tr.* **1** to dose, to measure out **2** (*distribuire con parsimonia*) to dole out
dòse *s. f.* dose, quantity, amount
dòsso *s. m.* (*di strada*) hump
dotàre *v. tr.* **1** to endow **2** (*fornire*) to equip, to furnish
dotazióne *s. f.* **1** (*rendita*) endowment **2** (*attrezzatura*) equipment
dòte *s. f.* **1** dowry **2** (*dono naturale*) gift, quality
dòtto *agg.* learned
dottóre *s. m.* **1** (*medico*) doctor, physician **2** (*laureato*) graduate
dottrìna *s. f.* doctrine
dóve *avv.* where
dovére (1) **A** *v. serv.* **1** (*obbligo*) must, to have (got) to, to be to, shall (ES: **devo correre se non voglio essere in ritardo a scuola** I must run if I don't want to be late at school, **devi imparare a controllarti** you've got to learn to control yourself, **che cosa devo fare?** what am I to do?) **2** (*necessità, opportunità, convenienza*) to have to, must, need; (*in frasi neg. e interr. neg.*) not to need, need not, not to have (got) to (ES: **a che ora devi essere all'aeroporto?** what time must you be at the airport?, **questa sera non devo uscire** I needn't get out tonight) **3** (*certezza, probabilità, supposizione, inevitabilità*) must, to be bound to, to have to (ES: **Paolo deve essere sordo** Paul must be deaf **4** (*accordo, programma stabilito*) to be to, to be due (to) (ES: **chi deve arrivare adesso?** who is to come next?, **l'aereo deve atterrare alle 12,15** the plane is due to land at 12,15) **5** (*devo?, dobbiamo?, nel senso di 'vuoi che?', 'volete che?'*) shall (ES: **devo aspettarti?** shall I wait for you?) **6** (*al condiz.*) should, ought to (ES: **dovreste aiutarlo** you ought to help him, **non avrebbe dovuto farlo** he shouldn't have done it) **7** (*al congiuntivo imperfetto*) should, were to (ES: **se dovessi tardare, precedetemi** if I should be late, just go ahead) **8** (*essere costretto, obbligato*) to be compelled to, to be forced to, to feel bound to (ES: **il ministro dovette dimettersi** the minister was forced to resign) **9** (*consiglio, suggerimento*) should have, ought to have (*con p. p.*) (ES: **dovevamo pensarci prima** we ought to have thought of it before) **B** *v. tr.* **1** (*essere debitore di*) to owe **2** (*derivare*) to take **3** (*esser dovuto*) to be due
dovére (2) *s. m.* duty ♦ **a d.** properly; **chi di d.** the person responsible
doveróso *agg.* right (and proper)
dovùnque **A** *avv.* (*dappertutto*) everywhere, (*in qualsiasi luogo*) anywhere **B** *cong.* wherever
dozzìna *s. f.* dozen
dozzinàle *agg.* cheap, ordinary
dragàre *v. tr.* to dredge
dràgo *s. m.* dragon
dràmma *s. m.* **1** drama, play **2** (*fig.*) tragedy
drammàtico *agg.* dramatic
drammatùrgo *s. m.* dramatist, playwright
drappeggiàre *v. tr.* to drape
drappéggio *s. m.* drapery
drappèllo *s. m.* **1** (*mil.*) squad **2** (*est.*) group
dràstico *agg.* drastic
drenàggio *s. m.* drainage, drain
drenàre *v. tr.* to drain
drìtto **A** *agg.* **1** straight **2** (*eretto*) upright **3** (*fam.*) (*furbo*) smart **B** *s. m.* **1** right side **2** (*fam.*) (*furbo*) smart person **3** (*maglia*) plain **C** *avv.* straight
drìzza *s. f.* halyard
drizzàre *v. tr.* **1** (*raddrizzare*) to straighten **2** (*rizzare*) to prick up
dròga *s. f.* **1** (*spezie*) spice **2** (*stupefacente*) drug, (*fam.*) dope
drogàre **A** *v. tr.* to drug **B** *v. rifl.* to take drugs

drogàto *s. m.* drug addict
drogherìa *s. f.* grocery, grocer's shop
dromedàrio *s. m.* dromedary
dualìsmo *s. m.* dualism
dùbbio **A** *agg.* **1** doubtful, uncertain **2** (*ambiguo*) dubious **B** *s. m.* doubt ♦ **senza d.** no doubt, without doubt
dubbioso *agg.* doubtful
dubitàre *v. intr.* **1** to doubt, to have doubts **2** (*temere*) to suspect **3** (*diffidare*) to distrust
dùca *s. m.* duke
ducàto *s. m.* **1** dukedom, duchy **2** (*moneta*) ducat
duchéssa *s. f.* duchess
due *agg. num. card. e s. m. inv.* two
duecènto *agg. num. card. e s. m. inv.* two hundred
duèllo *s. m.* duel
duétto *s. m.* duet
dùna *s. f.* dune
dùnque *cong.* **1** (*conclusione, conseguenza*) so, therefore **2** (*rafforzativo*) so, then, well ♦ **venire al d.** to come to the point
dùo *s. m. inv.* duo, duet
duòmo *s. m.* cathedral
duplex *agg. e s. m. inv.* (*tel.*) shared
duplicàto *s. m.* duplicate
duplicazióne *s. f.* duplication
dùplice *agg.* double, twofold
duraménte *avv.* **1** hard **2** (*aspramente*) harshly, roughly
durànte *prep.* during, in, throughout
duràre *v. intr.* **1** to last, to go on **2** (*resistere*) to hold out, (*di tessuto*) to wear **3** (*conservarsi*) to keep
duràta *s. f.* **1** duration, length **2** (*di tessuto*) wear **3** (*di motore*) life
duratùro *agg.* **1** lasting **2** (*di materiale*) durable **3** (*di colore*) fast
durévole *agg.* lasting, durable
durézza *s. f.* **1** hardness **2** (*asprezza*) harshness **3** (*rigidità*) stiffness
dùro **A** *agg.* **1** hard **2** (*rigido*) tough, stiff **B** *avv.* hard
dùttile *agg.* ductile, pliable

E

e o **ed** *cong.* and
èbano *s. m.* ebony
ebbène *cong.* well, so
ebbrézza *s. f.* **1** drunkenness, intoxication **2** (*fig.*) elation, thrill
èbete *agg.* stupid
ebollizióne *s. f.* boiling
ebràico **A** *agg.* (*della lingua*) Hebrew, Hebraic, (*della religione*) Jewish **B** *s. m.* (*lingua*) Hebrew
ebrèo **A** *agg.* Hebrew, Jewish **B** *s. m.* Jew, Hebrew
ebùrneo *agg.* ivory (*attr.*)
ecatómbe *s. f.* **1** hecatomb **2** (*fig.*) mass slaughter
eccedènte *agg. e s. m.* excess (*attr.*), surplus (*attr.*)
eccedènza *s. f.* excess, surplus
eccèdere **A** *v. tr.* to exceed, to surpass **B** *v. intr.* to go too far
eccellènte *agg.* excellent, first-rate
eccellènza *s. f.* **1** excellence **2** (*titolo*) Excellency ♦ **per e.** par excellence
eccèllere *v. intr.* to excel
eccèlso *agg.* lofty, sublime
eccèntrico *agg. e s. m.* eccentric
eccepìre *v. tr.* to object
eccessìvo *agg.* excessive
eccèsso *s. m.* excess, surplus
eccètera *avv.* etcetera, etc., and so on
eccètto *prep.* except (for), but, save (for) ♦ **e. che** unless
eccettuàre *v. tr.* to except, to leave out
eccezionàle *agg.* **1** exceptional **2** (*straordinario*) extraordinary
eccezionalménte *avv.* **1** exceptionally **2** (*straordinariamente*) extraordinarily
eccezióne *s. f.* **1** exception **2** (*obiezione*) objection ♦ **a e. di** with the exception of, except
ecchìmosi *s. f.* ecchymosis, bruise
eccìdio *s. m.* slaughter
eccitàbile *agg.* excitable
eccitànte *agg.* exciting, excitant
eccitàre **A** *v. tr.* **1** to excite **2** (*provocare*) to rouse, to stir up **B** *v. intr. pron.* to get excited
eccitazióne *s. f.* excitement
ecclesiàstico **A** *agg.* ecclesiastic(al), clerical **B** *s. m.* ecclesiastic
ècco *avv.* **1** (*qui*) here, (*là*) there **2** (*rafforzativo*) so there, there ♦ **e. fatto** that's that; **eccomi!** here I am!; **e. tutto** that's all
eccóme *avv. e inter.* rather, yes indeed
echeggiàre *v. tr. e intr.* to echo
eclèttico *agg.* eclectic
eclettismo *s. m.* eclecticism
eclissàre **A** *v. tr.* **1** to eclipse **2** (*fig.*) to eclipse, to outshine **B** *v. intr. pron.* **1** to be eclipsed **2** (*fig.*) to disappear, to vanish
eclìssi *s. f.* eclipse
eclìttico *agg.* ecliptic
èco *s. m. e f.* echo
ecografìa *s. f.* echography
ecologìa *s. f.* ecology
ecològico *agg.* ecological
economìa *s. f.* **1** economy, (*scienza*) economics *pl.* (*v. al sing.*) **2** *al pl.* (*risparmi*) savings *pl.* ♦ **fare e. su q.c.** to save money on st.
econòmico *agg.* **1** economic **2** (*poco costoso*) cheap, economic(al)
economìsta *s. m. e f.* economist
economizzàre *v. intr.* to economize
ecònomo *agg.* sparing, thrifty
ecosistèma *s. m.* ecosystem
ecumènico *agg.* (o)ecumenical
eczèma *s. m.* eczema
edèma *s. m.* (o)edema
édera *s. f.* ivy
edìcola *s. f.* **1** news-stand, kiosk, bookstall **2** (*arch.*) aedicule
edificàbile *agg.* building (*attr.*)
edificànte *agg.* edifying
edificàre *v. tr.* **1** to build **2** (*fig.*) to set up
edifìcio *s. m.* building
edìle *agg.* building (*attr.*)
edilìzia *s. f.* building
edilìzio *agg.* building (*attr.*) ♦ **licenza edilizia** planning permission
editóre *s. m.* **1** publisher **2** (*curatore*) editor
editorìa *s. f.* publishing
editoriàle **A** *agg.* publishing **B** *s. m.* (*articolo*) editorial
edìtto *s. m.* edict
edizióne *s. f.* edition

edonìsmo *s. m.* hedonism
educàre *v. tr.* **1** to bring up **2** (*esercitare*) to train, to educated
educatìvo *agg.* educational
educàto *agg.* well-mannered, polite
educazióne *s. f.* **1** upbringing **2** (*istruzione*) education, training **3** (*buone maniere*) (good) manners *pl.*, courtesy
efèbico *agg.* ephebic
effemèride *s. f.* ephemeris
effeminàto *agg.* effeminate
efferàto *agg.* brutal, ferocious, savage
effervescènte *agg.* sparkling, fizzy
effettivamente *avv.* really, actually
effettivo *agg.* **1** real, actual, effective **2** (*di personale*) permanent
effètto *s. m.* **1** effect **2** (*impressione*) impression, effect **3** (*comm.*) bill ♦ **effetti personali** personal belongings
effettuàbile *agg.* practicable
effettuàre **A** *v. tr.* to effect, to carry out, to make **B** *v. intr. pron.* to take place
efficàce *agg.* effective
efficàcia *s. f.* effectiveness, efficacy
efficiènte *agg.* efficient
efficiènza *s. f.* efficiency
effìgie *s. f.* effigy
effìmero *agg.* ephemeral
efflùvio *s. m.* scent, effluvium
effrazióne *s. f.* housebreaking, burglary
effusióne *s. f.* effusion
egemonìa *s. f.* hegemony
egemonizzàre *v. tr.* to monopolize
egittologìa *s. f.* Egyptology
egiziàno *agg. e s. m.* Egyptian
egìzio *agg. e s. m.* Egyptian
égli *pron. pers. 3ª sing. m.* he ♦ **e. stesso** he himself
egocèntrico *agg.* egocentric, self-centred
egoìsmo *s. m.* selfishness, egoism
egoìsta *s. m. e f.* egoist, selfish person
egrègio *agg.* **1** excellent, remarkable **2** (*nelle lettere*) dear
eiaculàre *v. tr. e intr.* to ejaculate
elaboràre *v. tr.* **1** to elaborate, to work out **2** (*inf.*) to process
elaboratóre *s. m.* computer
elaborazióne *s. f.* **1** elaboration **2** (*inf.*) processing
elargizióne *s. f.* donation
elasticità *s. f.* **1** elasticity **2** (*agilità*) agility, flexibility
elàstico **A** *agg.* elastic **B** *s. m.* rubber band
elefànte *s. m.* elephant
elegànte *agg.* elegant, smart
elèggere *v. tr.* to elect
elegìaco *agg.* elegiac
elementàre *agg.* **1** elementary **2** (*di base*) basic
eleménto *s. m.* **1** element **2** (*componente*) constituent, ingredient, element **3** (*persona*) member, person **4** *al pl.* (*rudimenti*) rudiments *pl.*
elemòsina *s. f.* alms ♦ **chiedere l'e.** to beg
elencàre *v. tr.* to list
elènco *s. m.* list ♦ **e. telefonico** telephone directory
elettoràle *agg.* electoral
elettoràto *s. m.* **1** (*insieme degli elettori*) electorate **2** (*diritto di voto*) franchise, (*diritto a essere eletto*) eligibility
elettóre *s. m.* elector, voter
elettràuto *s. m. inv.* car electrician, (*officina*) car electrical repairs
elettricìsta *s. m.* electrician
elettricità *s. f.* electricity
elèttrico *agg.* electric(al) ♦ **centrale elettrica** ower station
elettrizzànte *agg.* electrifying, thrilling
elettrizzàre **A** *v. tr.* to electrify **B** *v. intr. pron.* to be electrified
elettrocardiogràmma *s. m.* electrocardiogram
elèttrodo *s. m.* electrode
elettrodomèstico *s. m.* household appliance
elettroencefalogràmma *s. m.* electroencephalogram
elettromagnètico *agg.* electromagnetic
elettróne *s. m.* electron
elettrònica *s. f.* electronics *pl.* (*v. al sing.*)
elettrònico *agg.* electronic
elettrotècnico *agg.* electrotechnical
elevàre **A** *v. tr.* **1** to raise, to lift up **2** (*erigere*) to erect **3** (*mat.*) to raise **B** *v. intr. pron.* to rise, to overlook
elezióne *s. f.* election
èlica *s. f.* propeller
elicòttero *s. m.* helicopter
eliminàre *v. tr.* to eliminate
eliminatòrio *agg.* preliminary
èlio *s. m.* helium
elioterapìa *s. f.* heliotherapy
elipòrto *s. m.* heliport
elisabettiàno *agg.* Elizabethan
elitàrio *agg.* elitist
élite *s. f. inv.* elite

élla *pron. pers. 3ª sing. f.* she ♦ **e. stessa** she herself
ellènico *agg.* Hellenic
ellenìstico *agg.* Hellenistic
ellìsse *s. f.* ellipse
ellìttico *agg.* elliptic
elmétto *s. m.* helmet
élmo *s. m.* helmet
elogiàre *v. tr.* to praise
elògio *s. m.* praise
eloquènte *agg.* eloquent
eloquènza *s. f.* eloquence
elucubrazióne *s. f.* lucubration
elùdere *v. tr.* to evade, to elude
elusìvo *agg.* elusive
emaciàto *agg.* emaciated
emanàre **A** *v. tr.* **1** (*esalare*) to exhale **2** (*ordini, leggi*) to issue **B** *v. intr.* to emanate, to proceed
emancipàre **A** *v. tr.* to emancipate **B** *v. rifl.* to become emancipated, to free oneself
emancipazióne *s. f.* emancipation
emarginàre *v. tr.* to emarginate, to exclude
emàtico *agg.* hematic
ematòlogo *s. m.* haematologist
ematòma *s. m.* hematoma
embargo *s. m.* embargo
emblèma *s. m.* emblem
emblematico *agg.* emblematic
embolìa *s. f.* embolism
embrióne *s. m.* embryo
emendaménto *s. m.* amendment
emendàre *v. tr.* **1** (*dir.*) to amend **2** (*correggere*) to emend, (*migliorare*) to improve
emergènte *agg.* emergent
emergènza *s. f.* emergency
emèrgere *v. intr.* to emerge
emersióne *s. f.* emergence, emersion
eméttere *v. tr.* **1** to give out, (*suono*) to utter **2** (*esprimere*) to express, to deliver **3** (*mettere in circolazione*) to issue, to draw
emettitóre *s. m.* emitter
emicrània *s. f.* migraine
emigrànte *s. m. e f.* emigrant
emigràre *v. intr.* to emigrate
emigrazióne *s. f.* emigration
eminènte *agg.* eminent, distinguished
emiràto *s. m.* emirate
emìro *s. m.* emir
emisfèro *s. m.* hemisphere
emissióne *s. f.* **1** (*fis.*) emission **2** (*econ.*) issue
emittènte **A** *agg.* **1** (*banca*) issuing **2** (*radio, TV*) broadcasting **B** *s. m. e f.* (*di cambiale*) drawer, (*di titolo*) issuer **C** *s. f.* (*radio, TV*) transmitter, broadcaster
emodiàlisi *s. f.* hemodialysis
emofilìa *s. f.* hemophilia
emorragìa *s. f.* hemorrhage
emorròidi *s. f. pl.* hemorrhoids *pl.*
emostàtico *agg.* hemostatic
emotìvo *agg.* emotional
emottìsi *s. f.* hemoptysis
emozionànte *agg.* moving, exciting
emozionàre **A** *v. tr.* to move, to excite **B** *v. intr. pron.* to get excited
emozióne *s. f.* emotion, excitement
émpio *agg.* impious
empìrico *agg.* empiric
empòrio *s. m.* emporium, trade center, general shop
emulàre *v. tr.* to emulate
èmulo *s. m.* emulator
emulsióne *s. f.* emulsion
enciclopedìa *s. f.* encyclop(a)edia
encomiàbile *agg.* praiseworthy
endèmico *agg.* endemic
endocrinòlogo *s. m.* endocrinologist
endovéna *s. f.* intravenous injection
energètico *agg.* **1** energetic, energy (*attr.*) **2** (*di sostanza alimentare*) energy-giving
energìa *s. f.* energy
enèrgico *agg.* energetic, vigorous
ènfasi *s. f.* emphasis, stress
enfàtico *agg.* emphatic
enfisèma *s. m.* emphysema
enìgma *s. m.* enigma, (*indovinello*) riddle
enigmàtico *agg.* enigmatic
enigmìstica *s. f.* enigmatography, puzzles *pl.*
ennèsimo *agg.* **1** nth **2** (*fig.*) umpteenth
enologìa *s. f.* oenology
enórme *agg.* enormous, huge
enormità *s. f.* enormity, hugeness
ènte *s. m.* body, board, (*ufficio*) office, bureau, (*società*) company, agency, corporation
entràmbi **A** *agg.* both, either **B** *pron. pl.* both
entràre *v. intr.* **1** to go in, to come in, to get in, to enter **2** (*unirsi a*) to join **3** (*avere a che fare*) to have to do
entràta *s. f.* **1** entrance, entry **2** *spec. al pl.* (*econ.*) income, revenue, receipts *pl.*, earnings *pl.* ♦ **e. libera** admission free; **entrate e uscite** debit and credit
éntro *prep.* in, within, before, by ♦ **e. oggi** by this evening

entrotèrra *s. m. inv.* inland
entusiasmàre **A** *v. tr.* to arouse enthusiasm in, to carry away **B** *v. intr. pron.* to become enthusiastic
entusiàsmo *s. m.* enthusiasm
entusiàsta *agg.* enthusiastic
enumeràre *v. tr.* to enumerate
enunciàre *v. tr.* to enunciate
enurèsi *s. f.* enuresis
eòlico *agg.* aeolian
epàtico *agg.* hepatic ♦ **colica epatica** liver attack
epatìte *s. f.* hepatitis
epicèntro *s. m.* epicentre
èpico *agg.* epic
epicureìsmo *s. m.* epicurism
epidemìa *s. f.* epidemic
epidèmico *agg.* epidemic(al)
epidèrmico *agg.* epidermic
epidèrmide *s. f.* epidermis
epìgono *s. m.* imitator, follower
epìgrafe *s. f.* epigraph
epilessìa *s. f.* epilepsy
epìlogo *s. m.* epilogue
episcopàle *agg.* episcopal
episòdico *agg.* episodic(al)
episòdio *s. m.* episode
epistàssi *s. f.* epistaxis
epitàffio *s. m.* epitaph
epìteto *s. m.* **1** epithet **2** (*insulto*) insult
època *s. f.* **1** epoch, age **2** (*tempo, periodo*) time, period
epònimo **A** *agg.* eponymous **B** *s. m.* eponym
epopèa *s. f.* epos
eppùre *cong.* and yet
epuràre *v. tr.* to purge
epurazióne *s. f.* purge
equatóre *s. m.* equator
equatoriàle *agg.* equatorial
equazióne *s. f.* equation
equèstre *agg.* equestrian ♦ **circo e.** circus
equidistànte *agg.* equidistant
equilibràre *v. tr. e rifl. rec.* to equilibrate, to balance
equilibràto *agg.* balanced
equilibratùra *s. f.* balancing
equilìbrio *s. m.* balance, equilibrium
equìno *agg.* equine, horse (*attr.*)
equinòzio *s. m.* equinox
equipaggiaménto *s. m.* equipment
equipaggiàre **A** *v. tr.* to equip **B** *v. rifl.* to equip oneself, to kit oneself out
equipàggio *s. m.* crew
equiparàre *v. tr.* to make equal, to level
équipe *s. f. inv.* team
equità *s. f.* equity
equitazióne *s. f.* riding
equivalènte *agg. e s. m.* equivalent
equivalènza *s. f.* equivalence
equivalére *v. intr. e rifl. rec.* to be equivalent, to be equal in value
equivocàre *v. intr.* to misunderstand, to mistake
equìvoco **A** *agg.* **1** equivocal, ambiguous **2** (*sospetto*) dubious **B** *s. m.* equivocation, misunderstanding
èquo *agg.* fair
èra *s. f.* era, age
èrba *s. f.* grass, (*medicinale, aromatica*) herb, (*infestante*) weed
erbàrio *s. m.* herbarium, (*libro*) herbal
erbìvoro *agg.* herbivorous
erboristerìa *s. f.* herbalist's shop
erède *s. m. e f.* heir
eredità *s. f.* **1** (*dir.*) inheritance **2** (*fig.*) heritage **3** (*biol.*) heredity ♦ **lasciare in e.** to bequeath
ereditàre *v. tr.* to inherit
ereditàrio *agg.* hereditary
eremìta *s. m.* hermit
èremo *s. m.* hermitage
eresìa *s. f.* heresy
erètico *agg.* heretical
erètto *agg.* **1** erect, upright **2** (*costruito*) erected, built **3** (*istituito*) founded
erezióne *s. f.* erection
ergàstolo *s. m.* life sentence
èrica *s. f.* heather
erìgere **A** *v. tr.* **1** to erect, to build **2** (*innalzare*) to raise **3** (*istituire*) to found **B** *v. rifl.* **1** (*drizzarsi*) to stand up **2** (*fig.*) to claim to be
eritèma *s. m.* erythema
ermafrodìto *agg.* hermaphrodite
ermellìno *s. m.* ermine
ermètico *agg.* **1** hermetic, airtight **2** (*fig.*) obscure
èrnia *s. f.* hernia
eròe *s. m.* hero
erogàre *v. tr.* to supply, (*somma*) to disburse
eròico *agg.* heroic
eroìna (1) *s. f.* heroine
eroìna (2) *s. f.* (*chim.*) heroin
eroìsmo *s. m.* heroism
erosióne *s. f.* erosion
eròtico *agg.* erotic
erotìsmo *s. m.* erotism

erràre *v. intr.* **1** (*vagare*) to wander (about), to roam **2** (*sbagliare*) to be mistaken, to make mistakes
erróre *s. m.* mistake, error ♦ **e. di stampa** misprint
erudìto *s. m.* scholar
eruttàre *v. tr.* to throw out
eruzióne *s. f.* **1** eruption **2** (*med.*) rash
esacerbàre *v. tr.* to exacerbate, to exasperate
esageràre **A** *v. tr.* to exaggerate **B** *v. intr.* to overdo, to go too far
esagerazióne *s. f.* exaggeration
esagonàle *agg.* hexagonal
esàgono *s. m.* hexagon
esalàre *v. tr.* to exhale
esalazióne *s. f.* exhalation
esaltàre **A** *v. tr.* **1** to extol, to celebrate **2** (*entusiasmare*) to thrill **B** *v. intr. pron.* to become elated
esàme *s. m.* examination, exam, test
esaminàre *v. tr.* to examine
esànime *agg.* lifeless
esasperàre **A** *v. tr.* **1** to exasperate, to irritate **2** (*esacerbare*) to exacerbate, to aggravate **B** *v. intr. pron.* to become bitter
esasperazióne *s. f.* **1** exasperation, irritation **2** (*inasprimento*) aggravation
esattaménte *avv.* **1** (*in maniera esatta*) exactly, precisely, (*correttamente*) correctly **2** (*proprio*) just
esattézza *s. f.* **1** exactness **2** (*accuratezza*) accuracy
esàtto **A** *agg.* **1** exact, correct **2** (*accurato*) careful **B** *avv.* exactly
esattóre *s. m.* collector
esaudìre *v. tr.* to grant, to fulfil
esauriènte *agg.* exhaustive
esauriménto *s. m.* exhaustion, depletion ♦ **e. nervoso** nervous breakdown
esaurìre **A** *v. tr.* to exhaust **B** *v. rifl. e intr. pron.* **1** to get exhausted **2** (*di merci*) to run out, to sell out
esàusto *agg.* exhausted, worn out
esautoràre *v. tr.* to deprive of authority
esbórso *s. m.* disbursement
ésca *s. f.* bait
escatològico *agg.* eschatologic
eschimése **A** *agg.* Eskimo (*attr.*) **B** *s. m. e f.* Eskimo, Husky
esclamàre *v. tr. e intr.* to exclaim, to cry (out)
esclùdere **A** *v. tr.* to exclude, to leave out **B** *v. rifl. rec.* to exclude one another
esclusìva *s. f.* exclusive right, sole right
esclusivaménte *avv.* exclusively
esclusìvo *agg.* exclusive
escogitàre *v. tr.* to contrive, to devise
escoriazióne *s. f.* excoriation, graze
escursióne *s. f.* **1** excursion, tour **2** (*scient.*) range
escursionìsmo *s. m.* tourism
esecràre *v. tr.* to execrate
esecutìvo *agg. e s. m.* executive
esecutóre *s. m.* **1** executor **2** (*mus.*) performer
esecuzióne *s. f.* **1** execution **2** (*mus.*) performance
esèdra *s. f.* exedra
eseguìre *v. tr.* to execute, to carry out, to perform
esèmpio *s. m.* **1** example, instance **2** (*modello*) model, paragon ♦ **per e.** for example, for instance
esemplàre **A** *agg.* exemplary, model (*attr.*) **B** *s. m.* **1** (*modello*) model **2** (*elemento di serie*) specimen, (*copia*) copy
esemplificàre *v. tr.* to exemplify
esemplificazióne *s. f.* exemplification
esentàre *v. tr.* to exempt, to excuse
esènte *agg.* exempt, free
esenzióne *s. f.* exemption
esèquie *s. f. pl.* funeral rites *pl.*
esercitàre **A** *v. tr.* **1** to exercise **2** (*una professione*) to practise **3** (*addestrare*) to train **B** *v. rifl.* to practise, to train oneself
esercitazióne *s. f.* exercise, practice
esèrcito *s. m.* army
esercìzio *s. m.* **1** exercise **2** (*pratica*) practice **3** (*azienda commerciale*) concern, (*negozio*) shop ♦ **e. fisico** physical training
esibìre **A** *v. tr.* to exhibit, to show **B** *v. rifl.* **1** to show off **2** (*in spettacoli*) to perform
esibizióne *s. f.* **1** show, display, exhibition **2** (*di spettacolo*) performance
esibizionìsmo *s. m.* exhibitionism
esigènte *agg.* exacting, demanding
esigènza *s. f.* demand, need
esìgere *v. tr.* **1** to demand, to require, to insist on **2** (*riscuotere*) to collect, (*pretendere*) to exact
esìguo *agg.* scarce, exiguous, scanty
esilarànte *agg.* exhilarating ♦ **gas e.** laughing gas
èsile *agg.* **1** thin, slender **2** (*debole*) weak, faint
esiliàre *v. tr.* to exile, to banish
esìlio *s. m.* exile, banishment
esìmere **A** *v. tr.* to exempt **B** *v. rifl.* to get

out of
esistènte *agg.* existing
esistènza *s. f.* existence
esìstere *v. intr.* to exist, to be
esitàre *v. intr.* to hesitate
esitazióne *s. f.* hesitation
èsito *s. m.* result, outcome, issue
èsodo *s. m.* exodus, flight
esoneràre *v. tr.* to exonerate, to free, to extempt
esorbitànte *agg.* exorbitant
esorcizzàre *v. tr.* to exorcize
esòrdio *s. m.* **1** (*inizio*) beginning **2** (*debutto*) debut
esordìre *v. intr.* to begin, to start
esortàre *v. tr.* to exhort, to urge
esortazióne *s. f.* exhortation
esotèrico *agg.* esoteric
esòtico *agg.* exotic
espàndere A *v. tr.* to expand, to extend **B** *v. intr. pron.* to expand, to spread out
espansióne *s. f.* expansion
espansìvo *agg.* expansive
espatriàre *v. intr.* to expatriate
espediènte *s. m.* expedient, device
espèllere *v. tr.* **1** to expel, to turn out **2** (*emettere*) to eject, to discharge
esperiènza *s. f.* experience
esperiménto *s. m.* experiment, trial
espèrto *agg. e s. m.* expert
espiàre *v. tr.* to expiate
espiràre *v. tr. e intr.* to expire, to breathe out
espletàre *v. tr.* to dispatch
esplicativo *agg.* explanatory, explicative
esplìcito *agg.* explicit
esplòdere *v. intr.* to explode, to burst
esploràre *v. tr.* **1** to explore **2** (*mil.*) to scout
esploratóre *s. m.* **1** explorer **2** (*mil.*) scout ♦ **giovane e.** boy scout
esplorazióne *s. f.* exploration, scouting
esplosióne *s. f.* explosion
esplosìvo *agg. e s. m.* explosive
esponènte *s. m. e f.* exponent
espórre A *v. tr.* **1** to expose **2** (*mettere fuori*) to put out, to expose **3** (*mettere in mostra*) to show, to display **4** (*spiegare*) to expound, to explain **B** *v. rifl.* to expose oneself
esportàre *v. tr.* to export
esportazióne *s. f.* export
esposìmetro *s. m.* exposure meter
esposizióne *s. f.* **1** exposure **2** (*mostra*) exhibition, exposition, show **3** (*lo spiegare*) exposition
espósto *s. m.* petition, (*denuncia*) complaint
espressaménte *avv.* **1** (*esplicitamente*) explicitly **2** (*apposta*) on purpose, specially
espressióne *s. f.* expression
espressionìsmo *s. m.* expressionism
espressìvo *agg.* expressive
esprèsso A *agg.* **1** expressed **2** (*esplicito*) express, explicit **3** (*su richiesta*) express, made to order **4** (*veloce*) fast, express **B** *s. m.* **1** (*lettera*) express letter, (*USA*) fast letter **2** (*treno*) express **3** (*caffè*) espresso
esprìmere A *v. tr.* to express **B** *v. intr. pron.* to express oneself
espròprio *s. m.* expropriation
espulsióne *s. f.* expulsion
éssa *pron. pers. 3ª sing. f.* **1** (*sogg.*) (*riferito a cosa o animale di sesso imprecisato*) it (*riferito ad animale femmina o, fam., per 'ella, lei'*) she **2** (*compl.*) (*riferito a cosa o animale di sesso imprecisato*) it, (*riferito ad animale femmina o, fam., per 'lei'*) her
ésse *pron. pers. 3ª pl. f.* **1** (*sogg.*) they **2** (*compl.*) them ♦ **e. stesse** they themselves
essènza *s. f.* essence
essenziàle *agg.* essential
essenzialménte *avv.* essentially
èssere (1) A *v. aus.* **1** (*copula, aus. del passivo*) to be (ES: **la porta è aperta** the door is open, **il presidente è eletto ogni 4 anni** the President is elected every four years) **2** (*aus. nella coniugazione attiva di v. intr., rifl. e impers.*) to have (ES: **sono già partito** I have already left) **3** (*con v. serv.*) to have (ES: **è dovuto partire improvvisamente** he has had to leave unexpectedly) **B** *v. intr.* **1** (*esistere*) to be **2** (*accadere*) to become, to happen, to be **3** (*consistere*) to consist **4** (*costare*) to be, to cost, (*valere*) to be, to be worth, (*pesare*) to be, to weigh **5** (*andare, arrivare, stare, trovarsi*) to be **6** (*diventare*) to be, to get **7** (*esserci*) to be ♦ **e. di** (*materia*) to be (made) of, (*appartenenza*) to be of, (*origine*) to be from
èssere (2) *s. m.* **1** being, (*esistenza*) existence **2** (*creatura*) creature **3** (*stato*) state, condition
éssi *pron. pers. 3ª pl. m.* **1** (*sogg.*) they **2** (*compl.*) them ♦ **e. stessi** they them-

selves
essiccàre **A** *v. tr.* **1** to dry (up) **2** (*prosciugare*) to drain **B** *v. intr. pron.* to become dray, to dry up
ésso *pron. pers. 3ª sing. m.* **1** (*sogg.*) (*riferito a cosa o animale di sesso imprecisato*) it (*riferito ad animale maschio o, fam., per 'egli, lui'*) he **2** (*compl.*) (*riferito a cosa o animale di sesso imprecisato*) it, (*riferito ad animale maschio o, fam., per 'lui'*) him
èst *s. m.* east
èstasi *s. f.* ecstasy
estàte *s. f.* summer
estemporàneo *agg.* extemporary
estèndere **A** *v. tr.* to extend, to expand **B** *v. intr. pron.* to extend, to spread, to stretch
estensióne *s. f.* **1** extension **2** (*distesa*) expanse, extent
estenuànte *agg.* exhausting, weary
esterióre *agg.* external, outer (*attr.*), outward (*attr.*)
esternaménte *avv.* externally
esternàre *v. tr.* to express, to disclose
estèrno **A** *agg.* external, outer, outside (*attr.*) **B** *s. m.* outside ♦ **per uso e.** for external use only
èstero **A** *agg.* foreign **B** *s. m.* foreign countries *pl.* ♦ **all'e.** abroad
esteròfilo **A** *agg.* xenophilous **B** *s. m.* xenophile
estéso *agg.* large, wide, extensive
estètica *s. f.* aesthetics *pl.* (*v. al sing.*)
estètico *agg.* aesthetic(al)
estetìsmo *s. m.* aestheticism
estetìsta *s. m. e f.* beautician
estimatóre *s. m.* admirer
èstimo *s. m.* estimate
estìnguere *v. tr.* **1** to extinguish, to put out **2** (*saldare*) to settle
estìnto *s. m.* deceased
estintóre *s. m.* extinguisher
estinzióne *s. f.* extinction
estirpàre *v. tr.* to extirpate
estìvo *agg.* summer (*attr.*)
estòrcere *v. tr.* to extort
estorsióne *s. f.* extortion
estradizióne *s. f.* extradition
estraìbile *agg.* extractable, pull-out (*attr.*)
estràneo **A** *agg.* extraneous, foreign, unrelated (to) **B** *s. m.* stranger, outsider, foreigner
estràrre *v. tr.* **1** to extract, to pull out **2** (*a sorte*) to draw **3** (*minerale*) to mine
estrazióne *s. f.* **1** extraction **2** (*sorteggio*) drawing **3** (*da miniera*) mining
estremaménte *avv.* extremely
estremìsmo *s. m.* extremism
estremìsta *s. m. e f.* extremist
estremità *s. f.* **1** extremity, end **2** *al pl.* (*degli arti*) limbs *pl.*
estrèmo **A** *agg.* **1** (*nello spazio*) extreme, farthest **2** (*nel tempo*) last, final **B** *s. m.* **1** extreme **2** *al pl.* terms, essential data ♦ **l'E. Oriente** the Far East
estrìnseco *agg.* extrinsic
èstro *s. m.* **1** inspiration **2** (*capriccio*) whim, fancy
estróso *agg.* whimsical, fanciful
estrovèrso *agg.* extroverted
estuàrio *s. m.* estuary
esuberànte *agg.* exuberant
esulàre *v. intr.* **1** to go into exile **2** (*fig.*) to lie outside
èsule *s. m. e f.* exile
esultàre *v. intr.* to exult
età *s. f.* age
etèreo *agg.* ethereal
eternaménte *avv.* eternally
eternità *s. f.* eternity
etèrno *agg.* eternal
eterodòsso *agg.* heterodox
eterogèneo *agg.* heterogeneous
eterosessuàle *agg. e s. m. e f.* heterosexual
ètica *s. f.* ethics *pl.* (*v. al sing.*)
etichétta (1) *s. f.* label
etichétta (2) *s. f.* (*cerimoniale*) etiquette
ètico *agg.* ethical
etilìsmo *s. m.* alcoholism
etilìsta *s. m. e f.* alcoholic
etimologìa *s. f.* etymology
ètnico *agg.* ethnic(al)
etnologìa *s. f.* ethnology
etrùsco *agg.* Etruscan
èttaro *s. m.* hectare
ètto *s. m.* hectogram
eucaristìa *s. f.* Eucharist, Holy Communion
eufemìstico *agg.* euphemistic
euforìa *s. f.* euphoria, elation
eurìstico *agg.* heuristic
europeìsmo *s. m.* Europeanism
europèo *agg. e s. m.* European
eurovisióne *s. f.* Eurovision
eutanasìa *s. f.* euthanasia
evacuàre *v. tr. e intr.* to evacuate
evàdere **A** *v. tr.* **1** (*sbrigare*) to dispatch **2** (*sottrarsi a*) to evade **B** *v. intr.* to escape, to get away
evangèlico *agg.* evangelical

evaporàre *v. tr. e intr.* to evaporate
evaporazióne *s. f.* evaporation
evasióne *s. f.* **1** escape, getaway **2** (*fiscale*) evasion
evasìvo *agg.* evasive
evàso *s. m.* fugitive, runaway
evenienza *s. f.* event, eventuality
evènto *s. m.* event
eventuàle *agg.* possible
eventualménte *avv.* in case
evidènte *agg.* evident, plain
evidènza *s. f.* evidence, obviousness
evitàre **A** *v. tr.* **1** to avoid **2** (*sfuggire a*) to escape **3** (*risparmiare*) to spare **B** *v. rifl. rec.* to avoid each other
èvo *s. m.* age, ages *pl.*, era ♦ **il Medio E.** the Middle Ages
evocàre *v. tr.* to evoke
evolutìvo *agg.* evolutive
evolùto *agg.* advanced, fully-developed
evoluzióne *s. f.* evolution
evòlvere *v. intr. e intr. pron.* to evolve
evvìva *inter.* hurrah!
ex *pref.* ex, former
extra **A** *agg.* **1** (*speciale*) superior, first rate **2** (*in più*) extra, additional **B** *s. m.* extra
extraconiugàle *agg.* extramarital
extraeuropèo *agg.* non-European
extraterrèstre *agg.* extraterrestrial

F

fa *avv.* ago ♦ **un mese fa** a month ago
fabbisógno *s. m.* needs *pl.*, requirements *pl.*
fàbbrica *s. f.* factory, works
fabbricànte *s. m.* manufacturer, producer
fabbricàre *v. tr.* **1** to manufacture, to produce **2** (*costruire*) to build
fàbbro *s. m.* smith
faccènda *s. f.* **1** matter, affair, business **2** *al pl.* (*di casa*) housework
facchìno *s. m.* porter
fàccia *s. f.* **1** face **2** (*espressione*) look, expression **3** (*lato*) face, side
facciàta *s. f.* **1** (*arch.*) front, façade, face **2** (*pagina*) page
facèto *agg.* facetious, witty
facèzia *s. f.* witty remark, joke
fachìro *s. m.* fakir
fàcile *agg.* **1** easy **2** (*incline*) inclined, prone **3** (*probabile*) likely, probable
facilità *s. f.* **1** ease, facility **2** (*l'esser facile*) easiness **3** (*attitudine*) aptitude
facilitàre *v. tr.* to make easy
facilitazióne *s. f.* **1** facilitation **2** (*agevolazione*) facility
facinoróso *s. m.* ruffian
facoltà *s. f.* **1** faculty **2** (*autorità*) power, authority, right **3** (*università*) faculty, school
facoltatìvo *agg.* optional ♦ **fermata facoltativa** request stop
facoltóso *agg.* wealthy, well-to-do
facsìmile *s. m. inv.* facsimile
fàggio *s. m.* beech
fagiàno *s. m.* pheasant
fagiolìno *s. m.* French bean, (*USA*) string bean
fagiòlo *s. m.* bean
fagocitàre *v. tr.* **1** (*biol.*) to phagocytize **2** (*fig.*) to absorb, to engulf
fagòtto *s. m.* bundle
falànge *s. f.* phalanx
fàlce *s. f.* sickle
falciàre *v. tr.* to sickle, to cut down
fàlco *s. m.* hawk
falcóne *s. m.* falcon
fàlda *s. f.* **1** (*geol.*) stratum, layer **2** (*di abito*) tail **3** (*di cappello*) brim **4** (*di tetto*) pitch **5** (*di monte*) foot
falegnàme *s. m.* joiner, carpenter
falèsia *s. f.* cliff
fàlla *s. f.* leak
fallàce *agg.* fallacious, misleading
fallimentàre *agg.* **1** bankruptcy (*attr.*) **2** (*fig.*) ruinous
falliménto *s. m.* **1** bankruptcy **2** (*fig.*) failure
fallìre **A** *v. intr.* **1** to go bankrupt **2** (*fig.*) to fail **B** *v. tr.* to miss
fallìto *s. m.* **1** bankrupt **2** (*fig.*) failure
fàllo *s. m.* **1** error, fault, mistake **2** (*difetto*) defect, flaw **3** (*sport*) foul
falò *s. m.* bonfire
falsàre *v. tr.* **1** to distort, to misrepresent **2** (*falsificare*) to forge
falsàrio *s. m.* forger, falsifier
falsifioàre *v. tr.* to falsify, to fake, (*firme e sim.*) to forge
falsificàre *v. tr.* to falsify, to forge
falsificazióne *s. f.* falsification, forgery
fàlso **A** *agg.* false **B** *s. m.* **1** falsehood **2** (*oggetto falsificato*) forgery, fake
fàma *s. f.* **1** (*reputazione*) reputation, repute **2** (*rinomanza*) fame, renown
fàme *s. f.* **1** hunger **2** (*carestia*) famine ♦ **avere f.** to be hungry
famèlico *agg.* ravenous, greedy
famìglia *s. f.* family
familiàre *agg.* **1** domestic, family (*attr.*) **2** (*conosciuto*) familiar, well-know **3** (*semplice*) informal, homely
familiarità *s. f.* familiarity
familiarizzàre **A** *v. tr.* to familiarize **B** *v. intr. pron.* to become familiar, to familiarize oneself
famóso *agg.* famous
fan *s. m. e f. inv.* fan
fanàle *s. m.* laight, lamp
fanalìno *s. m.* tail-lamp
fanàtico **A** *agg.* fanatical **B** *s. m.* fanatic
fanciùllo *s. m.* child
fandònia *s. f.* lie
fanfàra *s. f.* **1** fanfare **2** (*banda*) brass-band
fàngo *s. m.* mud
fannullóne *s. m.* idler, lounger
fantascientìfico *agg.* science-fiction (*attr.*)
fantasciènza *s. f.* science-fiction
fantasìa *s. f.* **1** (*fantasticheria*) fantasy, daydream **2** (*immaginazione*) fancy, im-

agination
fantàsma *s. m.* ghost, phantom
fantasticàre *v. intr.* to daydream
fantàstico *agg.* **1** fantastic(al), imaginary, fanciful **2** (*straordinario*) incredible, fantastic
fànte *s. m.* **1** infantryman **2** (*carte da gioco*) jack
fanterìa *s. f.* infantry
fantòccio *s. m.* puppet
farabùtto *s. m.* rascal
faraóne *s. m.* Pharaoh
faraònico *agg.* pharaonic
farcìre *v. tr.* to stuff, to fill
fardèllo *s. m.* bundle, burden
fàre A *v. tr.* **1** (*in generale e in senso astratto*) to do (ES: **che cosa fai?** what are you doing?) **2** (*creare, produrre, realizzare, confezionare, cucinare, ecc.*) to make (ES: **f. soldi** to make money) **3** (*di professione*) to be **4** (*dire*) to say **5** (*reputare*) to think **6** (*scrivere*) to write, (*dipingere*) to paint **7** (*indicare*) to make, to be **8** (*rappresentare*) to perform, (*agire da, impersonare*) to act **9** (*pulire*) to clean **10** (*dedicarsi a*) to go in for, (*giocare a*) to play **11** (*generare*) to bear, to have **12** (*percorrere*) to go **13** (*trascorrere*) to spend **14** (*con valore causativo, seguito da inf.*) to have, to get, (*causare*) to cause, to make, (*lasciare*) to let **B** *v. intr.* **1** (*impers.*) to be **2** (*essere adatto*) to suit **3** (*stare per*) to be about **C** *v. rifl. e intr. pron.* **1** (*diventare*) to become **2** (*movimento*) to go, to come **3** (*con l'inf.*) to make oneself, to get
farètra *s. f.* quiver
farfàlla *s. f.* butterfly
farìna *s. f.* flour, meal
farinàceo A *agg.* farinaceous **B** *s. m. al pl.* starches *pl.*
farìnge *s. f. o m.* pharynx
faringìte *s. f.* pharyngitis
farmacìa *s. f.* **1** (*scienza e tecnica*) pharmacy **2** (*negozio*) chemist's shop, (*USA*) pharmacy, drugstore
farmacìsta *s. m. e f.* chemist, pharmacist
fàrmaco *s. m.* drug, medicine
farneticàre *v. intr.* to rave
fàro *s. m.* **1** (*naut.*) lighthouse **2** (*aer*) beacon, light **3** (*autom.*) headlight
fàrsa *s. f.* farce
fàscia *s. f.* **1** band, strip **2** (*benda*) bandage **3** (*geogr*) zone, strip **4** (*fig.*) sector, band
fasciàre *v. tr.* **1** to bind, to bandage **2** (*avvolgere*) to wrap
fasciatùra *s. f.* bandage, dressing
fascìcolo *s. m.* **1** (*incartamento*) dossier, file **2** (*di rivista*) issue, number, instalment **3** (*libretto*) booklet
fàscino *s. m.* fascination, charm
fàscio *s. m.* **1** bundle, sheaf **2** (*di luce*) beam
fascìsmo *s. m.* Fascism
fàse *s. f.* **1** (*scient.*) phase **2** (*stadio*) phase, stage **3** (*mecc.*) stroke
fastìdio *s. m.* **1** nuisance, bother, trouble **2** (*irritazione*) annoyance **3** (*avversione*) disgust
fastidióso *agg.* maddening, tiresome
fàsto *s. m.* pomp
fastóso *agg.* pompous
fàta *s. f.* fairy
fatàle *agg.* **1** fatal **2** (*inevitabile*) fated, destined
fatalìsta *s. m. e f.* fatalist
fatalità *s. f.* **1** fate, destiny, fatality **2** (*disgrazia*) mishap
fatica *s. f.* **1** (*lavoro faticoso*) labour, hard work, toil **2** (*sforzo*) effort, exertion **3** (*stanchezza*) weariness, fatigue **4** (*difficoltà*) difficulty **5** (*mecc.*) fatigue
faticàre *v. intr.* **1** to work hard, to toil **2** (*stentare*) to have difficulty
faticàta *s. f.* exertion, effort
faticóso *agg.* **1** tiring, hard **2** (*difficile*) difficult
fatìdico *agg.* fateful
fàto *s. m.* fate
fattìbile *agg.* feasible
fàtto A *agg.* **1** done, made **2** (*adatto*) fit **B** *s. m.* **1** fact, deed **2** (*avvenimento*) event **3** (*faccenda*) affair, matter ♦ **in f. di** as regard
fattóre (1) *s. m.* factor
fattóre (2) *s. m.* (*di campagna*) bailiff, farmer
fattorìa *s. f.* farm, (*càsa*) farmhouse
fattorìno *s. m.* messanger, office boy
fattùra *s. f.* **1** (*fabbricazione*) making, manufacture, (*lavorazione*) workmanship **2** (*comm.*) invoice, bill **3** (*fam.*) (*maleficio*) spell
fatturàre *v. tr.* to invoice
fàtuo *agg.* fatuous, vain
fàuna *s. f.* fauna
fàuno *s. m.* faun
fautóre *s. m.* supporter

fàva *s. f.* broad bean
favèlla *s. f.* speech
favìlla *s. f.* spark
fàvola *s. f.* **1** tale, story, fairy story, fable **2** (*fandonia*) tall story
favolóso *agg.* fabulous
favóre *s. m.* favour ♦ **per f.** please
favorévole *agg.* favourable
favorìre *v. tr.* **1** to favour, to support **2** (*promuovere*) to promote, to encourage
favoritìsmo *s. m.* favouritism
favorìto *agg. e s. m.* favourite
fazióso *agg.* factious
fazzolétto *s. m.* handkerchief ♦ **f. di carta** paper tissue
febbràio *s. m.* February
fèbbre *s. f.* fever ♦ **f. da fieno** hay-fever
febbricitànte *agg.* feverish
féccia *s. f.* dregs *pl.*
fèci *s. f. pl.* faeces
fècola *s. f.* flour ♦ **f. di patate** potato flour
fecondàre *v. tr.* to fertilize
fecondazióne *s. f.* fecundation, fertilization
fecóndo *agg.* fertile, prolific
féde *s. f.* **1** faith **2** (*anello*) wedding ring
fedéle *agg.* **1** faithful, loyal **2** (*veritiero*) true, exact
fedeltà *s. f.* fidelity, faithfulness
fèdera *s. f.* pillowcase
federàle *agg.* federal
federazióne *s. f.* federation
fégato *s. m.* **1** liver **2** (*fig.*) courage, guts *pl.*
félce *s. f.* fern
felìce *agg.* **1** happy, pleased, glad **2** (*fortunato*) lucky
felicità *s. f.* happiness
felicitàrsi *v. intr. pron.* to congratulate
felicitazióni *s. f. pl.* congratulations
felìno A *agg.* feline, catlike **B** *s. m.* feline
félpa *s. f.* **1** (*tessuto*) plush **2** (*indumento*) sweatshirt
féltro *s. m.* felt
fémmina *s. f.* **1** female **2** (*bambina, ragazza*) girl **3** (*di animale*) she-, (*di grande mammifero*) cow-
femminìle *agg.* **1** (*di sesso*) female **2** (*di donna*) feminine, woman's **3** (*gramm.*) feminine
femminìsmo *s. m.* feminism
fèmore *s. m.* femur, thigh-bone
fendinébbia *agg. e s. m.* fog-light
fenìcio *agg. e s. m.* Phoenician
fenicòttero *s. m.* flamingo
fenomenàle *agg.* phenomenal
fenòmeno *s. m.* **1** phenomenon **2** (*oggetto di meraviglia*) wonder
fèretro *s. m.* coffin
ferìàle *agg.* weekday (*attr*), working (*attr*)
fèrie *s. f. pl.* holidays *pl.*, vacation
feriménto *s. m.* wounding
ferìre A *v. tr.* to wound, to injure, to hurt **B** *v. rifl. e intr. pron.* to hurt oneself, to wound oneself
ferìta *s. f.* wound, hurt
feritóia *s. f.* loophole
férma *s. f.* (*mil.*) service
fermàglio *s. m.* clasp, clip
fermàre A *v. tr.* **1** to stop, to halt **2** (*interrompere*) to stop, to interrupt **3** (*dir*) to hold **4** (*fissare*) to fix, to fasten **B** *v. intr.* to stop **C** *v. rifl. e intr. pron.* **1** to stop **2** (*trattenersi*) to stay **3** (*fare una pausa*) to make a pause **4** (*mecc.*) to stall
fermàta *s. f.* stop, halt ♦ **divieto di f.** no stopping; **f. obbligatoria/a richiesta** regular/request stop
fermentazióne *s. f.* fermentation
ferménto *s. m.* ferment
ferméżza *s. f.* firmness
férmo A *agg.* **1** still, motionless **2** (*saldo*) firm, steady **B** *s. m.* **1** (*blocco*) lock, stop **2** (*arresto*) (provisional) arrest
fermopòsta *agg. e avv.* poste restante, (*USA*) general delivery
feróce *agg.* ferocious, fierce, wild
ferragósto *s. m.* feast of the Assumption
ferraménta *s. f.* **1** hardware, ironware, ironmongery **2** (*negozio*) hardware store, ironmonger's shop
fèrreo *agg.* iron (*attr*)
fèrro *s. m.* **1** iron **2** *al pl.* (*ceppi*) irons *pl.*, chains *pl.* **3** (*attrezzi*) instruments *pl.*, tools *pl.* ♦ **f. da calza** knitting-needle; **f. da stiro** iron; **f. di cavallo** horseshoe
ferrovìa *s. f.* railway, (*USA*) railroad ♦ **per f.** by rail
ferroviàrio *agg.* railway (*attr*), (*USA*) railroad (*attr*) ♦ **orario f.** train timetable
ferrovière *s. m.* railwayman, (*USA*) railroader
fèrtile *agg.* fertile, fruitful
fertilizzànte A *agg.* fertilizing **B** *s. m.* fertilizer
fèrvido *agg.* fervent
fervóre *s. m.* fervour, heat
fesserìa *s. f.* **1** nonsense, rubbish **2** (*ine-*

zia) trifle, nothing
fésso *agg.* stupid, foolish
fessùra *s. f.* crack, slit, fissure, (*per gettone*) slot
fèsta *s. f.* **1** (*solennità religiosa*) feast, festivity **2** (*giorno di vacanza*) holiday **3** (*ricevimento*) party
festeggiaménto *s. m.* celebration
festeggiàre *v. tr.* **1** to celebrate **2** (*accogliere festosamente*) to give a hearty welcome to
festività *s. f.* festivity, holiday ♦ **f. civile** public holiday
festìvo *agg.* holiday (*attr*), Sunday (*attr*)
festóso *agg.* joyful, merry, hearty
fetìccio *s. m.* fetish
feticìsmo *s. m.* fetishism
fèto *s. m.* f(o)etus
fétta *s. f.* slice
feudàle *agg.* feudal
feudalésimo *s. m.* feudalism
fèudo *s. m.* fief, feud
fiàba *s. f.* fairy tale, tale, story
fiabésco *agg.* **1** fairy, fairy-tale (*attr*) **2** (*favoloso*) fabulous
fiàcca *s. f.* **1** (*stanchezza*) weariness **2** (*indolenza*) indolence, laziness
fiaccàre *v. tr.* to weaken, to exhaust
fiàcco *agg.* **1** (*stanco*) weary, slack **2** (*debole*) weak, limp
fiàccola *s. f.* torch
fiàla *s. f.* phial
fiàmma *s. f.* flame, (*viva*) blaze ♦ **alla f.** flambé; **ritorno di f.** backfire
fiammànte *agg.* **1** flaming, blazing **2** (*fig.*) bright
fiammàta *s. f.* burst of flame
fiammeggiàre **A** *v. intr.* to blaze, to flame **B** *v. tr.* (*cuc.*) to singe
fiammìfero *s. m.* match
fiammìngo **A** *agg.* Flemish **B** *s. m.* Fleming
fiancàta *s. f.* side, flank
fiancheggiàre *v. tr.* **1** to flank **2** (*sostenere*) to support
fiànco *s. m.* **1** side **2** (*anat.*) hip, (*zool.*) flank **3** (*mil.*) flank
fiàsco *s. m.* **1** flask **2** (*insuccesso*) fiasco, flop (*fam.*)
fiàto *s. m.* breath
fìbbia *s. f.* buckle
fìbra *s. f.* fibre, (*USA*) fiber
ficcàre **A** *v. tr.* **1** to thrust, to drive **2** (*mettere*) to put, to stuff **B** *v. rifl.* to dive, to hide
fìco *s. m.* fig
fidanzaménto *s. m.* engagement
fidanzàrsi *v. rifl. e rifl. rec.* to become engaged, to get engaged
fidanzàta *s. f.* fiancée
fidanzàto *s. m.* fiancé
fidàre **A** *v. intr.* to trust **B** *v. intr. pron.* to trust, to rely on
fidàto *agg.* trustworthy, reliable
fidùcia *s. f.* confidence, reliance, trust
fièle *s. m.* gall
fienìle *s. m.* barn, hayloft
fièno *s. m.* hay
fièra (1) *s. f.* **1** (*mostra*) fair, exhibition **2** (*festa*) fête ♦ **f. campionaria** trade fair
fièra (2) *s. f.* (*animale feroce*) wild beast
fierézza *s. f.* **1** (*orgoglio*) pride **2** (*audacia*) boldness
fierìstico *agg.* fair (*attr*)
fièro *agg.* **1** (*orgoglioso*) proud **2** (*audace*) bold **3** (*indomito*) untamed **4** (*severo*) severe
fìfa *s. f.* (*fam.*) fright
fìglia *s. f.* daughter
figliàstro *s. m.* stepson
fìglio *s. m.* son, child
figùra *s. f.* **1** figure **2** (*forma, sagoma*) shape, form **3** (*illustrazione*) picture ♦ **fare bella/brutta f.** to cut a fine/poor figure
figuràccia *s. f.* poor figure
figuràre **A** *v. tr.* **1** to represent **2** (*immaginare*) to imagine, to picture **B** *v. intr.* **1** (*apparire*) to appear, to be **2** (*far figura*) to make a good impression
figuratìvo *agg.* figurative
figurìna *s. m.* **1** (*statuetta*) figurine **2** (*da raccolta*) picture-card
fìla *s. f.* **1** line, file, row **2** (*coda*) queue, line **3** (*serie*) string, series ♦ **fare la f.** to queue (up)
filantropìa *s. f.* philanthropy
filàntropo *s. m.* philanthropist
filàre **A** *v. tr.* to spin **B** *v. intr.* **1** (*correre*) to run, to make off **2** (*di ragionamento*) to hang together **3** (*amoreggiare*) to flirt **4** (*comportarsi bene*) to behave
filarmònica *s. f.* philharmonic society
filastròcca *s. f.* rigmarole
filatelìa *s. f.* philately
filàto *s. m.* yarn
filétto *s. m.* **1** (*bordo*) border **2** (*mecc.*) thread **3** (*cuc.*) fillet

filiàle A *agg.* filial B *s. f.* branch
filifórme *agg.* filiform
filigràna *s. f.* 1 filigree 2 (*della carta*) watermark
film *s. m. inv.* 1 film, (motion) picture, (*USA*) movie 2 (*pellicola, strato*) film
filmàre *v. tr.* to film, to shoot
filo *s. m.* 1 thread, (*tess.*) yarn 2 (*di metallo*) wire 3 (*tel., elettr.*) cable, wire 4 (*di collana*) string 5 (*taglio*) edge ♦ **f. d'erba** blade of grass; **f. spinato** barbed wire
filobus *s. m.* trolleybus
filologìa *s. f.* philology
filóne *s. m.* 1 (*miner.*) vein 2 (*di pane*) long loaf 3 (*fig.*) trend, current
filosofìa *s. f.* philosophy
filosòfico *agg.* philosophic(al)
filòsofo *s. m.* philosopher
filtràre *v. tr. e intr.* to filter
fìltro *s. m.* filter
fìlza *s. f.* string
finàle A *agg.* final B *s. m.* end, conclusion C *s. f.* (*sport*) ending, finals *pl.*
finalìsta *s. m. e f.* finalist
finalità *s. f.* aim, purpose, end
finalménte *avv.* at last, (*da ultimo*) finally
finànza *s. f.* finance
finanziaménto *s. m.* financing, loan, (*somma*) fund
finanziàrio *agg.* financial
finanzière *s. m.* 1 financier 2 (*guardia di finanza*) customs officer, revenue officer
finché *cong.* 1 until, till 2 (*per tutto il tempo che*) as long as
fìne (1) A *s. f.* end, ending, conclusion B *s. m.* 1 (*scopo*) aim, purpose, object 2 (*risultato*) result, conclusion
fìne (2) *agg.* 1 fine, thin 2 (*raffinato*) refined 3 (*acuto*) subtle
finèstra *s. f.* window
finestrìno *s. m.* window
fìngere A *v. tr. e intr.* to pretend, to simulate, to feign B *v. rifl.* to pretend
finimóndo *s. m.* bedlam, pandemonium
finìre A *v. tr.* 1 to finish, to end 2 (*esaurire*) to finish, to sell out 3 (*uccidere*) to kill B *v. intr.* 1 to finish, to end (up) 2 (*smettere*) to stop 3 (*esaurirsi*) to run out, to sell out 4 (*cacciarsi*) to get to
finìto *agg.* 1 finished 2 (*limitato*) finite 3 (*rovinato*) done for
finitùra *s. f.* finish, finishing
fìno (1) *agg.* 1 (*sottile*) fine, thin 2 (*acuto*) subtle, sharp 3 (*puro*) fine, pure
fìno (2) A *prep.* 1 (*tempo*) until, till, up to 2 (*luogo*) as far as B *avv.* even ♦ **f. da** since
finòcchio *s. m.* fennel
finóra *avv.* till now, up to now, yet
fìnta *s. f.* pretence, feint
fìnto *agg.* 1 (*falso*) false, insincere 2 (*simulato*) feigned 3 (*artificiale*) dummy, artificial, false
finzióne *s. f.* 1 pretence, make-believe 2 (*invenzione*) fiction, invention
fiòcco *s. m.* 1 bow 2 (*bioccolo*) flock 3 (*cuc.*) flake 4 (*naut.*) jib ♦ **con i fiocchi** excellent; **f. di neve** snowflake
fiòcina *s. f.* harpoon
fiòco *agg.* 1 weak, (*di suono*) faint 2 (*rauco*) hoarse
fiónda *s. f.* catapult, sling
fioràio *s. m.* florist
fiordalìso *s. m.* cornflower
fiòrdo *s. m.* fiord
fióre *s. m.* 1 flower, (*di albero da frutto*) blossom 2 (*carte da gioco*) clubs *pl.* 3 (*parte scelta*) the best part, the flower
fiorènte *agg.* 1 blooming 2 (*fig.*) flourishing
fiorétto *s. m.* (*arma*) foil
fiorièra *s. f.* flower box
fiorìre *v. intr.* 1 to flower, to blossom, to bloom 2 (*fig.*) to flourish
fioritùra *s. f.* 1 flowering, blooming, (*di alberi da frutto*) blossoming 2 (*fig.*) flourishing
fìrma *s. f.* signature
firmaménto *s. m.* firmament
firmàre *v. tr.* to sign
fisarmònica *s. f.* accordion
fiscàle *agg.* 1 fiscal, tax (*attr.*) 2 (*fig.*) strict
fischiàre A *v. intr.* 1 to whistle, (*per disapprovazione*) to boo 2 (*di segnale acustico*) to hoot 3 (*di proiettile*) to whiz(z) 4 (*di orecchie*) to buzz B *v. tr.* to whistle, (*per disapprovazione*) to boo
fìschio *s. m.* 1 whistle, (*di disapprovazione*) boo 2 (*di segnale acustico*) hoot 3 (*di proiettile*) whiz(z) 4 (*nelle orecchie*) buzzing
fìsco *s. m.* revenue, (*ufficio*) tax office
fìsica *s. f.* physics *pl.* (*v. al sing.*)
fìsico A *agg.* physical B *s. m.* 1 (*scienziato*) physicist 2 (*costituzione*) physique, body
fisiologìa *s. f.* physiology
fisiològico *agg.* physiologic

fisionomìa *s. f.* physiognomy
fisionomìsta *s. m. e f.* physiognomist
fisioterapìa *s. f.* physiotherapy
fisioterapìsta *s. m. e f.* physiotherapist
fissàre A *v. tr.* **1** (*rendere fisso*) to fix, to fasten, to make firm **2** (*guardare fisso*) to stare, to gaze **3** (*stabilire*) to fix, to arrange, to set **4** (*prenotare*) to book, to reserve **B** *v. intr. pron.* **1** to be fixed **2** (*ostinarsi*) to set one's heart on **3** (*stabilirsi*) to settle
fissazióne *s. f.* **1** fixing, fixation **2** (*idea ossessiva*) obsession
fìsso A *agg.* fixed **B** *avv.* fixedly
fìtta *s. f.* sharp pain, pang
fittìzio *agg.* fictitious
fìtto *agg.* thick, packed ♦ **a capo f.** head downwards
fiumàna *s. f.* stream, flood
fiùme *s. m.* **1** river **2** (*fig.*) flood, stream
fiutàre *v. tr.* **1** to smell, to sniff **2** (*la selvaggina*) to scent **3** (*fig.*) to scent, to smell
fiùto *s. m.* **1** scent **2** (*fig.*) nose
flagellazióne *s. f.* flagellation, scourging
flagèllo *s. m.* scourge
flagrànte *agg.* flagrant
flanèlla *s. f.* flannel
flash *s. m. inv.* **1** (*fot.*) flash **2** (*notizia giornalistica*) newsflash
flàuto *s. m.* flute
flèbile *agg.* feeble
fleboclìsi *s. f.* phleboclysis
flemmàtico *agg.* phlegmatic, cool
flessìbile *agg.* flexible, supple
flessióne *s. f.* **1** flexion **2** (*calo*) decrease, drop
flessuóso *agg.* flexuous
flèttere *v. tr.* to bend, to bow
flogòsi *s. f.* phlogosis
flòra *s. f.* flora
floreàle *agg.* floral
floricoltùra *s. f.* floriculture
flòrido *agg.* flourishing, (*prosperoso*) buxom
florilègio *s. m.* florilegium, anthology
flòscio *agg.* flabby, soft
flòtta *s. f.* fleet
flottìglia *s. f.* flotilla
flùido A *agg.* fluid, flowing **B** *s. m.* fluid
fluìre *v. intr.* to flow
fluorescènte *agg.* fluorescent
fluòro *s. m.* fluorine
flùsso *s. m.* **1** flow, stream **2** (*fis.*) flux
fluttuànte *agg.* fluctuating, floating
fluttuàre *v. intr.* **1** to fluctuate, to rise and fall **2** (*econ.*) to fluctuate, to float
fluviàle *agg.* river (*attr*)
fobìa *s. f.* phobia
fòca *s. f.* seal
focalizzàre *v. tr.* to focus
fóce *s. f.* mouth
focolàio *s. m.* **1** (*med.*) focus **2** (*fig.*) hotbed
focolàre *s. m.* **1** hearth, fireplace **2** (*fig.*) home
fòdera *s. f.* (*interna*) lining, (*esterna*) cover
foderàre *v. tr.* (*internamente*) to line, (*esternamente*) to cover
fòdero *s. m.* sheath
fóga *s. f.* impetuosity, ardour
fòggia *s. f.* **1** manner, fashion **2** (*forma*) shape
fòglia *s. f.* leaf
fogliàme *s. m.* foliage
fogliétto *s. m.* slip of paper
fòglio *s. m.* **1** sheet **2** (*pagina*) leaf **3** (*banconota*) bank note **4** (*di metallo*) plate
fógna *s. f.* sewer, drain
fognatùra *s. f.* sewerage system, drainage system
föhn *s. m. inv.* (*asciugacapelli*) hairdryer
folclóre *s. m.* folklore
folclorìstico *agg.* folklore (*attr*), folk (*attr*)
folgoràre *v. tr.* **1** (*elettr*) to electrocute **2** (*fig.*) to dazzle
folgorazióne *s. f.* **1** (*elettr*) electrocution **2** (*fig.*) flash
fòlla *s. f.* crowd, throng
fòlle *agg.* **1** mad, insane **2** (*pazzesco*) foolish, wild **3** (*mecc.*) neutral
folleggiàre *v. intr.* to make marry, to frolic
folleménte *avv.* madly
follìa *s. f.* **1** madness, insanity **2** (*azione folle*) folly
fólto *agg.* **1** thick **2** (*est.*) large, great
fomentàre *v. tr.* to foment, to encourage, to foster
fóndaco *s. m.* warehouse
fondàle *s. m.* **1** (*teatro*) back-drop **2** (*naut.*) sounding, depth
fondamentàle *agg.* fundamental, basic
fondaménto *s. m.* foundation
fondàre A *v. tr.* **1** to found, to erect **2** (*istituire*) to found, to establish **3** (*basare*) to found, to base, to ground **B** *v. rifl. e intr. pron.* to base oneself, to be based on
fondatóre *s. m.* founder
fondazióne *s. f.* foundation

fondènte A *agg.* melting **B** *s. m.* (dolce) fondant ♦ **cioccolato f.** plain chocolate
fóndere A *v. tr.* **1** (*liquefare*) to melt, to fuse **2** (*metalli*) to cast, to mould **3** (*mescolare*) to blend, to merge **B** *v. intr. e intr. pron.* to melt **C** *v. rifl. e rifl. rec.* to merge
fonderìa *s. f.* foundry
fondiàrio *agg.* land (*attr*), landed
fondìsta *s. m. e f.* long-distance runner
fóndo A *agg.* deep **B** *s. m.* **1** bottom, (*estremità*) end **2** (*feccia*) dregs *pl.* **3** (*sfondo*) background **4** (*econ.*) fund ♦ **piatto f.** soup-plate; **sci di f.** cross-country skiing
fondovàlle *s. m.* valley bottom
fonètica *s. f.* phonetics *pl.* (*v. al sing.*)
fonètico *agg.* phonetic
fontàna *s. f.* fountain
fónte A *s. f.* source, spring **B** *s. m.* (*battesimale*) font ♦ **f. di energia** source of power
footing *s. m. inv.* jogging
foràggio *s. m.* forage, fodder
foràre A *v. tr.* to pierce, to punch **B** *v. intr.* (*pneumatico*) to get a flat tyre, to puncture
foratùra *s. f.* piercing, (*di pneumatico*) puncture
fòrbici *s. f. pl.* scissors *pl.*
fórca *s. f.* **1** fork **2** (*patibolo*) gallows *pl.*
forcèlla *s. f.* fork
forchétta *s. f.* fork
forcìna *s. f.* hairpin
forènse *agg.* forensic
forèsta *s. f.* forest
forestièro A *agg.* foreign, alien **B** *s. m.* foreigner
forfait *s. m. inv.* lump-sum ♦ **dichiarare f.** to default, to scratch
fórfora *s. f.* dandruff
forgiàre *v. tr.* **1** to forge **2** (*modellare*) to shape, to mould
fórma *s. f.* **1** shape, form **2** (*stampo*) mould **3** (*genere, tipo, stile, procedura*) form **4** (*formalità*) formality, form, appearance **5** *al pl.* (*di persona*) figure **6** (*forma fisica*) form, fitness
formàggio *s. m.* cheese ♦ **f. magro** skimmed cheese; **f. piccante** strong cheese
formàle *agg.* formal
formalìsmo *s. m.* formalism
formalità *s. f.* formality, form ♦ **senza f.** informally
formalizzàre A *v. tr.* to formalize **B** *v. intr. pron.* to be shocked
formàre A *v. tr.* **1** to form, to make **2** (*modellare*) to shape, to mould **B** *v. intr. pron.* to form
formazióne *s. f.* **1** formation **2** (*addestramento*) training
formìca *s. f.* ant
formicàio *s. m.* anthill
formicolàre *v. intr.* **1** (*brulicare*) to swarm, to be full **2** (*prudere*) to tingle
formicolìo *s. m.* **1** swarming **2** (*intorpidimento*) tingling, pins and needles
formidàbile *agg.* **1** formidable, terrible **2** (*straordinario*) wonderful
formóso *agg.* buxom, shapely
fòrmula *s. f.* formula
formulàre *v. tr.* **1** to formulate **2** (*esprimere*) to express
formulàrio *s. m.* formulary, form
fornàce *s. f.* furnace, (*per laterizi*) kiln
fornàio *s. m.* baker, (*negozio*) bakery
fornèllo *s. m.* stove, cooker
fòrnice *s. m.* fornix
fornìre A *v. tr.* to furnish, to supply, to provide **B** *v. rifl.* to stock up
fornitóre *s. m.* supplier
fórno *s. m.* **1** oven **2** (*negozio*) bakery
fóro (1) *s. m.* hole
fóro (2) *s. m.* (*dir*) forum, court of justice
fórse *avv.* **1** perhaps, maybe **2** (*probabilmente*) probably **3** (*circa*) about
forsennàto *s. m.* madman, lunatic
fòrte A *agg.* **1** strong **2** (*di suono*) loud **3** (*di malattia*) bad, severe **4** (*considerevole*) large, heavy **5** (*profondo*) deep **B** *avv.* **1** strongly, hard **2** (*a volume alto*) loudly, loud **3** (*velocemente*) fast **4** (*con intensità*) hard, hardly
fortézza *s. f.* fortress
fortificàre *v. tr.* to fortify
fortificazióne *s. f.* fortification
fortìno *s. m.* blockhouse
fortùito *agg.* fortuitous, chance (*attr*)
fortùna *s. f.* **1** fortune, luck **2** (*successo*) success **3** (*emergenza*) emergency
fortunataménte *avv.* luckily
fortunàto *agg.* lucky, fortunate
fòrza *s. f.* **1** strength, force **2** (*potere*) power **3** (*mil., fis.*) force **4** (*violenza*) force
forzàre A *v. tr.* **1** to force, to compel **2** (*sforzare*) to strain **B** *v. rifl.* to force oneself
forzàto *agg.* forced
forzatùra *s. f.* forcing
forzière *s. m.* coffer

foschìa *s. f.* haze, mist
fósco *agg.* gloomy, dark
fosforescènte *agg.* phosphorescent
fòsforo *s. m.* phosphor(us)
fòssa *s. f.* **1** ditch, trench **2** (*tomba*) grave
fossàto *s. m.* ditch
fòssile *agg. e s. m.* fossil
fossilizzàrsi *v. tr. e intr. pron.* to fossilize
fòsso *s. m.* ditch, trench
fòto *s. f.* → **fotografia**
fotocèllula *s. f.* photocell
fotocolor *s. m. inv.* colour photograph
fotocòpia *s. f.* photocopy
fotocopiàre *v. tr.* to photocopy
fotogènico *agg.* photogenic
fotografàre *v. tr.* to photograph, to take a picture
fotografìa *s. f.* **1** (*arte*) photography **2** (*immagine*) photo(graph)
fotogràfico *agg.* photographic ♦ **macchina fotografica** camera
fotògrafo *s. m.* photographer
fotomodèlla *s. f.* model
fotomontàggio *s. m.* photomontage
fotorepòrter *s. m. inv.* photoreporter, press-photographer
fra *prep.* **1** (*fra due termini*) between, (*fra più di due termini*) among **2** (*in mezzo*) amid, amidst **3** (*partitivo e dopo un sup. rel.*) among, of **4** (*tempo*) in, within (*distrib.*) among
fracassàre **A** *v. tr.* to smash, to shatter **B** *v. intr. pron.* to break up
fracàsso *s. m.* din, racket
fràdicio *agg.* **1** (*marcio*) rotten **2** (*zuppo*) wet through, soaked ♦ **ubriaco f.** dead drunk
fràgile *agg.* **1** fragile, brittle **2** (*fig.*) frail, fragile
fràgola *s. f.* strawberry
fragóre *s. m.* uproar, rumble
fragoróso *agg.* loud, rumbling
fragrànte *agg.* fragrant
fraintèndere *v. tr. e intr.* to misunderstand
frammentàre **A** *v. tr.* to split up, to subdivide **B** *v. intr. pron.* to fragment, to split
frammentàrio *agg.* fragmentary
framménto *s. m.* fragment, splinter
fràna *s. f.* landslide
franàre *v. intr.* **1** to slide down **2** (*est.*) to collapse, to fall in
francaménte *avv.* frankly, openly
francése **A** *agg.* French **B** *s. m. e f.* (*abitante*) Frenchman *m.*, Frenchwoman *f.* **C** *s. m.* (*lingua*) French
franchézza *s. f.* frankness, openness
franchìgia *s. f.* immunity, franchise
frànco (1) *agg.* **1** frank, open, sincere **2** (*comm.*) free, franco
frànco (2) *s. m.* (*moneta*) franc
francobóllo *s. m.* stamp
francòfono *agg.* Francophone
frangènte *s. m.* **1** breaker **2** (*situazione difficile*) predicament, awkward situation
frangétta *s. f.* fringe
fràngia *s. f.* fringe
frangiflùtti *agg. e s. m. inv.* breakwater
franóso *agg.* subject to landslides
frantóio *s. m.* crusher, (*per olive*) oil mill
frantumàre *v. tr.* to shatter, to crush
frappé *s. m.* shake
frappórre **A** *v. tr.* to interpose, to put **B** *v. rifl. e intr. pron.* to intervene, to interfere
fràsca *s. f.* branch
fràse *s. f.* **1** sentence, period **2** (*locuzione, espressione*) phrase ♦ **f. fatta** cliché
fraseològico *agg.* phraseologic(al) ♦ **verbo f.** phrasal verb
fràssino *s. m.* ash
frastagliàto *agg.* indented, jagged
frastornàre *v. tr.* to confuse, to daze
frastornàto *agg.* confused, dazed
frastuòno *s. m.* noise, din
fràte *s. m.* friar, monk, (*appellativo*) Brother
fratellànza *s. f.* brotherhood, fraternity
fratellàstro *s. m.* half-brother
fratèllo *s. m.* brother
fraternizzàre *v. intr.* to fraternize
fratèrno *agg.* fraternal
frattàglie *s. f. pl.* chitterlings *pl.*, entrails *pl.*
frattànto *avv.* meanwhile
frattùra *s. f.* **1** fracture **2** (*est.*) break, rupture
fratturàre *v. tr. e intr. pron.* to fracture, to break
frazionàre **A** *v. tr.* to divide, to split **B** *v. rifl. o intr. pron.* to split
frazióne *s. f.* **1** fraction **2** (*di comune*) hamlet
fréccia *s. f.* **1** arrow **2** (*autom.*) indicator
freddaménte *avv.* coldly, coolly
freddàre **A** *v. tr.* **1** to cool **2** (*ammazzare*) to kill **B** *v. intr. pron.* to become cold
freddézza *s. f.* coldness
fréddo **A** *agg.* cold, chilly, (*fresco*) cool **B** *s. m.* cold, coldness, chilliness
freddolóso *agg.* sensitive to cold
freddùra *s. f.* witticism
fregàre *v. tr.* **1** to rub **2** (*fam.*) (*rubare*) to

pinch, to nick **3** (*fam.*) (*imbrogliare*) to cheat ♦ **fregarsene** not to give a damn
fregàta *s. f.* (*naut.*) frigate
fregatùra *s. f.* cheat, swindle
frégio *s. m.* **1** (*arch.*) frieze **2** ornament
frèmere *v. intr.* to tremble, to quiver, to throb
frenàre **A** *v. tr.* **1** to brake **2** (*fig.*) to restrain, to check **B** *v. intr.* to brake **C** *v. rifl.* to restrain oneself
frenàta *s. f.* braking
frenesìa *s. f.* frenzy
frenètico *agg.* frantic, frenzied
fréno *s. m.* **1** brake **2** (*fig.*) restraint, check
frequentàre **A** *v. tr.* **1** to frequent, to go often to, (*scuola*) to attend **2** (*persone*) to frequent, to go round with, to associate with **B** *v. rifl. rec.* to see one another
frequènte *agg.* frequent
frequenteménte *avv.* frequently, often
frequènza *s. f.* **1** frequency **2** (*assiduità*) attendance
frèsa *s. f.* cutter
freschézza *s. f.* **1** freshness **2** (*di temperatura*) coolness
frésco **A** *agg.* **1** fresh **2** (*di temperatura*) cool, fresh, chilly **B** *s. m.* cool, coolness ♦ **tenere in f.** to keep in a cool place
frétta *s. f.* hurry, haste
frettolóso *agg.* hasty, hurried
friàbile *agg.* friable
frìggere *v. tr. e intr.* to fry
frìgido *agg.* frigid
frìgo → **frigorifero**
frigorìfero **A** *agg.* refrigerating, freezing **B** *s. m.* fridge
fringuèllo *s. m.* finch
frittàta *s. f.* omelette
frìtto **A** *agg.* fried **B** *s. m.* fry
frittùra *s. f.* fry
frìvolo *agg.* frivolous
frizióne *s. f.* **1** (*sulla pelle*) rubbing, friction **2** (*fis.*) friction **3** (*mecc., autom.*) clutch
frizzànte *agg.* **1** (*di bevanda*) fizzy, sparkling **2** (*di aria*) crisp
frodàre *v. tr.* to defraud, to cheat
fròde *s. f.* fraud, cheating
frollàre *v. tr.* to hang
frónda *s. f.* branch
frontàle *agg.* frontal
frónte **A** *s. f.* **1** forehead **2** (*di edificio*) front, frontage **B** *s. m.* front ♦ **di f. a** opposite, in front of, (*paragone*) in comparison with
fronteggiàre **A** *v. tr.* to face up, **B** *v. rifl. rec.* to face each other
frontespìzio *s. m.* frontispiece, title-page
frontièra *s. f.* frontier, boundary
frontóne *s. m.* pediment, fronton
frónzolo *s. m.* frill, frippery
fròttola *s. f.* fib
frugàle *agg.* frugal
frugàre *v. tr. e intr.* to rummage, to ransack
fruìre *v. intr.* to enjoy
frullàre *v. tr.* to whip, to whisk
frullàto *s. m.* shake
frullatóre *s. m.* mixer
fruménto *s. m.* wheat
frusciàre *v. intr.* to rustle
fruscìo *s. m.* rustle
frùsta *s. f.* **1** whip **2** (*cuc.*) whisk
frustàre *v. tr.* to whip, to flog
frustìno *s. m.* crop
frustràre *v. tr.* to frustrate
frustrazióne *s. f.* frustration
frùtta *s. f.* fruit
fruttàre **A** *v. tr.* to yield, to make **B** *v. intr.* to bear fruit
fruttéto *s. m.* orchard
fruttificàre *v. intr.* to fructify, to bear fruit
fruttivéndolo *s. m.* greengrocer
frùtto *s. m.* **1** fruit **2** (*econ.*) interest, return ♦ **frutti di mare** shellfish, (*USA*) seafood
fu *agg.* late
fucilàre *v. tr.* to shoot
fucilàta *s. f.* (gun)shot
fucìle *s. m.* gun, rifle
fucìna *s. f.* forge
fùga *s. f.* **1** flight, escape **2** (*fuoriuscita*) leak **3** (*mus.*) fugue **4** (*sport*) sprint
fugàce *agg.* fleeting, short-lived
fugacità *s. f.* transiency
fuggévole *agg.* fleeting
fuggiàsco *agg. e s. m.* fugitive
fuggìre **A** *v. intr.* to flee, to run away, to escape **B** *v. tr.* to avoid
fùlcro *s. m.* fulcrum
fùlgido *agg.* shining
fulgóre *s. m.* brightness, splendour
fulìggine *s. f.* soot
fulminànte *agg.* fulminant
fulminàre **A** *v. tr.* **1** to strike by lightning **2** (*colpire*) to strike down, to strike dead **B** *v. intr. pron.* (*di lampadina*) to burn out
fùlmine *s. m.* lightning, thunderbolt
fulmìneo *agg.* lightning, instantaneous
fumaiòlo *s. m.* funnel
fumàre **A** *v. tr.* to smoke **B** *v. intr.* **1** to smoke **2** (*emettere vapore*) to fume, to

steam
fumàta *s. f.* **1** smoke **2** (*segnale*) smoke signal
fumatóre *s. m.* smoker
fumétto *s. m.* strip cartoon, comics *pl.*
fùmo *s. m.* **1** smoke **2** (*il fumare*) smoking **3** (*vapore*) fume, steam
fumóso *agg.* **1** smoky, smoking **2** (*fig.*) obscure
funàmbolo *s. m.* tigh-trope walker
fùne *s. f.* rope, cable
fùnebre *agg.* **1** funeral (*attr*) **2** (*lugubre*) funereal, mournful
funeràle *s. m.* funeral
funeràrio *agg.* funerary
funestàre *v. tr.* to devastate
fùngere *v. intr.* to act (as)
fùngo *s. m.* mushroom, (*bot.*, *med.*) fungus ♦ **f. velenoso** toadstool
funicolàre *s. f.* funicular, cable rail
funivìa *s. f.* cableway
funzionàle *agg.* **1** functional **2** (*pratico*) practical, useful
funzionalismo *s. m.* functionalism
funzionalità *s. f.* functionality
funzionaménto *s. m.* working, operation
funzionàre *v. intr.* to work, to operate, to run ♦ **far f. q.c.** to operate st., to make st. work
funzionàrio *s. m.* official, functionary
funzióne *s. f.* **1** (*ruolo, scopo*) function, role, task **2** (*carica*) function, office, position **3** (*funzionamento*) operation, working **4** (*relig.*) ceremony, service **5** (*scient.*) function
fuòco *s. m.* **1** fire **2** (*fornello*) burner **3** (*fis.*, *fot.*) focus
fuorché **A** *cong.* except, but **B** *prep.* except (for), excepting
fuòri **A** *avv.* **1** out, outside, (*all'aperto*) outdoors **2** (*lontano*) away **B** *prep.* **f. da/di** out of, outside ♦ **f. orario** out of hours; **f. servizio** out of order
fuoribórdo *s. m. inv.* outboard
fuoriclàsse *agg. e s. m. e f.* champion
fuorilégge **A** *agg.* illegal **B** *s. m. e f.* outlaw
fuoristràda *s. m. inv.* cross-country vehicle
fuoriuscìre *v. intr.* to come out
fuoriuscita *s. f.* discharge, emission
fùrbo *agg.* cunning, shrewd
furènte *agg.* raging, furious
furfànte *s. m. e f.* rascal
furgóne *s. m.* van
fùria *s. f.* **1** fury, rage **2** (*fretta*) rush ♦ **a f. di** by dint of; **in fretta e f.** in a rush
furibóndo *agg.* **1** furious, enraged **2** (*violento*) violent
furióso *agg.* **1** furious, raging **2** (*violento*) violent, wild
furóre *s. m.* fury, rage
furtìvo *agg.* furtive
fùrto *s. m.* theft
fùsa *s. f. pl.* purr
fuscèllo *s. m.* twig
fusìbile **A** *agg.* fusible **B** *s. m.* fuse (*elettr.*)
fusióne *s. f.* **1** fusion **2** (*econ.*) merger, merging
fùso (1) *agg.* fused, melted
fùso (2) *s. m.* **1** (*tess.*) spindle **2** (*orario*) time zone
fusolièra *s. f.* fuselage
fustàgno *s. m.* fustian
fustigazióne *s. f.* flogging
fustìno *s. m.* box
fùsto *s. m.* **1** (*bot.*) stem, (*tronco*) trunk **2** (*arch.*) shaft **3** (*recipiente*) drum
fùtile *agg.* trifling
futilità *s. f.* futility
futurìsmo *s. m.* futurism
futùro *agg. e s. m.* future

G

gabbàre A *v. tr.* to cheat B *v. intr. pron.* to make fun
gabbia *s. f.* cage
gabbiàno *s. m.* sea-gull
gabinétto *s. m.* 1 consulting room, (*med.*) surgery, (*scient.*) laboratory 2 (*pol.*) cabinet 3 (*servizi igienici*) toilet, lavatory, wc
gaffe *s. f. inv.* blunder
gagliardétto *s. m.* pennant
gagliàrdo *agg.* strong, vigorous
gàio *agg.* gay
gàla *s. f.* 1 (*festa*) gala 2 (*trina*) frill
galànte *agg.* 1 gallant 2 (*amoroso*) love (*attr*), amorous
galanterìa *s. f.* gallantry
galantuòmo *s. m.* gentleman
galàssia *s. f.* galaxy
galatèo *s. m.* etiquette, (good) manners *pl.*
galeóne *s. m.* galleon
galeòtto *s. m.* convict
galèra *s. f.* 1 (*naut.*) galley 2 (*prigione*) jail, prison
gàlla *s. f.* gall
gàlla, a *loc. avv.* afloat, floating ♦ **stare a g.** to float; **venire a g.** to surface
galleggiànte A *agg.* floating B *s. m.* float
galleggiàre *v. intr.* to float
gallerìa *s. f.* 1 (*traforo*) tunnel 2 (*di miniera*) gallery, tunnel 3 (*per esposizione*) gallery 4 (*teatro, cin.*) circle, balcony 5 (*strada coperta*) arcade
gallése A *agg.* Welsh B *s. m. e f.* (*abitante*) Welshman *m.*, Welshwoman *f.* C *s. m.* (*lingua*) Welsh
gallétta *s. f.* biscuit
gallicìsmo *s. m.* Gallicism
gallìna *s. f.* hen
gàllo *s. m.* cock
gallóne (1) *s. m.* 1 galloon 2 (*mil.*) stripe
gallóne (2) *s. m.* (*unità di misura*) gallon
galoppàre *v. intr.* to gallop
galoppatóio *s. m.* riding track
galòppo *s. m.* gallop
gàmba *s. f.* 1 leg 2 (*di lettera, di nota musicale*) stem ♦ **essere in g.** to be smart
gamberétto *s. m.* prawn, (*di mare*) shrimp
gàmbero *s. m.* crayfish
gàmbo *s. m.* stem, stalk
gàmma *s. f.* range
ganàscia *s. f.* jaw
gàncio *s. m.* hook
gànghero *s. m.* hinge
gàra *s. f.* 1 competition, contest 2 (*sport*) competition, race, match 3 (*comm.*) tender
garage *s. m. inv.* garage
garànte *s. m.* guarantee, warranter
garantìre A *v. tr.* 1 to guarantee, to warrant 2 (*rendersi garante per*) to vouch for 3 (*assicurare*) to assure B *v. rifl.* to secure oneself
garanzìa *s. f.* guarantee, warrant, security
garbàto *agg.* polite, well-mannered
gàrbo *s. m.* politeness
gardènia *s. f.* gardenia
gareggiàre *v. intr.* to compete
gargarìsmo *s. m.* gargle
garìtta *s. f.* sentry box
garòfano *s. m.* carnation ♦ **chiodi di g.** cloves
gàrza *s. f.* gauze
garzóne *s. m.* 1 (*garzone*) boy 2 (*apprendista*) apprentice
gas *s. m.* gas ♦ **a tutto g.** at full speed; **g. di scarico** exhaust gas
gasàto *agg.* fizzy
gasòlio *s. m.* gas oil, diesel oil
gassóso *agg.* gaseous
gàstrico *agg.* gastric
gastrìte *s. f.* gastritis
gastrointestinàle *agg.* gastroenteric
gastronomìa *s. f.* gastronomy
gastronòmico *agg.* gastronomic
gattìno *s. m.* kitten
gàtto *s. m.* cat
gattopàrdo *s. m.* ocelot
gàudio *s. m.* joy
gavétta *s. f.* mess tin
gavitèllo *s. m.* buoy
gay *agg. e s. m. e f. inv.* gay
gàzza *s. f.* magpie
gazzèlla *s. f.* gazelle
gazzétta *s. f.* gazette
gel *s. m. inv.* gel
gelàre *v. tr. e intr.* to freeze
gelàta *s. f.* frost
gelatàio *s. m.* ice-cream man

gelaterìa *s. f.* ice-cream shop
gelatìna *s. f.* **1** (*cuc.*) jelly, gelatine **2** (*chim.*) gelatin(e)
gelàto **A** *agg.* icy, frozen **B** *s. m.* ice-cream
gèlido *agg.* icy, freezing
gèlo *s. m.* **1** cold **2** (*brina*) frost
gelóne *s. m.* chilblain
gelosìa *s. f.* **1** jealousy **2** (*invidia*) envy **3** (*cura scrupolosa*) solicitude
gelóso *agg.* **1** jealous **2** (*invidioso*) envious **3** (*possessivo*) particular, jealous
gèlso *s. m.* mulberry
gelsomìno *s. m.* jasmin(e)
gemellàggio *s. m.* twinning
gemèllo *agg. e s. m.* twin
gèmere *v. intr.* to moan, to groan
gèmito *s. m.* moan, groan
gèmma *s. f.* **1** gem, jewel **2** (*bot.*) bud
gène *s. m.* gene
genealogìa *s. f.* genealogy
generàle *agg. e s. m.* general
generalità *s. f.* **1** generality **2** (*maggior parte*) majority **3** *al pl.* personal particulars
generalizzàre *v. tr. e intr.* to generalize
generalménte *avv.* generally, as a rule
generàre **A** *v. tr.* **1** to give birth to, to procreate **2** (*produrre*) to produce **3** (*causare*) to beget **4** (*scient.*) to generate **B** *v. intr. pron.* to be generated
generatóre *s. m.* generator
generazionàle *agg.* generational
generazióne *s. f.* generation
gènere *s. m.* **1** kind, type, sort, family **2** (*biol.*) genus **3** (*gramm.*) gender **4** (*letter.*) genre **5** (*prodotto*) product, goods *pl.* ♦ **generi alimentari** foodstuff
genèrico *agg.* generic, general
gènero *s. m.* son-in-law
generosità *s. f.* generosity
generóso *agg.* generous, liberal
gènesi *s. f.* genesis, origin
genètica *s. f.* genetics *pl.* (*v. al sing.*)
genètico *agg.* genetic
gengìva *s. f.* gum
genìale *agg.* ingenious
genialità *s. f.* ingeniousness, genius
gènio *s. m.* **1** genius **2** (*inclinazione*) talent, gift **3** (*folletto*) genie, genius
genitàle **A** *agg.* genital **B** *s. m. al pl.* genitals, genitalia
genitóre *s. m.* parent
gennàio *s. m.* January
gentàglia *s. f.* rabble
gènte *s. f.* people
gentìle *agg.* **1** kind, courteous **2** (*delicato*) gentle
gentilézza *s. f.* **1** kindness **2** (*favore*) favour
gentilìzio *agg.* noble
gentiluòmo *s. m.* gentleman
genuinità *s. f.* genuineness
genuìno *agg.* genuine, authentic
geocentrismo *s. m.* geocentricism
geografìa *s. f.* geography
geogràfico *agg.* geographic(al) ♦ **carta geografica** map
geologìa *s. f.* geology
geològico *agg.* geologic(al)
geometrìa *s. f.* geometry
geomètrico *agg.* geometric(al)
geòrgico *agg.* georgic
geotèrmico *agg.* geothermal
gerànio *s. m.* geranium
gerarchìa *s. f.* hierarchy
geràrchico *agg.* hierarchic(al)
gerènte *s. m. e f.* manager
gergàle *agg.* slang (*attr.*)
gèrgo *s. m.* slang, (*professionale*) jargon
geriatrìa *s. f.* geriatrics *pl.* (*v. al sing.*)
germànico *agg.* Germanic
gèrme *s. m.* germ
germogliàre *v. intr.* to sprout, to germinate
germóglio *s. m.* bud, sprout
geroglìfico *s. m.* hieroglyph
gerùndio *s. m.* gerund
gerundìvo *s. m.* gerundive
gèsso *s. m.* **1** chalk **2** (*med., edil., scultura*) plaster
gèsta *s. f. pl.* deeds *pl.*
gestànte *s. f.* pregnant woman
gestazióne *s. f.* gestation
gestióne *s. f.* management
gestìre (1) *v. tr.* to run, to manage
gestìre (2) *v. intr.* (*gesticolare*) to gesticulate
gèsto *s. m.* **1** gesture, sign, (*del capo*) nod, (*della mano*) wave **2** (*azione*) act, deed
gestóre *s. m.* manager
gesuìta *s. m.* Jesuit
gettàre **A** *v. tr.* **1** to throw, (*con forza*) to hurl **2** (*tecnol.*) to cast **B** *v. rifl. e intr. pron.* **1** to throw oneself **2** (*di fiume*) to flow
gettàta *s. f.* **1** (*tecnol.*) cast, casting **2** (*di molo*) jetty
gèttito *s. m.* yield, revenue ♦ **g. fiscale** tax revenue
gètto *s. m.* **1** jet, spurt, shoot **2** (*bot.*) sprout **3** (*tecnol.*) casting **4** (*aer.*) jet
gettóne *s. m.* **1** token **2** (*per giochi*)

counter
ghétto *s. m.* ghetto
ghiacciàia *s. f.* ice-box
ghiacciàio *s. m.* glacier
ghiacciàre *v. intr. e intr. pron.* to freeze
ghiacciàto *agg.* **1** frozen **2** (*freddissimo*) icy, freezing
ghiàccio *s. m.* ice
ghiacciòlo *s. m.* **1** icicle **2** (*gelato*) ice lolly
ghiàia *s. f.* gravel
ghiaióso *agg.* gravelly
ghiànda *s. f.* acorn
ghiàndola *s. f.* gland
ghigliottìna *s. f.* guillotine
ghignàre *v. intr.* to sneer
ghiótto *agg.* **1** gluttonous, greedy **2** (*appetitoso*) delicious
ghiottóne *s. m.* glutton
ghiribìzzo *s. m.* fancy, caprice
ghirigòro *s. m.* scribble
ghirlànda *s. f.* garland, wreath
ghìro *s. m.* dormouse
ghìsa *s. f.* cast iron
già *avv.* **1** already **2** (*prima di ora, prima di allora*) before, already, (*nelle frasi interr.*) yet **3** (*un tempo*) once, (*precedentemente*) formerly **4** (*da questo, quel momento*) (ever) since, from **5** (*per indicare consenso*) yes, of course, that's right
giàcca *s. f.* jacket ♦ **g. a vento** windcheater, anorak
giacché *cong.* as, since
giacére *v. intr.* to lie
giaciménto *s. m.* layer, body, deposit
giacìnto *s. m.* hyacinth
giacobìno *s. m.* Jacobin
giàda *s. f.* jade
giaggiòlo *s. m.* iris
giaguàro *s. m.* jaguar
giàllo **A** *agg.* yellow **B** *s. m.* **1** (*colore*) yellow **2** (*libro, film*) thriller **3** (*di semaforo*) amber light
giammài *avv.* never
giapponése *agg. e s. m. e f.* Japanese
giardinàggio *s. m.* gardening
giardinière *s. m.* gardener
giardìno *s. m.* garden ♦ **g. d'infanzia** kindergarten; **g. pensile** roof garden; **g. pubblico** park
giarrettièra *s. f.* garter
giavellòtto *s. m.* javelin
gigànte **A** *agg.* gigantic, giant (*attr.*) **B** *s. m.* giant
gigantésco *agg.* gigantic, huge
gigantìsmo *s. m.* gigantism
gigionìsmo *s. m.* hamming
gìglio *s. m.* lily
gilè *s. m. inv.* waistcoat
gin *s. m. inv.* gin
ginecologìa *s. f.* gynaecology
ginecòlogo *s. m.* gynaecologist
ginepràio *s. m.* **1** (*bot.*) juniper bush **2** (*fig.*) fix, nole
ginépro *s. m.* juniper
ginèstra *s. f.* broom
gingillàrsi *v. intr. pron.* to dawdle, to fiddle
gingìllo *s. m.* knick-knack
ginnàsio *s. m.* (*stor.*) gymnasium
ginnàsta *s. m. e f.* gymnast
ginnàstica *s. f.* **1** gymnastics *pl.* (*v. al sing.*), (*fam.*) gym **2** (*attività fisica*) exercise
ginòcchio *s. m.* knee ♦ **stare in g.** to kneel
giocàre **A** *v. intr.* **1** to play **2** (*d'azzardo*) to gamble **3** (*scommettere*) to bet **4** (*in Borsa*) to speculate **5** (*aver peso*) to play a part **B** *v. tr.* **1** to play **2** (*scommettere*) to bet on, to gamble on **3** (*ingannare*) to fool **4** (*rischiare*) to risk
giocatóre *s. m.* **1** player **2** (*d'azzardo*) gambler
giocàttolo *s. m.* toy
giòco *s. m.* **1** (*svago*) game, amusement **2** (*con regole*) game **3** (*modo di giocare*) play **4** (*giocattolo*) toy **5** (*d'azzardo*) gambling **6** (*scherzo*) fun, joke **7** (*mecc.*) clearance, play ♦ **carte da g.** playing cards; **doppio g.** double-cross; **g. di prestigio** conjuring tricks; **g. di società** parlour game
giocolière *s. m.* juggler
giocóso *agg.* playful, merry
giógo *s. m.* yoke
giòia (1) *s. f.* joy
giòia (2) *s. f.* (*pietra preziosa*) jewel
gioiellerìa *s. f.* jewellery, (*negozio*) jeweller's shop
gioiellière *s. m.* jeweller
gioièllo *s. m.* jewel
gioióso *agg.* joyful
gioìre *v. intr.* to rejoice
giornalàio *s. m.* newsagent
giornàle *s. m.* **1** newspaper, paper **2** (*periodico*) journal, magazine **3** (*registro*) journal **4** (*diario*) diary ♦ **g. di bordo** log; **g. radio** news
giornalièro *agg.* **1** (*di tutti i giorni*) daily, day-to-day **2** (*di un giorno*) day (*attr.*)

giornalismo *s. m.* journalism
giornalista *s. m. e f.* journalist
giornalménte *avv.* daily
giornàta *s. f.* day ♦ **g. festiva/lavorativa** holiday/workday
giórno *s. m.* **1** day **2** (*luce del giorno*) daylight, day ♦ **al g. d'oggi** nowadays; **buon g.!** good morning!
giòstra *s. f.* **1** (*stor.*) joust **2** merry-go-round, roundabout
giovaménto *s. m.* benefit
gióvane **A** *agg.* **1** young **2** (*giovanile*) youthful, youth (*attr.*) **B** *s. m. e f.* young man *m.*, young woman *f.* ♦ **i giovani** young people, the young; **vino g.** new wine
giovanìle *agg.* **1** youthful, youth (*attr.*) **2** (*di aspetto*) young-looking
giovanòtto *s. m.* young man
giovàre **A** *v. intr.* **1** (*essere utile*) to be useful **2** (*far bene*) to be good (for) **B** *v. intr. pron.* to take advantage
giovedì *s. m.* Thursday
gioventù *s. f.* youth, (*i giovani*) young people
gioviàle *agg.* jovial, jolly
giovinézza *s. f.* youth
giradìschi *s. m.* record-player
giràffa *s. f.* **1** (*zool.*) giraffe **2** (*cin.*, *TV*) boom
giraménto *s. m.* (*di capo*) giddiness
giramóndo *s. m. e f. inv.* globe trotter
giràndola *s. f.* **1** (*fuoco d'artificio*) catherine-wheel **2** (*giocattolo*) windmill **3** (*banderuola*) weathercock
girànte *s. f.* (*mecc.*) impeller, rotor
giràre **A** *v. tr.* **1** to turn **2** (*fare il giro, visitare*) to go round, to tour **3** (*mescolare*) to stir **4** (*avvolgere*) to wind **5** (*banca*) to endorse **6** (*cin.*) to shoot, to make **B** *v. intr.* **1** to turn **2** (*sul proprio asse*) to turn, to rotate, (*rapidamente*) to spin **3** (*andare in giro*) to go round **4** (*vagare*) to wander **C** *v. rifl.* to turn (round)
girarròsto *s. m.* spit
girasóle *s. m.* sunflower
giràta *s. f.* **1** (*giro*) turn **2** (*passeggiata*) walk, stroll **3** (*banca*) endorsement
giravòlta *s. f.* twirl
girévole *agg.* turning, revolving ♦ **ponte g.** swing bridge
girìno *s. m.* tadpole
giro *s. m.* **1** (*rotazione*) turn **2** (*percorso*) round **3** (*cerchio, cerchia*) circle **4** (*viaggio*) trip, tour, **5** (*passeggiata*) stroll, walk, (*in bici, treno, ecc.*) ride, (*in auto*) drive **6** (*mecc.*) turn, revolution ♦ **a g. di posta** by mail return; **g. d'affari** turnover; **prendere in g. qc.** to make fun of sb.
girocónto *s. m.* bank giro
gironzolàre *v. intr.* to wander about, to stroll about
girotóndo *s. m.* ring-a-ring-o'-roses
girovagàre *v. intr.* to wander about, to stroll about
giròvago *s. m.* vagrant
gìta *s. f.* trip, excursion
gitàno *agg.* gipsy
gitànte *s. m. e f.* excursionist
giù *avv.* down, (*al piano inferiore*) downstairs ♦ **in g.** down, downwards; **su per g.** more or less
giubbòtto *s. m.* **1** jacket **2** (*antiproiettile*) bullet-proof vest **3** (*di salvataggio*) life jacket
giubilèo *s. m.* jubilee
giùbilo *s. m.* joy
giudicàre **A** *v. tr.* **1** to judge **2** (*dir.*) to try **3** (*considerare*) to consider, to think **B** *v. intr.* **1** to judge **2** (*dir.*) to pass sentence
giùdice *s. m. e f.* judge
giudiziàrio *agg.* judicial
giudìzio *s. m.* **1** (*dir.*) judgment, (*causa*) trial, (*sentenza*) sentence **2** (*opinione*) judgment, opinion **3** (*discernimento*) wisdom, good sense
giudizióso *agg.* sensible
giùgno *s. m.* June
giullàre *s. m.* jester
giuménta *s. f.* mare
giùnco *s. m.* reed, rush
giùngere **A** *v. intr.* **1** to arrive, to reach, to come, to get **2** (*riuscire*) to succeed **B** *v. tr.* (*congiungere*) to join
giùngla *s. f.* jungle
giunònico *agg.* Junoesque
giùnta (1) *s. f.* addition ♦ **per g.** in addition
giùnta (2) *s. f.* (*comitato*) council, committee
giuntàre *v. tr.* to join
giùnto *s. m.* joint, coupling
giuntùra *s. f.* joint
giunzióne *s. f.* junction
giuraménto *s. m.* oath ♦ **sotto g.** on oath
giuràre *v. tr. e intr.* to swear ♦ **g. il falso** to perjure oneself
giuràto *s. m.* juror

giurìa *s. f.* jury
giuridicaménte *avv.* juridically
giurìdico *agg.* juridical
giurisdizionàle *agg.* jurisdictional
giurisdizióne *s. f.* jurisdiction
giurisprudènza *s. f.* jurisprudence, law
giurìsta *s. m. e f.* jurist
giustapposizióne *s. f.* juxtaposition
giustézza *s. f.* **1** justness **2** (*esattezza*) exactness
giustificàbile *agg.* justifiable
giustificàre **A** *v. tr.* **1** to justify **2** (*scusare*) to excuse **B** *v. rifl.* **1** to justify oneself **2** (*scusarsi*) to excuse oneself
giustificazióne *s. f.* justification, excuse
giustìzia *s. f.* justice
giustiziàre *v. tr.* to execute
giùsto **A** *agg.* **1** (*equo*) just, fair **2** (*esatto*) right, correct, exact **3** (*adatto*) right, suitable **B** *s. m.* the right **C** *avv.* **1** (*esattamente*) right, correctly **2** (*proprio*) just
glaciàle *agg.* glacial
glàssa *s. f.* icing
gli (1) *art. determ. m. pl.* → **i**
gli (2) *pron pers. 3ª m.* **1** *sing.* (*riferito a persona o animale di sesso maschile*) (to, for) him; (*riferito a cosa o animale di sesso non specificato*) (to, for) it **2** *pl.* (to, for) them
glicemìa *s. f.* glycemia
glicerìna *s. f.* glycerin
glìcine *s. m.* wistaria
globàle *agg.* global, total
glòbo *s. m.* globe
glòbulo *s. m.* (*anat.*) corpuscle
glòria *s. f.* glory
glorióso *agg.* glorious
glossàrio *s. m.* glossary
glottologìa *s. f.* glottology
glucòsio *s. m.* glucose
glùteo *s. m.* gluteus
gnòmo *s. m.* gnome
goal *s. m. inv.* goal
gòbba *s. f.* hump
gòbbo **A** *agg.* **1** humpbacked **2** (*curvo*) bent **B** *s. m.* **1** humpback **2** (*gobba*) hump
góccia *s. f.* drop
góccio *s. m.* drop
gocciolàre *v. tr. e intr.* to drip
godére **A** *v. tr.* to enjoy **B** *v. intr.* **1** (*rallegrarsi*) to be glad, to be delighted, to take delight in, to enjoy **2** (*fruire*) to enjoy
godiménto *s. m.* enjoyment
gòffo *agg.* awkward, clumsy
góla *s. f.* **1** throat **2** (*golosità*) gluttony **3** (*geogr.*) gorge
golétta *s. f.* schooner
gòlf (1) *s. m. inv.* jumper, sweater, jersey
gòlf (2) *s. m. inv.* (*sport*) golf
gólfo *s. m.* gulf
golosità *s. f.* **1** gluttony, greediness **2** (*boccone prelibato*) titbit
golóso *agg.* greedy, gluttonous
gómito *s. m.* **1** elbow **2** (*di strada*) sharp bend **3** (*mecc.*) crank
gomìtolo *s. m.* ball
gómma *s. f.* **1** rubber **2** (*resina*) gum **3** (*per cancellare*) eraser **4** (*pneumatico*) tyre ♦ **forare una g.** to get a puncture
gommapiùma *s. f.* foam-rubber
gommìsta *s. m.* tyre repairer
gommóne *s. m.* rubber dinghy
gonfalóne *s. m.* banner
gonfiàre **A** *v. tr.* **1** to swell, (*con aria*) to blow (up), to inflate **2** (*fig.*) to swell, to exaggerate **B** *v. intr. pron.* to swell
gónfio *agg.* swollen, (*d'aria*) inflated
gonfióre *s. m.* swelling
gongolàre *v. intr.* to be overjoyed
gònna *s. f.* skirt ♦ **g. a pieghe** pleated skirt; **g. pantalone** divided skirt
gorgheggiàre *v. intr.* to trill
górgo *s. m.* whirlpool
gorgogliàre *v. intr.* to gurgle
gorìlla *s. m.* gorilla
gòtico *agg.* Gothic
gòtta *s. f.* gout
governànte **A** *s. m.* governor, ruler **B** *s. f.* (*di casa*) housekeeper, (*bambinaia*) nurse
governàre **A** *v. tr.* **1** to govern, to rule **2** (*dirigere*) to run, to conduct **3** (*prendersi cura di*) to take care of **4** (*controllare*) to control **B** *v. intr.* (*naut.*) to steer
governatìvo *agg.* government (*attr*), state (*attr*)
governatóre *s. m.* governor
govèrno *s. m.* **1** government, rule **2** (*direzione*) direction, running **3** (*cura*) care
gozzovigliàre *v. intr.* to guzzle
gracchiàre *v. intr.* to crake, (*di corvo*) to caw
gracidàre *v. intr.* to croak
gràcile *agg.* weak, frail
gradàsso *s. m.* boaster
gradazióne *s. f.* **1** gradation **2** (*sfumatura*) shade ♦ **g. alcolica** alcoholic content
gradévole *agg.* pleasant, agreeable
gradiménto *s. m.* **1** pleasure, liking **2** (*ap-*

provazione) approval, acceptance
gradinàta *s. f.* **1** steps *pl.* **2** (*di teatro, stadio*) stands *pl.*, tiers *pl.*
gradìno *s. m.* step
gradìre *v. tr.* **1** to like **2** (*accogliere con piacere*) to appreciate, to be pleased with
gradìto *agg.* **1** pleasant **2** (*bene accetto*) welcome, appreciated
gràdo *s. m.* **1** degree **2** (*posizione*) rank, grade **3** (*mil.*) rank, (*gallone*) stripe ♦ **essere in g. di fare q.c.** to be able to do st.
graduàle *agg.* gradual
gradualménte *avv.* gradually
graduàre *v. tr.* to graduate
graduàto A *agg.* **1** graded **2** (*provvisto di scala graduata*) graduated **B** *s. m.* (*mil.*) non-commissioned officer
graduatòria *s. f.* classification, list
graffètta *s. f.* clip
graffiànte *agg.* biting
graffiàre A *v. tr.* **1** to scratch **2** (*fig.*) to bite **B** *v. intr. pron.* to be scratched
gràffio *s. m.* scratch
graffìto *s. m.* graffito
grafìa *s. f.* handwriting
gràfica *s. f.* graphics *pl.* (*v. al sing.*)
graficaménte *avv.* graphically
gràfico A *agg.* graphic **B** *s. m.* **1** graph, (*statistico*) chart **2** (*disegnatore*) graphic designer
grafologìa *s. f.* graphology
gramàglie *s. f. pl.* mourning
gramìgna *s. f.* spear grass, weed
grammàtica *s. f.* grammar
grammaticàle *agg.* grammatical
gràmmo *s. m.* gram
gràna *s. f.* **1** (*struttura*) grain **2** (*fam.*) (*problema*) trouble **3** (*pop.*) (*quattrini*) money
granàio *s. m.* barn, granary
granàta *s. f.* (*mil.*) grenade
granàto *s. m.* garnet
grànchio *s. m.* **1** crab **2** (*fig.*) (*errore*) blunder
grandàngolo *s. m.* wide-angle lens
grànde A *agg.* **1** (*di dimensioni*) big, large, (*largo*) wide **2** (*elevato*) high, (*di statura*) tall **3** (*numeroso*) large, great **4** (*notevole, intenso*) great **5** (*fuori misura*) large, big **6** (*adulto*) grown-up **B** *s. m.* **1** (*adulto*) adult, grown-up **2** (*personalità*) great man
grandézza *s. f.* **1** (*dimensione*) size **2** (*ampiezza*) width, breadth **3** (*fig.*) greatness **4** (*grandiosità*) grandeur **5** (*scient.*) quantity
grandinàre *v. intr. impers.* to hail
grandinàta *s. f.* hailstorm
gràndine *s. f.* hail ♦ **chicco di g.** hailstone
grandiosità *s. f.* grandeur, magnificence
grandióso *agg.* grand, magnificent
grandùca *s. m.* grand duke
granducàto *s. m.* grand duchy
granèllo *s. m.* grain, (*di polvere*) speck
granìto *s. m.* granite
gràno *s. m.* **1** (*frumento*) wheat **2** (*granello*) grain
grantùrco *s. m.* maize, (*USA*) corn ♦ **pannocchia di g.** corn-cob
granulóso *agg.* grainy, granular
gràppolo *s. m.* cluster, bunch ♦ **un g. d'uva** a bunch of grapes
gràsso A *agg.* **1** fat **2** (*unto*) greasy, fatty **3** (*di pianta*) succulent **B** *s. m.* **1** fat **2** (*lubrificante*) grease
grassòccio *agg.* plump
gràta *s. f.* grating
gratìcola *s. f.* grill
gratìfica *s. f.* bonus
gratificàre *v. tr.* to be rewarding, to gratify
gratin *s. m. inv.* gratin
gratis *avv.* free, gratis
gratitùdine *s. f.* gratitude
gràto *agg.* grateful
grattacàpo *s. m.* trouble
grattacièlo *s. m.* skyscraper
grattàre A *v. tr.* **1** to scratch, (*raschiare*) to scrape **2** (*grattugiare*) to grate **3** (*fam.*) (*rubare*) to pinch **B** *v. intr.* to grate **C** *v. rifl.* to scratch oneself
grattùgia *s. f.* grater
grattugiàre *v. tr.* to grate
gratùito *agg.* **1** free **2** (*ingiustificato*) gratuitous ♦ **ingresso g.** admission free
gravàme *s. m.* burden
gravàre A *v. intr.* to weigh, to lie **B** *v. tr.* to burden
gràve *agg.* **1** (*pesante*) heavy **2** (*duro*) harsh, severe, grievous **3** (*serio, importante*) serious **4** (*solenne*) solemn, grave **5** (*fon.*) grave **6** (*mus.*) low, grave
gravidànza *s. f.* pregnancy ♦ **analisi di g.** pregnancy test
gràvido *agg.* **1** pregnant **2** (*fig.*) laden
gravità *s. f.* **1** gravity, seriousness **2** (*fis.*) gravity
gravóso *agg.* heavy, burdensome
gràzia *s. f.* **1** grace **2** (*favore*) favour **3** (*dir.*) mercy

grazìare *v. tr.* to pardon
gràzie *inter.* thank you!, thanks! ♦ **g. mille!** many thanks; **no, g.** no, thanks; **sì, g.** yes, please
grazióso *agg.* **1** pretty **2** (*piacevole*) pleasant
grecìsmo *s. m.* Grecism
grèco *agg. e s. m.* Greek
gregàrio *s. m.* follower
grégge *s. m.* flock
gréggio *agg.* raw, crude
grembiùle *s. m.* apron, smock, (*da bambino*) pinafore
grèmbo *s. m.* **1** lap **2** (*ventre materno*) womb
gremìto *agg.* full, packed
gréto *s. m.* pebbly shore
grétto *agg.* mean, narrow-minded
grézzo → **greggio**
gridàre *v. tr. e intr.* to shout, to cry, to scream
grìdo *s. m.* cry, shout, scream
grifóne *s. m.* griffin
grìgio *agg.* grey
grìglia *s. f.* **1** grill **2** (*scient.*) grid ♦ **pesce alla g.** grilled fish
grigliàta *s. f.* grill ♦ **g. mista** mixed grill
grillétto *s. m.* trigger
grìllo *s. m.* **1** cricket **2** (*fig.*) whim, fancy
grimaldèllo *s. m.* pick
grìnta *s. f.* grit
grìnza *s. f.* wrinkle, (*su stoffa*) crease
grinzóso *agg.* wrinkled, (*di stoffa*) creased
grippàre *v. intr. e intr. pron.* to seize, to bind
grissìno *s. m.* breadstick
grondàia *s. f.* gutter
grondàre **A** *v. tr.* to pour **B** *v. intr.* to stream, to drip
gròppa *s. f.* back
gróppo *s. m.* **1** knot **2** (*di vento*) squall
grossézza *s. f.* **1** largeness, bigness **2** (*dimensione*) size **3** (*spessore*) thickness
grossìsta *s. m. e f.* wholesaler
gròsso *agg.* **1** big, large, great **2** (*grave*) big, serious **3** (*importante*) big, important
grossolàno *agg.* **1** coarse, rough **2** (*madornale*) gross
grossomòdo *avv.* roughly, approximately
gròtta *s. f.* cave
grottésco *agg.* grotesque
grovìglio *s. m.* tangle
gru *s. f.* crane
grùccia *s. f.* **1** crutch **2** (*per abiti*) coat-hanger
grugnìre *v. intr.* to grunt
grugnìto *s. m.* grunt
grùgno *s. m.* snout
grùllo *agg. e s. m.* stupid
grùmo *s. m.* **1** clot **2** (*di farina*) lump
grùppo *s. m.* **1** group, (*di persone*) party **2** (*mecc.*) unit, set ♦ **g. di lavoro** working party; **lavoro di g.** team work
grùzzolo *s. m.* hoard
guadagnàre **A** *v. tr.* to earn, to gain **B** *v. intr.* to earn
guadàgno *s. m.* gain, profit, earnings *pl.*
guadàre *v. tr.* to ford, to wade
guàdo *s. m.* ford
guaìna *s. f.* sheath
guàio *s. m.* trouble, fix
guaìre *v. intr.* to yelp, to cry
guaìto *s. m.* yelp, cry
guància *s. f.* cheek
guanciàle *s. m.* pillow
guànto *s. m.* glove
guardabòschi *s. m.* forester
guardacàccia *s. m. inv.* gamekeeper
guardàre **A** *v. tr.* **1** to look at **2** (*dare un'occhiata*) to have a look **3** (*guardare fisso*) to gaze at, to stare **4** (*guardare di sfuggita*) to glance at **5** (*guardare furtivamente*) to peep **6** (*osservare*) to watch, to look, to observe, (*scrutare*) to eye **7** (*custodire, sorvegliare*) to look after, to watch over **8** (*difendere*) to defend, (*proteggere*) to protect **9** (*considerare*) to consider, to view, to look at **10** (*esaminare*) to look over, to look into **B** *v. intr.* **1** to look at **2** (*essere orientato*) to face, to look out on **3** (*considerare*) to look on **4** (*cercare*) to try **5** (*badare*) to see, to mind, to be careful **C** *v. rifl.* **1** to look at oneself **2** (*stare in guardia*) to beware, to mind **3** (*astenersi*) to forbear, to abstain **D** *v. rifl. rec.* to look at each other
guardaròba *s. m. inv.* **1** wardrobe **2** (*stanza*) linen-room **3** (*di locale pubblico*) cloak-room, (*USA*) checkroom
guàrdia *s. f.* **1** (*sorveglianza*) guard, watch **2** (*persona*) guard
guardiàno *s. m.* keeper, warden ♦ **g. notturno** night-watchman
guardìngo *agg.* cautious
guardiòla *s. f.* **1** (*mil.*) guardroom **2** (*di portinaio*) porter's lodge
guarìbile *agg.* curable, (*di ferita*) healable
guarigióne *s. f.* recovery, (*di ferita*) healing
guarìre **A** *v. intr.* **1** to recover, (*di ferita*) to heal **2** (*fig.*) to get out **B** *v. tr.* to cure, to

heal
guarnigióne *s. f.* garrison
guarnìre *v. tr.* **1** (*ornare*) to trim **2** (*cuc.*) to garnish
guarnizióne *s. f.* **1** (*ornamento*) trimming **2** (*mecc.*) washer, gasket
guastafèste *s. m.* spoilsport
guastàre **A** *v. tr.* to spoil, to damage, to ruin **B** *v. intr. pron.* to break down, to fail
guàsto **A** *agg.* **1** (*danneggiato*) damaged, out of order **2** (*marcio*) rotten **B** *s. m.* breakdown, fault, failure, damage
guazzabùglio *s. m.* muddle, hotch-potch
guàzzo *s. m.* (*arte*) gouache
guèrcio *s. m.* squinter
guèrra *s. f.* war, warfare
guerreggiàre *v. intr.* to wage war, to fight
guerrièro **A** *agg.* warlike **B** *s. m.* warrior
guerrìglia *s. f.* guerrilla
gùfo *s. m.* owl
gùglia *s. f.* spire, (*di campanile*) steeple
guìda *s. f.* **1** guide **2** (*libro*) guide, handbook **3** (*direzione*) direction, leadership **4** (*mecc.*) guide, slide **5** (*autom.*) steering, drive, driving
guidàre *v. tr.* **1** to guide **2** (*amministrare*) to run, to manage **3** (*essere a capo*) to lead **4** (*un veicolo*) to drive
guidatóre *s. m.* driver
guinzàglio *s. m.* lead, leash
guizzàre *v. intr.* to dart
gùscio *s. m.* **1** shell **2** (*di legumi*) pod, husk
gustàre *v. tr.* **1** to enjoy **2** (*assaggiare*) to taste
gùsto *s. m.* **1** taste **2** (*aroma*) flavour **3** (*voglia*) fancy **4** (*piacere*) relish, gusto, enjoyment
gustóso *agg.* **1** tasty **2** (*divertente*) amusing
gutturàle *agg.* guttural

H

habitat *s. m. inv.* habitat
hall *s. f. inv.* hall, foyer
handicap *s. m. inv.* handicap
handicappàto **A** *agg.* handicapped **B** *s. m.* handicapped person, disabled person
hascìsc *s. m.* hashish
hawaiàno *agg. e s. m.* Hawaiian
herpes *s. m. inv.* herpes
hobbìsta *s. m. e f.* hobbyst
hobby *s. m. inv.* hobby
hockey *s. m.* hockey ♦ **h. su ghiaccio** ice hockey; **h. su pista** roller hockey
holliwoodiano *agg.* Hollywood (*attr.*)
hostess *s. f. inv.* (air-)hostess
hotel *s. m. inv.* hotel
hurrà *inter.* hurrah

I

i o **gli** *art. determ. m. pl.* the (*spesso non si traduce o si rende con un agg. poss. o un partitivo*) (ES: **i dolci fanno ingrassare** sweets make you fat, **ho comprato i biscotti** I have bought some cookies)
iàto *s. m.* hiatus
ibernazióne *s. f.* hibernation
ìbrido *agg. e s. m.* hybrid
icòna *s. f.* icon
iconoclàsta *agg. e s. m. e f.* iconoclast
iconografìa *s. f.* iconography
iconogràfico *agg.* iconographic(al)
idèa *s. f.* **1** idea **2** (*intenzione*) mind, intention **3** (*ideale*) ideal
ideàle *agg. e s. m.* ideal
idealìsmo *s. m.* idealism
idealizzàre *v. tr.* to idealize
idealménte *avv.* ideally
ideàre *v. tr.* **1** to conceive **2** (*progettare*) to plan
idem *avv.* so, too
idèntico *agg.* identical
identificàbile *agg.* identifiable
identificàre **A** *v. tr.* to identify **B** *v. rifl.* to identify oneself **C** *v. intr. pron.* to be identical
identificazióne *s. f.* identification
identità *s. f.* identity ♦ **carta d'i.** identity card
ideogràmma *s. m.* ideogram
ideologìa *s. f.* ideology
ideològico *agg.* ideological
idillìaco *agg.* idyllic
idiòma *s. m.* language, idiom
idiomàtico *agg.* idiomatic
idiosincrasìa *s. f.* idiosyncrasy
idiòta **A** *agg.* idiotic, stupid **B** *s. m. e f.* idiot
idiozìa *s. f.* **1** idiocy **2** (*azione idiota*) stupid thing
idolatràre *v. tr.* to worship
idolatrìa *s. f.* idolatry
ìdolo *s. m.* idol
idoneità *s. f.* fitness, suitability
idòneo *agg.* fit, suitable
idrànte *s. m.* hydrant
idratànte *agg.* **1** hydrating **2** (*di cosmetico*) moisturizing
idràulica *s. f.* hydraulics *pl.* (*v. al sing.*)
idràulico **A** *agg.* hydraulic **B** *s. m.* plumber
ìdrico *agg.* water (*attr*)
idrobiologìa *s. f.* hydrobiology
idrocarbùro *s. m.* hydrocarbon
idrocoltùra *s. f.* hydroponics *pl.* (*v. al sing.*)
idroelèttrico *agg.* hydroelectric
idròfilo *agg.* hydrophilic ♦ **cotone i.** cotton wool
idrofobìa *s. f.* hydrophobia
idròfobo *agg.* hydrophobic
idrògeno *s. m.* hydrogen
idrografìa *s. f.* hydrography
idrorepellènte *agg.* water-repellent
idroscàlo *s. m.* water airport
idrostàtico *agg.* hydrostatic
idrotermàle *agg.* hydrothermal
idrovolànte *s. m.* seaplane
ièlla *s. f.* (*fam.*) bad luck
ièna *s. f.* hyena
ieràtico *agg.* **1** hieratic **2** (*fig.*) solemn
ièri *avv. e s. m.* yesterday ♦ **i. mattina/sera** yesterday morning/evening; **i. l'altro, l'altro i.** the day before yesterday
iettatùra *s. f.* evil-eye
igiène *s. f.* **1** hygiene **2** (*salute*) health ♦ **i. dentale** dental care
igiènico *agg.* **1** hygienic, sanitary **2** (*salutare*) healthy ♦ **carta igienica** toilet paper
ignàro *agg.* unaware
ignìfugo *agg.* fireproof
ignòbile *agg.* ignoble, base
ignorànte *agg.* **1** ignorant, uneducated **2** (*maleducato*) rude, impolite
ignorànza *s. f.* ignorance
ignoràre **A** *v. tr.* **1** not to know, to be unaware of **2** (*trascurare*) to ignore **B** *v. rifl. rec.* to ignore each other
ignòto **A** *agg.* unknown **B** *s. m.* **1** the unknown **2** (*persona*) unknown person
igròmetro *s. m.* hygrometer
il o **lo** *art. determ. m. sing.* the (*spesso non si traduce o si rende con un agg. poss, con l'art. indef. o con un partitivo*) (ES: **adoro il vino bianco** I love white wine, **ho perso il portafoglio** I lost my wallet, **la rosa è un fiore profumato** a rose is a fragrant flower, **vai a comprare il pane** go and buy some bread)
ìlare *agg.* cheerful

ilarità *s. f.* hilarity, cheerfulness
illanguidìre **A** *v. intr.* to languish, to grow weak **B** *v. intr. pron.* to become weak, to fade
illazióne *s. f.* illation, inference
illècito *agg.* illicit
illegàle *agg.* illegal, unlawful
illegalità *s. f.* illegality
illegìttimo *agg.* illegitimate
illéso *agg.* **1** unhurt, unharmed **2** (*fig.*) intact
illetteràto *agg.* illiterate, ignorant
illibàto *agg.* pure, virgin
illimitàto *agg.* boundless, unlimited
illògico *agg.* illogical
illùdere **A** *v. tr.* to deceive, to delude **B** *v. rifl.* to deceive oneself, to delude oneself
illuminàre **A** *v. tr.* **1** to light up, to illuminate **2** (*fig.*) to enlighten **B** *v. intr. pron.* to lighten
illuminazióne *s. f.* **1** lighting, illumination **2** (*fig.*) flash of inspiration
illuminìsmo *s. m.* Enlightenment
illusióne *s. f.* illusion, delusion ♦ **farsi illusioni** to delude oneself; **i. ottica** optical illusion
illusionìsmo *s. m.* illusionism, conjuring
illustràre *v. tr.* to illustrate
illustratìvo *agg.* illustrative
illustràto *agg.* illustrated ♦ **cartolina illustrata** picture-postcard
illustrazióne *s. f.* **1** (*spiegazione*) illustration, explanation **2** (*figura*) picture, illustration
illùstre *agg.* distinguished, famous
imbacuccàre **A** *v. tr.* to wrap up **B** *v. rifl.* to wrap oneself up
imballàggio *s. m.* **1** (*l'imballare*) packing **2** (*involucro*) package
imballàre *v. tr.* **1** to pack **2** (*motore*) to race
imbalsamàre *v. tr.* to embalm, (*animali*) to stuff
imbandieràre *v. tr.* to deck with flags
imbandìre *v. tr.* to prepare, (*la tavola*) to lay
imbarazzànte *agg.* embarrassing
imbarazzàre **A** *v. tr.* **1** to embarrass **2** (*ostacolare*) to hamper **B** *v. intr. pron.* to be embarrassed
imbaràzzo *s. m.* **1** (*disagio*) embarrassment **2** (*disturbo, impaccio*) trouble, obstacle
imbarbariménto *s. m.* barbarization
imbarcàre **A** *v. tr.* to embark, to take on board **B** *v. rifl.* **1** to embark, to go aboard, to board **2** (*prendere servizio su una nave*) to sign on **3** (*fig.*) to embark on, to engage in **C** *v. intr. pron.* (*deformarsi*) to warp
imbarcazióne *s. f.* boat, craft
imbàrco *s. m.* **1** embarkation, embarking, shipping **2** (*aer*) boarding
imbastìre *v. tr.* **1** to tack, to baste **2** (*fig.*) to outline
imbàttersi *v. intr. pron.* to run into, to run up
imbattìbile *agg.* **1** unbeatable **2** (*insuperabile*) unsurpassable
imbavagliàre *v. tr.* to gag
imbeccàta *s. f.* prompt
imbecìlle *s. m. e f.* stupid, imbecile
imbellìre **A** *v. tr.* to make beautiful, to embellish **B** *v. intr. pron.* to become beautiful
imbèrbe *agg.* beardless
imbestialìre **A** *v. tr.* to enrage **B** *v. intr. pron.* to get enraged, to become furious
imbiancàre **A** *v. tr.* to whiten, (*muro*) to whitewash **B** *v. intr. pron.* to become white
imbianchìno *s. m.* (house-)painter
imboccàre *v. tr.* **1** to feed **2** (*entrare in*) to enter, to come on to, to turn into **3** (*portare alla bocca*) to put to one's mouth
imboccatùra *s. f.* **1** mouth **2** (*di strada, galleria*) entrance **3** (*di strumento a fiato*) mouthpiece
imbócco *s. m.* entrance
imbonitóre *s. m.* barker
imboscàre **A** *v. tr.* to put into safe keeping **B** *v. rifl.* **1** (*evitare il servizio militare*) to evade military service **2** (*eludere*) to shirk **3** (*scomparire*) to disappear
imboscàta *s. f.* ambush
imboschìre *v. tr.* to afforest
imbottigliàre **A** *v. tr.* **1** to bottle **2** (*bloccare*) to blockade **B** *v. intr. pron.* (*nel traffico*) to get caught in a traffic jam
imbottìre *v. tr.* **1** to stuff, to pad **2** (*farcire*) to fill
imbottitùra *s. f.* stuffing, padding
imbrattàre *v. tr.* to dirty, to soil
imbrigliàre *v. tr.* to bridle
imbroccàre *v. tr.* **1** to hit **2** (*fig.*) to guess
imbrogliàre **A** *v. tr.* **1** to cheat **2** (*confondere*) to mix up **3** (*arruffare*) to tangle, to entangle **B** *v. intr. pron.* **1** (*confondersi*) to get confused **2** (*arruffarsi*) to get tangled, to get entangled
imbròglio *s. m.* **1** (*inganno*) cheat, swindle **2** (*impiccio*) scrape, fix **3** (*intrico*) tangle
imbroglióne *s. m.* cheat, swindler
imbronciàto *agg.* sulky

imbrunìre *s. m.* nightfall
imbruttìre **A** *v. tr.* to make ugly **B** *v. intr. e intr. pron.* to become ugly
imbucàre *v. tr.* to post
imburràre *v. tr.* to butter
imbùto *s. m.* funnel
imitàre *v. tr.* **1** to imitate, to copy **2** (*fare l'imitazione*) to mimic **3** (*contraffare*) to forge
imitatóre *s. m.* **1** imitator **2** (*attore*) mimic
imitazióne *s. f.* **1** imitation **2** (*contraffazione*) fake **3** (*di attore*) impersonation, imitation
immacolàto *agg.* immaculate, spotless
immagazzinàre *v. tr.* to store (up)
immaginàre *v. tr.* **1** to imagine, to fancy **2** (*supporre*) to suppose, to think **3** (*inventare*) to invent, to think up
immaginàrio *agg.* imaginary, fictitious
immaginazióne *s. f.* imagination, fancy
immàgine *s. f.* **1** image **2** (*disegno, illustrazione*) figure, picture, illustration
immancàbile *agg.* unfailing
immàne *agg.* **1** enormous **2** (*spaventoso*) appalling, tremendous
immanènte *agg.* immanent
immangiàbile *agg.* uneatable
immatricolàre **A** *v. tr.* **1** (*persona*) to enrol **2** (*veicolo*) to register **B** *v. rifl.* to enrol oneself
immatricolazióne *s. f.* (*di persona*) enrolment, (*di veicolo*) registration
immatùro *agg.* **1** (*frutto*) unripe **2** (*fig.*) immature **3** (*prematuro*) premature, untimely
immedesimàrsi *v. rifl.* to identify oneself (with)
immediataménte *avv.* immediately
immediàto *agg.* immediate, prompt
immemoràbile *agg.* immemorial
immèmore *agg.* forgetful
immensità *s. f.* immensity
immènso *agg.* immense, huge
immèrgere **A** *v. tr.* to immerse, to dip, to plunge **B** *v. rifl.* **1** to plunge, (*di subacqueo*) to dive, (*di sottomarino*) to submerge **2** (*dedicarsi*) to immerse oneself, to give oneself up
immeritàto *agg.* undeserved
immeritévole *agg.* unworthy
immersióne *s. f.* **1** immersion, dip, plunge **2** (*di subacqueo*) dive, (*di sottomarino*) submersion **3** (*naut.*) draft
imméttere **A** *v. tr.* to introduce, to put in, to put on **B** *v. intr.* to lead to **C** *v. rifl.* to get into, to get onto
immigràto *agg. e s. m.* immigrant
immigrazióne *s. f.* immigration
imminènte *agg.* imminent, forthcoming
immischiàre **A** *v. tr.* to involve **B** *v. intr. pron.* to meddle in, to interfere
immissàrio *s. m.* tributary
immissióne *s. f.* immission, input
immòbile **A** *agg.* immovable, (*fermo*) still, motionless **B** *s. m.* real estate immovable, (*palazzo*) building
immobiliàre *agg.* immovable ♦ **agenzia i.** (real) estate agency; **proprietà i.** real estate, real property
immobilità *s. f.* immobility
immobilizzàre **A** *v. tr.* **1** to immobilize **2** (*econ.*) to lock up, to tie up **B** *v. rifl. e intr. pron.* to freeze
immolàre **A** *v. tr.* to sacrifice **B** *v. rifl.* to sacrifice oneself
immondìzia *s. f.* garbage, rubbish, trash ♦ **vietato depositare i.** no dumping
immóndo *agg.* filthy
immoràle *agg.* immoral
immortalàre *v. tr.* to immortalize
immortàle *agg. e s. m. e f.* immortal
immortalità *s. f.* immortality
immùne *agg.* **1** immune **2** (*libero*) free, (*esente*) exempt
immunità *s. f.* **1** immunity **2** (*esenzione*) exemption
immunizzàre **A** *v. tr.* to immunize **B** *v. rifl.* to immunize oneself, to become immune
immutàbile *agg.* immutable
impacchettàre *v. tr.* to wrap up, to package
impacciàre *v. tr.* to hamper, to hinder
impacciàto *agg.* **1** (*goffo*) awkward **2** (*a disagio*) uneasy
impàccio *s. m.* **1** hindrance, obstacle **2** (*situazione difficile*) scrape, trouble **3** (*imbarazzo*) embarrassment
impàcco *s. m.* compress
impadronìrsi *v. intr. pron.* **1** to take possession, to appropriate, (*con la violenza*) to seize **2** (*fig.*) to master
impagàbile *agg.* priceless
impaginàre *v. tr.* to paginate
impagliàre *v. tr.* to stuff with straw
impalàto *agg.* stiff
impalcatùra *s. f.* **1** scaffolding **2** (*struttura*) framework
impallidìre *v. intr.* **1** to turn pale **2** (*svanire*) to fade

impalpàbile *agg.* impalpable
impanàre *v. tr.* (*cuc.*) to crumb, to bread
impantanàrsi *v. intr. pron.* to stick in the mud, (*fig.*) to get bogged down
impappinàrsi *v. intr. pron.* to get flustered, to falter
imparàre *v. tr.* to learn
impareggiàbile *agg.* incomparable
imparentàrsi *v. intr. pron.* to become related to
ìmpari *agg.* unequal, uneven
impartìre *v. tr.* to impart, to give
imparziàle *agg.* impartial
imparzialità *s. f.* impartiality
impasse *s. f. inv.* impasse
impassìbile *agg.* impassive, unmoved (*pred.*)
impastàre **A** *v. tr.* to knead, to mix **B** *v. intr. pron.* to merge
impàsto *s. m.* mixture
impàtto *s. m.* impact
impaurìre **A** *v. tr.* to frighten, to scare **B** *v. intr. pron.* to get frightened, to be scared
impaziènte *agg.* impatient
impaziènza *s. f.* impatience
impazzàta, all' *loc. avv.* wildly, madly
impazzìre *v. intr.* **1** to go mad, to go crazy **2** (*di apparecchio*) to go haywire **3** (*di salsa*) to curdle ♦ **far i. qc.** to drive sb. crazy; **i. per q.c./qc.** to be mad about st./sb.
impeccàbile *agg.* impeccable
impediménto *s. m.* impediment
impedìre *v. tr.* **1** to prevent, to keep (from) **2** (*ostruire*) to obstruct, to bar **3** (*impacciare*) to hamper, to hinder
impegnàre **A** *v. tr.* **1** (*dare in pegno*) to pawn, to pledge **2** (*investire*) to invest **3** (*vincolare*) to bind **4** (*prenotare*) to reserve, to book **5** (*mil.*) to engage **6** (*occupare*) to take up, to keep busy **B** *v. rifl.* **1** (*prendersi un impegno*) to undertake, to commit oneself, to engage oneself **2** (*dedicarsi*) to devote oneself **3** (*farsi garante*) to go bail **4** (*essere coinvolto*) to be involved
impegnatìvo *agg.* **1** binding **2** (*che richiede impegno*) exacting
impégno *s. m.* **1** engagement, (*promessa*) promise, (*obbligo*) obligation, pledge **2** (*applicazione*) care, diligence
impellènte *agg.* impelling, urgent
impenetràbile *agg.* impenetrable
impennàrsi *v. intr. pron.* **1** (*di cavallo*) to rear up **2** (*aer.*) to nose up, to zoom
impennàta *s. f.* **1** (*di cavallo*) rearing up **2** (*aer.*) zoom **3** (*rialzo*) sudden rise
impensàbile *agg.* unthinkable
impensierìre *v. tr. e intr. pron.* to worry
imperatìvo *agg. e s. m.* imperative
imperatóre *s. m.* emperor
imperatrìce *s. f.* empress
impercettìbile *agg.* imperceptible
imperdonàbile *agg.* unforgivable
imperfètto *agg. e s. m.* imperfect
imperfezióne *s. f.* imperfection, flaw
imperiàle *agg.* imperial
imperialìsmo *s. m.* imperialism
imperióso *agg.* imperious
imperìzia *s. f.* unskilfulness
impermeàbile **A** *agg.* impermeable, (*all'acqua*) waterproof **B** *s. m.* mackintosh, raincoat
imperniàre **A** *v. tr.* **1** to hinge, to pivot **2** (*fig.*) to base **B** *v. intr. pron.* **1** to hinge, to pivot **2** to be based
impèro *s. m.* empire
imperscrutàbile *agg.* inscrutable
impersonàle *agg.* **1** impersonal **2** (*banale*) banal
impersonàre *v. tr.* **1** to personify **2** (*interpretare*) to play, to impersonate
impertèrrito *agg.* imperturbable, impassive
impertinènte *agg.* impertinent, cheeky
imperturbàbile *agg.* imperturbable
imperversàre *v. intr.* **1** to rage **2** (*essere diffuso*) to be the rage
ìmpeto *s. m.* **1** impetus, violence **2** (*impulso*) fit, impulse
impettìto *agg.* stiff
impetuóso *agg.* **1** violent, forceful **2** (*impulsivo*) impetuous, impulsive
impiantàre *v. tr.* **1** to install **2** (*fondare*) to establish, to set up
impiànto *s. m.* **1** plant, system, installation **2** (*costituzione*) establishment **3** (*struttura*) framework
impiastricciàre **A** *v. tr.* to smear, to dirty **B** *v. rifl.* to smear oneself, to dirty oneself
impiàstro *s. m.* **1** poultice **2** (*fam.*) (*seccatore*) bore, nuisance **3** (*fam.*) (*persona malaticcia*) weakling
impiccagióne *s. f.* hanging
impiccàre **A** *v. tr.* **1** to hang **2** (*fig.*) to put on the spot **B** *v. rifl.* to hang oneself
impicciàre **A** *v. tr. e intr.* to hinder, to be in the way **B** *v. intr. pron.* to meddle, to interfere

impìccio *s. m.* **1** hindrance, nuisance **2** (*seccatura*) fix, trouble, mess
impiegàre **A** *v. tr.* **1** (*usare*) to use, to make use of **2** (*spendere*) to use, to spend **3** (*di tempo, metterci*) to take **4** (*assumere*) to take on, to employ **5** (*investire*) to invest **B** *v. rifl.* to get a job
impiegàto *s. m.* employee, office-worker, clerk
impiègo *s. m.* **1** (*uso*) use **2** (*lavoro*) job, position, employment **3** (*investimento*) investment
impietosìre **A** *v. tr.* to move to pity **B** *v. intr. pron.* to be moved
impietóso *agg.* pitiless
impietrìre **A** *v. tr.* to petrify **B** *v. intr. e intr. pron.* to become petrified
impigliàre **A** *v. tr.* to entangle **B** *v. intr. pron.* to get caught
impigrìre **A** *v. tr.* to make lazy **B** *v. intr. e intr. pron.* to become lazy
implacàbile *agg.* implacable
implicàre *v. tr.* **1** to involve, to implicate **2** (*comportare*) to imply
implicazióne *s. f.* implication
implìcito *agg.* implicit
implùvio *s. m.* impluvium
impollinazióne *s. f.* pollination
imponènte *agg.* imposing
imponìbile **A** *agg.* taxable **B** *s. m.* taxable income
impopolàre *agg.* unpopular
impórre **A** *v. tr.* **1** to impose **2** (*ordinare*) to order, to force, to make **3** (*stabilire*) to fix **4** (*esigere*) to call for **B** *v. rifl. e intr. pron.* **1** to impose oneself, to stand out **2** (*farsi valere*) to assert oneself **3** (*avere successo*) to become popular, to be successful **4** (*rendersi necessario*) to be called for
importànte *agg.* important
importànza *s. f.* importance
importàre **A** *v. tr.* to import **B** *v. intr.* **1** (*avere importanza*) to matter, to care **2** (*essere necessario*) to be necessary ♦ **non importa!** it doesn't matter!
importazióne *s. f.* importation, import
impòrto *s. m.* amount, sum
importunàre *v. tr.* to bother
importùno *agg.* **1** boring **2** (*inopportuno*) untimely
imposizióne *s. f.* **1** imposition **2** (*ordine*) order, command ♦ **i. fiscale** taxation
impossessàrsi *v. intr. pron.* **1** to take possession, to seize **2** (*fig.*) to master
impossìbile **A** *agg.* impossible **B** *s. m.* (the) impossible ♦ **fare l'i.** to do one's best
impossibilità *s. f.* impossibility
impossibilitàto *agg.* unable
impòsta (1) *s. f.* tax, duty
impòsta (2) *s. f.* (*di finestra*) shutter
impostàre (1) *v. tr.* **1** (*gettare le basi*) to set up, to lay down **2** (*formulare*) to set out, to lay out, to formulate
impostàre (2) *v. tr.* (*corrispondenza*) to post, to mail
impostazióne *s. f.* definition, formulation, statement
impostùra *s. f.* imposture
impotènte *agg.* impotent
impoverìre **A** *v. tr.* to impoverish **B** *v. intr. pron.* to become poor
impraticàbile *agg.* impracticable, (*di strada*) impassable
impratichìre **A** *v. tr.* to train **B** *v. intr. pron.* to practise, to get to know
imprecàre *v. intr.* to curse
imprecazióne *s. f.* curse
imprecisàto *agg.* unspecified
impregnàre **A** *v. tr.* **1** to soak, to impregnate **2** (*fig.*) to fill **B** *v. intr. pron.* **1** to become impregnated, to become soaked **2** (*fig.*) to be filled
imprenditóre *s. m.* entrepreneur
impreparàto *agg.* unprepared
imprésa *s. f.* **1** enterprise, undertaking **2** (*azione*) exploit **3** (*ditta*) business, enterprise, firm, concern
impresàrio *s. m.* (*teatro*) manager
impressionàbile *agg.* sensitive
impressionànte *agg.* impressive, striking, shocking
impressionàre **A** *v. tr.* **1** to impress, to strike, to shock **2** (*turbare*) to move, to upset **3** (*fot.*) to expose **B** *v. intr. pron.* **1** to be struck, to be shocked **2** (*fot.*) to be exposed
impressióne *s. f.* **1** impression **2** (*sensazione*) sensation, feeling **3** (*impronta*) impress, imprint
impressionìsmo *s. m.* impressionism
imprestàre *v. tr.* to lend
imprevedìbile *agg.* unforeseeable
imprevìsto **A** *agg.* unforeseen, unexpected **B** *s. m.* unexpected event
impreziosìre *v. tr.* to make precious
imprigionàre *v. tr.* **1** to imprison, to put in

prison **2** (*rinchiudere*) to confine, to trap
imprìmere **A** *v. tr.* **1** to impress, to imprint **2** (*comunicare*) to give, to impart **B** *v. intr. pron.* to be impressed
improbàbile *agg.* improbable, unlikely
imprónta *s. f.* **1** imprint, impression, mark **2** (*di piede*) footprint **3** (*traccia*) track **4** (*fig.*) stamp, mark ♦ **impronte digitali** fingerprints
impropèrio *s. m.* abuse
impròprio *agg.* improper
improrogàbile *agg.* that cannot be postponed, final
improvvisaménte *avv.* suddenly
improvvisàre **A** *v. tr. e intr.* to improvise **B** *v. rifl.* to play
improvvisàta *s. f.* surprise
improvvìso *agg.* sudden
imprudènte *agg.* imprudent, rash
imprudènza *s. f.* imprudence, rashness
impudènte *agg.* impudent, shameless
impudènza *s. f.* impudence
impudìco *agg.* immodest, indecent
impugnàre *v. tr.* **1** to grasp, to grip **2** (*dir*) (*contestare*) to impugn, to contest
impulsìvo *agg.* impulsive
impùlso *s. m.* impulse
impuneménte *avv.* with impunity
impuntàrsi *v. intr. pron.* **1** to jib, to stop dead **2** (*ostinarsi*) to be obstinated
impuntùra *s. f.* back-stitch
impurità *s. f.* impurity
impùro *agg.* impure
imputàre *v. tr.* **1** (*attribuire*) to impute, to ascribe **2** (*accusare*) to accuse, to charge
imputàto *s. m.* defendant
imputazióne *s. f.* imputation
imputridìre *v. intr.* to rot, to putrefy
in *prep.* **1** (*stato in luogo*) in, at, (*sopra*) on (ES: **in forno** in the oven, **stare in casa** to stay at home, **in prima pagina** on the front page) **2** (*moto a luogo*) to, (*verso l'interno*) into (ES: **andare in Inghilterra** to go to England, **entrare nella stanza** to get into the room) **3** (*moto per luogo*) through, across, round (ES: **correre nei campi** to run across the fields) **4** (*trasformazione*) in, into (ES: **tradurre dall'inglese in italiano** to translate from English into Italian) **5** (*tempo*) in, on, at (ES: **in primavera** in spring, **in questo momento** at this moment, **in quel giorno** on that day) **6** (*modo, condizione*) in, on, at (ES: **in fretta** in a hurry, **stare in piedi** to stand on one's feet) **7** (*limitazione*) in, at (ES: **è bravo nel lavoro** he's good at work) **8** (*mezzo*) by, in, on (ES: **viaggiare in treno** to travel by train, **pagare in dollari** to pay in dollars) **9** (*materia*) *idiom.* (ES: **una borsa in pelle** a leather bag)
inàbile *agg.* unable, unfit
inabissàrsi *v. intr. pron.* to sink
inabitàbile *agg.* uninhabitable
inaccessìbile *agg.* inaccessible
inaccettàbile *agg.* unacceptable
inacidìre **A** *v. tr.* to sour **B** *v. intr. e intr. pron.* to turn sour
inadàtto *agg.* unsuitable, unfit
inadeguàto *agg.* inadequate
inadempiènza *s. f.* default
inafferràbile *agg.* elusive
inaffidàbile *agg.* unreliable
inalàre *v. tr.* to inhale
inalberàre **A** *v. tr.* to hoist **B** *v. rifl.* to get angry
inalienàbile *agg.* inalienable
inalteràbile *agg.* unalterable
inamidàre *v. tr.* to starch
inammissìbile *agg.* **1** inadmissible **2** (*ingiustificabile*) unjustifiable
inanimàto *agg.* inanimate
inappellàbile *agg.* **1** (*dir*) unappealable **2** (*est.*) final, irrevocable
inappetènza *s. f.* lack of appetite
inappuntàbile *agg.* faultless
inarcàre *v. tr., rifl. e intr. pron.* to bend, to curve
inaridìre *v. tr. e intr. pron.* to dry up, to wither
inarrestàbile *agg.* unrestrainable
inarrivàbile *agg.* **1** unattainable, unreachable **2** (*incomparabile*) incomparable
inascoltàto *agg.* unheard
inaspettàto *agg.* unexpected
inasprìre **A** *v. tr.* **1** to embitter, to exacerbate **2** (*aggravare*) to sharpen, to aggravate **B** *v. intr. pron.* to become embittered, to become harsher
inattaccàbile *agg.* **1** unassailable, proof (*pred.*) **2** (*irreprensibile*) irreproachable
inattendìbile *agg.* unreliable
inattéso *agg.* unexpected
inattìvo *agg.* inactive, idle
inattuàbile *agg.* impracticable
inaudìto *agg.* unprecedented
inauguràle *agg.* inaugural, opening
inauguràre *v. tr.* to inaugurate, to open
inaugurazióne *s. f.* inauguration, opening
inavvertènza *s. f.* inadvertence, oversight
inavvertitaménte *avv.* inadvertently

inavvicinàbile *agg.* unapproachable
incagliàre *v. intr. e intr. pron.* **1** (*naut.*) to run aground, to strand **2** (*fig.*) to get stuck, to come to a standstill
incalcolàbile *agg.* incalculable
incallìto *agg.* **1** hardened, callous **2** (*fig.*) inveterate
incalzàre **A** *v. tr.* **1** to follow closely **2** (*fig.*) to press, to urge **B** *v. intr.* to press, to be imminent
incameràre *v. tr.* to appropriate
incamminàrsi **A** *v. tr.* to start up **B** *v. intr. pron.* to set out, to start
incanalàre **A** *v. tr.* **1** to canalize **2** (*fig.*) to direct **B** *v. intr. pron.* to flow
incandescènte *agg.* incandescent, white-hot
incantàre **A** *v. tr.* to charm, to bewitch **B** *v. intr. pron.* **1** to be charmed, to be spell-bound **2** (*incepparsi*) to jam
incantésimo *s. m.* spell, charm
incantévole *agg.* enchanting, charming
incànto (1) *s. m.* spell, enchantment
incànto (2) *s. m.* (*asta*) auction
incanutìre *v. intr.* to turn white
incapàce **A** *agg.* unable, incompetent **B** *s. m. e f.* incompetent
incapacità *s. f.* incapacity, incompetence
incaponìrsi *v. intr. pron.* to get obstinate
incappàre *v. intr.* to run into, to get into
incapricciàrsi *v. intr. pron.* to take a fancy
incarceràre *v. tr.* to imprison
incaricàre **A** *v. tr.* to charge, to entrust **B** *v. rifl.* to undertake, to take upon oneself
incaricàto *s. m.* delegate, appointee
incàrico *s. m.* **1** task, job **2** (*nomina*) appointment
incarnàre **A** *v. tr.* to incarnate, to embody **B** *v. intr. pron.* **1** to become incarnate **2** (*di unghia*) to grow in
incartaménto *s. m.* file, dossier
incartàre *v. tr.* to wrap up
incassàre *v. tr.* **1** (*merce*) to pack **2** (*mecc., edil.*) to embed, to build in **3** (*incastonare*) to set **4** (*riscuotere*) to cash, to collect **5** (*fig.*) to get, to take
incàsso *s. m.* collection, (*somma incassata*) proceeds *pl.*, takings *pl.*
incastonàre *v. tr.* to set
incastonatùra *s. f.* setting
incastràre **A** *v. tr.* **1** to fix, to embed, to fit in **2** (*intrappolare*) to set up **B** *v. intr. pron.* **1** to fit **2** (*impigliarsi*) to get stuck
incàstro *s. m.* joint
incatenàre *v. tr.* **1** to chain (up), to enchain **2** (*fig.*) to tie down
incattivìre **A** *v. tr.* to make wicked **B** *v. intr. pron.* to become wicked
incàuto *agg.* incautious
incavàre *v. tr.* to hollow out
incavàto *agg.* hollow
ìncavo *s. m.* **1** hollow **2** (*scanalatura*) groove **3** (*tecnol.*) dap, notch
incendiàre **A** *v. tr.* to set fire to, to set on fire **B** *v. intr. pron.* to catch fire
incendiàrio **A** *agg.* incendiary **B** *s. m.* arsonist
incèndio *s. m.* fire ♦ **i. doloso** arson
incenerìre **A** *v. tr.* to reduce to ashes **B** *v. intr. pron.* to be reduced to ashes
incènso *s. m.* incense
incensuràto *agg.* uncensured ♦ **essere i.** to have a clean record
incentivàre *v. tr.* to stimulate, to boost
incentìvo *s. m.* incentive
incentràre **A** *v. tr.* to centre, to base **B** *v. intr. pron.* to be based
inceppàre **A** *v. tr.* to hinder, to obstruct **B** *v. intr. pron.* to jam, to stick
incertézza *s. f.* **1** uncertainty, doubt **2** (*indecisione*) indecision
incèrto *agg.* **1** uncertain, doubtful **2** (*indeciso*) undecided, irresolute **3** (*indefinito*) unclear **4** (*instabile*) unsettled
incespicàre *v. intr.* to stumble
incessànte *agg.* unending, unceasing
incèsto *s. m.* incest
incètta *s. f.* buying up
inchièsta *s. f.* **1** inquiry, survey **2** (*investigazione*) inquiry, investigation **3** (*giornalistica*) report
inchinàre **A** *v. tr.* to bow, to bend **B** *v. rifl.* to bend down
inchìno *s. m.* bow
inchiodàre **A** *v. tr.* **1** to nail **2** (*fig.*) to fix **B** *v. intr. pron.* (*bloccarsi*) to pull up short
inchiòstro *s. m.* ink
inciampàre *v. intr.* **1** to stumble, to trip up **2** (*imbattersi*) to run into
inciàmpo *s. m.* obstacle
incidentalménte *avv.* incidentally
incidènte **A** *agg.* incident **B** *s. m.* **1** (*infortunio*) accident **2** (*questione*) incident
incidènza *s. f.* influence, effect
incìdere (1) *v. tr.* **1** to engrave, to carve **2** (*registrare*) to record **3** (*med.*) to incise **4** (*fig.*) to impress
incìdere (2) *v. intr.* **1** (*gravare*) to weigh

(on) **2** (*influenzare*) to affect, to influence
incìnta *agg.* pregnant
incìrca, all' *avv.* about, approximately
incisióne *s. f.* **1** (*taglio*) cut, incision **2** (*tacca*) notch **3** (*arte*) engraving **4** (*registrazione*) recording
incisìvo **A** *agg.* incisive **B** *s. m.* incisor
incisóre *agg.* engraver
incitàre *v. tr.* to incite
incivìle *agg.* **1** uncivilized, barbaric **2** (*scortese*) rude
incivilìre **A** *v. tr.* to civilize **B** *v. intr. pron.* to grow civilized
inciviltà *s. f.* **1** barbarity **2** (*maleducazione*) rudeness, incivility
inclinàre **A** *v. tr.* to tilt, to incline **B** *v. intr.* **1** to slope, to be inclined **2** (*fig.*) to incline, to be disposed **C** *v. rifl. e intr. pron.* **1** to tilt, to slope **2** (*piegarsi*) to bend **3** (*naut.*) to list
inclinàto *agg.* inclined, sloping
inclinazióne *s. f.* inclination
inclìne *agg.* inclined
inclùdere *v. tr.* **1** to include **2** (*allegare*) to enclose
inclusìvo *agg.* inclusive
inclùso *agg.* **1** included, inclusive **2** (*allegato*) enclosed
incoerènte *agg.* inconsistent
incògnita *s. f.* unknown quantity
incògnito **A** *agg.* unknown **B** *s. m.* incognito
incollàre **A** *v. tr.* to stick, to glue **B** *v. intr. pron.* to stick
incolonnàre *v. tr.* to put in a column
incolóre *agg.* colourless
incolpàre **A** *v. tr.* to charge, to blame **B** *v. rifl.* to blame oneself
incólto *agg.* **1** (*di terreno*) uncultivated, fallow **2** (*trascurato*) neglected **3** (*ignorante*) uneducated
incòlume *agg.* unscathed, unharmed
incombènte *agg.* **1** impending **2** (*spettante*) incumbent
incómbere *v. intr.* **1** to impend over, to hang over **2** (*spettare*) to be incumbent on
incominciàre *v. tr. e intr.* to begin, to start
incomparàbile *agg.* incomparable
incompetènte *agg.* incompetent
incompiùto *agg.* unfinished
incomplèto *agg.* incomplete
incomprensìbile *agg.* incomprehensible
incompréso *agg.* **1** not understood **2** (*non apprezzato*) unappreciated
inconcepìbile *agg.* inconceivable
inconciliàbile *agg.* irreconcilable
inconcludènte *agg.* inconclusive, ineffectual
incondizionàto *agg.* unconditional
inconfondìbile *agg.* unmistakable
inconfutàbile *agg.* irrefutable
incongruènte *agg.* inconsistent
inconsapévole *agg.* unaware
incònscio *agg. e s. m.* unconscious
inconsistènte *agg.* insubstantial, unfounded
inconsuèto *agg.* unusual
inconsùlto *agg.* rash
incontenìbile *agg.* uncontrollable
incontràre **A** *v. tr.* **1** to meet **2** (*imbattersi in*) to meet with, to come up against **B** *v. intr.* (*aver successo*) to be popular, to be a success **C** *v. intr. pron.* to meet, to see **D** *v. rifl. rec.* **1** to meet **2** (*coincidere*) to coincide
incóntro (1) *s. m.* **1** meeting **2** (*sport*) match
incóntro (a) (2) *prep.* toward(s), up to
inconveniènte *s. m.* **1** inconvenience, drawback **2** (*contrattempo*) mishap, snag
incoraggiaménto *s. m.* encouragement
incoraggiàre *v. tr.* to encourage
incorniciàre *v. tr.* to frame
incoronàre *v. tr.* to crown
incoronazióne *s. f.* coronation
incorporàre **A** *v. tr.* **1** to incorporate **2** (*territorio*) to annex **3** (*econ.*) to merge, to incorporate **B** *v. rifl. rec.* to merge
incórrere *v. intr.* to incur
incorruttìbile *agg.* incorruptible
incosciènte *agg.* **1** unconscious **2** (*irresponsabile*) irresponsible
incosciènza *s. f.* **1** unconsciousness **2** (*irresponsabilità*) irresponsability, recklessness
incostànte *agg.* inconstant, variable
incredìbile *agg.* incredible, unbelievable
incrèdulo *agg.* incredulous
incrementàre *v. tr.* to increase
increménto *s. m.* increase, increment
increspàre *v. tr. e intr. pron.* (*di acqua*) to ripple, (*di capelli*) to frizz, (*di stoffa*) to gather
incriminàre *v. tr.* to incriminate
incrinàre **A** *v. tr.* **1** to crack **2** (*fig.*) to damage, to spoil **B** *v. intr. pron.* **1** to crack **2** (*fig.*) to break up, to deteriorate
incrinatùra *s. f.* **1** crack **2** (*fig.*) rift

incrociàre A *v. tr.* **1** to cross **2** (*incontrare*) to meet **B** *v. intr.* (*naut., aer*) to cruise **C** *v. rifl. rec.* **1** to cross, to intersect **2** (*biol.*) to interbreed
incrociatóre *s. m.* cruiser
incrócio *s. m.* **1** (*di strade*) crossing, crossroads *pl.* **2** (*biol.*) crossbreed
incrostàre A *v. tr.* to encrust **B** *v. intr. pron.* to be encrusted
incrostazióne *s. f.* encrustation
incubatrìce *s. f.* incubator
ìncubo *s. m.* nightmare
incùdine *s. f.* anvil
inculcàre *v. tr.* to inculcate, to instil
incunàbolo *s. m.* incunabulum
incuràbile *agg. e s. m. e f.* incurable
incurànte *agg.* careless
incùria *s. f.* carelessness
incuriosire A *v. tr.* to make curious, to excite curiosity **B** *v. intr. pron.* to become curious
incursióne *s. f.* raid
incurvàre *v. tr. e intr. pron.* to bend
incustodito *agg.* unattended
incùtere *v. tr.* to arouse, to strike
ìndaco *s. m.* indigo
indaffaràto *agg.* busy
indagàre *v. tr. e intr.* to investigate, to inquire into
indàgine *s. f.* **1** investigation, inquiry **2** (*ricerca*) research, survey
indebitàre A *v. tr.* to get into debt **B** *v. rifl.* to run into debt
indébito *agg.* **1** (*non dovuto*) not due, undue **2** (*immeritato*) undeserved **3** (*illegittimo*) illegal, unlawful
indebolìre *v. tr. e intr. pron.* to weaken
indecènte *agg.* **1** indecent **2** (*sporco*) dirty
indecènza *s. f.* **1** indecency **2** (*vergogna*) shame
indecifràbile *agg.* **1** indecipherable **2** (*illeggibile*) illegible **3** (*incomprensibile*) unintelligible
indecisióne *s. f.* indecision
indecìso *agg.* **1** undecided, unsettled **2** (*irresoluto*) irresolute
indefèsso *agg.* indefatigable
indefinìbile *agg.* indefinable
indefinìto *agg.* **1** indefinite **2** (*non risolto*) undefined
indeformàbile *agg.* non-deformable
indégno *agg.* **1** unworthy **2** (*vergognoso*) shameful
indelèbile *agg.* indelible
indènne *agg.* unhurt, unharmed, undamaged
indennità *s. f.* allowance, indemnity, compensation
indennizzàre *v. tr.* to compensate, to indemnify
indennìzzo *s. m.* indemnity, refund ♦ **domanda d'i.** claim for damages
inderogàbile *agg.* unbreakable
indesideràbile *agg.* undesirable
indeterminatézza *s. f.* indeterminateness
indeterminàto *agg.* indeterminate ♦ **a tempo i.** indefinitely
indiàno *agg. e s. m.* Indian
indiavolàto *agg.* **1** furious **2** (*frenetico*) frenzied
indicàre *v. tr.* **1** to indicate, to show, to point out, (*col dito*) to point at/to **2** (*denotare*) to be indicative of, to show, to denote **3** (*significare*) to mean **4** (*consigliare*) to suggest, to recommend **5** (*prescrivere*) to prescribe
indicatìvo *agg.* **1** indicative **2** (*approssimativo*) approximate
indicatóre A *agg.* indicative **B** *s. m.* indicator, gauge
indicazióne *s. f.* **1** indication, sign **2** (*istruzione*) direction, instruction
ìndice *s. m.* **1** (*dito*) forefinger **2** (*lancetta*) indicator, pointer **3** (*fig.*) (*indizio*) sign, indication **4** (*di libro*) (table of) contents *pl.*, (*i. analitico*) index **5** (*scient.*) index **6** (*econ.*) index, ratio
indicìbile *agg.* inexspressible
indietreggiàre *v. intr.* to draw back, to withdraw
indiètro *avv.* **1** back, behind **2** (*di orologio*) slow ♦ **all'i.** backwards
indiféso *agg.* undefended
indifferènte *agg.* **1** indifferent **2** (*disinteressato*) uninterested **3** (*insensibile*) cold, impassible
indifferènza *s. f.* indifference
indifferenziàto *agg.* undifferentiated
indìgeno *agg. e s. m.* native
indigènte *agg.* indigent, poor
indigènza *s. f.* indigence, poverty
indigestióne *s. f.* indigestion
indigèsto *agg.* indigestible
indignàre A *v. tr.* to shock, to offend **B** *v. intr. pron.* to be shocked, to get angry
indimenticàbile *agg.* unforgettable
indipendènte *agg.* independent
indipendenteménte *avv.* independently

indipendènza *s. f.* independence
indìre *v. tr.* to call, to declare
indirètto *agg.* indirect
indirizzàre **A** *v. tr.* **1** to address **2** (*dirigere*) to direct **B** *v. rifl.* **1** (*dirigersi*) to direct one's step towards **2** (*rivolgersi*) to apply, to address oneself
indirìzzo *s. m.* **1** address **2** (*fig.*) direction, trend, turn
indiscréto *agg.* indiscreet, tactless
indiscùsso *agg.* undisputed
indiscutìbile *agg.* unquestionable
indispensàbile *agg.* indispensable
indispettìre **A** *v. tr.* to vex, to annoy **B** *v. intr. pron.* to become vexed, to become annoyed
indisposizióne *s. f.* indisposition
indissolùbile *agg.* indissoluble
indistìnto *agg.* indistinct
indistruttìbile *agg.* indestructible
indisturbàto *agg.* undisturbed
indìvia *s. f.* endive
individuàle *agg.* individual
individualìsmo *s. m.* individualism
individualménte *avv.* individually
individuàre *v. tr.* **1** (*caratterizzare*) to individualize **2** (*localizzare*) to locate **3** (*distinguere*) to single out, to identify
indivìduo *s. m.* individual
indivisìbile *agg.* indivisible
indiziàto *agg. e s. m.* suspect
indìzio *s. m.* **1** indication, sign, clue **2** (*dir.*) circumstantial evidence
indoeuropèo *agg. e s. m.* Indo-European
ìndole *s. f.* nature
indolènte *agg.* indolent, lazy
indolenziménto *s. m.* stiffening
indolóre *agg.* painless
indomàni *s. m.* (the) following day, (the) next day
indoràre *v. tr.* to gild
indossàre *v. tr.* **1** (*portare addosso*) to wear, to have on **2** (*mettere addosso*) to put on
indossatóre *s. m.* model
indossatrìce *s. f.* model
indottrinàre *v. tr.* to indoctrinate
indovinàre *v. tr.* **1** to guess **2** (*prevedere, immaginare*) to foresee, to imagine
indovinèllo *s. m.* riddle
indovìno *s. m.* fortune-teller
indubbiaménte *avv.* undoubtedly
indùbbio *agg.* undoubted
indugiàre *v. intr.* **1** to delay **2** (*trattenersi*) to loiter, to linger
indùgio *s. m.* delay
indulgènte *agg.* indulgent
indulgènza *s. f.* indulgence
indùlgere *v. intr.* to indulge
indùlto *s. m.* pardon
induménto *s. m.* garment, clothes *pl.*
indurìre **A** *v. tr.* to harden **B** *v. intr. e intr. pron.* to harden, to become hard, (*di cemento, colla, ecc.*) to set
indùrre *v. tr.* to induce, to persuade
indùstria *s. f.* industry
industriàle **A** *agg.* industrial, manufacturing **B** *s. m.* industrialist, manufacturer
industrializzazióne *s. f.* industrialization
industriàrsi *v. intr. pron.* to try
induzióne *s. f.* induction
inebetìto *agg.* dazed
inebriàre **A** *v. tr.* to intoxicate **B** *v. intr. pron.* to become intoxicated
ineccepìbile *agg.* unexceptionable
inèdia *s. f.* starvation
inèdito *agg.* unpublished
inefficàce *agg.* ineffective
inefficiènza *s. f.* inefficiency
ineluttàbile *agg.* ineluctable
inequivocàbile *agg.* unequivocal
inerènte *agg.* inherent, concerning
inèrme *agg.* unarmed
inerpicàrsi *v. intr. pron.* to climb
inèrte *agg.* **1** inert **2** (*immobile*) motionless
inèrzia *s. f.* **1** inertia **2** (*inattività*) inactivity
inesattézza *s. f.* inexactitude, inaccuracy
inesàtto *agg.* incorrect, inaccurate
inesaurìbile *agg.* inexhaustible
inesistènte *agg.* inexistent
inesoràbile *agg.* inexorable
inesperiènza *s. f.* inexperience
inespèrto *agg.* inexperienced, (*senza pratica*) inexpert
inesploràto *agg.* unexplored
inespugnàbile *agg.* inexpugnable, impregnable
inestimàbile *agg.* invaluable, priceless
inètto *agg.* **1** unfit, unsuitable **2** (*incapace*) incompetent
inevàso *agg.* outstanding
inevitàbile *agg.* unavoidable, inevitable
inèzia *s. f.* trifle
infagottàre *v. tr. e rifl.* to wrap up
infallìbile *agg.* infallible
infamàre *v. tr.* to defame, to disgrace
infàme *agg.* infamous
infantìle *agg.* children's (*attr.*), infantile

infànzia *s. f.* childhood, infancy
infarcìre *v. tr.* to stuff, to cram
infarinàre *v. tr.* to flour
infarinatùra *s. f.* **1** flouring **2** (*fig.*) smattering
infàrto *s. m.* infarct
infastidìre A *v. tr.* to annoy **B** *v. intr. pron.* to get annoyed
infaticàbile *agg.* tireless
infàtti *cong.* in fact, as a matter of fact
infatuàre A *v. tr.* infatuate **B** *v. intr. pron.* to become infatuated
infatuazióne *s. f.* infatuation
infàusto *agg.* unfavourable
infecóndo *agg.* sterile, infertile
infedéle *agg.* unfaithful
infedeltà *s. f.* unfaithfulness
infelìce *agg.* **1** unhappy, wretched **2** (*inappropriato*) unfortunate, inappropriate **3** (*malfatto*) bad
infelicità *s. f.* **1** unhappiness **2** (*inopportunità*) inappropriateness
inferióre *agg.* **1** inferior **2** (*più basso*) lower **3** (*sottostante*) lower, below
inferiorità *s. f.* inferiority
infermerìa *s. f.* infirmary
infermièra *s. f.* nurse
infermière *s. m.* male nurse
infermità *s. f.* infirmity ♦ **i. mentale** insanity
infermo *agg.* invalid
infernàle *agg.* **1** infernal, hellish **2** (*fig.*) awful
infèrno *s. m.* hell
inferocìto *agg.* enraged
inferriàta *s. f.* bars *pl.*
infervoràre A *v. tr.* to animate, to arouse enthusiasm **B** *v. intr. pron.* to grow fervent, to get excited
infestàre *v. tr.* to infest
infettàre A *v. tr.* to infect **B** *v. intr. pron.* to become infected
infettìvo *agg.* infectious, catching
infètto *agg.* infected
infezióne *s. f.* infection
infiacchìre *v. tr. e intr. pron.* to weaken
infiammàbile *agg.* inflammable
infiammàre A *v. tr.* **1** to set on fire **2** (*fig.*) to inflame **B** *v. intr. pron.* **1** to take fire **2** (*fig.*) to become inflamed
infiammazióne *s. f.* inflammation
infìdo *agg.* treacherous
infierìre *v. intr.* **1** to be pitiless **2** (*imperversare*) to rage
infìggere *v. tr.* to drive, to fix
infilàre A *v. tr.* **1** to thread, to string **2** (*introdurre*) to insert, to slip in **3** (*infilzare*) to run through, to transfix **4** (*indossare*) to slip on, to put on **B** *v. rifl.* **1** (*farsi largo*) to thread one's way **2** (*introdursi*) to slip **3** (*indossare*) to slip on, to put on
infiltràrsi *v. intr. pron.* to infiltrate
infiltrazióne *s. f.* infiltration
infilzàre *v. tr.* **1** to run through, to transfix **2** (*conficcare*) to stick
ìnfimo *agg.* lowest
infìne *avv.* **1** (*alla fine*) at last **2** (*da ultimo*) finally **3** (*in fondo*) after all **4** (*insomma*) in short
infinità *s. f.* infinity
infinitesimàle *agg.* infinitesimal
infinìto A *agg.* **1** infinite **2** (*interminabile*) endless **3** (*innumerevole*) innumerable, endless **4** (*gramm.*) infinitive **B** *s. m.* **1** infinity **2** (*gramm.*) infinitive
infinocchiàre *v. tr.* (*fam.*) to make a fool of
infischiàrsi *v. intr. pron.* (*fam.*) not to care, to care nothing
infìsso *s. m.* frame
infittìre *v. tr. e intr. pron.* to thicken
inflazionàre *v. tr.* **1** to inflate **2** (*fig.*) to overdo
inflazióne *s. f.* inflation
inflessìbile *agg.* inflexible
inflìggere *v. tr.* to inflict
influènte *agg.* influential
influènza *s. f.* **1** influence **2** (*med.*) influenza, flu ♦ **prendere l'i.** to catch flu
influìre *v. intr.* to influence
inflùsso *s. m.* influence
infondàto *agg.* groundless
infóndere *v. tr.* to infuse
inforcàre *v. tr.* **1** to pitchfork **2** (*bicicletta, cavallo, ecc.*) to get on **3** (*occhiali*) to put on
informàle *agg.* informal
informàre A *v. tr.* **1** to inform, to acquaint **2** (*pervadere*) to pervade, to characterize **B** *v. intr. pron.* **1** to inquire **2** (*essere pervaso*) to be informed, to be pervaded
informàtica *s. f.* informatics *pl.* (*v. al sing.*)
informatìvo *agg.* informative
informatóre *s. m.* informer, informant
informazióne *s. f.* information
infórme *agg.* shapeless
infortunàrsi *v. intr. pron.* to get injured
infortùnio *s. m.* accident
infossàrsi *v. intr. pron.* **1** to become hollow

2 (*affondare*) to sink
infràngere A *v. tr.* 1 to break, to shatter 2 (*violare*) to infringe B *v. intr. pron.* to break, to shatter
infrangìbile *agg.* unbreakable
infraróssо *agg. e s. m.* infrared
infrasettimanàle *agg.* midweek (*attr*)
infrazióne *s. f.* infraction, infringement
infreddatùra *s. f.* cold
infreddolìto *agg.* cold
infruttuóso *agg.* 1 unfruitful, fruitless 2 (*improduttivo*) unprofitable 3 (*vano*) vain, unsuccessful
infuòri *avv.* out, outwards ♦ **all'i. di** except, apart from
infuriàre A *v. intr.* to rage B *v. intr. pron.* to fly into a rage, to flare up
infusióne *s. f.* infusion
infùso *s. m.* infusion
ingabbiàre *v. tr.* 1 to cage 2 (*fig.*) to enclose, to coop up
ingaggiàre *v. tr.* 1 to engage, to hire, to sign (up) 2 (*mil.*) to enlist 3 (*iniziare*) to start
ingannàre A *v. tr.* to deceive, to cheat, to swindle B *v. intr. pron.* to be mistaken, to be wrong ♦ **i. il tempo** to while away the time
ingannévole *agg.* deceitful, deceptive
ingànno *s. m.* deceit, deception
ingarbugliàre A *v. tr.* 1 to entangle 2 (*fig.*) to complicate, to confuse B *v. intr. pron.* to get entangled
ingegnàrsi *v. intr. pron.* to do one's best
ingegnère *s. m.* engineer
ingegnerìa *s. f.* engineering
ingégno *s. m.* intelligence
ingegnosità *s. f.* ingenuity, cleverness
ingegnóso *agg.* ingenious, clever
ingelosìre A *v. tr.* to make jealous B *v. intr. pron.* to become jealous
ingènte *agg.* great, huge
ingenuità *s. f.* ingenuousness, naïvety
ingènuo *agg.* ingenuous, naïve
ingerènza *s. f.* interference
ingerìre A *v. tr.* to swallow, to ingest B *v. intr. pron.* to interfere
ingessàre *v. tr.* to plaster
ingessatùra *s. f.* plaster
inghiottìre *v. tr.* to swallow
ingiallìre *v. tr. e intr. pron.* to yellow
ingigantìre A *v. tr.* to magnify B *v. intr. pron.* to become gigantic
inginocchiàrsi *v. intr. pron.* to kneel (down)
ingiù *avv.* down, downwards
ingiùria *s. f.* 1 insult, abuse 2 (*dir*) slander, offence
ingiuriàre A *v. tr.* to insult, to abuse B *v. rifl. rec.* to insult each other
ingiurióso *agg.* insulting, abusive
ingiustificàto *agg.* unjustified
ingiustìzia *s. f.* 1 injustice, unfairness 2 (*torto*) wrong
ingiùsto *agg.* unjust, unfair
inglése A *agg.* English B *s. m. e f.* Englishman *m.*, Englishwoman *f.* C *s. m.* (*lingua*) English
inglesìsmo *s. m.* Anglicism
ingoiàre *v. tr.* to swallow
ingolfàre A *v. tr.* to flood B *v. intr. pron.* 1 (*impelagarsi*) to plunge into 2 (*autom.*) to flood
ingombrànte *agg.* 1 cumbersome 2 (*fig.*) awkward
ingombràre *v. tr.* 1 to encumber, to block 2 (*fig.*) to stuff
ingòmbro *s. m.* 1 encumbrance, obstruction 2 (*mole*) bulk, (*dimensione*) size
ingórdo *agg.* greedy
ingorgàre A *v. tr.* to clog, to block (up) B *v. intr. pron.* to become blocked up, to clog up
ingórgo *s. m.* obstruction, (*del traffico*) jam
ingozzàre A *v. tr.* (*far mangiare*) to stuff, to fatten B *v. rifl.* to gobble, to gulp down
ingranàggio *s. m.* 1 gear 2 (*fig.*) mechanism, workings *pl.*
ingranàre A *v. tr.* to put into gear, to engage B *v. intr.* 1 to be in gear, to engage 2 (*fig.*) to get on (well)
ingrandiménto *s. m.* enlargement ♦ **lente d'i.** magnifying glass
ingrandìre A *v. tr.* 1 to enlarge, to expand 2 (*fis.*) to magnify 3 (*fig.*) to exaggerate B *v. intr. pron.* to become larger, to grow, to expand
ingrassàggio *s. m.* greasing
ingrassàre A *v. tr.* 1 to fatten, to make fat 2 (*lubrificare*) to grease B *v. intr. e intr. pron.* to put on weight, to fatten (up)
ingratitùdine *s. f.* ungratefulness
ingràto *agg.* ungrateful
ingraziàre *v. tr.* to ingratiate oneself with
ingrediènte *s. m.* ingredient
ingrèsso *s. m.* 1 entry 2 (*entrata*) entrance 3 (*accesso*) entry, admittance, admission ♦ **vietato l'i.** no entry
ingrossàre A *v. tr.* 1 to enlarge, to increase 2 (*gonfiare*) to swell B *v. intr. pron.* 1 to

become bigger, to increase **2** (*gonfiarsi*) to swell up **3** (*ingrassare*) to become fat **4** (*di mare*) to rise
ingròsso, all' *loc. avv.* wholesale
inguarìbile *agg.* incurable
ìnguine *s. m.* groin
inibìre **A** *v. tr.* **1** to inhibit **2** (*proibire*) to forbid **B** *v. rifl.* to restrain oneself
inibizióne *s. f.* inhibition
iniettàre *v. tr.* to inject
iniettóre *s. m.* injector
iniezióne *s. f.* injection
inimicàre **A** *v. tr.* to alienate, to make an enemy of, to antagonize **B** *v. intr. pron.* to fall out with
inimicìzia *s. f.* enmity, hostility
inimitàbile *agg.* inimitable
inimmaginàbile *agg.* unimaginable
ininfluènte *agg.* irrelevant
ininterrótto *agg.* continuous, uninterrupted
iniquità *s. f.* iniquity
inizìale **A** *agg.* initial, starting **B** *s. f.* initial
iniziàre **A** *v. tr.* **1** to begin, to start **2** (*instradare*) to initiate, to introduce **B** *v. intr.* to begin, to start
iniziatìva *s. f.* initiative
iniziàto *s. m.* initiate
iniziatóre *agg.* initiator
inìzio *s. m.* beginning, start
innaffiàre *v. tr.* to water
innalzàre **A** *v. tr.* to raise **B** *v. intr. pron.* to rise
innamoràre **A** *v. tr.* to charm **B** *v. intr. pron. e rifl. rec.* to fall in love
innamoràto *agg.* in love (*pred.*), loving
innànzi **A** *avv.* **1** (*prima*) before **2** (*poi*) on, onwards **B** *agg.* previous **C** *prep.* **i. (a)** **1** (*davanti a*) before, in front of **2** (*prima*) before ♦ **i. tutto** above all, first of all
innàto *agg.* innate, inborn
innaturàle *agg.* unnatural
innegàbile *agg.* undeniable
innervosìre **A** *v. tr.* to get on (sb.'s) nerves, to annoy **B** *v. intr. pron.* to get nervous, to get annoyed
innescàre **A** *v. tr.* **1** (*tecnol.*) to prime **2** (*fis.*) to trigger **B** *v. intr. pron.* to start
innésco *s. m.* **1** primer **2** (*fis., fig.*) trigger
innestàre **A** *v. tr.* **1** (*bot.*) to graft **2** (*inserire*) to insert, to plug in (*elettr.*) **3** (*mecc.*) to engage **B** *v. intr. pron.* to be inserted, to join
innèsto *s. m.* **1** (*bot.*) graft **2** (*mecc.*) connection, joint
ìnno *s. m.* hymn ♦ **i. nazionale** national anthem
innocènte *agg.* **1** innocent **2** (*dir.*) not guilty
innocènza *s. f.* innocence
innòcuo *agg.* innocuous, harmless
innovàre *v. tr.* to innovate, to renew
innovatìvo *agg.* innovative
innovatóre *s. m.* innovator
innumerévole *agg.* innumerable, countless
inoculàre *v. tr.* to inoculate
inodóre *agg.* odourless
inoffensìvo *agg.* harmless, inoffensive
inoltràre **A** *v. tr.* to forward, to send, (*per posta*) to mail **B** *v. rifl.* to advance, to go forward
inóltre *avv.* besides, too, moreover
inondàre *v. tr.* to flood
inondazióne *s. f.* flooding, flood, inundation
inoperóso *agg.* inactive
inopportùno *agg.* inopportune, untimely
inorgànico *agg.* inorganic
inorgoglìre **A** *v. tr.* to make proud **B** *v. intr. pron.* to become proud
inorridìre **A** *v. tr.* to horrify **B** *v. intr.* to be horrified
inospitàle *agg.* inhospitable
inosservàto *agg.* **1** unobserved, unnoticed **2** (*inadempiuto*) not observed, unfulfilled
inossidàbile *agg.* stainless
input *s. m. inv.* input
inquadràre **A** *v. tr.* **1** to organize, to arrange **2** (*fot., cin.*) to frame **B** *v. intr. pron.* to fit in, to form part of
inqualificàbile *agg.* **1** unmarkable **2** (*fig.*) deplorable
inquietànte *agg.* worrying, disturbing
inquietàre **A** *v. tr.* to worry, to disturb **B** *v. intr. pron.* **1** (*arrabbiarsi*) to get angry **2** (*preoccuparsi*) to worry
inquièto *agg.* **1** (*agitato*) restless **2** (*preoccupato*) uneasy, worried
inquietùdine *s. f.* **1** (*agitazione*) restlessness **2** (*preoccupazione*) anxiety, worry
inquilìno *s. m.* tenant
inquinaménto *s. m.* pollution
inquinàre *v. tr.* to pollute
inquisìre *v. tr.* to investigate
inquisizióne *s. f.* inquisition
insabbiàre **A** *v. tr.* **1** to sand **2** (*fig.*) to shelve **B** *v. intr. pron. e rifl.* **1** to get covered with sand **2** (*arenarsi*) to run aground **3** (*fig.*) to be shelved

insaccàti *s. m. pl.* sausages
insalàta *s. f.* salad
insalùbre *agg.* unhealthy
insanàbile *agg.* **1** incurable **2** (*irrimediabile*) irremediable
insanguinàre *v. tr.* **1** to stain with blood **2** (*funestare*) to bathe in blood
insaponàre **A** *v. tr.* to soap **B** *v. rifl.* to soap oneself
insapóre *agg.* flavourless, tasteless
insaziàbile *agg.* insatiable
inscatolàre *v. tr.* to box, to tin, to can
inscenàre *v. tr.* to stage
insediaménto *s. m.* **1** settlement **2** (*in una carica*) installation
insediàre **A** *v. tr.* to install **B** *v. intr. pron.* **1** to take office, to install oneself **2** (*stabilirsi*) to settle
inségna *s. f.* **1** (*di locale*) sign **2** (*bandiera*) banner, flag
insegnaménto *s. m.* teaching
insegnànte **A** *agg.* teaching **B** *s. m. e f.* teacher
insegnàre *v. tr.* **1** to teach **2** (*indicare*) to show
inseguiménto *s. m.* pursuit, chase
inseguìre *v. tr.* **1** to chase, to run after **2** (*fig.*) to pursue
insenatùra *s. f.* inlet
insensàto *agg.* senseless
insensìbile *agg.* **1** insensitive **2** (*impercettibile*) imperceptible **3** (*indifferente*) indifferent
inseparàbile *agg.* inseparable
inseriménto *s. m.* insertion
inserìre **A** *v. tr.* **1** to insert, to put in, to include **2** (*elettr.*) to connect, to plug in **B** *v. rifl. e intr. pron.* to enter
insèrto *s. m.* insert
inservìbile *agg.* useless
inserviènte *s. m. e f.* attendant
inserzióne *s. f.* **1** insertion **2** (*su giornale*) advertisement, ad
insetticìda *s. m.* insecticide
insètto *s. m.* insect
insicurézza *s. f.* insecurity
insìdia *s. f.* **1** snare, trap **2** (*pericolo*) peril, danger
insidiàre *v. tr.* to lay a trap for
insidióso *agg.* insidious
insième **A** *s. m.* **1** whole **2** (*assortimento*) set **3** (*mat.*) set **B** *avv.* **1** together **2** (*congiuntamente*) together, jointly **3** (*contemporaneamente*) together, at the same time **C** *prep.* **i. a/con** (together) with
insìgne *agg.* eminent, distinguished
insignificànte *agg.* **1** insignificant, negligible **2** (*inespressivo*) inexpressive
insignìre *v. tr.* to confer
insincèro *agg.* insincere
insindacàbile *agg.* unquestionable
insinuàre **A** *v. tr.* **1** to slip, to insert **2** (*fig.*) to insinuate, to suggest **B** *v. intr. pron. e rifl.* **1** to insinuate oneself **2** (*penetrare*) to creep
insìpido *agg.* **1** (*senza sale*) lacking in salt **2** (*insapore*) tasteless, insipid
insistènte *agg.* **1** insistent **2** (*ripetuto*) persistent **3** (*incessante*) unceasing
insìstere *v. intr.* to insist
insoddisfacènte *agg.* unsatisfactory
insoddisfàtto *agg.* **1** unsatisfied **2** (*scontento*) dissatisfied
insoddisfazióne *s. f.* dissatisfaction
insofferènte *agg.* **1** (*irritabile*) impatient, irritable **2** (*intollerante*) intolerant
insolazióne *s. f.* **1** insolation **2** (*colpo di sole*) sunstroke
insolènte *agg.* insolent
insolentìre *v. intr.* to be insolent to
insolènza *s. f.* insolence
insòlito *agg.* unusual
insolùbile *agg.* insoluble
insolùto *agg.* **1** unsolved **2** (*non pagato*) unpaid
insolvènte *agg.* insolvent
insómma *avv.* **1** (*in breve*) in short **2** (*in conclusione*) in conclusion **3** (*dunque*) then, well **4** (*esclamativo*) well (then)
insònne *agg.* sleepless
insònnia *s. f.* insomnia, sleeplessness
insonnolìto *agg.* sleepy, drowsy
insopportàbile *agg.* unbearable, insufferable
insórgere *v. intr.* **1** (*ribellarsi*) to rise (up) **2** (*protestare*) to protest **3** (*manifestarsi*) to arise
insórto *s. m.* rebel, insurgent
insospettàbile *agg.* beyond suspicion
insospettìre **A** *v. tr.* to make suspicious, to arouse suspicions **B** *v. intr. pron.* to become suspicious
insostenìbile *agg.* **1** unsustainable, untenable **2** (*insopportabile*) unbearable
insostituìbile *agg.* irreplaceable
inspiegàbile *agg.* inexplicable
inspiràre *v. tr.* to breathe in
instàbile *agg.* **1** unstable, unsteady **2** (*mu-*

tevole) changeable
installàre **A** *v. tr.* to install **B** *v. rifl.* to settle (oneself) in
installazióne *s. f.* installation
instancàbile *agg.* indefatigable, untiring
instauràre **A** *v. tr.* to set up, to establish **B** *v. intr. pron.* to begin
insù *avv.* up, upwards
insuccèsso *s. m.* failure, flop
insudiciàre **A** *v. tr.* to dirty, to soil **B** *v. rifl.* to dirty oneself, to get dirty
insufficiènte *agg.* insufficient, inadequate
insufficienza *s. f.* **1** insufficiency, inadequacy **2** (*mancanza*) lack, shortage **3** (*med.*) insufficiency **4** (*a scuola*) low mark
insulàre *agg.* insular
insulina *s. f.* insulin
insùlso *agg.* insipid, dull
insultàre *v. tr.* to insult, to abuse
insùlto *s. m.* insult, abuse
insuperàbile *agg.* insuperable
insurrezióne *s. f.* insurrection, rising
intaccàre *v. tr.* **1** (*fare tacche*) to notch **2** (*corrodere*) to corrode, to eat into **3** (*cominciare a consumare*) to draw up, to dip into **4** (*danneggiare*) to damage, to spoil
intagliàre *v. tr.* **1** to incise, to engrave **2** (*scolpire*) to carve
intàglio *s. m.* **1** (*arte*) intaglio **2** (*tacca*) notch
intangìbile *agg.* untouchable
intànto *avv.* **1** meanwhile, in the meantime, at the same time **2** (*avversativo*) but ♦ **i. che** while, as
intàrsio *s. m.* inlay
intasaménto *s. m.* stoppage, block, (*nel traffico*) jam
intasàre **A** *v. tr.* to obstruct, to block **B** *v. intr. pron.* to become blocked, to get stopped up
intascàre *v. tr.* to pocket
intàtto *agg.* **1** intact, untouched **2** (*illeso*) undamaged, uninjured
intavolàre *v. tr.* to start, to enter into
integràle *agg.* **1** integral, complete, comprehensive **2** (*di edizione*) unabridged **3** (*non raffinato*) wholemeal, unrefined
integralménte *avv.* in full
integrànte *agg.* integrant
integràre **A** *v. tr.* **1** to integrate **2** (*completare*) to supplement **B** *v. rifl.* to integrate
integrità *s. f.* integrity
intelaiatùra *s. f.* framework, (*di finestra*) sash
intellètto *s. m.* intellect
intellettuàle *agg.* intellectual
intellettualìsmo *s. m.* intellectualism
intelligènte *agg.* intelligent, clever
intelligènza *s. f.* intelligence, cleverness
intelligìbile *agg.* intelligible
intempèrie *s. f. pl.* bad weather
intempestìvo *agg.* untimely
intèndere **A** *v. tr.* **1** (*capire*) to understand **2** (*significare*) to mean, to intend **3** (*avere intenzione*) to intend, to propose, to be going to **4** (*udire*) to hear **B** *v. intr. pron.* to know about, to be an expert **C** *v. rifl. rec.* **1** (*mettersi d'accordo*) to come to an agreement, to agree **2** (*andare d'accordo*) to get on with
intendiménto *s. m.* **1** understanding **2** (*intenzione*) intention
intenditóre *s. m.* connoisseur, expert
intenerìre **A** *v. tr.* **1** to soften **2** (*fig.*) to move (to pity) **B** *v. intr. pron.* **1** to soften **2** to be moved
intensificàre *v. tr. e intr. pron.* to intensify
intensità *s. f.* intensity
intensìvo *agg.* intensive
intènso *agg.* intense
intènto **A** *agg.* intent **B** *s. m.* aim, purpose
intenzionàle *agg.* intentional
intenzióne *s. f.* intention
interaménte *avv.* entirely, wholly
interazióne *s. f.* interaction
intercalàre *s. m.* stock phrase
intercapèdine *s. f.* hollow space
intercèdere *v. intr.* to intercede, to plead
intercessióne *s. f.* intercession
intercettàre *v. tr.* to intercept, (*conversazione telefonica*) to tap
intercolùnnio *s. m.* intercolumn
intercomunicànte *agg.* communicating
intercontinentàle *agg.* intercontinental
interdétto *agg.* **1** (*vietato*) forbidden **2** (*dir.*) interdicted, disqualified **3** (*sorpreso*) dumbfounded
interdìre *v. tr.* **1** (*proibire*) to forbid **2** (*dir.*) to interdict, to disqualify
interdisciplinàre *agg.* interdisciplinary
interdizióne *s. f.* **1** (*proibizione*) prohibition **2** (*dir.*) interdiction, disqualification
interessaménto *s. m.* interest, concern
interessànte *agg.* interesting ♦ **essere in stato i.** to be with child, to be expecting
interessàre **A** *v. tr.* **1** to interest **2** (*riguardare*) to concern, to affect **B** *v. intr.* **1** to

interest, to be of interest **2** (*importare*) to matter **C** *v. intr. pron.* to be interested in, to care
interèsse *s. m.* interest
interferènza *s. f.* interference
interferire *v. intr.* to interfere
interfòno *s. m.* intercom
interiezióne *s. f.* interjection
interióra *s. f. pl.* entrails *pl.*
interióre *agg.* interior, inner
interlocutóre *s. m.* interlocutor
interlùdio *s. m.* interlude
intermediàrio *s. m.* **1** intermediary **2** (*econ.*) broker
intermèdio *agg.* intermediate
intermèzzo *s. m.* **1** (*intervallo*) break, interval **2** (*mus., teatro*) intermezzo
interminàbile *agg.* interminable
intermittènte *agg.* intermittent
internaménte *avv.* internally, inside
internàre *v. tr.* to intern
internazionàle *agg.* international
intèrno **A** *agg.* **1** internal, inner (*attr.*), inside (*attr.*) **2** (*geogr.*) inland **3** (*interiore*) inner (*attr.*), inward (*attr.*) **4** (*econ.*) (*nazionale*) home (*attr.*) **B** *s. m.* **1** interior, inside **2** (*tel.*) extension **3** (*alunno*) boarder **4** (*fodera*) lining
intéro *agg.* **1** (*tutto*) whole, all **2** (*completo*) entire, whole, complete ♦ **per i.** in full
interpellàre *v. tr.* to consult, to ask
interpórre **A** *v. tr.* **1** to interpose **2** (*frapporre*) to present **B** *v. rifl. e intr. pron.* to interpose, to intervene
interpretàre *v. tr.* **1** to interpret **2** (*teatro, mus.*) to play, to interpret
interpretazióne *s. f.* interpretation
intèrprete *s. m. e f.* interpreter
interrogàre *v. tr.* **1** to ask questions to **2** (*studente*) to examine, to test **3** (*dir.*) to question, to interrogate
interrogatìvo **A** *agg.* interrogative, questioning **B** *s. m.* **1** question **2** (*fig.*) mistery ♦ **punto i.** question mark
interrogatòrio **A** *agg.* interrogatory **B** *s. m.* interrogation, examination
interrogazióne *s. f.* **1** question, interrogation **2** (*a scuola*) test
interrómpere **A** *v. tr.* **1** to interrupt, to break off, to cut off **2** (*un discorso*) to interrupt **3** (*bloccare*) to block **B** *v. intr. pron.* to stop, to break off
interruttóre *s. m.* switch
interruzióne *s. f.* interruption
intersecàre *v. tr. e rifl. rec.* to intersect
intersezióne *s. f.* intersection
interstìzio *s. m.* interstice
interurbàno *agg.* interurban ♦ **telefonata interurbana** trunk call
intervàllo *s. m.* interval
intervenìre *v. intr.* **1** to intervene **2** (*prender parte*) to be present, to attend
intervènto *s. m.* **1** intervention **2** (*discorso*) speech **3** (*presenza*) presence, attendance **4** (*med.*) operation
intervìsta *s. f.* interview
intervistàre *v. tr.* to interview
intésa *s. f.* **1** (*comprensione*) unterstanding **2** (*accordo*) agreement **3** (*pol.*) entente
intestàre **A** *v. tr.* **1** (*mettere l'intestazione*) to head **2** (*una proprietà*) to register in sb.'s name, (*un assegno*) to make out **B** *v. intr. pron.* to persist, to insist
intestazióne *s. f.* **1** heading **2** (*registrazione*) registration
intestinàle *agg.* intestinal
intestìno **A** *agg.* intestine, civil **B** *s. m.* intestine
intiepidìre **A** *v. tr.* **1** (*scaldare*) to warm **2** (*raffreddare*) to cool **B** *v. intr. pron.* **1** (*scaldarsi*) to warm up **2** (*raffreddarsi*) to cool down
intimàre *v. tr.* to order, to command, to summon
intimazióne *s. f.* order, command, summons
intimidìre **A** *v. tr.* **1** to overawe, to make shy **2** (*impaurire*) to indimidate **B** *v. intr. pron.* **1** to become shy **2** (*impaurirsi*) to be intimidate
intimìsta *agg.* intimist
intimità *s. f.* **1** intimacy, privacy **2** (*familiarità*) familiarity
ìntimo **A** *agg.* **1** intimate, close **2** (*privato*) private, intimate, **3** (*il più profondo*) inner, innermost **4** (*profondo*) profound, deep **B** *s. m.* **1** (*parte interiore*) bottom **2** (*amico*) intimate friend, close friend **3** (*animo*) hearth, soul
intimorìre **A** *v. tr.* to intimidate, to frighten **B** *v. intr. pron.* to be frightened
intìngolo *s. m.* sauce
intirizzìre **A** *v. tr.* to numb, to make stiff **B** *v. intr. pron.* to grow numb, to grow stiff
intitolàre **A** *v. tr.* **1** to entitle, to give a title to, to call **2** (*dedicare*) to dedicate, to name after **B** *v. intr. pron.* to be entitled, to be called, to be named

intolleràbile *agg.* intolerable, unbearable
intollerànte *agg.* intolerant
intolleranza *s. f.* intolerance
intònaco *s. m.* plaster
intonàre **A** *v. tr.* **1** (*strumento*) to tune **2** (*incominciare a cantare, suonare*) to strike up **3** (*accordare*) to match **B** *v. intr. pron.* to be in tune, to match, to fit
intontìre **A** *v. tr.* to stun, to daze **B** *v. intr. pron.* to be stunned, to be dazed
intòppo *s. m.* obstacle
intórno **A** *avv.* round, around, about **B** *prep.* **i. (a)** **1** round, around **2** (*circa*) about **3** (*riguardo a*) about, on
intorpidìre **A** *v. tr.* to numb **B** *v. intr. pron.* to grow numb
intossicàre **A** *v. tr.* to poison **B** *v. rifl. e intr. pron.* to be poisoned
intossicazióne *s. f.* poisoning
intradòsso *s. m.* intrados
intraducìbile *agg.* untranslatable
intralciàre *v. tr.* to hinder, to hamper
intransigènte *agg.* intransigent
intransitìvo *agg. e s. m.* intransitive
intraprendènte *agg.* enterprising
intraprèndere *v. tr.* to undertake, to begin
intrattàbile *agg.* intractable
intrattenère **A** *v. tr.* to entertain **B** *v. intr. pron.* **1** (*trattenersi*) to stop **2** (*soffermarsi*) to dwell (upon)
intravedére *v. tr.* **1** (*vedere di sfuggita*) to catch a glimpse of **2** (*prevedere*) to foresee
intrecciàre **A** *v. tr.* **1** to twist, to intertwine **2** (*capelli*) to plait **3** (*fig.*) to weave together **B** *v. rifl. rec.* **1** to intertwine **2** to cross each other
intréccio *s. m.* **1** intertwinement, weaving **2** (*trama*) plot
intrìco *s. m.* tangle
intrìgo *s. m.* intrigue
intrìnseco *agg.* intrinsic
introdùrre **A** *v. tr.* **1** to introduce **2** (*inserire*) to put in, to insert **3** (*far entrare*) to show in, to usher **B** *v. intr. pron.* to get in
introduzióne *s. f.* introduction
intròito *s. m.* income, revenues *pl.*
introméttere **A** *v. tr.* to interpose **B** *v. rifl.* **1** to intervene, to come between **2** (*ingerirsi*) to interfere
introspettìvo *agg.* introspective
introvàbile *agg.* not to be found
introvèrso *agg. e s. m.* introvert
intrùglio *s. m.* concoction
intrusióne *s. f.* intrusion
intrùso *s. m.* intruder
intuìre *v. tr.* to perceive by intuition, to guess
intuitìvo *agg.* intuitive
intuizióne *s. f.* intuition
inumidìre **A** *v. tr.* to damp, to moisten **B** *v. intr. pron.* to moisten, to become damp
inùtile *agg.* **1** useless, unusable, pointless **2** (*non necessario*) unnecessary
inutilità *s. f.* uselessness, pointlessness
inutilizzàbile *agg.* unusable
inutilménte *avv.* uselessly, in vain
invadènte *agg.* intrusive
invàdere *v. tr.* to invade
invaghìrsi *v. intr. pron.* **1** to take a fancy of **2** (*innamorarsi*) to fall in love with
invalidità *s. f.* **1** invalidity **2** (*di persona*) disability
invàlido **A** *agg.* **1** invalid **2** (*di persona*) disabled, invalid **B** *s. m.* disabled person
invàno *avv.* in vain, to no purpose
invasióne *s. f.* invasion
invasóre **A** *agg.* invading **B** *s. m.* invader
invecchiaménto *s. m.* ag(e)ing
invecchiàre **A** *v. tr.* **1** to age, to make old **2** (*far sembrare vecchio*) to make look older **B** *v. intr.* to age, to grow old, to get old
invéce **A** *avv.* instead, on the contrary, but **B** *prep.* **i. di** instead of **C** *cong.* **i. che** instead of
inveìre *v. intr.* to rail against, to shout abuse at
invendìbile *agg.* unsaleable
inventàre *v. tr.* to invent
inventàrio *s. m.* **1** inventory **2** (*elenco*) list
inventìva *s. f.* inventiveness
inventìvo *agg.* inventive
inventóre *s. m.* inventor
invenzióne *s. f.* **1** invention **2** (*bugia*) lie, story
invernàle *agg.* winter (*attr.*)
invèrno *s. m.* winter
inverosìmile *agg.* unlikely, improbable
inversióne *s. f.* inversion, reversal ♦ **i. di marcia** U-turn
invèrso **A** *agg.* **1** opposite, contrary, reverse **2** (*mat.*) inverse **B** *s. m.* opposite, contrary
invertebràto *agg. e s. m.* invertebrate
invertìre **A** *v. tr.* to reverse, to invert **B** *v. intr.* pron. to be inverted
investigàre *v. tr. e intr.* to investigate
investigazióne *s. f.* investigation, inquiry

investiménto *s. m.* **1** investment **2** (*autom.*) collision, accident
investìre **A** *v. tr.* **1** (*econ.*) to invest **2** (*autom.*) to run over **3** (*assalire*) to assail **4** (*conferire una carica*) to invest, to give **B** *v. rifl. rec.* to collide
investitóre *s. m.* (*econ.*) investor
inviàre *v. tr.* to send, to forward
inviàto *s. m.* **1** messenger, envoy **2** (*giornalista*) correspondent
invìdia *s. f.* envy
invidiàre *v. tr.* to envy
invidióso *agg.* envious
invincìbile *agg.* invincible
invìo *s. m.* **1** (*di merce*) dispatch, forwarding **2** (*di denaro*) remittance **3** (*per posta*) mailing
invischiare **A** *v. tr.* (*fig.*) to involve in **B** *v. intr. pron.* to get involved
invisìbile *agg.* invisible
invitànte *agg.* tempting, attractive
invitàre *v. tr.* to invite, to ask
invitàto *s. m.* guest
invìto *s. m.* invitation
invocàre *v. tr.* **1** to invoke **2** (*chiedere*) to demand **3** (*fare appello a*) to appeal to
invogliàre *v. tr.* to tempt
involontàrio *agg.* unintentional, involuntary
involtìno *s. m.* roulade
invòlucro *s. m.* wrapping, cover
involuzióne *s. f.* **1** involution **2** (*declino*) decline, regression
inzaccheràre **A** *v. tr.* to splash with mud **B** *v. rifl.* to get splashed with mud
inzuppàre **A** *v. tr.* **1** to soak **2** (*immergere*) to dip **B** *v. intr. pron.* to get soaked
ìo *pron. pers. 1ª sing.* (*sogg.*) I, (*pred.*) me ◆ **io stesso** I myself
iòdio *s. m.* iodine
iònico (1) *agg.* Ionic
iònico (2) *agg.* (*chim.*) ionic
iperbòlico *agg.* hyperbolic(al)
ipercrìtico *agg.* hypercritical
ipermercàto *s. m.* hypermarket
ipermetropìa *s. f.* hypermetropia
iperrealìsmo *s. m.* hyper-realism
ipertensióne *s. f.* hypertension
ipnòsi *s. f.* hypnosis
ipnotìsmo *s. m.* hypnotism
ipnotizzàre *v. tr.* to hypnotize
ipocrisìa *s. f.* hypocrisy
ipòcrita **A** *agg.* hypocritical **B** *s. m. e f.* hypocrite
ipogèo *s. m.* hypogeum
ipotèca *s. f.* **1** mortgage **2** (*fig.*) claim
ipotecàre *v. tr.* **1** to mortgage **2** (*fig.*) to stake a claim on
ipòtesi *s. f.* **1** hypothesis **2** (*congettura*) conjecture, supposition
ipotètico *agg.* **1** hypothetical **2** (*presunto*) presumed, supposed
ìppica *s. f.* horse racing
ìppico *agg.* horse (*attr.*)
ippocàmpo *s. m.* sea-horse
ippocastàno *s. m.* chestnut
ippòdromo *s. m.* race-course
ippopòtamo *s. m.* hippopotamus
ìra *s. f.* rage, anger
irachèno *agg. e s. m.* Iraqi
iraniàno *agg. e s. m.* Iranian
irascìbile *agg.* irascible, quick-tempered
ìride *s. f.* iris
irlandése **A** *agg.* Irish **B** *s. m. e f.* Irishman *m.*, Irishwoman *f.* **C** *s. m.* (*lingua*) Irish
ironìa *s. f.* irony
irònico *agg.* ironic(al)
ironizzàre *v. tr. e intr.* to be ironic (about)
irradiàre **A** *v. tr. e intr.* to irradiate **B** *v. intr. pron.* to radiate, to spread out
irradiazióne *s. f.* irradiation
irraggiungìbile *agg.* unattainable
irragionévole *agg.* unreasoning, unreasonable
irrazionàle *agg.* irrational
irreàle *agg.* unreal
irrealtà *s. f.* unreality
irrecuperàbile *agg.* irretrievable
irredentìsmo *s. m.* irredentism
irregolàre *agg.* irregular
irremovìbile *agg.* inflexible
irreparàbile *agg.* irreparable
irreperìbile *agg.* not to be found
irrequièto *agg.* restless
irresistìbile *agg.* irresistible
irrespiràbile *agg.* unbreathable
irresponsàbile *agg.* irresponsible
irriducìbile *agg.* irreducible
irrigàre *v. tr.* to irrigate
irrigazióne *s. f.* irrigation
irrigidìre **A** *v. tr.* to stiffen **B** *v. intr. pron.* to become stiff
irrìguo *agg.* **1** (*che irriga*) irrigation (*attr.*) **2** (*irrigato*) irrigated, (*ricco d'acqua*) (well-)watered
irrilevànte *agg.* insignificant, trifling
irrimediàbile *agg.* irremediable
irripetìbile *agg.* unrepeatable

irrisòrio *agg.* **1** derisive **2** (*inadeguato*) trifling, ridiculous
irritàbile *agg.* irritable
irritànte *agg.* **1** irritating, annoying **2** (*med.*) irritant
irritàre **A** *v. tr.* **1** to irritate, to annoy **2** (*med.*) to irritate **B** *v. intr. pron.* to become irritated
irritazióne *s. f.* irritation
irrómpere *v. intr.* to burst into, to break into
irroràre *v. tr.* to sprinkle, to spray
irruènte *agg.* impetuous
irruènza *s. f.* impetuosity
irruzióne *s. f.* **1** (*polizia*) raid **2** (*est.*) irruption
iscrìtto *s. m.* member
iscrìvere **A** *v. tr.* **1** (*una persona*) to enrol(l), to enter **2** (*registrare*) to record, to enter **3** (*geom.*) to inscribe **4** (*scolpire*) to inscribe, to engrave **B** *v. rifl.* to enrol(l) oneself, to enter
iscrizióne *s. f.* **1** enrol(l)ment, registration, entry **2** (*su pietra*) inscription
islàmico *agg.* Islamic
islamìsmo *s. m.* Islamism
islandése **A** *agg.* Icelandic **B** *s. m. e f.* Icelander
isòbara *s. f.* isobar
isòbata *s. f.* isobath
ìsola *s. f.* island, isle
isolaménto *s. m.* **1** isolation **2** (*tecnol.*) insulation
isolàno *agg.* island (*attr.*)
isolànte *agg.* insulating
isolàre **A** *v. tr.* **1** to isolate **2** (*tecnol.*) to insulate **B** *v. intr. pron.* to isolate oneself, to cut oneself off
isolàto **A** *agg.* **1** isolated, secluded **2** (*tecnol.*) insulated **B** *s. m.* (*di case*) block
ispànico *agg.* Hispanic
ispettóre *s. m.* inspector, surveyor
ispezionàre *v. tr.* to inspect
ispezióne *s. f.* inspection
ìspido *agg.* bristly
ispiràre **A** *v. tr.* to inspire **B** *v. intr. pron.* to draw inspiration
ispiratóre *s. m.* inspirer
ispirazióne *s. f.* inspiration
israeliàno *agg. e s. m.* Israeli
israelìtico *agg.* Israelite
issàre *v. tr.* to hoist
istantaneaménte *avv.* instantly
istantàneo *agg.* instant, sudden
istànte *s. m.* instant, moment
istànza *s. f.* **1** (*richiesta*) request, application, petition **2** (*esigenza*) need, demand
istèrico *agg.* hysteric
isterìsmo *s. m.* hysteria
istigàre *v. tr.* to instigate, to incite
istigazióne *s. f.* instigation, incitement
istintìvo *agg.* instinctive
istìnto *s. m.* instinct
istituìre *v. tr.* to institute, to establish, to set up
istitùto *s. m.* institute, institution ♦ **i. di bellezza** beauty parlour
istituzionàle *agg.* institutional
istituzióne *s. f.* institution
ìstmo *s. m.* isthmus
ìstrice *s. m.* porcupine
istrióne *s. m.* actor, (*spreg.*) ham
istruìre *v. tr.* **1** to educate, to instruct **2** (*addestrare*) to train **3** (*dare istruzioni*) to direct, to give instructions to
istruttìvo *agg.* instructive
istruttóre *s. m.* instructor
istruttòria *s. f.* inquest
istruzióne *s. f.* **1** education, training **2** (*cultura*) learning, culture **3** *al pl.* instructions *pl.*, directions *pl.* **4** (*inf.*) statement ♦ **i. obbligatoria** compulsory education
italianìsta *s. m. e f.* Italianist
italiàno *agg. e s. m.* Italian
itàlico *agg.* Italic
iter *s. m. inv.* course, procedure
iteratìvo *agg.* iterative
itinerànte *agg.* itinerant, wandering
itineràrio *s. m.* itinerary, route
itterìzia *s. f.* jaundice
ìttico *agg.* ichthyic, fish (*attr.*) ♦ **mercato i.** fish market
ittiologìa *s. f.* ichthyology
ittìta *agg.* Hittite
iugoslavo *agg. e s. m.* Yugoslav
iùta *s. f.* jute

J

jazz *s. m.* jazz ♦ **orchestra j.** jazz band
jazzista *s. m. e f.* jazz player
jazzistico *agg.* jazz (*attr*)
jeans *s. m. pl.* jeans *pl.*
jeep *s. f.* jeep
jet *s. m. inv.* jet
jogging *s. m. inv.* jogging
jolly *s. m. inv.* joker
judo *s. m. inv.* judo

K

karatè *s. m. inv.* karate
keniòta *agg. e s. m. e f.* Kenyan
kermesse *s. f. inv.* kermess
ketch *s. m. inv.* ketch
killer *s. m. e f. inv.* killer
kitsch *agg. e s. m. inv.* kitsch
kiwi *s. m. inv.* kiwi
koala *s. m. inv.* koala

L

la (1) *art. determ. f. sing.* the (*spesso non si traduce o si rende con un agg. poss, con l'art. indef. o con il partitivo*) (ES: **mi piace la cioccolata** I like chocolate, **dammi il cappello, per favore** give me my hat, please, **la rosa è un fiore profumato** a rose is a fragrant flower, **hai comprato la cannella?** did you buy some cinnamon?)
la (2) *pron. pers. 3ª f. sing.* **1** (*oggetto*) (*riferito a donna o animale di sesso femminile*) her, (*riferito a cosa o animale di sesso indefinito*) it **2** (*oggetto, dando del Lei*) you
là *avv.* there
làbbro *s. m.* lip
labirìnto *s. m.* labyrinth, maze
laboratòrio *s. m.* **1** (*di ricerca*) laboratory, lab (*fam.*) **2** (*di artigiano*) workshop, workroom
laborióso *agg.* **1** (*industrioso*) hard-working, industrious **2** (*faticoso*) laborious, toilsome
laburìsta *agg.* Labour (*attr*)
làcca *s. f.* **1** lacquer, lake **2** (*per capelli*) hair spray **3** (*per unghie*) nail polish
lacchè *s. m.* lackey
làccio *s. m.* **1** lace, string **2** (*trappola*) snare ♦ **l. emostatico** tourniquet; **prendere al l.** to snare
laceràre *v. tr. e intr. pron.* to tear, to lacerate
lacerazióne *s. f.* laceration, tearing
làcero *agg.* **1** torn **2** (*med.*) lacerated
lacònico *agg.* laconic
làcrima *s. f.* **1** tear **2** (*goccia*) drop
lacrimàre *v. intr.* **1** (*per irritazione*) to water **2** (*versare lacrime*) to shed tears **3** (*stillare*) to drip
lacrimògeno *agg.* lachrymatory ♦ **gas l.** tear gas

lacrimóso *agg.* tearful
lacuàle *agg.* lake (*attr.*)
lacùna *s. f.* gap
lacùstre *agg.* lake (*attr.*), lacustrine
làdro *s. m.* thief, (*scassinatore*) burglar, (*rapinatore*) robber ♦ **al l.!** stop thief!
ladrocìnio *s. m.* robbery
laggiù *avv.* **1** (*in basso*) down there **2** (*lontano*) over there
lagnànza *s. f.* complaint
lagnàrsi *v. intr. pron.* to complain, to moan
làgo *s. m.* lake
lagùna *s. f.* lagoon
lagunàre *agg.* lagoon (*attr.*)
laicìsmo *s. m.* laicism
làico *agg.* lay, laic(al)
làma (1) *s. f.* blade
làma (2) *s. m.* (*zool.*) llama
lambìre *v. tr.* to lick
lamèlla *s. f.* (*anat., bot., zool.*) lamella, (*di fungo*) gill
lamentàre **A** *v. tr.* **1** to mourn, to lament **2** (*esprimere protesta per*) to complain **B** *v. intr. pron.* **1** to moan, to lament **2** (*lagnarsi*) to complain about
lamentèla *s. f.* complaint
laménto *s. m.* **1** lament, moan **2** (*lagnanza*) complaint **3** (*suono*) wail
lamentóso *agg.* mournful
lamétta *s. f.* razor-blade
lamièra *s. f.* plate, (*sottile*) sheet
làmina *s. f.* **1** (*anat., bot.*) lamina **2** (*metall.*) thin layer, leaf
laminàre *v. tr.* to laminate, to roll
laminàto *s. m.* **1** (*metall.*) rolled section **2** (*plastico*) laminate
làmpada *s. f.* lamp
lampadàrio *s. m.* chandelier
lampadìna *s. f.* bulb, lamp
lampànte *agg.* clear, evident
lampeggiàre **A** *v. intr.* **1** (*sfolgorare*) to flash **2** (*con luce intermittente*) to flash, to blink, to wink **B** *v. intr. impers.* to lighten
lampeggiatóre *s. m.* indicator, blinker
lampióne *s. m.* street lamp
làmpo **A** *s. m.* **1** lightning **2** (*guizzo di luce*) flash **B** *s. f.* (*cerniera*) zip (fastener)
lampóne *s. m.* raspberry
làna *s. f.* wool ♦ **di l.** woollen; **gomitolo di l.** ball of wool; **pura l.** pure wool
lancétta *s. f.* **1** (*di strumento*) pointer, needle **2** (*di orologio*) hand
lància *s. f.* **1** lance **2** (*tecnol.*) nozzle **3** (*naut.*) ship's boat, tender, launch ♦ **l. di salvataggio** lifeboat
lanciafiàmme *s. m.* flame-thrower
lanciàre **A** *v. tr.* **1** to throw, to hurl, to fling **2** (*un prodotto*) to launch **B** *v. rifl.* **1** to throw oneself, to fling, to dash **2** (*fig.*) to launch
lancinànte *agg.* piercing
làncio *s. m.* **1** throw, hurl, fling **2** (*sport*) throwing **3** (*pubblicitario*) launch, launching
lànda *s. f.* moor
lànguido *agg.* languid, faint
languìre *v. intr.* **1** to languish **2** (*venir meno*) to slacken, to drag
languóre *s. m.* weakness, languor
lanifìcio *s. m.* woollen mill
lantèrna *s. f.* lantern
lanùgine *s. f.* down
lapalissiàno *agg.* evident
lapidàre *v. tr.* to stone
lapidàrio *agg.* lapidary
làpide *s. f.* (*tombale*) tombstone, (*commemorativa*) memorial tablet
lapis *s. m. inv.* pencil
lapsus *s. m. inv.* slip
làrdo *s. m.* bacon fat, lard
larghézza *s. f.* **1** width, breadth **2** (*abbondanza*) largeness, abundance **3** (*ampiezza*) largeness, breadth
làrgo **A** *agg.* **1** broad, wide **2** (*di vestito*) loose-fitting, (*troppo grande*) big, loose **3** (*abbondante*) large **B** *s. m.* **1** width **2** (*naut.*) open sea ♦ **al l.** offshore; **farsi l.** to make one's way
làrice *s. m.* larch
larìnge *s. f.* larynx
laringìte *s. f.* laryngitis
laringoiàtra *s. m. e f.* laryngologist
làrva *s. f.* **1** (*zool.*) larva, grub **2** (*apparenza*) phantom
larvàle *agg.* larval
lasciapassàre *s. m. inv.* pass
lasciàre **A** *v. tr.* **1** to leave **2** (*abbandonare*) to abandon, to quit **3** (*permettere*) to let **4** (*lasciar andare*) to let go **5** (*lasciare da parte*) to keep **B** *v. rifl.* to let oneself **C** *v. rifl. rec.* to leave each other
làscito *s. m.* legacy
laser *s. m. inv.* laser
lassatìvo *agg. e s. m.* laxative
làsso *s. m.* lapse, period
lassù *avv.* up there
làstra *s. f.* slab, (*di metallo e fot.*) plate, (*di vetro*) sheet
lastricàre *v. tr.* to pave

làstrico *s. m.* paving ♦ **essere sul l.** to be on the rocks
lastróne *s. m.* (large) slab
latènte *agg.* latent
lateràle *agg.* lateral, side (*attr*)
lateralménte *avv.* laterally
laterìzi *s. m. pl.* bricks *pl.*
latifòglio *agg.* broad-leaved
latifondìsmo *s. m.* latifundism
latifóndo *s. m.* latifundium, large estate
latinìsmo *s. m.* Latinism
latinìsta *s. m. e f.* Latinist
latinità *s. f.* Latinity
latìno *agg. e s. m.* Latin
latìno-americàno *agg. e s. m.* Latin American
latitànte *s. m. e f.* absconder
latitùdine *s. f.* latitude
làto *s. m.* side ♦ **da un l. ..., dall'altro** on the one hand ..., on the other hand
latràre *v. intr.* to bark
làtta *s. f.* **1** tin **2** (*recipiente*) can, tin
lattàio *s. m.* milkman
lattànte *s. m.* (unweaned) baby
làtte *s. m.* milk ♦ **l. in polvere** powdered milk; **l. intero** whole milk; **l. scremato** skimmed milk
làtteo *agg.* milk (*attr*)
latterìa *s. f.* dairy
latticìnio *s. m.* dairy product
lattina *s. f.* tin, can
lattùga *s. f.* lettuce
làurea *s. f.* degree ♦ **l. ad honorem** honorary degree
laureàre **A** *v. tr.* to confer a degree **B** *v. intr. pron.* to graduate, to take a degree
laureàto *s. m.* graduate
làuro *s. m.* laurel, bay-tree
làuto *agg.* large, lavish
làva *s. f.* lava
lavabiancherìa *s. f. inv.* washing-machine
lavàbile *agg.* washable
lavàbo *s. m.* washbasin
lavàggio *s. m.* washing
lavàgna *s. f.* blackboard
lavànda (1) *s. f.* (*bot.*) lavender
lavànda (2) *s. f.* (*med.*) lavage ♦ **l. gastrica** gastric lavage
lavanderìa *s. f.* laundry, (*automatica*) laund(e)rette
lavandìno *s. m.* sink
lavapiàtti *s. m. e f. inv.* dish-washer
lavàre **A** *v. tr.* to wash **B** *v. rifl.* to wash oneself
lavastovìglie *s. f. inv.* dish-washer
lavàta *s. f.* wash
lavatrìce *s. f.* washing machine
làvico *agg.* lavic
lavorànte *s. m. e f.* worker, assistant
lavoràre **A** *v. intr.* **1** to work **2** (*funzionare*) to operate, to work **3** (*di ditta*) to do business **B** *v. tr.* to work
lavoratìvo *agg.* working
lavoratóre **A** *agg.* working **B** *s. m.* worker
lavorazióne *s. f.* working, manufacturing, (*metodo*) processing, (*fattura*) workmanship, (*realizzazione*) production
lavóro *s. m.* **1** work, (*spec. manuale*) labour **2** (*occupazione*) job, employment, work **3** (*fis.*) work **4** (*opera*) (piece of) work
lazzarétto *s. m.* lazaretto
le (1) *art. determ. f. pl.* the (*spesso non si traduce o si rende con l'agg. poss. o con il partitivo*) (ES: **battere le mani** to clap hands, **lavati le mani** wash your hands, **hai comprato le mele?** did you buy some apples?)
le (2) **A** *pron pers, 3ª sing. f.* **1** (*compl. ind.*) (to) her, (for) her (*riferito a donna o animale di sesso femminile*) (to) her, (for) her, (*riferito a cosa o animale di sesso indefinito*) (to) it, (for) it **2** (*compl. ind., dando del Lei*) (to) you, (for) you **B** *pron. pers. 3ª pl. f.* (*compl. ogg.*) them
leàle *agg.* **1** loyal **2** (*onesto*) fair
lealtà *s. f.* **1** loyalty **2** (*onestà*) fairness
lébbra *s. f.* leprosy
lebbrosàrio *s. m.* leper hospital
leccapièdi *s. m. e f.* bootlicker
leccàre *v. tr.* to lick, to lap
léccio *s. m.* ilex, holm-oak
leccornìa *s. f.* delicacy, titbit
lécito **A** *agg.* **1** (*dir*) licit, lawful **2** (*concesso*) allowed (*pred.*), right **B** *s. m.* right
lèdere *v. tr.* to damage
léga *s. f.* **1** league, alliance **2** (*metall.*) alloy
legàccio *s. m.* string
legàle **A** *agg.* **1** legal **2** (*conforme alla legge*) lawful **B** *s. m.* lawyer ♦ **ora l.** summer time
legalizzàre *v. tr.* **1** to legalize **2** (*autenticare*) to authenticate
legàme *s. m.* **1** tie, bond **2** (*connessione*) link, connection
legàre **A** *v. tr.* to tie, to bind, to fasten **B** *v. intr.* **1** (*accordarsi*) to go well, to get on well **2** (*aver connessione*) to be connected **C** *v. rifl.* to bind oneself

legàto *s. m.* (*dir*) legacy
legatorìa *s. f.* bookbindery
legatùra *s. f.* **1** fastening, binding **2** (*mus.*) ligature, slur
légge *s. f.* law ♦ **proposta di l.** bill
leggènda *s. f.* legend
leggendàrio *agg.* legendary
lèggere *v. tr.* to read
leggerézza *s. f.* **1** lightness **2** (*agilità*) nimbleness **3** (*mancanza di serietà*) thoughtlessness
leggèro *agg.* **1** light **2** (*lieve*) slight, (*di suono*) faint **3** (*non forte*) light, weak
leggiàdro *agg.* graceful
leggìbile *agg.* legible, readable
leggìo *s. m.* book-rest, (*mus.*) music-stand
legióne *s. f.* legion
legislatìvo *agg.* legislative
legislatùra *s. f.* legislature
legislazióne *s. f.* legislation, laws *pl.*
legittimàre *v. tr.* **1** to legitimize **2** (*giustificare*) to justify
legìttimo *agg.* lawful, legitimate, legal
légna *s. f.* wood, (*da ardere*) firewood
legnàme *s. m.* wood, (*da costruzione*) timber
légno *s. m.* **1** wood **2** (*mus.*) *al pl.* woodwinds *pl.* ♦ **di l.** wooden
legnóso *agg.* wooden, woody
legùme *s. m.* **1** (*pianta*) legume **2** *al pl.* (*semi*) pulse
lèi *pron. pers. 3ª sing. f.* **1** (*oggetto*) her **2** (*sogg.*) she **3** (*nella forma di cortesia*) you
lémbo *s. m.* **1** edge **2** (*zona*) strip
lèmma *s. m.* headword, entry
léna *s. f.* vigour
leninìsmo *s. m.* Leninism
lenìre *v. tr.* to soothe
lenitìvo *agg.* lenitive, soothing
lènte *s. f.* lens ♦ **lenti a contatto** contact lenses
lentézza *s. f.* slowness
lentìcchia *s. f.* lentil
lentìggine *s. f.* freckle
lènto *agg.* **1** slow **2** (*allentato*) slack
lènza *s. f.* fishing line
lenzuòlo *s. m.* sheet ♦ **l. da bagno** bath-towel
leóne *s. m.* lion
leonéssa *s. f.* lioness
leopàrdo *s. m.* leopard
lèpre *s. f.* hare
lèrcio *agg.* dirty
lèsbica *s f.* lesbian
lesèna *s. f.* pilaster
lesinàre *v. tr. e intr.* to skimp
lesionàre **A** *v. tr.* to damage **B** *v. intr. pron.* to be damaged
lesióne *s. f.* **1** (*med.*) lesion **2** (*dir*) injury **3** (*danno*) damage
lessàre *v. tr.* to boil
lèssico *s. m.* **1** lexicon, language **2** (*dizionario*) dictionary, lexicon
lésso **A** *agg.* boiled **B** *s. m.* boiled beef, boiled meat
lèsto *agg.* quick
letàle *agg.* lethal
letamàio *s. m.* **1** dung-hill **2** (*fig.*) pigsty
letàme *s. m.* manure, dung
letàrgo *s. m.* **1** (*med.*, *fig.*) lethargy **2** (*zool.*) dormancy
letìzia *s. f.* joy
lèttera *s. f.* letter ♦ **l. maiuscola/minuscola** capital/small letter
letteràle *agg.* literal
letteralménte *avv.* literally
letteràrio *agg.* literary, bookish
letteràto *s. m.* man of letters
letteratùra *s. f.* literature
lettìga *s. f.* stretcher
lètto *s. m.* bed ♦ **camera da l.** bedroom; **l. a castello** bunk bed; **l. a una piazza** single bed; **l. matrimoniale** double bed; **vagone l.** sleeping car
lettóre *s. m.* reader
lettùra *s. f.* reading
leucemìa *s. f.* leukaemia
lèva (1) *s. f.* lever
lèva (2) *s. f.* **1** (*mil.*) call-up, (*USA*) draft **2** (*est.*) generation
levànte **A** *agg.* rising **B** *s. m.* east
levàre **A** *v. tr.* **1** (*sollevare*) to raise, to lift **2** (*togliere*) to remove, to take away, to take off **3** (*abolire*) to remove, to abolish **B** *v. rifl. e intr. pron.* **1** (*togliersi*) to get out **2** (*alzarsi dal letto*) to get up, (*alzarsi in piedi*) to stand up, (*alzarsi in volo*) to take off **3** (*sorgere*) to rise
levàta *s. f.* **1** (*del sole*) rising **2** (*della posta*) collection
levatrìce *s. f.* midwife
levatùra *s. f.* stature, calibre
levigàre *v. tr.* to smooth
levigatézza *s. f.* smoothness
levrière *s. m.* greyhound
lezióne *s. f.* lesson, (*all'università*) lecture ♦ **ora di l.** period
lezióso *agg.* affected

lézzo *s. m.* stink
li *pron. pers. 3ª pl. m.* (*compl. ogg.*) them
lì *avv.* there ♦ **di lì a poco** shortly after; **lì per lì** (*dapprima*) at first, (*sul momento*) there and then; **lì vicino** near there
libagióne *s. f.* libation
libanése *agg. e s. m.* Lebanese
lìbbra *s. f.* pound
libèllo *s. m.* libel
libèllula *s. f.* dragon-fly
liberàle *agg.* liberal
liberalìsmo *s. m.* liberalism
liberalità *s. f.* liberality
liberalizzàre *v. tr.* to liberalize
liberalizzazióne *s. f.* liberalization
liberaménte *avv.* **1** freely **2** (*francamente*) frankly
liberàre **A** *v. tr.* **1** to free, to liberate, to release **2** (*sgombrare*) to clear **B** *v. rifl.* to free oneself, to get rid
liberatóre *s. m.* liberator
liberazióne *s. f.* liberation
lìbero *agg.* **1** free **2** (*non occupato*) clear, vacant, empty **3** (*aperto*) open
libertà *s. f.* freedom, liberty
libertìno *agg.* libertine
lìberty *agg. e s. m. inv.* art nouveau
lìbico *agg. e s. m.* Libyan
libìdine *s. f.* **1** lechery **2** (*desiderio*) lust, thirst
libràio *s. m.* bookseller
libràrio *agg.* book (*attr*)
libràrsi *v. rifl.* to hover
librerìa *s. f.* **1** bookshop, (*USA*) bookstore **2** (*mobile*) bookcase
librettìsta *s. m. e f.* librettist
librétto *s. m.* **1** booklet, book **2** (*d'opera*) libretto ♦ **l. degli assegni** chequebook; **l. di lavoro** employment card
lìbro *s. m.* book ♦ **l. di bordo** logbook; **l. di testo** text-book; **l. giallo** thriller
liceàle *agg.* high-school (*attr*)
licènza *s. f.* **1** (*concessione*) licence, authorization **2** (*scolastica*) (*esame*) school-leaving examination, (*diploma*) school-leaving certificate **3** (*libertà*) liberty, licence
licenziaménto *s. m.* dismissal
licenziàre **A** *v. tr.* to dismiss **B** *v. rifl.* to resign
licenzióso *agg.* dissolute, licentious
licèo *s. m.* high school
lìdo *s. m.* shore, beach
lièto *agg.* glad, happy
liève *agg.* **1** light **2** (*debole*) gentle, slight, soft
lievitàre *v. intr.* **1** to rise, to ferment **2** (*aumentare*) to grow
lièvito *s. m.* yeast
lìgio *agg.* faithful
lìgneo *agg.* (*di legno*) wooden, (*simile al legno*) woody
lìlla *agg. e s. m.* lilac
lìma *s. f.* file
limaccióso *agg.* muddy
limàre *v. tr.* **1** to file **2** (*fig.*) to polish
lìmbo *s. m.* limbo
limétta *s. f.* nail-file
limitàre **A** *v. tr.* **1** (*circoscrivere*) to bound **2** (*restringere*) to limit, to restrict **B** *v. rifl.* to limit oneself, to restrict oneself
limitatìvo *agg.* limitative, restrictive
limitazióne *s. f.* limitation, restriction
lìmite *s. m.* limit, bound
limìtrofo *agg.* neighbouring
limonàta *s. f.* lemonade
limóne *s. m.* lemon
limpidézza *s. f.* clearness, limpidity
lìmpido *agg.* clear, limpid
lìnce *s. f.* lynx
linciàggio *s. m.* lynching
linciàre *v. tr.* to lynch
lìndo *agg.* neat
lìnea *s. f.* **1** line **2** (*del corpo*) figure ♦ **in l. d'aria** as the crow flies; **l. aerea** airline; **servizio di linea** regular service
lineaménti *s. m. pl.* **1** features *pl.* **2** (*fig.*) outlines *pl.*
lineàre *agg.* **1** linear **2** (*fig.*) straightforward, consistent
linearità *s. f.* **1** linearity **2** (*fig.*) straightforwardness, consistency
lineétta *s. f.* dash
lìnfa *s. f.* lymph
lingòtto *s. m.* bar
lìngua *s. f.* **1** tongue **2** (*linguaggio*) language, tongue
linguàggio *s. m.* language, speech
linguétta *s. f.* tongue, spline
linguìstica *s. f.* linguistics *pl.* (*v. al sing.*)
linguìstico *agg.* linguistic
lìno *s. m.* **1** (*bot.*) flax **2** (*tessuto*) linen
liofilizzàre *v. tr.* to freeze-dry, to lyophilize
lipìde *s. m.* lipid
liquefàre *v. tr. e intr. pron.* to liquefy
liquidàre *v. tr.* **1** (*sciogliere*) to liquidate, to wind up **2** (*saldare*) to settle, to clear, to pay off **3** (*svendere*) to sell off **4** (*sbarazzarsi*) to get rid of

liquidazióne *s. f.* **1** liquidation, winding-up **2** (*pagamento*) settlement, payment **3** (*indennità di fine rapporto*) severance pay **4** (*svendita*) clearance sale
liquidità *s. f.* liquidity
lìquido **A** *agg.* liquid **B** *s. m.* **1** liquid, fluid **2** (*denaro*) cash
liquirìzia *s. f.* licorice
liquóre *s. m.* liquor, spirits *pl.*
lìra (1) *s. f.* (*mus.*) lyre
lìra (2) *s. f.* (*moneta*) lira ♦ **l. sterlina** pound sterling
lìrica *s. f.* **1** lyric poetry **2** (*componimento*) lyric **3** (*mus.*) opera
lìrico *agg.* **1** lyric(al) **2** (*mus.*) opera (*attr.*)
lirìsmo *s. m.* lyricism
lìsca *s. f.* fishbone
lisciàre *v. tr.* **1** to smooth **2** (*accarezzare*) to stroke **3** (*lusingare*) to flatter
lìscio *agg.* **1** smooth **2** (*semplice*) plain ♦ **ballo l.** ballroom dance
lìso *agg.* worn out
lìsta *s. f.* list
listìno *s. m.* list ♦ **l. prezzi** price-list
litanìa *s. f.* **1** litany **2** (*sequela*) string
lìte *s. f.* **1** quarrel, row **2** (*dir.*) lawsuit
litigàre *v. intr.* to quarrel, to have a row
litìgio *s. m.* quarrel, row
litigióso *agg.* quarrelsome
litografìa *s. f.* (*procedimento*) lithography, (*riproduzione*) lithograph
litoràle *s. m.* coast
litoràneo *agg.* coast (*attr.*), coastal
lìtro *s. m.* litre, (*USA*) liter ♦ **mezzo l.** half a litre
liturgìa *s. f.* liturgy
litùrgico *agg.* liturgical
liutàio *s. m.* lute-maker
liùto *s. m.* lute
livèlla *s. f.* level
livellàre **A** *v. tr.* to level, to even up **B** *v. intr. pron.* to level out, to even out
livèllo *s. m.* **1** level **2** (*grado*) standard, level, degree ♦ **passaggio a l.** level crossing
lìvido **A** *agg.* livid **B** *s. m.* bruise
livóre *s. m.* spite
livrèa *s. f.* **1** livery **2** (*di uccello*) plumage
lìzza *s. f.* lists *pl.*
lo (1) *art. determ. m. sing.* → **il**
lo (2) *pron. pers. 3ª sing. m.* **1** (*compl. ogg.*) (*riferito a uomo o animale maschio*) him, (*riferito a cosa o animale di sesso non determinato*) it **2** (*questo, ciò*) it, that (*spesso idiom.*) (ES: **lo so** I know)
lòbo *s. m.* lobe
locàle **A** *agg.* local **B** *s. m.* **1** (*stanza*) room, premises *pl.* **2** (*treno*) slow train
località *s. f.* resort
localizzàre **A** *v. tr.* **1** to locate **2** (*circoscrivere*) to localize **B** *v. intr. pron.* to become localized
locànda *s. f.* inn
locandìna *s. f.* playbill
locatàrio *s. m.* tenant, renter
locatóre *s. m.* lessor
locazióne *s. f.* lease
locomotìva *s. f.* locomotive
locomozióne *s. f.* locomotion
locùsta *s. f.* locust
locuzióne *s. f.* locution, expression
lodàre *v. tr.* to praise
lòde *s. f.* praise
lodévole *agg.* praiseworthy
logarìtmo *s. m.* logarithm
lòggia *s. f.* **1** (*arch.*) loggia **2** (*massonica*) lodge
loggiàto *s. m.* open gallery
loggióne *s. m.* gallery
lògica *s. f.* logic
logicaménte *avv.* **1** logically **2** (*naturalmente*) obviously
lògico *agg.* logical
logoràre *v. tr. e intr. pron.* to wear out
logorìo *s. m.* wearing out
lógoro *agg.* worn-out
logorròico *agg.* logorrheic
logoterapìa *s. f.* speech therapy
lombàggine *s. f.* lumbago
lómbo *s. m.* loin
lombrìco *s. m.* earthworm
londinése **A** *agg.* London (*attr.*) **B** *s. m. e f.* Londoner
longèvo *agg.* long-lived
longilìneo *agg.* long-limbed
longitudinàle *agg.* longitudinal
longitùdine *s. f.* longitude
lontanànza *s. f.* distance
lontàno **A** *agg.* **1** (*nello spazio*) far-off (*attr.*), far-away (*attr.*), distant (*attr.*), far off (*pred.*), far away (*pred.*), far apart (*pred.*), far (*attr.*) **2** (*nel tempo*) distant (*attr.*), far-away (*attr.*), far off (*pred.*), far away (*pred.*) **3** (*assente*) absent **4** (*vago*) faint, slight **B** *avv.* far away, a long way, in the distance, far **C** *prep.* **l. da** far from, away from
lóntra *s. f.* otter
loquàce *agg.* loquacious

lórdo *agg.* **1** dirty **2** (*valore*) gross
lordùra *s. f.* filth
lóro (1) A *agg. poss. 3ª pl. m. e f.* **1** their, (*loro proprio*) their own **2** (*pred.*) theirs **3** (*nella forma di cortesia*) your, yours (*pred.*) **B** *pron. poss. m. e f.* **1** theirs **2** (*nella forma di cortesia*) yours
lóro (2) *pron. pers. 3ª pl. m. e f.* **1** (*compl. ogg. e ind.*) them **2** (*sogg.*) they **3** (*pred.*) them, they **4** (*nella forma di cortesia, sogg. e compl.*) you
losànga *s. f.* lozenge
lósco *agg.* **1** (*bieco*) sly **2** (*di dubbia onestà*) suspicious, shady
lòtta *s. f.* **1** struggle, fight **2** (*sport*) wrestling
lottàre *v. intr.* **1** to struggle, to fight **2** (*sport*) to wrestle
lottatóre *s. m.* **1** fighter **2** (*sport*) wrestler
lotterìa *s. f.* lottery, (*di beneficenza*) raffle
lottizzàre *v. tr.* **1** to lot out **2** (*pol.*) to carve up
lozióne *s. f.* lotion
lubrificànte A *agg.* lubricating **B** *s. m.* lubricant
lubrificàre *v. tr.* to lubricate, to oil
lubrificazióne *s. f.* lubrication
lucchétto *s. m.* padlock
luccicàre *v. intr.* to glitter, to sparkle, to twinkle
lùccio *s. m.* pike
lùcciola *s. f.* firefly
lùce *s. f.* **1** light **2** (*apertura*) opening, (*arch.*) span **3** (*finestra, vetrina*) (light) window
lucènte *agg.* shining
lucèrna *s. f.* oil-lamp
lucernàrio *s. m.* skylight
lucèrtola *s. f.* lizard
lucidàre *v. tr.* to polish
lucidatrìce *s. f.* polisher
lucidità *s. f.* lucidity
lùcido A *agg.* **1** bright, shiny, (*lucidato*) polished **2** (*fig.*) lucid **B** *s. m.* **1** brightness, sheen **2** (*materiale lucidante*) polish
lucràre *v. tr.* to gain, to make a profit
lùcro *s. m.* gain, profit
lucróso *agg.* lucrative
ludìbrio *s. m.* mockery
lùdico *agg.* ludic, playful
lùglio *s. m.* July
lùgubre *agg.* gloomy, dismal
lùi *pron. pers. 3ª sing. m.* **1** (*compl. ogg. e ind.*) him **2** (*sogg.*) he **3** (*pred.*) he, him
lumàca *s. f.* snail
lùme *s. m.* lamp, light
luminària *s. f.* illuminations *pl.*
luminosità *s. f.* brightness, luminosity
luminóso *agg.* **1** bright, luminous **2** (*fig.*) brilliant
lùna *s. f.* moon ♦ **l. di miele** honeymoon
lùna park *loc. sost. m. inv.* funfair
lunàre *agg.* lunar, moon (*attr.*)
lunàrio *s. m.* almanac
lunàtico *agg.* moody
lunedì *s. m.* Monday
lunétta *s. f.* lunette
lungàggine *s. f.* slowness
lunghézza *s. f.* **1** length **2** (*edil.*) run
lùngi *avv.* far
lungimirànte *agg.* farsighted
lùngo A *agg.* **1** long **2** (*alto*) tall **3** (*lento*) slow **4** (*diluito*) weak, thin **B** *prep.* **1** along, by the side of **2** (*durante*) during, over
lungolàgo *s. m.* lakeside
lungomàre *s. m.* seafront, promenade
lunòtto *s. m.* rear window, back window
luògo *s. m.* **1** place, spot **2** (*di azione*) scene, site **3** (*di scritto*) passage
luogotenènte *s. m.* lieutenant
lùpo *s. m.* wolf
lùppolo *s. m.* hop
lùrido *agg.* filthy, dirty
lusìnga *s. f.* allurement, flattery
lusingàre *v. tr.* to allure, to flatter
lusinghièro *agg.* flattering, tempting
lussàre *v. tr.* to dislocate
lussazióne *s. f.* dislocation
lùsso *s. m.* luxury
lussuóso *agg.* luxurious
lussureggiànte *agg.* luxuriant
lussùria *s. f.* lust
lussurióso *agg.* lustful
lustràre A *v. tr.* to polish **B** *v. intr.* to shine
lustrascàrpe *s. m. e f. inv.* shoeshine
lustrìno *s. m.* sequin
lùstro (1) A *agg.* bright, shining, (*lucidato*) polished **B** *s. m.* **1** shine, gloss **2** (*fig.*) lustre, splendour
lùstro (2) *s. m.* (*periodo di 5 anni*) five-year period
luteranésimo *s. m.* Lutheranism
luteràno *agg. e s. m.* Lutheran
lùtto *s. m.* mourning
luttuóso *agg.* **1** mournful **2** (*che causa lutto*) tragic, distressing

M

ma *cong.* but, (*invece*) only that, (*tuttavia*) yet, still
màcabro *agg.* macabre
macché *inter.* of course not!
màcchia (1) *s. f.* stain, spot, blot
màcchia (2) *s. f.* (*boscaglia*) bush, copse
macchiàre A *v. tr.* to stain, to spot **B** *v. intr. pron.* **1** to get stained **2** (*fig.*) to sully
macchiétta *s. f.* **1** speck **2** (*persona*) character
màcchina *s. f.* **1** machine, engine **2** (*autom.*) car ♦ **m. per scrivere** typewriter
macchinàre *v. tr.* to plot
macchinàrio *s. m.* machinery
macchinazióne *s. f.* machination, plot
macchinista *s. m.* (*ferr.*) engine-driver, (*naut.*) engineer
macchinóso *agg.* intricate, complex
macedònia *s. f.* fruit-salad
macellàio *s. m.* butcher
macellàre *v. tr.* to slaughter
macellerìa *s. f.* butcher's shop
macèllo *s. m.* slaughter
maceràre A *v. tr.* **1** to soak, to steep **2** (*tecnol.*) to macerate **B** *v. rifl.* (*struggersi*) to waste away
macèrie *s. f. pl.* rubble, ruins *pl.*
macìgno *s. m.* boulder, rock
macilènto *agg.* emaciated
màcina *s. f.* millstone
macinacaffè *s. m.* coffee grinder
macinapépe *s. m. inv.* pepper-mill
macinàre *v. tr.* to grind, to mill, (*carne*) to mince
macinìno *s. m.* grinder, mill
macrobiòtico *agg.* macrobiotic
macroscòpico *agg.* **1** macroscopic **2** (*fig.*) gross, glaring
maculàto *agg.* spotted, (*zool.*) dappled
màdia *s. f.* kneading-trough
màdido *agg.* wet
madornàle *agg.* enormous, gross
màdre A *s. f.* **1** mother **2** (*matrice*) counterfoil, stub **B** *agg.* mother (*attr.*) ♦ **scena m.** crucial scene
madrelìngua A *agg. e s. f.* mother tongue **B** *s. m. e f.* native speaker
madrepàtria *s. f.* mother land, mother country
madrepèrla *s. f.* mother-of-pearl
madrigàle *s. m.* madrigal
madrìna *s. f.* **1** godmother **2** (*di cerimonia*) patroness
maestà *s. f.* majesty
maestóso *agg.* majestic, magnificent
maèstra *s. f.* teacher, (school) mistress
maestràle *s. m.* mistral
maestrànze *s. f. pl.* hands *pl.*, workers *pl.*
maestrìa *s. f.* **1** mastery, skill **2** (*accortezza*) cunning
maèstro A *agg.* **1** (*principale*) main **2** (*abile*) masterly, skilful **B** *s. m.* master, teacher, (*di scuola*) schoolteacher
màga *s. f.* sorceress
magàgna *s. f.* **1** (*imperfezione*) flaw, defect **2** (*problema*) catch **3** (*acciacco*) infirmity
magàri A *inter.* and how!, you bet! **B** *cong.* **1** (*desiderativo*) if only **2** (*concessivo*) even if **C** *avv.* **1** (*forse*) perhaps, maybe **2** (*persino*) even
magazzìno *s. m.* **1** (*deposito*) warehouse **2** (*negozio*) shop, store ♦ **grande m.** department store
màggio *s. m.* May
maggioràna *s. f.* marjoram
maggiorànza *s. f.* majority ♦ **la m. di** the greater part of, most
maggioràre *v. tr.* to increase, to put up
maggiorazióne *s. f.* **1** (*aumento*) increase **2** (*sovrapprezzo*) surcharge, extra charge
maggiordòmo *s. m.* butler
maggióre A *agg. comp.* **1** (*più grande*) greater, (*più grosso*) larger, bigger, (*più alto*) higher, taller, (*più lungo*) longer, (*più largo*) wider **2** (*più importante*) major **3** (*più anziano*) older, (*tra figli*) elder **B** *agg. sup. rel.* **1** (*il più grande*) the greatest, (*il più grosso*) the largest, the biggest, (*il più alto*) the highest, the tallest, (*il più lungo*) the longest, (*il più largo*) the widest **2** (*il più importante*) major, main **3** (*il più anziano*) oldest, (*tra figli*) eldest **C** *s. m. e f.* **1** (*il più anziano*) the oldest, (*tra figli*) the eldest **2** (*di grado*) superior **3** (*mil.*) major
maggiorènne *s. m. e f.* major, adult ♦ **diventare m.** to come of age

maggioritàrio *agg.* majority (*attr.*)
maggiorménte *avv.* **1** (*di più*) more **2** (*più di tutto*) most
magìa *s. f.* **1** magic **2** (*incantesimo*) spell
màgico *agg.* magical
magistèro *s. m.* teaching
magistràle *agg.* masterly
magistràto *s. m.* **1** (*dir.*) magistrate, judge **2** (*funzionario*) official
magistratùra *s. f.* **1** magistrature, magistracy **2** (*insieme dei magistrati*) the Bench
màglia *s. f.* **1** (*di filo*) stitch, (*di rete*) mesh, (*di catena*) link **2** (*lavoro a maglia*) knitting **3** (*indumento*) sweater, (*intima*) vest, (*maglietta*) T-shirt, (*sport*) shirt
maglierìa *s. f.* knitwear
magliétta *s. f.* T-shirt, (*intima*) vest
màglio *s. m.* hammer
magnànimo *agg.* magnanimous, noble
magnàte *s. m.* magnate, tycoon
magnèsio *s. m.* magnesium
magnète *s. m.* **1** (*fis.*) magnet **2** (*mecc.*) magneto
magnètico *agg.* magnetic
magnetìsmo *s. m.* magnetism
magnificaménte *avv.* magnificently
magnìfico *agg.* magnificent
màgno *agg.* great
magnòlia *s. f.* magnolia
màgo *s. m.* magician, wizard
màgra *s. f.* **1** (*di fiume*) minimum flow **2** (*scarsezza*) shortage **3** (*fam.*) (*figuraccia*) poor figure
magrézza *s. f.* thinness, leanness
màgro **A** *agg.* **1** thin, lean, slim **2** (*scarso*) poor, scanty **3** (*misero*) meagre, scant **B** *s. m.* (parte magra) lean (meat)
mài *avv.* never, ever (*in frasi interr., comparative e in presenza di negazione*) ♦ **caso m.** if; **come m.?** why?; **m. più** never again; **più che m.** more than ever
maiàle *s. m.* **1** pig **2** (*cuc.*) pork ♦ **braciole di m.** pork chops
maiòlica *s. f.* majolica
maionése *s. f.* mayonnaise
màis *s. m.* maize, (*USA*) corn
maiuscòlo *agg.* capital
malaccòrto *agg.* ill-advised, imprudent
malaféde *s. f.* bad faith
malaménte *avv.* badly
malandàto *agg.* in bad condition
malànno *s. m.* **1** (*malattia*) illness, (*acciacco*) infirmity **2** (*disgrazia*) misfortune
malapéna, a *loc. avv.* hardly
malària *s. f.* malaria
malatìccio *agg.* sickly
malàto **A** *agg.* **1** sick (*attr.*), ill (*pred.*) **2** (*di pianta*) diseased **3** (*fig.*) unsound, morbid, unhealthy **B** *s. m.* sick person, patient
malattìa *s. f.* **1** sickness, illness, disease **2** (*di piante*) disease
malaugurataménte *avv.* unfortunately
malaugùrio *s. m.* ill omen
malavìta *s. f.* (the) underworld
malcóncio *agg.* battered
malcontènto **A** *agg.* dissatisfied **B** *s. m.* discontent
malcostùme *s. m.* immorality
maldèstro *agg.* **1** clumsy **2** (*inesperto*) inexperienced
maldicènza *s. f.* **1** slander **2** (*pettegolezzo*) gossip
maldispósto *agg.* ill-disposed
màle **A** *s. m.* **1** (*in senso morale*) evil, wrong **2** (*dolore*) pain, ache, (*malattia*) sickness, illness, disease **3** (*sventura*) ill, misfortune, (*guaio*) trouble **4** (*danno*) harm **B** *avv.* badly, not well ♦ **capire m.** to misunderstand; **farsi m.** to hurt oneself; **non c'è m.** not too bad; **stare m.** (*di salute*) to be ill, (*non adattarsi*) not to suit
maledétto *agg.* cursed, damned
maledìre *v. tr.* to curse, to damn
maledizióne *s. f.* curse, malediction
maleducàto *agg.* rude, ill-bred, impolite
maleducazióne *s. f.* rudeness
malefàtta *s. f.* misdeed
malefìcio *s. m.* spell
malèfico *agg.* harmful
maleodorànte *agg.* stinking
malèssere *s. m.* **1** ailment, malaise **2** (*fig.*) uneasiness
malèvolo *agg.* malevolent
malfamàto *agg.* ill-famed
malfàtto *agg.* badly done
malfattóre *s. m.* criminal
malférmo *agg.* **1** unsteady, shaky **2** (*di salute*) poor, delicate
malformazióne *s. f.* malformation, deformity
malgovèrno *s. m.* misrule, bad government, (*cattiva amministrazione*) mismanagement
malgràdo **A** *prep.* notwithstanding, in spite of **B** *cong.* (al)though, even though ♦ **mio/tuo m.** against my/your will
malìa *s. f.* **1** spell **2** (*fig.*) charm

malignàre *v. intr.* to malign, to speak badly
malignità *s. f.* malignity, malice
malìgno *agg.* **1** malicious, malevolent **2** (*malefico*) evil, malignant, malign **3** (*med.*) malignant
malinconìa *s. f.* **1** melancholy, sadness **2** (*pensiero*) gloom
malincònico *agg.* melancholy, sad, gloomy
malincuòre, a *loc. avv.* unwillingly
malintenzionàto *agg.* ill-intentioned
malintéso **A** *agg.* mistaken **B** *s. m.* misunderstanding
malìzia *s. f.* **1** malice **2** (*astuzia*) cunning **3** (*espediente*) trick
malizióso *agg.* **1** malicious **2** (*astuto*) artful
malleàbile *agg.* malleable
mallèolo *s. m.* malleolus
malmenàre *v. tr.* **1** (*picchiare*) to beat up **2** (*trattare male*) to ill-treat, to mishandle
malmésso *agg.* shabby
malnutrìto *agg.* malnourished
malnutrizióne *s. f.* malnutrition
malòcchio *s. m.* evil eye
malóra *s. f.* ruin ♦ **andare in m.** to go to the dogs (*fam.*)
malóre *s. m.* (sudden) illness
malsàno *agg.* **1** unhealthy, sickly **2** (*non salutare*) unhealthy, unwholesome **3** (*fig.*) morbid, sick
malsicùro *agg.* **1** (*poco stabile*) unsteady **2** (*privo di sicurezza*) unsafe **3** (*incerto*) uncertain **4** (*inattendibile*) unreliable
màlta *s. f.* mortar
maltèmpo *s. m.* bad weather
màlto *s. m.* malt
maltrattaménto *s. m.* abuse
maltrattàre *v. tr.* to ill-treat, to maltreat
malumóre *s. m.* **1** bad temper, bad mood **2** (*dissapore*) bad feeling **3** (*scontento*) unrest ♦ **essere di m.** to feel blue
màlva **A** *s. f.* (*bot.*) mallow **B** *s. m.* (*colore*) mauve
malvàgio *agg.* wicked, evil
malversazióne *s. f.* misappropriation
malvìsto *agg.* disliked, unpopular
malvivènte *s. m.* delinquent
malvolentièri *avv.* unwillingly, against one's will
màmma *s. f.* mother, mummy (*fam.*)
mammèlla *s. f.* (*anat.*) mamma, (*fam.*) breast, (*di femmina d'animale*) udder
mammìfero **A** *agg.* mammalian **B** *s. m.* mammal, mammalian
manager *s. m. e f.* manager
manageriàle *agg.* managerial
manàta *s. f.* **1** (*manciata*) handful **2** (*colpo*) slap
mancaménto *s. m.* faint
mancànza *s. f.* **1** want, lack **2** (*assenza*) absence **3** (*fallo*) fault **4** (*difetto*) defect
mancàre **A** *v. intr.* **1** (*non avere a sufficienza*) to lack, to be lacking, to want, to be wanting **2** (*non esserci*) to be absent, (*non essere reperibile*) to be missing, (*essere lontano*) to be away **3** (*per arrivare a un termine stabilito*) to be (ES: **manca un quarto alle dieci** it is a quarter to ten) **4** (*per completare q.c.*) to be needed **5** (*venire meno*) to fail **6** (*agire male*) to wrong, (*sbagliare*) to make a mistake **7** (*omettere*) to omit, to fail **8** (*morire*) to pass away **9** (*essere rimpianto*) to miss (*costruzione pers.*) **B** *v. tr.* to miss
mància *s. f.* tip
manciàta *s. f.* handful
mancino *agg.* **1** left-handed **2** (*fig.*) treacherous
mandàre *v. tr.* **1** to send, to forward, to dispatch **2** (*emettere*) to give off, to emit ♦ **m. a chiamare** to send for; **m. a rotoli, a monte** to upset; **m. giù** to swallow; **m. in onda** to broadcast
mandarino *s. m.* tangerine
mandàto *s. m.* **1** (*incarico*) mandate, task, commission **2** (*dir., comm.*) warrant, order
mandìbola *s. f.* mandible, jaw
mandolino *s. m.* mandolin(e)
màndorla *s. f.* almond
màndria *s. f.* herd
mandrino *s. m.* mandrel, spindle, chuck
maneggévole *agg.* handy, manageable
maneggiàre *v. tr.* **1** (*strumenti*) to handle, to use **2** (*pasta, cera*) to knead, to mould **3** (*amministrare*) to manage
manéggio *s. m.* **1** (*il maneggiare*) handling, use **2** (*gestione*) management **3** *al pl.* (*intrighi*) intrigue **4** (*equitazione*) manège
manétte *s. f. pl.* handcuffs *pl.*
manfòrte *s. f.* help
manganèllo *s. m.* club
manganése *s. m.* manganese
mangeréccio *agg.* edible
mangiàbile *agg.* eatable
mangianàstri *s. m. inv.* cassette player
mangiàre **A** *v. tr.* **1** to eat, to take one's meals **2** (*consumare*) to eat up, to consume **3** (*nei giochi*) to take **B** *s. m.* **1** eating **2**

(*cibo*) food
mangiàta *s. f.* square meal, bellyful
mangiatóia *s. f.* manger
mangìme *s. m.* feedstuff, (*foraggio*) fodder
mangióne *s. m.* big eater
mangiucchiàre *v. tr.* to nibble at
màngo *s. m.* mango
manìa *s. f.* mania ♦ **m. di persecuzione** persecution complex
manìaco *agg.* **1** maniac(al) **2** (*fissato*) mad, crazy
mànica *s. f.* **1** sleeve **2** (*fam.*) (*combriccola*) gang ♦ **maniche corte/lunghe** short/long sleeves
manicarétto *s. m.* dainty, delicacy
manichìno *s. m.* dummy
mànico *s. m.* handle
manicòmio *s. m.* mental hospital, madhouse (*fam.*)
manicòtto *s. m.* muff
manicùre *s. f. e m.* **1** manicure **2** (*persona*) manicurist
manièra *s. f.* **1** manner, way **2** *al pl.* (*comportamento*) manners **3** (*stile*) style, manner
manieràto *agg.* affected
manierìsmo *s. m.* mannerism
manifattùra *s. f.* **1** manufacture **2** (*lavorazione*) workmanship **3** (*fabbrica*) factory
manifestàre **A** *v. tr.* to manifest, to show, to display, to express **B** *v. intr.* to demonstrate **C** *v. rifl. e intr. pron.* to manifest oneself, to reveal oneself, to show oneself
manifestazióne *s. f.* **1** manifestation, display **2** (*dimostrazione*) demonstration
manifèsto **A** *agg.* clear, obvious **B** *s. m.* **1** (*affisso*) placard, poster, (*avviso*) notice **2** (*ideologico, artistico*) manifesto
manìglia *s. f.* handle, (*appiglio sui mezzi pubblici*) strap
manipolàre *v. tr.* **1** to manipulate, to handle **2** (*adulterare*) to adulterate, (*falsificare*) to falsify **3** (*condizionare*) to manipulate
manipolazióne *s. f.* **1** manipulation, handling **2** (*adulterazione*) adulteration, (*falsificazione*) falsification, fiddling **3** (*condizionamento*) manipulation
maniscàlco *s. m.* horseshoer
mànna *s. f.* **1** manna **2** (*fig.*) blessing
mannàia *s. f.* axe, cleaver
màno *s. f.* **1** hand **2** (*lato*) side **3** (*tocco*) touch, hand **4** (*di vernice*) coat ♦ **contro m.** on the wrong side of the road; **di seconda m.** second-hand; **fatto a m.** handmade; **stringersi la m.** to shake hands
manodòpera *s. f.* labour
manòmetro *s. m.* manometer, gauge
manométtere *v. tr.* to tamper with
manòpola *s. f.* **1** grip, handle **2** (*girevole*) knob
manoscrìtto **A** *agg.* handwritten **B** *s. m.* manuscript
manovàle *s. m.* labourer
manovèlla *s. f.* crank, handle
manòvra *s. f.* **1** (*mil.*) manoeuvre **2** (*movimento*) monoeuvring, working **3** (*naut.*) rigging **4** (*fig.*) manoeuvre
manovràre **A** *v. tr.* **1** to manoeuvre, to handle, to control **2** (*fig.*) to manage, to manipulate **B** *v. intr.* **1** to manoeuvre **2** (*fig.*) to scheme
mansàrda *s. f.* mansard
mansióne *s. f.* function, task, duty
mansuèto *agg.* mild, meek
mantecàre *v. tr.* to whisk
mantèlla *s. f.* mantle, cloak
mantèllo *s. m.* **1** mantle, cloak **2** (*di animale*) coat
mantenére **A** *v. tr.* **1** to maintain, to keep, to preserve **2** (*sostenere*) to maintain, to support, to keep **3** (*rispettare*) to keep **B** *v. rifl.* to earn one's living, to keep oneself **C** *v. intr. pron.* to keep
manteniménto *s. m.* **1** maintenance **2** (*sostentamento*) support **3** (*manutenzione*) upkeep
màntice *s. f.* **1** bellows *pl.* **2** (*di carrozza*) hood
mànto *s. m.* mantle, cloak ♦ **m. stradale** road surface
manuàle **A** *agg.* manual **B** *s. m.* manual, handbook
manualità *s. f.* **1** manual character **2** (*destrezza*) manual dexterity
manualménte *avv.* manually, by hand
manùbrio *s. m.* **1** handle, (*di veicolo*) handle bar **2** (*attrezzo ginnico*) dumb-bell
manufàtto *s. m.* handwork, handmade article
manutenzióne *s. f.* maintenance, upkeep, (*tecnica*) service
mànzo *s. m.* **1** steer **2** (*cuc.*) beef
maomettàno *agg.* Mohammedan
màppa *s. f.* map, plan
mappamóndo *s. m.* **1** (*globo*) globe **2** (*planisfero*) map of the world
maràsma *s. m.* **1** (*decadenza*) decay **2**

(*caos*) chaos
maratóna *s. f.* marathon
màrca *s. f.* **1** brand, mark, (*fabbricazione*) make **2** (*bollo*) stamp **3** (*contromarca*) check **4** (*fig.*) kind, character
marcàre *v. tr.* **1** to mark, to brand **2** (*sport*) to score **3** (*accentuare*) to emphasize
marchése *s. m.* marquis, marquess
marchiàre *v. tr.* to brand, to mark, to stamp
màrchio *s. m.* **1** brand, mark, stamp **2** (*fig.*) mark ♦ **m. di fabbrica** trademark; **m. registrato** registered trademark
màrcia *s. f.* **1** march **2** (*sport*) walk **3** (*autom.*) gear, speed **4** (*mus.*) march
marciapiède *s. m.* **1** pavement, (*USA*) sidewalk **2** (*ferr.*) platform
marciàre *v. intr.* to march, to walk
màrcio *agg.* rotten
marcìre *v. intr.* to rot, to go bad
marciùme *s. m.* rot
màrco *s. m.* mark
màre *s. m.* sea ♦ **andare al m.** to go to the seaside; **frutti di m.** seafood
marèa *s. f.* tide
mareggiàta *s. f.* seastorm
maremòto *s. m.* seaquake
margarìna *s. f.* margarine
margherìta *s. f.* daisy
marginàle *agg.* marginal
màrgine *s. m.* **1** (*orlo, bordo*) edge **2** (*di foglio*) margin **3** (*econ.*) margin
margòtta *s. f.* layer
mariàno *agg.* Marian
marìna **A** *s. f.* **1** navy **2** (*arte*) seascape **B** *s. m. inv.* (*naut.*) marina
marinàio *s. m.* seaman, sailor, mariner
marinàre *v. tr.* **1** (*cuc.*) to marinate, to pickle **2** (*la scuola*) to play truant
marinarésco *agg.* sailor (*attr.*)
marìno *agg.* marine, sea (*attr.*)
marionétta *s. f.* puppet
maritàre **A** *v. tr.* to marry **B** *v. rifl. e rifl. rec.* to get married
marìto *s. m.* husband
marìttimo *agg.* maritime, marine, sea (*attr.*)
marmàglia *s. f.* rabble
marmellàta *s. f.* jam ♦ **m. di arance** marmalade
marmìtta *s. f.* silencer (*autom.*)
màrmo *s. m.* marble
marmòcchio *s. m.* kid
marmòreo *agg.* marble (*attr.*)
marmòtta *s. f.* marmot
marocchìno *agg. e s. m.* Moroccan
maróso *s. m.* breaker
marróne **A** *agg.* brown **B** *s. m.* (*castagna*) chestnut
marsìna *s. f.* tails *pl.*
marsùpio *s. m.* **1** (*zool.*) marsupium, pouch **2** (*per bambini*) baby sling
martedì *s. m.* Tuesday
martellaménto *s. m.* pounding
martellàre **A** *v. tr.* **1** to hammer **2** (*fig.*) to pound **B** *v. intr.* to throb
martèllo *s. m.* hammer
martinétto *s. m.* jack
màrtire *s. m. e f.* martyr
martìrio *s. m.* **1** martyrdom **2** (*fig.*) torment
màrtora *s. f.* marten
martoriàre *v. tr.* to torment
marxìsmo *s. m.* Marxism
marxista *agg. e s. m. e f.* Marxist
marzapàne *s. m.* marzipan
marziàle *agg.* martial
marziàno *s. m.* Martian
màrzo *s. m.* March
mascalzóne *s. m.* rascal, scoundrel
mascàra *s. m. inv.* mascara
mascèlla *s. f.* jaw
màschera *s. f.* **1** mask **2** (*travestimento*) fancy dress **3** (*persona mascherata*) masker **4** (*di commedia*) stock character **5** (*inserviente di teatro, cinema*) usher *m.*, usherette *f.* ♦ **ballo in m.** masked ball; **m. di bellezza** face mask
mascheràre **A** *v. tr.* **1** to mask **2** (*travestire*) to dress up **3** (*nascondere*) to conceal, to disguise **B** *v. rifl.* **1** to put on a mask, (*vestirsi da*) to dress as **2** (*fig.*) to pass oneself off
mascheràta *s. f.* masquerade
maschìle *agg.* **1** male, men's **2** (*virile*) masculine, manly **3** (*gramm.*) masculine
maschilìsta *agg.* male chauvinist
màschio (1) **A** *agg.* male **B** *s. m.* male, (*ragazzo*) boy, (*uomo*) man, (*figlio*) son
màschio (2) *s. m.* (*di castello*) donjon
mascolìno *agg.* masculine
mascotte *s. f. inv.* mascot
masochìsmo *s. m.* masochism
màssa *s. f.* **1** mass, body **2** (*grande quantità*) heap, load **3** (*folla*) mass, crowd **4** (*fis.*) mass **5** (*elettr.*) earth, ground
massacrànte *agg.* exhausting
massacràre *v. tr.* **1** to massacre, to slaughter **2** (*picchiare*) to beat **3** (*rovinare*) to spoil
massàcro *s. m.* **1** massacre, slaughter **2**

(*fig.*) disaster
massaggiàre *v. tr.* to massage
massàggio *s. m.* massage
massàia *s. f.* housewife, housekeeper
masserìzie *s. f. pl.* household goods *pl.*
massicciàta *s. f.* roadbed, ballast
massìccio **A** *agg.* massive **B** *s. m.* massif
massificazióne *s. f.* standardization
màssima (1) *s. f.* **1** (*principio*) principle, rule **2** (*detto*) saying, maxim
màssima (2) *s. f.* (*temperatura*) maximum
massimàle *s. m.* limit, ceiling
massimalìsmo *s. m.* maximalism
màssimo **A** *agg.* **1** maximum, the greatest **2** (*mat.*) highest, maximum **B** *s. m.* maximum, top, peak ♦ **al m.** (*tutt'al più*) at most, (*al più tardi*) at the latest; **m. livello** top level; **tempo m.** time limit
màsso *s. m.* mass of stone, block, rock ♦ **caduta massi** falling rocks
massóne *s. m.* Freemason
massonerìa *s. f.* Freemasonry
masticàre *v. tr.* **1** to chew, to masticate **2** (*borbottare*) to mumble
màstice *s. m.* mastic, putty
mastìno *s. m.* mastiff
mastodòntico *agg.* colossal, enormous
masturbazióne *s. f.* masturbation
matàssa *s. f.* **1** skein, hank **2** (*fig.*) tangle
matemàtica *s. f.* mathematics *pl.* (*v. al sing.*), (*fam.*) maths *pl.* (*v. al sing.*)
matemàtico *agg.* mathematic(al)
materassìno *s. m.* **1** (*gonfiabile*) inflatable mattress, airbed **2** (*sport*) mat
materàsso *s. m.* mattress
matèria *s. f.* **1** matter, (*materiale*) material (*sostanza*) substance **2** (*argomento*) matter, subject, theme **3** (*disciplina*) subject ♦ **materie prime** raw materials
materiàle **A** *agg.* **1** material **2** (*rozzo*) rough **B** *s. m.* material, stuff
materialìsmo *s. m.* materialism
materialménte *avv.* materially
maternità *s. f.* maternity, motherhood ♦ **congedo per m.** maternity leave
matèrno *agg.* maternal, motherly, mother (*attr.*)
matìta *s. f.* pencil
matriarcàle *agg.* matriarchal
matrìce *s. f.* **1** matrix **2** (*di registro, libretto*) counterfoil, stub **3** (*metall.*) mould, die **4** (*fig.*) root
matrìcola *s. f.* **1** (*registro*) roll list, register **2** (*numero*) (matriculation) number **3** (*studente*) fresher
matrìgna *s. f.* stepmother
matrimoniàle *agg.* matrimonial, marriage (*attr.*), wedding (*attr.*) ♦ **camera/letto m.** double room/bed
matrimònio *s. m.* **1** marriage **2** (*cerimonia*) wedding ♦ **pubblicazioni di m.** banns
matròna *s. f.* matron
matronèo *s. m.* women's gallery
matronìmico *agg.* matronymic
mattatóio *s. m.* slaughter-house
mattìna *s. f.* morning
mattinàta *s. f.* morning
mattinièro *agg.* early-rising
mattìno *s. m.* morning
màtto **A** *agg.* mad, crazy **B** *s. m.* madman, lunatic ♦ **scacco m.** checkmate
mattóne *s. m.* **1** brick **2** (*fig.*) bore
mattonèlla *s. f.* tile
mattutìno *agg.* **1** morning (*attr.*) **2** (*mattiniero*) early-rising
maturàre **A** *v. tr.* **1** to mature, to ripen **2** (*raggiungere*) to reach gradually **B** *v. intr.* **1** (*di frutto*) to ripe **2** (*di persona, cosa*) to mature **3** (*comm.*) to fall due, (*di interessi*) to accrue **C** *v. intr. pron.* to mature, to become mature
maturazióne *s. f.* **1** maturation, ripening **2** (*comm.*) maturity, expiry, (*di interessi*) accrual
maturità *s. f.* maturity
matùro *agg.* mature, ripe
mausolèo *s. m.* mausoleum
màzza *s. f.* club
mazzàta *s. f.* blow
mazzétto *s. m.* (little) bunch
màzzo *s. m.* bunch ♦ **m. di carte** pack of cards
me *pron. pers. 1ª sing. m. e f.* **1** (*compl. ogg. e ind.*) me **2** (*con funzione di sogg.*) I
meàndro *s. m.* meander
meccànica *s. f.* **1** mechanics *pl.* (*v. al sing.*) **2** (*meccanismo*) mechanism
meccanicaménte *avv.* mechanically
meccànico **A** *agg.* mechanical **B** *s. m.* mechanic, (*tecnico*) engineer
meccanìsmo *s. m.* **1** mechanism, works *pl.* **2** (*fig.*) mechanism
meccanizzàre **A** *v. tr.* to mechanize **B** *v. intr. pron.* to become mechanized
meccanizzazióne *s. f.* mechanization
mecenàte *s. m. e f.* patron
mecenatìsmo *s. m.* patronage

mèda *s. f.* seamark, beacon
medàglia *s. f.* medal
medaglióne *s. m.* locket, medallion
medésimo **A** *agg. dimostr.* same **B** *pron. dimostr.* (*persona*) the same (one), (*cosa*) the same (thing)
mèdia *s. f.* average, mean
mediàno *agg.* medial, middle (*attr*)
mediànte *prep.* by, by means of, through
mediàre *v. tr. e intr.* to mediate
mediatóre *s. m.* **1** mediator, middleman **2** (*comm.*) broker
medicaménto *s. m.* medicament
medicàre **A** *v. tr.* to medicate, to treat **B** *v. rifl.* to medicate oneself
medicazióne *s. f.* dressing, medication
medicìna *s. f.* **1** medicine **2** (*medicamento*) medicine, medicament, (*USA*) drug
medicinàle **A** *agg.* medicinal **B** *s. m.* medicine, medicament, (*USA*) drug
mèdico **A** *agg.* medical **B** *s. m.* doctor
medievàle *agg.* medieval
mèdio **A** *agg.* **1** (*di mezzo*) middle, medium **2** (*conforme alla media*) average (*attr*), mean (*attr*) **3** (*scient.*) medium **B** *s. m.* (*dito*) middle finger
mediòcre *agg.* mediocre, second-rate, ordinary
mediocrità *s. f.* mediocrity
medioevo *s. m.* Middle Ages *pl.*
meditàre **A** *v. tr.* **1** to meditate, to ponder **2** (*progettare*) to plan, to intend **B** *v. intr.* to meditate (on), to brood (over), to ponder
meditazióne *s. f.* meditation
mediterràneo *agg.* Mediterranean
medùsa *s. f.* jelly-fish, medusa
megàfono *s. m.* megaphone
megalìtico *agg.* megalithic
megalòmane *agg.* megalomaniac
megalòpoli *s. f.* megalopolis
mèglio **A** *avv.* **1** (*comp.*) better **2** (*sup. rel.*) best **B** *agg. inv.* **1** (*migliore, preferibile*) better **2** (*sup. rel.*) best **C** *s. m. e f. inv.* (the) best (thing) ♦ **avere la m. su qc.** to have the better of sb.; **di bene in m.** better and better; **m. ancora** better still
méla *s. f.* apple ♦ **m. cotogna** quince
melagràna *s. f.* pomegranate
melanzàna *s. f.* aubergine, (*USA*) eggplant
melènso *agg.* dull
mellìfluo *agg.* honeyed, sugary
mélma *s. f.* slime, mud
melmóso *agg.* slimy, muddy
melodìa *s. f.* melody
melodióso *agg.* melodious
melodrammàtico *agg.* **1** (*mus.*) operatic **2** (*fig.*) melodramatic
melóne *s. m.* melon
membràna *s. f.* membrane
mèmbro *s. m.* **1** member **2** (*arto*) limb
memoràbile *agg.* memorable
memòria *s. f.* **1** memory **2** (*ricordo*) memory, remembrance, recollection **3** (*oggetto*) memento, (*di famiglia*) heirloom **4** (*scritto*) memoir ♦ **sapere q.c. a m.** to know st. by heart
memoriàle *s. m.* **1** (*dir*) memorial **2** (*memorie*) memoirs *pl.*
menadìto, a *loc. avv.* perfectly
mendicànte *s. m. e f.* beggar
mendicàre *v. tr. e intr.* to beg
menefreghìsmo *s. m.* indifference
menìnge *s. f.* meninx
meningìte *s. f.* meningitis
menisco *s. m.* meniscus
méno **A** *avv.* **1** less, not so ... (as) **2** (*comp.*) less ... than, not so ... as, not as ... as **3** (*sup.*) the least, (*fra due*) the less **4** (*mat.*) minus **B** *agg. inv.* less, not so much, (*con s. pl.*) fewer **C** *s. m. inv.* **1** less, not as much **2** (*il minimo*) the least, as little as **3** (*mat.*) minus ♦ **a m. che** unless; **fare a m. di** to do without; **venire m.** to fail
menomàre *v. tr.* to disable, to damage
menomazióne *s. f.* disablement
menopàusa *s. f.* menopause
mènsa *s. f.* **1** table **2** (*di università*) refectory, (*di fabbrica*) canteen, (*di soldati*) cookhouse, (*di ufficiali*) mess
mensìle **A** *agg.* monthly **B** *s. m.* **1** (*salario*) salary **2** (*pubblicazione*) monthly
mensilménte *avv.* monthly
mènsola *s. f.* **1** shelf **2** (*arch.*) console, bracket
ménta *s. f.* mint
mentàle *agg.* mental
mentalità *s. f.* mentality, outlook
mentalménte *avv.* mentally
ménte *s. f.* mind
mentìre *v. intr.* to lie
ménto *s. m.* chin
mentòlo *s. m.* menthol
méntre **A** *cong.* **1** (*temporale*) while, (*quando*) as **2** (*avversativo*) whereas, while **3** (*finché*) while, as long as **B** *s. m. inv.* moment, meantime, meanwhile

menù *s. m. inv.* menu
menzionàre *v. tr.* to mention
menzógna *s. f.* lie
meravìglia *s. f.* **1** wonder **2** (*sorpresa*) astonishment, surprise **3** (*cosa meravigliosa*) wonder, marvel
meravigliàre **A** *v. tr.* to astonish, to amaze, to surprise **B** *v. intr. pron.* to be astonished, to be amazed, to wonder
meraviglióso *agg.* wonderful, marvellous
mercànte *s. m.* merchant, trader, dealer
mercanteggiàre **A** *v. tr.* to traffic in **B** *v. intr.* to bargain, to haggle
mercantìle **A** *agg.* merchant (*attr*), mercantile, commercial **B** *s. m.* merchant ship
mercantilìsmo *s. m.* mercantilism
mercanzìa *s. f.* **1** (*merce*) merchandise, goods *pl.* **2** (*roba*) stuff
mercatìno *s. m.* flea market
mercàto *s. m.* market, (*luogo*) market-place ♦ **a buon m.** cheap
mèrce *s. f.* goods *pl.*
mercé *s. f.* mercy
mercenàrio *agg. e s. m.* mercenary
mercerìa *s. f.* haberdashery
mercoledì *s. m.* Wednesday
mercùrio *s. m.* mercury, quicksilver
mèrda *s. f.* shit
merènda *s. f.* snack
meridiàna *s. f.* sun-dial
meridiàno *agg. e s. m.* meridian
meridionàle **A** *agg.* southern, south (*attr*) **B** *s. m. e f.* southerner
meridióne *s. m.* south
merìnga *s. f.* meringue
meritàre *v. tr.* **1** to deserve, to merit **2** (*valere*) to be worth **3** (*procurare*) to earn
meritévole *agg.* deserving, worthy
mèrito *s. m.* merit ♦ **in m. a** as regards, as to
meritòrio *agg.* praiseworthy
merlétto *s. m.* lace
mèrlo (1) *s. m.* (*zool.*) blackbird
mèrlo (2) *s. m.* (*arch.*) merlon
merlùzzo *s. m.* cod
meschìno *agg.* **1** poor, miserable **2** (*gretto*) mean, wretched
mescolànza *s. f.* mixture, blend
mescolàre **A** *v. tr.* **1** to mix, to blend **2** (*rimestare*) to stir **3** (*confondere*) to confuse **4** (*mettere in disordine*) to muddle **5** (*le carte*) to shuffle **B** *v. intr. pron., rifl. e rifl. rec.* to mix, to get mixed up
mése *s. m.* month
méssa (1) *s. f.* (*relig.*) mass
méssa (2) *s. f.* (*il mettere*) placing, setting ♦ **m. a fuoco** focusing; **m. a punto** setting up; **m. a terra** grounding; **m. in opera** installation; **m. in piega** set
messaggèro *s. m.* messenger
messàggio *s. m.* **1** message **2** (*discorso*) address
messàle *s. m.* missal
mèsse *s. f.* harvest
messiànico *agg.* Messianic
messicàno *agg. e s. m.* Mexican
messinscèna *s. f.* **1** (*teatro*) staging **2** (*fig.*) sham, act
mésso *s. m.* messenger
mestàre **A** *v. tr.* to stir, (*mescolare*) to mix **B** *v. intr.* to plot
mestière *s. m.* **1** trade, profession, job **2** (*esperienza*) craft, experience
mèsto *agg.* sad
méstolo *s. m.* ladle
mestruazióne *s. f.* menstruation
mèta *s. f.* **1** destination **2** (*fine*) goal, aim
metà *s. f.* **1** half **2** (*parte di mezzo*) middle
metabolìsmo *s. m.* metabolism
metafìsico *agg.* metaphysical
metàfora *s. f.* metaphor
metafòrico *agg.* metaphoric(al)
metàllico *agg.* metal (*attr*), metallic
metallizzàto *agg.* metallized
metàllo *s. m.* metal
metallùrgico *agg.* metallurgic(al)
metalmeccànico **A** *agg.* engineering **B** *s. m.* metalworker
metamorfismo *s. m.* metamorphism
metamòrfosi *s. f.* metamorphosis
metàno *s. m.* methane
metèora *s. f.* meteor
meteorologìa *s. f.* meteorology
meteorològico *agg.* meteorologic(al) ♦ **bollettino m.** weather report
meticolóso *agg.* meticulous, scrupulous
metòdico *agg.* methodical
metodìsta *s. m. e f.* Methodist
mètodo *s. m.* method
metodològico *agg.* methodological
mètopa *s. f.* metope
mètrico *agg.* metric
mètro *s. m.* **1** metre, (*USA*) meter **2** (*strumento*) rule **3** (*fig.*) criterion ♦ **m. cubo** cubic metre; **m. quadrato** square metre
metropolìta *s. m.* metropolitan
metropolitàna *s. f.* underground, tube

(*fam.*), (*USA*) subway
metropolitàno *agg.* metropolitan
méttere **A** *v. tr.* **1** to put, (*collocare*) to set, to place, (*disporre*) to arrange **2** (*indossare*) to put on, to wear **3** (*impiegare*) to take **4** (*investire*) to put, (*scommettere*) to bet **5** (*far pagare*) to charge **6** (*supporre*) to suppose **7** (*paragonare*) to compare **8** (*causare*) to cause, to make, to inspire **9** (*emettere*) to put forth **10** (*installare*) to lay on, to put in **B** *v. rifl. e intr. pron.* **1** to put oneself, to place oneself **2** (*cominciare*) to start, to begin, to set to **3** (*indossare*) to wear, to put on
mezzadrìa *s. f.* métayage, share-cropping
mezzalùna *s. f.* half-moon, crescent
mezzàno **A** *agg.* middle (*attr*) **B** *s. m.* pimp
mezzanòtte *s. f.* midnight
mèzzo (1) **A** *agg.* **1** half **2** (*medio*) middle, medium (*attr*) **B** *s. m.* **1** (*metà*) half **2** (*centro*) middle, centre **C** *avv.* half
mèzzo (2) *s. m.* **1** (*strumento*) means, equipment **2** (*di trasporto*) (means of) transport **3** (*fis.*) medium **4** *al pl.* (*mezzi economici*) means, money
mezzogiòrno *s. m.* **1** midday, noon, twelve o'clock **2** (*sud*) south ♦ **a m.** at noon
mezzóra *s. f.* half an hour
mi **A** *pron. pers. 1ª sing. m. e f.* **1** (*compl. ogg.*) me **2** (*compl. ind.*) (to, for) me **B** *pron. rifl. 1ª sing.* myself (*o idiom.*)
miagolàre *v. intr.* to mew, to miaow
mìccia *s. f.* fuse
micenèo *agg.* Mycenaean
micidiàle *agg.* deadly, lethal
mìcio *s. m.* pussy(cat)
mìcrobo *s. m.* microbe
microcòsmo *s. m.* microcosm
microfìlm *s. m. inv.* microfilm
micròfono *s. m.* microphone, mike (*fam.*)
microrganìsmo *s. m.* microorganism
microscòpico *agg.* microscopic(al)
microscòpio *s. m.* microscope
midóllo *s. m.* marrow ♦ **m. spinale** spinal marrow
mièle *s. m.* honey ♦ **luna di m.** honeymoon
miètere *v. tr.* to reap, to harvest
mietitùra *s. f.* **1** reaping **2** (*raccolto*) harvest **3** (*tempo*) reaping time
migliàio *s. m.* thousand
mìglio (1) *s. m.* (*bot.*) millet
mìglio (2) *s. m.* (*unità di misura*) mile ♦ **m. marino** nautical mile
miglioraménto *s. m.* improvement
miglioràre **A** *v. tr.* to improve, to better **B** *v. intr.* to improve, to get better
miglióre **A** *agg.* **1** (*comp.*) better **2** (*sup.*) the best, (*fra due*) the better **B** *s. m. e f.* the best
migliorìa *s. f.* improvement
mìgnolo *s. m.* little finger, (*del piede*) little toe
migràre *v. intr.* to migrate
migratòrio *agg.* migratory
miliardàrio *agg. e s. m.* multimillionaire, (*USA*) billionaire
miliàrdo *s. m.* one thousand millions, milliard, (*USA*) billion
milionàrio *agg. e s. m.* millionaire
milióne *s. m.* million
militànte *agg. e s. m. e f.* militant
militàre (1) **A** *agg.* military **B** *s. m.* soldier
militàre (2) *v. intr.* **1** (*fare il soldato*) to serve in the army **2** (*fig.*) to militate
militarésco *agg.* military
millantàre *v. tr.* to boast of
millantatóre *s. m.* boaster, braggart
mìlle *agg. num. card. e s. m. inv.* (one) thousand
millenàrio *agg.* millenary
millènnio *s. m.* millennium
millepièdi *s. m. inv.* millepede
millèsimo *agg. num. ord. e s. m.* thousandth
milligràmmo *s. m.* milligram(me)
millìmetro *s. m.* millimetre, (*USA*) millimeter
mìlza *s. f.* spleen
mimàre *v. tr. e intr.* to mime
mimètico *agg.* mimetic(al)
mimetizzàre **A** *v. tr.* to camouflage **B** *v. rifl.* to camouflage oneself
mìmica *s. f.* **1** (*teatro*) mime **2** (*il gesticolare*) gestures *pl.*
mìmo *s. m.* mime
mimósa *s. f.* mimosa
mìna *s. f.* **1** mine **2** (*di matita*) lead
minàccia *s. f.* menace, threat
minacciàre *v. tr.* to threaten, to menace
minacciόso *agg.* threatening, menacing
minàre *v. tr.* **1** to mine **2** (*insidiare*) to undermine
minaréto *s. m.* minaret
minatóre *s. m.* miner
minatòrio *agg.* threatening, minatory
mineràle **A** *agg.* mineral **B** *s. m.* mineral, (*da cui si estrae un metallo*) ore ♦ **acqua m.** mineral water
mineralogìa *s. f.* mineralogy
mineràrio *agg.* mining, mineral, mine (*attr*),

ore (*attr*)

minèstra *s. f.* soup ♦ **m. di verdura** vegetable soup

mingherlìno *agg.* thin

miniatùra *s. f.* miniature, (*di manoscritti*) illumination

miniaturìsta *s. m. e f.* miniaturist, (*di manoscritti*) illuminator

minièra *s. f.* mine, pit

minigònna *s. f.* miniskirt

mìnima *s. f.* **1** (*temperatura*) minimum temperature **2** (*mus.*) minim

minimizzàre *v. tr.* to minimize

mìnimo A *agg.* **1** (the) least, the smallest, the slightest, minimum (*attr*) **2** (*molto piccolo*) very small, very slight, minimal **B** *s. m.* **1** minimum **2** (*di motore*) lowest gear **3** (*la minima cosa*) the least

ministèro *s. m.* **1** (*funzione*) office, function, (*relig.*) ministry **2** (*insieme dei ministri*) Ministry, Board, (*USA*) Department

minìstro *s. m.* minister

minorànza *s. f.* minority

minóre A *agg.* **1** (*più piccolo*) smaller, (*più corto*) shorter, (*più basso*) lower **2** (*meno*) less(er) **3** (*meno importante*) minor **4** (*più giovane*) younger **B** *agg. sup. rel.* **1** (*il più piccolo*) the smallest, (*il più corto*) the shortest, (*il più basso*) the lowest **2** (*il minimo*) the least **3** (*il meno importante*) minor **4** (*il più giovane*) the youngest, (*tra due*) the younger **C** *s. m. e f.* **1** (*il più giovane*) the youngest, (*fra due*) the younger **2** (*di grado*) junior

minorènne A *agg.* underage **B** *s. m. e f.* minor

minuétto *s. m.* minuet

minùscolo *agg.* **1** (*di lettera*) small, (*tip.*) lower case **2** (*piccolo*) tiny

minùta *s. f.* draft, rough copy

minùto (1) A *agg.* **1** minute, small, tiny **2** (*delicato*) delicate, frail **3** (*particolareggiato*) detailed, minute **4** (*di poco conto*) petty, small **B** *s. m.* (*comm.*) retail

minùto (2) *s. m.* minute ♦ **lancetta dei minuti** minute hand

minùzia *s. f.* **1** trifle **2** (*meticolosità*) meticulousness

mìo A *agg. poss. 1ª sing.* **1** my **2** (*pred.*) mine **B** *pron. poss.* mine **C** *s. m.* **1** (*denaro, averi*) my own money, my income **2** *al pl.* (*parenti*) my family, (*genitori*) my parents

mìope *agg.* myopic, shortsighted

mìra *s. f.* **1** aim **2** (*fig.*) target, aim, goal, design ♦ **prendere di m. qc.** to pick on sb.

miràbile *agg.* admirable

miràcolo *s. m.* miracle

miracolóso *agg.* miraculous

miràggio *s. m.* mirage

miràre *v. intr.* to aim

mirìade *s. f.* myriad

mirìno *s. m.* **1** sight **2** (*fot.*) finder

mirtìllo *s. m.* bilberry

misàntropo A *agg.* misanthropic **B** *s. m.* misanthrope

miscèla *s. f.* mixture, blend

miscelatóre *s. m.* mixer

miscellànea *s. f.* miscellany

mìschia *s. f.* scuffle, fray

mischiàre A *v. tr.* to mix, to mingle, to blend **B** *v. rifl.* **1** to mix, to mingle **2** (*intromettersi*) to meddle, to interfere

miscredènte A *agg.* misbelieving **B** *s. m. e f.* misbeliever

miscùglio *s. m.* mixture

miseràbile *agg.* **1** miserable, wretched **2** (*scarso*) poor, scanty **3** (*spregevole*) despicable, mean

miseràndo *agg.* miserable

misèria *s. f.* **1** poverty **2** (*meschinità*) meanness **3** (*inezia*) trifle **4** *al pl.* (*disgrazie*) troubles *pl.*, misfortunes *pl.*

misericòrdia *s. f.* mercy

mìsero *agg.* **1** poor, miserable, wretched **2** (*scarso*) poor, scanty **3** (*meschino*) mean, miserable **4** (*infelice*) unfortunate

misfàtto *s. m.* misdeed, crime

misògino A *agg.* misogynous **B** *s. m.* misogynist

mìssile *s. m.* missile

missionàrio *agg. e s. m.* missionary

missióne *s. f.* mission

misterióso *agg.* mysterious

mistèro *s. m.* mystery

mìstica *s. f.* **1** mystical theology **2** (*est.*) mystique

misticìsmo *s. m.* mysticism

mìstico *agg.* mystic(al)

mistificàre *v. tr.* to mystify, to hoax

mistificatóre *s. m.* mystifier, hoaxer

mìsto A *agg.* mixed **B** *s. m.* mixture

mistùra *s. f.* mixture, blend

misùra *s. f.* **1** measure, measurement **2** (*taglia*) size **3** (*limite*) limit, proportion, (*moderazione*) moderation **4** (*provvedimento*) measure, step

misuràbile *agg.* measurable
misuràre **A** *v. tr.* **1** to measure, (*tecnol.*) to gauge **2** (*valutare*) to estimate, to judge **3** (*provare indossando*) to try on **4** (*limitare*) to limit, to moderate **B** *v. intr.* to measure **C** *v. rifl.* **1** (*contenersi*) to limit oneself **2** (*cimentarsi*) to measure oneself
misuràto *agg.* measured
misuratóre *s. m.* meter, gauge
misurìno *s. m.* (small) measure
mìte *agg.* **1** mild, meek **2** (*moderato*) moderate **3** (*di clima*) mild
mìtico *agg.* mythical, legendary
mitigàre **A** *v. tr.* to mitigate, to alleviate **B** *v. intr. pron.* **1** to calm down **2** (*del clima*) to become mild
mìtilo *s. m.* mussel
mitizzàre *v. tr.* to mythicize
mìto *s. m.* myth
mitologìa *s. f.* mythology
mitològico *agg.* mythologic(al)
mitòmane *agg. e s. m. e f.* mythomaniac
mìtra (1) *s. f.* (*relig.*) mitre
mìtra (2) *s. m.* (*arma*) submachine gun
mitragliatrìce *s. f.* machine gun
mittènte *s. m. e f.* sender
mnemònico *agg.* mnemonic
mòbile **A** *agg.* **1** (*che si muove*) mobile, moving, (*che può essere mosso*) movable **2** (*mutevole*) changeable, mutable, unstable **B** *s. m.* piece of furniture, *al pl.* furniture ♦ **s. mobile** escalator
mobìlia *s. f.* furniture
mobiliàre *agg.* movable, personal
mobilità *s. f.* **1** mobility **2** (*mutevolezza*) inconstancy
mobilitàre *v. tr. e rifl.* to mobilize
mobilitazióne *s. f.* mobilization
mocassìno *s. m.* moccasin
mòccolo *s. m.* **1** (*di candela*) candle-end **2** (*fam.*) (*bestemmia*) oath
mòda *s. f.* **1** fashion, style **2** (*maniera*) manner, custom, fashion **3** (*mat.*) mode ♦ **alla m.** fashionable; **fuori m.** out of fashion
modalità *s. f.* modality, (*procedura*) formality
modanatùra *s. f.* moulding
modèlla *s. f.* model
modellàre **A** *v. tr.* to model, to mould **B** *v. rifl.* to model oneself
modellìsmo *s. m.* model-making, modelling
modèllo **A** *s. m.* **1** model **2** (*stampo*) mould **3** (*di abito*) pattern **B** *agg.* model, exemplary
modem *s. m. inv.* modem
moderàre **A** *v. tr.* **1** to moderate, to check, to curb **2** (*contenere*) to reduce, to regulate **B** *v. rifl.* to moderate oneself
moderàto *agg.* moderate
moderatóre **A** *agg.* moderating **B** *s. m.* moderator
moderazióne *s. f.* moderation
modernariàto *s. m.* modern antiques *pl.*
modernìsmo *s. m.* modernism
modernità *s. f.* modernity
modernizzàre **A** *v. tr.* to modernize, to update **B** *v. rifl.* to bring oneself up-to-date
modèrno *agg.* modern, up-to-date (*attr.*)
modèstia *s. f.* modesty
modèsto *agg.* modest
mòdico *agg.* moderate, reasonable
modìfica *s. f.* modification
modificàbile *agg.* modifiable
modificàre *v. tr. e intr. pron.* to modify, to change
mòdo *s. m.* **1** way, manner **2** (*mezzo*) means, (*occasione*) way **3** (*maniera*) manners *pl.*, (*misura*) measure **4** (*gramm.*) mood **5** (*locuzione*) expression **6** (*mus.*) mode ♦ **in che m.?** how?; **in m. che/da** so that, in such a way as to; **in ogni m.** anyway, in any case; **in qualche m.** somehow; **per m. di dire** so to say
modulàre *agg.* modular
modulazióne *s. f.* modulation
mòdulo *s. m.* **1** form, (*USA*) blank **2** (*arch., tecnol.*) module **3** (*mat., fis.*) modulus
mògano *s. m.* mahogany
mògio *agg.* dejected, depressed
móglie *s. f.* wife ♦ **prender m.** to get married
moìna *s. f.* simpering ♦ **fare le moine** to simper
mòla *s. f.* **1** (*di mulino*) millstone **2** (*molatrice*) grinder
molàre (1) *agg. e s. m.* (*dente*) molar
molàre (2) *v. tr.* **1** to grind **2** (*tagliare*) to cut
mòle *s. f.* **1** bulk, mass **2** (*dimensione*) size, dimension
molècola *s. f.* molecule
molestàre *v. tr.* to molest, to bother, to tease
molèstia *s. f.* nuisance, bother
molèsto *agg.* troublesome, annoying, bothering
mòlla *s. f.* **1** spring **2** (*fig.*) incentive, main-

spring **3** *al pl.* (*per afferrare*) tongs *pl.*
mollàre A *v. tr.* **1** (*allentare*) to slacken **2** (*lasciar andare*) to let go **3** (*fam.*) (*abbandonare*) to quit, to leave **4** (*fam.*) (*appioppare*) to give **B** *v. intr.* to give in
mòlle *agg.* **1** soft **2** (*debole*) weak, flabby
mollétta *s. f.* **1** (*per bucato*) clothes-peg, clothes-pin **2** (*per capelli*) hair-grip **3** (*per afferrare*) tongs *pl.*
mollìca *s. f.* crumb
mollùsco *s. m.* mollusc, shellfish
mòlo *s. m.* mole, pier, wharf
moltéplice *agg.* manifold, various
moltiplicàre *v. tr., rifl. e intr. pron.* to multiply
moltiplicazióne *s. f.* multiplication
moltìssimo A *agg. indef. sup.* **1** very much, (*in frasi afferm.*) a great deal of **2** (*tempo*) very long **3** *al pl.* very many, (*in frasi afferm.*) a great many **B** *pron. indef.* **1** very much, (*in frasi afferm.*) a grat deal **2** (*tempo*) a very long time **3** *al pl.* very many, (*in frasi afferm.*) a great many **C** *avv.* very much
moltitùdine *s. f.* multitude, (*folla*) crowd
mólto A *agg. indef.* **1** much, a lot of, lots of, a great deal of, a great quantity of **2** (*tempo*) long **3** (*grande*) great **4** *al pl.* many, a lot of, lots of, a great many **B** *pron. indef.* **1** much, a great deal, a lot **2** (*molto tempo*) a long time **3** *al pl.* many, a lot of, (*molta gente*) many people, a lot of people **C** *avv.* **1** (*con agg. e avv. di grado positivo, con participio pres.*) very **2** (*con agg. e avv. di grado comp.*) much **3** (*con p. p.*) much, greatly, **4** (*con verbo*) much, very much, a lot **5** (*a lungo*) long, (*spesso*) often
momentaneaménte *avv.* at the moment, at present
momentàneo *agg.* momentary, temporary
moménto *s. m.* **1** moment **2** (*circostanza, tempo*) time **3** (*opportunità*) opportunity, chance
mònaca *s. f.* nun
monacàle *agg.* monastic
monachésimo *s. m.* monasticism
mònaco *s. m.* monk
monàrca *s. m.* monarch
monarchìa *s. f.* monarchy
monàrchico *agg.* **1** monarchic(al) **2** (*fautore della monarchia*) monarchist
monastèro *s. m.* monastery, (*di monache*) convent
monàstico *agg.* monastic
mónco *agg.* **1** maimed **2** (*fig.*) incomplete
moncóne *s. m.* stump
mondàno *agg.* **1** worldly, earthly, mundane **2** (*della società elegante*) worldly, society (*attr.*) ♦ **vita mondana** society life
mondàre *v. tr.* to clean
mondiàle *agg.* world (*attr.*), world-wide
móndo *s. m.* **1** world **2** (*grande quantità*) a world of, a lot of
monèllo *s. m.* rascal
monéta *s. f.* **1** coin, piece **2** (*denaro*) money **3** (*spicciolo*) change
monetàrio *agg.* monetary
mongolfièra *s. f.* hot-hair balloon
mònito *s. m.* warning
monitor *s. m. inv.* monitor
monitoràre *v. tr.* to monitor
monocoltùra *s. f.* monoculture
monocòrde *agg.* monotonous
monocromàtico *agg.* monochrome, monochromatic
monogamìa *s. f.* monogamy
monografìa *s. f.* monograph
monolìtico *agg.* monolithic
monolocàle *s. m.* bedsitter, studio
monòlogo *s. m.* monologue
monomanìaco *agg.* monomaniac
monopòlio *s. m.* monopoly
monopósto *agg. inv.* single-seater (*attr.*)
monosìllabo *s. m.* monosyllable
monoteìsmo *s. m.* monotheism
monotonìa *s. f.* monotony
monòtono *agg.* monotonous
monsóne *s. m.* monsoon
montacàrichi *s. m. inv.* goods-lift, (*USA*) elevator
montàggio *s. m.* **1** assembly **2** (*cin.*) editing
montàgna *s. f.* mountain
montagnóso *agg.* mountainous
montàno *agg.* mountain (*attr.*)
montàre A *v. tr.* **1** (*salire*) to mount, to climb **2** (*cavalcare*) to ride **3** (*mettere insieme*) to assemble, (*un film*) to edit **4** (*gonfiare*) to exaggerate **5** (*incastonare*) to mount, to set **B** *v. intr.* **1** to mount, to climb, to get on **2** (*salire*) to rise **C** *v. intr. pron.* to get big-headed
montatùra *s. f.* **1** (*di occhiali*) frame, (*di pietra*) setting, mounting **2** (*fig.*) stunt
mónte *s. m.* mountain, mount (*davanti a nome proprio*) ♦ **andare a m.** to fail; **m. di pietà** pawnshop; **m. premi** prize money

montgomery *s. m. inv.* duffel coat
montóne *s. m.* ram, (*carne*) mutton ♦ **pelle di m.** sheepskin
montuóso *agg.* mountainous
monumentàle *agg.* monumental
monuménto *s. m.* monument
moquette *s. f. inv.* moquette, carpet
mòra (1) *s. f.* **1** (*di rovo*) blackberry **2** (*di gelso*) mulberry
mòra (2) *s. f.* (*ritardo*) delay, (*dilazione*) extension
moràle A *agg.* moral **B** *s. f.* morals *pl.* **C** *s. m.* morale, spirits *pl.*
moralìsmo *s. m.* moralism
moralità *s. f.* morality
moralizzàre *v. tr.* to moralize
moralménte *avv.* morally
mòrbido *agg.* soft, smooth
morbìllo *s. m.* measles *pl.* (*v. al sing.*)
mòrbo *s. m.* disease, illness
morbóso *agg.* morbid
mordàce *agg.* biting, cutting
mordènte *s. m.* **1** (*chim.*) mordant **2** (*fig.*) bite, drive
mòrdere *v. tr.* to bite, to bite into
morèna *s. f.* moraine
morènte *agg.* dying
morfologìa *s. f.* morphology
morfològico *agg.* morphologic(al)
moribóndo *agg.* dying
morigeràto *agg.* moderate, sober
morìre *v. intr.* **1** to die **2** (*cessare, spegnersi*) to die out, to go out, (*di suono*) to die away **3** (*terminare*) to end
mormoràre A *v. tr.* **1** to murmur, to whisper **2** (*borbottare*) to mutter **B** *v. intr.* **1** to murmur **2** (*parlar male*) to speak ill
morosità *s. f.* arrearage
mòrsa *s. f.* vice, (*USA*) vise
morsétto *s. m.* **1** (*mecc.*) clamp **2** (*elettr.*) terminal
morsicàre *v. tr.* to bite
mòrso *s. m.* **1** bite **2** (*boccone*) bit, scrap **3** (*puntura*) sting **4** (*del cavallo*) bit
mortàio *s. m.* mortar
mortàle A *agg.* **1** (*che è soggetto a morte*) mortal **2** (*che cagiona morte*) mortal, deadly **3** (*come la morte*) deathlike, deathly **B** *s. m. e f.* mortal
mortalità *s. f.* mortality ♦ **indice di m.** death rate
mòrte *s. f.* death
mortificàre A *v. tr.* to mortify **B** *v. rifl.* to mortify oneself **C** *v. intr. pron.* to feel mortified
mortificazióne *s. f.* mortification
mòrto A *agg.* dead **B** *s. m.* dead person, (*cadavere*) corpse ♦ **i morti** the dead; **natura morta** still life; **stagione morta** off season
mortòrio *s. m.* funeral
mosàico *s. m.* mosaic
mósca *s. f.* fly
moscerìno *s. m.* midge, gnat
moschèa *s. f.* mosque
moschétto *s. m.* musket
móscio *agg.* **1** flabby **2** (*fig.*) limp
moscóne *s. m.* bluebottle
mòssa *s. f.* **1** movement **2** (*nel gioco*) move
móstra *s. f.* **1** show, exhibition **2** (*ostentazione*) display
mostràre A *v. tr.* **1** to show, to display **2** (*ostentare*) to show off **3** (*indicare*) to show, to point out **4** (*dimostrare*) to prove **B** *v. rifl. e intr. pron.* **1** to show oneself **2** (*apparire*) to appear
móstro *s. m.* monster
mostruóso *agg.* **1** monstrous **2** (*enorme*) enormous
motel *s. m. inv.* motel
motivàre *v. tr.* **1** to justify **2** (*causare*) to cause **3** (*suscitare interesse*) to motivate
motivazióne *s. f.* motivation, reason
motìvo *s. m.* **1** motive, reason, ground **2** (*mus.*) motif, theme **3** (*elemento decorativo*) pattern, motif ♦ **m. conduttore** leitmotif
mòto (1) *s. m.* **1** motion, movement **2** (*esercizio fisico*) exercise **3** (*sommossa*) rebellion, revolt **4** (*impulso*) impulse
mòto (2) *s. f.* motorcycle
mòtocicletta *s. f.* motorcycle
motociclìsmo *s. m.* motorcycling
motociclìsta *s. m. e f.* motorcyclist
motóre A *agg.* motor, driving, propelling **B** *s. m.* engine, motor
motorìno *s. m.* moped ♦ **m. d'avviamento** starter
motorizzàre *v. tr. e rifl.* to motorize
motoscàfo *s. m.* motorboat
mòtto *s. m.* **1** saying **2** (*facezia*) witticism
movènte *s. m.* motive
movimentàre *v. tr.* to enliven, to animate
moviménto *s. m.* **1** movement **2** (*moto*) motion **3** (*andirivieni*) flow, bustle
mozióne *s. f.* motion
mozzàre *v. tr.* to cut off ♦ **m. il fiato** to

take breath away
mozzicóne *s. m.* stub, end
mózzo (1) *s. m.* **1** (*naut.*) ship boy **2** (*di stalla*) stable boy
mòzzo (2) *s. m.* (*mecc.*) hub
mùcca *s. f.* cow
mùcchio *s. m.* heap, stack ♦ **un m. di gente** a lot of people
mùco *s. m.* mucus
mucósa *s. f.* mucosa, mucous membrane
mùffa *s. f.* mould
muggìre *v. intr.* **1** to moo, to low **2** (*mugghiare*) to bellow
muggìto *s. m.* moo, lowing
mughétto *s. m.* **1** lily of the valley **2** (*med.*) thrush
mugnàio *s. m.* miller
mugolàre *v. intr.* to howl, to whimper
mulattièra *s. f.* muletrack
mulinàre **A** *v. tr.* **1** to whirl **2** (*fig.*) to brood over **B** *v. intr.* to whirl around
mulinèllo *s. m.* **1** (*d'acqua*) whirpool, (*d'aria*) whirlwind **2** (*per canna da pesca*) reel
mulìno *s. m.* mill ♦ **m. a vento** windmill
mùlo *s. m.* mule
mùlta *s. f.* fine
multàre *v. tr.* to fine
multicolóre *agg.* multicoloured
multifórme *agg.* multiform
multinazionàle *agg.* multinational
mùltiplo *agg. e s. m.* multiple
mùmmia *s. f.* mummy
mùngere *v. tr.* to milk
municipàle *agg.* municipal, town (*attr*)
municipalità *s. f.* municipality
municìpio *s. m.* **1** municipality, town council **2** (*palazzo*) town hall
munificènza *s. f.* munificence, liberality
munìre **A** *v. tr.* **1** (*fortificare*) to fortify **2** (*provvedere*) to provide, to supply **B** *v. rifl.* to equip oneself, to supply oneself
munizióni *s. f. pl.* munitions *pl.*
muòvere **A** *v. tr.* **1** to move **2** (*suscitare*) to move, to induce **3** (*sollevare*) to raise, to bring up **B** *v. intr.* to move **C** *v. rifl.* to move, to stir, to go
muràglia *s. f.* wall
muràle *agg.* mural, wall (*attr*)
muràre *v. tr.* **1** to wall up **2** (*circondare di mura*) to wall
muratóre *s. m.* bricklayer, mason
murèna *s. f.* moray
mùro *s. m.* **1** wall **2** *al pl.* (*mura*) walls *pl.*
mùschio *s. m.* **1** musk **2** (*bot.*) moss
muscolàre *agg.* muscular
mùscolo *s. m.* **1** muscle **2** (*mitilo*) mussel
muscolóso *agg.* muscular, brawny
musèo *s. m.* museum
museruòla *s. f.* muzzle
mùsica *s. f.* music
musicàle *agg.* musical
musicassétta *s. f.* cassette
musicìsta *s. m. e f.* musician
mùso *s. m.* **1** (*di animale*) snout, muzzle **2** (*di auto, aereo*) nose **3** (*di persona*) mug **4** (*broncio*) long face
musóne *s. m.* (*fam.*) sulky person
mùssola *s. f.* muslin
musulmàno *agg. e s. m.* Muslim, Moslem
mùta *s. f.* **1** (*di uccelli*) moult, (*di serpenti*) shedding **2** (*di cani*) pack **3** (*tuta per immersioni*) wet suit
mutaménto *s. m.* change
mutànde *s. f. pl.* briefs *pl.*, (*da uomo*) pants *pl.*, underpants *pl.*, (*da donna*) panties *pl.*
mutàre *v. tr., intr. e intr. pron.* to change
mutazióne *s. f.* change, mutation
mutévole *agg.* changeable, variable
mutilàre *v. tr.* to maim, to mutilate
mutilàto *s. m.* cripple
mutilazióne *s. f.* maiming, mutilation
mutìsmo *s. m.* mutism, silence
mùto *agg.* dumb, mute ♦ **film m.** silent film
mùtuo (1) *agg.* mutual, reciprocal
mùtuo (2) *s. m.* loan

N

nabàbbo *s. m.* nabob
nàcchere *s. f. pl.* castanets *pl.*
nàfta *s. f.* diesel oil, naphta
naftalìna *s. f.* (*tarmicida in palline*) mothballs *pl.*
nàiade *s. f.* naiad
naïf *agg. inv.* naive, naïf
nailon *s. m. inv.* nylon
nànna *s. f.* (*fam.*) bye-bye
nàno *agg. e s. m.* dwarf
napoletàno *agg. e s. m.* Neapolitan
nàppa *s. f.* **1** (*fiocco*) tassel **2** (*pelle*) soft leather
narcisìsmo *s. m.* narcissism
narcisìsta *s. m. e f.* narcissist
narcìso *s. m.* (*bot.*) narcissus
narcòsi *s. f.* narcosis
narcòtico *agg. e s. m.* narcotic
narìce *s. f.* nostril
narràre *v. tr. e intr.* to tell, to narrate
narratìva *s. f.* fiction
narratìvo *agg.* narrative
narratóre *s. m.* **1** narrator, story-teller **2** (*scrittore*) writer
narrazióne *s. f.* **1** narration, telling **2** (*racconto*) tale, story
nartèce *s. m.* narthex
nasàle *agg.* nasal
nascènte *agg.* rising
nàscere *v. intr.* **1** to be born **2** (*trarre origine*) to come, (*derivare*) to arise, to derive, to be due **3** (*sorgere*) to rise **4** (*di piante*) to spring up, to come up, to grow **5** (*di capelli, unghie, corna*) to sprout **6** (*di fiume*) to rise ♦ **far n.** to give rise to, to originate
nàscita *s. f.* **1** birth **2** (*origine*) origin, extraction ♦ **luogo di n.** birthplace
nascitùro *agg.* unborn
nascóndere **A** *v. tr.* to hide, to conceal **B** *v. rifl. e intr. pron.* to hide (oneself), to be hidden
nascondìglio *s. m.* hiding-place
nascondìno *s. m.* hide-and-seek
nascósto *agg.* hidden
nasèllo *s. m.* hake
nàso *s. m.* nose
nàstro *s. m.* **1** ribbon **2** (*tecnol.*) tape, ribbon, band ♦ **n. di partenza** starting tape
natàle **A** *agg.* native **B** *s. m.* **1** (*Natale*) Christmas **2** (*giorno natale*) birthday **3** *al pl.* (*nascita*) birth ♦ **buon N.** merry Christmas
natalità *s. f.* natality, birthrate
natalìzio *agg.* Christmas (*attr.*)
natànte *s. m.* boat, craft
nàtica *s. f.* buttock
natìo *agg.* native
natività *s. f.* nativity
natìvo *agg. e s. m.* native
nàto *agg.* born
natùra *s. f.* **1** nature **2** (*genere*) type, kind, nature **3** (*carattere*) nature, character ♦ **pagare in n.** to pay in kind
naturàle *agg.* natural
naturalézza *s. f.* **1** truthfulness **2** (*semplicità*) simplicity
naturalìsmo *s. m.* naturalism
naturalìsta *s. m. e f.* naturalist
naturalizzàre **A** *v. tr.* to naturalize **B** *v. rifl.* to become naturalized
naturalménte *avv.* **1** naturally **2** (*certamente*) of course
naturìsmo *s. m.* naturism
naturìsta *s. m. e f.* naturist
naufragàre *v. intr.* **1** (*di nave*) to be wrecked, (*di persona*) to be shipwrecked **2** (*fig.*) to be wrecked, to fail
naufràgio *s. m.* **1** shipwreck, wreck **2** (*fig.*) wreck, failure
nàufrago *s. m.* shipwrecked person
naumachìa *s. f.* naumachia
nàusea *s. f.* nausea ♦ **avere la n.** to feel sick
nauseabóndo *agg.* nauseating, sickening
nauseàre *v. tr. e intr.* to nauseate, to make sick
nàutica *s. f.* **1** nautical science **2** (*attività*) boating
nàutico *agg.* nautical
navàle *agg.* naval
navàta *s. f.* (*centrale*) nave, (*laterale*) aisle
nàve *s. f.* ship, vessel, boat
navétta *s. f.* shuttle
navigàbile *agg.* navigable
navigabilità *s. f.* navigability
navigàre *v. tr. e intr.* to sail, to navigate
navigatóre **A** *agg.* seafaring **B** *s. m.* **1**

navigator **2** (*marinaio*) sailor
navigazióne *s. f.* **1** navigation, (*a vela*) sailing **2** (*viaggio*) voyage, (*traversata*) crossing ♦ **compagnia di n.** shipping line
navìglio *s. m.* ships *pl.*, fleet
nazionàle **A** *agg.* national **B** *s. f.* (*sport*) national team
nazionalìsmo *s. m.* nationalism
nazionalìsta *agg. e s. m. e f.* nationalist
nazionalità *s. f.* nationality
nazionalizzàre *v. tr.* to nationalize
nazióne *s. f.* nation, country
nazìsmo *s. m.* Nazism
né *cong.* neither, nor ♦ **né ... né** (neither) ... nor; **né l'uno né l'altro** neither; **né più né meno** exactly
ne **A** *pron. m. e f., sing. e pl.* **1** (*specificazione, argomento*) of, about (him, her, them, this, that) (ES: **che ne sai?** what do you know about it?) **2** (*poss.*) his, her, its, their (ES: **quale ragazza? non ne ricordo il nome** which girl? I don't remember her name) **3** (*partitivo*) some, any (ES: **chi ne vuol comprare?** who wants to buy some?, **non ne ho** I haven't any) **4** (*causale*) for it, about it (ES: **ne sono felice** I'm very happy about it) **5** (*pleonastico*) (ES: **me ne vado** I'm going away) **B** *avv.* (*moto da luogo*) from it, from here, out of it (ES: **andiamocene da qui** let us go away from here)
neànche **A** *avv.* **1** neither, nor **2** (*rafforzativo di altra negazione*) even (ES: **non l'ho n. visto** I haven't even seen him) **B** *cong.* **n. a/se** even if
nébbia *s. f.* fog, (*leggera*) mist
nebbióso *agg.* foggy, misty
nebulósa *s. f.* nebula
nebulóso *agg.* nebulous, vague
nécessaire *s. m. inv.* toilet-case ♦ **n. per barba** shaving set
necessariaménte *avv.* necessarily, of necessity
necessàrio *agg.* necessary, indispensable
necessità *s. f.* necessity, (*bisogno*) need
necessitàre **A** *v. tr.* to necessitate **B** *v. intr.* **1** (*aver bisogno*) to need **2** (*essere necessario*) to be necessary
necrològio *s. m.* obituary
necròpoli *s. f.* necropolis
nefàndo *agg.* wicked
nefàsto *agg.* inauspicious, fateful
negàre *v. tr.* **1** to deny **2** (*rifiutare*) to refuse
negativaménte *avv.* negatively
negatìvo *agg. e s. m.* negative
negazióne *s. f.* **1** denial, (*rifiuto*) refusal **2** (*gramm.*) negative **3** (*contrario*) negation
negligènte *agg.* negligent
negligènza *s. f.* **1** negligence **2** (*trascuratezza*) shabbiness
negoziànte *s. m. e f.* dealer, trader, (*esercente*) shop-keeper
negoziàre *v. tr.* **1** to deal in, to trade in **2** (*trattare*) to negotiate
negoziàto *s. m.* negotiation
negòzio *s. m.* shop, (*USA*) store
négro *agg. e s. m.* black
nemìco **A** *agg.* **1** (*ostile*) adverse, inimical, opposed **2** (*che detesta*) fearful **3** (*del nemico*) enemy (*attr*) **B** *s. m.* enemy
nemméno *avv. e cong.* → **neanche**
nènia *s. f.* **1** sing-song **2** (*funebre*) dirge
nèo *s. m.* **1** spot, mole, (*med.*) naevus **2** (*fig.*) flaw
neoclassicìsmo *s. m.* neoclassicism
neoclàssico *agg.* neoclassic(al)
neòfita *s. m. e f.* neophyte, novice
neolatìno *agg.* neo-Latin
neolìtico *s. m.* Neolithic
neologìsmo *s. m.* neologism
neon *s. m. inv.* neon
neonàto *s. m.* (newborn) baby
neorealìsmo *s. m.* neorealism
neozelandése **A** *agg.* New Zealand (*attr*) **B** *s. m. e f.* New Zealander
nepotìsmo *s. m.* nepotism
neppùre *avv. e cong.* → **neanche**
nèrbo *s. m.* **1** scourge **2** (*fig.*) strength
nerborùto *agg.* brawny
nerétto *s. m.* (*tip.*) boldface
néro **A** *agg.* **1** black **2** (*scuro*) dark **3** (*tetro*) gloomy **4** (*profondo*) dire **B** *s. m.* black
nervatùra *s. f.* **1** (*arch., mecc.*) ribs *pl.* **2** (*bot.*) nervation
nèrvo *s. m.* nerve ♦ **avere i nervi** to be in a bad mood
nervosìsmo *s. m.* nervousness, irritation
nervóso **A** *agg.* **1** nervous **2** (*irritabile*) irritable, nervy **3** (*incisivo*) incisive **B** *s. m.* nervousness ♦ **avere il n.** to be on edge; **esaurimento n.** nervous breakdown
nèspola *s. f.* medlar
nèsso *s. m.* connection, nexus
nessùno **A** *agg. indef.* **1** no, (*con altra negazione*) any **2** (*qualche*) any **B** *pron.*

indef. **1** (*persona*) nobody, no one, (*cosa*) none; (*con partitivo*) none; (*con altra negazione*) anybody, anyone, any **2** (*qualcuno*) anybody, anyone, (*con partitivo*) any **C** *s. m.* nobody, no one
nèttare *s. m.* nectar
nettézza *s. f.* **1** cleanness **2** (*precisione*) clarity
nétto *agg.* **1** clean **2** (*preciso*) clear, clear-cut, sharp **3** (*comm.*) net ♦ **di n.** clean through; **prezzo n.** net price
netturbìno *s. m.* dustman, (*USA*) garbage collector
neurologìa *s. f.* neurology
neuròlogo *s. m.* neurologist
neuropsichiàtra *s. m. e f.* neuropsychiatrist
neuropsichiatrìa *s. f.* neuropsychiatry
neutràle *agg.* neutral
neutralità *s. f.* neutrality
neutralizzàre *v. tr.* to neutralize
nèutro *agg.* **1** neutral **2** (*biol., gramm.*) neuter
neutróne *s. m.* neutron
nevàio *s. m.* snowfield
néve *s. f.* snow ♦ **fiocco di n.** snowflake
nevicàre *v. intr. impers.* to snow
nevicàta *s. f.* snowfall
nevìschio *s. m.* sleet
nevóso *agg.* snowy, (*coperto di neve*) snow-covered
nevralgìa *s. f.* neuralgia
nevrastènico *agg.* **1** neurasthenic **2** (*irritabile*) irritable
nevròsi *s. f.* neurosis
nevròtico *agg.* neurotic
nìbbio *s. m.* kite
nìcchia *s. f.* niche
nicchiàre *v. intr.* to hedge, to hesitate
nichilìsmo *s. m.* nihilism
nicotìna *s. f.* nicotine
nidiàta *s. f.* nestful, brood
nidificàre *v. intr.* to nest
nìdo *s. m.* **1** nest **2** (*covo*) den ♦ **n. d'infanzia** crèche, nursery
niènte **A** *pron. indef.* **1** nothing, (*con altra negazione*) anything **2** (*qualcosa*) anything **B** *s. m.* nothing **C** *agg. inv.* no, (*con altra negazione*) any **D** *avv.* not at all
nienteméno *avv.* no less than
nìnfa *s. f.* nymph
ninfèa *s. f.* waterlily
ninfèo *s. m.* nymphaeum
ninnanànna *s. f.* lullaby
nìnnolo *s. m.* knick-knack
nipóte *s. m. e f.* (*di zii*) nephew *m.*, niece *f.*, (*di nonni*) grandson *m.*, granddaughter *f.*
nirvàna *s. m. inv.* nirvana
nìtido *agg.* clear, limpid
nitràto *s. m.* nitrate
nìtrico *agg.* nitric
nitrìre *v. intr.* to neigh
nitrìto (1) *s. m.* neigh, whinny
nitrìto (2) *s. m.* (*chim.*) nitrite
nitroglicerìna *s. f.* nitroglycerine
no **A** *avv.* no, not **B** *s. m. inv.* no, (*rifiuto*) refusal ♦ **dire di no** to say no; **un giorno sì e uno no** every other day; **sì e no** (*circa*) about
nòbile *agg. e s. m. e f.* noble
nobiliàre *agg.* nobiliary, noble
nobiltà *s. f.* nobility
nòcca *s. f.* knuckle
nocciòla *s. f.* hazel(-nut)
nòcciolo *s. m.* **1** stone **2** (*fig.*) heart, kernel
nóce *s. f.* walnut ♦ **n. di cocco** coconut; **n. moscata** nutmeg
nocìvo *agg.* harmful, noxious
nòdo *s. m.* **1** knot **2** (*ferr.*) junction **3** (*scient.*) node **4** (*del legno*) knag **5** (*punto cruciale*) crux **6** (*unità di misura*) knot
nodóso *agg.* knotty
nói *pron. pers. 1ª pl. m. e f.* **1** (*sogg.*) we **2** (*compl.*) us ♦ **n. stessi** we ourselves
nòia *s. f.* **1** boredom **2** (*fastidio*) annoyance, nuisance, bother
noióso *agg.* **1** boring, tiresome **2** (*fastidioso*) annoying, troublesome
noleggiàre *v. tr.* **1** (*prendere a noleggio*) to hire, to rent, (*naut., aer.*) to charter **2** (*dare a noleggio*) to hire out, to rent, to let out
noleggiatóre *s. m.* hirer, renter, charterer
noléggio *s. m.* **1** hire, rent, charter **2** (*prezzo*) hire (rate), rental
nòmade **A** *agg.* nomadic **B** *s. m. e f.* nomad
nóme *s. m.* **1** name **2** (*gramm.*) noun **3** (*soprannome*) nickname ♦ **farsi un n.** to make one's name; **n. commerciale** trade name; **n. e cognome** full name
nomèa *s. f.* reputation
nomìgnolo *s. m.* nickname
nòmina *s. f.* nomination, appointment
nominàle *agg.* nominal
nominàre *v. tr.* **1** (*menzionare*) to mention **2** (*designare*) to designate, to appoint, to name
nominatìvo *agg.* **1** (*gramm.*) nominative **2** (*comm.*) registered
non *avv.* not

non- *pref.* (*davanti ad agg. e s.*) non-, un-, in-
nonché *cong.* **1** (*tanto meno*) let alone, still less **2** (*e inoltre*) as well as
noncurànte *agg.* careless
noncurànza *s. f.* carelessness, nonchalance
nondiméno *cong.* nevertheless
nònna *s. f.* grandmother, (*fam.*) grandma
nònno *s. m.* grandfather, (*fam.*) grandpa
nonnùlla *s. m. inv.* trifle
nòno *agg. num. ord.* ninth
nonostànte **A** *prep.* in spite of, despite, notwithstanding **B** *cong.* **n. che** (even) though, although
nontiscordardimé *s. m.* forget-me-not
nòrd *s. m.* north ♦ **n.-est** northeast; **n.-ovest** northwest
nòrdico *agg.* **1** northern **2** (*dell'Europa settentrionale*) Nordic
nòrma *s. f.* **1** rule, norm, standard **2** (*avvertenza*) instruction, direction **3** (*consuetudine*) custom, norm
normàle *agg.* normal, standard (*attr.*)
normalità *s. f.* normality
normalizzàre *v. tr.* to normalize
normalménte *avv.* normally
normànno *agg. e s. m.* Norman
normatìva *s. f.* set of rules
norvegése *agg. e s. m. e f.* Norwegian
nosocòmio *s. m.* hospital
nostalgìa *s. f.* longing (for), nostalgia, (*di casa*) homesickness
nostàlgico *agg.* nostalgic, (*di casa*) homesick
nostràno *agg.* local, home (*attr.*)
nòstro **A** *agg. poss. 1ª pl.* **1** our **2** (*pred.*) ours **B** *pron. poss.* **1** ours **2** *al pl.* (*la nostra famiglia*) our family, our relatives, (*i nostri amici*) our friends
nòta *s. f.* **1** (*segno*) sign, mark **2** (*appunto, commento*) note **3** (*mus.*) note **4** (*lista*) list **5** (*conto*) bill
notàbile *s. m.* notable
notàio *s. m.* notary (public)
notàre *v. tr.* **1** (*annotare*) to note, to take note of **2** (*osservare*) to notice, to observe
notévole *agg.* **1** (*pregevole*) remarkable, notable **2** (*grande*) considerable
notìfica *s. f.* notification, notice
notificàre *v. tr.* **1** (*dir*) to notify, to serve **2** (*render noto*) to advise, to announce
notìzia *s. f.* **1** piece of news, news **2** (*informazione*) information
notiziàrio *s. m.* news
nòto *agg.* well-known, known
notorietà *s. f.* notoriety, renown
notòrio *agg.* well-known, (*spreg.*) notorious
nottàmbulo *s. m.* night bird
nottàta *s. f.* night
nòtte *s. f.* night ♦ **buona n.** good night; **di n.** by night; **la n. scorsa** last night; **questa n.** tonight
nottùrno *agg.* nocturnal, night (*attr.*)
novànta *agg. num. card. e s. m. inv.* ninety
novantèsimo *agg. num. ord. e s. m.* ninetieth
nòve *agg. num. card. e s. m. inv.* nine
novecentésco *agg.* twentieth-century (*attr.*)
novecènto *agg. num. card. e s. m. inv.* nine hundred ♦ **il N.** the twentieth century
novèlla *s. f.* tale, short story
novellìno *agg.* raw, green
novèllo *agg.* **1** new, spring **2** (*secondo*) second
novèmbre *s. m.* November
novilùnio *s. m.* new moon
novità *s. f.* **1** novelty **2** (*innovazione*) change, innovation **3** (*notizia*) news
novìziato *s. m.* novitiate
novìzio *s. m.* novice
nozióne *s. f.* knowledge, notion
nòzze *s. f. pl.* wedding, marriage ♦ **n. d'oro** golden wedding; **viaggio di n.** honeymoon
nùbe *s. f.* cloud
nubifràgio *s. m.* cloudburst
nùbile *agg.* unmarried, single
nùca *s. f.* nape
nucleàre *agg.* nuclear ♦ **energia n.** nuclear power
nùcleo *s. m.* **1** nucleus **2** (*gruppo*) group, (*squadra*) squad, team ♦ **n. familiare** family unit
nudìsmo *s. m.* nudism
nudìsta *agg. e s. m. e f.* nudist
nùdo *agg.* bare, naked, nude, (*svestito*) unclothed ♦ **a piedi nudi** barefoot; **mezzo n.** half-nacked
nùgolo *s. m.* cloud
nùlla → **niente**
nullaòsta *s. m. inv.* permit, authorization
nullità *s. f.* **1** nullity **2** (*cosa o persona*) nonentity **3** (*non validità*) invalidity
nùllo *agg.* **1** (*dir*) null, invalid **2** (*di nessuna importanza*) of no importance
numeràle *agg. e s. m.* numeral
numeràre *v. tr.* to number
numeràto *agg.* numbered ♦ **posti nume-**

rati numbered seats
numerazióne *s. f.* numbering, numeration
numericaménte *avv.* numerically
numèrico *agg.* numerical
nùmero *s. m.* **1** number **2** (*cifra*) figure, digit **3** (*taglia, misura*) size **4** (*di spettacolo*) turn ♦ **n. civico** street number; **n. di telefono** telephon number
numeróso *agg.* numerous, large
numismàtica *s. f.* numismatics *pl.* (*v.* *al sing.*)
nùnzio *s. m.* nuncio
nuòcere *v. intr.* to damage, to do harm (to), to harm
nuòra *s. f.* daughter-in-law
nuotàre *v. intr.* to swim
nuotàta *s. f.* swim
nuotatóre *s. m.* swimmer
nuòto *s. m.* swimming
nuòva *s. f.* news
nuovaménte *avv.* again
nuòvo *agg. e s. m.* new ♦ **di n.** again; **n. di zecca** brand-new
nutriènte *agg.* nourishing
nutriménto *s. m.* nourishment, food
nutrìre **A** *v. tr.* to feed, to nourish **B** *v. intr.* to be nutritious **C** *v. rifl.* to feed (on)
nutritìvo *agg.* **1** nutritive **2** (*nutriente*) nourishing
nutrizióne *s. f.* nourishment
nùvola *s. f.* cloud
nuvolóso *agg.* cloudy, overcast
nuziàle *agg.* wedding (*attr*), nuptial

O

o o **od** *cong.* or ♦ **o ... o** either ... or
òasi *s. f.* oasis
obbediènte *agg.* obedient
obbediènza *s. f.* obedience
obbedìre *v. intr.* to obey, to comply
obbligàre **A** *v. tr.* **1** to oblige, to compel **2** (*costringere*) to force, to make **3** (*impegnare*) to bind **B** *v. rifl.* to bind oneself, to engage oneself
obbligatòrio *agg.* compulsory
obbligazióne *s. f.* **1** obligation **2** (*fin.*) bond, debenture
òbbligo *s. m.* obligation
obbròbrio *s. m.* disgrace
obelìsco *s. m.* obelisk
oberàre *v. tr.* to overload
oberàto *agg.* overburdened
obesità *s. f.* obesity
obèso *agg.* obese
obiettàre *v. tr. e intr.* to object
obiettività *s. f.* objectivity
obiettìvo **A** *agg.* objective **B** *s. m.* **1** objective **2** (*scopo*) aim, goal, target, objective **3** (*fot.*) lens
obiettóre *s. m.* objector ♦ **o. di coscienza** conscientious objector
obiezióne *s. f.* objection
obitòrio *s. m.* mortuary, morgue
oblìo *s. m.* oblivion
oblìquo *agg.* **1** oblique, (*inclinato*) slanting **2** (*indiretto*) indirect
obliteràre *v. tr.* **1** to obliterate **2** (*biglietto*) to stamp
oblò *s. m.* bull's eye
oblùngo *agg.* oblong
òboe *s. m.* oboe
òbolo *s. m.* mite
obsolescènza *s. f.* obsolescence
obsolèto *agg.* obsolete
òca *s. f.* goose
occasionàle *agg.* **1** immediate **2** (*casuale*) fortuitous, chance (*attr.*) **3** (*saltuario*) occasional
occasionalménte *avv.* **1** occasionally **2** (*per caso*) by chance
occasióne *s. f.* **1** occasion **2** (*opportunità*) opportunity, chance, occasion **3** (*affare*) bargain
occhiàie *s. f. pl.* shadows *pl.*
occhialàio *s. m.* optician
occhiàli *s. m. pl.* glasses *pl.* ♦ **o. da sole** sun-glasses
occhiàta (1) *s. f.* look, glance
occhiàta (2) *s. f.* (*zool.*) saddled bream
occhieggiàre **A** *v. tr.* to eye **B** *v. intr.* to peep
occhièllo *s. m.* **1** buttonhole **2** (*tecnol.*) eye
òcchio *s. m.* **1** eye **2** (*vista*) sight **3** (*sguardo*) look, glance, eye ♦ **a o. nudo** with the nacked eye; **a quattr'occhi** in private; **chiudere un o. su q.c.** to turn a blind eye on st.; **dare nell'o.** to attract attention
occidentàle *agg.* west (*attr.*), western, (*da occidente*) westerly
occidènte *s. m.* west
occipitàle *agg.* occipital
occlùdere *v. tr.* to occlude
occlusióne *s. f.* occlusion
occorrènte **A** *agg.* necessary, required **B** *s. m.* the necessary
occorrènza *s. f.* necessity ♦ **all'o.** in case of need
occórrere **A** *v. intr.* **1** to need, to want, to be needed, to be wanted (ES: **occorrono molti più soldi** much more money is needed) **2** (*tempo*) to take (ES: **per cuocere una torta di mele occorre mezz'ora** it takes half an hour to cook an apple pie) **B** *v. intr. impers.* to be necessary, to need, to must, to have to (ES: **non occorre che ti muova** you needn't move)
occultàre *v. tr.* to hide, to conceal, (*astr.*) to occult
occùlto *agg.* **1** (*nascosto*) hidden **2** (*magico*) occult
occupàre **A** *v. tr.* **1** to occupy, to take possession of **2** (*spazio*) to take up **3** (*tempo*) to spend, to occupy **4** (*carica*) to hold **5** (*impiegare*) to employ **6** (*impegnare*) to keep busy **B** *v. intr. pron.* **1** to attend to, to be responsible for, (*come lavoro*) to do as a job, (*commerciare*) to deal in **2** (*interessarsi*) to be interested in, to be concerned with **3** (*prendersi cura*) to look after, to see to **4** (*impicciarsi*) to get involved in **5** (*trovar lavoro*) to find a job

occupàto *agg.* **1** (*impegnato*) busy, engaged **2** (*non libero*) taken, engaged **3** (*soggetto a occupazione*) occupied **4** (*impiegato*) employed
occupazióne *s. f.* **1** occupation **2** (*attività*) job, employment, occupation **3** (*dir*) occupancy
oceànico *agg.* oceanic, ocean (*attr*)
ocèano *s. m.* ocean
oceanografia *s. f.* oceanography
òcra *s. f.* ochre
oculàre *agg.* ocular, eye (*attr*) ♦ **testimone o.** eye-witness
oculàto *agg.* cautious, shrewd
oculìsta *s. m. e f.* oculist
òde *s. f.* ode
odiàre **A** *v. tr.* to hate **B** *v. rifl. rec.* to hate each other
odièrno *agg.* today's (*attr*)
òdio *s. m.* hatred, hate
odióso *agg.* hateful, hideous, detestable
odissèa *s. f.* odyssey
odontoiatrìa *s. f.* odontology
odontotècnico *s. m.* dental mechanic
odoràre *v. tr. e intr.* to smell
odoràto *s. m.* smell
odóre *s. m.* **1** smell, odour, scent **2** (*piacevole*) perfume, scent **3** (*fig.*) odour **4** *al pl.* (*cuc.*) herbs
odoróso *agg.* sweet-smelling, fragrant
offèndere **A** *v. tr.* **1** to offend **2** (*danneggiare*) to damage, to injure **3** (*violare*) to break, to infringe **B** *v. intr. pron.* to be offended, to take offence **C** *v. rifl. rec.* to offend each other, to insult each other
offensiva *s. f.* offensive
offensìvo *agg.* offensive
offerènte *s. m. e f.* offerer, (*a un'asta*) bidder
offèrta *s. f.* **1** offer **2** (*donazione*) offering, donation **3** (*comm.*) offer, (*econ.*) supply, (*a un'asta*) bidding
offésa *s. f.* **1** offence, insult **2** (*torto*) wrong
offéso *agg.* **1** offended, hurt **2** (*ferito*) injured
officiàre *v. tr.* to serve
officina *s. f.* workshop, shop ♦ **o. meccanica** machine-shop
offrìre **A** *v. tr.* **1** to offer **2** (*a un'asta*) to bid **3** (*esporre*) to expose **B** *v. rifl.* to offer oneself **C** *v. intr. pron.* (*presentarsi*) to offer oneself, to occur, to arise ♦ **offrirsi volontario** to volunteer
offuscàre **A** *v. tr.* to darken, to dim **B** *v. intr. pron.* to darken, to get dark, to grow dark, to become obscured
oftàlmico *agg.* ophthalmic
oftalmologìa *s. f.* ophthalmology
oggettivàre *v. tr.* to objectify
oggettività *s. f.* objectivity
oggettìvo *agg.* objective
oggètto *s. m.* **1** object, thing **2** (*argomento*) subject, subject matter **3** (*motivo*) object, subject **4** (*scopo*) object, purpose **5** (*gramm.*) object ♦ **oggetti preziosi** valuables; **oggetti personali** personal belongings
òggi *avv. e s. m.* today ♦ **a tutt'o.** till today; **o. stesso** this very day
oggigiórno *avv.* nowadays
ogìva *s. f.* ogive
ógni *agg. indef.* **1** (*ciascuno*) every, each, (*tutti*) all **2** (*qualsiasi*) any, all **3** (*distributivo*) every ♦ **o. due giorni** every two days, every second day; **o. giorno** every day; **o. tanto** every now and then
ognùno *pron. indef.* **1** everybody, everyone **2** (*con partitivo*) each (one), every (single) one, all
olandése **A** *agg.* Dutch **B** *s. m. e f.* Dutchman *m.*, Dutchwoman *f.* **C** *s. m.* (*lingua*) Dutch
oleodótto *s. m.* oil pipeline
oleóso *agg.* oily, oil (*attr*)
olfàtto *s. m.* (sense of) smell
oliàre *v. tr.* to oil
oliatóre *s. m.* oiler
oligarchìa *s. f.* oligarchy
olimpìadi *s. f. pl.* Olympic games *pl.*, Olympics *pl.*
olìmpico *agg.* **1** (*dell'Olimpo*) Olympian **2** (*delle Olimpiadi*) Olympic
olimpiònico *agg.* Olympic
òlio *s. m.* oil ♦ **o. d'oliva/di semi** olive/seed oil; **quadro a o.** oil painting; **sott'o.** in oil
olìva *s. f.* olive
olivàstro *agg.* olive
olìvo *s. m.* olive tree
ólmo *s. m.* elm
olocàusto *s. m.* holocaust
oltraggiàre *v. tr.* to outrage, to insult
oltràggio *s. m.* outrage
oltraggióso *agg.* outrageous
oltrànza, a *loc. avv.* to the death, to the bitter end
óltre **A** *avv.* **1** (*di luogo*) farther (on), further (on) **2** (*di tempo*) longer, more, over **3** (*di quantità*) over, more **B** *prep.* **1** (*di*

luogo) beyond, on the other side of, over **2** (*più di*) more than, over **3 o. a** (*in aggiunta*) besides, in addition to, as well as ♦ **o. tutto** and besides
oltremàre *avv.* overseas
oltrepassàre *v. tr.* **1** to go beyond **2** (*eccedere*) to exceed
omàggio *s. m.* **1** (*ossequio*) homage **2** *al pl.* (*saluto*) regards *pl.*, compliments *pl.* **3** (*offerta*) (free) gift, (*comm.*) free sample, giveaway ♦ **biglietto in o.** complimentary ticket
ombelicàle *agg.* umbilical
ombelìco *s. m.* navel
ómbra *s. f.* **1** shade, shadow **2** (*parvenza*) shadow, hint **3** (*spettro*) shade
ombreggiàre *v. tr.* to shade
ombreggiatùra *s. f.* shading
ombrellàio *s. m.* umbrella-maker, (*venditore*) umbrella-seller
ombrèllo *s. m.* umbrella ♦ **o. da sole** sunshade, parasol
ombrellóne *s. m.* beach-umbrella
ombrétto *s. m.* eye shadow
ombrìna *s. f.* (*zool.*) umbrine
ombróso *agg.* **1** shady, shadowy **2** (*di cavallo*) skittish **3** (*di persona*) touchy
omelette *s. f. inv.* omelette
omelìa *s. f.* homily
omeopatìa *s. f.* hom(o)eopathy
omeopàtico *agg.* hom(o)eopathic
òmero *s. m.* humerus
ométtere *v. tr.* to omit, to leave out
omicìda *s. m. e f.* homicide, murderer
omicìdio *s. m.* homicide, murder
omissióne *s. f.* omission
omogeneità *s. f.* homogeneity
omogeneizzàto *s. m.* homogenized food
omogèneo *agg.* homogeneous
omologàre *v. tr.* **1** to homologate, to approve, to validate **2** (*riconoscere*) to recognize
omologìa *s. f.* homology
omònimo A *agg.* homonymous **B** *s. m.* **1** homonym **2** (*persona*) namesake
omosessuàle *agg. e s. m. e f.* homosexual
óncia *s. f.* ounce
ónda *s. f.* wave
ondàta *s. f.* wave ♦ **o. di caldo** heat-wave
ónde *cong.* **1** (*affinché*) in order that, so that **2** (*cosicché*) so that
ondeggiàre *v. intr.* **1** to rock, to roll **2** (*oscillare*) to wave, to sway
ondulàto *agg.* **1** wavy, undulating **2** (*di lamiera, cartone*) corrugated
ondulatòrio *agg.* undulatory
ondulazióne *s. f.* **1** undulation **2** (*di capelli*) wave
ònere *s. m.* burden, (*dovere*) duty, (*spesa*) charge
oneróso *agg.* onerous, burdensome
onestà *s. f.* honesty
onèsto *agg.* honest
ònice *s. f.* onyx
onìrico *agg.* oneiric
onnipotènte *agg.* **1** (*di Dio*) omnipotent, almighty **2** (*di persona*) all-powerful
onnipresènte *agg.* omnipresent, ubiquitous
onnìvoro *agg.* omnivorous
onomàstico *s. m.* name-day
onorànze *s. f. pl.* honour
onoràre A *v. tr.* **1** to honour **2** (*conferire onore*) to do honour to **B** *v. rifl.* to be honoured
onoràrio (1) *agg.* honorary
onoràrio (2) *s. m.* fee, emolument
onóre *s. m.* honour
onorificènza *s. f.* honour, (*decorazione*) decoration
onorìfico *agg.* honorary
ónta *s. f.* **1** (*disonore*) dishonour, disgrace **2** (*offesa*) offence ♦ **a o. di** in spite of
opàco *agg.* opaque
opàle *s. m.* opal
opalescènte *agg.* opalescent
òpera *s. f.* **1** work **2** (*melodramma*) opera **3** (*ente*) institution
operàio A *agg.* (*che lavora*) worker (*attr.*), (*di operai*) working, workers' **B** *s. m.* workman, worker, hand ♦ **o. specializzato** skilled worker
operàre A *v. tr.* **1** to do, to work, to perform **2** (*med.*) to operate on **B** *v. intr.* to operate, to work, to act **C** *v. intr. pron.* **1** (*accadere*) to occur **2** (*farsi operare*) to be operated on
operatìvo *agg.* **1** (*in vigore*) operative **2** (*pratico*) operating
operatóre *s. m.* operator
operatòrio *agg.* operating
operazióne *s. f.* **1** operation **2** (*econ.*) transaction, operation
operétta *s. f.* operetta
operóso *agg.* industrious, active
opinàbile *agg.* debatable
opinióne *s. f.* opinion
òppio *s. m.* opium

oppórre *v. tr., intr. pron. e rifl.* to oppose
opportunaménte *avv.* opportunely, suitably
opportunìsmo *s. m.* opportunism
opportunìsta *s. m. e f.* opportunist
opportunità *s. f.* **1** timeliness, advisability **2** (*occasione*) opportunity, occasion, chance
opportùno *agg.* opportune, timely, (*appropriato*) appropriate
oppositóre *s. m.* opponent
opposizióne *s. f.* opposition
oppósto **A** *agg.* **1** opposite **2** (*contrario*) opposite, opposing, contrary **B** *s. m.* opposite, contrary ♦ **all'o.** on the contrary
oppressióne *s. f.* oppression
oppressìvo *agg.* oppressive
oppressóre *s. m.* oppressor
opprimènte *agg.* oppressive
opprìmere *v. tr.* to oppress, to weigh down
oppugnàre *v. tr.* to impugn, to refute
oppùre *cong.* **1** or **2** (*altrimenti*) or else, otherwise
optàre *v. intr.* to opt (for), to decide (for)
opulènza *s. f.* wealth, opulence
opùscolo *s. m.* booklet
opzionàle *agg.* optional
opzióne *s. f.* option, choice
óra (1) *s. f.* **1** hour **2** (*nel computo del tempo*) time **3** (*tempo*) time, (*momento*) moment ♦ **che o. è?** what time is it?; **o. di chiusura** closing time; **ore dei pasti** meal time; **ore di punta** peak hours; **o. legale** summer time; **un'o. e mezza** an hour and a half
óra (2) **A** *avv.* **1** (*adesso*) now, at present **2** (*poco fa*) just **3** (*tra poco*) in a minute, shortly **B** *cong.* **1** (*allora*) now **2** (*invece*) but ♦ **d'o. in poi** from now on; **o. che** now that; **or o.** just now; **prima d'o.** before
oràcolo *s. m.* oracle
òrafo *s. m.* goldsmith
oràle *agg.* oral
oràrio **A** *agg.* hourly, hour (*attr.*) **B** *s. m.* **1** time, hours *pl.*, schedule **2** (*tabella*) timetable
oràta *s. f.* (*zool.*) gilthead
oratóre *s. m.* orator, speaker
oratòrio *s. m.* oratory
orazióne *s. f.* **1** (*preghiera*) prayer **2** (*discorso*) oration
òrbita *s. f.* **1** orbit **2** (*anat.*) eye-socket, orbit
orchèstra *s. f.* orchestra, (*piccola*) band ♦ **direttore d'o.** conductor
orchestràre *v. tr.* to orchestrate
orchidèa *s. f.* orchid
òrco *s. m.* ogre
òrda *s. f.* horde
ordìgno *s. m.* device, contrivance
ordinàle *agg.* ordinal
ordinaménto *s. m.* **1** order, arrangement **2** (*regolamento*) regulations *pl.*, rules *pl.*
ordinànza *s. f.* ordinance, order, injunction
ordinàre **A** *v. tr.* **1** (*mettere in ordine*) to put in order, to arrange **2** (*comandare*) to order, to command, to direct **3** (*commissionare*) to order **4** (*prescrivere*) to prescribe **5** (*relig.*) to ordain **B** *v. rifl.* to arrange oneself, to draw oneself up
ordinàrio *agg.* **1** ordinary, usual **2** (*grossolano*) common
ordinazióne *s. f.* **1** order **2** (*relig.*) ordination
órdine *s. m.* order ♦ **di prim'o.** first-class, first-rate; **o. del giorno** agenda; **o. professionale** professional association; **parola d'o.** password
ordìre *v. tr.* to plot, to plan
ordìto *s. m.* warp
orecchiàbile *agg.* catchy
orecchìno *s. m.* ear-ring
orécchio *s. m.* ear
orecchióni *s. m. pl.* (*fam.*) mumps *pl.*
oréfice *s. m.* goldsmith, (*gioielliere*) jeweller
oreficerìa *s. f.* **1** (*arte*) jeweller's art, goldsmith's art **2** (*negozio*) jeweller's (shop), goldsmith's (shop)
òrfano *agg. e s. m.* orphan
orfanotròfio *s. m.* orphanage
organétto *s. m.* barrel organ
organicità *s. f.* organicity
orgànico **A** *agg.* **1** organic **2** (*sistematico*) organized, systematic **B** *s. m.* staff
organigràmma *s. m.* organization chart
organìsmo *s. m.* **1** organism **2** (*organizzazione*) organization, body
organizzàre **A** *v. tr.* to organize **B** *v. rifl.* to organize oneself
organizzatóre **A** *agg.* organizing **B** *s. m.* organizer
organizzazióne *s. f.* organization
òrgano *s. m.* **1** organ **2** (*apparato, ente*) body, branch, organ **3** (*mecc.*) part, unit
orgàsmo *s. m.* **1** orgasm **2** (*agitazione*) excitement

òrgia *s. f.* orgy
orgóglio *s. m.* pride
orgogliόso *agg.* proud
orientàbile *agg.* adjustable
orientàle *agg.* oriental, eastern, east (*attr*), (*da oriente*) easterly
orientaménto *s. m.* **1** orientation **2** (*tendenza*) trend ♦ **senso dell'o.** sense of direction
orientàre **A** *v. tr.* **1** to orient, to orientate **2** (*indirizzare*) to steer **B** *v. rifl.* **1** to orientate oneself, to take one's bearings **2** (*tendere*) to tend **3** (*intraprendere*) to take up
orientatìvo *agg.* indicative
orïènte *s. m.* east
orìgano *s. m.* oregano, origanum, wild marjoram
originàle **A** *agg.* **1** original **2** (*nuovo*) new, original **3** (*non contraffatto*) genuine, real **4** (*strano*) strange, queer **B** *s. m.* **1** original **2** (*persona*) eccentric
originalità *s. f.* **1** originality **2** (*novità*) novelty **3** (*stranezza*) strangeness
originàre **A** *v. tr.* to originate, to cause **B** *v. intr. e intr. pron.* to originate, to arise, to spring
originàrio *agg.* **1** original, primary **2** (*nativo*) native
orìgine *s. f.* origin
origliàre *v. tr.* to eavesdrop
orìna *s. f.* urine
orinàre *v. tr. e intr.* to urinate
orizzontàle *agg.* horizontal
orizzontalménte *avv.* horizontally
orizzontàrsi *v. rifl.* **1** to orientate oneself, to get one's bearings **2** (*raccapezzarsi*) to find one's way
orizzónte *s. m.* horizon
orlàre *v. tr.* **1** to hem **2** (*bordare*) to border, to edge
órlo *s. m.* **1** (*di vestito, tenda, ecc.*) hem **2** (*margine*) border, edge, brink, rim, lip
órma *s. f.* **1** footprint, track **2** (*fig.*) trace, mark
ormài *avv.* **1** by now, by this time, (*riferito al pass.*) by then, by that time **2** (*quasi*) almost, nearly
ormeggiàre *v. tr. e intr. pron.* to moor
orméggio *s. m.* mooring
ormóne *s. m.* hormone
ornamentàle *agg.* ornamental
ornaménto *s. m.* ornament
ornàre **A** *v. tr.* to adorn, to decorate **B** *v. rifl.* to adorn oneself
ornitologìa *s. f.* ornithology
òro *s. m.* gold ♦ **o. zecchino** fine gold; **placcato in o.** gold plated
orografìa *s. f.* orography
orologiàio *s. m.* watchmaker, (*riparatore*) watch-repairer
orològio *s. m.* clock, (*da polso, da tasca*) watch
oròscopo *s. m.* horoscope
orrèndo *agg.* horrible, dreadful
orrìbile *agg.* horrible, dreadful
òrrido *agg.* horrid, horrible
orripilànte *agg.* horrifying
orróre *s. m.* horror ♦ **film dell'o.** horror film
orsacchiòtto *s. m.* (*giocattolo*) teddy bear
órso *s. m.* bear ♦ **o. bruno** brown bear; **o. grigio** grizzly; **o. polare** sea bear
ortàggio *s. m.* vegetable
ortìca *s. f.* nettle
orticària *s. f.* nettle rash
orticoltùra *s. f.* horticulture
òrto *s. m.* vegetable garden, kitchen garden ♦ **o. botanico** botanical garden
ortodossìa *s. f.* orthodoxy
ortodòsso *agg. e s. m.* orthodox
ortogonàle *agg.* orthogonal
ortografìa *s. f.* orthography ♦ **errore di o.** spelling mistake
ortopedìa *s. f.* orthop(a)edics *pl.* (*v. al sing.*)
ortopèdico **A** *agg.* orthop(a)edic(al) **B** *s. m.* orthop(a)edist
orzaiòlo *s. m.* sty(e)
òrzo *s. m.* barley
osannàre *v. tr.* to acclaim
osàre **A** *v. intr.* to dare **B** *v. tr.* to risk, to attempt
oscenità *s. f.* obscenity
oscèno *agg.* obscene
oscillàre *v. intr.* **1** to swing, to sway, to rock, to oscillate **2** (*variare*) to fluctuate **3** (*essere dubbioso*) to waver **4** (*elettr.*) to oscillate
oscillazióne *s. f.* **1** swinging, oscillation **2** (*variazione*) fluctuation **3** (*fis.*) oscillation
oscuraménto *s. m.* **1** darkening, obscuring **2** (*mil.*) blackout
oscurantìsmo *s. m.* obscurantism
oscuràre **A** *v. tr.* to darken, to obscure, to black out **B** *v. intr. e intr. pron.* to darken, to become obscure
oscurità *s. f.* darkness, obscurity
oscùro **A** *agg.* **1** dark, obscure **2** (*poco noto*) obscure, unknown **B** *s. m.* dark ♦

essere all'o. di q.c. to be in the dark about st.
ospedàle *s. m.* hospital
ospedalièro *agg.* hospital (*attr.*)
ospitàle *agg.* hospitable
ospitalità *s. f.* hospitality
ospitàre *v. tr.* **1** to give hospitality to, to put up, to take in **2** (*di albergo*) to accommodate **3** (*contenere*) to house
òspite *s. m. e f.* **1** (*chi ospita*) host *m.*, hostess *f.* **2** (*persona ospitata*) guest ♦ **camera degli ospiti** guest-room; **o. d'onore** special guest; **o. pagante** paying guest
ospìzio *s. m.* hospice, home
ossatùra *s. f.* **1** skeleton, bones *pl.* **2** (*struttura*) framework, structure
òsseo *agg.* bony, osseous
ossèquio *s. m.* **1** (*omaggio*) homage **2** *al pl.* (*saluti*) regards *pl.*, respects *pl.* **3** (*obbedienza*) obedience
ossequióso *agg.* deferential, respectful
osservàbile *agg.* noticeable, visible
osservànza *s. f.* observance
osservàre *v. tr.* **1** to observe, to watch, to examine **2** (*rispettare*) to keep, to observe, to respect **3** (*notare*) to notice, to point out **4** (*obiettare*) to object
osservatóre *s. m.* observer
osservatòrio *s. m.* observatory
osservazióne *s. f.* **1** observation **2** (*rimprovero*) reproach
ossessionàre *v. tr.* to haunt, to obsess
ossessióne *s. f.* obsession
ossessìvo *agg.* haunting, obsessive
ossìa *cong.* **1** (*cioè*) that is, id est, (*abbr.* i.e.), or **2** (*o meglio*) or rather
ossidàre *v. tr. e intr. pron.* to oxidize
òssido *s. m.* oxide
ossigenàre *v. tr.* **1** to oxygenate **2** (*i capelli*) to peroxide, to bleach
ossìgeno *s. m.* oxygen
òsso *s. m.* **1** bone **2** (*nocciolo*) stone, pit
ossùto *agg.* bony
ostacolàre *v. tr.* to hinder, to hamper
ostàcolo *s. m.* **1** obstacle, hindrance, handicap **2** (*ippica*) jump, (*atletica*) hurdle
ostàggio *s. m.* hostage
òste *s. m.* host, innkeeper
osteggiàre *v. tr.* to oppose, to be hostile to
ostèllo *s. m.* (youth) hostel
ostensòrio *s. m.* ostensory
ostentàre *v. tr.* **1** to show off, to parade **2** (*fingere*) to feign
ostentazióne *s. f.* ostentation, showing off
osterìa *s. f.* tavern, pub
ostetrìcia *s. f.* obstetrics *pl.* (*v. al sing.*)
ostètrico **A** *agg.* obstetric(al) **B** *s. m.* obstetrician
òstia *s. f.* **1** (*relig.*) host **2** (*cialda*) wafer
òstico *agg.* hard, difficult
ostìle *agg.* hostile
ostilità *s. f.* hostility
ostinàrsi *v. intr. pron.* to persist, to insist
ostinàto *agg.* obstinate, stubborn
ostinazióne *s. f.* obstinacy, stubbornness
ostracìsmo *s. m.* ostracism
òstrica *s. f.* oyster
ostruìre **A** *v. tr.* to obstruct, to block (up) **B** *v. intr. pron.* to become obstructed
ostruzióne *s. f.* obstruction
ostruzionìsmo *s. m.* obstructionism, (*USA*) filibustering
otìte *s. f.* otitis
otorinolaringoiàtra *s. m. e f.* otorhinolaryngologist
ótre *s. m.* wineskin
ottagonàle *agg.* octagonal
ottànta *agg. num. card. e s. m. inv.* eighty
ottantèsimo *agg. num. ord. e s. m.* eightieth
ottàva *s. f.* octave
ottàvo *agg. num. ord. e s. m.* eighth
ottemperàre *v. intr.* to comply, to observe
ottenebràre *v. tr. e intr. pron.* to darken, to cloud
ottenére *v. tr.* **1** to obtain, to get **2** (*ricavare*) to obtain, to extract
òttica *s. f.* **1** optics *pl.* (*v. al sing.*) **2** (*fig.*) point of view
òttico **A** *agg.* optic(al) **B** *s. m.* optician
ottimàle *agg.* optimal, optimum (*attr.*)
ottimaménte *avv.* very well
ottimìsmo *s. m.* optimism
ottimìsta **A** *agg.* optimistic **B** *s. m. e f.* optimist
ottimizzàre *v. tr.* to optimize
òttimo **A** *agg. sup. rel.* **1** very good, excellent, first-rate **2** (*ottimale*) optimal, optimum (*attr.*) **B** *s. m.* **1** the best **2** (*l'optimum*) optimum
òtto *agg. num. card. e s. m. inv.* eight
ottóbre *s. m.* October
ottocentésco *agg.* nineteenth-century (*attr.*)
ottocènto *agg. num. card. e s. m. inv.* eight hundred ♦ **l'O.** the nineteenth century
ottomàno *agg. e s. m.* Ottoman
ottóne *s. m.* brass

otturàre **A** *v. tr.* **1** to block (up), to stop (up) **2** (*un dente*) to fill **B** *v. intr. pron.* to get blocked up, to clog

otturatóre *s. m.* **1** (*arma*) breech-block **2** (*fot.*) shutter

otturazióne *s. f.* **1** blocking (up), stopping **2** (*di dente*) filling

ottùso *agg.* **1** obtuse **2** (*fig.*) dull, obtuse

ovàia *s. f.* ovary

ovàle *agg. e s. m.* oval

ovàtta *s. f.* cotton wool, (*per imbottitura*) padding

ovattàre *v. tr.* **1** to pad **2** (*fig.*) to attenuate, to muffle

ovazióne *s. f.* ovation

òvest *s. m.* west

ovìle *s. m.* sheepfold, pen

ovìno **A** *agg.* ovine, sheep (*attr.*) **B** *s. m.* sheep

ovìparo *agg.* oviparous

ovoidàle *agg.* ovoid(al)

òvulo *s. m.* (*biol.*) ovum, ovule

ovùnque *avv.* → **dovunque**

ovvéro *cong.* **1** (*ossia*) or, that is **2** (*o meglio*) or rather

ovviaménte *avv.* obviously

ovviàre *v. intr.* to get out of

òvvio *agg.* clear, obvious, evident

oziàre *v. intr.* to idle about, to laze about

òzio *s. m.* **1** idleness, laziness **2** (*riposo*) leisure

ozióso *agg.* idle

ozòno *s. m.* ozone

P

pacàto *agg.* calm, quiet
pacchétto *s. m.* packet
pacchiàno *agg.* garish, showy
pàcco *s. m.* parcel, pack, package
pàce *s. f.* peace
pachidèrma *s. m.* pachyderm
pacificàre **A** *v. tr.* **1** to pacify, to appease **2** (*riconciliare*) to reconcile **B** *v. intr. pron.* **1** to make it up **2** (*calmarsi*) to calm down **C** *v. rifl. rec.* to reconcile oneself
pacificazióne *s. f.* **1** pacification **2** (*riconciliazione*) reconciliation
pacìfico *agg.* peaceful, pacific
pacifìsmo *s. m.* pacifism
pacifìsta *s. m. e f.* pacifist
padèlla *s. f.* frying pan
padiglióne *s. m.* **1** pavilion **2** (*anat.*) auricle
pàdre *s. m.* father
padrìno *s. m.* godfather
padronàle *agg.* master's, (*principale*) main
padronànza *s. f.* mastery, command, control ♦ **p. di sé** self-control
padróne *s. m.* **1** master **2** (*proprietario*) owner **3** (*di casa*) landlord
padroneggiàre **A** *v. tr.* to master, to command, to control **B** *v. rifl.* to control oneself
paesàggio *s. m.* landscape, scenery, view
paesaggìsta *s. m. e f.* landscape painter
paesàno *agg.* **1** country (*attr*), rural **2** (*di paese*) village (*attr*)
paése *s. m.* **1** (*nazione*) country **2** (*territorio*) land, country **3** (*villaggio*) village
paffùto *agg.* chubby
pàga *s. f.* pay, wages *pl.*
pagàbile *agg.* payable
pagàia *s. f.* paddle
pagaménto *s. m.* payment ♦ **condizioni di p.** terms of payment; **p. alla consegna** cash on delivery; **p. a saldo** settlement
paganésimo *s. m.* paganism, heathenism
pagàno *agg. e s. m.* pagan, heathen
pagàre *v. tr. e intr.* to pay ♦ **p. da bere a qc.** to stand sb. a drink
pagèlla *s. f.* (school) report
pagèllo *s. m.* sea-bream
pàggio *s. m.* pageboy
pagherò *s. m. inv.* (*comm.*) I owe you (*abbr.* IOU)
pàgina *s. f.* page ♦ **p. bianca** blank page; **prima p.** front page
pàglia *s. f.* straw
pagliaccétto *s. m.* rompers *pl.*
pagliàccio *s. m.* clown, buffoon
pagliàio *s. m.* straw-stack
pagliétta *s. f.* **1** (*cappello*) straw hat **2** (*per pulire*) steel wool
pagnòtta *s. f.* loaf
pagòda *s. f.* pagoda
pàio *s. m.* **1** pair **2** (*circa due*) couple
paiòlo *s. m.* pot
pàla *s. f.* **1** shovel **2** (*di remo, elica, ventilatore*) blade, (*di mulino*) vane **3** (*d'altare*) altar-piece
paladìno *s. m.* paladin, champion
palafìtta *s. f.* **1** palafitte **2** (*edil.*) pilework
palàmito *s. m.* boulter
palàto *s. m.* palate
palàzzo *s. m.* **1** palace **2** (*casa signorile*) mansion **3** (*edificio*) building ♦ **p. dello sport** stadium
pàlco *s. m.* **1** (*teatro*) box **2** (*tribuna*) stand, platform **3** (*palcoscenico*) stage
palcoscènico *s. m.* stage
paleoantropologìa *s. f.* paleoanthropology
paleocristiàno *agg.* early Christian
paleografìa *s. f.* pal(a)eography
paleolìtico *agg.* Pal(a)eolithic
palesàre **A** *v. tr.* to reveal, to disclose **B** *v. rifl. o intr. pron.* to show oneself
palése *agg.* evident, manifest, clear
palestinése *agg. e s. m. e f.* Palestinian
palèstra *s. f.* gymnasium
palétta *s. f.* **1** (small) shovel, (*per la spazzatura*) dustpan **2** (*del capostazione*) bat
palétto *s. m.* **1** stake, pole, post **2** (*chiavistello*) bolt
palizzàta *s. f.* fence
pàlla *s. f.* ball
pallacanèstro *s. f.* basketball
pallamàno *s. f.* handball
pallanuòto *s. f.* water polo
pallavólo *s. f.* volleyball
palliatìvo *agg. e s. m.* palliative
pàllido *agg.* **1** pale **2** (*fig.*) faint, dim, slight
pallìno *s. m.* **1** (*bocce*) jack **2** (*biliardo*) cue ball **3** (*da caccia*) shot **4** (*fig.*) mania

♦ **disegno a pallini** polka-dot pattern
pallóne *s. m.* **1** ball **2** (*calcio*) football **3** (*aerostato*) balloon
pallóre *s. m.* pallor
pallòttola *s. f.* **1** pellet **2** (*proiettile*) bullet
pallottolière *s. m.* abacus
pàlma *s. f.* palm ♦ **p. da cocco** coconut-palm; **p. da datteri** date-palm
palmìpede *agg.* web-footed
palmìzio *s. m.* palm(-tree)
pàlmo *s. m.* **1** (*della mano*) palm **2** (*spanna*) span ♦ **a p. a p.** inch by inch
pàlo *s. m.* **1** pole, post, stake **2** (*fam.*) (*complice*) lookout
palombàro *s. m.* diver
palómbo *s. m.* smooth hound
palpàre *v. tr.* to feel, to finger, (*med.*) to palpate
pàlpebra *s. f.* eyelid
palpitàre *v. intr.* to palpitate, to throb
palpitazióne *s. f.* palpitation, throbbing
pàlpito *s. m.* throb
paltò *s. m.* overcoat
palùde *s. f.* marsh, bog, swamp, fen
paludóso *agg.* marshy, boggy, swampy
palùstre *agg.* marsh (*attr.*), fen (*attr.*)
pànca *s. f.* bench, form, (*di chiesa*) pew
pancétta *s. f.* **1** (*pancia*) paunch, belly **2** (*cuc.*) bacon
panchìna *s. f.* bench
pància *s. f.* belly, stomach, tummy (*fam.*) ♦ **mal di p.** belly-ache
panciòtto *s. m.* waistcoat, (*USA*) vest
pàncreas *s. m.* pancreas
pànda *s. m. inv.* panda
pandemònio *s. m.* pandemonium, uproar
pàne *s. m.* **1** bread **2** (*fig.*) (*il necessario*) bread, living, food **3** (*forma*) block, cake, loaf ♦ **p. fresco** fresh bread; **p. integrale** wholemeal bread; **p. tostato** toast
panegìrico *s. m.* panegyric
panellenìsmo *s. m.* Panhellenism
panetterìa *s. f.* bakery, (*negozio*) baker's (shop)
panettière *s. m.* baker
pànfilo *s. m.* yacht
pangrattàto *s. m.* breadcrumbs *pl.*
pànico *s. m.* panic
panière *s. m.* basket
panifìcio *s. m.* bakery, baker's (shop)
panìno *s. m.* roll, (*imbottito*) sandwich
pànna *s. f.* cream ♦ **caffè con p.** coffee with cream; **p. montata** whipped cream
panne *s. f. inv.* breakdown
pannéggio *s. m.* drapery
pannèllo *s. m.* panel
pànno *s. m.* cloth ♦ **mettersi nei panni di qc.** to put oneself in sb.'s shoes
pannòcchia *s. f.* cob
pannolìno *s. m.* napkin, (*USA*) diaper
panoràma *s. m.* **1** view, panorama **2** (*fig.*) survey, outline
panoràmica *s. f.* **1** (*panorama*) view, panorama **2** (*fig.*) survey **3** (*cin.*) panning
panoràmico *agg.* panoramic ♦ **schermo p.** wide screen; **strada panoramica** panoramic drive
pansé *s. f.* pansy
pantagruèlico *agg.* Pantagruelian
pantalóni *s. m. pl.* trousers *pl.*, pants *pl.* ♦ **p. corti** shorts; **un paio di p.** a pair of trousers
pantàno *s. m.* morass, quagmire
panteìsmo *s. m.* pantheism
pantèra *s. f.* panther
pantòfola *s. f.* slipper
pantomìma *s. f.* pantomime
panzàna *s. f.* fib, lie
paonàzzo *agg.* purple, violet
pàpa *s. m.* pope
papà *s. m.* daddy, dad, pa
papàia *s. f.* papaya
papàle *agg.* papal
papàto *s. m.* papacy
papàvero *s. m.* poppy
pàpera *s. f.* **1** duckling, gosling **2** (*errore*) slip
pàpero *s. m.* gosling
papìro *s. m.* papyrus
papìsmo *s. m.* papism
pàppa *s. f.* pap, baby food
pappagàllo *s. m.* parrot
pappagòrgia *s. f.* double chin
pàra *s. f.* para rubber
paràbola (1) *s. f.* (*racconto*) parable
paràbola (2) *s. f.* **1** (*geom.*) parabola **2** (*fig.*) course
parabrézza *s. m. inv.* windscreen, (*USA*) windshield
paracadùte *s. m. inv.* parachute
paracadutìsmo *s. m.* parachuting ♦ **p. acrobatico** skydiving
paracàrro *s. m.* kerbstone
paradìso *s. m.* paradise, heaven
paradossàle *agg.* **1** paradoxical **2** (*bizzarro*) strange
paradòsso *s. m.* paradox
parafàngo *s. m.* mudguard, (*USA*) fender

paraffìna *s. f.* paraffin
paràfrasi *s. f.* paraphrase
parafùlmine *s. m.* lightning-rod
paràggi *s. m. pl.* neighbourhood
paragonàbile *agg.* comparable
paragonàre **A** *v. tr.* to compare **B** *v. rifl.* to compare oneself
paragóne *s. m.* **1** comparison **2** (*esempio*) analogy
paràgrafo *s. m.* paragraph
paràlisi *s. f.* paralysis
paralìtico *agg. e s. m.* paralytic
paralizzàre *v. tr.* to paralyse
parallelepìpedo *s. m.* parallelepiped
parallelìsmo *s. m.* parallelism
parallèlo *agg. e s. m.* parallel
paralùme *s. m.* lampshade
paràmetro *s. m.* parameter
paranòia *s. f.* paranoia
paranòico *agg. e s. m.* paranoiac
paranormàle *agg.* paranormal
paraòcchi *s. m.* blinkers *pl.*
parapètto *s. m.* parapect, (*naut.*) bulwark
parapìglia *s. m.* turmoil, confusion
parapsicologìa *s. f.* parapsychology
paràre *v. tr.* **1** (*addobbare*) to adorn, to decorate **2** (*riparare*) to shield **3** (*evitare*) to parry, (*calcio*) to save ♦ **andare a p.** to drive at
parasóle **A** *agg. inv.* sun (*attr*) **B** *s. m. inv.* parasol, sunshade
parassìta **A** *agg.* parasitic(al) **B** *s. m.* parasite
paràta (1) *s. f.* parade
paràta (2) *s. f.* (*sport*) parry
paratìa *s. f.* bulkhead
paraùrti *s. m.* bumper
paravènto *s. m.* screen
parcèlla *s. f.* fee, bill
parcheggiàre *v. tr.* to park
parchéggio *s. m.* **1** parking **2** (*posteggio*) (car) park ♦ **divieto di p.** no parking
parchìmetro *s. m.* parking-meter
pàrco (1) *s. m.* park
pàrco (2) *agg.* frugal, moderate
parécchio **A** *agg. indef.* **1** (quite a) lot of, rather a lot of, plenty of **2** (*tempo*) (quite) a long, rather a long **3** *al pl.* several, quite a lot of, rather a lot of **B** *pron. indef.* **1** quite a lot, rather a lot **2** *al pl.* several, quite a few, quite a lot **C** *avv.* quite, very, quite a lot
pareggiàre **A** *v. tr.* **1** to equalize, to make equal **2** (*comm.*) to balance, to square, to settle **3** (*uguagliare*) to match **4** (*livellare*) to level **5** (*tagliando*) to trim **B** *v. intr.* (*finire pari*) to draw, to tie
paréggio *s. m.* **1** (*comm.*) balance, squaring **2** (*sport*) draw, tie
parentàdo *s. m.* relatives *pl.*
parènte *s. m. e f.* relative, relation
parentèla *s. f.* **1** relationship, kinship **2** (*insieme dei parenti*) relatives *pl.*
parèntesi *s. f.* **1** (*segno*) parenthesis, bracket **2** (*inciso*) digression **3** (*intervallo*) interval, period
parére (1) *v. intr.* **1** to seem, to appear, to look (like) **2** (*impers.*) to seem, (*credere*) to think ♦ **mi pare di sì** I think so; **pare impossibile che ...** it seems impossible that ...
parére (2) *s. m.* opinion, advice ♦ **a mio p.** in my opinion
paréte *s. f.* **1** wall **2** (*superficie*) side, surface **3** (*di montagna*) face
pàri **A** *agg.* **1** equal, same, (*simile*) like, similar **2** (*di punteggio, conto*) equal, even **3** (*di numero*) even **4** (*allo stesso livello*) level, equal **5** (*equivalente*) equivalent, equal **B** *s. m.* **1** (*pareggio*) draw, tie **2** (*numero pari*) even number **3** (*persona*) equal, peer ♦ **alla p.** at the same level, (*presso famiglia*) au pair, (*fin.*) at par; **fare p. e dispari** to play odds and evens
parigìno *agg. e s. m.* Parisian
parìglia *s. f.* pair ♦ **rendere la p.** to give tit for tat
parità *s. f.* **1** parity, equality **2** (*pareggio*) draw, tie
parlamentàre *agg.* parliamentary
parlaménto *s. m.* Parliament
parlantìna *s. f.* talkativeness
parlàre **A** *v. intr.* to speak, to talk **B** *v. tr.* to speak **C** *v. rifl. rec.* to speak to each other
parlàta *s. f.* way of speaking, (*dialetto*) dialect
parlatòrio *s. m.* parlour
parodía *s. f.* parody
paròla *s. f.* **1** word **2** (*facoltà di parlare*) speech **3** (*promessa*) word, promise **4** (*discorso*) words *pl.*, speech **5** *al pl.* (*di canzone*) lyrics *pl.* ♦ **p. d'ordine** password; **parole incrociate** crossword puzzle; **rivolgere la p. a qc.** to address sb.
parolàccia *s. f.* swearword, four-letter word
parossìstico *agg.* paroxysmal
parricìda *s. m.* parricide

parròcchia *s. f.* parish
parrocchiàle *agg.* parish (*attr.*), parochial
pàrroco *s. m.* (*cattolico*) parish priest, (*protestante*) parson, vicar
parrùcca *s. f.* wig
parrucchière *s. m.* hairdresser
parsimònia *s. f.* thriftiness, parsimony
parsimonióso *agg.* thrifty
pàrte *s. f.* **1** (*porzione*) part, share, portion **2** (*luogo, regione*) parts *pl.*, region **3** (*lato*) side, part **4** (*direzione*) way, direction **5** (*ruolo*) part, rôle **6** (*partito, fazione*) party, faction ♦ **a p. ciò** apart from that; **d'altra p.** on the other side; **farsi da p.** to step aside; **p. civile** plaintiff
partecipàre A *v. intr.* **1** to participate (in), to share, to take part (in) **2** (*essere presente*) to be present (at), to attend **B** *v. tr.* (*annunciare*) to announce, to inform
partecipazióne *s. f.* **1** participation **2** (*presenza*) presence, attendance **3** (*fin.*) holding, interest **4** (*annuncio*) announcement, (*scritto*) card ♦ **p. di nozze** wedding card
partécipe *agg.* participating ♦ **essere p. di q.c.** to take part in st., to share st.; **rendere p. qc. di q.c.** to acquaint sb. with st.
parteggiàre *v. intr.* to side (with), to support
partènza *s. f.* **1** departure **2** (*sport*) start ♦ **essere in p.** to be about to leave
particèlla *s. f.* particle
particìpio *s. m.* participle
particolàre A *agg.* **1** particular, special, peculiar **2** (*privato*) particular, private **3** (*strano*) peculiar, strange **4** (*accurato*) detailed **B** *s. m.* particular, detail
particolarità *s. f.* particularity, peculiarity
partigiàno *agg. e s. m.* partisan
partìre *v. intr.* **1** to leave, to go away **2** (*decollare*) to take off, (*salpare*) to sail **3** (*mettersi in moto*) to start **4** (*iniziare*) to start **5** (*provenire*) to come **6** (*fam.*) (*rompersi*) to go ♦ **a p. da** beginning from, as from; **p. per l'estero** to go abroad
partìta *s. f.* **1** (*comm.*) lot, parcel, stock **2** (*giocata*) game, (*sport*) match **3** (*scrittura contabile*) entry
partìto *s. m.* **1** party **2** (*risoluzione*) decision, resolution **3** (*occasione di matrimonio*) match
partitùra *s. f.* score
partizióne *s. f.* partition, division
pàrto *s. m.* (child)birth, delivery ♦ **p. cesareo** caesarian birth; **sala p.** delivery room
partorìre *v. tr.* to bear, to give birth to
parvènza *s. f.* **1** appearance **2** (*traccia*) semblance
parziàle *agg.* partial
pascolàre *v. tr. e intr.* to graze, to pasture
pàscolo *s. m.* pasture, grazing
pàsqua *s. f.* Easter
pasquàle *agg.* Easter (*attr.*)
pasquétta *s. f.* Easter Monday
passàbile *agg.* fairly good
passàggio *s. m.* **1** passage, passing **2** (*transito*) transit **3** (*luogo dove si passa*) passage, way, (*attraversamento*) crossing **4** (*su veicolo*) lift **5** (*letter., mus.*) passage **6** (*fig.*) (*cambiamento*) shift, (*trasferimento*) handing, transfer ♦ **p. pedonale** pedestrian crossing; **vietato il p.** no transit
passànte A *s. m. e f.* passer-by **B** *s. m.* (*di cintura*) loop ♦ **p. ferroviario** railway link
passapòrto *s. m.* passport ♦ **mettere il visto su un p.** to visa a passport; **p. scaduto** expired passport
passàre A *v. intr.* **1** to pass, (*attraverso*) to pass through, to go through, (*vicino*) to pass by, to go by **2** (*trascorrere*) to pass, to go by, to elapse **3** (*cessare*) to pass away, to cease **4** (*fare visita*) to call on, to call at **5** (*diventare*) to become **6** (*essere considerato*) to be considered, (*essere scambiato*) to pass off as, to be taken for **7** (*essere approvato*) to be passed, to get through **8** (*intercorrere*) to be **9** (*a carte*) to pass **B** *v. tr.* **1** (*attraversare*) to pass, to cross, (*valicare*) to go beyond **2** (*trascorrere*) to pass, to spend **3** (*far passare*) to pass **4** (*dare*) to give, to hand, to pass **5** (*cospargere di*) to put, to spread **6** (*sopportare*) to go through, to pass through **7** (*trafiggere*) to pass through **8** (*promuovere*) to pass
passatèmpo *s. m.* pastime, (*il p. preferito*) hobby
passàto A *agg.* **1** past **2** (*scorso*) last **B** *s. m.* **1** past **2** (*gramm.*) past, perfect **3** (*cuc.*) soup
passaverdùra *s. m. inv.* vegetable mill
passeggèro A *agg.* passing, transitory **B** *s. m.* passenger
passeggiàre *v. intr.* to walk, to take a walk, to stroll

passeggiàta *s. f.* **1** walk, (*in bici, a cavallo*) ride **2** (*luogo*) walk, promenade
passeggìno *s. m.* pushchair, (*USA*) stroller
passéggio *s. m.* walk, stroll
passerèlla *s. f.* **1** (*per imbarco e sbarco*) gangway **2** (*teatro*) parade **3** (*per sfilate di moda*) catwalk
pàssero *s. m.* sparrow
passìbile *agg.* liable
passionàle *agg.* **1** of passion, passional **2** (*appassionato*) passionate
passióne *s. f.* passion
passìvo **A** *agg.* passive **B** *s. m.* **1** (*econ.*) deficit, liabilities *pl.* **2** (*gramm.*) passive
pàsso (1) *s. m.* **1** step, pace **2** (*andatura*) pace, walk **3** (*rumore*) footstep, (*orma*) footprint **4** (*brano*) passage **5** (*tecnol.*) pitch
pàsso (2) *s. m.* **1** (*passaggio*) passage, way **2** (*valico*) pass
pàsta *s. f.* **1** (*impasto*) dough, pastry **2** (*pasticcino*) pastry, cake **3** (*per minestra*) pasta **4** (*sostanza pastosa*) paste **5** (*fig.*) nature ♦ **p. frolla** short pastry; **p. sfoglia** puff pastry
pastasciùtta *s. f.* pasta
pastèlla *s. f.* batter
pastèllo *agg. e s. m.* pastel
pastìcca *s. f.* tablet, lozenge
pasticcerìa *s. f.* **1** confectionery **2** (*negozio*) pastry-shop, confectioner's shop
pasticciàre *v. tr. e intr.* to mess up, to make a mess
pasticcière *s. m.* confectioner
pasticcìno *s. m.* pastry, cake
pastìccio *s. m.* **1** mess **2** (*cuc.*) pie
pastìglia *s. f.* **1** pastille, lozenge, sweet, drop **2** (*di freni*) pad
pastinàca *s. f.* parsnip
pàsto *s. m.* meal
pastoràle *agg.* pastoral
pastóre *s. m.* **1** shepherd **2** (*relig.*) pastor, minister
pastorìzia *s. f.* sheep-farming
pastorizzàre *v. tr.* to pasteurize
pastóso *agg.* mellow, soft
pastràno *s. m.* overcoat
pastùra *s. f.* pasture
patàta *s. f.* potato ♦ **p. americana** sweet potato, batata; **patate fritte** fried potatoes, chips, (*USA*) French fries
paté *s. m. inv.* paté
patèma *s. m.* anxiety
patènte *s. f.* licence, permit ♦ **p. di guida** driving licence
paternalìsmo *s. m.* paternalism
paternità *s. f.* paternity, fatherhood
patèrno *agg.* paternal, (*da padre*) fatherly
patètico *agg.* pathetic
pàthos *s. m.* pathos
patìbolo *s. m.* gallows, scaffold
pàtina *s. f.* patina
patio *s. m.* patio
patìre **A** *v. intr.* to suffer **B** *v. tr.* **1** to suffer, to undergo **2** (*sopportare*) to bear, to stand
patìto **A** *agg.* sickly **B** *s. m.* fan
patologìa *s. f.* pathology
patològico *agg.* pathologic(al)
pàtria *s. f.* **1** (native) country, homeland **2** (*luogo di nascita*) birthplace, home
patriàrca *s. m.* patriarch
patriarcàto *s. m.* **1** patriarchy **2** (*relig.*) patriarchate
patrìgno *s. m.* stepfather
patrimoniàle *agg.* patrimonial ♦ **imposta p.** property tax
patrimònio *s. m.* **1** patrimony, property **2** (*somma considerevole*) fortune **3** (*fig.*) heritage
patriòta *s. m. e f.* patriot
patriòttico *agg.* patriotic
patriottìsmo *s. m.* patriotism
patrocinàre *v. tr.* **1** (*dir*) to plead, to defend **2** (*sponsorizzare*) to sponsor, to support
patrocìnio *s. m.* **1** (*dir*) pleading, defence **2** (*sponsorizzazione*) patronage, sponsorship
patronàto *s. m.* patronage
patronìmico *agg. e s. m.* patronymic
patròno *s. m.* **1** (*dir*) counsel **2** (*protettore*) patron, supporter **3** (*santo*) patron saint
pàtta *s. f.* flap, (*di pantaloni*) fly
patteggiàre *v. tr. e intr.* to negotiate
pattinàggio *s. m.* skating ♦ **p. artistico** figure-skating; **p. a rotelle** roller-skating; **p. su ghiaccio** ice-skating; **pista di p.** skating-rink
pattinàre *v. intr.* to skate
pattinatóre *s. m.* skater
pàttino *s. m.* skate
pàtto *s. m.* **1** agreement, pact **2** (*condizione*) term, condition ♦ **a p. che** on condition that; **venire a patti** to come to terms
pattùglia *s. f.* patrol
pattuìre *v. tr.* to agree upon, to stipulate
pattumièra *s. f.* dustbin, (*USA*) garbage-can
paùra *s. f.* fear, dread, (*spavento*) fright,

scare ♦ **aver p. di q.c.** to be afraid of st.
pauróso *agg.* **1** (*che ha paura*) fearful, timorous **2** (*che incute paura*) frightening
pàusa *s. f.* **1** pause, (*nel lavoro*) break **2** (*mus.*) rest
pavimentàre *v. tr.* **1** (*di casa*) to floor **2** (*di strada*) to pave
pavimentazióne *s. f.* **1** (*di casa*) flooring **2** (*di strada*) paving
paviménto *s. m.* floor
pavóne *s. m.* peacock
pavoneggiàrsi *v. intr. pron.* to strut about
pazientàre *v. intr.* to be patient
pazіènte *agg. e s. m.* patient
pazіènza *s. f.* patience ♦ **p.!** never mind!
pazzésco *agg.* **1** mad, crazy, foolish **2** (*eccessivo*) absurd, senseless
pazzìa *s. f.* madness
pàzzo **A** *agg.* **1** mad, crazy, insane, lunatic **2** (*eccessivo*) wild **B** *s. m.* madman, lunatic
pècca *s. f.* fault
peccaminóso *agg.* sinful
peccàre *v. intr.* **1** (*fare peccato*) to sin **2** (*essere difettoso*) to be faulty, to lack
peccàto *s. m.* sin ♦ **che p.!** what a pity!
peccatóre *s. m.* sinner
péce *s. f.* pitch
pècora *s. f.* sheep
peculàto *s. m.* peculation
peculiàre *agg.* peculiar, characteristic
peculiarità *s. f.* peculiarity
pedàggio *s. m.* toll
pedagogìa *s. f.* pedagogy
pedalàre *v. intr.* to pedal, to cycle
pedàle *s. m.* pedal
pedàna *s. f.* **1** footboard, (*della cattedra*) dais **2** (*salto*) springboard, (*lancio*) circle, (*scherma*) piste
pedànte **A** *agg.* pedantic **B** *s. m. e f.* pedant
pedanterìa *s. f.* pedantry
pedàta *s. f.* **1** kick **2** (*impronta*) footprint
pedèstre *agg.* pedestrian, dull
pediàtra *s. m. e f.* p(a)ediatrician
pediatrìa *s. f.* p(a)edriatrics *pl.* (*v. al sing.*)
pedicùre *s. m. e f. inv.* pedicure, chiropodist
pedìna *s. f.* (*dama*) man, (*scacchi, fig.*) pawn
pedinàre *v. tr.* to tag after, to tail
pedonàle *agg.* pedestrian (*attr*) ♦ **isola p.** pedestrian precinct; **passaggio p.** pedestrian crossing
pedonalizzàre *v. tr.* to pedestrianize
pedóne *s. m.* **1** pedestrian **2** (*pedina*) pawn
pèggio **A** *agg. inv.* worse **B** *s. m. e f. inv.* the worst (thing) **C** *avv.* **1** (*comp.*) worse **2** (*sup. rel.*) worst, (*tra due*) worse ♦ **alla meno p.** anyhow, somehow; **alla p.** at worst; **p. che mai** worse than ever
peggioraménto *s. m.* worsening
peggioràre **A** *v. tr.* to worsen, to make worse **B** *v. intr.* to get worse
peggioratìvo *agg. e s. m.* pejorative
peggióre *agg.* **1** (*comp.*) worse **2** (*sup. rel.*) the worst, (*tra due*) the worse
pégno *s. m.* pawn, pledge
pelàme *s. m.* coat
pelàre *v. tr.* **1** (*sbucciare*) to peel, (*spellare*) to skin **2** (*fig., fam.*) to fleece
pelàto *agg.* **1** (*calvo*) bald, hairless **2** (*sbucciato*) peeled
pellàme *s. m.* skins *pl.*
pèlle *s. f.* **1** skin, (*carnagione*) complexion **2** (*cuoio*) hide, leather **3** (*buccia*) peel, skin, rind
pellegrinàggio *s. m.* pilgrimage
pellegrìno *s. m.* pilgrim
pellerόssa *s. m. e f.* American Indian
pelletterìa *s. f.* **1** leather goods *pl.* **2** (*negozio*) leather goods shop
pellicàno *s. m.* pelican
pellicceria *s. f.* **1** furs *pl.* **2** (*negozio*) furrier's shop
pellìccia *s. f.* **1** fur **2** (*indumento*) fur coat
pellìcola *s. f.* **1** (*membrana*) film, pellicle **2** (*fot., cin.*) film
pélo *s. m.* **1** hair **2** (*pelame*) coat, hair, (*pelliccia*) fur **3** (*di tessuto*) pile
pelóso *agg.* hairy
péltro *s. m.* pewter
pelùria *s. f.* down
péna *s. f.* **1** (*dir*) punishment, penalty **2** (*sofferenza*) pain, suffering, sorrow **3** (*fatica*) trouble ♦ **a mala p.** hardly; **mi fa p.** I feel sorry for him; **non ne vale la p.** it isn't worth it; **p. capitale** capital punishment
penàle **A** *agg.* penal **B** *s. f.* penalty, fine ♦ **codice p.** criminal code
penalità *s. f.* penalty
penalizzàre *v. tr.* **1** to penalize **2** (*danneggiare*) to damage
penàre *v. intr.* **1** to suffer **2** (*far fatica*) to find it difficult
pendènte **A** *agg.* **1** hanging **2** (*inclinato*) leaning **3** (*dir*) pending, outstanding **B** *s. m.* pendant, (*orecchino*) ear-drop
pendènza *s. f.* **1** slope, incline **2** (*grado d'inclinazione*) gradient **3** (*dir*) pending suit **4** (*comm.*) outstanding account

pèndere *v. intr.* **1** to hang (down) **2** (*inclinare*) to lean **3** (*di superficie*) to slant, to slope **4** (*incombere*) to hang over **5** (*propendere*) to be inclined, to tend **6** (*dir.*) to be pending
pendìce *s. f.* slope
pendìo *s. m.* slope, slant
pèndola *s. f.* pendulum-clock
pendolàre **A** *agg.* **1** pendular **2** (*di lavoratore*) commuting **B** *s. m. e f.* commuter
pèndolo *s. m.* pendulum ♦ **orologio a p.** pendulum-clock
pène *s. m.* penis
penetràre **A** *v. tr.* **1** to seep into, to penetrate, to pierce **2** (*fig.*) to penetrate **B** *v. intr.* **1** to penetrate into, to pierce into **2** (*entrare*) to enter, (*furtivamente*) to steal into
penetrazióne *s. f.* penetration
penicillìna *s. f.* penicillin
peninsulàre *agg.* peninsular
penìsola *s. f.* peninsula
penitènte *agg. e s. m. e f.* penitent
penitènza *s. f.* **1** penance **2** (*castigo*) punishment **3** (*nei giochi*) forfeit
penitenziàrio **A** *agg.* penitentiary **B** *s. m.* prison, (*USA*) penitentiary
pénna *s. f.* **1** (*per scrivere*) pen **2** (*di uccello*) feather **3** (*scrittore*) writer ♦ **p. a sfera** ballpoint pen; **p. stilografica** fountain-pen
pennàcchio *s. m.* plume
pennarèllo *s. m.* felt-tip pen
pennellàta *s. f.* brush stroke
pennèllo *s. m.* brush ♦ **p. da barba** shaving-brush; **stare a p.** to fit perfectly
pennìno *s. m.* nib
pennóne *s. m.* **1** (*naut.*) yard **2** (*stendardo*) pennon
penómbra *s. f.* gloom, semi-darkness
penóso *agg.* painful
pensàre **A** *v. tr.* **1** to think **2** (*proporsi, decidere*) to think, to decide **3** (*considerare*) to consider, to bear in mind **4** (*immaginare*) to think, to imagine **B** *v. intr.* **1** to think (of) **2** (*badare*) to mind, to take care of, to see to **3** (*giudicare*) to think
pensatóre *s. m.* thinker
pensièro *s. m.* **1** thought **2** (*opinione*) opinion, mind **3** (*attenzione*) thought, care **4** (*preoccupazione*) trouble, worry **5** (*dono*) gift
pensieróso *agg.* thoughtful, pensive
pènsile *agg.* pensile, hanging, suspended ♦ **giardino p.** roof garden
pensilìna *s. f.* cantilever roof, shelter
pensionaménto *s. m.* retirement
pensionànte *s. m. e f.* boarder
pensionàto *s. m.* **1** (*persona*) pensioner, retired person **2** (*istituto*) boarding-house, hostel, (*per anziani*) rest home
pensióne *s. f.* **1** (*assegno*) pension, annuity **2** (*vitto e alloggio*) board and lodging **3** (*luogo*) boarding-house, guest-house ♦ **andare in p.** to retire
pensóso *agg.* thoughtful, pensive
pentagonàle *agg.* pentagonal
pentàgono *s. m.* pentagon
pentagràmma *s. m.* pentagram, stave
pentecòste *s. f.* Whitsunday
pentiménto *s. m.* repentance
pentìrsi *v. intr. pron.* to repent, to regret
péntola *s. f.* pot, pan, saucepan ♦ **p. a pressione** pressure cooker
penùltimo *agg.* penultimate, second-last, last but one
penùria *s. f.* scarcity, shortage
penzolàre *v. intr.* to dangle, to hang down
penzolóni *avv.* hanging
pepàre *v. tr.* to pepper
pepàto *agg.* **1** peppery **2** (*fig.*) sharp
pépe *s. m.* pepper ♦ **p. in grani** whole pepper
peperoncìno *s. m.* hot pepper, paprika
peperóne *s. m.* pepper
pepìta *s. f.* nugget
pèplo *s. m.* peplum, peplos
pér **A** *prep.* **1** (*moto per luogo*) through, (*senza direzione fissa*) about, around, (*lungo*) along, up, (*sopra*) over, all over (ES: **passare per Londra** to pass through London) **2** (*moto a luogo*) for, to (ES: **partire per Roma** to leave for Rome) **3** (*stato in luogo*) in, on (ES: **incontrare qc. per la città** to meet sb. in the town) **4** (*estensione, misura*) for (ES: **camminare per miglia e miglia** to walk for miles and miles) **5** (*per un certo periodo, per una data precisa*) for, (*entro un termine*) by, (*per un intero periodo di tempo*) (all) through, throughout (ES: **per due ore** for two hours, **saranno di ritorno per le cinque** they'll be back by five o'clock) **6** (*mezzo*) by, through (ES: **per via aerea** by air mail) **7** (*modo*) by, in (ES: **chiamare per nome** to call by name, **per iscritto** in writing) **8** (*prezzo*) for (ES: **comprare q.c. per 50 sterline** to buy st. for fifty pounds)

9 (*causa*) for, owing to, because of, on account of, out of, through (ES: **assente per malattia** absent owing to illness, **fare q.c. per amore** to do st. out of love) **10** (*termine, vantaggio, utilità, interesse*) for (ES: **fatelo per me** do it for me) **11** (*fine, scopo*) for (ES: **la lotta per la vita** the struggle for life) **12** (*limitazione*) for (ES: **è troppo difficile per me** it's too difficult for me) **13** (*colpa*) for (ES: **fu processato per furto** he was tried for theft) **14** (*distributivo*) by, at, in, per, for (ES: **il tre per cento** three per cent, **uno per uno** one by one, **due per volta** two at a time) **15** (*mat.*) by (ES: **divisione per due** division by two) **16** (*come, in qualità di*) as (ES: **avere un cane per amico** to have a dog as a friend) **17** (*scambio, sostituzione*) for (ES: **ti ho scambiata per la moglie di Mario** I'd taken you for Mario's wife) **B** *cong.* **1** (*finale*) for, (in order) to **2** (*causale*) for **3** (*concessivo*) however ♦ **stare per fare q.c.** to be about to do st.

péra *s. f.* pear

peràltro *avv.* moreover, what is more

perbàcco *inter.* by Jove!, (*certo!*) of course

perbène **A** *agg.* respectable **B** *avv.* well

perbenìsmo *s. m.* respectability

percènto *avv. e s. m. inv.* percent

percentuàle **A** *agg.* percent (*attr*), proportional **B** *s. f.* **1** percentage, (*tasso*) rate **2** (*commissione*) commission

percepìre *v. tr.* **1** to perceive, to feel **2** (*ricevere*) to collect, to cash, to receive

percezióne *s. f.* perception

perché **A** *avv.* why, what for **B** *cong.* **1** (*esplicativo*) because, for, since, as **2** (*finale*) so (that), so as, in order that **3** (*correlativo di 'troppo'*) for, to **C** *s. m. inv.* **1** (*motivo*) reason, motive **2** (*dubbio*) question

perciò *cong.* so, for this/that reason, therefore

percórrere *v. tr.* **1** (*una distanza*) to cover, to go along **2** (*in lungo e in largo*) to travel, to scour **3** (*attraversare*) to run through, to go across

percórso *s. m.* **1** (*tratto*) way, journey **2** (*distanza*) run, distance **3** (*tracciato*) route, course

percòssa *s. f.* blow, stroke

percuòtere *v. tr.* to strike, to hit, to beat, to knock

percussióne *s. f.* percussion

pèrdere **A** *v. tr.* **1** to lose **2** (*lasciarsi sfuggire*) to miss **3** (*sprecare*) to waste **4** (*lasciar uscire*) to leak, to lose **5** (*rovinare*) to ruin **B** *v. intr.* **1** to lose **2** (*far uscire liquido*) to leak **C** *v. intr. pron.* **1** (*smarrirsi*) to get lost, to lose oneself **2** (*svanire*) to fade away, (*sparire*) to disappear **3** (*andare smarrito*) to be mislaid, to get lost **4** (*rovinarsi*) to be ruined

perdigiórno *s. m. e f.* idler

pèrdita *s. f.* **1** loss **2** (*spreco*) waste **3** (*falla*) leak

perditèmpo *s. m. e f.* timewaster

perdonàbile *agg.* excusable

perdonàre **A** *v. tr.* **1** to forgive, to pardon **2** (*scusare*) to excuse, to pardon **3** (*risparmiare*) to spare **B** *v. intr.* to forgive

perdóno *s. m.* **1** forgiveness, pardon **2** (*esclamativo*) sorry

perduràre *v. intr.* **1** to continue, to go on **2** (*persistere*) to persist

perdutaménte *avv.* desperately, hopelessly

peregrinàre *v. intr.* to wander

peregrinazióne *s. f.* wandering

perènne *agg.* perennial, perpetual, (*eterno*) everlasting

perentòrio *agg.* peremptory

perfettaménte *avv.* perfectly

perfètto *agg.* perfect

perfezionaménto *s. m.* **1** perfecting, improvement **2** (*completamento*) completion **3** (*specializzazione*) specialization

perfezionàre **A** *v. tr.* to perfect, (*migliorare*) to improve **B** *v. intr. pron. e rifl.* **1** to perfect oneself **2** (*specializzarsi*) to specialize

perfezióne *s. f.* perfection

perfezionìsta *s. m. e f.* perfectionist

pèrfido *agg.* perfidious, treacherous

perfìno *avv.* even

perforàre **A** *v. tr.* to perforate, to pierce, to punch **B** *v. intr. pron.* to be pierced

perforazióne *s. f.* perforation

pergamèna *s. f.* parchment

pergolàto *s. m.* pergola, bower

pericolànte *agg.* tumbledown, unsafe, precarious

perìcolo *s. m.* danger, peril, hazard

pericolosità *s. f.* danger, dangerousness

pericolóso *agg.* dangerous

periferìa *s. f.* **1** (*zona esterna*) periphery **2** (*di città*) outskirts *pl.*, suburbs *pl.*

perifèrico *agg.* **1** (*esterno*) peripheral **2** (*di quartiere*) suburban

perìfrasi *s. f.* periphrasis

perimetràle *agg.* perimetric(al), (*esterno*) outer
perìmetro *s. m.* perimeter
periodicaménte *avv.* periodically
periodicità *s. f.* periodicity
periòdico **A** *agg.* periodic(al), recurring **B** *s. m.* periodical, magazine
perìodo *s. m.* period
peripezìa *s. f.* vicissitudes *pl.*, adventure
perìre *v. intr.* to perish, to die
periscòpio *s. m.* periscope
perìto *s. m.* expert
peritonìte *s. f.* peritonitis
perìzia *s. f.* **1** (*abilità*) skill, ability **2** (*valutazione*) appraisal, survey, examination, (*tecnica*) expert report, expertise
pèrla *s. f.* pearl
perlàceo *agg.* pearly
perloméno *avv.* at least
perlopiù *avv.* **1** (*per la maggior parte*) mainly, mostly **2** (*di solito*) usually
perlustràre *v. tr.* to search, to patrol
perlustrazióne *s. f.* **1** (*mil.*) patrol, reconnaissance **2** (*est.*) searching
permalóso *agg.* touchy
permanènte **A** *agg.* permanent, standing **B** *s. f.* permanent wave, perm
permanènza *s. f.* **1** permanence, persistence **2** (*soggiorno*) stay
permanére *v. intr.* to remain, (*perdurare*) to persist
permeàre *v. tr.* to permeate
permésso *s. m.* **1** permission, leave, permit **2** (*dal lavoro*) leave **3** (*licenza*) licence, permit
perméttere *v. tr.* **1** to allow, to permit, to let **2** (*rendere possibile*) to enable **3** (*autorizzare*) to authorize **4** (*concedersi*) to afford, to allow
permissìvo *agg.* permissive
pèrmuta *s. f.* exchange, permutation
pernàcchia *s. f.* raspberry
pernìce *s. f.* partridge
perniciόso *agg.* pernicious, noxious
pèrno *s. m.* **1** pivot, pin **2** (*cardine*) hinge **3** (*fig.*) mainstay, support
pernottaménto *s. m.* overnight stay
pernottàre *v. intr.* to stay overnight
péro *s. m.* pear
però *cong.* **1** (*avversativo*) but, however, yet **2** (*concessivo*) nevertheless
peróne *s. m.* perone, fibula
peroràre **A** *v. tr.* to plead, to defend **B** *v. intr.* to perorate
perpendicolàre *agg. e s. f.* perpendicular
perpetràre *v. tr.* to perpetrate, to commit
perpetuàre **A** *v. tr.* to perpetuate **B** *v. intr. pron.* to last
perpètuo *agg.* perpetual
perplessità *s. f.* perplexity
perplèsso *agg.* perplexed, puzzled
perquisìre *v. tr.* to search
perquisizióne *s. f.* perquisition, search ♦ **mandato di p.** search-warrant
persecutóre *s. m.* persecutor
persecuzióne *s. f.* persecution
perseguìre *v. tr.* **1** to pursue, to follow **2** (*dir*) to prosecute
perseguitàre *v. tr.* to persecute, to pursue
perseverànte *agg.* perseverant
perseverànza *s. f.* perseverance
perseveràre *v. intr.* to persevere, to persist
persiàna *s. f.* shutter
persiàno *agg. e s. m.* Persian
pèrsico (1) *agg.* Persian
pèrsico (2) *agg. e s. m.* (*zool.*) perch, bass
persìno *avv.* → **perfino**
persistènte *agg.* persistent
persìstere *v. intr.* to persist
persóna *s. f.* **1** (*essere umano*) person (*pl.* people) **2** (*qualcuno*) someone, somebody **3** (*corpo*) body, figure **4** (*gramm., dir*) person ♦ **in/di p.** personally; **p. di servizio** servant
personàggio *s. m.* **1** personage, personality **2** (*teatro, letter*) character, person **3** (*tipo strano*) character
personàle **A** *agg.* personal **B** *s. m.* **1** staff **2** (*corporatura*) figure **3** (*sfera privata*) privacy
personalità *s. f.* **1** personality **2** (*persona importante*) personage, personality
personalizzàre *v. tr.* to personalize
personalménte *avv.* personally
personificàre *v. tr.* to personify
personificazióne *s. f.* personification
perspicàce *agg.* perspicacious, shrewd
perspicàcia *s. f.* perspicacity, shrewdness
persuadére **A** *v. tr.* to persuade, to convince **B** *v. rifl.* to persuade oneself, to convince oneself
persuasióne *s. f.* persuasion, conviction
persuasìvo *agg.* persuasive, convincing
pertànto *cong.* therefore, so
pèrtica *s. f.* perch
pertinènte *agg.* pertinent
pertósse *s. f.* whooping-cough
pertùgio *s. m.* hole, opening

perturbàre **A** *v. tr.* to perturb, to upset **B** *v. intr. pron.* to become upset, (*di tempo*) to worsen
perturbazióne *s. f.* perturbation, disturbance
pervàdere *v. tr.* to pervade
pervenìre *v. intr.* to reach, to attain, to achieve, to arrive at
perversióne *s. f.* perversion
pervèrso *agg.* perverse
pervertìre **A** *v. tr.* to pervert **B** *v. intr. pron.* to become perverted
pésa *s. f.* **1** (*pesatura*) weighing **2** (*pesa pubblica*) weigh-house
pesànte *agg.* **1** heavy **2** (*noioso*) boring, dull, heavy **3** (*faticoso*) tyring **4** (*di aria*) close, stuffy **5** (*duro*) hard, rough
pesantézza *s. f.* heaviness, weight
pesàre **A** *v. tr.* to weigh **B** *v. intr.* **1** to weigh, to be heavy **2** (*esser gravoso*) to bother, to be a burden **3** (*aver importanza*) to count **C** *v. rifl.* to weigh oneself
pèsca (1) *s. f.* (*frutto*) peach
pésca (2) *s. f.* **1** (*il pescare*) fishing **2** (*il pescato*) catch, haul ♦ **p. a strascico** trawling; **p. con la lenza** angling; **p. di beneficenza** lucky dip
pescàre **A** *v. tr.* **1** to fish for, (*prendere*) to fish, to catch **2** (*trovare*) to get hold of **3** (*cogliere sul fatto*) to catch **4** (*estrarre*) to draw, to pick up **B** *v. intr.* (*naut.*) to draw
pescatóre *s. m.* fisherman
pésce *s. m.* fish
pescecàne *s. m.* shark
pescespàda *s. m.* swordfish
pescheréccio **A** *agg.* fishing **B** *s. m.* fishing boat
pescherìa *s. f.* fishmonger's, fish-shop
peschièra *s. f.* fishpond
pescivéndolo *s. m.* fishmonger
pèsco *s. m.* peach(-tree) ♦ **fiori di p.** peach-blossom
pescóso *agg.* abounding in fish
péso *s. m.* **1** weight **2** (*importanza*) weight, importance **3** (*onere*) burden, load ♦ **essere di peso a qc.** to be a burden for sb.; **lancio del p.** shot put
pessimìsmo *s. m.* pessimism
pessimìsta *s. m. e f.* pessimist
pèssimo *agg.* very bad, awful, terrible
pestàre *v. tr.* **1** to crush, to pound, (*ridurre in polvere*) to grind **2** (*calpestare*) to tread on, to trample on **3** (*picchiare*) to beat
pèste *s. f.* plague
pestèllo *s. m.* pestle
pestìfero *agg.* **1** pestiferous **2** (*puzzolente*) stinking, (*disgustoso*) disgusting **3** (*fastidioso*) pestilent
pestilènza *s. f.* pestilence, plague
pètalo *s. m.* petal
petàrdo *s. m.* firecracker
petizióne *s. f.* petition
petrolièra *s. f.* tanker
petrolière *s. m.* oilman
petrolìfero *agg.* oil (*attr.*) ♦ **pozzo p.** oil-well
petròlio *s. m.* petroleum, oil
pettegolàre *v. intr.* to gossip
pettegolézzo *s. m.* gossip
pettégolo **A** *agg.* gossipy **B** *s. m.* gossip
pettinàre **A** *v. tr.* to comb **B** *v. rifl.* to comb one's hair
pettinàta *s. f.* combing
pettinatùra *s. f.* **1** hairstyle, hair-do **2** (*tess.*) combing
pèttine *s. m.* **1** comb **2** (*zool.*) pecten, scallop
pettirósso *s. m.* robin
pètto *s. m.* chest, breast
petulànza *s. f.* insolence, tiresomeness
pèzza *s. f.* **1** (*di stoffa*) roll, piece **2** (*toppa*) patch **3** (*straccio*) rag **4** (*macchia*) spot
pezzènte *s. m.* tramp
pèzzo *s. m.* piece, bit, part
phon *s. m. inv.* hair dryer
piacènte *agg.* pleasant
piacére **A** *s. m.* **1** pleasure, delight **2** (*divertimento*) pleasure, amusement **3** (*favore*) favour, kindness **4** (*volontà*) will **B** *v. intr.* to like, to be fond of ♦ **a p.** at will; **chiedere un p. a qc.** to ask a favour of sb.; **per p.** please
piacévole *agg.* pleasant, agreeable
piàga *s. f.* **1** sore **2** (*flagello*) plague, scourge, curse **3** (*persona*) pain, nuisance
piagnistèo *s. m.* whine, whining
piagnucolàre *v. intr.* to whine, to whimper
piàlla *s. f.* plane, planer
piallàre *v. tr.* to plane
piàna *s. f.* plain, flat
pianeggiànte *agg.* level, flat
pianeròttolo *s. m.* landing
pianéta *s. m.* planet
piàngere **A** *v. intr.* to cry, to weep **B** *v. tr.* **1** to cry, to weep **2** (*lamentare*) to grieve for, to mourn
pianificàre *v. tr.* to plan
pianificazióne *s. f.* planning

pianìsta *s. m. e f.* pianist
piàno (1) **A** *agg.* **1** flat, level, even **2** (*liscio*) smooth **3** (*chiaro*) clear, plain **4** (*semplice*) simple **5** (*geom.*) plane **B** *avv.* **1** (*sommessamente*) softly, quietly, (*a bassa voce*) in a low voice **2** (*lentamente*) slowly, slow **3** (*con cautela*) gently, carefully
piàno (2) *s. m.* **1** (*terreno pianeggiante*) plain, flat land, level land **2** (*superficie piana*) plane **3** (*di casa*) floor, storey, (*di nave, bus*) deck **4** (*progetto*) plan, scheme, project, programme **5** (*mus.*) piano
pianofòrte *s. m.* piano ♦ **p. a coda** grand piano
pianotèrra *s. m. inv.* ground floor, (*USA*) first floor
piànta *s. f.* **1** plant, (*albero*) tree **2** (*del piede, della scarpa*) sole **3** (*disegno di edificio*) plan, (*mappa*) map ♦ **di sana p.** completely: **in p. stabile** on the regular staff
piantagióne *s. f.* plantation
piantàre **A** *v. tr.* **1** to plant **2** (*conficcare*) to thrust, to drive **3** (*abbandonare*) to leave, to quit, to abandon **B** *v. intr. pron.* **1** (*conficcarsi*) to stick, to get stuck in **2** (*piazzarsi*) to plant oneself, to place oneself **C** *v. rifl. rec.* to leave each other, to part ♦ **piantarla** to stop
pianterréno *s. m.* ground floor, (*USA*) first floor
piànto *s. m.* **1** weeping, crying **2** (*lacrime*) tears *pl.* ♦ **scoppiare in p.** to burst into tears
pianùra *s. f.* plain, flat land, lowland
piàstra *s. f.* **1** (*mecc.*) plate **2** (*edil.*) slab
piastrèlla *s. f.* tile
piattafórma *s. f.* platform
piattèllo *s. m.* disk ♦ **tiro al p.** trap-shooting, clay-pigeon shooting
piattìno *s. m.* saucer
piàtto **A** *agg.* flat **B** *s. m.* **1** (*stoviglia*) plate, (*grande*) dish **2** (*vivanda*) dish **3** (*portata*) course **4** *al pl.* (*mus.*) cymbals *pl.* **5** (*nel gioco delle carte*) kitty **6** (*di bilancia*) plan ♦ **lavare i piatti** to wash up
piàzza *s. f.* **1** square **2** (*comm.*) market **3** (*posto*) place ♦ **letto a una p.** single bed; **p. di pagamento** place of payment
piazzàle *s. m.* large square
piazzaménto *s. m.* placing
piazzàre **A** *v. tr.* **1** to place, to put **2** (*comm.*) to sell, to market **B** *v. rifl.* **1** (*mettersi*) to settle oneself **2** (*sport*) to be placed, to come
piazzìsta *s. m.* commercial traveller
piazzòla *s. f.* lay-by
piccànte *agg.* **1** spicy, hot **2** (*fig.*) bawdy, spicy, risqué
piccàrsi *v. rifl.* **1** to pride oneself **2** (*impermalosirsi*) to be offended
picchétto *s. m.* **1** (*paletto*) peg **2** (*mil., di scioperanti*) picket
picchiàre **A** *v. tr.* to beat, to hit, to strike **B** *v. intr.* **1** (*battere*) to strike, to tap **2** (*bussare*) to knock **C** *v. rifl. rec.* to fight, to come to blows
picchiàta *s. f.* (*aer*) dive
picchiettàre **A** *v. intr.* to patter **B** *v. tr.* to spot, to dot
pìcchio *s. m.* (*zool.*) woodpecker
piccìno **A** *agg.* **1** tiny, small, little **2** (*meschino*) mean **B** *s. m.* child
piccionàia *s. f.* pigeon-house
piccióne *s. m.* pigeon ♦ **p. viaggiatore** carrier-pigeon
pìcco *s. m.* peak ♦ **a p.** vertically
pìccolo **A** *agg.* **1** small, little, tiny **2** (*basso*) short **3** (*giovane*) young **4** (*di poco conto*) sligh, small, trifling **5** (*meschino*) mean, petty **6** (*breve*) short, brief **B** *s. m.* **1** child, little one **2** (*di animale*) joey, (*di cane*) pup ♦ **da p.** as a child
piccóne *s. m.* pick
piccòzza *s. f.* axe
picnic *s. m. inv.* picnic
pidòcchio *s. m.* louse
piède *s. m.* foot ♦ **a piedi** on foot; **a piedi nudi** barefoot; **in punta di piedi** on tiptoe; **p. di porco** jemmy; **prendere p.** to get a footing
piedistàllo *s. m.* pedestal
pièga *s. f.* **1** fold, wrinkle **2** (*fatta ad arte*) pleat, (*dei pantaloni*) crease **3** (*dei capelli*) set **4** (*andamento*) turn **5** (*geol.*) fold
piegàre **A** *v. tr.* **1** to fold (up), (*flettere*) to bend **2** (*sottomettere*) to bend, to subdue **B** *v. intr.* to bend, to turn **C** *v. rifl. e intr. pron.* **1** to bend **2** (*cedere*) to yield, to give in
pieghettàre *v. tr.* to pleat
pieghévole **A** *agg.* **1** (*flessibile*) pliable, pliant **2** (*atto a essere piegato*) folding **B** *s. m.* brochure
pièna *s. f.* **1** flood, spate **2** (*folla*) crowd ♦ **fiume in p.** river in flood
pièno **A** *agg.* **1** full, filled **2** (*non cavo*)

solid **3** (*in carne*) full, plump **4** (*sazio*) full up **B** *s. m.* **1** (*colmo*) height, (*mezzo*) middle **2** (*carico completo*) full load, (*di nave*) full cargo ♦ **fare il p.** (*di benzina*) to fill up

pietà *s. f.* **1** pity, compassion, mercy **2** (*devozione*) piety, devotion

pietànza *s. f.* **1** dish **2** (*portata*) course

pietóso *agg.* **1** (*che sente pietà*) pitiful, merciful **2** (*che muove a pietà*) pitiful, pitiable, piteous, (*miserevole*) wretched **3** (*brutto*) awful

piètra *s. f.* stone

pietrificàre **A** *v. tr.* to petrify **B** *v. intr. pron.* to become petrified, to petrify

pìffero *s. m.* fife, pipe

pigiàma *s. m.* pyjamas *pl.*

pigiàre *v. tr.* to press, to push

pigliàre → **prendere**

pìglio *s. m.* manner, look

pigmentazióne *s. f.* pigmentation

pigménto *s. m.* pigment

pigmèo *s. m.* pigmy

pìgna *s. f.* pine-cone

pignolerìa *s. f.* pedantry, fussiness

pignòlo **A** *agg.* pedantic, fussy **B** *s. m.* pedant, fastidious person

pignoràre *v. tr.* to distrain on, to attach

pigolàre *v. intr.* to peep

pigrìzia *s. f.* laziness

pìgro *agg.* **1** lazy **2** (*lento*) sluggish

pìla *s. f.* **1** (*di oggetti*) pile, heap, stack **2** (*elettr.*) battery, pile **3** (*torcia*) torch

pilàstro *s. m.* pillar

pìllola *s. f.* pill

pilóne *s. m.* **1** (*di ponte*) pier **2** (*di linea elettrica*) pylon

pilòta *agg. e s. m.* pilot

pilotàre *v. tr.* to pilot

pinacotèca *s. f.* picture-gallery

pinéta *s. f.* pinewood

ping-pong *s. m. inv.* table tennis, ping-pong

pìngue *agg.* **1** (*grasso*) fat **2** (*fertile*) fertile, rich **3** (*grosso*) large, big

pinguìno *s. m.* penguin

pìnna *s. f.* **1** (*di pesce*) fin, (*di mammifero acquatico*) flipper **2** (*per nuotare*) flipper **3** (*naut., aer.*) fin

pinnàcolo *s. m.* pinnacle

pìno *s. m.* pine

pinòlo *s. m.* pine-seed

pìnza *s. f.* pliers *pl.*, pincers *pl.*, tongs *pl.*

pinzétta *s. f.* tweezers *pl.*

pìo *agg.* **1** pious, devout **2** (*misericordioso*) compassionate **3** (*benefico*) charitable

pioggerèlla *s. f.* drizzle

piòggia *s. f.* **1** rain **2** (*est.*) shower

piòlo *s. m.* peg

piombàre *v. intr.* **1** (*cadere a piombo*) to plunge, to plump, to fall **2** (*gettarsi su*) to pounce, to swoop **3** (*arrivare all'improvviso*) to rush

piómbo *s. m.* lead

pionière *s. m.* pioneer

piòppo *s. m.* poplar

piovàno *agg.* rain (*attr.*)

piòvere *v. intr.* **1** (*impers.*) to rain **2** (*fig.*) to rain, to pour

piovigginàre *v. intr. impers.* to drizzle

piovosità *s. f.* rainfall

piovóso *agg.* rainy

piòvra *s. f.* octopus

pìpa *s. f.* pipe

pipì *s. f.* (*fam.*) pee ♦ **fare p.** to pee

pipistrèllo *s. m.* bat

piramidàle *agg.* pyramidal

piràmide *s. f.* pyramid

piràta *s. m.* pirate ♦ **p. della strada** road-hog

piraterìa *s. f.* piracy

pirìte *s. f.* pyrite

piròga *s. f.* pirogue

piròmane *s. m. e f.* pyromaniac

piròscafo *s. m.* steamer

pirotècnico *agg.* pyrotechnic(al)

piscicoltùra *s. f.* fish breeding

piscìna *s. f.* swimming pool

pisèllo *s. m.* pea

pisolìno *s. m.* nap, snooze, doze ♦ **fare un p.** to take a nap

pìsta *s. f.* **1** (*traccia*) track, (*di animale*) trail, scent **2** (*percorso*) track **3** (*sport*) track, race-track **4** (*aer.*) strip ♦ **p. da ballo** dance floor; **p. da sci** ski run

pistàcchio *s. m.* pistachio

pistòla *s. f.* **1** (*arma*) pistol **2** (*tecnol.*) gun

pistóne *s. m.* piston, (*idraulico*) ram

pitóne *s. m.* python

pittóre *s. m.* painter

pittorésco *agg.* picturesque

pittòrico *agg.* pictorial

pittùra *s. f.* **1** painting **2** (*dipinto*) picture **3** (*vernice*) paint ♦ **p. fresca** wet paint

pitturàre *v. tr.* to paint

più **A** *agg. comp. inv.* **1** more (ES: **hai più amici di me** you have more friends than I have) **2** (*parecchi*) several (ES: **più volte** several times) **B** *avv. comp.* **1** (*in maggior* *quantità*) more, (*in frasi neg.*) no more, (*con altra negazione*) any more (ES: **dovresti dormire di più** you should sleep more, **non c'è più pane** there's no more bread, **non ne voglio più** I don't want any more) **2** (*comp. di maggioranza*) more, -er (*suffisso aggiunto ad avv. e agg.*) (ES: **più difficile** more difficult, **più facile** easier, **più alto** taller) **3** (*sup. rel.*) the most, (*tra due*) the more; the -est, (*tra due*) the -er (*suffisso aggiunto ad agg. e avv.*) (ES: **è la più bella** she is the most beautiful, **il giorno più lungo** the longest day, **sei il più felice di tutti noi** you are the happiest of us all) **4** (*in frasi neg. per indicare la cessazione di un fatto*) no longer, not any longer, not any more (ES: **non siete più studenti** you are no longer students, **non abitano più qui** they don't live here any longer) **5** (*mat.*) plus (ES: **due più due** two plus two) **C** *s. m.* **1** (*comp.*) more, (*sup.*) most (ES: **ha bevuto più del solito** he drank more than usual, **il più è fatto** most of it is done) **2** (*la maggioranza*) the majority **D** *prep.* plus

piuccheperfètto *s. m.* past perfect

piùma *s. f.* feather, plume

piumìno *s. m.* **1** (*d'oca*) down **2** (*coperta*) quilt **3** (*giacca*) padded jacket **4** (*per cipria*) powder puff **5** (*per spolverare*) feather duster

piuttòsto **A** *avv.* **1** (*preferibilmente*) rather, sooner, (*o meglio*) better **2** (*alquanto*) rather, somewhat, quite **3** (*invece*) instead **B** *cong.* **p. che/di** rather than, better than

pivèllo *s. m.* greenhorn

pìzza *s. f.* **1** (*cuc.*) pizza **2** (*cin.*) film can **3** (*noia*) nuisance, bore

pizzicàre **A** *v. tr.* **1** to pinch, to nip **2** (*di insetti*) to bite, to sting **3** (*di sostanza*) to burn **4** (*cogliere di sorpresa*) to catch **5** (*mus.*) to pluck **B** *v. intr.* **1** (*prudere*) to itch **2** (*essere piccante*) to be hot **3** (*di insetti*) to bite, to sting

pìzzico *s. m.* **1** pinch, nip **2** (*piccola quantità*) bit **3** (*puntura d'insetto*) bite

pizzicòtto *s. m.* pinch, nip

pìzzo *s. m.* **1** (*merletto*) lace **2** (*barba*) pointed beard

placàre **A** *v. tr.* **1** (*calmare*) to placate, to calm (down) **2** (*mitigare*) to soothe **B** *v. intr. pron. e rifl.* to calm down

plàcca *s. f.* **1** plate **2** (*med.*) plaque

placcàre *v. tr.* to plate

plàcido *agg.* placid, calm

plagiàre *v. tr.* to plagiarize

plàgio *s. m.* plagiarism

planàre *v. intr.* to glide, (*naut.*) to plane

planàta *s. f.* glide, (*naut.*) plane

plància *s. f.* (*naut.*) bridge

planetàrio *agg.* **1** planetary **2** (*del mondo*) worldwide

planimetrìa *s. f.* planimetry

planisfèro *s. m.* planisphere

plàsma *s. m.* plasma

plasmàre *v. tr.* to mould, to shape

plàstica *s. f.* **1** (*arte del modellare*) plastic art **2** (*med.*) plastic surgery, plastics *pl.* (*v. al sing.*) **3** (*materia*) plastic

plasticità *s. f.* plasticity

plàstico **A** *agg.* plastic **B** *s. m.* **1** (*modello*) plastic model **2** (*esplosivo*) plastic

plastificàre *v. tr.* to plasticize

plàtano *s. m.* plane

platèa *s. f.* **1** (*teatro*) stalls *pl.* **2** (*est.*) audience

plateàle *agg.* blatant

plàtino *s. m.* platinum

platònico *agg.* Platonic

plausìbile *agg.* plausible

plàuso *s. m.* approval

plebàglia *s. f.* mob

plèbe *s. f.* (*stor.*) plebs, (*spreg.*) mob

plebèo *agg.* plebeian

plenàrio *agg.* plenary

plenilùnio *s. m.* full moon

pleonàstico *agg.* pleonastic, unnecessary

plèttro *s. m.* plectrum

pleurìte *s. f.* pleurisy

plìco *s. m.* (*busta*) cover

plìnto *s. m.* plinth

plotóne *s. m.* platoon, squad

plùmbeo *agg.* **1** leaden **2** (*opprimente*) oppressive

pluràle *agg. e s. m.* plural

pluralìsmo *s. m.* pluralism

pluralità *s. f.* plurality

plusvalóre *s. m.* surplus(-value)

plutocrazìa *s. f.* plutocracy

pluviàle *agg.* pluvial, rain (*attr.*)

pneumàtico **A** *agg.* pneumatic, air (*attr.*) **B** *s. m.* tyre

po' → **poco**

pòco **A** *agg. indef.* **1** little, not much **2** (*di tempo*) short **3** (*scarso*) scant, little **4** *al pl.* few, not many, (*alcuni*) a few **B** *pron. indef.* **1** little, not much **2** (*un poco*) a little, some, a few **3** *al pl.* few, very few, not many,

(*poche persone*) few people **C** *s. m.* little **D** *avv.* **1** (*con agg. e avv. di grado positivo, con part. pres. e part. pass. in funzione di agg.*) not very **2** (*con agg. e avv. comp.*) not much, little **3** (*con verbi*) little, not ... very much **4** (*un p., un po'*) rather, quite, a little, a bit ♦ **fra p.** very soon; **per p. non ...** nearly; **p. fa** a short time ago
podére *s. m.* farm, (*proprietà terriera*) estate
poderóso *agg.* powerful, mighty
pòdio *s. m.* podium, platform
podìsmo *s. m.* walking, (*gara sportiva*) track events *pl.*
poèma *s. m.* poem
poesìa *s. f.* **1** poetry **2** (*componimento*) poem, piece of poetry
poèta *s. m.* poet
poètica *s. f.* poetics *pl.* (*v. al sing.*)
poètico *agg.* poetic
poggiàre **A** *v. tr.* to lean, to rest **B** *v. intr.* to rest, to be based **C** *v. rifl.* to rely, to base oneself
poggiatèsta *s. m. inv.* headrest
pòggio *s. m.* knoll, hillock
pòi **A** *avv.* **1** (*successivamente*) then, (*dopo*) after(wards), (*più tardi*) later on **2** (*inoltre*) and then, besides, (*in secondo luogo*) secondly **3** (*avversativo*) but **4** (*conclusivo*) finally, then, after all **B** *s. m.* future ♦ **d'ora in p.** from now on; **prima o p.** sooner or later
poiché *cong.* **1** as, since, for **2** (*dopo che*) after, when
poker *s. m. inv.* poker
polàcco **A** *agg.* Polish **B** *s. m.* **1** (*abitante*) Pole **2** (*lingua*) Polish
polàre *agg.* polar
polarizzàre *v. tr.* **1** to polarize **2** (*fig.*) to focus
polèmica *s. f.* **1** polemic, controversy **2** (*spreg.*) argument
polèmico *agg.* polemic
policlìnico *s. m.* polyclinic, general hospital
policromàtico *agg.* polychromatic
polièdrico *agg.* **1** polyhedric **2** (*fig.*) versatile
polièstere *s. m.* polyester
polifònico *agg.* polyphonic
polìgamo **A** *agg.* polygamous **B** *s. m.* polygamist
poliglòtta *agg. e s. m. e f.* polyglot
poligonàle *agg.* polygonal
polìgono *s. m.* polygon ♦ **p. di tiro** rifle-range
polimòrfo *agg.* polymorphous
poliomielìte *s. f.* poliomyelitis
pòlipo *s. m.* **1** (*zool.*) polyp, (*polpo*) octopus **2** (*med.*) polypus
polistiròlo *s. m.* polystyrene
politècnico *agg. e s. m.* polytechnic
politeismo *s. m.* polytheism
polìtica *s. f.* **1** politics *pl.* (*v. al sing.*) **2** (*linea di condotta*) policy **3** (*diplomazia*) diplomacy ♦ **p. interna/estera** home/foreign politics
politicaménte *avv.* politically
politicizzàre *v. tr.* to politicize
polìtico **A** *agg.* **1** political **2** (*diplomatico*) diplomatic **B** *s. m.* politician
politòlogo *s. m.* political expert
polìttico *s. m.* polyptych
polivalènte *agg.* **1** (*chim.*) polyvalent **2** (*est.*) multi-purpose (*attr.*)
polizìa *s. f.* police ♦ **agente di p.** policeman; **p. stradale** traffic police; **posto di p.** police station
poliziésco *agg.* **1** police (*attr.*) **2** (*di libro, film*) detective (story)
poliziòtto *s. m.* policeman
pòlizza *s. f.* **1** (*assicurativa*) policy **2** (*ricevuta*) bill, receipt ♦ **p. sulla vita** life insurance policy
pollàio *s. m.* poultry-pen, hen-house
pollàme *s. m.* poultry
pòllice *s. m.* **1** thumb **2** (*unità di misura*) inch
pòlline *s. m.* pollen
póllo *s. m.* chicken ♦ **p. arrosto** roast chicken
polmonàre *agg.* pulmonary
polmóne *s. m.* lung
polmonìte *s. f.* pneumonia
pòlo (1) *s. m.* (*fis., geogr.*) pole
pòlo (2) *s. m.* (*sport*) polo
pólpa *s. f.* **1** (*di frutto*) pulp **2** (*carne*) lean meat
polpàccio *s. m.* calf
polpastrèllo *s. m.* fingertip
polpétta *s. f.* rissole, (*di carne*) meatball
polpettóne *s. m.* **1** meatloaf **2** (*fig.*) mishmash
pólpo *s. m.* octopus
polpóso *agg.* pulpy
polsìno *s. m.* cuff
pólso *s. m.* **1** (*anat.*) wrist **2** (*pulsazione*) pulse **3** (*polsino*) cuff **4** (*fig.*) energy, nerve
poltìglia *s. f.* **1** mash, mush **2** (*fango*) mud,

slush
poltrìre *v. intr.* to laze (about)
poltróna *s. f.* **1** armchair **2** (*teatro*) stall **3** (*fig.*) position
poltróne *s. m.* idler, lazy-bones (*fam.*)
pólvere *s. f.* **1** dust **2** (*sostanza polverulenta*) powder ♦ **in p.** powdered; **p. da sparo** gunpowder
polverièra *s. f.* **1** powder magazine **2** (*fig.*) powder keg
polverizzàre **A** *v. tr.* to pulverize **B** *v. intr. pron.* **1** to pulverize **2** (*svanire*) to melt away
polveróne *s. m.* **1** dust cloud **2** (*fig.*) uproar
polveróso *agg.* **1** dusty **2** (*simile a polvere*) powdery
pomàta *s. f.* ointment, cream
pomèllo *s. m.* knob
pomeridiàno *agg.* **1** afternoon (*attr.*) **2** (*di ore*) p.m. (*post meridiem*)
pomerìggio *s. m.* afternoon
pómice *s. f.* pumice
pómo *s. f.* **1** (*bot.*) pome, (*mela*) apple **2** (*pomello*) knob
pomodòro *s. m.* tomato ♦ **salsa di p.** tomato sauce; **succo di p.** tomato juice
pómpa (1) *s. f.* (*fasto*) pomp
pómpa (2) *s. f.* pump
pompàre *v. tr.* to pump, to draw up
pompèlmo *s. m.* grapefruit
pompière *s. m.* fireman
pompóso *agg.* pompous
ponderàre **A** *v. tr.* to ponder, to weigh up **B** *v. intr.* to reflect
ponderazióne *s. f.* reflection, consideration
ponderóso *agg.* **1** (*pesante*) heavy, ponderous **2** (*gravoso*) weighty
ponènte *s. m.* west
pónte *s. m.* **1** bridge **2** (*naut.*) deck **3** (*impalcatura*) scaffold ♦ **p. aereo** air lift; **p. levatoio** drawbridge
pontéfice *s. m.* pontiff
pontificàre *v. intr.* to pontificate
pontificàto *s. m.* pontificate
pontificio *agg.* papal ♦ **Stato Pontificio** Papal States
pontìle *s. m.* wharf
pony *s. m. inv.* pony
popolàre (1) *agg.* **1** popular **2** (*tradizionale*) folk (*attr.*)
popolàre (2) **A** *v. tr.* to populate, to people **B** *v. intr.* to become populated
popolarità *s. f.* popularity
popolazióne *s. f.* **1** population **2** (*popolo*) people
pòpolo *s. m.* people
popolóso *agg.* populous, densely populated
póppa *s. f.* stern ♦ **a p.** aft
poppàre *v. tr. e intr.* to suck
populìsmo *s. m.* populism
porcellàna *s. f.* china, porcelain
porcellìno *s. m.* little pig, piglet ♦ **p. da latte** sucking-pig; **p. d'India** guinea pig
porcherìa *s. f.* **1** (*sudiciume*) filth, dirt **2** (*azione disonesta*) dirty trick **3** (*indecenza*) obscenity **4** (*cibo schifoso*) disgusting food **5** (*cosa fatta male*) rabbish, trash
porcìle *s. m.* pigsty
porcìno *s. m.* pore mushroom
pòrco *s. m.* **1** pig, swine **2** (*cuc.*) pork
porcospìno *s. m.* hedgehog
pòrfido *s. m.* porphyry
pòrgere *v. tr.* to hand, to pass, to give
pornografìa *s. f.* pornography
pornogràfico *agg.* pornographic
pòro *s. m.* pore
poróso *agg.* porous
pórpora *s. f.* **1** purple **2** (*med.*) purpura
pórre **A** *v. tr.* **1** to put, to place, (*posare*) to lay (down) **2** (*supporre*) to suppose **3** (*imporre*) to set, to put **B** *v. rifl.* **1** to put oneself, to place oneself **2** (*accingersi*) to set to ♦ **poniamo che ...** let us suppose that ...
pòrro *s. m.* **1** (*bot.*) leek **2** (*med.*) wart
pòrta *s. f.* **1** door **2** (*di città*) gate **3** (*calcio*) goal ♦ **abitare p. a p.** to live next door to; **a porte chiuse** (*dir*) in camera
portabagàgli *s. m.* **1** (*facchino*) porter **2** (*autom.*) boot, (*USA*) trunk, (*sul tetto*) roof rack
portabandièra *s. m. e f.* standard-bearer
portàbile *agg.* portable
portacénere *s. m. inv.* ashtray
portachiàvi *s. m. inv.* key-ring
portacìpria *s. m. inv.* (powder) compact
portaèrei *s. f. inv.* aircraft-carrier
portafinèstra *s. f.* French-window
portafòglio *s. m.* **1** wallet, (*USA*) pocketbook **2** (*banca*) portfolio
portafortùna *s. m. inv.* lucky charm, mascot
portàle *s. m.* portal
portalèttere *s. m. inv.* postman
portaménto *s. m.* bearing
portamonéte *s. m. inv.* purse

portànte *agg.* (*tecnol.*) load-bearing
portantìna *s. f.* **1** sedan (chair) **2** (*lettiga*) litter
portaombrèlli *s. m. inv.* umbrella-stand
portapàcchi *s. m. inv.* carrier, rack
portàre **A** *v. tr.* **1** (*verso chi parla*) to bring, (*andare a prendere*) to fetch **2** (*lontano da chi parla, accompagnare*) to take **3** (*portare con fatica, d'abitudine, trasportare*) to carry **4** (*prendere con sé*) to take, to bring **5** (*indossare*) to wear **6** (*condurre*) to lead **7** (*provare, nutrire sentimenti*) to nourish, to bear **8** (*causare*) to cause, to bring about **9** (*produrre*) to bear, to bring forth, to produce **10** (*avere*) to have, to bear **11** (*sopportare*) to bear, to endure **12** (*addurre*) to adduce, to bring forward **13** (*avere una portata di*) to have a range of **B** *v. rifl. e intr. pron.* **1** (*spostarsi*) to move **2** (*andare*) to go, (*venire*) to come ♦ **p. avanti** to carry out, to maintain; **p. fortuna** to bring luck; **p. via** to take away
portasapóne *s. m. inv.* (*supporto*) soap-dish, (*contenitore*) soap-box
portascì *s. m. inv.* ski-rack
portasciugamàno *s. m.* towel-rack
portàta *s. f.* **1** (*di pranzo*) course **2** (*capacità di carico*) capacity, (*di nave*) tonnage **3** (*raggio d'azione*) range **4** (*di corso d'acqua*) flow, discharge, (*di pompa*) delivery capacity **5** (*importanza*) importance ♦ **a p. di mano** within reach, to hand
portàtile *agg.* portable
portatóre *s. m.* **1** (*comm.*) bearer **2** (*med.*) carrier
portavóce *s. m. e f. inv.* spokesman *m.*, spokeswoman *f.*
portènto *s. m.* **1** portent, wonder **2** (*persona*) prodigy
porticàto *s. m.* arcade, colonnade
pòrtico *s. m.* porch, portico, (*porticato*) arcade
portièra *s. f.* **1** (*portinaia*) porter, concierge, doorkeeper **2** (*autom.*) door
portière *s. m.* **1** (*portinaio*) porter, concierge, doorkeeper **2** (*calcio*) goal-keeper
portinàio *s. m.* porter, concierge, doorkeeper
portinerìa *s. f.* porter's lodge
pòrto (1) *s. m.* port, harbour ♦ **capitano di p.** harbour master; **p. franco** free port; **p. militare** naval port
pòrto (2) *s. m.* **1** (*prezzo del trasporto*) carriage, freight **2** (*licenza*) licence ♦ **p. assegnato** carriage forward; **p. d'armi** gun licence
portoghése *agg. e s. m. e f.* Portuguese
portolàno *s. m.* pilot-book
portóne *s. m.* main entrance
portuàle *agg.* port (*attr.*), harbour (*attr.*)
porzióne *s. f.* **1** part, portion, share **2** (*di cibo*) helping
pòsa *s. f.* **1** (*il porre*) laying, placing **2** (*per un ritratto*) sitting, pose **3** (*atteggiamento affettato*) pose **4** (*posizione*) posture **5** (*fot.*) exposure ♦ **teatro di p.** studio
posacénere *s. m. inv.* ashtray
posàre **A** *v. tr.* to put (down), to lay (down), to place **B** *v. intr.* **1** (*essere basato*) to rest, to stand **2** (*per ritratto, foto*) to pose, to sit **3** (*atteggiarsi*) to pose **C** *v. rifl. e intr. pron.* **1** (*di uccello, cosa*) to alight, to settle, (*appollaiarsi*) to perch **2** (*aer.*) to land **3** (*soffermarsi*) to stay
posàta *s. f.* (piece of) cutlery
posàto *agg.* composed
positivìsmo *s. m.* positivism
positìvo *agg.* positive
posizionàre *v. tr.* to position
posizióne *s. f.* position
posologìa *s. f.* posology, dosage
pospórre *v. tr.* **1** (*porre dopo*) to place after **2** (*posticipare*) to postpone
possedére *v. tr.* to possess, to own, to have
possediménto *s. m.* possession, (*proprietà immobiliare*) property, estate
possessìvo *agg.* possessive
possèsso *s. m.* **1** possession, ownership **2** (*padronanza*) mastery
possessóre *s. m.* possessor, owner, (*detentore*) holder
possìbile *agg.* possible
possibilìsmo *s. m.* possibilism
possibilità *s. f.* **1** possibility, opportunity, chance **2** *al pl.* (*mezzi*) means *pl.*
possibilménte *avv.* if possible
possidènte *s. m. e f.* property owner
pòsta *s. f.* **1** post, mail **2** (*ufficio*) post office **3** (*al gioco, fig.*) stake ♦ **fare la p. a qc.** to waylay sb.; **per p.** by mail; **p. aerea** air mail
postàle *agg.* postal, post (*attr.*), mail (*attr.*) ♦ **cartolina p.** postcard; **casella p.** POB (*postal office box*); **cassetta p.** letter box; **pacco p.** parcel
postazióne *s. f.* post, position
postbèllico *agg.* postwar (*attr.*)

postdatàre *v. tr.* to postdate
posteggiàre *v. tr. e intr.* to park
posteggiatóre *s. m.* car park attendant
postéggio *s. m.* car park, (*USA*) parking lot ♦ **p. di taxi** rank, (*USA*) stand
poster *s. m. inv.* poster
posterióre *agg.* **1** back, rear, hind, posterior **2** (*nel tempo*) later, following
posterità *s. f.* posterity
postìccio *agg.* artificial, false
posticipàre *v. tr.* to postpone
postìlla *s. f.* (marginal) note, gloss
postìno *s. m.* postman
postmodèrno *agg. e s. m.* postmodern
pósto *s. m.* **1** (*luogo*) place, spot **2** (*collocazione*) place **3** (*spazio*) space, room **4** (*posto a sedere*) seat **5** (*lavoro*) job, position **6** (*luogo con particolare funzione*) station, post ♦ **al p. di** instead of; **a p.** in order, tidy; **fuori p.** out of place, in the wrong place; **p. di blocco** roadblock
postrìbolo *s. m.* brothel
postulàto *s. m.* postulate
pòstumo **A** *agg.* posthumous **B** *s. m.* aftereffect
potàbile *agg.* drinkable
potàre *v. tr.* to prune, to cut down
potàssio *s. m.* potassium
potènte *agg.* **1** powerful, mighty **2** (*efficace*) potent, effective
potènza *s. f.* **1** power, might, (*forza*) strength **2** (*efficacia*) potency **3** (*stato*) power **4** (*mat.*) power **5** (*fis., tecnol.*) power, rating
potenziàle *agg.* potential
potenziàre *v. tr.* to strengthen, (*sviluppare*) to develop
potére (1) **A** *v. serv.* **1** (*avere la capacità, la forza, la facoltà di fare*) can (*indicativo e congiuntivo pres.*), could (*indicativo e congiuntivo pass., condiz.*), to be able (ES: **posso mangiare tutto ciò che voglio** I can eat all I like, **ieri notte non ho potuto dormire** yesterday night I could not sleep, **se parlasse italiano, potrei capirlo** if he should speak Italian, I could understand him) **2** (*avere la possibilità, il permesso di fare*) may, can (*indicativo e congiuntivo pres.*), might, could (*condiz., indicativo pass. nel discorso ind.*), to be able, to be allowed, to be permitted (ES: **posso entrare?** may I come in?, **chiese se poteva vederlo** he asked if he might (*o* could) see him) **3** (*essere probabile, possibile*) may, might, can, could, to be possible, to be likely (ES: **potrebbe esserci un errore** there might be a mistake, **posso avere torto** I may be wrong) **4** (*augurio, esortazione*) may, might, could (ES: **potrebbe almeno rispondere!** he might at least reply!) **B** *v. tr.* to have an effect
potére (2) *s. m.* **1** power **2** (*influenza*) influence, sway
pòvero **A** *agg.* **1** poor, needy **2** (*miserabile*) poor, unfortunate, wretched **3** (*scarso*) scanty, poor **4** (*semplice*) plain, bare **5** (*defunto*) late **B** *s. m.* poor man
povertà *s. f.* **1** poverty, indigence **2** (*scarsezza*) shortage, scarcity, lack
pozzànghera *s. f.* puddle
pózzo *s. m.* **1** well **2** (*miner.*) shaft
pragmàtico *agg.* pragmatic
pranzàre *v. intr.* to dine, to have dinner, (*a mezzogiorno*) to lunch, to have lunch ♦ **p. in casa/fuori** to dine in/out
prànzo *s. m.* dinner, (*di mezzogiorno*) lunch ♦ **dopo p.** after lunch
pràssi *s. f.* praxis, usual procedure
praterìa *s. f.* grassland, (*USA*) prairie
pràtica *s. f.* **1** practice **2** (*esperienza*) experience **3** *al pl.* (*trattative*) negotiations **4** (*incartamento*) file, dossier
praticàbile *agg.* practicable, (*fattibile*) feasible
praticaménte *avv.* practically
praticànte **A** *agg.* practising **B** *s. m. e f.* apprentice
praticàre **A** *v. tr.* **1** (*mettere in pratica*) to practise, to put into practice **2** (*esercitare*) to practice, to follow **3** (*frequentare*) to frequent **4** (*fare*) to make **B** *v. intr.* **1** to practise **2** (*frequentare*) to associate with
praticità *s. f.* practicality
pràtico *agg.* **1** practical **2** (*esperto*) experienced, skilled
pràto *s. m.* meadow, grass, (*all'inglese*) lawn
preàmbolo *s. m.* preamble
preannunciàre *v. tr.* to announce
preavvisàre *v. tr.* to inform in advance, to forewarn
preavvìso *s. m.* notice, forewarning
prebèllico *agg.* prewar (*attr.*)
precarietà *s. f.* precariousness
precàrio *agg.* **1** precarious **2** (*temporaneo*) temporary
precauzióne *s. f.* **1** precaution **2** (*cautela*) caution, care
precedènte **A** *agg.* preceding, previous,

former **B** *s. m.* **1** precedent **2** *al pl.* record
precedènza *s. f.* **1** precedence, priority **2** (*di traffico*) right of way
precèdere **A** *v. tr.* to precede, to come before **B** *v. intr.* to precede, to come first
precètto *s. m.* rule, precept
precettóre *s. m.* tutor
precipitàre **A** *v. tr.* **1** to precipitate, to throw down **2** (*affrettare*) to rush, to hasten **B** *v. intr.* **1** to fall, (*aer.*) to crash **2** (*evolvere negativamente*) to come to a head **C** *v. intr. pron.* **1** to throw oneself **2** (*affrettarsi*) to rush, to dash
precipitazióne *s. f.* precipitation
precipitóso *agg.* **1** precipitous, headlong **2** (*avventato*) hasty, rash
precipìzio *s. m.* precipice ♦ **correre a p.** to run headlong
precisaménte *avv.* **1** precisely **2** (*esattamente*) exactly
precisàre *v. tr.* to specify, to tell precisely
precisazióne *s. f.* precise statement, precise information
precisióne *s. f.* **1** precision, accuracy **2** (*esattezza*) preciseness
precìso *agg.* **1** (*accurato*) careful **2** (*esatto*) precise, exact **3** (*definito*) definite, particular **4** (*identico*) identical **5** (*in punto*) sharp
preclùdere *v. tr.* to preclude, to bar
preclusióne *s. f.* preclusion
precòce *agg.* **1** precocious, (*anticipato*) early **2** (*prematuro*) premature
precocità *s. f.* precocity
precolombiàno *agg.* pre-Columbian
preconcètto **A** *agg.* preconceived **B** *s. m.* preconception
precórrere *v. tr.* to anticipate
precursóre *s. m.* precursor, forerunner
prèda *s. f.* **1** prey, quarry **2** (*bottino*) booty
predatóre **A** *agg.* predatory **B** *s. m.* (*solo animale*) predator
predecessóre *s. m.* predecessor
predèlla *s. f.* platform, dais, (*di altare*) predella
predellìno *s. m.* footboard
predestinàre *v. tr.* to destine, to predestinate
predestinazióne *s. f.* predestination
predeterminàre *v. tr.* to predetermine
predétto *agg.* above-mentioned, aforesaid
prèdica *s. f.* **1** sermon **2** (*ramanzina*) telling-off, lecture
predicàre *v. tr. e intr.* to preach
predicàto *s. m.* predicate
predicatóre *s. m.* preacher
predicazióne *s. f.* preaching
predilètto *agg. e s. m.* favourite
predilezióne *s. f.* fondness, partiality
predilìgere *v. tr.* to prefer
predìre *v. tr.* to foretell, to predict
predispórre **A** *v. tr.* **1** to predispose, to induce **2** (*preparare in anticipo*) to arrange in advance, to plan **B** *v. rifl.* to prepare oneself
predisposizióne *s. f.* **1** (*med.*) predisposition **2** (*inclinazione*) bent **3** (*preparazione*) arrangement
predizióne *s. f.* prediction
predominànte *agg.* predominant, prevailing
predominàre *v. intr.* to predominate, to prevail
predomìnio *s. m.* predominance, (*supremazia*) supremacy
preesistènte *agg.* preexistent
preesìstere *v. intr.* to preexist
prefabbricàto *agg.* prefabricated
prefazióne *s. f.* preface, foreword
preferènza *s. f.* preference
preferenziàle *agg.* preferential
preferìbile *agg.* preferable
preferibilménte *avv.* preferably
preferìre *v. tr.* to prefer, to like better
prefètto *s. m.* prefect
prefettùra *s. f.* prefecture
prefìggere *v. tr.* to fix, to establish (in advance)
prefiguràre *v. tr.* to prefigure
prefisso *s. m.* **1** prefix **2** (*tel.*) (area) code
pregàre *v. tr.* **1** to pray **2** (*chiedere*) to ask, to beg
pregévole *agg.* valuable
preghièra *s. f.* **1** prayer **2** (*richiesta*) request
pregiàto *agg.* valuable
prègio *s. m.* **1** (*stima*) esteem, regard **2** (*valore*) value **3** (*buona qualità*) (good) quality, (*merito*) merit
pregiudicàre *v. tr.* to prejudice, to compromise, (*danneggiare*) to harm, to damage
pregiudicàto *s. m.* previous offender
pregiudìzio *s. m.* prejudice
pregnànte *agg.* pregnant
prégno *agg.* **1** pregnant **2** (*fig.*) full, rich
prègo *inter.* **1** (*rispondendo a chi ringrazia*) don't mention it!, you're welcome **2** (*per invitare a ripetere*) pardon? **3** (*per invitare*

ad accomodarsi) please **4** (*cedendo il passo*) after you
pregustàre *v. tr.* to foretaste, to anticipate
preistòria *s. f.* prehistory
preistòrico *agg.* prehistoric
prelàto *s. m.* prelate
prelevàre *v. tr.* to take, to draw, (*danaro*) to withdraw
prelibàto *agg.* delicious
prelièvo *s. m.* **1** (*banca*) withdrawal, drawing **2** (*med.*) sample
preliminàre *agg. e s. m.* preliminary
prelùdio *s. m.* prelude
prematrimoniàle *agg.* premarital, pre-marriage (*attr.*)
prematùro *agg.* premature
premeditazióne *s. f.* premeditation
prèmere A *v. tr.* **1** to press **2** (*incalzare*) to bear down on **B** *v. intr.* **1** to press **2** (*importare*) to matter, to be of interest
preméssa *s. f.* introduction, preamble, premise
preméttere *v. tr.* **1** to state beforehand **2** (*mettere prima*) to put before, to place before ♦ **premesso che ...** granted that ...
premiàre *v. tr.* **1** to give a prize to, to award a prize to **2** (*ricompensare*) to reward, to recompense
premiazióne *s. f.* prize-giving
preminènte *agg.* pre-eminent, prominent
prèmio *s. m.* **1** prize, award **2** (*ricompensa*) reward **3** (*di assicurazione*) premium **4** (*indennità*) bonus ♦ **p. Nobel** Nobel prize
premistóppa *s. m. inv.* stuffing box
premonitóre *agg.* premonitory
premorìre *v. intr.* to die before (sb. else), to predecease
premunìre A *v. tr.* **1** to fortify **2** (*fig.*) to protect, to preserve **B** *v. rifl.* to protect oneself
premùra *s. f.* **1** (*sollecitudine*) care **2** (*gentilezza*) kindness **3** (*fretta*) hurry, haste
premuróso *agg.* solicitous
prenatàle *agg.* antenatal, prenatal
prèndere A *v. tr.* **1** to take, (*acchiappare*) to catch, (*afferrare*) to seize **2** (*assumere*) to take over, to assume, (*personale*) to employ, to engage **3** (*ottenere, guadagnare*) to get, to earn **4** (*sorprendere*) to catch, to take **5** (*comprare*) to buy, (*far pagare*) to charge **6** (*occupare*) to take up **7** (*una malattia*) to catch, to get **B** *v. intr.* **1** to take **2** (*attecchire*) to take root **3** (*far presa*) to set
prenotàre *v. tr.* to book, to reserve ♦ **p. una stanza in un albergo** to book a room at a hotel; **p. un posto in treno** to book a seat on a train
prenotazióne *s. f.* booking, reservation ♦ **annullare una p.** to cancel a booking
preoccupànte *agg.* worrying
preoccupàre A *v. tr.* to worry, to trouble **B** *v. intr. pron.* **1** to worry, to be troubled **2** (*occuparsi*) to make sure
preoccupàto *agg.* worried, troubled
preoccupazióne *s. f.* worry, care
preparàre A *v. tr.* to prepare, to make ready, (*predisporre*) to arrange **B** *v. rifl.* **1** to prepare oneself, to get ready **2** (*accingersi*) to be about to **C** *v. intr. pron.* (*essere prossimo*) to be in store
preparatìvo *s. m.* preparation
preparazióne *s. f.* **1** preparation **2** (*esperienza*) qualification
preponderànte *agg.* preponderant, predominant
prepórre *v. tr.* **1** to place before **2** (*mettere a capo*) to put at the head of, to put in charge
preposizióne *s. f.* preposition
prepotènte *agg.* overbearing
prepotére *s. m.* excessive power
prerogatìva *s. f.* prerogative
présa *s. f.* **1** taking **2** (*cattura*) seizure, capture **3** (*stretta*) hold **4** (*pizzico*) pinch **5** (*d'acqua, d'aria*) intake **6** (*elettr.*) tap, socket ♦ **far p.** (*di cemento*) to set, (*di ancora*) to hold; **macchina da p.** camera; **p. di posizione** stand; **p. in giro** joke
presàgio *s. m.* presage, omen
presagìre *v. tr.* **1** (*prevedere*) to foresee, to predict **2** (*essere presagio di*) to forebode
prèsbite *agg.* long-sighted
presbiteriàno *agg.* Presbyterian
presbitèrio *s. m.* presbytery
prescégliere *v. tr.* to select, to choose
prescìndere *v. intr.* to leave aside ♦ **a p. da ciò** apart from this
prescrìvere *v. tr.* to prescribe
prescrizióne *s. f.* **1** (*dir., med.*) prescription **2** (*precetto*) precept, regulation
presentàbile *agg.* presentable
presentàre A *v. tr.* **1** (*mostrare*) to present, to show, (*esibire*) to produce **2** (*inoltrare*) to put in, to present, (*proporre*) to propose **3** (*offrire, porgere*) to present, to offer **4**

(*far conoscere*) to introduce, to present **5** (*uno spettacolo*) to present **B** *v. rifl.* **1** to present oneself **2** (*farsi conoscere*) to introduce oneself **C** *v. intr. pron.* **1** (*offrirsi*) to arise, (*capitare*) to occur **2** (*sembrare*) to seem, to appear
presentatóre *s. m.* presenter
presentazióne *s. f.* **1** presentation **2** (*il far conoscere una persona a un'altra*) introduction
presènte (1) A *agg.* **1** present **2** (*attuale*) present, current **3** (*questo*) this **B** *s. m.* **1** (*tempo*) present (time), (*gramm.*) present (tense) **2** *al pl.* those present
presènte (2) *s. m.* (*dono*) present, gift
presentiménto *s. m.* foreboding, presentiment
presènza *s. f.* **1** presence **2** (*frequenza*) attendance
presenziàre *v. tr. e intr.* to be present (at)
presèpe *s. m.* crib
preservàre *v. tr.* to preserve, to keep
preservatìvo A *agg.* preservative **B** *s. m.* prophylactic, condom
prèside *s. m. e f.* head, (*di facoltà*) dean
presidènte *s. m.* president, (*di assemblea*) chairman
presidènza *s. f.* presidency, (*di assemblea*) chairmanship
presidenziàle *agg.* presidential
presidiàre *v. tr.* **1** (*mil.*) to garrison **2** (*est.*) to protect, to guard
presìdio *s. m.* **1** (*mil.*) garrison **2** (*salvaguardia*) protection, defence **3** (*ausilio*) aid
presièdere *v. tr. e intr.* to preside, to be at the head of, to act as chairman of
prèssa *s. f.* press
pressappochìsmo *s. m.* inaccuracy
pressappòco *avv.* about, more or less
pressàre *v. tr.* to press
pressióne *s. f.* pressure ♦ **p. del sangue** blood pressure; **pentola a p.** pressure cooker
prèsso A *avv.* nearby, near, close (at hand) **B** *prep.* **1** (*vicino a*) near, not far from **2** (*accanto, a fianco a*) beside, next to, by **3** (*a casa di, da*) with, in, at, (*negli indirizzi*) c/o (*care of*) **4** (*fra*) among, with **C** *s. m. al pl.* (*vicinanze*) neighbourhood, (*dintorni*) outskirts *pl.*
pressoché *avv.* almost, nearly, all but, practically
pressurizzàre *v. tr.* to pressurize
prestabilìre *v. tr.* to arrange beforehand, to fix
prestànte *agg.* good-looking, handsome
prestàre A *v. tr.* **1** (*dare in prestito*) to lend **2** (*dare*) to give **B** *v. rifl.* **1** (*essere disponibile*) to lend oneself, (*rendersi utile*) to help **2** (*acconsentire*) to consent **C** *v. intr. pron.* (*essere adatto*) to be fit
prestazióne *s. f.* performance
prestigiatóre *s. m.* conjurer
prestìgio *s. m.* **1** (*influenza*) prestige **2** (*fascino*) glamour **3** (*prestidigitazione*) sleight-of-hand ♦ **giochi di p.** conjuring tricks
prestigióso *agg.* prestigious
prèstito *s. m.* loan ♦ **dare in p.** to lend; **prendere in p.** to borrow
prèsto *avv.* **1** (*in breve tempo*) soon, in a short time, before long **2** (*di buon'ora*) early **3** (*in fretta*) quickly ♦ **p.!** quick!, hurry up!
presùmere *v. tr.* to presume, to think
presuntuóso *agg.* presumptuous, conceited
presunzióne *s. f.* **1** (*supposizione*) presumption **2** (*boria*) conceit
presuppórre *v. tr.* **1** to presuppose **2** (*supporre*) to suppose, to assume
presuppósto *s. m.* **1** (*premessa*) assumption **2** (*condizione necessaria*) presupposition, requirement
prète *s. m.* priest
pretendènte *s. m. e f.* **1** pretender **2** (*corteggiatore*) suitor
pretèndere A *v. tr.* **1** to claim, to pretend **2** (*esigere*) to expect, to require **B** *v. intr.* to pretend
pretenzióso *agg.* pretentious
pretésa *s. f.* **1** pretension, claim **2** (*richiesta*) claim, demand ♦ **senza pretese** unpretentious
pretèsto *s. m.* **1** pretext **2** (*occasione*) occasion, opportunity
prevalènte *agg.* prevalent, prevailing
prevalènza *s. f.* prevalence, priority
prevalére *v. intr.* **1** to prevail **2** (*essere in numero superiore*) to outnumber
prevaricàre *v. intr.* to abuse (one's office)
prevedére *v. tr.* **1** to foresee, to foretell, to anticipate, (*di tempo atmosferico*) to forecast **2** (*stabilire*) to provide (for)
prevedìbile *agg.* predictable
prevenìre *v. tr.* **1** (*precedere*) to precede, to arrive before, (*anticipare*) to anticipate, to

forestall **2** (*cercare di evitare*) to prevent **3** (*preavvertire*) to inform, to forewarn **4** (*influenzare negativamente*) to prejudice
preventivo A *agg.* **1** preventive, **2** (*econ.*) extimated **B** *s. m.* estimate, budget
prevenùto *agg.* prejudiced
prevenzióne *s. f.* **1** prevention, (*di malattia*) prophylaxis **2** (*pregiudizio*) prejudice, bias
previdènte *agg.* provident, wise
previdènza *s. f.* providence ♦ **p. sociale** social security
previsióne *s. f.* forecast, prevision, expectation ♦ **previsioni del tempo** weather forecast
preziosìsmo *s. m.* preciosity
prezióso *agg.* precious
prezzémolo *s. m.* parsley
prèzzo *s. m.* price, (*costo*) cost, (*tariffa*) rate, fee
prigióne *s. f.* **1** prison, jail **2** (*pena*) imprisonment
prigionìa *s. f.* imprisonment
prigionièro A *agg.* imprisoned **B** *s. m.* prisoner
prìma (1) A *avv.* **1** (*nel tempo*) before **2** (*in anticipo*) beforehand, in advance **3** (*più presto*) earlier, sooner **4** (*un tempo*) formerly, once **5** (*per prima cosa*) first, (*in primo luogo*) first of all **6** (*nello spazio*) first, before **B** *prep.* **p. di** before, ahead of **C** *cong.* **p. che** before
prìma (2) *s. f.* **1** (*prima classe*) first class **2** (*teatro*) first night, (*cin.*) première **3** (*autom.*) first gear **4** (*sport*) basic position
primàrio A *agg.* **1** primary **2** (*principale*) main, leading **B** *s. m.* head physician
primàte *s. m.* primate
primàto *s. m.* **1** primacy, supremacy **2** (*sport*) record
primavèra *s. f.* spring
primaverìle *agg.* spring (*attr.*)
primeggiàre *v. intr.* to excel
primitivìsmo *s. m.* primitivism
primitìvo *agg.* **1** primitive **2** (*precedente*) original
primìzia *s. f.* firstling
prìmo A *agg. num. ord.* **1** first **2** (*principale*) main, principal, chief **3** (*iniziale*) early, first **4** (*prossimo*) next **B** *s. m.* **1** (the) first, (*fra due*) the former **2** (*il migliore*) (the) best, (the) top **3** (*primo piatto*) first course **4** (*minuto primo*) minute
primogènito *agg. e s. m.* first-born
primordiàle *agg.* **1** primordial **2** (*est.*) early
prìmula *s. f.* primula, primrose
principàle A *agg.* principal, chief, main **B** *s. m.* master, manager
principalménte *avv.* principally, chiefly, mainly
principàto *s. m.* principality
prìncipe *s. m.* prince
principéssa *s. f.* princess
principiànte *s. m. e f.* beginner
princìpio *s. m.* **1** (*inizio*) beginning **2** (*norma*) principle **3** *al pl.* (*rudimenti*) principles *pl.* **4** (*origine, causa*) origin, cause **5** (*chim.*) principle
prióre *s. m.* prior
priorità *s. f.* priority
prìsma *s. m.* prism
privàre A *v. tr.* to deprive **B** *v. rifl.* to deprive oneself, (*negarsi*) to deny oneself
privataménte *avv.* in private
privàto A *agg.* **1** private **2** (*privo*) deprived, bereft **B** *s. m.* private person
privazióne *s. f.* **1** (*il privare*) deprivation **2** (*perdita*) loss **3** (*disagio*) hardship, privation
privilegiàre *v. tr.* to favour
privilègio *s. m.* **1** privilege **2** (*onore*) honour
prìvo *agg.* deprived (of), devoid (of), (*mancante*) lacking (in)
pro (1) *prep.* for, for the benefit of
pro (2) *s. m.* advantage, benefit ♦ **il p. e il contro** the pros and cons
probàbile *agg.* probable, likely
probabilità *s. f.* probability, chance
probabilménte *avv.* probably, likely
problèma *s. m.* problem
problemàtica *s. f.* problems *pl.*
problemàtico *agg.* problematic
probòscide *s. f.* trunk
procacciàre *v. tr.* to procure, to get
procèdere *v. intr.* **1** to proceed, to go on, to advance **2** (*accingersi*) to start **3** (*comportarsi*) to behave, (*trattare*) to deal
procediménto *s. m.* **1** (*corso*) course **2** (*metodo*) process, procedure **3** (*dir.*) proceedings *pl.*
procedùra *s. f.* procedure
processàre *v. tr.* to try
processióne *s. f.* procession
procèsso *s. m.* **1** (*dir.*) trial, action, proceedings *pl.* **2** (*fase, metodo*) process

procióne *s. m.* racoon
proclàma *s. m.* proclamation
proclamàre *v. tr.* to proclaim
proclamazióne *s. f.* proclamation, declaration
procreàre *v. tr.* to procreate, to beget
procùra *s. f.* proxy
procuràre *v. tr.* **1** to procure, to get, to obtain **2** (*causare*) to cause, to bring about **3** (*fare in modo che*) to try
procuratóre *s. m.* **1** proxy **2** (*dir.*) attorney
prodézza *s. f.* feat, exploit
prodigalità *s. f.* prodigality, extravagance
prodigàre **A** *v. tr.* to lavish **B** *v. rifl.* to do all one can
prodìgio *s. m.* prodigy, marvel, wonder
prodigióso *agg.* prodigious, portentous, wonderful
pròdigo *agg.* prodigal, extravagant
prodótto *s. m.* product, produce
prodùrre **A** *v. tr.* **1** (*generare*) to produce, to yield, to bear **2** (*fabbricare*) to produce, to make **3** (*causare*) to cause **B** *v. rifl.* to appear **C** *v. intr. pron.* to happen, to occur
produttività *s. f.* productivity
produttìvo *agg.* productive
produttóre *s. m.* producer
produzióne *s. f.* production
profanàre *v. tr.* to profane
profanatóre **A** *agg.* profaning **B** *s. m.* profaner
profàno **A** *agg.* **1** (*non sacro*) profane, secular **2** (*inesperto*) ignorant **B** *s. m.* layman
proferìre *v. tr.* to utter
professàre **A** *v. tr.* **1** to profess, to declare **2** (*esercitare*) to practise **B** *v. rifl.* to profess oneself
professionàle *agg.* professional, (*derivante da professione*) occupational
professióne *s. f.* profession
professionìsmo *s. m.* professionalism
professionìsta *s. m. e f.* professional
professóre *s. m.* teacher, (*di università*) professor
profèta *s. m.* prophet
profètico *agg.* prophetic(al)
profezìa *s. f.* prophecy
profìcuo *agg.* profitable
profilàre **A** *v. tr.* **1** to profile **2** (*orlare*) to border, to edge **B** *v. intr. pron.* **1** to be outlined **2** (*fig.*) to loom up
profilàssi *s. f.* prophylaxis
profilàttico **A** *agg.* prophylactic **B** *s. m.* prophylactic, condom
profìlo *s. m.* **1** (*del volto*) profile **2** (*linea di contorno*) outline **3** (*scient.*) profile **4** (*descrizione*) sketch
profittàre *v. tr.* to profit, to take advantage
profìtto *s. m.* **1** profit, benefit, advantage **2** (*econ.*) profit, gain
profondìmetro *s. m.* depth-gauge
profondità *s. f.* depth
profóndo *agg.* deep, profound
pròfugo *agg. e s. m.* refugee
profumàre **A** *v. tr.* to perfume, to scent **B** *v. intr.* to smell, to be fragrant **C** *v. rifl.* to put on scent, to perfume oneself
profumataménte *avv.* profusely, (*a caro prezzo*) dearly
profumàto *agg.* scented, fragrant
profumerìa *s. f.* **1** perfumery **2** (*negozio*) perfume shop
profùmo *s. m.* perfume, scent
profusióne *s. f.* profusion
progenitóre *s. m.* progenitor, ancestor
progettàre *v. tr.* **1** to plan **2** (*fare il progetto*) to plan, to design
progettazióne *s. f.* design
progettìsta *s. m. e f.* planner, designer
progètto *s. m.* plan, project, design
prògnosi *s. f.* prognosis
progràmma *s. m.* **1** programme, (*USA*) program, plan **2** (*scolastico*) syllabus, programme **3** (*inf.*) program
programmàre *v. tr.* to plan, to programme, to program
programmazióne *s. f.* programming, planning
progredìre *v. intr.* **1** to advance **2** (*fare progressi*) to progress, to make progress, to get on **3** (*migliorare*) to improve
progressióne *s. f.* progression
progressivaménte *avv.* progressively
progressìvo *agg.* progressive
progrèsso *s. m.* progress, (*sviluppo*) development
proibìre *v. tr.* **1** to forbid, to prohibit **2** (*impedire*) to prevent
proibitìvo *agg.* prohibitive
proibìto *agg.* forbidden, prohibited
proibizióne *s. f.* prohibition
proiettàre *v. tr.* **1** to project, to cast, to throw **2** (*geom.*) to project **3** (*film*) to show
proièttile *s. m.* bullet, shell
proiettóre *s. m.* **1** (*sorgente luminosa*) searchlight, floodlight **2** (*autom.*) light **3** (*fot., cin.*) projector
proiezióne *s. f.* projection

pròle *s. f.* children *pl.*
proletàrio *agg. e s. m.* proletarian
proliferàre *v. intr.* to proliferate
prolìfico *agg.* prolific
prolìsso *agg.* prolix, verbose
pròlogo *s. m.* prologue
prolùnga *s. f.* extension
prolungaménto *s. m.* prolongation, extension
prolungàre **A** *v. tr.* **1** to prolong, to extend **2** (*prorogare*) to delay **B** *v. intr. pron.* **1** to extend, to continue **2** (*dilungarsi*) to dwell
promemòria *s. m. inv.* memorandum, memo
proméssa *s. f.* promise
prométtere *v. tr. e intr.* to promise
prominènte *agg.* prominent
promiscuità *s. f.* promiscuity
promìscuo *agg.* promiscuous, mixed
promontòrio *s. m.* promontory, headland
promotóre *s. m.* promoter
promozióne *s. f.* promotion
promulgàre *v. tr.* to promulgate
promuòvere *v. tr.* **1** to promote **2** (*uno studente*) to pass
prònao *s. m.* pronaos
pronipóte *s. m. e f.* **1** (*di bisnonno*) great grandchild, (*di prozio*) grandnephew *m.*, granddaughter *f.* **2** *al pl.* (*discendenti*) descendants
pronóme *s. m.* pronoun
pronosticàre *v. tr.* to forecast, to prognosticate
pronòstico *s. m.* forecast, prognostic
prontaménte *avv.* readily, quickly
prontézza *s. f.* readiness, quickness
prónto *agg.* **1** ready, prepared **2** (*svelto*) prompt, quick, ready **3** (*incline*) inclined ♦ **p.!** (*al telefono*) hello!; **p. soccorso** first aid
prontuàrio *s. m.* manual, handbook
pronùncia *s. f.* pronunciation
pronunciàre **A** *v. tr.* **1** to pronounce, (*proferire*) to utter **2** (*dire*) to say, (*recitare*) to deliver **B** *v. intr. pron.* to pronounce, to declare one's opinion
pronunciàto *agg.* pronounced, (*spiccato*) strong
propagànda *s. f.* propaganda, (*pubblicità*) advertising
propagàre *v. tr. e intr. pron.* to propagate, to spread
propàggine *s. f.* **1** layer **2** (*diramazione*) offshoot
propèndere *v. intr.* to incline, to be inclined, to tend
propensióne *s. f.* propensity, propension, inclination
propènso *agg.* disposed, inclined
propilèo *s. m.* propylaeum
propinàre *v. tr.* to administer, (*cibo*) to dish up
propiziàre *v. tr.* to propitiate
propìzio *agg.* propitious
proponìbile *agg.* proposable
propórre *v. tr.* **1** to propose, (*suggerire*) to suggest **2** (*decidere*) to decide, to set **3** (*offrire*) to offer
proporzionàle *agg.* proportional
proporzionàre *v. tr.* to proportion
proporzióne *s. f.* **1** proportion, (*rapporto*) ratio **2** (*dimensione*) dimension, size
propòsito *s. m.* **1** purpose, intention, design **2** (*argomento*) subject ♦ **a p. di** with regard to
proposizióne *s. f.* clause
propósta *s. f.* proposal, (*offerta*) offer
proprietà *s. f.* **1** property, ownership **2** (*possedimento*) property, estate **3** (*caratteristica*) property, characteristic **4** (*i proprietari*) owners *pl.*
proprietàrio **A** *agg.* proprietary **B** *s. m.* owner
pròprio **A** *agg.* **1** (*possessivo*) one's (own), (*di lui*) his (own), (*di lei*) her (own), (*di cosa o animale*) its (own), (*di loro*) their (own) **2** (*caratteristico*) characteristic, particular, typical **3** (*appropriato, conveniente*) appropriate, suitable **4** (*letterale*) literal, exact **5** (*gramm., mat.*) proper **B** *pron. poss.* one's (own), (*di lui*) his (own), (*di lei*) hers, her (own), (*di cosa o animale*) its (own), (*di loro*) theirs, their (own) **C** *s. m.* one's own **D** *avv.* **1** (*davvero*) really, quite **2** (*precisamente*) just, exactly **3** (*affatto, in frasi neg.*) at all
propulsióne *s. f.* propulsion
pròroga *s. f.* **1** extension, delay **2** (*rinvio*) adjournment
prorogàre *v. tr.* **1** to extend, to prolong **2** (*rinviare*) to postpone, to delay
prorómpere *v. intr.* to burst (out)
pròsa *s. f.* **1** prose **2** (*opera in prosa*) prose work **3** (*teatro*) drama
prosàico *agg.* prosaic
prosciògliere *v. tr.* to release, to absolve
prosciugàre **A** *v. tr.* **1** to dry up, to drain **2** (*fig.*) to exhaust **B** *v. intr.* to dry up
prosciùtto *s. m.* ham

prosecuzióne *s. f.* prosecution, continuation
proseguiménto *s. m.* continuation
proseguìre **A** *v. tr.* to continue, to carry on **B** *v. intr.* to continue, to go on, to pursue
prosperàre *v. intr.* to prosper, to flourish, to boom
prosperità *s. f.* prosperity, affluence
pròspero *agg.* prosperous, flourishing
prosperóso *agg.* prosperous, flourishing
prospettàre **A** *v. tr.* to show, to point out **B** *v. intr. pron.* to appear
prospèttico *agg.* perspective
prospettìva *s. f.* **1** perspective **2** (*possibilità*) prospect
prospètto *s. m.* **1** (*facciata*) front **2** (*tabella*) table, (*riassunto*) summary
prospiciènte *agg.* facing, overlooking
prossimaménte *avv.* in a short time, before long
prossimità *s. f.* closeness, proximity
pròssimo **A** *agg.* **1** (*molto vicino*) near, close, at hand (*pred.*) **2** (*successivo*) next **B** *s. m.* neighbour
pròstilo *s. m.* prostyle
prostituìre **A** *v. tr.* to prostitute **B** *v. rifl.* to prostitute oneself, to sell oneself
prostitùta *s. f.* prostitute
prostituzióne *s. f.* prostitution
prostràre **A** *v. tr.* to prostrate, to exhaust **B** *v. rifl.* to prostrate oneself
protagonìsta *s. m. e f.* **1** protagonist **2** (*attore*) leading actor
protèggere **A** *v. tr.* **1** to protect, to shield, to shelter, to take care of **2** (*favorire*) to favour, to promote **B** *v. rifl.* to protect oneself
proteìna *s. f.* protein
protèndere **A** *v. tr.* to stretch out, to hold out **B** *v. rifl. e intr. pron.* to stretch out, to lean forward
pròtesi *s. f.* prothesis ♦ **p. dentaria** dental prothesis
protèsta *s. f.* protest
protestànte *agg. e s. m.* Protestant
protestantésimo *s. m.* Protestantism
protestàre *v. tr. e intr.* to protest
protettìvo *agg.* protective
protettóre *s. m.* protector, patron
protezióne *s. f.* **1** protection **2** (*patrocinio*) patronage
protezionìsmo *s. m.* protectionism
protocollàre *agg.* protocol (*attr.*)
protocòllo *s. m.* **1** protocol **2** (*registro*) record, register
protòtipo *s. m.* prototype
protràrre **A** *v. tr.* **1** to prolong, to extend **2** (*differire*) to postpone, to defer **B** *v. intr. pron.* to continue
protuberànza *s. f.* protuberance
pròva *s. f.* **1** (*esperimento, controllo*) trial, test **2** (*dimostrazione*) proof, (*elemento di prova*) evidence **3** (*tentativo*) try **4** (*risultato*) result **5** (*di abito*) fitting **6** (*teatro*) rehearsal ♦ **a prova di** proof (*attr.*)
provàre **A** *v. tr.* **1** (*dimostrare*) to prove, to demonstrate, to show **2** (*tentare*) to try, (*sperimentare*) to experience **3** (*sentire*) to feel **4** (*mettere alla prova*) to try, to test **5** (*un vestito*) to try on **6** (*teatro*) to rehearse **7** (*assaggiare*) to taste **B** *v. intr. pron.* to try, to attempt
provenièenza *s. f.* **1** origin, provenance **2** (*fonte*) source
provenìre *v. intr.* **1** to come **2** (*avere origine*) to derive, to originate
provènto *s. m.* proceeds *pl.*, income
provenzàle *agg.* Provençal
proverbiàle *s. m.* **1** proverbial **2** (*notorio*) notorious
provèrbio *s. m.* proverb, saying
provétta *s. f.* test tube
provìncia *s. f.* province, district
provinciàle *agg. e s. m. e f.* provincial
provincialìsmo *s. m.* provincialism
provocànte *agg.* provocative
provocàre *v. tr.* **1** to provoke **2** (*suscitare*) to cause, to induce
provocatòrio *agg.* provocative
provocazióne *s. f.* provocation
provvedére **A** *v. tr.* **1** (*fornire*) to provide, to supply **2** (*disporre*) to prepare, to get ready **B** *v. intr.* **1** to provide (for), to arrange for **2** (*prendersi cura*) to take care of **C** *v. rifl.* to provide oneself
provvediménto *s. m.* measure, action, provision
provvidènza *s. f.* **1** providence **2** (*provvedimento*) provision
provvidenziàle *agg.* providential
provvigióne *s. f.* commission
provvisòrio *agg.* provisional, temporary
provvìsta *s. f.* provision, supply
prùa *s. f.* bow
prudènte *agg.* prudent, cautious
prudènza *s. f.* prudence, caution
prùdere *v. intr.* to itch, to be itchy
prùgna *s. f.* plum ♦ **p. secca** prune

prùno *s. m.* blackthorn
pruriginóso *agg.* **1** itchy **2** (*fig.*) exciting
prurìto *s. m.* itch
pseudònimo *s. m.* pseudonym, (*di scrittore*) pen name
psìche *s. f.* psyche
psichiàtra *s. m. e f.* psychiatrist
psichiatrìa *s. f.* psychiatry
psichiàtrico *agg.* psychiatric
psìchico *agg.* psychic(al), mental
psicoanàlisi *s. f.* psychoanalysis
psicoanalìsta *s. m. e f.* psychoanalyst
psicofàrmaco *s. m.* psychotropic drug
psicologìa *s. f.* psychology
psicologicaménte *avv.* psychologically
psicològico *agg.* psychological
psicòlogo *s. m.* psychologist
psicòsi *s. f.* psychosis
pubblicàre *v. tr.* to publish, to issue
pubblicazióne *s. f.* publication, issue
pubblicità *s. f.* **1** publicity **2** (*propaganda commerciale*) advertising
pubblicitàrio *agg.* advertising ♦ **annuncio p.** ad; **spazio p.** spot
pubblicizzàre *v. tr.* to publicize, to advertize
pùbblico **A** *agg.* public, (*dello stato*) state (*attr.*) **B** *s. m.* **1** public **2** (*uditorio*) audience **3** (*vita pubblica*) public life
pùbe *s. m.* pubis
pubertà *s. f.* puberty
pudìco *agg.* modest
pudóre *s. m.* modesty, decency, (*vergogna*) shame
puericultùra *s. f.* puericulture
puerìle *agg.* childish
pugilàto *s. m.* boxing
pùgile *s. m.* boxer
pugnalàre *v. tr.* to stab
pugnàle *s. m.* dagger
pùgno *s. m.* **1** fist **2** (*colpo*) punch, blow **3** (*manciata*) fistful, handful
pùlce *s. f.* flea
pulcìno *s. m.* chick
pulédro *s. m.* colt
puléggia *s. f.* pulley
pulìre *v. tr.* to clean
pulìta *s. f.* clean, cleaning
pulìto *agg.* **1** clean **2** (fig.) clear, honest
pulizìa *s. f.* **1** (*il pulire*) cleaning **2** (*l'essere pulito*) cleanliness, cleanness
pùllman *s. m. inv.* coach
pullòver *s. m. inv.* pullover
pullulàre *v. intr.* **1** to spring up **2** (*essere gremito*) to swarm, to teem
pulmìno *s. m.* minibus
pùlpito *s. m.* pulpit
pulsànte **A** *agg.* pulsating **B** *s. m.* pushbutton
pulsàre *v. intr.* to pulsate, to beat
pulsazióne *s. f.* pulsation, throbbing
pulvìno *s. m.* dosseret, pulvino
pulvìscolo *s. m.* (fine) dust ♦ **p. atmosferico** motes
pùma *s. m.* puma
pungènte *agg.* **1** prickly **2** (*fig.*) biting, sharp
pùngere *v. tr.* to prick, to sting
pungiglióne *s. f.* sting
punìre *s. f.* to punish
punizióne *s. f.* **1** punishment **2** (*sport*) penalty
pùnta *s. f.* **1** point **2** (*estremità*) tip, end **3** (*cima*) top, peak **4** (*promontorio*) cape, headland **5** (*di trapano*) drill **6** (*massima intensità*) peak **7** (*piccola quantità*) touch, pinch
puntàle *s. m.* ferrule
puntàre **A** *v. tr.* **1** (*dirigere*) to point, to direct **2** (*mirare*) to point, to aim **3** (*poggiare, spingere*) to put, to push **4** (*scommettere*) to bet, to wager **5** (*di cane*) to set, to point **6** (*guardare fissamente*) to stare at **B** *v. intr.* **1** (*dirigersi*) to head **2** (*aspirare a*) to aim **3** (*fare assegnamento*) to count (on)
puntàta (1) *s. f.* **1** (*somma scommessa*) bet, stake **2** (*breve visita*) flying visit
puntàta (2) *s. f.* (*di scritto*) instalment, (*TV, radio*) episode
punteggiatùra *s. f.* punctuation
puntéggio *s. m.* score
puntellàre *v. tr.* **1** to prop (up) **2** (*fig.*) to back up, to support
puntèllo *s. m.* prop, support
puntìglio *s. m.* stubbornness ♦ **per p.** out of pique
puntiglióso *agg.* stubborn, obstinate
puntìna *s. f.* **1** (*da disegno*) drawing pin **2** (*mecc.*) point
puntìno *s. m.* dot
pùnto *s. m.* **1** point **2** (*cucito, maglia*) stitch **3** (*macchiolina*) dot **4** (*segno d'interpunzione*) full stop ♦ **due punti** colon; **mettere a p.** to set up, to adjust; **p. e virgola** semicolon
puntuàle *agg.* **1** punctual, on time (*pred.*) **2** (*accurato*) precise, careful
puntualità *s. f.* **1** punctuality **2** (*preci-*

sione) precision
puntùra *s. f.* **1** (*di ago, spina*) prick, (*di insetto*) sting, bite **2** (*iniezione*) injection, shot (*fam.*)
punzecchiàre **A** *v. tr.* **1** to sting, to bite **2** (*stuzzicare*) to tease **B** *v. rifl. rec.* to tease each other
pupàzzo *s. m.* puppet
pupìlla *s. f.* pupil
pupìllo *s. m.* **1** (*dir*) ward **2** (*favorito*) favourite
puraménte *avv.* **1** purely, merely **2** (*solamente*) just, only
purché *cong.* provided (that), on condition that, as long as
pùre **A** *avv.* **1** also, too, as well, (*perfino*) even **2** (*concessivo*) please, as you like, certainly **B** *cong.* **1** (*anche se*) even if, (*sebbene*) even though **2** (*tuttavia, eppure*) but, yet ♦ **entra p.!** please come in!; **pur di** just to
purè *s. m.* mash, purée ♦ **p. di patate** mashed potatoes
purézza *s. f.* purity
pùrga *s. f.* **1** laxative **2** (*fig.*) purge
purgànte *agg. e s. m.* laxative
purgàre *v. tr.* **1** to give a laxative to **2** (*purificare*) to purge, to purify **3** (*espurgare*) to expurgate
purgativo *agg.* laxative
purgatòrio *s. m.* purgatory
purificàre *v. tr.* to purify
purìsmo *s. m.* purism
puritanésimo *s. m.* Puritanism
puritàno *agg. e s. m.* Puritan
pùro *agg.* **1** pure **2** (*semplice*) sheer, mere ♦ **per p. caso** by mere chance
purtròppo *avv.* unfortunately
pus *s. m. inv.* pus
pùstola *s. f.* pustule
putifèrio *s. m.* row, mess
putrefàre *v. intr. e intr. pron.* to putrefy, to go bad, to decompose
putrefazióne *s. f.* putrefaction, rot, corruption
pùtrido *agg.* rotten, putrid
puttàna *s. f.* whore
pùtto *s. m.* putto
pùzza *s. f.* stench, stink, bad smell
puzzàre *v. intr.* to stink, to smell bad
pùzzo *s. m.* stench, stink, bad smell
pùzzola *s. f.* polecat
puzzolènte *agg.* stinking, bad-smelling

Q

qua *avv.* here ♦ **al di q. di** on this side of; **eccomi q.** here I am; **q. e là** here and there; **q. fuori** out here; **q. giù** down here
quàcchero *agg. e s. m.* Quaker
quadèrno *s. m.* exercise-book, copy-book
quadrangolàre *agg.* quadrangular
quadrànte *s. m.* quadrant, (*di orologio*) dial
quadràre **A** *v. tr.* **1** to square **2** (*i conti*) to balance **B** *v. intr.* **1** (*essere esatto*) to balance **2** (*essere pertinente*) to fit, to suit
quadràto **A** *agg.* **1** square **2** (*fig.*) well-balanced, sound **B** *s. m.* **1** square **2** (*box*) ring
quadrétto *s. m.* **1** small square, small check **2** (*scenetta*) scene ♦ **a quadretti** (*di carta*) squared, (*di stoffa*) check(ed)
quadricromìa *s. f.* four-colour process
quadriennàle *agg.* **1** quadriennial, four-year (*attr*) **2** (*che si svolge ogni 4 anni*) quadriennial, four-yearly (*attr*)
quadrifòglio *s. m.* **1** four-leaved clover **2** (*arch.*) quatrefoil
quadrimestràle *agg.* **1** four-monthly (*attr*) **2** (*che si compie ogni quadrimestre*) quarterly
quadrimèstre *s. m.* period of four months
quadrimotóre *s. m.* four-engined aircraft
quàdro (1) *agg.* square
quàdro (2) *s. m.* **1** (*pittura*) picture, painting **2** (*descrizione*) picture, description, outline **3** (*vista, spettacolo*) sight, scene **4** (*quadrato*) square **5** (*tabella*) table **6** (*tecnol.*) board, panel **7** *al pl.* (*mil., pol.*) cadre, (*d'azienda*) management **8** *al pl.* (*carte da gioco*) diamonds
quadrùpede *agg. e s. m.* quadruped
quadruplicàre *v. tr. e intr. pron.* to quadruple
quàdruplo *agg. e s. m.* quadruple
quaggiù *avv.* down here
quàglia *s. f.* quail
quàlche *agg. indef.* **1** a few, some, (*in frasi interr.*) any **2** (*un certo*) some, a certain amount of **3** (*quale che sia*) some, (*in frasi interr.*) any ♦ **da q. parte** somewhere, anywhere; **fra q. minuto** in a few minutes; **in q. modo** somehow or other; **q. altro** some/any other, (*in più*) some/any more; **q. volta** sometimes
qualcòsa *pron. indef.* **1** (*in frasi afferm. o interr. con valore positivo*) something **2** (*in frasi neg. e dubit.*) anything
qualcùno **A** *pron. indef.* **1** (*in frasi afferm. o interr. con valore positivo*) (*persona*) somebody, someone, (*persona o cosa*) some **2** (*in frasi interr. e dubit.*) (*persona*) anybody, anyone, (*persona o cosa*) any **3** (*alcuni*) (*persona*) some (people), any (people), a few (people), (*persona o cosa*) some, any **B** *s. m.* (*persona importante*) somebody ♦ **q. altro** some/any other, (*un'altra persona*) somebody/anybody else, (*uno in più*) some/any more
quàle **A** *agg.* **1** (*interr.*) (*fra un numero limitato*) which, (*fra un numero indeterminato*) what **2** (*escl.*) what **3** (*rel.*) (*spesso correlato con 'tale'*) (just) as **4** (*qualunque*) whatever **B** *pron.* **1** (*interr.*) (*fra un numero limitato*) which, (*fra un numero indeterminato*) what **2** (*rel. riferito a persone*) (*sogg.*) who, that, (*compl. ogg. e ind.*) who, that, whom, (*poss.*) whose **3** (*rel. riferito a cose o animali*) which, that, (*poss.*) of which, whose **C** *avv.* (*in qualità di*) as
qualìfica *s. f.* **1** qualification **2** (*giudizio*) appraisal **3** (*titolo*) title
qualificàre **A** *v. tr.* **1** to qualify **2** (*definire*) to describe **3** (*caratterizzare*) to characterize **B** *v. rifl.* **1** to qualify **2** (*presentarsi*) to introduce oneself
qualificatìvo *agg.* qualifying
qualificazióne *s. f.* qualification
qualità *s. f.* **1** quality, (*proprietà*) property **2** (*genere*) kind, sort **3** (*ufficio, carica*) capacity
qualóra *cong.* if, in case
qualsìasi *agg. indef.* → **qualunque**
qualùnque *agg. indef.* **1** any **2** (*mediocre*) ordinary, common **3** (*quale che sia*) whatever, (*riferito a un numero limitato*) whichever
quàndo **A** *avv.* when **B** *cong.* **1** when **2** (*ogni volta che*) whenever **3** (*mentre*) while **4** (*condizionale o causale*) when, since, if ♦ **da q.** since; **da q.?** since when?; **fino a q.** till, as long as
quantità *s. f.* quantity ♦ **una (grande) q. di** a lot of

quantitatìvo **A** *agg.* quantitative **B** *s. m.* quantity, amount

quànto **A** *agg.* **1** (*interr.*) how much, *pl.* how many, (*quanto tempo?*) how long (ES: **q. pane c'è?** how much bread is there?, **q. tempo ci vuole per arrivare alla stazione?** how long does it take to get to the station?) **2** (*in frasi ellittiche*) how much, (*di tempo*) how long (o *idiom.*) (ES: **q. costa?** how much is it?, **q. c'è da Milano a Venezia?** how far is it from Milan to Venice?, **quanti ne abbiamo oggi?** what is the date today?) **3** (*escl.*) what (a lot of), how (ES: **quanti dischi hai!** what a lot of records you have!) **4** (*tutto quello che*) as ... as (ES: **avrai tanto aiuto q. te ne serve** you'll have as much help as you need) **B** *avv.* **1** (*interr.*) (*con agg. e avv.*) how, (*con v.*) how much (ES: **q. è grande la casa?** how big is the house?, **q. hai studiato oggi?** how much have you studied today?) **2** (*escl.*) (*con agg.*) how, (*con v.*) how (much) (ES: **q. è bello!** how beautiful it is!, **q. mi piace!** how I love it!) **3** (*correlativo di 'tanto'*) as ... as, (*sia ... sia*) both ... and, (*quanto più ... tanto meno*) the more ... the less, the ...-er ... the less, (*quanto più, tanto più*) the more ... the more, the ...-er ... the ...-er (ES: **ne so (tanto) q. prima** I know as much as I did before, **mangerò tanto il dolce q. la macedonia** I'll have both the dessert and the fruit salad, **q. più freddo è il tempo, tanto meno mi piace** the colder the weather is, the less I like it, **q. più mangi, tanto più ingrassi** the more you eat, the fatter you become) **C** *pron.* **1** (*interr.*) how much, *pl.* how many (ES: **q. ne vuoi?** how much do you want of it?, **quanti ne hai letti?** how many did you read?) **2** (*escl.*) what a lot (of) (ES: **q. ne hai consumato!** what a lot you've used!) **D** *pron. rel.* **1** (*ciò che*) what, (*tutto quello che*) all (that) (ES: **ho q. mi occorre** I have all I need) **2** *al pl.* (*tutti coloro che*) all those (who), whoever (ES: **quanti credono in Dio** all those who believe in God) **3** (*correlativo di 'tanto'*) as (ES: **ho dormito (tanto) q. ho potuto** I've slept as much as I could) **4** (*in frasi comp.*) than (ES: **meno di q. pensassimo** less than we expected) ♦ **in q.** (*poiché*) since, as, (*in qualità di*) as; **per q.** however, although; **q. a** as for

quantùnque *cong.* **1** (*benché*) (al)though **2** (*anche se*) even if

quarànta *agg. num. card. e s. m. inv.* forty

quarantèna *s. f.* quarantine

quarantésimo *agg. num. ord. e s. m.* fortieth

quarésima *s. f.* Lent

quartétto *s. m.* **1** quartet **2** (*fam.*) foursome

quartière *s. m.* **1** (*di città*) quarter, area, neighbourhood **2** (*mil.*) quarters *pl.*

quartìna *s. f.* (*letter.*) quatrain

quàrto **A** *agg. num. ord.* fourth **B** *s. m.* **1** quarter, fourth **2** (*di ora*) quarter

quàrzo *s. m.* quartz ♦ **orologio al q.** quartz watch

quàsi **A** *avv.* **1** almost, nearly, (*con significato neg.*) hardly **2** (*forse*) perhaps **3** (*per poco non*) very nearly **B** *cong.* **q. che** as if ♦ **q. mai** hardly ever; **q. sempre** almost always

quassù *avv.* up here

quattórdici *agg. num. card. e s. m. inv.* fourteen

quattrìno *s. m.* penny, *al pl.* money

quàttro *agg. num. card. e s. m. inv.* four

quattrocentésco *agg.* fifteenth-century (*attr.*)

quattrocènto *agg. num. card. e s. m. inv.* four hundred

quattromìla *agg. num. card. e s. m. inv.* four thousand

quéllo **A** *agg. dimostr.* **1** that, those *pl.* **2** (*come art. determ.*) the **B** *pron. dimostr.* **1** that (one), those *pl.* **2** (*prima di un agg. qualif., di un'espressione attributiva o di una frase relativa*) the one (ES: **prenderò q. che mi piace di più** I'll take the one I like best) **3** (*con un poss. non si traduce*) (ES: **questa non è la mia macchina, è quella di mia moglie** this isn't my car, it's my wife's **4** (*seguito da un pron. relativo*) (*colui*) the man, the one, (*colei*) the woman, the one, (*coloro*) those, the people, (*chiunque*) whoever, anyone, (*ciò che*) what (ES: **quelli che hai incontrato sono miei amici** the people you met are friends of mine) **5** (*con valore di pron. pers.*) he, *f.* she, *pl.* they, (*con valore di 'ciò'*) that ♦ **questo ... q.** one ... one, some ... some, (*tra due già menzionati*) the former ... the latter

quèrcia *s. f.* oak

querèla *s. f.* action

querelàre *v. tr.* to bring an action against, to sue

quesìto *s. m.* question

questionàre *v. intr.* to argue, to quarrel
questionàrio *s. m.* questionnaire
questióne *s. f.* **1** (*discussione*) question, issue **2** (*faccenda*) question, matter, (*punto della questione*) point **3** (*litigio*) quarrel
quésto **A** *agg. dimostr.* this, *pl.* these **B** *pron. dimostr.* **1** this (one), *pl.* these **2** (*con valore di pron. pers.*) he, *f.* she, *pl.* they, (*con valore di 'ciò'*) that, this ♦ **q. ... quello** one ... one, some ... some, (*tra due già menzionati*) the latter ... the former
quèstua *s. f.* begging, (*in chiesa*) collection
qui *avv.* **1** here **2** (*temporale*) now ♦ **q. dentro/fuori** in/out here
quietànza *s. f.* receipt
quietàre **A** *v. tr.* to quiet, to calm **B** *v. intr. pron.* to quiet down, to calm down
quiète *s. f.* **1** quiet, calm **2** (*riposo*) rest
quièto *agg.* quiet, calm
quìndi **A** *avv.* then, afterwards **B** *cong.* so, therefore
quìndici *agg. num. ord. e s. m. inv.* fifteen
quindicinàle *agg.* **1** fortnight's (*attr*) **2** (*che ricorre ogni 15 giorni*) fortnightly
quinquènnio *s. m.* period of five years
quìnta *s. f.* **1** (*teatro*) wing, side-scene **2** (*mus.*) fifth ♦ **dietro le quinte** behind the scenes
quintàle *s. m.* quintal
quintétto *s. m.* **1** quintet **2** (*fam.*) fivesome
quìnto *agg. num. ord. e s. m.* fifth
quòta *s. f.* **1** (*somma*) share, amount, (*rata*) instalment, (*contributo*) dues *pl.* **2** (*altezza*) altitude, height **3** (*nel disegno tecnico*) dimension ♦ **a 3000 metri di q.** at 3000 metres above sea level
quotàre **A** *v. tr.* **1** (*valutare*) to value, to assess **2** (*Borsa*) to quote, to list **B** *v. rifl.* to subscribe
quotazióne *s. f.* **1** (*prezzo*) quotation prize, (*valutazione*) evaluation **2** (*Borsa*) quotation **3** (*di moneta*) exchange rate **4** (*reputazione*) reputation
quotidianaménte *avv.* daily
quotidiàno **A** *agg.* daily, everyday **B** *s. m.* daily
quozièнте *s. m.* quotient

R

rabàrbaro *s. m.* rhubarb
ràbbia *s. f.* **1** anger, rage, fury **2** (*med.*) rabies
rabbìno *s. m.* rabbi
rabbióso *agg.* **1** furious, angry **2** (*accanito*) violent, furious **3** (*med.*) rabid
rabbonìre *v. tr. e intr. pron.* to calm down
rabbrividìre *v. intr.* to shudder, to shiver
rabbuiàrsi *v. intr. pron.* **1** to darken, to grow dark **2** (*corrucciarsi*) to grow gloomy
raccapricciànte *agg.* horrifying
raccattàre *v. tr.* to pick up
racchétta *s. f.* **1** (*da tennis*) racket, (*da ping-pong*) bat, (*da sci*) ski-stick, ski-pole **2** (*del tergicristallo*) windscreen wiper
racchiùdere *v. tr.* to contain, to hold
raccògliere A *v. tr.* **1** to pick (up) **2** (*mettere insieme*) to gather, to collect **3** (*fare collezione*) to collect, to make a collection of **4** (*ricevere*) to receive **5** (*mietere*) to reap, to harvest **6** (*dare rifugio*) to shelter, to take in **7** (*accettare*) to accept **B** *v. intr. pron.* to gather **C** *v. rifl.* to collect one's thoughts, to concentrate
raccogliménto *s. m.* concentration
raccoglitóre *s. m.* (*per documenti*) folder
raccòlta *s. f.* **1** collection, raising **2** (*di frutti della terra*) harvesting, (*raccolto*) harvest **3** (*collezione*) collection **4** (*adunata*) gathering
raccòlto A *agg.* **1** (*colto*) picked **2** (*adunato*) gathered **3** (*assorto*) absorbed, engrossed **4** (*intimo*) cosy **B** *s. m.* crop, harvest
raccomandàre A *v. tr.* **1** to recommend **2** (*affidare*) to entrust, to commit **3** (*esortare*) to exhort **4** (*corrispondenza*) to register **B** *v. rifl.* to implore, to beg
raccomandàta *s. f.* registered letter
raccomandàto *agg.* **1** recommended **2** (*di corrispondenza*) registered
raccomandazióne *s. f.* **1** recommendation **2** exhortation, advice
raccontàre *v. tr.* to tell
raccónto *s. m.* **1** story, tale, (*novella*) short story **2** (*resoconto*) relation, account
raccòrdo *s. m.* **1** connection, link **2** (*mecc.*) connector, connection **3** (*ferr.*) sidetrack ♦ **r. stradale** link road
rachìtico *agg.* **1** (*med.*) rachitic **2** (*stentato*) stunted
racimolàre *v. tr.* to scrape up, to collect
ràda *s. f.* roadstead
radar *s. m. inv.* radar
raddolcìre A *v. tr.* **1** to sweeten **2** (*fig.*) to soften **B** *v. intr. pron.* to soften, to mellow
raddoppiàre *v. tr. e intr.* to double, to redouble
raddóppio *s. m.* redoubling
raddrizzàre A *v. tr.* **1** to straighten **2** (*fig.*) to correct, to settle **B** *v. rifl.* to straighten oneself
radènte *agg.* grazing
ràdere A *v. tr.* **1** to shave **2** (*abbattere*) to raze **3** (*sfiorare*) to graze **B** *v. rifl.* to shave (oneself)
radiàle *agg.* radial
radiànte *s. m.* radiant
radiàre *v. tr.* to expell, to strike off
radiatóre *s. m.* radiator
radiazióne *s. f.* radiation
ràdica *s. f.* briar-root
radicàle *agg. e s. m. e f.* radical
radicàre *v. intr. e intr. pron.* to root, to take root
radìcchio *s. m.* chicory
radìce *s. f.* root
ràdio (1) *s. m.* (*anat.*) radius
ràdio (2) *s. m.* (*chim.*) radium
ràdio (3) *s. f.* radio
radioamatóre *s. m.* radio-amateur, ham (*fam.*)
radioattività *s. f.* radioactivity
radioattìvo *agg.* radioactive
radiocrònaca *s. f.* radio commentary
radiocronìsta *s. m. e f.* radio commentator
radiofàro *s. m.* (radio) beacon
radiografìa *s. f.* **1** radiography **2** (*immagine*) X-ray
radiòlogo *s. m.* radiologist
radioscopìa *s. f.* radioscopy
radiosegnàle *s. m.* radio signal
radióso *agg.* radiant, bright
radiosvèglia *s. f.* radio alarm
radiotàxi *s. m. inv.* radiotaxi
radiotècnico *s. m.* radio engineer
radiotelèfono *s. m.* radio telephone
radiotrasmissióne *s. f.* broadcast

ràdo *agg.* **1** (*sparso*) thin, sparse **2** (*non frequente*) infrequent, occasional ♦ **di r.** rarely
radunàre **A** *v. tr.* **1** to gather, to assemble **2** (*raccogliere*) to amass **B** *v. intr. pron.* to gather, to assemble
radùno *s. m.* gathering, meeting
radùra *s. f.* clearing, glade
ràfano *s. m.* horseradish
raffazzonàre *v. tr.* to patch up
rafférmo *agg.* stale
ràffica *s. f.* **1** (*di vento*) gust **2** (*di proiettili*) burst **3** (*fig.*) hail
raffiguràre *v. tr.* **1** (*rappresentare*) to represent, to show **2** (*simboleggiare*) to symbolize, to be a symbol of **3** (*immaginare*) to imagine
raffigurazióne *s. f.* representation, depiction
raffinàre *v. tr. e intr. pron.* to refine
raffinatézza *s. f.* refinement
raffinàto *agg.* refined
raffinerìa *s. f.* refinery
rafforzàre **A** *v. tr.* to reinforce, to strengthen **B** *v. intr. pron.* to get stronger
raffreddaménto *s. m.* cooling
raffreddàre **A** *v. tr.* to cool, to make cold **B** *v. intr. pron.* **1** to cool down, to become cold **2** (*fig.*) to die down, to cool off **3** (*prendere un raffreddore*) to catch a cold
raffreddóre *s. m.* cold
raffrónto *s. m.* comparison
ràfia *s. f.* raffia
ragàzza *s. f.* **1** girl **2** (*fidanzata*) girlfriend
ragàzzo *s. m.* **1** boy, (*giovane*) youth **2** (*garzone*) boy **3** (*fidanzato*) boyfriend
raggiànte *agg.* radiant
raggièra *s. f.* rays *pl.*
ràggio *s. m.* **1** ray, beam **2** (*geom.*) radius **3** (*di ruota*) spoke **4** (*fis.*) ray **5** (*portata*) range
raggiràre *v. tr.* to deceive, to cheat, to swindle
raggìro *s. m.* cheat, swindle, trick
raggiùngere *v. tr.* **1** to reach, to get to, to arrive at **2** (*riunirsi con qc.*) to join, to catch up **3** (*conseguire*) to attain, to achieve
raggomitolàre **A** *v. tr.* to roll up **B** *v. rifl.* to curl up
raggranellàre *v. tr.* to scrape up
raggrinzìre **A** *v. tr.* to wrinkle (up) **B** *v. intr. pron.* to become wrinkled
raggruppàre *v. tr. e intr. pron.* to group, to assemble
ragguàglio *s. m.* information, details *pl.*
ragguardévole *agg.* **1** (*ingente*) considerable, substantial **2** (*importante*) distinguished
ragionaménto *s. m.* reasoning, argument
ragionàre *v. intr.* **1** to reason, to think **2** (*discutere*) to argue
ragióne *s. f.* **1** reason **2** (*causa*) reason, motive **3** (*diritto*) right, reason **4** (*argomentazione*) reason, justification **5** (*rapporto*) ratio, proportion, (*tasso*) rate ♦ **a maggior r.** even more so; **avere r.** to be right; **r. sociale** corporate name
ragionerìa *s. f.* accounting
ragionévole *agg.* reasonable
ragionière *s. m.* accountant
ragliàre *v. intr.* to bray
ràglio *s. m.* braying
ragnatéla *s. f.* cobweb, (spider's) web
ràgno *s. m.* spider
ragù *s. m.* meat sauce
rallegraménti *s. m. pl.* congratulations *pl.*
rallegràre **A** *v. tr.* to cheer up, to make glad **B** *v. intr. pron.* **1** to cheer up, to rejoice **2** (*congratularsi*) to congratulate
rallentaménto *s. m.* slowing down
rallentàre **A** *v. tr.* to slow down, to slacken **B** *v. intr.* **1** to slow down **2** (*ridurre*) to slacken, to die down
ramanzìna *s. f.* telling-off
ramàrro *s. m.* green lizard
ramàzza *s. f.* broom
ràme *s. m.* copper
ramificare **A** *v. intr.* to branch **B** *v. intr. pron.* to branch out
ramìno *s. m.* rummy
rammaricàre **A** *v. tr.* to afflict **B** *v. intr. pron.* to regret, to be sorry
rammàrico *s. m.* regret
rammendàre *v. tr.* to darn, to mend
rammentàre *v. tr. e intr. pron.* to remember, to recall
rammollìre *v. tr. e intr. pron.* to soften
ràmo *s. m.* branch
ramoscèllo *s. m.* twig, sprig
ràmpa *s. f.* **1** ramp, slope **2** (*di scale*) flight ♦ **r. di lancio** launching pad
rampànte *agg.* **1** rampant **2** (*fig.*) go-getting
rampicànte **A** *agg.* climbing, creeping **B** *s. m.* climber, creeper
rampìno *s. m.* hook
rampóllo *s. m.* offspring

rampóne *s. m.* crampon
ràna *s. f.* frog ♦ **nuoto a r.** breast-stroke
ràncido *agg.* rancid
ràncio *s. m.* mess
rancóre *s. m.* grudge
rànda *s. f.* mainsail
randàgio *agg.* stray
randèllo *s. m.* cudgel, club
ràngo *s. m.* rank
rannicchiàre **A** *v. tr.* to curl up **B** *v. rifl.* to crouch
rannuvolàrsi *v. intr. pron.* **1** to become cloudy **2** (*fig.*) to darken, to become gloomy
ranòcchio *s. m.* frog
ràntolo *s. m.* wheeze
ranùncolo *s. m.* ranunculus, buttercup
ràpa *s. f.* turnip
rapàce **A** *agg.* **1** predaceous, predatory **2** (*fig.*) greedy **B** *s. m.* bird of prey
rapàre **A** *v. tr.* to crop **B** *v. rifl.* to have one's hair cropped
ràpida *s. f.* rapid
rapidità *s. f.* swiftness, rapidity
ràpido **A** *agg.* swift, rapid, quick **B** *s. m.* express (train)
rapiménto *s. m.* **1** kidnapping **2** (*fig.*) rapture
rapìna *s. f.* robbery
rapinàre *v. tr.* to rob
rapinatóre *s. m.* robber
rapìre *v. tr.* **1** to kidnap, (*portar via*) to carry off, to steal **2** (*fig.*) to ravish
rapitóre *s. m.* kidnapper
rappacificàre **A** *v. tr.* to reconcile, to pacify **B** *v. rifl. rec.* to become reconciled
rapportàre *v. tr. e intr. pron.* to relate
rappòrto *s. m.* **1** (*resoconto*) report, statement **2** (*relazione, connessione*) relation, connection **3** (*sessuale*) intercourse **4** (*scient.*) ratio **5** (*confronto*) comparison ♦ **in r. a** in relation to, with reference to
rapprèndere *v. intr. e intr. pron.* to coagulate, to congeal, to set
rappresàglia *s. f.* retaliation, reprisal
rappresentànte *s. m. e f.* **1** representative **2** (*comm.*) agent
rappresentàre *v. tr.* **1** to represent, to depict **2** (*fare le veci di*) to act for, to represent, (*comm.*) to be an agent for **3** (*simboleggiare*) to symbolize, to stand for **4** (*teatro*) to perform, to stage, (*cin.*) to show **5** (*significare*) to mean
rappresentatìvo *agg.* representative
rappresentazióne *s. f.* **1** representation **2** (*teatro*) performance
rapsodìa *s. f.* rhapsody
raraménte *avv.* seldom, rarely
rarefàre *v. tr. e intr. pron.* to rarefy
rarità *s. f.* rarity
ràro *agg.* **1** rare **2** (*non comune*) uncommon, exceptional
rasàre **A** *v. tr.* **1** (*radere*) to shave **2** (*siepe*) to trim, (*prato*) to mow **B** *v. rifl.* to shave
raschiàre *v. tr.* to scrape
rasentàre *v. tr.* **1** to graze, to skim **2** (*fig.*) to border on
rasènte a *prep.* close to
ràso *s. m.* satin
rasóio *s. m.* razor ♦ **r. elettrico** electric razor
ràspa *s. f.* rasp
rasségna *s. f.* **1** (*mil.*) review, inspection **2** (*resoconto*) review, survey, (*rivista*) review **3** (*mostra*) show, exhibition
rassegnàre **A** *v. tr.* (*presentare*) to hand in **B** *v. intr. pron.* to resign oneself ♦ **r. le dimissioni** to hand in one's resignation
rassegnazióne *s. f.* resignation
rasserenàre *v. tr. e intr. pron.* **1** to clear up **2** (*fig.*) to cheer up
rassettàre *v. tr.* to tidy up, to put in order
rassicuràre **A** *v. tr.* to reassure **B** *v. intr. pron.* to be reassured
rassodàre **A** *v. tr.* to harden, to firm up **B** *v. intr. pron.* to harden, to set
rassomigliànte *agg.* similar, like
rassomigliànza *s. f.* likeness, resemblance
rassomigliàre **A** *v. intr.* to be like, to resemble **B** *v. rifl. rec.* to be similar, to be alike
rastrellàre *v. tr.* **1** to rack **2** (*mil.*) to mop up, (*di polizia*) to comb (out) **3** (*econ.*) to rake up
rastrèllo *s. m.* rake
rastremazióne *s. f.* taper
ràta *s. f.* instalment ♦ **comprare a rate** to buy by instalments; **vendita a rate** hire purchase
rateàle *agg.* instalment (*attr*)
rateazióne *s. f.* division into instalments
ratìfica *s. f.* ratification
ratificàre *v. tr.* to ratify, to confirm
ràtto (1) *s. m.* abduction, rape
ràtto (2) *s. m.* (*zool.*) rat
rattoppàre *v. tr.* to patch, to mend
rattòppo *s. m.* **1** patching, mending **2** (*toppa*) patch

rattrappìre **A** *v. tr.* to make numb **B** *v. intr. pron.* **1** to become numb **2** (*contrarsi*) to contract
rattristàre **A** *v. tr.* to sadden **B** *v. intr. pron.* to become sad, to be sad
raucèdine *s. f.* hoarseness
ràuco *agg.* hoarse, raucous
ravanèllo *s. m.* radish
ravvedérsi *v. intr. pron.* to mend one's way
ravvisàre *v. tr.* to recognize
ravvivàre *v. tr. e intr. pron.* **1** to revive **2** (*rallegrare*) to brighten (up)
raziocìnio *s. m.* **1** reason **2** (*buon senso*) common sense
razionàle *agg.* rational
razionalìsmo *s. m.* rationalism
razionaménto *s. m.* rationing
razionàre *v. tr.* to ration
razióne *s. f.* ration, (*porzione*) portion, share
ràzza *s. f.* **1** race, (*di animali*) breed **2** (*genere*) kind, sort
razzìa *s. f.* raid, foray
razziàle *agg.* racial
razzìsmo *s. m.* racism
razzìsta *agg. e s. m. e f.* racist
ràzzo *s. m.* rocket
razzolàre *v. intr.* to scratch about
re *s. m. inv.* king
reagènte *s. m.* reagent
reagìre *v. intr.* to react
reàle (1) *agg.* real
reàle (2) *agg.* (*di re*) royal
realìsmo *s. m.* realism
realìstico *agg.* realistic
realizzàre **A** *v. tr.* **1** to carry out, to achieve, to fulfil, to accomplish **2** (*econ.*) to realize **3** (*sport*) to score **4** (*comprendere*) to realize **B** *v. intr. pron.* to come off, to come true **C** *v. rifl.* to fulfil oneself
realizzazióne *s. f.* **1** carrying out, achievement **2** (*econ.*) realization **3** (*produzione*) production
realménte *avv.* really, (*effettivamente*) actually, (*veramente*) truly
realtà *s. f.* reality
reàto *s. m.* offence, crime
reattività *s. f.* reactivity
reattóre *s. m.* reactor
reazionàrio *agg. e s. m.* reactionary
reazióne *s. f.* reaction
rébbio *s. m.* prong
recapitàre *v. tr.* to deliver
recàpito *s. m.* **1** (*indirizzo*) address **2** (*consegna*) delivery
recàre **A** *v. tr.* **1** to bring, to carry **2** (*arrecare*) to cause, to bring **B** *v. intr. pron.* to go
recèdere *v. intr.* to withdraw
recensióne *s. f.* review
recensìre *v. tr.* to review
recensóre *s. m.* reviewer
recènte *agg.* recent, late ♦ **di r.** recently
recentemènte *avv.* recently, lately
recessióne *s. f.* recession
recìdere *v. tr.* to cut (off)
recidìvo **A** *agg.* recidivous **B** *s. m.* recidivist
recìnto *s. m.* **1** (*per animali*) pen, corral **2** (*per bambini*) playpen **3** (*recinzione*) fence
recipiènte *s. m.* container, vessel
recìproco *agg.* reciprocal
rècita *s. f.* performance
recitàre **A** *v. tr.* **1** to recite, to say aloud **2** (*teatro*) to perform, to act, to play **B** *v. intr.* to act, to play
recitazióne *s. f.* **1** recitation **2** (*di attore*) acting ♦ **scuola di r.** drama(tic) school
reclamàre **A** *v. tr.* **1** to claim, to ask for **2** (*aver bisogno di*) to need **B** *v. intr.* to protest, to make a complaint
réclame *s. f. inv.* advertising, (*annuncio*) advertisement
reclàmo *s. m.* claim, complaint
reclinàre *v. tr.* to recline, to bend (down)
reclusióne *s. f.* **1** seclusion **2** (*dir.*) imprisonment
rècluta *s. f.* recruit
reclutàre *v. tr.* to recruit
recòndito *agg.* hidden, (*profondo*) innermost
record *s. m. inv.* record
recriminazióne *s. f.* **1** recrimination **2** (*lagnanza*) complaint
recrudescènza *s. f.* fresh outbreak
recuperàre → **ricuperare**
redarguìre *v. tr.* to scold, to reproach
redattóre *s. m.* **1** (*estensore*) compiler, drafter **2** (*di casa editrice*) editor **3** (*di giornale*) copyreader, member of the editorial staff
redazionàle *agg.* editorial
redazióne *s. f.* **1** (*stesura*) drafting **2** (*di libro, giornale*) editing **3** (*insieme dei redattori*) editorial staff
redditività *s. f.* profitability
redditìzio *agg.* profitable
rèddito *s. m.* income
redentóre *s. m.* redeemer

redenzióne *s. f.* redemption
redìgere *v. tr.* **1** to draw up, to write, to compile **2** (*curare come redattore*) to edit
redìmere *v. tr.* to redeem
rèdine *s. f.* rein
rèduce **A** *agg.* back, returned **B** *s. m. e f.* **1** veteran **2** (*sopravvissuto*) survivor
referèndum *s. m. inv.* referendum
referènza *s. f.* reference
refèrto *s. m.* report
refettòrio *s. m.* refectory
refezióne *s. f.* meal
refrattàrio *agg.* refractory
refrigeràre *v. tr.* to refrigerate, to cool
refrigèrio *s. m.* refreshment, relief
refurtìva *s. f.* stolen goods *pl.*
refùso *s. m.* misprint
regalàre *v. tr.* to give, to present
regàle *agg.* regal, royal
regàlo *s. m.* present, gift
regàta *s. f.* regatta, race
reggènte *s. m. e f.* regent
règgere **A** *v. tr.* **1** to bear, to support, (*tenere*) to hold **2** (*sopportare*) to stand **3** (*governare*) to rule **4** (*dirigere*) to run, to manage **5** (*gramm.*) to govern, to take **B** *v. intr.* **1** (*resistere*) to hold out, to resist **2** (*sopportare*) to stand, to bear **3** (*durare*) to last, to hold out **4** (*essere plausibile*) to stand up, to be consistent **C** *v. rifl. e intr. pron.* **1** (*sostenersi*) to stand, (*aggrapparsi*) to hold on **2** (*governarsi*) to be ruled
règgia *s. f.* royal palace
reggicàlze *s. m. inv.* suspender belt
reggiménto *s. m.* regiment
reggiséno *s. m.* brassière, bra
regìa *s. f.* **1** (*di spettacolo*) direction **2** (*est.*) organization
regìme *s. m.* **1** regime, system **2** (*dieta*) diet **3** (*tecnol.*) running, condition, (*velocità*) speed
regìna *s. f.* queen
règio *agg.* royal
regionàle *agg.* regional
regióne *s. f.* region, district
regìsta *s. m. e f.* **1** (*di spettacoli*) director **2** (*est.*) organizer
registràre *v. tr.* **1** to record, to enter, to register **2** (*suoni, immagini*) to record
registratóre *s. m.* recorder
registrazióne *s. f.* **1** (*annotazione*) record, entry **2** (*di suoni, immagini*) recording
regìstro *s. m.* register
regnànte **A** *agg.* reigning, ruling **B** *s. m. e f.* sovereign
regnàre *v. intr.* to reign
régno *s. m.* **1** reign **2** (*paese*) kingdom
règola *s. f.* rule ♦ **a r. d'arte** duly
regolàbile *agg.* adjustable
regolaménto *s. m.* **1** rule, regulation, rules *pl.* **2** (*pagamento*) settlement
regolàre (1) *agg.* **1** regular **2** (*uniforme*) even, smooth
regolàre (2) **A** *v. tr.* **1** to regulate **2** (*ridurre*) to reduce, (*controllare*) to control **3** (*tecnol.*) to adjust, to set **4** (*definire*) to settle **B** *v. rifl.* **1** (*comportarsi*) to act **2** (*moderarsi*) to control oneself
regolarità *s. f.* regularity
regolarménte *avv.* regularly
regolazióne *s. f.* regulation
regredìre *v. intr.* **1** to go back **2** (*fig.*) to regress
regrèsso *s. m.* regress, regression
reincàrico *s. m.* reappointment
reincarnazióne *s. f.* reincarnation
reinserìre *v. tr.* to reinstate, to reinsert
reintegràre *v. tr.* to reintegrate
relativìsmo *s. m.* relativism
relatività *s. f.* relativity
relatìvo *agg.* **1** relative, related **2** (*non assoluto*) relative, comparative **3** (*attinente*) relevant, pertinent **4** (*gramm.*) relative
relatóre *s. m.* **1** (*di conferenza*) speaker, lecturer **2** (*di tesi universitaria*) supervisor
relazionàre *v. tr.* to report, to inform
relazióne *s. f.* **1** (*resoconto*) report, account **2** (*nesso*) connection, relation **3** (*conoscenza*) acquaintance **4** (*contatto*) touch **5** (*legame amoroso*) (love) affair
relegàre *v. tr.* to relegate, to exile
religióne *s. f.* religion
religióso *agg. e s. m.* religious
relìquia *s. f.* relic
reliquiàrio *s. m.* reliquary, shrine
relìtto *s. m.* **1** wreckage, wreck **2** (*fig.*) outcast
remàre *v. intr.* to row
rematóre *s. m.* rower, oar
reminiscènza *s. f.* reminiscence
remissióne *s. f.* remission
remissìvo *agg.* submissive
rèmo *s. m.* oar
remòto *agg.* distant, remote
rèndere **A** *v. tr.* **1** (*restituire*) to give back, to return, to restore **2** (*contraccambiare*)

to render, to return, to repay **3** (*dare, fare*) to render, to give, to make **4** (*produrre*) to produce, to return, (*fruttare*) to yield **5** (*rappresentare*) to render, to reproduce **B** *v. rifl.* to become, to make oneself
rendicónto *s. m.* statement, report
rendiménto *s. m.* **1** (*produzione*) yield, production, output **2** (*efficienza*) efficiency **3** (*fin.*) yield, return
rèndita *s. f.* **1** (*privata*) income, (*pubblica*) revenue **2** (*dir.*) annuity
rène *s. m.* kidney
réni *s. f. pl.* loins *pl.*, back
rènna *s. f.* **1** (*zool.*) reindeer **2** (*pelle conciata*) buckskin
rèo *s. m.* offender
repàrto *s. m.* **1** department, division, (*di ospedale*) ward **2** (*mil.*) detachment
repellènte *agg.* repellent, repulsive
repentìno *agg.* sudden
reperìre *v. tr.* to find
repèrto *s. m.* **1** find **2** (*med.*) report
repertòrio *s. m.* **1** (*elenco*) list, inventory **2** (*teatro*) repertory, repertoire
rèplica *s. f.* **1** (*risposta*) reply, answer **2** (*teatro*) performance **3** (*copia*) copy, (*di opera d'arte*) replica **4** (*ripetizione*) repetition
replicàre *v. tr.* **1** (*rispondere*) to replay, to answer **2** (*ripetere*) to repeat
repressióne *s. f.* repression
reprìmere *v. tr.* to repress, to restrain
repùbblica *s. f.* republic
repubblicàno *agg. e s. m.* republican
reputàre *v. tr.* to consider, to deem
reputazióne *s. f.* reputation
requisìre *v. tr.* to requisition
requisìto *s. m.* requisite, requirement
requisizióne *s. f.* requisition
résa *s. f.* **1** (*mil.*) surrender **2** (*restituzione*) return **3** (*rendimento*) yield, return, profit
rescìndere *v. tr.* to rescind, to cancel
residènte *agg. e s. m. e f.* resident
residènza *s. f.* residence
residenziàle *agg.* residential
resìduo **A** *agg.* residual **B** *s. m.* remainder, remnant
rèsina *s. f.* resin
resistènte *agg.* **1** resistant, proof **2** (*forte*) strong, tough ♦ **r. al calore** heatproof; **r. al fuoco** fireproof
resistènza *s. f.* resistance
resìstere *v. intr.* **1** to resist, to withstand, to hold out **2** (*sopportare*) to endure, to stand
resocónto *s. m.* account, report, statement
respingènte *s. m.* buffer, (*USA*) bumper
respìngere *v. tr.* **1** to repel, to repulse **2** (*rimandare*) to return, to send back **3** (*rifiutare*) to reject, to refuse **4** (*bocciare*) to fail
respiràre *v. tr. e intr.* to breathe
respiratóre *s. m.* aqualung
respirazióne *s. f.* respiration, breathing
respìro *s. m.* **1** breath, breathing **2** (*fig.*) respite, rest
responsàbile **A** *agg.* responsible, liable **B** *s. m. e f.* person in charge
responsabilità *s. f.* responsibility
respònso *s. m.* response, answer
rèssa *s. f.* throng, crowd
restàre *v. intr.* **1** to stay, to remain **2** (*essere, diventare*) to be, to become **3** (*esser lasciato*) to be left **4** (*avanzare*) to remain, to be left **5** (*resistere*) to stay, to last
restauràre *v. tr.* to restore
restauratóre *s. m.* restorer
restaurazióne *s. f.* restoration
restàuro *s. m.* restoration, repair
restìo *agg.* unwilling, reluctant
restituìre *v. tr.* **1** to return, to give back, to restore **2** (*contraccambiare*) to return, to repay
rèsto *s. m.* **1** remainder, rest **2** (*di denaro*) change **3** (*mat.*) remainder **4** *al pl.* (*rovine*) ruins *pl.*, remains *pl.* **5** *al pl.* (*di cibo*) leftovers *pl.*
restrìngere **A** *v. tr.* **1** to tighten, to narrow, (*vestito*) to take in **2** (*limitare*) to restrict, to limit **B** *v. intr. pron. e rifl.* **1** to narrow, to get narrower, (*contrarsi*) to contract **2** (*di tessuto*) to shrink **3** (*limitarsi*) to limit oneself
restrittivo *agg.* restrictive
restrizióne *s. f.* restriction
réte *s. f.* **1** net **2** (*complesso, sistema*) network, system **3** (*inganno*) snare, trap ♦ **r. da pesca** fishing-net
reticènte *agg.* reticent
reticènza *s. f.* reticence
reticolàto *s. m.* wire-netting, (*di filo spinato*) barbed-wire work
retìcolo *s. m.* network, grid
rètina *s. f.* retina
retòrica *s. f.* rhetoric
retòrico *agg.* rhetorical
retràttile *agg.* retractile
retribuìre *v. tr.* to pay, to remunerate
retribuzióne *s. f.* pay, remuneration

rètro *s. m. inv.* back
retrocèdere **A** *v. tr.* **1** (*degradare*) to demote, (*mil.*) to degrade **2** (*dir.*) to recede **B** *v. intr.* to retreat, to recede, to withdraw
retrògrado *agg.* retrograde
retromàrcia *s. f.* (*mecc.*) reverse gear
retroscèna **A** *s. f.* (*teatro*) backstage **B** *s. m.* (*fig.*) underhand work
retrospettìva *s. f.* retrospective
retrospettìvo *agg.* retrospective
retrotèrra *s. m. inv.* **1** hinterland **2** (*fig.*) background
retrovisóre *s. m.* rearview mirror
rètta (1) *s. f.* (*geom.*) straight line
rètta (2) *s. f.* (*di pensione*) charge
rettangolàre *agg.* rectangular
rettàngolo *s. m.* rectangle
rettìfica *s. f.* **1** correction, adjustment **2** (*chim.*) rectification **3** (*mecc.*) grinding
rettificàre *v. tr.* **1** to correct, to adjust **2** (*chim.*) to rectify **3** (*mecc.*) to grind
rèttile *s. m.* reptile
rettilìneo **A** *agg.* rectilinear, straight **B** *s. m.* straight stretch
rettitùdine *s. f.* rectitude
rètto *agg.* **1** straight, right **2** (*onesto*) upright, honest
rettóre *s. m.* **1** (*relig.*) rector **2** (*di università*) chancellor, (*USA*) president
reumàtico *agg.* rheumatic
reumatìsmo *s. m.* rheumatism
reverèndo *agg. e s. m.* reverend
reversìbile *agg.* reversible, (*dir.*) reversionary
reversibilità *s. f.* reversibility
revisionàre *v. tr.* **1** to revise, to check **2** (*comm.*) to audit **3** (*mecc.*) to overhaul
revisióne *s. f.* **1** revision, review **2** (*di conti*) audit, auditing **3** (*mecc.*) overhaul
revisionìsta *s. m. e f.* revisionist
revisóre *s. m.* **1** reviser **2** (*contabile*) auditor
rèvoca *s. f.* revocation, repeal
revocàre *v. tr.* to revoke, to repeal
revòlver *s. m. inv.* revolver
riabilitàre **A** *v. tr.* **1** to rehabilitate **2** (*reintegrare*) to reinstate **B** *v. rifl.* to rehabilitated oneself
riabilitazióne *s. f.* rehabilitation
riabituàre **A** *v. tr.* to reaccustom **B** *v. rifl.* to reaccustom oneself
riaccèndere *v. tr.* **1** to light again **2** (*motore, luce*) to switch on again
riaccompagnàre *v. tr.* to take back
riacquistàre *v. tr.* **1** to buy back **2** (*recuperare*) to recover
riadattàre *v. tr.* to readapt
riaddormentàre **A** *v. tr.* to put to sleep again **B** *v. intr. pron.* to fall asleep again
riaffermàre *v. tr.* **1** to reaffirm **2** (*confermare*) to confirm
rialzàre *v. tr.* **1** to raise, to lift up **2** (*far aumentare*) to increase, to raise
riàlzo *s. m.* **1** rise, increase **2** (*di terreno*) elevation
rianimàre **A** *v. tr.* **1** to reanimate, to revive **2** (*rallegrare*) to cheer up **B** *v. intr. pron.* **1** to recover oneself **2** (*riprendere coraggio*) to take heart again **3** (*rallegrarsi*) to cheer up
rianimazióne *s. f.* **1** reviving **2** (*med.*) resuscitation
riannodàre **A** *v. tr.* **1** to knot again **2** (*fig.*) to renew **B** *v. intr. pron.* to renew
riaprìre *v. tr., intr. e intr. pron.* to reopen
riassùmere *v. tr.* **1** to re-engage, to take on again **2** (*riprendere*) to reassume **3** (*riepilogare*) to sum up
riassùnto *s. m.* summary
riavére **A** *v. tr.* **1** to have again **2** (*recuperare*) to get back, to recover **B** *v. intr. pron.* to recover, to get over
ribadìre *v. tr.* **1** (*mecc.*) to clinch **2** (*confermare*) to confirm, to repeat
ribàlta *s. f.* **1** (*piano ribaltabile*) flap **2** (*teatro*) front of the stage **3** (*fig.*) limelight
ribaltàbile *agg.* folding, (*di sedile*) tip-up (*attr.*)
ribaltaménto *s. m.* overturning
ribaltàre *v. tr. e intr. pron.* to overturn, to capsize
ribassàre **A** *v. tr.* to lower, to reduce **B** *v. intr.* to fall, to drop
ribàsso *s. m.* fall, drop, decrease, (*sconto*) discount
ribàttere **A** *v. tr.* **1** to beat again **2** (*mecc.*) to clinch **3** (*confutare*) to refute **4** (*riscrivere a macchina*) to retype **B** *v. intr.* **1** to beat again **2** (*replicare*) to retort, to answer back
ribellàrsi *v. intr. pron.* to rebel, to revolt
ribèlle **A** *agg.* rebellious, rebel (*attr.*) **B** *s. m. e f.* rebel
ribellióne *s. f.* rebellion
rìbes *s. m.* currant, (*nero*) blackcurrant, (*rosso*) redcurrant
ribollìre **A** *v. tr.* to boil again **B** *v. intr.* **1** to boil again **2** (*fig.*) to boil, to seethe

ribrézzo *s. m.* disgust
ributtànte *agg.* disgusting
ricadére *v. intr.* **1** to fall again, to fall back **2** (*avere una ricaduta*) to relapse **3** (*scendere*) to fall down, to hang (down) **4** (*gravare*) to fall, to rest
ricadùta *s. f.* **1** relapse **2** (*fis.*) fallout
ricamàre *v. tr.* to embroider
ricambiàre *v. tr.* **1** to change again **2** (*contraccambiare*) to return, to repay
ricàmbio *s. m.* **1** replacement **2** (*pezzo di ricambio*) spare part **3** (*avvicendamento*) turnover
ricàmo *s. m.* embroidery
ricapitolàre *v. tr.* to sum up, to recapitulate
ricàrica *s. f.* reloading, (*di batteria*) recharging
ricaricàre **A** *v. tr.* **1** to reload **2** (*orologio*) to rewind **3** (*batteria*) to recharge **B** *v. rifl.* to buck up
ricattàre *v. tr.* to blackmail
ricattatóre *s. m.* blackmailer
ricàtto *s. m.* blackmail
ricavàre *v. tr.* **1** (*dedurre*) to deduce, to come to **2** (*ottenere*) to obtain, to get **3** (*estrarre*) to extract **4** (*guadagnare*) to gain, to earn
ricàvo *s. m.* proceeds *pl.*, return
ricchézza *s. f.* **1** wealth **2** (*abbondanza*) abundance, richness
rìccio (1) **A** *agg.* curly **B** *s. m.* curl
rìccio (2) *s. m.* **1** (*zool.*) hedgehog **2** (*di castagna*) (chestnut) husk ♦ **r. di mare** sea urchin
rìcciolo *s. m.* curl
ricciùto *agg.* curly
rìcco **A** *agg.* **1** rich, wealthy **2** (*di valore*) valuable, precious **3** (*sfarzoso*) sumptuous **4** (*abbondante*) full, rich, abounding **B** *s. m.* rich person
ricérca *s. f.* **1** search, quest **2** (*il perseguire*) pursuit **3** (*scientifica*) research **4** (*indagine*) investigation, inquiry **5** (*richiesta*) demand
ricercàre *v. tr.* **1** to look for, to seek (for), to search for **2** (*perseguire*) to pursue **3** (*investigare*) to investigate, to inquire into
ricercàto *agg.* **1** (*dir*) wanted **2** (*richiesto*) sought-after **3** (*raffinato*) refined **4** (*affettato*) affected
ricercatóre *s. m.* **1** searcher **2** (*scientifico*) researcher
ricetrasmittènte *s. f.* transceiver
ricètta *s. f.* **1** (*cuc.*) recipe **2** (*med.*) prescription **3** (*fig.*) formula
ricettàrio *s. m.* **1** (*cuc.*) recipe book, cookbook **2** (*med.*) book of prescriptions
ricettazióne *s. f.* receiving of stolen goods
ricévere *v. tr.* **1** to receive, to get **2** (*accettare*) to accept, to take **3** (*ammettere*) to admit **4** (*prendere, avere*) to take, to get, to have, to receive **5** (*accogliere*) to receive, to welcome **6** (*ammettere a visitare*) to receive, to be at home to, (*a un'udienza*) to grant audience to
ricevimènto *s. m.* **1** receiving, receipt **2** (*accoglienza*) reception **3** (*festa*) reception, party
ricevitorìa *s. f.* receiving office
ricevùta *s. f.* receipt
ricezióne *s. f.* reception
richiamàre **A** *v. tr.* **1** to call again **2** (*far tornare*) to call back, to recall **3** (*attirare*) to attract **B** *v. intr. pron.* **1** (*far riferimento*) to refer **2** (*appellarsi*) to appeal
richiàmo *s. m.* recall, call
richièdere *v. tr.* **1** to ask for again, to ask for back **2** (*domandare*) to ask, to request **3** (*fare domanda*) to apply for **4** (*esigere*) to demand, (*necessitare*) to require
richièsta *s. f.* request, demand, (*scritta*) application
riciclàre *v. tr.* to recycle
rìcino *s. m.* castor-oil plant
ricognizióne *s. f.* reconnaissance
ricominciàre *v. tr. e intr.* to begin again, to start again
ricompènsa *s. f.* reward
ricompensàre *v. tr.* to reward, to repay
ricompràre *v. tr.* to buy back
riconciliàre **A** *v. tr.* to reconcile **B** *v. rifl.* to be reconciled, to make (it) up **C** *v. rifl. rec.* to make friends again, to make (it) up
riconciliazióne *s. f.* reconciliation
ricondùrre *v. tr.* to bring again, to bring back, to take back
riconférma *s. f.* reconfirmation
riconfermàre *v. tr.* to reconfirm, to confirm (again)
ricongiùngere *v. tr. e intr. pron.* to rejoin
ricongiunzióne *s. f.* rejoining
riconoscènte *agg.* thankful, grateful
riconoscènza *s. f.* thankfulness, gratitude
riconóscere **A** *v. tr.* **1** to recognize **2** (*ammettere ufficialmente*) to acknowledge, to recognize **3** (*ammettere*) to admit, to own **4** (*apprezzare*) to appreciate, to recognize **5** (*identificare*) to identify **B** *v. rifl.* to re-

cognize oneself **C** *v. rifl. rec.* to recognize each other
riconoscìbile *agg.* recognizable
riconosciménto *s. m.* **1** recognition, (*ufficiale*) acknowledgement **2** (*identificazione*) identification **3** (*ammissione*) admission, avowal
riconsideràre *v. tr.* to reconsider
ricopiàre *v. tr.* to copy, to recopy
ricoprìre **A** *v. tr.* **1** to cover, (*di nuovo*) to cover again **2** (*tecnol.*) to plate **3** (*colmare*) to load **4** (*occupare*) to hold, to fill **B** *v. rifl. e intr. pron.* to cover oneself
ricordàre **A** *v. tr.* **1** to remember, to recall **2** (*richiamare alla memoria altrui*) to remind **3** (*menzionare*) to mention **B** *v. intr. pron.* to remember
ricòrdo *s. m.* **1** memory, recollection, remembrance **2** (*oggetto*) souvenir
ricorrènte *agg.* recurrent
ricorrènza *s. f.* **1** recurrence **2** (*anniversario*) anniversary
ricórrere *v. intr.* **1** (*rivolgersi*) to apply, to go to **2** (*fare appello*) to appeal **3** (*ripetersi*) to recur **4** (*accadere*) to occur, (*di anniversario*) to fall
ricórso *s. m.* **1** resort, recourse **2** (*dir.*) petition, appeal
ricostituènte *agg. e s. m.* tonic
ricostruìre *v. tr.* to reconstruct, to rebuild
ricostruzióne *s. f.* reconstruction, rebuilding
ricoveràre **A** *v. tr.* to shelter, to take in **B** *v. rifl.* to take shelter ♦ **r. all'ospedale** to hospitalize
ricóvero *s. m.* **1** shelter **2** (*in ospedale*) admission, hospitalization **3** (*ospizio*) poor-house, (*per anziani*) old people's home
ricreàre **A** *v. tr.* **1** to recreate **2** (*rinvigorire*) to revive **B** *v. rifl.* to relax
ricreatìvo *agg.* recreative, recreational
ricreazióne *s. f.* recreation
ricrédersi *v. intr. pron.* to change one's mind
ricucìre *v. tr.* **1** to resew, to sew again, to restitch, (*una ferita*) to sew up **2** (*ricomporre*) to re-estabilish
ricuòcere *v. tr.* to recook
ricuperàre *v. tr.* **1** to recover, to get back **2** (*riguadagnare*) to make up for **3** (*riabilitare*) to rehabilitate **4** (*riciclare*) to recycle
ricùpero *s. m.* **1** recovery **2** (*salvataggio*) rescue **3** (*riabilitazione*) rehabilitation **4** (*riutilizzo*) reutilization, (*riciclo*) recycling **5** (*rimonta*) making up
ricùrvo *agg.* bent
ridacchiàre *v. intr.* to giggle, to snigger
ridàre *v. tr.* **1** to give again **2** (*restituire*) to give back, to return
ridere *v. intr.* to laugh (at)
ridìcolo **A** *agg.* **1** ridiculous, absurd **2** (*esiguo*) paltry **B** *s. m.* **1** ridicule **2** (*ridicolaggine*) ridiculousness
ridimensionàre *v. tr.* **1** (*riorganizzare*) to reorganize, (*ridurre*) to reduce **2** (*fig.*) to reconsider, to reappraise
ridipìngere *v. tr.* to repaint
ridìre *v. tr.* **1** to tell again, to say again **2** (*obiettare*) to object to, to find fault (with)
ridondànte *agg.* redundant
ridòsso *s. m.* shelter ♦ **a r. di** under (the) lee of, at the back of, behind
ridùrre **A** *v. tr.* **1** to reduce, to cut down **2** (*trasformare*) to turn into, to reduce **3** (*spingere, portare*) to drive, to reduce **4** (*adattare*) to adapt **B** *v. intr. pron.* **1** to reduce oneself **2** (*diventare*) to be reduced, to become **3** (*diminuire*) to decrease, (*restringersi*) to shrink
riduzióne *s. f.* **1** reduction, cut **2** (*sconto*) discount **3** (*adattamento*) adaptation
riecheggiàre *v. intr.* to resound
rielaboràre *v. tr.* to revise, to work out again
rielèggere *v. tr.* to re-elect
rielezióne *s. f.* re-election
riempìre **A** *v. tr.* **1** to fill (up), to stuff **2** (*compilare*) to fill in **B** *v. rifl. e intr. pron.* **1** to be filled **2** (*rimpinzarsi*) to stuff oneself
rientrànza *s. f.* recess
rientràre *v. intr.* **1** to re-enter, to enter again, (*tornare*) to go back, to return **2** (*far parte*) to be included in, to be part of
riepilogàre *v. tr.* to recapitulate, to sum up
riepìlogo *s. m.* recapitulation, summary
riesumàre *v. tr.* **1** to exhume **2** (*fig.*) to unearth
rievocàre *v. tr.* **1** to recall **2** (*commemorare*) to commemorate
rievocazióne *s. f.* **1** recalling **2** (*commemorazione*) commemoration
rifaciménto *s. m.* **1** remaking, (*di film*) remake **2** (*ricostruzione*) reconstruction
rifàre **A** *v. tr.* **1** to do again, to make again, to remake **2** (*ripristinare*) to restore, (*ricostruire*) to rebuild **3** (*riparare*) to repair **4** (*imitare*) to imitate, to ape **5** (*ripercorrere*) to retrace **B** *v. rifl. e intr. pron.* **1** to make up **2** (*vendicarsi*) to revenge oneself

3 (*risalire*) to go back to
riferiménto *s. m.* reference
riferìre A *v. tr.* **1** to report, to tell, to relate **2** (*ascrivere*) to attribute, to connect **B** *v. intr. pron.* **1** (*alludere*) to refer, to make reference **2** (*concernere*) to concern, to refer
rifilàre *v. tr.* **1** (*tagliare*) to trim **2** (*dare*) to give, (*appioppare*) to palm off
rifinìre *v. tr.* to finish off
rifinitùra *s. f.* finishing touch
rifiorìre *v. intr.* **1** to blossom again **2** (*fig.*) to flourish again
rifiutàre A *v. tr.* **1** to refuse, (*respingere*) to reject **2** (*non concedere*) to deny, to refuse **B** *v. intr. pron.* to refuse
rifiùto *s. m.* **1** refusal, rejection **2** (*diniego*) denial **3** (*scarto*) refuse, *al pl.* waste, rubbish
riflessióne *s. f.* reflection
riflessìvo *agg.* **1** reflective, thoughtful **2** (*gramm., mat.*) reflexive
riflèsso *s. m.* **1** reflection **2** (*fig.*) influence, effect **3** (*med.*) reflex
riflèttere A *v. tr.* to reflect **B** *v. intr.* to think over, to reflect, to consider **C** *v. rifl.* to be reflected
riflettóre *s. m.* **1** reflector **2** (*proiettore*) searchlight
riflùsso *s. m.* reflux, (*di acqua*) ebb
rifocillàre A *v. tr.* to give refreshment to **B** *v. rifl.* to take refreshment
rifóndere *v. tr.* **1** to melt again **2** (*rimborsare*) to refund
rifórma *s. f.* reform, reformation
riformàre *v. tr.* **1** to re-form **2** (*sottoporre a riforma*) to reform, to amend
riformatóre A *agg.* reforming **B** *s. m.* reformer
riformatòrio *s. m.* approved school, (*USA*) reformatory
riforniménto *s. m.* **1** supplying, (*di carburante*) refuelling **2** (*scorta*) supply ♦ **fare r. di benzina** to fill up the tank
rifornìre A *v. tr.* to supply, to stock **B** *v. rifl.* to stock up
rifrazióne *s. f.* refraction
rifuggìre A *v. intr.* **1** to flee again **2** (*fig.*) to shrink, to avoid **B** *v. tr.* to avoid
rifugiàrsi *v. intr. pron.* to shelter, to take refuge
rifùgio *s. m.* refuge, shelter
rìga *s. f.* **1** line **2** (*fila*) row **3** (*da disegno*) rule **4** (*striscia*) stripe **5** (*scriminatura*) parting
rigattière *s. m.* junk dealer
rigettàre *v. tr.* **1** to throw again, to throw back **2** (*respingere*) to reject
rigètto *s. m.* rejection
rigidità *s. f.* **1** rigidity **2** (*fig.*) severity, strictness
rìgido *agg.* **1** rigid, stiff **2** (*di clima*) rigorous, harsh **3** (*severo*) strict, severe, rigid
rigiràre A *v. tr.* **1** to turn again, to turn over **2** (*distorcere*) to twist, to distort **B** *v. rifl.* to turn round
rìgo *s. m.* **1** line **2** (*mus.*) stave, staff
rigogliόso *agg.* luxuriant, flourishing
rigonfiaménto *s. m.* swelling, bulge
rigóre *s. m.* **1** (*freddo*) rigours *pl.* **2** (*austerità*) uprightness **3** (*severità*) rigour, strictness, severity **4** (*precisione*) exactness ♦ **calcio di r.** penalty (kick)
rigoróso *agg.* rigorous, strict
rigovernàre *v. tr.* to wash up
riguardàre A *v. tr.* **1** to look at, to examine **2** (*considerare*) to regard, to concern **3** (*custodire*) to take care of **B** *v. rifl.* to take care of oneself
riguàrdo *s. m.* **1** (*cura*) care **2** (*rispetto*) respect, regard, consideration **3** (*relazione*) regard, respect
rilasciàre A *v. tr.* **1** to leave again **2** (*liberare*) to release, to set free **3** (*concedere*) to grant, to give **4** (*allentare*) to relax **B** *v. rifl. e intr. pron.* to relax
rilàscio *s. m.* **1** release **2** (*concessione*) granting, issue
rilassàre *v. tr. e rifl.* to relax
rilegàre *v. tr.* to bind
rilegatùra *s. f.* binding
rilèggere *v. tr.* to read again
rilevaménto *s. m.* **1** survey **2** (*naut.*) bearing
rilevànte *agg.* considerable
rilevàre *v. tr.* **1** (*notare*) to notice, to point out **2** (*ricavare*) to take **3** (*dare il cambio*) to relieve **4** (*subentrare*) to take over, (*comprare*) to buy **5** (*topografia*) to survey, (*geogr*) to map **6** (*naut.*) to take a bearing of
rilièvo *s. m.* **1** relief **2** (*importanza*) importance, stress **3** (*osservazione*) remark **4** (*rilevamento*) survey **5** (*altura*) height, high ground ♦ **mettere in r.** to point out
rilòga *s. f.* curtain rod
riluttànte *agg.* reluctant, unwilling
riluttànza *s. f.* reluctance, unwillingness

rìma *s. f.* **1** rhyme **2** *al pl.* (*versi*) rhymed verses *pl.*, poetry
rimandàre *v. tr.* **1** to send again **2** (*restituire, mandare indietro*) to send back **3** (*rinviare*) to postpone, to put off **4** (*far riferimento*) to refer
rimaneggiàre *v. tr.* to (re)adapt, to revise
rimanènte **A** *agg.* remaining **B** *s. m.* **1** remainder, leftovers *pl.* **2** *al pl.* (*persone*) the others *pl.*, the rest
rimanènza *s. f.* remainder, rest, leftovers *pl.*
rimanère *v. intr.* **1** to remain, to stay **2** (*avanzare*) to be left, to remain **3** (*persistere*) to remain, to last **4** (*essere situato*) to be located **5** (*mantenersi*) to keep, to remain **6** (*stupirsi*) to be astonished ♦ **r. male** to be disappointed
rimarchévole *agg.* remarkable, notable
rimarginàre *v. tr. e intr. pron.* to heal
rimasùglio *s. m.* remainder, *al pl.* leftovers *pl.*
rimbalzàre *v. intr.* to rebound, to bounce back
rimbàlzo *s. m.* rebound
rimboccàre *v. tr.* to tuck up, to turn down
rimbombàre *v. intr.* to rumble, to resound
rimbómbo *s. m.* rumble
rimborsàbile *agg.* refundable, repayable
rimborsàre *v. tr.* to reimburse, to refund, to repay
rimbórso *s. m.* reimbursement, refund, repayment
rimboschiménto *s. m.* reafforestation
rimediàre **A** *v. tr.* **1** (*porre rimedio a*) to remedy, to put right **2** (*racimolare*) to scrape up **B** *v. intr.* to remedy, to make up for
rimèdio *s. m.* remedy, cure
rimescolàre *v. tr.* **1** to mix up, to stir up **2** (*carte da gioco*) to shuffle **3** (*rinvangare*) to rake up
riméssa *s. f.* **1** (*di denaro*) remittance, transfert **2** (*deposito di autobus*) (bus) depot, garage **3** (*calcio*) throw-in
riméttere **A** *v. tr.* **1** to put again, to replace **2** (*affidare*) to refer, to leave **3** (*mandare*) to remit, (*consegnare*) to deliver **4** (*perdonare, condonare*) to remit, to forgive **5** (*rimetterci*) to lose, to ruin **B** *v. rifl. e intr. pron.* **1** (*ristabilirsi*) to recover **2** (*affidarsi*) to rely (on) **3** (*rasserenarsi*) to clear up ♦ **r. a nuovo** to do up
rimmel *s. m. inv.* mascara
rimónta *s. f.* recovery
rimontàre **A** *v. tr.* **1** to go up **2** (*ricomporre*) to reassemble **B** *v. intr.* **1** to remount **2** (*risalire*) to go back, to date back **3** (*ricuperare uno svantaggio*) to move up, to catch up
rimorchiàre *v. tr.* to tow
rimorchiatore *s. m.* tug
rimòrchio *s. m.* **1** tow **2** (*veicolo*) trailer ♦ **prendere a r.** to take in tow
rimòrso *s. m.* remorse, regret
rimozióne *s. f.* **1** removal **2** (*da un incarico*) dismissal, discharge ♦ **zona a r. forzata** towaway zone
rimpàsto *s. m.* reshuffle
rimpatriàre *v. tr. e intr.* to repatriate
rimpàtrio *s. m.* repatriation
rimpiàngere *v. tr.* to regret
rimpiànto *s. m.* regret
rimpiazzàre *v. tr.* to replace
rimpicciolìre **A** *v. tr.* to make smaller **B** *v. intr. pron.* to become smaller
rimpinguàre **A** *v. tr.* **1** to fatten (up) **2** (*arricchire*) to enrich **B** *v. rifl.* **1** to grow fat **2** (*arricchirsi*) to grow rich
rimpinzàre **A** *v. tr.* to fill, to stuff **B** *v. rifl.* to stuff oneself
rimproveràre *v. tr.* **1** to reproach, to rebuke, (*sgridare*) to scold **2** (*biasimare*) to blame, to reproach **3** (*rinfacciare*) to grudge
rimpròvero *s. m.* reproach, rebuke, (*sgridata*) scolding
rimuginàre *v. tr. e intr.* to turn over in one's mind
rimuneràre *v. tr.* to remunerate
rimunerazióne *s. f.* remuneration, payment
rimuòvere *v. tr.* **1** to remove **2** (*destituire*) to dismiss, to discharge **3** (*dissuadere*) to dissuade, to deter
rinàscere *v. intr.* to revive
rinascimentàle *agg.* Renaissance (*attr.*)
rinasciménto *s. m.* Renaissance
rinàscita *s. f.* renaissance, revival
rincaràre *v. tr.* to raise (the price of)
rincasàre *v. intr.* to go back home
rinchiùdere **A** *v. tr.* to shut up **B** *v. rifl.* to shut oneself up
rincominciàre *v. tr.* to begin again, to start again
rincórrere *v. tr.* to run after
rincórsa *s. f.* run-up
rincréscere *v. intr.* **1** to be sorry, to regret **2** (*dispiacere*) to mind
rincresciménto *s. m.* regret
rinculàre *v. intr.* to recoil

rinforzàre **A** *v. tr.* to strengthen, to reinforce **B** *v. intr.* (*di vento*) to grow stronger **C** *v. intr. pron.* to become stronger
rinfòrzo *s. m.* strengthening, reinforcement
rinfrancàre **A** *v. tr.* to encourage, to hearten **B** *v. intr. pron.* to take heart again
rinfrescànte *agg.* refreshing
rinfrescàre **A** *v. tr.* **1** to cool **2** (*rinnovare*) to do up, to restore **B** *v. intr.* to cool, (*di vento*) to freshen **C** *v. rifl.* to cool down, to refreshen up
rinfrésco *s. m.* **1** (*festa*) party **2** (*cibi e bevande*) refreshments *pl.*
rinfùsa, àlla *loc. avv.* in confusion, higgledy-piggledy
ringhiàre *v. intr.* to growl, to snarl
ringhièra *s. f.* railing, (*di scala*) banister
ringhióso *agg.* snarling
ringiovanìre **A** *v. tr.* **1** to make young (again) **2** (*far sembrare più giovane*) to make look younger **B** *v. intr.* **1** to grow young again **2** (*sembrare più giovane*) to look younger
ringraziaménto *s. m.* thanks *pl.*
ringraziàre *v. tr.* to thank
rinnegàre *v. tr.* to disown, to deny
rinnovaménto *s. m.* renewal
rinnovàre **A** *v. tr.* **1** to renew **2** (*ripetere*) to repeat **3** (*cambiare*) to change, to renew **B** *v. intr. pron.* **1** to be renewed **2** (*ripetersi*) to happen again
rinnòvo *s. m.* renewal
rinocerónte *s. m.* rhinoceros
rinomàto *agg.* renowned, famous
rinsaldàre *v. tr.* to strengthen, to consolidate
rintoccàre *v. intr.* (*di campana*) to toll, (*di orologio*) to strike
rintócco *s. m.* (*di campana*) toll, (*di orologio*) stroke
rintracciàre *v. tr.* to trace, to track down, (*trovare*) to find
rintronàre **A** *v. tr.* **1** (*assordare*) to deafen **2** (*stordire*) to stun **B** *v. intr.* to resound
rinùncia *s. f.* renunciation
rinunciàre *v. intr.* to renounce, to give up
rinvenìre **A** *v. tr.* to find out, to discover **B** *v. intr.* **1** (*ricuperare i sensi*) to recover one's senses, to come to **2** (*ricuperare freschezza*) to revive
rinviàre *v. tr.* **1** (*mandare indietro*) to send back, to return **2** (*posporre*) to put off, to postpone
rinvìo *s. m.* **1** postponement, adjournment **2** (*restituzione*) return, sending back **3** (*riferimento*) cross-reference
rionàle *agg.* local
rióne *s. m.* district, quarter
riordinàre *v. tr.* **1** to put in order again, to tidy up **2** (*riorganizzare*) to reorganize
riorganizzàre *v. tr.* to reorganize
ripagàre *v. tr.* **1** to pay again **2** (*ricompensare*) to repay, to reward **3** (*risarcire*) to pay, to refund
riparàre **A** *v. tr.* **1** (*aggiustare*) to repair **2** (*proteggere*) to shelter, to protect **3** (*rimediare*) to redress, to make amends for **B** *v. intr.* to make up (for) **C** *v. rifl.* to protect oneself
riparazióne *s. f.* repair, fixing
ripàro *s. m.* shelter, cover, protection
ripartìre (1) *v. tr.* (*dividere*) to split up, to divide, (*distribuire*) to share out
ripartìre (2) *v. intr.* (*partire di nuovo*) to leave again, (*riavviarsi*) to start again
ripartizióne *s. f.* division, distribution
ripensàre *v. intr.* **1** (*tornare a pensare*) to think again **2** (*riandare col pensiero*) to recall **3** (*cambiare parere*) to change one's mind
ripercórrere *v. tr.* to run through again, to go over again
ripercuòtersi *v. intr. pron.* **1** to reverberate **2** (*fig.*) to have repercussions, to affect
ripercussióne *s. f.* repercussion
ripescàre *v. tr.* **1** (*tirare fuori dall'acqua*) to fish out **2** (*trovare*) to find (again)
ripètere **A** *v. tr.* to repeat **B** *v. rifl.* to repeat oneself **C** *v. intr. pron.* to recur
ripetizióne *s. f.* **1** repetition **2** (*lezione privata*) private lesson
ripiàno *s. m.* **1** (*di scaffale*) shelf **2** (*terreno*) level ground
ripìcca *s. f.* spite, pique
rìpido *agg.* steep
ripiegàre **A** *v. tr.* **1** to bend again, to refold **2** (*piegare*) to fold up **3** (*abbassare*) to lower **B** *v. intr.* **1** (*ritirarsi*) to withdraw, to retreat **2** (*fig.*) to fall back **C** *v. intr. pron.* to bend
ripiègo *s. m.* expedient, makeshift
ripièno **A** *agg.* (*pieno*) full, (*riempito, farcito*) stuffed, filled **B** *s. m.* stuffing, filling
ripopolàre *v. tr.* to repopulate
ripórre *v. tr.* **1** to put away **2** (*collocare*) to place, to put
riportàre **A** *v. tr.* **1** to bring again, to take again, to bring back, to take back, to carry

back **2** (*riferire*) to report, (*citare*) to quote **3** (*ricevere, ottenere*) to get, to receive, to carry off **4** (*mat.*) to carry **B** *v. intr. pron.* **1** (*tornare*) to go back **2** (*riferirsi*) to refer
riposàre *v. tr., intr. e rifl.* to rest
ripòso *s. m.* rest
ripostìglio *s. m.* lumber-room, store-room, closet
riprèndere **A** *v. tr.* **1** to take again, (*riacchiappare*) to catch again, (*riconquistare*) to retake **2** (*prendere indietro*) to take back, to get back, (*ricuperare*) to recover **3** (*rincominciare*) to begin again, to start again, to resume **4** (*rimproverare*) to tell off, to reprove **5** (*cin.*) to shoot **B** *v. intr.* (*ricominciare*) to start again, to begin again **C** *v. intr. pron.* to recover
riprésa *s. f.* **1** restarting, resumption, renewal **2** (*rinascita*) revival **3** (*da malattia, emozioni*) recovery **4** (*teatro*) revival **5** (*cin.*) shot, take **6** (*autom.*) pick-up **7** (*di partita*) second half, (*pugilato*) round
ripristinàre *v. tr.* to restore, to re-estabilish
riproducìbile *agg.* reproducible
riprodùrre *v. tr., rifl. e intr. pron.* to reproduce
riproduzióne *s. f.* reproduction
riprovàre **A** *v. tr.* **1** to try again **2** (*sentire di nuovo*) to feel again **B** *v. intr. e intr. pron.* to try again
riprovévole *agg.* reprehensible, despicable
ripudiàre *v. tr.* to repudiate, to disown
ripugnànte *agg.* repulsive, disgusting
ripugnàre *v. intr.* to disgust, to dislike
ripulìre **A** *v. tr.* **1** to clean again **2** (*pulire*) to clean up **3** (*dirozzare*) to refine **4** (*svuotare*) to clean out, to ransack **B** *v. rifl.* to clean oneself up
riquàdro *s. m.* square
risàcca *s. f.* backwash
risàia *s. f.* rice-field
risalìre **A** *v. tr.* **1** to go up again, to climb up again **2** (*contro corrente*) to go up **B** *v. intr.* **1** to go up again, to climb up again **2** (*aumentare*) to rise again, to go up again **3** (*nel tempo*) to go back, to date back
risaltàre *v. intr.* **1** (*spiccare*) to stand out, to show up **2** (*sporgere*) to stick out
risàlto *s. m.* prominence, relief
risanàre *v. tr.* **1** (*guarire*) to cure, to restore **2** (*bonificare*) to reclaim **3** (*riequilibrare*) to balance, (*riorganizzare*) to reorganize
risapùto *agg.* well-known
risarciménto *s. m.* compensation, refund ♦ **richiesta di r.** claim for damages
risarcìre *v. tr.* to repay, to refund, to indemnify
risàta *s. f.* laughter, laugh
riscaldaménto *s. m.* **1** heating **2** (*sport*) warming up ♦ **impianto di r.** heating system; **r. centrale** central heating
riscaldàre **A** *v. tr.* **1** to warm, to heat **2** (*scaldare di nuovo*) to heat up, to warm up **3** (*fig.*) to stir up **B** *v. intr.* to give heat **C** *v. rifl.* **1** to warm oneself, to get warm **2** (*fig.*) to warm up, to get excited
riscattàre *v. tr.* to ransom, to redeem
riscàtto *s. m.* **1** redemption **2** (*prezzo richiesto*) ransom
rischiaràre *v. tr. e intr. pron.* to light up
rischiàre *v. tr.* to risk, to venture
rìschio *s. m.* risk
rischióso *agg.* risky
risciacquàre *v. tr.* to rinse
riscontràre *v. tr.* **1** (*verificare*) to check, to verify **2** (*trovare*) to find, to notice **3** (*confrontare*) to compare
riscóntro *s. m.* **1** (*controllo*) check **2** (*confronto*) comparison **3** (*conferma*) confirmation
riscoprìre *v. tr.* to rediscover
riscossióne *s. f.* collection
riscrìvere *v. tr.* to write again, to rewrite
riscuòtere **A** *v. tr.* **1** to collect, to draw, to cash **2** (*conseguire*) to earn, to win **3** (*scuotere*) to shake **B** *v. intr. pron.* **1** (*trasalire*) to start **2** (*risvegliarsi*) to come to
risentiménto *s. m.* resentment
risèrbo *s. m.* reserve, discretion
risèrva *s. f.* **1** (*scorta*) reserve **2** (*restrizione*) reserve, reservation **3** (*di caccia, pesca*) reserve, preserve
riservàre **A** *v. tr.* **1** to reserve, to keep **2** (*prenotare*) to book **B** *v. intr. pron.* to intend, to propose
riservatézza *s. f.* **1** privacy **2** (*carattere*) reserve, discretion
riservàto *agg.* **1** (*chiuso*) reserved, restrained **2** (*prenotato*) reserved, booked **3** (*segreto*) confidential
risguàrdo *s. m.* flyleaf
risièdere *v. intr.* to reside, to live
rìsma *s. f.* **1** (*di carta*) ream **2** (*fig.*) kind, quality
rìso (1) *s. m.* laugh, laughter
rìso (2) *s. m.* (*bot.*) rice
risolutìvo *agg.* resolutive, decisive
risolùto *agg.* resolute
risoluzióne *s. f.* **1** resolution, decision **2**

(*mat.*) solution **3** (*dir.*) cancellation
risòlvere **A** *v. tr.* **1** to solve, to work out, to resolve **2** (*definire*) to settle **3** (*rescindere*) to cancel **B** *v. intr. pron.* **1** (*decidersi*) to decide, to make up one's mind **2** (*trasformarsi*) to change, to turn into **3** (*di malattia*) to resolve, to clear up
risonànza *s. f.* resonance, echo
risórgere *v. intr.* to rise again, to revive
risorgìva *s. f.* resurgence
risórsa *s. f.* resource
risparmiàre **A** *v. tr.* **1** to save (up) **2** (*evitare, salvare*) to spare **B** *v. rifl.* to spare oneself
risparmiatóre *s. m.* saver
rispàrmio *s. m.* **1** saving **2** (*somma risparmiata*) savings *pl.*
rispecchiàre *v. tr.* to reflect
rispedìre *v. tr.* **1** (*spedire di nuovo*) to send again **2** (*spedire indietro*) to send back
rispettàbile *agg.* **1** respectable **2** (*considerevole*) considerable
rispettabilità *s. f.* respectability
rispettàre *v. tr.* **1** to respect, to honour **2** (*osservare*) to comply with, to observe
rispettìvo *agg.* respective
rispètto *s. m.* respect
rispettóso *agg.* respectful
risplèndere *v. intr.* to shine
rispóndere **A** *v. intr.* **1** to answer, to reply **2** (*ribattere*) to answer back **3** (*farsi garante*) to be responsible for, to answer for **4** (*corrispondere*) to meet **5** (*obbedire*) to respond **B** *v. tr.* **1** to answer **2** (*a carte*) to reply
rispósta *s. f.* **1** answer, reply **2** (*reazione*) response
rìssa *s. f.* brawl
rissóso *agg.* brawling, quarrelsome
ristabilìre **A** *v. tr.* to re-establish, to restore **B** *v. intr. pron.* **1** to settle again **2** (*rimettersi*) to recover, to get well again
ristagnàre *v. intr.* to be stagnant
ristàgno *s. m.* stagnation
ristàmpa *s. f.* reprint
ristampàre *v. tr.* to reprint
ristorànte *s. m.* restaurant
ristoràre **A** *v. tr.* to refresh, to restore **B** *v. rifl.* to refresh oneself
ristoratóre *s. m.* restaurateur
ristrettézza *s. f.* **1** narrowness **2** (*meschinità*) meanness **3** (*insufficienza*) lack, shortage **4** *al pl.* (*condizioni economiche disagiate*) financial straits *pl.*
ristrétto *agg.* **1** narrow **2** (*meschino*) mean **3** (*limitato*) narrow, limited **4** (*condensato*) condensed ♦ **caffè r.** strong coffee
ristrutturàre *v. tr.* to restructure, to renovate
ristrutturazióne *s. f.* restructuration, renovation
risucchiàre *v. tr.* to suck
risultàre *v. intr.* **1** to result, to come out, to follow, to ensue, to spring **2** (*essere noto, impers.*) to understand, to know ♦ **risulta chiaro che ...** it is clear that ...
risultàto *s. m.* result, outcome
risuolàre *v. tr.* to resole
risuonàre *v. intr.* to resound
risurrezióne *s. f.* resurrection
risuscitàre **A** *v. tr.* to resuscitate, to revive **B** *v. intr.* to rise again, to revive
risvegliàre **A** *v. tr.* to awake, to awaken **B** *v. intr. pron.* **1** to wake up **2** (*fig.*) to revive
risvéglio *s. m.* **1** (re)awakening, waking up **2** (*fig.*) revival
risvòlto *s. m.* **1** (*di giacca*) lapel, (*di pantaloni*) turn-up **2** (*fig.*) implication, consequence
ritagliàre *v. tr.* to cut out
ritàglio *s. m.* (*pezzetto*) scrap, (*di giornale*) cutting, clipping
ritardàre **A** *v. tr.* to delay, to retard, to put off **B** *v. intr.* to delay, to be late
ritardatàrio *s. m.* late-comer
ritàrdo *s. m.* delay ♦ **essere in r.** to be late
ritégno *s. m.* reserve, restraint
ritenére **A** *v. tr.* **1** (*trattenere*) to hold, to keep, to retain **2** (*credere*) to think, to believe **B** *v. rifl.* to consider oneself
ritiràre **A** *v. tr.* **1** (*tirare di nuovo*) to throw again **2** (*tirare indietro*) to withdraw, to draw back, to retract **3** (*farsi consegnare*) to collect, to pick up, (*riscuotere*) to draw **B** *v. rifl.* to retire, to withdraw **C** *v. intr. pron.* **1** (*di tessuto*) to shrink **2** (*di acque*) to subside, to recede
ritiràta *s. f.* **1** retreat, withdrawal **2** (*in caserma*) tattoo
ritìro *s. m.* **1** withdrawal, retirement **2** (*luogo appartato*) retreat
rìtmo *s. m.* **1** rhythm **2** (*tasso*) rate
rìto *s. m.* **1** rite **2** (*usanza*) custom
ritoccàre *v. tr.* **1** to retouch **2** (*prezzi*) to readjust
ritócco *s. m.* **1** touch-up, finishing touch **2** (*di prezzi*) adjustment, revision
ritornàre **A** *v. intr.* **1** to return, to go back,

to come back **2** (*ricorrere*) to recur **3** (*tornare a essere*) to become again **B** *v. tr.* to return, to give back
ritornèllo *s. m.* refrain
ritórno *s. m.* return
ritràrre A *v. tr.* **1** (*tirare indietro*) to withdraw, to draw back **2** (*distogliere*) to divert **3** (*rappresentare*) to represent, to portray, to depict **B** *v. rifl.* **1** to withdraw **2** (*sottrarsi*) to get out **3** (*rappresentarsi*) to portray oneself
ritrattàre *v. tr.* **1** (*trattare di nuovo*) to treat again **2** (*ritirare*) to retract, to withdraw
ritràtto *s. m.* portrait
ritróso *agg.* **1** (*riluttante*) reluctant **2** (*timido*) shy ♦ **a r.** backwards
ritrovaménto *s. m.* finding, (*scoperta*) discovery
ritrovàre A *v. tr.* **1** to find (again) **2** (*scoprire*) to find, to discover **3** (*ricuperare*) to recover **4** (*incontrare di nuovo*) to meet (again) **B** *v. intr. pron.* to find oneself **C** *v. rifl. rec.* (*incontrarsi di nuovo*) to meet again **D** *v. rifl.* **1** (*raccapezzarsi*) to see one's way **2** (*sentirsi a proprio agio*) to feel at ease
ritròvo *s. m.* meeting, (*luogo*) meeting-place
rìtto *agg.* upright, erect
rituàle *s. m.* ritual
riunióne *s. f.* meeting
riunìre A *v. tr.* **1** to reunite, to put together **2** (*adunare*) to gather, to collect together **3** (*riconciliare*) to bring together again **B** *v. rifl.* **1** to come together again **2** (*adunarsi*) to gather, to meet
riuscìre *v. intr.* **1** to succeed, to manage, (*essere capace*) to be able **2** (*avere esito*) to come out, to turn out, (*avere esito positivo*) to be successful, to succeed **3** (*avere attitudine*) to be clever at, to be good at **4** (*apparire, risultare*) to be, (*dimostrarsi*) to prove **5** (*uscire di nuovo*) to go out again
riuscìta *s. f.* result, outcome, (*successo*) success
rìva *s. f.* (*di fiume*) bank, (*di lago, mare*) shore
rivàle *agg. e s. m. e f.* rival
rivalità *s. f.* rivalry
rivàlsa *s. f.* **1** (*rivincita*) revenge **2** (*risarcimento*) compensation
rivalutàre *v. tr.* to revalue
rivalutazióne *s. f.* revaluation
rivedére A *v. tr.* **1** (*vedere di nuovo*) to see again, (*incontrare di nuovo*) to meet again **2** (*correggere*) to revise, to correct, (*controllare*) to check **3** (*ripassare*) to look over again **B** *v. rifl. rec.* to see each other again, to meet again
rivelàre A *v. tr.* **1** to reveal, to disclose **2** (*mostrare*) to show **B** *v. rifl.* to reveal oneself, to show oneself
rivelazióne *s. f.* revelation
rivéndere *v. tr.* **1** to resell, to sell again **2** (*vendere al dettaglio*) to retail
rivendicàre *v. tr.* to claim
rivèrbero *s. m.* reverberation
riverènza *s. f.* **1** reverence **2** (*inchino*) bow, curtsey
riverìre *v. tr.* **1** to revere, to respect **2** (*salutare*) to pay one's respects to
riverniciàre *v. tr.* to repaint
riversàre A *v. tr.* to pour (again) **B** *v. intr. pron.* **1** to flow **2** (*fig.*) to pour (out)
rivestiménto *s. m.* covering, coating, (*interno*) lining
rivestìre A *v. tr.* **1** (*vestire di nuovo*) to dress again **2** (*provvedere di abiti*) to dress, to provide with clothes **3** (*ricoprire*) to cover, to coat, (*foderare*) to line **4** (*una carica*) to hold **B** *v. rifl.* to dress again
rivièra *s. f.* coast
rivìncita *s. f.* **1** (*sport*) return match, (*gioco*) return game **2** (*rivalsa*) revenge
rivisitàre *v. tr.* to revisit
rivista *s. f.* **1** (*mil.*) review **2** (*periodico*) review, (*rotocalco*) magazine **3** (*teatro*) revue, show ♦ **passare in r.** to review
rivìvere A *v. tr.* to live again **B** *v. intr.* to live again, (*tornare in vita*) to come to life again
rivòlgere A *v. tr.* **1** to turn, to direct **2** (*indirizzare*) to address **B** *v. rifl.* **1** to turn, to address **2** (*ricorrere*) to apply
rivòlta *s. f.* revolt, rebellion
rivoltàre A *v. tr.* **1** to turn (over) again **2** (*rovesciare*) to turn (over), (*con l'interno verso l'esterno*) to turn inside out, (*capovolgere*) to turn upside down **B** *v. rifl.* to turn round, to turn over **C** *v. intr. pron.* (*ribellarsi*) to revolt, to rebel
rivoltèlla *s. f.* revolver
rivoluzionàre *v. tr.* to revolutionize
rivoluzionàrio *agg. e s. m.* revolutionary
rivoluzióne *s. f.* revolution
rizzàre A *v. tr.* to raise, to erect **B** *v. intr. pron.* (*di capelli, peli*) to bristle
ròba *s. f.* stuff, things *pl.*
robùsto *agg.* strong, sturdy
ròcca *s. f.* fortress, stronghold
roccafòrte *s. f.* fortress, stronghold

rocchétto *s. m.* **1** reel, spool **2** (*elettr*) coil
ròccia *s. f.* rock
rocciatóre *s. m.* rock-climber
roccióso *agg.* rocky
rococò *agg. e s. m.* rococo
rodàggio *s. m.* **1** (*autom.*) running-in, (*USA*) breaking-in **2** (*fig.*) trial stage
rodeo *s. m. inv.* rodeo
ródere **A** *v. tr.* **1** to gnaw **2** (*corrodere*) to eat into, to corrode **B** *v. rifl.* to worry
roditóre *s. m.* rodent
rododèndro *s. m.* rhododendron
rógna *s. f.* **1** (*med.*) scabies, (*bot., zool.*) scab **2** (*fastidio*) nuisance, trouble
rognóne *s. m.* kidney
rògo *s. m.* **1** (*supplizio*) stake **2** (*pira*) (funeral) pyre **3** (*incendio*) fire
rollìo *s. m.* rolling
romànico *agg.* Romanesque
romàno *agg. e s. m.* Roman
romanticìsmo *s. m.* Romanticism
romàntico *agg. e s. m.* romantic
romànza *s. f.* romance
romanzésco *agg.* **1** novel (*attr*) **2** (*fig.*) fantastic
romanzière *s. m.* novelist
romànzo *s. m.* **1** novel **2** (*medievale*) romance **3** (*novellistica*) fiction **4** (*fig.*) fantasy, romance
rómbo (1) *s. m.* (*geom.*) rhombus
rómbo (2) *s. m.* (*zool.*) rhombus
rómbo (3) *s. m.* (*rumore*) rumble, roar
romboidàle *agg.* rhomboidal
roméno *agg. e s. m.* Rumanian
rómpere **A** *v. tr.* **1** to break, to burst, to smash **2** (*interrompere*) to break off **B** *v. intr.* **1** (*interrompere i rapporti*) to break up **2** (*fam.*) (*seccare*) to bother **C** *v. intr. pron.* to break
rompicàpo *s. m.* riddle, puzzle
rompighiàccio *s. m.* ice breaker
rompiscàtole *s. m. e f. inv.* nuisance, pest
rónda *s. f.* rounds *pl.*, patrol
rondèlla *s. f.* washer
róndine *s. f.* swallow
rondóne *s. m.* swift
ronzàre *v. intr.* **1** to buzz, to hum **2** (*girare*) to hang round
ronzìno *s. m.* nag
ròsa (1) *agg. e s. m.* pink
ròsa (2) *s. f.* **1** (*bot.*) rose **2** (*gruppo di persone*) group ♦ **r. dei venti** compass card
rosàrio *s. m.* rosary
ròseo *agg.* rosy
rosicchiàre *v. tr.* to nibble, to gnaw
rosmarìno *s. m.* rosemary
rosolàre **A** *v. tr.* to brown **B** *v. intr. pron.* **1** to get brown **2** (*fig.*) to bask in the sun
rosolìa *s. f.* German measles *pl.*, rubella
rosóne *s. m.* rose-window
ròspo *s. m.* toad
rossétto *s. m.* lipstick
rósso *agg. e s. m.* red
rossóre *s. m.* flush
rotàia *s. f.* rail
rotatìva *s. f.* rotary press
rotatòria *s. f.* roundabout
rotazióne *s. f.* **1** rotation **2** (*di personale, scorte*) turnover
roteàre **A** *v. tr.* to swing, (*occhi*) to roll **B** *v. intr.* to wheel
rotèlla *s. f.* small wheel, (*di pattino*) roller
rotocàlco *s. m.* magazine
rotolàre *v. tr. e intr.* to roll
ròtolo *s. m.* roll, (*di corda*) coil
rotónda *s. f.* **1** (*arch.*) rotunda **2** (*terrazza*) round terrace
rotondità *s. f.* rotundity, roundness
rotóndo *agg.* round
rótta (1) *s. f.* (*sconfitta*) rout, retreat ♦ **a r. di collo** headlong; **essere in r. con qc.** to be on bad terms with sb.
rótta (2) *s. f.* (*naut., aer*) course, route
rottàme *s. m.* scrap
rottùra *s. f.* break, breaking
ròtula *s. f.* kneecap, rotula
roulotte *s. f. inv.* caravan, (*USA*) trailer
rovènte *agg.* red-hot
róvere *s. m. o f.* durmast
rovesciàre **A** *v. tr.* **1** to upset, to knock over, to overturn **2** (*rivoltare*) to turn inside out **3** (*versare*) to pour, (*accidentalmente*) to spill **4** (*abbattere*) to overthrow **B** *v. intr. pron.* **1** to overturn, (*capovolgersi*) to capsize **2** (*versarsi*) to spill **3** (*riversarsi*) to pour
rovèscio **A** *agg.* (*capovolto*) upside down, (*con l'interno all'esterno*) inside out **B** *s. m.* **1** reverse, back, other side **2** (*opposto*) opposite **3** (*lavoro a maglia*) purl (stitch) **4** (*tennis*) backhand **5** (*di pioggia*) heavy shower **6** (*dissesto*) setback
rovìna *s. f.* ruin
rovinàre **A** *v. tr.* **1** to ruin, (*guastare*) to spoil **2** (*abbattere*) to demolish, to pull down **B** *v. intr.* to crash, to collapse **C** *v. rifl. e intr. pron.* to be ruined

rovinóso *agg.* ruinous, disastrous
rovistàre *v. tr. e intr.* to ransack
róvo *s. m.* bramble
rózzo *agg.* rough, coarse
rubàre *v. tr.* to steal
rubinétto *s. m.* tap, (*USA*) faucet
rubìno *s. m.* ruby
rubrìca *s. f.* **1** (*quaderno*) index-book, (*per indirizzi*) address-book **2** (*di giornale*) column, survey
rùde *agg.* rough, harsh
rùdere *s. m.* ruin
rudimentàle *agg.* rudimentary
rudiménto *s. m.* rudiment
rùga *s. f.* wrinkle
rùggine *s. f.* rust
rugginóso *agg.* rusty
ruggìre *v. intr.* to roar
ruggìto *s. m.* roar
rugiàda *s. f.* dew
rugosità *s. f.* roughness, (*di viso*) wrinkledness
rugóso *agg.* **1** (*di viso*) wrinkled **2** (*scabro*) rough
rùllo *s. m.* roll, (*di macchina per scrivere*) platen
ruminànte *agg. e s. m.* ruminant
ruminàre *v. tr. e intr.* to ruminate
rumóre *s. m.* noise
rumoróso *agg.* noisy
ruòlo *s. m.* role
ruòta *s. f.* wheel ♦ **r. di scorta** spare wheel
ruotàre **A** *v. tr.* to rotate, (*occhi*) to roll **B** *v. intr.* **1** to rotate, to revolve **2** (*roteare*) to circle (round), to wheel about
rùpe *s. f.* cliff, rock
rupèstre *agg.* rocky
ruràle *agg.* rural, country (*attr.*)
ruscèllo *s. m.* brook
rùspa *s. f.* scraper, bulldozer
ruspànte *agg.* farmyard
russàre *v. intr.* to snore
rùsso *agg. e s. m.* Russian
rùstico *agg.* **1** country (*attr.*), rustic, rural **2** (*rozzo*) rough
rùvido *agg.* rough, coarse
ruzzolàre *v. intr.* **1** (*cadere*) to tumble down **2** (*rotolare*) to roll
ruzzolóne *s. m.* tumble

S

sàbato *s. m.* Saturday
sabbàtico *agg.* sabbatical
sàbbia *s. f.* sand
sabbiatùra *s. f.* **1** sand-bath **2** (*tecnol.*) sand-blasting
sabbióso *agg.* sandy
sabotàggio *s. m.* sabotage
sabotàre *v. tr.* to sabotage
sàcca *s. f.* bag, knapsack
saccarìna *s. f.* saccharine
saccaròsio *s. m.* saccharose
saccènte **A** *agg.* pedantic, (*presuntuoso*) conceited **B** *s. m. e f.* know-all
saccheggiàre *v. tr.* to sack, to pillage, to plunder, to loot
saccheggiatóre *s. m.* pillager, plunderer
sacchèggio *s. m.* sack, pillage, plunder
sacchétto *s. m.* bag
sàcco *s. m.* **1** sack, bag **2** (*grande quantità*) a lot, lots *pl.*, a great deal, heaps *pl.* ♦ **s. a pelo** sleeping bag
sacerdòte *s. m.* priest
sacerdotéssa *s. f.* priestess
sacerdòzio *s. m.* priesthood
sacralgìa *s. f.* sacralgia
sacraménto *s. m.* sacrament
sacràrio *s. m.* **1** (*archeol.*) sacrarium **2** (*dei caduti*) memorial
sacrificàre **A** *v. tr.* **1** to sacrifice **2** (*sprecare*) to waste **B** *v. intr.* to offer sacrifices **C** *v. rifl.* to sacrifice oneself
sacrificio *s. m.* sacrifice
sacrilègio *s. m.* sacrilege
sàcro *agg.* **1** sacred, holy **2** (*consacrato*) consecrated, dedicated
sàdico **A** *agg.* sadistic **B** *s. m.* sadist
sadomasochìsmo *s. m.* sadomasochism
saétta *s. f.* **1** (*freccia*) arrow **2** (*fulmine*) thunderbolt, flash of lightning
safàri *s. m. inv.* safari
sàga *s. f.* saga
sagàce *agg.* shrewd, sagacious
saggézza *s. f.* wisdom
saggiàre *v. tr.* **1** (*analizzare*) to assay **2** (*fig.*) to test, to try out
sàggio (1) **A** *agg.* wise **B** *s. m.* wise man
sàggio (2) *s. m.* **1** (*prova*) test, trial, (*metall.*) assay **2** (*campione*) sample **3** (*dimostrazione*) proof **4** (*scritto*) essay
saggìsta *s. m. e f.* essayist
sàgola *s. f.* line
sàgoma *s. f.* **1** (*forma*) shape, outline, profile **2** (*tecnol.*) template **3** (*bersaglio*) target **4** (*fam.*) (*persona stramba*) character
sàgra *s. f.* festival, feast
sagràto *s. m.* church-square
sagrestìa *s. f.* sacristy
sàio *s. m.* habit
sàla *s. f.* hall, room ♦ **s. da pranzo** dining room; **s. d'aspetto** waiting room; **s. operatoria** operating theatre
salàme *s. m.* salami
salamòia *s. f.* brine, pickle
salàre *v. tr.* to salt, (*per conservare*) to corn
salàrio *s. m.* wage, salary
salàsso *s. m.* **1** bleeding **2** (*fig.*) drain
salàto *agg.* **1** salt, salty **2** (*sotto sale*) corned, salted **3** (*costoso*) expensive, stiff **4** (*salace*) biting
saldàre **A** *v. tr.* **1** (*metall.*) to weld **2** (*unire*) to link up with, to join **3** (*comm.*) to settle, to pay off, to balance **B** *v. intr. pron.* **1** (*metall.*) to weld **2** (*di ossa*) to knit **3** (*unirsi*) to tie up, to link
saldatóre *s. m.* welder
saldatrice *s. f.* welder
saldatùra *s. f.* **1** (*metall.*) welding **2** (*fig.*) link, connection
saldézza *s. f.* firmness, strenght
sàldo *s. m.* **1** (*importo residuo*) settlement, balance **2** (*resto*) rest, balance **3** (*svendita*) sale
sàle *s. m.* salt ♦ **s. grosso** coarse salt; **senza s.** saltless; **sotto s.** salted
salesiàno *agg. e s. m.* Salesian
sàlice *s. m.* willow ♦ **s. piangente** weeping willow
saliènte *agg.* important, main
salièra *s. f.* saltcellar
salina *s. f.* (*deposito*) salt pan, salina
salìno *agg.* saline, salt (*attr.*)
salire **A** *v. intr.* **1** to rise, to climb, to go up, to come up **2** (*su un mezzo di trasporto*) to get on **3** (*fig.*) to rise, to go up **B** *v. tr.* to climb, to go up, to ascend
salita *s. f.* **1** slope, ascent **2** (*il salire*) climbing, ascent **3** (*aumento*) rise, in-

crease
salìva *s. f.* saliva, spittle
sàlma *s. f.* corpse
salmì *s. m.* salmi
sàlmo *s. m.* psalm
salmóne *s. m.* salmon ♦ **s. affumicato** smoked salmon
salmonellòsi *s. f.* salmonellosis
salóne *s. m.* **1** hall **2** (*per esposizione*) showroom
salòtto *s. m.* **1** drawing room, sitting room **2** (*letterario*) salon
salpàre **A** *v. tr.* to weigh **B** *v. intr.* **1** to (set) sail, to set out **2** (*l'ancora*) to weigh (anchor)
sàlsa *s. f.* sauce
salsèdine *s. f.* saltness, (*salinità*) salinity
salsìccia *s. f.* sausage
salsièra *s. f.* sauce boat, gravy boat
saltàre **A** *v. tr.* to jump (over), to leap (over), to skip **B** *v. intr.* **1** to jump, to leap, to spring **2** (*esplodere*) to blow up, to pop out
saltatóre *s. m.* jumper
saltellàre *v. intr.* to skip, to hop
saltimbànco *s. m.* acrobat, tumbler
sàlto *s. m.* **1** jump, leap, spring **2** (*omissione*) gap
saltuariaménte *avv.* occasionally
saltuàrio *agg.* irregolar, occasional
salùbre *agg.* salubrious, wholesome, healthy
salubrità *s. f.* wholesomeness, healthiness
salumerìa *s. f.* delicatessen (shop)
salùmi *s. m. pl.* cold cuts *pl.*
salumière *s. m.* delicatessen seller
salutàre (1) **A** *v. tr.* **1** to greet, to say hallo to, (*partendo*) to say goodbye to **2** (*mil.*) to salute **3** (*fare visita*) to call (in) **B** *v. rifl. rec.* to greet each other, to say goodbye to each other
salutàre (2) *agg.* wholesome, healthy, salutary
salùte *s. f.* health
salutìsta *s. m. e f.* hygienist
salùto *s. m.* greeting, salutation
salvacondótto *s. m.* safe-conduct
salvadanàio *s. m.* money-box
salvagènte *s. m.* (*ciambella*) life buoy, (*giubbotto*) life jacket, (*cintura*) life belt
salvagócce *s. m. inv.* drip-catcher
salvaguardàre *v. tr.* to safeguard, to protect
salvàre **A** *v. tr.* **1** to save, (*trarre in salvo*) to rescue **2** (*mettere da parte*) to put aside, to save **B** *v. rifl.* **1** to save oneself, to survive **2** (*evitare*) to be spared
salvatàggio *s. m.* rescue ♦ **battello di s.** life boat; **cintura di s.** life belt
salvatóre *s. m.* saver, rescuer, (*spirituale*) saviour
sàlve *inter.* hello!, hi!
salvézza *s. f.* **1** salvation **2** (*sicurezza*) safety **3** (*scampo*) escape
sàlvia *s. f.* sage
salviétta *s. f.* **1** (*tovagliolo*) napkin **2** (*asciugamano*) towel
sàlvo (1) *agg.* **1** safe **2** (*al sicuro*) secure ♦ **mettersi in s.** to reach safety
sàlvo (2) **A** *prep.* **1** (*tranne*) except (for), but **2** (*a parte*) apart from **B** *cong.* **s. che** except that, (*a meno che*) unless
sambùco *s. m.* elder
sanàre *v. tr.* **1** to cure **2** (*correggere*) to rectify, to correct **3** (*econ.*) to balance, to put right
sanatòrio *s. m.* sanatorium
sancìre *v. tr.* to sanction
sàndalo (1) *s. m.* (*bot.*) sandal, sandalwood
sàndalo (2) *s. m.* (*calzatura*) sandal
sàngue *s. m.* blood ♦ **al s.** (*di carne*) underdone, rare; **a s. freddo** in cold blood
sanguìgno *agg.* blood (*attr*), sanguineous
sanguinàre *v. intr.* to bleed
sanguisùga *s. f.* leech
sanità *s. f.* **1** soundness, (*salubrità*) wholesomeness **2** (*ente sanitario*) health board
sanitàrio *agg.* sanitary, health (*attr*) ♦ **certificato s.** health certificate
sàno *agg.* **1** healthy, wholesome, (*senza difetto*) sound **2** (*salubre*) healthy, healthful, wholesome **3** (*saggio*) sound ♦ **s. e salvo** safe and sound
santìno *s. m.* holy picture
santità *s. f.* holiness, sanctity
sànto **A** *agg.* holy, (*seguito da nome proprio*) Saint **B** *s. m.* saint
santóne *s. m.* guru (*fig.*)
santuàrio *s. m.* sanctuary, shrine
sanzióne *s. f.* sanction
sapére (1) **A** *v. tr.* **1** to know **2** (*venire a sapere*) to hear, to learn, to know **3** (*essere capace*) can, to be able, to know how **B** *v. intr.* **1** to know **2** (*venire a conoscenza*) to hear, to learn **3** (*aver sapore*) to taste, (*aver odore*) to smell **4** (*pensare*) to think
sapére (2) *s. m.* knowledge, (*cultura*) learning
sàpido *agg.* sapid

sapiènte *agg.* **1** (*saggio*) wise **2** (*colto*) learned **3** (*abile*) skilful
sapiènza *s. f.* **1** (*saggezza*) wisdom **2** (*cultura*) learning **3** (*sapere*) knowledge
sapóne *s. m.* soap ♦ **s. da barba** shaving soap
saponétta *s. f.* cake of soap
sapóre *s. m.* **1** taste, flavour **2** (*fig.*) spice
saporìto *agg.* tasty, savoury
saracinésca *s. f.* (rolling) shutter
sarcàsmo *s. m.* sarcasm
sarcàstico *agg.* sarcastic
sarcòfago *s. m.* sarcophagus
sardìna *s. f.* sardine
sàrdo *agg. e s. m.* Sardinian
sàrta *s. f.* dressmaker
sàrtia *s. f.* shroud
sartiàme *s. m.* shrouds *pl.*, rigging
sàrto *s. m.* tailor
sartorìa *s. f.* tailor's (workshop), dressmaker's
sàsso *s. m.* stone, rock, (*ciottolo*) pebble
sassofonista *s. m. e f.* saxophonist
sassòfono *s. m.* saxophone, sax
sàssola *s. f.* bailer
sassóso *agg.* stony
satànico *agg.* satanic
satèllite *s. m.* satellite
sàtira *s. f.* satire
satìrico *agg.* satiric(al)
saturazióne *s. f.* saturation
sàturo *agg.* **1** (*chim.*) saturated **2** (*pieno*) full, filled with
sàuna *s. f.* sauna
savàna *s. f.* savanna(h)
saziàre **A** *v. tr.* **1** to satisfy, to sate, to glut **2** (*riempire*) to fill **B** *v. rifl.* **1** to get full, to become satiated **2** (*fig.*) to get tired
sàzio *agg.* satiated, glutted, full (up) (*fam.*)
sbadatàggine *s. f.* carelessness, inadvertence
sbadàto **A** *agg.* careless **B** *s. m.* scatterbrain
sbadigliàre *v. intr.* to yawn
sbadìglio *s. m.* yawn
sbagliàre **A** *v. tr.* to mistake, to go wrong in **B** *v. intr. e intr. pron.* to make a mistake, to be wrong, to be mistaken
sbàglio *s. m.* mistake, error ♦ **per s.** by mistake
sballottàre *v. tr.* to toss (about), to push (about)
sbalordìre **A** *v. tr.* to amaze, to astonish **B** *v. intr. e intr. pron.* to be amazed, to be astonished
sbalorditìvo *agg.* amazing, astonishing
sbalzàre *v. tr.* **1** to throw, to toss, to fling **2** (*lavorare a sbalzo*) to emboss
sbàlzo *s. m.* **1** jolt, jerk **2** (*cambiamento*) sudden change, jump **3** (*sporgenza*) overhang **4** (*rilievo*) embossment
sbandaménto *s. m.* **1** (*autom.*) sliding, veering **2** (*naut.*) heeling **3** (*fig.*) leaning, disorientation
sbandàre **A** *v. intr.* **1** (*autom.*) to slide **2** (*naut.*) to heel **3** (*fig.*) to lean **B** *v. intr. pron.* to disperse, to disband
sbandieràre *v. tr.* **1** to wave **2** (*fig.*) to display, to show off
sbaragliàre *v. tr.* to rout
sbarazzàre **A** *v. tr.* to clear up **B** *v. rifl.* to get rid
sbarbàre *v. tr. e rifl.* to shave
sbarcàre **A** *v. tr.* to disembark, (*da aereo*) to land, (*da autobus*) to put down, (*merci*) to unload **B** *v. intr.* to land, to get off
sbàrco *s. m.* landing, (*di merci*) unloading
sbàrra *s. f.* bar
sbarraménto *s. m.* **1** blockage, obstruction **2** (*mil.*) barrage
sbarràre *v. tr.* **1** to bar, to block, to obstruct **2** (*gli occhi*) to open wide **3** (*segnare con barra*) to cross
sbàttere **A** *v. tr.* **1** (*battere*) to knock, to bang, to beat **2** (*sbatacchiare*) to bang, to slam **3** (*gettare*) to hurl, to fling, (*buttare fuori*) to throw out **4** (*agitare*) to shake, to toss **B** *v. intr.* **1** (*di porta, finestra*) to bang, to slam **2** (*di ali, vele*) to flap
sbattùto *agg.* **1** (*frullato*) beaten **2** (*stanco*) tired out
sbavàre *v. intr.* **1** to dribble **2** (*di inchiostro*) to smudge
sbèrla *s. f.* slap, cuff
sberlèffo *s. m.* grimace
sbiadìre *v. tr., intr. e intr. pron.* to fade
sbiadìto *agg.* **1** faded **2** (*scialbo*) dull
sbiancàre **A** *v. tr.* to whiten, (*tessuto*) to bleach **B** *v. intr. pron.* **1** to turn white **2** (*impallidire*) to go pale
sbièco *agg.* sloping, aslant, oblique
sbigottìre **A** *v. tr.* to bewilder, to astonish, (*turbare*) to dismay **B** *v. intr. e intr. pron.* to be bewildered, to be astonished, (*turbarsi*) to be dismayed
sbilanciàre **A** *v. tr.* to unbalance, to throw off the balance **B** *v. intr. pron.* to lose one's balance

sbirciàre *v. tr.* to peep, to glance at
sbìrro *s. m.* (*spreg.*) cop
sbloccàre **A** *v. tr.* **1** to unblock, to free **2** (*mecc.*) to unlock, to release **3** (*econ.*) to decontrol **B** *v. rifl. e intr. pron.* **1** to reopen, to restart **2** (*psic.*) to get over
sboccàre *v. intr.* **1** (*di corso d'acqua*) to flow into **2** (*di strada*) to lead to, to come out
sbocciàre *v. intr.* to blossom, to bloom
sbócco *s. m.* outlet, (*di fiume*) mouth, (*uscita*) way out
sbollìre *v. intr.* **1** to stop boiling **2** (*fig.*) to cool down
sbòrnia *s. f.* drunkenness
sborsàre *v. tr.* to pay out, to spend
sbottàre *v. intr.* to burst out
sbottonàre **A** *v. tr.* to unbutton **B** *v. rifl.* **1** to undo one's buttons **2** (*fam., fig.*) to open one's heart
sbraitàre *v. intr.* to shout
sbranàre *v. tr.* to tear to pieces
sbriciolàre *v. tr. e intr. pron.* to crumble
sbrigàre **A** *v. tr.* to dispatch, to get through, to finish off **B** *v. intr. pron.* to hurry up, to be quick
sbrigatìvo *agg.* speedy, (*affrettato*) hasty
sbrinaménto *s. m.* defrosting
sbrinàre *v. tr.* to defrost
sbrinatóre *s. m.* defroster
sbrindellàto *agg.* tattered
sbrodolàre **A** *v. tr.* to soil **B** *v. rifl.* to soil oneself
sbrogliàre **A** *v. tr.* to disentangle, to unravel **B** *v. rifl.* to extricate oneself, to get oneself out of
sbrónza *s. f.* drunkenness
sbronzàrsi *v. rifl.* to get drunk
sbrónzo *agg.* drunk (*pred.*)
sbruffóne *s. m.* boaster
sbucàre *v. intr.* **1** to come out of **2** (*fig.*) to spring
sbucciàre *v. tr.* **1** to peel **2** (*sgranare*) to shell **3** (*produrre un'abrasione*) to graze
sbuffàre *v. intr.* **1** to puff, to pant **2** (*per noia*) to grumble, to snort **3** (*gettare sbuffi di fumo*) to puff away
sbùffo *s. m.* puff
scàbbia *s. f.* scabies
scabróso *agg.* **1** rough **2** (*fig.*) scabrous, delicate
scacchièra *s. f.* (*per scacchi*) chess-board, (*per dama*) draught-board
scacciacàni *s. m. o f. inv.* blank pistol
scacciàre *v. tr.* to drive away, to drive out, to expel
scàcco *s. m.* **1** (*quadratino di scacchiera*) square, (*disegno*) check **2** *al pl.* (*gioco*) chess **3** (*sconfitta*) loss, setback
scaccomàtto *s. m.* checkmate ♦ **dare s.** to checkmate
scadènte *agg.* poor, second-rate
scadènza *s. f.* expiry, (*ultima data utile*) deadline ♦ **data di s.** expiry date, due date
scadenzàrio *s. m.* due register, bill-book
scadére *v. intr.* **1** to expire, to be due, to mature **2** (*peggiorare*) to fall off
scafàndro *s. m.* diving suit
scaffàle *s. m.* shelf, bookcase
scàfo *s. m.* hull
scagionàre *v. tr.* to exculpate
scàglia *s. f.* scale, (*di sapone*) flake
scagliàre **A** *v. tr.* to hurl, to throw **B** *v. rifl.* to hurl oneself, to throw oneself, to rush
scaglionàre *v. tr.* to space out, to spread
scaglióne *s. m.* **1** (*gruppo*) group, batch **2** (*mil.*) echelon **3** (*classe*) bracket
scàla *s. f.* **1** staircase, stairs *pl.*, (*portatile*) ladder **2** (*mus., geogr., mat.*) scale ♦ **s. a pioli** rung ladder; **s. mobile** escalator
scalàre *v. tr.* **1** to scale, to climb (up) **2** (*detrarre*) to scale down, to take off
scalàta *s. f.* climbing
scalatóre *s. m.* climber
scaldabàgno *s. m.* water heater
scaldalètto *s. m.* warming pan
scaldàre **A** *v. tr.* to heat, to warm **B** *v. intr.* to warm, to give out heat **C** *v. rifl.* to warm oneself **D** *v. intr. pron.* **1** to heat up, to warm up **2** (*eccitarsi*) to get excited
scaldavivànde *s. m. inv.* chafing-dish
scalétta *s. f.* **1** list **2** (*cin.*) treatment
scalfìre *v. tr.* **1** to scratch **2** (*fig.*) to touch, to affect
scalfittùra *s. f.* scratch
scalinàta *s. f.* flight of steps
scalìno *s. m.* step
scàlo *s. m.* **1** call **2** (*porto*) port, (*aeroporto*) airport **3** (*impalcatura per navi*) slip ♦ **s. merci** goods yard; **volo senza s.** non-stop flight
scalógna *s. f.* bad luck
scalóne *s. m.* great staircase
scaloppìna *s. f.* escalope
scalpèllo *s. m.* chisel, (*med.*) scalpel
scalpóre *s. m.* noise, sensation
scàltro *agg.* shrewd, sly, cunning

scalzàre *v. tr.* **1** to bare the roots of **2** (*fig.*) to undermine
scàlzo *agg.* barefoot
scambiàre **A** *v. tr.* **1** to exchange, to swap **2** (*confondere*) to mistake **B** *v. rifl. rec.* to exchange ♦ **s. una visita** to return a visit
scambiévole *agg.* reciprocal
scàmbio *s. m.* **1** exchange **2** (*ferr*) points *pl.*, (*USA*) switch
scamosciàto *agg.* chamois (*attr*), suède
scampagnàta *s. f.* outing, picnic
scampanellata *s. f.* long loud ring
scampanìo *s. m.* pealing
scampàre **A** *v. tr.* **1** to save, to rescue **2** (*evitare*) to avoid, to escape **B** *v. intr.* **1** to escape **2** (*rifugiarsi*) to take refuge
scàmpo (1) *s. m.* escape, safety
scàmpo (2) *s. m.* (*zool.*) prawn
scàmpolo *s. m.* remnant
scanalatùra *s. f.* **1** groove **2** (*arch.*) flute, fluting
scandagliàre *v. tr.* to sound, to fathom
scandalìstico *agg.* scandalmongering
scandalizzàre **A** *v. tr.* to scandalize **B** *v. intr. pron.* to be scandalized
scàndalo *s. m.* scandal
scandalóso *agg.* scandalous, shocking
scandìnavo *agg. e s. m.* Scandinavian
scandìre *v. tr.* **1** (*versi*) to scan **2** (*parole*) to articulate, to pronounce **3** (*mus.*) to stress
scansafatìche *s. m. e f.* lazybones
scansàre **A** *v. tr.* **1** (*spostare*) to move aside **2** (*evitare*) to avoid, to escape **B** *v. rifl.* to step aside
scantinàto *s. m.* basement
scantonàre *v. intr.* to turn the corner, (*svignarsela*) to slip away
scàpito *s. m.* detriment
scàpola *s. f.* scapula, shoulder-blade
scàpolo **A** *agg.* unmarried, single **B** *s. m.* bachelor
scappaménto *s. m.* exhaust ♦ **tubo di s.** exhaust pipe
scappàre *v. intr.* **1** (*fuggire*) to flee, to run away, to get away, to escape **2** (*andarsene in fretta*) to rush **3** (*sfuggire*) to slip
scappàta *s. f.* call, short visit
scappatèlla *s. f.* escapade
scappatóia *s. f.* way out, loophole
scarabèo *s. m.* beetle
scarabocchiàre *v. tr.* to scribble, to scrawl
scarabòcchio *s. m.* scribble, scrawl
scarafàggio *s. m.* cockroach
scaramùccia *s. f.* skirmish
scaraventàre *v. tr.* to hurl, to fling
scarceràre *v. tr.* to release, to set free
scarcerazióne *s. f.* release
scardinàre *v. tr.* to unhinge
scàrica *s. f.* discharge, (*di proiettili*) volley
scaricàre **A** *v. tr.* **1** to unload, to discharge, to release, (*deporre*) to set down **2** (*riversare*) to discharge, to empty **3** (*registrare in uscita*) to write down, to cancel **4** (*detrarre*) to deduct **B** *v. rifl.* **1** to relieve oneself **2** (*rilassarsi*) to unwind **C** *v. intr. pron.* **1** (*perdere la carica*) to run down **2** (*sfociare*) to flow
scàrico **A** *agg.* unloaded, (*di orologio*), run-down, (*di batteria*) flat **B** *s. m.* **1** unloading, discharging **2** (*di rifiuti*) dumping **3** (*registrazione in uscita*) cancellation **4** (*di motore*) exhaust ♦ **tubo di s.** wastepipe, drainpipe
scarlattìna *s. f.* scarlatina, scarlet fever
scarlàtto *agg.* scarlet
scarmigliàto *agg.* ruffled
scàrno *agg.* **1** (*magro*) lean, skinny **2** (*inadeguato*) meagre, inadequate **3** (*spoglio*) bare
scàrpa *s. f.* shoe ♦ **lucido da scarpe** shoe polish; **scarpe basse** flat shoes; **scarpe da ginnastica** sneakers, gymshoes
scarpàta *s. f.* slope, escarpment
scarpièra *s. f.* shoe-rack
scarpinàre *v. intr.* to tramp, to trek
scarpinàta *s. f.* long walk, tramp
scarpóne *s. m.* boot
scarseggiàre *v. intr.* to be lacking, to be short, to run out
scarsézza *s. f.* scarceness, scarcity, shortage, (*mancanza*) lack
scarsità *s. f.* scarceness, scarcity, shortage, (*mancanza*) lack
scàrso *agg.* scarce, scanty, poor, (*manchevole*) lacking
scartaménto *s. m.* gauge
scartàre (1) *v. tr.* **1** to unwrap **2** (*rifiutare*) to discard, to reject
scartàre (2) *v. intr.* (*deviare*) to swerve
scàrto (1) *s. m.* **1** discard, waste, scrap **2** (*al gioco delle carte*) discard
scàrto (2) *s. m.* **1** (*deviazione*) swerve, (*di cavallo*) shy **2** (*margine*) spread, margin **3** (*differenza*) difference
scartòffie *s. f. pl.* (heap of) papers, (*d'ufficio*) paperwork
scassàre *v. tr.* to break, to smash

scassinàre *v. tr.* to break open
scassinatóre *s. m.* burglar, (*di banche*) bank-robber, (*di cassaforte*) safebreaker
scatenàre **A** *v. tr.* **1** (*suscitare*) to rouse, to set off **2** (*aizzare*) to stir up **B** *v. intr. pron.* **1** to break out, to burst out **2** (*sfrenarsi*) to run wild
scàtola *s. f.* box, case, (*di cartone*) carton, (*di latta*) tin, can
scatolàme *s. m.* tins *pl.*, cans *pl.*, (*di generi alimentari*) tinned food, canned food
scattàre **A** *v intr.* **1** (*di congegno*) to go off, to be released **2** (*balzare*) to spring **3** (*adirarsi*) to lose one's temper **4** (*iniziare*) to start, to begin **B** *v. tr.* (*fot.*) to take, to snap
scattìsta *s. m. e f.* sprinter
scàtto *s. m.* **1** (*mecc.*) click, (*pezzo*) release **2** (*balzo*) spring, burst **3** (*impulso*) impulse, (*scatto d'ira*) fit **4** (*aumento*) increase **5** (*tel.*) unit
scaturìre *v. intr.* **1** to spring **2** (*derivare*) to originate, to result
scavalcàre *v. tr.* **1** to pass over, to climb over **2** (*soppiantare*) to supplant **3** (*superare*) to go ahead, to overtake
scavàre *v. tr.* to dig, to excavate
scavatrìce *s. f.* excavator, digger
scàvo *s. m.* **1** digging out, excavation **2** *al pl.* (*archeol.*) excavation, (*miner*) workings *pl.*
scègliere *v. tr.* **1** to choose, to pick out, to select **2** (*preferire*) to choose, to prefer
sceìcco *s. m.* sheik(h)
scelleràto *agg.* wicked
scellìno *s. m.* shilling
scélta *s. f.* choice, selection
scemàre *v. intr.* to diminish, to lessen
scémo *agg.* stupid, silly
scémpio *s. m.* ruin
scèna *s. f.* **1** scene **2** (*scenario*) scenery **3** (*palcoscenico*) stage, (*teatro*) theatre **4** (*finzione*) act
scenàrio *s. m.* **1** (*teatro*) scenery **2** (*ambiente*) background
scenàta *s. f.* scene, row
scéndere **A** *v. intr.* **1** to go down, to get down, to come down **2** (*da un mezzo*) to get off, to get out **3** (*presentare pendenza*) to descend, to slope, to run down **4** (*calare, diminuire*) to fall, to drop, to decrease **5** (*pendere*) to come down, to fall, to hang down **6** (*di astro*) to go down, to sink **7** (*fig.*) (*abbassarsi*) to lower oneself **B** *v. tr.* to go down, to come down
scendilètto *s. m. inv.* bedside carpet
sceneggiàre *v. tr.* to dramatize
sceneggiàto *s. m.* (*TV*) serial
sceneggiatóre *s. m.* scriptwriter
sceneggiatùra *s. f.* script
scenétta *s. f.* sketch
scènico *agg.* stage (*attr*)
scenografìa *s. f.* set designing, setting
scenogràfico *agg.* **1** set (*attr*), stage (*attr*), scenographic(al) **2** (*fig.*) spectacular
scenògrafo *s. m.* set designer, scene painter
scervellàrsi *v. intr. pron.* to rack one's brains
scèttico *agg.* sceptical
scèttro *s. m.* sceptre
schèda *s. f.* **1** card **2** (*elettorale*) voting paper
schedàre *v. tr.* to record, to register, to card index
schedàrio *s. m.* card index, file
schedìna *s. f.* coupon
schéggia *s. f.* splinter
schèletro *s. m.* skeleton
schèma *s. m.* **1** scheme, pattern, outline, draft **2** (*tecnol.*) diagram
schemàtico *agg.* schematic
schérma *s. f.* fencing
schermàglia *s. f.* skirmish
schermàre *v. tr.* to screen, to shield
schermatùra *s. f.* screening, shielding
schérmo *s. m.* screen, shield
schermografìa *s. f.* x-rays *pl.*
schernìre *v. tr.* to scoff at, to mock at
schérno *s. m.* mockery, sneer
scherzàre *v. intr.* **1** to joke **2** (*prendere alla leggera*) to trifle, to joke, to make light of
schérzo *s. m.* **1** joke, jest, (*tiro*) trick **2** (*inezia*) child's play, trifle ♦ **per s.** for fun, for a joke
scherzóso *agg.* joking, laughing
schettinàre *v. intr.* to roller-skate
schèttino *s. m.* roller-skate
schiaccianóci *s. m. inv.* nutcracker
schiacciàre *v. tr.* **1** to crush, to squeeze, to squash, (*premere*) to press **2** (*ridurre in poltiglia*) to mash **3** (*sopraffare*) to crush, to overwhelm ♦ **s. un sonnellino** to have a nap
schiaffeggiàre *v. tr.* to slap, to smack, to cuff
schiàffo *s. m.* slap, smack, cuff
schiamazzàre *v. intr.* to make a din, to kick up a row
schiamàzzo *s. m.* din, row, racket

schiantàre *v. tr. e intr. pron.* to break
schiànto *s. m.* crash
schiarìre **A** *v. tr.* **1** to clear, to make clear **2** (*sbiadire*) to fade **B** *v. intr.* **1** to clear up, (*illuminarsi*) to brighten up **2** (*sbiadire*) to fade
schiarìta *s. f.* clearing up
schiavitù *s. f.* slavery
schiàvo *agg. e s. m.* slave
schièna *s. f.* back ♦ **mal di s.** backache
schienàle *s. m.* back
schièra *s. f.* **1** (*mil.*) formation **2** (*gruppo*) group, crowd
schieraménto *s. m.* **1** array, formation **2** (*fig.*) line-up
schieràre **A** *v. tr.* **1** (*mil.*) to marshal, to draw up **2** (*disporre in ordine*) to line up **B** *v. rifl.* **1** to draw up, to line up **2** (*parteggiare*) to side
schiètto *agg.* **1** pure **2** (*franco*) frank, open
schifézza *s. f.* filth, disgusting thing
schìfo *s. m.* disgust
schifóso *agg.* **1** disgusting, revolting **2** (*pessimo*) awful, dreadful
schioccàre *v. tr. e intr.* (*frusta*) to crack, (*le dita*) to snap, (*le labbra*) to smack
schiodàre *v. tr.* to unrivet, to unnail
schiòppo *s. m.* gun, rifle, shotgun
schiùdere **A** *v. tr.* to open (a little) **B** *v. intr. pron.* **1** to open, (*bot.*) to unfold **2** (*di uova*) to hatch
schiùma *s. f.* foam, froth, (*di sapone*) lather
schiumóso *agg.* foamy, frothy, (*di sapone*) lathery
schivàre *v. tr.* to avoid, to dodge
schìvo *agg.* averse, reluctant, shy
schizofrenìa *s. f.* schizophrenia
schizofrènico *agg. e s. m.* schizophrenic
schizzàre **A** *v. tr.* **1** to splash, to spatter, to squirt (out), to spurt (out) **2** (*abbozzare*) to sketch **B** *v. intr.* **1** to spurt, to squirt **2** (*saltar fuori*) to jump, to spring **C** *v. rifl.* to splash oneself
schizzinóso *agg.* fussy
schìzzo *s. m.* **1** squirt, spurt **2** (*macchia*) splash, stain **3** (*disegno*) sketch **4** (*abbozzo*) draft
sci *s. m.* (*attrezzo*) ski, (*attrività*) skiing ♦ **s. d'acqua** water-ski
scìa *s. f.* **1** wake **2** (*traccia*) trail, track
scià *s. m.* shah
sciàbola *s. f.* sabre
sciacàllo *s. m.* (*zool.*) jackal
sciacquàre *v. tr.* to rinse
sciacquóne *s. m.* flush, flushing device
sciagùra *s. f.* disaster
sciaguràto *agg.* **1** (*sfortunato*) unlucky, (*miserevole*) wretched **2** (*malvagio*) wicked
scialacquàre *v. tr.* to squander, to waste
scialàre *v. intr.* to squander money
sciàlbo *agg.* **1** pale, faint **2** (*fig.*) dull
sciàlle *s. m.* shawl
scialùppa *s. f.* tender ♦ **s. di salvataggio** lifeboat
sciàme *s. m.* swarm
sciaràda *s. f.* charade
sciàre *v. intr.* to ski
sciàrpa *s. f.* scarf
sciàtica *s. f.* sciatica
sciatóre *s. m.* skier
sciàtto *agg.* slovenly
scientìfico *agg.* scientific
sciènza *s. f.* science, (*conoscenza*) knowledge
scienziàto *s. m.* scientist
scìmmia *s. f.* monkey
scimmiottàre *v. tr.* to ape
scimpanzé *s. m.* chimpanzee
scimunìto *agg.* silly, stupid
scìndere **A** *v. tr.* to divide, to separate **B** *v. intr. pron.* to split
scintigrafìa *s. f.* scintigraphy
scintìlla *s. f.* spark
scintillàre *v. intr.* **1** (*mandare scintille*) to spark **2** (*risplendere*) to shine, to sparkle, to twinkle
scintillìo *s. m.* sparkling, twinkling
sciocchézza *s. f.* **1** foolishness, stupidity **2** (*azione, parole*) folly, foolish thing, nonsense **3** (*inezia*) trifle
sciòcco **A** *agg.* silly, stupid **B** *s. m.* fool
sciògliere **A** *v. tr.* **1** to melt, to dissolve **2** (*slegare*) to loose, to untie, to undo **3** (*liberare*) to release, to set free **4** (*risolvere*) to resolve, to solve **5** (*porre fine a, annullare*) to dissolve, to annul, to wind up **B** *v. rifl. e intr. pron.* **1** (*slegarsi*) to loosen **2** (*terminare*) to be dissolved, to break up **3** (*liquefarsi*) to melt, to dissolve, (*di neve*) to thaw
scioglilìngua *s. m. inv.* tongue-twister
sciolìna *s. f.* ski wax
scioltézza *s. f.* **1** nimbleness, agility **2** (*nel parlare*) fluency
sciòlto *agg.* **1** (*liquefatto*) melted **2** (*slegato*) untied, loose **3** (*agile*) nimble **4** (*disinvolto*) easy **5** (*non confezionato*)

loose **6** (*annullato, concluso*) dissolved, closed
scioperànte *s. m. e f.* striker
scioperàre *v. intr.* to strike, to go on strike
sciòpero *s. m.* strike
sciovìa *s. f.* ski-lift
scippàre *v. tr.* to snatch, to bag-snatch
scippatóre *s. m.* bag-snatcher
scìppo *s. m.* bag-snatching
sciròcco *s. m.* sirocco
sciròppo *s. m.* syrup
scìsma *s. m.* schism
scissióne *s. f.* split, division
sciupàre A *v. tr.* **1** (*danneggiare*) to damage, to spoil **2** (*sprecare*) to waste, to squander **B** *v. intr. pron.* to spoil, to get damaged
scivolàre *v. intr.* **1** to slide, to glide **2** (*involontariamente*) to slip **3** (*autom.*) to skid
scìvolo *s. m.* **1** slide **2** (*naut., aer.*) slipway **3** (*tecnol.*) chute
scivolóne *s. m.* slip
scivolóso *agg.* slippery
scleròsi *s. f.* sclerosis
scoccàre A *v. tr.* to shoot **B** *v. intr.* **1** (*scattare*) to be released **2** (*di ore*) to strike **3** (*balenare*) to flash
scocciàre A *v. tr.* to bother, to pester **B** *v. intr. pron.* to be annoyed, to be fed up
scocciatóre *s. m.* pest, bother, nuisance
scocciatùra *s. f.* bother, nuisance
scodèlla *s. f.* bowl, (*piatto fondo*) soup bowl
scodinzolàre *v. intr.* to wag its tail
scoglièra *s. f.* cliff, reef
scòglio *s. m.* **1** rock, reef **2** (*fig.*) difficulty
scoiàttolo *s. m.* squirrel
scolapàsta *s. m. inv.* colander
scolapiàtti *s. m. inv.* plate-rack
scolàre (1) *agg.* school (*attr.*)
scolàre (2) *v. tr. e intr.* to drain
scolarésca *s. f.* pupils *pl.*
scolàro *s. m.* schoolchild, pupil
scolàstico *agg.* scholastic, school (*attr.*) ♦ **tasse scolastiche** school fees
scoliòsi *s. f.* scoliosis
scollàre A *v. tr.* to unglue, to unstick **B** *v. intr. pron.* to get unstuck
scollatùra *s. f.* (*di abito*) neckline, neckhole
scólo *s. m.* drainage
scolorìre A *v. tr.* to discolour, to bleach **B** *v. intr. e intr. pron.* to fade, to lose colour
scolpìre *v. tr.* to sculpt, to engrave, to cut, to carve

scombinàre *v. tr.* to upset, to mess up
scombussolàre *v. tr.* to upset, to unsettle
scomméssa *s. f.* **1** bet, wager **2** (*somma scommessa*) stake ♦ **fare una s.** to make a bet
scomméttere *v. tr.* to bet, to wager ♦ **s. alle corse** to bet on horses
scommettitóre *s. m.* better, bettor
scomodàre A *v. tr.* to trouble, to disturb **B** *v. intr.* to be inconvenient **C** *v. rifl.* to trouble oneself
scomodità *s. f.* discomfort, inconvenience
scòmodo *agg.* uncomfortable, inconvenient
scompagnàto *agg.* unmatched, odd
scomparìre *v. intr.* to disappear
scompàrsa *s. f.* **1** disappearance **2** (*morte*) death
scompàrso *agg.* missing
scompartiménto *s. m.* compartment, section
scompàrto *s. m.* compartment, section
scompigliàre *v. tr.* **1** (*sconvolgere*) to upset **2** (*mettere in disordine*) to disarrange **3** (*arruffare*) to ruffle
scompìglio *s. m.* mess, confusion
scomponìbile *agg.* decomposable, dismountable
scomponibilità *s. f.* decomposability
scompórre A *v. tr.* **1** (*smontare*) to take to pieces **2** (*decomporre*) to decompose, to resolve **3** (*scompigliare*) to disarrange, to upset, (*arruffare*) to ruffle **B** *v. intr. pron.* to get upset
scomposizióne *s. f.* **1** decomposition, resolution **2** (*mat.*) factorization
scomùnica *s. f.* excommunication
scomunicàre *v. tr.* to excommunicate
sconcertànte *agg.* disconcerting
sconcertàre A *v. tr.* to disconcert, to bewilder **B** *v. intr. pron.* to be disconcerted, to be bewildered
scóncio A *agg.* indecent, obscene **B** *s. m.* disgrace
scondìto *agg.* plain, undressed
sconfessàre *v. tr.* to disavow, to repudiate
sconfìggere *v. tr.* **1** to defeat **2** (*eliminare*) to eliminate
sconfinàre *v. intr.* **1** to cross the frontier, (*in una proprietà*) to trespass **2** (*fig.*) to digress from
sconfìtta *s. f.* **1** defeat **2** (*eliminazione*) elimination
sconfortànte *agg.* discouraging

persona) haughty
sdentàto *agg.* toothless
sdoganàre *v. tr.* to clear (through the customs)
sdolcinàto *agg.* mawkish, cloying
sdoppiàre *v. tr. e intr. pron.* to divide, to split
sdraiàre *v. tr. e rifl.* to lie down
sdràio *s. f. inv.* deckchair
sdrucciolévole *agg.* slippery
se *cong.* **1** (*condizinale, causale, concessivo*) if **2** (*dubitativo*) whether, if **3** (*desiderativo*) if only ♦ **come se** as if, as though; **se mai** if (ever), (*nel caso che*) in case; **se non** (*eccetto*) but, except
sé *pron. pers. rifl. 3ª sing. e pl.* **1** (*compl. ogg. e ind.*) oneself, him(self) *m.*, her(self) *f.*, it(self) *n.*, them(selves) *pl.* **2 di sé, da sé** self- (ES: **padronanza di sé** self-control)
sebàceo *agg.* sebaceous
sebbène *cong.* (al)though, even though
sécca *s. f.* shoal, shallows *pl.* ♦ **fiume in s.** dry river
seccànte *agg.* annoying, tiresome
seccàre A *v. tr.* **1** to dry (up) **2** (*annoiare*) to bore, (*irritare*) to annoy **B** *v. intr. pron.* **1** (*diventare secco*) to dry (up) **2** (*annoiarsi*) to get bored, (*irritarsi*) to get annoyed
seccatóre *s. m.* bore, nuisance
seccatùra *s. f.* bother, nuisance, bore
secchièllo *s. m.* bucket
sécchio *s. m.* pail, bucket
sécco *agg.* **1** dry **2** (*seccato*) dried, (*ap*
passito) withered **3** (*magro*) thin **4** (*bru*
sco) sharp, (*freddo*) cold
secessióne *s. f.* secession
secessionìsta *s. m. e f.* secessionist
secolàre *agg.* secular
sècolo *s. m.* century
secónda *s. f.* **1** (*autom.*) second gear
(*seconda classe*) second class
secondariaménte *avv.* secondly
secondàrio *agg.* secondary
secondìno *s. m.* jailer
secóndo (1) A *agg. num. ord.* second
m. **1** (*minuto secondo*) second **2** (*sec*
piatto) second course
secóndo (2) *prep.* in accordance wi
cording to
secondogènito *agg.* second-born
secrezióne *s. f.* secretion
sèdano *s. m.* celery
sedativo *agg. e s. m.* sedative
sède *s. f.* **1** seat **2** (*comm.*) offic

sconfòrto *s. m.* discouragement, dejection
scongelàre *v. tr.* **1** to defrost, to thaw out **2** (*sbloccare*) to unpeg, to unfreeze
scongiuràre *v. tr.* **1** (*supplicare*) to beseech, to implore **2** (*evitare*) to avoid, to avert
scongiùro *s. m.* incantation, spell
sconnèsso *agg.* **1** disconnected **2** (*fig.*) incoherent
sconosciùto A *agg.* unknown **B** *s. m.* stranger
sconquassàre *v. tr.* **1** to shatter, to smash **2** (*sconvolgere*) to upset
sconsacràre *v. tr.* to deconsecrate
sconsideràto *agg.* thoughtless, rash
sconsigliàre *v. tr.* to advise against
sconsolànte *agg.* discouraging
sconsolàto *agg.* disconsolate, dejected
scontàre *v. tr.* **1** (*banca*) to discount **2** (*detrarre*) to deduct **3** (*fare uno sconto*) to reduce **4** (*espiare*) to pay for, to atone for, (*in carcere*) to serve
scontàto *agg.* **1** (*banca*) discounted **2** (*ribassato*) reduced **3** (*espiato*) paid for **4** (*previsto*) foregone, expected
scontentàre *v. tr.* to displease, to dissatisfy
scontentézza *s. f.* discontent, dissatisfaction
scontènto A *agg.* discontented, displeased **B** *s. m.* discontent
scónto *s. m.* discount, rebate
scontràrsi *v. intr. pron.* **1** to clash **2** (*urtarsi*) to collide **3** (*incontrarsi*) to run into
scontrìno *s. m.* ticket, coupon, voucher
scóntro *s. m.* **1** (*combattimento*) encounter, fight **2** (*urto di veicoli*) collision, crash **3** (*contrasto*) clash
scontróso *agg.* sullen, peevish
sconveniènte *agg.* improper, unsuitable
sconvolgènte *agg.* upsetting, disturbing
sconvòlgere *v. tr.* to upset, to disturb, to throw into confusion
scópa *s. f.* broom
scopàre *v. tr.* to sweep
scopèrta *s. f.* discovery ♦ **andare alla s.** to scout
scopèrto A *agg.* **1** uncovered **2** (*non vestito*) bare **3** (*aperto*) open **4** (*di conto, assegno*) overdrawn, uncovered **B** *s. m.* (*banca*) overdraft
scòpo *s. m.* aim, end, object, purpose
scoppiàre *v. tr.* **1** to burst, to explode **2** (*manifestarsi improvvisamente*) to break out
scoppiettàre *v. intr.* to crackle
scòppio *s. m.* **1** burst, explosion **2** (*rumore*) bang, crash **3** (*manifestazione improvvisa*) outbreak
scoprìre A *v. tr.* **1** (*togliere ciò che copre*) to uncover, to bare **2** (*mostrare*) to disclose, to show **3** (*arrivare a conoscere*) to discover, to find (out) **4** (*scorgere*) to sight, to descry **5** (*mil.*) to expose **B** *v. rifl.* **1** (*di abiti, coperte*) to throw off one's clothes **2** (*manifestarsi*) to show oneself
scopritóre *s. m.* discoverer
scoraggiàre A *v. tr.* to discourage **B** *v. intr. pron.* to be discouraged
scorbùtico *agg.* cantankerous, peevish
scorciàre *v. tr.* to shorten
scorciatóia *s. f.* short cut
scórcio *s. m.* **1** (*arte*) foreshortening **2** (*visuale*) (partial) view **3** (*di tempo*) end, close
scordàre *v. tr. e intr. pron.* to forget
scòrgere *v. tr.* to make out, to see, to notice
scòria *s. f.* scoria, slag ♦ **scorie radioattive** radioactive waste
scorpacciàta *s. f.* bellyful
scorpióne *s. m.* **1** scorpion **2** (*astr.*) Scorpio
scorrazzàre A *v. intr.* to run about **B** *v. tr.* to take around
scórrere A *v. tr.* **1** to run, to glide, to slide **2** (*fluire*) to flow, to stream **3** (*di tempo*) to roll by, to pass **B** *v. tr.* (*leggere in fretta*) to look through, to glance over
scorrettézza *s. f.* **1** incorrectness, (*errore*) mistake **2** (*maleducazione*) rudeness **3** (*atto sconveniente*) impropriety
scorrètto *agg.* **1** incorrect **2** (*maleducato*) improper
scorrévole *agg.* **1** flowing, fluent **2** (*mecc.*) sliding
scorrevolézza *s. f.* fluency
scórsa *s. f.* quick look
scórso *agg.* last, past
scorsóio *agg.* running
scòrta *s. f.* **1** escort **2** (*provvista*) store, supply
scortàre *v. tr.* to escort
scortése *agg.* rude, impolite
scortesìa *s. f.* **1** rudeness, impoliteness **2** (*azione scortese*) rude act
scorticàre *v. tr.* **1** to skin **2** (*produrre un'abrasione in*) to graze
scòrza *s. f.* rind, peel, skin, (*di albero*) bark ♦ **s. d'arancia** orange peel
scoscéso *agg.* steep

degree ♦ **tiro a s.** target-shooting
segregàre *v. tr.* to segregate, to isolate
segregazióne *s. f.* segregation, isolation
segréta *s. f.* dungeon
segretariàto *s. m.* secretariat(e)
segretàrio *s. m.* secretary
segreterìa *s. f.* **1** secretariat **2** (*ufficio*) secretary's office ♦ **s. telefonica** answering machine
segretézza *s. f.* secrecy
segréto *agg. e s. m.* secret
seguàce *s. m. e f.* follower
seguènte *agg.* following, next
segùgio *s. m.* (*zool.*) bloodhound
seguìre **A** *v. tr.* **1** to follow **2** (*sorvegliare*) to supervise **3** (*frequentare*) to attend **B** *v. intr.* **1** to follow **2** (*continuare*) to continue **3** (*accadere*) to occur, to happen
seguitàre *v. tr. e intr.* to continue
séguito *s. m.* **1** (*scorta*) retinue, train, suite **2** (*insieme di seguaci*) followers *pl.* **3** (*sequela*) succession, series **4** (*continuazione*) continuation **5** (*effetto*) sequel, consequence **6** (*consenso*) following ♦ **in s.** later on; **in s. a** in consequence of
sèi *agg. num. card. e s. m. inv.* six
seicentésco *agg.* seventeenth-century (*attr*)
seicènto *agg. num. card. e s. m. inv.* six hundred
sélce *s. f.* flint
selciàto *s. m.* pavement
selettìvo *agg.* selective
selezionàre *v. tr.* to select, to pick out
selezióne *s. f.* selection
sèlla *s. f.* saddle
sellàre *v. tr.* to saddle
sellìno *s. m.* saddle
sélva *s. f.* wood
selvaggìna *s. f.* game
selvàggio *agg.* wild, savage
selvàtico *agg.* wild
semàforo *s. m.* traffic-lights *pl.*, (*ferr.*) semaphore
sembiànza *s. f.* **1** (*fattezze*) countenance, face **2** (*apparenza*) appearance
sembràre *v. intr.* **1** to seem, to appear, to look (like) **2** (*impers.*) to seem, (*credere*) to think
séme *s. m.* **1** seed, (*di frutto*) pip **2** (*fig.*) seed, cause **3** (*delle carte da gioco*) suit
semènza *s. f.* seed
semestràle *agg.* **1** (*che dura un semestre*) six-month (*attr*) **2** (*che avviene ogni sei mesi*) six-monthly, half-yearly
semèstre *s. m.* semester, half-year
semiàsse *s. m.* axle-shaft
semiautomàtico *agg.* semiautomatic
semicérchio *s. m.* semicircle
semicircolàre *agg.* semicircular
semiconduttóre *s. m.* semiconductor
semifinàle *s. f.* semifinal
semilavoràto *agg.* semifinished
sémina *s. f.* sowing
seminàre *v. tr.* **1** to sow **2** (*spargere*) to scatter, to spread **3** (*lasciare indietro*) to leave behind
seminàrio *s. m.* **1** (*relig.*) seminary **2** (*università*) seminar
seminarìsta *s. m.* seminarist
seminfermità *s. f.* partial infirmity, (*mentale*) partial insanity
seminterràto *s. m.* basement
semioscurità *s. f.* half-darkness
semmài *cong.* if (ever), (*nel caso che*) in case
sémola *s. f.* bran
semolìno *s. m.* semolina
sémplice *agg.* **1** (*di un solo elemento*) simple, single **2** (*solo*) simple, mere **3** (*non ricercato*) simple, plain **4** (*facile*) easy, simple **5** (*di basso grado*) common, ordinary
sempliceménte *avv.* simply
semplicità *s. f.* simplicity
semplificàre *v. tr.* to simplify
sèmpre **A** *avv.* **1** always, all the time **2** (*senza interruzione*) always, throughout, ever **3** (*ancora*) still **B** *cong.* **s. che** provided (that), as long as ♦ **per s.** for ever; **s. meglio** better and better
sempreverde *agg.* evergreen
sènape *s. f.* mustard
senàto *s. m.* senate
senatóre *s. m.* senator
senilità *s. f.* senility
sénno *s. m.* sense, judgment
séno *s. m.* **1** breast, bosom **2** (*mat.*) sine **3** (*anat.*) sinus
sensàto *agg.* sensible
sensazionàle *agg.* sensational, thrilling
sensazióne *s. f.* **1** sensation, feeling **2** (*scalpore*) sensation
sensìbile *agg.* **1** (*che ha sensibilità*) sensitive **2** (*che si percepisce coi sensi*) sensible **3** (*rilevante*) notable, considerable
sensibilità *s. f.* **1** sensitiveness **2** (*scient.*) sensibility
sènso *s. m.* **1** sense **2** (*sensazione*) sensa-

tion, feeling **3** (*significato*) sense, meaning **4** (*direzione*) direction, way ♦ **buon s.** common sense; **s. unico** one-way only
sensuàle *agg.* sensual
sensualità *s. f.* sensuality
sentènza *s. f.* **1** (*dir.*) sentence **2** (*massima*) saying
sentièro *s. m.* path, track
sentimentàle *agg.* sentimental
sentiménto *s. m.* sentiment, feeling
sentìna *s. f.* bilge
sentinèlla *s. f.* sentry
sentìre **A** *v. tr.* **1** to feel **2** (*gustare*) to taste **3** (*odorare*) to smell **4** (*udire*) to hear, (*ascoltare*) to listen to **B** *v. intr.* (*udire*) to heart **C** *v. rifl.* to feel ♦ **sentirsi bene/male/stanco** to feel well/ill/tired
sènza **A** *prep.* **1** (*mancanza*) without **2** (*negazione*) un-, in-, -less (*con agg. e avv.*) **3** (*esclusione*) excluding **B** *cong.* **s. (che)** without (*col gerundio*) (ES: **s. mangiare** without eating)
separàre **A** *v. tr.* to separate, to divide, to part **B** *v. rifl. e rifl. rec.* to separate, to part
separàto *agg.* separate
separatóre *s. m.* separator
separazióne *s. f.* separation
sepolcràle *agg.* sepulchral
sepólcro *s. m.* grave, sepulchre
sepólto *agg.* buried
sepoltùra *s. f.* **1** burial **2** (*sepolcro*) grave
seppellìre *v. tr.* to bury
séppia *s. f.* cuttlefish ♦ **nero di s.** sepia; **osso di s.** cuttlebone
sequènza *s. f.* sequence
sequestràbile *agg.* sequestrable, seizable
sequestràre *v. tr.* **1** (*dir.*) to seize, to sequestrate, to confiscate **2** (*portar via*) to take away **3** (*rapire una persona*) to kidnap
sequèstro *s. m.* **1** sequestration, seizure **2** (*di persona*) kidnapping
sequòia *s. f.* redwood, sequoia
séra *s. f.* evening, night
seràle *agg.* evening (*attr.*), night (*attr.*)
seràta *s. f.* evening, night
serbàre **A** *v. tr.* **1** (*mettere da parte*) to lay aside **2** (*conservare*) to keep **B** *v. rifl.* to keep, to remain
serbatóio *s. m.* tank, reservoir
sèrbo *agg. e s. m.* Serbian
serenità *s. f.* serenity
seréno **A** *agg.* **1** clear, serene **2** (*fig.*) calm, tranquil **B** *s. m.* clear sky
sergènte *s. m.* sergeant
seriàle *agg.* serial
sèrie *s. f.* **1** series **2** (*assortimento*) set **3** (*fila*) row, line **4** (*sport*) division ♦ **di s. B** (*fig.*) second-rate; **numero di s.** serial number; **produzione in s.** mass production
serietà *s. f.* **1** seriousness **2** (*gravità*) gravity
serigrafìa *s. f.* silk-screen printing, serigraphy
sèrio *agg.* **1** serious, earnest **2** (*grave*) serious, grave
sermóne *s. m.* sermon
serpeggiàre *v. intr.* **1** to wind, to meander **2** (*insinuarsi*) to spread
serpènte *s. m.* snake
sèrra *s. f.* greenhouse
serrànda *s. f.* shutter
serràre **A** *v. tr.* **1** to shut, to close, (*a chiave*) to lock **2** (*stringere*) to tighten, to clasp **3** (*incalzare*) to press hard upon **B** *v. rifl.* to lock oneself **C** *v. intr. pron.* to tighten
serràta *s. f.* lock-out
serratùra *s. f.* lock
servìle *agg.* **1** servile, slavish **2** (*gramm.*) auxiliary
servìre **A** *v. tr.* **1** to serve, to attend **2** (*di persona di servizio*) to wait on **3** (*offrire cibi*) to serve, to help **4** (*dare le carte*) to deal **B** *v. intr.* **1** (*prestare servizio*) to serve **2** (*a tavola*) to serve, to wait **3** (*giovare*) to serve, to be of use **4** (*fare l'ufficio di*) to serve, to act as **5** (*tennis*) to serve **6** (*occorrere*) to need **C** *v. intr. pron.* **1** (*usare*) to use, to make use **2** (*a tavola*) to help oneself **3** (*fornirsi*) to buy, to get, (*abitualmente*) to be a steady customer
servitù *s. f.* **1** servitude, slavery **2** (*personale di servizio*) servants *pl.*
serviziévole *agg.* helpful
servìzio *s. m.* **1** service **2** (*mil.*) service, duty **3** (*favore*) favour **4** (*serie di oggetti*) set, service **5** (*giornalistico*) report **6** *al pl.* services *pl.* ♦ **donna di s.** maid; **fuori s.** out of order; **servizi igienici** bathroom
sèrvo *s. m.* servant
servocomàndo *s. m.* servocontrol
servofréno *s. m.* servobrake
servomeccanìsmo *s. m.* servomechanism
servomotóre *s. m.* servomotor
servostèrzo *s. m.* power steering
sessànta *agg. num. card. e s. m. inv.* sixty

sessantésimo *agg. num. ord. e s. m.* sixtieth
sessióne *s. f.* session
sèsso *s. m.* sex
sessuàle *agg.* sexual, sex (*attr*)
sessualità *s. f.* sexuality
sestànte *s. m.* sextant
sèsto *agg. num. ord. e s. m.* sixth
séta *s. f.* silk
setàccio *s. m.* sieve
séte *s. f.* thirst ♦ **avere s.** to be thirsty
setificio *s. m.* silk mill
sétola *s. f.* bristle
sètta *s. f.* sect
settànta *agg. num. card. e s. m. inv.* seventy
settantèsimo *agg. num. ord. e s. m.* seventieth
settàrio *s. m.* sectarian, (*fazioso*) factious
sètte *agg. num. card. e s. m. inv.* seven
settecènto *agg. num. card. e s. m. inv.* seven hundred
settèmbre *s. m.* September
settentrionàle *agg.* northern, north (*attr*)
settentrióne *s. m.* north
sèttico *agg.* septic
settimàna *s. f.* week ♦ **la prossima s.** next week; **la scorsa s.** last week
settimanàle **A** *agg.* weekly, week (*attr*) **B** *s. m.* weekly (magazine)
settimanalménte *avv.* weekly
sèttimo *agg. num. ord. e s. m.* seventh
sètto *s. m.* septum
settóre *s. m.* **1** sector **2** (*fig.*) field, area, sector
severità *s. f.* severity, strictness, rigour
sevèro *agg.* **1** severe, strict **2** (*sobrio*) austere
sevìzia *s. f.* torture
seviziàre *v. tr.* to torture
sezionàre *v. tr.* to dissect
sezióne *s. f.* **1** section **2** (*reparto*) division, department
sfaccendàto *s. m.* idler
sfacciatàggine *s. f.* impudence, cheekiness
sfacciàto *agg.* **1** impudent, cheeky **2** (*di colore*) gaudy
sfacèlo *s. m.* breakup, ruin
sfaldàre **A** *v. tr.* to flake **B** *v. intr. pron.* **1** to flake off, to scale off **2** (*fig.*) to break up
sfamàre **A** *v. tr.* to feed **B** *v. rifl.* to appease one's hunger, to feed oneself
sfàrzo *s. m.* pomp, magnificence
sfasaménto *s. m.* **1** (*elettr*) phase displacement **2** (*stordimento*) bewilderment, confusion
sfasciàre (1) *v. tr.* (*sbendare*) to unbandage
sfasciàre (2) **A** *v. tr.* **1** (*rompere*) to shatter, to smash **2** (*fig.*) to break upon **B** *v. intr. pron.* to fall to pieces
sfatàre *v. tr.* to discredit
sfavillàre *v. intr.* to shine, to sparkle
sfavorévole *agg.* unfavourable
sfèra *s. f.* **1** sphere **2** (*mecc.*) ball ♦ **cuscinetto a sfere** ball bearing
sfèrico *agg.* spheric(al)
sferragliàre *v. intr.* to clang
sferràre *v. tr.* to land, to deliver
sferzàre *v. tr.* **1** to whip **2** (*fig.*) to lash out at, (*incitare*) to drive
sfìda *s. f.* challenge
sfidàre **A** *v. tr.* **1** to challenge, to defy **2** (*affrontare*) to face, to brave **B** *v. rifl. rec.* to challenge each other
sfidùcia *s. f.* mistrust, distrust, (*politica*) no confidence
sfiguràre **A** *v. tr.* to disfigure, to spoil **B** *v. intr.* to cut a poor figure
sfilàre **A** *v. tr.* **1** to unthread **2** (*togliere di dosso*) to slip off **B** *v. intr. pron.* to get unthreaded
sfilàta *s. f.* **1** parade **2** (*serie*) string
sfìnge *s. f.* sphinx
sfinìre **A** *v. tr.* to exhaust, to wear out **B** *v. intr. pron.* to wear oneself out
sfioràre *v. tr.* **1** to graze, to skim **2** (*fig.*) to touch on **3** (*stare per raggiungere*) to be on the verge of
sfiorìre *v. intr.* to fade, to wither
sfocàto *agg.* **1** (*fot.*) out of focus, blurred **2** (*fig.*) hazy, vague
sfociàre *v. intr.* **1** to flow (into) **2** (*fig.*) to result (in)
sfoderàre *v. tr.* **1** (*togliere la fodera*) to remove the lining **2** (*sguainare*) to unsheathe **3** (*ostentare*) to make a display (of)
sfoderàto *agg.* unlined
sfogàre **A** *v. tr.* to give vent to, to let out **B** *v. intr.* to come out **C** *v. intr. pron.* **1** to relieve one's feelings **2** (*prendersela*) to take it out **3** (*levarsi la voglia*) to take one's fill
sfoggiàre *v. tr.* to show off
sfòglia *s. f.* **1** (*lamina*) foil **2** (*pasta sfoglia*) puff pastry
sfogliàre (1) **A** *v. tr.* (*togliere le foglie*) to strip the leaves off, (*un fiore*) to pluck the petals off **B** *v. intr. pron.* to lose leaves, (*di fiore*) to shed petals
sfogliàre (2) **A** *v. tr.* (*scorrere frettolo-*

samente) to leaf through, to turn over the pages of **B** *v. rifl.* (*sfaldarsi*) to flake
sfógo *s. m.* **1** vent, outlet **2** (*eruzione cutanea*) rash
sfolgorànte *agg.* blazing, shining
sfollagènte *s. m. inv.* truncheon, baton
sfollàre **A** *v. tr.* to disperse, to clear, to evacuate **B** *v. intr.* to disperse, to evacuate
sfoltìre *v. tr.* **1** to thin (out) **2** (*fig.*) to cut, to reduce
sfondàre **A** *v. tr.* **1** (*rompere il fondo di*) to knock the bottom out of, to break the bottom of **2** (*rompere passando*) to break through, to break down **3** (*mil.*) to break through **B** *v. intr.* to make a name for oneself, to have success **C** *v. intr. pron.* to break at the bottom
sfóndo *s. m.* background
sformàre **A** *v. tr.* **1** (*togliere la forma*) to put out of shape **2** (*togliere dalla forma*) to remove from the mould, to turn out **B** *v. intr. pron.* to lose one's shape
sfornàre *v. tr.* **1** to take out of the oven **2** (*produrre*) to bring out
sfornito *agg.* deprived, (*di merci*) unstocked
sfortùna *s. f.* bad luck, ill luck, (*disgrazia*) misfortune
sfortunataménte *avv.* unfortunately, unluckily
sfortunàto *agg.* **1** unlucky, unfortunate **2** (*con esito negativo*) unsuccessful
sforzàre **A** *v. tr.* to force, to strain **B** *v. intr. pron.* to strive
sfòrzo *s. m.* **1** effort, strain **2** (*mecc.*) stress, strain
sfrattàre *v. tr.* to turn out, to evict
sfràtto *s. m.* turning out, eviction
sfrecciàre *v. intr.* to speed
sfregàre *v. tr.* **1** to rub, (*per pulire*) to polish **2** (*graffiare*) to scratch
sfregiàre *v. tr.* to slash, to disfigure
sfrégio *s. m.* slash, cut
sfrenàto *agg.* unbridled, unrestrained
sfrontàto *agg.* impudent
sfruttaménto *s. m.* exploitation
sfruttàre *v. tr.* **1** to exploit, to overwork, to utilize **2** (*approfittare di*) to exploit, to take advantage of, to profit by **3** (*utilizzare al meglio*) to make the most of
sfruttatóre *s. m.* exploiter
sfuggìre **A** *v. intr.* to escape **B** *v. tr.* to avoid
sfumàre **A** *v. intr.* **1** to vanish, to disappear, to fade away **2** (*andare in fumo*) to come in nothing **3** (*di colore*) to shade **B** *v. tr.* to shade
sfumatùra *s. f.* **1** shade, nuance **2** (*tocco*) touch, hint **3** (*di capelli*) tapering
sfuocàto *agg.* → **sfocato**
sfuriàta *s. f.* **1** fit of anger **2** (*rimprovero*) tirade
sgabèllo *s. m.* stool
sgabuzzìno *s. m.* closet, store-room
sganciàre **A** *v. tr.* **1** to unhook, (*staccare*) to disconnect **2** (*fam.*) (*denaro*) to stump up **B** *v. rifl. e intr. pron.* **1** to be unhooked **2** (*liberarsi*) to get away
sgangheràto *agg.* ramshackle
sgarbàto *agg.* rude
sgàrbo *s. m.* rudeness
sgargiànte *agg.* showy, gaudy
sgattaiolàre *v. intr.* to slip away
sgelàre *v. tr. e intr.* to thaw, to defrost
sghémbo *agg.* oblique
sghignazzàre *v. intr.* to laugh scornfully
sgobbàre *v. intr.* to work hard, to grind away
sgocciolàre **A** *v. intr.* to drip, to trickle **B** *v. tr.* **1** to drip **2** (*svuotare*) to drain, to empty
sgocciolatóio *s. m.* drip
sgolàrsi *v. intr. pron.* to shout oneself hoarse
sgombràre **A** *v. tr.* **1** to clear, to clear away **2** (*un alloggio*) to vacate, to move out of **B** *v. intr.* to clear out
sgómbro *s. m.* mackerel
sgomentàre **A** *v. tr.* to dismay, to frighten **B** *v. intr. pron.* to be frightened
sgoménto *s. m.* dismay, fright
sgonfiàre *v. tr. e intr. pron.* to deflate
sgónfio *agg.* deflated, flat
sgòrbio *s. m.* scrawl, scribble
sgorgàre **A** *v. intr.* to gush out, to flow **B** *v. tr.* to unclog
sgozzàre *v. tr.* to cut the throat of
sgradévole *agg.* disagreeable, unpleasant
sgradìto *agg.* unpleasant, unwelcome
sgranàre *v. tr.* to shell, to hull
sgranchìre *v. tr. e rifl.* to stretch
sgranocchiàre *v. tr.* to munch
sgrassàre *v. tr.* to degrease
sgraziàto *agg.* awkward, clumsy
sgretolàre *v. tr. e intr. pron.* to crumble
sgridàre *v. tr.* to scold, to rebuke
sgridàta *s. f.* scolding, telling-off
sguaiàto *agg.* coarse
sgualcire *v. tr. e intr. pron.* to crease
sguàrdo *s. m.* look, glance ♦ **dare uno s. a q.c.** to have a look at st.
sguazzàre *v. intr.* to wallow

sguinzagliàre *v. tr.* to let loose, (*dietro a qc.*) to set on
sgusciàre (1) *v. tr.* (*togliere il guscio*) to shell, to hull
sgusciàre (2) *v. intr.* (*sfuggire*) to slip away
shampoo *s. m. inv.* shampoo
shock *s. m. inv.* shock
si A *pron. rifl. 3ª* **1** (*con i v. rifl.*) himself *m.*, herself *f.*, itself *n.*, themselves *pl.*, (*con sogg. impers.*) oneself (ES: **vestirsi** to dress oneself, **egli si vestì** he dressed himself, **essi si vestirono** they dressed themselves) **2** (*con i v. rifl. impropri, in funzione di compl. di termine) si rende con l'agg. poss.* (ES: **si è fatto male a un ginocchio** he hurt his knee) **3** (*con i v. intr. pron.*) *idiom.* (ES: **si dimentica sempre di chiudere la finestra** he always forgets to close the window) **B** *pron. rec.* one another, (*tra due*) each other (ES: **i miei genitori si amano** my parents love each other) **C** *pron. indef.* **1** one, they, people, we, you, man (ES: **si vede che ...** one can see ..., **si dice che ...** people say that ..., **in Inghilterra si beve molta birra** in England they drink a lot of beer) **2** (*con valore passivo*) (ES: **si parla inglese** English is spoken here) **3** (*con valore pleonastico*) *idiom.* (ES: **si è mangiato un dolce intero** he ate a whole cake)
sì A *avv.* yes **B** *s. m. inv.* **1** yes **2** (*voto favorevole*) ay
sìa ... sìa *cong.* **1** (*tanto ... quanto*) both ... and **2** (*o ... o*) whether ... or, either ... or
sibilàre *v. intr.* to whistle
sìbilo *s. m.* whistle
sicàrio *s. m.* hired killer
sicché *cong.* **1** (*perciò*) so **2** (*così che*) so that
siccità *s. f.* drought
siccóme *cong.* as, since, because
siciliàno *agg. e s. m.* Sicilian
sicuraménte *avv.* certainly, of course
sicurézza *s. f.* **1** security, safety **2** (*l'esser sicuro*) assurance, (self-)confidence **3** (*certezza*) certainty ♦ **uscita di s.** emergency exit
sicùro A *agg.* **1** safe, secure **2** (*certo*) sure, certain **3** (*saldo*) steady **4** (*esperto*) skilful, expert, confident **5** (*affidabile*) reliable, trusty **B** *s. m.* safety, safety place ♦ **di s.** certainly
siderurgìa *s. f.* iron metallurgy
sìdro *s. m.* cider
sièpe *s. f.* hedge
sièro *s. m.* serum, (*del latte*) whey
sieroterapìa *s. f.* serotherapy
sièsta *s. f.* siesta, nap
sifóne *s. m.* siphon
sigarétta *s. f.* cigarette
sìgaro *s. m.* cigar
sigillàre *v. tr.* to seal
sigìllo *s. m.* seal
sìgla *s. f.* **1** initials *pl.*, abbreviation **2** (*mus.*) signature tune
siglàre *v. tr.* to initial, to sign
significàre *v. tr.* **1** to mean, to signify **2** (*valere*) to mean, to matter, (*simboleggiare*) to stand for
significativo *agg.* **1** significant, expressive **2** (*importante*) important
significàto *s. m.* **1** meaning, sense **2** (*importanza*) importance, significance
signóra *s. f.* **1** lady, woman **2** (*davanti al nome*) Mrs, (*vocativo, senza nome*) madam
signóre *s. m.* **1** gentleman, man **2** (*davanti al nome*) Mr, (*vocat. senza nome*) sir
signorìa *s. f.* rule, dominion
signorìle *agg.* elegant, luxury
signorìna *s. f.* **1** young lady, girl **2** (*davanti al nome*) Miss, (*vocativo, senza nome*) madam, miss
silenziatóre *s. m.* silencer
silènzio *s. m.* silence
silenzióso *agg.* **1** silent **2** (*senza rumori*) quiet
silìcio *s. m.* silicon
sìllaba *s. f.* syllable
siluràre *v. tr.* **1** to torpedo **2** (*licenziare*) to oust
silùro *s. m.* torpedo
silvèstre *agg.* silvan
simbiòsi *s. f.* symbiosis
simboleggiàre *v. tr.* to symbolize
simbòlico *agg.* symbolic(al)
simbolìsta *s. m. e f.* symbolist
sìmbolo *s. m.* symbol
sìmile A *agg.* **1** similar, like, alike (*pred.*) **2** (*tale*) such **B** *s. m.* (*prossimo*) fellow
similitùdine *s. f.* **1** (*letter.*) simile **2** (*mat.*) similitude **3** (*rassomiglianza*) likeness
simmetrìa *s. f.* symmetry
simmètrico *agg.* symmetric(al)
simpatìa *s. f.* liking, attraction
simpàtico *agg.* **1** nice, pleasant **2** (*anat.*) sympathetic
simpatizzànte *s. m.* sympathizer
simpatizzàre *v. intr.* **1** to take a liking to

each other **2** (*sostenere*) to sympathize with
simpòsio *s. m.* symposium
simulàre **A** *v. tr.* to simulate, to sham **B** *v. intr.* to pretend
simulazióne *s. f.* simulation
simultàneo *agg.* simultaneous
sinagòga *s. f.* synagogue
sincerità *s. f.* sincerity
sincèro *agg.* sincere, true
sìncope *s. f.* syncope
sincronìa *s. f.* synchrony
sindacàle *agg.* union (*attr*)
sindacalista *s. m. e f.* trade unionist
sindacàto *s. m.* **1** trade union, (*USA*) labour union **2** (*fin.*) syndicate, pool
sìndaco *s. m.* **1** mayor **2** (*di società*) auditor
sìndrome *s. f.* syndrome
sinfonìa *s. f.* symphony
sinfònico *agg.* symphonic
singhiozzàre *v. intr.* **1** (*avere il singhiozzo*) to hiccup **2** (*piangere*) to sob
singhiózzo *s. m.* **1** hiccup **2** (*di pianto*) sob
singolàre **A** *agg.* **1** (*gramm.*) singular **2** (*strano*) singular, unusual, strange **3** (*raro*) rare **B** *s. m.* **1** (*gramm.*) **2** (*tennis*) singles
sìngolo **A** *agg.* **1** single, individual, separate **2** (*unico*) single, sole **B** *s. m.* individual
sinìstra *s. f.* left
sinìstro **A** *agg.* **1** left **2** (*minaccioso*) sinister, grim **B** *s. m.* accident
sìno → **fino (2)**
sinònimo *s. m.* synonym
sintàssi *s. f.* syntax
sìntesi *s. f.* synthesis
sintètico *agg.* **1** synthetic(al) **2** (*conciso*) concise ♦ **fibre sintetiche** synthetic fibres
sintetizzàre *v. tr.* **1** to synthetize **2** (*riassumere*) to summarize
sintomàtico *agg.* **1** symptomatic(al) **2** (*significativo*) significant, indicative
sintomatologìa *s. f.* symptomatology
sìntomo *s. m.* symptom
sinuóso *agg.* winding
sinusìte *s. f.* sinusitis
sipàrio *s. m.* curtain
sirèna *s. f.* siren
sirìnga *s. f.* syringe
sìsma *s. m.* seism, earthquake
sìsmico *agg.* seismic(al)
sismògrafo *s. m.* seismograph
sismòlogo *s. m.* seismologist
sistèma *s. m.* system
sistemàre **A** *v. tr.* **1** (*ordinare*) to arrange, to put in order **2** (*definire*) to settle, to resolve **3** (*collocare*) to place, (*in un alloggio*) to accomodate, to put up **4** (*procurare lavoro, far sposare*) to fix up **B** *v. rifl.* **1** (*trovare alloggio*) to settle **2** (*trovare lavoro*) to find a job **3** (*mettersi a posto*) to settle down
sistemàtico *agg.* systematic
sistemazióne *s. f.* **1** organization, arrangement, (*collocazione*) placing, layout **2** (*definizione*) settlement **3** (*in alloggio*) accomodation **4** (*impiego*) job
sìto *s. m.* place, site
situàre **A** *v. tr.* to site, to place **B** *v. intr. pron.* to be situated
situazióne *s. f.* situation
skipper *s. m. e f. inv.* skipper
slacciàre *v. tr.* to unlace, to loosen
slàncio *s. m.* **1** rush, run **2** (*fig.*) impulse, fit
slavàto *agg.* **1** washed out, (*pallido*) pale **2** (*fig.*) dull
slavìna *s. f.* snowslide
slàvo *agg. e s. m.* Slav
sleàle *agg.* disloyal, (*non corretto*) unfair
slegàre **A** *v. tr.* to untie, to unfasten **B** *v. rifl.* to untie oneself, to loosen
slip *s. m. inv.* panties *pl.*, briefs *pl.*
slìtta *s. f.* **1** sleigh, sledge, (*USA*) sled **2** (*mecc.*) slide
slittàre *v. intr.* **1** (*scivolare*) to skid, (*mecc.*) to slip **2** (*perdere valore*) to slide, to fall **3** (*essere rinviato*) to be postponed
slogàre *v. tr. e intr. pron.* to dislocate
slogatùra *s. f.* dislocation
sloggiàre **A** *v. tr.* to drive out, (*sfrattare*) to evict **B** *v. intr.* to clear out
smacchiàre *v. tr.* to clean
smacchiatóre *s. m.* stain remover
smàcco *s. m.* blow
smagliànte *agg.* dazzling
smagliatùra *s. f.* **1** (*di calza*) ladder **2** (*di pelle*) stretch mark **3** (*fig.*) gap
smaliziàto *agg.* knowing
smaltàre *v. tr.* to enamel, (*ceramica*) to glaze
smaltatùra *s. f.* enamelling, (*di ceramica*) glazing
smaltìre *v. tr.* **1** (*digerire*) to digest, (*fig.*) to swallow **2** (*vendere*) to sell off, to clear **3**

(*eliminare*) to take off, (*acque*) to drain, (*rifiuti*) to dispose of **4** (*sbrigare*) to finish off
smàlto *s. m.* **1** enamel **2** (*per unghie*) nail varnish **3** (*fig.*) shine
smània *s. f.* **1** (*desiderio*) longing, craving **2** (*frenesia*) agitation, frenzy
smantellàre *v. tr.* to dismantle
smarriménto *s. m.* **1** loss, (*di lettera, pacco*) miscarriage **2** (*confusione*) confusion, bewilderment
smarrìre **A** *v. tr.* to lose, to mislay **B** *v. intr. pron.* **1** (*perdere la strada*) to lose one's way **2** (*andare perduto*) to get lost **3** (*confondersi*) to get confused
smarrìto *agg.* **1** lost, mislaid **2** (*fig.*) bewildered
smascheràre *v. tr.* to unmask
smentìre **A** *v. tr.* **1** to belie, to deny **2** (*ritrattare*) to withdraw **B** *v. rifl.* to contradict oneself
smentìta *s. f.* denial
smeràldo *s. m.* emerald
smerciàre *v. tr.* to sell
smèrlo *s. m.* scallop
sméttere *v. intr.* to stop, to leave off, to give up
smìlzo *agg.* thin
sminuìre *v. tr.* to belittle, to play down
sminuzzàre *v. tr.* to mince, to crumble
smistaménto *s. m.* **1** sorting, clearing **2** (*ferr.*) shunting, switching
smistàre *v. tr.* **1** to sort **2** (*ferr.*) to shunt, to switch
smisuràto *agg.* immeasurable, immense
smodàto *agg.* immoderate
smoking *s. m. inv.* dinner jacket
smontàggio *s. m.* disassembly
smontàre **A** *v. tr.* **1** to disassemble, to take in pieces **2** (*scoraggiare*) to discourage **3** (*demolire*) to demolish **B** *v. intr.* **1** (*da un mezzo*) to get off, (*da cavallo*) to dismount **2** (*finire il turno*) to go off duty, to stop work
smòrfia *s. f.* grimace
smorfióso *agg.* simpering
smòrto *agg.* pale, faded, dull
smorzàre **A** *v. tr.* **1** (*luce*) to shade, to dim, (*suono*) to deaden, (*colore*) to tone down **2** (estinguere) to slake, (*fig.*) to appease **B** *v. intr. pron.* **1** to grow fainter, to fade **2** (*fig.*) to be appeased
smottaménto *s. m.* landslip
smùnto *agg.* (*pallido*) pale, (*emaciato*) lean, emaciated
smuòvere *v. tr.* **1** to move, to shift **2** (*dissuadere*) to dissuade, to budge **3** (*commuovere*) to move, to touch
smussàre *v. tr.* **1** to round off **2** (*fig.*) to soften, to smooth
snaturàto *agg.* heartless
snèllo *agg.* slender, slim
snervànte *agg.* enervating
snidàre *v. tr.* to flush, to dislodge
snobbàre *v. tr.* to snob
snobìsmo *s. m.* snobbery
snocciolàre *v. tr.* **1** to stone **2** (*spiattellare*) to tell
snodàre **A** *v. tr.* **1** (*sciogliere*) to loosen **2** (*rendere agile*) to make supple **B** *v. intr. pron.* **1** to come loose **2** (*di strada*) to wind
snòdo *s. m.* **1** articulated joint **2** (*svincolo*) junction
soàve *agg.* sweet
sobbalzàre *v. intr.* **1** to jerk, to jolt **2** (*trasalire*) to start
sobbàlzo *s. m.* jerk, jolt
sobbarcàrsi *v. rifl.* to take upon oneself
sobbórgo *s. m.* suburb
sobillàre *v. tr.* to stir up
sòbrio *agg.* **1** sober, moderate **2** (*semplice*) simple, plain
socchiùdere *v. tr.* **1** (*chiudere*) to half-close, to close a little **2** (*aprire*) to half-open, to leave ajar
soccórrere *v. tr.* to help, to aid, to assist
soccorritóre *s. m.* helper, rescuer
soccórso *s. m.* **1** help, aid, (*salvataggio*) rescue **2** (*med.*) aid ♦ **pronto s.** first aid; **s. stradale** breakdown service
socialdemocràtico *agg.* Social Democratic
sociàle *agg.* **1** social **2** (*di società*) corporate, company (*attr.*) **3** (*di associazione*) club (*attr.*) ♦ **assistente s.** social worker; **previdenza s.** social security
socialìsmo *s. m.* Socialism
socialìsta *agg. e s. m. e f.* Socialist
società *s. f.* **1** society **2** (*dir., econ.*) company, partnership, firm, (*USA*) corporation
sociévole *agg.* sociable
sòcio *s. m.* **1** member **2** (*di accademia, società scientifica*) fellow **3** (*dir., econ.*) partner, associate
sociologìa *s. f.* sociology
sociòlogo *s. m.* sociologist

sòda *s. f.* soda
sodalìzio *s. m.* **1** association **2** (*legame amichevole*) fellowship
soddisfacènte *agg.* satisfactory
soddisfàre A *v. tr.* **1** to satisfy, to please, to gratify **2** (*adempiere*) to fulfil, to meet, to discharge, (*pagare*) to pay off **B** *v. intr.* to fulfil, to discharge
soddisfazióne *s. f.* **1** satisfaction, pleasure **2** (*adempimento*) fulfilment
sòdio *s. m.* sodium
sòdo *agg.* solid, firm, hard ♦ **uovo s.** hard-boiled egg
sofà *s. m.* sofa
sofferènte *agg.* **1** suffering **2** (*che mostra sofferenza*) painstricken
sofferènza *s. f.* suffering, pain
soffiàre A *v. intr.* to blow **B** *v. tr.* **1** to blow, to puff **2** (*fam.*) (*portar via*) to steal
sòffice *agg.* soft
sóffio *s. m.* **1** puff, whiff, breath **2** (*med.*) murmur
soffitta *s. f.* attic
soffitto *s. m.* ceiling
soffocaménto *s. m.* choking, suffocation
soffocànte *agg.* choking, stifling
soffocàre *v. tr. e intr.* to choke, to suffocate, to stifle
soffrìggere *v. tr. e intr.* to fry slightly
soffrìre A *v. tr.* **1** to suffer, to endure **2** (*sopportare*) to stand, to bear **B** *v. intr.* to suffer
sofisticàto *agg.* **1** sophisticated **2** (*adulterato*) adulterated
software *s. m. inv.* software
soggettivo *agg.* subjective
soggètto (1) *agg.* **1** (*sottoposto*) subject **2** (*incline*) subject, prone **3** (*dipendente*) dependent
soggètto (2) *s. m.* **1** (*argomento*) subject, (subject) matter, topic **2** (*individuo*) subject, person, (*spreg.*) character **3** (*gramm.*) subject
soggezióne *s. f.* **1** subjection **2** (*timore*) awe, (*imbarazzo*) uneasiness
sogghignàre *v. intr.* to sneer
soggiornàre *v. intr.* to stay
soggiórno *s. m.* **1** stay **2** (*stanza*) living-room ♦ **permesso di s.** residence permit
soggiùngere *v. tr. e intr.* to add
sòglia *s. f.* threshold
sògliola *s. f.* sole
sognànte *agg.* dreamy
sognàre *v. tr. e intr.* to dream
sognatóre *s. m.* dreamer
sógno *s. m.* dream
sòia *s. f.* soya-bean
solàio *s. m.* attic
solaménte *avv.* only, just
solàre *agg.* solar, sun (*attr*)
sólco *s. m.* furrow, (*traccia*) track
soldàto *s. m.* soldier
sòldo *s. m.* **1** (*moneta*) coin, penny **2** *al pl.* money
sóle *s. m.* sun, (*luce, calore*) sunshine
soleggiàto *agg.* sunny
solènne *agg.* solemn
solennità *s. f.* **1** solemnity **2** (*festività*) holiday
solfàto *s. m.* sulphate
solféggio *s. m.* solfeggio
solidàle *agg.* **1** united, solidly behind (*pred.*) **2** (*dir*) jointly liable **3** (*mecc.*) integral
solidarietà *s. f.* solidarity
solidità *s. f.* solidity
sòlido A *agg.* **1** (*fis., geom.*) solid **2** (*stabile*) solid, stable, (*di colore*) fast **3** (*saldo*) sound **B** *s. m.* solid
solilòquio *s. m.* soliloquy
solìsta A *agg.* solo **B** *s. m. e f.* soloist
solitaménte *avv.* usually
solitàrio A *agg.* **1** (*di persona*) solitary, lone (*attr*) **2** (*di luogo*) lonely **B** *s. m.* **1** (*brillante*) solitaire **2** (*con le carte*) patience
sòlito *agg.* usual, customary
solitùdine *s. f.* solitude
sollecitàre *v. tr.* **1** to urge, to press for, to solicit **2** (*mecc.*) to stress
sollecitazióne *s. f.* **1** solicitation **2** (*comm.*) request **3** (*mecc.*) stress
sollécito A *agg.* prompt, ready **B** *s. m.* request, reminder
sollecitùdine *s. f.* **1** promptness, speed **2** (*interessamento*) concern, care **3** (*attenzione*) kindness
solleticàre *v. tr.* to tickle
sollético *s. m.* tickle, tickling
sollevàre A *v. tr.* **1** to raise, to lift **2** (*fig.*) to relieve, to comfort **3** (*far sorgere*) to raise **4** (*far insorgere*) to stir up **B** *v. rifl. e intr. pron.* **1** to rise, to arise **2** (*riprendersi*) to get over **3** (*insorgere*) to rise
sollièvo *s. m.* relief
sólo A *agg.* **1** alone (*pred.*) **2** (*unico*) only **3** (*esclusivo*) sole **B** *s. m.* only one **C** *avv.* only, just ♦ **da s.** by oneself

soltànto *avv.* only, just
solùbile *agg.* **1** soluble **2** (*risolvibile*) solvable ♦ **caffè s.** instant coffee
soluzióne *s. f.* **1** (*chim.*) solution **2** (*spiegazione*) solution, solving
solvènte *agg. e s. m.* solvent
sòma *s. f.* load
somàro *s. m.* ass, donkey
somigliànza *s. f.* resemblance, likeness
somigliàre **A** *v. tr. e intr.* to resemble, to be like, to look like **B** *v. rifl. rec.* to be like each other, to be alike
sómma *s. f.* **1** (*mat.*) sum, total, amount, (*operazione*) addition **2** (*di denaro*) sum (of money), amount
sommàre **A** *v. tr.* to add, to sum **B** *v. intr.* (*ammontare*) to amount ♦ **tutto sommato** all things considered, all in all
sommàrio **A** *agg.* **1** summary, brief **2** (*dir.*) summary **3** (*approssimativo*) perfunctory **B** *s. m.* summary
sommèrgere *v. tr.* **1** to submerge, (*inondare*) to flood **2** (*colmare*) to overwhelm
sommergìbile *s. m.* submarine
somméssso *agg.* **1** humble **2** (*di suono*) low, soft
somministràre *v. tr.* to give (out), to administer
sommità *s. f.* top, summit, peak
sómmo **A** *agg.* **1** highest **2** (*fig.*) supreme, (*grande*) great **B** *s. m.* summit, top, peak ♦ **per sommi capi** briefly
sommòssa *s. f.* rising, revolt
sommozzatóre *s. m.* scuba diver, frogman
sonàglio *s. m.* rattle
sonàre → **suonare**
sónda *s. f.* **1** (*med.*) probe **2** (*meteor.*) sonde **3** (*miner.*) drill
sondàggio *s. m.* **1** sounding **2** (*med.*) probing **3** (*indagine*) poll, survey
sondàre *v. tr.* to sound, to probe
sonétto *s. m.* sonnet
sonnàmbulo *agg.* sleepwalker
sonnecchiàre *v. intr.* to doze
sonnìfero *s. m.* sleeping pill, sleeping draught
sónno *s. m.* sleep
sonnolènza *s. f.* sleepiness, drowsiness
sonorità *s. f.* sonority, acoustics *pl.*
sonòro **A** *agg.* **1** sonorous, resonant **2** (*rumoroso*) loud **3** (*cin.*) sound (*attr.*) **4** (*fon.*) voiced **B** *s. m.* **1** (*cin.*) talkie **2** (*audio*) sound
sontuóso *agg.* sumptuous
soporìfero *agg.* soporific
soppesàre *v. tr.* **1** to weigh in one's hand **2** (*fig.*) to consider carefully, to weigh
soppiàtto, di *loc. avv.* stealthily
sopportàbile *agg.* bearable, endurable
sopportàre **A** *v. tr.* to support, to bear, to endure, to stand, to put up with **B** *v. rifl. rec.* to stand each other
sopprìmere *v. tr.* **1** to suppress, to abolish, to cancel **2** (*uccidere*) to kill, to put down
sópra **A** *avv.* **1** up, on, above **2** (*al piano superiore*) upstairs **3** (*precedentemente*) above **B** *prep.* **1** (*sovrapposizione con contatto*) on, upon, up, on to, (*in cima a*) on top of **2** (*sovrapposizione senza contatto, rivestimento*) over **3** (*più in alto di*) above **4** (*oltre*) over **5** (*di seguito*) after **6** (*riguardo*) on
sopràbito *s. m.* overcoat
sopraccìglio *s. m.* eyebrow
sopraddétto *agg.* above-mentioned, aforesaid (*attr.*)
sopraffàre *v. tr.* to overcome, to overwhelm
sopraffìno *agg.* first-rate, excellent
sopraggiùngere *v. intr.* **1** to arrive, to come **2** (*accadere*) to happen, to turn up
sopralluògo *s. m.* on-the-spot investigation, inspection
soprammòbile *s. m.* knick-knack
soprannóme *s. m.* nickname
sopràno *s. m. e f.* soprano
soprassedére *v. intr.* to put off, to wait
soprattùtto *avv.* above all
sopravvalutàre *v. tr.* to overestimate, to overvalue
sopravvènto *s. m.* upper hand
sopravvissùto *s. m.* survivor
sopravvivènza *s. f.* survival
sopravvìvere *v. intr.* to survive
soprùso *s. m.* abuse of power
soqquàdro *s. m.* confusion
sorbétto *s. m.* water ice, sorbet
sorbìre *v. tr.* **1** to sip **2** (*sopportare*) to put up with
sòrdido *agg.* sordid, dirty
sordìna *s. f.* mute ♦ **in s.** on the sly
sordità *s. f.* deafness
sórdo **A** *agg.* **1** deaf **2** (*di suono*) dull, muffled **B** *s. m.* deaf person
sordomùto *agg.* deaf and dumb
sorèlla *s. f.* sister
sorellàstra *s. f.* half-sister, stepsister
sorgènte **A** *agg.* rising **B** *s. f.* spring, source

sórgere *v. intr.* **1** (*levarsi*) to rise **2** (*scaturire*) to rise, to arise, to spring out **3** (*elevarsi*) to stand, to rise
soriàno *s. m.* tabby (cat)
sormontàre *v. tr.* to surmount
sornióne *agg.* sly, crafty
sorpassàre *v. tr.* **1** to go beyond, to exceed to surpass **2** (*autom.*) to overtake
sorpàsso *s. m.* overtaking ♦ **divieto di s.** no overtaking
sorprendènte *agg.* surprising
sorprèndere A *v. tr.* **1** (*cogliere di sorpresa*) to catch **2** (*meravigliare*) to surprise **B** *v. intr. pron.* to be surprised
sorprésa *s. f.* surprise
sorpréso *agg.* surprised
sorrèggere *v. tr.* to support, to hold up
sorridènte *agg.* **1** smiling **2** (*benevolo*) good-natured
sorrìdere *v. intr.* **1** to smile **2** (*attrarre*) to make happy
sorriso *s. m.* smile
sorseggiàre *v. tr.* to sip
sórso *s. m.* **1** sip, gulp, draught **2** (*goccio*) drop
sòrta *s. f.* kind, sort
sòrte *s. f.* **1** fate, destiny, fortune **2** (*caso*) chance
sorteggiàre *v. tr.* to draw
sortéggio *s. m.* draw
sortilègio *s. m.* sorcery, witchcraft
sorveglianza *s. f.* watch, surveillance, supervision
sorvegliàre *v. tr.* **1** to guard, to watch, (*sovrintendere*) to supervise **2** (*tenere d'occhio*) to look after, to watch
sorvolàre *v. tr. e intr.* **1** to fly over, to overfly **2** (*fig.*) to pass over, to skip
sòsia *s. m. e f. inv.* double
sospèndere *v. tr.* **1** (*attaccare*) to suspend, to hang **2** (*interrompere*) to suspend, to stop, to interrupt **3** (*da una carica, da scuola*) to suspend
sospensióne *s. f.* **1** suspension **2** (*interruzione*) suspension, interruption, stoppage
sospéso A *agg.* **1** hanging, suspended **2** (*interrotto*) suspended, interrupted **3** (*trepidante*) in suspence **B** *s. m.* (*pagamento*) outstanding payment ♦ **in s.** pending, in abeyance
sospettàre *v. tr. e intr.* to suspect
sospètto A *agg.* **1** suspicious **2** (*discutibile*) suspect, questionable **3** (*di cui si teme l'esistenza*) suspected **B** *s. m.* suspicion
sospettóso *agg.* suspicious
sospìngere to drive, to push
sospiràre A *v. intr.* to sigh **B** *v. tr.* to sigh for, to long for
sospìro *s. m.* sigh
sòsta *s. f.* **1** (*fermata*) halt, stop **2** (*pausa*) pause **3** (*interruzione*) interruption, break ♦ **divieto di s.** no parking
sostantìvo *s. m.* substantive
sostànza *s. f.* **1** substance, essence **2** (*materia*) substance, matter, material, stuff **3** (*nutrimento*) nourishment **4** *al pl.* (*ricchezze*) property, possessions *pl.*
sostanzióso *agg.* substantial
sostàre *v. intr.* **1** to stop, to stay **2** (*fare una pausa*) to have a break
sostégno *s. m.* support, prop
sostenére A *v. tr.* **1** (*tenere su*) to support, to sustain, to hold up **2** (*portare su di sé*) to carry, to take **3** (*sopportare*) to bear, to stand, (*reggere*) to stand up to **4** (*resistere a*) to withstand **5** (*appoggiare*) to support, to uphold, (*difendere*) to defend **6** (*affermare*) to maintain, to assert **7** (*mantenere*) to keep up, to support **B** *v. rifl. e intr. pron.* **1** (*reggersi in piedi*) to stand up, (*appoggiarsi*) to support oneself **2** (*sostentarsi*) to sustain oneself
sostenitóre *s. m.* supporter
sostentaménto *s. m.* sustenance, maintenance
sostenùto *agg.* **1** (*riservato*) reserved, distant **2** (*solenne*) elevated **3** (*elevato*) fast
sostituìbile *agg.* replaceable
sostituìre A *v. tr.* **1** (*rimpiazzare*) to replace, to substitute **2** (*prendere il posto di*) to take the place of, to substitute for, to replace **B** *v. rifl.* to take sb.'s place
sostitùto *s. m.* substitute
sostituzióne *s. f.* replacement, substitution
sottacéto A *agg.* pickled **B** *s. m.* pickle
sottàna *s. f.* skirt
sotterfùgio *s. m.* trick, expedient
sotterràneo A *agg.* underground **B** *s. m.* basement, cellar
sotterràre *v. tr.* to bury
sottigliézza *s. f.* **1** thinness **2** (*acutezza*) sharpness **3** (*cavillo*) quibble
sottìle *agg.* **1** thin **2** (*acuto*) sharp, subtle
sottilizzàre *v. intr.* to subtilize, to split hairs
sottintèndere *v. tr.* to understand, to imply
sottintéso A *agg.* understood, implied **B**

s. m. implicit meaning, allusion

sótto A *avv.* **1** down, under, below, beneath, underneath **2** (*al piano sotto*) downstairs **3** (*più avanti*) below **4** (*in perdita*) short **B** *prep.* **1** (*in posizione inferiore*) under, beneath, underneath **2** (*più in basso*) below **3** (*meno di*) under **C** *s. m.* bottom, underside

sottobicchière *s. m.* coaster, (*piattino*) saucer

sottobòsco *s. m.* undergrowth

sottobràccio *avv.* arm in arm

sottocòsto *avv.* below cost ♦ **vendere s.** to sell off

sottocutàneo *agg.* subcutaneous

sottofóndo *s. m.* **1** (*edil.*) foundation **2** (*fig.*) substratum **3** (*di suoni*) background

sottolineàre *v. tr.* **1** to underline, to underscore **2** (*fig.*) to underline, to stress

sottomarìno *agg. e s. m.* submarine

sottoméSSo *agg.* **1** (*soggiogato*) subdued, subject **2** (*remissivo*) submissive, respectful

sottométtere A *v. tr.* **1** (*assoggettare*) to subdue, to subject **2** (*subordinare*) to subordinate **3** (*presentare*) to submit **B** *v. rifl.* to submit

sottopassàggio *s. m.* underpass, subway

sottopórre A *v. tr.* **1** (*assoggettare*) to subdue, to subject **2** (*presentare*) to submit, to present **3** (*costringere a subire*) to subject, to put through **B** *v. rifl.* **1** to submit **2** (*subire*) to undergo

sottoprodótto *s. m.* by-product

sottoscàla *s. m. inv.* understairs

sottoscrìtto *agg. e s. m.* undersigned

sottoscrìvere *v. tr.* **1** (*firmare*) to sign, to undersign, (*aderire a*) to subscribe **2** (*approvare*) to support, to subscribe to

sottoscrizióne *s. f.* subscription

sottosópra *avv.* upside down

sottostànte *agg.* below

sottosvilùppo *s. m.* underdevelopment

sottotèrra *avv.* underground

sottotìtolo *s. m.* subtitle

sottovèste *s. f.* petticoat

sottovóce *avv.* in a low voice

sottovuòto *agg. e avv.* vacuum-packed

sottràrre A *v. tr.* **1** (*portare via*) to take away, to remove, (*rubare*) to steal **2** (*liberare*) to save, to rescue **3** (*mat.*) to subtract **4** (*dedurre*) to deduct **B** *v. rifl.* to get out, to evade, to shirk

sottrazióne *s. f.* **1** (*mat.*) subtraction **2** (*il portar via*) taking away, (*furto*) abstraction

sovièticO *agg. e s. m.* Soviet

sovraccaricàre *v. tr.* to overload, to overburden

sovraespórre *v. tr.* to overexpose

sovraffollàto *agg.* overcrowded

sovràno *agg. e s. m.* sovereign

sovrapponìbile *agg.* superimposable

sovrappórre A *v. tr.* to put on, to place on, to superimpose **B** *v. intr. pron.* **1** to be superimposed, to overlap **2** (*aggiungersi*) to arise in addition

sovrastànte *agg.* overhanging

sovrastàre *v. tr. e intr.* **1** to stand above, to overlook, to overhang **2** (*essere imminente*) to be imminent, to hang over **3** (*essere superiore*) to surpass

sovrumàno *agg.* superhuman

sovvenzionàre *v. tr.* to finance

sovvenzióne *s. f.* subvention, aid

sovversìvo *agg. e s. m.* subversive

sózzo *agg.* dirty

spaccàre *v. tr. e intr. pron.* to break, to split

spaccatùra *s. f.* split

spacciàre A *v. tr.* **1** (*vendere*) to sell (off), **2** (*mettere in circolazione*) to circulate, (*clandestinamente*) to peddle, to utter, (*droga*) to push **3** (*divulgare*) to spread **B** *v. rifl.* to pretend (to be)

spacciatóre *s. m.* dealer, utterer, (*di droga*) pusher

spàccio *s. m.* **1** (*negozio*) shop **2** (*vendita*) sale **3** (*traffico illegale*) traffic

spàcco *s. m.* **1** slit, cleft, (*taglio*) tear **2** (*di vestito*) vent

spaccóne *s. m.* boaster

spàda *s. f.* sword

spaesàto *agg.* lost

spagnòlo A *agg.* Spanish **B** *s. m.* **1** (*abitante*) Spaniard **2** (*lingua*) Spanish

spàgo *s. m.* string, twine

spaiàto *agg.* odd

spalancàre A *v. tr.* to open wide **B** *v. intr. pron.* to be throw open

spalàre *v. tr.* to shovel away

spàlla *s. f.* **1** shoulder **2** *al pl.* (*schiena*) back

spalleggiàre *v. tr.* to back, to support

spallièra *s. f.* **1** (*di sedia*) back **2** (*di letto*) head (of the bed) **3** (*di piante*) espalier **4** (*attrezzo ginnico*) wall bar

spalmàre *v. tr.* to spread, to smear ♦ **s. di burro** to butter

spanàre *v. tr. e intr. pron.* to strip

spàndere *v. tr. e intr. pron.* to spread

spànna *s. f.* span
sparàre *v. tr. e intr.* to shoot, to fire
sparatòria *s. f.* shooting
sparecchiàre *v. tr.* to clear
sparéggio *s. m.* **1** (*sport*) play-off **2** (*squilibrio*) unbalance
spàrgere **A** *v. tr.* **1** to scatter, to strew **2** (*divulgare*) to spread **3** (*versare*) to shed **B** *v. intr. pron.* **1** to scatter, to disperse **2** (*diffondersi*) to spread
sparìre *v. intr.* to disappear, to vanish
sparizióne *s. f.* disappearance
sparlàre *v. intr.* to run down, to talk behind sb.'s back
spàro *s. m.* shot
sparpagliàre *v. tr. e intr. pron.* to scatter
spartiàcque *s. m. inv.* watershed
spartìre *v. tr.* **1** (*separare*) to separate **2** (*distribuire*) to share out, to divide
spartìto *s. m.* score
spartitràffico *s. m. inv.* traffic divider
sparùto *agg.* **1** (*emaciato*) lean **2** (*esiguo*) small
sparvièro *s. m.* sparrow-hawk
spàsimo *s. m.* pang
spàsmo *s. m.* spasm
spasmòdico *agg.* **1** (*med.*) spasmodic(al) **2** (*angoscioso*) agonizing
spassionàto *agg.* impartial, unbiased
spàsso *s. m.* amusement, fun ♦ **andare a s.** to go for a walk
spassóso *agg.* funny
spàstico *agg. e s. m.* spastic
spauràcchio *s. m.* bugbear
spavàldo *agg.* bold, arrogant
spaventapàsseri *s. m.* scarecrow
spaventàre **A** *v. tr.* to frighten, to scare **B** *v. intr. pron.* to be frightened, to get scared
spavènto *s. m.* fright, fear
spaventóso *agg.* frightful, frightening, deadful
spaziàle *agg.* spatial, space (*attr.*)
spazientìre **A** *v. tr.* to try the patience of **B** *v. intr. pron.* to lose one's patience
spàzio *s. m.* space
spazióso *agg.* spacious
spazzacamìno *s. m.* chimney-sweep
spazzanéve *s. m. inv.* snowplough
spazzàre *v. tr.* **1** to sweep **2** (*portar via*) to sweep away, to wipe out
spazzatùra *s. f.* garbage, rubbish, (*USA*) trash
spazzìno *s. m.* street-sweeper
spàzzola *s. f.* brush ♦ **s. per capelli** hair-brush
spazzolàre *v. tr.* to brush
spazzolìno *s. m.* brush, (*da denti*) tooth-brush
spazzolóne *s. m.* mop
specchiàrsi *v. rifl. e intr. pron.* **1** to look at oneself (in a mirror) **2** (*riflettersi*) to be reflected
specchiétto *s. m.* **1** hand-mirror **2** (*autom.*) rear-view mirror **3** (*tabella*) table
spècchio *s. m.* mirror
speciàle *agg.* **1** special **2** (*particolare*) peculiar **3** (*di qualità*) first-class
specialìsta *s. m. e f.* specialist
specialìstico *agg.* specialized
specialità *s. f.* speciality
specializzàre *v. tr., rifl. e intr. pron.* to specialize
specializzàto *agg.* specialized, skilled ♦ **non s.** unskilled
specialménte *avv.* especially
spècie *s. f. inv.* **1** kind, sort **2** (*scient.*) species
specificàre *v. tr.* to specify
specìfico *s. m.* specific
speculàre (1) *agg.* specular
speculàre (2) *v. intr.* **1** (*indagare*) to speculate **2** (*approfittare*) to trade on
speculazióne *s. f.* speculation
spedìre *v. tr.* to send, to mail, to dispatch, (*via mare*) to ship
spedìto *agg.* **1** quick, prompt **2** (*sciolto*) fluent
spedizióne *s. f.* **1** (*invio*) sending, forwarding, dispatch **2** (*scientifica, mil.*) expedition
spedizionière *s. m.* carrier, forwarder, (*marittimo*) shipping agent
spègnere **A** *v. tr.* to extinguish, (*fuoco*) to put out, (*luce, radio*) to turn off, to switch off **B** *v. intr. pron.* **1** to be extinguished, to go out, (*di fuoco*) to burn out **2** (*scomparire*) to die down, to fade **3** (*morire*) to pass away
speleologìa *s. f.* spel(a)eology
speleòlogo *s. m.* spel(a)eologist
spellàre **A** *v. tr.* to skin **B** *v. intr. pron.* to peel, to get skinned
spellatùra *s. f.* graze, excoriation, (*da sole*) peeling
spèndere *v. tr.* **1** to spend **2** (*impiegare*) to spend, to put in
spennàre *v. tr.* **1** to pluck **2** (*fig.*) to rip off
spensieràto *agg.* thoughtless

spènto *agg.* **1** extinguished, out (*pred.*), (*di apparecchi*) turned off (*pred.*), switched off (*pred.*) **2** (*scialbo*) dull
sperànza *s. f.* hope
speràre **A** *v. tr.* **1** to hope **2** (*aspettarsi*) to expect **B** *v. intr.* to hope, to trust in
sperdùto *agg.* **1** dispersed **2** (*isolato*) secluded, lonely **3** (*smarrito*) lost
spergiuràre *v. intr.* to perjure oneself
spergiùro *s. m.* **1** (*chi spergiura*) perjurer **2** (*falso giuramento*) perjury
spericolàto *agg.* reckless
sperimentàle *agg.* experimental
sperimentàre *v. tr.* **1** to experiment with, to test, to try **2** (*fare esperienza di*) to experience
spèrma *s. m.* sperm
speronàre *v. tr.* to ram
speróne *s. m.* **1** spur **2** (*naut.*) ram
sperperàre *v. tr.* to squander, to waste
spésa *s. f.* **1** expense, (*costo*) charge, cost **2** (*acquisto*) buy, purchase **3** (*compera*) shopping ♦ **fare la s.** to do the shopping; **fare spese** to go shopping
spésso **A** *agg.* thick **B** *avv.* often
spessóre *s. m.* **1** thickness **2** (*fig.*) depth
spettacolàre *agg.* spectacular
spettàcolo *s. m.* **1** show, spectacle, sight **2** (*teatro*) performance, (*cin.*) showing
spettacolóso *agg.* spectacular
spettàre *v. intr.* **1** to be for, to be up to **2** (*competere*) to be due
spettatóre *s. m.* **1** spectator, *al pl.* audience **2** (*testimone*) bystander, witness
spettinàre **A** *v. tr.* to mess up hair **B** *v. rifl. e intr. pron.* to ruffle one's hair
spèttro *s. m.* **1** ghost **2** (*scient.*) spectrum
spèzie *s. f. pl.* spices *pl.*
spezzàre *v. tr. e intr. pron.* to break
spezzatìno *s. m.* stew
spezzettàre *v. tr.* to break into pieces
spìa *s. f.* **1** spy, informer, (*riferito a bambini*) sneak **2** (*indizio*) indication, sign **3** (*luminosa*) (warning) light
spiacènte *agg.* sorry
spiacére **A** *v. intr.* **1** to be sorry **2** (*nelle frasi di cortesia*) to mind **B** *v. intr. pron.* to be sorry
spiacévole *agg.* **1** unpleasant **2** (*increscioso*) regrettable
spiàggia *s. f.* beach, shore
spianàre *v. tr.* **1** to level, to make level **2** (*radere al suolo*) to raze **3** (*appianare*) to smooth
spiantàto *s. m.* penniless person
spiàre *v. tr.* **1** to spy on **2** (*aspettare ansiosamente*) to wait for
spiàta *s. f.* tip-off
spiazzàre *v. tr.* to wrongfoot
spiàzzo *s. m.* open space
spiccàre **A** *v. tr.* **1** (*staccare*) to pick, to pluck **2** (*emettere*) to issue **B** *v. intr.* to stand out, to show up ♦ **s. un salto** to jump
spiccàto *agg.* **1** marked, strong **2** (*nitido*) distinct, clear
spìcchio *s. m.* slice, (*di agrume*) segment, (*di aglio*) clove
spicciàre **A** *v. tr.* to finish off **B** *v. intr. v. intr. pron.* to hurry up
spìcciolo *s. m.* change
spiedìno *s. m.* skewer
spièdo *s. m.* spit ♦ **allo s.** on the spit
spiegàre **A** *v. tr.* **1** (*svolgere*) to unfold, to spread out **2** (*far capire*) to explain **B** *v. rifl.* to explain oneself **C** *v. intr. pron.* to spread out, to open out
spiegazióne *s. f.* explanation
spiegazzàre **A** *v. tr.* to crumple **B** *v. intr. pron.* to get crumpled
spietàto *agg.* pitiless, cruel
spifferàre *v. tr.* to blurt out, to blab
spìffero *s. m.* draught
spìga *s. f.* ear, spike
spigliàto *agg.* easy
spìgola *s. f.* bass
spìgolo *s. m.* edge, corner
spìlla *s. f.* **1** pin **2** (*gioiello*) brooch
spillàre *v. tr.* **1** to tap, to draw off **2** (*fig.*) to worm, to get out
spìllo *s. m.* pin ♦ **tacchi a s.** stiletto heels
spilòrcio *s. m.* miser
spìna *s. f.* **1** thorn **2** (*di pesce*) fishbone **3** (*elettr*) plug ♦ **s. dorsale** backbone
spinàcio *s. m.* spinach
spinàle *agg.* spinal
spinétta *s. f.* spinet
spìngere **A** *v. tr.* **1** to push, to shove, (*ficcare*) to drive, to thrust **2** (*condurre*) to drive, (*indurre*) to induce, (*stimolare*) to urge **B** *v. intr.* to push **C** *v. intr. pron.* **1** to push **2** (*arrivare*) to go
spinóso *agg.* thorny
spìnta *s. f.* **1** push, shove, thrust **2** (*aiuto*) helping hand, (*stimolo*) incentive, spur **3** (*fis. tecnol.*) thrust
spinterògeno *s. m.* distributor
spìnto *agg.* **1** pushed, driven **2** (*audace*)

risqué
spintóne *s. m.* shove
spionàggio *s. m.* espionage, spying
spiovènte **A** *agg.* sloping **B** *s. m.* slope
spiòvere **A** *v. intr.* (*ricadere*) to come down **B** *v. intr. impers.* (*cessare di piovere*) to stop raining
spìra *s. f.* coil
spiràglio *s. m.* **1** (small) opening, crack, vent **2** (*di luce*) glimmer
spiràle *s. f.* spiral
spiràre (1) **A** *v. intr.* (*soffiare*) to blow **B** *v. tr.* **1** (*emanare*) to give off **2** (*fig.*) to express
spiràre (2) *v. intr.* (*morire*) to pass away
spiritìsmo *s. m.* spiritualism
spìrito *s. m.* **1** spirit **2** (*fantasma*) spirit, ghost **3** (*mente, intelligenza*) mind **4** (*disposizione d'animo*) spirit, attitude **5** (*significato essenziale*) spirit, sense **6** (*arguzia*) wit, (*umorismo*) humour **7** (*vivacità*) life, liveliness **8** (*chim.*) spirit, alchool
spiritosàggine *s. f.* **1** wittiness **2** (*detto spiritoso*) witticism
spiritóso *agg.* witty
spirituàle *agg.* spiritual
splendènte *agg.* bright, shining
splèndere *v. intr.* to shine
splèndido *agg.* splendid, wonderful
splendóre *s. m.* **1** (*luce*) brilliance, brightness **2** (*fig.*) splendour
spodestàre *v. tr.* to deprive of power, (*un re*) to dethrone
spogliàre **A** *v. tr.* **1** to undress, to strip **2** (*privare*) to deprive, to strip **B** *v. rifl. e intr. pron.* **1** (*svestirsi*) to undress, to strip **2** (*privarsi*) to deprive oneself, to strip oneself **3** (*di albero*) to shed
spogliarèllo *s. m.* striptease
spogliatóio *s. m.* changing room, dressing room
spòglie *s. f. pl.* **1** (*vesti*) dress **2** (*preda di guerra*) spoils *pl.*, booty
spòglio **A** *agg.* **1** (*nudo*) bare **2** (*libero*) free **B** *s. m.* **1** (*conto*) counting **2** (*esame*) examination
spòla *s. f.* shuttle
spolpàre *v. tr.* to strip the flesh off
spolveràre *v. tr.* to dust
spónda *s. f.* **1** (*bordo*) edge **2** (*riva*) bank, side, (*di mare, lago*) shore **3** (*parapetto*) parapet
sponsor *s. m. inv.* sponsor
sponsorizzàre *v. tr.* to sponsor
spontaneità *s. f.* spontaneity
spontàneo *agg.* spontaneous, natural
spopolàre **A** *v. tr.* to depopulate **B** *v. intr.* (*avere successo*) to be a big hit **C** *v. intr. pron.* to become depopulated
sporadicità *s. f.* sporadicity
sporàdico *agg.* sporadic
sporcàre **A** *v. tr.* to dirty, to soil, to stain **B** *v. rifl. e intr. pron.* to dirty oneself, to get dirty
sporcìzia *s. f.* **1** (*l'essere sporco*) dirtiness, filthiness **2** (*cosa sporca*) dirt, filth
spòrco *agg.* dirty, filthy
sporgènte *agg.* projecting, protruding, protuberant
sporgènza *s. f.* projection
spòrgere **A** *v. tr.* to put out, to stretch out **B** *v. intr.* to jut out, to stick out **C** *v. rifl.* to lean out
sport *s. m. inv.* sport
spòrta *s. f.* shopping bag
sportèllo *s. m.* **1** door **2** (*di ufficio*) counter, window
sportìvo **A** *agg.* sporting, sport (*attr.*) **B** *s. m.* sportsman, (*appassionato*) (sports) fan
spòsa *s. f.* bride ♦ **abito da s.** wedding dress
sposalìzio *s. m.* wedding
sposàre **A** *v. tr.* **1** to marry, to get married to **2** (*dare in matrimonio*) to marry (off) **3** (*abbracciare, sostenere*) to embrace **B** *v. rifl. e rifl. rec.* **1** to marry, to get married **2** (*armonizzarsi*) to go well
spòso *s. m.* **1** bridegroom **2** *al pl.* (*marito e moglie*) newlyweds *pl.*
spossànte *agg.* exhausting
spostàre **A** *v. tr.* **1** to move, to shift **2** (*cambiare*) to change **3** (*differire*) to postpone **B** *v. rifl. e intr. pron.* to move, to shift
sprànga *s. f.* bar, (*catenaccio*) bolt
spràzzo *s. m.* flash
sprecàre **A** *v. tr.* to waste, to squander **B** *v. intr. pron.* **1** to waste one's energy **2** (*ironicamente*) to put oneself out
sprèco *s. m.* waste
spregévole *agg.* despicable
spregiativo *agg.* pejorative
spregiudicàto *agg.* unprejudiced, unconventional
sprèmere *v. tr.* to squeeze
spremiagrùmi *s. m. inv.* citrus-fruit squeezer
spremùta *s. f.* juice
sprezzànte *agg.* scornful
sprigionàre **A** *v. tr.* to emit, to give off **B**

v. intr. pron. to emanate, to burst out
sprizzàre *v. tr. e intr.* to squirt, to spray, to spurt
sprofondàre A *v. intr.* **1** (*di terreno*) to subside, to give away **2** (*affondare*) to sink **B** *v. intr. pron.* to sink
spronàre *v. tr.* to spur
spróne *s. m.* spur
sproporzionàto *agg.* disproportionate
sproporzióne *s. f.* disproportion
spropositàto *agg.* enormous
spropòsito *s. m.* **1** (*errore*) mistake, blunder **2** (*eccesso*) enormous quantity
sprovvedùto *agg.* unprepared, inexperienced
sprovvìsto *agg.* devoid, unprovided ♦ **alla sprovvista** unawares
spruzzàre *v. tr.* **1** to spray, to sprinkle **2** (*inzaccherare*) to splash
sprùzzo *s. m.* spray, sprinkling, (*di fango*) splash
spùgna *s. f.* **1** sponge **2** (*tessuto*) sponge-cloth, terry-cloth
spùma *s. f.* foam, froth
spumànte *s. m.* sparkling wine
spumeggiàre *v. intr.* to foam, to froth
spuntàre A *v. tr.* **1** (*rompere la punta di*) to blunt, to break the point of **2** (*tagliare la punta di*) to cut the tip of, to trim **3** (*controllare*) to check (off) **4** (*ottenere*) to obtain, to get **B** *v. intr.* **1** (*di astro*) to rise, (*di pianta*) to sprout, (*di capelli, ecc.*) to begin to grow, (*di lacrime*) to well up **2** (*apparire*) to appear, to come out **3** (*sporgere*) to stick out **C** *v. intr. pron.* to get blunt
spuntìno *s. m.* snack
spùnto *s. m.* **1** (*suggerimento*) cue, hint **2** (*punto di partenza*) starting point
spurgàre *v. tr.* to purge, to clean
sputàre *v. tr. e intr.* to spit
spùto *s. m.* spit
squàdra *s. f.* **1** (*sport*) team **2** (*mil.*) squad **3** (*gruppo*) team, (*di operai*) gang **4** (*mecc., da disegno*) square
squadràre *v. tr.* **1** to square **2** (*guardare*) to look up and down
squadrìglia *s. f.* squadron
squagliàre A *v. tr.* to melt, to liquefy **B** *v. intr. pron.* **1** to melt, to liquefy **2** (*svignarsela*) to make off, to clear off
squalìfica *s. f.* disqualification
squalificàre A *v. tr.* to disqualify **B** *v. rifl.* to bring discredit
squàllido *agg.* **1** bleak, dreary **2** (*triste*) dismal **3** (*abietto*) wretched
squallóre *s. m.* dreariness, squalor
squàlo *s. m.* shark
squàma *s. f.* scale
squamàre *v. tr. e intr. pron.* to scale
squarciagóla, a *loc. avv.* at the top of one's voice
squattrinàto *agg.* penniless
squilibràre A *v. tr.* to unbalance, to put out of balance **B** *v. intr. pron.* to lose one's balance
squilibràto A *agg.* **1** unbalanced **2** (*pazzo*) insane, mad **B** *s. m.* madman, lunatic
squilìbrio *s. m.* **1** imbalance **2** (*mentale*) derangement, insanity
squillànte *agg.* shrill, (*di colore*) bright
squillàre *v. intr.* to ring
squìllo *s. m.* ring, (*di tromba*) blare
squisìto *agg.* exquisite, delicious
squittìre *v. intr.* to squeak
sradicàre *v. tr.* to uproot
srotolàre *v. tr.* to unroll
stàbile A *agg.* **1** stable, steady **2** (*permanente*) permanent, durable **B** *s. m.* house, building
stabiliménto *s. m.* **1** factory, plant, works **2** (*edificio pubblico*) establishment ♦ **s. balneare** bathing establishment
stabilìre A *v. tr.* **1** to establish, to fix, to set **2** (*accertare*) to estabilish, to ascertain **3** (*decidere*) to decide, to arrange **B** *v. rifl.* to settle, to estabilish oneself
stabilità *s. f.* stability, steadiness
staccàre A *v. tr.* **1** to take off, to detach, to cut off, (*strappare*) to tear off, to pull off, (*tirare giù*) to take down **2** (*slegare*) to loosen, (*sganciare*) to unhook **3** (*scostare*) to move away **4** (*separare*) to separate **5** (*togliere*) to disconnect **6** (*lasciare indietro*) to leave behind **B** *v. intr.* **1** (*spiccare*) to stand out **2** (*smettere di lavorare*) to knock off **C** *v. intr. pron.* **1** to come off, to come out, to get detached **2** (*slegarsi*) to break away, (*sganciarsi*) to get unhooked **3** (*scostarsi*) to move away **4** (*separarsi*) to leave **5** (*abbandonare*) to detach oneself, to give up **6** (*distanziarsi*) to pull ahead **7** (*essere differente*) to be different
staccionàta *s. f.* fence
stàdio *s. m.* **1** (*sport*) stadium, ground **2** (*fase*) stage
stàffa *s. f.* stirrup

staffétta *s. f.* **1** courier **2** (*sport*) relay
stagionàle *agg.* seasonal
stagionàre **A** *v. tr.* to season, to let age **B** *v. intr. pron.* to age
stagionatùra *s. f.* seasoning
stagióne *s. f.* season
stagliàrsi *v. intr. pron.* to stand out
stàgno (1) *s. m.* (*chim.*) tin
stàgno (2) *agg.* watertight
stàgno (3) *s. m.* pond, pool
stagnòla *s. f.* tinfoil
stalagmìte *s. f.* stalagmite
stalattìte *s. f.* stalactite
stàlla *s. f.* shed, (*per cavalli*) stable, (*per bovini*) cowshed
stallière *s. m.* stableman, groom
stallóne *s. m.* stallion
stamattìna *avv.* this morning
stambécco *s. m.* rock-goat
stàmpa *s. f.* **1** print, printing **2** (*giornali, giornalisti*) press **3** (*riproduzione*) print **4** *al pl.* (*nelle spedizioni postali*) printed matter
stampànte *s. f.* printer
stampàre *v. tr.* **1** to print **2** (*pubblicare*) to publish **3** (*imprimere*) to imprint
stampatèllo *s. m.* block letters *pl.*
stampatóre *s. m.* printer
stampèlla *s. f.* crutch
stàmpo *s. m.* **1** die, mould **2** (*genere*) kind, sort
stanàre *v. tr.* to drive out
stancàre **A** *v. tr.* **1** to tire, to weary **2** (*infastidire*) to bore, to annoy **B** *v. rifl.* to get tired
stanchézza *s. f.* tiredness
stànco *agg.* tired
standard *agg. e s. m. inv.* standard
standardizzàre *v. tr.* to standardize
stànga *s. f.* bar, shaft
stangàta *s. f.* blow, squeeze
stanòtte *avv.* tonight, (*appena trascorsa*) last night
stantìo *agg.* stale
stantùffo *s. m.* piston
stànza *s. f.* room
stanziàre **A** *v. tr.* to allocate, to appropriate **B** *v. intr. pron.* to settle, to establish oneself
stappàre *v. tr.* to uncork
stàre *v. intr.* **1** to stay, (*rimanere*) to remain **2** (*essere*) to be **3** (*abitare*) to live **4** (*andare*) to go, to be **5** (*dipendere*) to depend **6** (*spettare*) to be up ♦ **come stai?** how are you?; **starci** (*essere d'accordo*) to count in, (*esserci spazio*) to have room for; **s. per fare q.c.** to be going to do st.
starnutìre *v. intr.* to sneeze
starnùto *s. m.* sneeze
staséra *avv.* this evening, tonight
statàle *agg.* state (*attr*), government (*attr*)
statìsta *s. m.* statesman
statìstica *s. f.* statistics *pl.* (*v. al sing.*)
stàto *s. m.* **1** state, condition **2** (*posizione sociale*) position, standing **3** (*politico*) state **4** (*dir*) status **5** (*fis.*) state ♦ **s. civile** civil status; **s. d'assedio** state of siege
stàtua *s. f.* statue
statuniténse **A** *agg.* United States (*attr*) **B** *s. m. e f.* United States citizen
statùra *s. f.* height
statùto *s. m.* statute, charter
stavòlta *avv.* this time
stazionàrio *agg.* stationary
stazióne *s. f.* station ♦ **s. balneare** seaside resort
stécca *s. f.* **1** stick, rod, (*da biliardo*) cue, (*di ombrello*) rib **2** (*mus.*) false note **3** (*confezione di sigarette*) carton **4** (*tangente*) bribe
steccàto *s. m.* fence
stèle *s. f.* stele
stélla *s. f.* star ♦ **s. di mare** starfish; **s. filante** streamer
stellàto *agg.* starry
stèlo *s. m.* **1** (*bot.*) stalk, stem **2** (*sostegno*) stand
stèmma *s. m.* coat of arms
stemperàre *v. tr. e intr. pron.* to dissolve, to melt
stendàrdo *s. m.* standard, banner
stèndere **A** *v. tr.* **1** (*distendere, allungare*) to stretch (out) **2** (*spiegare*) to spread (out), to lay out **3** (*mettere a giacere*) to lay **4** (*spalmare*) to spread **5** (*mettere per iscritto*) to draw up, to draft **B** *v. intr. pron.* (estendersi) to stretch **C** *v. rifl.* (*sdraiarsi*) to lie down
stenografàre *v. tr.* to take down in shorthand
stenografìa *s. f.* shorthand
stentàre *v. intr.* to find it hard, to have difficult
stéppa *s. f.* steppe
stèrco *s. m.* dung
stèreo *agg. e s. m. inv.* stereo
stèrile *agg.* **1** sterile, barren **2** (*inutile*) vain, fruitless **3** (*med.*) sterile, sterilized

sterilità *s. f.* **1** barrenness, sterility **2** (*med.*) sterility
sterilizzàre *v. tr.* to sterilize
sterilizzatóre *s. m.* sterilizer
sterilizzazióne *s. f.* sterilization
sterlìna *s. f.* pound, sterling
sterminàre *v. tr.* to exterminate, to wipe out
sterminàto *agg.* (*smisurato*) endless
stermìnio *s. m.* extermination
stèrno *s. m.* breast-bone
sterzàre *v. intr.* to steer
stèrzo *s. m.* steering (gear), (*volante*) steering wheel
stésso **A** *agg.* **1** (*identico*) same **2** (*dopo un pron. pers. o un s.*) (*io s.*) I myself, (*tu s.*) you yourself, (*egli s.*) he himself, (*ella stessa*) she herself, (*esso s.*) it itself, (*noi stessi/stesse*) we ourselves, (*voi stessi/stesse*) you yourselves, (*essi stessi/esse stesse*) they themselves (ES: **Io farò io s.** I'll do it myself, **l'artista s. presenziò all'inaugurazione** the artist himself presided over the opening) **3** (*rifl.*) -self, -selves *pl.* **4** (*proprio, esattamente*) very (ES: **oggi s.** this very day) **5** (*uguale*) same, like **B** *pron. dimostr.* **1** (*la stessa persona*) same **2** (*la stessa cosa*) the same **C** *avv.* the same
stesùra *s. f.* drawing up
stilàre *v. tr.* to draw up, to draft
stìle *s. m.* style
stilìsta *s. m. e f.* stylist
stillàre *v. tr. e intr.* to drip
stillicìdio *s. m.* dripping
stilòbate *s. m.* stylobate
stilogràfica *s. f.* fountain pen
stìma *s. f.* **1** (*valutazione*) estimate, evaluation, appraisal **2** (*prezzo stimato*) valuation **3** (*buona opinione*) esteem
stimàre *v. tr.* **1** (*valutare*) to estimate, to appraise, to value **2** (*tenere in considerazione*) to esteem **3** (*giudicare*) to consider, to think
stimolàre *v. tr.* to stimulate, to spur
stìmolo *s. m.* stimulus
stìnco *s. m.* shin, (*cuc.*) shank
stìngere *v. tr. e intr.* to fade
stipàre *v. tr. e intr. pron.* to cram, to pack
stipèndio *s. m.* salary, pay
stìpite *s. m.* jamb
stipulàre *v. tr.* to stipulate, (*redigere*) to draw up
stiràre **A** *v. tr.* **1** to stretch **2** (*col ferro*) to iron **3** (*i capelli*) to straighten **B** *v. rifl.* **1** to stretch (oneself) **2** (*procurarsi uno stiramento*) to strain a muscle
stiratùra *s. f.* ironing
stìrpe *s. f.* **1** birth, family, descent **2** (*prole*) offspring
stitichézza *s. f.* constipation
stìtico *agg.* constipated
stìva *s. f.* hold
stivàle *s. m.* boot
stivalétto *s. m.* ankle-boot
stìzza *s. f.* anger
stizzìre **A** *v. tr.* to irritate **B** *v. intr. pron.* to get angry
stoccafìsso *s. m.* stockfish
stoccàta *s. f.* **1** thrust **2** (*fig.*) gibe
stòffa *s. f.* **1** cloth, material, fabric **2** (*fig.*) stuff
stoìno *s. m.* (door)mat
stòla *s. f.* stole
stólto *agg.* foolish
stòmaco *s. m.* stomach
stonàre *v. intr.* **1** (*mus.*) to be out of tune **2** (*fig.*) to be out of place, (*di colori*) to clash
stop *s. m. inv.* **1** (*segnale*) stop signal **2** (*luci*) stop-light
stóppa *s. f.* tow
stoppìno *s. m.* wick
stòrcere **A** *v. tr.* to twist, to wrench **B** *v. rifl. e intr. pron.* to twist, to writhe
stordìre **A** *v. tr.* **1** to stun, to daze **2** (*assordare*) to deafen **3** (*sbalordire*) to stun, to stupefy **B** *v. rifl.* to dull one's senses
stòria *s. f.* **1** history **2** (*racconto*) story, tale **3** (*faccenda*) affair, business **4** (*bugia*) story, fib **5** (*pretesto*) pretext, excuse **6** (*smanceria*) fuss
stòrico **A** *agg.* historic(al) **B** *s. m.* historian
storièlla *s. f.* funny story, joke
storiografìa *s. f.* historiography
storióne *s. m.* sturgeon
stormìre *v. intr.* to rustle
stórmo *s. m.* flight
stornàre *v. tr.* **1** to avert, to divert, to turn aside **2** (*fin.*) to transfer **3** (*cancellare*) to cancel, to write off
stórno *s. m.* **1** (*trasferimento*) transfer, diversion **2** (*cancellazione*) reversal, cancellation
storpiàre *v. tr.* **1** to cripple **2** (*deformare*) to mangle
stòrpio **A** *agg.* crippled **B** *s. m.* cripple
stòrta *s. f.* sprain, twist
stòrto *agg.* crooked, twisted
stovìglie *s. f. pl.* dishes *pl.*

stràbico **A** *agg.* squinting **B** *s. m.* squinter
strabiliànte *agg.* amazing
strabìsmo *s. m.* squint
stracciàre *v. tr.* to tear, to rip
stràccio *s. m.* rag, cloth, (*per la polvere*) duster
stracòtto *s. m.* stew
stràda *s. f.* **1** road, (*di città*) street **2** (*tragitto, cammino*) way ♦ **s. a senso unico** one-way street; **s. dissestata** uneven road
stradàle *agg.* road (*attr*)
strafalcióne *s. m.* blunder
strafàre *v. intr.* to overdo it
strafottènte *agg.* arrogant
stràge *s. f.* **1** (*massacro*) slaughter, carnage **2** (*distruzione*) destruction
stràllo *s. m.* stay
stralunàto *agg.* **1** (*di occhi*) rolling **2** (*sconvolto*) bewildered
stramazzàre *v. intr.* to fall heavily
stràmbo *agg.* strange, odd, eccentric
strampalàto *agg.* odd, eccentric
stranézza *s. f.* **1** strangeness **2** (*atto, parola strana*) eccentricity
strangolàre *v. tr.* to strangle, (*soffocare*) to choke
stranièro **A** *agg.* foreign **B** *s. m.* foreigner
stràno *agg.* strange, odd, queer
straordinàrio **A** *agg.* **1** extraordinary, special **2** (*enorme*) immense, enormous **3** (*di lavoro*) overtime **B** *s. m.* **1** (*cosa straordinaria*) extraordinary thing **2** (*lavoro straordinario*) overtime
strapazzàre **A** *v. tr.* **1** to ill-treat, to mistreat **2** (*trattare senza cura*) to take no care of **B** *v. rifl.* to tire oneself out
strapiómbo *s. m.* cliff, overhang ♦ **a s.** sheer
strapotére *s. m.* excessive power
strappàre **A** *v. tr.* **1** to tear **2** (*togliere tirando*) to pull up, to pull away, to rip **B** *v. intr. pron.* to tear, to get torn
stràppo *s. m.* **1** tear, rent, rip **2** (*tirata, strattone*) pull, snatch, jerk **3** (*infrazione*) infringement **4** (*muscolare*) sprain **5** (*fig.*) split **6** (*passaggio in auto*) lift
strapuntìno *s. m.* folding seat
straripaménto *s. m.* overflowing
straripàre *v. intr.* to overflow
strascicàre **A** *v. tr.* to trail, to drag, (*i piedi*) to shuffle **B** *v. intr.* to trail **C** *v. rifl.* to drag oneself
stràscico *s. m.* **1** train **2** (*conseguenza*) after-effect ♦ **pesca a s.** trawling; **rete a s.** trawl-net
stratagèmma *s. m.* stratagem, trick
stratèga *s. m.* strategist
strategìa *s. f.* strategy
stratègico *agg.* strategic(al)
stràto *s. m.* layer, stratum, (*di rivestimento*) coat
stratosfèra *s. f.* stratosphere
stravagànte *agg.* queer, odd, eccentric
stravagànza *s. f.* oddness, strangeness
stravècchio *agg.* very old
stravìzio *s. m.* excess, intemperance
stravòlgere *v. tr.* **1** (*torcere*) to twist **2** (*fig.*) to distort, (*snaturare*) to change radically **3** (*turbare*) to upset
straziàre *v. tr.* **1** to lacerate, to torture **2** (*fig.*) to murder
stràzio *s. m.* torment, torture
stréga *s. f.* witch, hag
stregàre *v. tr.* to bewitch
stregóne *s. m.* wizard
stregonerìa *s. f.* witchcraft, sorcery
strègua *s. f.* standard, rate
stremàre *v. tr.* to exhaust
strèmo *s. m.* extreme limit
strènna *s. f.* gift, present
strènuo *agg.* **1** brave, courageous **2** (*infaticabile*) tireless
strepitóso *agg.* uproarious, resounding, clamorous
stress *s. m. inv.* stress
stressànte *agg.* stressful
strétta *s. f.* **1** grasp, hold, grip **2** (*dolore*) pang **3** (*situazione difficile*) dire straits *pl.* **4** (*momento culminante*) climax **5** (*econ.*) squeeze ♦ **mettere qc. alle strette** to put sb. with his back against the wall; **s. di mano** handshake
strétto **A** *agg.* **1** narrow **2** (*di abito*) tight **3** (*serrato*) tight, fast, (*di denti*) clenched **4** (*rigoroso*) strict, firm, close **5** (*intimo*) close **6** (*preciso*) exact, precise **7** (*chiuso*) close **8** (*pigiato*) packed **B** *s. m.* straits *pl.*
strettóia *s. f.* narrow passage, bottleneck
striàto *agg.* striped, striated
strìdere *v. intr.* **1** to creak, to squeak **2** (*contrastare*) to clash
strìdulo *agg.* shrill
strillàre *v. tr. e intr.* to scream, to shout
strìllo *s. m.* scream, cry, shout
strillóne *s. m.* newspaper seller
striminzìto *agg.* stunted
strimpellàre *v. tr.* to strum, to bang away

strìnga *s. f.* **1** lace **2** (*inf.*) string
stringàto *agg.* **1** (*di scarpa*) laced-up **2** (*di stile*) concise
strìngere **A** *v. tr.* **1** to grip, to clasp, to grasp, to clench **2** (*rendere più stretto*) to tighten, (*un abito*) to take in **3** (*concludere, stipulare*) to make, to draw up **4** (*accelerare*) to quicken **B** *v. intr.* **1** (*incalzare*) to press **2** (*essere stretto*) to be tight **3** (*condensare*) to make it brief
strìscia *s. f.* **1** strip, stripe **2** (*scia*) streak, trail **3** (*di fumetti*) (comic) strip ♦ **strisce pedonali** zebra crossing
strisciàre **A** *v. tr.* to drag **B** *v. intr.* **1** to crawl, to creep **2** (*sfregare*) to scrape **3** (*fig.*) to grovel **C** *v. rifl.* to rub oneself
strìscio *s. m.* **1** graze **2** (*segno*) scrape **3** (*med.*) smear ♦ **colpire di s.** to graze
striscióne *s. m.* banner
stritolàre *v. tr.* to grind, to crush, to smash
strizzàre *v. tr.* to squeeze, (*panni*) to wring (out) ♦ **s. l'occhio** to wink
stròfa *s. f.* strophe
strofinàccio *s. m.* cloth, (*per spolverare*) duster, (*per asciugare piatti*) tea cloth, (*per pavimenti*) floor cloth
strofinàre **A** *v. tr.* **1** to rub **2** (*pulire*) to clean, (*lucidare*) to polish **B** *v. rifl.* to rub oneself
strombatùra *s. f.* splay
strombazzàre **A** *v. tr.* to trumpet **B** *v. intr.* (*suonare il clacson*) to toot
stroncàre *v. tr.* **1** to break off, to cut off **2** (*reprimere*) to put down, to crush **3** (*criticare*) to slash, to pan, to tear apart
stroncatùra *s. f.* harsh criticism, slating
stropicciàre **A** *v. tr.* **1** to rub **2** (*sgualcire*) to crumple, to crease **B** *v. intr. pron.* to get creased
strozzàre **A** *v. tr.* **1** to strangle, (*soffocare*) to choke **2** (*occludere*) to block **B** *v. intr. pron.* **1** to choke **2** (*restringersi*) to narrow
strozzatùra *s. f.* narrowing, bottleneck
strumentàle *agg.* **1** instrumental **2** (*che serve da strumento*) exploitable
strumentalizzàre *v. tr.* to exploit, to manipulate
strumentìsta *s. m. e f.* instrumentalist
struménto *s. m.* **1** tool, instrument, implement **2** (*mus.*) instrument
strùtto *s. m.* lard
struttùra *s. f.* structure, frame
strutturalìsmo *s. m.* structuralism
strutturàre **A** *v. tr.* to structure **B** *v. intr. pron.* to be structured
strùzzo *s. m.* ostrich
stuccàre **A** *v. tr.* **1** (*decorare con stucco*) to stucco **2** (*riempire di stucco*) to plaster, to putty **3** (*nauseare*) to sicken **4** (*annoiare*) to bore **B** *v. intr. pron.* to get fed up
stucchévole *agg.* sickening, nauseating
stùcco *s. m.* (*per decorazioni*) stucco, (*riempitivo*) plaster, putty, filler
studènte *s. m.* student
studentésco *agg.* student (*attr*), students' (*attr*)
studiàre **A** *v. tr.* **1** to study, (*all'università*) to read **2** (*esaminare*) to study, to examine **B** *v. intr. pron.* to try
stùdio *s. m.* **1** study, studying **2** (*indagine*) study, analysis **3** (*progetto*) plan **4** (*stanza*) study **5** (*ufficio di professionista*) office, (*di artista*) studio **6** (*cin., TV*) studio
studióso **A** *agg.* studious **B** *s. m.* scholar
stùfa *s. f.* stove, (*elettrica*) heater
stufàre **A** *v. tr.* **1** (*cuc.*) to stew **2** (*annoiare*) to bore **B** *v. intr. pron.* to get tired
stufàto *s. m.* stew
stùfo *agg.* bored, fed up
stuòia *s. f.* mat
stupefacènte **A** *agg.* **1** stupefying, amazing **2** (*med.*) stupefacient **B** *s. m.* drug
stupèndo *agg.* stupendous, marvellous, wonderful
stupidàggine *s. f.* **1** stupidity **2** (*cosa, azione stupida*) stupid thing, piece of nonsense **3** (*inezia*) trifle
stupidità *s. f.* stupidity
stùpido **A** *agg.* stupid, foolish **B** *s. m.* idiot, fool
stupìre **A** *v. tr.* to astonish, to amaze **B** *v. intr. pron.* to be astonished, to be amazed
stupóre *s. m.* astonishment, amazement
stupràre *v. tr.* to rape
stupratóre *s. m.* rapist
stùpro *s. m.* rape
sturàre *v. tr.* **1** to unblock, to unplug **2** (*bottiglie*) to uncork
stuzzicadènti *s. m. inv.* toothpick
stuzzicàre *v. tr.* **1** to prod, to poke, to pick **2** (*molestare*) to tease **3** (*eccitare*) to excite, to whet
su **A** *avv.* **1** up **2** (*al piano superiore*) upstairs **3** (*indosso*) on **B** *prep.* **1** (*sovrapposizione con contatto*) on, upon, up, on to, (*in cima a*) on top of **2** (*sovrapposizione senza contatto, rive-*

stimento, protezione, dominio, superiorità) over **3** (*più in alto di*) above **4** (*lungo*) on, (*affacciato su*) on to **5** (*verso, intorno a*) about, at **6** (*in direzione di*) to(wards), (*contro*) on, at **7** (*riguardo a*) on, about ♦ **due su tre** two out of three; **in su** upwards, (*in avanti*) onwards
subàcqueo A *agg.* subaqueous, underwater (*attr.*) **B** *s. m.* skin diver
subaffittàre *v. tr.* to sublet
subbùglio *s. m.* confusion, mess
subcosciènte *agg. e s. m.* subconscious
sùbdolo *s. m.* sly, devious
subentràre *v. intr.* to take the place of, to replace
subìre *v. tr.* to undergo, to suffer
subissàre *v. tr.* to overwhelm
subitàneo *agg.* sudden
sùbito *avv.* **1** at once, immediately **2** (*in breve tempo*) soon ♦ **s. prima** just before
sublìme *agg.* sublime
subodoràre *v. tr.* to suspect
subordinàto *agg. e s. m.* subordinate
suburbàno *agg.* suburban
subùrbio *s. m.* suburb
succedàneo *agg. e s. m.* substitute
succèdere A *v. intr.* **1** (*subentrare*) to succeed **2** (*seguire*) to follow **3** (*accadere*) to happen, to occur **B** *v. rifl. rec.* to follow one another
successióne *s. f.* **1** succession **2** (*serie*) succession, series, sequence ♦ **imposta di s.** inheritance tax
successivaménte *avv.* subsequently
successìvo *agg.* following
succèsso *s. m.* **1** success, (*esito*) outcome **2** (*opera di successo*) hit
successóre *s. m.* successor
succhiàre *v. tr.* to suck
succìnto *agg.* **1** (*di vestito*) scanty **2** (*conciso*) concise
sùcco *s. m.* **1** juice **2** (*fig.*) essence, point
succóso *agg.* juicy
succursàle *s. f.* branch
sud *s. m.* south
sudafricàno *agg. e s. m.* South African
sudamericàno *agg. e s. m.* South American
sudàre *v. tr. e intr.* to sweat
sudàta *s. f.* sweat
sudàto *agg.* sweaty
suddétto *agg.* above-mentioned, aforesaid
sùddito *agg. e s. m.* subject
suddivìdere *v. tr.* to subdivide, to split up
sùdicio *agg.* dirty, filthy
sudóre *s. m.* sweat, perspiration
sufficiènte A *agg.* **1** sufficient, enough **2** (*altezzoso*) arrogant, haughty **B** *s. m.* sufficient, enough
sufficiènza *s. f.* **1** sufficiency **2** (*alterigia*) arrogance, conceit **3** (*voto scolastico*) pass mark ♦ **a s.** enough
suffìsso *s. m.* suffix
suffràgio *s. m.* suffrage
suggellàre *v. tr.* to seal
suggeriménto *s. m.* suggestion, hint
suggerìre *v. tr.* **1** to suggest **2** (*teatro, scuola*) to prompt
suggeritóre *s. m.* prompter
suggestionàbile *agg.* suggestible
suggestionàre A *v. tr.* to influence **B** *v. intr. pron.* to persuade oneself
suggestióne *s. f.* **1** suggestion **2** (*fascino*) awesomeness
suggestìvo *agg.* suggestive, striking
sùghero *s. m.* cork
sùgo *s. m.* **1** juice **2** (*cuc.*) sauce **3** (*fig.*) essence
suicìda A *agg.* suicidal **B** *s. m. e f.* suicide
suicidàrsi *v. rifl.* to commit suicide
suicìdio *s. m.* suicide
suìno *s. m.* swine
sulfamìdico *s. m.* sulphamide
sultanàto *s. m.* sultanate
sultàno *s. m.* sultan
sùo A *agg. poss. 3ª sing.* **1** (*di lui*) his, (*di lei*) her, (*di cosa o animale*) its, (*s. proprio*) his own, her own, its own **2** (*nella forma di cortesia*) your **3** (*con sogg. impers.*) one's, (*s. proprio*) one's own **B** *pron. poss.* (*di lui*) his, (*di lei*) hers, (*nella forma di cortesia*) yours **C** *s. m.* **1** (*denaro, averi*) his/her own money **2** *al pl.* (*familiari*) his/her family, (*i suoi seguaci*) his/her supporters
suòcera *s. f.* mother-in-law
suòcero *s. m.* father-in-law
suòla *s. f.* sole
suòlo *s. m.* soil, ground, land
suonàre A *v. tr.* **1** to sound, (*campanello, campane*) to ring **2** (*strumenti musicali*) to play **3** (*di orologio*) to strike **B** *v. intr.* **1** to sound, (*di campanello, campane*) to ring **2** (*eseguire musica*) to play **3** (*scoccare*) to strike **4** (*risuonare*) to ring, to resound
suonatóre *s. m.* player
suòno *s. m.* sound
suòra *s. f.* nun, sister

superàre *v. tr.* **1** to exceed, to go over, to be over, (*di persona*) to surpass, to outdo **2** (*passare al di là di*) to get over, (*di veicolo*) to overtake **3** (*vincere, sormontare*) to overcome, to get over, to get through
superàto *agg.* outdated, old-fashioned
supèrbia *s. f.* arrogance, pride, conceit
supèrbo *agg.* **1** proud, arrogant, haughty **2** (*magnifico*) superb, magnificent
superconduttività *s. f.* superconductivity
superficiàle *agg.* **1** superficial, surface (*attr.*) **2** (*fig.*) superficial, shallow
superficie *s. f.* surface
supèrfluo *agg.* superfluous
superióre **A** *agg.* **1** superior **2** (*più alto*) higher **3** (*sovrastante*) upper **4** (*al di sopra*) above **5** (*di grado*) senior **6** (*avanzato*) advanced **B** *s. m.* superior
superiorità *s. f.* superiority
superlatìvo *agg. e s. m.* superlative
supermercàto *s. m.* supermarket
supèrstite **A** *agg.* surviving **B** *s. m. e f.* survivor
superstizióne *s. f.* superstition
superstizióso *agg.* superstitious
superstràda *s. f.* highway, motorway
supìno *agg.* supine
suppellèttile *s. f.* furnishings *pl.*
suppergiù *avv.* about, nearly, roughly
supplementàre *agg.* supplementary, additional, extra
suppleménto *s. m.* supplement, (*di spesa*) extra (charge)
supplènte **A** *agg.* temporary, substitute **B** *s. m. e f.* substitute, (*insegnante*) supply teacher
sùpplica *s. f.* petition
supplicàre *v. tr.* to beg, to implore
supplìre **A** *v. tr.* to replace, to stand in for **B** *v. intr.* to make up, to compensate
supplìzio *s. m.* torture, torment
suppórre *v. tr.* to suppose
suppòrto *s. m.* support, stand, bearing
supposizióne *s. f.* supposition, assumption
suppósta *s. f.* suppository
suprèmo *agg.* **1** supreme **2** (*principale*) prime, chief, (*straordinario*) extraordinary **3** (*massimo*) great(est), highest **4** (*estremo*) last
surgelàre *v. tr.* to (deep-)freeze
surgelàto *s. m.* frozen food
surrealìsmo *s. m.* surrealism
surrealìsta *s. m. e f.* surrealist
surriscaldàre *v. tr. e intr. pron.* to overheat
surrogàto *s. m.* surrogate, substitute
suscettìbile *agg.* **1** susceptible **2** (*permaloso*) touchy
suscitàre *v. tr.* to stir up, to excite, to arouse
susìna *s. f.* plum
susseguìrsi *v. intr. pron.* to follow one another
sussidiàrio *agg.* subsidiary
sussìdio *s. m.* subsidy, grant, (*aiuto*) aid
sussistènza *s. f.* **1** (*esistenza*) existence **2** (*sostentamento*) subsistence
sussìstere *v. intr.* **1** to exist, to subsist **2** (*esser valido*) to be valid
sussultàre *v. intr.* **1** to start **2** (*di cose*) to shake
sussurràre *v. tr.* to whisper, to murmur
sussurrìo *s. m.* whispering
sussùrro *s. m.* whisper, murmur
sutùra *s. f.* suture
suturàre *v. tr.* to suture
svagàre **A** *v. tr.* **1** to divert, to distract attention **2** (*divertire*) to amuse, to entertain **B** *v. rifl.* **1** to distract one's mind **2** (*divertirsi*) to amuse oneself
svàgo *s. m.* **1** relaxation, (*passatempo*) hobby **2** (*divertimento*) amusement
svaligiàre *v. tr.* to rob, (*una casa*) to burgle
svalutàre **A** *v. tr.* **1** to devalue, to depreciate **2** (*sminuire*) to undervalue **B** *v. intr. pron.* to be devalued, to depreciate
svalutazióne *s. f.* devaluation
svanìre *v. intr.* **1** (*sparire*) to disappear, to vanish **2** (*venir meno*) to be lost, to fade
svantàggio *s. m.* **1** disadvantage, drawback **2** (*danno*) detriment
svantaggióso *agg.* **1** disadvantageous **2** (*dannoso*) detrimental
svaporàre *v. intr.* **1** to lose scent **2** (*fig.*) to fade
svariàto *agg.* **1** (*vario*) varied **2** *al pl.* various, different
svasatùra *s. f.* flare
svàstica *s. f.* swastika
svedése **A** *agg.* Swedish **B** *s. m. e f.* Swede **C** *s. m.* (*lingua*) Swedish
svéglia *s. f.* **1** call **2** (*orologio*) alarm-clock
svegliàre **A** *v. tr.* **1** to wake (up), to awake **2** (*fig.*) to stir, to arouse **B** *v. rifl.* to wake (up), to awake **C** *v. intr. pron.* to reawaken, to be roused
svéglio *agg.* **1** awake (*pred.*) **2** (*fig.*) wide-awake, quick
svelàre *v. tr.* to reveal, to disclose

sveltézza *s. f.* quickness, speed
svèlto *agg.* **1** quick, fast, rapid **2** (*fig.*) quick-witted, smart
svéndere *v. tr.* to sell off
svéndita *s. f.* (clearance) sale
sveniménto *s. m.* faint
svenìre *v. intr.* to faint
sventàre *v. tr.* to foil
sventolàre *v. tr. e intr.* to wave, to flutter
sventùra *s. f.* misfortune
sventuràto *agg.* unfortunate
svergognàto *agg.* shameless
svernàre *v. intr.* to winter
svestìre *v. tr. e rifl.* to undress
svettàre *v. intr.* to stand out
svezzaménto *s. m.* weaning
svezzàre *v. tr.* to wean
sviàre **A** *v. tr.* **1** to divert, to turn aside **2** (*distrarre*) to distract **3** (*traviare*) to lead astray **B** *v. intr. pron.* to go astray, to deviate
svignàrsela *v. intr. pron.* to slink off
sviluppàre **A** *v. tr.* **1** (*far crescere*) to develop, to expand **2** (*rinvigorire*) to strengthen **3** (*elaborare*) to develop, to work out **4** (*produrre*) to generate, to produce **5** (*fot., mat.*) to develop **B** *v. rifl. e intr. pron.* **1** to develop **2** (*crescere*) to grow, (*rinvigorirsi*) to strengthen **3** (*espandersi*) to expand, to develop
svilùppo *s. m.* development
svisceràto *agg.* passionate
svìsta *s. f.* oversight
svitàre **A** *v. tr.* to unscrew **B** *v. intr. pron.* to come unscrewed
svìzzero *agg. e s. m.* Swiss
svogliàto *agg.* unwilling, indolent
svolazzàre *v. intr.* to flutter, to fly about
svòlgere **A** *v. tr.* **1** to unwind, to unroll **2** (*sviluppare*) to develop **3** (*eseguire*) to carry out, to do **B** *v. rifl.* **1** to unwind, to unroll **2** (*svilupparsi*) to develop **C** *v. intr. pron.* (*accadere*) to happen, to occur
svolgiménto *s. m.* **1** unwinding, unrolling **2** (*esecuzione*) execution **3** (*sviluppo*) development, progress
svòlta *s. f.* **1** (*lo svoltare*) turning **2** (*di strada*) turn, bend
svoltàre *v. intr.* to turn
svuotàre *v. tr.* to empty

T

tabaccàio *s. m.* tobacconist
tabaccherìa *s. f.* tobacconist's (shop)
tabàcco *s. m.* tobacco, (*da fiuto*) snuff
tabèlla *s. f.* table, schedule
tabellóne *s. m.* notice-board
tabernàcolo *s. m.* tabernacle
tabù *s. m.* taboo
tabulàto *s. m.* printout
tàcca *s. f.* notch
taccàgno **A** *agg.* miserly, stingy **B** *s. m.* miser
taccheggiàre *v. tr. e intr.* to shoplift
taccheggiatóre *s. m.* shoplifter
tacchéggio *s. m.* shoplifting
tacchìno *s. m.* turkey
tacciàre *v. tr.* to accuse
tàcco *s. m.* heel
taccuìno *s. m.* notebook
tacére **A** *v. intr.* **1** to be silent, to keep silent **2** (*non far rumore*) to be still **B** *v. tr.* to pass over in silence, to leave out
tachicardìa *s. f.* tachycardia
tachìmetro *s. m.* speedometer
tàcito *agg.* **1** tacit, implicit **2** (*quieto*) still
tacitùrno *agg.* taciturn
tafàno *s. m.* horse-fly
tafferùglio *s. m.* brawl, scuffle
tàglia *s. f.* **1** (*misura*) size **2** (*ricompensa*) reward
tagliacàrte *s. m. inv.* paper knife
tagliàndo *s. m.* coupon, slip
tagliàre **A** *v. tr.* **1** to cut **2** (*attraversare*) to cut across, (*intersecare*) to intersect **3** (*interrompere, staccare*) to cut off, to interrupt **4** (*escludere*) to cut out **5** (*ridurre*) to cut down **6** (*mescolare*) to blend **B** *v. intr. e intr. pron.* to cut **C** *v. rifl.* to cut oneself, to get cut
tagliàto *agg.* **1** cut **2** (*portato*) cut out **3** (*di vino*) blended
tagliènte *agg.* cutting, sharp
taglière *s. m.* chopping-board
tàglio *s. m.* **1** cut, cutting **2** (*ferita*) cut **3** (*parte tagliente*) edge **4** (*tono*) tone **5** (*pezzo*) cut, (*di stoffa*) length, (*di banconota*) denomination **6** (*dimensione*) size **7** (*di vite*) slot
tagliòla *s. f.* trap
tàlco *s. m.* talc ◆ **t. in polvere** talcum powder
tàle **A** *agg.* **1** (*simile*) such, like that (*pred.*) (ES: **tali sono i suoi problemi** such are his problems, **tali fatti accadono ogni giorno** things like that happen every day) **2** (*intensivo*) so, such (ES: **c'era una t. confusione!** there was such a caos!) **3** (*un certo*) a, certain (ES: **un t. signor Smith** a Mr Smith) **4** (*preceduto dall'art. determ.*) such and such (ES: **il t. giorno alla t. ora** on such and such day, at such and such time) **5** (*dimostr*) this, that (ES: **in t. caso** in that case) **B** *pron.* **1** (*dimostr*) he *m.*, she *f.*, the/that person, the/that fellow (ES: **è lui il t. che cercavi** that's the fellow you were looking for) **2** (*indef.*) (*preceduto dall'art. indeterm.*) someone, (*preceduto da 'quel', 'quella'*) the man, the woman (ES: **c'è un t. che ti aspetta** there's someone waiting for you, **c'è quel t. dell'assicurazione** the insurance man is here)
talènto *s. m.* talent
talismàno *s. m.* talisman
talloncìno *s. m.* coupon, slip
tallóne *s. m.* heel
talménte *avv.* **1** (*con agg. e avv.*) so **2** (*con v.*) so much. in such a way
talóra → **talvolta**
tàlpa *s. f.* mole
talvòlta *avv.* sometimes, at times
tamarìndo *s. m.* tamarind
tamburellàre *v. intr.* to drum
tamburèllo *s. m.* tambourine
tambùro *s. m.* **1** drum **2** (*arch.*) tambour
tamponaménto *s. m.* **1** (*il tamponare*) plugging **2** (*autom.*) collision, (*a catena*) pile-up **3** (*med.*) tamponage
tamponàre *v. tr.* **1** to stop up, to plug **2** (*med.*) to tampon **3** (*autom.*) to collide with, to crash into
tampóne *s. m.* **1** plug, stopper **2** (*med., assorbente*) tampon **3** (*per timbri*) pad **4** (*chim., inf., elettr*) buffer
tàna *s. f.* den
tandem *s. m. inv.* tandem
tànfo *s. m.* stench
tangènte **A** *agg.* tangent **B** *s. f.* **1** tangent **2** (*quota*) share, percentage, (*illegale*) rake-off, cut

tangenziàle **A** *agg.* tangential **B** *s. f.* (*strada*) bypass, ring road
tàngo *s. m.* tango
tànica *s. f.* can, tank
tànto **A** *agg. indef.* **1** (*intensivo*) so much, such, so many *pl.*, (*così grande*) so great (ES: **te l'ho detto tante volte** I've told you so many times) **2** (*molto*) much, many *pl.*, a lot of, lots of (ES: **hanno t. denaro** they have lots of money) **3** (*comp., spesso in correlazione con 'quanto'*) as much, as many *pl.*, (*in frasi neg.*) so much, so many *pl.* (ES: **ho tanti soldi quanto te** I have as much money as you, **non hai tanti giocattoli quanti ne ho io** you have not so many toys as I have) **4** (*altrettanto*) as much, as many *pl.* **B** *avv.* **1** (*così, talmente*) (*con agg. e avv.*) so, (*con v.*) such a lot, so (much) (ES: **sono t. felice che non riesco a stare fermo** I am so happy that I cannot keep still, **l'amava t.!** he loved her so much!) **2** (*in correlazione con 'quanto'*) (*con agg. e avv.*) as, so, (*con v.*) as much, so much (ES: **lavoro t. quanto mi basta** I work as hard as I need) **3** (*molto*) (*con agg. e avv.*) so, (*con v.*) so much (ES: **gli era t. affezionato** he was so fond of him) **4** (*temporale*) (for) a long time, long, so long (ES: **l'ho aspettato t.** I waited for him a long time) **5** (*moltiplicativo*) as much (ES: **due volte t.** twice as much) **6** (*soltanto*) just (ES: **t. per cambiare** just for a change) **7** (*comunque*) in any case (ES: **parla pure, t. faccio come voglio** you can go on talking, I'll do as I please in any case) **C** *pron. indef.* **1** (*molto*) much, many *pl.*, a lot, (*molte persone*) many people, a lot of people (ES: **tanti guidano in modo pericoloso** many people drive dangerously) **2** (*comparativo in correlaz. con 'quanto'*) as much, as many *pl.*, so much, so many *pl.* (ES: **prendine t. quanto basta** take as much as is necessary) **D** *s. m.* so much (ES: **un t. per cento** so much per cent) ♦ **ogni t.** every now and then; **t. più che ...** all the more that ...; **t. ... quanto** (*sia ... sia*) both ... and; **una volta ogni t.** once in a while
tàppa *s. f.* **1** (*luogo di sosta*) stopping place **2** (*fermata*) halt, stop, stay **3** (*parte di percorso*) stage, leg, (*di gara sportiva*) lap **4** (*momento fondamentale*) stage
tappàre **A** *v. tr.* to plug, to cork, to stop (up) **B** *v. rifl.* to shut oneself up
tapparèlla *s. f.* roll-up shutter
tappéto *s. m.* **1** carpet **2** (*sport*) mat, (*boxe*) canvas
tappezzàre *v. tr.* **1** to paper **2** (*coprire*) to cover **3** (*foderare*) to upholster
tappezzerìa *s. f.* **1** (*arte, professione*) upholstery **2** (*di tessuto*) tapestry, (*di carta*) wall-paper, (*per mobili, auto*) upholstery
tappezzière *s. m.* **1** (*di mobili*) upholsterer **2** (*di pareti*) paperhanger, decorator
tàppo *s. m.* plug, stopper, (*di bottiglia*) cap, (*di sughero*) cork
tàra *s. f.* **1** (*comm.*) tare **2** (*difetto*) defect, blemish
tarchiàto *agg.* stocky
tardàre **A** *v. tr.* to delay, to put off **B** *v. intr.* to be late, to be long, to delay
tàrdi *avv.* late
tardìvo *agg.* **1** late **2** (*che arriva tardi*) tardy, belated
tàrdo *agg.* **1** (*lento*) slow **2** (*ottuso*) dull **3** (*di tempo*) late
tàrga *s. f.* **1** plate **2** (*autom.*) numberplate, (*USA*) license plate
targhétta *s. f.* plate
tarìffa *s. f.* tariff, rate, price, (*di biglietto*) fare
tariffàrio *s. m.* tariff, price list, rate table
tàrlo *s. m.* woodworm
tàrma *s. f.* moth
tarmicìda *s. m.* moth-killer
taròcco *s. m.* tarot, tarok
tarsìa *s. f.* marquetry, tarsia
tartagliàre *v. intr.* to stutter, to stammer
tàrtaro *s. m.* tartar
tartarùga *s. f.* tortoise, (*di mare*) turtle
tartìna *s. f.* canapé
tartùfo *s. m.* truffle
tàsca *s. f.* pocket
tascàbile **A** *agg.* pocket (*attr.*) **B** *s. m.* (*libro*) paperback
taschìno *s. m.* breast-pocket
tàssa *s. f.* tax, duty, dues *pl.*, (*per iscrizione*) fee
tassàbile *agg.* taxable
tassàmetro *s. m.* meter
tassàre *v. tr.* to tax, to assess
tassatìvo *agg.* peremptory
tassazióne *s. f.* taxation
tassèllo *s. m.* plug
tassì → **taxi**
tassìsta *s. m. e f.* taxi driver, cabdriver
tàsso (1) *s. m.* (*zool.*) badger
tàsso (2) *s. m.* (*bot.*) yew

tàsso (3) *s. m.* rate ♦ **t. di natalità** birthrate
tastàre *v. tr.* **1** to touch, to feel **2** (*fig.*) to sound out
tastièra *s. f.* keyboard
tastierìsta *s. m. e f.* keyboard operator, (*mus.*) keyboard player
tàsto *s. m.* key
tastóni, a *loc. avv.* gropingly
tàttica *s. f.* tactics *pl.* (*v. al sing.*)
tàttico *agg.* tactical
tàtto *s. m.* **1** touch **2** (*fig.*) tact
tatuàggio *s. m.* tattoo
tatuàre *v. tr.* to tattoo
tauromachìa *s. f.* bullfight
tavèrna *s. f.* tavern, inn
tàvola *s. f.* **1** (*asse*) board, plank **2** (*tavolo*) table **3** (*illustrazione*) plate **4** (*tabella*) table ♦ **t. a vela** windsurfer; **t. calda** snack bar
tavolàta *s. f.* table, tableful
tavolàto *s. m.* **1** (*pavimento*) wood(en) floor **2** (*geogr.*) plateau
tavolétta *s. f.* tablet, bar
tavolìno *s. m.* small table
tàvolo *s. m.* table
tavolòzza *s. f.* palette
tàxi *s. m. inv.* taxi, cab
tàzza *s. f.* cup
tazzìna *s. f.* (small) cup
te *pron pers. 2ª sing.* you ♦ **fai da te** do it yourself; **se fossi in te** if I were you; **tocca a te** it's your turn
tè *s. m.* tea
teatràle *agg.* theatrical
teàtro *s. m.* theatre, (*USA*) theater
tèca *s. f.* reliquary
tècnica *s. f.* **1** technique **2** (*tecnologia*) technics *pl.* (*v. al sing.*)
tècnico **A** *agg.* technical **B** *s. m.* technician, engineer, (*esperto*) expert
tecnologìa *s. f.* technology
tedésco *agg. e s. m.* German
tèdio *s. m.* tedium, boredom
tegàme *s. m.* pan
téglia *s. f.* baking-tin
tégola *s. f.* tile
teièra *s. f.* tea-pot
téla *s. f.* cloth, canvas
telàio *s. m.* **1** loom, (*da ricamo*) tambour **2** (*ossatura*) frame
telecàmera *s. f.* telecamera
telecomàndo *s. m.* remote control
telecomunicazióne *s. f.* telecommunication
telecrònaca *s. f.* television report
telecronìsta *s. m. e f.* commentator
telefèrica *s. f.* cableway
telefonàre *v. tr. e intr.* to telephone, to phone, to ring up, to call
telefonàta *s. f.* (phone) call
telefònico *agg.* telephone (*attr.*)
telefonìsta *s. m. e f.* (telephone) operator
telèfono *s. m.* telephone, phone ♦ **colpo di t.** call; **elenco del t.** telephone directory
telegiornàle *s. m.* news
telègrafo *s. m.* telegraph
telegràmma *s. m.* telegram, (*USA*) wire
telemàtica *s. f.* telematics *pl.* (*v. al sing.*)
telepatìa *s. f.* telepathy
teleschérmo *s. m.* telescreen
telescòpio *s. m.* telescope
teleselezióne *s. f.* direct dialling
telespettatóre *s. m.* televiewer
televisióne *s. f.* television, (*apparecchio*) television set
televisivo *agg.* television (*attr.*)
televisóre *s. m.* television set
telex *s. m. inv.* telex
tellìna *s. f.* clam
télo *s. m.* length of cloth
telóne *s. m.* tarpaulin
tèma *s. m.* **1** subject, topic, theme **2** (*scolastico*) composition **3** (*mus.*) theme
temeràrio *agg.* temerarious
temére *v. tr.* to fear, to be afraid of ♦ **temo di no/sì** I fear not/so
tèmpera *s. f.* tempera, distemper
temperamatìte *s. m. inv.* pencil sharpener
temperaménto *s. m.* temperament, disposition
temperàre *v. tr.* **1** (*mitigare*) to temper, to mitigate **2** (*fare la punta*) to sharpen
temperàto *agg.* **1** temperate, moderate **2** (*mus.*) tempered
temperatùra *s. f.* temperature
temperìno *s. m.* **1** (*coltellino*) penknife **2** (*temperamatite*) pencil sharpener
tempèsta *s. f.* storm, tempest
tempestàre *v. tr.* **1** (*colpire*) to batter, to pound **2** (*subissare*) to annoy, to pester **3** (*ornare*) to stud
tempestività *s. f.* opportuneness, timeliness
tempestìvo *agg.* opportune, timely
tempestóso *agg.* stormy
tèmpia *s. f.* temple
tèmpio *s. m.* temple
tempìsmo *s. m.* sense of timing

templàre *s. m.* Templar
tèmpo *s. m.* **1** time **2** (*atmosferico*) weather **3** (*mus.*) tempo, time **4** (*gramm.*) tense **5** (*fase*) stage, phase ♦ **t. fa** some time ago; **t. libero** spare time; **t. morto** idle time; **t. pieno** full time; **un t.** (*nel passato*) once
temporàle *s. m.* storm
temporàneo *agg.* temporary
temporeggiàre *v. intr.* to play for time
tempràre **A** *v. tr.* **1** (*metall.*) to temper, to harden **2** (*fortificare*) to strengthen **B** *v. rifl. e intr. pron.* to be strengthened
tenàce *agg.* tenacious
tenàglie *s. f. pl.* tongs *pl.*, pincers *pl.*, pliers *pl.*
tènda *s. f.* **1** tent **2** (*di finestra*) curtain
tendènza *s. f.* **1** trend, tendency **2** (*attitudine*) disposition, bent
tendenziàle *agg.* tendential
tendenzióso *agg.* tendentious
tèndere **A** *v. tr.* **1** (*porgere*) to stretch (out), to hold out **2** (*mettere in tensione*) to stretch, to tighten **3** (*predisporre*) to lay, to set **B** *v. intr.* **1** to tend, to be inclined **2** (*mirare*) to aim, to intend
tendìna *s. f.* curtain
tèndine *s. m.* tendon, sinew
tendóne *s. m.* awning, (*impermeabile*) tarpaulin, (*da circo*) tent, big top
tènebre *s. f. pl.* dark, darkness
tenebróso *agg.* dark, gloomy
tenènte *s. m.* lieutenant
tenére **A** *v. tr.* **1** to hold, to keep **2** (*prendere*) to take **3** (*occupare*) to take up **4** (*contenere*) to contain **5** (*considerare, ritenere*) to consider, to regard **6** (*organizzare*) to hold, to deliver **B** *v. intr.* **1** (*resistere*) to hold **2** (*essere a tenuta stagna*) to be watertight **3** (*dare importanza*) to care, (*avere caro*) to value, (*volere*) to like, to want **4** (*parteggiare*) to be for, to support **C** *v. rifl.* **1** to keep oneself, to hold oneself **2** (*trattenersi*) to help (*col gerundio*) **3** (*attenersi*) to stick, to follow
tenerézza *s. f.* tenderness
tènero *agg.* **1** tender, soft **2** (*fig.*) tender, loving, (*di parole*) fond
tènia *s. f.* tapeworm, taenia
tènnis *s. m. inv.* tennis
tennìsta *s. m. e f.* tennis player
tenóre *s. m.* **1** (*modo*) tenor, way **2** (*contenuto*) tenor, contents *pl.* **3** (*mus.*) tenor
tensióne *s. f.* **1** tension **2** (*elettr.*) voltage
tentàre *v. tr.* **1** to try, to attempt **2** (*indurre in tentazione*) to tempt
tentatìvo *s. m.* attempt, try
tentazióne *s. f.* temptation
tentennàre **A** *v. intr.* **1** to stagger, to totter, (*oscillare*) to swing **2** (*fig.*) to waver, to hesitate **B** *v. tr.* to shake
tènue *agg.* **1** slender, slight **2** (*delicato*) soft
tenùta *s. f.* **1** (*proprietà agricola*) estate, farm **2** (*capacità*) capacity **3** (*abbigliamento*) clothes *pl.*, (*uniforme*) uniform **4** (*tecnol.*) seal ♦ **a t. d'acqua** watertight; **t. di strada** roadholding
teologìa *s. f.* theology
teòlogo *s. m.* theologian
teorèma *s. m.* theorem
teorìa *s. f.* theory
teòrico **A** *agg.* theoretic(al) **B** *s. m.* theorist, theorician
tepóre *s. m.* warmth
tèppa *s. f.* mob
teppìsmo *s. m.* hooliganism
teppìsta *s. m. e f.* hooligan
terapèutico *agg.* therapeutic(al)
terapìa *s. f.* therapy
tergicristàllo *s. m.* windscreen wiper
tergiversàre *v. intr.* to prevaricate
tèrgo *s. m.* back ♦ **a t.** overleaf
termàle *agg.* thermal ♦ **sorgenti termali** hot springs; **stabilimento t.** spa
tèrme *s. f. pl.* **1** thermal baths *pl.*, hot springs *pl.*, spa **2** (*archeol.*) thermae *pl.*
tèrmico *agg.* thermic, thermal
terminàle *agg. e s. m.* terminal
terminàre *v. tr. e intr.* to end, to finish
tèrmine *s. m.* **1** (*fine*) end, close **2** (*limite*) limit **3** (*confine*) boundary **4** (*scadenza*) expiry, date, time **5** (*condizione, rapporto*) term **6** (*parola*) term, word **7** (*mat.*) term
terminologìa *s. f.* terminology
tèrmite *s. f.* termite
termodinàmica *s. f.* thermodynamics *pl.* (*v. al sing.*)
termòmetro *s. m.* thermometer
termosifóne *s. m.* radiator
termòstato *s. m.* thermostat
tèrra *s. f.* **1** (*pianeta*) earth, (*mondo*) world **2** (*opposto ad acqua*) land **3** (*terreno*) ground, (*materiale terroso*) earth, (*suolo coltivabile*) soil, (*pavimento*) floor **4** (*paese, regione*) land, country **5** (*proprietà*) land, estate, property

terracòtta *s. f.* terracotta ♦ **vasellame di t.** earthenware
terraférma *s. f.* dry land, (*continente*) mainland
terràglia *s. f.* earthenware
terrapièno *s. m.* bank, (*mil.*) rampart
terràzza *s. f.* terrace
terrazzaménto *s. m.* terracing
terràzzo *s. m.* terrace
terremòto *s. m.* **1** earthquake **2** (*fig.*) upheaval
terréno A *agg.* earthly **B** *s. m.* **1** ground, (*suolo*) soil **2** (*proprietà, porzione di terra*) land **3** (*campo*) field ♦ **piano t.** ground floor, first floor
terrèstre *agg.* terrestrial, earthly, land (*attr*)
terrìbile *agg.* terrible, awful, dreadful
terrificànte *agg.* terrifying, appalling
territoriàle *agg.* territorial
territòrio *s. m.* territory, region
terróre *s. m.* terror, dread
terrorìsmo *s. m.* terrorism
terrorìsta *s. m. e f.* terrorist
tèrso *agg.* clear
terziàrio *s. m.* tertiary
terzìno *s. m.* back
tèrzo *agg. num. ord. e s. m.* third
terzùltimo *agg.* last but two
tésa *s. f.* brim
tèschio *s. m.* skull
tèsi *s. f.* thesis
téso *agg.* **1** tigh, stretched, tense **2** (*mirante*) aimed
tesorerìa *s. f.* treasury
tesorière *s. m.* treasurer
tesòro *s. m.* treasure
tèssera *s. f.* **1** card, ticket, pass **2** (*di mosaico*) tessera
tèssere *v. tr.* to weave
tèssile *agg.* textile
tessitóre *s. m.* weaver
tessitùra *s. f.* weaving, (*disposizione dei fili*) texture
tessùto *s. m.* **1** fabric, material, cloth **2** (*biol.*) tissue ♦ **t. di lana** woollen fabric; **t. di seta** silk material
test *s. m. inv.* test
tèsta *s. f.* head ♦ **a t.** per head, each; **essere in t.** to be in the lead; **mal di t.** headache
tèsta-códa *loc. sost. m. inv.* spin, about-face
testaménto *s. m.* will, testament
testàrdo *agg.* stubborn
testàta *s. f.* **1** head **2** (*di giornale*) heading, (*giornale*) newspaper **3** (*mil.*) warhead **4** (*colpo*) butt
testatóre *s. m.* testator
tèste *s. m. e f.* witness
testìcolo *s. m.* testicle
testimòne *s. m. e f.* witness
testimoniànza *s. f.* **1** testimony, witness **2** (*prova*) evidence, proof
testimoniàre *v. tr. e intr.* to testify
testìna *s. f.* head
tèsto *s. m.* text
testuàle *agg.* **1** textual **2** (*preciso*) exact, precise
testùggine *s. f.* tortoise, (*di mare*) turtle
tètano *s. m.* tetanus
tètro *agg.* gloomy
tétto *s. m.* **1** roof **2** (*livello massimo*) ceiling
tettóia *s. f.* roofing, canopy
tettùccio *s. m.* roof, (*apribile*) sunroof
ti *pron. pers. 2ª sing. m. e f.* **1** (*compl. ogg.*) you, (*compl. ind.*) (to) you, (for) you **2** (*rifl.*) yourself
tiàra *s. f.* tiara
tìbia *s. f.* tibia, shin-bone
tibùrio *s. m.* lantern
tic *s. m. inv.* tic
ticchettìo *s. m.* ticking
tièpido *agg.* tepid, lukewarm
tifàre *v. intr.* to be a fan of
tìfo *s. m.* **1** (*med.*) typhus **2** (*sport*) support, fanaticism ♦ **fare il t. per** to be a fan of
tifóne *s. m.* typhoon
tifóso *s. m.* fan, supporter
tìglio *s. m.* linden
tignòla *s. f.* moth
tìgre *s. f.* tiger
timbàllo *s. m.* timbale, pie
timbràre *v. tr.* to stamp, (*lettera*) to postmark ♦ **t. il cartellino** to clock in/out
tìmbro *s. m.* **1** stamp, (*postale*) postmark **2** (*mus.*) timbre
timidézza *s. f.* shyness
tìmido *agg.* shy, timid
tìmo (1) *s. m.* (*bot.*) thyme
tìmo (2) *s. m.* (*anat.*) thymus
timóne *s. m.* rudder, helm ♦ **ruota del t.** steering wheel
timonière *s. m.* helmsman, steersman
timóre *s. m.* fear, dread
timoróso *agg.* fearful, afraid (*pred.*)
tìmpano *s. m.* **1** (*anat.*) tympanum, eardrum **2** (*mus.*) kettledrum **3** (*arch.*) tympanum, gable
tìnca *s. f.* tench

tìngere *v. tr.* **1** to dye **2** (*colorare*) to colour, to stain, (*lievemente*) to tinge
tìno *s. m.* tub, vat
tinòzza *s. f.* tub
tìnta *s. f.* **1** (*sostanza colorante*) dye, (*pittura*) paint **2** (*colore*) colour
tintarèlla *s. f.* (sun-)tan
tinteggiàre *v. tr.* to paint
tintinnàre *v. intr.* to tinkle
tintorìa *s. f.* dry cleaner's
tintùra *s. f.* dyeing, dye, (*per capelli*) hair dye
tìpico *agg.* typical
tìpo *s. m.* **1** type, model, pattern **2** (*varietà*) kind, sort **3** (*individuo*) fellow, chap, character, (*USA*) guy
tipografìa *s. f.* **1** (*procedimento*) typography **2** (*stamperia*) printing works *pl.*
tipogràfico *agg.* typographic(al)
tipògrafo *s. m.* printer, typographer
tipologìa *s. f.* typology
tiràggio *s. m.* draught
tirànno *s. m.* tyrant
tirànte *s. m.* **1** tie-rod **2** (*edil.*) tie-beam
tiràre **A** *v. tr.* **1** to pull, to draw, (*trascinare*) to drag **2** (*lanciare*) to throw **3** (*tendere*) to draw **4** (*stampare*) to print **B** *v. intr.* **1** (*avere tiraggio*) to draw **2** (*soffiare*) to blow **3** (*sparare*) to shoot **4** (*tendere*) to tend **5** (*di vestito*) to be tight **6** (*essere teso*) to feel tight **C** *v. rifl.* to draw, to drag ♦ **t. a lucido** to polish; **t. di boxe** to box; **t. fuori** to draw out; **t. giù** to pull down, (*abbassare*) to lower; **t. su** to pull up, (*raccogliere*) to pick up; **t. sul prezzo** to bargain
tiratóre *s. m.* shooter, shot
tiratùra *s. f.* **1** printing, edition **2** (*numero di copie*) circulation
tìrchio **A** *agg.* mean, stingy **B** *s. m.* miser
tìro *s. m.* **1** (*trazione*) draught **2** (*lancio*) throw, cast **3** (*di arma*) shot, fire, (*lo sparare*) shooting **4** (*muta*) team **5** (*scherzo*) trick **6** (*di sigaretta*) puff ♦ **t. alla fune** tug-of-war; **t. a segno** target-shooting; **t. con l'arco** archery
tirocìnio *s. m.* apprenticeship, training
tiròide *s. f.* thyroid
tisàna *s. f.* infusion, (herb) tea
titolàre **A** *agg.* regular, (*che ha solo il titolo*) titular **B** *s. m. e f.* (*proprietario*) owner, (*detentore*) holder
tìtolo *s. m.* **1** title, (*di giornale*) headline **2** (*onorifico, accademico*) title, (*qualifica*) qualification **3** (*ragione*) reason, (*diritto*) title, right **4** (*fin.*) bond, security
titubànte *agg.* hesitant
tìzio *s. m.* person, someone
tizzóne *s. m.* brand
toccànte *agg.* touching, moving
toccàre **A** *v. tr.* **1** to touch, (*sfiorare*) to touch in, (*tastare*) to feel, (*maneggiare*) to handle **2** (*raggiungere*) to reach **3** (*commuovere*) to touch, to move **4** (*riguardare*) to concern, to affect **5** (*colpire*) to hurt **B** *v. intr.* **1** (*capitare*) to happen, to fall **2** (*spettare*) to fall, to be up to, (*essere di turno*) to be turn **3** (*dovere*) to have **C** *v. rifl. rec.* to touch each other
toccasàna *s. m. inv.* cure-all
tócco *s. m.* touch, (*di pennello*) stroke
tòga *s. f.* robe, gown
tògliere **A** *v. tr.* **1** to take away, to take out, (*vestiti*) to take off **2** (*rimuovere*) to remove **3** (*sottrarre*) to take **4** (*liberare*) to relieve, to free **5** (*interrompere l'erogazione di*) to cut off **B** *v. rifl.* to go away, to get out
toilette *s. f.* **1** (*bagno*) toilet, lavatory **2** (*mobile*) dressing table
tolleránte *agg.* **1** tolerant **2** (che sopporta) enduring
tolleránza *s. f.* **1** tolerance **2** (*capacità di sopportazione*) endurance, tolerance **3** (*scarto*) allowance
tolleràre *v. tr.* **1** to tolerate, to bear, to stand **2** (*concedere*) to allow
tomàia *s. f.* upper
tómba *s. f.* tomb, grave
tombàle *agg.* tomb (*attr*), grave (*attr*)
tombìno *s. m.* manhole
tómbola *s. f.* **1** tombola **2** (*ruzzolone*) tumble
tòmo *s. m.* tome, volume
tomografìa *s. f.* tomography
tònaca *s. f.* (*di frate*) cowl, frock, (*di prete*) soutane
tonalità *s. f.* **1** tonality **2** (*sfumatura*) tone, shade
tóndo **A** *agg.* round **B** *s. m.* **1** round, (*cerchio*) circle, ring **2** (*arte*) tondo
tónfo *s. m.* **1** thud, (*in acqua*) splash **2** (*fig.*) fall, crash
tònico **A** *agg.* tonic **B** *s. m.* **1** tonic **2** (*cosmetico*) toner
tonificànte *agg.* tonic, bracing
tonificàre *v. tr.* to tone (up), to brace
tonnellàggio *s. m.* tonnage

tonnellàta *s. f.* ton
tónno *s. m.* tuna, tunny, (*in scatola*) tuna fish
tòno *s. m.* **1** tone **2** (*mus.*) tone, key, (*intonazione*) tune **3** (*accordo*) tune
tonsìlla *s. f.* tonsil
tonsillìte *s. f.* tonsillitis
tónto **A** *agg.* stupid, dull **B** *s. m.* foolish, dunce
top *s. m. inv.* top
topàzio *s. m.* topaz
topicìda *s. m.* rat-poison
topless *s. m. inv.* topless
tòpo *s. m.* mouse
topografia *s. f.* topography
topònimo *s. m.* toponym
tòppa *s. f.* **1** (*pezza*) patch **2** (*della serratura*) keyhole
toràce *s. m.* chest, thorax
tórba *s. f.* peat
tórbido *agg.* **1** (*di liquido*) turbid, cloudy **2** (*fosco*) gloomy **3** (*inquieto*) troubled
tòrcere **A** *v. tr.* **1** to twist, to wring **2** (*curvare*) to bend **B** *v. rifl.* to twist, to writhe
torchiàre *v. tr.* **1** to press **2** (*fig.*) to grill
tòrchio *s. m.* press
tòrcia *s. f.* torch
torcicòllo *s. m.* stiff neck
tórdo *s. m.* thrush
torménta *s. f.* snow storm
tormentàre **A** *v. tr.* to torture, to torment, (*annoiare*) to pester **B** *v. rifl.* to be tormented, to worry
torménto *s. m.* torment, agony, (*seccatura*) nuisance
tornacónto *s. m.* advantage, profit
tornàdo *s. m. inv.* tornado
tornànte *s. m.* hairpin bend
tornàre *v. intr.* **1** to return, (*andare di nuovo*) to go back, (*venire di nuovo*) to come back, (*essere di ritorno*) to be back **2** (*ridiventare*) to become again **3** (*quadrare*) to balance, to square
tornasóle *s. m.* litmus
tornèo *s. m.* tournament
tórnio *s. m.* lathe
tòro *s. m.* **1** bull **2** (*astr*) Taurus
torpèdine *s. f.* torpedo
torpedinièra *s. f.* torpedo boat
torpóre *s. m.* torpor, numbness
tórre *s. f.* **1** tower **2** (*scacchi*) castle, rook
torrefazióne *s. f.* torrefaction, (*di caffè*) roasting
torrènte *s. m.* stream, torrent
torrenziàle *agg.* torrential
torrétta *s. f.* turret
torrióne *s. m.* keep, tower
torsióne *s. f.* torsion
tórso *s. m.* trunk, torso ♦ **a t. nudo** bare-chested
tórsolo *s. m.* core
tórta *s. f.* cake, pie, tart ♦ **t. di mele** apple-pie
tortièra *s. f.* baking-tin
tortìno *s. m.* pie
tòrto *s. m.* **1** wrong **2** (*colpa*) fault ♦ **a t.** wrongly
tórtora *s. f.* turtledove
tortuóso *agg.* **1** winding, tortuous **2** (*fig.*) tortuous, devious
tortùra *s. f.* **1** torture **2** (*fig.*) agony, torment
torturàre **A** *v. tr.* to torture **B** *v. rifl.* to torment oneself, to worry
tórvo *agg.* grim
tosaèrba *s. m. inv.* lawn mower
tosàre *v. tr.* to shear, to clip
toscàno *agg. e s. m.* Tuscan
tósse *s. f.* cough
tòssico *agg.* toxic
tossicodipendènte *s. m. e f.* (drug) addict
tossicodipendènza *s. f.* drug addiction
tossicòmane *s. m. e f.* (drug) addict
tossìna *s. f.* toxin
tossìre *v. intr.* to cough
tostapàne *s. m. inv.* toaster
tostàre *v. tr.* to toast, (*caffè*) to roast
totàle **A** *agg.* total, complete, whole, utter **B** *s. m.* total
totalità *s. f.* **1** totality **2** (*numero complessivo*) mass, whole
totalizzàre *v. tr.* to total, (*punteggio*) to score
tòtano *s. m.* tattler
tournée *s. f. inv.* tour
tovàglia *s. f.* tablecloth
tovagliòlo *s. m.* napkin
tòzzo **A** *agg.* squat **B** *s. m.* piece
tra *prep.* → **fra**
traballàre *v. intr.* to stagger, to totter
traboccàre *v. intr.* to overflow
trabocchétto *s. m.* trap
tracannàre *v. tr.* to gulp down
tràccia *s. f.* **1** trace, sign, (*impronta*) track, trail, (*di uomo*) footprint **2** (*schema*) outline
tracciàre *v. tr.* **1** to trace (out), to mark out, to draw, to plot **2** (*delineare*) to outline
tracciàto *s. m.* plan, route
trachèa *s. f.* trachea, windpipe

tracòlla *s. f.* shoulder-belt, baldric ♦ **borsa a t.** shoulder-bag
tracòllo *s. m.* collapse, ruin, crash
tracotànte *agg.* overbearing
tradiménto *s. m.* **1** treason, (*inganno*) betrayal **2** (*slealtà*) treachery
tradìre A *v. tr.* **1** to betray **2** (*essere infedele a*) to be unfaithful to **3** (*ingannare*) to deceive **4** (*venir meno a*) to fail **B** *v. rifl.* to betray oneself
traditóre A *agg.* treacherous **B** *s. m.* traitor, betrayer
tradizionàle *agg.* traditional
tradizióne *s. f.* tradition
tradùrre *v. tr.* **1** to translate **2** (*esprimere*) to express **3** (*dir.*) to transfer
traduttóre *s. m.* translator
traduzióne *s. f.* **1** translation **2** (*dir.*) transfer
trafelàto *agg.* out of breath
trafficànte *s. m. e f.* dealer, trafficker
trafficàre *v. intr.* **1** to trade, to deal **2** (*fare traffici illeciti*) to traffic, (*spacciare*) to push **3** (*affaccendarsi*) to bustle about
tràffico *s. m.* **1** traffic **2** (*commercio*) trade, (*illecito*) traffic
trafìggere *v. tr.* to stab, to pierce through
trafìla *s. f.* procedure
trafilétto *s. m.* paragraph
traforàre *v. tr.* to bore, to drill
trafóro *s. m.* **1** perforation, boring, tunneling **2** (*galleria*) tunnel
trafugàre *v. tr.* to purloin, to steal
tragèdia *s. f.* tragedy
traghettàre *v. tr.* to ferry
traghétto *s. m.* ferry(boat)
tràgico *agg.* tragic(al)
tragicòmico *agg.* tragicomic(al)
tragitto *s. m.* **1** (*percorso*) way **2** (*viaggio*) journey, (*per mare*) passage, crossing
traguàrdo *s. m.* **1** finishing line **2** (*fig.*) goal, aim
traiettòria *s. f.* trajectory
tràina *s. f.* towrope ♦ **pescare alla t.** to troll
trainàre *v. tr.* to tow, to draw
tràino *s. m.* haulage, drawing
tralasciàre *v. tr.* **1** to leave out, to omit **2** (*desistere da*) to give up
tràlcio *s. m.* shoot
tralìccio *s. m.* trellis, pylon
tram *s. m.* tram, (*USA*) streetcar
tràma *s. f.* **1** (*di tessuto*) weft **2** (*intreccio*) plot, plan **3** (*macchinazione*) plot, conspiracy
tramandàre *v. tr.* to hand down
tramàre *v. tr.* to plot, to intrigue
trambùsto *s. m.* confusion, bustle
tramestìo *s. m.* rummaging
tramezzìno *s. m.* sandwich
tramèzzo *s. m.* partition wall
tramontàna *s. f.* north wind
tramontàre *v. intr.* **1** to set **2** (*fig.*) to fade, to wane
tramónto *s. m.* **1** (*del sole*) sunset, (*di astri*) setting **2** (*fig.*) decline, fading
tramortìre *v. tr.* to stun
trampolière *s. m.* wading-bird, wader
trampolìno *s. m.* spring board, diving board, (*per sci*) ski-jumping board
tràmpolo *s. m.* stilt
tramutàre A *v. tr.* to change, to convert **B** *v. intr. pron.* to change into, to turn into
tràncio *s. m.* slice
tranèllo *s. m.* trap, snare
trangugiàre *v. tr.* to gulp down
trànne *prep.* except, save, but
tranquillànte A *agg.* tranquillizing **B** *s. m.* tranquillizer
tranquillità *s. f.* quiet, calm, (*di spirito*) tranquillity
tranquillizzàre A *v. tr.* to tranquillize, to calm down **B** *v. intr. pron.* to calm down
tranquìllo *agg.* peaceful, calm, quiet, (*di spirito*) tranquil
transatlàntico *s. m.* (trasatlantic) liner
transazióne *s. f.* **1** arrangement **2** (*dir., comm.*) transaction
transènna *s. f.* **1** barrier **2** (*arch.*) transenna
transessuàle *s. m. e f.* transsexual
transètto *s. m.* transept
transìgere *v. intr.* **1** to come to an agreement, to come to terms **2** (*dir.*) to come to a transaction
transistor *s. m. inv.* transistor
transitàbile *agg.* practicable
transitàre *v. intr.* to travel, to pass
transitìvo *agg.* transitive
trànsito *s. m.* transit ♦ **divieto di t.** no thoroughfare; **t. interrotto** road up
transitòrio *agg.* temporary
tranvìa *s. f.* tramway, (*USA*) streetcar line
tranvière *s. m.* tram driver, (*USA*) streetcar operator
trapanàre *v. tr.* to drill, to bore
tràpano *s. m.* drill
trapassàre A *v. tr.* to pierce, to run through

B *v. intr.* **1** (*passare*) to pass **2** (*morire*) to pass away
trapàsso *s. m.* **1** transition **2** (*dir*) transfer
trapelàre *v. intr.* to leak out
trapèzio *s. m.* **1** (*geom.*) trapezium **2** (*anat.*) trapezius **3** (*ginnastica, vela*) trapeze
trapezìsta *s. m. e f.* trapezist
trapiantàre **A** *v. tr.* to transplant **B** *v. rifl.* to settle
trapiànto *s. m.* transplant, transplantation
tràppola *s. f.* trap
trapùnta *s. f.* quilt
tràrre **A** *v. tr.* **1** to draw, to pull **2** (*derivare*) to derive, to get **3** (*condurre*) to lead **B** *v. rifl.* to draw
trasalìre *v. intr.* to start, to jump
trasandàto *agg.* careless, shabby
trasbordàre **A** *v. tr.* (*naut.*) to tranship, (*ferr.*) to transfer **B** *v. intr.* to change
trascéndere **A** *v. tr.* to transcend, to go beyond **B** *v. intr.* to let oneself go, to lose control
trascinàre **A** *v. tr.* **1** to drag, to trail **2** (*avvincere*) to fascinate **B** *v. rifl.* to draw oneself along **C** *v. intr. pron.* to drag on
trascórrere **A** *v. tr.* to spend, to pass **B** *v. intr.* to pass, to elapse
trascrìvere *v. tr.* **1** to transcribe **2** (*registrare*) to register
trascrizióne *s. f.* **1** transcription **2** (*registrazione*) registration
trascuràbile *agg.* negligible
trascuràre **A** *v. tr.* **1** to neglect **2** (*tenere in poco conto*) to disregard, to ignore **B** *v. rifl.* to let oneself go
trascuratézza *s. f.* **1** carelessness **2** (*svista*) oversight
trascuràto *agg.* **1** careless, negligent **2** (*non curato*) neglected
trasecolàre *v. intr.* to be astounded
trasferiménto *s. m.* transfer
trasferìre **A** *v. tr.* to move, to transfer **B** *v. intr. pron. e rifl.* to move
trasfèrta *s. f.* **1** transfer **2** (*indennità*) travelling allowance ♦ **partita in t.** away game
trasfiguràre **A** *v. tr.* to transfigure **B** *v. intr. pron.* to become transfigured
trasformàre **A** *v. tr.* to transform, to change **B** *v. intr. pron.* to transform oneself, to turn into
trasformatóre *s. m.* transformer
trasfusióne *s. f.* transfusion
trasgredìre *v. tr. e intr.* to infringe, to transgress
trasgressióne *s. f.* transgression, infringement
traslàto *agg.* metaphorical
traslitterazióne *s. f.* transliteration
traslocàre *v. tr. e intr.* to move
traslòco *s. m.* removal, move
trasméttere **A** *v. tr.* **1** to pass, to transfer, to convey **2** (*mandare*) to send, to pass on **3** (*TV, radio*) to broadcast, to transmit **B** *v. intr. pron.* to be transmitted
trasmettitóre *s. m.* transmitter
trasmissióne *s. f.* transmission
trasmittènte *s. f.* transmitter
trasognàto *agg.* dreamy
trasparènte *agg.* transparent
trasparènza *s. f.* transparency
trasparìre *v. intr.* to shine through ♦ **lasciar t.** to betray
traspiràre **A** *v. tr.* to transpire **B** *v. intr.* **1** to perspire **2** (*bot., fig.*) to transpire
traspirazióne *s. f.* perspiration, transpiration
trasportàbile *agg.* transportable
trasportàre *v. tr.* **1** to transport, to carry, to convey **2** (*spostare*) to move, (*trasferire*) to transfer
trasportatóre *s. m.* carrier, conveyor
traspòrto *s. m.* **1** transport, conveyance, carriage, (*di merce*) freight **2** *al pl.* transport **3** (*fig.*) transport
trastullàre **A** *v. tr.* to amuse **B** *v. rifl. e intr. pron.* **1** to play **2** (*perdere tempo*) to waste time
trasudàre **A** *v. tr.* to ooze with **B** *v. intr.* to trasude, (*sudare*) to perspire, (*umidità*) to ooze
trasversàle **A** *agg.* **1** transversal, cross (*attr.*) **2** (*indiretto*) indirect **B** *s. f.* **1** transversal **2** (*via*) cross street
trasvolàre *v. tr.* to fly across
trasvolàta *s. f.* flight, (air) crossing
tràtta *s. f.* **1** (*traffico*) trade **2** (*banca*) draft, bill **3** (*tratto*) distance, (*ferr.*) section
trattàbile *agg.* **1** tractable **2** (*di prezzo*) negotiable
trattaménto *s. m.* **1** treatment, service **2** (*med., tecnol.*) treatment **3** (*economico*) pay, wages *pl.*
trattàre **A** *v. tr.* **1** to treat, to deal with **2** (*maneggiare*) to handle **3** (*discutere*) to deal with, to discuss **4** (*contrattare*) to handle, to transact, to negotiate **5** (*com-*

merciare) to deal in, to handle **6** (*chim., med.*) to treat **B** *v. intr.* **1** (*di un argomento*) to deal with, to be about **2** (*avere a che fare*) to deal **3** (*condurre trattative*) to negotiate **4** (*essere*) to be (about), (*essere questione*) to be a question **C** *v. rifl.* to treat oneself ♦ **di che si tratta?** what is it about?

trattativa *s. f.* negotiation, talks *pl.*

trattàto *s. m.* **1** (*libro*) treatise **2** (*accordo*) treaty

trattazióne *s. f.* treatment

tratteggiàre *v. tr.* **1** to outline **2** (*disegnare a tratti*) to dash **3** (*descrivere*) to describe

trattenére **A** *v. tr.* **1** (*far rimanere*) to keep, to retain **2** (*frenare*) to hold back, to keep, to restrain **3** (*intrattenere*) to entertain **4** (*fare una trattenuta*) to deduct **B** *v. rifl.* **1** (*rimanere*) to stop, to stay, to remain **2** (*frenarsi*) to restrain oneself, to keep oneself

trattenimènto *s. m.* entertainment, party

trattenùta *s. f.* deduction

trattìno *s. m.* dash, (*nelle parole*) hyphen

tràtto *s. m.* **1** (*di penna, matita*) stroke **2** (*frazione di spazio*) part, tract, stretch, (*di tempo*) period, while **3** (*caratteristica*) trait, feature **4** *al pl.* feature ♦ **d'un t.** suddenly

trattóre *s. m.* tractor

trattorìa *s. f.* restaurant

tràuma *s. m.* trauma ♦ **t. psichico** mental shock

traumàtico *agg.* traumatic

traumatòlogo *s. m.* traumatologist

travàglio *s. m.* **1** trouble, pain, suffering **2** (*del parto*) labour

travasàre *v. tr.* to pour off

tràve *s. f.* beam

travèrsa *s. f.* **1** crossbar **2** (*via*) side road, cross road

traversàre *v. tr.* to cross

traversàta *s. f.* crossing, passage

traversìa *s. f.* misfortune

travèrso **A** *agg.* **1** transverse, cross **2** (*obliquo*) oblique **B** *s. m.* width ♦ **andare di t.** (*di cibo*) to go the wrong way

travertìno *s. m.* travertin(e)

travestimènto *s. m.* disguise

travestìre **A** *v. tr.* to disguise **B** *v. rifl.* to disguise oneself

travïàre **A** *v. tr.* to mislead, to lead astray **B** *v. intr. pron.* to go astray

travisàre *v. tr.* to distort, to alter, to misinterpret

travolgènte *agg.* overwhelming

travòlgere *v. tr.* **1** to sweep away, to carry away **2** (*sopraffare*) to overwhelm **3** (*investire*) to run over

trazióne *s. f.* **1** traction **2** (*autom.*) drive

tre *agg. num. card. e s. m. inv.* three

trebbiàre *v. tr.* to tresh

tréccia *s. f.* plait, braid

trecènto *agg. num. card. e s. m. inv.* three hundred

trédici *agg. num. card. e s. m. inv.* thirteen

trégua *s. f.* **1** truce **2** (*riposo*) respite, rest

tremàre *v. intr.* to tremble, to shake, to quiver, (*di freddo*) to shiver, (*di paura*) to quake

tremèndo *agg.* frightful, awful, terrible

tremìla *agg. num. card. e s. m. inv.* three thousand

trèmito *s. m.* tremble, shake, quiver

tremolàre *v. intr.* to tremble, (*di luce*) to flicker

tremóre *s. m.* **1** trembling, shaking **2** (*med.*) tremor

trèno *s. m.* train ♦ **t. accelerato** slow train; **t. diretto** through train; **t. espresso** fast train; **t. rapido** express train

trénta *agg. num. card. e s. m. inv.* thirty

trentésimo *agg. num. ord. e s. m.* thirtieth

trèpidare *v. intr.* to be anxious

trésca *s. f.* intrigue

tréspolo *s. m.* trestle, (*per pappagallo*) perch

triangolàre *agg.* triangular

triangolazióne *s. f.* triangulation

triàngolo *s. m.* triangle

tribù *s. f.* tribe

tribùna *s. f.* **1** (*per oratori*) tribune, platform **2** (*per uditori*) gallery **3** (*sport*) stand **4** (*arch.*) apse

tribunàle *s. m.* court, tribunal

tributàre *v. tr.* to bestow, to grant

tribùto *s. m.* tribute

trichèco *s. m.* walrus

triciclo *s. m.* tricycle

triclìnio *s. m.* triclinium

tricòlogo *s. m.* trichologist

tricolóre *agg.* tricolo(u)r

tricuspidàle *agg.* tricuspid(al)

tridènte *s. m.* trident

tridimensionàle *agg.* tridimensional, three-dimensional

trielìna *s. f.* trichloroethylene

trifòglio *s. m.* clover

trìglia *s. f.* mullet

trìglifo *s. m.* triglyph
trillàre *v. intr.* to trill
trilobàto *agg.* trilobal
trimestràle *agg.* quarterly, three-monthly
trimèstre *s. m.* quarter, three-month period
trimotóre *s. m.* three-engined aircraft
trìna *s. f.* lace
trincèa *s. f.* trench
trinceràre **A** *v. tr.* to entrench **B** *v. intr. pron.* to entrench oneself
trinciàre *v. tr.* to cut (up)
trinità *s. f.* trinity
trìo *s. m.* trio
trionfàle *agg.* triumphal
trionfàre *v. intr.* to triumph
triónfo *s. m.* triumph
triplicàre *v. tr. e intr. pron.* to triple, to treble
trìplice *agg.* triple, treble
trìplo *agg. e s. m.* triple, treble
trìppa *s. f.* tripe
trìste *agg.* **1** sad, unhappy **2** (*cupo*) gloomy, bleak
tristézza *s. f.* **1** sadness, unhappiness **2** (*cupezza*) gloominess
tritacàrne *s. m. inv.* mincer
tritaghiàccio *s. m. inv.* ice-crusher
tritàre *v. tr.* to mince, to chop up, to grind
tritatùtto *s. m. inv.* mincer, food-grinder
trìto *agg.* **1** (*tritato*) minced, chopped **2** (*comune, stranoto*) trite, worn-out
trìttico *s. m.* triptych
trivellàre *v. tr.* to bore, to drill
triviàle *agg.* coarse, vulgar
trofèo *s. m.* trophy
troglodìta *s. m.* troglodyte
trómba *s. f.* **1** trumpet **2** (*delle scale*) well ♦ **t. d'aria** tornado
trombettista *s. m. e f.* trumpet (player)
trombóne *s. m.* **1** trombone **2** (*fanfarone*) braggart
trombòsi *s. f.* thrombosis
troncàre *v. tr.* to cut off, to break off
tronchése *s. m. o f.* (cutting) nippers *pl.*
trónco *s. m.* **1** trunk, (*d'albero abbattuto*) log **2** (*ceppo*) stock **3** (*tratto*) section **4** (*geom.*) frustum
troneggiàre *v. intr.* to tower, to stand out
tròno *s. m.* throne
tropicàle *agg.* tropical
tròpico *s. m.* tropic
tròppo **A** *agg. indef.* (*quantità*) too much, too many *pl.*, (*durata*) too long, (*estensione*) too far **B** *pron. indef.* too much, too many *pl.* **C** *avv.* **1** (*con avv. e agg.*) too, (*con v.*) too much **2** (*molto*) too, so (very)
tròta *s. f.* trout
trottàre *v. intr.* to trot
trottatóre *s. m.* trotter
trotterellàre *v. intr.* to trot along
tròtto *s. m.* trot
tròttola *s. f.* spinning-top
trovàre **A** *v. tr.* **1** to find **2** (*scoprire*) to find out, to discover **3** (*incontrare*) to meet **4** (*sorprendere*) to catch **5** (*far visita a*) to see **B** *v. intr. pron.* **1** to find oneself **2** (*essere*) to be **3** (*sentirsi*) to feel **C** *v. rifl. rec.* to meet
trovàta *s. f.* trick
truccàre **A** *v. tr.* **1** to make up **2** (*mascherare*) to disguise **3** (*falsificare*) to fix, to rig, to falsify **B** *v. rifl.* **1** to make oneself up **2** (*travestirsi*) to disguise oneself
truccatóre *s. m.* make-up man, visagiste
trùcco *s. m.* **1** trick **2** (*con cosmetici*) make-up
trùce *agg.* grim
trucidàre *v. tr.* to slaughter
trùciolo *s. m.* chip, shaving
trùffa *s. f.* fraud, swindle, cheat
truffàre *v. tr.* to defraud, to cheat, to swindle
trùppa *s. f.* troop
tu *pron. pers. 2ª sing.* you ♦ **tu stesso** you yourself
tùba *s. f.* tuba
tubàre *v. intr.* to coo
tubatùra *s. f.* piping, pipes *pl.*
tubazióne *s. f.* piping, pipes *pl.*
tubétto *s. m.* tube
tùbo *s. m.* tube, pipe ♦ **t. digerente** alimentary canal; **t. di scappamento** exhaust-pipe
tuffàre **A** *v. tr.* to plunge, to dip **B** *v. rifl.* to dive, to plunge
tuffatóre *s. m.* diver
tùffo *s. m.* dive, plunge
tùfo *s. m.* tuff
tùga *s. f.* deckhouse
tugùrio *s. m.* hovel
tulipàno *s. m.* tulip
tumefàre *v. tr. e intr. pron.* to tumefy
tumefazióne *s. f.* tumefaction
tumóre *s. m.* tumour, (*USA*) tumor
tùmulo *s. m.* **1** (*archeol.*) tumulus **2** (*cumulo di terra*) mound
tumùlto *s. m.* **1** tumult, uproar **2** (*sommossa*) riot
tumultuóso *agg.* tumultuous, riotous
tùndra *s. f.* tundra

tùnica *s. f.* tunic
tunnel *s. m. inv.* tunnel
tùo **A** *agg. poss. 2ª sing* your **B** *pron. poss.* yours **C** *s. m.* **1** (*ciò che è tuo*) your property, what you own **2** *al pl.* (*i tuoi familiari*) your family, (*i tuoi sostenitori*) your supporters
tuonàre *v. intr.* to thunder
tuòno *s. m.* thunder
tuòrlo *s. m.* yolk
turàcciolo *s. m.* cork
turàre *v. tr.* to plug, to stop
turbaménto *s. m.* **1** disturbing **2** (*agitazione*) perturbation
turbànte *s. m.* turban
turbàre **A** *v. tr.* to upset, to trouble **B** *v. intr. pron.* to get upset, to become agitated
turbìna *s. f.* turbine
turbinàre *v. intr.* to whirl
tùrbine *s. m.* whirl
turbolènto *agg.* **1** turbulent, stormy **2** (*di bambino*) boisterous
turchése *agg. e s. m.* turquoise
turchìno *agg. e s. m.* deep blue
tùrco **A** *agg.* Turkish **B** *s. m.* **1** (*abitante*) Turk **2** (*lingua*) Turkish
turìsmo *s. m.* tourism
turìsta *s. m. e f.* tourist
turìstico *agg.* tourist (*attr.*)
tùrno *s. m.* **1** turn **2** (*di lavoro*) shift, (*di servizio*) duty
tùrpe *agg.* **1** base, vile, shameful **2** (*osceno*) obscene, filthy
turpilòquio *s. m.* foul language
tùta *s. f.* overalls *pl.*, (*sportiva*) tracksuit ♦ **t. mimetica** camouflage
tutèla *s. f.* **1** (*dir.*) guardianship, tutelage **2** (*protezione*) protection, (*difesa*) defence, safeguard
tutelàre *v. tr.* to protect, to defend
tutóre *s. m.* **1** (*dir.*) guardian **2** (*bot.*) stake
tutt'al più *loc. avv.* **1** (*al massimo*) at (the) most **2** (*alla peggio*) at (the) worst
tuttavìa *cong.* but, yet, nevertheless, however
tùtto **A** *agg. indef.* **1** all, (*intero*) (the) whole (of) (ES: **t. l'anno** all the year, the whole year) **2** *al pl.* all, (*ogni*) every, (*ciascuno*) each, (*qualsiasi*) any (ES: **tutti gli uomini sono uguali** all men are equal, **ci vediamo tutti i giorni** we see each other every day) **3** (*completamente*) all, quite (ES: **sei t. bagnato** you're all wet) **B** *pron. indef.* **1** all, (*ogni cosa*) everything, (*qualsiasi cosa*) anything (ES: **t. dipende da te** everything is up to you) **2** *al pl.* all, (*ognuno*) everybody, everyone, (*ciascuno*) each one (ES: **lo sanno tutti** everybody knows) **C** *s. m.* whole, total, (*ogni cosa*) everything (ES: **mescolate il t.** mix everything) ♦ **a tutta velocità** at full speed; **a t. spiano** all out; **di t. punto** completely; **prima di t.** first of all; **tutt'altro!** not at all!; **t. intorno** all around
tuttofàre *agg.* general
tuttóra *avv.* still
tutù *s. m.* tutu

U

ubbidiènte *agg.* obedient
ubbidìre *v. intr. e tr.* to obey
ubicazióne *s. f.* location, site
ubiquità *s. f.* ubiquity
ubriacàre **A** *v. tr.* to make drunk **B** *v. rifl. e intr. pron.* to get drunk
ubriachézza *s. f.* drunkenness ♦ **in stato di u.** in a drunken state
ubriàco *agg. e s. m.* drunk
uccellièra *s. f.* aviary
uccèllo *s. m.* bird
uccìdere **A** *v. tr.* to kill **B** *v. rifl.* **1** (*rimanere ucciso*) to get killed **2** (*suicidarsi*) to kill oneself
uccisióne *s. f.* killing, (*assassinio*) murder
uccisóre *s. m.* killer, (*assassino*) murderer
udìbile *agg.* audible
udiènza *s. f.* **1** audience, hearing, (*colloquio*) interview **2** (*dir.*) hearing, sitting ♦ **u. a porte chiuse** sitting in camera
udìre *v. tr.* to hear
uditivo *agg.* auditory
udìto *s. m.* hearing
uditòrio *s. m.* audience
uffa *inter.* ooh, phew
ufficiàle **A** *agg.* official, formal **B** *s. m.* officer
uffìcio *s. m.* **1** office, bureau, (*reparto*) department, (*edificio*) premises *pl.* **2** (*carica*) office, task, function **3** (*dovere*) duty ♦ **orario d'u.** office hours; **u. postale** post office; **u. turistico** tourist office
ufficióso *agg.* unofficial
ugèllo *s. m.* nozzle, jet
ùggia *s. f.* boredom, nuisance
uggióso *agg.* boring, tiresome, (*di tempo*) gloomy
uguagliànza *s. f.* equality
uguagliàre *v. tr.* **1** (*rendere uguale*) to equalize, to make equal, (*livellare*) to level **2** (*essere uguale a*) to equal, to be equal **3** (*sport*) to equal **4** (*paragonare*) to compare
uguàle **A** *agg.* **1** equal, (*identico*) same, like, identical **2** (*uniforme*) even, regular, uniform **B** *s. m.* **1** equal **2** (*la stessa cosa*) the same
ugualménte *avv.* **1** equally **2** (*malgrado tutto*) all the same
ùlcera *s. f.* ulcer ♦ **u. duodenale** duodenal ulcer; **u. gastrica** gastric ulcer
ùlna *s. f.* ulna
ulterióre *agg.* further
ultimaménte *avv.* lately
ultimàre *v. tr.* to complete, to finish
ùltimo **A** *agg.* **1** last, final **2** (*il più recente*) latest, last **3** (*estremo*) farthest, utmost **4** (*principale*) ultimate **B** *s. m.* **1** last **2** (*momento finale*) end
ultrasuòno *s. m.* ultrasound
ultraviolétto *agg. e s. m.* ultraviolet
ululàre *v. intr.* to howl, (*di sirena*) to hoot
ululàto *s. m.* howl, (*di sirena*) hoot
umanésimo *s. m.* humanism
umanìsta *s. m. e f.* humanist
umanità *s. f.* **1** humanity, (*genere umano*) mankind **2** (*bontà*) humanity
umanitàrio *agg.* humanitarian
umàno *agg.* **1** human **2** (*gentile*) humane
umidificàre *v. tr.* to humidify
umidificatóre *s. m.* humidifier
umidità *s. f.* dampness, moisture, humidity
ùmido *agg.* damp, moist, humid
ùmile *agg.* humble, modest
umiliànte *agg.* humiliating
umiliàre **A** *v. tr.* to humiliate, to humble **B** *v. rifl.* to humble oneself
umiliazióne *s. f.* humiliation
umiltà *s. f.* **1** (*virtù*) humility **2** (*l'essere di modesta condizione*) humbleness
umóre *s. m.* **1** humour **2** (*stato d'animo*) mood, temper ♦ **essere di cattivo/buon u.** to be in a bad/good mood
umorìsmo *s. m.* humour
umorìsta *s. m. e f.* humorist
umorìstico *agg.* humorous, comic, (*divertente*) funny
un → **uno**
unànime *agg.* unanimous
unanimità *s. f.* unanimity
uncinétto *s. m.* crochet
uncìno *s. m.* hook
ùngere **A** *v. tr.* **1** to grease, to oil **2** (*sporcare di grasso*) to make greasy **3** (*fig.*) to flatter, to butter up **B** *v. rifl. e intr. pron.* to grease oneself
ungherése *agg. e s. m. e f.* Hungarian
ùnghia *s. f.* **1** nail **2** (*artiglio*) claw

unghiàta *s. f.* scratch
unguènto *s. m.* ointment
unicaménte *avv.* only, solely
ùnico **A** *agg.* **1** only, one **2** (*esclusivo*) sole **3** (*singolo*) single **4** (*senza pari*) unique **B** *s. m.* only, one
unifamiliàre *agg.* one-family (*attr.*)
unificàre **A** *v. tr.* **1** to unify **2** (*uniformare*) to standardize **B** *v. rifl. rec.* to join (together)
unificazióne *s. f.* **1** unification, union **2** (*uniformazione*) standardization
uniformàre **A** *v. tr.* **1** (*conformare*) to conform, to adapt, to fit **2** (*rendere uniforme*) to standardize, to make uniform **B** *v. rifl.* to conform, to comply
unifórme **A** *agg.* uniform, even **B** *s. f.* uniform
uniformità *s. f.* uniformity
unilateràle *agg.* unilateral, one-sided
unióne *s. f.* **1** union **2** (*accordo, armonia*) unity, agreement **3** (*associazione*) union, association
unìre **A** *v. tr.* **1** to unite, to join (together), to put together **2** (*collegare*) to connect, to link **3** (*aggiungere*) to add **B** *v. rifl. e rifl. rec.* **1** (*mettersi insieme*) to join, (*fondersi*) to merge **2** (*legarsi*) to unite, to join up, to come together
unità *s. f.* **1** unity **2** (*misura, valore, mil., inf.*) unit **3** (*mat.*) unity, unit
unitàrio *agg.* unitary, unit (*attr.*)
unìto *agg.* **1** united **2** (*accluso*) enclosed **3** (*uniforme*) uniform, even
universàle *agg.* **1** universal, general **2** (*multiuso*) multipurpose
università *s. f.* university
universitàrio *agg.* university (*attr.*)
univèrso *s. m.* universe
unìvoco *agg.* univocal, unambiguous
ùno **A** *agg. num. card. e s. m.* one **B** *art. indeterm.* **1** a an **2** (*circa*) some, about **C** *pron. indef.* **1** (*qualcuno*) someone, (*un tale*) a man, a fellow, (*con partitivo*) one **2** (*ciascuno*) each **3** (*impersonale*) one, you ♦ **l'u. e l'altro** both; **l'un l'altro** one another, each other; **né l'u. né l'altro** neither; **(l')u. ... l'altro** one ... the other
ùnto **A** *agg.* greasy, oily **B** *s. m.* grease
untuóso *agg.* greasy, oily
uòmo *s. m.* man
uòvo *s. m.* egg
ùpupa *s. f.* hoopoe
uragàno *s. m.* hurricane
urànio *s. m.* uranium
urbanìsta *s. m. e f.* city-planner, town-planner
urbanìstica *s. f.* city-planning, town-planning
urbanizzazióne *s. f.* urbanization
urbàno *agg.* **1** urban, city (*attr.*), town (*attr.*) **2** (*cortese*) urbane, polite
urèa *s. f.* urea
urètra *s. f.* urethra
urgènte *agg.* urgent, pressing
urgènza *s. f.* **1** urgency, (*fretta*) hurry **2** (*emergenza*) emergency
ùrgere *v. intr.* to be urgent
urìna *s. f.* urine
urlàre *v. tr. e intr.* to shout, to yell
ùrlo *s. m.* cry, shout, yell
ùrna *s. f.* **1** urn **2** (*elettorale*) ballot-box ♦ **andare alle urne** to go to the polls
urografìa *s. f.* urography
urologìa *s. f.* urology
uròlogo *s. m.* urologist
urtàre **A** *v. tr.* **1** to bump (into), to knock (against), to crash (into), to collide with **2** (*infastidire*) to irritate, to annoy, (*offendere*) to hurt, to offend **B** *v. intr.* to knock, to strike **C** *v. rifl. rec.* **1** to collide, to bump into one another **2** (*fig.*) to quarrell
urticànte *agg.* urticant
ùrto *s. m.* **1** (*spinta*) push, shove **2** (*collisione*) bump, knock, collision **3** (*attacco*) attack **4** (*contrasto*) clash, collision
usànza *s. f.* **1** custom, usage **2** (*abitudine*) habit
usàre **A** *v. tr.* **1** to use, to make use of **2** (*essere solito*) to be accustomed (to), to be used (to) **B** *v. intr.* **1** (*servirsi*) to make use of **2** (*essere di moda*) to be in fashion, to be fashionable
usàto **A** *agg.* **1** (*non nuovo*) second-hand (*attr.*) **2** (*in uso*) in use (*pred.*) **B** *s. m.* (*cose usate*) second-hand goods *pl.*
uscière *s. m.* usher
ùscio *s. m.* door
uscìre *v. intr.* **1** to get out, (*andare fuori*) to go out, (*venire fuori*) to come out **2** (*di pubblicazione*) to come out, to be issued **3** (*lasciare*) to leave **4** (*essere prodotto*) to be turned out **5** (*essere estratto*) to be drawn **6** (*provenire*) to come **7** (*cavarsela*) to get out ♦ **u. di strada** to go off the road
uscìta *s. f.* **1** going out, coming out **2** (*passaggio*) exit, way out **3** (*sbocco*) outlet **4** (*spesa*) expense, outlay **5** (*motto di

spirito) witty remark **6** (*desinenza*) ending ♦ **u. di sicurezza** emergency exit
usignòlo *s. m.* nightingale
ùso *s. m.* **1** use **2** (*usanza*) usage, custom, (*abitudine*) habit ♦ **fuori u.** out of order
ustionàre **A** *v. tr.* to burn, to scald **B** *v. rifl.* to burn oneself, to scald oneself
ustióne *s. f.* burn, scald
usuàle *agg.* usual, customary
usufruìre *v. intr.* to take advantage, to benefit
usufrùtto *s. m.* usufruct
usùra (1) *s. f.* usury
usùra (2) *s. f.* (*logorio*) wear and tear
utensìle *s. m.* tool, (*domestico*) utensil
utènte *s. m. e f.* user, (*consumatore*) consumer
utènza *s. f.* **1** use, consumption **2** (*insieme degli utenti*) users *pl.*, consumers *pl.*
ùtero *s. m.* uterus
ùtile **A** *agg.* **1** useful, helpful **2** (*utilizzabile*) usable **B** *s. m.* **1** (*econ.*) profit, benefit, (*interesse*) interest, (*guadagno*) gains *pl.* **2** (*fig.*) profit
utilità *s. f.* **1** utility, usefulness **2** (*vantaggio*) profit, benefit
utilitària *s. f.* runabout, compact car
utilitàrio *agg.* utilitarian
utilizzàre *v. tr.* to use, to make use of, to utilize
utilizzatóre *s. m.* user, utilizer
utilìzzo *s. m.* use, utilization
utopìa *s. f.* utopia
utopista *s. m. e f.* utopian
utopìstico *agg.* utopian
ùva *s. f.* grapes *pl.* ♦ **u. passa** raisin; **u. spina** gooseberry
uxoricìda *s. m.* uxoricide
uxoricìdio *s. m.* uxoricide

V

vacànte *agg.* vacant, empty
vacànza *s. f.* **1** holiday, vacation **2** (*assenza*) vacuum ♦ **vacanze estive** summer holidays
vàcca *s. f.* cow
vaccinàre *v. tr.* to vaccinate
vaccinazióne *s. f.* vaccination
vaccìno *s. m.* vaccine
vacillàre *v. intr.* **1** to totter, to stagger, to wobble **2** (*di luce*) to flicker **3** (*essere incerto*) to waver, to vacillate
vàcuo *agg.* vacuous, inane
vagabondàre *v. intr.* to wander about
vagabóndo *s. m.* **1** vagrant, tramp **2** (*fannullone*) loafer
vagàre *v. intr.* to wander, to roam
vagheggiàre *v. tr.* to long for, to dream of
vagìna *s. f.* vagina
vaginìte *s. f.* vaginitis
vagìre *v. intr.* to cry, to whimper
vàglia *s. m. inv.* money order ♦ **v. postale** postal order; **v. telegrafico** telegraphic money order
vagliàre *v. tr.* **1** to riddle, to screen **2** (*considerare*) to examine, to weigh
vàglio *s. m.* **1** riddle, screen **2** (*fig.*) sifting, examination
vàgo **A** *agg.* vague, faint **B** *s. m.* vagueness
vagóne *s. m.* wagon, car, van, coach ♦ **v. letto** sleeping car
vaiólo *s. m.* smallpox
valànga *s. f.* avalanche
valènte *agg.* clever, skilful
valére **A** *v. intr.* **1** (*avere valore*) to be worth **2** (*esser valido*) to be valid, (*essere in vigore*) to be in force **3** (*aver peso*) to count, to be of account, to have weight **4** (*servire, giovare*) to be of use, to be of avail **5** (*equivalere*) to be worth, to be equal to **B** *v. tr.* to win **C** *v. intr. pron.* to make use, to take advantage, to avail oneself
valeriàna *s. f.* valerian
valévole *agg.* valid
valicàre *v. tr.* to cross
vàlico *s. m.* (mountain) pass
validità *s. f.* **1** validity **2** (*valore*) value **3** (*efficacia*) effectiveness
vàlido *agg.* **1** valid **2** (*fondato*) sound, well-grounded **3** (*di pregio*) valid, good **4** (*efficace*) efficient, effective
valigerìa *s. f.* leather-goods shop
valìgia *s. f.* suitcase ♦ **fare/disfare le valigie** to pack/to unpack
vallàta *s. f.* valley
vàlle *s. f.* valley
vallétto *s. m.* page
vallóne *s. m.* deep valley
valóre *s. m.* **1** value, worth **2** (*econ., mat., mus.*) value **3** (*coraggio*) valour, bravery, courage **4** (*validità*) value, validity **5** *al pl.* (*oggetti preziosi*) valuables *pl.*, (*titoli*) securities *pl.*
valorizzàre *v. tr.* **1** (*aumentare il valore di*) to increase the value of, to appreciate, (*migliorare*) to improve **2** (*sfruttare*) to exploit **3** (*mettere in risalto*) to set off
valoróso *agg.* valiant, brave
valùta *s. f.* currency
valutàre *v. tr.* **1** (*giudicare il valore di*) to value, to estimate, to appraise **2** (*considerare*) to consider, to weigh **3** (*calcolare*) to calculate, to reckon **4** (*stimare*) to value, to esteem
valutazióne *s. f.* **1** valuation, estimation **2** (*valore attribuito*) estimate **3** (*giudizio, considerazione*) judgement, consideration
vàlvola *s. f.* valve
vàlzer *s. m. inv.* waltz
vàmpa *s. f.* **1** blaze, flame **2** (*al viso*) flush, blush
vampàta *s. f.* **1** blaze, burst of flame **2** (*folata*) blast **3** (*al viso*) flush, blush
vampìro *s. m.* vampire
vandàlico *agg.* vandalic
vandalìsmo *s. m.* vandalism
vàndalo *s. m.* vandal
vaneggiàre *v. intr.* to rave
vanèsio **A** *agg.* foppish **B** *s. m.* fop
vànga *s. f.* spade
vangàre *v. tr.* to spade
vangèlo *s. m.* Gospel
vanìglia *s. f.* vanilla
vanità *s. f.* **1** vanity **2** (*inutilità*) vainness, uselessness
vanitóso *agg.* vain
vàno **A** *agg.* **1** (*inutile*) vain, useless **2** (*privo di fondamento*) vain, empty **3**

(*vanitoso*) vain **B** *s. m.* **1** (*parte vuota*) space, hollow, (*apertura*) opening **2** (*stanza*) room

vantàggio *s. m.* **1** advantage, benefit **2** (*sport*) lead, (*tennis*) advantage

vantaggióso *agg.* advantageous, favourable

vantàre **A** *v. tr.* **1** to boast **2** (*esaltare*) to extol, to praise **3** (*millantare*) to boast of **4** (*pretendere*) to claim **B** *v. rifl. e intr. pron.* to boast, to show off

vanterìa *s. f.* boasting

vànto *s. m.* **1** boast(ing) **2** (*motivo d'orgoglio*) pride, merit

vànvera, a *loc. avv.* haphazardly ♦ **parlare a v.** to talk nonsense

vapóre *s. m.* **1** vapour, (*acqueo*) steam **2** *al pl.* (*fumi*) fumes *pl.* **3** (*nave a vapore*) steamer ♦ **ferro a v.** steam iron

vaporétto *s. m.* ferry, water bus

vaporizzàre **A** *v. tr.* to vaporize **B** *v. intr. pron.* to evaporate

vaporizzatóre *s. m.* vaporizer, atomizer

vaporóso *agg.* gauzy, (*di capelli*) fluffy

varàre *v. tr.* to launch

varcàre *v. tr.* to cross, to pass

vàrco *s. m.* opening, passage

variàbile **A** *agg.* variable, changeable, (*volubile*) fickle **B** *s. f.* variable

variàre **A** *v. tr.* to vary, to change **B** *v. intr.* **1** to vary, to change **2** (*fluttuare*) to fluctuate

variatóre *s. m.* variator, (*elettr.*) converter

variazióne *s. f.* variation, (*cambiamento*) change, (*fluttuazione*) fluctuation

varìce *s. f.* varix, varicose vein

varicèlla *s. f.* chicken-pox, varicella

varicóso *agg.* varicose

variegàto *agg.* **1** variegated, multi-coloured, (*screziato*) streaked **2** (*fig.*) diversified

varietà (1) *s. f.* **1** (*diversità*) variety, (*differenziazione*) variedness **2** (*gamma*) assortment, variety **3** (*specie*) kind, type

varietà (2) *s. m.* (*teatro*) variety (show), vaudeville

vàrio *agg.* **1** (*variato*) varied **2** (*differente*) various, different **3** *al pl.* (*parecchi*) several

variopìnto *agg.* multi-coloured

vàro *s. m.* **1** (*naut.*) launch, launching **2** (*di legge*) passing

vasàio *s. m.* potter

vàsca *s. f.* **1** basin, tank **2** (*da bagno*) bath, (*USA*) bathtub, tub

vascèllo *s. m.* vessel, ship

vaselìna *s. f.* vaseline

vasellàme *s. m.* earthenware

vàso *s. m.* **1** pot, jar, (*ornamentale*) vase **2** (*bot., anat.*) vessel **3** (*tecnol.*) bowl, tank

vassóio *s. m.* tray

vàsto *agg.* wide, large, vast

vecchiàia *s. f.* old age

vècchio **A** *agg.* **1** old **2** (*maggiore*) (*comp.*) older, (*sup.*) oldest **3** (*antico*) ancient, old **4** (*stantio*) stale **5** (*stagionato*) seasoned **B** *s. m.* **1** old man **2** (*ciò che è vecchio*) the old

véce *s. f.* place, stead ♦ **fare le veci di qc.** to take sb.'s place

vedére **A** *v. tr.* **1** to see **2** (*incontrare*) to meet, to see **3** (*esaminare*) to examine, to have a look at **4** (*capire*) to see, to understand **5** (*fare in modo che*) to see, to try, to take care **6** (*decidere*) to decide **B** *v. intr.* to see **C** *v. rifl.* **1** to see oneself **2** (*sentirsi*) to feel **D** *v. rifl. rec.* to meet

vedétta *s. f.* look-out, vedette

védova *s. f.* widow

védovo *s. m.* widower

vedùta *s. f.* **1** (*panorama*) view, sight **2** (*quadro, fot.*) picture **3** *al pl.* (*opinioni*) view, idea

veemènte *agg.* vehement

veemènza *s. f.* vehemence

vegetàle *agg. e s. m.* vegetable

vegetàre *v. intr.* **1** to grow **2** (*fig.*) to vegetate

vegetariàno *agg. e s. m.* vegetarian

vegetazióne *s. f.* vegetation

vègeto *agg.* **1** thriving **2** (*di persona*) vigorous, strong

veggènte *s. m. e f.* seer, clairvoyant

véglia *s. f.* watch, vigil

vegliàre **A** *v. tr.* to watch over **B** *v. intr.* **1** to stay awake **2** (*fare la veglia*) to keep watch

veglióne *s. m.* party, dance ♦ **v. di fine d'anno** New Year's Eve dance

veìcolo *s. m.* **1** vehicle **2** (*mezzo*) carrier, vehicle, medium

véla *s. f.* sail, (*il fare vela*) sailing ♦ **barca a v.** sailing boat

velàre **A** *v. tr.* **1** to veil **2** (*offuscare*) to dim, to cover **3** (*nascondere*) to conceal **B** *v. intr. pron.* to mist

velàto *agg.* veiled

veleggiàre *v. intr.* to sail

veléno *s. m.* poison

velenóso *agg.* **1** poisonous, venomous **2** (*fig.*) venemous
velièro *s. m.* sailing ship
velìna *s. f.* tissue paper
velìsta *s. m. e f.* sailor
velìvolo *s. m.* aircraft
velleità *s. f.* foolish aspiration
vèllo *s. m.* fleece
vellùto *s. m.* velvet
vélo *s. m.* **1** veil **2** (*strato sottile*) film
velóce *agg.* fast, quick, swift
velocìsta *s. m. e f.* sprinter
velocità *s. f.* speed, velocity ♦ **eccesso di v.** speeding; **limite di v.** speed limit
velòdromo *s. m.* velodrome, cycle-track
véna *s. f.* **1** vein **2** (*filone*) vein, lode, stringer **3** (*d'acqua*) spring **4** (*ispirazione*) inspiration **5** (*umore*) mood
venàle *agg.* **1** sale (attr.), saleable **2** (*fig.*) venal, mercenary
venatùra *s. f.* vein
vendémmia *s. f.* vintage, grape harvest
vendemmiàre *v. tr. e intr.* to harvest grapes
véndere *v. tr.* **1** to sell **2** (*esercitare il commercio di*) to deal in
vendétta *s. f.* revenge, vengeance
vendìbile *agg.* saleable, marketable
vendicàre **A** *v. tr.* to revenge **B** *v. rifl.* to revenge oneself
vendicatìvo *agg.* revengeful, vindictive
véndita *s. f.* **1** selling, sale **2** (*negozio*) shop ♦ **in v.** on sale, for sale; **v. all'asta** auction; **v. per corrispondenza** mail-order selling
venditóre *s. m.* seller, vendor
venèfico *agg.* poisonous, venomous
veneràbile *agg.* venerable
veneràndo *agg.* venerable
veneràre *v. tr.* to revere, to venerate
venerdì *s. m.* Friday
venèreo *agg.* venereal
vèneto *agg. e s. m.* Venetian
veneziàno *agg. e s. m.* Venetian
veniàle *agg.* venial
venìre *v. intr.* **1** to come **2** (*derivare*) to derive **3** (*manifestarsi*) to have got **4** (*risultare, riuscire*) to come out, to turn out **5** (*costare*) to cost **6** (*spettare*) to be due, to be owed **7** (*aus. nella forma passiva*) to be ♦ **mi viene da ridere** I feel like laughing; **v. a conoscenza** to hear; **v. avanti** to come on; **v. in mente** to occur; **v. meno** (*svenire*) to faint, (*svanire*) to fail; **v. via** to come away, (*staccarsi*) to come off
venóso *agg.* venous
ventàglio *s. m.* **1** fan **2** (*gamma*) range, spread
ventàta *s. f.* **1** gust of wind **2** (*fig.*) wave
ventèsimo *agg. num. ord. e s. m.* twentieth
vénti *agg. num. card. e s. m. inv.* twenty
ventilàre *v. tr.* to air, to ventilate
ventilàto *agg.* airy, windy
ventilatóre *s. m.* fan
vènto *s. m.* wind
vèntola *s. f.* **1** (*per fuoco*) fire-fan **2** (*mecc.*) fan
ventósa *s. f.* sucker
ventóso *agg.* windy
vèntre *s. m.* stomach, belly, tummy (*fam.*)
ventùra *s. f.* chance, luck
venùta *s. f.* coming, arrival
véra *s. f.* **1** (*di pozzo*) well-curb **2** (*anello*) wedding ring
veraménte *avv.* **1** really, truly, indeed **2** (*a dire il vero*) actually
verànda *s. f.* veranda, (*USA*) porch
verbàle **A** *agg.* **1** spoken, oral **2** (*gramm.*) verbal **B** *s. m.* minutes *pl.*, record
verbalizzàre *v. tr.* to record, to minute
verbèna *s. f.* vervain, verbena
vèrbo *s. m.* verb
vérde *agg. e s. m.* green ♦ **v. pubblico** parks and gardens, green
verdeggiànte *agg.* verdant
verdétto *s. m.* verdict
verdùra *s. f.* greens *pl.*, vegetables *pl.*
vérga *s. f.* rod, staff
vérgine *agg. e s. f.* virgin
verginità *s. f.* virginity
vergógna *s. f.* **1** shame, (*disonore*) disgrace **2** (*imbarazzo*) embarrassment, (*timidezza*) shyness
vergognàrsi *v. intr. pron.* **1** to be ashamed, to feel ashamed **2** (*per timidezza*) to be shy, to feel embarrassed
vergognóso *agg.* **1** shameful, disgraceful **2** (*timido*) shy
verìfica *s. f.* **1** verification, control, check **2** (*contabile*) audit
verificàbile *agg.* verifiable
verificàre **A** *v. tr.* to verify, to check, to control **B** *v. intr. pron.* **1** (*accadere*) to happen **2** (*avverarsi*) to come true
verìsmo *s. m.* verism, realism
verìsta *s. m. e f.* verist
verità *s. f.* truth
veritièro *agg.* truthful

vèrme *s. m.* worm
vermìglio *agg. e s. m.* vermilion
vernàcolo *s. m.* vernacular
vernìce *s. f.* **1** paint, (*trasparente*) varnish **2** (*apparenza*) veneer **3** (*pelle lucida*) patent leather
verniciàre *v. tr.* to paint, (*con vernice trasparente*) to varnish ♦ **v. a spruzzo** to spray
vernissage *s. f. inv.* varnishing day
véro **A** *agg.* **1** true, real **2** (*completo, perfetto*) perfect, absolute **B** *s. m.* truth
verosimigliànte *agg.* likely, probable
verosìmile *agg.* likely, probable
verricèllo *s. m.* winch
verrùca *s. f.* verruca, wart
versaménto *s. m.* **1** pouring, spilling **2** (*deposito*) deposit, (*pagamento*) payment **3** (*med.*) effusion
versànte *s. m.* side
versàre **A** *v. tr.* **1** to pour **2** (*rovesciare*) to spill **3** (*spargere*) to shed **4** (*depositare*) to deposit, (*pagare*) to pay **B** *v. intr.* (*trovarsi*) to be **C** *v. intr. pron.* (*sfociare*) to flow
versàtile *agg.* versatile
versétto *s. m.* verse
versióne *s. f.* version
vèrso (1) *prep.* **1** (*direzione*) toward(s), -ward(s) (*suffisso*) **2** (*in prossimità*) near **3** (*tempo*) about, toward(s) **4** (*nei confronti di*) to, towards, (*contro*) against
vèrso (2) *s. m.* **1** (*riga di poesia*) line **2** (*poesia*) verse, poetry **3** (*suono*) sound, (*di animali*) call, cry **4** (*direzione*) direction, way **5** (*modo, maniera*) way **6** (*smorfia*) grimace, face
vèrso (3) *s. m.* (*retro*) verso, reverse, back
vèrtebra *s. f.* vertebra
vertebràle *agg.* vertebral, spinal
vertebràto *agg. e s. m.* vertebrate
vertènza *s. f.* controversy, dispute ♦ **v. sindacale** grievance
verticàle *agg. e s. f.* vertical
verticalménte *avv.* vertically
vèrtice *s. m.* **1** top, summit **2** (*geom.*) vertex **3** (*direzione*) top management **4** (*incontro*) summit
vertìgine *s. f.* dizziness, giddiness
vertiginóso *agg.* dizzy, giddy
vérza *s. f.* savoy cabbage
vescìca *s. f.* **1** (*anat.*) bladder **2** (*della pelle*) blister
vescovìle *agg.* episcopal, bishop's (*attr.*)
véscovo *s. m.* bishop
vèspa *s. f.* wasp
vespàio *s. m.* wasps' nest
vèspro *s. m.* vespers *pl.*
vessìllo *s. m.* standard, banner
vestàglia *s. f.* dressing gown
vèste *s. f.* **1** garment, clothes *pl.* **2** (*apparenza*) guise, appearance, (*aspetto*) format **3** (*funzione*) capacity ♦ **in v. di** as
vestiàrio *s. m.* clothes *pl.*, clothing
vestìbolo *s. m.* **1** (*atrio*) hall **2** (*anat., archeol.*) vestibule
vestìre **A** *v. tr.* **1** to dress, (*provvedere di vestiti*) to clothe **2** (*fare vestiti a*) to make sb.'s clothes **3** (*indossare*) to wear **B** *v. intr.* to dress, to be dressed **C** *v. rifl.* to dress (oneself), to get dressed
vestìto *s. m.* (*da uomo*) suit, (*da donna*) dress
veteràno *s. m.* veteran
veterinària *s. f.* veterinary science
veterinàrio *s. m.* veterinarian
vèto *s. m.* veto
vetràio *s. m.* glass-worker
vetràta *s. f.* **1** (*finestra*) glass-window **2** (*porta*) glass-door
vetrerìa *s. f.* glassworks
vetrìna *s. f.* (shop) window
vetrinìsta *s. m. e f.* window dresser
vetriòlo *s. m.* vitriol
vétro *s. m.* glass, (*di finestra*) window-pane
vétta *s. f.* top, summit, peak
vettóre *s. m.* **1** (*geom., fis., biol.*) vector **2** (*corriere*) carrier
vettovàglie *s. f. pl.* provisions *pl.*, supply
vettùra *s. f.* **1** (*carrozza*) coach, (*automobile*) car **2** (*ferr.*) carriage, coach
vetustà *s. f.* ancientness
vezzeggiàre *v. tr.* to fondle, to pamper
vezzeggiatìvo *s. m.* **1** term of endearment **2** (*nomignolo*) pet name
vézzo *s. m.* **1** (*abitudine*) habit **2** *al pl.* (*moine*) mincing ways *pl.*
vezzóso *agg.* **1** (*grazioso*) charming **2** (*lezioso*) mincing
vi (1) *pron. pers. 2ª pl.* **1** (*compl. ogg.*) you, (*compl. di termine*) (to) you (ES: **vi aiuterò volentieri** I'll help you with pleasure) **2** (*rifl.*) yourselves (ES: **vi siete vestiti?** have you dressed yourselves?) **3** (*rec.*) one another, each other (ES: **vi amate davvero?** do you really love each other?)
vi (2) *avv.* → **ci (2)**
vìa (1) *s. f.* **1** (*strada*) road, street **2** (*percorso, cammino*) way, path **3** (*modo*) way,

(*mezzo*) means **4** (*anat.*) duct, tract
vìa (2) *s. m.* (*segnale di partenza*) start, starting signal
vìa (3) **A** *avv.* away, off **B** *inter.* go!, (*scacciando*) go away!, off with you!, (*coraggio!*) come on! ♦ **e così v.** and so on
viadótto *s. m.* viaduct
viaggiàre *v. intr.* to travel, to make a trip, to journey ♦ **v. per lavoro** to travel on business
viaggiatóre **A** *agg.* travelling **B** *s. m.* **1** traveller **2** (*passeggero*) passenger
viàggio *s. m.* journey, trip (*per mare*) voyage, (*giro turistico*) tour ♦ **agenzia di viaggi** travel agency; **buon v.!** have a nice journey!; **v. organizzato** package tour
viàle *s. m.* avenue, boulevard, (*di giardino*) path
viandànte *s. m. e f.* wayfarer
viavài *s. m. inv.* coming and going
vibràre **A** *v. tr.* **1** (*agitare*) to brandish **2** (*colpi*) to strike **3** (*lanciare*) to hurl **B** *v. intr.* to vibrate, (*mecc.*) to chatter
vibrazióne *s. f.* vibration
vicàrio **A** *agg.* vicarious **B** *s. m.* **1** (*sostituto*) deputy, substitute **2** (*relig.*) vicar
vìce *s. m. e f.* deputy, assistant
vicènda *s. f.* event, vicissitude ♦ **a v.** each other, one another, (*alternatamente*) in turn
vicendévole *agg.* mutual, reciprocal
vicepresidènte *s. m.* vice-president
viceré *s. m.* viceroy
vicevèrsa *avv.* **1** vice versa **2** (*invece*) but
vicinànza *s. f.* **1** closeness, nearness, proximity **2** *al pl.* neighbourhood, (*dintorni*) outskirts *pl.*
vicinàto *s. m.* **1** neighbourhood **2** (*insieme dei vicini*) neighbours *pl.*
vicìno **A** *agg.* **1** near, nearby, close, near at hand (*pred.*) **2** (*adiacente*) adjoining, adiacent, next, (*limitrofo*) neighbouring (*attr*) **3** (*affine*) close **B** *s. m.* neighbour **C** *avv.* near (by), nearby, close (by) **D** *prep.* near (to), close to
vìcolo *s. m.* alley
vìdeo *s. m. inv.* video
videocassétta *s. f.* videocassette
videocitòfono *s. m.* videointercom
videoregistratóre *s. m.* video recorder
vietàre *v. tr.* to forbid, to prohibit, to prevent
vietàto *agg.* forbidden ♦ **senso v.** no entry
vigènte *agg.* current, effective, in force
vigilànte *s. m. e f.* guard
vigilànza *s. f.* supervision, vigilance, surveillance
vigilàre **A** *v. tr.* to watch over, to supervise **B** *v. intr.* to keep watch
vìgile **A** *agg.* vigilant, watchful **B** *s. m.* **1** (*urbano*) policeman **2** (*del fuoco*) fireman
vigìlia *s. f.* eve
vigliàcco **A** *agg.* cowardly **B** *s. m.* coward
vìgna *s. f.* vineyard
vignéto *s. m.* vineyard
vignétta *s. f.* cartoon
vignettìsta *s. m. e f.* cartoonist
vigógna *s. f.* vicugna
vigóre *s. m.* **1** vigour, strength **2** (*validità*) force, effectiveness ♦ **in v.** in force, effective
vigoróso *agg.* vigorous, strong
vìle *agg.* **1** cowardly **2** (*meschino*) base, vile **3** (*senza valore*) worthless, filthy
vilipèndio *s. m.* scorn, contempt, (*dir.*) public insult
vìlla *s. f.* villa
villàggio *s. m.* village
villanìa *s. f.* **1** rudeness **2** (*azione da villano*) rude action
villàno **A** *agg.* rude, impolite **B** *s. m.* lout
villeggiànte *s. m. e f.* holiday-maker, (*USA*) vacationer
villeggiatùra *s. f.* holiday, (*USA*) vacation ♦ **luogo di v.** holiday resort
villóso *agg.* hairy
viltà *s. f.* **1** cowardice **2** (*azione meschina*) mean action
vìmine *s. m.* wicker
vincènte **A** *agg.* winning **B** *s. m. e f.* winner
vìncere **A** *v. tr.* **1** to win **2** (*sconfiggere*) to beat, to defeat **3** (*sopraffare*) to overcome **B** *v. intr.* to win **C** *v. rifl.* to control oneself
vìncita *s. f.* **1** win **2** (*ciò che si vince*) winnings *pl.*
vincitóre **A** *agg.* winning, victorious **B** *s. m.* winner
vincolàre *v. tr.* **1** to bind **2** (*fin.*) to tie up **3** (*mecc.*) to constrain
vìncolo *s. m.* bond, tie
vinìcolo *agg.* wine (*attr.*)
vìno *s. m.* wine ♦ **v. spumante** sparkling wine
viòla (1) **A** *s. f.* (*bot.*) viola, violet **B** *agg. e s. m.* (*colore*) violet, purple
viòla (2) *s. f.* (*mus.*) viola
violàre *v. tr.* **1** (*trasgredire*) to break, to infringe, to violate **2** (*profanare*) to profane **3** (*violentare*) to rape

violazióne *s. f.* **1** violation, infringement **2** (*profanazione*) profanation ♦ **v. di domicilio** housebreaking
violentàre *v. tr.* **1** to rape **2** (*fig.*) to do violence to
violènto *agg.* violent
violènza *s. f.* violence ♦ **non v.** non-violence; **v. carnale** rape
violétta *s. f.* violet
violinìsta *s. m. e f.* violinist
violìno *s. m.* violin, fiddle (*fam.*)
violoncellìsta *s. m. e f.* (violon)cellist
violoncèllo *s. m.* (violon)cello
viòttolo *s. m.* path, lane
vìpera *s. f.* viper
viràle *agg.* viral
viràre *v. intr.* **1** (*naut.*) to veer **2** (*aer.*) to turn **3** (*chim.*) to change colour
viràta *s. f.* veer
vìrgola *s. f.* comma ♦ **v. decimale** point
virgolétte *s. f. pl.* inverted commas *pl.*, quotation marks *pl.*
virìle *agg.* manly, masculine, virile
virilità *s. f.* manliness, virility
virtù *s. f.* **1** virtue **2** (*potere*) power, property ♦ **in v. di** by virtue of
virtuàle *agg.* virtual ♦ **realtà v.** virtual reality
virtuóso **A** *agg.* virtuous **B** *s. m.* **1** virtuous man **2** (*mus.*) virtuoso
vìrus *s. m. inv.* virus
visagìsta *s. m. e f.* beautician
visceràle *agg.* visceral
vìscere *s. m.* **1** internal organ **2** *al pl.* viscera *pl.*, (*intestino*) bowels *pl.*, (*di animale*) entrails *pl.* **3** *al pl.* (*fig.*) bowels *pl.*
vìschio *s. m.* mistletoe
vischióso *agg.* viscous
vìscido *agg.* **1** viscid, slimy **2** (*scivoloso*) slippery **3** (*fig.*) slimy, oily
viscónte *s. m.* viscount
viscontéssa *s. f.* viscountess
visìbile *agg.* visible
visibilità *s. f.* visibility ♦ **scarsa v.** poor visibility
visièra *s. f.* peak
visionàrio *agg. e s. m.* visionary
visióne *s. f.* **1** vision **2** (*vista*) sight
vìsita *s. f.* **1** visit, (*breve*) call **2** (*ispezione*) inspection, control **3** (*med.*) examination **4** (*persona che visita*) visitor ♦ **biglietto da v.** visiting card; **v. medica** medical examination
visitàre *v. tr.* **1** to visit **2** (*andare a trovare*) to visit, to call on, to see **3** (*med.*) to examine
visitatóre *s. m.* visitor
visìvo *agg.* visual
vìso *s. m.* face
visóne *s. m.* mink
vìspo *agg.* lively, sprightly
vissùto *agg.* lived
vìsta *s. f.* **1** sight **2** (*veduta*) sight, view **3** (*campo visivo*) view
vistàre *v. tr.* to endorse, (*passaporto*) to visa
vìsto *s. m.* approval, endorsement, (*su passaporto*) visa
vistóso *agg.* **1** showy **2** (*grande*) big, large
visuàle **A** *agg.* visual **B** *s. f.* **1** (*vista*) sight, view **2** (*campo visivo*) view
vìta (1) *s. f.* **1** life, (*durata*) lifetime **2** (*modo di vivere*) life, living **3** (*necessario per vivere*) living **4** (*animazione*) animation, (*vitalità*) vitality
vìta (2) *s. f.* (*parte del corpo*) waist
vitàle *agg.* vital
vitalità *s. f.* vitality
vitalìzio **A** *agg.* for life, life (*attr.*) **B** *s. m.* life annuity
vitamìna *s. f.* vitamin
vìte (1) *s. f.* (*bot.*) vine
vìte (2) *s. f.* (*mecc.*) screw
vitèllo *s. m.* **1** calf **2** (*cuc.*) veal **3** (*pelle*) calf(skin)
vitìccio *s. m.* tendril
viticoltóre *s. m.* vine-grower
vitìgno *s. m.* vine
vìtreo *agg.* vitreous
vìttima *s. f.* victim
vìtto *s. m.* **1** (*cibo*) food **2** (*pasti*) board ♦ **v. e alloggio** board and lodging
vittòria *s. f.* **1** victory **2** (*sport*) win
vittorióso *agg.* victorious, winning
vìva *inter.* hurrah, up with
vivàce *agg.* **1** lively, vivacious **2** (*sveglio*) quick **3** (*di colore*) bright
vivacità *s. f.* **1** liveliness **2** (*prontezza*) quickness **3** (*di colore*) brightness
vivàio *s. m.* (*di piante*) nursery, (*di pesci*) fish farm
vivànda *s. f.* **1** food **2** (*pietanza*) dish
vivandière *s. m.* sutler
vivènte **A** *agg.* living **B** *s. m. e f.* living being
vìvere (1) *v. tr. e intr.* to live
vìvere (2) *s. m.* life, living
vìveri *s. m. pl.* food, supplies *pl*, victuals *pl.*, provisions *pl.*

vìvido *agg.* vivid
vivisezióne *s. f.* vivisection
vìvo **A** *agg.* **1** living, alive (*pred.*), live (*attr.*) **2** (*vivace*) lively **3** (*profondo*) deep, sharp **4** (*vivido*) vivid **5** (*di colore*) bright **B** *s. m.* **1** living person **2** (*parte viva*) living part, heart
viziàre *v. tr.* **1** to spoil **2** (*dir.*) to vitiate
viziàto *agg.* **1** spoilt **2** (*guasto*) faulty **3** (*dir.*) vitiated ♦ **aria viziata** foul air
vìzio *s. m.* **1** vice **2** (*cattiva abitudine*) bad habit **3** (*difetto*) fault, defect
vizióso *agg.* vicious, corrupt
vocabolàrio *s. m.* **1** (*insieme di termini*) vocabulary **2** (*dizionario*) dictionary
vocàbolo *s. m.* word, term
vocàle **A** *agg.* vocal **B** *s. f.* vowel
vocalìzzo *s. m.* vocalism
vocazióne *s. f.* vocation, calling
vóce *s. f.* **1** voice **2** (*diceria*) rumour **3** (*parola*) word, (*di dizionario*) entry **4** (*gramm.*) voice, part **5** (*mus.*) voice, part **6** (*contabile*) item, entry ♦ **a v. alta/bassa** in a loud/low voice
vociàre *v. intr.* to shout
vóga *s. f.* **1** (*il vogare*) rowing **2** (*moda*) fashion ♦ **essere in v.** to be in fashion
vogàre *v. intr.* to row
vogatóre *s. m.* **1** rower, oarsman **2** (*attrezzo*) rowing machine
vòglia *s. f.* **1** (*desiderio*) wish, longing, fancy, desire **2** (*volontà*) will **3** (*macchia della pelle*) birthmark **4** (*di gestante*) craving
vói *pron. pers. 2ª pl. m. e f.* you ♦ **v. stessi** you ... yourselves
volàno *s. m.* **1** (*gioco*) badminton **2** (*mecc.*) flywheel
volànte (1) **A** *agg.* **1** flying **2** (*movibile*) movable **B** *s. f.* (*polizia*) flying squad
volànte (2) *s. m.* (*autom.*) wheel
volantìno *s. m.* leaflet
volàre *v. intr.* **1** to fly **2** (*librarsi*) to blow **3** (*passare velocemente*) to fly by, to pass quickly **4** (*precipitare*) to fall off
volàtile *s. m.* bird
volenteróso *agg.* willing, keen
volentièri *avv.* willingly, with pleasure
volére (1) *v. tr.* **1** to want (ES: **voglio restare qui** I want to stay here) **2** (*gradire*) to like (*spec. al condiz.*) (ES: **fai come vuoi** do as you like, **volete andare al cinema stasera?** would you like to go to the movies tonight?) **3** (*desiderare*) to wish (ES: **vorrei saper risolvere questo problema** I wish I could solve this problem) **4** (*nelle richieste*) will, can, would, (*nelle offerte*) will have, would like (ES: **vorresti chiudere la porta?** would you close the door?, **vuoi un po' di zucchero?** will you have some sugar?) **5** (*essere intenzionato a*) to intend, to be going (to), (*essere disposto*) to be willing (to) (ES: **cosa volete fare adesso?** what are you going to do now?) **6** (*disporre, stabilire*) to will (ES: **il destino ha voluto così** fate has willed it so) **7** (*permettere*) to let, to allow (ES: **mio padre non vuole che ti veda** my father doesn't allow me to meet you) **8** (*pretendere, aspettarsi*) to expect, to want, to demand (ES: **tu vuoi troppo da lei** you're expecting too much of her) **9** (*richiedere, aver bisogno di*) to need, to require, to want (ES: **è un animale che vuole molte attenzioni** it's an animal that requires much care) **10** (*seguito da v. impers.*) to be going (to), to look (like) (ES: **secondo me vuole piovere** I think it's going to rain) **11** (*volerci, impers.*) to take, to be required, to need (ES: **quanto ci vuole da qui a casa di Mary?** how long does it take from here to Mary's?) ♦ **v. dire** to mean; **vuoi ... vuoi** both ... and
volére (2) *s. m.* will
volgàre **A** *agg.* **1** vulgar, common, coarse **2** (*bot., zool.*) trivial **B** *s. m.* vernacular
volgarizzàre *v. tr.* **1** (*tradurre in volgare*) to translate into the vernacular **2** (*divulgare*) to popularize
vòlgere *v. tr., intr. e rifl.* to turn
vólgo *s. m.* common people
volièra *s. f.* aviary
volitìvo *agg.* volitive
vólo *s. m.* flight ♦ **v. acrobatico** stunt flying; **v. a vela** soaring, gliding
volontà *s. f.* will, wishes *pl.*
volontariaménte *avv.* voluntarily
volontàrio **A** *agg.* voluntary **B** *s. m.* volunteer
volovelìsta *s. m. e f.* glider
vólpe *s. f.* fox
vòlta (1) *s. f.* **1** time **2** (*turno*) turn ♦ **a mia v.** in my turn; **C'era una v. ...** Once upon a time there was ...; **una v. o due** once or twice
vòlta (2) *s. f.* (*arch.*) vault
voltafàccia *s. m. inv.* about-turn
voltàggio *s. m.* voltage

voltàre *v. tr., intr. e rifl.* to turn
volteggiàre *v. intr.* to circle, to twirl
voltéggio *s. m.* vaulting
vólto *s. m.* **1** face **2** (*aspetto*) aspect, appearance
volùbile *agg.* fickle, inconstant
volùme *s. m.* volume
voluminóso *agg.* voluminous, bulky
volùta *s. f.* **1** (*arch.*) volute **2** (*spira*) spiral
voluttà *s. f.* voluptuousness, (*piacere*) delight
voluttuàrio *agg.* unnecessary
voluttuóso *agg.* voluptuous, sensual
vomitàre *v. tr.* to vomit, to retch, to throw up
vòmito *s. m.* vomit ♦ **conato di v.** retching
vóngola *s. f.* clam
voràce *agg.* voracious
voràgine *s. f.* chasm
vòrtice *s. m.* **1** whirl **2** (*fis.*) vortex ♦ **v. d'acqua** whirlpool, eddy; **v. d'aria** whirlwind
vòstro **A** *agg. poss. 2ª pl.* your **B** *pron. poss.* yours **C** *s. m.* **1** (*ciò che è vostro*) what is yours, your property **2** *al pl.* (*i vostri parenti*) your relatives *pl.*, (*i vostri seguaci*) your supporters *pl.*
votànte **A** *agg.* voting **B** *s. m. e f.* voter
votàre **A** *v. tr.* **1** to vote, (*approvare*) to pass **2** (*dedicare*) to offer, to dedicate **B** *v. intr.* to vote **C** *v. rifl.* to devote oneself
votazióne *s. f.* **1** voting, poll **2** (*scolastica*) marks *pl.*
votìvo *agg.* votive
vóto *s. m.* **1** (*promessa*) vow **2** (*per elezione*) vote **3** (*scolastico*) mark
vulcàno *s. m.* volcano
vulcanòlogo *s. m.* volcanologist
vulneràbile *agg.* vulnerable
vuotàre *v. tr. e intr. pron.* to empty
vuòto **A** *agg.* empty **B** *s. m.* **1** empty space, gap **2** (*bottiglia*) empty **3** (*fis.*) vacuum ♦ **a v.** in vain

W

wafer *s. m. inv.* wafer
water *s. m. inv.* toilet bowl
watt *s. m. inv.* watt
western *agg. e s. m. inv.* western
whisky *s. m. inv.* whisky, (*USA, Irlanda*) whiskey
windsurf *s. m. inv.* **1** (*tavola*) (windsurf) board **2** (*sport*) windsurfing
würstel *s. m. inv.* frankfurter

X

xenofobìa *s. f.* xenophobia
xenòfobo *s. m.* xenophobe
xerocòpia *s. f.* xerographic copy
xerografìa *s. f.* xerography
xilofonista *s. m. e f.* xylophone player
xilòfono *s. m.* xilophone
xilografìa *s. f.* xylography, (*stampa*) xilograph

Y

yacht *s. m.* yacht ♦ **y. a motore** motor yacht; **y. a vela** sailing yacht
yarda *s. f.* yard
yoga *s. m. inv.* yoga
yògurt *s. m.* yoghurt
yùcca *s. f.* yucca

Z

zabaióne *s. m.* egg-flip
zaffàta *s. f.* whiff, (*tanfo*) stench
zafferàno *s. m.* saffron
zaffìro *s. m.* sapphire
zàino *s. m.* backpack, knapsack, rucksack
zàmpa *s. f.* (*arto di animale*) leg, (*parte terminale*) paw, hoof, (*di uccello*) claw ♦ **a quattro zampe** four-footed
zampettàre *v. intr.* **1** to trot **2** (*di bambino*) to toddle
zampillànte *agg.* gushing
zampillàre *v. intr.* to gush
zampìllo *s. m.* gush, spurt
zampiróne *s. m.* fumigator
zampógna *s. f.* bagpipes *pl.*
zampognàro *s. m.* piper
zànna *s. f.* tusk, (*di carnivori*) fang
zanzàra *s. f.* mosquito
zanzarièra *s. f.* mosquito-net
zàppa *s. f.* mattock, hoe
zappàre *v. tr.* to hoe, to dig
zar *s. m. inv.* czar
zarìna *s. f.* czarina
zarìsta *agg. e s. m.* czarist
zàttera *s. f.* raft ♦ **z. di salvataggio** life raft
zavòrra *s. f.* ballast
zàzzera *s. f.* long hair, mop
zèbra *s. f.* **1** zebra **2** *al pl.* (*passaggio pedonale*) zebra crossing
zécca (1) *s. f.* mint
zécca (2) *s. f.* (*zool.*) tick
zèlo *s. m.* zeal
zènit *s. m.* zenith
zénzero *s. m.* ginger
zéppa *s. f.* wedge
zéppo *agg.* packed, crammed
zerbìno *s. m.* doormat
zèro *s. m.* zero, nought ♦ **vincere due a z.** to win two-nil
zìa *s. f.* aunt
zibellìno *s. m.* sable
zigàno *agg. e s. m.* tzigane
zìgomo *s. m.* cheekbone
zigzag *s. m. inv.* zigzag ♦ **andare a z.** to zigzag
zimbèllo *s. m.* laughing-stock
zìnco *s. m.* zinc
zingarésco *agg.* gipsy (*attr.*)
zìngaro *s. m.* gipsy
zìo *s. m.* uncle
zircóne *s. m.* zircon
zitèlla *s. f.* spinster
zittìre **A** *v. tr.* to hiss, to boo **B** *v. intr.* to fall silent
zìtto *agg.* silent ♦ **sta' z.!** be quiet!
zizzània *s. f.* **1** (*bot.*) darnel **2** (*fig.*) discord
zòccolo *s. m.* **1** (*calzatura*) clog, sabot **2** (*di equino*) hoof **3** (*piedistallo*) base, plinth **4** (*battiscopa*) skirting (board)
zodiacàle *agg.* zodiacal
zodìaco *s. m.* zodiac
zolfanèllo *s. m.* (sulphur) match
zólfo *s. m.* sulphur
zòlla *s. f.* sod, turf
zollétta *s. f.* lump ♦ **zucchero in zollette** lump sugar
zòna *s. f.* zone
zòo *s. m. inv.* zoo
zoologìa *s. f.* zoology
zoòlogo *s. m.* zoologist
zootecnìa *s. f.* zootechny
zoppicàre *v. intr.* **1** to limp **2** (*essere instabile*) to be shaky **3** (*mancare di rigore*) to be weak
zòppo **A** *agg.* lame, limping **B** *s. m.* lame person
zoticóne s. m. boor, lout
zùcca *s. f.* **1** (*bot.*) pumpkin **2** (*testa*) head, pate (*fam.*)
zuccàta *s. f.* blow with the head
zuccheràre *v. tr.* to sugar, to sweeten
zuccheràto *agg.* sugared, sweetened
zuccherièra *s. f.* sugar-bowl
zuccherìno **A** *agg.* sugary, sweet **B** *s. m.* **1** sweet **2** (*contentino*) sop
zùcchero *s. m.* sugar ♦ **z. a velo** icing sugar; **z. filato** candyfloss
zucchìno *s. m.* courgette, (*USA*) zucchini
zuccóne *s. m.* (*testardo*) stubborn person, (*ottuso*) blockhead
zùffa *s. f.* scuffle, fight
zùfolo *s. m.* flageolet
zùppa *s. f.* soup ♦ **z. di pesce** fish soup; **z. di verdura** vegetable soup
zuppièra *s. f.* soup-tureen
zùppo *agg.* wet (through)

USEFUL PHRASES

EN ROUTE

AIRPLANES

Devo andare a... Può darmi orari e tariffe dei voli?
I must go to... Can you give me the flight times and prices?

Ci sono quattro posti disponibili sul volo... per... del giorno...?
Are there four seats available on flight... for... on...?

Vorrei un biglietto per...
I'd like a ticket for...

Vorrei prenotare un posto per... sul volo... del...
I'd like to book a seat for... on flight... on...

Vorrei spostare/annullare/confermare la mia prenotazione
I'd like to change/to cancel/to confirm my booking

A che ora dobbiamo trovarci all'aeroporto?
What time must we be at the airport?

Come si può raggiungere l'aeroporto?
What's the best way to get to the airport?

Quanto dista l'aeroporto dal centro della città?
How far is the airport from the city center (downtown)?

A che ora e da dove parte il bus per l'aeroporto?
What time and where does the bus leave for the airport?

A che ora parte il volo numero... per...?
What time does flight number... for... leave?

Vorrei un posto...	I'd like...
al finestrino	a window seat
corridoio	an aisle seat
non fumatori	a no smoking seat
fumatori	a smoker's seat

Ho smarrito la carta d'imbarco
I've lost my boarding card

Mi può dare una coperta/un cuscino, per favore?
Can you give me a blanket/a pillow, please?

I miei bagagli non sono arrivati; a quale ufficio devo rivolgermi?
My luggage (baggage) hasn't arrived; which office must I go to?

Recapitateml i bagagli a questo indirizzo
Send my luggage (baggage) to this address

Dov'è il deposito bagagli?
Where is the left-luggage office?

Dove posso trovare un taxi/un autobus?
Where can I get a taxi/a bus?

Arrivals	Arrivi
Baggage claim	Ritiro bagagli
Boarding now	Imbarco immediato
Cancelled flight	Volo cancellato
Check-in	Check-in
Customs	Dogana
Delayed flight	Volo ritardato
Departures	Partenze
Destination	Destinazione
Domestic flights	Nazionali
Gate	Uscita
International flights	Internazionali
Left-luggage office	Deposito bagagli

TRAINS, BUSES, AND TAXIS

Dove è la fermata del bus numero... per...?
Where does bus number... for... stop?

Dov'è la stazione della metropolitana?
Where's the underground/tube (subway) station?

Dove posso acquistare un biglietto per il bus?
Where can I buy a bus ticket?

Quale bus/metro devo prendere per...?
Which bus/underground must I take for...?

Questo bus/treno passa per...?
Does this bus/train go past...?

Dove devo scendere per andare a...?
Where must I get off to go to...?

È questa la direzione giusta per andare a...?
Is this the right direction to go to...?

Dove posso trovare un taxi?
Where can I get a taxi?

Quanto costa un taxi fino a...?
How much does a taxi to... cost?
Può aspettarmi qualche minuto?
Can you wait for me for a few minutes, please?
Quanto le devo?
How much do I owe you?
Dove si trova la stazione ferroviaria?
Where's the railway station?
Mi porti alla stazione. Ho molta fretta!
Can you take me to the station? I'm in a great hurry!
Vorrei un biglietto di prima/seconda classe per...
I'd like a first/second class ticket to...
Vorrei un biglietto di andata e ritorno per...
I'd like a return ticket to...
Posso fare il biglietto sul treno?
Can I buy the ticket on the train?
Vorrei fare una prenotazione sul treno per... delle... del...
I'd like to book a seat on the... train to... on...
Vorrei prenotare una cuccetta per... sul treno delle... del...
I'd like to book a couchette to... on the... train on...
C'è una coincidenza per...? A che ora parte?
Is there a connection for...? What time does it leave?

AUTOMOBILES

Il pieno, per favore
Fill up, please

Può controllare...?	Can you check...?
l'acqua	the water level
l'olio	the oil level
l'acqua della batteria	the battery water
il liquido dei freni	the brake fluid
la pressione dei pneumatici	the tyre pressures
Può sostituire...?	Can you change...?
l'olio	the oil
il filtro dell'olio	the oil filter
il filtro dell'aria	the air filter
i pneumatici	the tyres
le spazzole del tergicristallo	the windscreen wiper blades
un fusibile	a fuse

Può dare una pulita al parabrezza?
Could you clean the windscreen?
Può darmi un recipiente vuoto?
Could you give me an empty container?
Può mettere un po' di benzina in un recipiente? Sono rimasto a secco
Could you put a little petrol in a container? I've run out
Può indicarmi la strada giusta per...?
Can you tell me which is the right way for...?
Qual è la strada più breve per...?
Which is the shortest road to...?
Può dirmi dove mi trovo?
Can you tell me where I am?
Può accompagnarmi a..., per favore?
Could you take me to..., please?
È asfaltata/percorribile la strada per?
Has the road for... got a hard surface?/Is the road to... passable?
Quanti chilometri ci sono per arrivare...?
How far is it to...?

a un distributore	a petrol station/a service station
al prossimo paese	the nearest town
a un telefono	a telephone
alla prossima uscita	the next exit

Posso parcheggiare qui?
Can I park here?
Quanto tempo posso lasciare la macchina?
How long can I leave my car here?
Quanto costa il parcheggio?
How much does the car park cost?
Può indicarmi un meccanico/gommista?
Can you tell me where I can find a mechanic/tyre repairer?
Può indicarmi un'officina per far controllare la mia auto?
Can you tell me where I can find a garage to check my car?
La mia macchina è guasta: può darmi una mano?
My car has broken down: could you give me a hand?
Può mandare un carro attrezzi?
Can you send a breakdown lorry?
Può trainare la macchina fino a...?
Can you tow my car to...?

La macchina... The car...
non parte won't start
fa un fumo nero/ blu/bianco gives off black/ blue/white smoke
Il motore... The engine...
non si avvia won't start
si avvia ma si spegne subito starts but stops at once
non tiene il minimo won't tick over
consuma/perde olio/ acqua uses too much/leaks oil/water
perde colpi misfires
fa uno strano rumore makes a funny noise

Si sente odore di benzina
I can smell petrol

Non entrano le marce
The gears won't engage

La frizione strappa/slitta
The clutch engages suddenly/slips

Non si accendono le luci
The lights don't come on

I freni non funzionano
The brakes don't work

Ho perso le chiavi
I've lost the keys

Si è rotta la chiave nella serratura
The key has broken off in the lock

Non funziona/è rotto il...
The.... doesn't work/is broken

Riesce a ripararlo subito?
Can you mend it at once?

Quanto tempo ci vuole per la riparazione?
How long will it take to mend it?

Ha scoperto il guasto?
Have you found out what's wrong?

Quanto pensa possa venire a costare la riparazione?
How much do you think the repair will cost?

Molte grazie per il suo aiuto!
Thank you very much for your help!

Dove posso noleggiare una macchina?
Where can I rent a car?

Vorrei noleggiare una macchina per.. giorni/settimane
I'd like to rent a car for... days/weeks

Vorrei una macchina di piccola/media/grande cilindrata
I'd like a car with a small/medium/large engine

C'è un extra per il chilometraggio?
Must I pay extra for mileage?

È possibile lasciare la macchina a....?
Can I leave the car at...?

Entro che ora devo riportare la macchina?
What time must I return the car by?

Avete una macchina più grande/piccola?
Have you got a larger/smaller car?

AT THE HOTEL

Potete raccomandarmi un albergo...?
Could you recommend a...?
economico cheap hotel
centrale central hotel
non distante da... hotel not far from....
con garage hotel with a garage

Ho prenotato una camera... a nome...
I have a room booked under the name of...

Posso vedere la camera?
Can I see the room?

Vorrei una camera...
I'd like a...
singola single room
doppia double room
a tre letti room with three beds
con bagno room with a bathroom
con doccia room with a shower

Quanto cosa...?
How much does... cost?
la camera e la prima colazione the room with breakfast/bed and breakfast
la mezza pensione/ half board
la pensione completa full board

La prima colazione è compresa nel prezzo?
Is breakfast included in the price?

Il prezzo è per la camera o per persona?
Is the price for the room or per person?

C'è l'ascensore?
Is there a lift?

A che piano si trova?
Which floor is it on?

La camera non mi piace; vorrei cambiarla
I don't like the room; I'd like to change it

Va bene, la prendo
OK, I'll take it

Intendo fermarmi...
I mean to stay for...

una notte	one night
una settimana	one week
quindici giorni	fifteen days

Le devo lasciare un acconto?
Must I leave you an advance payment?

Posso riavere il mio passaporto/la mia carta d'identità?
Could I have my passport/identity card back?

È possibile aggiungere un letto?
Is it possible to put another bed in?

Può portarmi la colazione in camera?
Could you bring my breakfast to my room?

Dove posso parcheggiare la macchina?
Where can I park my car?

C'è il servizio lavanderia?
Is there a laundry service?

La camera è ancora in disordine!
The room hasn't been made up!

Mi mandi la cameriera!
Could you send me the chambermaid?

Mi faccia parlare con il direttore!
I'd like to speak to the manager!

A che ora viene servito/a...?
What time is... served?

la prima colazione	breakfast
il pranzo	lunch
la cena	dinner

Vorrei essere svegliato alle..., per favore
I'd like to be woken at..., please

Per favore, mi può portare i bagagli in camera?
Could you carry my luggage (baggage) to my room, please?

Posso depositare dei documenti/dei valori?
Can I leave my documents/some valuables with you?

Può cambiarmi questa banconota?
Can you change this note for me?

Ci sono messaggi per me?
Are there any messages for me?

Attendo una telefonata. Me la può passare in camera?
I'm waiting for a telephone call. Can you put it through to my room?

Mi ha cercato qualcuno?
Has anyone called for me/telephoned me?

Mi dia la chiave numero..., per favore
Could you give me the key number..., please?

Rientrerò tardi: posso avere la chiave del portone?
I'll be coming back late: can I have the front door key?

Vorrei fare una telefonata
I'd like to make a telephone call

Può chiamare questo numero a mio nome?
Can you telephone this number for me?

Ho lasciato i bagagli in camera
I've left my luggage (baggage) in my room

Ho deciso di partire domani
I've decided to leave tomorrow

Può prepararmi il conto?
Can you prepare my bill for me?

Accettate carte di credito?
Do you accept credit cards?

Posso pagare con traveller's cheque?
Can I pay by traveller's cheques?

Posso lasciare i bagagli fino a stasera?
Can I leave my luggage (baggage) here until this evening?

Può chiamarmi un taxi?
Can you call a taxi for me?

BANK, POST OFFICE, AND TELEPHONE

Può indicarmi una banca?
Can you tell me where I can find a bank?

Qual è l'orario di apertura delle banche?
When are the banks open?/What are the banking hours?

Vorrei cambiare questa somma di denaro
I'd like to change this sum of money

Vorrei cambiare un traveller's cheque
I'd like to change a traveller's cheque

Ho perso i traveller's cheque: cosa devo fare?
I've lost my traveller's cheques: what should I do?
Mi hanno rubato i traveller's cheque e la ricevuta d'acquisto!
My traveller's cheques and the receipt have been stolen!
È possibile avere del contante con la mia carta di credito?
Is it possible to have cash with my credit card?
Dov'è l'ufficio postale?
Where's the Post Office?
Qual è l'orario di apertura degli uffici postali?
What time are the Post Office's open?
Dove posso comprare dei francobolli?
Where can I buy some stamps?
Qual è l'affrancatura per una lettera/cartolina?
What's the postage for a letter/postcard?
Devo spedire questo pacco
I must post this parcel
A quale sportello devo rivolgermi?
Which window should I go to?
Vorrei incassare questo vaglia
I'd like to cash this money order (postal order)
Vorrei fare un versamento
I'd like to make a payment
Dov'è il fermo posta?
Where is the poste restante (general delivery)?
Desidero fare una telefonata a carico del destinatario
I'd like to make a collect call
Non ho moneta per telefonare: può aiutarmi?
I'd haven't got any change for the telephone: can you help me?
Vorrei una scheda per telefonare
I'd like a card for the telephone
C'è un posto telefonico pubblico?
Is there a public telephone?
Vorrei chiamare questo numero
I'd like to call this number
Qual è il prefisso per...?
What's the code number (area code) for...?
Può riprovare?
Can you try again?
Riprovo più tardi
I'll try again later
Può richiamarmi a questo numero?
Can you call me back at this number?
Non capisco, può parlare più lentamente?
I don't understand, could you speak more slowly?
La linea è occupata
The line is engaged
La linea è disturbata. Parli più forte
The line is bad. Could you speak louder?
È caduta la linea
I've lost the line
Il telefono è guasto
The telephone is broken

BAR AND RESTAURANT

C'è un bar/ristorante qui vicino?
Is there a bar/restaurant near here?
Vorrei fare colazione (prima colazione)
I'd like breakfast
Può farmi un panino?
Can you make me a sandwich/a roll?
Vorrei prenotare un tavolo per... persone per le ore...
I'd like to book a table for... people for...
È libero questo tavolo?
Is this table free?
C'è molto da aspettare?
Will I (we) have to wait long?
Abbiamo molta fretta
We're in a great hurry
Aspetto degli amici
I'm waiting for some friends
Dov'è il guardaroba?
Where's the cloakroom (coatroom)?
Dov'è la toilette?
Where's the toilet/bathroom?
Mi porti un aperitivo
Could you bring me an aperitif?
Può portarmi il menù/la carta dei vini?
Can you bring me the menu/the wine list?

Potete consigliarmi qualcosa di speciale?
Could you suggest something special?

Qual è il vostro piatto caratteristico?
What is your local dish?

Qual è il piatto del giorno?
What is the dish of the day?

Vorrei bere... I'd like to drink...
acqua minerale gasata/non gasata sparkling/still mineral water
acqua naturale tap water
...ghiacciata iced...
...non fredda not too cold

Cameriere!
Waiter!

Può aggiungere un altro coperto?
Could you lay another place?

Questo... è sporco! Me lo può cambiare, per favore?
This... is dirty! Could you bring me another, please?

Quali sono gli ingredienti?
What are the ingredients of this dish?

Cosa vuol dire...?
What does.... mean?

Mi porti un altro...
Could you bring me another...?

Vorrei solo una mezza porzione
I'd like just a half portion

Questa pietanza è fredda/poco cotta
This dish is cold/underdone

Me la può scaldare?
Could you heat it for me?

Me la può cuocere di più?
Could you cook it a little more?

Vorrei della carne... I'd like some...
al sangue rare meat
ben cotta well-cooked meat
molto cotta very well-cooked meat

Che contorni/dessert avete?
What vegetables/desserts have you got?

Mi porti della frutta fresca
Could you bring me some fresh fruit?

Mi faccia il conto, per favore
Could you bring me the bill (check), please?

Quanto pago?
How much do I owe you?

Accettate carte di credito?
Do you accept credit cards?

Ho bisogno della ricevuta
I need the receipt

Tenga il resto
Keep the change

Questo è per lei
This is for you

Mi può chiamare un taxi?
Can you call a taxi for me?

C'è un telefono?
Have you got a telephone?

CULTURE

Dov'è...? Where is...?
il museo the museum
la galleria d'arte moderna the gallery of modern art
la pinacoteca the art gallery

A che ora apre/chiude il museo?
What time does the museum open/close?

Qual è il giorno di chiusura?
Which day is it closed?

Il museo è sempre aperto?
Is the museum always open?

Vorrei un catalogo del museo in italiano
I'd like an Italian catalogue of the museum

C'è una guida che parla italiano?
Is there a guide who speaks Italian?

Quanto costa l'ingresso?
How much does it cost to get in?

L'ingresso è libero?
Is it free to get in?

C'è uno sconto per studenti?
Is there a student reduction?

È possibile visitare...?
Is it possible to visit...?
la chiesa the church
il palazzo the palace
la sacrestia the sacrity
il chiostro the cloister
la cripta the crypt

A che ora inizia lo spettacolo?
What time does the show/play/film start?

HEALTH

Può consigliarmi un...?
Can you recommend a/an?

cardiologo	cardiologist
dentista	dentist
ginecologo	gynaecologist
oculista	oculist
ortopedico	orthopaedist
pediatra	paediatrician
traumatologo	traumatologist

Conosce un medico che parla italiano?
Do you know a doctor who speaks Italian?

Posso parlare col dottore?
Can I speak to the doctor?

Vorrei fissare un appuntamento col dottore...
I'd like to make an appointment with Doctor...

Posso venire subito? È urgente!
Can I come at once? It's urgent!

Dov'è l'ambulatorio del dottor...?
Where is Doctor...'s surgery?

A che ora arriva il dottore?
What time does the doctor arrive?

Il dottore può venire a visitarmi?
Can the doctor come and visit me?

Può chiamare un medico?
Can you call a doctor?

Dov'è l'ospedale più vicino?
Where's the nearest hospital?

Mi porti al pronto soccorso
Can you take me to the First Aid Centre?

Non mi sento bene
I dont't feel well

Mi sento...	I feel...
male	ill
meglio	better
peggio	worse
Mi fa male qui	It hurts here
Mi/gli fa male...	My/his/her... hurts
Ho...	I ....
l'influenza	have got flu
voglia di vomitare	want to be sick
la febbre	have got a temperature
la diarrea	have got diarrhoea
mal di denti	have got toothache
una ferita	am injured/ wounded
un'infezione	have got an infection
le vertigini	am suffering from dizzy spells
una scottatura	have burnt myself

Non riesco a dormire
I can't sleep

Soffro di diabete
I've got diabetes

Porto lenti corneali
I wear contact lenses

Aspetto un bambino
I'm expecting a baby

Sono alla... settimana di gravidanza
I'm in my... week of pregnancy

Sono allergico a...
I'm allergic to...

Può prescrivermi un...?
Could you prescribe me a...?

Credo di essermi rotto...
I think I've broken my...

Non posso muovere...
I can't move my...

Posso continuare il viaggio?
Can I continue my journey?

Quando potrò riprendere il viaggio?
When will I be able to continue my journey?

Devo prendere delle precauzioni?
Are there any precautions I should take?

Quant'è il suo onorario?
How much is your fee?

Può farmi la ricetta?
Can you make me out a prescription?

Dov'è la farmacia più vicina?
Where's the nearest chemist (drugstore)?

Vorrei qualcosa contro...
I'd like something for...

il raffreddore	a cold
la febbre	a temperature
la tosse	a cough
il mal di denti	toothache
il mal di testa	a headache
una scottatura	a burn
la diarrea	diarrhoea
la stitichezza	constipation
l'insonnia	insomnia

Vorrei... ma non ho la ricetta
I'd like..., but I haven't got a prescription

ITALIAN PRONUNCIATION FOR ENGLISH SPEAKERS

Accent Marks

Italian spelling provides most of the information needed to pronounce Italian correctly. This dictionary uses additional accents, both grave and acute, to indicate the stressed syllable in each multisyllabic word. Accents are also used to distinguish "open" and "closed" vowels. In this dictionary, é = International Phonetic Alphabet [e] (closed and stressed), è = IPA [ɛ] (open and stressed), ó = IPA [o] (closed and stressed), and ò = IPA [ɔ] (open and stressed). Unstressed vowels do not have accents. Outside of dictionaries, the only accents written or printed are grave accents used (1) to mark a final stressed vowel, and (2) to distinguish otherwise identical single-syllable words.

Vowels

The five Italian vowels have a clear-cut sound; they are never drawn out or slurred as in English. Italian vowels correspond approximately to the following English sounds.

a	like *a* in "father": **casa**, **ama**, **lana**
e (*closed*)	like *a* in "make": **sera**, **mela**, **vedere**
e (*open*)	like *e* in "let": **sedia**, **festa**, **bene**
i	like *ee* in "feet": **liti**, **tini**, **piccolo**
o (*closed*)	like *o* in "note": **coda**, **molto**, **conto**
o (*open*)	like *aw* in "law": **cosa**, **toro**, **donna**
u	like *oo* in "mood": **luna**, **uno**, **lupo**

Consonants

b	like English *b* in "boy": **bello**, **bianco**, **abete**
c	before *a*, *o*, *u*, or a consonant, like English *k* in "kind": **cura**, **come**, **casa**
c	before *e* and *i*, like English *ch* in "cherry": **cento**, **celeste**, **baci**
cc	before *e* and *i*, like a double English *ch*: **accento**, **accidenti**
ch	(used only before *e* or *i*) like English *k* in "kick": **perchè**, **chiaro**, **bianchi**
ci	before *a*, *o*, and *u*, like English *ch* in "cherry": **ciao**, **cioccolata**, **ciuffo**
d	like English *d* in "dance": **dedalo**, **davanti**, **dove**
g	before *a*, *o*, and *u*, like English *g* in "go": **gara**, **lago**, **gufo**
g	before *e* and *i*, like English *g* in "gem": **gelo**, **giro**, **vagito**. If the *i* is unstressed and followed by another vowel, its sound is unheard (Italian *gio* would sound like English *jo* in "joke"): **giovane**, **giacca**, **giocare**, **giugno**.

gh	(used only before *e* and *i*) like English *g* in "go": **ghirlanda, fughe, laghi**
gli	sounds somewhat like *-lli-* in "million": **egli, migliore, figlia**. However, *gli* is pronounced hard as in English "negligence" (1) when it is initial (except in the article *gli*) as in *glioma*, (2) when it is preceded by a consonant as in *ganglio*, and (3) when it is followed by a consonant as in *negligenza*.
gn	sounds approximately like *ni* in "onion": **lavagna, signore, legno**.
gu	before a vowel, sounds like English *gw* in "Gwen": **guerra, guida, guasto**.
h	is always silent: **ho, hai, ha, ah**.
l	like English *l* in "lamb": **lana, lavoro, levare**
m	like English *m* in "money": **male, merito, moto**
n	like English *n* in "net": **nano, nebbia, nido**
p	like English *p* in "pot," but without the aspiration that sometimes accompanies the English sound: **porta, ape, lupa**
qu	like English *qu* in "quart": **questo, quasi, quinto**
r	is well trilled and pronounced with the tip of the tongue against the upper front teeth: **rosa, mare, ora**.
s	has two sounds: (1) when it is followed by a vowel, it is called "pure" and sounds like English hard *s* in "some": **sale, falso**; (2) when it is followed by a consonant (except *p*), especially at the beginning of a word, it is called "impure" and sounds like English *s* in "rose" or *z* in "zero": **sbaglio, svenire, snello**.
sc	before *a*, *o*, and *u*, like English *sk* in "skip": **scatola, scopo, scusa**
sc	before *e* or *i*, like English *sh* in "ship": **scena, scelta, scivolare**
sch	has the sound of English *sc* in "scope" or English *sch* in "school": **schiavo, dischi, mosche, schema, maschio**.
t	like English *t* in "table": **tale, tutto, patire**
z	sometimes sounds like English *ts* in "nuts": **grazia, forza, zucchero**; sometimes like English *dz* in "adze": **zero, mezzo, zelo**.

Double Consonants

In Italian, double consonants are longer and more emphatic than single consonants. It takes much more time and force to pronounce them: **mamma fratello battaglia cappello atto pello bocca tetto**.

Stress

Generally, Italian words are stressed on the last syllable but one—that is, on the penultimate syllable: **cu*ci*na vo*ta*na col*la*na ma*ti*ta**.

Sometimes the words are stressed on the last syllable but two—that is, on the antepenultimate syllable: ***ma*gico** ***lo*gico** ***al*bero** **dif*fi*cile**.

Rarely, the words are stressed on the last syllable but three: **an*dan*dosene** ***col*locano** **por*ta*temelo** ***ec*cotelo**.

When a word is stressed on the last syllable, an accent mark is always written: **cit*tà*** **volon*tà***.

ENGLISH PHONETICS FOR ITALIAN SPEAKERS

L'alfabetico fonetico adottato è quello approvato dall'Associazione fonetica internazionale.

Vocali

[ɑː]	car, father
[æ]	and, man
[ɛ]	bed, yes
[ʌ]	cup, up
[ə]	a, mother
[ɜː]	girl, word
[ɪ]	pig, it
[iː]	tree, please
[ɒ]	box, not
[ɔː]	wall, horse
[ʊ]	book, full
[uː]	shoe, fool

Dittonghi

[aɪ]	five, fly
[aʊ]	how, house
[eɪ]	train, name
[ɛə]	there, care
[ɪə]	ear, here
[əʊ]	go, boat
[ɔɪ]	toy, oil
[ʊə]	poor, sure

Consonanti

[p]	pencil, stop
[b]	book, boy
[t]	train, pot
[d]	dog, kind
[k]	car, black
[g]	go, egg
[f]	floor, off
[v]	very, seven
[θ]	thin, mouth
[ð]	this, with
[s]	sun, place
[z]	zoo, noise
[ʃ]	fish, ship
[ʒ]	pleasure, measure
[tʃ]	church, chair
[dʒ]	judge, age
[l]	leg, full
[m]	match, him
[n]	name, pen
[ŋ]	ring, song
[r]	room, very
[j]	yes, you
[w]	wind, away
[h]	hat, hand
[x]	loch (in parole gaeliche)

Segni particolari

[ː]	indica un prolungamento della vocale che lo precede
[ˈ]	l'accento tonico principale cade sulla sillaba successiva
[ˌ]	l'accento tonico secondario cade sulla sillaba successiva
[ʳ]	indica la presenza di una **r** muta a fine parola

I caratteri posti tra parentesi tonde si riferiscono a suoni opzionali

ABBREVIATIONS

Abbreviation	Italian	English
abbr.	*abbreviazione*	abbreviation
acrt.	*accorciativo*	shortened form
aer.	*aeronautica*	aeronautics
afferm.	*affermativo*	affirmative
agg.	*aggettivo*	adjective
anat.	*anatomia*	anatomy
arald.	*araldica*	heraldry
arc.	*arcaico*	archaic
arch.	*architettura*	architecture
archeol.	*archeologia*	archaeology
art.	*articolo*	article
arte	*arte*	art
astr.	*astronomia, astrologia*	astronomy, astrology
attr.	*attributivo*	attributive
autom.	*automobilismo*	automobiles
avv.	*avverbio, avverbiale*	adverb, adverbial
banca	*banca*	banking
biol.	*biologia*	biology
bot.	*botanica*	botany
card.	*cardinale*	cardinal
chim.	*chimica*	chemistry
cin.	*cinematografia*	cinematography
comm.	*commercio*	commerce
comp.	*comparativo*	comparative
compl.	*complemento*	complement
compl. ind.	*complemento indiretto*	indirect object
compl. ogg.	*complemento oggetto*	direct object
condiz.	*condizionale*	conditional
cong.	*congiunzione*	conjunction
cuc.	*cucina*	cooking
determ.	*determinativo*	definite
difett.	*difettivo*	defective
dimostr.	*dimostrativo*	demonstrative
dir.	*diritto*	law
dubit.	*dubitativo*	dubitative
econ.	*economia*	economics
edil.	*edilizia*	building
elettr.	*elettricità*	electricity
elettron.	*elettronica*	electronics
enf.	*enfatico*	emphatic

Abbreviation	**Italian**	**English**
ES	*esempio*	example
escl.	*esclamativo*	exclamatory
est.	*esteso*	extended
f.	*femminile*	feminine
fam.	*familiare*	informal, colloquial
ferr.	*ferrovia*	railway
fig.	*figurato*	figurative
fin.	*finanza*	finance
fis.	*fisica*	physics
fon.	*fonologia*	phonology
fot.	*fotografia*	photography
fut.	*futuro*	future
geogr.	*geografia*	geography
geol.	*geologia*	geology
geom.	*geometria*	geometry
gramm.	*grammatica*	grammar
idiom.	*idiomatico*	idiomatic
impers.	*impersonale*	impersonal
ind.	*indiretto*	indirect
indef.	*indefinito*	indefinite
indeterm.	*indeterminativo*	indefinite
inf.	*infinito,* *informatica*	infinitive, computer science
inter.	*interiezione*	interjection
interr.	*interrogativo*	interrogative
intr.	*intransitivo*	intransitive
inv.	*invariato*	invariant
iron.	*ironico*	ironic
letter.	*letterario*	literary
loc.	*locuzione*	expression, phrase
m.	*maschile*	masculine
mat.	*matematica*	mathematics
mecc.	*meccanica*	mechanics
med.	*medicina*	medicine
metall.	*metallurgia*	metallurgy
meteor.	*meteorologia*	meteorology
mil.	*militare*	military
miner.	*mineralogia*	mineralogy
mitol.	*mitologia*	mythology
mus.	*musica*	music
naut.	*nautica*	nautical
neg.	*negativo*	negative
num.	*numerale*	numeral
ord.	*ordinale*	ordinal
ogg.	*oggetto*	object
pass.	*passato*	past

Abbreviation	Italian	English
pers.	*personale*	personal
pl.	*plurale*	plural
pol.	*politica*	politics
pop.	*popolare*	popular, informal
poss.	*possessivo*	possessive
p. p.	*participio passato*	past participle
pred.	*predicato, predicativo*	predicate, predicative
pref.	*prefisso*	prefix
prep.	*preposizione*	preposition
pres.	*presente*	present
pron.	*pronome, pronominale*	pronoun, pronominal
psic.	*psicologia*	psychology
q.c.	*qualche cosa*	something
qc.	*qualcuno*	someone
radio	*radio*	radio
rec.	*reciproco*	reciprocal
rel.	*relativo*	relative
relig.	*religione*	religion
rifl.	*riflessivo*	reflexive
s.	*sostantivo*	substantive, noun
sb.		somebody
scient.	*scientifico*	scientific
serv.	*servile*	auxiliary
sing.	*singolare*	singular
sogg.	*soggetto*	subject
sost.	*sostantivato*	used as a substantive
spec.	*specialmente*	especially
sport.	*sport*	sports
spreg.	*spregiativo*	pejorative
st.		something
stor.	*storia*	history
sup.	*superlativo*	superlative
teatro	*teatro*	theater
tecnol.	*tecnologia*	technology
tel.	*telefonia*	telephones
tess.	*industria tessile*	textile industry
tip.	*tipografia*	typography
tr.	*transitivo*	transitive
TV	*televisione*	television
USA	*americano*	American
v.	*verbo*	verb
volg.	*volgare*	vulgar
zool.	*zoologia*	zoology